MW01194071

THE HISTORICAL JESUS OF THE GOSPELS

The Historical Jesus of the Gospels

Craig S. Keener

WILLIAM B. EERDMANS PUBLISHING COMPANY
GRAND RAPIDS, MICHIGAN

Wm. B. Eerdmans Publishing Co.
2140 Oak Industrial Drive NE, Grand Rapids, Michigan 49505
www.eerdmans.com

Library of Congress Cataloging-in-Publication Data

Keener, Craig S., 1960-
    The historical Jesus of the Gospels / Craig Keener.
       p.   cm.
    ISBN 978-0-8028-6888-6 (pbk.: alk. paper)
    1. Jesus Christ — Historicity.   I. Title.

    BT303.2.K45   2009
    232.9'08 — dc22

                  2009029275

To E. P. Sanders and James H. Charlesworth

Contents

Abbreviations

Abbreviations employed in the Bibliography of Sources Cited

AARAS	American Academy of Religion Academy Series
AB	Anchor Bible
ABD	*Anchor Bible Dictionary*
ABR	*Australian Biblical Review*
ABRL	Anchor Bible Reference Library
AbrN	*Abr-Nahrain*
ABW	*Archaeology in the Biblical World*
ACR	*Australasian Catholic Record*
AcT	*Acta Theologica*
AJA	*American Journal of Archaeology*
AJBS	*African Journal of Biblical Studies*
AJET	*Africa Journal of Evangelical Theology*
AJP	*American Journal of Philology*
AJSR	*Association for Jewish Studies Review*
AJT	*Asia Journal of Theology*
ALW	*Archiv für Liturgiewissenschaft*
AnBib	Analecta Biblica
ANRW	*Aufstieg und Niedergang der Römischen Welt*
ANTC	Abingdon New Testament Commentaries
Anton	*Antonianum*
ANZSTR	Australian and New Zealand Studies in Theology and Religion
APB	*Acta Patristica et Byzantina*
ASCSA	American School of Classical Studies at Athens
ASDE	*Annali di storia dell' esegesi*
ASNU	Acta Seminarii Neotestamentici Upsaliensis
ASTI	*Annual of the Swedish Theological Institute*
ATR	*Anglican Theological Review*
AUSS	*Andrews University Seminary Studies*
BA	*Biblical Archaeologist*
BAGB	*Bulletin de l'Association Guillaume Budé*

BAIAS	*Bulletin of the Anglo-Israel Archaeological Society*
BAR	*Biblical Archaeology Review*
BASOR	*Bulletin of the American Schools of Oriental Research*
BBR	*Bulletin of Biblical Research*
BECNT	Baker Exegetical Commentary on the New Testament
BEDS	*Bulletin Ecclésiastique du diocèse de Strasbourg*
BeO	*Bibbia e Oriente*
BETL	Bibliotheca Ephemeridum Theologicarum Lovaniensium
Bib	*Biblica*
BiBh	*Bible Bhashyam (Biblebhashyam)*
BibInt	*Biblical Interpretation*
BibSp	*Bible and Spade*
BibT	*The Bible Today*
BibUnt	Biblische Untersuchungen
Bijdr	*Bijdragen*
BIOSCS	*Bulletin of the International Organization for Septuagint and Cognate Studies*
BJRL	*Bulletin of the John Rylands University Library*
BJS	Brown Judaic Studies
BK	*Bibel und Kirche*
BL	*Bibel und Liturgie*
BLE	*Bulletin de Littérature Ecclésiastique*
BN	*Biblische Notizen*
BNTC	Black's New Testament Commentaries
BR	*Biblical Research*
BRev	*Bible Review*
BSac	*Bibliotheca Sacra*
BTB	*Biblical Theology Bulletin*
BTr	*Bible Translator*
BurH	*Buried History*
BZ	*Biblische Zeitschrift*
CaÉ	Cahiers Évangiles
CathW	*Catholic World*
CB	*Cultura Bíblica*
CBC	Cambridge Bible Commentary
CBNTS	Coniectanea Biblica: New Testament Series
CBQ	*Catholic Biblical Quarterly*
CBQMS	Catholic Biblical Quarterly Monograph Series
CBull	*Classical Bulletin*
CCWJCW	Cambridge Commentaries on Writings of the Jewish and Christian World 200 BC to AD 200
CHB	*Christian History & Biography*
ChrCent	*Christian Century*
ChSt	*Chicago Studies*
CJ	*Classical Journal*
Colloq	*Colloquium*
ColT	*Collectanea Theologica*
CommCog	*Communication and Cognition*

ConsJud	*Conservative Judaism*
CP	*Classical Philology*
CQ	*Classical Quarterly*
CRBR	*Critical Review of Books in Religion*
CSER Review	*Committee for the Scientific Examination of Religion*
CTM	*Concordia Theological Monthly*
CTQ	*Concordia Theological Quarterly*
CTSR	*Chicago Theological Seminary Register*
CuadTeol	*Cuadernos de Teología*
CurBS	*Currents in Research: Biblical Studies*
CurTM	*Currents in Theology and Mission*
CV	*Communio Viatorum*
CW	*Classical World*
DBM	*Deltion Biblikon Meleton*
Di	*Dialog*
DJG	*Dictionary of Jesus and the Gospels.* Ed. Joel B. Green, Scot McKnight, and I. Howard Marshall. Downers Grove, IL: InterVarsity, 1992.
DNTB	*Dictionary of New Testament Background.* Ed. Craig A. Evans and Stanley E. Porter. Downers Grove, IL: InterVarsity, 2000.
DPL	*Dictionary of Paul and His Letters.* Ed. Gerald F. Hawthorne, Ralph P. Martin, and Daniel G. Reid. Downers Grove, IL: InterVarsity Press, 1993.
DRev	*Downside Review*
DSD	*Dead Sea Discoveries*
DTT	*Dansk Teologisk Tidsskrift*
EHRel	Études d'Histoire des Religions
EKKNT	Evangelisch-Katholischer Kommentar zum Neuen Testament
Enc	*Encounter*
EphLit	*Ephemerides Liturgicae*
ÉPROER	Études préliminaires aux religions orientales dans l'empire romain
EpwRev	*Epworth Review*
ErAuf	*Erbe und Auftrag*
ErIsr	*Eretz-Yisrael*
ESEC	Emory Studies in Early Christianity
EspV	*Esprit et Vie*
EstBib	*Estudios Bíblicos*
ETL	*Ephemerides Theologicae Lovanienses*
ETR	*Études Théologiques et Religieuses*
EvK	*Evangelische Kommentare*
EvQ	*Evangelical Quarterly*
ExpT	*Expository Times*
F&M	*Faith & Mission*
FoiVie	*Foi et Vie*
FR	*Fourth R*
FreiRund	*Freiburger Rundbrief*
FRLANT	Forschungen zur Religion und Literatur des Alten und Neuen Testaments
FZPhTh	*Freiburger Zeitschrift für Philosophie und Theologie*
GNS	Good News Studies

GosPersp	*Gospel Perspectives.* 6 vols. Ed. R. T. France and David Wenham. Sheffield: JSOT Press, 1980-1986.
GR	*Greece & Rome*
GRBeit	*Grazer Beiträge*
GRBS	*Greek, Roman and Byzantine Studies*
GTT	*Gereformeerd Theologisch Tijdschrift*
HDBull	*Harvard Divinity Bulletin*
HDR	Harvard Dissertations in Religion
Hen	*Henoch*
Hermeneia	Hermeneia — A Critical and Historical Commentary on the Bible
HeyJ	*Heythrop Journal*
Hok	*Hokhma*
Hor	*Horizons*
HR	*History of Religions*
HS	*Hebrew Studies*
HSS	Harvard Semitic Studies Series
HThKNT	Herders theologischen Kommentar zum Neuen Testament
HTR	*Harvard Theological Review*
HTS	Harvard Theological Studies
HTS/TS	*HTS Teologiese Studies/Theological Studies*
HUCA	*Hebrew Union College Annual*
HvTSt	*Hervormde Teologiese Studies*
IBR	Institute for Biblical Research
IBS	*Irish Biblical Studies*
ICC	International Critical Commentaries
IEJ	*Israel Exploration Journal*
IgViv	*Iglesia Viva*
IJSocLang	*International Journal of the Sociology of Language*
Imm	*Immanuel*
Int	*Interpretation*
IsNumR	*Israel Numismatic Research*
ITS	*Indian Theological Studies*
JAAR	*Journal of the American Academy of Religion*
JANESCU	*Journal of the Ancient Near Eastern Society of Columbia University*
JATS	*Journal of the Adventist Theological Society*
JBL	*Journal of Biblical Literature*
JBLMS	Journal of Biblical Literature Monograph Series
JBQ	*Jewish Bible Quarterly*
Jeev	*Jeevadhara*
JerPersp	*Jerusalem Perspective*
JES	*Journal of Ecumenical Studies*
JESHO	*Journal of the Economic and Social History of the Orient*
JETS	*Journal of the Evangelical Theological Society*
JExpPsyc	*Journal of Experimental Psychology*
JFSR	*Journal of Feminist Studies in Religion*
JGRCJ	*Journal of Greco-Roman Christianity and Judaism*
JHC	*Journal of Higher Criticism*
JHS	*Journal of Hellenic Studies*

JIHist	*Journal of Interdisciplinary History*
JJS	*Journal of Jewish Studies*
JJT	*Josephinum Journal of Theology*
JNSL	*Journal of Northwest Semitic Languages*
JPFC	*The Jewish People in the First Century: Historial Geography, Political History, Social, Cultural and Religious Life and Institutions.* 2 vols. Ed. S. Safrai and M. Stern with D. Flusser and W. C. van Unnik. Section 1 of Compendia Rerum Iudaicarum ad Novum Testamentum. Vol. 1: Assen: Van Gorcum & Comp., B.V., 1974; Vol. 2: Philadelphia: Fortress, 1976.
JPJ	*Journal of Progressive Judaism*
JQR	*Jewish Quarterly Review*
JR	*Journal of Religion*
JRS	*Journal of Roman Studies*
JSHJ	*Journal for the Study of the Historical Jesus*
JSJ	*Journal for the Study of Judaism in the Persian, Hellenistic, and Roman Periods*
JSNT	*Journal for the Study of the New Testament*
JSNTSup	Journal for the Study of the New Testament Supplements
JSOTSup	Journal for the Study of the Old Testament Supplements
JSP	*Journal for the Study of the Pseudepigrapha*
JSQ	*Jewish Studies Quarterly*
JSS	*Journal of Semitic Studies*
JTS	*Journal of Theological Studies*
JTSA	*Journal of Theology for Southern Africa*
KEKNT	Kritisch-exegetischer Kommentar über das Neue Testament, begründet von H. A. W. Meyer
LCL	Loeb Classical Library
LD	Lectio Divina
LEC	Library of Early Christianity
LNTS	Library of New Testament Studies
LPSt	Library of Pauline Studies
LS	*Louvain Studies*
LTP	*Laval Théologique et Philosophique*
LTQ	*Lexington Theological Quarterly*
LUOSM	Leeds University Oriental Society Monograph
MBPS	Mellen Biblical Press Series
MNTC	Moffatt New Testament Commentary
MT	*Ministry Today*
NAC	New American Commentary
NCamBC	New Cambridge Bible Commentary
NCBC	New Century Bible Commentary
NEA	*Near Eastern Archaeology*
NedTT	*Nederlands Theologisch Tijdschrift*
Neot	*Neotestamentica*
NHLE	Nag Hammadi Library in English
NICNT	New International Commentary on the New Testament
NIGTC	New International Greek Testament Commentary
NIVAC	NIV Application Commentary

NovT	*Novum Testamentum*
NovTSup	Supplements to Novum Testamentum
NRTh	*Nouvelle Revue Théologique*
NTG	New Testament Guides
NTIC	New Testament in Context
NTS	*New Testament Studies*
NTT	*Norsk Teologisk Tidsskrift*
NTTS	New Testament Tools and Studies
Numen	*Numen: International Review for the History of Religions*
NV	*Nova et Vetera*
OBT	Overtures to Biblical Theology
OCD	*The Oxford Classical Dictionary: The Ultimate Reference Work on the Classical World.* 3rd rev. ed. Ed. Simon Hornblower and Antony Spawforth. Oxford: Oxford University Press, 2003.
OCPHS	Oxford Centre for Postgraduate Hebrew Studies
OEANE	*The Oxford Encyclopedia of Archaeology in the Near East.* Ed. Eric M. Meyers. 5 vols. New York: Oxford University Press, 1997.
OJRS	*Ohio Journal of Religious Studies*
OTP	*The Old Testament Pseudepigrapha.* 2 vols. Ed. James H. Charlesworth. Garden City, NY: Doubleday & Company, 1983-1985.
PAAJR	*Proceedings of the American Academy for Jewish Research*
PAST	Pauline Studies
PastPsy	*Pastoral Psychology*
PEQ	*Palestine Exploration Quarterly*
Phil	*Philologus*
PIBA	*Proceedings of the Irish Biblical Association*
POTTS	Pittsburgh Original Texts and Translations Series
PSB	*Princeton Seminary Bulletin*
PTMS	Pittsburgh Theological Monograph Series
PzB	*Protokolle zur Bibel*
Qad	*Qadmoniot*
QC	*Qumran Chronicle*
R&T	*Religion & Theology*
RB	*Revue Biblique*
RBL	*Review of Biblical Literature*
RefR	*Reformed Review*
REJ	*Revue des Études Juives*
RelSRev	*Religious Studies Review*
ResQ	*Restoration Quarterly*
RevExp	*Review and Expositor*
RevFSoc	*Revue française de Sociologie*
RevQ	*Revue de Qumran*
RevRabbJud	*Review of Rabbinic Judaism*
RevScRel	*Revue des Sciences Religieuses*
RHPR	*Revue d'histoire et de philosophie religieuses*
RHR	*Revue de l'histoire des religions*
RivB	*Rivista Biblica*
RMPhil	*Rheinisches Museum für Philologie*

RocT	*Roczniki Teologiczne*
RocTK	*Roczniki Teologiczno-Kanoniczne (= RocT)*
RRéf	*Revue Réformée*
RRT	*Reviews in Religion and Theology*
RSLR	*Rivista di Storia e Letteratura Religiosa*
RSPT	*Revue des Sciences Philosophiques et Théologiques*
RSR	*Recherches de Science Religieuse*
RTL	*Revue Théologique de Louvain*
RuBL	*Ruch Biblijny i Liturgiczny*
SBET	*Scottish Bulletin of Evangelical Theology*
SBFLA	*Studii Biblici Franciscani Liber Annuus*
SBLAcBib	Society of Biblical Literature Academia Biblica
SBLBMI	Society of Biblical Literature Bible and Its Modern Interpreters Series
SBLDS	Society of Biblical Literature Dissertation Series
SBLMS	Society of Biblical Literature Monograph Series
SBLSBS	Society of Biblical Literature Sources for Biblical Study/SBL Resources for Biblical Study
SBLSemS	Society of Biblical Literature Semeia Studies
SBLSP	Society of Biblical Literature Seminar Papers
SBLSymS	Society of Biblical Literature Symposium Series
SBLTT	Society of Biblical Literature Texts and Translations
SBLWGRW	Society of Biblical Literature Writings from the Greco-Roman World
SBT	Studies in Biblical Theology
ScEs	*Science et esprit*
SCI	*Scripta Classica Israelica*
ScrB	*Scripture Bulletin*
ScrTh	*Scripta Theologica*
SEÅ	*Svensk Exegetisk Årsbok*
SecCent	*Second Century*
Sem	*Semitica*
SJFWJ	Studia Judaica: Forschungen zur Wissenschaft des Judentums
SHR	Studies in the History of Religions, Supplements to Numen
SIDIC	Journal of the Service Internationale de Documentation Judeo-chrétienne
SJLA	Studies in Judaism in Late Antiquity
SJOT	*Scandinavian Journal of the Old Testament*
SJT	*Scottish Journal of Theology*
SLJT	*Saint Luke's Journal of Theology*
SNTSMS	Society for New Testament Studies Monograph Series
SNTSU	*Studien zum Neuen Testament und seiner Umwelt*
SocAn	*Sociological Analysis*
SP	Sacra Pagina
SPhilA	*Studia Philonica Annual (Studia Philonica)*
SPhilMon	Studia Philonica Monographs
SR/SR	*Studies in Religion/Sciences religieuses*
SSAMD	Sage Series on African Modernization and Development
ST	*Studia Theologica*
STDJ	Studies on the Texts of the Desert of Judah
STK	*Svensk Teologisk Kvartalskrift*

StPB	Studia Post-Biblica
SUNT	Studien zur Umwelt des Neuen Testaments
SWJT	*Southwestern Journal of Theology*
T&K	*Texte & Kontexte*
TANZ	Texte und Arbeiten zum neutestamentlichen Zeitalter
TBei	*Theologische Beiträge*
TDNT	*Theological Dictionary of the New Testament.* 10 vols. Ed. Gerhard Kittel and Gerhard Friedrich. Trans. Geoffrey W. Bromiley. Grand Rapids: Eerdmans, 1964-1976.
ThTo	*Theology Today*
TJ	*Trinity Journal*
TJT	*Toronto Journal of Theology*
TLZ	*Theologische Literaturzeitung*
TNTC	Tyndale New Testament Commentaries
TQ	*Theologische Quartalschrift*
TTE	*The Theological Educator*
TTKi	*Tidsskrift for Teologi og Kirke*
TUMSR	Trinity University Monograph Series in Religion
TynBul	*Tyndale Bulletin*
TZ	*Theologische Zeitschrift*
UNDCSJCA	University of Notre Dame Center for the Study of Judaism and Christianity in Antiquity
USFISFCJ	University of South Florida International Studies in Formative Christianity and Judaism
USQR	*Union Seminary Quarterly Review*
VC	*Vigiliae Christianae*
VT	*Vetus Testamentum*
WBC	Word Biblical Commentary
WTJ	*Westminster Theological Journal*
WUNT	Wissenschaftliche Untersuchungen zum Neuen Testament
WW	*Word and World*
YCS	*Yale Classical Studies*
ZABR	*Zeitschrift für Altorientalische und Biblische Rechtsgeschichte*
ZAW	*Zeitschrift für die Alttestamentliche Wissenschaft*
ZDMG	*Zeitschrift der Deutschen Morgenländischen Gesellschaft*
ZDPV	*Zeitschrift des Deutschen Palästina-Vereins*
ZNT	*Zeitschrift für Neues Testament*
ZNW	*Zeitschrift für die Neutestamentliche Wissenschaft*
ZPE	*Zeitschrift für Papyrologie und Epigraphik*
ZRGG	*Zeitschrift für Religions- und Geistesgeschichte*

Acknowledgements

Special thanks to Eerdmans and especially Michael Thomson for welcoming this manuscript; to Jenny Hoffman and others for their editorial work; also to Diane Chen, my esteemed colleague in New Testament at Palmer Seminary, for her helpful feedback on it. I am also grateful to Richard Bauckham, Craig Evans, and others whose comments prompted me to undertake this book. I also gratefully acknowledge permission from Hendrickson Publishers to reuse relevant material from my John and (forthcoming) Acts commentaries (especially, though not exclusively, in chs. 6-8, 10). Many other parts of this volume build on material found in my Matthew commentary for Eerdmans.

Preface

When scholars speak of "historical Jesus research," they mean especially what we can infer about Jesus from purely historical study. Yet a major key to how we reconstruct the historical Jesus involves the sources we use to decide what we know about him. Scholars who depend largely on sources from the second century (such as the *Gospel of Thomas*) or later (such as the *Secret Gospel of Mark*, probably a twentieth-century forgery) will reconstruct the Jesus of history differently than scholars who depend primarily on Mark, Luke, and Matthew. The central and most important part of this book thus focuses especially on the questions of our sources, particularly on the potential reliability of our earliest sources.

Beyond that, this book samples some key themes, sayings, and actions that we can attribute to Jesus with a high degree of probability. It should be understood that when historians speak in terms of probability, we speak only of what can be ascertained by historical methods. We lack historical evidence for most of what has happened in history; no one claims that nothing happened except what we can demonstrate by historical means. As scholars often point out, studies concerning the historical Jesus merely sort available historical evidence according to historical methods; they cannot bring us fully face-to-face with the Jesus who lived, taught, and died in the first century CE. They are useful, however, in providing a way that historians *as* historians can talk about Jesus, and a critical minimum of assumptions that both Christians and non-Christians can use in dialogue about Jesus.

Dedication

I have dedicated this book to Ed Sanders and Jim Charlesworth. I had once dreamed of studying with Geza Vermes and especially E. P. Sanders at Oxford, but, knowing that this dream was financially impossible for me, I applied instead to Princeton, Duke, and Yale. Of the three, Princeton was initially my first choice, because I desired to study with James Charlesworth; yet I ended up at Duke, which had its own strong set of advantages (not least of which was that they accepted me into their program). Providentially (from my perspective), Ed later interviewed at Duke, and I met him when, as Orval Wintermute was giving him a tour of the campus, they visited the classics reading room where I was then working through Epictetus.

After Ed took the position at Duke, I had the privilege of being his graduate assistant, hence hearing him engage undergraduates as well as my fellow graduate students. From one of his earlier books, I had expected him to be harsh, but soon discovered that some of his more graphic statements were intended rhetorically, to hold attention (not infrequently in a humorous way). He was thoroughly supportive of his students, fair toward us when we disagreed, and has remained kind and supportive in the years following. I do not expect him to agree with everything in this book (though I think I have agreed with him more often than disagreed), but I trust that he will recognize his seminal influence on me, as well as on a generation of scholars working in Jesus research from an especially Jewish context.

I met James Charlesworth briefly when I visited Princeton before my doctoral work, but have gotten to know him more fully in more recent years. Although I did not have the privilege of studying with him in person, he has nevertheless shown great kindness and generosity in welcoming my scholarship. His work on different aspects of early Judaism and Jesus research, as well as his collaboration with and organization of a broad range of scholars for numerous important projects, has likewise helped to shape the current generation of scholarship in these areas. (Not least, Jim's industry in organizing the massive Pseudepigrapha project has preserved many of us from depending too much on earlier translations published nearly a century ago.) Again, I do not presume that either scholar will agree with every decision I have made in the book (no two scholars agree on everything anyway),[1] but I remain grateful for their example and support.

This Book's Genesis

A range of ancient sources from treaties to forensic speeches often opened with a narrative explaining the events leading up to the present situation. Such an explanatory narrative seems in order here.

This book would not exist apart from conversations with Richard Bauckham and Craig Evans in April 2007. This book rests especially on detailed research into the Gospels, research with which some of my earlier readers will be familiar. I had already invested considerable time in historical Jesus scholarship, but (despite a publisher's urging) had long refused to add to the plethora of books on the subject. Instead, I published my research on the subject in my Matthew and John commentaries (in the introduction and appropriate passages).[2] Nevertheless, I hoped that my research would provide useful fodder for others working in the discipline, including those addressing some of the misinformation popularly propagated about Jesus in recent years, which has often ignored his Jewish setting.

Over the years, though, I discovered that new historical Jesus research often neglects commentators' contributions (sometimes even while offering the same arguments). It took me a few years to realize that the field is too overwhelmed with explicit discussions of "Jesus research" for many specialists to have time to explore most commentaries in depth, despite the textual nature of most of our best sources.[3] As I myself am learning, it is impossible for a readable book to engage all that has been published on the subject.

Soon after I began to recognize this situation, James Charlesworth kindly invited me to present a paper synopsis on "Luke-Acts and the Historical Jesus" at the Second Princeton-Prague Symposium on the Historical Jesus. I profited from dialogue with many other scholars there (too many for me to mention here individually, though the published works of some are cited in this book), but it was a stray comment behind me that compelled me to write on the topic. "He just writes commentaries," one scholar noted. "If you want those in the historical Jesus field to read your work, you don't stick it in commentaries." I am not certain that he was referring to me; I was not the only commentator present. But I found the remark's truth applicable to myself in any case.

As I conversed afterward separately with Craig Evans and Richard Bauckham, I suggested that the usefulness of my historical Jesus research was proving limited because I had dealt with it only text-by-text in commentaries, or in my commentary introductions. I had written more than a single book's worth of discussion on the subject, but not in a discrete book devoted to the topic. These two friends each honestly challenged me to put such research into a "historical Jesus" book. Their urging proved persuasive, against my prior inclination (I had been hoping to start work on another project, now unhappily deferred).

This book at numerous points thus often develops, sometimes at greater or lesser length, research found in my commentaries on Matthew, John, and Acts, as well as adding newer material focused on this topic. (I am grateful to both Eerdmans and Hendrickson for permitting me to recycle and augment relevant material in my commentaries published by them.) Some of my insights, put into this book now in 2008, may not seem as "new" or "fresh" as they would have in the mid-90s (e.g., on matters of oral transmission in Mediterranean antiquity or ancient historiography).[4] I ask the reader only to keep in mind that most of those particular insights do appear in my earlier commentaries, although I have since developed them. I believe that the combination of arguments here will in any case prove useful.

When I began planning this work, I had intended a style in some ways comparable to John Dominic Crossan's *Historical Jesus*, except much shorter and with much fuller documentation. Although providing fuller documentation would not be difficult, I have failed to achieve the brevity I had intended, despite some limitations noted in the following introduction. I might thus revisit this material in a more popular work at a later time.

Introduction

Some more skeptical scholars consider "uncritical" other scholars who believe that much of the story of Jesus happened anything like how it appears in the traditional Gospels. Yet these skeptical scholars have often uncritically accepted sources or hypotheses on far less evidence than the reports available in our traditional Gospels. (Some of these scholars built much, for example, on the *Secret Gospel of Mark,* now shown to be a recent forgery.)

For a scholar who disagrees with more skeptical scholars to be genuinely uncritical would mean that she is unaware of the skeptical scholars' arguments and has never thought through her own. For more skeptical scholars to deride less skeptical scholars as uncritical simply because the latter do not find the former's arguments persuasive is to substitute name-calling for dialogue. This is what we call an "ad hominem argument," and ad hominem arguments certainly are not good logic (sometimes employed most vociferously, in fact, where the evidence is weakest). Some leading scholars in the field warn that no one is free from assumptions, and that the presuppositions of skeptics are no more value-free than those of believers.[1]

In fact, as most scholars recognize, we cannot know anything very specific about Jesus (excluding, say, his Palestinian Jewish environment) apart from the earliest documents that tell us about him.[2] Reports about Jesus include a brief report in Josephus, mention in two Roman historians, perhaps a few snippets of information here and there, but especially and at significant length early Christian tradition. That is, those most apt to preserve reports about Jesus were those to whom he most mattered — his followers. (We know far less about various other Judean prophets like Theudas precisely because no movement persisted interested in preserving their teachings. Why a movement persisted in the case of Jesus rather than Theudas is a different question worthy of mention in ch. 22.) We may talk about his followers' "biases" toward him, but ultimately we have little beyond these sources to work with, and if we want to talk about the "historical Jesus," we must focus on the nature of our sources.

In the end, our most complete sources are the traditional ones, though we must approach them with critical acumen. How historically reliable are these "best" sources? That question is the primary subject of this book.

Limitations of This Book

Given the size of the book, I have had to defer one major topic (questions concerning Gospel reports of miracles) for a separate work. Moreover, to keep the book within its promised size constraints, I have focused on several key themes, rather than trying to treat the subject exhaustively. That is, I have neither tried to survey all that has been written (I confess this with genuine apologies to those with whose works I have failed to engage) nor tried to evaluate every incident or saying in the gospel tradition (despite offering a number of examples).[3] In contrast to my more detailed work on the Gospels, I am not working pericope by pericope here.

Nor am I taking time to challenge attempts to harmonize all details in the Gospels; I am taking for granted that my readers know better. Students regularly consult synopses on the Gospels, comparing and contrasting parallel pericopes; they are thus aware that the Gospel writers both draw on a common pool of information at many points, and also exercise literary freedoms uncharacteristic of modern (though, I will argue, not ancient) writers on historical topics. To take one graphic example, whereas Mark (reflecting his Palestinian tradition) reports supplicants digging through a roof to reach Jesus, in Luke they tear off the roof tiles — an image more understandable to Luke's northern Mediterranean audience.[4] I think it is fair to surmise that those who protest the theological impossibility of such differences have never taken time to honestly and closely compare parallel texts in the Gospels.

For the sake of space, I will not seek to demonstrate such points that are self-evident in the Gospels themselves and barely ever in dispute among biblical scholars. Rather, I will argue instead that such adaptations appear within the acceptable bounds of ancient biography, historiography, and oral tradition. Yet I also wish to emphasize that the Gospels, like comparable ancient works, contain such adaptations *in contrast to* a novelistic, wholesale creation of events. Because works with historical interest and focused on recent events were expected to report genuine events, but had some flexibility in how they reported them, my focus is largely on events and patterns of teaching rather than on details. The clear evidence for historical tradition in the Gospels (not least being the conspicuous dependence of Luke and Matthew on sources) rules out assigning them to the genre category of novel, and thus invites us to explore the ways they used historical tradition where we can test this use.

I am not attempting to survey all works on the historical Jesus, which continue to be published at a rapid rate. While interacting with secondary literature on a subject is an important scholarly enterprise, it is not the purpose of this book. Some important works (such as A.-J. Levine's *Misunderstood Jew*) came to my attention too late in the research process; many others are excluded neither for reasons of chronology nor content, but simply because interacting with further conversation partners than I already had would have taken this book in a direction different from its intended purpose.

I also do not intend to interact with Bart Ehrman's textual objections to the reliability of the early Christian sources that include the Gospels, since these objections are not relevant to the main thrust of this book. One need not argue that the entire text of the Gospels as we have them is accurate; most scholars, in fact (including most conservative ones), will agree with most of Ehrman's major textual decisions (e.g., the inauthenticity of Mk 16:9-20 or Jn 7:53–8:11).[5] Observing that most scholars have not been driven to agnosticism by these textual issues, one scholar suggests that Ehrman's agnostic response to them reflects his rigidly conservative background; if the text is *either* completely right *or* completely wrong, Ehrman's skepticism is a logical conclusion. Most biblical scholars do not insist on such a forced choice, just as most historians would not.[6] (Ehrman himself has more recently attributed his agnosticism to the problem of suffering in the world, which appears to me to make far more understandable sense as an objection, though not one that draws on his text-critical expertise.)

Even if the textual situation were far more muddled than it is, what we have is *sufficient* for general conclusions. For example, this book will later point to a number of Jewish parallels with Jesus' teachings, parallels hardly introduced to the Gospels by later Egyptian Christian scribes![7]

The Book's Objective

Although the book involves scholarly work in ancient sources, I have tried to avoid extensive technical jargon from my guild (at least without explaining it first). I have tried to keep the book short and understandable enough to be useful not only to scholars but to students and former students of the subject, as well as others sufficiently interested in the topic to engage ancient sources.[8]

Let me explain first what I am *not* doing. First, my focus will be on the historical sources more than reconstructing yet another new portrait of Jesus. In the second part of the book I will provide a sketch of some of what we can say about Jesus historically based on our sources. Before turning to that, however, I must first establish which sources are genuinely reliable, the extent to which they are reliable, and why they are reliable to that extent. Even in the second part of the book, one of my primary objectives is to show that our sources frequently fit Jesus' context and the most plausible historical reconstructions of Jesus' ministry and plan.

Second, in contrast to my attempts in some of my more detailed scholarly work to interact with the majority of scholars writing on the subject, I have drawn the net more narrowly here in hopes of keeping this work briefer and more readable. The interested reader can find many other useful works that survey Jesus scholarship,[9] work I do not seek to duplicate here.

Third, although I have elsewhere defended the likelihood of substantial historical information in the Fourth Gospel,[10] I draw on that argument very rarely here, for two reasons: (1) The book already has grown longer than my prospectus to the publisher promised, and readers have access to my arguments concerning John's Gospel elsewhere; and (2) There is sufficient material in the more widely accepted Synoptic sources to make the book's point. John's Gospel is different from the others and poses special problems, and there are enough issues of controversy involved in the present discussion that it seemed superfluous to add another one.[11]

Fourth, I should make clear for other readers what scholars often take for granted. As scholars often point out,[12] claims based on research concerning the "historical Jesus" are not intended to be identical to claiming a complete or even representative knowledge of the Jesus who lived in the first century. What can be known of Jesus through historical methods, like what can be known of almost anyone by means of such methods, is only a shadow of how the person would have been experienced by those who knew the person.[13]

The historical enterprise proceeds based on probabilities and works from a limited base of evidence; it is therefore limited in the claims it makes. (It is certainly not identical with what most believers mean by a "faith" perspective, although this difference of approach does not mean that historians must denigrate a faith perspective in its own sphere.)[14] As Gerd Theissen and Annette Merz point out, historical research by virtue of its character does not "say, 'That's what it was', but, 'It could have been like that on the basis of the sources.'"[15] Or as James Charlesworth puts it, "Historical research is scientific by method but not by conclusion; the historian at best can provide us not with certainty but with probability."[16] John Meier, too, reckons that the historical method can give us only a partial picture of the Jesus who lived in history.[17]

Beyond this observation, reconstructions vary widely based on whether we use minimalist historical criteria (admitting only the most certain evidence), a more maximalist approach (admitting any evidence not clearly inadmissible), or some approach in between these two extremes. Minimalists and maximalists both keep us honest about the outer limits of our historical evidence. The former, for example, help us not to assume more certainty for the elements used for our reconstruction than is publicly defensible; the latter invite us to work creatively with as much evidence as possible to produce a cohesive portrait rather than arguing from silence beyond the boundaries of our knowledge. Scholars may hold various personal convictions (whether religious or not), but we use the constraints of historical method so that we can dialogue with others who may differ from our other assumptions while we nevertheless work together academically on the basis of shared methodological assumptions.

Like all scholars (though I think not *more* than most scholars), I write with my own presuppositions. For those who are interested in the question, I began my interest in questions about religion and, to a much lesser extent, biblical perspectives from a position of extreme (though not totally closed-minded) skepticism, as an atheist. As one who is now a Christian I approach the subject with a special interest I previously lacked, but an interest that I believe makes me more rather than less committed to investigating genuine historical information about Jesus. When I was an atheist I never imagined that my life would take this turn, but I harbor no regrets that it has. Even when I was an atheist I valued pursuing truth, regardless of where it might lead.

Jesus and Judaism

I believe that reasons for my emphasis on Jewish sources in this volume should be evident. Whatever else scholars may say about Jesus with confidence, we certainly can say that Jesus was Jewish. One problem in much modern New Testament scholarship is that scholars tend to be particularly competent *either* in the early Jewish context *or* in the larger Greco-Roman context of the New Testament. I trust that those who see my work on Acts (Hendrickson) or Paul's Corinthian correspondence (Cambridge) will recognize that I work in non-Jewish Greco-Roman sources as well as in Jewish ones. I trust that the early chapters of this book will demonstrate the same; while Jesus was a Galilean Jew, the finished form of our Gospels reflects approaches to genre that prevailed in the writers' own Diaspora (non-Palestinian) setting. Yet the more Diaspora-friendly Gospels, written in Greek, are to at least that extent removed from the specific milieu in which Jesus primarily ministered. One therefore expects more Palestinian Jewish elements to reflect prior tradition.

I prefer a more specifically Jewish context for studying Jesus historically not because I have not studied the other sources, but for two methodological reasons: First, Jesus was a Galilean Jew, for whom Palestinian Jewish sources provide the closest cultural context. Second, as I inductively worked through ancient literature over the years, I often found much closer Palestinian Jewish parallels to Jesus' speech and actions (sometimes down to turns of phrase) than in other sources. (By contrast, my non-Jewish sources proved more helpful for understanding early Christian writers addressing audiences with a larger Gentile membership.) Because Hellenism influenced Judaism far more than the reverse, sources with *mixed* influences (apart from some magical texts) are typically *Jewish,* not non-Jewish.

Of course, even Judean Judaism had a larger Greco-Roman context that should be taken into account, but scholars who have worked through only the non-Jewish sources are at a disadvantage in understanding Jesus in his context. (To give a specific example: most "Cynic" parallels for Jesus fit the image of a Jewish prophet better.) For the Gospels, written in Greek and addressing a more cosmopolitan audience, I do draw on the wider range of sources.

Although I employ the entire range of Jewish sources in seeking to understand Jesus' teaching, current debates compel me to offer a brief word of justification for one circle of these sources. Some scholars today are particularly skeptical of employing material from ancient rabbis, a skepticism that I must here briefly acknowledge and hence to which I must respond. It is certainly true that all rabbinic sources in their written form come from after the time of Jesus. (No rabbinic documents precede the early third century, although many traditions are earlier, especially from c. 70-c. 200.) Nevertheless, Jesus was a sage, and consequently some striking parallels appear with sayings of rabbis that are recorded only in later sources (as well as parallels with earlier sage material such as Sirach). Given the limitations of what sources have remained extant, close parallels in material that cannot depend on the Gospels may suggest common sources in earlier Jewish customs, story lines, figures of speech, reasoning patterns and so forth. I have argued at length elsewhere that these sources can be used to help us understand such early ideas or customs. (Later rabbis certainly were not normally deliberately echoing Jesus, and many commonalities prove too close for coincidence.) I have also suggested that New Testament scholars who avoid this material completely for chronological reasons have for the most part misunderstood the warnings about their abuse (which pertain to more particular kinds of information).[18] No major argument in the book rests on the dating of this material, however, and these remain simply one source of information among many. (Sometimes I cite them purely as illustrations of how early Jewish traditions documented elsewhere came to be fleshed out more concretely in these voluminous collections.)

Most importantly, it should be noted, even for those who disagree with my approach, that using such material to suggest that some customs or ideas were traditional in some Jewish circles differs substantially from a much greater anachronism I critique at some points in this book — namely, taking later Christian documents (whether gnostic or otherwise) and using them to reconstruct sources alleged to be superior to our extant first-century ones. I seek to give preference to the earlier sources (such as Josephus, Qumran or the Gospels), and secondarily to those later sources (here including rabbinic literature) that are independent (or almost completely independent) from Christian sources.

Notes about Style

In capitalizing the titles of "Gospels," I am following current literary convention, not asserting a theological position. My use of "c.e." refers to the "common era," a phrase many scholars use for the same period popularly designated as "a.d.," but without thereby implying a theological position ("Anno domini," "in the year of the Lord"). In using "Palestine," I am following the standard literary convention of most works in biblical studies for Judea, Galilee, and Samaria; I am not, as a reviewer once complained, making any political statement about modern Middle Eastern affairs. (This is also the case when in some contexts I employ the biblical designation "Israel" for the Jewish people.) Although some now use "Judean" for all first-century Jews (including those in the Diaspora), I simply follow the common usage here that is current at the moment without entering that debate.

Nonspecialist readers should also take note of some essential terms that will recur repeatedly in this book: "Synoptics" refers to the Gospels of Matthew, Mark, and Luke (called "synoptic" because they overlap so much). "Eschatology" usually refers to what pertains to the "end time," or to a future era distinct from the present one. "Tradition" refers to information passed on over time, typically orally. When historians speak of "prophets" and "healers," they normally are using categories from the movements they describe, rather than offering statements of their own belief.

Conclusion

My primary goal in this book is not so much to add another reconstruction of the "historical Jesus" (although I will expend much of the second half of the book suggesting where I believe the evidence of the best sources points in that regard). My primary goal is rather to investigate how much we can know from the best sources available, and to offer examples of how these sources provide us more adequate information about Jesus than many scholars think we have. If we focus on the earliest sources and approach them with the increased confidence that I believe they warrant, we will arrive at a fuller, more multifaceted picture of Jesus than some single-emphasis portraits of earlier scholarship have permitted.

SECTION I

DISPARATE VIEWS ABOUT JESUS

"Those who are fond of talking about negative theology can find their account here. There is nothing more negative than the result of the critical study of the Life of Jesus."

ALBERT SCHWEITZER[1]

"Even under the discipline of attempting to envision Jesus against his own most proper Jewish background, it seems we can have as many pictures as there are exegetes. . . . [Their] stunning diversity is an academic embarrassment. It is impossible to avoid the suspicion that historical Jesus research is a very safe place to do theology and call it history, to do autobiography and call it biography."

JOHN DOMINIC CROSSAN[2]

In this section I will merely summarize and evaluate some sample proposals in Jesus research. It is not my intention to engage all authors who have written important works on the subject;[3] others have provided more detailed, book-length surveys of the historical and present "quests" for Jesus.[4] For me to repeat their work, except as at most a thumbnail sketch, would digress too long from this book's primary purpose. I offer this survey of several views primarily to show the diversity of scholarly opinion, hence to demonstrate why one's choice of sources and methodology is extremely important.

Despite the limits of my survey, however, we can learn from history, including the history of scholarship, and this history in turn includes its record of failures. Academic history has passed a negative verdict on most of the past two centuries of "historical Jesus" research, which has more often than not replaced earlier conclusions with newer ones, only to find the newer ones themselves displaced.[5] While quests for the historical Jesus start with the reasonable assumption that later orthodox christology should not be read into our earliest accounts about Jesus, they have too often read Jesus in light of too narrow a background (e.g., only a revolutionary, solely a teacher, just a prophet, or exclusively some other category, but often not more than one at a time) or as a reflection of their own values.[6]

More recent scholarship has sometimes (though as we shall see, not always) avoided the pitfall of narrow reconstructions.[7] In our own partial reconstruction later in the book, we shall endeavor to avoid the forced category-choices and welcome whatever aspects of Jesus' activity the evidence of our best sources yields. Nevertheless, even such attempts to synthesize earlier insights inevitably inherit and make use of the categories of previous scholarship. Most helpfully, recent scholarship has increasingly (though not always) focused on the Galilean Jewish setting of Jesus, a perspective invaluable for reconstructing Jesus' true message and activity.

CHAPTER 1

The Development of Jesus Scholarship

Each of the next three chapters offers only the briefest summary of views, by way of introducing some of the diverse ideas about Jesus in the past few centuries of academic discussion. Although outsiders sometimes think of scholarship as monolithic (depending on how many books on the subject they have read), "historical Jesus" research has proved to be anything but monolithic. The "assured results" of one generation or school are usually challenged in the next.

John Dominic Crossan put the matter well nearly two decades ago: "*Historical Jesus research* is becoming something of a scholarly bad joke," due, he noted, to "the number of competent and even eminent scholars producing pictures of Jesus at wide variance with one another."[1] Consensus has been elusive,[2] as our summary of views in these next three chapters is intended to illustrate.

Likewise, whereas outsiders often think of scholarship as dispassionate and objective, scholarship is in fact often driven by scholars' assumptions, which are in turn often the product of the ideas dominant in their own era. Biographers and historians addressing other ancient figures might interpret their subjects sympathetically, but Jesus scholarship has developed this tendency more than most. In an era that emphasized Christian ethics, writers about Jesus often portrayed him as the epitome of such ethics. In a setting that emphasized a form of existentialism, some scholars presented him as existentialism's greatest voice. Today, too, we have our variety of contextually packaged, readily marketable "Jesus" figures.

While such mundane contextualizations are to be preferred to the Third Reich's "Aryan" Jesus, they still run a serious risk of distorting and malforming what we know about Jesus. Indeed, if we are interested in the Jesus who lived and died in first-century Galilee, we would do better to read him in the very context that the Reich Church most abhorred — Jesus' Judaism.[3]

Earlier Modern "Historical Jesus" Studies

The current quest — today almost a market — in "Jesus" research builds on a long modern tradition. Some of that tradition bespeaks the courage of inquirers willing to suffer for their convictions (whether against the hostility of theologians or that of skeptics); some of it warns of authors pandering to their market niches in the most profitable manner.

The Renaissance emphasis on a return to the sources invited scholars to look for the "original" Jesus behind the portrayals of Medieval dogma. While this inquiry initially remained a pious quest, it was inevitably shaped by the presuppositions about the nature of history with which its scholars worked. Thus sixteenth-century English Deists[4] worked with different presuppositions about what was "possible" than did those of more traditional Christian persuasion.

The radical Enlightenment's prejudice against divine or supernatural causation eventually shaped much of Jesus research. Although the reason that Albert Schweitzer's famous history of the Jesus quest[5] starts with Hermann Samuel Reimarus (1694-1768) may be that Reimarus fits the trajectory Schweitzer wished to emphasize, Reimarus offers an adequate beginning for our summary. Reimarus' work was a polemic rather than an objective historical study, and his work circulated openly only after his death.[6] Today scholars regard most of Reimarus' views as wrong, but we can appreciate at least his emphasis on Jesus' Jewish context (introduced by others before him).[7]

Yet once Reimarus' work pried open previously repressed academic possibilities, some others soon joined attempts to explain the gospel tradition without regard to the miracle claims so offensive to the radical Enlightenment understanding of "reason." Thus Karl Friedrich Bahrdt wrote of Essenes as a secret society that offered medical and psychosomatic cures. They and Jesus accommodated superstition, Bahrdt supposed, merely to communicate rational truth.[8] Likewise, Karl Heinrich Venturini opined that Jesus healed with medicaments, always carrying his medicine chest as he traveled around.[9] Both Bahrdt and Venturini seem to have conveniently overestimated ancient medical capabilities.

More influentially, David Friedrich Strauss (1808-74) endeavored to "demythologize" the gospel portrait of Jesus, seeking to recover the original story behind the later descriptions by stripping or explaining away what he deemed impossible. The "Jesus" such writers produced was a modern rational Jesus amenable to their own tastes.[10] Schweitzer contends that scholars in this "rational phase" of Jesus research sometimes made historically irrational choices (such as preferring John's testimony to that of the Synoptics) to achieve their portrait.[11]

Shaped by Romanticism, most nineteenth-century authors of "lives of Jesus" produced a romantic Jesus, a Jesus of noble sentiment who appealed to like-minded audiences (and, coincidentally, helped sell many of the authors' books). (Schweitzer complains that one of the most famous of these authors, Ernest Renan, was more interested in his literary public than in scientific objectivity.)[12] Although writers produced a vast number of these "lives," their basic character remained substantially the same.[13]

An Example: Adolf von Harnack's Civilized Jesus

One of the last great works in the tradition of nineteenth-century "liberal" lives of Jesus was that of Adolf von Harnack (1851-1930), one of the most revered academicians of his era. Harnack's work on the "essence of Christianity" (now available as *What Is Christianity?*) offered essentially an apologetic for liberal Christianity, that is, a Christianity that could accommodate the claims of his era's modernity.[14] Thus he sought to present the "gospel" in a form relevant to his own time, addressing objections posed by his milieu.[15] He placed heavy emphasis on cultural religion, regarding Protestantism as a notably German contribution to civilization.[16]

In keeping with the spirit of his day, he reduced the essential gospel to ethics,[17] and demythologized Jesus' message of the kingdom to God's rule in the individual heart[18] or religious enlightenment. Producing a Jesus in keeping with the values of his day, he notes that the true kernel of Jesus' teaching was far more modern than the ancient husk through which it came.[19] This quest for the true (modern) kernel seems to constitute his historical criterion for establishing the "oldest tradition" about Jesus.[20]

Harnack does view the more Jewish portrait of Jesus as earlier and more authentic to Jesus.[21] Nevertheless, he argues that the goal of Jesus' teachings, while nurtured in Judaism,[22] is safely beyond it.[23] Accommodating "modern" perspectives, he regards the belief that life has vanquished death as more important than anything that might have happened historically at Jesus' grave;[24] like many after him, he distinguishes between an objective, historical resurrection and the Easter faith.[25] Yet whatever Harnack's view of the matter theologically, his interpretation of the evidence is quite different from that of the "primitive" apostolic church he in some other respects valued. Historically, they did not separate their Easter faith from the claim that Jesus returned from the dead; mere hope in afterlife or returned spirits offended almost no one and would not have provided a defining boundary for the movement. Unfortunately, divesting the Jesus movement of such elements foreign to modern thought appears to have been part of the price of eliminating the offensive Jewish eschatology of Jesus and his first followers. While Harnack notes that Jesus and his disciples were bounded by their time,[26] it seems also the case that, despite occasional forays against the assumptions of his milieu,[27] Harnack was no less a child of his own, and unapologetically so.[28]

For all the positive elements in Harnack's perspectives, he could not have guessed the dangers that such enculturated Christianity would lead to with the "Aryan Christianity" of the Reich Church a generation later. Individualistic, inward religion may have its value, but it proved more malleable to the cultural demands of anti-Semitic nationalism than respect for a first-century Jewish sage would have.[29] This is not to blame Harnack or his peers for an outcome they could not have foreseen; it is to object to a vision of Jesus so wedded to our own cultural settings that we lose sight of Jesus' original historical (Jewish and Middle Eastern) setting. Harnack's optimistic Jesus, designed for modern western readers, perished in the bloodshed of the first world war.[30]

The Apocalyptic Jesus of Weiss and Schweitzer

In 1906 Albert Schweitzer's survey and devastating[31] critique of previous modern Jesus scholarship[32] put an end to much of the "Jesus" industry of his day. (Schweitzer was also a good marketer: he presented his own view as the natural product of the evolution of sound thinking.)[33] Although Schweitzer's survey of previous Jesus research was selective and somewhat tendentious, it was sufficient to establish his central point regarding the history of scholarship. His point was that Jesus scholars had produced a Jesus in their own image, to their own liking. Not unlike some preachers and perhaps a few scholars today,[34] they had used respect for Jesus to promulgate their own ideology.

Schweitzer's own portrait of Jesus drew from recent work by Johannes Weiss (1863-1914), who had argued, against his nineteenth-century predecessors, that Jesus proclaimed the world's imminent end, a prediction that then failed to occur. His emphasis on the future character of the "kingdom" Jesus proclaimed, based on Jesus' early Jewish context, offered an important challenge to his predecessors' "liberal" lives of Jesus.[35] Weiss was not ignorant of his era's scholarship;[36] rather, he addressed particular questions precisely because these questions were being answered differently in his milieu.[37]

Eschatology (emphasis on the impending end of the age) was central in Weiss's reconstruction of Jesus' teaching. For example, he notes that Jesus' expression "Son of man" is eschatological imagery;[38] this perspective coheres with Jesus' proclamation of God's end-time kingdom. Weiss believes that Jesus expected the kingdom to come immediately (cf. Mk 13:32)[39] or in the next generation.[40]

Granted, Weiss sometimes overplayed eschatology. For example, he sometimes[41] may play down too much the rarer texts that could emphasize the presence of the kingdom;[42] for example, "entering the kingdom" in the present becomes for him merely "entering the way that leads to the kingdom."[43] Like some other "Jesus" scholars, Weiss sometimes draws the net of context too narrowly, in this case exploiting only apocalyptic background. Thus, for example, he traces Jesus' messianic consciousness to his consciousness of his sonship[44] in an apocalyptic context,[45] even though God's Fatherhood is a pervasive theme throughout Jesus' Jewish environment.[46]

Like Weiss, Schweitzer drew on Jesus' Jewish, and especially eschatological ("end-time"), environment to portray a more Jewish Jesus than the one embraced by some of his contemporaries, who were generally more interested in "relevant" theology or preaching. Similarly, Schweitzer shared many of the critical assumptions of his era's biblical scholarship,[47] though like Weiss, not always consistently.[48] He regards Jesus as apocalyptic rather than as a modern rationalist,[49] and observes that an eschatological outlook often suggests the authenticity of early traditions.[50] Unfortunately, like Weiss, he defines ancient Jewish perspectives too narrowly in terms of apocalyptic pseudepigrapha.[51] Nevertheless, scholars have often observed that, regardless of their excesses, "there is no going back behind Weiss and Schweitzer."[52]

Yet Schweitzer's own conclusions seemed disillusioning for both his own faith and that of many other liberal Christians: Jesus was a deluded (if heroic) apocalyptist dreamer.[53] Of course, Schweitzer found a friendlier way to put this: Jesus' spirit, in his useful teachings, lives on among his followers.[54] Schweitzer's emphasis on eschatology or Jesus' Jewish context would not necessarily have the same effect today. Whereas his generation had little use for eschatology, two world wars, rampant genocide and other factors have since reinvigorated it;[55] oppressed people naturally often resonate with the hopes of a better world more than content people do.[56] This was not, however, Schweitzer's milieu, and his emphasis on Jesus' eschatological framework was for him an act of brutal academic honesty. Eschatology did not "preach" well in his circles.

Bultmann

For some time after Schweitzer's critique, scholars generally showed much less interest in producing "lives" of Jesus or even producing much scholarship about Jesus' life.[57] Schweitzer's argument had decisively altered western liberal Jesus scholarship by producing a Jesus that seemed less useful to the theologians who made Jesus their primary concern. No longer did it appear possible to deny that Jesus' worldview was apocalyptic; yet liberal western academia deemed the apocalyptic worldview no longer relevant. (In fact this worldview was flourishing outside those circles, especially since the spread of dispensational premillennialism in the U.S.; but when academia took notice of such circles, its notice was not positive.) How could theologians reclaim a Jesus whose message was deemed so irrelevant to good theology?

Rudolf Bultmann sought to find a way.[58] He employed the critical tools of his day[59] (though, like most of his predecessors, he did use material in addition to "Q" and Mark).[60] Nevertheless, he remained deeply interested in relevance.[61] Whereas the "Aryan Christians" had tried to make Christianity relevant to a German nationalism recovering from international abuse after the first world war, Bultmann sought a different tack.[62] Bultmann's apologetic strategy was to demythologize Jesus' message to make it "relevant" for his day. Yes, the form of Jesus' message was apocalyptic, but the real nature of that message was existential: God coming as the demander.[63]

The Existential Jesus

While acknowledging Schweitzer's apocalyptic Jesus, Bultmann theologically circumvented it. Perhaps insufficiently heedful of Schweitzer's critique of non-apocalyptic Jesuses made in the interpreters' image,[64] Bultmann created a Jesus relevant to the reigning philosophic paradigm of his own day, especially at the University of Marburg, where he taught.[65] His Jesus preached an existential message akin to that of the university's renowned philosopher, Martin Heidegger.[66] Bultmann could then accommodate historical skepticism to the fullest, welcoming skeptics to the fold, because he had nothing theologically to lose from it.[67] History could not affect Jesus' existential message, and this translation for Bultmann's secular audience could make his Jesus appealing even to those for whom philosophic assumptions had rendered traditional faith impossible.

Bultmann felt that realized eschatology (the future promises fulfilled in the present) within the New Testament itself showed that the delay of Jesus' "return" had already led to this process of reinterpretation in the first century.[68] The problem, of course, is that in most NT documents this realized eschatology stands alongside and anticipates future eschatology as well (see e.g., Rom 8:23; 1 Cor 2:9-10; 15:50-54; Phil 1:23; 3:20-21). Bultmann often deployed a form of "content criticism" in which texts that disagreed with his interpretation were declared in conflict with the *genuine* spirit of New Testament theology.[69]

One danger in producing a Jesus relevant primarily to one's own era, whether "conservative," "liberal," or something else, is that this Jesus is ultimately not very relevant to other cultures or other eras.[70] It has not surprisingly proved much easier to recontextualize the Jesus of the Gospels for other settings than to recontextualize Bultmann's Jesus. Indeed, Bultmann's largely skeptical approach to history did not even leave enough information about the "original" Jesus for scholars to rework. Bultmann's critics complain that the existential approach to Jesus "dehistoricizes" Jesus, taking him out of his first-century context;[71] the relevance of an existential Jesus has naturally faded with the marketability of existentialism. Many have argued that Bultmann was obsessed with a now out-of-date worldview.[72]

De-Judaizing Jesus?

Just as earlier Jesus scholars selected those elements of the Gospels that fit their ideal portrait of Jesus, Bultmann could do much the same. While a better historical scholar than most of his predecessors, all he actually *needed* for his portrait of Jesus was the "existential" core of his teaching. He wondered if Palestinian Jewish Christianity would have really preserved much information about Jesus[73] (contrary to what we will observe about oral tradition in ch. 10). Although Bultmann allowed more of Jesus' "Jewishness" than had some of his predecessors,[74] his criterion of dissimilarity laid heavier emphasis on points where he thought that Jesus differed from his Jewish environment.[75] Thus, for example, his Jesus attacked the law as a formal legal authority[76] and is antithetical to the OT and contemporary Judaism.[77]

Moreover, although Bultmann had more knowledge of Judaism than some of his critics have implied,[78] it appears to have been limited and either second-hand or (often) sifted through severely distorted assumptions.[79] Most critically, the view of (rabbinic) Judaism he inherited from some of his teachers was excessively legalistic,[80] and no more than a shadow of what can now be known about real Judaism in Jesus' day (as many scholars would agree that Bultmann's Jesus was only a shadow of what can be known about the historical Jesus). Worse, Bultmann often uncritically stressed non-Jewish, "gnostic" elements in Christian origins, including a gnostic redeemer myth pieced together from disparate, much later sources.[81] If his minimalist historical Jesus was Jewish, nevertheless he spawned a movement the substance of which became unrecognizable to Judaism with astonishing swiftness.

When some lines of Jesus research today deemphasize Jesus' Jewishness in favor of Greek philosophic and other background, often producing a portrait of Jesus particularly "relevant" to its modern philosophic audience, one wonders how far we have come beyond either Bultmann or his pre-Schweitzer predecessors.[82] One need not agree with all of Schweitzer's views to appreciate his historical honesty.

While Bultmann's historical skepticism reduced interest in historical Jesus research among his followers, some of them revisited the subject. In 1953 Ernst Käsemann announced a new quest for the historical Jesus, and in 1956 another

Bultmannian, Günther Bornkamm, wrote a work about Jesus.[83] Such "Second Questers" did not venture as far beyond Bultmann as most of the so-called[84] "Third Questers" have, but returning to interest in the Jesus of history was at least an improvement (from historians' standpoint).

We will introduce recent views in the next two chapters, but will first turn our attention to what has usually been considered an idiosyncratic view from the 1960s. The purpose of this digression is to reinforce our larger portrait of the diversity within Jesus research.

Jesus the Revolutionary?

Several decades ago, S. G. F. Brandon envisioned Jesus as a zealot.[85] Such an approach was not entirely new; two centuries earlier, Reimarus had interpreted the kingdom against the backdrop of Jewish resistance against Roman oppression.[86] While viewing Jesus as a revolutionary would make sense of Jesus' execution and "kingdom" language, it is hardly the best explanation of these features. Most extant Jewish use of "kingdom" language is *not* linked to revolutionaries, and a number of prophetic figures (most obviously John the Baptist, as noted in Josephus)[87] managed to get martyred without leading military revolts. (Romans also suppressed most rebels *militarily,* unlike Jesus.)

Brandon's view is important to us not because it is widely held today; in its fullest form of "Jesus as zealot" it is in fact virtually dead. But Brandon's view illustrates the diversity within Jesus research, and also serves as a warning about the politics of the academy. Today, for example, there are scholars who make Jesus virtually a Cynic sage. Brandon's thesis may have been mistaken, but at least it exhibited the virtue of placing Jesus within a genuine first-century Jewish context, rather than importing a context that existed in Galilee barely if at all.

Was Jesus a Revolutionary?

Was Jesus a revolutionary? Against Brandon,[88] little evidence connects Jesus with insurrectionist activity; one can unfortunately argue almost any case when one rejects as unreliable the only historical evidence we have.[89] Revolutionary sentiments may have been widespread, shared even by many Pharisees and (before the war of 66-73 CE) some younger Sadducean priests. With that said, those actually directly involved in insurrectionary-type activity or even brigandage around the time of Jesus' ministry must have been at most a small percentage of the population (see Appendix 1).

Nevertheless, it is not difficult to see how some would have understood his popular appeal to the masses and open challenges to some social customs as potential political threats.[90] Indeed, his preaching about God's "kingdom" could not but have some sort of political implications,[91] whether achieved in the present or the (possibly near) future, through human agents or without them.[92] Contrary to the assumptions of some western academicians today, theology and politics were not mutually exclusive interests in antiquity[93] (or in some parts of the world today).

Yet Jesus' actions (discussed later in the book) place him closer to another category of activity of his day, namely, the paradigm that depended on God to intervene supernaturally to consummate his kingdom. Josephus reports several prophetic figures who sought not to attack Rome but to produce signs of divine deliverance; apparently they expected God to act on their behalf. Nevertheless, because they (in contrast to John or Jesus) had armed followers, Rome's soldiers intervened militarily; Jesus may have been more nonresistant than they. Similarly, Sanders[94] cites the repeated expectation in some strands of early Jewish literature that God would bring down a new Temple,[95] or fight for Israel and bring in the kingdom by his own power.[96] Jesus may have overturned tables in and pronounced judgment on the temple of his day to prepare the way for a new one, yet done so as a prophetic sign, expecting God himself to bring about the kingdom.

Assuming that Jesus waited on God to act, submitting (as we will argue later in the book) even to an execution that he might have been able to avoid, those interested in Jesus for theological questions will ask, "Did God act as Jesus expected?" Some, following Schweitzer's line of argument, contend that Jesus went to the cross as a deluded visionary, vainly hoping to provoke God's hand. (In this, he would be like prophetic figures soon after him who expected God to make the Jordan part or Jerusalem's walls collapse.)

Others, impressed by his teaching about a hidden kingdom (Mk 4:30-32) or the value of martyrdom (Mk 8:34-38), affirm instead that Jesus by dying accomplished exactly what he intended. One can affirm this much without asking the further theological question about whether God acted as Jesus expected, beyond Jesus' execution. Jesus presumably expected to be raised; most Palestinian Jews apparently expected resurrection and reward at the end of the age. If Jesus expected a vindication earlier than this, one cannot answer the theological question without examining the question of his resurrection (introduced in ch. 22; Appendix 8). In any case, we must at least leave open the possibility that Jesus intended to die a martyr's death in Jerusalem, and that he believed that this death would activate an important phase in God's plan.

Popular Views about Jesus

The context Brandon offers for Jesus may be inadequate, but it is not without all merit. Whatever Jesus' own intentions, some followers were likely attracted to the possibility of a charismatic figure strong enough not only to produce healings and exorcisms but to lead the people to political liberation (cf. Jn 6:15). In many cultures, oppressed peasants naturally sympathize with resistance movements, and some scholars have argued for such a situation in Judea,[97] most clearly in the first Judean revolt.[98]

This proposal is also useful in reminding us that Jesus was in fact executed as a revolutionary;[99] this role was a natural way for the elite to view, or at least to dispose of, a wilderness or Galilean prophet. That Jesus was executed on the charge of claiming "kingship" is virtually certain (see discussion in chs. 18, 21); and even a prophet figure passively awaiting God's intervention (as perhaps some of Josephus' sign-prophets were) could threaten the stability of society by stirring hopes of Rome's overthrow.

Yet at least some Judeans, like Josephus, apparently did not share this view of Jesus.[100] Josephus presents John the Baptist and Jesus differently from the wilderness prophets whose armed followers suggested a threat to the authorities. This evidence suggests that John and Jesus did not advocate violent revolution, despite the charge conveniently leveled against the popular teacher Jesus.[101] What survived of Jesus' teachings confirms this suggestion. As we shall argue later in the book, Jesus expected both a kingdom and a role for himself in that kingdom. But he expected this to occur solely by God's intervention, and voluntarily offered himself for martyrdom in expectation of that intervention.

Jesus on Nonresistance

The preserved sayings of Jesus do not naturally lend themselves to the interpretation that Jesus was a revolutionary,[102] apart from a few sayings that fit Jesus' use of hyperbole and shocking metaphor.[103] For example, the words that Mark attributes to Jesus on the week before his crucifixion, "Render to Caesar what is Caesar's" (Mk 12:17), do not sound like a revolutionary. Jesus' beatitudes may criticize oppression, but they emphasize the way of dependence on God rather than resistance or any attempt to seize the kingdom (Lk 6:20-23; especially Matt 5:3-12). Jesus teaches radical nonretaliation (Matt 5:38-47; 7:1; Lk 6:27-37). Although he was not unique in teaching against avenging oneself,[104] he was certainly emphatic about it.

Yet Jesus takes this ethic of nonretaliation to its furthest possible length when he invites disciples not only to refuse to strike back, but to rejoice when persecuted (Matt 5:10-12; Lk 6:22-23). One should accommodate oppressors[105] for the sake of peace, trusting in divine reward and vindication (Matt 5:39-48; 7:1//Lk 6:27-37). In enduring persecution, his disciples would follow the model of the earlier prophets (Matt 5:12//Lk 6:23),[106] a model amplified in Jewish tradition.[107] Linked with his other teachings about radical dependence on God (e.g., Matt 6:25-33//Lk 12:22-31), such passages suggest nonretaliation not simply for its own sake, but as an act of radical dependence on God rather than oneself.

As we shall see later, accepting suffering is precisely the behavior that Jesus himself models in the passion tradition; the gospel tradition as a whole is coherent on this point. At Gethsemane he refuses to resist (cf. the apparently multiply attested warning in Matt 26:52 and Jn 18:11).[108] Jesus and those of the Pharisees who advocated peace rather than revolution were ultimately vindicated when Rome brutally crushed the aspirations of the Jewish resistance in 66-73.[109]

Conclusion

The history of Jesus scholarship illustrates the wide range of views scholars have articulated about Jesus in recent centuries. Biases and the demands of constituency affect not only popular religion, but also academic Jesus research. The presuppositions with which we start tend to dictate the way that we select our evidence about Jesus, the context in which we read that evidence about Jesus, and consequently the conclusions to which we come about Jesus.

We have noted these tendencies in the liberal Jesus frequent in the Romantic era; in the apocalyptic Jesus of Weiss and Schweitzer; in the existential Jesus of Bultmann; and in the revolutionary Jesus of Brandon. Some of these approaches have offered more useful historical perspective on Jesus than others have, but all illustrate that the context in which we read our sources affects how we understand them. The following two chapters offer a few more examples of this diversity and this problem.

CHAPTER 2

Jesus the Cynic Sage?

"The historical Jesus was, then, a peasant Jewish Cynic. His peasant village was close enough to a Greco-Roman city like Sepphoris that sight and knowledge of Cynicism are neither inexplicable nor unlikely."

JOHN DOMINIC CROSSAN[1]

"Jesus' use of parables, aphorisms, and clever rejoinders is very similar to the Cynics' way with words. Many of his themes are familiar Cynic themes."

BURTON MACK[2]

". . . especially among certain authors now or formerly connected with the Jesus Seminar, emphasis on the Jewishness of Jesus is hardly a central concern. Whether one looks at the more serious works of writers like John Dominic Crossan and Burton L. Mack or the sensationalist popular works of authors like Robert W. Funk, one finds Jesus the Cynic philosopher or Jesus the generic Mediterranean peasant . . . largely overshadowing the specific 1st-century Palestinian Jew named Jesus."

JOHN P. MEIER[3]

Most of the approaches sampled in this chapter will be echoed later in this book less often than those treated in the following chapter. The authors surveyed here portray a Jesus who does not fit a first-century Jewish context nearly as convincingly as views to which we will turn in ch. 3. Not all of the sample views surveyed here are equally widely held among scholars, but they do illustrate the wide range of proposals that scholars have offered in recent decades.

Although the "Jesus Seminar" is somewhat of an amorphous group, it has popularized the idea of Jesus as a noneschatological sage, an image that can appeal to much of our modern culture without much translation. I use the Jesus Seminar to introduce my discussion of the Cynic Jesus of Crossan and especially that of Burton Mack.

The Noneschatological Jesus Seminar

If a revolutionary view of Jesus (such as we find in S. G. F. Brandon) takes Jesus' kingdom language too narrowly in one way, some others manage to take it still more narrowly in a different way. Indeed, whereas Brandon at least situated Jesus in a Jewish environment, these scholars have often severed him from that environment.

Marketable Relevance

In recent years, the "often-maligned Jesus Seminar"[4] has produced a non-eschatological Jesus that many scholars criticize as taking insufficient account of Schweitzer's critique of earlier "lives of Jesus." That is, their Jesus is not very Jewish,[5] not very eschatological (i.e., does not talk much about God's distinctly future activity), and suspiciously resembles the values of the scholars who depict him.[6] The divergence from Schweitzer proves to be no mere oversight, however; the Seminar admits an agenda to displace "Schweitzer's eschatological Jesus."[7]

The Jesus Seminar is popularly known for having voted with marbles on Jesus' sayings. (Although voting makes some sense,[8] the use of marbles in particular was probably designed partly for marketability, since it could readily attract media attention.)[9] More critically, the method of calculating these votes has been critiqued for its subjectivity. One critic offers an example: whereas 25% of the scholars voting on the assigned day thought that Jesus surely said Matt 25:29, and another 11% thought that he likelier than not said it (for over one-third in favor), a majority thought that he either did not or probably did not say it. Thus the Seminar's published conclusion was that Jesus did not utter the saying, even though a third of even the Seminar itself disagreed with that verdict.[10]

Emory professor Luke Timothy Johnson argues that the Jesus Seminar is "an entrepreneurial venture" that speaks not for major scholarly associations (such as SBL or SNTS) but is a "self-selected" group based largely on shared "goals and methods."[11] He notes that most major graduate academic institutions are unrepresented, that the Seminar lacks significant European representation, and that most participants have not produced major academic work in Jesus research. Moreover, well over half of the members have their doctorates from the five specific institutions where such ideas have flourished (especially from three of them, although certainly by no means do all the faculty at these institutions, still less all their graduates, hold such views).[12] (A member of the Jesus Seminar himself also laments the predominant cultural and gender homogeneity of the group.)[13] Johnson complains that the process is biased against the authenticity of Jesus' sayings[14] and that it has garnered attention by seeking the media coverage that most scholars have ignored.[15]

Whatever one makes of several aspects of Johnson's critique (some of the Seminar's "criteria" are more mainstream than others),[16] he is certainly correct that the Jesus Seminar's claim to speak for the broader range of scholarship is inaccurate. Unfortunately, the Seminar *does* publicly claim to speak for scholarship. Thus they hail their version as "the Scholars' Version," in contrast to other English translations (which they charge are theologically controlled).[17] They thereby concisely dismiss the scholarly integrity of hundreds of other NT scholars. Likewise, they contend, their acceptance of only 16% of the gospel accounts as historically accurate will not surprise "critical scholars," whom they define as "those whose evaluations are not predetermined by theological considerations."[18] Apparently they do not regard as genuinely critical or open-minded the majority of NT scholars who accept much larger amounts of the gospel material as reliable than the Seminar does. These "noncritical" scholars would include many who have published more extensive scholarly work on the subject (including many of the influential volumes cited in this book) than the vast majority of Jesus Seminar members have.

The Seminar in fact can accurately represent only its own narrower range of scholarship, though for much of the public its dominant voices apparently deliberately conflate its claims with the voice of scholarship more generally. For this radical group to claim to speak for Jesus scholarship more generally would be like a group of professors from fundamentalist institutions issuing a portrait of Jesus that would then be hailed as "the scholarly portrait." The problem is not such professors summarizing the views of their own group (which is their right), but the presentation of those views as a scholarly consensus. The Jesus Seminar does not have the right to speak for scholarship as a whole.[19]

The End for the End-Times?

I will not treat the Jesus Seminar in detail here, since its target audience has been the general public (especially through popular media); the scholarly guild advances ideas in different ways. But the Jesus Seminar does help introduce one of the issues on the table in this chapter. The Jesus Seminar claims to be representative of mainstream Gospels scholarship particularly in its skepticism concerning Jesus' eschatology — a claim that many other scholars reject.[20]

Johnson complains about a particular scholar's claim that most scholars today regard Jesus as noneschatological, pointing out that this supposed majority scholarly opinion is simply based on 59% of the Jesus Seminar, "a self-selected group of like-minded scholars (at most, seventy out of the 6,900 members of the Society of Biblical Literature)."[21] Indeed, a member of the Seminar helps explain how the Seminar's own perspective became so emphatically noneschatological: "When the cynic school prevailed, for example, in the voting at the Jesus Seminar, the apocalyptists quit coming; this further skewed the vote."[22]

Many scholars argue that, while scholarship after Schweitzer for a time abandoned Jesus the comfortable, noneschatological sage, the pre-Schweitzer position has made its comeback in circles like the Jesus Seminar.[23] The resulting experience of déjà vu has prompted one critic to remark, "There is something disturbingly familiar about a mildly reforming, sagacious teacher, who . . . does not use language and imagery that promises the reversal of the rulers of the world."[24] As John Meier, one of the most textually thorough scholars in Jesus research,[25] complains:

> A tweady poetaster who spent his time spinning out parables and Japanese koans, a literary aesthete who toyed with 1st-century deconstructionism, or a bland Jesus who simply told people to look at the lilies of the field — such a Jesus would threaten no one, just as the university professors who create him threaten no one.[26]

The Seminar's critics suggest that its view fails to explain how its harmless, noneschatological sage, like that of the nineteenth-century lives of Jesus, would get himself crucified.[27] E. P. Sanders complains that those uncomfortable with an eschatological Jesus who fit his milieu, followed John and left an eschatological church must instead resort to claiming "that everybody misunderstood Jesus completely." This is, he opines, a position based on wishful thinking without evidence.[28]

Ignoring Jewish Environment

In addition to challenging the eschatological content of some of Jesus' securest sayings (see ch. 17), the noneschatological Jesus suggested by such scholars ignores basic historical constraints such as Jesus' historical context. Jesus' radically eschatological predecessor John and his eschatological subsequent followers make a noneschatological Jesus highly improbable.[29] Some scholars try to counter this observation by making Jesus an opponent of John's eschatological approach. Since no extant saying of Jesus repudiates John's eschatology, they must make this argument by means of inference. They do so particularly by contending that Matt 11:11//Lk 7:28 denigrates John.[30] But this interpretation of the saying rests on inadequate understanding of ancient Jewish speech patterns; as we shall argue in our chapter on John the Baptist, this saying simply reflects standard Jewish rhetoric of praising others not by *denigrating* the point of comparison but by choosing a *positive* object of comparison.[31] Later Christians would not likely have conformed Jesus to John (the competition),[32] but his own contemporaries sometimes compared him with John (Mk 6:14-16; 8:28) or with Elijah (Mk 6:15; 8:28).[33]

Doubting Jesus' eschatological orientation is just a symptom of the larger problem of insufficient attention to Jesus' immediate Jewish environment. The older liberal view that the earliest views about Jesus' identity evolved from a Palestinian Jewish apocalyptist to a hellenistic divine man does not fit all the evidence (see ch. 19), but certainly fits better than the contemporary "Jesus Seminar's" essential reversal of the sequence, which must assume that later Christians Judaized Jesus.[34] Such an approach makes no sense of their world: in view of Roman anti-Judaism and the growing influence of Diaspora Christianity as years passed, inventing greater attachments to Judaism would be counterproductive to the movement.[35] Indeed, Paul, an early missionary to the Greek world, shares an apocalyptic worldview with much of Palestinian Judaism as much as two decades before Mark, our first extant Gospel.[36] Jesus' Jewish movement proclaimed a coming eschatological kingdom from the beginning. And apocalyptic and eschatological ideology was largely Jewish in the forms in which we have it in the Jesus movement.

Crossan's "Peasant Cynic"

Later in this chapter (and in ch. 4), we will treat a particularly extreme exponent of the "Cynic Jesus" thesis, namely Burton Mack. Here I will survey instead a position of John Dominic Crossan, namely that Jesus was a "peasant Jewish Cynic." This description of Jesus does not actually summarize all of Crossan's approach to Jesus,[37] and in critiquing it I do not imply disagreement with every contribution of Crossan to the historical Jesus discussion. Nevertheless, it constitutes one of Crossan's own summaries of his view in his most widely used "historical Jesus" book.[38] It thus provides a particularly useful illustration of a pole in the wide range of disparate views on the "Jesus" market today.

An assorted survey of basic but well-written information about the ancient Mediterranean world dominates the first part of Crossan's book.[39] Here Crossan simply lays the background for his approach to Jesus. Most of this background is unobjectionable, although some elements are closer to Jesus' specifically Judean context than others.[40] Crossan then turns to a survey of various types of ancient leaders: visionaries, teachers, revolutionaries, leaders of peasant protest, healers, magicians, prophets, bandits and would-be kings.[41] After this survey he finally turns to Jesus' teachings and activities,[42] his death,[43] and the resurrection experiences.[44] Thus perhaps 190 pages (less than 40% of the book) focus primarily on ancient sources about Jesus in particular, as opposed to the ancient world in general.[45] My point here is that Crossan, like many scholars today (including myself), places a heavy weight on Jesus' context. But on what aspects of Jesus' context does he focus?

We return now to Crossan's description of Jesus as a "peasant Jewish Cynic." By now it will be obvious that at least one element of Crossan's reconstruction is unobjectionable, namely, that Jesus was Jewish. It is thus the two other elements of the description that we must investigate. While scholars may debate whether or not Jesus was a "peasant" (depending largely on the meaning they assign to that designation), the title "Jewish Cynic" runs strongly against what we know of the first-century world. If Jesus was a "Jewish Cynic" (in contrast to a Jewish sage, signs-worker and/or eschatological prophet), he is the only one we know about. Since the main point of placing Jesus in categories is to help us understand him in context, this proposal therefore proves particularly unhelpful.

Peasants in the Ancient Mediterranean World

Extrapolating from traditional societies today, some scholars contend that peasants must have constituted at least 90% of the empire's, and Jewish Palestine's, population.[46] These estimates could be high, but everyone agrees that peasants comprised the majority of the population of Judea and Galilee. Indeed, if we define "peasant" broadly as simply an agrarian worker without much land, the estimates could well be accurate. Most of the empire was rural,[47] and the infrastructure of the Mediterranean economy could not support many massive urban centers like Rome (which depended on its empire for its needs).[48] Most of the empire's labor force thus consisted of subsistence-level agricultural labor.[49]

In a system that persisted and developed in Medieval Europe, much of this agricultural force worked other people's estates; although some smallholders remained, in regions like Italy and Asia Minor most poor people no longer owned their own land.[50] Those who lived on and worked the estates of the rich were poor tenant farmers,[51] who were often subject to exploitation.[52]

There is also no question that most of the rural empire was poor,[53] so that the connotations readers today often assign to the designation "peasants" are apt for these agrarian laborers. One ancient composer of fables, himself a former slave, opined that it made little difference whether one was a peasant or a slave; it was merely a matter of changing masters.[54] Subsistence for the poor was minimal, so that most died young; in parts of the empire, most peasants probably made barely enough to stay alive.[55] That rich landowners oppressed the poor was widely enough known.[56]

The letters of a Roman aristocrat writing the better part of a century later illustrates how aristocrats viewed the problem. Pliny fancies himself a benevolent absentee landowner, but his tenants have fallen so far into debt, despite his reducing the rent, that they no longer even try to catch up on it.[57] (Meanwhile, his urban servants supervise the peasants to make sure they are working while he enjoys a bit of leisure.)[58] He complains about a former landowner who sold the peasants' possessions to compensate for their debt, thereby diminishing their future resources. This, he reasoned, foolishly diminished their future ability to pay.[59] His response is to consider completely displacing the tenants by some more profitable labor such as slaves.[60] The aristocrat's strongest concern, of course, is how to guard his own economic interests.[61]

The difficulties that farmers endured throughout much of the rest of the empire presumably impacted Galilee as well. Agriculture was central to the Palestinian Jewish economy;[62] with only two large cities, Galilee's population primarily resided in agrarian villages and towns.[63] Although much land was fertile,[64] the peasant farmers held few concerns more pressing than harvest,[65] an image frequent enough in Jesus' parables (Mk 4:29; 12:2; Matt 20:1-7). Probably most Galileans, while not destitute, lived challenging lives.[66]

Was Jesus a Peasant?

We may thus agree fully with Crossan (and others) that peasant culture is an essential part of the background for the Gospels. Regardless of how one defines "peasant," Jesus of Nazareth grew up in a rural village setting. As we shall note again in ch. 12, Nazareth is too insignificant a site[67] for tradition to have invented.[68] Indeed, detractors might even count this location against Jesus' credibility (cf. Jn 1:46).[69] (It is rarely disputed today; that Jesus was from Nazareth is multiply, independently attested.)[70]

Much of Jesus' audience must have also consisted of rural, agrarian peasants. In contrast to the settings of later rabbinic parables, the settings of the majority of Jesus' extant parables reflect an agrarian environment.[71] That such a setting generates perspectives that differ from an urban setting should go without saying. (For example, my wife, a Congolese professor who spent much of her childhood in rural village settings, was able to make more sense of many details in Genesis' patriarchal narratives on the basis of her personal background than I was with my academic training in biblical studies.)

But was Jesus *himself* a peasant? Leaders of movements do not always arise from the same socioeconomic status as most of their followers (although they sometimes do). The answer to the question of Jesus' peasanthood may depend largely on how we define "peasant," but if we define it in its basic sense as an agrarian laborer, Jesus was probably not a peasant himself.[72]

Our only concrete sources for Jesus' occupation preceding his teaching career portray him as a carpenter, a woodworker. This was not a despised profession like some others,[73] but neither was it a sufficiently prestigious occupation (such as, say, a scribe) to suggest that later members of the Jesus movement would have invented it. Conjoined with the near certainty that Jesus spent most of his childhood in Nazareth, this occupation readily fits what we know of Jesus' period and location, knowledge probably absent to most non-Galilean Christians. From 6 CE, when Jesus was perhaps a boy approaching adolescence, Antipas immediately began rebuilding the devastated Galilean capital of Sepphoris[74] — from which Nazareth was a distance of only four miles.[75] That Joseph (Matt 13:55) and Jesus (Mk 6:3)[76] were carpenters fits this situation quite well, since precisely that work (along with stonemasons) would have been in high demand.[77] Yet carpenters were artisans, not peasants, and many assign them to the upper ten percent of nonaristocratic Galilean society.[78]

The few disciples whose backgrounds are mentioned in the Gospels are also not agrarian peasants: four fishermen and one or more tax gatherers (Mk 1:16, 19; 2:14; cf. Lk 19:8).[79] Perhaps the Gospels specify only those with striking occupations; or perhaps fishermen could better afford to follow Jesus than farmers could (though the latter could probably travel seasonally, especially outside harvest and planting times).[80] In the final analysis, the dominant element in the crowds that followed Jesus most likely consisted of peasants; but they did not comprise all of Jesus' followers, at least not if we mean "peasant" in any technical sense.

Thus, although general studies of peasant culture shed some light on Galilean agriculturalists,[81] the picture of Jesus as a "peasant"[82] is not very nuanced, dependent as it is on a rather broad definition of "peasant."[83] Some could also use the title to detract from more specifically Jewish characteristics of Jesus' identity.[84]

Was Jesus a Cynic?

Though most of Jesus' Galilean followers would have been peasants, no one would make the claim that most of them were Cynics. Some have compared Jesus' demands on disciples to those of wandering Cynics (usually without claiming direct Cynic influence).[85] The comparison of Cynics to elements in the early Jesus movement (often offered negatively by outsiders) is not unreasonable; Diaspora missionaries like Paul[86] may have helped make this model acceptable.

Nevertheless, one may claim with confidence that Crossan's "peasant Jewish Cynic"[87] type never existed. Aside from the lack of any Jewish Cynics known to us (and appeal to unknown ones argues from silence against all our extant evidence to the contrary), Cynics were (as Crossan also concurs)[88] characteristically urban,[89] whereas peasants were by definition rural.

Jesus' Non-Cynic Environment

Despite some similarities, Jesus' itinerant ministry in Galilee is hardly distinctly Cynic (even in Luke, who is most apt to present Jesus to his readers in such culturally relevant terms).[90] For example, Jesus may have had a home, probably in Capernaum (cf. perhaps Matt 4:13; Mk 2:1; 9:33; Jn 1:38-39), from which most of Galilee was in walking distance.[91] Further, Cynics were not the only sages, even among Greek philosophers, who traveled.[92] Jewish Torah teachers also could travel "from place to place to speak."[93]

Most telling, Cynics were surely too rare in Jewish Palestine to provide the primary model.[94] Although rightly placing the emphasis of Jesus' ministry in Galilean villages, Crossan opines that Jesus' "peasant village was close enough to a Greco-Roman city like Sepphoris that sight and knowledge of Cynicism are neither inexplicable nor unlikely."[95] How plausible is this view about Sepphoris? Sepphoris was hellenized in many respects,[96] was the most pro-Roman city in Galilee,[97] and refused to participate in the revolt against Rome in 66 CE.[98]

Sepphoris was, however, a thoroughly *Jewish* city, and remained faithful to Judaism as its inhabitants understood it.[99] Archaeology shows that though many pork-eating Gentiles later settled in Sepphoris, pig remains are absent from the city of Jesus' day.[100] Later rabbis emphasize (admittedly probably partly for propagandistic reasons, given their own work there) that Sepphoris was particular about the purity of Israelite lineage[101] and acknowledge the surrounding region to be Jewish.[102]

Moreover, Nazareth may have existed in the shadow of the wealthy Hellenized Jewish city of Sepphoris, but Galilean villages and towns were not severely economically dependent on the two Hellenized cities.[103] Whatever other drawbacks Nazareth may have had (Jn 1:46), its inhabitants seem to have been entirely "orthodox," as attested by priests probably a generation later.[104] Sepphoris' prominence and later Christian tradition about it make its absence in the Gospels all the more striking; Jesus probably had little contact with it,[105] certainly during his ministry.[106] Traditions about Jesus ignore these cities even when Jesus denounces sites that had not responded adequately to Jesus' ministry among them (Matt 11:21, 23//Lk 10:13, 15).[107] This neglect is not surprising: large cities usually were economically parasitic on the countryside,[108] and most Galileans hated the two cities.[109]

The Character of *Real* Cynics

What were *real* Cynics like? Despite complaints we will note below, Stoics sometimes respected Cynics,[110] and others also followed the example of "good" Cynics.[111] Stoic views toward Cynics in this period are typically ambivalent, with both positive and negative characteristics.[112]

Nevertheless, Cynics got their name from being compared with "dogs" (*kunes,* pl. of *kuōn),*[113] and not without reason. Their indecent, private acts in public gained them this reputation; thus Diogenes, while preaching, squatted and did something considered dishonorable, leading the crowds to denounce him as crazy.[114] Even most other philosophers despised such behavior: for them, being "bestial" meant being led by passions instead of by reason.[115] They and others thus ridiculed Cynics' "doggishness."[116]

Some philosophers denounced fake Cynics and other philosophers,[117] accusing them of greed[118] or of abandoning real work for the easier job of preaching.[119] Many viewed excess Cynics as demagogues;[120] the masses, some complained, could not distinguish between true and false philosophers[121] (the sort of complaint many scholars offer today about public voices on the historical Jesus!).

Cynics were known for their uninvited public preaching.[122] Lucian gives us a sample of the style of preaching attributed to harsh Cynics.[123] He mentions Cynics harshly and indiscriminately abusing passersby.[124] They were loud and boisterous,[125] and might rant angrily if contradicted by another speaker.[126] One comic portrayal presents Cynics hitting each other with their staffs.[127]

Cynics were known for their rudeness and especially their disrespect for social rank and status.[128] When a person of status warned the famous Cynic Diogenes not to spit in the wealthy home where he had brought him, Diogenes allegedly spat in the man's face, explaining that nothing of poorer quality was available.[129] They were also antisocial enough to criticize rulers, but given their established tradition, they usually got away with it. In stories about Diogenes, he desired as much honor as Alexander of Macedon[130] (a clear example of Cynic hubris). A Cynic could, of course, go too far; when Demetrius the Cynic in Rome denounced baths on the day that Nero dedicated his new baths, Tigellinus allegedly had him banished from Rome.[131]

Comparing Jesus with Real Cynics

While Jesus speaks boldly in the Gospels, the traditional Jewish model of prophet seems a closer parallel than such socially alienated Cynics. Unlike Cynics, Jesus had close friends and many followers. Jesus' miraculous ministry likewise recalls some biblical prophets, but not the activities of Cynics, who did not perform miracles but lived on the street and harangued passersby on urban street corners.

It was the Cynic's lifestyle that above all distinguished one as a Cynic rather than something else.[132] Granted, elements of Cynic behavior were adapted by others without adopting the Cynic tradition wholesale.[133] In the case of Jesus, however, we must ask whether Cynic models are the nearest cultural sources for similar elements in Jesus' behavior and teaching.

The radical lifestyle of the Cynics does provide a historical analogy for the wider sort of traveling sages in the first-century eastern Mediterranean world. These other sorts of teachers also used witty sayings for often analogous purposes. Radical Greek teachers, including Cynics, used humor, shock and incongruity to hold attention.[134] But of course so did the biblical prophets (see e.g., the Hebrew puns in Mic 1:10-16) and, as we shall see later in the book, Palestinian Jewish sages (to varying degrees). Jesus used rhetoric meant to attract attention; in this he resembled Cynics, but also a wide range of other ancient sages. It thus seems more profitable to explore analogies closer at hand to his culture, the sort of analogies with which he may have actually had some contact (in contrast to Cynics).

Cynics and other radical teachers shared with Jesus a notable departure from established societal roles and readiness to critique the social order. Yet Jesus did not obscenely defecate or stimulate himself sexually in public as Cynics were known to do. He did not cajole hearers while begging for money, threaten anyone with a staff, or even spit on a host. He and his disciples are not said to live on the street, or in the shadow of temples. In contrast to Cynics and even John the Baptist (Jesus' explicit, and Jewish prophetic, foil),[135] Jesus was not completely antisocial (Matt 11:18-19//Lk 7:33-34). Jesus was not interested merely in critiquing the social order for the sake of philosophy; like some other Palestinian Jews, he prophesied a new order to be established by God.

Moreover, Jesus' itinerancy is explained more simply without recourse to the example of Cynics. Those most apt to wander from town to town were socially dislocated people, like landless persons seeking work.[136] Some point to a more particular model of wandering prophets.[137] Itinerancy — perhaps a feature of ancient mobility in general — was hardly a central or distinctive feature of early Christian prophecy.[138] Nevertheless, the most relevant background for Jesus' itinerant mission widely known in Jewish Palestine is that of the Old Testament prophets;[139] Jesus and his followers did, after all, have a prophetic mission (see ch. 17).

Some compare with Cynics Jesus' instructions that his disciples should travel lightly on their mission (Mk 6:8-9). Urban Cynics voluntarily limited themselves to a single cloak; they chose a simple and toilsome lifestyle living on the street (unlike Jesus' disciples) to prepare themselves for hardships.[140] But the very passage that some use for this comparison reveals that Jesus forbade his disciples to carry a pouch for begging (Mk 6:8),[141] in *contrast* to Cynics![142] Some even think that the prohibition is designed to *distinguish* the disciples from typical wandering preachers (probably similar to Cynics in the Greek world) "whose questionable reputation they did not want to share."[143]

Far more relevant to Jesus' immediate environment were the abundant rural peasants; at least in the poorest parts of the empire some might own only one cloak.[144] Some Jews known as Essenes also showed their devotion to God by a simple lifstyle; those who lived in the wilderness devoted all their goods to the community.[145] Josephus also indicates that Essenes did not take provisions when they traveled, expecting hospitality from fellow-Essenes in every city, fitting Jesus' instructions in this passage.[146] Likewise, Israel's ancient prophets (the relevance of which we have already noted) lived simply in times of national apostasy.[147]

Most scholars note that, whatever the parallels with Cynics in Jesus' teaching and ministry, the differences are far greater;[148] they were not known, for example, "for healings and exorcisms."[149] Even one scholar who does portray Jesus in Cynic terms elsewhere offers a sound methodological warning that, in light of the foregoing evidence, should bring any extensive use of Cynic parallels into question: many abuse the comparative method by simply "seizing a few elements in diverse cultures, describing them in very general and similar terms, and then positing a causal connection."[150]

Gerd Theissen and Annette Merz put the matter well from a German perspective (although as an American I would hesitate to blame our state of California for this idea). Noting that the current Jesus "quest" divides between those advocating a non-eschatological, Cynic-type Jesus and a Jewish Jesus focused on restoration eschatology, they complain that the former view "seems to have more Californian than Galilean local colouring."[151]

Greek Background Is Not the Problem

I should clarify at this point that I am not minimizing the value of Greek background for the study of the Gospels or the historical Jesus. First, the Gospels are written in Greek and presumably bear marks of literary adaptation for Greek and Diaspora Jewish audiences. We must take these features into account when working back to the historical Jesus. But second, and more important for the study of the historical Jesus, much evidence suggests that Palestinian Judaism was hellenized[152] (influenced by the pervasive Greek culture), though of course less thoroughly than Judaism in the Greek-speaking Diaspora.[153] (On the limits to this approach, see our warnings about Sepphoris, above.) By contrast, the Greco-Roman world on the whole was far less Judaized.

Yet this clear direction of Greek influence in Jewish culture but mostly negligible Jewish influence on Greek culture invites another conclusion. Wherever we have a mixture of Jewish and hellenistic motifs we must be dealing with something primarily Jewish, not something primarily Gentile (since the latter would exhibit much less Jewish influence).[154] This observation has serious implications for some theories proposed today. Thus, for example, Burton Mack's view that Jesus, though Jewish by birth, was more "hellenistic" in his behavior,[155] has nothing historically to commend it. James D. G. Dunn is right to complain that the "neo-liberal quest" of Crossan and Mack still treats Jesus' Jewishness as not central to his identity.[156] It is to Mack's views, generally less grounded or nuanced than Crossan's, that we now turn.

A More Extreme Example

Like Crossan and others, Burton Mack's Jesus is a teacher of wisdom without an embarrassing eschatological agenda.[157] As we have noted, the nineteenth century liberal "lives of Jesus" pursued such a noneschatological, wise Jesus created in the image of each writer's ethical ideal. Like the Jesus Seminar,[158] Mack agrees with these sources in finding a noneschatological Jesus. But Mack goes beyond Crossan and some members of the Jesus Seminar.

What Kind of Sage?

Mack portrays a more pervasively Cynic Jesus than Crossan does. He does so by isolating and focusing exclusively on a very slender element of our sources for Jesus, namely, what he considers the earliest part of the source "Q." This leaves him with only seven pages of wisdom sayings to work with for who Jesus was and what he taught. ("Q" is scholars' label for a source no longer extant, which Matthew and Luke shared. It is reconstructed on the basis of Matthew and Luke. I will deal with Mack's perspective on Q in ch. 4, but for now I simply mention that his method of determining the "earliest" part of this hypothetical document is astonishingly subjective.)

The traditions Mack counts earliest (based on his premise that Jesus was only a sage) not surprisingly portray Jesus as a sage. Since Jesus was certainly a sage (whatever else he may have been as well), Mack has no trouble finding genuine "sage" aspects of Jesus. Whereas eschatology tends to be distinctively

Jewish,[159] highlighting Jesus' "sage" features can allow for a less ethnic-specific feel to Jesus.

By itself, the observation that Jesus was a sage would not prove particularly profound, controversial or problematic. By definition, everyone recognizes that both Jewish sages and Cynic sages were "sages." The problem is Mack's faulty assumption that such sage characteristics must make Jesus like a Cynic, when we know that *Jewish* sages abounded in Galilee, and we lack evidence for any Cynic ones there![160] As I will show later in this book (in chs. 13-15), Jesus' teachings show abundant parallels to specifically *Jewish* teachers.

As Cynic parallels to what he thinks is the earliest layer of Q, Mack adduces Jesus' "aphoristic style, unconventional behavior," bold straightforwardness, and so forth.[161] But as we have noted, most of these characteristics appear in other wisdom traditions and beyond wisdom traditions, and certainly beyond Cynics.[162] The biblical Book of Proverbs, cited regularly among Palestinian Jews, is full of "aphorisms"; aphorisms also characterize Jewish wisdom teaching more generally.[163] Many other philosophers besides Cynics were known for their impudent boldness,[164] and the same was true for Jewish biblical prophets (e.g., 1 Kgs 21:20-24; 22:28; 2 Kgs 3:13-14). Geza Vermes focuses on similar behavior among Galilean "charismatic sages," who preserved ancient Jewish prophetic traditions, not new Cynic ones.[165] If Vermes' examples are a bit limited (see our next chapter), they are at least more common in Galilee and much more relevant for a Galilean Jew than Mack's are.

Either Sage or?

To argue against Jesus being an eschatological prophet, Mack forces an illogical choice: if Jesus was a sage, Mack contends, then he was not an eschatological prophet.[166] Because Mack accepts only the "wisdom" "layer" of Q as early, he argues that its image represents the real Jesus, suppressed by a church antagonistic to this image of Jesus. (As noted above, I shall deal later with the subjective way that he defines which part of "Q" is early, but a central factor seems to be that whatever fits his thesis about the authentic Jesus is early.)

Mack contends that the later canon purposely excluded "Q" to destroy evidence of the earliest Christian genre of instruction.[167] In reality, we lack any evidence that "Q" even remained extant in the second century. (Christians probably simply did not feel a need to keep using "Q" independently because they found most of it incorporated in more complete Gospels.) By contending that the church did away with the instruction genre, Mack must ignore the inconvenient fact that the church actually continued to use this genre, even more frequently than it appears in the New Testament. (Compare the "Two Ways" instruction format in Barnabas and the Didache.) Contrary to Mack's conspiratorial thesis, the catechetical model probably *increased* rather than declined in subsequent centuries.

Mack suggests that for the "first followers of Jesus . . . What mattered most was the body of instructions that circulated in his name"; only later, he contends, did "groups in different locations" produce varied mythologies of his life somehow harmonized with his teachings in the later gospels.[168] After Mack has eliminated the context of Jesus' prophetic life (contrast our ch. 17), it is much easier to reinterpret his sayings that remain.

Simply comparing other ancient sources would ruin Mack's thesis, however: his forced-choice logic cannot work in any document where it may be tested objectively. His assumption that the roles of wisdom teacher and eschatological prophet are incompatible[169] does not fit all ancient Jewish teachers. That a figure expecting the imminent end of the age might also provide rules for a community expected to survive that final holocaust or endure for some time is evident in the conjunction of both modes of thought in the Dead Sea Scrolls, which are pre-Christian.[170]

The Dead Sea Scrolls moreover include wisdom texts as well as eschatology, showing that the same people could accept both approaches.[171] Some also contend that even the eschatological *Similitudes of Enoch* (no later than the first century) blend "wisdom and apocalyptic or eschatological sayings."[172] Similarly, that Rabbi Akiba (early second-century) was purportedly a mystic and also among the most vocal supporters of Bar Kochba suggests that even the early rabbinic trajectory did not absolutely separate revelatory, rabbinic, and revolutionary streams of thought.

First-century Judaism does not allow us to simply force a choice among options such as teachers, prophets, healers, and messiahs, as if such categories were logically incompatible. While these categories did not always overlap, they sometimes did so.[173] Recognizing (rightly) that Jesus was a sage thus affords us no license to automatically infer that he was not also a prophet (or whatever other category we might conceive for him). We must grapple fairly with all potential roles for Jesus claimed by the texts without assuming that demonstrating one refutes another, except in cases of true contradiction (e.g., a pacifist versus an armed revolutionary).

Cynic parallels for the study of Jesus prove useful only when placed in a larger context of ancient sages, especially the closer and more abundant Jewish cultural parallels. Likewise, Jewish wisdom parallels should be pursued heavily but not to the exclusion of Jewish apocalyptic, legal and "charismatic" parallels. Early traditions about Jesus also attribute these roles to him (see chs. 13, 17-18), and our sources indicate that these categories were no less a part of Judaism nor incompatible with the wisdom tradition.

A Cynic Kingdom?

Mack's assumption that noting Jesus' role as a teacher makes him like a Cynic sage (incompatible with an end-time prophet) is astonishing enough. Yet still more astonishing is Mack's comparison of Jesus' clearly authentic "kingdom" teaching to Cynic teaching about rulership.[174] When Mack tries to defend this quite distant comparison by denying that the "kingdom of God" is a pre-Christian Jewish conception,[175] he ignores several important points.

First, he ignores with but brief argument the consensus of most Jewish and New Testament scholarship on the question. A consensus can be and sometimes is mistaken, but that claim should be argued rather than assumed.[176] Second, Mack ignores the precise parallels in wording between the opening lines of the "Lord's Prayer"[177] ("Hallowed be your name; your kingdom come . . .") and the regularly uttered Jewish prayer known as the Kaddish. Most commentators familiar with Judaism recognize this prayer as the background of, or at least derived from the same milieu as, the opening lines of the Lord's Prayer.[178] In its earliest form, the Kaddish runs something like, ". . . hallowed be his great name . . . may his kingdom reign . . ."[179] The parallel between the *Kaddish* and the first stanza of Jesus' model prayer was so obvious in a Jewish setting that an eighth-century translation of the Lord's Prayer from Latin into Hebrew borrows some of its wording directly from the *Kaddish*.[180] Third and most significantly, as we note below, Mack ignores the Bible known and regularly quoted by Jesus and his Jewish hearers.

Because the kingdom is the most pervasive element in Jesus' teaching, Mack must make it a Greek idea to maintain his thesis. But consider the evidence. Which is closer to Jesus' teaching about God's kingdom: the ideal of wise philosophers' right to rule,[181] to which Mack appeals, or the common Jewish expression "kingdom of God"? Let us for the sake of argument exclude from consideration our earliest rabbinic sources that employ the expression and all other Jewish sources (including pre-Christian Qumran scrolls)[182] from the first centuries of this era. When Mack excludes from consideration all Jewish evidence as too late, did he think to first check the Jewish Scriptures, used widely by Jewish people?

Jewish people regularly employed the psalms in worship, and the psalms praise the reign ("kingdom") of God (Ps 22:28; 145:11-13; cf. Ps 47:8; 93:1; 96:10; 97:1). The expected Davidic king would rule over David's kingdom (Is 9:7). Daniel 2:44, 47, even implies the "mystery" of God's future "kingdom," just as in Mk 4:11. Is not the Jewish conception of the one, Jewish God's kingdom closer to Jesus' message about God's kingdom than a Cynic sage claiming that sages have the right to rule? Why would a scholar bend over backwards to avoid that conclusion?

Jesus' Gentile Movement Became Jewish?

Mack's view of how Jesus' movement developed must presuppose that Jesus (though a Galilean Jew) spawned a movement that was essentially Gentile in character, some part of which later became conservatively Jewish. Since an ancient Gentile movement would not likely respect a conservative Jewish trajectory, it is not surprising that we have no parallels to any such phenomenon in antiquity.[183]

More specifically, Mack claims that the Christ cult quickly evolved "on the model of the mystery religions, complete with entrance baptisms, rites of recognition (the holy kiss), ritualized meals (the lord's supper)," as well as a new emphasis on conversion.[184] I will return at the end of this section to Mack's logic of preferring Gentile to Jewish parallels, but for the moment want to survey these specific examples. Mystery cults were non-Jewish and polytheistic, hence do not provide ready background to Jesus' early movement. Had Mack looked elsewhere, he would have seen that the parallels he suggests were in no wise limited to mystery religions. Thus, for example, kisses were standard greetings for family or close associates throughout the ancient Mediterranean world,[185] in no way limited to cult associations.

Likewise, Jewish parallels to conversion (also "with entrance baptisms") are much closer than joining various mystery cults.[186] Mystery "baptisms" were simply an initial lustration — like the regular cultic lustrations many temples required on normal occasions — that were part but not the center of cultic initiation.[187] By contrast, Jewish proselyte baptism *was* a rite of initiation-conversion, known even in Greek writers like Epictetus.[188] Even if one rejects the priority or influence of Jewish proselyte baptism, as some do, the Jewish initial lustrations at Qumran[189] are at least closer to the milieu in which Jesus' movement originated and initially grew than are pagan mystery lustrations.

Mack's suggested origin of the "lord's supper" also ignores closer parallels for more distant ones. It is easy to understand how a cult meal modeled after the Jewish Passover Seder could be adapted in a Greek context to resemble a Greek banquet or cultic meal,[190] but difficult to see why Jewish Christians (who were influenced by Greek culture but mistrusted Gentile religious practices) would have transformed a Greek cultic celebration into a Passover meal. (We discuss the last supper later, in ch. 20.)

Certainly Diaspora Jewish missionaries to Greeks adapted Greek language and Mediterranean Christianity became increasingly hellenized over the next few centuries. But as we have noted, Judaism was heavily influenced by Greek culture, and the reverse was not true (apart from magical texts). Texts that share both Jewish and Greek elements — as all New Testament documents in varying degrees do — are thus primarily Jewish rather than non-Jewish texts.

One cannot be certain of a writer's motives, but Mack at least seems to suggest that part of his motivation for writing is to disabuse Christians of faulty thinking (an agenda one can certainly appreciate). He seeks to force them to see that they alone (he opines) of all religions demand that their adherents believe their myth to be history, and he summons them to recognize that their myth is not history. By such a procedure, Mack hopes to make Christians "multicultural," able to dialogue evenhandedly with other faiths.[191] Regardless of what one thinks of this agenda (most of us favor true multiculturalism), Mack's agenda, like that of the Jesus Seminar, seems to drive his reading of historical data.

Pagan Origins Again

Mack is not alone in suggesting a Gentile context for much of the Jesus tradition. For example, another scholar charges that modern scholars usually prefer a Jewish setting for the gospel materials due to ecumenical and apologetic motives: that is, a Jewish setting is useful for Christian-Jewish dialogue and for "defending" the Jesus traditions.[192] Many scholars using Jewish sources would be surprised to find their work characterized in such terms. (Many historical scholars lack strong ecumenical commitments, and even more lack apologetic interests. Some indeed profess no religious faith.)

In any case, this scholar considers his own alternative less "biased": some of the purported sayings of Jesus make better sense, he thinks, from backgrounds in Cynicism, gnosticism, or Hellenistic mystery religions.[193] While later sources did create some Jesus-sayings relevant to their setting (particularly clear in gnosticism), and Gospel writers reworded and reframed sayings for their own audiences, we shall argue later in the book that we possess a great abundance of gospel material that makes the best sense in a specifically Jewish context.

We will treat gnostic materials in ch. 4, and have treated Cynic parallels (the most plausible of the three suggestions) above. As we have suggested, a background in mystery cults suffers from the same drawbacks as the Cynic proposal: these cults are far removed from Jesus' milieu.[194] They were also less publicly accessible than knowledge of Cynics, even in urban settings. Jewish people did not need to appeal to Gentile mystery cults for their concept of "mystery," which already appears long before Jesus' day in Daniel and possibly *1 Enoch*,[195] as well as in Qumran Scrolls dependent on them.[196] Today, even most works on early Diaspora Christianity place little emphasis on the mysteries, because their secretive character made them less relevant for informing discourse shared with any not initiated to the mysteries.[197]

To conclude this section, I return to the problem of any portrayal in which the earliest Jesus movements' context was hellenistic and Jewish ideas (like Jewish eschatology or messiahship) entered later. Does it not make more sense to start from the Galilean Jewish framework of Jesus and his first disciples and regard non-Jewish ideas as the later adaptations? (Jesus' ministry also developed in the context of the prior ministry of the Jewish prophet John, attested in the Jewish historian Josephus.)[198] After all, even Paul, working in a Diaspora environment, recognizes that Palestinian Jewish apostles (whose prominence rested on their association with Jesus) with conservative Jewish sentiments or constituencies dominated the Jerusalem church (Gal 2:9-12). The Jesus movement originated in Jewish Palestine, not in the Diaspora, and Jews would hardly have adapted a pagan cult (that happened to exalt a Galilean Jew!). Pagan anti-Judaism was common enough that hellenizers would not have made their message more Palestinian Jewish (e.g., more eschatological), hence less acceptable in the Diaspora, to commend it to their audiences! Clearly a Palestinian Jewish context makes the most sense for Jesus of Nazareth, as we shall argue more fully in following chapters. We shall also argue that the substance of a large amount of the tradition preserved about Jesus in the Synoptics reflects that same context rather than a later one.

Conclusion

Scholars who argue for a non-eschatological Jesus usually (though not always) resort to primarily Gentile contexts for Jesus rather than the most obvious context we know to be true of him: Jesus was a Jewish Galilean. In their most extreme form, the non-Jewish portrayals of Jesus place him in the context of Cynic philosophers, and seek to explain away the Jewish character of even specifically Jewish language such as "kingdom of God."

A much nearer context for Jesus, one more often preferred in the current so-called "Third Quest" for him, is his known setting as a Galilean Jew. Scholars adopting this approach have come to a higher degree of consensus about Jesus, although, as we shall note in the following chapter, some disparity (even about his eschatological message) persists.

CHAPTER 3

Jesus and Judaism

"When the Third Quest was launched, one of the main characteristics that distinguished it from the First Quest of 19th-century German Protestantism and the Second (existentialist) Quest of the students of Rudolf Bultmann in the 1950s and 1960s was its determination to take the Jewishness of Jesus with utter seriousness and to situate him squarely within Palestinian Judaism at the turn of the era."

JOHN P. MEIER[1]

"The chief finding of Jesus the Jew is the recognition of Jesus within the earliest Gospel tradition . . . as a charismatic prophetic preacher and miracle-worker, the outstanding 'Galilean Hasid.'"

GEZA VERMES[2]

The discussion of Jesus' Jewish context is close to the heart of most current Jesus scholarship. A major earlier phase of Jesus research pursued the Gospels' sources; Bultmann's phase, more interested in the early church's preaching than in what could be known historically about Jesus, asked how the traditions were shaped by preaching. By contrast, Jesus' historical context dominates the present discussion.[3] Partly for this reason, Jesus research today is on the whole less skeptical about what we can know about Jesus than mid-twentieth-century scholarship was.[4]

The largest divide today is between the view that Jesus was a Cynic-type wisdom teacher and the view that he was an eschatological prophet.[5] The latter remains the majority view,[6] although if one subtracts the specifically Cynic element these categories need not be mutually exclusive. What most unites the *majority* of Jesus researchers today (including some scholars who deny Jesus' eschatological approach) is an emphasis on Jesus' Jewish context.[7] The pictures of Jesus this scholarship produces are more plausible than other reconstructions because they are more accurately grounded in what we can know historically about Jesus' setting. Nevertheless, a range of views exist, depending partly on the aspects of Jesus' Jewish setting selected for attention.

The handful of representative views selected in this chapter each work to build a cohesive picture of Jesus around a key theme or themes. In so doing, they leave out some evidence, but also offer more of a distinctive thesis about Jesus' mission than one would gather from works focused on methodology, sayings traditions, and so forth. They also overlap on many points despite their distinctive emphases. Thus Borg insists on Jesus as a sage, prophet, and founder of a renewal movement, though not a strictly end-time prophet. Vermes compares the perspectives of Sanders (and Martin Hengel) to his own, suggesting that Jesus was "charismatic healer — teacher — prophet."[8] For heuristic purposes, however, I shall highlight some characteristic and relatively distinctive features of each of these portrayals.

Some Third Quest Views

The so-called Third Quest includes a diverse range of views, but its dominant expression among scholars today is a recognition of Jesus' Jewish context.[9] This approach represents a significant improvement over most previous discussions, retaining the Jewish (and in the majority of cases the eschatological) emphasis of Weiss and Schweitzer, while reflecting a much fuller understanding of first-century Judaism than was available to earlier generations of scholars.

In practice, this means closer attention to first-century, firsthand Judean sources like the Jewish historian Josephus (despite his Hellenistic apologetic approach) and the Dead Sea Scrolls (despite their sectarian perspective), as well as archaeological and other data. (Even those who portray Jesus as more Cynic than Jewish reflect the trend to take into account Jesus' environment; they simply choose a different and, in my view, much less plausible environment.) Several "Third Quest" scholars, among them E. P. Sanders, Geza Vermes, and James Charlesworth, are well known for their work in Jewish sources more generally.

Beyond a common emphasis on reading Jesus in his context, however, these scholars have produced a wide array of views. The Jesus of Richard Horsley is notably political; the distinctive feature of the Jesus of Marcus Borg is more like a mystic or (in cross-cultural terms) a shaman (though he is also prophet and teacher); the Jesus of Geza Vermes is a signs-working prophet like Elijah or Honi; and the Jesus of E. P. Sanders is an eschatological prophet. Naturally, some of these perspectives overlap, and (as some of their proponents acknowledge) they are not all incompatible. For example, those who wanted Jesus killed undoubtedly saw his activity as politically threatening, and shamanism provides a crosscultural rubric for discussing the activity of a prophetic healer. Signs-working and eschatological prophets were also compatible, as some of their proponents concur (although Josephus' eschatological and politically problematic "sign-prophets" differed starkly from a mere wonder-worker like Honi).

In addition to different pictures of Jesus, scholars pursue different approaches in their scholarly task. N. T. Wright and John Dominic Crossan, for example, synthesize a wide range of other scholarship into (very different) coherent pictures of Jesus' mission. Whereas they are particularly noteworthy for their skillful big-picture approach, John Meier (like Raymond Brown on Jesus' passion) focuses on detail, painstakingly and voluminously examining each line of evidence.[10] E. P. Sanders works from particular historical data that are undisputed to construct a portrait of what can probably be known about Jesus. Whereas Sanders starts with Jesus' actions, many others start with his teaching (an approach reflected earlier in e.g., T. W. Manson or Joachim Jeremias). Ideally one would like to synthesize the best of all these approaches, although ideally this could also invite an enormous range of competence (and perhaps a team of scholars working together from complementary angles).

Although not all the "historical Jesus" scholars writing today reflect this emphasis, the third quest on the whole reflects an increasing recognition of Jesus' Jewish context. While one could have sampled any of the perspectives mentioned briefly above (or others), and I could have surveyed other carefully thought-out approaches below (such as Horsley, Meier, Gerd Theissen, Amy-Jill Levine, or Tom Holmén, among many others), my purpose here is merely to offer some samples, so I have elected to treat only three works here that have been influential in my own continent's academic circles for some time. The first, Marcus Borg's approach, is one that could have been placed in the preceding chapter, because he questions Jesus' eschatology in the traditional sense. Nevertheless, the Jewish context of his basic approach seems sufficient to justify placing it here as well.

The second, the Jewish scholar Geza Vermes, helpfully sets Jesus' healing ministry in a Jewish context. Because I have deferred most discussion of Jesus' healing activity for another book, it is helpful for me to introduce the influential approach of Vermes here. Vermes has long been a major voice in scholarship on early Judaism and is among the best-known early scholars on the Dead Sea Scrolls. The third is the approach of E. P. Sanders, whose research also leaves its imprint on this book (especially in my understanding of Jesus as an eschatological prophet). Sanders is also well known for his work in early Judaism as well as early Christianity. Despite my affinity for Sanders in most respects (as suggested in the book's dedication), I shall try to engage what I feel are weaknesses as well as strengths in his approach.[11]

Jesus as Charismatic Healer, Prophet and Sage

Of the sample views here, Borg is the one who could in some sense most easily have fit either this chapter or the previous one. Borg's Jesus challenged injustices in the present rather than promising an urgent future kingdom (although he did warn of impending judgment). Borg emphasizes the side of Jesus that "preaches" best in a modern framework,[12] but to what extent is this the Jesus of history? I believe that Borg does in fact correctly emphasize one side of the Jesus tradition, and that we can profit from his work on that aspect even if we find it less helpful with some other aspects of the sources.

Although Borg's *Jesus: A New Vision* and other works are useful, I focus here most frequently on a seminal academic work revised from his doctoral thesis, *Conflict, Holiness & Politics in the Teachings of Jesus*. If eschatology is not limited to the literal sense emphasized by Weiss and Schweitzer, he notes, it need not exclude Jesus' interest in his nation's political situation.[13] He shows that resistance against Rome was widespread, rather than limited to a single Jewish movement;[14] he also views what he calls the "quest for holiness" in terms of resistance against gentile oppression.[15] Jesus, he believes, challenged this ethos of exclusivist holiness used for resistance.[16]

Unlike some scholars who force a choice between Jesus as a sage and Jesus as a prophet, Borg recognizes Jesus as both sage[17] and prophet.[18] Like Sanders and some others,[19] he argues that Jesus intended a renewal movement, exemplified by choosing twelve disciples as the nucleus of a new community.[20] (We will address some of these points more fully in ch. 17.) He combines the miracle-working "holy man" model (similar to Vermes' charismatic that we summarize in the next section) with "a prophet who spoke of the consequences of his people's present course."[21] He rightly emphasizes how the tradition reveals Jesus' intimacy with God[22] and radical dependence on, or faith in, God.[23] Like Sanders, Borg views Jesus' action in the temple as a prophetic act, though unlike Sanders, he treats Jesus' recorded pronouncement as the key to understanding it.[24]

He argues that Jesus had to defend his behavior (such as table fellowship with sinners) against pious detractors. Whereas some scholars play down Jesus' conflicts with Pharisees, Borg emphasizes such conflicts that are so central to the tradition,[25] and contends that these focused on the correct interpretation of Torah.[26] On Borg's view, Jesus posed mercy as an alternative to exclusivist holiness.[27] He believes that Jesus' merciful interpretation of the law led to a distinctive approach to the Torah regarding the sabbath[28] and the temple.[29] Thus, for example, he thinks that Jesus condemned the Pharisees' practice of extrabiblical tithes.[30] His Jesus treats holiness in terms of humility and self-death[31] rather than in terms of separatism, in contrast to Pharisaism.[32]

Borg rightly critiques some traditional critical assumptions.[33] He is intensely concerned with Jesus' social settings,[34] and rightly emphasizes Jesus' continuity with Judaism.[35] Although he does not draw the net of ancient sources as widely as some, he makes heavy use of Josephus, a first-century Jewish historian who is one of our most useful sources.

More problematic is his reduction of traditional eschatology, as we have noted.[36] Whereas many scholars see Jesus as an "eschatological prophet," Borg envisions him as a social prophet.[37] Borg relates "the future threat" to Israel to its misguided present course, a course that Jesus' mission challenged.[38] The alternative perspective on Jesus' message, he says, is "apocalyptic calculation . . . that the end of all was near," a view he claims is now rejected by "most scholars."[39]

Expectation of the imminent end need not entail calculations of its precise timing (some ancient sources even include multiple estimates), but in any case one need not pose alternatives so starkly. However one counts the number of scholars (I believe that Borg is mistaken on this point),[40] is the "alternative" perspective so incompatible with his own evidence? Some alternatives are not mutually exclusive in ancient Jewish sources. For example, Jewish sources could lay side by side the alternatives of the end coming at a foreordained time[41] or at a time contingent on Israel's repentance.[42] Such alternatives were no more inconsistent than God's sovereignty factoring in human responsibility, a combination many or most Jews accepted.[43] However subsequent believers might temporally separate the temple's destruction from cosmic destruction or transformation after 70 CE, distinguishing coming catastrophes may have been no more necessary for a prophet c. 30 CE than comparable earlier prophets' warnings of imminent judgment in light of the coming day of the Lord. Likewise, the Qumran scrolls did not distinguish the two; apocalyptic sources sometimes allowed for stages of transition to the kingdom, but we might count all the future ones as eschatological in some sense.

While I do agree with Borg about the impending crisis in Israel, I would argue that the early gospel tradition also suggests a climactic future kingdom (cf. Mk 9:47; 10:23, 25; Matt 6:9//Lk 11:2; Matt 8:11-12//Lk 13:28-29) that was imminent at least in the sense of being potentially near (Mk 1:15; 9:1).[44] Likewise Jesus' promise about the twelve reigning on twelve thrones suggests the future kingdom (Matt 19:28//Lk 22:30). Our earliest extant Christian source, Paul, seems to suggest a form of imminent eschatology different from what Borg envisions for Jesus (1 Thess 4:13–5:11; 2 Thess 1:5–2:15), although including trouble in the temple (2 Thess 2:3-4).[45] I will argue later (ch. 17 and especially appendix 4) that Paul here is directly echoing Jesus' end-time teachings, hence providing our earliest extant interpretation of Jesus' future message (within two decades after Jesus' teaching). Nor was Paul's interpretation, offered to many confused Gentile Christians for whom it was clearly not originally designed, eccentric;

scholars have often shown that Jesus' language resembles that of other Jewish eschatological sources,[46] hence would naturally be understood by his followers in that light.

Still, the heart of Jesus' eschatological teaching undoubtedly did involve imminent historical crisis. The old order was collapsing; his people could no longer take for granted the continuance of any structures on which they depended. Such announcements from society's fringe could not but disturb anyone with political, economic, or other interests in the old order. Indeed, Jesus must have calculated such warnings to dislodge his hearers' comfort and security, and must have been aware that it would provoke hostility from the elite. It did so when other prophets challenged the old order (and would undoubtedly have similar effect on modern western hearers as well). Healings and exorcisms could point people to depend on God rather than the old order for their most fundamental needs. But while all of this squares well with envisioning Jesus as a social prophet of impending crisis (such as the war with Rome a generation later), it does not rule out the possibility of eschatological transformation, whether at that time or later. In Joel, for example, a locust plague foreshadows the judgment of the nations. Apart from specifying the end as unknown and expecting judgment within a generation (see ch. 17), quantifying the times was not Jesus' primary interest.

Borg's appeal to shamanism (what he more often calls the "holy man" model) provides a cross-cultural model for examining Jesus' activity as a healer.[47] Nevertheless, as a context for understanding Jesus' use of "kingdom of God"[48] it is inadequate, since close Jewish parallels for Jesus' terminology exist. For the most part, he doubts that Jesus' kingdom teaching is clearly future eschatology, depicting it more in terms of experiential reality[49] and numinous presence.[50] Although Borg does not in this work rule out the possibility of future elements absolutely,[51] on this point, at least, he comes close to forcing a choice that perhaps need not be forced.

Jesus as Jewish Charismatic Healer

In chs. 13-17 we will examine in greater detail the evidence that many of Jesus' Jewish contemporaries understood him as a sage and prophet; these views fit our textual evidence much better than proposals that neglect first-century Jewish sources. Nevertheless, we must introduce such categories briefly here lest some readers suppose that our position is a novel or idiosyncratic one.

I will revisit Vermes' work briefly in ch. 17 (though trying not to repeat all that I have said here). Moreover, because I have deferred most questions about Jesus' miracles to a separate book, I will not treat Vermes' approach here as thoroughly as if I had tried to include all my material in one volume. Nevertheless, it is valuable to introduce his work here, as illustrative of a key element of the current discussion.[52]

The brief way in which scholars usually summarize other scholars' views may be too rigid. Although Vermes emphasizes the "charismatic" rather than "eschatological" character of Jesus' ministry, he recognizes that Jesus probably expected God's imminent kingdom.[53] Nevertheless, Vermes is best known for his comparing Jesus to "charismatic" sages,[54] and it is to this comparison that we now turn.

Jesus as Charismatic Sage

Vermes doubts that Jesus was a "rabbi" in the later sense of that term.[55] By this he does not mean that we cannot find fruitful comparisons between Jesus' teaching and that of later rabbis. Vermes himself draws these at numerous points, since rabbinic sources preserve some wider Jewish traditions, and certainly did not borrow ideas corresponding to the Gospels from the Gospels themselves.[56] Nevertheless, he envisions a closer model for first-century Galilee: that of the charismatic holy man.

In his early work, Vermes can envision Judean Pharisees having a difficult time with Jesus.[57] Following the form critics, however, Vermes attributes the Gospels' particular stories about Jesus' *interpretive* conflicts with Pharisees, involving Scripture debates, to later Christian tradition.[58] Although I believe that this approach oversimplifies our data, Vermes is not apparently denying that conflicts occurred. On Vermes' reading, Jesus was devoted to the law, but was interested more in fulfilling its larger purpose than in observing its specific regulations.[59] While I believe that Jesus may have engaged in more midrashic (traditional Jewish interpretive) treatment of the law than Vermes allows, one can well imagine how even Jesus' frequently non-Pharisaic approach to the law would have brought him into conflict with Pharisees at times. Vermes notes such conflict between Jewish charismatics and Pharisees.[60]

Nevertheless, Vermes is undoubtedly right that Jesus was crucified not for challenging interpretations of Jewish law nor for leading an insurrection, but for having caused a commotion in the temple during Passover season.[61] (We will return to this idea in chs. 20-21.) Vermes strikes a useful balance: "There is little doubt that the Pharisees disliked his nonconformity" on matters like healing on the sabbath; "There is no evidence, however, of an active and organized participation on the part of the Pharisees in the planning and achievement of Jesus' downfall."[62]

Even here, he allows that "some individual Pharisees bore a measure of responsibility," but he lays most of the blame on "representatives of the political establishment — Herod Antipas and his supporters in Galilee, and the chief priests and Pilate in the capital."[63] This perspective, incidentally, fits well what we find in our Gospels; even the Fourth Gospel, known for its polemical relationship to Pharisaism, shifts the focus to the chief priests and Pilate in the passion narrative.[64]

Honi and Hanina

Most scholars today accept the claim that Jesus was a healer and exorcist, as his contemporaries would have understood such categories.[65] Vermes naturally looks for the closest parallels to miracle workers not among Gentiles but among Jewish sages, and cites the most prominent, namely Honi and Hanina. He probably goes too far in suggesting that holy men like Hanina ben Dosa dominated first-century Galilean religious experience more than the priests or scribes did;[66] we do not hear of many other miracle-working sages,[67] especially from Jesus' era. This observation conflicts with what we would expect if such miracle workers were as common as Vermes allows.[68] Still, he is surely correct to emphasize that many people would have followed such charismatic leaders.[69]

Vermes appropriately looked to the most obvious context for understanding Jesus as a miracle-working sage, namely those available in his Palestinian Jewish setting. Hanina was a Galilean, like Jesus, although he is the only other Galilean we know of to whom signs are attributed.[70] Nevertheless, the value of these sources is more limited than we might hope, if taken by themselves. Thus rain-making is the only miracle common to both Honi and Hanina, yet it is absent from Jesus' ministry.[71] Relatively few of the divine interventions reported involve healing.[72]

We also have a more difficult time knowing as much about these sages' miracles as we would like because most sources for them come from centuries after their time. While Honi (Onias) was earlier than Jesus and undoubtedly known for getting answered prayer regarding rain,[73] most of the details we hear about him surface only perhaps half a millennium after he lived.[74] Most scholars place Hanina ben Dosa in the first century,[75] but his association with miracles is mild in early rabbinic sources.[76] Later material about Hanina is much more abundant, but was transmitted and developed over the course of three or four centuries.[77] Many scholars also conclude that while Jewish wonder-workers offer closer parallels than pagan ones do, they differ significantly from Jesus (especially because they operate only through prayer and because they lack an explicitly eschatological context for their miracles).[78]

But Vermes and others have also appealed to the biblical model of Elijah's signs.[79] However relevant Honi and Hanina are for understanding Jesus' prophetic ministry, Jesus and most of his Jewish contemporaries knew very well the model of Elijah. (Vermes shows that the rabbinic portrait of Hanina ben Dosa is also modeled on Elijah.)[80] Some biblical prophets like Elijah and Elisha were particularly emphasized as healers;[81] some others, like Isaiah, might heal occasionally (Is 38:21);[82] and Jewish sources continued to link miracles with many of the biblical prophets.[83]

Elijah's Model

The observation that some of Jesus' activity resembles Elijah allows us to bring together both an emphasis on Jesus' signs and an emphasis on his end-time approach, that is, the best of both Vermes' and Sanders' insights. Vermes himself notes Jewish future expectations for Elijah, suspecting that some Galilean sympathizers probably viewed Jesus in this manner.[84]

Jewish tradition naturally developed the biblical promise of Elijah's return found in Mal 4:5-6 (MT 3:23-24). This development appears quite early, in pre-Christian sources like Ben Sira (Sir 48:10);[85] some also find reference to Elijah as forerunner in *1 En.* 90:31.[86] *4 Ezra* 6:26 assumes him among historic figures with special roles at the end of the age.[87] Moreover, the obviously knowledgeable Jewish writer Matthew (Matt 17:10) unhesitatingly follows Mark (Mk 9:11) in presupposing that this role was widely known in Jewish circles.

Later rabbis also seized on this feature of eschatological expectation, although they more heavily emphasized Elijah's present activity.[88] The rabbis were clearly aware of Malachi's prophecy and anticipated Elijah's return at the end of the age,[89] destined to appear alongside rabbinism's other eschatological figures.[90] In ch. 17, we shall explore in more detail ancient Jewish expectations of an eschatological Mosaic prophet. Some sources appear to coalesce the end-time Elijah with the promised prophet like Moses.[91]

Jesus as an Eschatological Prophet

Although a number of scholars have argued that Jesus functioned as an eschatological prophet, E. P. Sanders has offered one of the seminal and most influential cases for this position in our generation. I am addressing in this section especially Sanders' seminal work on Jesus research, *Jesus and Judaism,* even though I believe that his later work for a broader audience, *The Historical Figure of Jesus,* works out some earlier inconsistencies and in some respects presents a more coherent picture of Jesus.

Sanders shows clear evidence that Jesus anticipated a future kingdom.[92] For example, the Son of man will be ashamed of those who are ashamed of Jesus and his message (e.g., Mk 8:38).[93] He accepts the pervasive evidence from the tradition that people believed that Jesus worked miracles.[94] Given Jesus' eschatological message (such as the kingdom and apparently the new temple), Sanders thinks Jesus' healing activity was closer to the promised signs of eschatological prophets (like Theudas) than to charismatic sages like Honi (Vermes' view) or to the magical papyri (Morton Smith's view, usually treated as eccentric today).[95] (One cannot simply object to this that the sign-prophets were not known for healing in contrast to Honi or magicians, since Honi and magicians were also not known primarily for this.)

I believe (and will argue in ch. 17) that Sanders and other like-minded scholars have a solid case for viewing Jesus as an eschatological prophet. As we have noted above, Elijah and Moses were both miracle-working prophets expected to return at the time of the end. Especially because some miracles attributed to Jesus resemble those of such prophets (e.g., Mk 6:41-42), it appears that even from an early point in the tradition Jesus' followers envisioned him at least in some way along such lines. Indeed, he may be the source of their perception on this point.

In the decades immediately after Jesus' ministry, Josephus reports a prophet who wanted to make city walls collapse or the Jordan to part[96] — like Joshua, Moses' original successor.[97] These prophets apparently depended not on military might but on an anticipated eschatological miracle to deliver them and their people.[98] The expectation of signs-working prophets is thus relevant for understanding Jesus, and we will return to it more fully in ch. 17.

Jesus in Context

Unlike most of his predecessors, Sanders starts with some fairly certain historical information about Jesus' life, rather than with the sayings.[99] For example, he seeks to learn about Jesus' expectations and mission based on his act in the temple, which he regards as historically secure.[100] Working from this secure point, he compares expectation of a new temple and restoration in early Jewish literature,[101] to which Jesus' views seem comparable, and finds other indications of Jesus' Jewish restoration eschatology.[102] (Many or most scholars do now view Jesus as somehow a prophet of Israel's restoration.)[103]

These indications include the continuity of thought regarding eschatological restoration from John the Baptist to Paul — implying the intervening influence of Jesus.[104] By comparing contemporary sources, Sanders shows that Jesus' choice of a special group of twelve disciples also marks his movement as a remnant movement interested in Israel's restoration.[105] Such features would have readily marked Jesus out to his contemporaries as an eschatological preacher.

Some of Jesus' other behavior contrasts with contemporary expectations. Sanders presents Jesus' fellowship with "sinners" as highly unusual, a practice neither borrowed from contemporary Judaism nor fully endorsed by his followers. It is, he contends, thus both authentic and revealing about Jesus' mission.[106] Sanders connects Jesus' welcome of sinners with his view that Jesus was not calling for national repentance.[107] I would view the evidence differently: on my view, national repentance was so urgent that Jesus went out of his way to seek sinners, and his mission as an agent of the kingdom was so central that embracing his message counted for more before God than did conventional forms of expressing repentance. (I will return to that subject in ch. 14.)

He doubts most supposed cases of Jesus rejecting the law (e.g., the sabbath), but does find evidence that Jesus allowed the law to be set aside in some cases, probably related to the emergency situation of the impending kingdom.[108] He doubts much conflict with the Pharisees, but given Jesus' action in the temple, he (like Vermes and others) allows the more lethal opposition of the aristocratic priests.[109]

Forced Choices?

Although the reader will recognize that I agree with Sanders' basic thesis and agree with most of his approach, I wish at this point to note some areas where I think Sanders has treated the evidence too narrowly.[110] Like many other scholars, Sanders sometimes presents alternatives in such a way as to force choices, offering two alternatives without allowing for the possibility of other options. For example, he argues that Jesus either attacks purity or the necessary business arrangements in the temple, if he is attacking anything at all;[111] but a detractor could (if one wished) suggest that Jesus' complaint had some other basis than these two alternatives (for example, the location of the trade).

More importantly, while I believe that Sanders is right to argue for the future kingdom, he may too readily play down some evidence for its presence in Jesus' ministry. In the gospel tradition, the kingdom is received as a gift, entered as a child (Mk 10:14-15), and apparently parabled as a current, smaller foretaste of the future (Mk 4:26-32). Here again, the division of options seems part of the culprit in excluding potential evidence. Dividing material about the kingdom into six categories, Sanders includes this "present" material in two other categories (covenant[112] and the kingdom's character).[113] Because he includes each piece of evidence in only one category, he thus excludes them from the category of the kingdom-as-present in Jesus, a category that consequently has so little remaining in it that Sanders can essentially reject it.[114] Yet many of these sayings could belong to multiple categories, a possibility excluded only by the arbitrary choice of including them in only one category each. Even so, Sanders does allow it as at least conceivable that Jesus believed that the kingdom was breaking in through his message,[115] in the same way that some other prophets of his day may have thought this for their own activity.[116]

Repentance and Conflict

Sanders doubts the tradition's portrayal of Jesus' call to public repentance.[117] Yet I believe that his helpful approach to Jesus as an eschatological prophet may challenge his own suggestion that Jesus did not emphasize public repentance. Sanders distinguishes this repentance aspect of Jesus' mission too sharply from that of John the Baptist. But repentance's occurrence in John's teaching and that of many of Jesus' followers provides an argument from continuity, the very sort of argument he elsewhere accepts in the case of restoration eschatology.[118]

If Mark portrays Jesus as calling Israel to repent (Mk 1:14-15) or sending his disciples to do so (Mk 6:12), Sanders thinks that the evangelists "felt it necessary to remedy" the lack of Jesus' teaching on the subject, hence concludes that "the sayings were added."[119] By this line of argument, one could account for any evidence in the tradition that conflicts with one's thesis as proof that one's thesis is correct! He doubts that Jesus required restitution.[120] His case is somewhat stronger at this point; the Gospels do not offer extensive evidence for Jesus demanding restitution. Nevertheless, one can argue against Jesus' concern for restitution completely only by discounting a story like Zaccheus (Lk 19:8) and by ignoring Matt 5:24 (which he elsewhere seems to accept as authentic).[121]

While Jesus surely ate with sinners (hence accepted them on a social level), to claim that he accepted them without repentance and moral reformation[122] seems to exclude a large amount of the Jesus tradition solely on the grounds of its content (at least, if Jesus' acceptance is construed as making them his followers without transformation). Not only does Jesus' message of repentance appear in multiple strata of the tradition (e.g., Mk 1:15; 6:12; Lk 13:3-5; 15:7, 10), but Jesus' demands for discipleship are radical. Sanders could be right that Jesus did not require sacrifice with repentance[123] and perhaps limited restitution; but in a different context Sanders accepts the force of Matt 8:21-22//Lk 9:59-60,[124] which necessarily involves radical obedience for converts. As we shall note in ch. 14, many other texts also emphasize radical discipleship (e.g., Mk 1:16-20; 8:34; 10:21-30). Limited use of the term "repentance" need not entail any denial that Jesus demanded radical change.

Part of the conflict here is a matter of definition; "repentance" in first-century Judaism required restitution and sacrifice, which Sanders finds lacking in Jesus' teaching.[125] (He may not hold John the Baptist to the same standard; although he allows that John preached repentance, we find no requirement of restitution or sacrifice in John's teaching.)[126] We should not argue against a practice from silence when ancient hearers may have simply assumed it, but it does seem that Jesus' interests differed from those of priests and even Pharisees.

Moreover, Sanders does allow that Jesus would have believed in repentance in the general sense, but argues that, unlike other Jewish restoration sources, Jesus did not emphasize *national* repentance.[127] It seems to me more likely, however, that this very context in early Judaism supports the probability that Jesus did call for national repentance, like John. I believe that this call would support rather than detract from Sanders' larger emphasis on Jesus' restoration eschatology. Indeed, in "Q" material that is difficult to doubt, Jesus laments entire towns that have not adequately repented (Matt 11:21//Lk 10:13), and perhaps Israel as well (Matt 12:41//Lk 11:32). (In a later work, Sanders also contends that Jesus probably concurred with John's message of repentance because of coming judgment,[128] though he continues to believe that "repentance" was not a prominent theme for Jesus.)[129]

Just as Jesus should be more in continuity with John's mission on the matter of repentance, it would not be surprising if his mission led to conflict with Jewish teachers who disagreed with him. While Sanders rightly reacts against Christian scholarship that has traditionally demonized ancient Judaism as a foil for Jesus, I believe that he too often minimizes or eliminates tensions in the tradition between Jesus and the Pharisees.[130] Although we must read Jesus within Judaism, we do know that most Jewish groups did in fact have conflicts with others. Of course, Sanders' emphasis is appropriate: the Pharisees did not go around trying to kill people who differed with their interpretation of the law. Even in the Gospels, where some Pharisees "plotted" against Jesus, it is, as Sanders notes, Jerusalem's priestly leaders who get Jesus executed, and that within a few days of their decision.[131] But interpretive conflict with some Pharisees and/or scribes pervades the tradition, appearing in every level of it.[132] We address these issues in ch. 16.

Jesus and Eschatology

What of Sanders' contention that Jesus was an eschatological prophet? Many, probably most, scholars find this conclusion difficult to evade (despite differences among themselves on what they mean by "eschatology"). Jesus is eschatologically oriented in Mark, Q (in our current and least speculative form), and in our earliest Pauline sources that probably reflect Jesus' teaching on the subject (a point we will address more fully in ch. 17 and appendix 4). Only the Fourth Gospel emphasizes realized eschatology while playing down the future, and even that gospel includes some future eschatology.[133]

Further, Jesus historically followed an eschatological prophet (John) and generated an enthusiastically eschatological movement. The closest parallels to his earliest movement are found among Palestinian Jews who expected an imminent divine intervention of some sort. (I include in this comparison those who expected divinely enabled political deliverance from Rome through protest or revolt, and the "sign" prophets depending on divine intervention.)[134]

Why then are some scholars today skeptical of an eschatological Jesus? It is noteworthy that some of the scholars who do so appeal to non-Jewish analogies to support their understanding of Jesus, even though no one can seriously deny that Jesus was Jewish. There is also more intellectual cultural appeal today in a non-eschatological Jesus, as was the case before (as well as for most of the years since) Weiss and Schweitzer. Most scholars who emphasize Jesus' Jewish framework recognize that Jesus spoke prophetically about the future, whether as a matter of an imminent crisis in the political order (which did materialize), a more cosmic cataclysm, or both.

Conclusion

We have surveyed several approaches to Jesus with an emphasis on his Jewish context, and suggested that these offer a more satisfactory framework for understanding Jesus' ministry. Although I have focused here on Borg's early work and especially the approaches of Vermes and Sanders, many other scholars could have been named. My primary objective in this book is not to survey earlier literature, however, but to argue for a synthesis that also draws on some additional information offered in the following chapters. My point has been to illustrate the diverse range of views in Jesus scholarship and provide a sense of where this book will fit within that range.

Before I turn to various traditions about Jesus, I need to explore the written sources that have preserved them. What are the most dependable sources? That is, which ancient gospels or other works provide generally useful information about Jesus? To this question we turn in the following chapter.

CHAPTER 4

Other Gospels?

"I propose a single stream of tradition for the passion-resurrection traditions from the [Gospel of Peter's] Cross Gospel into Mark. . . . My theory, then, is that canonical Mark dismembered Secret Mark's story of the young man's resurrection and initiation."

JOHN DOMINIC CROSSAN[1]

"The claims that these writings contain independent valuable historical evidence for the life and teaching of Jesus do not stand up to scrutiny."

GRAHAM STANTON[2]

". . . the Gospel of Thomas and the Gospel of Peter, to cite just two examples . . . drip with indications of lateness, yet some scholars hope to date forms of these writings to the first century. They do this by attempting to extract early, hypothetic forms of the text from the actual texts that we have. But they do this without any evidence."

CRAIG EVANS[3]

Whether due to theological dissatisfaction with the canonical Gospels or due to historical curiosity, talk of "lost Gospels" is in vogue today. Fortunately for such interest, we have good reason to believe, as we shall note more fully later, that many accounts of Jesus' life did circulate in the first century (as noted in Lk 1:1). I doubt that there is a New Testament scholar alive today who could contain her or his excitement should one of these documents come to light.

Nevertheless, and *un*fortunately for our interest, none of the noncanonical "gospels" currently circulating are authentic first-century works. This deficiency proves especially unfortunate for scholars who have reconstructed alternative pictures of Jesus and his earliest followers to a significant extent based on these documents.[4] In the case of at least some of these scholars, the wish may be mother to the thought. As Craig Evans, a scholar who has worked extensively in these sources, warns, "In marked contrast to the hypercritical approach many scholars take to the canonical Gospels, several scholars are surprisingly uncritical in their approach to the extracanonical Gospels."[5] On the whole these works bear all the signs of lateness rather than reflecting early Palestinian Jewish tradition.[6] At the end of the chapter we shall briefly survey some other noncanonical evidence, though the results of that examination also prove slender.

Constantine's Canon?

Not many years ago parts of the media hyped the "lost" Gospel of Judas.[7] While this "gospel" is valuable for understanding beliefs in the era from which it emerged, however, for the most part neither the scholars who worked on it nor New Testament scholars found it very relevant for understanding the historical Jesus. The work is simply too late to preserve reliable traditions about Jesus.[8]

Some popular writers today have spoken of scores of ancient "gospels" competing with the canonical gospels until purged by Constantine.[9] This claim is either disingenuous or stems from ignorance of the facts.[10]

If we count as a "gospel" any "life of Jesus" regardless of the date of its composition, we would have to include the plethora of nineteenth-century "lives of Jesus" (along with a few movies about Jesus today). Clearly, however, the only "lives of Jesus" that can be counted on to give us independently reliable information are those that were composed within the earliest generations of the church. As we shall argue, of the "gospels" that survive today, for better or for worse only the four preserved and accepted by the mainstream second-century church into their functioning canon can lay a solid claim to stem from the first few generations (i.e., from the first century, although the Fourth Gospel probably meets this criterion by less than a decade). For the most part, what they failed to preserve failed to survive.

We will argue later that far more works about Jesus circulated in the first century than the four now in the Christian canon; apart from these four, however, none was circulated widely enough to survive. The other extant works are later, some from the second century, but many from centuries following. One can in fact find scores of extant (most of them barely extant) works that can be called "gospels," but only a few of these date even to the second century, and many stem from long *after* Constantine.

The popular claim is also disingenuous because matters were settled for the vast *majority* of the church long before Constantine. By 170 CE, Tatian in Syria harmonized the four gospels now accepted as canonical, probably developing earlier work from the mid-second century. From the same generation Irenaeus in the western Empire, far from Syria and addressing a culturally quite different form of the Christian movement than Tatian addressed, also emphasized these four gospels. Toward the end of the second century, Irenaeus treats Matthew, Mark, Luke and John as the only gospels universally accepted by the "orthodox" circle of churches.[11] Irenaeus' modern detractors may dispute his claims about how early these works were accepted, but they were certainly widely accepted by his day, and to place other works on an equal footing with the four as late as Constantine is simply inaccurate. Works circulating in some minority circles never attained sufficient readership to become standard or displace their earlier public competitors.[12]

Most importantly, the popular claim is disingenous because it compares apples and oranges under the rubric "gospels." The other works that we call gospels mostly fall into two broad categories: "apocryphal gospels" and "gnostic gospels."[13] Neither of the two are exactly "lives" of Jesus (in the sense of ancient biography), and gnostic gospels are especially disqualified. Most gnostic gospels are simply collections of sayings.

Apocryphal Gospels and Acts

Until recent times most scholars agreed with Bultmann's assessment of the apocryphal gospels as legendary and historically valueless.[14] The apocryphal gospels tend to display second-century tendencies far removed from a Palestinian tradition; they exhibit many more clearly secondary and tendentious features than the earlier Gospels ultimately received as canonical by the Church.[15]

The Genre of the Apocryphal Gospels

The apocryphal gospels seem concerned to fill in missing details of Jesus' life,[16] and are closer in genre to novels than to biographies.[17] Novels generally reflected the milieu of their readership more than that of their characters,[18] and this characteristic fits these apocryphal gospels' cultural horizons. Thus the apocryphal gospels did not even need to draw extensively on earlier gospels,[19] although there are some parallels.[20]

Ancient readers knew the genre of novel, but in the overwhelming majority of cases could distinguish between historical and fictitious narratives.[21] Although this distinction was probably somewhat less obvious once the apocryphal works became widely circulated beyond their original audiences, there is little indication that they offered any serious competition with the four gospels ultimately deemed canonical. Distinctions in genre revealed distinctions in purpose. Even when historical works have incorrect facts they do not become fiction, and a novel that depends on historical information does not become history;[22] what distinguishes the two genres is the nature of their truth claims.[23] (We address the contrast between novel and history further in our following chapter.)

Most scholars recognize that the apocryphal gospels and acts bear various similarities to ancient novels.[24] The apocryphal acts include "faked documentation and other devices used in ancient fiction to create an atmosphere of verisimilitude."[25] One scholar points out such apocryphal works' "large ration of the absurd," such as "talking dogs and competitive displays of magic, sky travels and a miracle competition (Acts of Peter), obedient bed-bugs (Acts of John), baptized lions (Acts of Paul)," and "cannibals (Andrew and Matthew among the *anthropophagoi*)."[26] Needless to say, many are enjoyable to read.

In contrast to Luke's Acts, the apocryphal acts date from the period of the heyday of the Greek romances.[27] At least some of them, most obviously the *Acts of Paul*, appear dependent in content on Luke's Acts.[28] Just as later apocryphal gospels diverge significantly from Palestinian and Semitic traits in the early strata of the Jesus tradition, so these apocryphal acts often diverge much further from the undisputed epistles' portrait of Paul than Luke's Acts does.[29]

Most novelistic gospels and acts were theologically compatible with the majority of the church of their day, and simply appealed to the popular imaginations of many Christians eager to fill in gaps of what was known about Jesus' earthly life. Still, their narrative form came too close to canonical forms for some critics' comfort, and not everyone took well to composing fiction under the guise of fact: the church defrocked the well-meaning presbyter in Asia Minor who compiled the *Acts of Paul.* (And it should be admitted that, from a literary perspective, these early Christian novelists were hardly forerunners of John Bunyan, G. K. Chesterton, Dorothy Sayers, C. S. Lewis, J. R. Tolkien or Anne Rice.)

Nevertheless, a work can be harmless or even edifying and widely recommended, without meeting the ancient church's criteria for canonicity. (To my knowledge, no one has recommended C. S. Lewis' *Chronicles of Narnia* for canonization, at least not officially.) Many early churches viewed their gospels as "memoirs" of Jesus;[30] novels might be good or bad, but they were not memoirs. Simply because someone wrote a religious work, even in the first century, would not automatically invite early Christians to treat it as Scripture.

The church felt that its canon's Gospels had to stem from those who knew Jesus directly or through close association with those who did, to guarantee accurate information. While scholars debate the authorship of the four Gospels today, most place all four within the first century (within three to six-and-a-half decades of the events they narrate). Works that appeared suddenly at a later time, claiming a previously "hidden" tradition of apostolic authorship (such as some apocryphal gospels do), would naturally be suspect. When these later works contradicted the long-circulated, publicly preserved traditions of Jesus' teachings, as gnostic sources did, they could hardly command a widespread hearing outside their own circles.

Examples from the Apocryphal Gospels

The character of Jesus in some of these "gospels" differs noticeably from the character of the Jesus in our extant first-century sources. Thus, for example, in the *Infancy Story of Thomas* (not the same as the earlier Gospel of Thomas), Jesus strikes dead a boy who bumped him. When the deceased boy's parents complain to Joseph, Jesus strikes them blind, to his stepfather's dismay.[31] When another observer complains because Jesus made clay sparrows on the Sabbath, Jesus claps his hands and the birds fly off.[32] A child died accidentally and when Jesus was accused of having pushed him, Jesus raised him to testify.[33]

The apocryphal gospels vary in kind,[34] including infancy gospels (such as those attributed to James and Thomas); a passion gospel *(Acts of Pilate)*; and the Gospels of Bartholomew; of Nicodemus; and so forth. For some, like the Gospels of Barnabas, the Ebionites, and the Hebrews, we possess only fragments quoted by other authors. Some of the apocryphal gospels are very late (the Apocryphal Gospel of John, for example, not to be confused with our canonical Gospel of John, may derive from the eleventh century). Others probably stem from the second century, though probably dependent on our canonical Gospels.[35]

A small minority of scholars think that the Gospel of Peter comes from the first century;[36] it is not docetic and has some apocalyptic elements. Thus Crossan, an "alternative gospel" advocate, dates part of it (the so-called Cross Gospel) earlier than any of the canonical Gospels, and relies on it for part of his reconstruction of events surrounding Jesus.[37] Its date, however, is surely later than the first century. The ninth-century document scholars today call the "Gospel of Peter" has no title, and its putative original is dated to the second century only because some have supposed it to be the work condemned (though not really described) by an ancient bishop later quoted by Eusebius. Some argue that our document is not in fact the one referred to in Eusebius; if they are correct, the original version of this work could date as late as the ninth century.[38]

In any case, it would be difficult to argue that this text, with its self-rolling stone, walking cross, and other features strikingly uncharacteristic of the securest Jesus tradition, is earlier than the canonical gospels.[39] It appears to draw on all four canonical Gospels, and sometimes apparently includes wording characteristic of those sources.[40] The level of anti-Jewish prejudice resembles some second-century works.[41] Most importantly, the work is so far removed from any knowledge of early Judaism as to portray Jewish leaders keeping watch in a cemetery at night (obviously violating Jewish belief and practice regarding ritual purity).[42] Our standards and expectations for novels, however, differ from those for biographies and histories.

Gnostic Gospels

As we have noted, comparing many other surviving "gospels" with the canonical ones is somewhat like comparing apples and oranges. If this observation is true regarding apocryphal gospels, which are essentially novels but at least share the canonical Gospels' narrative form, it is much more the case with regard to "gnostic gospels," most of which are largely collections of sayings. (While Jesus researchers are happy to study Jesus' teachings, what we could say about his "life" would be severely limited if these sources were all we had to work with.)

With regard to literary form, the gnostic gospels are nothing like the canonical Gospels; they are called gospels only because they purport to convey good news.[43] Thus at most we could look there for some of Jesus' sayings, not a biographic narrative about him (though some do frame sayings with narrative, the emphasis is normally on the sayings). Much of what we find in the gnostic "gospels" are in fact random sayings collections including both sayings of Jesus (often randomly arranged) and later gnosticizing words attributed to him.

Indeed, most of what appears in the gnostic gospels is not helpful even for reconstructing Jesus' teachings. Most sayings that first surface in the gnostic "gospels" are hardly early, though the earlier of these collections may preserve or adapt some authentic agrapha as well as sayings also reported in our canonical gospels.[44] The collections as a whole are tendentious in a gnosticizing (and hence later) direction and lack most of the sort of early Palestinian Jewish material frequently found in the Synoptics and even John.[45]

The leading gnostics for the most part represented an academic elite, and in their purely gnostic form never commanded a majority within ancient circles of Christians. It is also unclear to what degree the plethora of "gospels" and other works functioned as "canon" among them, and to what degree some gnostic schools appreciated the authority of other gnostic schools' revelations. Groups categorized as gnostic by the later church were more diverse than we usually assume;[46] today some scholars even regard our category as anachronistic, a neologism.[47] Gnostics emphasized the secrecy of their knowledge partly because they appealed to an elite class of "insiders,"[48] but probably also because they lacked any true sources that allowed them to claim earlier public traditions.

A Sign of Lateness

The absence of full gnosticism in any first-century sources is significant, since those extant sources from the early Empire report even prominent individual philosophers and orators in Greek cities. One could cite the gnostic claim of information passed on secretly, in contrast to the public transmission of information in philosophic schools or the apostolic church. Even to appeal to this secrecy, however, one must concede to a point that works against the likelihood of any pre-Christian gnostic sects: gnostics' appeal to secret traditions constituted their own tacit admission that their traditions lacked any demonstrably early, publicly testable special information.[49] When we find clearly gnostic elements in a work, therefore, these elements indicate that the work in its current form cannot predate the first century.

Many respected scholars have argued for a pre-Christian, pagan gnosticism,[50] but today an increasing number of them admit the scarcity of the evidence.[51] Certainly in the areas of NT scholarship with which I am most familiar (Synoptics, John, and Paul), appeals to gnostic backgrounds have declined substantially in recent years, supplanted by more concrete evidence from Jewish and Greco-Roman sources.

While "gnosticizing" tendencies as broadly defined clearly exist in pre-Christian middle Platonic and related traditions, the features unique to Christian gnosticism do not appear in any texts prior to the spread of Christianity. Alongside other elements in gnosticism, the Christian element is also clear in all extant bodies of gnostic literature.[52]

Many of the early gnostic texts found in the Nag Hammadi corpus depend on Christian tradition.[53] The individual texts that do not, might presuppose Christian or at least mixed gnostic influence by virtue of the collections in which they appear.[54] Despite the contention of many scholars that these texts preserve pre-Christian gnostic tradition,[55] the clear Christian influence in many of these texts shifts the burden of proof to the defender of this thesis. Regardless of proposed antecedents, the gnosticism found in these documents is from the Christian period and at times clearly polemicizes against more traditional Christian "orthodoxy."[56] The extant texts, therefore, do not prove a clear pre-Christian gnosticism.[57]

Still later are other collections like the Hermetica; scholars most familiar with the documents do not date them before the Christian period.[58] Comparing the Hermetica with the latest of the canonical Gospels, John, shows far less overlap than some have supposed. Whereas only about 4% of John's words do not appear in the most common Greek version of the Old Testament, 60% of John's words do not overlap with the Hermetica; all words shared by John and the Hermetica also appear in the Greek translation of the Old Testament.[59] This may suggest that John's vocabulary is derived most commonly from the Jewish Bible in its Greek form.[60]

Among the canonical Gospels, by contrast, even John's thinking is much farther from gnosticism than, say, the Jewish philosopher Philo's is. The discovery of the Qumran scrolls moved Johannine scholars to a greater appreciation for John's Palestinian Jewish elements; in chs. 14-16 we shall focus on various Palestinian Jewish elements of the traditions in the Synoptic Gospels. Even John includes substantial knowledge of Jerusalem's topography, long after Jerusalem's destruction;[61] most gnostic gospels, by contrast, would probably not *care* about topography.

The Gospel of Thomas

While most scholars do not go this far, the Jesus Seminar treats the Gospel of Thomas as an independent source.[62] Of the surviving works that we call "gospels" that were not accepted into the canon, the one thought to contain the largest amount of early tradition is the sayings Gospel of Thomas. This optimism seems likely correct, but if the post-canonical works include little of value, it could be true without saying much. More than likely, Thomas *does* contain some reliable traditions besides where it draws on the canonical Gospels (or, on some views, their sources); but given clearly later elements in Thomas alongside them, it is clear that much of Thomas is *not* original.[63] For most scholars, the later elements in Thomas bring into question how much we can be sure of the elements that are impossible for us to date.

Most scholars today agree that even the Gospel of Thomas in its present form (some argue as many as one-third of its sayings) involves gnostic influence,[64] even if it is less gnostic than many later documents. This state of affairs contrasts with the canonical Gospels, especially the Synoptics, which lack clearly gnostic elements. These canonical Gospels often retain Palestinian Jewish figures of speech, customs, and so forth (sometimes in spite of their authors' own tendencies) that point to early Palestinian tradition (see later chapters in this book). Although even the most obscure of Greek philosophical schools in this period stand well documented among our ancient sources, we lack evidence for full-blown gnosticism before the second century (although its constituent parts, such as Middle Platonism, were already evolving, as we have noted).[65] Thus Thomas represents a late document compared with the canonical Gospels.[66]

As in the case of the gnostic gospels in general, Thomas belongs to a different genre than the canonical gospels.[67] On the assumption that Q (common material behind both Matthew and Luke) is purely a sayings source, some wish to make Thomas as early as Q. But this argument depends on a disputed (though defensible) major premise and an indefensible, implicit minor premise. I address both more fully below, but let me comment on them briefly at this relevant point. First, not all scholars accept "Q" (though I accept it as very probable and employ it as a working hypothesis in this book), and not all who do so accept it as purely a sayings source.[68] But the second, implicit premise is the more astonishing one. Sayings collections existed for over a millennium before "Q" and for centuries afterward. Why must one first-century sayings source invite us to date Thomas (but not the many later gnostic sayings sources) to the same period?

Against a first-century date for Thomas is also the recognition, with probably the majority of scholars today, that Thomas in its current form depends on the Synoptics. This is because Thomas has parallels to every stratum of Gospel tradition (including John and distinctively Matthean redaction) and some of its sayings follow others solely because of the sequence in the canonical Gospels.[69] Such dependence may limit how much we can rely on Thomas as an independent source.[70] If Thomas or a collection that grew into Thomas existed in earlier stages,[71] it seems to me that trying to uncover these stages invites as much caution as it would if we tried to uncover preliminary stages in, say, Mark's Gospel — what most scholars today would consider a speculative exercise (see below our comments on stages within "Q").

Some scholars have gone further, reconstructing a specifically late-second-century date for Thomas. This thesis remains disputed, and I do not rest my more general argument on it; the consensus dating is already over a century after Jesus' execution, outside personal memory of the eyewitnesses, so adding an additional generation does not really change our point much. Nevertheless, it is a thesis currently under discussion and illustrates a possible milieu for the finished gospel.

Noting commonly recognized parallels with second-century Syrian ideas,[72] Nicholas Perrin recently reverted this Coptic document back into Syriac. Although "back translation" is always precarious, in this case it produced what appears to be a startling discovery: all but three of the couplets in the Gospel of Thomas are linked by 500 catchwords[73] (such links being a common practice in Syriac and other sources).[74] (Syriac puns often occur in adjacent verses as well;[75] for example, "fire" and "light" are similar Syriac terms.)[76] Thus Perrin argues that the work as we have it is clearly an "organic unity,"[77] composed (at least in its present form) all at one time.[78] In itself this discovery would not necessarily render Thomas late; it suggests, in fact, that the work is at least somewhat earlier than our earliest Coptic example of it.[79]

What is more troubling for an "early Thomas" hypothesis is that Thomas bears numerous characteristics of Syriac Christianity from the second half of the second century, more than of a Palestinian Jewish milieu well over a century earlier. Worse yet, the Gospel of Thomas sometimes follows the sequence and content of Tatian's *Diatessaron* (and other Syrian tradition from that period or later).[80] It sometimes shares readings with the Diatessaron that do not appear in the Greek manuscripts.[81] In some cases where some have regarded Thomas' readings as earlier than the canonical Gospels, they instead reflect precisely the later Syrian tradition (even to the mix of second and third person in *Thomas* 54).[82] Tatian's *Diatessaron* is a harmony of our four canonical Gospels dating to c. 170 CE (i.e., from shortly before Irenaeus was defending the church's commitment to these four Gospels).[83] If the Gospel of Thomas follows Tatian's *Diatessaron,* it would stem from some time after c. 170 CE.[84] In this case it could be assigned safely to the last quarter of the second century — roughly a century after the average date assigned to the canonical Gospels by critical scholars. This is the very latest at which one could possibly date this work, given most scholars' dating of *P.Oxy.* 1 (which attests it) to 200 CE.[85]

Against this conclusion, we could argue that Tatian and Thomas may simply reflect a common Syriac tradition.[86] Though the points of common sequence might suggest more than a common oral tradition, granting a common oral source would allow an earlier date than dependence on the *Diatessaron* would require. This solution is a possible one, but Perrin's most important observation would nevertheless remain. We would still have a Syriac provenance (probably not before the mid-second century) and dependence on mid- to late-second-century Syriac tradition, not the original Jesus tradition.[87] Even without dependence on the *Diatessaron,* most scholars date *Thomas* in its present form to the mid-second century;[88] dependence would simply make the case firmer and a few decades later. By contrast, very few scholars would try to date the Synoptics or John this late.[89]

Perhaps not surprisingly, the gospel's closing paragraph sounds more like some Greek philosophers than like the Jewish teacher and prophet we hear in the canonical Gospels. When Peter insists that Mary Magdalene, as a woman, is unworthy of spiritual life, Jesus responds, "I myself shall lead her in order to make her male, so that she too may become a living spirit resembling you males. For every woman who will make herself male will enter the Kingdom of Heaven."[90] One might compare such thinking in the first-century Jewish Middle Platonist thinker Philo, whose world of thought is almost universally recognized to differ substantially from Jesus' Palestinian Jewish milieu. Wishing to praise the intellectual ability of the empress Livia, Philo remarks that she became male in her intellect.[91] In contrast to some popular portrayals of this second-century gospel today, Thomas, like Philo, was no feminist. Nor do such remarks belong to the same conceptual world as the Palestinian Jewish sage and prophet of Synoptic tradition.

Some argue that the original Gospel of Thomas lacked all the late material found in its present form. One cannot of course rule out this possibility, but this approach's appeal to a hypothetical source constitutes a tacit admission that no concrete documentary evidence supports the "early Thomas" idea. (It offers the same problem as arguments for stages in Q: it becomes more speculative than most scholars can find persuasive.) All the concrete evidence that we *do* have suggests a later work simply drawing on some earlier sources (at least including the canonical Gospels). Moreover, if we do accept the catchwords thesis, they are so deeply embedded in the work's structure as to render quite difficult any attempt to reconstruct a mid-first-century original.

In some cases, Thomas may appeal to scholars of a particular bent today because of its noneschatological approach.[92] Some of the same scholars who appeal to Thomas, however, are fairly skeptical of much historical tradition in John's Gospel,[93] which also emphasizes the present experience of God much more than the future kingdom.[94] In such cases, the double standard is telling, for our textual evidence for John is earlier.

Mixing Types of Gospels

A minority of scholars have argued that apocryphal and gnostic gospels reflect a form earlier than that of the canonical Gospels and similar gospels no longer extant.[95] Working from the apocryphal gospels, for example, Helmut Koester has suggested that they reflect genres earlier than our canonical Gospels,

> . . . such as sayings collections, aretalogies (miracle collections), and apocalypses. As a result, the Coptic Gospel of Thomas should be seen in a trajectory from Q, the Infancy Gospel of Thomas from collections like the Johannine Semeia source, and the Apocryphon of John from revelations like the Apocalypse of John.[96]

In principle, such genre comparisons are not objectionable (regardless of whether or not they are correct). Any attempt to designate these later works as early based on such genre considerations, however, would reflect an illegitimate inference. All the relevant genres coexisted in the first century, so chronological inferences on the basis of such genres are unwarranted.

Some have compared even the canonical Gospels with a kind of writing called aretalogies (narratives celebrating marvelous deeds of heroes).[97] Aretalogies do have some features in common with some gospel narratives, but our ancient examples are normally brief narrations or lists of divine acts, hence do not provide the best analogies for the Gospels as whole works.[98] These narratives might support the hypothesis of early circulated miracle-collections, as Koester thinks (though they differ even from apocryphal gospels). But aretalogy was not even a clearly defined genre,[99] and, as we have already noted, the apocryphal gospels generally fit the genre of novels.

The Gospel of Thomas probably does intentionally follow the ancient form of a sayings collection; but acknowledging this form does not require us to retroject gnosticism into earlier Christian sayings collections, or to imply that Thomas must be as early as "Q." First, as we have noted, sayings collections are as old as Israelite and other ancient Near Eastern proverbs and also extend to Greek collections of philosophers' witticisms.[100] We thus cannot *date* a work based simply on its "sayings" genre.[101] Sayings collections hardly disappeared after the first century! The rabbinic collection Pirqe Abot and the Syrian *Sentences of Sextus* in fact date to the later period likely for the Gospel of Thomas.[102]

Moreover, as we have also noted, it is not clear that Q excluded all narrative (the matter is debated). Although Q is probably primarily sayings (some with narrative frames), it probably includes some narrative (especially in Matt 3:1-12// Lk 3:7-17; Matt 4:1-11//Lk 4:1-12; Matt 8:5-13//Lk 7:2-10);[103] we will address the issue of Q more fully below. Of course, some sayings sources could include narrative frames (even when simply, "so-and-so said") when needed. Reasonably assuming that Q was largely a sayings source, however, would still not clarify the relationship between these works and Q. Since various sayings sources existed, there is no reason to assume that gnostic sayings collections made Q their model unless they can be shown to draw substantially from Q material. In fact, they appear to have had access to "Q" material only the way we do — through Matthew and Luke. (As we have noted, even the Gospel of Thomas, the possible exception, includes sayings that include Matthew's or Luke's editing. Later works are even far more problematic than Thomas.)

We should also observe that the sayings form does not invite us to assume that the sayings genre was opposed in principle to narrative gospels, as some scholars have argued.[104] Both forms could exist simultaneously without representing competing "communities." Ancient collections of sayings of famous teachers did not preclude an interest in the deeds of those teachers; reports of sages' teachings frequently incorporated accounts of their lives or settings for their sayings;[105] and Ahiqar's wisdom sayings and narrative were probably already combined more than half a millennium before the Gospels were written.[106] Most of the proverbs in the Old Testament collection called Proverbs are traditionally attributed to Solomon (cf. Prov 1:1; 10:1; 25:1); but it hardly follows that those who followed this wisdom-genre therefore rejected the narrative reports concerning Solomon in 1 Kings (cf. 1 Kgs 4:32). Ancient rhetorical experts also addressed how to combine sayings with narrative.[107] Early Christian tradition and use of narrative genre were not likely isolated in a single stream; where Paul's incidental use attests Jesus traditions, they attest both Q and Mark, and some of the Q material is more like Matthew whereas some is more like Luke.[108] Historically, it is simply nonsense to pretend that writers and communities were limited to writing in a single literary genre.

While sayings collections, like narratives, could be either early or late, both the gnostic texts and their more "orthodox" second-century competitors are clearly later, expansive, and considerably farther removed from the Palestinian Jesus tradition than the canonical Gospels are.

Still Later Gospels

We will not explore in any detail gnostic "gospels" later than Thomas. This is because they tend to be more "gnostic" than Thomas, offering fewer parallels with authentic Jesus tradition and even fewer signs of Jesus' original milieu. In other words, few of their sayings offer much good claim to derive from the Jesus of history, however much they may teach us about what people were teaching in his name in a subsequent period. Such later "gospels" include the Gospel of Philip and the Gospel of Mary. The Gospel of Truth is a purely gnostic meditation, even further from a "gospel" form.

The majority of churches (what we might call the "mainstream" of churches, what has traditionally been called "orthodox") rejected gospels composed based on gnostic "revelation." They insisted instead on the standard established by first-century Gospels, composed by eyewitnesses or those who knew them. This reflects not simple bias on their part but their insistence on materials known to be early, publicly believed to be from the apostolic circle that knew Jesus, and those who learned from them directly. This was a claim that the later gnostic works, despite their attributions, could not meet; traditions supposedly passed on in "secret" were rightly suspected of being later inventions.

Thus, apart from some disputed sayings in Thomas, it is unlikely that any of the apocryphal or gnostic gospels reflect any degree of authentic Jesus tradition.[109] Groups that claim "secret" traditions, as the gnostics often did for their works, thereby concede their lack of public attestation, in contrast to the widely circulated Gospels accepted by the mainstream of early Christianity.[110]

As noted above, gnostic "gospels" constitute an entirely different genre than the "biographic" genre now generally assigned to the four Gospels later deemed canonical.[111] Conclusions concerning them should not, therefore, be read back into studies of the canonical Gospels.

A Twentieth-Century Forgery

The "Secret Gospel of Mark," not to be confused with the canonical Gospel of Mark, is an important source for John Dominic Crossan's reconstruction of the historical Jesus. But while some scholars have wished to use the "Secret Gospel of Mark," more scholars have cautiously warned against its use in reconstructing the life of Jesus.[112] In fact, Secret Mark, once hailed by some New Testament scholars (especially by its putative discoverer Morton Smith) as an early (even pre-Mark) source,[113] has come to be regarded by most as a forgery dating from anywhere between the late second and the twentieth century.[114] The most recent discussion suggests that a twentieth-century date is most likely for the forgery, offering New Testament scholarship's own version of science's famous "Piltdown Man."[115]

The only manuscript (actually, a photograph of a manuscript) seems to derive from a different provenance than the monastery where it was supposedly found, and evidence appears to suggest that it appeared at the monastery only in recent times.[116] Its attribution to Clement is stylistically open to question;[117] it also clearly presupposes modern idiom and perhaps modern custom.[118] In fact, recent analysis reveals the typical "forger's tremor" throughout the document,[119] as well as characteristics of Morton Smith's Greek handwriting style, convincing many that Smith himself was the forger.[120]

Smith's publications on Secret Mark reflect the same "cut-and-paste" excerpting techniques that characterize the composition of both Secret Mark and the allegedly Clementine document in which it is embedded.[121] Its understanding of homosexuality reflects that of Smith and his twentieth-century context rather than that held in the first century,[122] and some thus suggest that it may have been composed precisely to advance that twentieth-century perspective.[123]

The work may even reflect some twentieth-century literary models.[124] These include a novel about a fraudulent document discrediting Christianity, discovered at the very same monastery and exposed by one "Lord Moreton" — published one year before Morton Smith's first visit to this monastery![125] We are all capable of being taken in occasionally, and it is understandable that many scholars (including myself) would have been reticent to charge such a noted scholar as Morton Smith with forgery. Given the breadth of information today, we must depend on other scholars at many points. The evidence, however, now seems to be in on this case: the *Secret Gospel of Mark* is a forgery, hence any reconstructions based on it must be re-reconstructed.

"Q" as a Lost Gospel?

One proposed "lost gospel" is in a different category from the other ones for at least two reasons. First, "Q" is hypothetical — we have no actual manuscript of the document. I would not, however, for this reason make Q a less likely source than the others we have surveyed, and that is because of a second reason: Q is probably genuinely earlier than any of our extant, finished Gospels. Thus if there is a "Q," it is one of our *best* sources for reconstructing Jesus' teaching, although it must be taken in connection with other reasonably early sources.

The major problem in this case is not the date of the document, but that the *version* of "Q" some scholars are citing is essentially nothing more than a collection of sayings selected to fit their narrower reconstruction of Jesus. Since we concluded our survey of various approaches to Jesus research in ch. 2 by observing Burton Mack's approach, it seems consistent to conclude this chapter on "other gospels" by commenting on the hypothetical "early" version of Q on which much of his case rests.

Many scholars recoil at Burton Mack's announcement that "Q is . . . a new text that has recently come to light."[126] Scholars used the Q hypothesis through most of the twentieth century, so what Mack implies is that *his* circle's *understanding* of Q is a recent "discovery." To put the matter less charitably, the Q hypothesis has been coopted for a new agenda.[127]

I am among those who think the Q hypothesis quite likely (a number of respected scholars today do not even grant this point),[128] but acknowledging and working from the hypothesis of Q is not the same as building a speculative hypothesis on a speculative reconstruction of a hypothetical document.[129] Mack's particular *version* of Q is not a consensus document of NT scholarship.

I will address Q more fully in the chapter on the Gospels' sources, but should make a few comments about my own perspective here. I will draw on "Q" in my own reconstruction of sources about Jesus, but in doing so, I am clear that we know nothing about "Q" other than what we can reconstruct from Matthew and Luke ("Q" representing the material that they share in common). I had once considered "Q" simply a convenient label for any traditions (probably many of them oral) outside Mark that Matthew and Luke shared in common. It was working through the Synoptics together again in D. Moody Smith's Luke seminar that convinced me that at least much of the Q material represents some shared written source, because Matthew and Luke often follow it in the same sequence.[130] I should note, however, that some of my colleagues in that very seminar came to dispense with Q altogether. I suspect that none of us subscribed to the various editorial "layers" in "Q" that some scholars have found. Despite claims of consensus about Q in some circles, there is very much a *lack* of consensus about it.

Are Wise Sayings Incompatible with Everything Else?

Mack uses the form of "Q" as a sayings source to argue for a "Q community" that did not know accounts of Jesus' deeds. This proposal rests on at least four questionable premises: First, it assumes that we can reconstruct entire "communities" from documents (even documents just seven pages long) that use these documents, a premise that many scholars reasonably find problematic.[131]

Second, it assumes that when a community employs a brief document that omits mention of a particular belief, we can safely argue from that silence that the community did not accept (or know of) that belief. Yet any number of comparisons would demonstrate the logical falsehood of this assumption. (I could even use the premise to argue that different books I have written, some of which do not mention issues central to the other books, were produced by different "communities.")[132]

Third, it assumes that Q was exclusively a sayings-gospel.[133] This premise, not unique to Mack, is more plausible than any of the other premises involved in this case, but may be somewhat problematic in at least a few passages.[134] Fourth and more problematic, it offers a dramatic leap of logic on the basis of this third premise. It assumes that if "Q" (which it further assumes as the earliest source) was a sayings source, then Jesus must have been remembered originally for his teachings rather than his deeds.[135] The fourth premise does not follow from the third, even were the third true.

I will return to the other premises later, but let us start with the third, least objectionable, premise. Was Q a purely sayings gospel, completely lacking narrative? Many scholars argue that Q consisted mostly of sayings, yet concede that it included some narrative (certainly one need not assume that it proved hostile to narrative).[136] To argue that Q was exclusively a sayings-gospel, Mack eventually must inform the reader that he distinguishes layers within Q. Mack's "Q" is not simply shorthand for the common material shared by Matthew and Luke, the way many scholars use it. Rather, he refers to what he considers the *earliest* "layer" of "Q."

A Non-eschatological Wisdom Source?

Mack's reconstruction of the "early layer" of Q not only excludes Q's arguably few narratives, but also its many sayings about future judgment and a future figure, at least sometimes identified with Jesus. Omitting eschatology from Q requires some major surgery! It is "Q" (the shared material behind Matthew and Luke, apart from Mark) that mentions the Twelve reigning and judging Israel in the end-time (Matt 19:28; Lk 22:30); or the incomparably powerful end-time judge burning the wicked (Matt 3:7-12; Lk 3:7-9, 16-17); or Jesus rejecting the wicked at the judgment (Matt 7:21-23; Lk 13:26-27).[137]

Following the work of some of his colleagues, Mack's "early" version of Q not surprisingly presents Jesus as a nonapocalyptic, Cynic-type sage, just what Mack considers Jesus to be.[138] Yet the idea that wisdom sayings in "Q" constitute its earliest layer is hardly a consensus.[139] Indeed, some scholars, by contrast, have argued that the eschatological sayings are the earliest layer in Q and that wisdom sayings were later embedded in this apocalyptic framework![140] And any who regard even some of Jesus' eschatological sayings as authentic will come up with a completely different picture of Jesus than Mack does.[141]

Many other scholars are skeptical, I believe rightly, of the value of the quest for finding specific layers of editing in Q.[142] Literary critics outside the discipline consider such procedures even more eccentric.[143] Not only is the entire procedure of distinguishing "layers" based on emphases too speculative. Here it is also circular: the assertion that the "sage" layer is earliest rests on the very reconstruction of Jesus the argument is designed to prove!

A basic principle of historiography is that the more one builds hypotheses on other hypotheses, the less the overall probability of the additional hypotheses. If "Q" were (for example) 70% probable, and if one granted (which I would not) that some layers within Q were 70% likely, one would have already conceded that the overall likelihood of these layers is less than 50% (49%, to be exact). To then hypothetically reconstruct those layers and argue (as again I would not) that one's reconstruction was 70% likely, one would be left with an overall probability of 34.3% (about one-third). Of course, scholars differ on all the likelihood of each of these hypotheses, but my point is simply that the more one adds speculation to speculation, the further on a limb one's speculation goes. Inevitably the limb becomes unable to support the scholar's weight.[144]

Arguments from Silence

Mack assumes that ideas not present in what he identifies as the earliest recension of Q were not held by Q's compilers. If Mack wishes us to apply this methodological assumption consistently and rigorously, there was actually quite little the "Q community" believed. If we cannot assume their early Christian context on the basis of what they do clearly have in common with early Christianity, perhaps we cannot assume their broader Jewish or Greco-Roman context either. In short, a consistently minimalist approach must insist that they believed only seven pages of wisdom sayings and nothing else.[145]

If we assume Mack's document for the sake of argument, it originally focused primarily on ethics; but does a community that produced a manual of ethics believe in nothing other than ethics? No one would accept this thesis if it were applied to Qumran's Manual of Discipline (1QS) or to most of the later rabbinic tractate *Aboth*.

As an example of how Mack's approach functions, one may take his argument that the Q people did not accept Jesus' Messiahship, since his severely edited version of Q does not affirm that teaching.[146] But assuming that Jesus' Messiahship was not accepted by the earliest Jewish Christians, when did the idea arise? Diaspora Jews might believe in a messiah,[147] but our evidence generally indicates less messianic sentiment among Jews outside Palestine than among Jews within Palestine.[148] And messianic speculation certainly would not arise among Gentile Christians who had not first borrowed it from Jews: Gentiles had no messianic categories, and for Greeks "Christ" often simply became Jesus' last name. Who then invented Jesus' messiahship?[149]

If one argues that the authors of Q, as part of the early Jesus movement, accepted other tenets that all surviving evidence indicates that all Jesus' known followers believed, one offers an argument (rightly or wrongly) on the basis of some explicit evidence we do have.[150] By contrast, dismissing all the concrete evidence we do have and then constructing a hypothesis on the basis of silence offers only a specious argument.[151] What a document says may provide us some insights concerning the community it addresses, but what it does not say tells us very little, especially in a seven-page document addressing a particular issue (as Mack makes Q1 out to be).

Yale professor Leander Keck made this case rather strongly in an influential article in 1974.[152] As Keck puts it, given the randomly preserved and situation-specific character of the early Christian sources,

> . . . can we convert silence into absence? That is, can we argue that the "silence" with regard to certain forms and traditions in the literature in hand shows that the material itself was absent from the community? . . . Can the theology and ethics of a community be inferred from one strand of tradition? For example, was the church which developed and used Q dependent on this material alone?[153]

It is unfortunate that some scholars have continued to neglect this important methodological caution.

Forced-Choice Logic

The assumption that the earliest version of Q must include either eschatology or wisdom, but cannot include both, typically rests on the still less likely assumption that these genres of thought are theologically incompatible.[154] (We briefly addressed this sort of forced-choice logic with regard to genres, above.) Leander Keck bolsters his case against communities that believed only particular documents by appealing to first-century Jewish texts:[155]

> Surely Qumran has shown us that the same community uses and produces multiple forms which function side by side. It is tantalizing to imagine how the Qumran community would have been reconstructed if the total finds from the caves had been limited to the Hymns and the Genesis Apocryphon!

"Since Qumran shows us divergent ideas, as well as diverse forms," he contends, whoever seeks "to reconstruct discrete communities and theologies on the basis of rigorous logical coherence alone" must bear the burden of proof.[156] Other scholars have noted the blend of wisdom and eschatology in such early Jewish sources.[157] Ben Witherington similarly complains:[158]

> Arguing there was a Q community is rather like arguing there was a Proverbs community, or an Aboth community. Besides the fact that it is wholly an argument from silence, with no data outside of Q by which to check such a view, where is there any precedent in early Judaism for such a community?

The related view that Q must include only one outlook fails to fit what we know of much of either early Judaism or early Christianity.[159]

Single communities used different documents in multiple genres that expressed multiple interests. The Qumran community seems interested in its founder's teachings; many scholars have attributed many of the community's hymns to the same founder. Besides hymns, the same community employed a manual of discipline, eschatological texts like the War Scroll, and pesher interpretations of the Old Testament. More specifically, single documents sometimes freely mixed wisdom and apocalyptic thought;[160] no necessary boundary in antiquity rendered these categories mutually exclusive.[161]

Indeed, one need not search as distantly as Qumran to discern authors, documents or communities that combine divergent perspectives. Matthew, Mark, and Luke each freely combine narrative with sayings, and eschatology with wisdom (especially in Matthew). If Matthew did not find Mark and "Q" irreconcilable,[162] if Mark himself may have used Q at points,[163] why need the original users of Q have found narratives intolerable? Why need the first users of a first edition of "Q" have found wisdom and eschatology incompatible, when that edition's supposed editors felt free to add the alternative perspective to the same document? If "Q" were so incompatible with the canonical Gospels, why would Matthew and Luke make such abundant use of a source so dramatically antithetical to their theology?[164]

The wisdom version of Q that Mack accepts as the earliest recension seems more determined by the conclusion that he and some of his colleagues wish to arrive at than by any other consistent or objective method. He uses "Q" as an anti-"Gospel" that, by virtue of its greater antiquity, trumps claims to accurate Jesus tradition in the early Gospels we actually do have. Thus J. Andrew Overman, chair of classics at Macalaster College, understandably complains about Mack's earlier *Myth of Innocence:*[165]

> The data that constitute historically reliable information about Jesus are largely based on a particular version of Q. There is great trust in our ability to determine which traditions are "early" and which are "late." The selection of what is authentic material frequently seems arbitrary.

More Dependable "Noncanonical" Sources

Are there then no surviving non-Christian sources about Jesus? Indeed there are some, and several of these confirm some important points about the historical Jesus. Yet all are fragmentary, and some depend on the reports of Christians.[166] Some scholars note the brief but early comments of Thallus, apparently in the 50s CE, regarding darkness around the time of Jesus' crucifixion;[167] the Syrian Stoic Mara bar Serapion, who claimed (c. 73 CE) that Jesus was a "wise king of the Jews";[168] and various others.[169] It is helpful to note these sources, but the information available in them is slender.[170]

The most relevant material appears in the early-second-century Roman historians Tacitus and Suetonius and in the first-century Jewish historian Josephus. Tacitus notes that Pontius Pilate had "Christus" executed;[171] Suetonius' report may suggest that Jewish people in Rome were debating Jesus' identity within two decades of his execution.[172] We shall briefly discuss Josephus further below.

Why do these sources not comment more? These writers addressed only what was in their purview; the focus of Tacitus and Suetonius was on Rome itself, and on the provinces or foreign wars especially insofar as they affected matters in Rome. They had little reason to be interested in Jesus himself,[173] although the massive growth of his followers in Rome apparently twice called for comment. Both these passages mention Jesus only in connection with Rome.

This neglect is not a result of prejudice against Jesus (though of course such prejudice existed); these historians simply did not focus on figures that seemed irrelevant for their audience's interests. By comparison, Tacitus has little reason to discuss even the first-century Judean king Agrippa I.[174] Pontius Pilate appears in Tacitus *only* as the governor who ordered Jesus' execution.[175] Jesus does appear in these Roman historians more than any other "messianic" or pro-phetic leader of Palestine. Despite the prominence of Josephus' *War* as a first-hand Jewish account to the Roman world's elite, he is of no interest to later rab-binic sources (less, in fact, than Jesus was). Later rabbinic sources acknowledge Jesus as a wonder-worker, but view him with hostility, treating him as a magi-cian. The rabbis write over a century later than the Gospels (at the earliest nearly two centuries after Jesus), however, and where they have "information" it tends to be secondhand, based on Christian reports.[176]

Josephus offers more information about Jesus than Tacitus or Suetonius do, though diplomatically remaining silent on the troublesome popular movement that Jesus spawned.[177] While Josephus plays down potentially "messianic" ele-ments in recent history[178] and even in the OT,[179] Josephus does mention Jesus' brother James (*Ant.* 20.200) and likely does mention Jesus himself (*Ant.* 18.64). (For his treatment of John the Baptist, see ch. 11.)

Although three brief lines in Josephus' passage about Jesus seem to be later additions, the vast majority of scholars today believe that the passage is authen-tic once these additions are set aside.[180] (Only a few have defended its complete authenticity, without interpolations.)[181] One supporting factor is the passing mention of Jesus in the passage on James; a Christian interpolator would not mention Jesus only in passing, and Josephus would mention him in passing only if he had already (in 18.64) mentioned him.[182] Another factor is that the passage seems mostly neutral, not what an ancient Christian would likely write about Je-sus.[183] Interestingly, the Arabic version of Josephus, transmitted without the same tampering, independently confirms the hypothesis that the passage was genuinely from Josephus apart from these interpolated Christian remarks.[184]

When we examine what Josephus actually says about Jesus, he portrays him as a wise sage and apparently as a worker of miracles,[185] both features that recur in the Gospels that we will consider in greater detail there.

Why We Must Look Elsewhere

Even for Josephus, however, Jesus was not a central figure. He is treated far better than any of the leaders of movements considered a threat to the land's political stability, but is not accorded more space than those other popular lead-ers. Josephus is interested in government leaders and prominent members of the aristocracy. It was instead those who were interested in Jesus who would preserve his teachings and report more of his life. Not all who came to be inter-ested in Jesus began that way; at least some people began with hostility to Jesus yet became his followers (Paul being the best-known case in point).[186] But only those with interest are likely to focus on a person.

Jesus' group was like other groups in this regard. Qumran documents revere their founder, the teacher of righteousness; but no extant sources outside Qumran speak of him, not even those authors (like Philo, Josephus, and Pliny) who mention the Essenes.[187] Josephus claims to have been a Pharisee, and tells us much about the historic role of Pharisees. Yet he never mentions Hillel, founder of the Hillelite school revered in later rabbinic sources.[188] Dio Cassius reports the Judean revolt of 132-135 CE without ever mentioning Bar Kochba — its *leader*![189] Similarly, we would not expect to find much interest in Jesus himself in contemporary Gentile documents,[190] or in fact among anyone except his followers.

Similarly, Israeli scholar David Flusser points out, "We can hardly expect to find information about Jesus in non-Christian documents. He shares this fate with Moses, Buddha, and Mohammed, who likewise received no mention in the reports of non-believers."[191] Or as Flusser complains elsewhere, for most charismatic figures in history, outside sources provide a control, but we can know about them only through critically reading their followers' testimony. Thus

> All that is significant about Joseph Smith (1805-1844), founder of the Mormons, can be learned only from him, and from Mormon documents. Then there is the case of Simon Kimbangu, the African who performed miracles of healing in the Belgian Congo from March 18 to September 14, 1921. He died in exile [sic: prison] in 1950 . . . the testimony of the Belgian authorities in the Congo are [sic: is] as helpful in his case as the imagined archives of Pilate or records in the chancellery of the high priest would be in the case of Jesus.[192]

Similarly, only four works informative about Socrates and from his era survived, and the only three with any useful information derive from his followers.[193] (Even if one emphasizes divergences in these portrayals, the agreements point to elements of the common figure of Socrates behind them.)[194]

It is no surprise that it was those who followed his teachings, or came to follow his teachings, who had the greatest interest in preserving them. And, contrary to what some have said, ancient followers of a teacher *were* normally interested in what the teacher actually did and taught (especially in the first generation or two, the period in which the canonical Gospels were forming). (We shall argue for ancients' historical interest more fully in ch. 7.) Most Jesus scholars recognize the canonical Gospels as the earliest substantive sources for historical Jesus research.[195] It is thus to these more detailed sources that we must now turn.

Conclusion

Apart from minor comments about Jesus, the extracanonical sources scholars have used to reconstruct the story or teachings of Jesus date from the second century or later. These sources tend to be significantly later than the first-century Gospels that early Christians chose to preserve. Although the Gospel of Thomas may contain some authentic traditions, the Gospel of Peter may be very late and Secret Mark appears to be a modern forgery. The apocryphal gospels are novels mostly from the late second and early third century; the gnostic "gospels" differ starkly in genre from our canonical Gospels, and in any case reflect gnostic elements underlining their later date. These features are quite in contrast to the abundance of Palestinian Jewish elements that we shall note (e.g., chs. 11-16) in our canonical Gospels. The pre-Gospel source we can probably reconstruct to some degree, "Q," is helpful, but cannot easily be divided into "authentic" and "inauthentic" stages. It can be reconstructed only on the basis of our canonical Gospels. It is, then, the canonical Gospels to which we must look for our most secure information about the historical Jesus.

The rest of the book divides into two sections. First, we must examine the question of the canonical Gospels' genre and its implications for discovering substantial historical information in them. (This may be our most distinctive contribution to the discussion of historical Jesus research.) Second, we must explore sample forms and passages within these Gospels to evaluate how well their picture of Jesus fits his time and place (often in contrast to the time and place of their writing). (We will focus on the less controversial issue of the "Synoptic" Gospels — Matthew, Mark, and Luke — and their sources, rather than on John.) In the process, we will also ask how the most historically certain elements of their story about Jesus cohere to tell us something about the Jesus who lived in history.

THE CHARACTER OF THE GOSPELS

"Because the evidence offered by the gospels is hearsay evidence, scholars must be extremely cautious in taking the data at face value."

THE JESUS SEMINAR[1]

As we noted in the introduction, some scholars consider "uncritical" those who pay too much attention to the canonical Gospels. Nevertheless, some of these same "critical" scholars on far less evidence have treated the *Secret Gospel of Mark* (now shown to be a twentieth-century forgery) as earlier than our canonical Gospels. These scholars sometimes criticize other scholars for a "canonical bias," but the criticism is inaccurate. As Dale Allison points out, whereas nearly all documents in Crossan's "earliest layer" of tradition are hypothetical and none surely predate 70, the only works providing information about Jesus that we can surely date before 70 all are accessible in the New Testament: Paul, "Q" and Mark.[2]

In fact, the majority of scholars working in Jesus research focus far more on the canonical Gospels than on works like *Secret Mark* or even the *Gospel of Thomas.* This is not because the canonical Gospels are "canonical," but because they are simply all that we certainly have (apart from brief fragments here and there) to work with from the first century. The church's interest in these works led the church to preserve them; but for all our historical interest in works that the church did not preserve, unpreserved works do not remain available for our examination.

We cannot force later preserved works to make up for earlier unpreserved ones; we simply have to work around our disadvantage when dealing with early preserved ones. (Luke's lack of derision for earlier works in Lk 1:1, however, may suggest that most "Jesus books" in his day did not present a radically different Jesus, even if they were differently arranged.)[3] Neither can we simply reject as "biased" all the information that we have, then argue from the silence that remains for a contrary view. We must ascertain how accurate these sources can be based on what we know of ancient writing practices and the degree of tradition in these sources that corresponds to the earliest environment of Jesus. In this section we will look at ancient literary practice. In the book's later section, we will test sample gospel sources for correspondence to specifically Palestinian Jewish elements and try to offer elements for a cohesive picture of Jesus from these sources.

As noted earlier, we cannot know much very specific about Jesus (that would distinguish him from any other Galilean of his generation) apart from documents about him stemming from the generations immediately following him. Apart from a brief report in Josephus and mention in two Roman historians, we are dependent especially on those most apt to preserve reports about Jesus, that is, those to whom he most mattered — his followers. We may talk about their "biases" toward him, but ultimately we have little beyond these sources to work with, and if we want to talk about the "historical Jesus," we must focus on the nature of our sources.

How reliable are these sources? Contrary to what modern writers sometimes suppose, "bias" did not make biographies into novels. We take bias into account when we read works of ancient biography or history, yet at the same time we depend heavily on these sources to understand the persons about whom they are written (both because they are the only sources available, and because comparison shows such works to preserve substantial information). If this is true for other figures of antiquity, why should it be any less true of Jesus? (And if some of us assume that it must be less true of Jesus, what does that say about our own presuppositions?)[4]

This observation raises several questions. First, what is the genre of those gospels that we find most useful? We will argue (with the current majority of scholars) that it best fits ancient biography, a genre normally expected to deal in historical facts insofar as possible (albeit told from the writer's perspective).

Second, were ancient writers concerned with genuine history? Granted that three of the Gospel writers composed "biographies" rather than "histories," what does the historical substance of histories tell us about ancients' interests in historical facts? Our conclusions here will not support the common modern assumption that ancient thinkers were uncritical. Once we turn to apply these observations to the Gospels, we will explore as a particular example Luke-Acts, which *was* composed as a work of ancient historiography.

Afterward, we will turn to a discussion of the Gospels' sources, both written and oral. Granted historical interest and biographic intention, would ancient writers have made good use of their sources? How accurately would the reports of eyewitnesses be retold and preserved? Only after we have laid these foundations will we begin to examine samples of information from the Gospels, in the extensive later part of the book.

CHAPTER 5

The Gospels as Biographies

"The Gospels are biographies. They tell the story of the career of Jesus in order to persuade the reader of his significance."

GRAHAM STANTON[1]

". . . the very fact that they chose to adapt Greco-Roman biographical conventions to tell the story of Jesus indicates that they were centrally concerned to communicate what they thought really happened."

DAVID AUNE[2]

A work's "genre" is its literary "type" or classification. This classification provides the culturally conditioned, conventional expectations according to which a work would normally be read.[3] Ancient readers recognized various genre categories;[4] in fact, sometimes they sought to be *too* precise about such categories.[5] Although as categories genres are fluid and overlap,[6] they are not always completely artificial. Ancient writers could adapt them, but genre conventions did provide ranges of definition for those who chose to follow them.

Premeditated Literary Works

Although we will be more specific about Gospel genre below, we must first observe the broader significance of their narrative genre more generally. We shall examine the importance of oral tradition in ch. 10, and this history of transmission leaves an indelible mark on some of our Gospel sources. Notwithstanding this important observation, we must not underestimate the level of literary cohesiveness our works display. Literary critics have demonstrated that in their present form the Gospels are relatively polished and intricate works. The consequent cohesiveness characterizes literary works in general, regardless of their more particular genre (e.g., novels, biographies, and histories).[7]

Audiences in the ancient Mediterranean world would appreciate such literary preparation, even for many speeches.[8] Writers of Greek and Latin narratives typically began with a rough draft before producing their final work;[9] Jewish writers in Greek could do the same.[10] The Gospels are thus undoubtedly polished products of much effort, carefully arranged to communicate their points most adequately.[11]

The writers of the Synoptics, like writers of most ancient historical works, probably began with a basic draft of the material in roughly chronological order, to which they could later add a topical outline, speeches, and other rhetorical adjustments.[12] Luke and Matthew probably followed one main source at a time, incorporating a large block of Q material into Mark;[13] both Luke and Matthew make Mark the backbone and supplement this from other sources.[14] After completing the book, a writer might check copyists' manuscripts when possible, and then give the first copy to the dedicatee when appropriate[15] (perhaps Luke did this for his dedicatee Theophilus).

Large, premeditated narrative works like the Gospels are not mere occasional documents like letters. As Charles Talbert points out, "Foundation documents like the canonical gospels (and Acts) seemed more analogous to systematic theology, albeit in narrative form"; they are more shaped by the foundational events they report and less shaped by their local situations than letters are.[16]

Foundation documents can be largely fictitious (like Virgil's *Aeneid*), but they can also use the best historical traditions to which authors had access. Ancient historians often examined "foundations" in a way that encouraged and solidified loyalties or convictions, whether Livy's valedictory history of Rome or, more to the point, apologetic histories of marginalized peoples (by Josephus and others). Granted, foundation stories of the distant past might be mythical; but such suppositions are less relevant for recent foundations. To require an unimaginative choice between literary strategies and narrative cohesiveness on the one hand, and substantial genuine information on the other, is to impose categories unworkable in ancient literature (particularly historiography and biography).

Suggestions about Gospel Genre

Readers viewed the Gospels as biographies of some sort from the mid-second century through most of the nineteenth century. This view prevailed until Votaw in 1915,[17] when their differences from modern biography led most scholars to seek a new classification for them.[18] Thus Burton Mack claims that in the early twentieth century scholars realized "that the gospels were not biographies and that they sustained a very problematic relation to history."[19] Yet as we shall see, this early-twentieth-century verdict about gospel genre has proved premature.

Unique Genre?

The twentieth century generated a variety of proposals regarding the genre of the Gospels.[20] Some of these proposals have proved less helpful than others. Classifying the Gospels as "gospels" is self-evidently true, but such a classification does not reveal the broader literary expectations for reading them that a broader classification could. That is, if identifying a work's generic category guides the way the reader interprets a document, the earlier standard classification of the New Testament Gospels as "unique"[21] is of limited value. Granted, their focus on Jesus' character makes them unique,[22] but this is because of Jesus' distinctive character more than the literary techniques of the authors. Most works, including other Greco-Roman documents, are "unique" in some sense.[23] Even though the four canonical Gospels are closer to one another than they are to any other documents of antiquity,[24] they are also each distinct from the others[25] and all fit into a broader category of narrative.[26] While it is true that the Gospels tell a story that was unique in their time, their first audience would have been most familiar with coherent literary works surrounding primary characters in terms of Hellenistic "lives," or ancient biographies.[27]

Folk Literature?

Not much more helpful is the suggestion that the Gospels represent popular or "folk literature" of the lower classes in contrast to the stylish, sophisticated literature of the upper classes.[28] While the Gospels' oral sources were naturally transmitted in such a folk milieu, such forced categories prove unhelpful for genre criticism of the Gospels: they ignore the continuum between "folk literature" and the more stylish rhetoric and texts that strongly influenced them,[29] as well as differences among the Gospels themselves (Luke writes on a much more sophisticated Greek level than Mark).[30] Specific genre categories like "biographies" actually appear throughout the continuum.[31]

Memoirs?

The Gospels' sources may well include collections of "memoirs," personal recollections sometimes also polished in antiquity for publication.[32] Such memoirs could readily provide content for "folk" biographies.[33] Some or many second-century Christian writers viewed the Gospels[34] — alongside other apostolic works — as "memoirs," perhaps recalling Xenophon's *Memorabilia,* a "life" of Socrates. This comparison provides attestation that some saw the Gospels as a form of biography from an early period.[35] A common general pattern does exist, but the canonical Gospels may represent a different *kind* of biography than most collections of memoirs; they are complete literary narratives and not simply "folk" biographies as most such collections would be.[36]

Drama or Mythography?

Not all literary works concerning specific characters were biographies. At the same time, all four canonical Gospels are a far cry from some other genres. Whether or not influenced by drama, clearly they were not written as Greek plays, which were composed in poetry.[37]

Mythography could recycle oral tradition,[38] but involved the distant past, not recent historical individuals. Whatever one thinks of the Gospels' accounts of healings and a smattering of other miracles, they remain a far cry from the entertaining, fanciful metamorphosis stories, fantastic creatures, divine rapes, and so forth in a compilation like Ovid's *Metamorphoses.* If some writers today treat the Gospels' reports of healings as similar to mythography, it is because of modern western cultural biases that coalesce diverse kinds of paranormal claims, not a matter of genre. Ancient historians often included reports of unusual phenomena, yet most focused on the real world that differed significantly from mythographers' focus. Indeed, tens of thousands of people today claim eyewitness experience of supernaturally empowered recoveries, and whether or not we agree with their interpretation of their experience, the *genre* of their reports is not typically mythography.[39] Mythography in this period normally also addressed mythic topics (like Ovid's *Metamorphoses*) or primeval times (e.g., Apollodorus).[40]

Novels?

The primary literary alternative to viewing the Gospels as biography is to view them as intentional fiction,[41] a suggestion that I will argue has little to commend it.[42] (This observation is not meant to denigrate the value of ancient novels for insights regarding ancient writers' literary techniques; but these same techniques appear in historical genres as well.)[43]

The true heyday of novels begins in the late second century[44] (not surprisingly the period when apocryphal gospels began to flourish). Nevertheless, first-century readers recognized the genre of novel (the hellenistic "romance"),[45] occasionally (though not usually) including novels about historical characters.[46] At the same time, ancients usually distinguished between narratives that were intended as fictitious and those that were intended as historical.[47]

Whereas the apocryphal gospels and apocryphal acts betray characteristics of novels,[48] as we noted earlier, the four canonical Gospels much more closely resemble ancient biography.[49] Ancient novelists did not usually seek to write *historical* novels; most focused on fictitious characters.[50] A small minority of ancient novels[51] built them around historical characters, but *none* of the examples typically cited involve persons from recent history. This pattern does not at all fit what we find in the first-century Gospels.

Moreover, the use of historical characters and even some historical information was a far cry from historical research and sources (such as Luke's use of Mark and Q in his Gospel) that characterized biographies. The excesses of some forms of earlier source and redaction criticism notwithstanding, one would also be hard-pressed to find a novel so clearly tied to its sources as Matthew or Luke is.[52] Works with a historical prologue like Luke's (Lk 1:1-4; Acts 1:1-2) were historical works;[53] novels lacked such fixtures, although occasionally they could include a proem telling why the author made up the story.[54] As we shall show later (especially chs. 11-16), the extant first-century Gospels reflect too much authentic Palestinian Jewish background, sometimes including even obscure cultural details, to be ancient novels.

Further, novels typically reflected the milieu of their readership more than that of their characters,[55] a situation quite different from histories and biographies that were readily adapted for readers but focused on historical content. Greek novels often focused on ethnographically or geographically remote subjects not easily checked; this cultural distance allowed the appearance of greater plausibility without requiring genuine research.[56] Some novels were realistic,[57] but many were inconsistent or uninterested in local color.[58] By contrast, local color pervades the Gospels so thoroughly that we sometimes wonder how well Diaspora audiences understood some of the details.

The majority of ancient novels were also "romances," in which the two major characters were lovers who persevered in faithfulness despite obstacles, with erotic desire playing a leading role.[59] Even the Christian apocryphal acts work to accommodate this pattern (except within a framework of chastity),[60] but we see nothing of this interest in the earlier, canonical Gospels and Acts.

Finally, novels were written primarily to entertain rather to inform.[61] A few[62] functioned as religious propaganda as well as entertainment, but entertainment remained a key element, and religious propaganda certainly was in no wise restricted to the genre of novels.[63] Nor is entertainment the exclusive do-

main of novels; historical works intended primarily to inform were nevertheless typically written in an entertaining manner.[64] Most ancient works sought to
entertain; the question was whether they also sought to inform, which novels
did not.[65]

In contrast to novels, the Gospels do not present themselves as texts composed primarily for entertainment, but as true accounts of Jesus' ministry. Despite some differences in purpose among themselves, all four Gospels fit the
general genre of ancient biography: the "life" (often just the public life) of a
prominent person. Such biographies were normally written to praise the person and to communicate some point or points to the writer's generation. That
biographies, like novels, could seek to propagate particular moral and religious
perspectives does not challenge the distinction between them; biographies
were also often propagandistic in a more general sense, intended to provide
role models for moral instruction.[66]

Biographies

In more recent years scholars have been returning to the dominant historical
consensus that the Gospels represent biographies in the ancient sense of the
term.[67] Biography (the *bios*, or "life") was one of the more common literary
genres in antiquity; letters were even more so, hence it is not surprising that
much of the New Testament consists of these genres.[68] Graham Stanton regards
as "surprisingly inaccurate" the older views of Bultmann and others that the
Gospels were not biographies.[69]

To claim that the four canonical Gospels are biographies is not to limit the
distinctiveness of the character they portray (sometimes the basis for denial),[70]
but to contend that biography is the most obvious general category for an ancient audience approaching a volume about a single historical individual.[71]
Public "lives" *(bioi)* of important historical individuals include the lives of
sages. Surviving Greek examples focus on philosophers, honoring founders of
philosophic schools and preserving their teachings.[72]

We have numerous examples of surviving biographies from within a few
decades after the Gospels,[73] and others[74] much earlier. Other works related to
biography appear even earlier, but with respect to genre the more historically-
oriented works such as these biographies from roughly the Gospels' era provide
the most fruitful comparisons.

After carefully defining the criteria for identifying genre and establishing
the characteristic features of Greco-Roman *bioi*, or lives,[75] Richard Burridge's
dissertation shows how both the Synoptics and John fit this genre.[76] (For one
example, the lengths of all four canonical Gospels likewise fit the medium-

range length — 10,000-25,000 words — found in ancient biographies as opposed to many other kinds of works.)[77] So forceful is Burridge's work on gospel genre as biography that one reviewer concludes, "This volume ought to end any legitimate denials of the canonical Gospels' biographical character."[78] Arguments concerning the biographical character of the Gospels have thus come full circle: the Gospels, long viewed as biographies until the early twentieth century, now are widely viewed as biographies again.

Greco-Roman Biography and History

Classifying the Gospels as ancient biography is helpful for understanding the Gospels only if we define some of the characteristics of ancient biography, particularly (for our interests here) with respect to biographies' particular historical character. Although biographies were, as we shall argue, meant to be historical works in the general sense, we must first point out that their genre is distinct from history proper (while overlapping with it at points).

Because the Gospels include elements that connect them with historiography proper as well as with biography,[79] some scholars have argued that the Gospels fit the genre of history and not biography.[80] Thus one scholar argues that though the Gospels are "lives," they differ from Greek lives because they cannot trace moral development in one they regard as God incarnate.[81] He argues that in any case Roman biographies fall closer to history, starting with the second-century writer Suetonius.[82] This association, however, appears too narrow: did the Roman historian Tacitus (in his *Agricola*) suddenly develop a new, mixed genre in the same generation as Suetonius without prior models? Biographies of the Greek writer Plutarch also include considerable historical content. Moreover, historical works that focused on a particular individual were "lives" *(bioi)*, the most natural category in which ancient readers would place most of the Gospels.[83] Historical features in biographies are too pervasive to require us to simply transfer biographies from the narrower biographic genre to the wider historical one.

As noted above, although biographies could serve a wide range of literary functions,[84] ancient biographers intended their works to be more historical than novelistic.[85] This observation especially fits the forms of biography dominant in this era (writers like Nepos, Plutarch, Suetonius, and Tacitus). Thus some classicists treat biography as a particular "subdivision of history."[86] This classification respects both biography's particular attention to the life of an individual and the interest in the genuine past that it shares with historiography.

More generally, first-century historiography often focused on notable individuals.[87] This approach eventually moved historiography in a more biographic direction; thus "the Greco-Romans of the first century, chiefly prompted by the Roman habit of thinking in terms of models, . . . extended the definition of history by adding the life and character of famous men to speeches and deeds as the proper subject of history."[88] Some distinguish this approach from pure biography in terms of their distinct purposes.[89] As we have noted, the primary distinction is not biographic focus but whether the work is limited to a single character.[90] Such histories often tended to be "encomiastic," magnifying heroes,[91] but as we shall note in a subsequent chapter, such an emphasis does not make them fictitious.

The central difference between biography and history in this matter was that the former focused on a single character whereas the latter included a broader range of events.[92] Classicists often note that history thus contained many biographic elements, but normally lacked the sustained focus on a single person and emphasis on characterization.[93] Biographies were less exhaustive, focusing more on the models of character they provided.[94] Structured by the reigns of emperors, Roman historiography included increasing elements of "imperial autobiography" by the end of the first century.[95]

Biographies were normally essentially historical works (provided we allow for the differences between the ancient genres and their modern successors, noted below); thus the gospels would have an essentially historical as well as propagandistic function. To quote more fully the words of David Aune used above,

> . . . while biography tended to emphasize encomium, or the one-sided praise of the subject, it was still firmly rooted in historical fact rather than literary fiction. Thus while the Evangelists clearly had an important theological agenda, the very fact that they chose to adapt Greco-Roman biographical conventions to tell the story of Jesus indicates that they were centrally concerned to communicate what they thought really happened.[96]

Our most obvious and abundant examples of biography from the early empire are in Plutarch and Suetonius.[97] To what extent does their genre tether them to facts about the past? Plutarch does often work from memory but his notes are taken from a wide range of sources, and are usually even arranged fairly chronologically.[98] Plutarch sometimes takes liberties with his material, though elsewhere proves very accurate.[99] Suetonius took notes from official "libraries and archives," arranged his notes topically, but proved less critically discerning about his material than Plutarch. He includes various and sometimes varying accounts, but modern historians appreciate "his hesitation to impose his own judgments."[100] As we have noted, Suetonius seems to straddle the genres of biography and history.[101] While some mythical elements appear in both these writers (particularly when writing about the distant past), clearly both are biographies just as the Gospels are.[102]

Naturally we have a range of works sometimes classified as biography.[103] Yet where these biographies' information is inaccurate, they do not thereby become novels. As some literary critics have pointed out, even when historical works have incorrect facts they do not become fiction, and a novel that depends on historical information does not become history. Nevertheless, some scholars have argued that while many ancient biographers were mostly accurate, some were quite unreliable. While it is true that some biographers were less accurate than others, frequently cited examples like Ps.-Callisthenes' *Alexander Romance*[104] do not make the case; this work does not belong to the main biographic genre (especially as it existed in this period).[105] When biography involved deliberate falsification of events (as opposed to creative retelling of sources), it departed from the expected conventions of its genre.

Ancient biographies and histories were different genres, yet (as the contemporary debate over the genre of Luke-Acts shows) the former can draw on the principles of the latter enough to allow considerable overlap (hence I offer examples from ancient histories as well as biographies). While taken by itself Luke's Gospel is biography, as part of Luke's two-volume work the Gospel becomes a biographic component in a larger history, just as authors of multivolume histories could devote an entire volume or section to a particularly prominent character.[106] Luke's biography of Jesus is thus inseparable from his larger historical work.

Yet claiming a basically historical function by ancient standards does not mean that the gospel writers wrote history the way modern historians would; ancient historiography itself proceeded on different principles than modern historiography does, as we shall emphasize in a later chapter. This was also true of ancient biographers; thus Plutarch opines that some ancient writers added some missing details about Alexander's manner of death, inventing tragic scenes appropriate to the topic.[107] Naturally, over the centuries (as in the span of time between Alexander and Plutarch), such adaptations by less conservative writers would multiply. We would expect fewer such divergences from the eyewitness sources in the briefer span of time between Jesus' death and the appearance of first-century Gospels.

Different from Modern Biography

Ancient biography differed from modern biography in some respects, including in how it treated historical information.[108] For instance, ancient biographies sometimes differed from their modern namesake by beginning in the protagonist's adulthood, as in many political biographies,[109] the first-century Life of Aesop[110] or in Mark's Gospel.

In contrast to modern historical biography, ancient biographers also did not need to follow a chronological sequence; most felt free to rearrange their material topically.[111] This pattern is particularly obvious in Suetonius.[112] Some scholars maintain that one kind of biographies were literary biographies ordered chronologically, insofar as was possible;[113] they suggest that Alexandrian biographies were arranged more systematically or topically.[114] In practice, these types were never followed exactly and chronological biographies appear to have been rare.[115] Insofar as we employ such types, however, Luke seems to fall closer to the former category (following the order of Mark virtually exactly except for a few, perhaps two, very significant exceptions), whereas Matthew follows the more common topical format (compare e.g., his five topical discourse sections).

Lack of chronological sequence posed no problems for readers of ancient biographies. Many Jewish interpreters doubted that the biblical accounts of Moses at Sinai were arranged chronologically.[116] Nor did early Christians expect the Gospels to reflect chronological sequence: Augustine suggested the Evangelists wrote their Gospels as God recalled the accounts to their memory;[117] as early as the early second century some Christian leaders claimed that Mark wrote what he heard from Jesus' disciple Peter, but Peter did not narrate it (hence Mark did not write it) in the sequence in which it occurred.[118] The earliest traditions were oral, and oral performance can vary the sequence of events.[119]

Some also argue that ancient biography, in contrast to modern biography or novels, plays down characterization; this distinction, however, is not accurate. Characterization was often developed by how a story was told rather than specific comments,[120] but comments about a person's character do appear in many biographies.[121] Certainly ancient narrators in various genres did care about characterization.[122] We catch glimpses of even Jesus' struggles in the Gospels (e.g., Mk 14:32-42). Yet if Jesus is a "flat" rather than multidimensioned character in many Gospel accounts, it may be because he was considered consistently positive, and because the writers esteemed him too highly to tamper with the limited tradition on such matters.[123]

Ancient biographers were also often less embarrassed by their biases than are their modern counterparts. We shall note in a later chapter Greco-Roman (and Jewish) historians' emphasis on moral (and often political and theological) lessons. Like other kinds of historical writers, biographers frequently sought to teach moral lessons from their stories;[124] one might in a sense learn from great teachers of the past by proxy, as students of their recorded teachings.[125]

Biographers may in fact have felt a special obligation to provide such moral lessons. Thus the pre-Christian biographer Cornelius Nepos declares that biographers dwelt on the virtues of their subject in ways that historians did not, and intended their work for less technical audiences.[126] Ancients permitted biography more freedom to be one-sided in praise than was appropriate for academic history.[127] Biographers also could write for apologetic and polemical reasons.[128] Some ancient biographers emphasize moral lessons in their stories more than others do; some writers, like Plutarch, vary in their moralizing even from one biography to the next.[129]

At the same time, the particular perspectives of such documents do not destroy their historical value for us. As the Jewish scholar Geza Vermes points out, "a theological interest is no more incompatible with a concern for history than is a political or philosophical conviction," and we can allow for these in interpretation.[130] The better historians like Polybius felt that their work should include praise and blame for individuals, but that they should pursue truth and fairness,[131] properly evaluating the right distribution of praise and blame.[132] Biographers felt free to critique their heroes' shortcomings,[133] and most biographies mixed some measure of praise and blame.[134] Plutarch, for example, insists that it is necessary to include failings in the biography of a good person, but to give the right balance.[135]

Biographers of teachers could include a less than flattering story even about one's own teacher, though apt to report especially favorable matters about him.[136] One could also criticize some activities of other figures one regarded highly.[137] Of course some teachers were regarded as exceptional; the earlier writer Xenophon has only good to report about Socrates,[138] and it is hardly likely that early Christians would find flaws in one they worshiped.[139] But normally disciples respected their teachers enough to preserve and transmit their teachers' views accurately, even when they disagreed with them, rather than to distort their teachers' views to fit the disciples' own.[140] (This might be the more true with a teacher they venerated.) Further, when one's source could not recall the substance of a speech a biographer might not try to reproduce it.[141]

Conclusion

The Gospels are premeditated foundation documents. While foundation stories about the distant, legendary past were inevitably mythical, schools tended to preserve information about more recent founders, a more appropriate comparison for first-century Gospels about the recent figure Jesus. Scholars have proposed various genre forms for the Gospels; some (like "unique" or "folk literature") are not very helpful. Others, like "memoirs," are on the right track (even if "memoirs" underestimates the literary cohesiveness of Matthew, Luke and John). Clearly the Gospels are not mythography, novels, or pure drama. As works focused on a single, historical character, drawing on significant amounts of historical tradition, the Gospels are most readily recognized as ancient biography.

Although ancient biography differed from its modern heir and namesake, it was supposed to deal in historical information rather than the fanciful creation of events. Some biographies were more historically reliable than others (typically, those about recent generations were much more reliable than those about the distant past). We must examine the Gospels in greater detail to see where on this spectrum they lie.

Before turning to material about Jesus in the Gospels, however, we must address two issues. First, one of the Gospels shows a particularly clear overlap with the larger genre of history. Second, we must address an objection that some modern writers raise: did ancients even care about genuine historical information?

CHAPTER 6

Luke-Acts as History

". . . having acquired thorough knowledge I decided to compose carefully for you an orderly narrative from its beginning, honorable Theophilus, so that you may be fully assured about the matters in which you have been instructed."

LUKE 1:3-4[1]

"The reasons for regarding Luke-Acts as a History are obvious and, to most scholars, compelling."

LUKE TIMOTHY JOHNSON[2]

"[Luke] is not just an 'edifying writer', but a historian and theologian who needs to be taken seriously. His account always remains within the limits of what was considered reliable by the standards of antiquity. That means that the author's assurance in Luke 1:3 is more than mere convention; it contains a real theological and historical programme, though this cannot be measured by the standards of a modern critical historian."

MARTIN HENGEL[3]

We have treated the Gospels as biographies, but one Gospel invites a somewhat different approach, an approach that illustrates the often fine line between biography and history. Luke's Gospel is indeed a biography, but it is part of a two-volume work (Luke-Acts) that when taken together cannot easily be defined as biography.[4]

Although the two volumes may differ somewhat in genre,[5] the narrative unity of the two works[6] would invite any attentive auditors to hear them together. Many scholars suggest that Luke may combine elements of two genres,[7] especially in this case the related genres of history and biography. While taken by itself the Gospel is biography, as part of Luke's two-volume work the Gospel becomes a biographic component in a larger history. Ancient auditors would not find such a combination difficult to comprehend; authors of multivolume histories could devote an entire volume or section to a particularly prominent character.[8] Luke's biography of Jesus is thus inseparable from his larger historical work.

Just as most scholars today recognize the Gospels as biographies, the dominant view concerning Acts today, earlier argued by Lukan scholars such as Martin Dibelius and Henry Cadbury,[9] is that it is a work of ancient historiography.[10] Luke Timothy Johnson in the *Anchor Bible Dictionary* notes that most scholars today accept this assignment of genre for Luke-Acts as a whole.[11] Indeed, Hengel and Schwemer contend that those who deny Luke-Acts as acceptable first-century historiography need to read more ancient historiography "and less hypercritical and scholastic secondary literature."[12]

Luke-Acts as History

Various factors support the thesis that Luke conceives of his project as primarily a history. Unlike a novel, Luke uses sources abundantly in his first volume (usually agreed to be at least Mark and "Q") and presumably in his second volume as well, though we cannot distinguish the sources clearly in Acts.[13] Luke's claim to investigate or have close acquaintance with his information (Lk 1:3) fits historical works,[14] and his occasional use of the first-person plural (e.g., Acts 16:10) emphasizes the involvement considered ideal for a good Hellenistic historian.[15]

Other aspects of Luke-Acts fit the historical genre. Luke's extensive use of public monologues in Acts fits the conventions of ancient histories better than those of biographies or novels.[16] (Indeed, in Acts they may cumulatively consume a larger proportion of the work than in Thucydides or Sallust, though Luke's speeches are individually shorter than was typical in the multivolume histories.)[17] Likewise, neither a biography nor a romance should end the way Acts does, because they would focus on Paul the character (hence perhaps his death or release). But if Acts is a historical work, it can chronicle "the rise and spread of the gospel and of the social and religious movement to which that gospel gave birth," especially from Jerusalem to Rome.[18] We focus below on some historiographic features that include or are more specific to the Gospel.

Luke's Preface

Significantly, Luke-Acts also includes what appears very much like the prefaces found in histories.[19] Granted, they also show some features similar to the scientific treatise tradition,[20] a tradition that not surprisingly overlaps in some of its features with those of history works more narrowly defined (but not novels).[21] But some proposed parallels to scientific prefaces seem questionable,[22] and while Luke's preface could fit this tradition stylistically (and most kinds of prefaces share some similarities),[23] the stylistic criterion is inadequate without attention to the more important matter of content.[24] David Aune points out that Luke-Acts "is obviously not a scientific or technical treatise";[25] moreover, its prefaces do speak of historical matters (Lk 1:1; Acts 1:1).

Loveday Alexander, who originally pointed out the parallels in technical treatises, has clarified her understanding of the value of these parallels. She agrees that Luke is not writing a technical scientific work; her appeal to such parallels in prefaces was not intended to delineate his work's genre.[26] She explains further:

> Nor was I claiming that Luke did not intend his work to be read as 'history,' if by that we mean a reliable account of events in the recent past. In fact (paradoxically enough), casting Luke as a sober, pragmatic, writer of 'scientific prose' might give us a much more secure handle on his reliability. It is certainly evident (as I have made clear all along) that the preface shows a strong interest both in 'reliability' and in the preservation of authentic tradition.[27]

Where the conventions she cites appear in historiography, they appear in writers culturally marginal to the dominant Greek culture, such as Jewish authors.[28] In view of his preface, Alexander argues that Luke is clearly *not* writing *rhetorical* history or epic history;[29] if Acts is history, it is, she contends, the sort of history where scientific and historical traditions "intersect, i.e. on the more scholarly, less rhetorical side of history . . . , and perhaps especially where the author and/or subject is non-Greek."[30]

If Alexander debates whether Luke's preface is appropriate exclusively to history, nevertheless the majority of scholars argue that, in the most important respects, this preface is consistent with or even points to[31] historiography. As Terrance Callan notes, a good introduction should summarize what is to follow;[32] and Luke's summary of what will follow is explicitly historical: "an orderly narrative of the things fulfilled among us" (Lk 1:1, 3). Likewise, his explicit purpose is to confirm what Theophilus has learned about such events (1:4). "Given this statement of the question, it is almost obvious that the preface of Luke-Acts most resembles the prefaces of histories."[33] Luke focuses on "a narrative of events," as Herodotus "writes of 'the great and marvellous deeds done by Greeks and foreigners' (1.1)."[34]

Just as Luke's purpose is to confirm truth (Lk 1:4),[35] Lucian emphasizes that history's distinctive commitment is to truth.[36] That Luke also sees his work as useful (Lk 1:4)[37] would not conflict with this goal.[38] Given Luke's clear statements, especially in view of parallels to such claims in historical works, Luke-Acts would easily enough project a historical genre (especially in view of the following narratives) to a first-century audience.

Luke's language otherwise fits historical prefaces, as numerous scholars point out. David Moessner shows that Dionysius of Halicarnassus, writing perhaps a century before Luke, *"combines three technical terms that Luke will employ in his short prooemial period (Lk. 1.1-4),"* and they share also four other key terms.[39] Clare Rothschild[40] and Todd Penner[41] also list several comparisons with most historical prefaces. While not all these characteristics they note are limited to historiography, the conjunction of various features in historiography is significant.

Likewise, when possible Luke sets his events in the context of world history, just as historians (and almost exclusively historians) did in their histories (Lk 2:1-2; 3:1-2; Acts 18:12).[42] Moreover, where we can check Luke against extrinsic data, he fits far better than novels set in the past, like Chariton's romance or Judith.[43] Some have even found in Luke's work specific stylistic echoes of Polybius and his successors in Hellenistic historiography, suggesting that Luke imitates not only the Septuagint but also the style of eastern Mediterranean historians.[44]

A more specifically Jewish approach could point in the same direction. After surveying Luke's use of Old Testament historiography, Rosner suggests that Luke's use of analogous features implies that he "was writing what he conceived to be a historical work."[45] Some scholars even argue that Luke sought to write salvation history as he knew it from the Old Testament.[46] Certainly Luke cites the Septuagint far more than any other source, and it is in fact the only extant historical source (apart from Mark) that he quotes (and one that he in fact regularly quotes with marked citations). Nevertheless, as in the case of Josephus' *Antiquities,* use of biblical information would not prevent one from writing Hellenistic history at the same time.[47]

Luke's claims that have invited significant question are largely the sorts of issues on which we would expect Luke to have less information from his Christian sources (such as private conversations[48] or some events most geographically and chronologically remote).[49] Questions on such points should not be used to ignore Luke's record on the many other points where we can expect him to preserve the best evidence (just as we would not ignore the value of other historians' best evidence on account of their more questionable material). Indeed, in such places (for example, Acts' we-narratives) difficulties of this sort appear rare.

Luke's Claim of "thorough knowledge" (Lk 1:3)

For Greeks the very term used for research or investigation, *historia,* left "no doubt possible about what was early considered the defining characteristic of the genre"; it focused on "the interrogation of witnesses and other informed parties" and then weaving their responses into a cohesive narrative.[50] Even if some writers failed to travel to all the places their narratives covered, travel was apparently a familiar component of historical research. The early Greek historian Herodotus initiated this emphasis on research,[51] traveling widely; Thucydides, who cross-examined his sources, assumed this approach as the standard.[52] Diodorus Siculus[53] and Appian[54] both claim to have visited sites about which they wrote. Although most of the subjects for Philostratus' sophistic biographies were long deceased, he interviewed some who lived, even on multiple occasions;[55] in addition, he recorded information from those who had heard them.[56]

Polybius avers that investigation is "the *most* important part" of writing history.[57] His proposed method for conducting investigation, given the limitations of space and time, was to interview people, critically evaluate reports, and accept the most reliable sources.[58] Although interviews were impossible when dealing with the distant past,[59] writers preferred them when living witnesses remained available.[60] Greek historians often traveled to the locations of events and consulted those considered reliable oral sources.[61] Condemning writers who sought to make guesses sound plausible, Polybius noted that in his research he had also come across documentary evidence.[62] Probability is one helpful test, he conceded, but visiting a location and interviewing witnesses there is much better.[63]

Greek historians had their weaknesses, but primary research was one of their strengths. Klaus Meister observes,

> Although Greek historians usually referred to only one or two predecessors and quoted them uncritically (an 'unscholarly' practice according to modern understanding), their primary research was often superior to that of modern historians: they relied to a large degree on 'autopsy' and their own experiences, collected and examined the oral transmission, questioned eyewitnesses and sources, and visited the scenes of events in order to gather their information on the spot.[64]

In actual practice, not all historians in this period traveled.[65] Roman historians usually focused on Roman history, most of which was available locally through armies and legates sending word back to the senate. Thus they sometimes simply collected information without field research,[66] although they still expected accuracy in their writing.[67]

Did Luke Travel?

Was Luke more like a typical Greek historian or a typical Roman one on the matter of travel? Given Luke's Greek style and his focus on events in the Greek East, those who contend that Luke was primarily a "Hellenistic historian" rather than a Roman one easily have the stronger case. This observation need not mean that Luke traveled to all locations in his narrative, but it appears that he traveled sometimes. If, as apparently at least a slight majority of Acts scholars contend, the author of Acts also authored the "we" source,[68] Acts clearly stands much closer to the Hellenistic mold. Luke would not have traveled as widely as, say, Polybius,[69] but on this majority interpretation he would be acquainted firsthand with material and locations in his more detailed "we" material, including Jerusalem and especially Caesarea. He could have spent up to two years in Judea (Acts 24:27 with 21:15; 27:1). Probably most of it would have been in Caesarea on the coast rather than in Galilee, but he would have had access to believers there who had been part of the early Jerusalem church and were familiar with the earliest traditions (Acts 21:8, 10, 16). He may have had some contact with James the Lord's brother (Acts 21:18), though we cannot say how much.

Opinions do vary regarding his "we" sections, and one's approach to Luke's historical methodology does not rise or fall on this point alone. Nevertheless, I believe that evidence for his genuine participation in some later events in his second volume, Acts, is very strong.[70] "We" appears only sporadically, whereas a fictitious "we" in a novel normally appeared throughout the work. Without comment (as if the audience knows the identity of the narrator), the "we" appears incidentally in Troas, leaves off in Philippi (Acts 16:10-16), and resumes years later, again in Philippi (20:6–21:18; 27:1–28:16). It does not appear at more theologically pregnant points where it would be most useful (say in Acts 2, 10, or 15).[71] As one might expect for eyewitness material, the "we" sections tend to be among Luke's most detailed material.[72] (Detractors often cite differences from Paul; at least some of the more significant of these, however, may reflect a traditional Protestant misunderstanding of Paul.)[73]

Scholars offer various interpretations of this material. While the "we" material could reflect a travel itinerary, it would presumably be the narrator's own; why else would he preserve its first person narration only here, when he has other sources also reporting eyewitness material (Lk 1:2)?[74] Most current scholars believe that the proposal of a literary device for sea-voyages[75] misreads the evidence;[76] the proposal of a fictitious literary device more generally is also questionable. Although entire works could be pseudonymous,[77] Luke does not name himself, and his first audience seems (and Theophilus surely is) aware of his identity.[78] First-person narrators normally remain central to the action throughout the narrative in novels,[79] but (as we noted in ch. 5 and here) Luke-Acts is not a novel. More relevant is first-person narration in histories; like third-person narration naming the narrator, this narration nearly always indicated the actual presence of the author on the occasions noted.[80] Classicist Arthur Darby Nock noted that a fictitious "we" is extremely rare outside obvious fiction; he thus evaluated Luke's "we" narratives as authentic eyewitness memoirs.[81] For such reasons a majority of Lukan scholars concur that Luke here uses his own notes; that he indicates his presence on the occasions marked by "we"; and/or that this section includes the narrator's genuine personal reminiscences.[82] We would grant the accuracy of this claim to almost any other ancient historian who made it; that some NT scholars are skeptical in Luke's particular case may say more about the assumptions of NT criticism than about Luke himself.

What is the relevance of this connection to Luke's "research" for the gospel story? The "we" departs for Judea with Paul in 20:5–21:18 and departs from Judea up to two years later (see 24:17) in 27:1–28:16. The narrator probably spent most of the interim in Caesarea, but even this location would have afforded Luke the opportunity to become more "fully acquainted" with reports about the Judean events (if not geography) that he depicts.

More on "thorough familiarity"

Luke informs his audience that he "was thoroughly familiar with" the matters about which he writes (Lk 1:3). Although some translations render his verb *parakoloutheō* as if it denotes investigation or research, neither is necessarily implied, "although both these activities might be required in the process."[83] Nevertheless, the term does indicate *thorough* acquaintance by one means or another.[84] In view of other ancient prologues using the same language, Luke's wording suggests thorough familiarity with reports and that he is able to evaluate their accuracy.[85] One would use this terminology to display one's "impeccable credentials" for writing reliably.[86]

How extensive was Luke's firsthand acquaintance and/or his investigation? As we have noted, Roman historians typically consulted records; Greek historians in the tradition of Polybius traveled and consulted with witnesses.[87] Although Luke himself was not a witness to the events in the Gospels (as potentially opposed to some later parts of Acts),[88] his travels allowed him to confirm many of the oral traditions circulating (Lk 1:2), traditions already known to his audience (Lk 1:4). Presumably this confirmation would have at least included interviewing Jerusalem followers of Jesus who could confirm and augment the stories circulating among Diaspora Christians.[89] Luke's appeal to "eyewitnesses" (Lk 1:2)[90] fits the appreciation for research in Hellenistic historiography and has parallels in some histories.

The actual term *autopsia* (mentioned by Meister, above) is a rare one; but the convention of appeal to such sources is much more widespread.[91] While the term may not be common, the emphasis on visual observation that it implied was;[92] both Greek[93] and Roman[94] historians emphasized it. The *ideal* for ancient historians was to have seen events themselves;[95] since this was not always possible, they often had to depend on oral sources.[96] When they needed to defend their work, historians typically showed their reliance on oral sources and autopsy, from Polybius through the first century.[97] Tacitus sought information from witnesses where possible (and otherwise had access to imperial annals for numerous points).[98] When the term is used, it normally indicates "those with personal/first-hand experience: those who know the facts at first hand."[99] Luke emphasizes eyewitness attestation not only in his preface, but commonly enough to reinforce the preface's claim.[100]

Confirmation (Lk 1:4)

That Luke's research serves a primarily confirmatory purpose (1:4) suggests that Luke in the end does not arrive at conclusions far distant from his sources.[101] Ancient rhetoricians often appealed to common knowledge to make a point; though this information may have sometimes been gossip, it seems unlikely that it was typically simply a rhetorical deception.[102] Appeals to common knowledge suggest that the knowledge was in fact widespread; hence that what Luke reports in his Gospel (and, to a lesser extent, in Acts) was already in wide circulation at the time of his writing, probably within the lifetime of some who had known Jesus' public ministry.

Thus many stories Luke includes in his Gospel (as well as many that he did not) were probably widely disseminated among many churches. The early churches throughout the Empire were already informally networked long before Luke wrote, and certainly long before the more explicit network of bishops we recognize by the early second century. In Mediterranean antiquity in general, travelers regularly carried news from one location to another;[103] whenever one learned of someone traveling near a place where one had friends, one might prepare and send a letter.[104]

Clearly already in the third decade of the Christian movement, many churches knew what was happening with churches in other cities (Rom 1:8; 1 Cor 11:16; 14:33; 1 Thess 1:7-9), and even shared letters (Col 4:16). Missionaries could speak of some churches to others (Rom 15:26; 2 Cor 8:1-5; 9:2-4; Phil 4:16; 1 Thess 2:14-16) and send personal news by other workers (Eph 6:21-22; Col 4:7-

9). Urban Christians traveled (1 Cor 16:10, 12, 17; Phil 2:30; 4:18), carrying letters (Rom 16:1-2; Phil 2:25). They also relocated to other places (Rom 16:3, 5; perhaps 16:6-15 passim) and sent greetings to other churches (Rom 16:21-23; 1 Cor 16:19; Phil 4:22; Col 4:10-15).[105] Pauline scholarship works from a more objective basis for understanding early Christianity than some of the hypotheses circulated in sectors of Gospels scholarship. While different locations might have their own struggles or theological emphases, the idea that the early, geographically distinct Christian communities were theologically and socially isolated from one another (e.g., a "Q" community with a non-messianic, Cynic Jesus) is simply a fiction created by modern scholarship.

Apologetic Historiography

Most scholars concur that one of the primary functions of Luke-Acts is apologetic (that is, defending the faith). This purpose fits quite well into a well-known line of ancient historiography. Because apologetic involves a purpose rather than a specific literary form, it can overlap with various other types of historiography that are classified instead by form or topic.

Nevertheless, apologetic historiography was common for works by minority authors about their peoples (or in this case about an aspect of their movement). The literary elite of minority cultures sometimes wrote about their ancient traditions, seeking to counter Greek ethnocentrism.[106] Often they argued that their own civilizations predated the Greeks, hence that the Greeks borrowed from them.[107] Hellenistic Jewish historians followed this pattern, adapting their stories as best as possible to Greek literary and rhetorical forms to argue that their culture was older and greater than that of the Greeks.[108]

Although the apologetic element is not always dominant, all extant ancient Jewish historiography to some degree emphasized the antiquity and superiority of Israel's religion.[109] The most complete example of Jewish apologetic historiography is Josephus' retelling of sacred Jewish history in his *Antiquities;* Josephus seeks to demonstrate God's special providence in Israel's history.[110]

Many scholars contend that Luke-Acts fits the genre of apologetic historiography,[111] even if apologetic constitutes only one element of his objective. Part of Luke's apologetic is his argument that the Gentile Christian movement, far from being a recent innovation, is an appropriate outgrowth of Israel's ancient and sacred history. Luke indeed goes beyond other Hellenistic Jewish writers (like Artapanus, Demetrius, Eupolemus, and Pseudo-Eupolemus) in his overarching promise-fulfilment schema;[112] this approach naturally reflects his theological perspective that the promised messianic era has come. It claims to unify Luke's story with Israel's earlier story in a way that these earlier writers did not claim for their own stories, suggesting that Luke views Luke-Acts itself as a continuation of the biblical story.[113] As noted earlier, those writing "biblical" history could also be writing hellenistic historiography. Luke's adaptation of his recent sacred material (about Jesus) should not be greater than his adaptation of his "ancient," biblical material, as exemplified in Acts 7 (where even some of the changes reflect early Jewish traditions rather than Luke's imagination).

Conclusion

As the majority of scholars concur, Luke's preface, speeches, and other features support the assignment of his two-volume work to the genre of ancient historiography (without contesting that the first volume by itself is biographic in character). We shall examine the use of sources in a later chapter, but Luke's use of sources points in the same direction. Luke's claim of "thorough knowledge" fits the claims, and normally the research practices, of eastern Mediterranean historical writers. He would have had ample opportunity to learn from eyewitnesses and/or those who knew them. Luke's particular apologetic interests do not detract from, but strengthen his ties to the historical genre (see further discussion on writers' perspectives and commitments in ch. 8).

Some modern scholars recognize that ancient writers, whatever their human biases, were in a better historical position to evaluate matters of their day than we are today.[114] Luke was able to investigate or at least be aware of the information passed on to him. Roughly the same critical tools were available to him as are available to us, and much more information was available to him than is otherwise available to us. While we may recognize Luke's emphases and question him on matters of detail, we ultimately have little to work with for alternative reconstructions if we dismiss the Gospels' materials.

CHAPTER 7

Ancient Historiography as History

". . . ancient historians understood the narrative framework to be an intentional literary creation that would interpret the actions and events being described."

TODD PENNER[1]

"On balance, therefore, tendentiousness, though an omnipresent danger, probably threatened the integrity of [ancient] historiography no more than in present times."

C. W. FORNARA[2]

The view that ancient writers cared little for historical accuracy, or that blends all narrative genres as if all were equally novelistic, is misinformed. As we have noted, biography and history overlap in their interests, so historical method is relevant for understanding biographies. Because (as we have also noted) one of the Gospels, Luke, belongs to a larger historical project (Luke-Acts), comparisons with ancient historiography will prove especially relevant there.

Ancient historians were interested both in facts and in how they communicated them, both in what we today consider historical information and in delivery (conventional literary or rhetorical presentation). These concerns mingled inseparably in their work, but we shall try to separate them into two chapters here. The first will address mostly ancient historians' use of genuine information. The second will focus on how they dressed up that information for their audience. Both can inform how we understand the Gospel writers, since they will illustrate how these authors expected an ancient audience to hear their works.

Most historians did value historical accuracy regarding events where they

could achieve it; they often displayed critical thinking regarding sources (as often, though not always, exemplified in Polybius); and they recognized that
sources closer to the events were more apt to be accurate than later ones were.

Concerns for Historical Information

In ways that differed starkly from modern historians, ancient historians were
creative with speeches and moralistic adaptations.[3] Here, however, we examine
the more "conservative" side of ancient historiography: historians did not normally invent "events" in their sources. (Even those that accused others of extensive embellishment rarely accused them of inventing battles, deaths, and so
forth.) Rhetorical adaptation (in which some historians like Josephus apparently took great pride) was not novelistic composition from scratch, and events
tend to remain among different writers even as interpretations of those events
vary. Paul's letters suggest that the earliest Christians were interested in the
apostles and their advance of the gospel.[4]

Historians' Concern for Accuracy?

Contrary to what some have argued, ancient historians generally had concerns
for accuracy regarding events.[5] Although historians, especially elite historians,
were also concerned with rhetorical presentation, they did not consider factual
and rhetorical goals incompatible so long as rhetoric was kept within appropriate bounds (the verdict of appropriateness varying from one historian to another). Many historians did not achieve common ideals of accuracy, but objective accuracy remained an ideal by which other historians evaluated their
work.[6]

In one of the seminal studies a generation ago, A. W. Mosley examined the
claims and practice of various ancient historians and concluded that some (he
includes both Herodotus and Thucydides) followed their material as carefully
as they could, whereas others (he includes here Strabo and Plutarch) were
much less dependable.[7] Among Romans, Tacitus proved a more critical historian, though many were not.[8] The ideal, then, remained accuracy, although not
all writers achieved this goal equally well.

History was supposed to be truthful,[9] and historians harshly criticized
other historians whom they accused of promoting falsehood, especially when
they were thought to exhibit self-serving agendas.[10] To a lesser extent, historians critiqued those who unknowingly got their facts wrong.[11] More damag-
ingly, a writer who consistently presented the least favorable interpretation, ig-

noring the diverse views of his sources, could be accused of malice.[12] Even biographers, who had a bit more freedom to be one-sided,[13] might evaluate sources' or witnesses' motives.[14]

Ancients readily distinguished between the goals of history and those of less factual epic poetry. For example, the Greek thinker Aristotle noted that the difference between "history" and "poetry" was not their literary style, for one could put Herodotus into verse if one wished. Rather, he insisted, the former recounts what actually happened whereas the latter recounts what might happen.[15] Early Greek historians distinguished themselves from epic poets not only by prose but by explicitly identifying themselves and the limits of their knowledge.[16] Likewise, even rhetorical historians recognized that historical inquiry required not merely rhetorical skill but research,[17] and those thought guilty of inadequate research or firsthand acquaintance with their reports were likely to be doubted.[18]

The perspectives of Pliny the Younger are helpful here. Pliny was an orator who was alive during the writing of the Gospels; he valued history, even though his public speaking career never allowed leisure to write it himself.[19] Ideal subjects for history offered original and interesting material, he opined, but only provided that the material was based on genuine facts.[20] We shall explore later the role of rhetoric in historiography, but Pliny, a rhetorician, felt that history's *primary* goal, in contrast to that of some other genres, was truth and accuracy rather than rhetorical display.[21] He insisted that accuracy was praiseworthy.[22] Historians would insist that their duty was to present facts accurately, though acknowledging that some individuals discussed in their histories viewed the facts (and the political perspectives informing their presentation) quite differently.[23]

Still, he recognized that contemporary political exigencies could affect the telling of current history; eager to appear in Tacitus' history, Pliny reminds him of one of his own noteworthy deeds,[24] though the incident, the prosecution of one bad governor,[25] is barely worthy of mention. Tacitus can increase Pliny's fame, the latter urges. Yet his caveat is also significant: of course he ought not go beyond the facts, Pliny allows, since history must attend only to the truth.[26]

Although Pliny writes as a Roman, writers in the eastern Mediterranean (such as the Gospel writers) may have held a greater commitment to firsthand research than Roman historians did. Romans were often interested in history more for collections of moral examples than for its own sake (though both Greeks and Romans valued both uses for history). Thus because Livy valued history for its examples, he sometimes failed to research alternative perspectives on the character of those about whom he wrote.[27] But even among Romans, while some may have written something like fiction, "Such excess . . . for which there are enough modern parallels, was a gross evasion of the rules of historical responsibility."[28] In the first century BCE, Cicero noted that everyone expected historians to avoid falsehood and bias.[29] Accuracy was not always achieved, but the desire for it does distinguish the conventions of historiography from those for novels or epic.

C. W. Fornara, a scholar of ancient historiography, argues that despite the failures of some writers, objectivity remained the goal in history. For this reason modern scholars dispute which direction Sallust leaned; he produced "a designedly neutral text," "concealed his predilections," and, "for the sake of historical truth, he repressed his loyalties and took (or tried to take) an objective view."[30] "Honesty and objectivity" were part of the genre, Fornara contends, part of "the contract between author and reader."[31] He concludes, "On balance, therefore, tendentiousness, though an omnipresent danger, probably threatened the integrity of historiography no more than in present times."[32]

Fornara very likely plays down tendentiousness too much (see our discussion in the next chapter); yet he is surely correct to the extent that historians did not feel free to invent events, but only to interpret them. They were not always objective, but blatant fabrication of persons and events violated the rules of their genre, inviting severe criticism. Interests shaped the telling of history, but did not allow anything close to the same degree of factual freedom they normally afforded novels and epics.

As one sample of a range among earlier Greek historians, we may contrast Herodotus with Thucydides, perhaps the two most widely read historians in antiquity.[33] Ancients recognized that Herodotus wrote more for his audience's pleasure than Thucydides did;[34] his charm consisted especially in making readers feel that they were reading stories rather than history.[35] Thucydides, however, had a reputation for notably accurate history writing.[36]

Herodotus employed but sometimes misunderstood his oral sources in his travels, and could not read other nations' written ones.[37] Yet even Herodotus, who was largely pioneering[38] the sort of ethnographic research he undertook, was a genuine ancient historian. His depiction of the eastern Mediterranean coastal regions fits what we know of these regions from other sources.[39] One faction of modern scholars has made him out to be "a mere 'arm-chair scholar' who only feigned his journeys, his personal observation and his sources," but Klaus Meister judges this view an "aberration" that has been refuted yet really merits little refutation. It is unbelievable, he argues, that Herodotus simply invented the vast array of citations scattered throughout his work.[40] Herodotus does not, to be sure, work from the consensus methodology of critical scholarship laid down after his time, in that he offers little attempt to evaluate his sources; he does not, however, invent them.[41] Herodotus also displays far less Hellenic bias than we might expect.[42] Ancient historians' frequent use of sources is not simply an anachronistic supposition; we address some explicit evidence for their use of sources in chapter 9.

Historians and Critical Thinking

Although there were plenty of cases of historical credulity,[43] and ancient historians were less critical of their sources than their modern successors are,[44] most historians and biographers were capable of critically evaluating their sources. Thus, for example, Plutarch disputes a claim of Herodotus based on the numbers and an extant inscription.[45] Elsewhere he tries to distinguish more accurate from less accurate sources by using reason,[46] or questions a later source including information missing in an allegedly primary source.[47]

Such concerns are hardly rare. Livy opines that some numbers he found in early "annals" may be exaggerated, and simply concludes that in any case the slaughter was great.[48] Pausanias complains that many think that Theseus instituted democracy, despite the inconsistency of such a notion with the claim that he was in fact a king. Then he adds, "there are many false beliefs current among the mass of mankind, since they are ignorant of historical science and consider trustworthy whatever they have heard from childhood in choruses and tragedies."[49] Citing historical plausibility, the Jewish historian Josephus similarly argues against various claims.[50]

Dionysius of Halicarnassus,[51] himself a rhetorician, critiques not only Thucydides' style[52] but his failure to achieve the expected standard of historical accuracy. "Art," this rhetorician opines, "does not excuse history from such exaggeration."[53] Yet Thucydides himself was hardly oblivious to the need for critical evaluation. Thucydides recognizes that Greeks were not called "Hellenes" before the Trojan War, since Homer, writing long after that war, does not yet use the term.[54] He refused to dismiss Mycenae's past splendor based on remains in his day, noting that cities of his own day might hold power without impressive physical structures.[55] When a distinction between accurate and inaccurate sources proved impossible, writers often simply presented several different current opinions on what had happened.[56] A writer might simply admit that he did not *know* how something happened.[57]

Even Herodotus' methodology of reporting a range of sources without evaluating their accuracy[58] did not thereby assume or pronounce judgment in their favor, provided the audience would be duly warned to, or would understand that they were obligated to, make their own decisions. Thus Lucian advised that the historian should report a myth found in one's source without commiting oneself to it; "make it known for your audience to make of it what they will — you run no risk and lean to neither side."[59]

Polybius recognizes that myth may be helpful for bringing pleasure,[60] but argues that the goal of history is purely truth.[61] Dionysius of Halicarnassus warns that history involves truth rather than legends, and that one should pursue facts, "neither adding to nor subtracting from" them.[62] (Even if such historians underestimated the role of an author's presuppositions, the value of facticity they articulated for historiography is not one easily applied to novelistic or purely mythical narrative forms.) Herodian (perhaps somewhat rhetorically) criticizes earlier historians for preferring rhetorical style to truth[63] and emphasizes that he never depended on unconfirmed information.[64] Because of their obligation to truth, biographers and historians could report unflattering accounts of individuals they generally respected.[65] Historians might recognize exaggerations in an account, while averring that genuine historical tradition stood behind it,[66] or might regard an account as too implausible altogether.[67] Ancient historians were also aware that propaganda helped create legend.[68]

Such perspectives show us that some ancient historians criticized others for failing to live up to the ideals of the discipline. While it is also clear that the ideal was not always realized, these claims indicate how historians could expect to be evaluated by their peers and reveal the extent to which ancient historiography anticipated its modern namesake. Although some ancient historians were not consistently rigorous, ancient thinkers were as capable of critical thought as modern ones. The most vocal example of this principle, however, is Polybius.

Polybius' High Ideal Standard

Although not all historians shared Polybius' more rigorous standards, his work provides special opportunity to explore these questions because he raises them so frequently in his writing.[69] Polybius' invective against the rhetorical historian Timaeus[70] provides an example of the standards by which historians might be judged by their peers. To be sure, Polybius' peer review of Timaeus seems hardly objective itself; he impugns his motives,[71] even while opining that Timaeus warrants such harsh treatment because he has been harsh with others.[72] Fornara rightly questions the fairness of Polybius' critique; he polemicized "against Timaeus, by our standards an indefatigable and enterprising scholar," because the latter merely collected books rather than traveled.[73] We know that some writers (note here Lucian) could use hyperbole as part of their wit in satirizing "bad" historians; though bias may have been more acceptable, hence more pervasive, in antiquity than it is today, it was probably not commonly as severe or malicious as accusers (and perhaps competitors) like Polybius suggest. (However harsh some modern reviewers may be, modern scholars may be grateful that we did not write two millennia ago.)

Nevertheless, Polybius' critique illustrates the demands for accuracy to which ancient historians could be subjected, and the public consequences of leaving oneself open to the critique of having failed to achieve such accuracy.[74]

Polybius complains that Timaeus' work reveals that he was unacquainted with Africa, about which he writes.[75] Timaeus's errors are hardly surprising, Polybius opines, since he failed to do sufficient investigation,[76] and even when he did visit places and consult witnesses, he got his facts wrong.[77] When covering matters treated properly by other historians, Timaeus elaborates excessively and confuses the information that is there.[78] Polybius accuses Timaeus of fabricating sources where he fails to name them.[79] (This accusation is probably an unfair one, reflecting simply different approaches to style or different target audiences.)

As we have noted, Polybius is not above assuming that he can infer Timaeus' motives. Timaeus' problem, Polybius argues, is not ignorance but prejudice; Timaeus is more concerned with epideictic rhetoric (praise and blame) than with proper history.[80] One could forgive historians who merely erred, Polybius allows, but Timaeus' errors are deliberate lies.[81] Polybius charges that Timaeus slanders people by presenting them in a worse light than is appropriate.[82] This criticism may well unfairly impugn Timaeus' motives for his perspective, and may simply inform us that Polybius evaluated the data differently; one could not easily avoid rivals' criticisms. But from Polybius' description it appears likely that Timaeus did at least exaggerate.

More broadly, Polybius condemns authors who sensationalize their story to make it more graphic and provide cohesiveness;[83] Polybius himself might permit a little of this to tie the narrative together, but (he contends) he would not permit very much.[84] He complains that another historian, Phylarchus, records tragic scenes of women, children, and the aged wailing as they are enslaved. Polybius objects to this portrayal (even though we can suspect that it is a historically likely inference) because it is meant to arouse pity, i.e., pathos used for entertainment value.[85] The historian should not, Polybius opines, "try to thrill his readers" with exaggeration or tragic poetry endeavoring "to imagine the probable utterances of his characters."[86] A tragic poet should entertain and settle for verisimilitude, he contends, but a historian should stick with facts.[87]

On a more general level, however, these standards that Polybius cites are not exclusively his own, but are shared with Timaeus himself, however well or poorly he may live up to the standard in a given instance. Timaeus admits that falsehood is the worst vice in writing history, and that those who write falsehood should find a different name for their book than history.[88] Timaeus would also agree with Polybius that the truth of a book's content, rather than its style or length, confirms that a work is history.[89]

Likewise, Polybius has to defend himself in advance against others' criticisms. He feels compelled to explain why he himself depends on Aratus rather than the often contradictory accounts of his contemporary Phylarchus.[90] He contends that the latter "makes many random and careless statements,"[91] and promises to offer just the most relevant examples.[92]

Historians of the early empire continued to maintain such standards as the ideal; Tacitus declares that history should cater to leaders neither by flattering nor by attacking them.[93] Although political pressure might require some adjustments for current monarchs or dynasties (or even influence the selection process by which historians survived, published, and their works remained extant), this pressure did not permit wholesale invention of facts (nor ought we to imagine the Gospel writers constrained by such political pressures from their protagonists!). Historians who invented events (far more than sensational or rhetorical historians embellishing relevant details; see our next chapter) risked refutation and serious denunciation, and their works were unlikely to survive their patrons.[94]

Earlier Versus Later Sources

The question of how soon the gospel sources derive after the events that they report is essential to the discussion of their potential reliability. Ancient as well as modern historians valued firsthand sources most highly (all other factors being equal), and after these they valued those closest in date to the events reported.[95] On this count the Gospels fare better than many historians.[96]

Ancient historians were especially happy, when reporting recent events, to include oral tradition from eyewitnesses.[97] The second best source after the author being an eyewitness was the author's use of eyewitnesses.[98] Josephus concurs with Gentile historians in preferring this practice.[99] Of course, whether due to bias or memory lapse, even eyewitnesses did not always agree on details, requiring some weighing of individual testimony.[100] (Among logical principles deemed useful then as today, witnesses were considered most dependable shortly after the events they purported to attest.)[101]

Because oral traditions were most reliable in the generation they recounted, Greek historians liked to travel to compile oral sources in the generation of the current events they reported. Thus "the historians of each generation establish the record of their own time" most effectively.[102] Nevertheless, sources committed to writing often held a special authority;[103] even an eyewitness might even cite another eyewitness source written before his own work had been committed to writing.[104] Writers often recognized that whereas oral tradition could be modified over time, written sources were fixed.[105]

When historians or biographers were themselves eyewitnesses, they usually noted this.[106] Audiences naturally would give special credence also to writers whose works bore the approval of eyewitnesses. Josephus emphasizes that he wrote his autobiography while witnesses remained alive who could verify or falsify his claims,[107] and complains that Justus, one of his rivals, waited twenty years to publish, till after the eyewitnesses were dead.[108] Josephus thus contends that Justus should be less believable than himself, whose work was known to the eyewitnesses and never contradicted by them.[109]

Elsewhere also Josephus condemns Greek historians willing to write about events where they were neither present nor dependent on those with firsthand knowledge.[110] Some, he complained, wrote about the war without having been there, which he regarded as inadequate research for appropriate histories.[111] By contrast, Josephus says, he was present[112] and he alone understood the Jewish refugees and wrote the information down;[113] his accusers did not *know* the Jewish side of the story.[114] Justus was not present when the events he describes took place in Galilee, and those who could have supplied Justus with such information perished in the siege of Jerusalem.[115] Josephus himself was not present for most of his *Antiquities* or parts of his *War,* but the principle of dependence on eyewitness or early sources when possible is useful for considering the Gospels; they differ from works written centuries after the events they narrate. Most scholars date Matthew and Luke after 70 or even 80, hence over four or five decades after the events described in the Gospel, albeit while some eyewitnesses may remain alive. That some eyewitnesses remained alive when Mark was written is very likely; probably even more remained alive (and in church leadership, Gal 2:9) during the primary period of oral transmission.

The critical sensitivity of ancient historians about the proximity of sources to events especially affected their understanding of the remote past. Ancient historians were less accurate when they wrote about people of many centuries past than when they wrote about more recent events (as the Gospels do),[116] and they were themselves aware of this difference.[117] (Conversely, the advantage of writing about ancient history was that one could simply collect what earlier historians said, whereas writing about recent matters could lead to offense!)[118]

Ancient historians, like their modern successors, generally preferred not only witnesses but writers closer in time to the events reported rather than later sources.[119] Following the same principle, many ancient writers pointed out the obscurity of reports from centuries earlier, expecting a much higher standard of accuracy when handling reports closer to their own period.[120] Most writers recognized that the earliest period was shrouded in myth,[121] even if they sometimes found the myths' basic outline acceptable.[122]

Sources about characters who lived many centuries in the past often conflicted, a conflict that inadvertently attests to a proliferation of written historical sources no longer extant (see our discussion of sources in ch. 9). When writing about characters of the distant past, then, historians would have to sort through legendary as well as actual historical data,[123] and might well have difficulty ascertaining which was which.[124] Sometimes they simply repeated apparently incredible information and warned readers to use discretion;[125] often, however, they sought to "demythologize" their ancient reports.[126] We may take the example of Plutarch writing about Theseus, who was thought to have lived over a millennium before him. Plutarch proposes to purify "Fable, making her submit to reason and take on the semblance of History" by determining what is probable and credible.[127] This means that when depending on historically remote sources, ancient historiography sometimes had to settle for historical verisimilitude rather than high probability (by modern standards) concerning the events that ancient historians reported.[128]

Their criteria for distinguishing what was credible from what was not were often inadequate, but they illustrate ancient intellectuals' recognition of the problem and their critical intentions.[129] Sometimes writers employed a criterion of coherency with other evidence,[130] such as known customs of a report's day;[131] other historical context[132] (including chronological data);[133] coherence with documentary sources;[134] consistency of reported behavior with a person's other known behavior (something like modern form critics' criterion of coherence);[135] or even material remains.[136] Following the probability argument standard in the law courts,[137] a historian could challenge an event recounted in earlier histories because of intrinsic improbabilities in their accounts.[138] Another historian often evaluates various reports by comparing them; he notes that one story too prominent to ignore is not reported by any of the eyewitness writers, hence is likely unreliable.[139]

Historians' generally more cautious approach to early sources contrasts with their greater trust in more recent material, and we generally agree with their intuitions, which were informed by greater knowledge of their period. We respect Thucydides, Polybius, and (closer to the Gospels' era) Josephus as contemporaries of much of what they report (regardless of some rhetorical embellishments). We depend heavily on writers of the early empire like Tacitus and Suetonius, who report relatively recent events (of the past century to century and a half, with accuracy increasing further later in that period). Despite their biases, they provide an invaluable source for understanding the early empire (see discussion below on evaluating degrees of historical reliability). Barring convincing evidence to the contrary (such as much greater divergence from primary sources than we find in such historians), we should evaluate the Gospels analogously. They write about events fulfilled within the past century, mostly roughly half a century or so before they wrote.

Ancient as well as modern writers recognized that one could communicate truths through fictitious stories, whether Jewish sages' story parables, Greek fables, or philosophers' illustrations. But the stakes changed once authors made claims about history, thereby inviting historical falsification. Early Christians and their critics recognized the genre of gospels and Acts as offering public claims in the arena of history (cf. 1 Cor 15:3-8; Lk 1:1-4; 2:1-2; 3:1-2; Acts 26:26), and proceeded in their debate accordingly.

Sometimes the distinction between myth and history served polemic or apologetic purposes, but it did so precisely because many thinkers believed that the nature of foundational claims mattered. "The distinction between myth (or fiction) and history" became one crux in early Christianity's debates with its detractors; "Celsus describes the gospels as fictions (πλάσματα) and viewed them as largely unhistorical," and Christians took the same approach toward Philostratus' *Life of Apollonius*.[140] Celsus, Porphyry and Julian all claimed that the gospels were fictions, fabricating stories and not history,[141] apparently assuming "that one needs to show the falsity of the sources (e.g. the biblical literature) of the Christians' message before one can stop the religion."[142]

But using information for an agenda is not incompatible with the presence of genuine information. Contrary to what is sometimes assumed, early Christians did have historical interest, and this is what we might expect in their setting. In the context of a Jewish covenant understanding of history as the framework for God's revelation, the earliest Christians should have been interested in the history of Jesus.[143] Even apocalypses often provide "historical reviews."[144] Indeed, even the Qumran sect, whose teacher was important but much less central than in the Christian movement,[145] preserved at least some information about its teacher.[146] Interest in history distinguished the Christian movement[147] from both Mithraism, with its more cosmic emphasis,[148] and earlier mystery cults,[149] but fits the commitment of ancient historians.[150]

Limited Analogies with Josephus

As a Hellenistically educated monotheist steeped in Palestinian Judaism but writing history for a Diaspora audience,[151] Josephus may invite comparison with the Gospels. The comparison is less complete than some scholars might make it; the Gospels address a much less sophisticated, much more popular audience than Josephus does. As we shall see, Josephus appeals to an elite audience that demanded more rhetorical elaboration than some other historians thought fitting, and more than the Gospel writers were probably rhetorically capable of providing. Nevertheless, Josephus provides one among several possible analogies, and an analogy potentially valuable enough to warrant exploration.

Clearly Josephus both preserves and adapts prior material. Josephus does not uncritically affirm all his sources; he can note that some make a particular claim,[152] and can refuse to decide himself the cause of some events, diplomatically leaving final decisions to the reader's discretion.[153] He can also question a source's bias.[154] Yet we can best test Josephus' reliability where he is reproducing accounts to which we have ready access, most often biblical accounts.[155]

Josephus, like some other Jewish writers,[156] dramatizes, adds speeches, omits what appears counterproductive, and inserts his own apologetic slant.[157] Sometimes Josephus apparently "corrects" or adjusts biblical accounts based on other biblical passages.[158] This practice may not represent his method everywhere; he may strive for greater rhetorical sophistication in his magnum opus, the *Antiquities* (where we have most of his overlap with Scripture), than in his earlier *War*.[159] But even here Josephus tends to adapt events in his sources, not create them.[160] (Speeches are, as often noted, a different story.)[161]

Even when he adds extrabiblical events to biblical accounts (such as Moses' exploits as an Egyptian prince), our extant sources (such as Artapanus) often confirm that he is following earlier extrabiblical traditions, not composing from his imagination. Josephus also clearly depends on sources, for postbiblical as well as biblical events,[162] such as the work of the eyewitness Nicolas of Damascus,[163] although he critiques what he sees as Nicolas' bias.[164]

Like other extant historians, Josephus affirms his intention to write truth, in contrast to those historians he thinks are unconcerned for it.[165] This claim recalls the standard that historians demanded, but does not resolve the extent to which Josephus fulfills it.[166] He condemns those who wrote about events without any firsthand knowledge, contrasting them with his own knowledge of the Judean-Roman war.[167] Not only was he an eyewitness of much that he claims,[168] he claims to have even taken notes,[169] receiving reports also from deserters from the city.[170]

Yet whether due to conflicting sources,[171] careless composition, or neglecting to explain information that would resolve some of the tensions, Josephus sometimes contradicts himself.[172] Sometimes he does this even in some of his most rhetorically refined material, and in material closest to his own lifetime.[173] Josephus also sometimes forgets to include information; although promising to recount more about Helena's and Izates' benefactions during Jerusalem's famine,[174] he never returns to the subject (at least not in this extant volume).[175]

How does Josephus *usually* fare in his reports of the postbiblical period? Scholars on Josephus range from skepticism to appreciation, generally depending on the aspects of his historiography on which they focus their attention. I shall mention some of his weaknesses first. On a number of points he fails to impress,[176] for example, in his speeches.[177] Most historians today also argue that Josephus' population estimates are unreliable and that he is sometimes mistaken on distances.[178] Since it is unlikely that Josephus actually counted people or measured distances, such matters do not otherwise affect the substance of what he reports about events. Josephus occasionally makes mistakes on even his most public information,[179] although this appears to be the exception rather than the rule.[180]

Josephus' biases are, despite his claims of straightforwardness, difficult to miss. He is probably more accurate in many of his details than in his summaries; he does not fabricate events, but he puts his slant on them. Indeed, his overarching summaries[181] and apologetic perspectives[182] sometimes conflict with the information he himself reports. For example, he presents the Judean-Roman war as virtually an accident in which incompetent governors and a few Jewish "bandits" forced Judea into unwilling conflict with Rome.[183] His perspective is that of an aristocrat, favoring Jewish aristocrats;[184] some of his work may be biased toward Pharisees (a group to which he allegedly once belonged);[185] he may also exaggerate Jewish privileges in the Empire (albeit based on genuine precedents) to further his apologetic on their behalf; and he presented Jewish sects in terms of Greek philosophic ideals.[186]

Josephus' biases do not, however, significantly hamper our use of his work for historical reconstruction; as one historian notes: "These biases are to be expected" and are usually easy enough to recognize; "With proper allowance made for his special interests and recognition that he was sometimes misinformed, the reader will find Josephus on the whole reliable."[187]

If we leave aside examples of bias (including in summaries), speeches and difficult estimates, Josephus proves generally accurate on matters of historical detail. As noted above, whereas archaeology has challenged some of Josephus' claims, it has vindicated him on many detailed points.[188] Apart from distance estimates, Josephus proves otherwise generally reliable on geographic matters,[189] and archaeology confirms most of his observations about Jerusalem, which he knew well: here, despite some errors, he is often accurate in even quite minute details such as the measurements of columns.[190] One of Herod's three towers remains, 66 feet square and 66 feet high — just as Josephus claimed.[191]

Outside Jerusalem, the Caesarea Ancient Harbor Excavation Project has largely confirmed Josephus' description of Caesarea's harbor, despite some omissions in his description.[192] Josephus appears to confuse the directions of the theater and amphitheater from Caesarea's harbor, but supplies many correct details.[193]

As one Israeli archaeologist emphasized regarding the concrete physical data (where Josephus fares better than in his fairly blatant biases or rhetorical distortions):

> Before archaeological excavations, it was the vogue among historians — very serious historians — to argue that Josephus in many places relates sheer nonsense, that he is not historical, that he exaggerates, and so forth. But the more we dig in Jerusalem and at Masada and at Herodium and in [Herodian] Jericho, the greater respect we — both archaeologists and historians — have for the accuracy of Josephus. He is one of the greatest historians. Of course he had his own prejudices. But show me any historian without them. Josephus is accurate not only for his own period but for previous periods as well, for example, the Hellenistic period.[194]

Despite reservations, scholars normally accept his main outline of events as accurate.[195] Josephus not only claims accuracy[196] (itself no guarantee of it), but he presented copies to Vespasian, Titus, Herod of Chalchis, Agrippa — so he dared not have seriously misrepresented the events also known to them.[197] (By the same principle, we may doubt that Luke could have easily gotten away with fabricating new events contradicting those Theophilus had already heard; Lk 1:4.)

How do Matthew and Luke compare with Josephus? Their adaptation of Mark generally sticks close to Mark's stories and Luke (with very rare exceptions)[198] reproduces even his sequence. If this pattern is representative of their use of written sources, they may stay closer to their sources than Josephus stays to the Greek Bible in his *Antiquities*. Moreover, the Gospel writers are not "rhetorical" historians (Luke, the closest, is nowhere close to Josephus); by contrast, Josephus in his *Antiquities* (more than in his *War*) often is.[199] Historians frequently depend on Josephus, despite his biases and literary freedom, for historical information where he is our primary source. Although the Gospels address less politically significant information, they reflect more rigorous transmission methods and far less rhetorical adaptation. Because they remain our best source, we ought to give significant heed to them.

Conclusion

Ancient historians did show genuine concern for historical information. Some were more accurate than others, but obvious biases or misinformation invited critique from other historians. Historians did often critically evaluate their sources. While we may suspect that biographers were often less critical with information that suited their purposes, their historical interests (noted in the previous chapter) would have motivated them to make some use of such historical methods. We must, however, also examine the other side of ancient historical writing and assess its relevance for our subject.

CHAPTER 8

Ancient Historiography as Rhetoric

"Contrary to the conclusions of past scholarship, these literary tools [rhetorical techniques] do not undermine generic understandings of the work as historiography in favor of theological readings, rather they support the designation of Luke-Acts as Hellenistic historiography."

CLARE ROTHSCHILD[1]

We have noted historians' interest in historical information; now we must note their interest in rhetorically acceptable presentation. On the elite level of most of our extant sources, this interest involved techniques common to rhetoric; on the less elite level of the Gospels, it probably involved more techniques found in popular storytelling. (In this respect the Gospels probably resemble many other popular biographies.)

There was no academic discipline of "history" in antiquity; the two advanced disciplines were philosophy and rhetoric, and rhetoric (something like "communications" today) was more dominant in public discourse. Because of this, rhetoric pervaded Greco-Roman life, and many of the elite with most leisure to write history were orators. Their works consequently often reflect careful literary design meant to appeal to their audience's sophisticated tastes.

Modern Versus Ancient Historiography

Although it should go without saying, we must be careful to distinguish ancient historiography from modern historiography.[2] When we claim that a biblical (or other ancient) work is history or letter, modern readers often make the facile assumption (happily more difficult for apocalyptic texts) that we are talking about the same genres as modern history or modern letters.[3] Granted, there are considerable similarities; the ranges overlap; and modern analogies evolved from these ancient forms. But conventions differed, and only those who have done little reading in the ancient sources will simply equate them.

It is anachronistic to assume that ancient and modern histories would share all the same generic features (such as the way speeches should be composed) simply because we employ the same term today to describe both. Barring supernatural inspiration to write according to as-yet nonexistent historical conventions that no one expected (even when they *did* assume such inspiration), we should not demand that ancient historians conform precisely to modern historiography. Ancient historians sometimes fleshed out scenes and speeches to produce a coherent narrative in a way that their contemporaries expected but that modern academic historians would not consider acceptable when writing for their own peers. This contrast reflects the different interests of ancient and modern historiography: ancient writers (at least those whose works survived) emphasized a cohesive narrative more than simple recitation of facts. By contrast, modern scholars value accuracy in facts much more than the "flow" of the narrative for their audience.

Ancient historical writers varied in the degree of cohesiveness and attention to bare facts, just as modern historical writers do; but on the whole, the ancient range was far more concerned with fleshing out missing details for cohesive narratives than modern ones are.[4] Because of their focus on traditional, sacred content, the Synoptics differ from elite expectations. They are sometimes less cohesive, sometimes with more evidence of their sources, and do not develop scenes with elaborate descriptions. Nevertheless, it is helpful here to establish the options available to ancient writers and the degree of freedom within which they worked.

Perhaps the biggest difference between ancient and modern historiography would appear in the treatment of speeches. Rhetorically minded elite ancient historians augmented or adjusted information about speeches (or when necessary invented them) to fill out a full scene, as opposed to simply offering what would have been considered rhetorically inept tidbits of tradition.[5] (Thus one orator criticizes a historian who conveys much accurate information yet fails to achieve this eloquently.)[6] Because such speeches are not directly relevant to biographies (including the Synoptics),[7] and because the Synoptics generally involve sayings traditions rather than speeches, I will, for the sake of space, omit full discussion of speeches here. The interested reader may find my treatment of them elsewhere.[8]

Such differences do not mean that most historians made up "events." They do mean that where necessary historians had the generic freedom to fill in a missing detail to make sense of their sources, to flesh out a speech or even a scene, and so forth.[9] In such situations, plausible and probable inferences could be acceptable.[10] Having noted this general caveat, however, we do have good reason to believe (as we will show later) that the first Gospel writers had sources for the events and sayings they depict and wrote reasonably close in time to the events they narrate. After having written commentaries on Matthew, John, and Acts, I believe that Luke, in particular, while making some use of the ancient historian's freedoms for arrangement,[11] remained as careful as possible according to the standards typically expected for popular historiography.

Ancient Expectations

Lucian writes that good biographers avoid flattery that falsifies events[12] and only bad historians invent data.[13] By his criticism Lucian shows us two things: first, that some historians did fabricate data (or at least could be so accused by those who disagreed with them);[14] and second, that most historians agreed that the practice was unacceptable, at least for events (rather than, say, details of conversations or reports of emotions).[15]

The boundaries of genres were not, however, always clearly defined. Many ancient readers questioned the veracity of particular historians, and some used the trappings of history to recount fanciful tales.[16] Although most surviving histories are quite distinct from novels, we do have some novels about historical characters. Cicero reasonably opined that Xenophon's story of Cyrus was meant to teach about proper government, not history about Cyrus.[17] Most scholars allow that works such as Xenophon's *Cyropaedia* and Pseudo-Callisthenes' account of Alexander are exceptions to the usual division (novels about historical personages, sometimes employing some known traditions).[18] Such historical novelists were more interested in rhetorical effect and praising their protagonist, but as we noted in the previous chapter, this was hardly the desired norm for history.[19] (It should also be noted that Pseudo-Callisthenes wrote somewhere between 460 and 760 years after Alexander's death — i.e., likely over half a millennium later, a situation quite different from the Gospels.) Some other statements, however, suggest that even some true histories fell short of the ideal standard. Plutarch complains that some writers added details missing elsewhere, for example composing a proper tragic finale for Alexander's life.[20]

This practice reflected a wider use of historical information in speeches; the influence of rhetoric pervaded Greco-Roman intellectual life.[21] Rhetoricians were permitted to "adjust stories" to provide cohesiveness to their narrative; if Coriolanus died one way and a rhetorician was drawing a parallel between Coriolanus and Themistocles, the rhetorician could make use of a parallel account of the latter's death already invented by others. One could do this, Cicero claimed, knowing full well that the parallel account was not solid history.[22] Fornara complains that the view that Cicero here allows rhetors to "distort history" misreads his Latin; rather, he simply spoke of rhetors using historical illustrations in their speeches.[23] The context, however, at least suggests that Cicero expected some speakers to select their accounts on utilitarian grounds, that is, for what worked best rhetorically in their speeches. At the same time, it is true that Cicero was speaking about speeches, not about Greek historiography. Even when historical works embellished their story in a manner that modern historians would consider fictional, they were bound by the prior story in a way that novelists were not.[24]

Claiming that historical writers used sources (as we shall argue in ch. 9) and were concerned about genuine historical information does not mean that they did not place their own "twist" on the material. To the contrary, it was customary for writers to do so, and the more rhetorically sophisticated the expected audience, the greater the expectations of such displays of rhetorical prowess.

Because time has naturally preserved mostly the rhetorically respected historians of the elite class (who also had the most leisure and resources to publish their histories), these histories are typically more rhetorical (and certainly usually include fuller speeches than) Luke-Acts;[25] the other Gospel writers are not even comparable. Nevertheless, these observations reveal that ancient historiography was more reader- (better, hearer-) driven than its typical modern academic analogue, and we must take this factor into account when reading ancient works with historical content.

Historians and Rhetoric

Rhetorical techniques were pervasive in ancient historiography, so such elements do not detract from assigning any work to this genre.[26] Historians used rhetorical techniques to make their histories persuasive.[27] Greek historians knew how to present their material in an artistic way,[28] and rhetorical conventions affected the telling of good history.[29] This influence was especially prominent during the Empire, when rhetorical style affected not only speeches but even Roman literature.[30] Romans not only continued the Greek emphasis on argumentative history with an "interpretive superstructure" for the information; they mixed it far more deliberately with rhetoric.[31] Pliny the Younger declares that one orator's histories were as charming as the writer's speeches, though more concise.[32] Even Tacitus, one of the most respected Roman historians and our principal source for the early Empire, was a powerful orator in his own right.[33] Although Greek historians on the whole maintained a standard of accuracy in the events they told, rhetorical standards did influence the ways they told their stories and how they conceived historical verisimilitude.

Historians were interested not only in accuracy but also in plausibility and probability,[34] as in rhetoric more generally.[35] They might claim to prefer truth over style, but so did orators; such claims merely show that they dealt with information as well as style.[36] The measure of each of these elements varied from one historian to another, but historians in general both appealed to the historical research tradition and sought to represent the past persuasively.[37] Historians could draw on epic literary strategies and interests in how they told their narratives.[38]

Members of the elite class expected histories to conform to the appropriate historical style.[39] Readers noticed when the pre-Christian Roman historian Sallust regularly displayed rhetorical tropes in his historical writing.[40] A history written in a style between the normal historical and discursive styles could sell well among the rhetorically trained elite.[41]

Although some historians sought restraint in the use of rhetoric, no one opposed it entirely.[42] "Pleasure and beauty" remained important purposes for any work.[43] Not only Thucydides, but even the methodologically insistent Polybius could succumb to the temptation to exaggerate the unique importance of his subject matter.[44] Rhetorical conventions also appeared in ancient biography, though more so in rhetorical biographers like Isocrates than others.[45] If for no other reason, the prominent role of speeches in ancient histories made the heavy use of rhetoric inevitable.

Some ancient historians allowed rhetoric more control over their presentation of history than others did. As Clare Rothschild points out, ancient historians debated "not about *whether,* but about *how* methods of argumentation should be used": should the orator persuade by logical appeal or "inferior means (obsequy, amusement, sensationalism)"?[46] By the era of the Gospels, historians imitated and mixed the various types of earlier historical approaches, including "epic, tragic and scientific approaches." Some "sacrificed standards of critical research for the immediate gratification of their audiences," using especially epic and tragic techniques. Meanwhile, "others catering to more critical audiences imitated the more subtle argument strategies of Herodotus and his tradents." Most mixed techniques to some degree to reach the widest possible audience.[47]

We should not, however, use the rhetorical element to summarily dismiss the historical value of ancient historical writers; if Theopompus' rhetoric spoiled his history,[48] that of the orator Tacitus did not spoil his.[49] Even the best historians employed standards of rhetoric, but they used more restraint in rhetorical embellishment.[50] Moreover, though historians even as early as Herodotus employed rhetorical strategies, history was written quite differently "from poetry, drama, oratory, and forensic argument."[51] Most historians recognized that historical inquiry required not merely rhetorical skill but research.[52]

The historian's moral or political aims could weigh more heavily than literary artistry, and neither such aims nor rhetorical presentation meant that historians simply "'revised' the past to serve their own purposes."[53]

Some writers explicitly criticized those more interested in showing off rhetorical skill than in historical truth.[54] Lucian expresses this concern in a particularly emphatic manner, heavily criticizing those who overemphasize rhetorical embellishment in histories.[55] In his essay *How to Write History,* Lucian summarizes the expectations of at least the more stringent historical critics (the standards by which other historians could expect to be evaluated).[56] He complains about writers who wanted to praise their rulers and generals, but emphasizes that true history must not include any lies, unlike encomia.[57]

Such writers, Lucian warns, must recognize that history employs rules "different from poetry and poems," which can blame their excesses on inspiration.[58] "This . . . is the one thing peculiar to history, and only to Truth must sacrifice be made"; one writing history must ignore all other concerns.[59] Flatterers work for the present; historians preserve truth for the future.[60] History's purpose, he opined, should not be to give pleasure, but only to be *useful;* "and that comes from truth alone."[61]

Of course, not all ancient historians agreed with Lucian, who is among the most critical writers in this regard.[62] We have noted that Josephus was heavily rhetorical,[63] for example, composing some speeches freely. Likewise in narrative, comparing his *Antiquities* with the LXX reveals the degree of his rhetorical adaptation.[64]

At the same time, we should not obliterate the distinctions between pure rhetoric and the use of rhetoric in historiography (outside its speeches). Pliny the Younger points out that, for all their commonalities, history and oratory are different disciplines: rhetoric focuses on trivial narratives, and history on famous deeds.[65] He notes that in these different genres, style, vocabulary, rhythm, and subject-matter all differ.[66]

Various historians indicate the careful balance they often sought. Polybius recognized the epideictic function of historical writing, contending that historians must render judgments about whether peoples or individuals "are worthy of praise or blame."[67] Moral judgments and rhetorical artistry, however, did not require abandonment of historical responsibility; a history was not a speech (epideictic or otherwise). Thus Polybius at one point warns that in his history he had to differ from what he had earlier written about someone in an encomium. There he had exaggerated the person's "achievements," but "the present history, which distributes praise and blame impartially, demands a strictly true account and one which states the ground on which either praise or blame is based."[68] In a later period, Dio Cassius emphasizes that he has given attention to both tasteful literary style and historical accuracy in his narrative.[69]

Suetonius, though more disposed to credit scandals about some of his subjects than about others, avoids embellishment and would not easily be classed a "rhetorical" historian,[70] in spite of his considerable interest in rhetoric.[71] But his contemporary Tacitus, a renowned orator who also wrote about oratory,[72] was no less careful a historian (and in some respects was more so).

Gospels Distorted by Rhetoric?

The only Gospel writer likely influenced overtly by rhetorical conventions was Luke. (Later Christian writers who had every reason to find significant rhetorical expertise in the Gospels failed to discover it there.)[73] Was Luke heavily or only mildly influenced by models of dramatic rhetorical historians? Luke's preface indicates some concerns shared with rhetorical historiography: his emphasis on an "orderly" account suggests that he valued persuasive arrangement.[74]

Yet Luke was certainly no rhetorical historian like Theopompus; he was likewise certainly not as rhetorically trained as most extant historians and biographers, often members of the elite trained first of all in rhetoric. Modern scholars evaluating Luke-Acts in terms of Greco-Roman rhetoric thus sometimes come to strikingly different conclusions. On the one hand, some argue that classical rhetorical conventions deeply influenced Luke's literary techniques.[75] On the other hand, others argue that Luke's literary level would be considered low to educated Greeks, in contrast to refined hellenistic history.[76]

Both perspectives have some value, depending on which part of Luke-Acts we are reading and the foil with which we are contrasting Luke's work. Luke employs classical rhetoric where needed (e.g., Lk 1:1-4; Acts 17:22-31), including even some complex periodic sentences (Lk 1:1-4; Acts 15:24-26; cf. Lk 3:1-2).[77] He employs the same rhetorical authentication techniques we find in many of the more elite historians.[78] Luke fairly often employs the rhetorically clear technique of "inflection," though this was apparently one of the more basic exercises.[79] More significantly, Luke makes significant use of prose rhythm (based on vowel rhythm), which is otherwise rare in our earliest Christian documents.[80] The cumulative effect of rhetorical comparisons with speeches in Acts suggests that Luke was familiar with various rhetorical strategies and devices.[81]

Yet Luke writes for a more popular audience than most elite historians did.[82] Luke surely did not belong to the elite in the way that extant historians of the Roman senatorial class or equites did. Most Hellenistic historians had formal rhetorical training;[83] it is not clear that Luke did. From his preface in Lk 1:1-4, Loveday Alexander suggests that if Luke writes history, he writes it from the more scientific, less rhetorical side of historiography.[84] Though educated, Luke does not necessarily display advanced training in rhetoric. The ability to vary style, even in a single speech, was rhetorically important;[85] yet Luke does not even seek to vary style in speeches as much as one would expect of some rhetoricians.

The more detailed rhetorical exercise of elaborately describing scenes is missing in Luke-Acts; it uses rhetoric, as all literary works did, but is not intended as anything like an epideictic showpiece.[86] Even the shortest sort of example of the elaborative rhetorical device *ekphrasis*[87] is missing in Luke's work. Luke depicts action and itineraries, but hardly graphically; he offers physical descriptions of neither places[88] nor people, as all those who have wished they knew what Jesus or Paul looked like are well aware.

Second Sophistic orators appreciated earlier rhetorical historians like Sallust painting a vivid picture of details and feelings,[89] and thought that historians ought to describe the countryside,[90] lengths to which Luke never comes close. (This is true even in the "we" material, where Luke is most vivid and detailed. There is nothing, for example, about the famous 100-petaled roses around Philippi.)[91] Rhetors demanded graphic scenes providing visual horror fitting for the events;[92] that Luke, though reporting Jesus' and Stephen's executions, avoids depicting gore, places him toward the more restrained end of this continuum. Later elite writers shaped by the Second Sophistic[93] averred that historians should write in the "grand" style,[94] which is not Luke's preferred style.[95]

I thus differ from the scholars who see Luke's work as "dramatic" history in terms of such elaborations.[96] Still, Luke is "dramatic" in other ways, e.g., by including numerous "signs" reports.[97] Eckhard Plümacher sees miraculous elements as more dominant in "tragic-pathetic" history;[98] yet Luke is readier to report signs than to develop specifically tragic-pathetic elements at any length.[99] Popular literature often developed tales of exotic distant lands, unusual "natural phenomena," divine interventions, and wonders;[100] Luke's lands belong to the real world,[101] and he focuses on only those unusual phenomena (miracle reports) genuinely relevant to his story. Such features simply suggest that he wrote in a manner more consistent with an audience immersed in Scripture (which reported many such signs) than in elite Greco-Roman rhetorical conventions (and that he wrote more about miracle-workers, whose role he hardly invented; cf. 2 Cor 12:12).

John, Matthew, and especially Mark appear less conversant in Greco-Roman rhetoric than Luke is. We should not therefore expect significant distortion of information in the interest of rhetorical presentation (although Jewish storytelling conventions may have influenced John and Matthew).[102] Yet even if we did find significant rhetorical influence, we would not for this reason expect the Gospels to be less reliable sources than Suetonius or Plutarch.

Historical Perspectives, *Tendenz,* and Purpose

We have noted that most ancient historiography involved both an interest in information and an interest in pleasing rhetorical presentation. In histories, however, rhetorical presentation was meant not merely to entertain, but also to convey particular perspectives.[103] All historians, ancient and modern, write from some systems of values and perspectives, whether these systems reflect the larger culture, conventions of their guild, minority values, or idiosyncratic perspectives.[104] More than most historians today, ancient historians generally also wrote for cultural or moral edification (which often included nationalistic themes).

Just as most historical writers today also have particular interests (say, women's history; African-American history; modern military history; and so forth),[105] ancient historians could write with moral or political agendas. An ancient historical monograph (relevant to Luke-Acts) would normally include an even more particular focus.

History and Agendas

No close reader of the Gospels will deny that they communicate particular perspectives as well as information.[106] Does their "slant" reduce the value of the information they convey? An ancient audience would expect perspectives and agendas whenever they encountered biographies and histories. While modern historians take such agendas into account when they read ancient biographers and historians, they do not for this reason treat them as novelists who simply fabricated stories to communicate their views.

Ancient historians could write from particular overt moral or religious perspectives.[107] Indeed, it was an "interpretive superstructure"[108] that distinguished history as a literary work from mere chronicles. Whatever the boundaries between history and novel, modern traditional boundaries between history and theology are far less applicable to ancient texts. If anything, the emphasis on providing moral models and lessons is even clearer in succinct biographies than in the larger histories. It is certainly clearer in both of them than in the vast majority of novels (the primary objective of which was usually entertainment).

We recognize today that no historians, including modern ones, are disinterested reporters; historians select the events that they will report based on what they find to be of greatest interest or of greatest relevance to their focus (which again relates to interest).[109] (Interest shapes even journalists' reports and the editing of these reports for popular consumption.) Ancient historians, however, had less pressure from strict peer review in the direction of objectivity or in the direction of consensus among historians than is usual today. No less than biblical historians, Hellenistic historians "selectively reported the past in order to accomplish larger goals."[110]

While affirming the truth of their own perspectives, ancients also recognized the danger of biases (typically *others'* biases) distorting the historical enterprise. Thus for example Josephus complains about contemporary historians who distorted Nero's reign, either from favor because they benefited from it or from malice because they suffered under it.[111] He complains that such historians failed to avoid bias even when reporting earlier eras, because they do not care about truth.[112] Because his interest is in truth, he insists, he writes with greater accuracy.[113]

We may well dispute Josephus' accuracy at points, but we should also take note of the ideal that he expects his audience to embrace: bias should be avoided. That Josephus could appeal to such an ideal, while straightforwardly writing with an explicit focus and from an explicit vantage point, should caution us not to confuse perspective-shaped historical writing with novels. Perspectives and interests are to be expected, but the prospect of critics could engender at least some sense of accountability to fairness regarding the substance of events, and set some limits on how much bias was acceptable in a public forum.[114] As is the case today, historians could fiercely debate conflicting views, but being able to marshall genuine information would strengthen one's case.

Political and National Agendas

Historians often wrote to inculcate "good citizenship,"[115] hence usually displayed, in varying measures, national or ethnic biases. Polybius, for example, exhibits a pro-Roman *Tendenz*.[116] Thucydides, though a participant in the Peloponnesian War, proves surprisingly impartial; yet even he had his biases.[117] Livy claimed that history teaches a nation's greatness and what one may imitate.[118] One also thinks of Josephus' apologetic attempt to whitewash his people from excess complicity in the revolt while simultaneously appealing to the dignity of his Roman readership.[119]

It is of course true that history is usually written by the victors,[120] but even in ancient epic triumph[121] or national loyalties did not always dictate bias. Historians often report sympathetically both sides of a conflict.[122] Herodotus, one of the earliest historians, often regards Egyptians and others as superior to his fellow-Greeks[123] and describes other peoples fairly objectively; he criticizes Greek failings, and praises both Spartan and Athenian virtues.[124] Biographers, too, included both "flat" and "round" characters.[125] Lucian criticizes historians who praise their own leaders, while slandering the other side, as engaging merely in panegyric.[126] A historian who focuses on what is negative about a character can be accused of malice, unless this approach is necessary for the telling of the story.[127]

Yet political and ethnic agendas were not the only agendas in ancient historiography. Historians had moral and theological biases as well as political ones (political, moral and theological categories in fact sometimes overlapped). While we cannot draw a strict line between nationalistic and moralistic agendas (patriotism was generally viewed as a moral virtue itself), broader moral lessons sometimes even took precedence over nationalistic agendas. Despite Polybius' pro-Roman *Tendenz,* for example, he notes that he often praises both Romans and Carthaginians, but only so he can set before statesmen proper models for conduct.[128]

Moral Agendas

Most ancient historians felt responsible to certain standards of historical accuracy (whether or not they achieved them), but also felt responsible to arrange their histories in such a manner as to provide moral lessons.

Respectable members of ancient society in general reflected similar concerns in a variety of genres; for example, in letters about honorable people, writers could praise past figures' virtues as models inviting imitation.[129] The emphasis on imitating ancestral wisdom and learning from both positive and negative historical examples pervaded rhetoric from classical Athens through the late empire.[130] Orators could employ earlier biographies (such as Plutarch's *Lives*) this way.[131]

These objectives were clear in histories and biographies themselves. Contrary to what some modern interpreters suppose, moral agendas characterized ancient historiography and biography far more often than they characterized novels. The moral agenda constituted a paramount one for historians; one taught history not simply to memorize the past but to draw lessons from it.[132] Thus some historians felt that historians should choose a noble subject, so their work would contribute to good moral character as well as providing information.[133] No less a careful ancient historian than Polybius begins his multivolume history by observing its utilitarian value: people "have no more ready corrective of conduct than knowledge of the past."[134]

Likewise, Tacitus, one of our most reliable historical sources for the early empire, emphasizes that the biographic study of history promotes virtue.[135] Often lamenting the decline of traditional Roman values, he was (like his contemporaries) "a moralist, who regards it as his duty to hold vice up to scorn and to praise virtue."[136] Lucian, a stickler for historical accuracy, as we have noted, allows for history's edifying value, i.e., moral lessons, provided they flow from truth.[137]

Valerius Maximus was not the most careful historian, but his perspective on the utility of historical examples is representative: It is helpful to know history "so that a backward look . . . may yield some profit to modern manners."[138] Historians and biographers frequently included even moralizing narrative asides to interpret history's meaning more directly for their readers, to illustrate the fulfillment of prophetic utterances, or to provide the author's perspective.[139] Jewish historiography was certainly no less interpretive.[140]

The Value of Moral Examples

What such historians often meant by the instructive value of history was the positive and negative moral examples of other persons' behavior. Whereas one's own life was too brief to use one's own experience to guard against all faults, the collective memory of humanity offered greater wisdom. Historians generally believed that if one understood why events happened,[141] not merely historians but also statesmen[142] and orators[143] (both of which some of them were) could use these events as precedents.[144] When the pre-Christian rhetorical historian Dionysius of Halicarnassus lists purposes for writing history, its value as a model inviting honorable behavior is a significant one.[145]

Jewish people understood the Bible's narratives as providing moral lessons in the same manner: the writers recorded examples of virtue and vice for their successors to emulate or avoid.[146] They could likewise employ postbiblical models as examples of virtues.[147] Because Josephus repeats so much of the biblical narrative in the *Antiquities,* one can observe the way he adapts biblical characters to accentuate their value as positive (Lot;[148] Isaac;[149] Joseph;[150] Moses;[151] Ruth and Boaz;[152] Samuel;[153] Hezekiah;[154] Jehoshaphat;[155] Josiah;[156] Daniel;[157] Nehemiah),[158] negative (Jeroboam;[159] Ahab)[160] or intermediate moral models.[161] Such observations are relevant for understanding the Gospels as biographies applying their narratives.

The Role of Praise and Blame

Historians narrated accounts with a view to praise or blame.[162] Some historians might criticize other historians for getting the mixture wrong, but no one doubted that history provided moral lessons. Thus Polybius, who insists on the appropriate distribution of praise and blame,[163] criticizes some historians for praising Philip, noting that his actions warrant censure.[164] Polybius emphasizes that he himself does not praise or blame prominent people in his prefaces, but always while recounting their (praiseworthy or reproachable) behavior; that, he averred, was the appropriate place to express one's views.[165] Nor was Polybius alone in viewing praise and blame as important elements in selecting moral examples. History-writing preserves for immortality the fame of those who deserve it, Pliny opined, hence offers incentive for noble deeds.[166]

Historians' interest in these matters reflected the broader value assigned to imitating moral examples in antiquity. Thus rhetoricians invited hearers to learn from both positive and negative examples in history.[167] Histories that focused on individuals often tended to be "encomiastic," magnifying heroes.[168]

When reading ancient biographers and historians, modern historians can take into account their propensity to praise or blame, but we do not for such reasons discount the value of their evidence, as if they were novels. Most ancient biographers, for example, felt free to record negative as well as positive features of their protagonists, when appropriate.[169] Thus while Suetonius' *Vespasian* is mostly adulatory (a striking contrast to his biographies of Caligula, Nero or Domitian), he reports his love of money.[170] He reports Nero's good deeds first "to separate them from his shameful and criminal deeds, of which I shall proceed now to give an account."[171] Suetonius did not indiscriminately praise all, but assigned praise and blame on what he viewed as the preponderance of positive and negative actions — that is, based on an interpretation of, rather than free creation of, information.

Ancients were well aware that their affection or respect for a person could bias their judgments, but also recognized that such affection could be based on sound evaluations.[172] Certainly bias would influence presentation while praising an emperor's virtues, even if one avoided telling any untruths.[173] More common would be a case like Tacitus, a sober historian, who composes an encomiastic biography of his father-in-law Agricola. This example, however, involves perspective and interest rather than deliberate distortion. Tacitus' *Agricola* may praise his father-in-law, but it expresses no less historical interest than his *Annals* or *Histories.* Josephus' autobiography may include apologetic — but so do his less biographic, more strictly historical works.

Historians' "Theology"

Historians' moral illustrations, social commentary in speeches, and political interests often reveal their distinctive philosophic and theological perspectives.[174] Most importantly for understanding the gospels, most ancient historians also sought to interpret the divine will in some patterns in history.[175] Oracles and omens were said to reveal Rome's divine destiny.[176] Some deity helped the Greeks escape Persia, Xenophon decides.[177] Despite Herodotus' occasional rationalism, he reports dreams, omens, and other signs of divine activity, his ideal audience's consensus on the reality of which he seems to assume.[178]

Israelite historians also sought to interpret from a divine perspective the events they recited.[179] While postmodern critics may view history as useable for agendas, the thought that it included objectively recognizable patterns seems odd to both modern and postmodern readers; yet this was the dominant perspective in many other eras (albeit a perspective that could not preclude diverse opinions concerning what constituted those patterns).[180]

From a broader perspective, Hellenistic historians saw providence in history, so that Diodorus could describe "historians as 'ministers of divine providence' who arrange their accounts in the light of their understanding of providence in human events."[181] Dionysius of Halicarnassus includes among history's lessons the virtue of piety toward the gods.[182] Jewish historians naturally offered such an approach as well;[183] Josephus is often explicit about providence in human affairs.[184] Of the four Gospels, Luke, the most hellenistic, has been compared most frequently with this approach.[185]

Most Jews viewed God's communication to them in Old Testament narrative as historically true,[186] hence would have taken for granted that history could communicate theology.[187] Even most Hellenistic Jewish intellectuals viewed most of Scripture as historically as well as theologically true.[188] While foundation stories could use evocative mythology, some scholars rightly point out that the earliest Christian writers, grounded in this traditional Jewish framework, claimed to use genuine history as their "myth," purporting to announce historical truth in the public arena.[189] The Gospel writers, some or most writing within half a century after the events narrated, believed that they were communicating genuine historical information in a theologically relevant way.

Separating their history from their theology is not as simple as many modern readers assume. Part of the gospel writers' "theology" involves the proclamation of God's acts in history; thus if some modern readers reject their claim that God acted in history in Jesus of Nazareth, they are also disagreeing with the Gospels' theology (and not just with their historiography). Disagreeing with their theology may also lead to displeasure with how they frame their historiography. Attempts to screen out anything in the Gospels that is compatible with the writers' faith prejudice the case against their perspective, for the early Christians believed that their faith flowed from the faith-stimulating impact of Jesus.[190]

All other ancient historians and biographers, like many modern ones, had agendas they considered important; they used history to shed light on their own time, no less than did the Gospels.[191] But had the Gospel writers wished to communicate solely later Christian doctrine and not history, they could have readily chosen simpler forms than biography for this purpose.[192]

Is Theological Tendenz Compatible with "True" History?

Modern historians write from various perspectives, just as ancient ones did, as interpreters in postmodern times in particular emphasize.[193] (Dunn points to the varying estimates of Winston Churchill and Margaret Thatcher today as examples.)[194] No historian can escape subjective bias; but holding a perspective concerning events does not make the information about the events bad history, even if it may bias what information gets presented and preserved.[195] Similarly, even news outlets in different countries (and sometimes in the same country) select and "spin" news in different ways, but most (the vast majority of free media) are responsible enough to use genuine data.[196] We may evaluate the value of authors' perspectives (e.g., theodicy for the gods; capitalism; globalism) from our own perspectives (e.g., Enlightenment rationalism; Marxism; or nationalism). Recognizing writers' perspectives does not, however, require us to assume that they falsified their data. Another writer may select and emphasize the data differently without disagreeing in the main with the reliability of the specific data presented.

The Gospel writers' agendas are less often moralistic, and far less often nationalistic, than was frequent among their contemporaries, but no less often (and in fact generally more often) theological (in the stricter sense). At the same time, ancient historians and biographers normally communicated these agendas by recounting stories that they believed to be true.[197] As the Jewish scholar Geza Vermes points out, "a theological interest is no more incompatible with a concern for history than is a political or philosophical conviction," and we can allow for these interests in interpretation.[198]

Ancient History as Non-history?

We should not treat rhetorical or moral interests as inimical to historical information. Ancient historians developed many of the critical methodologies further refined and used by historians today.[199] We err when we treat ancient historians as if they were modern historians, but we also err when we treat them as lacking interest in historical information.

On one side, many scholars are anachronistic in holding ancient historians to modern standards. Some have done so in order to defend a particular theological understanding of how gospel authors should have written; others use these standards to discredit them.[200] Both approach the Gospels in an anachronistic manner in this regard.

By contrast, some scholars, in rightly emphasizing the differences between ancient and modern historiography (differences we have been noting), have overstated these differences.[201] While ancient biography and history need not have been accurate in all details, the genres generated expectations of some ideal standards. Granted that ancient historians write from locations of class, political and ethnic bias;[202] that they supplied (and historians cannot help but supply) interpretive grids in how they constructed their narratives;[203] that historians, especially elite historians, made abundant use of rhetoric, including epideictic rhetoric;[204] that historical intention does not guarantee the accuracy of one's sources: shall we for such reasons simply dismiss all historical value in Tacitus, Suetonius, or even Josephus, as if they wrote something historically on the level of novels about historical characters? Such a sweeping claim, if pressed fully, could easily eradicate most of what we claim to know about first-century history.[205] Ancient historiography was not modern historiography, but neither was it identical with novels.

Gerd Lüdemann appears to imply that such watering down the factual historical demands of ancient history represents modern apologists' attempt to *rescue* biblical writings by lowering historical standards.[206] Claims that ancient historians wrote history so differently from today that one cannot hold Luke (and other Gospel writers) to a high standard "are irrelevant, deceptive, or as false as the occasionally advanced claim that the ancients were not concerned about false attribution of writings"; ancients did in fact care about "what really happened."[207] "To say that the great Roman historians did not write what actually happened does not mean — as Haenchen seems to imply — that they could write almost anything."[208] Lüdemann may also overstate the case, but the fact that we find scholars on both sides of the debate probably reflects the diversity of our data regarding information and rhetoric: ancient historians endeavored to recount their information in rhetorically sensitive ways.

Thus when Josephus portrays Agrippa's death according to tragic conventions and uses the owl as an omen,[209] Josephus takes his full liberties as a rhetorical historian (much more interested in Hellenistic rhetorical and tragic conventions than any of our Gospel writers are); but he does not invent Agrippa's death on that occasion. Clare Rothschild offers a fairly balanced, centrist assessment: historians, who like orators claimed that they placed truth over style, varied in their preferences, but mostly dealt both in information and its persuasive presentation.[210]

While it is true that virtually all ancient historians exhibited both a degree of literary freedom and edifying agendas unacceptable to many modern (albeit perhaps less so to postmodern) historians, denying that most of the events they report derive from their sources is easily refuted by comparing them with their extant sources where both cover the same ground (e.g., Luke using Mark). Historians could exercise flexibility on details to provide coherent rhetorical presentation, but such flexibility did not normally entail wholesale creation of events (and not necessarily even of all details, when authentic details were available).

Conclusion

In the previous chapter, we established that writers on historical subjects did have historical interest. Here, we have examined some of their other interests. These included, first of all, communicating in an appealing form; for elite audiences this involved rhetoric (though for more popular audiences it may have simply meant recounting the stories in an entertaining manner). Ancient historical writers were also interested in offering positive or negative models, to provide moral, political, and even theological perspectives.

Ancient audiences did not regard such goals as incompatible with true history, though even they sometimes noted the tensions these competing goals raised. Although less overtly, modern historians and biographers also write from particular perspectives. We should take into account the liberties such ancient expectations would have allowed the Gospels' authors, though some (such as John) may have made more use of the liberty than others (such as Luke). Yet we should also not exaggerate the liberty, whether to defend or condemn the Gospel writers.

CHAPTER 9

The Gospels' Written Sources

"[I surveyed] about 2000 volumes . . . we have collected in 36 volumes 20,000 noteworthy facts obtained from one hundred authors that we have explored. . . . For you must know that when collating authorities I have found that the most professedly reliable and modern writers have copied the old authors word for word, without acknowledgement."

PLINY THE ELDER[1]

". . . many have set out to compose a narrative of the events fulfilled among us . . ."

LUKE 1:1 (PROBABLY WRITING IN THE 70S OR 80S CE)

Some of those who wish to reconstruct material about Jesus are very skeptical about the only real extensive sources available for such a quest: namely, the first-century Gospels. Some of these scholars, ironically, seem more prepared to advance their own hypotheses on the basis of relative silence (after they have excluded our concrete evidence) than to consider the actual evidence of our first-century sources. Classicists recognize the various weaknesses of their sources, but nevertheless find them more practical than modern alternative reconstructions offered without any extant evidence.[2] Historical Jesus scholars are at their best when they follow the same approach.

In preceding chapters we have argued for the likelihood that the Gospels, as ancient biographies from within two generations of the events (i.e., within the first century), preserve substantial information about Jesus. We have also argued that such writers would have historical interest and would likely preserve considerable historical information. In this chapter we examine more specifically some of the methods that scholars use to mine these sources.

126

Scholars have already offered detailed arguments regarding the sources of our present Synoptic Gospels. The predominant views have not achieved complete consensus, and I acknowledge that the minority views merit consideration. My views on Matthew and Luke using Mark and "Q" are the traditional and dominant ones in Gospels scholarship, although I leave them open to correction. Here, however, I will simply work with this majority view without supplying detailed arguments for it. I am doing so because this view has been argued extensively elsewhere; because I have nothing new to add to that particular discussion; because it is difficult to justify making this book longer for points that are already so widely held; because one must start the discussion somewhere (and a consensus position is the easiest place to start, especially when the writer agrees with it); and because most of those whose views I am challenging in this book also concede the existence of "Q."

Where I can add to the discussion is the broader methodological question, more often discussed among classicists, of how ancient biographers and historians used sources. This discussion will be relevant even for those who reconstruct the sources of the Gospels differently than I do.

Using Sources

Ancient historians and biographers exercised considerable literary liberties, as we have seen, yet they were hardly free to invent events, at least without encountering significant criticism from other historians. The same principle should have held true among early Christians who respected the apostles; Gospels and historical Jesus scholars often underestimate the networking of early Christians, a mistake Pauline scholars (dealing with more concrete information on the matter) cannot so easily repeat.

As we noted more extensively in a previous chapter, the early churches throughout the Empire were already informally networked long before the writing of the Gospels. Probably before any of our extant Gospels were written, urban Christians traveled (1 Cor 16:10, 12, 17; Phil 2:30; 4:18); relocated to other places (Rom 16:3, 5); sent greetings to other churches (Rom 16:21-23; 1 Cor 16:19; Phil 4:22; Col 4:10-15); and so forth. While different locations might have their own struggles or theological emphases, the idea that the early Christian communities were isolated from one another is a modern academic inference that conflicts with all our actual evidence.

Ancient Historical Writers' Use of Sources

Omniscient narrators, common in epic poetry,[3] were not common in history or biography. Historians, in fact, often felt constrained to indicate some of their sources,[4] especially if they depended on written sources and wrote for upper class readers who might have access to these various works. Accuracy of sources, unimportant in some genres, was known to be a concern of historians.[5] One could establish one's point better by naming various earlier sources supporting it.[6] A historical writer who does not include everything that has been written might need to explain that he had in fact read almost everything but did not judge it all suitable for inclusion.[7]

That ancient historians, biographers and anthologists[8] depended on earlier sources is not in question; both biblical[9] and Greco-Roman[10] writers frequently cite them. (Other means of detecting them, such as different textures within a narrative, are usually less dependable.)[11] They often cite varying accounts, even when preferring one above another.[12] Thus, for example, the biographer Arrian prefers above other sources his two earliest ones, which often agree, and he chooses between them when they diverge;[13] when sources diverge too much he frankly complains that the exact truth is unrecoverable.[14]

Likewise the biographer Philostratus notes a point where his sources diverge, and his research provided no definitive resolution;[15] such a complaint hardly implies that ancient biographers regularly practiced free invention![16] At one point the biographer Plutarch names five sources for a "majority" position and nine for a minority one,[17] plus an extant letter attributed to the person about whom he writes.[18] Occasionally historians also found ways to harmonize traditions,[19] or apparently smoothed out contradictions in their sources in their own rewriting.[20]

At the same time, lack of citation does not mean that sources are not used. As our opening quote from Pliny suggests, writers did not all acknowledge all of their sources. Historians usually mentioned sources, but generally did so only when they conflicted or the author disagreed or was unsure about their reliability[21] or about which sources were best.[22] Such conflicts arose more often when treating events of the more remote past than when treating the present. The Gospel writers do not identify specific sources (although they clearly had some available; Lk 1:1-2), probably at least partly because they discuss events of a recent generation on which sources have not yet diverged greatly.[23] They may also follow some Jewish conventions on this point; in some such works we can identify the sources only because they are extant.[24] The more popular audience anticipated may be a more important factor; popular works of various genres were less likely to cite sources, even when they clearly depend on them. Earlier exaggerated contrasts between elite and popular literature aside,[25] the Gospels do not reflect an elite audience.

Including material missing in earlier extant sources does not always betray fabrication. A writer providing information missing in some earlier historians sometimes was drawing from sources unavailable to the other historians, whether the sources were written, oral, or both.[26] Moreover, even writers who preserved their sources sometimes edited them, even in the case of sacred cultural texts[27] and philosophic works.[28] Some argue that such changes were more common at the written than the oral level,[29] perhaps because the former reflected literary urban culture and the latter more traditional society.

For one example of using sources we may return to Polybius, whom we have noted before. Polybius complains that Timaeus failed to make appropriate use of earlier historians' works, though living in Athens provided him access to them;[30] this complaint reinforces the picture that many sources were available and that good historians were expected to consult them when possible. For Polybius, real history requires a study of documents, though this must take a third place after visiting the locations in question and reviewing their historical context.[31]

We should not underestimate the research sources available to ancient writers, especially since (as in Lk 1:1) they often explicitly mention the existence of such works. Clearly an abundance of contemporary sources existed then that are no longer extant;[32] for example, Pliny the Elder, explaining that he could not survey everything,[33] notes that he surveyed about two thousand volumes (though focusing especially on a hundred), and supplemented them with other data.[34] Few of his sources remain extant, but we can appreciate Pliny's preservation of much of the content.

Luke's Relation to Earlier Sources

One of the Gospels, Luke, openly attests to the existence of a number of sources available before he wrote. Luke's original prologue (Lk 1:1-4) probably introduces the entire two-volume work,[35] although not necessarily every statement covers every section of his work equally. At least for his Gospel, Luke claims the availability of "many"[36] written documents covering the same events that he covers (Lk 1:1). Some of these documents were probably among his sources;[37] certainly they were not all written at once, and those he mentioned wrote before him, though we cannot say how early the first narratives were.[38]

Did Luke find most such first-generation sources about Jesus trustworthy or suspect? Luke's mention of these earlier works does not denigrate their information. Historians often cited inadequacies in earlier writers as reasons for writing,[39] though some explicitly disclaimed such reasons.[40] Some rhetorical critics also offered this claim of unique superiority for select historians before their time.[41] Many think that Luke thus finds fault with the work of his predecessors; thus elsewhere in Luke's work, a cognate to *asphaleia* in Lk 1:4 can address distinguishing truth among "competing claims" (Acts 21:34; 22:30; 25:26).[42]

But Luke's language is far less harsh than that of writers who genuinely criticized their predecessors, and need not imply that he is claiming that they lacked eyewitness sources that he has.[43] Some writers noted that they simply had a fresh perspective to add to the work of their predecessors.[44] Another writer could claim to prefer even his predecessors' style to his own, but to regard his own selectivity as an improvement;[45] or note that he has nothing new to add in terms of information, but offers it in a different way.[46]

Luke departs from the work of his predecessors not primarily in terms of accuracy of information but instead in terms of rhetorical superiority:[47] in 1:3, he promises *kathexēs,* which was the proper sequencing of events in terms of cause and effect, necessary to an accurate account.[48] The term need not specify chronological order, but rather logical and persuasive order;[49] for a history, however, logical order would include as much chronology as possible. Luke does in fact follow Mark's sequence closely, with two major exceptions.[50] In contrast to some other genres (usually including biography),[51] history should be written sequentially,[52] though often allowing for completing narratives begun at different times.

Other elements of Luke's prologue may point to a claim of either rhetorical or factual excellence. Some argue that his language in Lk 1:3 involves only literary completeness, providing an explanation for events.[53] While this reading of Luke 1:3 is possible, Luke's use of *akribōs* elsewhere could suggest accuracy instead of or *in addition to* completeness; accuracy was also part of the term's nuance,[54] including in Luke-Acts.[55] The term can suit an "exact" account elsewhere.[56]

Luke's rhetorical superiority to earlier Gospels of his day (though not to elite historians) is likely: as a comparison with our other extant Gospels may confirm, his Gospel is far closer to the general vein of extant Greco-Roman historiography. Nevertheless, his research and arrangement did not lead him to depart substantially from the *facts* of his predecessors; he saw his purpose as confirmatory (Lk 1:4). Their nearness in basic substance may reflect the relatively recent nature of the events they report.

Gospel Sources

As nineteenth- and early-twentieth-century scholars sought to test the historical reliability of the Gospels, their attention naturally turned to source criticism.[57] Source criticism asks the question: What written sources might the author of a Gospel have used? During some early forays into this question critics overindulged their imaginations, overconfidently but arbitrarily assigning various elements to numerous, speculative source layers. Scholars who study Greco-Roman literature have increasingly recognized the excesses of traditional source criticism,[58] and other literary disciplines have likewise rejected this often speculative nineteenth- and early-twentieth-century approach to uncovering sources.[59]

Nevertheless, the criteria appear somewhat more objective in Matthew and Luke, where we probably retain evidence for at least two of their sources. Although various source theories have come and gone, the majority of scholars today agree that Matthew and Luke used Mark, "Q" (i.e., a source Matthew and Luke shared), and some other material not employed by our other extant Gospels.[60] Scholars commonly call this view the "Two-Source Hypothesis."

While this remains the general consensus, however, scholars are no more unanimous on this subject than on most others. Some able scholars have made a defensible case for the older view that Mark used Matthew rather than the reverse, and their case merits fair consideration.[61] But for several reasons, and especially because so much of Mark appears in Matthew and Luke (and Mark lacks many useful sayings found in these Gospels), most scholars remain convinced that Matthew and Luke both used Mark and at least one other source that they shared in common.[62] Further, consistent patterns appear in Matthew's abbreviation of Mark,[63] and Matthew uses an eclectic text-type for his Old Testament quotations *except* where he overlaps with Mark, where he tends to follow Mark in employing the most common Greek version.[64]

Most scholars also agree that Matthew and Luke shared another source,[65] which is nicknamed "Q"[66] for lack of a better name. On this point, too (even more than on the use of Mark), scholarship lacks complete unanimity. Although some write as if fairly certain concerning the substance and extent of "Q,"[67] most scholars express skepticism to what degree of certainty it can be reconstructed.[68] Given questions about its precise extent and other factors, "Q" certainly should not be used to "reconstruct the whole theological outlook" of its community.[69] That Galilee (including Capernaum) is central in "Q" could reflect the milieu in which it was transmitted,[70] but could also simply reflect the milieu of Jesus whose sayings it contains.[71]

Still others have debated even "Q"'s existence as a concrete document.[72] Some envision it as purely oral tradition,[73] and still others as a composite of sources.[74] By contrast, most scholars do view "Q" as a whole document, which is in my opinion likely, given the common sequence of Q in Matthew and Luke.[75] (This does not, of course, require that all points shared by Matthew and Luke belong to this document. Further, we lack any parts of "Q" that one or both of these authors failed to use.)[76] "Q" was probably originally in Aramaic, and various translations of it into Greek may account for some of the variants between Matthew and Luke.[77]

Scholarship has become increasingly polarized between those who reconstruct "Q" in excessive detail and those who deny it altogether, although I think that the range of options between these positions remains the majority position. Some are able to dispense with a Q hypothesis altogether, suggesting that Luke (a smaller number here add Mark) simply used Matthew.[78] This final view, while more defensible than a collocation of different traditions, remains a distinctly minority (though respectable) position.[79] (A very few scholars deny even literary dependence among the extant Gospels.)[80] Nevertheless, I concur with the majority position that Matthew and Luke used a common source in addition to Mark. Because the point of this book is historical Jesus research rather than literary dependence among the Gospels, I am using this position (as opposed to the possibility that Luke used Matthew) as a default position, rather than expending space arguing for it.[81]

"Q" probably represents more than simply a tapestry of oral traditions. Since Matthew and Luke often follow their shared material in the same sequence, we concur with the most common theory about Q: it (or most of it) probably represents a single prominent written source. Although we acknowledge weaknesses in this position (and probably interaction with continuing oral tradition at every stage of writing), I will work here from the basic two-source hypothesis. Because the Q collection was probably edited in the 40s, less than two decades after the events it describes,[82] we may assume a high degree of reliability for its traditions.

Because Matthew and Luke follow Mark and Q closely (by ancient literary standards) where we can check them, the assumption held by many scholars that they simply invent material where we *cannot* check them[83] seems simply imagination run amuck.[84] Their basically conservative editing at most points will impress one if one begins with neither a thoroughgoing skepticism nor a naive fundamentalism, but the standards of ancient texts in general. As Ben Witherington puts it (1994: 214), Matthew

> takes over more than 90% of his Markan source (606 out of 661 Markan verses), while Luke takes over only a little over 50%. The difference in degree of word for word appropriation of Mark in the pericopes and sayings that Matthew and Luke take over is minimal. Luke uses about 53% of Mark's exact words in the material culled from that source, while the First Evangelist uses about 51% of Mark's exact words of the 606 verses he appropriates. This means that Luke and the First Evangelist are about equally likely to preserve the exact wording of their source, and they do so about half the time.

So "conservative" is Matthew's editing by ancient standards that Witherington suspects that Matthew "very likely saw himself as primarily an editor or redactor, not an author."[85] This suggestion surely overstates the case (Matthew edited his Gospel so tightly that it functions as a unified whole);[86] nevertheless, many changes that Matthew makes in some of his sources could depend on information his other sources supply.[87] Thus Matthew sometimes "corrects" ambiguities in Mark (e.g., Matt 12:3-4//Mk 2:25-26; Matt 3:3//Mk 1:2-3; Matt 14:1//Mk 6:14); sometimes "rejudaizes" his language (Matt 19:3, 9//Mk 10:2, 11-12; passim for "kingdom of heaven//God";); and at least on some occasions, Matthew makes his changes because of early tradition older than Mark (Matt 12:28//Lk 11:20; missing in Mk 3:23-29).

At the same time, these authors' relative conservatism need not render all of their *sources* of equal historical worth; and where the sources were oral, they might, for all we know, have exercised greater freedom in their retelling.[88] At any rate, Matthew's circle certainly had other Palestinian traditions beside Mark and Q, and these traditions had undoubtedly been interacting with Mark and Q long before he wrote his Gospel.[89] From the earliest period, Mediterranean storytellers regularly drew on a much larger body of oral traditions.[90]

Since Matthew and Luke depend on Mark, it is important whether or not Mark preserves some reliable information. Tradition from perhaps within half a century of Mark does in fact claim his dependence on Peter,[91] a claim that from the standpoint of the putative dates of the sources is not implausible.[92] We should remember that Luke believes that many written accounts as well as the oral material on which he depends reflect material passed down from eyewitnesses (Lk 1:1-2). Given his frequent use of Mark, Luke presumably believes that Mark depends on significant eyewitness material. Because (as we have suggested earlier) Luke may have earlier been in Judea for up to two years near 60 CE, Luke presumably had good reason to form this favorable opinion of Mark's substance and to confirm what Theophilus had heard (Lk 1:4), probably sources including such widely disseminated works as Mark's.

Expanding and Condensing Sources

Ancient writers freely expanded or abridged accounts without any thought that others might find this practice objectionable. Contrary to early form-critical studies of the Gospels, which supposed that the tradition's tendency was always expansive, it is impossible to predict whether the passage of time would lengthen or shorten accounts.[93] Expansion was in fact sometimes due to the passage of time and consequent growth of tradition;[94] in other cases, however, lengthy stories were sometimes progressively abbreviated in time.[95]

One ancient rhetorical exercise involved "expanding" and "condensing" fables.[96] When applied to other kinds of narrative, this approach need not tamper with historical substance. For example, aside from adding details known from other sources and adding some description that is either implicit in the narrative or inherently probable in itself, the same ancient writer's example for expanding a *chreia* does not make much change in its basic meaning.[97] Likewise, another writer explains amplification as adding more and more phrases to bring home the point increasingly forcefully.[98] One could expand a work by including more summaries and connections.[99] In rhetorical exercises one can elaborate a *chreia* by offering an encomium on a character; then paraphrasing; then explaining; and so forth.[100]

Hellenistic Jewish historians followed this practice. Josephus, for example, often follows accurately the sequence and substance of the biblical account, while expanding on some biblical narratives,[101] even though he could not but assume that many Jewish readers would readily recognize the addition. 2 Maccabees openly claims to be a careful abridgment of a five-volume work by Jason of Cyrene (2 Macc 2:24-25), noting that the author has followed the *rules* of abridgment (2:28). Most Synoptic scholars likewise believe that Matthew (and less frequently Luke) abridges Markan accounts. Few stylistic critics would have complained about abridgments. Greco-Roman writers and rhetoricians appreciated conciseness in a narrative, provided that it did not impair clarity or plausibility.[102] Perhaps more importantly for many ancient readers, longer works were not only more expansive, but also more expensive.

Many changes that writers made in their sources were matters of arrangement, which was of great importance to those trained in rhetoric.[103] Writers sometimes added clauses nonessential to the meaning or removed essential ones simply to make the arrangement sound better.[104] Also relevant to the Gospels, inserting sayings from sayings-collections into narrative, or narratives into sayings, was considered a matter of arrangement, not a matter of fabrication.[105] Linking sayings based on common points and wording was apparently common.[106] Thus, for example, while Matthew and Luke overlap a great deal in their initial lengthy "speech" of Jesus (Matt 5:3-7:27//Lk 6:20-49), an ancient audience would not be surprised that Matthew also apparently weaves in other material not from the same speech in his source (e.g., Matt 7:7-11//Lk 11:9-13; Matt 7:13//Lk 13:24).

As we have suggested, even writers intending to write accurate historical information could "spice up" or "enhance" their narratives for literary, moralistic, and political purposes.[107] Again, this is not to say that good biographers or historians fabricated events (sometimes in fact they simply repeated their sources);[108] but they did often alter or add explanatory details to events.[109] Given the importance of vividness for rhetorical style,[110] it is not surprising that some writers added details to augment dramatic effect.[111] Many interpreters through history have noticed divergences in the Gospels without feeling troubled by them; for example, Luther apparently considered concern over divergences among the sources on points of detail a pedantic exercise.[112]

Authors differed among themselves as to how much variation in detail they permitted, but some writers who wanted to guard the historical enterprise from distortion had strong feelings about those who permitted too much (as we noted earlier). Thus the second-century rhetorician Lucian objected to those historical writers who amplified and omitted merely for literary or encomiastic purposes (i.e., to make the character look better).[113] Even despite their divergences from one another, however, modern historians of the period regularly mine various ancient historians that conflict on various points.[114]

Palestinian Jewish haggadah about ancient persons permitted greater amplification than Hellenistic historiography,[115] but may be comparable in this respect to Greek mythography.[116] (A significant part of the difference between historical and mythical was often perceived as the difference between recent historical figures and remote characters of the mythical or legendary past.)[117] The process was probably often incremental, preserving earlier legendary accretions and speculations. Writers used amplification for various reasons (see appendix 3, on Palestinian Jewish biography). But while such traditional techniques may have influenced Hellenistic Jewish historians and particularly their sources, they did not characterize the genre of history per se. (Some early Christians also seem to have found the traditional haggadic approach problematic; cf. 1 Tim 1:4; Tit 1:14.)[118] What may therefore be more relevant for works written in Greek is the degree of variation among Hellenistic Jewish works involving historical traditions such as 2 Macc and 4 Macc[119] (though 4 Macc is a philosophic treatise more than a historical monograph) and probably especially the historian Josephus.[120]

But in general, one does not expect as free a treatment of recent characters (the sort covered in the Gospels or most of Josephus' report of the Jewish war) as with those of the distant past, where audience expectations for accuracy of details was less. Moreover, as we have noted, the Gospel writers did not write on the same rhetorical level as Josephus, who needed to impress the Greek and Roman elite with his rhetorical skills. What they lack in elite rhetoric, they make up for in the cohesiveness of their more popular and concise narrative.

Redaction Criticism

We will treat the history of "form criticism" more in our next chapter, but must offer a few comments about "redaction criticism" here. While source and form criticism were sometimes helpful in understanding the nature of Jesus' teachings and the way the Gospels are written, scholars asked these questions mainly to test the Gospel stories' reliability, not to understand the Gospels' message. Inevitably scholars began to ask, "Given that Matthew and Luke used Mark and Q, *why* do they edit them the way they do?" This question became the focus of the editorial critics, generally called redaction critics.[121]

More sober controls eventually checked the early excesses of some redaction critics. Some redaction critics assumed that any material Matthew or Luke added to their main sources was not historical. This view stemmed not from careful observations, but from some unlikely presuppositions: namely, that Matthew and Luke had no other information available except in Mark and Q, and that editing a source for literary style or theological emphasis renders one's information unhistorical.[122] Yet ancient writers often followed a main source that they checked or supplemented with other sources.[123]

Various other weaknesses characterize these assumptions. For example, the probable presence of substantial traditional material in Matthew besides Mark and Q weakens these premises.[124] (Certainly it is unreasonable to suppose that Matthew and Luke used historical sources only where we happen to be able to check them.) Further, characteristic diction or style do not make elements ahistorical;[125] indeed, writers could openly acknowledge their stylistic editing of earlier sources even for purely aesthetic reasons.[126] Some variation may simply reflect the sorts of adaptation familiar in "oral performance," for dramatic or phonetic purposes rather than theological ones.[127] Some note that, given the emphasis on memory in antiquity, many early Christians could have known sources like Mark by heart, and Matthew and Luke can be "redacting" more freely based on memory rather than a rigid text in front of them.[128] Current scholarship thus practices its redaction criticism more carefully, though it would be a mistake to abandon the method's insights altogether.[129]

I noticed a fairly consistent rhetorical pattern when I was working on my Matthew commentary. Where possible, Matthew has underlined Jesus' Jewish character more emphatically than Mark did. That is, where Mark adapted Jesus to a broader (more "universal") Greco-Roman audience, Matthew has fairly consistently re-Judaized Jesus. In some cases, Matthew may have been following the rhetorical practices of speech-in-character and historical verisimilitude,[130] making Jesus fit what was known about him in general (e.g., as a Jewish teacher, he should have introduced parables with the sorts of formulas used by Jewish teachers; he may have used "kingdom of heaven"). If Matthew lacked tradition on any of these points, his guesses are nevertheless more apt to be correct than ours, given his proximity to Jesus' situation. Sometimes Matthew also demonstrates a more sensitive understanding of Palestinian Jewish nuances than does Luke or his tradition.[131]

In other cases, however, I am reasonably sure that Matthew has re-Judaized Jesus based on solid traditions available to him. If the Didache is not dependent on Matthew, it may often cite some of this pre-Matthean tradition.[132] As we have noted, Matthew elsewhere "corrects" Mark's adaptations for Gentile readers to better accord with historical data available to him.[133] In any case, Vermes is correct to argue that Matthew has preserved much of the special Jewish coloring of Jesus, which fits with our picture of Jesus in undeniably authentic traditions[134] (as we shall see in some subsequent chapters).

For historical questions, redaction criticism remains useful in inviting us to observe the patterns of how writers adapt their material to make a particular point. This observation in turn helps us recognize both the extent to which they viewed adaptation as a legitimate part of their biographic task and which of our sources preserves the likeliest original tradition in particular cases.

It also helps us recognize that the Gospel writers we can test (Matthew and Luke) employed their sources in ways similar to those of other historical writers. If anything, a synopsis of the Gospels convinces us that they tended to be more conservative than many other historians writing about the recent past (the past two or three generations), and much more conservative than those writing about the distant past of earlier centuries. If this is true of the Gospels that we can test, and they trusted Mark, the earlier source, the burden of proof should rest on one arguing that Mark composed more in a novelistic way than based on tradition.

What we know of how historical writers composed their works (above) is relevant to how we should expect the Gospel writers to have employed their sources.[135] Historians frequently followed an earlier historian in the first draft;[136] 2 Maccabees, for example, abridges an earlier work by Jason of Cyrene (2 Macc 2:23). Such observations do fit the Gospel writers that we can concretely test, Matthew and Luke. Like other Greek writers, Luke mostly follows one source at a time, at least in his Gospel, where he incorporates a large block of Q material into Mark;[137] both he and Matthew make Mark the backbone and supplement this work from other sources.[138]

Some people viewed use of preexisting lines as plagiarism; yet even writers who regarded failure to credit sources as dishonest note that most ancient authors did so, frequently verbatim.[139] Even in elite circles, if one alluded to well-known works the hearers might recognize, the thought was not plagiarism but literary sophistication that flattered the source;[140] if one could assume one's audience's knowledge, one did not need to state the source of one's quotes. Given the pervasiveness of oral traditions about Jesus, the Gospels probably functioned as common property of the apostolic church, so that borrowing from an earlier one would sound more like flattering the source than like plagiarism. If much gospel tradition was "common property" of the early churches (cf. Lk

1:4), audiences might not expect particular identification.[141] (As noted above, even elite writers sometimes cited sources especially where they conflicted.)[142]

Conclusion

The Gospels that we can best test for their use of sources, Matthew and Luke, seem to have employed them at least as conservatively as other ancient historical and biographic writers. Some of these sources presumably represent written sources belonging to the first generation following Jesus' ministry. Most scholars date Mark within four decades, and many date "Q" to roughly two decades, after the bulk of events and sayings they report. By the standards we use for determining events in antiquity, such written sources are remarkably early. (Scholars who date the Gospels earlier than I do could assert this claim still more strongly.)

When we think in terms of these few decades, we should recognize a point that some more skeptical scholars often neglect: during most of this period, Jesus' closest disciples remained the Jesus movement's leading teachers.[143] Were we trying to reconstruct the public activity and teachings of another teacher from the period, and had sources from the first generation of his followers, we would be relatively confident that these sources preserved much reliable material (this is the case, for example, with regard to Musonius Rufus). If the teacher founded a school, we would normally assume that those interested in and trusted for writing about the teacher in the first generation either were disciples or would have derived information preserved by the disciples. Some scholars treat the Gospels and their sources in ways far more skeptical than classicists would treat other sources. We shall address the issue of oral traditions and disciples in the next chapter.

CHAPTER 10

The Gospels' Oral Sources

"Only sayings and parables that can be traced back to the oral period, 30-50 c.e., can possibly have originated with Jesus."

THE JESUS SEMINAR[1]

". . . the tradition in the Gospels is not strictly a folk tradition, derived from long stretches of time, but a tradition preserved by believing communities who were guided by responsible leaders, many of whom were eyewitnesses of the ministry of Jesus."

W. D. DAVIES[2]

". . . many have sought to compile a narrative of the acts fulfilled in our midst, just as those who were eyewitnesses and servants of the message have from the beginning transmitted them orally to us."

LUKE 1:1-2

We noted in ch. 7 that while Roman writers about the past often depended simply on written records, eastern Mediterranean writers about the past usually preferred consulting eyewitnesses and those within living memory of them, when this was possible. Written transmission was thus often secondary to oral transmission, which played an essential role in Greek circles and the primary role in later rabbinic circles.[3] One philosopher reportedly reproved a friend who lamented losing his notes: "You should have inscribed them . . . on your mind instead of on paper."[4]

Although we will survey the nature of oral transmission more generally, the observations below concerning disciples and teachers are paramount for the Jesus tradition. Few scholars doubt that Jesus had disciples, including close adherents that in ancient terms would have constituted his "school." Yet students were normally quite trustworthy with their mentors' teachings, even when they disagreed with these teachings. Why (except to negatively prejudice the discussion's outcome) should we assume that Jesus' disciples were distinctively incompetent in this regard? Moreover, these disciples were respected leaders and teachers in the Jesus movement during the critical period of oral transmission before written gospels appeared (cf. Gal 1:17-19; 2:1-2, 7-10; 1 Cor 15:5-7). Should this observation not have implications for our quest? Answers in the affirmative are increasing today, even more than when some of us were offering these observations more cautiously over a decade ago.

Orality

By Jesus' day, much of the Mediterranean world was literate as well as oral,[5] but even at this time only a minority could read, especially on a formal level, and orality remained an important part of the larger culture. Memory cultivation is particularly emphasized in oral cultures,[6] and there remained a bias toward orality and oral memory in the first-century world.[7]

Many cultures orally pass on information for centuries, maintaining accuracy in the points transmitted.[8] (Even in the transmission of Balkan ballads, where this pattern has been disputed, the basic story is fixed at the oral stage long before the words are fixed at the written stage.)[9] Many oral societies are now in transition due to westernization and the social dislocation caused by urbanization. My wife, who is Congolese and spent much of her childhood in villages, knows many stories about earlier generations (especially within her family). She also observes, however, that such stories are being lost as younger generations fail to repeat them and most stories fail to be written down.

In oral cultures the point of recall tends to be thematic rather than verbatim, but can include epics considered hopelessly long to modern western audiences.[10] Variation is to be expected in oral performances, perhaps explaining a number of variants in our gospel tradition as well.[11] Not all societies are equally careful with the details of their traditions, but oral history can supplement written records both in orally skilled and unskilled societies.[12] Oral historiography has therefore come into its own as a discipline,[13] although it is more useful (for historical information) when applied to figures in the recent memory of the informants[14] than when investigating the legendary past.[15]

Like some other societies, the ancient Mediterranean world highly prized oral memory. Bards recited Homeric epics and other poets from memory, though intellectuals generally regarded these bards as low-class, engaging in an elementary exercise.[16] Centuries before the Gospels, the best professional recit-ers could recite all of Homer by heart;[17] in the general era of the Gospels, Dio Chrysostom even claims a people who no longer were able to speak Greek well but most of whom knew "the *Iliad* by heart."[18] Many poems remained fluid, but the *Iliad* remained textually constant, because it became canonical for Greek culture.[19] Such feats of memory appear in some other oral societies.[20]

Oral Traditions Besides Written Sources

Even the Gospels that used written sources appear to have used oral sources as well. Over one third of the "Q" material shared by Matthew and Luke shows "less than 40 percent" verbal correspondence.[21] The content and often se-quence show that this is clearly the same material, yet the flexibility in commu-nicating it fits what we expect of "*oral* performance."[22] Certainly the Gospel writers must have had access to oral material beyond what appears in their written sources. As James D. G. Dunn warns, "What kind of failure in historical imagination could even suggest to us that Matthew, say, only knew the Lord's Prayer because he read it in Q? Or that Luke only knew the words of the Last Supper because he found them in Mark? The alternative explanation positively cries out for consideration: that these were living traditions, living because they were used in regular church assemblies."[23]

Dunn argues that features characteristic of oral tradition more generally also characterize the material in our Gospels.[24] Though a sufficient number of persons could read and write, the majority of people were illiterate and would know the stories about Jesus from hearing them repeatedly.[25]

From a comparative historical standpoint, it is surely nonsense to assume that the surviving documents represent the entirety of the stories told about Jesus, and that whatever Matthew and Luke did not find in Mark or Q they must have invented.[26] No one would assume such a position for other ancient sources. Thus, for example, our collection of orations by the famous ancient orator Dio Chrysostom (c. 40/50 to after 110 CE) includes only some of his ma-terial, as is made clear in the many additional fragments found in Stobaeus (c. 450 CE) and Maximus the Confessor (580-662 CE).[27] Pliny the Elder explored some two thousand volumes (focusing on about a hundred) as sources for his own encyclopedic *Natural History,*[28] yet barely any of these other sources have survived.

In the ancient Greek world, some writers felt free to add information from centuries-old oral traditions that did not appear in their written sources.[29] The countless allusions to other stories in Homer[30] lent themselves to later develop-ment, but clearly refer to fuller stories that Homer's works did not record, and which we have in forms developed from such traditions. In the case of the Gospels, the writers themselves assume knowledge of traditions about Jesus not recorded in their Gospels (e.g., Acts 20:35; Jn 20:30).

Jewish storytellers also passed on traditions informally over long stretches of time, ultimately contributing to many of the documents now collected as "Pseudepigrapha."[31] The careful preservation of details in such oral tradition is difficult to guarantee;[32] but within the first generation or two, one would expect more of the widely circulated oral sources to remain accurate than would be the case in a later period. It is clear, in any case, that many traditions and documents flourished for some time in antiquity besides those that have survived to this day.

Sayings Traditions

Although historians were known to invent speeches and conversations, biographers often preferred to draw on a teacher's sayings when these were available. Sayings collections (such as Arrian's *Diatribes,* a collection of Epictetus' teachings by one of his students) sometimes could even reflect the teacher's style (though the writer's interests could select which sayings were most relevant).

Remembering teachers' sayings was an expected part of the culture. Both attributed and unattributed maxims were memorized and passed on for centuries even in elementary educational settings.[33] Jewish sayings collections like Proverbs and Pirke Aboth consist primarily of short, pithy sayings, and some of Jesus' sayings were no doubt remembered and circulated in such a form.[34] Greco-Roman sayings collections likewise included sayings and brief contexts for them when necessary.[35] Outside such collections, sayings were often transmitted apart from one another,[36] although sayings could also be combined with narratives to make a work more cohesive. As we noted earlier, ancient readers considered inserting sayings from sayings-collections into narrative, or narratives into sayings, a matter of arrangement, not a matter of fabrication.[37]

Nevertheless, Jesus probably also used some sayings on more than one occasion, just as most speakers do.[38] Moreover, sayings for which context was necessary, such as in brief narratives climaxing in the protagonist's quip (a kind of *chreiai* today sometimes classified as pronouncement stories),[39] were often transmitted with narrative contexts.[40] Thus we probably have some sayings of Jesus in the Gospels in their original contexts, whereas others may appear in distinct contexts (cf. e.g., Matt 7:13-14//Lk 13:24; Matt 8:11//Lk 13:29).

Sayings traditions also may have grown, although in most cases this expansion became significant primarily over a period of generations or centuries.[41] Similar sayings could be attributed to different teachers; sometimes this simply indicated that both had uttered the same idea,[42] but in other cases sayings or even entire tales may have been transferred, deliberately (as common property cited by various teachers) or through mistake, from one teacher to another, as in Greek tradition.[43] Although ancients often assumed the accuracy of attributions, they were not always certain.[44] On other occasions, however, the famous speaker himself may have borrowed sayings from others.[45]

The relevance of this transfer of sayings to study of the Synoptic sayings-traditions is limited;[46] such transfer and composition began to happen regularly only long after the teachers' death, usually a number of generations (and most fully, centuries) after the teachers' death. By contrast, from the first generation the basic framework of the Jesus tradition was already established in the entire community that revered him, and quickly fixed in various written texts. Moreover, Jesus held a special status in early Christianity; there were not a number of other teachers with whom he could be confused or whose sayings the transfer of which would enhance his authority. He may have also himself used some sayings already in circulation (given the familiarity of his Jewish teaching style in other respects; see e.g., our ch. 13).

Ignoring such limitations, many early form critics applied to the gospel tradition principles of form criticism culled from studies of Old Testament traditions preserved for many centuries and various folk traditions developed over centuries.[47] Yet as W. D. Davies notes, probably only a single life span

> separates Jesus from the last New Testament document. And the tradition in the Gospels is not strictly a folk tradition, derived from long stretches of time, but a tradition preserved by believing communities who were guided by responsible leaders, many of whom were eyewitnesses of the ministry of Jesus. The Gospels contain materials remembered recently, at least as compared with other traditional literatures, so that the rules which governed the transmission of folk tradition do not always apply to the tradition found in the Gospels.[48]

Pierre Benoit similarly protests that many rabbinic apophthegms preserve some genuine reminiscences, but that beyond this, recollections no more than thirty to forty years old cannot be compared with the rabbis' "oral tradition stretching over several centuries which only very late in its life received a fixed form."[49] Others rightly emphasize that Jesus taught publicly as well as privately, and a "radical amnesia" that allowed his followers to forget even the substance of his teachings is quite unlike other schools, and is historically improbable.[50]

Further, early Christians plainly did not indulge the temptation to create answers for their own situations in the Jesus tradition preserved in the Synoptics: some significant conflicts that early Christians faced (such as circumcising

Gentiles) fail to turn up in the Gospels.[51] Meanwhile, many sayings imply a Palestinian setting more relevant to Jesus than to the later church.[52]

Thus Mark, who alone uses the words of Jesus to address the controversy about the purity of foods, resists the temptation to make Jesus explicitly *say* Mark's view; Mark provides this explicit interpretation only in an editorial aside (Mk 7:19, which Matthew, writing for a kosher audience, naturally feels free to omit). The gospel tradition nowhere addresses the later-burning issue (attested in Acts and Paul's letters) of whether Gentiles must be circumcised to join God's people. It provides only two examples of Jesus' ministry to Gentiles, and in both cases (if we read his initial response to the centurion as a question)[53] he first snubs the Gentile.[54] (This is most obvious where Jesus calls the Syrophoenician woman a "dog,"[55] a title recognized as an insult throughout the ancient Mediterranean world.)[56] One would not expect believers later involved in the Gentile mission to create the snubs, although they undoubtedly sought to make use of these stories about Gentiles available in the gospel tradition.

Although the Gospel writers and their sources felt free to adapt the gospel tradition in ways customary to their era, the tradition does not bear the marks of fabrication. As Secret Mark reflects its twentieth-century milieu and the apocryphal gospels reflect the late-second- to early-third-century heyday of Greek novels, the gospel tradition bears signs of forming earlier than the extant first-century Gospels that adapted it for their own day.

Memorization in Antiquity

In this section we will survey some conclusions from memory studies more generally, but then turn to more concretely relevant examples specific to the ancient Mediterranean and Middle Eastern world of which Jesus was a part. Antiquity provides much evidence of skilled memory, and we will find particularly relevant examples for ancient disciples. Both memory studies and ancient sources suggest that what was most accurately preserved for the longest time was the gist, the basic substance of the experience.[57]

Memory Studies More Generally

Studies of long-term memory show the character of information preservation by informal, untrained eyewitnesses in modern western culture.[58] Typically informal memory will include components rather than the whole, and lack a chronological framework for events.[59] (Thus, for example, various sayings of Jesus on different occasions could easily have been linked in memory reconstructions without regard for the specific sequence of occasions on which they were spoken.) Although memories can be imperfect, there are normally limits to this imperfection (i.e., they do not ordinarily involve free composition of events); even when some details are inaccurate, the "gist" is usually accurate.[60] The reconstruction and arrangement of memory do involve interpretive structures, but these structures would also be involved in the initial hearing.[61]

Studies of long-term memory also show the sorts of information apt to be preserved by eyewitnesses. These include, among other elements, unusual events;[62] consequential events;[63] events in which the eyewitness "is emotionally involved";[64] "vivid imagery";[65] and "frequent rehearsal."[66] Most of these factors are relevant for Jesus' followers' memories about him.[67] While memory studies in general are important, however, we must give special attention to what can be known about memory practices in the time of Jesus and the Gospels.

Skilled Memory in Antiquity

Because the majority of specifically Jewish sources addressing the issue are later, but the sources that we do have reflect patterns more widely distributed in Mediterranean antiquity, we cast the net for information on ancient Mediterranean memory as widely as possible. Such information suggests that issues of memory were relevant for historiography in antiquity as they are for historiography today.

The ancient historian Thucydides shows us the problems that both memory's limits and its interpretive structures impose, as suggested above. He complained about the difficulties involved in his quest to determine accurate details, "because those who were eyewitnesses of the several events did not give the same reports about the same things, but reports varying according to their championship of one side or the other, or according to their recollection."[68] Such limits from everyday witnesses must be taken into account. Nevertheless, Thucydides felt that, by noting commonalities among the various sources, he did manage to provide an accurate story. Although the gospel tradition may not have had many skilled interrogators like Thucydides, some other factors suggest that it preserves much historical information. Before turning to the Gospels, however, it is important to survey the prowess of some memories in antiquity.

Records abound of carefully trained memories. The elder Seneca was able to recount long sections of over a hundred declamations from his youth,[69] though Seneca was admittedly exceptional.[70] Difficult as it may seem to most readers today,[71] the elder Seneca testifies that in his younger days he could repeat back 2000 names in exactly the sequence in which he had just heard them, or recite up to 200 verses given to him, in reverse.[72] Even if his recollections of youthful prowess are exaggerated, they testify to an emphasis on memory that far exceeds standard expectations today.

Seneca also reports that another man, hearing a poem recited by its author, recited it back to the author verbatim (facetiously claiming the poem to be his own).[73] He also recalls the famous Hortensius, who listed back every purchaser and price at the end of a day-long auction, his accuracy attested by the bankers.[74] Another source claims that one sophist even in his old age could repeat back 50 names in sequence after hearing them just once.[75] Rhetoricians believed that artificial memory, augmented by discipline and training, could move far beyond natural memory,[76] and ancients developed mnemonic techniques to help them recall blocks of data astonishing to modern readers dependent on a continuous flow of information.[77]

Orators would memorize their speeches, often even of several hours' duration;[78] memoria, i.e., "learning the speech by heart in preparation for delivery," was one of the five basic tasks of an orator.[79] Rhetorical students practiced declamation, offering their practice speeches "from memory."[80] Pliny the Younger praises a rhetorician so skillful that he could repeat verbatim speeches that he had delivered extemporaneously.[81] One rhetor memorized his speech as he was writing it out, never needing to read it again;[82] he could remember every declamation he had ever delivered, word for word, making books unnecessary.[83]

At least rhetorically trained hearers could recall elements of speeches, even some that hearers might consider inferior, with memory strong enough even to supplement written sources.[84] Likewise, a deceased teacher's former disciples might also collectively remember bits and pieces of speeches, sewing them together,[85] a process relevant to communal memory and to other cases of groups of disciples carrying on their master's teachings.

Even if the early church altogether lacked those with the sort of exceptional memories noted by Seneca and some others (and it seems likely that they would have had at least a *few* members with exceptional memories), it requires far less exceptional *communal* memory to have preserved the basic substance of Jesus' message and the direction of his ministry. Communal memory is relevant where a group of hearers could remind one another of various points, with those whose memory was most exceptional taking the lead.[86] Whereas "chain" transmission might depend on a single person's memory, "net" transmission of a community could help guarantee larger amounts of tradition.[87] (I return to this concept briefly in discussing traditions passed on from other Jewish teachers to their disciples.) Although not directly relevant to the gospel tradition, communal memory also could preserve some central ideas for even several centuries; thus for example, Megarians retained ethnic hatred against Athens seven centuries after their late-fifth-century BCE conflicts.[88]

Disciples and Teachers

Memorization was the most pervasive form of ancient education.[89] The youngest learned by rote memorization at the elementary level.[90] Memorizing sayings of famous teachers was a regular school exercise at the basic level;[91] students at various levels also memorized examples.[92]

Although it was the youngest who learned by rote memorization at the elementary level, higher education (after about age 16) included memorizing many speeches and passages useful for speeches[93] — though the ultimate goal was both understanding and remembering.[94] Even at the stage of advanced education, which focused on rhetoric, students especially "memorized model speeches and passages" for their own use.[95]

Disciples were expected to be attentive; thus the philosopher Peregrinus rebuked an equestrian who seemed inattentive and yawning.[96] Teachers passed on their teachings to others,[97] language that could also be used for transmission of information through written histories.[98] Sayings attributed to founders of Greek schools were transmitted by members of each school from one generation to the next;[99] the practice seems to have been encouraged by the founders of the schools themselves.[100] Indeed, in all schools "teaching was passed down from master to pupils, who in turn passed it on to their own pupils";[101] the founder's teachings often functioned as canonical for their communities.[102] Of course, disciples passed on teachings, not speeches or extensive dialogues per se (hence more like what we find in the Synoptics than in John).[103]

A former student need not always agree with one's teacher,[104] but respect for teachers was paramount,[105] and in such a setting we would expect respectful preservation of teachings even when the transmitter registered disagreement.

Whether the emphasis was on memorizing texts or the teacher's words depended on the particular ancient school in question.[106] Lucian portrays an excellent philosophic student as rehearsing each of the points of the previous day's lectures in his mind.[107] Some schools were known for practicing particularly diligent training of their memories, training especially prominent in stories about the Pythagoreans.[108] One criterion for prospective Pythagorean disciples was said to be their ability to preserve what they were taught.[109] As a method of training their memories, the Pythagoreans reportedly would not rise from bed in the mornings until they had recited their previous days' works.[110] (Pythagorean emphasis on repetition for memorization[111] reflects a relatively effective method of preserving long-term memory.)[112] While stories about the Pythagoreans represent an extreme, they provide a graphic illustration of the value more generally placed on memory in ancient schools.

Although the emphasis lay on memorizing teachings, students studied and emulated teachers' behavior as well.[113] They further transmitted it: thus, for example, Eunapius learned a story about Iamblichus from Eunapius' teacher Chrysanthius, who learned it from Aedesius the disciple of Iamblichus himself;[114] Philostratus has oral information about a teacher two generations earlier through an expert from the previous generation.[115] Jews also learned from the behavior of their ancestors, i.e., from lessons drawn from narratives,[116] as students must also imitate their teachers.[117] (This reflects a broader practice; Greek disciples also often learned by imitating teachers' moral behavior.)[118]

Note-Taking

Emphasis on orality coexisted with literacy in Mediterranean school settings.[119] Orators often used written speeches or notes,[120] or wrote out, polished and published their speeches after delivery.[121] Hearers of speeches sometimes took notes to capture the gist of the speeches,[122] although some speakers wanted their hearers to be too spellbound to be able to take notes.[123] (Such notes were not, of course, verbatim transcripts, which were not available in this period.)[124] One could also takes notes[125] from which one would later arrange one's material for a composition, for the purpose of guarding memory.[126]

It is especially in academic settings, however, that note-taking prevailed. Disciples of advanced Greek teachers, both in philosophy and rhetoric, often took notes during their teachers' lectures.[127] Thus, for example, Quintilian mentions such taking of notes, even while emphasizing the use of memory.[128] Likewise, our collection of discourses from Musonius Rufus appears to depend on the writings of one of his students.[129] Many teachers left the matter of publication to their followers.[130]

From an early period those who took such notes sometimes published them.[131] The practice is attested close to the era of the Gospels by Arrian, a disciple of Epictetus. His accounts of Epictetus' teaching in Koine are so different from Arrian's own Atticizing diction in his other writings[132] that he feels it necessary to apologize for the rough style of these discourses: "whatever I heard him say I used to write down, word for word, as best I could, endeavouring to preserve it as a memorial, for my own future use, of his way of thinking and the frankness of his speech."[133] Records of teachings thus could preserve even the teacher's distinctive style (fitting distinctive style and language for Jesus often evident in our Gospels).

Quintilian, the famous Roman teacher of rhetoric, inadvertently attests the potential accuracy of such a practice. Some of the boys who were his students had published in his name their notes on his lectures. He attests that their notes were fairly accurate, though he clearly wished that he had had the opportunity to polish them for publication. His own published work overlapped with what they had written.[134]

While Jewish disciples may have taken fewer notes and emphasized orality much more highly than most Gentiles, they also were able to take notes and use them as initial mnemonic devices to recall larger blocs of material.[135] Certainly the supposition that few Palestinian Jews could write has been challenged and shown inaccurate.[136] Some suggest that at least one of Jesus' followers, a tax-collector (Mk 2:14),[137] would have had the skills to take such notes, and later Christian tradition in fact opined that the other disciples later made use of his notes.[138] Whatever the particulars, the possibility that some disciples took some notes during Jesus' ministry or soon afterward is a factor worth taking into account. Confronted with a classicist's evidence of note-taking in antiquity, one traditional form critic conceded that such evidence would require revision in the skepticism of radical form critics.[139]

Jewish Academic Memory

Jewish education emphasized memorization of Torah (through repeated reading and recitation).[140] Josephus likewise stressed memorization and understanding, though his focus (in contrast to that of Greeks) was the law rather than earlier Greek authors.[141] This method of learning was thus hardly limited to the circle of later rabbis; it was part of regular Jewish education in the home and basic school education all Jewish youths were to receive.[142]

But the most easily documented example, where the process was taken to its fullest extent and where we have the greatest volume of extant material, is among disciples of rabbis. Rabbis lectured to their pupils and expected them to memorize their teachings by laborious repetition.[143] Thus a rabbi might praise a student who, instead of trying to learn on his own, merely preserved his teacher's wisdom, like a good cistern.[144] This practice was all the more intense for those studying to be teachers of Torah.[145]

There is much emphasis in both Tannaitic and later Amoraic literature on careful traditioning.[146] Because this traditioning in practice tended toward "net transmission" rather than "chain transmission" (i.e., the sayings became the property of the rabbinic community, and not only of a single disciple of a teacher), transmission could be guarded more carefully in the first generation or two.[147] There is also evidence that Jewish teachers sometimes spoke in easily memorizable forms, as did Jesus.[148] Stylistic features of oral tradition (and perhaps a teaching style designed to facilitate such transmission) pervade Jesus' teachings recorded in the Gospels.[149]

Some have complained (technically correctly) that all the rabbinic evidence is later than the first century; but it is hardly likely that this evidence would be discontinuous with all the other Jewish and Greco-Roman evidence that we do have, especially given the particular focus on it in our later extant sources.[150]

Limited Adaptation

At the same time, teachings could be condensed and abridged,[151] and the very emphasis on the tradition could lead rabbis to portray their teaching as merely amplifying what preceded,[152] or to attempt harmonizations of earlier contradictory opinions attributed to a given rabbi.[153] Among Gentiles, standard rhetorical practice included paraphrasing sayings, as evidenced by the rhetorical exercises in which it features prominently.[154] (It is thus not surprising that a writer would praise a sophist who both "received" disciple-instruction accurately and "passed it on" eloquently.)[155] The standard of accuracy for ancient memory was the "gist";[156] memory often preserves the gist of matters even when details remain more obscure or inaccurate.[157]

Thus both faithfulness to and adaptation of oral sources characterize early rabbinic use of earlier tradition,[158] and the exact wording of Jesus' sayings could vary, for instance, from Matthew to Luke to the Didache.[159] E. P. Sanders concludes that "The gospel writers did not wildly invent material," though "they developed it, shaped it and directed it in the ways they wished."[160]

Implications

In light of the foregoing discussion, our starting assumption should be that disciples of Jesus would have learned and transmitted his teachings no less carefully than most ancient disciples transmitted the wisdom of their mentors.[161] If we must start with assumptions either way, should not the burden of proof rest on the assumptions of the radical skeptics, rather than on the assumption that Jesus' disciples were like other disciples in antiquity and hence sought to transmit their master's sayings accurately?

The views of the more extreme form critics that seem to presume that the church created rather than submitted to the substance of his teaching contrasts with our evidence, including our limited evidence about ancient Jewish traditioning. Birger Gerhardsson's initial work published in 1961 may have overstated his case,[162] but many now recognize that his severest critics have done the same.[163] As we have noted, memorization and transmission of famous teachers' sayings was not only a later rabbinic practice; it characterized elementary education throughout the Mediterranean. Further, most of the forms of traditions passed on in the Synoptic Gospels are the sort that would be passed on in circles less formal than Gerhardsson suggested yet more controlled than Bultmann suggested.[164] Studies of oral tradition suggest that the form of news and jokes was highly flexible; that of parables and narratives was somewhat flexible; and that of proverbs and poems allowed virtually no flexibility.[165] Most of Jesus' sayings would thus be conveyed with either some or virtually no flexibility, not with maximal flexibility.

Examining the early Christian data supports this likelihood that Jesus' teachings would have been transmitted substantially accurately. Paul, our earliest extant Christian source, attests even many of the purportedly "latest" developments of first-century Christian thought (such as wisdom Christology) within the first generation.[166] He attests even some elements of the Jesus sayings tradition in occasional letters like 1 Corinthians and 1 Thessalonians (though such attestation was plainly not his purpose).[167] In some of these cases, his language suggests that he was passing on to his many readers what he had received.[168] Paul seems to have known and expected his audience to recognize that he knew the Jesus tradition;[169] he explicitly distinguishes his teaching from that of Jesus (1 Cor 7:10, 12, 25).[170] Communities already schooled in the oral tradition would catch subtler allusions to that tradition than modern hearers who demand a greater degree of verbatim correspondence.[171]

Indeed, to assume from silence that Paul did not know the Jesus tradition because he does not cite it more explicitly and more often is almost analogous to assuming that the writer of 1 John was unaware of the Johannine Jesus tradition because the document presupposes rather than cites that tradition.[172] Despite clear differences in terms of target audience, Bultmann's radical dichotomy between Paul's Diaspora perspectives and Palestinian Jewish material in the Gospels is read into the evidence.[173] The writer of a probably post-70 Diaspora Gospel from the Pauline circle shows awareness of many earlier sources that he insists go back to the eyewitnesses (Lk 1:1-2); and he was probably in a position to know (Lk 1:3-4). The exclusively oral stage of the Jesus tradition, before the written sources of Lk 1:1, could not have been more than three or at most four decades,[174] and occurred while the eyewitnesses maintained a dominant position in early Christianity.[175]

As we shall note later, these eyewitnesses included the "twelve," a group that most scholars date to Jesus' lifetime.[176] Few scholars would question that Jesus had disciples, or that at least some of those most intimate followers (like Peter) rose to prominence in the early Jesus movement. Revolutionaries had followers without having disciples, but prophets could have both;[177] even eccentric wilderness ascetics could have disciples.[178] But most importantly, teachers and sages almost by definition had disciples; and whatever else Jesus was, he was surely a teacher (see ch. 13). Our extant first-century sources about the early Jesus movement emphasize continuity of testimony (cf. Acts 1:21-22),[179] with the "twelve" apparently maintaining a dominant position in the decades following Jesus' mission to Jerusalem (Gal 2:9; cf. 1 Cor 15:5).

The witnesses include also many others from the early period, including other apostles (1 Cor 15:7), Jesus' relatives (1 Cor 15:7),[180] a number of women prominent enough to be named (Mk 15:40-41),[181] and at least 500 others (1 Cor 15:6). The sources repeatedly emphasize the importance of witnesses for the tradition;[182] plenty of persons are named in the Gospels who could be sources and guarantors of the tradition.[183] Even the tradition in the Fourth Gospel, which we are not engaging much in this book, rests on the testimony of the "beloved disciple" (who claims to be an eyewitness of at least some of the key events; Jn 13:23; 19:26-27, 35; 21:24).[184]

Early Christian Creativity?

More skeptical scholars often overestimate the degree of early Christian creativity in the gospel tradition. Clearly early Christians resisted the temptation to read some major issues of their day into gospel materials (e.g., food laws and circumcision).[185] Some of Paul's occasional letters also inadvertently attest at an early date the accuracy of elements of the Jesus tradition (1 Cor 7:10-12; 11:23; 15:3; 1 Thess 4:15), whereas the Jesus tradition in the Gospels exhibits little influence from Paul.[186] Indeed, many sayings in the tradition imply a setting relevant only to Palestine and/or the specific time of Jesus.[187]

Even more significantly, written Gospels were appearing within three decades of Jesus' ministry, while eyewitnesses maintained positions of prominence in the Church;[188] as we noted in chs. 6 and 9, Luke attests his reader's awareness of many existing written sources (Lk 1:1-4). Had early traditioners and writers indulged in free invention in various geographical communities, we could have expected Gospels much more diverse than our Synoptics are[189] — more like the later Gnostic materials formed under such conditions.[190] That is, had Gospel writers composed freely without regard for their sources, we would have much more radically different works instead of the substantial overlap in content we find in our Synoptic Gospels. For this reason as well as those given above, it should be more when a scholar disputes a particular saying, rather than when one contends for its authenticity, that one should assume the burden of proof.[191]

Discerning "tradition" on the basis of spontaneous revelation[192] also appears to be a later practice. Although all concur that the early Christians prophesied, it is highly unlikely, against some scholars,[193] that many "sayings of the risen Jesus" were retroactively attributed to the historical Jesus.[194] The few clear examples of prophecies we have in the New Testament are always explicitly identified as such,[195] and again, issues of the later church rarely appear in collections of Jesus' teachings.[196] As we shall note later in the book, Jesus was a prophet who launched a prophetic movement; but he was also a sage who taught disciples to preserve and expound his teachings. The disciples probably were communicating the substance of Jesus' teaching even during his lifetime, if even so much as a historical kernel lies behind Jesus sending the Twelve in his lifetime.[197] On the antiquity of some end-times material and the extreme improbability that it originated in prophecy, see appendix 4.

Robert Price has suggested other objections to a reliable tradition. He rejects the analogy of rabbinic transmission, comparing instead the seventeenth-century messianic claimant Sabbatai Sevi or the twentieth-century African healer Simon Kimbangu, whose disciples within a generation made him out to be the Messiah.[198] Yet these comparisons are anachronistic and misplaced. Kimbangu did not train disciples by passing on easily memorizable sayings;[199] nor did all of his followers make such assertions about him;[200] nor do we have first-century Jewish examples of such rapid deification. Moreover, the labels given to Kimbangu and Sabbatai Sevi derived from analogies with Jesus — a claim more difficult to make for Jesus given the lack of contemporary parallels in his day. His early Palestinian Jewish followers lacked close models for rapid deification; his later Gentile followers in the Diaspora would hardly have invoked the category of "Messiah." Ancient sages could be deified, but not so quickly, and certainly not in Jewish monotheism, even in the Diaspora.

Price also suggests that the apostles would not have been concerned with others spreading invented tales, nor could they have stopped this practice if they were.[201] But where would the Gospel writers have sought their information? Who would have been considered the most reliable sources? To whom did ancient biographers of sages turn in other cases? Was it not more often to disciples and schools that passed on a founder's teaching, rather than to popular opinion? And to whom would the early Jesus movement have looked for leadership, but to Jesus' circle of closest followers, and to James his brother? In fact, Paul's undisputed letter to the Galatians confirms that precisely these persons were the leaders in the Jerusalem Jesus movement, and that they were also known to be such in the Diaspora. Price's skepticism thus seems excessive and unwarranted.

Traditional Form Criticism

As mentioned earlier, nineteenth- and twentieth-century scholars investigated the gospels' written sources. Because early Christians told and retold the stories about Jesus orally before writing Gospels, however, scholars also began to ask about the way early Christians transmitted them, and thus developed form criticism.[202]

Many form critics made observations difficult to dispute, for example, that Jesus used teaching forms popular among his contemporaries (such as parables and witty sayings), and that early Christians transmitted Jesus' sayings and deeds in forms used by other biographers and storytellers of their day. They also identified characteristic forms of various narrative units, such as controversy stories.[203]

Many form critics, however, speculated about the preaching settings of the various forms, opining that we know more about the preaching communities (though they are not explicitly mentioned in our sources) than about Jesus (the subject of the sources)! In a post-Schweitzer period of skepticism about the historical Jesus, Bultmann and many other New Testament scholars focused on the early communities that transmitted reports about Jesus, which they thought might prove more fruitful historically. But this approach has proved ironic, for we in fact know far less about the earliest transmitting communities than we know about the historical Jesus.[204] If pioneers in any discipline tend to exaggerate their discipline's importance, such early form critics were no doubt among them!

Some form critics started with skeptical presuppositions and consequently produced studies with predictably skeptical conclusions (Bultmann being the best-known example);[205] others started with less skeptical premises and accepted much more of the material as authentic to Jesus.[206]

The conclusions varied in part because of the varying premises with which different scholars started, and in part because flaws existed in the standard methodology.[207] Some criteria for authenticity the form critics developed were, however, reasonable: for instance, a saying of Jesus attested in a variety of independent sources or that would not have been made up by the later church was probably authentic.[208] At the same time, although these criteria could logically help to verify traditions, they could not logically help to falsify them. For example, one could hardly assume that a saying of Jesus preserved only once or that his followers agreed with is necessarily inauthentic! In other words, the best criteria of form criticism work much better to demonstrate the reliability of some material in the Gospels than to argue the reverse.[209]

The abuse of these criteria sometimes led to pure speculation grounded only in preexisting theories about the development of early Christianity.[210] Skepticism about the fidelity of oral tradition partly reflects the earlier form critics' print culture, which can predispose us to bias against orality.[211] If some early form critics were skeptical about what can be known about Jesus, their contrary confidence about their own ability to reconstruct the prehistory of traditions behind texts is widely viewed as eccentric by literary critics outside biblical studies.[212]

Form-critical Criteria

Twentieth-century form critics established some criteria that remain helpful today, although form criticism's serious weaknesses have rendered most contemporary scholars skeptical concerning the degree to which they remain valuable.[213] Some criteria are more helpful than others. We explore especially four traditional form-critical criteria briefly here: multiple attestation; coherence; dissimilarity; and Palestinian environment.

The Criteria of Multiple Attestation and Coherence

Negative uses of the form-critical criteria resemble arguments from silence. Given the dearth of two-millennia-old sources remaining extant, we have silence in abundance; nevertheless, we have what seem to be *representative* samples of enough *kinds* of sayings to reconstruct a great deal about Jesus with a high degree of historical probability.

Form critics pointed out that when multiple, early and independent sources attest a saying, that saying holds a greater claim to authenticity. This observation does not mean that sayings attested only once must be inauthentic; in fact, we can be quite sure that most things Jesus said during his lifetime are attested *nowhere* in our tradition. Apparently enough traditions remained by the late first century that we cannot expect any Gospel writer to feel obligated to include them all (cf. Jn 20:30; 21:25). But the principle does provide a guideline useful to those who want to find the most secure elements in the tradition, and for that purpose it seems a matter of common sense. Thus we can use the criterion positively (to support the likelihood of particular sayings) but not negatively (to screen them out). Ancients, too, used this criterion to support portraits of, say, Socrates.[214] Moreover, although many of Jesus' individual sayings are not repeated in all our sources, particular themes and emphases, many of them distinctive to Jesus, are.[215]

The criterion of coherence asks whether the sayings in question fit with other sayings or behavior that we regard as authentic. Again, this criterion was used even in antiquity.[216] Recent scholars, more critical of the negative use of all the form-critical criteria, have critiqued even the negative use of the criterion of coherence, since the same person need not always speak the same way.[217] Although less warranted than criticism of the dissimilarity criterion (below), the critique is at least somewhat deserved, given the unsystematic and sage-like character of Jesus' teaching. Moreover, as we have noted, we surely have only a fraction of Jesus' teaching, teaching that if available more fully might also provide context for assimilating a more diverse range of thoughts.

Writers' preferences also affect which diverse aspects of Jesus' personality appear. For example, one may compare two ancient collections of tradition about the philosopher Musonius Rufus, each of which portrays him quite differently.[218] Moreover, most who have used the criterion of coherence have traditionally based it on the criterion of dissimilarity: anything Jesus truly said must cohere with whatever was unique to Jesus.[219] If one doubts the criterion of dissimilarity (which is quite easy to doubt; see our discussion below), any criteria based on it will also collapse. Used positively, though, the criterion can be helpful; this includes coherence with broader themes in Jesus' teachings (such as the kingdom), and teachings or actions consistent with Jesus' "rejection and execution."[220] In fact, the Synoptic portrait of Jesus is probably more generally internally coherent than many modern scholarly reconstructions of Jesus are.[221]

The Criteria of "Dissimilarity" (Uniqueness) and Embarrassment

One criterion, that of dissimilarity, has particularly fallen on hard times. The criterion excludes the likelihood of Jesus having a high degree of continuity with his Jewish contemporaries and the likelihood of his disciples having a high degree of continuity with his teachings.[222] From what we know of ancient teachers and their schools, however, the reverse is far more likely. The criterion is therefore useful only in its positive role: what later Christians would not have invented is authentic tradition (this resembles what scholars currently call the criterion of embarrassment). This criterion of embarrassment can be useful.[223]

In recent years scholars in the discipline have thus seriously critiqued the negative use of this criterion and urged special caution regarding it.[224] The rising dissatisfaction easily evident a decade ago[225] is currently a relatively strong consensus against the feasibility of this particular form-critical approach, and not surprisingly so. Second Questers used the criterion to emphasize Jesus' uniqueness (a status they believed theologically useful);[226] most Third Questers set Jesus in his Jewish context, hence tend to emphasize a criterion of continuity.[227]

Finding a Jesus different from Judaism historically has anti-Semitic roots;[228] a historian's first focus should not be what is *distinctive* about Jesus, but what is *characteristic* of him.[229] If one applied this criterion to Luther, accepting about him only what differed from both contemporary Catholicism and subsequent Lutheranism, one's knowledge of Luther would prove meager indeed.[230] The negative use of this criterion thus can produce only a "skewed ... picture of Jesus," one that wrongly isolates him from his known context.[231]

Palestinian Environment

The criterion of Palestinian Jewish environment makes far more sense than the criterion of dissimilarity, and frequently cancels it out.[232] A sort of "similarity" criterion is thus more in vogue today: whatever situates Jesus in the continuum between contemporary Judaism and the movement that emerged from him offers the likeliest portrait of Jesus.[233] The Third Quest tends to highlight Jesus' Jewish environment,[234] but sometimes to the neglect of the movement that emerged from his teaching; a "continuum" approach seeks to integrate both contexts.[235] Noting Jesus' continuity with his environment also allows one to highlight areas of his discontinuity (genuine dissimilarity) more accurately and in a more nuanced manner.[236]

In its negative form, one would use this criterion to reject the authenticity of anything in the stories about Jesus that cannot plausibly fit in Jesus' environment, e.g., the idea that the temple was no longer standing (a post-70 development).[237] This does not mean that Jesus never said or did anything dissonant with his environment (his death on a Roman cross likely suggests significant dissonance regarding something). Others of his contemporaries, too, differed from the mainstream of their environment in various ways. But as we shall see in later chapters, a significant proportion of gospel tradition fits Jesus' own Galilean environment better than it fits the later urban and probably mostly Diaspora churches that provided the dominant first audiences for our Gospels.

We should note, of course, that Greek culture transformed Palestinian Judaism, but Palestinian Judaism exerted little influence on Greek culture. We thus regularly read Palestinian Jewish sources in light of their Greek context, and should not be surprised to discover Greek elements in the early gospel tradition. The passing on of these traditions and writing them down for Diaspora audiences would only increase such elements. When we find distinctively *Palestinian Jewish* features in the tradition, however, we must recognize these as marks that the tradition originated in Jewish Palestine. Palestinian Jewish features need not guarantee that a saying must have inevitably originated with Jesus, but they do take us back to the earliest circle of witnesses for Jesus, greatly increasing the probability that the saying is authentic.

The direction of hellenization (or at least more hellenistic ways of recounting matters) should have increased in later sources, and on average Palestinian elements should be earlier. As we noted in ch. 2, the older liberal view that the earliest christology evolved from a Palestinian Jewish apocalyptist to a hellenistic divine man does not fit our evidence adequately,[238] but certainly it comes closer to fitting it than does the contemporary "Jesus Seminar's" frequent apparent reversal of the sequence, which assumes that later Christians Judaized Jesus.[239] This later Judaization of less Jewish material makes no sense in view of Roman anti-Judaism and the growing influence of Diaspora Christianity as years passed.[240] Our earliest Christian sources support a Palestinian Jewish foundation for the movement: though writing to mixed churches in the Diaspora that may have struggled with his message, Paul shares an apocalyptic worldview with much of Palestinian Judaism as much as two decades before Mark wrote.[241]

Aramaisms

Scholars have often cited a particular linguistic feature of Palestinian environment as characteristic of Jesus.[242] Although our extant Gospels are written in Greek, that they contain Aramaic figures of speech also tends to suggest authentic Jesus material,[243] especially if the first translators into Greek frequently sought word-for-word fidelity as some scholars suggest.[244] Although reconstructing Aramaic behind gospel traditions seems more complex than often allowed, some have argued that the Aramaic original of as much as 80% of the Synoptic sayings material appears to fit a poetic or rhythmic form helpful for memorization.[245] Jesus' common phrase "Son of Man" (literally, "the son of the man") makes no more sense in Greek than it does in English, but such a phrase makes perfect sense in Hebrew or Aramaic, where it frequently occurs. Some divergences in Jesus' sayings in different Gospels may reflect different possible translations of these sayings from Aramaic.[246] (Various Semitic structural features of many sayings also suggest their antiquity, and perhaps that their sage uttered them in easily memorized form.)[247]

Although Greek was the universal trade language in the urban east (hence probably the one common language for even the Jerusalem church), the Aramaic vernacular would be dominant in rural settings, such as most of the settings where Jesus taught (especially in Galilee). (Although Aramaic was probably the first language of most Galileans outside the urban centers, even in Lower Galilee,[248] Greek was widespread in Palestine;[249] even the Semiticist Gustaf Dalman long ago recognized the use of Greek in Jerusalem.)[250] Aramaic was the diplomatic language of Israel in dialogue with Mesopotamia before the exile (2 Kgs 18:26; Is 36:11), and the dominant language of Israel before the Hellenistic period.[251] Many Qumran scrolls appear in Aramaic (despite the prejudice for Hebrew),[252] and Babylonian Jewry, which affected Palestinian Judaism just as the Mediterranean Diaspora did, used Aramaic.[253] Throughout western

Asia, Aramaic remained the vernacular of peoples (especially in rural areas or small towns) whose first language was not Greek or a small local language.

Material from Masada indicates that bilingualism (and even trilingualism) was common, but Aramaic was the common tongue for most Judeans, though Hebrew could be used in priestly and purity matters.[254] Aramaic was the dominant language for the masses even in Jerusalem.[255] Even Greek composition in Judea reflects abundant Aramaisms, especially for those scribes and translators whose Greek was weaker.[256] The Aramaic tradition apparently remained important enough that Paul seems to have taught some Aramaic words to his churches (Rom 8:15; 1 Cor 16:22; Gal 4:6).

Because most of Jesus' teachings in the Synoptics appear to have been delivered to Galilean villagers, they probably reflect Aramaic rather than Greek originals.[257] It is quite true that the earliest church, like Jesus, often spoke Aramaic; but the early presence of many Greek-speakers in the Jerusalem church means that, in Jerusalem at least, the shared language of the community understood by all was Greek. From an early period, the bilingual milieu of the Syrian and Palestinian churches undoubtedly facilitated the ready translation on a popular level of Jesus' sayings from Aramaic to Greek, probably sometimes in diverse forms.[258]

Some might therefore charge that the earliest Christians could have invented some sayings attributed to Jesus in this period.[259] But given all we know of Jewish and (for that matter) Greco-Roman traditioning and the growth of legends, this would be the *least* likely period in which sayings or stories would be invented.[260] (Paul attests two of the leading eyewitnesses — Peter and John — plus Jesus' brother in positions of leadership in the Jerusalem church — Gal 2:9; cf. 1 Cor 15:7.) At the same time, early Christians wrote our Gospels and probably their direct sources in Greek, and just as Matthew frequently adjusts Mark's Greek, his sources may have also adapted earlier language. So Aramaisms suggest traditions stemming from the earliest (hence most reliable) community; but[261] good Greek is not a mark *against* the reliability of the traditions (especially if most Palestinian Jews were bilingual, as is probably the case).[262] Aramaic could be translated into colloquial Greek just as it could be translated into Greek with Semitic interference in its syntax.

Narratives about Jesus

Ancient biographers generally felt that a record of the subject's deeds and words revealed the person's character far better than editorial comments might.[263] Jewish disciples cared about their teacher's lifestyle, which they normally sought to imitate,[264] and which in later sources might even function as legal precedent.[265] Even Jewish children learned by practice and *imitation* as well as by memorization, so a teacher's behavior was presumably a matter of careful observation.[266] In Greek as well as Jewish culture, students were eager to preserve the *deeds* and character of their masters as well as their teachings.[267]

Although the early Christians undoubtedly retold the stories in a variety of ways, the most common form of Synoptic pericopes suggests that early Christians adopted the sort of short narratives typically used to recount the deeds and deed-related sayings of famous teachers. These often bare-bones scenes offered the easiest form for remembering and transmitting the accounts. Even original eyewitness reports usually include a narrative element; the interpretive process of narrativizing occurs throughout the process of memory and is not inconsistent with even eyewitness reports.[268] The "forms" of stories that form critics assigned to early Christian homiletic use (perhaps based partly on their familiarity with the pericopes' later Christian usage) could thus as easily stem from the natural ways eyewitnesses could have constructed and developed their stories.[269] But we do not know the precise milieu in which any given unit of tradition in our Gospels assumed its basic present form.

Although our present Gospels are finished literary works intended to be read as such, they still reflect some of the process of oral tradition that stands behind their sources. For instance, many of our stories in the Synoptic Gospels are brief accounts of events in Jesus' ministry, often with a minimum of chronological links to their context. Some have compared these Synoptic accounts with *chreiai,* brief examples (often of heroes of history) recounted, memorized, and paraphrased in regular school exercises in the ancient Mediterranean world.[270] (The length and form of *chreiai* admittedly varied,[271] limiting the precision of the comparison.) It was natural for Jesus' disciples and their first hearers to remember stories about Jesus in the same way that they were accustomed to remembering stories about other important figures. The combination of such narratives with anecdotes, teaching material (sayings and speeches), plus an extended account of the protagonist's end, characterizes ancient biography in general, so we should not be surprised to find it in the Gospels.[272]

In the first half of the twentieth century form-critics pointed out some particular patterns in the Synoptic Gospels' accounts about Jesus. Some form-critics called one recurrent pattern "controversy-narratives," short accounts where Jesus debates with his opponents and proves his case. Although we may guess that the social repercussions of these debates continued long after the recorded narratives end, such narratives typically close with a rejoinder or quip from Jesus that shames and often silences his opponents. Some form-critics called narratives concluding with Jesus' witty retorts "pronouncement stories." Such stories about teachers were common in antiquity,[273] suggesting that Jesus shamed his opponents in a way understood by his disciples from their culture.[274] The use of such accounts also suggests why the disciples would have transmitted the stories as they did. Occasions on which restraint is shown in describing miracles suggest controls on these traditions similar to those on the sayings traditions.[275]

Because Jesus authored the sayings material but not the narratives about him, his disciples presumably transmitted the sayings more carefully while transmitting the narratives more in their own words;[276] hence Aramaisms predominate in the former. Other ancient writers also seem to have adapted narratives with some degree of freedom, as we have noted. Nevertheless, the historiographic considerations we noted for ancient sources in general apply here: sources from the first generation or two are likely to have often preserved the gist of the events they report.

Conclusion

Ancient Mediterranean culture valued orality more than modern western culture does. They could preserve oral traditions and could use collections of sayings in written or oral form, or in both. Many of Jesus' teachings are in the sort of readily memorizable forms in which sages often offered them to facilitate retention.

Ancient memories could be highly developed, as illustrated in oratory, storytelling, basic education and advanced education. Disciples normally preserved the substance of their masters' teachings and, where relevant, stories about their behavior. Disciples sometimes took notes that proved highly accurate. To assume that Jesus' disciples acted completely unlike other disciples with regard to transmitting their teacher's sayings — despite the comparatively early publication of sources about Jesus — is to value one's skepticism about Jesus more highly than the concrete comparative evidence.

Scholarship as a whole has become less impressed with some earlier form-critical criteria like the criterion of dissimilarity (meant to emphasize Jesus' uniqueness); today it often emphasizes the continuity between Jesus and his Palestinian Jewish environment. Jesus' sayings often reflect their original context in his Galilean ministry far better than they reflect the situations of the churches addressed in the Gospels. Such insights will help to shape the discussion involved in the rest of this book, where we hope to illustrate how well the Jesus of the Gospels fits his milieu.

WHAT WE LEARN ABOUT JESUS FROM THE BEST SOURCES

Jesus' Story in the Gospels

In this section we will examine aspects of Jesus' teaching and story in our most reliable sources, the Gospels. A maximalist approach to the sources grants as evidence whatever is possible; a mediating approach looks for whatever is most probable historically. "Historical Jesus" research sometimes, however, seeks to identify a critical minimum, the *least* that all scholars "should" be willing to accept in view of historical evidence.[1] There is nothing wrong with looking for a critical minimum, as long as it is clear that this is what we are doing. Yet some scholars speak as if they are looking for whatever is probable, when in fact they are seeking only a critical "minimum."

The danger of a minimum is that, if defined too narrowly, it can exclude so much evidence as to offer a skewed picture that is certainly distorted and easily manipulated. For some, a minimalist reconstruction of what we can know about Jesus is very little indeed, when they define the minimum in terms of historically proved certainty. This is an unfair standard, since historical reconstruction by its nature never reaches the levels of certainty possible in, say, theoretical mathematics. Most scholars accept a larger working framework, however, and admit in their "minimum" what is "almost certain" or even add what is "very probable."

Approaches vary partly on whether scholars' goal is whatever is historically probable or what is the critical minimum. Approaches also vary based on how particular scholars define "minimum," and they also vary depending on the value one assigns to various lines of evidence. We have already worked to establish that we can expect a high degree of reliable evidence for the substance of Jesus' life and ministry from the sources of the Synoptic Gospels. Our objective will be to build on this approach to note some of what is probable, rather than simply a minimum.

Nevertheless, because we focused more on Luke's approach earlier, we will focus more often on Mark, "Q," and to a lesser extent Matthew here. In reconstructing what we can know about Jesus to a great degree of probability by purely historical means, I depend heavily on Mark and "Q" material in this final section. It should be understood that I do not regard this material as the only potentially reliable material; I have already argued that we should expect otherwise based on the nature of our sources. But I am giving preference to these sources because I am appealing to a consensus of scholarship regarding the *most* accepted sources for reconstructing Jesus' life.

When we combine elements about Jesus for which the Gospels provide us much evidence, much of the picture that emerges becomes coherent, fitting a cohesive whole.[2] Jesus prophetically summoned his people to prepare for the kingdom, offering radical ethical demands to prepare them for it. But Jesus himself had a mission that would involve confronting the ruling elite, as the powerful figures of this present age, and lead to his martyrdom. This, too, was connected to the coming kingdom, a connection understood by his followers in terms of the resurrection.

CHAPTER 11

John the Baptist

". . . it may be that John the Baptist served [Jesus] not only as the reagent by which the elements of his distinctive Gospel were brought to precipitation but also as the inspiration for that line of thought that leads from the contemplation of his personal jeopardy toward the conception of his own place in God's plan."

CARL H. KRAELING[1]

"It seems likely, then, that in continuing John's message, Jesus also continued his immersion."

JOAN E. TAYLOR[2]

"At the beginning of Jesus' career, then, we find him accepting the mission of John the Baptist, who said that the climax of history was at hand. Within no more than a decade after Jesus' execution, we have firm proof that his followers expected this dramatic event very soon. Jesus must fit this context."

E. P. SANDERS[3]

Scholars today frequently depict John as Jesus' "mentor," or Jesus as John's "disciple."[4] Even if such explicit titles go beyond our extant evidence, Jesus certainly had some respectful relationship toward John. The Gospels, eager to exalt Jesus, would hardly have invented his submission to John's baptism or portrayed Jesus' ministry as chronologically following John's (at least in the Synoptics) if John did not genuinely play an important role in Jesus' ministry. Early sources compare Jesus with John (Mk 11:27-33; Q material in Matt 11:18-19//Lk 7:33-34), and some of John's known emphases (like baptism, also attested in Josephus' portrayal of John)[5] show up in the early Jesus movement probably because Jesus approved of such emphases.

Thus what we know about John affects what we can surmise about Jesus, as scholars often observe. This observation challenges the suppositions of those who think of Jesus opposing an eschatological message (in contrast to the explicit gospel evidence to the contrary), when we know that both John and Jesus' subsequent followers supported it.[6] To posit such a view is simply to dismiss all the evidence for Jesus' teaching and his context (in his own and John's movements) that we have and to argue the contrary based on inferences from silence. While such inferences satisfy particular audiences today, such an approach ends up trying to explain away more evidence than it explains.

A much larger number of scholars accept John's ministry as a positive context for that of Jesus.[7] As Robert Webb concludes, "We may conclude at the historical level what the early Christians concluded at a theological level: John the Baptist was the forerunner of Jesus."[8] Since I do not wish to expend much space on material already treated more thoroughly by others, this chapter will be quite brief. It is nevertheless important to offer a context for Jesus' mission as an end-time prophet as well as a sage.

John in Josephus

Even the Jesus Seminar almost unanimously recognized that John the Baptist invited repentance and baptized.[9] This recognition fits the portrait of John in Josephus, who cannot be accused of writing with any bias supporting the Gospels: John, "called the Baptist" (*Ant.* 18.116) and drawing great crowds (18.118), administered baptism in the following manner; John "was a good man, and commanded the Jews to exercise virtue, both regarding justice toward one another, and piety toward God, and thus to come to baptism." It would be acceptable if they used it to purify the body once the soul had been fully purified by "justice" or "righteousness" (*Ant.* 18.117).

Most scholars think Josephus' comments on John are authentic. Among other reasons, this confidence is because they fit the language of this section of Josephus' work[10] and a Christian interpolator would have harmonized them with the Gospels (which is not the case with this passage).[11] John's movement had an independent existence outside Jesus' movement, a status that seems to have generated some later confusion and ambivalence concerning the groups' relationship (cf. Acts 19:1-6).[12] Nevertheless, John remained important in the history of the early Christian movement because his movement provided an immediate context for that of Jesus. Early Christians viewed the connection as more important for historic than theological reasons; thus it is prominent in the Gospels, mentioned in historic references in Acts, and missing in the letters and Revelation.

Although the Gospels and Josephus agree on various points, where they differ the Gospels (which are slightly earlier) may actually be more authentic. Although Josephus presents the Baptist's mission like a moralizing philosopher for his Hellenized audience,[13] the Gospel accounts preserve a greater ring of authenticity: John was a wilderness prophet proclaiming impending judgment. That is, the Gospels, which flow from a community that embraced much of John's message, have changed the portrait of John (at least in this regard) less than Josephus did.

John's Mission in the Wilderness

That John historically baptized in the wilderness (Mk 1:4-5) is clearly early tradition, Mark's account citing a geographical situation (the narrow Jordan Valley in the wilderness) that obtained only in Palestine.[14] The meaning of John's location would not be lost on Syro-Palestinian Jews. Israel's prophets had predicted a new exodus in the wilderness.[15] Many of John's Jewish contemporaries acknowledged this as the appropriate place not only for renewal movements[16] but for prophets and Messiahs.[17]

Further, even the verse that the Gospels use to justify John's mission in the wilderness (Is 40:3) could reflect the self-identity of John's own early renewal movement in Palestine.[18] The Qumran sectarians, also located in the wilderness, already applied this very Isaiah text to their own mission in the wilderness.[19] Despite this similarity, however, John was not, at least at this time, part of the Qumran community. Rather than separating himself totally from Israel as the Qumran community did,[20] he preached directly to the crowds that came to him there (Mk 1:4-5; cf. Jos. *Ant.* 18.118).[21]

No less important to John's mission, the wilderness was likewise a natural place for fugitives from a hostile society,[22] including prophets like Elijah (1 Kgs 17:2-6; 2 Kgs 6:1-2). John could have safely drawn crowds there as he could have nowhere else (cf. Jos. *Ant.* 18.118), and it provided him the best accommodations for public baptisms that symbolically challenged the hegemony of establishment leaders (see Jos. *Ant.* 18.117).

Josephus confirms the image of John as a wilderness reformer, who sought to purify those who had first purified their souls (*Ant.* 18.117). This portrait fits the Gospels' picture of a baptism "of repentance"; Josephus merely employs more hellenistic (hence less likely original) language than the Gospels do.[23] That Josephus speaks favorably of John — in contrast to his condemnation of wilderness "prophets" urging insurrection against Rome — suggests that he knew the difference.[24] John's renewal movement was designed to bring Israel to repentance so that God would act on their behalf, not to challenge the authorities directly or militarily.

It is even plausible that some of John's more specific words in the "Q" tradition preserved in the Gospels reflect some of his original message, remembered by many of his followers who afterward joined Jesus' movement.[25] Thus God raising up stones for Abraham's children (Matt 3:9//Lk 3:8) may reflect a wordplay that worked only in John's Aramaic, not the later church's Greek.[26] That a prophet of renewal would challenge individual Jewish people's special status in order to secure their repentance fits earlier biblical expectations.[27]

That a prophet of the kingdom could speak of God's imminent judgment (as earlier prophets often did) is also not surprising.[28] The specific imagery John employs in "Q" fits his likely audience in rural Palestine better than that of the Gospels' likely urban Diaspora audiences, though it was probably intelligible to everyone.[29] "Q"'s John shares with earlier biblical writers the natural agricultural image of harvest and threshing-floor (Matt 3:12//Lk 3:17) as judgment and/or the end-time.[30] This image is also consistent with the rest of the Jesus tradition (Mk 4:29; cf. Mk 12:2; Matt 9:38//Lk 10:2; Matt 13:39) and early Judaism;[31] the wicked are destroyed "like straw in fire"[32] or like chaff.[33] Fire naturally symbolized future judgment (e.g., Is 26:11; 66:15-16, 24).[34]

John's imagery of threshing[35] and harvest fits agricultural practice, although he graphically extends the metaphor. But where the imagery departs from realism, it most starkly underlines the point. Chaff did not burn eternally (or even long),[36] yet John depicts the wicked's fire as "unquenchable." John does not simply echo the Jewish consensus of his day, because opinions divided on the character of hell.[37] Some believed that it was eternal for at least the worst sinners;[38] but some others believed that most sinners would endure hell only temporarily and would then be destroyed[39] or (on some views) released.[40] Thus John specifically affirmed the harshest image of his day: divine judgment involved eternal torment. Again, however, teaching about "Gehinnom" (hell), whether eternal or temporary, fits especially a Palestinian milieu (even linguistically), not the environment of the later Gospel writers.[41]

Announcing the Coming One?

That John announced impending judgment is very likely; but did he also announce a coming messianic figure or associate that figure with Jesus?[42] In support of the possibility, articulated in direct discourse in both Mark and "Q," we may note that prophets of impending judgment, like many other Jewish people, could believe in a messiah or end-time prophet, or could speak of the coming of God himself. Likewise, given the undeniable connection of some sort that Jesus had with John, it is certainly plausible that John knew of Jesus. Given the greater movement that ultimately arose from Jesus, his potential historical significance even before his independent prominence should not be underestimated. If John announced a coming one, whether or not he specifically associated that expectation with Jesus,[43] we would expect Jesus' early followers to have preserved this expectation as the confirmation of a reliable prophet. We thus examine some aspects of "Q"'s report of John's prophecy about the coming one.

Although the Gospel writers portray John as the expected end-time "Elijah," preparing the way for the Lord (Mal 3:1; 4:5-6), even John's reported message about the coming one may reflect tradition earlier than the purpose to which the Gospel writers put it. John may proclaim no mere human "messiah," but the expected intervention of God himself: "one is coming who . . . will baptize you in the holy Spirit and fire" (Matt 3:11//Lk 3:16). John was surely aware that in Scripture only God pours out the divine Spirit (e.g., Is 44:3; Ezek 39:29; Joel 2:28-29) and fiery end-time judgment. Because "Spirit" can also mean "wind," which was used to separate wheat from chaff during threshing,[44] this image would also fit as part of the preceding context.[45] Because the earlier biblical prophets we have just mentioned announced an outpouring of the Spirit connected with Israel's restoration, and because John was a prophet seeking Israel's restoration, it makes sense that this promise of both the Spirit and judgment belonged historically to his message. That Jesus' highly charismatic movement emerged in the context of John's preaching is also consistent with this notion.

Moreover, the coming one appears to be somehow divine in the sandal image: "I am not worthy to handle his sandals" (Mk 1:7//Jn 1:27; probably also Q in Matt 3:11//Lk 3:16). In ancient Mediterranean thought, a household servant's basest tasks involved the master's feet, such as washing his feet, carrying his sandals or unfastening his sandals' thongs.[46] Although ancient Jewish teachers often expected disciples to function as servants,[47] later rabbis made one exception explicit: disciples did not tend to the teacher's sandals.[48] Whereas Israel's prophets had called themselves "servants of God,"[49] John declares himself unworthy even to be the coming judge's slave![50]

Others, however, object that God does not wear sandals (although the image appears figuratively in Ps 60:8; 108:9, John would not touch God's figurative sandals). Webb suggests that the tension between the divine and human elements of John's proclamation makes some sense in the setting of other Jewish expectations of some exalted, coming figures.[51]

John's Doubts, Jesus' Praise (Matt 11:2-11//Lk 7:19-28)

Rather than conflicting with John's earlier proclamation about the coming one, his subsequent doubts about Jesus in "Q"[52] would fit it well. Jesus' ministry had so far fulfilled *none* of John's eschatological promises. A prophet who was merely healing the sick and driving out demons did not appear to fulfill John's vision of a divine immerser in God's Spirit and end-time fiery judgment.[53]

In any case, the "criterion of embarrassment" makes John's doubts even more plausible historically than the "Q" report about his message; one hardly expects Christian tradition to have invented his doubts! Although early Christians had reason to stress John's testimony for Jesus, this narrative reports John's doubts and does not even conclude with a clear statement of John's renewed faith.[54] The tradition here is thus likely authentic, not a creation of early Christian imagination.[55]

Jesus' recorded response to John's doubts (Matt 11:5-6//Lk 7:22-23) is to invite John's attention to the nature of Jesus' miracles as signs of the promised kingdom. Many scholars argue that Jesus interprets his miracles here by means of an allusion to Isaiah 35:5-6, which mentioned some of the same signs he was performing. In so doing Jesus reminded John's disciples that the works he was currently performing might be less dramatic than a fire-baptism, but that Isaiah had already offered them as signs of the messianic era.[56] Thus they were compatible with John's message. Some scholars have argued that the deeds Jesus lists were even already considered messianic in some streams of Jewish thought;[57] the biblical allusions that many scholars find in his words here suggest an early Palestinian interpretive tradition also attested at Qumran.[58] Whatever the particulars, Jesus' answer here does fit a Palestinian Jewish setting.

Most modern scholars, including even Bultmann, accept this response of Jesus as authentically reflecting the words of Jesus.[59] The saying does, after all, sound more like Jesus than like his later followers: Jesus' roundabout response to John is characteristic of Jesus' responses (fitting the Messianic secret, a Middle Eastern teaching style, and Jesus' penchant for riddles). The gospel for the "poor" coheres with other Q tradition about Jesus (cf. Matt 5:3//Lk 6:20); and the saying exhibits Semitic structure. The setting of the saying also seems likely authentic.[60] The account lacks specifically Christian understandings of Jesus (e.g., emphasizing atonement or Lordship) and traditional Christian titles ("coming one" hardly qualifies).[61]

After John's messengers leave, Jesus goes on to praise John to the crowds. Jesus' contrast here between John and a shaking reed or pampered prince also appears to reflect early Palestinian tradition. That John was plainly not a pampered prince (Matt 11:8//Lk 7:25) probably contrasts him with his persecutor, Herod Antipas, Galilee's best-known prince.[62] Jesus contrasts John with Antipas only implictly, as we would expect for an authentic saying from during Jesus' public ministry; to name this ruler openly during Antipas' tetrarchy would be indiscreet (given Antipas' contemporary abuse of John). Later Christians might not catch the allusion, but Jesus' Galilean contemporaries presumably would have.[63]

That this tradition reflects a setting during Jesus' ministry is made more likely by the observation that Jesus' claim that John was no easily bent reed (Matt 11:7; Lk 7:24) fits a setting in Jesus' own day.[64] The image reflects the literal setting of John's ministry: the banks of the Jordan, the site of John's baptism, hosted reeds growing as high as five meters.[65] Moreover, Theissen suggests that even this image might also allude more specifically (albeit again discreetly) to Antipas,[66] arguing for the reed as Antipas' emblem on coins before A.D. 26.[67] If Theissen is right, the saying must have originated in Palestine while the memory of Antipas' reed emblem remained fresh — probably in the late 20s, i.e., the time of John's ministry.[68]

After implicitly challenging Antipas, Jesus honors John. Jesus claims that John is a prophet (Matt 11:9//Lk 7:26), a role in which many would have viewed him, as we have noted. Scholars may be more apt to dispute Jesus' quotation of Mal 3:1 in the following lines (Matt 11:10//Lk 7:27), referring to a messenger who will prepare the way, since this tradition surely envisions Jesus as the one whose way John prepares.[69] Yet if Jesus continued John's mission of summoning Israel to repentance, and worked more signs than John, could he not have viewed himself as John's greater successor? We know of no other successor of John as popular as Jesus was. Whether or not the original saying refers to Jesus, it comports with "Q's" portrayal of the one John claimed would follow him (Matt 3:11//Lk 3:16). The text in context refers to preparing *God's* way (Mal 3:1), and ancient Jewish tradition *usually* viewed the end-time Elijah as preparing God's rather than the Messiah's way.[70]

Jesus' praise of the Baptist in Matt 11:9-11//Lk 7:26-28 is presumably authentic; the later church, sometimes concerned with John's undue popularity, would hardly have invented it.[71] Yet it is quite easy for those unfamiliar with ancient Jewish rhetorical practices to misunderstand the character of his praise.

Jesus' Repudiation of John?

After Jesus praises John, he observes that the least in the kingdom are greater than John. Some scholars suggest that Jesus denigrates John by claiming that "the least in the kingdom is greater than he"[72] (Matt 11:11//Lk 7:28). On the basis of this alleged criticism they then suggest a breach between the two that led to Jesus proclaiming a message contrary to John's, namely, that Jesus must have opposed John's eschatological message. (This hypothesis does invite those of us who understand the "kingdom" as eschatological to wonder why Jesus would have denigrated an eschatological message by referring to the kingdom.) This reading, however, imposes a foreign understanding on the account and employs that interpretation as a substitute for any genuine evidence that Jesus' message contradicted John's. The ministries of the two prophets certainly differed, but our sources indicate that Jesus, like John, continues to warn about repentance in the face of God's impending day of justice.

The view that Jesus broke with John, hence opposed John's message, hence did not speak of imminent judgment or the end, depends on a series of extrapolations. It also has to suppose that the extant gospel tradition consistently distorts the actual teaching of its "lord" to make it fit that of John (as if the gospel tradition owed more fidelity to John than to Jesus). This view uses an explanation of a saying that many consider obscure to explain away the only hard evidence we have, and then to argue from the silence that remains that Jesus believed the opposite of what both John believed and what Jesus' followers thought Jesus taught. Would later Christians have wrongly conformed Jesus to John (the competition)? His own contemporaries sometimes compared him with John or with Elijah (Mk 6:15; 8:28), who in gospel tradition was the background for John (Mk 1:6; 9:13; Matt 11:14; 17:12), *despite* John's lack of signs. They viewed both as prophets (e.g., Mk 6:4, 15; 11:32).

In fact, Jesus is not at all hostile toward John here; after all, he makes John the most significant figure of history so far (Matt 11:11//Lk 7:28)! He confronts John's question graciously in Matt 11:4-6//Lk 7:22-23, quite in contrast with how he addresses his opponents and even wayward disciples (Mk 8:33; 12:38-40; Matt 23:25-39//Lk 11:39-52); far from invoking judgment as on one who had seen much and believed little (Matt 11:21-24//Lk 10:13-15), he had John's disciples recount to John what they had now seen for the first time (Matt 11:4-5//Lk 7:21-22) and pronounced a blessing on him if he would persevere (Matt 11:6//Lk 7:23). He calls John his promised forerunner (Matt 11:10//Lk 7:27).[73] He further chides that generation for not receiving John (Matt 11:18-19//Lk 7:33-34).[74]

The suggestion that Jesus is criticizing John at all in these words reflects an inadequate understanding of ancient Jewish speech patterns (and even of broader Greco-Roman rhetoric).[75] Jesus' contemporaries and successors developed hyperbolic and superlative praise still further: rabbis called Johanan ben Zakkai "the least" of Hillel's eighty disciples not to demean Johanan but to praise Hillel as a teacher.[76] This observation fits the context. Over half a century ago Carl Kraeling's work on John the Baptist showed that the explicitly positive saying in Matt 11:11//Lk 7:28 (no one born of women is greater than John) exemplified standard Jewish rhetoric:[77]

In a single passage in the Mekhilta, for instance, we have statements about both Joseph and Moses that use the same expression. About Joseph it is said, 'there is not among his brethren one greater than he,' and about Moses 'there is not in Israel one greater than he.' As used in Jewish texts such statements are not to be taken as blanket judgments . . ."

The "least" in the kingdom is greater than John simply in the sense that anyone in the kingdom has access to a fuller revelation than those who spoke beforehand (Matt 13:16-17//Lk 10:23-24).[78] It exalts Jesus' followers not by denigrating John but by comparing them with someone great, just as the context interprets it.

Further, when Jesus divides time into eras by making John transitional between earlier prophets and the kingdom (Matt 11:12-13//Lk 16:16), he cannot mean that John would be excluded from the future kingdom. In "Q" tradition, the righteous who precede the era of the kingdom nevertheless would participate in it (Matt 8:11//Lk 13:28). Jesus' language is meant to envision the promised eschatological blessing, not John's failure to be saved.

That the prophets continued their ministry until or through the time of Jesus' predecessor John (Matt 11:13//Lk 16:16) suggests that the saying envisions both John and Jesus highly, making John the climactic prophet and Jesus' promised forerunner. Jesus might allude to a traditional Jewish recognition that the law and prophets pointed to the coming messianic era,[79] which had now confronted them in his own ministry. Far from necessarily being later Christian language, such a claim fits Jesus' vision of himself as special revealer of the kingdom (Matt 12:28//Lk 11:20).

Seeking to emphasize differences between Jesus and John, Crossan points out that Jesus further contrasts John with himself also in Matt 11:18-19//Lk 7:33-34.[80] The point of the contrast, however, denigrates not John but the hostile critics that John shares with Jesus: they reject the message whether it comes through the style of John or of Jesus, neither of which styles Jesus condemns.[81] The charge that John the prophet "has a demon" could suggest a familiar spirit, such as those that belonged to magicians.[82] Although his accusers could not enforce any punishment in the relatively pluralistic Judaism of first-century Palestine, under Jewish law such a charge involved a capital offense. Likewise, the charge that Jesus was a "glutton and a drunkard" alludes to the "rebellious son" of Deuteronomy 21:20 — also a capital offense.[83] Jesus and John, despite their different styles, were God's servants with a common opposition.

John's Execution

The accounts of John's martyrdom in Josephus and the Gospels are clearly independent, and their overlap is limited. Where they overlap, however, they mutually attest that Herod Antipas imprisoned and subsequently executed this popular prophet.[84] Indeed, they agree even in their portrayal of Herodias' character, though this portrayal appears in a different connection in the two sources.[85]

Views vary concerning the historicity of Mark's account of John's execution. Even John Meier is skeptical of the account, citing Mark's "legendary tone" plus differences with Josephus.[86] But "legendary" is a tricky category; if we allow the Gospels to tell a story about the Herodian court to begin with, many items will support historical verisimilitude (including the character of Herodias in Mark), though some details of the account[87] appear more questionable. By contrast, Gerd Theissen thinks that the story behind Mark was a popular account, originally not preserved just among Christians, a tradition also standing behind Josephus.[88]

Rather than either of these alternatives, however, I believe that Josephus and Mark depend on different traditions of a common event. Josephus' sources are probably more Herodian, Mark's perhaps from Christians who once circulated among the Baptist's disciples (cf. e.g., Acts 19:3-5), who may have received explanation from contacts within the Herodian court. The source for Mark's story of John's martyrdom could also easily come from within Antipas' household via Joanna or Manaen, who became disciples (possibly also among Luke's sources — Lk 8:3; 24:10; Acts 13:1).[89] From a purely historical standpoint, we can be fairly certain that Antipas had John executed for preaching what he took as undermining his honor.

Antipas, son of Herod the Great and a Samaritan wife, had functioned as "tetrarch" over Galilee and Perea since about 4 BCE (not a "king" as in Mark).[90] He had engaged in a politically prudent marriage with a Nabatean princess, perhaps seeking to secure further loyalty from Nabatean subjects within his territory of Perea.[91] Yet Antipas's lust undercut his political prudence. When Antipas divorced his first wife to take his brother's wife Herodias,[92] he violated the Mosaic law concerning incest (Lev 18:16; 20:21), as Josephus also points out.[93]

These were fresh issues in the time when John the Baptist was arrested, not when the Gospels were written. Mark's account that the prophet publicly reproached a public example of immorality is thus quite plausible. Josephus' portrayal of Antipas suggests that he was doubtless little concerned about Jewish morality,[94] but what John viewed in moral terms, Antipas undoubtedly saw as a potential political threat, undermining the security of his people's allegiance.[95] The political threat was particularly acute because it was his very affair with Herodias that was already destabilizing his kingdom; Antipas' plans to divorce his first wife had provoked trouble with her father, the powerful Nabatean king Aretas IV. This trouble later led to war and public humiliation for Antipas, which his own people then attributed to divine judgment for executing John.[96]

That many Nabateans in Perea presumably remained loyal to Aretas rather than Herod Antipas the tetrarch further extended the embarrassing political implications of the affair.

According to Josephus' briefer account of John's execution, it must have occurred at Herod's famous fortress Machaerus in Perea,[97] where Antipas' first wife had escaped to her father,[98] where many Nabateans lived, and near where John had often preached.[99] This fortress included a dungeon where John was kept, and apparently separate dining facilities for men and women (thus Mark notifies us that Herodias' daughter "went out" to confer with her mother).[100]

Josephus says nothing of the dance of Herodias' daughter (presumably the one he calls Salome), mentioned in Mark, but it is not as implausible as some contend.[101] According to some accounts the girl, Salome, may have been between six and eight years old; more likely, she was a virgin of marriageable age (twelve to fourteen), but possibly already betrothed or married to Philip the tetrarch.[102] Apart from Antipas' drunkenness, one would hardly expect him to invite another member of the royal family to engage in a sensuous Hellenistic dance.[103] Her dance is, as one commentator notes, "an improbably bizarre touch, which could forthwith be dismissed as fictional, were it not a known fact that the excesses of the Herodian court were in most respects quite notorious."[104] Ancient historical literature is sufficiently replete with such scenes — even the display of freshly severed heads during banquets — to warn against facile assumptions of what is possible.[105]

If Mark knew of it, he relinquishes the opportunity to report the eventual outcome of Antipas' marriage to Herodias. Josephus, however, cannot be accused of the same neglect. He recounts that when Antipas, prompted by his wife Herodias, later sought the title "king" that had been granted to her brother Herod Agrippa I,[106] he was deposed and banished to Gaul for his arrogance.[107]

Historically, John's execution must have affected Jesus and his movement. John's execution cast a shadow over Jesus' ministry: if the elite could silence one prophet, they could silence others. In fact, most prophetic figures of the era were suppressed or killed, according to Josephus (who counts as false prophets most of them, excluding John, Jesus, Joshua ben Ananiah and a few others). In such a context, that Jesus would challenge the temple authorities in Jerusalem without an armed following could suggest that, contrary to many scholars' views, he too expected martyrdom.

Jesus' Baptism by John

The most telling explicit connection with John in the Gospels is that Jesus accepted baptism under John's ministry. This baptism indicates, at the least, that Jesus knew and accepted John's message, which involved summoning Israel to turn back to God.[108] That indication in turn supports the likelihood that Jesus' message stood in continuity with John's, even if their approach differed.[109] The traditions about Jesus' message in our Gospels do in fact confirm this expectation.

Given the embarrassment of some early Christian traditions (both in the canonical Gospels and in the early Gospel of the Nazoreans) that Jesus accepted baptism from one of lower spiritual status than himself, it is virtually inconceivable that early Christians made up the story of John baptizing Jesus.[110] It was established rhetorical practice to hurry most quickly over points that might disturb the audience.[111] Matthew appropriately hastens over the baptism itself in a participle (Matt 3:16); the Fourth Gospel omits it altogether! The Gospel writers did not wish to emphasize that Jesus had been subordinate to John's ministry in some way, especially so close to the beginning of Jesus' own. Following their sources, however, the Synoptics retain this information, albeit in the barest form.

John as the Source of Baptism for the Jesus Movement

If Jesus followed John, and Jesus' disciples baptized, the most probable connection between these facts is a line of continuity running through Jesus himself, as in our opening quotation from Joan Taylor above.[112] This practice seems likely even though the Gospels make little of it, perhaps because for them it was only Jesus' anticipated Spirit baptism that would radically transform John's water baptism. The Fourth Gospel's portrait of baptism by Jesus' disciples (Jn 3:26) thus makes sense. Because Christian baptism is presupposed in our earliest sources (Paul, e.g., Rom 6:3-4; 1 Cor 1:14-17) and our depictions of the earliest events (Jesus' postresurrection commission in Matt 28:19; the first Christian sermon in Acts 2:38), it seems more likely that Jesus, who moved in the Baptist's circle, actually urged on his followers the rite, than that later urban Jerusalem Christians or Galilean Christians more chronologically and geographically distant from the Baptist would have done so.

The Synoptic tradition does omit mention of the practice. Whether the Synoptics deemphasize it to avoid comparisons with the Baptist, or whether Christian baptism represents a postresurrection mandate, is unclear. At the same time, the Fourth Gospel appears to have more reason to downplay it than the Synoptics do, yet reports it. This Gospel thus may report accurate historical tradition that in the earliest stage of Jesus' ministry, which overlapped with John in a comparable region, Jesus' disciples supervised others' baptisms under his instruction. The author is careful to report that Jesus himself did not practice baptism (Jn 4:2), which might help explain why it does not appear in Synoptic tradition. Further, to outsiders the baptism of Jesus' followers at this stage would have appeared as merely a continuation of the Baptist's practice by one of his former disciples.[113] Even in baptism, the context of John and the subsequent Jesus movement sheds light on Jesus.

Conclusion

Our information from Josephus supports the Gospels' basic portrayals of John's baptism of repentance and martyrdom. That John announced another eschatological figure after him is also consistent with our knowledge of ancient Jewish thought.

Jesus' recent submission to John suggests that he at least in part envisions himself as carrying on his mission. Although we should not rule out originality on Jesus' part, the respective chronologies of John's and Jesus' ministries do not provide for much time for radical shifts in the message and mission between John's execution and that of Jesus. Both prophets summon Israel to repentance, and Jesus follows John's prophetic road to martyrdom at the hands of corrupt authorities over his people.

We turn now to Jesus' Galilean context and his teachings. As we shall see, despite the differences between the two prophets, the bulk of Jesus' teachings in the gospel tradition fit our expectation of one who continues John's mission. Both as sage and prophet, Jesus calls for a new standard of righteousness before God, in the process sometimes challenging the norms of the current political elite and of the traditional religious establishment.

CHAPTER 12

Jesus the Galilean Jew

"At that time Jesus came from Nazareth in Galilee and was baptized in the Jordan under John's supervision."

MARK 1:9[1]

Whatever else we can say about Jesus historically, those who emphasize Jesus' traditional Jewish environment certainly have a far better case than those who compare him especially with Cynic philosophers. Virtually no one today disputes or has any reason to dispute that Jesus was a Jew from Galilee. The later church lacked incentive to invent either his ethnicity or his apparently unpromising origins on Judea's "frontier." In this section I introduce some aspects of Jesus' Galilean Jewish context[2] that I believe are difficult to dispute.

Jesus from Jewish Galilee

Theissen and Merz rightly note that local, Palestinian Jewish coloring pervades our Gospel accounts about Jesus.[3] This color suggests that this material originated not in the Diaspora (or, given its often Galilean and rural character, even in Jerusalem), but most likely during Jesus' ministry, circulated among his earliest Galilean followers. As the Israeli scholar David Flusser noted, "The early Christian accounts about Jesus are not as untrustworthy as scholars today often think. The first three Gospels not only present a reasonably faithful picture of Jesus as a Jew of his own time," but "portray him quite plausibly as a Jewish miracle-worker and preacher"[4] rather than as the object of the church's proclamation.

No one would have invented Jesus' Galilean background. Such a background was obscure to most people in the Diaspora, and Judean critics could employ it as a matter of scorn. This was true partly because of the urban/rural divide in antiquity; Jerusalem and the urban centers where Jesus' movement first spread in the Diaspora would not be predisposed to appreciate the intellectual or cultural world of the Galilean countryside.[5] This contrast even supports the rural, Galilean features of Jesus' ministry by way of the positive use of the "criterion of dissimilarity," since after Jesus' disappearance his movement spread quickly from Jerusalem to other urban centers with less use for rural tradition.

Further, some Judean rabbis questioned Galileans' observance of the law.[6] As we shall note below, their perspective stems especially from prejudice;[7] nevertheless, it suggests that inventing an origin in Galilee would hurt the Jesus movement in Judea. According to the rabbis, regional differences helped determine whether one could trust that food had been properly tithed.[8] As we shall note, Galileans tended to be loyal to the law — but not always to Pharisaic interpretations of the law. In any case, the urban Jerusalem and Diaspora branches of the Jesus movement would hardly have served their own cause by inventing a rural Galilean background for Jesus.[9]

If Jesus was from Jewish Galilee, we may also assume Jesus' Jewish culture and ethnicity.[10] Although a de-Judaized Galilee appealed to "Aryan Christians" who wanted an Aryan Jesus,[11] Jewish sources always portray Galileans (in contrast to the force-converted Idumeans) as full, genuine Jews.[12] Archaeological surveys indicate that Galilee became heavily populated only after the Hasmonean conquests, suggesting Judean settlement there.[13]

In our earlier chapter responding to the "Cynic Jesus" thesis, we noted the Jewishness of even the Galilean city Sepphoris, and still more the countryside around it.[14] Granted, Gentile cities abounded around Galilee[15] and social intercourse occurred.[16] The Upper Galilee had robust commercial ties with Tyre.[17] But Gentiles did not predominate,[18] and Greek cultural influence was far less in Galilee's villages than in urban Jerusalem before 70 CE.[19] Whereas the Upper Galilee included both Jewish and Syrian elements, lower Galilee was nearly completely Jewish by the time of Josephus.[20]

Whereas the Lower Galilee may reflect more hellenized art and speech due to its contact with larger cities,[21] it has been questioned whether it was appreciably more hellenized in other respects.[22] The theater of Sepphoris seated only five thousand, hence at most half of Sepphoris's own population; it was not intended for, nor did it likely attract, Galilean villagers.[23] I suspect that some scholars have overstated the case against hellenization, but their emphasis offers a welcome counterbalance to portraits of rural Galilee that in principle virtually equate it with Athens or Corinth.[24]

What is preserved about Jesus' own ministry reinforces still further this connection with a traditional Palestinian Jewish context. Jesus himself restricted his ministry almost entirely to the Jewish parts of Galilee, apparently avoiding even the two more hellenized Jewish cities Tiberias and Sepphoris.[25]

Galileans and the Law

There is no reason to doubt Jesus' Jewish orthodoxy based on his environment. Later rabbinic opposition to Galilee derives especially from later Babylonian texts[26] (notably after the Palestinian rabbis had settled in Galilee following the abortive Bar Kochba revolt of 132-135 CE), though, as we have noted, some earlier rabbinic texts also question Galileans' observance of the law.[27]

By contrast, first-century sources indicate Galileans' loyalty to the law,[28] and later Palestinian sources can approve Galilean customs even when they differed from the norms of respected rabbis.[29] Moreover, Josephus indicates that most Galileans were loyal to Jerusalem and the priesthood.[30] Although Jerusalem exercised no political control over Galilee, Josephus shows that its status as Judaism's center gave it special influence.[31]

Archaeology confirms Jewish Galileans' "Jewishness" and "orthodox" practice.[32] Stone vessels, which were considered less susceptible to impurity,[33] predominate, and are common even in pre-70 Sepphoris.[34] Distinctly Jewish purification pools are common, again even in Sepphoris; so are distinctive Jewish burial practices such as ossuaries.[35] Studies of Galilean bones show pork-free diets, and pig remains are missing in pre-70 Jewish Galilee.[36]

Galileans apparently shared with Judeans religious customs and some elements of material culture, but differed in some other aspects of culture, such as wealthy Jerusalemites' decorations and foreign styles.[37] That is, they were likely if anything more culturally conservative, rather than more culturally liberal, than Judeans.

Galileans and Jesus vs. Pharisees?

Some argue that charismatic teachers, less amenable to traditional restrictions than Pharisaic scribes were, may have been more common in Galilee than Pharisees were.[38] Galileans were loyal to the Jerusalem Temple, but not particularly loyal to the Pharisees or their successors (probably accounting for some subsequent rabbinic calumnies).[39] Even in the second century, Galilee did not accept the predominantly Judean Pharisees' or rabbis' leadership.[40] The rabbis tried to control Galilean Jewry purely in religious matters, but Galileans generally did not accommodate them even here.[41] Jesus was probably not the only conservative Galilean Jew to run into conflicts with Pharisees or the Jerusalem elites, though he may have had one of the larger followings.

Galileans and the Zealot Jesus?

If Jesus' Galilean context might explain some of his popularity vis-à-vis the usual Judean popularity of the Pharisees, it does not lend any specific support to the idea, briefly surveyed early in this book, that Jesus was a revolutionary. "Judas the Galilean" (Acts 5:37), leader of the infamous and ill-fated tax revolt during Jesus' childhood, was naturally considered Galilean (though not actually born there).[42] This association does not, however, mean that Galileans were particularly predisposed toward revolution, as some have suggested.[43]

The "revolutionary Galilean" approach neglects considerable evidence.[44] When Josephus' rhetoric is taken into account,[45] Galilee was clearly unprepared at the time of the first revolt; it hardly proved an ideal base for Zealot sympathizers.[46] Sepphoris, in fact, refused to join the revolt of 66-70 (perhaps recalling its earlier destruction under the Roman governor Varus). Further, the messianic uprisings of Theudas, the Samaritan, and the Egyptian prophet that Josephus reports neither transpired near Galilee nor boasted explicit Galilean support.[47]

Life in Galilee

Although ancient population estimates are always precarious, estimates of Galilee's population around three-quarters of a million[48] probably at least offer a general order of magnitude to work with.[49]

Literary and archaeological sources both suggest a cultural distinction between upper Galilee (the Golan) and lower Galilee. The latter included larger and more culturally mixed urban areas; although most of its inhabitants lived in villages, the wider cultural diversity in Galilee's cities must have regularly influenced the villages to some degree.[50] Nevertheless, Galilee as a whole had some homogenous cultural characteristics.[51] Moreover, archaeological and literary evidence confirm that the heavy population of the lower Galilee was primarily rural and agricultural,[52] and villages, despite outside cultural influences, were mainly autonomous politically and economically.[53] The wider ancient Mediterranean clash between urban and rural life obtained in Galilee as well,[54] though it should not be exaggerated.[55]

Virtually Certain Information about Jesus

Our knowledge about Galilee constitutes part of Jesus' context. Some information the Gospels offer specifically about Jesus' Galilean environment provides an even more detailed context for what we can say about him.

Jesus Was from Nazareth

No one would *invent* Nazareth as a background for Jesus. As we noted earlier in the book, Nazareth is too insignificant a site[56] for tradition to have invented;[57] indeed, such a place of origin could count against one's credibility (cf. Jn 1:46).[58] (It is rarely disputed today; that Jesus was from Nazareth is multiply, independently attested.)[59]

Likewise, despite the appeal to the rejected-prophet motif after the fact, no one would invent Jesus' rejection in his home town. Nevertheless, this home-village disdain may fit its village gossip lifestyle just as Jerusalem's less informed but swift execution of Jesus would have fit the city's expected disdain for a country prophet.

Jesus Ministered among Fishing Villages

No one would make up fishing villages as sites of a great person's ministry. Granted, they had at least more strategic value than most Galilean villages, but this is not saying much. Capernaum proved a more suitable site for Jesus' ministry than smaller Nazareth would have. Capernaum was walking distance from both Perea and Philip's territories across the Jordan.[60] But while Capernaum may have been locally significant, it would not appear particularly significant to urban audiences elsewhere in the Roman Empire. Estimates for Capernaum's population have ranged as high as 12,000,[61] but the current estimate is closer to 1000-2000 people.[62] No one in either Jerusalem or the Diaspora would make up such a town as a strategic site for the Messiah's ministry.[63]

That Capernaum appears so often in stories about Jesus (e.g., Matt 8:5//Lk 7:1; Mk 2:1) may suggest that someone was interested in preserving tradition about this small town — perhaps some of Jesus' own disciples who lived there.[64] Jesus' denunciation of Capernaum's limited responsiveness in "Q" (Matt 11:23// Lk 10:15) would also hardly appear relevant to later believers and is unlikely to have been invented.

Jesus' association with Capernaum is multiply attested in various strata of tradition (e.g., Mk 1:21; 2:1; Matt 4:13; Lk 4:31; Jn 2:12), including "Q" (Matt 8:5//Lk 7:1). Although Jesus continued to be identified by his place of reputed origin (Nazareth), as was customary, Jewish tradition supports the notion that even outsiders could also come to view him as a resident of Capernaum in time.[65] That Capernaum appears in later rabbinic accounts solely in connection with "schismatics," presumably in this case Jesus' followers,[66] suggests that Jesus' missionary strategy there was ultimately successful. Archaeology attests the early Christian presence there, including a house that many scholars believe is the actual house of Peter that figures in the Gospels.[67]

In "Q," Jesus denounces "Chorazin" and "Bethsaida" (Matt 11:21; Lk 10:13).[68] Theissen[69] notes that whereas Bethsaida was well known,[70] Chorazin is otherwise barely known apart from modern excavations there.[71] Some argue that few Greek and Roman authors except Pausanias knew much of the cities around the Lake of Galilee, including Bethsaida;[72] others contend that Bethsaida was forgotten after the Roman destruction in 70.[73] Later Christians would lack incentive to invent such a tradition about either site.

Moreover, Bethsaida was renamed "Julia" after 30 CE. Whereas Josephus in the late first century calls it by both names, the Gospels call it only "Bethsaida," its name during Jesus' public ministry. That is, the Gospels do not switch to the name current in the period when the tradition was being passed on, but preserve only and precisely the name that was used during Jesus' Galilean ministry, which ended about 30 CE.[74]

Nor is the oracle against these villages easily attributed to the later church on other grounds. The prophecy does not reflect later Christian preaching[75] and may reflect signs of an Aramaic origin.[76] Because the same oracle claims that Tyre and Sidon would have repented had they had the same opportunities as these villages, it may presuppose lack of Christian communities in Tyre and Sidon, in contrast to the situation that obtained by the late 50s at the latest.[77] That Jesus uttered such oracles against these Galilean fishing villages seems the most logical conclusion.

Returning to Capernaum: what is true of these villages is also true of the oracle against Capernaum in the same context in "Q" (Matt 11:23//Lk 10:15). Later Christians probably would have been loath to fabricate opposition to Jesus' ministry in his adopted town.[78] Indeed, far from testifying that the saying is a later Christian invention,[79] Capernaum's unrepentance suggests that the saying dates to Jesus' lifetime, since, as we have noted, Capernaum later became a center of Galilean Christianity.

Jesus Called Fishermen

No one would invent rural Galilee, fishermen, or tax gatherers. We have already noted that the elites of the empire held little respect for peasants. Fishermen were not peasants,[80] but probably often were, like tax-gatherers, "among the more economically mobile of the village culture."[81] Nevertheless, they were not elite. Mere propagandists wishing to impress outsiders might have been happy to cite respectable adherents close to Herod (cf. Lk 8:3; Acts 13:1), who might have impressed the entire range of ancient society. By contrast, the example of fishermen could appeal only to the working class themselves.

Yet fishermen involved with Jesus also fit the criterion of Palestinian environment (here more narrowly the "criterion" of Galilean fishing villages such as Capernaum and Bethsaida). Although the primary occupation even on the lake of Galilee was agricultural,[82] fishing remained a major industry there,[83] and fish was a primary staple of the first-century Palestinian diet,[84] as elsewhere in Mediterranean antiquity.[85] Fishing imagery in Jesus' parables fits a Galilean setting. (Thus, for example, the parable about the end-time involving a seine net and the separation of edible, perhaps kosher fish from inedible ones; Matt 13:47-50.)[86]

That Jesus would call fishermen, therefore, should arouse no skepticism. Davies and Allison list a number of points favoring the historical tradition behind the section,[87] which I adapt only slightly below:

(1) The Synoptics and John attest, probably independently, that Peter and Andrew followed Jesus in Galilee.

(2) Other "Q" narratives confirm that Jesus, in contrast to most rabbis, called his own disciples (Matt 8:19-22//Lk 9:57-62), Jesus' practice here probably follows the model of Elijah (1 Kgs 19:19-21), which plays a comparatively minimal role in rabbinic texts.[88]

(3) The tradition of the Twelve attests that he did choose disciples whom he expected to aid his mission (like other teachers, he expected disciples to propagate the work).

(4) The structure of Mk 1:17 is "recognizably Semitic" and the saying makes sense only as part of the narrative.

(5) No one had reason to invent the four's occupation as fishermen (Mk 1:16; cf. Jn 21:3), and Andrew, who is not central in Synoptic or Pauline tradition, must appear for more historical reasons.

Ben Witherington adds some other observations. For example, "fishers of humans" is hardly a later Christian image for mission, yet the metaphor makes sense if some of Jesus' earliest disciples were fishermen. The narrative also hardly drew the image of Jesus recruiting disciples from Jewish practice (it was neither traditional Jewish nor subsequent Christian practice); finally, Luke 5:10 attests the "fishers of humans" saying in a different context and form, perhaps supporting the saying's authenticity by means of multiple attestation.[89] Some of the above arguments are more convincing than others, but cumulatively the most convincing of them offer a very strong case.

Conclusion

Most of the Gospels' portraits of Jesus fit his Galilean milieu. He likely grew up in Nazareth and moved to Capernaum. We cannot infer from such a milieu that Jesus was extremely hellenized, that he was disloyal to the law, or even that he was predisposed toward revolution. From this milieu we can conclude, with the Gospels, that some of Jesus' first disciples were likely fishermen. This Galilean Jew was not a Cynic and not likely a Pharisee (despite some shared common ground with Pharisees); he was, however, a sage, and plausibly a charismatic one.

CHAPTER 13

Jesus the Teacher

"A disciple does not outrank his teacher, nor a slave his or her slaveholder; it suffices for a disciple to become like his teacher, and a slave like a master . . ."

MATTHEW 10:24-25

When people in antiquity spoke or wrote about teachers, one of the main subjects of discussion was naturally the teachers' sayings. Ancient historians rarely could provide more than plausible reconstructions of speeches, offering the semblance of what was known or supposed to have been said on a particular occasion. By contrast, notable sayings of famous sages often circulated and were memorized and passed on. Interested followers or admirers sometimes gathered these sayings into collections or included them in related narratives. When the sages were recent, one could expect the sayings to reflect genuine tradition about the speaker (though not usually in order).

In this chapter I will introduce Jesus the sage, a role that the majority of scholars today accept regardless of their views on other issues (such as Jesus' eschatology). I will focus especially on Jesus' use of parables, a form distinctive to Jesus in our first-century Christian sources, and show how these parables fit a first-century Palestinian Jewish context. Indeed, examining other Jewish parables demonstrates that even the parable *interpretations* in the Gospels can be understood within a first-century Jewish context much more readily than many earlier scholars supposed.

We know much about Jesus' teachings. Scholars differ over the details, but without reconstructing Jesus' precise words, scholars can gather enough evidence from our sources to speak of Jesus' purpose and mission.[1]

Jesus as a Sage

Although a gap exists between prototypical sages of traditional wisdom like Joshua ben Sira on one hand and local legal experts on the other,[2] many people apparently expected popular teachers to straddle the continuum, and many teachers accommodated such expectations.[3] But while Jesus does debate the law with legal experts in our sources, the dominant ethos of his teaching seems to focus less on legal and scribal matters than it combines the role of wisdom teacher with (as we shall see later) that of prophet.

The case should not be overstated. Some scholars today, emphasizing that Jesus was a charismatic leader of some sort, are reticent to call Jesus a teacher of the law.[4] It is true that Jesus was not part of what later became the rabbinic movement, nor was he *merely* a Jewish scribe or ancient Near Eastern wisdom sage.[5] But many other early sages traveled,[6] and it is unlikely that Galilean Jews who saw themselves as faithful to God's law would have made a hard-and-fast distinction among categories like charismatic sage, teacher of wisdom and teacher of Scripture.[7]

Some doubt that Jesus would have used implicit quotations, opining that few Galileans would have been educated enough to catch them.[8] Yet this view probably underestimates the biblical literacy of Galileans (perhaps acceding too much to Judean propaganda in early rabbinic sources), who presumably regularly heard Scripture in local synagogues. Jesus' contemporaries did not shun such allusions aimed for those who would catch them;[9] given his movement's direction over time, it seems implausible that later *Gentile* Christians added the allusions.[10] By contrast, and, I think, more accurately, other scholars have shown that Jesus did use Scripture extensively.[11]

Although many others besides scribes undoubtedly expounded Scripture in first-century synagogues,[12] Jesus' frequent teaching in synagogues suggests that many viewed him as an authoritative teacher, though not as an ordained rabbi in the later sense.[13] Most scholars note that many characteristics of Jesus' ministry fit expectations for sages and scribes, and whatever else Jesus may have been, he was clearly a Jewish teacher of one or both types as well.[14]

Jesus and Sages' Style

Jesus was distinctive in some respects.[15] Each teacher had some unique or characteristic elements in his style,[16] and many scholars have commented on specific characteristics of Jesus' teaching style, some unique to him and others common to ancient Jewish teachers in general.[17] (For instance, few if any other teachers sometimes prefaced their words with, "Amen [Truly], I tell you.")[18]

By contrast, some other elements of Jesus' style are characteristic of his

contemporaries in general.[19] Most rhetorical forms in biblical wisdom literature, such as proverbs and riddles, continued among sages of Jesus' day.[20] Jewish teachers typically employed the rhetorical techniques of hyperbole and rhetorical overstatement.[21]

Unfortunately for some of his subsequent interpreters, Jesus employed this
same evocative, engaging teaching style, regularly seeking to evoke specific responses rather than to provide direct proof-texts for subsequent theological
systems.[22] Modern interpreters often find his sayings hopelessly contradictory
and incoherent when we fail to familiarize ourselves with catchy figures of Jewish speech, expecting instead developed doctrinal pronouncements.

We find even exact parallels to some of his language among Jewish teachers.[23] For example, Jesus often introduces parables with precisely the same language documented in later rabbis. Jesus' phrases like "To what shall I compare . . . ?" (Matt 11:16//Lk 7:31; also Lk 13:18, 20)[24] and "So-and-so is like" (e.g.,
Mk 4:26, 31; 13:34; Matt 11:16; 13:24; 25:1; Lk 6:48-49)[25] both appear regularly in
later Jewish sources. These later sources undoubtedly did not borrow them
from Jesus, so Jesus and the later rabbis undoubtedly reflect a common pattern
already used by sages in Jesus' era.

As we noted earlier, much of Jesus' audience must have also consisted of
rural, agrarian peasants. More than in the settings of many later rabbinic parables,[26] the settings of the majority of Jesus' extant parables reflect an agrarian
environment.[27]

The Teller of Jewish Parables

Although some styles of rhetoric spanned numerous cultures, one sort of Jewish teaching style is fairly distinctively Jewish.[28] Greek animal fables are somewhat comparable, but Jesus' stories are almost always about human (rather than
animal) actors, and bear many traits reflecting their Jewish and often even rural
Galilean flavor.[29] Although later Christians employed illustrations, they were
usually the sort of illustrations characteristic of the Greek world, not the sort of
story parables at home specifically in Jewish Palestine.[30]

By normal historical standards, then, we should give special attention to
parables in the Gospels as among the least debatable, most securely authentic
elements of the Jesus tradition.[31] In this section, I will spend more time showing Jewish elements in some of the parables than in discussing Jesus' message,
which has been amply done by others. For most Gospels scholars, however, it
can almost go without saying that a major theme in many of the Gospel parables (and certainly in our first extant Gospel, Mark) is God's kingdom, a theme
that we will explore briefly later.

Story Parables as a Jewish Form

What is a parable? The range for the Greek term for "parable" in the Gospels roughly translates the sense of the Hebrew term *mashal.*[32] The Septuagint (the standard Greek version of the Old Testament dominant in Jesus' day) translates *mashal* in different ways, but in several texts it translates it as *parabolē.*[33] The *mashal* includes a variety of types of discourse, including stories (e.g., Ezek 24:2-5; cf. fable in Judg 9:7-15), proverbs (e.g., 1 Sam 24:13), taunt-songs (Is 14:4), and riddles (Ezek 17:2).[34] Jewish hearers were thus accustomed to a variety of parables, and this range of forms overlaps significantly with those teachings of Jesus designated "parables" in the Gospels. But in rabbinic literature, the *mashal* specifically includes the kind of story parables told by both Jesus (e.g., Mk 4:3-8; 12:1-9) and later rabbis.[35] This suggests that between the Septuagint and the time of the rabbis, a parable of the sort that Jesus told would already be recognized as a *mashal* (as attested later by the rabbis), which would naturally be rendered into Greek as *parabolē* (as attested by the Septuagint).[36]

Although Gentiles also used analogies, metaphor, allegory, and riddles,[37] the source of Jesus' storytelling style is plainly not primarily Greek.[38] Story parables are a largely Jewish phenomenon.[39] Parables appear in the biblical prophets (2 Sam 12:1-7; Is 5:1-7),[40] in some apocalyptic literature[41] and some other Jewish texts,[42] but were especially common property of the sages.[43]

The closest formal and linguistic parallels to Jesus' parables, however, occur in Middle Eastern rabbinic texts, i.e., later records of how Jewish teachers customarily reasoned and taught.[44] This close similarity seems the consensus of scholars directly familiar with both sets of parables.[45] Although rabbinic parables are midrashic, hence more stereotyped, examination demonstrates considerable formal similarities between rabbinic and Gospel parables, especially morphological but often extending even to stock metaphors and characters.[46]

Our rabbinic parables are admittedly all later than Jesus, though this could not be otherwise, since all rabbinic literature is later than Jesus, as are most of the sages it cites.[47] But because Jesus probably did not influence directly most later rabbis,[48] it appears most logical to infer that both Jesus and these rabbis drew on and adapted standard Palestinian Jewish teaching techniques of their day.[49] Jesus probably occasionally even developed earlier sages' parabolic story lines.[50]

Some differences between the two groups of parables reflect the different sorts of environments addressed by the respective tellers of parables. Whereas the later rabbinic parables often focus on settings such as royal courts, however (as in Matt 18:23; 22:2; 25:34), Jesus most often told stories about agriculture and the daily life of his common hearers,[51] a characteristic that supports authenticity in his Galilean context. Another contrast with rabbinic parables is that Jesus' parables tend to subvert conventional values, whereas those of the rabbis tend to reinforce them.[52] This difference may reflect also the contrast between Jesus' prophetic role and the function of educated legal experts. Jesus' parables are also far more apt to emphasize eschatology,[53] though it is possible that this difference might reflect the situation of Palestinian Jewish thought after the failure of the Bar Kochba revolt more than it reflects a divergence of interests in Jesus' day.

Except when reporting Jesus' parables, other New Testament writers, usually addressing urban communities outside Palestine, do not employ such parables. Because later Christians would therefore not have invented Jesus' parables, most scholars accept their authenticity as genuine teachings of Jesus.[54]

Limited Adaptation, not Wholesale Creation

Authenticity, of course, does not preclude adaptation, which was common in retelling stories. Later tellers altered characters in earlier rabbinic parables and otherwise adapted them to speak to new situations.[55] Likewise, embellishment was natural to the folklorish context in which parables were transmitted.[56] But rabbinic literature preserved parables primarily because of the story lines and morals themselves, whereas the gospel tradition preserved parables because they were *Jesus'* parables. Thus we should not expect the same measure of adaptation in Jesus' recorded parables.

Moreover, rabbinic tradition preserved and recycled some parables over the course of many generations and even centuries, a period of transmission not comparable to the period informing our written Gospels. As noted in our discussion of the Gospels' sources, the process of transmission behind our extant Gospels was much briefer than that in rabbinic literature, and the relatively controlled conditions do not lend themselves to a great deal of folklorish embellishment. In this early period we should probably usually think of more conservative adaptations[57] (compare Matthew's and Luke's conservative adaptations of Mk 4:3-20), while allowing for reapplication of parables in new contexts (e.g., Matt 5:15 with Mk 4:21//Lk 8:16). These observations do not suggest that the evangelists invented wholly new parables that they then attributed to Jesus.

Parable Settings in the Gospels

Some scholars suggest that some of the parable settings may have been transmitted along with the traditions to which they were attached.[58] In rabbinic parables one might expect an attribution and an application, but rarely a description of the setting in which the teaching was uttered; still, rabbinic analogies may break down here, since rabbinic texts usually stress the rabbis' teaching more than their person, whereas the gospel tradition is interested in both. It is thus possible that Jesus may have spoken many parables on specific occasions mentioned in the Gospels. An inductive approach would test this best, and one such study concludes that Synoptic writers almost invariably claim the same audience for the same parables, with but two exceptions that could conceivably represent different parables.[59] Some settings also make good local sense; like a cove near Capernaum, many natural acoustic settings existed in Galilee that would enable thousands to hear the voice of someone properly positioned.[60]

At the same time, it is likely that Jesus spoke parables in a variety of settings (e.g., Mk 3:23; 4:2; 7:15, 17; 12:1; 13:28), and many of his parables were collected into arrangements like those in the Gospels. Parables tend to occur in bunches in later Jewish texts as well.[61] Neither the Gospels nor their sources were under obligation to report the occasions on which Jesus told parables, and ancient writers had considerable freedom to rearrange material to fit their purposes.[62] Also some parables scholars note that, "Like the gospel parables, the same rabbinic parable may appear in different contexts far removed from one another."[63]

Parable Interpretations in the Gospels

Where the Gospels offer interpretations for Jesus' parables, many scholars have traditionally argued that those interpretations are later elements in the reports about Jesus. While this perspective dominated much of the twentieth-century consensus on Jesus' parables, it completely conflicted with the most thorough research on Jewish parables: other Jewish parables frequently include interpretations. As scholars have increasingly worked with early Jewish parables, they have increasingly recognized the likelihood that Jesus could have offered interpretations alongside his parables.

Jewish teachers normally used parables as sermon illustrations to explain a point they were teaching.[64] By contrast, some writers attribute many of the Gospels' parables to Jesus but many of the interpretations of the parables to later editors. In light of contemporary Jewish models, their presupposition for this approach is almost certainly mistaken.[65] Even the more distant Greek analogies would tend to challenge skepticism about the interpretations. Many Greek and Roman fables include explicit moral lessons at the beginning[66] or end[67] of the fables; occasionally fables include morals at the beginning and the end.[68]

Of more direct relevance, however, are the Jewish models. Though some are riddles,[69] our earliest Israelite parables usually have interpretations (e.g., Judg 9:16-20; 2 Sam 12:7-9), and rabbinic parables nearly always occur alongside the points they illustrate.[70] Rabbinic parables typically begin with the point to be illustrated and include the nimshal (application or explanation) near the end.[71] Rabbinic sources often include explicit interpretations.[72]

What is *unusual* about Jesus' teaching is not that it includes interpretations, as at times in the Gospels, but that it so often does *not* include them. To offer an illustration without stating the point was like presenting a riddle instead.[73] Yet Jesus was not completely alone even in this practice.[74] Jewish sages sometimes spoke of the "hidden things."[75] The Qumran community believed that God had revealed to its leaders mysteries hidden from other readers of Scripture.[76] Although most mainstream Jewish teachings were available to the public, many Jewish teachers apparently held particular teachings to be too esoteric for public teaching.[77]

Perhaps most relevant for comparison with the case of Jesus' parables are other eschatological Jewish parables. Here explanations can appear, but do not always appear. Even the parable of *4 Ezra* 4:13-18 includes some sort of explanation in 4:20-21. Enoch's eschatological Similitudes[78] remain more mysterious, however, like most of Jesus' public parables about the Kingdom.[79]

"Allegorical" Interpretations

Some complain that several interpretations in the Gospels (such as those in the parable of the four soils, Mk 4:14-20) include multiple points of reference. Many parables scholars traditionally viewed these correspondences as problematic because they followed Adolf Jülicher, who in the late nineteenth and early twentieth century insisted (against previous interpreters) that parables must have one main point.[80] By contrast, against Jülicher's categorization of parables in these strict Aristotelian terms,[81] others drew attention to rabbinic parallels, which revealed weaknesses in Jülicher's line of argument.[82] Jülicher began with deductive categories and imposed them on the Gospel data, whereas his critics' approach was inductive, based on concrete parables.[83] The influential parables scholar C. H. Dodd followed Jülicher, but as one expert in rabbinic parables points out, Dodd's own work unfortunately "betrays not the slightest first-hand acquaintance with rabbinic parables."[84] Another influential parables scholar, Joachim Jeremias, whose knowledge of rabbinic sources might have protected him from the error, admits that he follows Dodd.[85]

Biblical parables could include multiple points of contact with the original audience's situation (e.g., 2 Sam 12:1-6). Noting these correspondences is legitimate and need not be confused with the wanton allegorization practiced in much of Christian history.[86] Rabbinic parables likewise often have allegorical features, with multiple points of interpretation,[87] just as in Jesus' parable of the four soils.

Robert M. Johnston, toward the end of his massive study of the earliest layer of rabbinic parables, thus complains that "The demand that we must choose between one-point-of-comparison 'parable' and every-feature-must-be-decoded 'allegory' is artificial, arbitrary, and unreasonable."[88] The vast majority of these Tannaitic parables would be "allegories, by Jülicher's definition."[89] One of his most important conclusions bears quotation:[90]

> Most importantly, the study of rabbinic parables renders unusable the distinction between parable and allegory in respect to the parables of the gospels: if the parables of Jesus are generically the same as those of the rabbis, which seems inescapable from the standpoint of morphology and inner structure, then the classical Jülicherian model must be discarded as inapplicable to the gospel parables.

There is thus no historical reason to deny the authenticity of parable interpretations of Jesus based on allegorization or multiple extrinsic referents.[91]

Galilean Imagery in Jesus' Parables

As for the Palestinian Jewish setting of the *content* of Jesus' parables, a few images may suffice. The woman baking bread (Matt 13:33//Lk 13:21) can fit Jesus' rural setting: although Roman cities had bakeries, Galilean village women baked their own families' bread.[92] Jesus' use of harvest for the end of the age is likewise relevant: thus one later Jewish writer depicts the end-time as a harvest when the seed of the evil ones and of the good ones is ripe for harvest;[93] a later rabbinic tradition depicts Israel as wheat gathered at the age's end but the wicked nations as the field's straw and stubble to be burned and scattered.[94] In some other Jewish texts, the final harvest would be when God will gather the wicked for judgment.[95]

Although we could look at parables in Mark, I will cite here a few parables that appear only in Matthew to illustrate that, even when not multiply attested, Jesus' parables often show signs of authentic Palestinian tradition. The farmer who sold everything to buy a field with buried treasure in it (Matt 13:44) may fit Palestinian custom revealed in some legal contracts, which could specify the sale of not only the land but of "all that is in it,"[96] freeing him to later "rediscover" the treasure.[97] Jewish teachers also recounted stories that included items like the pearl of great price (Matt 13:46).[98]

More extensively, the parable of laborers in the vineyard appears only in Matthew, but Matthew did not likely invent it. He frames it with a principle in Mk 10:31, that the first will be last and the last first (Matt 19:30; 20:16);[99] yet starting with the principle alone, one could have created a parable that would have illustrated it with a much closer correspondence than a parable about equal pay for unequal labor!

Whatever this parable's point, it clearly resembles the parables of some other Jewish sages. One may for example compare one early rabbinic parable: a king paid other workers a modest wage, but to an especially hard worker, symbolizing Israel, he provided much pay. The rabbis concluded that God repaid Gentiles for their little good in this life, but would repay Israel all she deserved in the coming world.[100]

The setting also fits Galilean life; although some of the following features could fit rural life anywhere in the Empire, the Christian movement outside Galilee started in cities throughout the Empire, only gradually and slowly spreading to the countryside. Rural features of the Jesus tradition would thus tend to be early.

Other features in this parable tend to fit this setting. Vineyards[101] and hirelings were important features of Galilean life in this period.[102] Other Jewish teachers also laid heavy emphasis on fieldowners showing concern for the poor,[103] and, more to the point, could portray God as the master of one's labor, who would pay the reward of one's work.[104] While many Galileans seem to have worked their own fields or crafts,[105] many others were peasants working the estates of a handful of well-to-do absentee landlords.[106] The harvest required an influx of extra workers,[107] for which landowners typically drew on the ranks of the landless poor for such brief and urgent tasks.[108] In Jesus' day the average harvest wages may have been a half drachma or lower,[109] so it could be understood that the landowner in this parable has been generous to all the laborers.[110]

Urban writers who lived on rural estates could write accurately about rural life, but one would not expect as much insight from non-elite Christians in cities outside Galilee as from a storyteller genuinely in touch with the Galilean countryside. Nor would one expect later writers to look for authentic rural features to add to Jesus' teachings; one would not even expect them to focus on such matters. By way of comparison, the later gnostic sayings collections do not typically concern themselves with accumulating such features.

Conclusion

In this chapter I have argued that Jesus' parable-telling practice is authentic, and that we should also accept most parables attributed to him in the Gospels as authentic, barring strong evidence to the contrary. I have not explored the message of Jesus' parables, some of which I will subsume under some general themes regarding Jesus' teaching, to be treated especially in ch. 14.

But it bears mention here that such themes include the kingdom (Mk 4:11). In parables, Jesus' articulation of this theme probably included how it was already at work in Jesus' ministry but yet to be fully consummated. This point appears in Mark's parables of the gradual growth of seed for harvest, and of the mustard seed (Mk 4:26-32). It is probably also the point of Q's parable of the woman's leaven (Matt 13:33//Lk 13:20-21).[111] Parables also proclaimed both that the end (or at least, some sort of judgment) was imminent (Mk 13:28-29; perhaps Matt 5:25-26//Lk 12:58-59), although that the precise time was unknown (Mk 13:33-37). As we shall see later, a surely authentic parable also includes the conviction that Jesus as God's agent, more special than earlier prophets, would meet a prophet's fate in confronting the guardians of Israel, i.e., the Jerusalem elite (Mk 12:1-12). This seems to suggest a connection between Jesus' beliefs about his identity and the inauguration of God's kingdom.

CHAPTER 14

Kingdom Discipleship

"Whoever wants to belong to my movement must deny themselves, accepting their shameful execution and following me [to death]."

MARK 8:34

Putting Jesus in his Palestinian Jewish context will help us to recognize that the later Gospels do in fact preserve much of the voice of the "historical Jesus." I sought to provide an early Jewish setting for most of Jesus' words in Matthew in my commentary on that work; here I merely survey some important examples from that and other research.

Because there are too many available examples for a single chapter, I am treating some themes relating to the kingdom and the radical demands of discipleship in this chapter, while deferring Jesus' ethical teaching and legal controversies for the next two chapters. The distinction is artificial: ethics belong to Jesus' demands for discipleship, and the priority of preparing the kingdom undoubtedly exercises at least some effect on the other categories.

Preaching the Kingdom

Because virtually every stratum of Gospel tradition testifies that Jesus regularly announced the kingdom, there should be no doubt that this was a characteristic emphasis of Jesus' teaching.[1]

We do not need to separate preaching of a coming kingdom from its "political" ramifications.[2] Those expecting God to intervene and establish a new order could not but expect the passing of the old, whether or not the proclaimers had a role (direct or indirect) in that transition. Many others who believed that their activity was part of God's end-time plan (probably including insurgents who rose in the countryside in later decades) could be even more hostile to the present order, which appeared to them as clearly *not* an expression of God's reign.

Background for Jesus' Kingdom Preaching

Palestinian Jews were quite familiar with the concept of the kingdom.[3] The Hebrew, Aramaic and Greek terms generally translated "kingdom" usually signify the concept "reign" or "authority" or "rule."[4] Like the Old Testament, Jewish teachers could speak of God's present rule (especially among the people who obeyed his law).[5] But Jewish people also looked for the kingdom as God's future rule, when he would reign unchallenged,[6] as attested in regular Jewish prayers.[7] Because "heaven" was a common Jewish periphrasis for "God,"[8] some other Jewish texts use "kingdom of heaven" as a periphrasis for "kingdom of God."[9] Sometimes they also seem to use "kingdom" as a periphrasis for the divine name.[10]

Jesus' picture of the kingdom, as well as of the Son of Man, might derive especially from Daniel 7, a passage less frequently mined by Jesus' followers than in the Jesus tradition itself.[11] With its collocation of language such as a "mystery" about God's "kingdom," "Son of man," and God's kingdom ending worldly empires, Daniel provided the most fertile (and immediately available) background for Jesus' teachings about the kingdom.[12] In Daniel, God's kingdom intervened at the climax of all earthly kingdoms, in the time of the fourth human kingdom, which ancient interpreters (at least in the Roman period)[13] widely understood as the Roman empire.[14]

Present or Future?

Scholars have often debated whether Jesus emphasized a present or future kingdom. More of the clearest evidence may favor Jesus announcing a future (impending) kingdom.[15] Certainly many of Jesus' contemporaries believed that the current age was drawing to a close and a new era was dawning.[16] Yet many have also noted an emphasis on the presence of the kingdom in the Gospels, especially in the kingdom parables and sayings like the one about entering the kingdom as a child (e.g., Lk 13:18-21; 18:17; Mk 4:26-32; 10:15).[17]

The kingdom's imminence contributed to its present demand. Climaxing the introduction to his Gospel, Mark summarizes Jesus' teaching, as Mark (and perhaps his sources) understood it: "The promised time is now fulfilled! The kingdom has drawn near, so turn to God and trust this promised good news!" (Mk 1:15). Jesus' proclamation here probably implies that the kingdom "has drawn near"[18] rather than "has arrived,"[19] but in either case the sense of its intrusive imminence compels an immediate response.[20]

Elsewhere, in "Q" material,[21] Jesus claims that his expulsion of demons by God's finger (Lk 11:20; cf. Matt 12:28)[22] proves that God's kingdom has come on them.[23] Some think that the kingdom has already "come" in some sense in this verse;[24] those who disagree often view it as at least quite imminent.[25] This means that the earlier gospel tradition, and probably Jesus himself, envisioned Jesus' exorcisms as a sign of God's impending reign.[26] This end-time interpretation of Jesus' exorcisms lacks parallels in magical exorcism texts.[27] That it also lacks substantial parallels in Jewish messianic and end-time expectation[28] may support the authenticity of the saying; early Christians had no other available source for the idea than Jesus himself, whom all our strata portray as an innovator.[29]

One of the clear texts supporting a future kingdom appears in the pre-Synoptic form of Jesus' kingdom prayer (Matt 6:9-13//Lk 11:2-4), which most scholars accept as authentic.[30] A minority of scholars, like Crossan, deny the prayer's authenticity, suggesting that if Jesus taught this prayer to his followers it should show up in more than two Gospels and in "a more uniform version."[31] Yet *how* wide the attestation we should expect for any given tradition is a subjective judgment. Indeed, we should count ourselves fortunate to have any attestation for the prayer since we have no early Christian hymnbook. By comparison, Qumran hymns from the Teacher of Righteousness (the community's founder) turn up only rarely outside Qumran's liturgical documents.

The prayer cannot be an invention of the later Gentile church; it closely echoes the Kaddish (as well as the language of other early Jewish prayers).[32] For that matter, we do have the prayer in another fairly early Christian source (*Did.* 8.2), although this form (unlike the briefer form in Luke) probably depends on Matthew. Yet Crossan needs the prayer to be inauthentic, or at least (as he says) for none of it to be eschatological, to defend his argument that Jesus did not teach a future kingdom.[33] Those not bound to that conclusion need not accept the argument designed to produce it.

If this prayer is authentic, as I believe it is, I believe that we should construe the first lines as eschatological. When Jewish people prayed for God's kingdom to "come," they were not simply invoking God's mystical presence among them for the present time; they were praying for God's future reign to come. If Jesus meant something different from these prayers, it is surprising that he would use precisely the same language they do, leaving the disciples confused regarding his point.[34]

In Mk 8:38–9:1, Jesus is reported to claim, "For anyone who is ashamed of me and my words in this unfaithful and wicked generation, the Son of man will also be ashamed of that person when he comes in his Father's glory with the holy angels. . . . some of those standing here will not taste death until they have witnessed the kingdom having been inaugurated with power." The Synoptics apply the last part of the saying to the transfiguration (Mk 9:2); perhaps it should be understood in terms of inaugurated eschatology. Despite such plausible approaches to the saying, its straightforward sense (some of Jesus' disciples surviving until the kingdom comes) does not as easily fit the experience of the later church. They would not likely have invented a saying so easily construed as contrary to their experience regarding at least most of the original disciples.[35] Some contend that multiple attestation also supports the authenticity of this saying.[36]

Balancing Present and Future Aspects

If one examines the entire evidence available in the Gospels, the kingdom appears to exhibit both present and future elements, as is widely recognized today.[37] Eventually Jesus' first followers, once they believed that Jesus would need to come back to establish his kingdom fully, affirmed that the anticipated kingdom would arrive in two stages corresponding to Jesus' first and second coming. But could Jesus have conceptualized both present and future aspects of the kingdom? His teachings seem to imply that God's reign was already at work in his ministry (including his exorcisms; Matt 12:28//Lk 11:20) in a comparatively obscure way, yet one that not only foreshadowed but would eventuate in the mighty rule of God on earth (Mk 4:26-32; Matt 13:33//Lk 13:20-21).

If Jesus implied his messiahship in any sense,[38] and spoke of a future son of man, we may thus assume that when he announced the kingdom, he undoubtedly announced God's imminent rule in the final sense (rather than simply God's providential and generally noncontroversial rule over creation or over Israel through the law). He also expected to play a role in this kingdom,[39] already active in a hidden way in the present (because he was a key agent to usher it in). That he both proclaimed an imminent kingdom and trained his disciples to carry on his work suggests that the tension between present and future in the gospel tradition's kingdom teaching may go back to Jesus himself.

Jesus' Community for the Kingdom

Could Jesus have envisioned a community carrying on in an interim between two phases of the kingdom? It is understandable that many scholars believe that he did not, and that the disciples "discovered" this perspective only gradually. One could infer this from Jesus' apparent belief that the end was imminent. Yet while many of Jesus' extant sayings do seem to proclaim an imminent end of the age (at the least in terms of *potential* imminence), other sayings of Jesus suggest a period between his initial mission and the end of the age (Mk 4:15-20, 26-32; 13:5-13 [vs. 13:14-27]).[40] We suggested above that Jesus' own teaching may contain this tension. Perhaps Jesus envisioned a brief period of transition to the future kingdom, common enough in apocalyptic texts.[41]

Ancient teachers regularly established communities of followers to perpetuate their teachings;[42] other Jewish groups planned communities;[43] and culturally relevant evidence (like Jesus' choice of *twelve* disciples) supports the notion that Jesus did as well.[44] Some doubt that Jesus, who expected the kingdom in the near future, could have founded a community;[45] yet Qumran's Teacher of Righteousness, who expected the end of the age in the near future, did just that.

Indeed, we may have a more explicit saying in this regard. Although many scholars find the saying implausible (it appears only in Matthean material), others think that Jesus may have even spoken of building a "community" of followers (Matt 16:18).[46] Some argue that "a Messiah without a Messianic Community" would have been "unthinkable" to contemporary Judaism,[47] and Davies and Allison offer a number of cumulatively noteworthy arguments for the passage's authenticity.[48] Indeed, the example of Qumran shows that a Jewish renewal movement could have employed the very language Jesus does in this passage.[49] We treat this passage in greater detail in discussing Jesus and the twelve in ch. 17.

Modern interpreters' resistance to Jesus' announcement of a future kingdom is sometimes theological. Although most scholars concur that Jesus taught about the kingdom, many find it a concept difficult to translate for those interested in Jesus' teaching today. Some contemporary scholars, who maintain that Jesus' future kingdom is an unrealistic hope for modern people, label the kingdom a myth and translate it into existential language more appropriate for their own academic circles of thought.[50] But their position presupposes modern contempt for apocalyptic thought rather than a detailed historical argument.[51] Further, even on theological terms, a future kingdom hardly appears irrelevant to the persecuted and oppressed, who nurture hope that God's justice will ultimately triumph and vindicate them.[52] Finally, on the historical level, whatever modern readers' application of such passages, it would be naïve to presuppose that the early Jesus movement shared modernity's non-eschatological perspective; had they wanted a noneschatological mode for expressing their convictions, Sadducees and much of Diaspora Judaism offered much more relevant models.[53]

Son of Man

In early Christian literature, "Son of man" appears almost exclusively in sayings attributed to Jesus;[54] it is clearly not a designation for Jesus invented by the later church. In view of the patently Semitic, non-Hellenistic figure of speech involved,[55] the view that the expression originated later, among Hellenists,[56] should be rejected.

Some scholars propose a distinction between the "Son of Man" and Jesus himself based on some of his sayings (Mk 8:38; Lk 12:8). This supposed distinction, however, ignores the common polite Aramaic use of third-person speech for oneself.[57] Sometimes the more generic use of "son of man" might even mean "I" in common usage.[58] Indeed, the alleged distinction can be found in only four sayings; if even one of the many other "Son of Man" sayings is authentic, this distinction between Jesus and the Son of Man would be untenable.[59] Jesus' use of the term allows some ambiguity,[60] however, which might help him to maintain the "messianic secret" (see ch. 18) and delay his own conflict with the politically powerful authorities.

Normally, "Son of Man" was simply good Hebrew and Aramaic for "human one,"[61] and sometimes was used as a circumlocution like "that one."[62] While this broader usage allowed Jesus to maintain sufficient ambiguity to protect himself officially, his eschatological usage probably points to a more specific biblical allusion. On the basis of the more general usage, some scholars reject its eschatological sense in the Gospels.[63] Most, however, recognize that at least some of the Son of Man sayings use the title eschatologically,[64] whether they derive the title's background from Daniel[65] or, on somewhat more debatable evidence, from the Similitudes of *1 Enoch.*[66]

Yet the Similitudes are of uncertain date,[67] and even the phrase's meaning in these sayings is debated. Some argue that Enoch is himself the "son of man" (human one; see *1 En.* 71:14),[68] or even that "son of man" there represents humanity in general.[69] Still, whether representing Enoch or not, the figure in most passages in the Similitudes is an exalted one: the Son of Man was chosen before creation of world,[70] will be worshiped by the whole earth,[71] and will be a light to the Gentiles;[72] he appears to be identified with "my Elect"[73] and "God's Anointed."[74] He sits on the throne of glory as a judge.[75]

In any case, an eschatological usage in the *Similitudes* would probably reflect an interpretation of Daniel,[76] which (as part of common Judaism's basic "canon") circulated even more widely than the widely known traditions of *1 Enoch.* The "Son of Man" in *1 En.* 46:3, the first occurrence in the *Similitudes,* reflects the language of Dan 7.[77]

Meanwhile, scholars debate also the precise sense of Dan 7:13. Some think that the figure of Dan 7:13 is angelic;[78] this is not clear, since the figure is closely identified with the suffering saints of the most high God (Dan 7:18, 21-22). The figure in Daniel 7 may be corporate,[79] but probably reflects a sort of corporate identity between the people (Dan 7:18, 21-22) and their ruler (7:13-14).[80] In any case, the passage was certainly amenable to such an interpretation in the first century.[81]

When the Pharisees think that Jesus "blasphemes" because he forgives sins, Jesus demonstrates the "Son of Man's authority on earth" (Mk 2:10); he likewise claims authority for the Son of Man as "Lord of the Sabbath" (Mk 2:28). The Son of Man's "authority" here may refer to Dan 7:14; in the previous verse the "Son of Man" receives the kingdom and authority. But Jesus' allusion to Daniel 7:13-14 becomes most explicit in Mk 13:26 (addressed to Jesus' disciples) and in Mk 14:62 (address to Jesus' opponents, fully ending Mark's "messianic secret"). It is clear that Mark views the background of Jesus' usage as in Daniel.

Although some scholars have argued that the later church created many or all of Jesus' "Son of Man" sayings,[82] "Son of Man" in early Christian texts appears almost exclusively, as we have noted, on Jesus' lips. The proper, positive use of the criterion of dissimilarity thus would suggest that if *any* title of Jesus is authentic, this one is.[83] Although many scholars agree that Jesus used the title, they dispute the authenticity of one or more of the groups of sayings (especially either suffering or reigning Son of man sayings) in which the title is used. Yet if the title is authentic and barely used by anyone except Jesus, one need not a priori exclude any of the groups of sayings. If Jesus proclaimed a kingdom and implied his messiahship, one especially need not exclude the eschatological sayings.

If the Gospels provide any indication at all, as we have observed, Jesus apparently defined his mission — both its suffering and exaltation — in terms of the Son of Man of Daniel 7:13-14.[84] Daniel's context would explain *both* the suffering and exaltation aspects of the title (cf. Dan. 7:21-22, 25-27), rendering irrelevant any forced choice between their uses.[85] For Mark, the Son of Man who suffered before his exaltation is the forerunner of the community of faith, his audience, now suffering great tribulation at the hands of hostile world-rulers (Mk 13:9-20, 26).[86] Yet because of its more common idiomatic associations, "Son of Man" retains an ambiguity that "Son of God" as a title for a specific person would lack.

The Diaspora audience likely for most or all of our extant Gospels was likely less familiar with Enoch's Similitudes than they would have been with Daniel. The mention of clouds with the Son of man's coming in Mk 13:26 and 14:62 deliberately recalls Dan 7:13.

Radical Demands of Discipleship

Jesus summoned disciples to follow him, making this call more pressing than kin or other social ties, than possessions, or even their lives. To illustrate this emphasis, we will briefly examine his sayings about letting the dead bury their dead; about it being easier to get a camel through a needle's eye than a rich person into the kingdom; and the demand to take up the cross and follow Jesus to death.

The urgency of the kingdom message risked subverting the social order. Yet if Jesus held a prominent role in the kingdom, and if he expected to reign as the "son of man" in any sense, the demand to follow him might prepare for the kingdom in another way. Most of Jesus' demands could fit those of a radical sage, but they would be even more appropriate if he were an eschatological prophet or ruler.

Jesus Summons Disciples

That Jesus actually called disciples to follow him, regardless of the conse-quences for livelihood and social ties (Mk 1:20; 2:14), suggests a perception of his identity quite different from that of the normal Jewish teacher. Normally disciples chose teachers; only the most radical teachers (here a comparison with Cynics and their ilk becomes more relevant than usual) called their own disciples, with the expectation that the disciples would follow.

While Jesus was a traditional Jewish teacher in some respects,[87] he was not *merely* a traditional teacher.[88] As one scholar observes, no one can question that Jesus called disciples;[89] but the evidence indicates that, unlike other teachers, he never trained his disciples to replace him in all respects.[90]

Mark portrays Jesus calling his own disciples rather than waiting for them to come to him (Mk 1:16-20); as we have noted in ch. 12, this call of fishermen probably reflects authentic tradition. Jesus' activity in this narrative differs from the most common practice, since disciples normally chose their teachers rather than the reverse.[91] Early Jewish and Greek tradition most frequently as-sume that disciples are responsible for acquiring their own teachers of the law or philosophy.[92] Despite exceptions, the more radical teachers who, like Jesus, sometimes even rejected prospective disciples (Mk 10:21-22), probably consid-ered the disciple's responsibility so weighty that many of them would have felt it dishonorable for the teacher to seek out the disciple.

Some scholars thus opine that Jesus' seeking out disciples himself thus rep-resents a serious breach of custom, "coming down to their level" socially.[93] Al-though discipleship language in the Gospels is roughly the same as in other ex-tant streams of Jewish tradition,[94] some of Jesus' methods mark him out as a radical teacher on the periphery of the more usual social institution. Probably Jesus selects as his model the prophetic way of choosing one's successor found in 1 Kgs 19:19-21, as at least part of the gospel tradition may have recognized (cf. Lk 9:61-62). As "fishers for people," their mission was primarily to "win back" the lost sheep of Israel,[95] i.e., to serve as the nucleus for Jesus' renewal movement.

Relinquishing Family Ties

The claim that the disciples abandoned their livelihoods to follow Jesus would offer a useful lesson for early hearers of the gospel tradition, like similar accounts in antiquity (many of them likely true).[96] Biographers, historians, and often even rhetoricians used stories that were true to illustrate these lessons, so there is likely historical information here as well as hortatory value.

James and John left behind not only their fishing boat, representing their livelihood, but their father and the family business (Mk 1:20). Likewise, though the disciples apparently later took wives with them on their travels (1 Cor 9:5), this was probably not the case during Jesus' public ministry; none of the women traveling with Jesus' group (Mk 15:40-41; Lk 8:2-3) are said to be the male disciples' wives.[97] Although Galilee was small enough that the disciples could have conceivably returned home regularly, these narratives suggest a style of discipleship more demanding than usual.

Although disciples of rabbis normally remained with their wives during study,[98] later rabbis did praise those who stayed away from home for years of Torah study.[99] The stories are probably fictitious — many teachers forbade leaving one's wife for more than thirty days to engage in Torah study[100] — but the stories probably do presuppose that some Jewish men went away from home to study with famous teachers of the Law.[101] Jesus apparently demanded more in this way than the vast majority of his contemporaries.

In a culture emphatic about familial respect, Jesus taught his disciples that following him took precedence over the approval or even civility of one's family.[102] Some radical philosophers demanded such loyalty to philosophy and some rabbis to Torah, but few teachers demanded such loyalty to *themselves*. Jesus told disciples that whoever loved parents or children more than him were unworthy of him (Matt 10:37//Lk 14:26). Luke's harsher wording ("hating" them) could mean "love less" (Matt 10:37),[103] but is probably original; Jesus undoubtedly employed the more graphic expression as hyperbole, and Matthew has communicated the sense less offensively. Many viewed honoring one's parents as the highest social obligation;[104] even if some spoke of honoring one's teacher more,[105] no Jewish teacher would speak of "hating" one's parents by comparison. God alone was worthy of that role.[106]

Nor did Jesus merely apply such social demands to his disciples; in tradition coherent with his teaching, he followed such demands himself. Jesus relativizes his loyalty to his own family, defining kinship by adherence to God's will more than by genetic relationship (Mk 3:33-35). Because such language could have invited censure against Jesus from later Christians' critics as well as from his own contemporaries,[107] it seems unlikely that later Christians invented it. (That Jesus himself did not mind offending critics may be suggested by other stark sayings familiar in the Jesus tradition; his prophetic role; and the relative brevity of his ministry prior to his execution.)

Moreover, the context of the saying involves the unbelief of Jesus' immediate family. Given the role of "James the Lord's brother" in the later church (Acts 12:17; 15:13; 21:18; 1 Cor 15:7; Gal 1:19; 2:9; Jude 1), one would rather expect the early Christians to have emphasized his virtues and so to avoid the charge of nepotism.[108] The stark portrayal here is not apt to reflect an invention of the early Jewish Christians who honored James. Thus it is likely that Jesus had some conflict with his immediate family regarding his mission, as Mark indicates.

Let the Dead Bury Their Dead

In "Q" material, Jesus declares that following him takes precedence over all social obligations, even those family obligations one's society and religion declare to be ultimate (Matt 8:21-22//Lk 9:59-60). This saying is widely accepted as authentic, particularly due to the positive application of the criterion of dissimilarity; it does not fit the mainstream of early Judaism, Christianity, or Greco-Roman thought.[109]

In this passage, when a prospective disciple requests permission to simply attend to his father's burial before following Jesus, the latter replies, "Let the dead bury their dead." This striking response may represent a typically sage-like sort of catchy saying[110] probably meaning, "Let the 'spiritually dead' see to such concerns."[111] Others suggest, "Let the other physically dead persons in the tombs see to your physically dead father," a manifest impossibility characteristic of Jesus' typically shocking and graphic style to emphasize that this is no business of the living disciple's.[112]

Despite the graphic language, Jesus' demand may prove less harsh in some respects than it sounds at first. The prospective disciple is probably not asking permission to attend his father's funeral later that day; his father more likely either was not yet dead or had been buried once already. When a person died, mourners would gather, the body would be prepared, and a funeral procession would take the body to the tomb immediately (cf. Mk 5:35, 38; Lk 7:12), leaving little opportunity for family members to be away making promises to sages. For a week afterward, the family would remain mourning at home and not go out in public.[113] But father and son might wish to be together before the father died,[114] and Semitic idioms in other languages might suggest that "I must first bury my father" could function as a request to wait until one's father dies — perhaps for years — so that one may fulfill the ultimate filial obligation before leaving home.[115]

A custom practiced only in the decades immediately surrounding the time of Jesus might illumine this passage more directly, however. In Jesus' day the eldest son would return to the tomb a year after the father's death to "rebury" his father by arranging his now bare bones in a container and sliding it into a slot on the wall. If the father has died, this young man cannot refer to his father's initial burial (which would be underway at that moment), hence must be asking for as much as a year's delay for a secondary burial.[116]

Then again, if Jesus' demand sounds less urgent than we might suppose, in respect to priorities it proves more demanding than it at first sounds to modern western readers. The offense lies not in the immediacy of the demand but in the priority the demand takes over family obligations,[117] the kind of demand God made of biblical prophets.[118] Many Jewish people considered honoring parents the supreme commandment,[119] and considered burial of one's parents one of the most important implications of that commandment regardless of the circumstances.[120]

A few teachers did insist that disciples honor their teachers above their parents,[121] but for a young man in his thirties (as Jesus apparently was)[122] to seek such honor would be considered presumptuous and shameful.[123] Moreover, such teachers never envisioned anything as dramatic as neglecting the parents' burial. When sages figuratively placed demands for the honor of sages higher than those of one's parents, it was to emphasize the importance of Torah study, but they would never have placed even the urgency of Torah study above the urgency of burying a parent who had died,[124] and presumably would have avoided dishonoring or disobeying living parents by any means possible.[125]

In most current interpretations of biblical law, only one person's honor took precedence over the honor shown to parents: God's.[126] Jesus does insist on honoring parents (Mk 7:6-13); yet he demands a greater affection toward himself. A disciple cannot simply "move on" from him after several years, as with some other teachers, and count it a profitable learning experience.[127] In a saying generally deemed authentic, Jesus scandalously claims the supreme position of attention in his followers' lives.

Relinquishing Belongings

Jesus urged someone with many possessions to sell them and give the proceeds to the poor (Mk 10:17-22, what we often call the story of the "rich young ruler"). This demand coheres with Jesus' invitation to disciples to give their resources and store up treasures in heaven (Matt 6:19-21//Lk 12:33) and various other sayings (e.g., Matt 10:9//Lk 9:3; Mk 4:19; 10:25; Lk 12:16-21; 14:33), including an almost indisputable one using Aramaic (Matt 6:24//Lk 16:13).[128] It coheres also with the calling of the disciples (treated above) and other narratives in the Gospels (Mk 1:16-20; 10:28).[129]

The particular story in question probably reflects authentic tradition, with a sufficiently graphic point to invite some disciples' memory of the occasion. The ruler's opening question, "What shall I do to obtain eternal life?" (Mk 10:17) seems to have been the sort of practical question one could address to a religious teacher.[130] That Jesus appears to reject the title "good" in this story, attributing that title to God alone, is not likely a response that the later church would have invented.[131]

The demands also fit the positive use of the criterion of dissimilarity. While some later Christians did take Jesus' words literally, these again are probably not the sort of words that the Christian community designed for itself. It would also sound radical in a mainstream Jewish context in the first century (though not among the wilderness Essenes).[132] Nevertheless, as general advice (rather than the specific call to a wealthy person), it would make sense within an eschatological and/or wisdom framework.[133]

A Needle's Eye

When Jesus' demand dissuades the prospective disciple from following, Jesus warns that a rich person can enter the kingdom no more easily than a camel can pass through a needle's eye (Mk 10:25). The multiplicity of subsequent attempts to tone down Jesus' radical language here[134] shows the discomfort with this saying among subsequent Christians (who often had means or valued supporters who did). Granted that Jesus' saying may be intended as shocking hyperbole to seize attention on a particular occasion,[135] it is also characteristic of Jesus' teaching style.

Jesus apparently employs a common figure of speech when he speaks of a camel passing through a needle's eye. In Babylonia, where the largest land animals were elephants, Jewish teachers could depict what was impossible or close to impossible as "an elephant passing through a needle's eye";[136] in Palestine, where the largest land animal and beast of burden was a camel,[137] describing the impossible as a "camel passing through a needle's eye" may have been a common expression as well.[138] The criterion of Palestinian environment supports the wording; the criterion of coherency with Jesus' other radical sayings supports Jesus speaking in this way. Given the eschatological urgency (characteristic of the Jesus tradition) that adapts the more traditional saying, Vermes thinks the saying authentic.[139]

Taking Up the Cross

"Taking up one's cross" (Mk 8:34; Matt 10:38//Lk 14:27; cf. Jn 12:25) in antiquity hardly meant the relatively minor burdens assumed by many popular readers of the text today. It meant marching on the way to one's execution, shamefully carrying the heavy horizontal beam (the *patibulum*) of the instrument of one's own execution through the midst of a sometimes jeering mob.[140] Under less controlled circumstances, the mobs themselves could tear people apart.[141] Jesus anticipated literal martyrdom for himself (Mk 8:31) and many of his followers by the Romans' standard means of executing lower-class criminals and slaves; talk about his kingdom could appear ultimately incompatible with Rome's claims.[142] If disciples "come after" and imitate their teacher, their lives are forfeit from the moment they begin following him.

Jesus added that his followers must abandon preserving their life in this world if they hoped to preserve it in the world to come (Mk 8:35-38). Jesus' contemporaries would understand that losing one's life in this age would be a small price to preserve it in the eternal age to come.[143]

Together, such radical demands of Jesus regarding relinquishing or relativizing family ties, possessions and one's own life suggest the urgency of the kingdom that overturns the ordinary worldly expectations. (Even some more traditional Jewish teachers allowed that prophets could temporarily overturn regulations of the law for national emergencies.[144] The imminence of the kingdom would certainly constitute such an emergency.) Moreover, most of these demands specifically involve following Jesus himself, suggesting that he viewed his ministry as more than that of an ordinary sage or even healer. Following him was an urgent demand of the kingdom; presumably he believed that he acted as a divine agent of God's impending kingdom. Following God in this time thus would include following Jesus himself. Such demands would fit expectations of a new Moses or other eschatological prophetic leader (cf. ch. 17; as well as some other eschatological roles such as the messianic king, discussed in ch. 18).

Eschatological Inversion

Mark and "Q" cohere in emphasizing Jesus' teaching about an eschatological inversion — the exaltation of the lowly and the humbling of the proud. In Mark, Jesus warned that the first would be last, and the last first (Mk 10:31; cf. Matt 19:30; 20:8, 16; Lk 13:30). In the saying's context, those who sacrificed everything for the kingdom in the present would be exalted in the kingdom, supplanting the prosperous of this age (Mk 10:21-30).[145]

In "Q," Jesus claimed that whoever exalted themselves would be humbled, and whoever humbled themselves would be exalted (Matt 23:12//Lk 14:11). In both Matthew and Luke, the contexts involve seating and personal honor.[146] Jesus here evokes a biblical concept, including prophetic imagery involving impending judgment in Isaiah,[147] and the language does fit Jesus' contemporary Jewish environment as well.[148] Eschatological inversion more generally was also a widespread Jewish expectation.[149]

It is Jesus' particular application of this expectation in his ministry that is frequently distinctive. For example, Jesus declares that the kingdom belongs to children (Mk 9:37; 10:14-15) — to those lowly in status and dependent on the heavenly Father (cf. Matt 6:8-9//Lk 11:2; Matt 7:7-11//Lk 11:11-13). This portrait fits many texts about depending on God the way that flowers or birds do (Matt 6:28-30; Lk 12:27-28) — a complete trust in God that also fits the Gospels' portrait of Jesus as a worker of miracles. (So prominent in Jesus' parables and wisdom sayings are his emphasis on utter faith in God and relinquishment of possessions that Vermes considers "detachment from possessions, unquestioning trust in God and absolute submission to him" as the central thrust of Jesus' teaching.)[150] This picture may tell us something about Jesus' own relationship with the Father in terms of his radical dependence on him. The kingdom belonging to children seems to be an idea distinctive to Jesus, yet in keeping with his radical approach to the Jewish idea of end-time inversion.

Jesus' teachings about outsiders to power also cohere well with his healing ministry and his later confrontation with the authorities (treated in ch. 20). Jesus did not busy himself with impressing the elite, but with healings and exorcisms — with the needy rather than the powerful. Since what mattered was divine approval at the judgment and not human rank in this age, he could not respect the honor boundaries of his culture. His growing popularity would therefore inevitably lead to collision with some members of the elite concerned with preserving their own superior honor in this age. Some others did share this disdain for those honored in this age; whereas Josephus shows that some responded violently (targeting the aristocratic priests), many would have looked to God for vindication. Jesus' healing ministry, however, seems a fairly distinctive application of this priority (we address Jesus' healings briefly in ch. 17 and more fully in a separate, forthcoming book).

Less distinctive is Jesus' expectation of God's concern for the economically marginal. Although Jesus apparently had some supporters with means (Lk 8:3 [cf. Mk 15:41]), he had special interest in preaching good news to the poor, which he describes in language (in Matt 11:5//Lk 7:22) that clearly evokes Is 61:1 (as appears more fully in Lk 4:18). Jesus' teaching on God's concern with the poor coheres well with his Jewish environment,[151] but also with the importance of those who had possessions relinquishing them for others (e.g., Mk 10:21), an emphasis noted above.

In "Q," God's favor for the poor is expressed also in terms of eschatological inversion: it is the poor who would receive the kingdom (Matt 5:3//Lk 6:20; cf. Jms 2:5). Although the corresponding "woe" to the rich appears characteristically and explicitly only in Luke (Lk 6:24; cf. Lk 1:53), the idea is certainly consistent with Jesus' teaching, both concerning the wealthy (Mk 10:25) and concerning the use of eschatological inversion, sometimes in the context of woes (e.g., Matt 11:21-23//Lk 10:13-15; Matt 23:12-13).[152]

Jesus' ministry to the marginalized led him to transgress some expectations for ritual purity (cf. our discussion in chs. 15-16). Although the matter is too controversial today to make it a central point here, Jesus also seems to have been less apt to enforce traditional gender restrictions than the majority of his ancient Mediterranean contemporaries.[153] The conception may also cohere with and inform Jesus' expectation of impending martyrdom, depending on divine vindication and exaltation.

One place where Jesus' application of the principle of eschatological inversion is particularly unusual is that he does not speak of Israel's exaltation over the nations, but welcomes the spiritually and morally marginalized through repentance in light of the kingdom. Among those he welcomes are tax-gatherers, sometimes viewed as collaborators with the Gentile occupation.

Welcoming Tax-collectors

That Jesus welcomed tax gatherers into the kingdom, ate with them, and even invited one or more to follow him as disciples is multiply attested (Mk 2:14-15; Lk 19:2; Matt 11:19//Lk 7:34).[154] In doing so, Jesus was not merely playing to his primary audience of nonelite Galileans, but was expressing a controversial conviction about the kingdom. The common people and nonaristocratic pietists alike despised tax-gatherers as agents of the Romans and their aristocratic pawns.[155]

Like the parable in Lk 18:10-11 (cf. Mk 2:16), later rabbinic texts sometimes contrast tax-gatherers and Pharisees, the least and most pious people one might expect to meet in daily life.[156] Later rabbinic tradition likewise continues the common people's disdain for the profession.[157] (Perhaps not surprisingly, those directly involved with taxation were not popular elsewhere in the Empire either.)[158]

The average Jewish person in ancient Palestine had several reasons to dislike tax-gatherers. *First,* Palestine's local Jewish aristocracies undoubtedly arranged for this tax-collection.[159] *Second,* that the Empire sometimes had to take precautions against tax-gatherers overcharging people[160] suggests that some taxgatherers did just that.[161] Extant documents indicate that to avoid such problems people sometimes paid tax gatherers bribes, in one case as high as 2200 drachmas "for extortion."[162] *Further,* nearly all scholars concur that taxes were exorbitant even without overcharging.[163] To illustrate in an extreme manner (though matters were probably less severe in Galilee), in some parts of the Empire taxation was so oppressive that laborers fled their land, occasionally depopulating entire villages.[164]

In Mk 2:14-15, Jesus calls the tax gatherer Levi to follow him, and eats in his home along with many other tax gatherers and "sinners" who were following him. Levi's office would have made him locally well-known. Levi probably either taxed local fishermen or acted as a customs agent charging levies on merchandise leaving Philip's tetrarchy for that of Herod Antipas.[165] Because Capernaum was ideally located for significant customs revenue, many scholars today lean toward the view that Levi here is a customs officer.[166] Customs officers[167] probably generated less local discontent, however, so this interpretation might have greater problems explaining the contextual association with despised sinners (Mk 2:15-17).[168]

For Jesus to welcome tax collectors into God's kingdom suggests a radical rethinking of the character of the kingdom. Jesus, like John, called all Israel to repent in light of the coming kingdom; repentance along the lines of Jesus' movement would grant one a place in the kingdom regardless of one's past sins. The matter of the kingdom was apparently also urgent enough to welcome whoever would embrace it (Matt 22:9; Lk 14:23).[169]

Supping with Sinners

Tax-collectors represent a striking example of a larger category of people welcomed in Jesus' ministry. Although the negative use of the dissimilarity criterion has been discredited, the positive version can remain useful, especially when supplemented by multiple attestation (which does support Jesus' eating with tax gatherers and other sinners). On a positive use of the criterion of dissimilarity, most scholars concur that Jesus sometimes ate with those whom others considered sinful.[170] Certainly the later church would not have invented a practice it found difficult to carry out itself (cf. already Gal 2:12-13). Nor would the church have invented the "glutton-and-drunkard" charge (Matt 11:19//Lk 7:34), which we treated in our chapter on John the Baptist, and which coheres with Mark's portrayal of Jesus eating with sinners (Mk 2:16-17).[171]

That most of Jesus' religious contemporaries did not share Jesus' practice is not difficult to understand. Table fellowship established something of a covenant relationship;[172] eating with sinners thus would appear to connote acceptance of them. By contrast, a pious person normally preferred to eat with scholars.[173]

Scholars debate what the Gospels mean by "sinners." Some have taken "sinners" here to mean the *am haaretz,* common people whom the Pharisees despised for their lack of adherence to Pharisaic food laws.[174] Others have responded that the Pharisees did not despise the common people as sinners.[175] Pharisees seem to have been often annoyed by these people who did not share their concern for and understanding of the laws;[176] most people certainly failed to tithe on their foods according to Pharisaic standards.[177] Yet if the *am haaretz* comprised the vast majority of Palestinian Jews in the first century,[178] the Pharisees could hardly have viewed them as fully excluded from the covenant.[179]

The label "sinners" usually specifies blatant violators of the law,[180] and that seems the most natural way to take it here. The Gospels do not explain the general title "sinners," and Mark's and Luke's probably largely Gentile audiences would not naturally associate "sinner" (Mk 2:17) with *am haaretz.*[181] The Gospels thus presumably interpret the term more generally,[182] and their authors were likely in a better position to know the particular meaning of the term than we are. If we take the approach that Jesus referred to more blatant "sinners," we can understand Pharisaic concerns with Jesus' choice of dining companions all the better. Pharisees were concerned about with whom they ate, and if they were careful about meals merely with *am haaretz,*[183] one can be certain they would suspect a teacher who ate with blatant "sinners."

Pure table-fellowship was a primary defining characteristic of the Pharisaic movement.[184] Scripture was already clear that one should not have fellowship with sinners (Ps 1:1; 119:63; Prov 13:20; 14:7; 28:7), though the point in each instance was to warn against being influenced by sinners. Jewish tradition developed this warning against improper association with the wicked.[185] Jesus' behavior thus thoroughly violated his contemporaries' understanding of holiness.[186] Yet had the Pharisees valued his objective more than his method they should not have been annoyed. In Jesus' case the influence was going one way — from Jesus to the sinners (Mk 2:15, 17; Lk 15:1; cf. Ps 25:8).[187]

Although later Jewish tradition remarks that it would be difficult for a tax-gatherer to repent,[188] it allowed that God can forgive this sin like any other[189] and emphasized God's love toward the repentant;[190] Jewish tradition already warned not to reproach one who had turned from sin (Sir 8:5). In actually *seeking out* tax gatherers and sinners, however, Jesus goes beyond the traditions of his contemporaries. Even John, who called for Israel to repent, allowed people to come to him in the wilderness. Jesus goes even to the most obviously sinful and seeks their repentance. This behavior was so shocking that it left an indelible mark in the traditions about him, traditions that may have been less than comfortable even to some of his later followers (cf. Acts 11:3; *Barn.* 4.2; 10.10; 11.7).

Conclusion

Jesus taught about God's impending kingdom, and demanded that people get their lives in order to be ready for it, even as signs of the kingdom were breaking in around them. In view of the coming kingdom, his followers needed to be ready to relinquish family ties, possessions, and even their lives for the greater prize of the kingdom. Many of these sayings also indicate that the followers need to relinquish these goods for Jesus, who therefore clearly holds a role more prominent than that of a mere sage. Jesus perceives following him as a necessary part of preparing for the kingdom (hence presumably views himself at least as a significant eschatological prophet).

In light of the coming kingdom, Jesus also spoke and acted as if God would invert the present order, exalting the lowly and casting down the proud. Many others also expected such an inversion, but Jesus acted on it in sometimes distinctive ways in his ministry, welcoming children, focusing on healing the sick and disabled, and even welcoming those marginalized from society for moral reasons. Such values also cohere with his impending confrontation with some elite persons of status in the present age and his submission to a shameful death in expectation of God's vindication.

CHAPTER 15

Jesus' Jewish Ethics

> *"The chief demand in God's law is: 'Heed, O Israel, the Lord, our God, the Lord is one. You must love the Lord your God with every fabric and fiber of your being.' The demand that comes second to this one is, 'You must love your neighbor as you love yourself.'"*
>
> MARK 12:29-31

Jesus' ethics are inseparable from his demands for discipleship, and the priority of preparing for the kingdom that pervades his teaching. This chapter is thus, in a sense, a continuation of the previous one. Here we survey some more of Jesus' teaching on possessions; love; divorce; korban; and the beatitudes. We conclude with some other randomly selected sayings that illustrate how pervasively the criterion of Jewish environment supports the earliness of this sayings material.

Last of all I will survey some of Jesus' purity practices. I reserve these for the end because my examples here focus on Jesus' behavior more than on his sayings, and because purity practices provide the best transition to the controversy narratives in the following chapter.

Jesus on Possessions

We have already noted Jesus' demands on some potential disciples' resources (e.g., Mk 10:21-22). Such examples cohere with a larger emphasis in Jesus' teaching, one that appears in multiple layers of the tradition and is undoubtedly authentic to Jesus.

Some of Jesus' teachings on discipleship appear too radical to have been conveniently invented by more sedentary later followers.[1] For example, we noted that Jesus' emphasis on utter faith in God and relinquishment of possessions is so recurrent that Vermes considers it the central thrust of his teaching.[2] Jesus' teaching on possessions coheres on the one hand with his radical dependence on the Father, and on the other with Jesus' demands for discipleship and the absolute priority of the kingdom. In light of the coming kingdom, matters considered valuable in the present lose all their value (Mk 10:21; Matt 6:20//Lk 12:33; Matt 13:44-46).[3]

Although only the more radical sages of antiquity shared Jesus' view that earthly possessions were essentially worthless,[4] his *illustrations* of the point fit their Jewish environment. Thus for example Jesus invites his hearers to lay up their treasures in heaven rather than on earth, where they remain susceptible to moths, rust and thieves (Matt 6:19-21//Lk 12:33). Jesus employs images that were probably familiar to most of his audience. They would recognize the corruptibility of wealth,[5] that obedience on earth led to treasure in heaven,[6] and that laying up treasures according to God's commandments was better than letting one's resources rust (Sir 29:10-11).

Jesus warned against being divided between two masters, God and Mammon (Matt 6:24//Lk 16:13). Everyone must serve someone, but one whose service is divided will love one master and hate the other.[7] "Mammon" here was a common Aramaic term for money or property,[8] but its contrast with God as an object of service here might suggest that it has been deified (by its worshipers) as well as personified.[9] The Aramaic term tends to support authenticity; the graphic image, characteristic of Jesus' teaching style, reinforces that support.

Jesus sometimes used a standard type of Jewish argument traditionally called *qal vaomer:* "how much more?" (e.g., Matt 7:11//Lk 11:13; Matt 10:25; 12:12).[10] This figure of speech appears also in Jesus' teaching about trusting God regarding possessions. For example, if God cares for birds and for perishable flowers, how much more for people in his image, and for his own beloved children (Matt 6:26, 30//Lk 12:24, 28)! Even Jesus' claim that one should not worry about tomorrow's food (Matt 6:31-34//Lk 12:28-31) is compatible with his Jewish environment,[11] including his language chiding his disciples for their "little faith" (Matt 6:30//Lk 12:28).[12]

The Love Command (Mk 12:29-31)

Mark reports Jesus as teaching that the greatest commandments in the law are whole-hearted love for the only true God and loving one's neighbor as oneself (Mk 12:29-31). The positive use of the double "similarity" criterion (the continuum approach) comes into play here: that is, the teaching fits Jesus' environment as well as left a conspicuous imprint on the church. Jesus' teaching here, as well as the question about the greatest commandment that it answers, readily fit the criterion of Palestinian environment. They reveal Jesus as a sage still in dialogue with Judean teachers of the law. At the same time, they explain the centrality of a "law of love" in diverse parts of early Christianity in a way best explained by dependence on the single authority figure shared by that entire movement.

This passage surely reflects Palestinian Jewish tradition.[13] Some Pharisees ask a question with which they had sufficient practice, since their own teachers debated among themselves which commandment was the "greatest."[14] Although all commandments were equally weighty in one sense,[15] teachers had to distinguish between "light" and "heavy" commandments in practice.[16] Although many opted for the command to obey one's parents as the "greatest," other Jewish teachers stressed love as the preeminent commandment.[17]

In the late first century R. Akiba, in contrast to some of his colleagues, regarded love of neighbor in Lev 19:18 as the greatest commandment in the law.[18] Although Jesus ranked it only second,[19] their rankings were close.[20] Other Jewish teachers also conjoined love of God with love of neighbor,[21] following the natural Jewish interpretive principle[22] of linking two commandments on the basis of the common opening word we'ahavta ("You shall love").[23] (Others also looked for summaries or epitomes of the law.)[24]

Yet as Vermes notes, there is also something distinctive about Jesus' combination of the two as the greatest commandments.[25] This link exercised an authoritative influence on subsequent Christian formulations.[26] In the multiplicity of other proposals concerning the greatest commandment among other Jewish teachers, only Jesus wielded the moral authority among his followers to focus their ethics so profoundly around a single theme.[27] The distinctive primacy that love plays in virtually all early Christian ethics would not have been possible had the Christians not derived this primacy from the mouth of the one Teacher who united them. Thence comes the early Christian "law of love," attested not only in Mark's tradition but in Paul (Rom 13:8-10; Gal 5:14), James (Jas 2:8), and Johannine tradition (Jn 13:34-35).[28]

From Jesus' teaching on the subject we see him engaged with Jewish discussions of his day and devoted to the Torah, especially on matters of foundational principle. The first passage Jesus cites in fact portrays the love of God as a summary of the law (Deut 6:1-7); one who loved God would fulfill the whole Torah (Deut 5:29). This passage about loving God was the central and best-known text of Judaism, the shema.[29] Likewise, the command to love one's neighbor as oneself (Lev 19:18) expresses a general principle (cf. Lev 19:34), though its original context applied it to a more specific situation.

The love command coheres with some of Jesus' other teachings, such as the "Q" saying about treating one's neighbor as one would wish to be treated (Matt 7:12//Lk 6:31).[30] This saying fits its Jewish environment,[31] although not in a distinctive way (being a sentiment shared with other cultures as well,[32] even as far away as China).³³ That both Matthew (Matt 7:12; but not Luke) and a later report about Jesus' predecessor Hillel³⁴ cite it as fulfilling the law is surely more than coincidence.³⁵ The love command coheres particularly well with Jesus' extension of the command to love of enemy in "Q" (Matt 5:44//Lk 6:27, 35).³⁶

Divorce

Many of Jesus' radical sayings better reflect the wisdom of a sage shocking hearers to attention than that of a community creating a behavior code. This observation is obviously true concerning Jesus' teaching on divorce. The church would hardly have invented a saying that it had so much trouble implementing: although Mark and Luke simply include brief versions of the saying, Matthew and Paul both qualify it for practical situations such as a spouse's infidelity or abandonment.³⁷

Moreover, multiple attestation makes Jesus' divorce teaching (in various forms) one of his most assuredly attested teachings.³⁸ It appears in Mark (Mk 10:11-12; cf. Matt 19:9); "Q" (Matt 5:32; Lk 16:18); and already in Paul (1 Cor 7:10-12).

Although the language comes closer to the debate of first-century Pharisaic schools in Matt 19:3-9 than in Mark 10:2-12, both passages can be understood as evoking a debate among the two Pharisaic schools known to have been current precisely in Jesus' day.³⁹ In a manner resembling other first-century Jewish teachers, Jesus counters his interlocutors' standard text in Deut 24 by appealing to a countertext. Since other Jewish teachers of this period looked to the creation narrative for God's ideal purposes on various issues,⁴⁰ including the Pharisaic schools we have just noted,⁴¹ Jesus' argument would be difficult to ignore.⁴² Based on the citation of Scripture in CD 4.20-5.2, Sanders regards the tradition that Jesus cited the creation narrative in defense of his divorce position as likely.⁴³ I have treated Jesus' teaching on divorce more extensively in other works (especially regarding its hyperbolic function),⁴⁴ but the survey of evidence here should be sufficient to establish that the teaching is one of the most securely grounded, clearly authentic elements of traditions preserved about Jesus.

Korban Teaching

Although Jesus demanded allegiance to himself over family, as we have noted, he also resisted religious arrangements by which one sought freedom from responsibility for caring for aged parents. This concern appears in a passage where he is accusing religious teachers of focusing on external purity concerns while ignoring deeper principles of the law such as caring for parents. Apparently some were devoting resources to the temple that were needed to care for their parents.

Mark seems to imply that this was being arranged through what his tradition calls "Korban," a distinctly Jewish oath meaning "gift."[45] The term was applied to an offering to God, including what was vowed to the temple.[46] One could dedicate an object for sacred use, and even if Pharisaic teachers agreed with Jesus that the vow turned out to be inappropriate, given what we know about their views on vows they probably would not have used their authority to cancel it.[47] As far away as Alexandria some Jewish teachers could use such vows to keep property from other family members.[48] By exploiting some commonly held traditional practices, an unscrupulous person could have circumvented some biblical principles.

Jesus' portrayal of the issue and his response both fit his environment. A Pharisaic teacher could have offered the same sort of argument that Jesus offers here, since Pharisees could argue by laying one text against the interpretation of another. As much as or more than in surrounding cultures, Judaism heavily stressed honoring[49] and obeying[50] one's parents. They likewise highly emphasized the obligation to support one's parents in their old age.[51] Not only Jesus, but Pharisaic tradition also unremorsefully criticizes Pharisees who fell short of what they considered virtue.[52]

Beatitudes

Beatitudes appear elsewhere in the Mediterranean world,[53] but were a characteristically Jewish rhetorical form. They appear most obviously throughout the Hebrew Bible and Septuagint[54] and afterward continued in use in early Judaism.[55]

Although back-translation into another language is always precarious, it is likely more than coincidence that some of the verbal differences between Matthew's and Luke's beatitudes reflect different possible ways of translating Aramaic expressions into Greek.[56] A common Aramaic original would suggest that these particular beatitudes, at least, go back to our earliest traditions about Jesus.

Many of Jesus' beatitudes resemble traditional Jewish formulations and ideas; thus his claim that the merciful would receive mercy (i.e., from God; Matt 5:7) fits the traditional Jewish notion that "God is merciful to the merciful."[57] It has been argued that Jesus' same beatitude, when translated back into Aramaic, reflects a particular rhythm characteristic of some of Jesus' teaching.[58]

Some Other Sayings Supported by the
Jewish Environment Criterion

Sayings supported by the criterion of Jewish environment are too many to re-count here (without becoming like a commentary), but we can offer a sample. Jesus offered many witty sayings and riddles in the gospel tradition, so fre-quently that they may be safely considered fairly characteristic of his teaching. Some of these sayings can be understood fully only in Jesus' original environ-ment or among his Jewish followers familiar with the traditions of Judean sages (i.e., especially for those who lived in greater Judea). If these sayings come from the first generation (before 70 CE), and/or if they come from Jewish Palestine, they come from the time and place where Jesus' words would be most clearly remembered and understood, and in a period when oral tradition was most likely to get their attribution correct.

In one case, Jesus asks rhetorically how one should re-season salt that has lost its saltiness, a striking image. The image is striking both because salt tech-nically cannot become unsalty,[59] and because seasoning that needs to be sea-soned is absurdly pointless. That this graphic image would have struck his con-temporaries forcefully is clear; a late-first-century Palestinian rabbi reportedly answered the same absurd question with an equally absurd answer (one should salt it with the afterbirth of a mule),[60] suggesting that he understood its rhetori-cal force.

Likewise, Jesus underlines the permanence of Scripture's authority in a graphic, hyperbolic manner, declaring that not even the smallest letter would pass away (Matt 5:18//Lk 16:17). His recorded language apparently alludes to a more widely known story, probably known to Jesus' original hearers, but per-haps not to most of Matthew's and surely not to most of Luke's audiences. Jesus' "letter" (NRSV), "smallest letter" (NIV), "jot" (KJV), or (literally) *iota* (the smallest Greek letter) undoubtedly refers to the Hebrew letter *yod*,[61] which Jew-ish teachers said would not pass from the law. Some said that when Sarai's name was changed to Sarah, the *yod* removed from her name cried out from one gen-eration to another, protesting its removal from Scripture, until finally, when Moses changed Oshea's name to Joshua, the *yod* was returned to Scripture. "So you see," the teachers would say, "not even this smallest letter can pass from the Bible."[62] Likewise, sages declared that when Solomon threatened to uproot a *yod* from the law, God responded that he would uproot a thousand Solomons rather than a word of his law.[63]

While not multiply attested, Jesus' saying that follows this one in Matthew (Matt 5:19) fits only a distinctly eastern, Jewish milieu. Jesus claims that one who keeps and leads others to keep the least commandment will be greatest in the kingdom.[64] Jesus again employs hyperbolic rhetoric characteristic of sages:

his words do not seem to allow for the possibility of many who would keep or break the least commandment (hence vie for the same status), nor of some who would break some commandments while keeping others. Jewish teachers typically depicted various persons as "greatest," rather than only a single one; the emphasis was not on numerical precision but on praising worthy people.[65] When Jesus speaks of the "least" commandment, he also reflects Jewish legal language. Jewish teachers regularly distinguished "light" and "heavy" commandments,[66] and in fact determined which commandments were the "least" and "greatest."

Noting that both the "greatest" commandment about honoring parents[67] (Ex 20:12; Deut 5:16) and the "least" commandment about the bird's nest (Deut 22:6-7) bore the same promise, "Do this and you will live," some later rabbis decided that "live" meant "in the world to come," and said God would reward equally for any commandment. One who kept the law regulating the bird's nest merited eternal life, whereas one who broke it merited damnation.[68]

Jesus here likely employs the rhetoric in a manner analogous to that of his contemporaries. As some ancient Jewish teachers put it, "one should be as careful with regard to a light commandment as you would be with a heavy one, since you do not know the allotment of the reward."[69] Likewise one who keeps a single commandment keeps his life, but one who neglects such a commandment neglects his life.[70] The sages were not suggesting that they never broke commandments,[71] but rather felt that one who cast off any commandment or principle of the law was discarding the authority of the law as a whole.[72] Likewise, accepting some commandments implied recognizing the validity of them all.[73]

One could pile up countless other samples of Jesus' sayings fitting a Palestinian Jewish environment: for example, Jesus' teaching (limited to Matthew) that lust constitutes adultery (Matt 5:28);[74] his demand for integrity rather than oaths (Matt 5:33-37);[75] the abuse of oaths in his environment (cf. Matt 5:34-36; 23:16-22);[76] the kingdom prayer of Matt 6:9-13 and Lk 11:2-4;[77] the warning that it would be "measured" to one as one measured to others (Matt 7:2; Lk 6:38);[78] removing the beam from one's eye before trying to remove the chip from another's (Matt 7:3-5//Lk 6:41-42);[79] the confidence that the heavenly Father would provide for his children no less than an earthly one would (Matt 7:11; Lk 11:13);[80] admonishing another privately before public reproof (Matt 18:15-17; cf. Lk 17:3);[81] and possibly the allusion to a heavenly "Sanhedrin" or court (Matt 5:22).[82]

So many other possible examples of Jesus' teachings making their best sense in a Palestinian Jewish framework could be offered that there is no point merely listing them here.[83] Because Matthew amplifies traditional Jewish formulations even in the wording that he adds to Mark and "Q," we cannot rule out Matthew and other Jewish disciples of Jesus presenting his words in a manner most in keeping with their Jewish context. That is, some elements suggesting a Palestinian Jewish environment in Jesus' collected sayings could potentially stem from others besides Jesus. Nevertheless, adapting sayings is not the same as creating them, and the preponderance of such sayings in early tradition suggests that they do in fact reflect Jesus' message and style. And again, the sources most in touch with Palestinian Jewish traditions are also the sources apt to be closest to the historical Jesus.

Purity Practices

Although a longer book could devote an extensive section to exploring Jesus' treatment of levitical impurity, we simply pause to note it briefly here. The kingdom was so all-consuming that it took precedence not only over one's possessions, kinship ties and moral past but even over levitical purity practices (and certainly their postbiblical expansion). From our limited extant sources, it does not appear that Jesus regarded such practices as wrong (cf. in fact Mk 1:44), but rather that he believed that, in view of the kingdom, the heart of the law must take precedence (cf. Matt 23:25-26//Lk 11:39-41; Matt 23:23//Lk 11:42).

Narratives reflecting Jesus' practice cohere with collections of his sayings and conflicts with rival teachers. Jesus' violation of his contemporaries' conventional purity boundaries appears throughout the gospel tradition.[84] In the Gospels, however, Jesus does not explicitly address contracting impurity so much as he removes the impurity (hence addresses it far more effectively than levitical separation from it does). Gospel narratives portray Jesus touching the unclean, including lepers (Mk 1:41)[85] and (most impure of all) corpses (Mk 5:41; cf. Lk 7:14). They also portray him publicly acknowledging the touch of a bleeding woman (Mk 5:31-33), which should have rendered him impure (Lev 15:25-27).[86] Presumably the writers viewed such cases the way they viewed Jesus' contact with sinners: the true influence flowed from Jesus to others, not the reverse. Nevertheless, they are no more likely to have deliberately invented this pervasive yet potentially controversial emphasis in Jesus' behavior toward the impure than they are to have invented his welcome of sinners.

We may illustrate this unlikelihood by way of comparison with a related issue. We have no saying of Jesus explicitly claiming all foods to be pure (suggesting that the Gospel writers did not invent such sayings to address the issues with which the church soon struggled; cf. Acts 10:13-15; Rom 14:14; Col 2:16, 21; Heb 13:9). We have one saying that could be interpreted that way,[87] and Mark's interpretation (rather than adaptation) of the saying along these lines. But whereas Matthew reports Jesus' saying found in Mark, he omits Mark's interpretation (Mk 7:19), with which he apparently either disagreed or found unhelpful in his setting.[88] Since the Gospel writers did not invent sayings of Jesus purifying foods, which became an issue for them, they had little reason to invent Jesus touching the unclean. Matthew omits Mark's interpretation about unclean foods, but he nevertheless allows Jesus to touch the unclean.[89]

As we shall see in the next chapter, a number of Jesus' sayings (particularly conspicuous in Q) do show that he emphasized inward purity over outward purity (a sentiment shared by some of his contemporaries),[90] and disagreed with some of his contemporaries over purity and other matters.

CHAPTER 16

Conflicts with Other Teachers

"It will be bad for you Pharisees, for strict though you are in tithing even products like mint and rue and every sort of herb, you overlook justice and the love of God. You should have done the latter without neglecting the former."

LUKE 11:42 (PARALLELED IN MATTHEW 23:23)

Although Jesus' teachings fit their Palestinian Jewish environment, that Jewish environment included a range of perspectives. The diversity of perspectives regularly led to disagreements, often produced harsh rhetoric between competing groups, and reportedly occasionally even led to violence. If Jesus taught some ideas that differed from those of some other teachers of the law, we would expect some disagreements. This is, in fact, what we find in the tradition. Although valuing and calling his people back to the message of Scripture, Jesus failed to lay the emphasis where some of his contemporaries expected. If Jesus' other activities (such as healings) augmented his popularity beyond that of most other teachers, others may have viewed him as undermining the sound teachings they were laboring to cultivate among the people.[1]

Doubting Conflict with Pharisees

Some scholars attribute stories about Jesus' conflicts with the Pharisees only to the imagination or experience of later Christians.[2] Elsewhere some of the same scholars concede that disputes occurred, but "not necessarily between Jesus and the scribes and Pharisees."[3] To this perspective we must make three concessions. A simple comparison of the extant Gospels will reveal that Matthew and especially John do at least sometimes intensify the specifically Pharisaic opposition in their narratives (e.g., Matt 3:7;[4] Jn 1:24; 7:32, 45). At least some-

223

times, therefore, more general disputes were later assigned specifically to the Pharisees.

Nevertheless, we must qualify this concession; we should not assume on the basis of these few examples that every mention of Pharisees was added later (even Matthew and John do not do it all the time). It seems more likely instead that Matthew and John felt free to adapt these "opponents" based on the presence of Pharisees already in many of the accounts. Opposition, including Pharisaic opposition, appears already in Mark (Mk 2:16, 18, 24; 3:6; 7:1, 3, 5; 8:11, 15; 10:2; 12:13), and Jesus harshly criticizes the Pharisees in "Q" (Matt 23:6, 23-28//Lk 11:39-44). To argue that every layer of tradition must be misrepresenting Jesus values a theory about how Jesus "should" have acted, without any supporting documentary evidence, against all the documentary evidence we do have.

As a second concession, Pharisees probably were rare in Galilee. Josephus mentions the Pharisees primarily in Jerusalem in our sources, not in Galilee.[5] Still, Josephus' interest focuses on Jerusalem in any case,[6] so we would not expect him to tell us as much about any individual Pharisees living in Galilee. One could thus argue that more Pharisees lived in Galilee than some of our sources suggest, though they presumably predominated in Jerusalem.[7] Local elites, at least, presumably did have significant contact with Jerusalem.

Further, the Pharisees could be visitors from Jerusalem rather than local.[8] Indeed, if Jesus was becoming well-enough known, Pharisees could have visited to evaluate and dialogue with him; Josephus reports such measures in his own case in Galilee.[9] Moreover, keeping in mind that ancient biographers were more interested in anecdotes than in chronology, we can allow for the possibility that Jesus had some of these conflicts in Judea. We have every reason from Jesus' context to believe the Gospels' claim that Jesus, like most Galileans, did travel to Judea for festivals.[10] (Nevertheless, this final objection by itself could account for only some of the stories.)[11]

A third caveat is that the Pharisees did not go around trying to kill or even arrest people who differed with their interpretation of the law — at least not in this period.[12] Even in the Gospels, where some Pharisees "plotted" against Jesus, it is Jerusalem's priestly leaders who get Jesus executed, and that within a few days of their decision.[13] The Fourth Gospel, which most often combines "Pharisees" with (and perhaps occasionally substitutes them for) other groups elsewhere in the gospel tradition, also lays the blame for Jesus' execution mostly on the priestly elite.[14]

Authenticity of the Conflict Accounts

Now that we have registered and qualified these caveats, however, the substance of these accounts is likely authentic. First of all, the accounts must predate the major Jewish-Christian conflicts to which some wish to attribute them. Mark's accounts clearly precede the major breaches in the post-70 era;[15] because they appear in Mark, they could not have been composed far enough after 70 merely to respond to Pharisaic dominance after the temple's destruction. Further, such stories would not have arisen in a period when Pharisees were not the Christians' primary enemies, and perhaps were on good terms, in the late 40s (Acts 15:5)[16] through the early 60s.[17] These stories probably would not have arisen much in most of the early period of the Jerusalem church, either (cf. Acts 5:17, 33-34).

Second, *some* Pharisaic opposition in the early period existed and probably had earlier roots: at least *some* Pharisees in the very earliest part of this period joined ranks with the Sadducees to persecute Christians (Phil 3:5-6),[18] and it is unlikely that the conflicts simply began shortly after Jesus' cruxifixion. Jesus' movement was popular before his execution as well as afterward, so we need not infer, against the only documentary evidence we have either way, that conflict must reflect the disciples' rather than Jesus' life-setting.

Moreover, some other early persecution by some Judean opponents against Jesus' Jewish followers is certain (e.g., 1 Thess 2:14-16).[19] We know that some of Jesus' followers were whipped as a form of synagogue discipline; while the tradition could have transferred the attitudes of synagogue leaders more generally to Pharisees, it is also possible that some Pharisees may have been involved. Paul, maintaining his solidarity with the synagogue, suffered this public disgrace at least five times (2 Cor 11:24).[20] Although the fair-minded Pharisees apparently officially opposed corporal punishment for matters of theological disagreement,[21] popular sentiments sometimes could yield to violent actions (cf. Jer 20:1-2; 37:15), and even Pharisees might permit floggings for disrupting public order.[22] The persecution started at some point, and accepting the claims of some of the documents that it started in Jesus' own lifetime is just as reasonable as placing it afterward. Regarding the Pharisees, Gospel reports of the conflict are generally more verbal than violent anyway, which is even less problematic.

Together these first two observations suggest authenticity: Some sort of conflicts appeared in the earliest Jesus tradition, but these were not all conformed to the *primary* opponents of Christians in the early years after the resurrection (Sadducees), nor were they all added after 70 when the heirs of Pharisaism are thought to have become the dominant competition. Thus it is reasonable to suppose that the original opponents in these traditions may have been usually correctly transmitted.

Third, multiple attestation supports the thesis that Jesus did have Sabbath conflicts.[23] They appear in Mark (e.g., Mk 2:23-28), apparently independently in John (Jn 5:1-9), and perhaps independently in special Lukan material (Lk 13:10-17). Lack of clear narrative attestation in Q (unless Matthew simply omits the tradition of Lk 13:10-17) is not surprising given how few narratives from Q appear in our Gospels, but as we have noted, Jesus clearly denounces Pharisees in Q material (Matt 23:6, 23-28//Lk 11:39-44), and such a challenge to honor would initiate conflict even if none existed beforehand. Because Pharisees were the most "meticulous" interpreters and non-priestly observers of the law with whom Jesus would have come in contact,[24] it is reasonable to trust the Gospels' claim that these conflicts were with Pharisees.

Fourth, conflict over the interpretation of the law was common.[25] Vermes thinks that Jesus' lack of halakic (though not biblical) concern would lead to the situation that he "cannot have been greatly loved by the Pharisees."[26] He notes that in normal times Jesus' debates with the Pharisees would seem mere "infighting" of related "factions," but eschatological tension meant that times were not normal.[27]

Indeed, surprising as it may be to readers in some parts of the twenty-first century world, such conflicts sometimes even turned violent, whether this behavior had any official sanction or not. Not only in intra-Jewish strife nearly two centuries earlier (during the civil war during Alexander Jannaeus' reign),[28] but also during the subsequent war with Rome, Judeans massacred fellow-Judeans of rival parties. Josephus faced life-threatening opposition from rivals within his own social class,[29] and both such passages in Josephus and the history of other early Jewish groups such as the Essenes (violent conflicts with the priesthood)[30] and Pharisees[31] indicate the pervasiveness of intra-Jewish strife.

Finally, Jesus' theological kinship with the populist Pharisees may have led to open disagreements. One may note that Jesus' teaching more closely resembles that of the Pharisees than any of the other "parties" mentioned by Josephus (Sadducees, Essenes, or revolutionaries); yet dissimilarities are also striking.[32] But like most of his contemporaries, Jesus undoubtedly did not belong to any of these "parties," and in any case such a marginal kinship would hardly preclude conflict. Social conflict theory illustrates that conflicts become most severe among groups most closely connected.[33]

The Gospels charge the elite, mainly Sadducees, with abuse of power and engineering Jesus' execution. But while the Pharisees were probably not violently against Jesus, it is likely that they sometimes had conflict with him.

Coherence of the Conflict Tradition

Tom Holmén shows that Jesus' conflicts appear in every layer of tradition (i.e., they are "multiply attested"), and that they frequently involve the same issues (i.e., they fit the criterion of cohesiveness). He notes that contemporary Judaism emphasized various "covenant markers" (such as sabbath, circumcision, temple, and purity, including kashrut) as signs of loyalty to the covenant.[34] He argues that Jesus was not against these practices, but neither did he treat them as path markers or loyalty tests.[35]

For example, sabbath conflicts appear throughout the traditions about Jesus, hence are multiply attested.[36] The later church did not invent these, because its question was not relaxed Jewish observance (as apparently in Jesus' case) but whether Gentiles needed to observe the sabbath.[37] Various layers of gospel tradition also multiply attest Jesus' conflicts with some of his contemporaries over issues of purity.[38] Jesus criticized the temple and its cult, despite their centrality to his contemporaries.[39] Jesus' approach to tithing (Matt 23:23// Lk 11:42 Q; Lk 18:9-14) differed from its emphatic use as a path marker among Pharisees and some others.[40] Some apparently treated regular fasting as a covenant marker as well, in contrast to Jesus (Mk 2:17-20).[41]

We have noted Pharisaic concern with Jesus' distinctive practice of eating with sinners; they would have seen this behavior as challenging their understanding of path markers.[42] Holmén notes that "sinners" were not pervasive in Galilee, hence argues that Jesus was deliberately *violating* his contemporaries' holiness conventions.[43] (While this might be true, I believe that Jesus may have additional reasons for reaching out to even the alienated of Israel,[44] while he believed that those who rejected his kingdom message and authority would be excluded because they were rejecting the gift of God's kingdom.) Jesus' command to love enemies was (in that emphatic form) distinctive,[45] which might challenge the nationalism implicit in path markers.

Holmén concludes that these covenant markers are so prominent in the stories about Jesus because they were so central to Palestinian Judaism in his day, but the stories consistently portray Jesus refusing to emphasize such features.[46] He proposes that Jesus may have shared covenant belief and expected loyalty, but approached them in terms of the internal law of Jer 31:31-34 and Ezek 36:27 rather than path markers,[47] as suggested by his possible allusion to the new covenant at the last supper.[48] I am less inclined than Holmén to think that Jesus relaxed the law,[49] but I think he has firmly established his case that conflict over key issues of the law, emphasized by Jesus' contemporaries, pervades the traditions about Jesus.

Differing Interpretations of the Sabbath

Jewish people held some views of the Sabbath universally, but many, including many Pharisees, recognized diverse interpretations of Sabbath practice. The Sabbath was central to Jewish practice throughout the ancient world.[50] It was part of Jewish life, not restricted merely to the most pious.[51] The rest of the Roman world marked its calendar with market-days rather than a weekly religious day of rest,[52] but they were widely aware of the Jewish Sabbath.[53]

The seventh day was already important in the Genesis creation narrative, but it became still more so in later tradition,[54] which declared that angels kept the Sabbath and that this day was holier than any other holy day.[55] (Some later rabbis even said, in notoriously hyperbolic language, that the Sabbath outweighed all other commandments of the Torah.)[56] A well-educated first-century Jew like Josephus could assume that Moses commanded Jewish people to assemble to learn the law together each Sabbath[57] (the law actually commanded no such thing). Josephus also claims that Jewish laws required, and even the laxer Jews of Tiberias observed, retiring to one's home for a dinner when the Sabbath began around 6 p.m.[58] Later teachers meticulously detailed a protective "fence" around the Sabbath law.[59]

Most Jewish people allowed some exceptions, especially for saving a life (including defensive warfare).[60] But any activity that could be done before the Sabbath was prohibited on the Sabbath.[61] Although matters of life and death remained exceptions and common people were probably less particular, most Pharisees probably opposed minor medical cures on the Sabbath, generating conflict with Jesus' healing activities.[62]

It is doubtful that Jesus himself rejected the Sabbath, though he clearly interpreted and applied it quite differently from many of his contemporaries. Even in the Fourth Gospel, Jesus defends his Sabbath practice with a good halakic argument (Jn 7:22-23).[63] As Vermes notes, "If, as is often claimed, the evangelists aimed at inculcating . . . Christian doctrine such as the annulment of the Sabbath legislation . . . they did a pitiful job which falls far short of proving their alleged thesis."[64] One may suspect that wishful thinking of later Gentile Christianity generated some of the later antinomian or partly antinomian traditions of interpretation.[65]

Conflicts about the Sabbath

Under later rabbinic rules, which may or may not reflect earlier Pharisaic ideals, Sabbath violation was in theory worthy of death.[66] Nevertheless, under the same rules it would have been impossible in practice to have found someone sufficiently guilty of Sabbath violation to warrant execution.[67] The Essenes observed the Sabbath more strictly than others,[68] probably sharing the view of the document *Jubilees* that death was appropriate for even minor infractions such as intercourse with one's wife[69] or fasting[70] on the Sabbath.[71] Nevertheless, in practice they commuted the biblical death sentence for its violation.[72]

Jesus' conflicts in the Synoptics with his contemporaries concerning the Sabbath were relatively minor by the standards of Sabbath controversies of the period.[73] Even in later rabbinic sources, divergent opinions flourished,[74] including in probably first-century houses-debates.[75] Some other groups did apparently come to blows,[76] and individual representatives of some groups might wish Jesus' death in contradiction to their own group's ethical teachings;[77] Josephus attests that some aristocrats went so far as seeking to kill a fellow aristocratic rival for influence (in this instance, himself).[78] Jesus' conflicts with Pharisees concerning the Sabbath are (as we have noted) multiply attested in the tradition and are likely historically.[79]

Some scholars challenge the settings of some of the Gospel sabbath conflict narratives. One would not usually expect to find Pharisees in a Galilean wheatfield on the Sabbath;[80] this was hardly their usual habitat[81] and makes sense only if they were looking for grounds to accuse the disciples.[82] But as we have noted, the case against allowing any Galilean Pharisees in the Gospels argues only from silence in very limited sources; and we cannot rule out the possibility of Judean visitors or other factors. It is not even impossible that these Pharisees were traveling with Jesus or seeking to test him, although this is not the most obvious interpretation. Apart from the narrative's unusual setting, however, the rest of its portrayal of these Pharisees' reasoning makes sense without much explanation.[83]

If Jesus' disciples picked heads of grain on a sabbath so they could eat, it is plausible that controversy would arise. The law explicitly forbade work on the Sabbath (e.g., Ex 31:13-14; 35:2; Ezek 20:20), and some of the pious might construe gleaning as work, as a form of "reaping."[84] But Jesus and his disciples could also make a contrary case from the law and Jewish tradition. Scripture did not explicitly prohibit their specific action,[85] and Jewish tradition celebrated the Sabbath with joyous feasting.[86] Such a principle might even invite Jesus' disciples to glean provided that the urgency of their mission had detained them from preparing food the previous day.[87]

Like any good Jewish teacher, Jesus responds to his detractors from Scripture. Although his critics may have insisted on beginning with an explicit legal text,[88] Jesus appeals instead to inspired narrative to show how God expected the legal statements to be qualified in practice, "a precedent for allowing hunger to override the law."[89] The Pharisees could have objected that the David story addressed forbidden food rather than the Sabbath,[90] but Jesus extrapolates from principle.[91]

Why would some Pharisees have objected to Jesus healing on the sabbath in other Gospel accounts? Some teachers considered applying medicine to be work justifiable on the Sabbath only if a person's life was in danger.[92] But the teachers themselves found ways to circumvent some of their regulations,[93] and many teachers probably permitted medicine if it had been prepared before the Sabbath[94] or if the act was medically urgent.[95] This act, however, was not medically urgent.[96] But Jesus acted as a man of prayer, not a pharmacist, and in Mk 3:5, Jesus does not even lay hands on the man, which *some* might have considered work. Instead, he simply orders the man to stretch forth his hand, an act that was not considered work by anyone's standard; God alone performs "work" in this scene.[97]

Even the strict majority Pharisaic school in this period, the Shammaites, would have violated their own standards of ethics to have punished Jesus harshly (at most a later rabbinic judge would have fined him or ordered a beating, which one rabbi occasionally — but rarely — levied against another). Although they prohibited prayer for the sick on the Sabbath, they never sought to kill the minority school at the time, Hillelite Pharisees, for permitting prayer on the Sabbath.[98] Why then might Mark infer that they wished to kill Jesus (Mk 3:6)?

We can say certainly that Pharisaic ethics would have prohibited killing Jesus for such arguments. We cannot rule out the possibility that, humans being what we are, some wished him harm; but we also should note that, whatever their inferences about Pharisees' anger, the Gospels never accuse the Pharisees of carrying out such wishes (by contrast, cf. their attempt even to warn Jesus in Lk 13:31). The passion narrative blames Jesus' execution primarily on the largely Sadducean Jerusalem elite who, once they decided Jesus was a threat, acted efficiently and within days. There is thus a difference in kind between the sorts of conflicts that Jesus had with Pharisees and those he had with Jerusalem's rulers. This difference does not offer us license, however, to deny any conflict.

Why Conflicts with Pharisees?

The passion narrative is clear that largely Sadducean Jerusalem aristocrats engineered Jesus' execution; first-century sources also suggest that Jesus' Jerusalem followers and the Pharisees sometimes made common cause in subsequent decades.[99] Moreover, Jesus' ethical teachings and even belief in the resurrection closely resemble that of the Pharisees. Why then would conflict arise between them?

We have noted that social conflict theory shows that disagreeing groups sharing the most ideology in common often experience the greatest friction.[100]

Indeed, some later rabbis even thought that debates between Shammaites and Hillelites (two schools of Pharisees in Jesus' day) occasionally brought them to blows![101]

What we can know of Jesus' actions suggests that his ministry would have generated at the least vigorous debate with many of his Pharisaic contemporaries.[102] Although some scholars today have viewed Jesus' denunciations of Pharisees as anti-Jewish because of their subsequent abuse, in Jesus' lifetime these controversies were "in-house" Jewish controversies, part of a larger pattern of many debates among Jewish groups in that period. Even the harshest of polemic against scribes and/or Pharisees in the Gospels (Mk 12:38-40; "Q" material in Lk 11:39-52 and, more extensively, Matt 23:1-36) was intra-Jewish polemic, the sort elsewhere offered by one Jewish group against another.

Jesus was not alone in criticizing some fellow Jews for hypocrisy. Rabbinic Judaism, which probably sprang in large measure from Pharisaism, harshly condemned hypocrisy.[103] Indeed, these later rabbis were quick to condemn the hypocrisy of some kinds of Pharisees whose motives were less than holy,[104] and acknowledged hypocrisy among scholars[105] and within Israel.[106] They regarded hypocrisy in general as morally reprehensible and deserving of judgment.[107] The Synoptic writers' critiques, like these, are Jewish critiques within Judaism, "no more 'anti-Semitic' than the Dead Sea Scrolls,"[108] and not intended for exploitation by Gentile anti-Judaism. (The Qumran scrolls in fact treat most of Israel as followers of Belial.)[109] They are demonstrably quite different from the sort of Gentile anti-Judaism exemplified by Tacitus or Apion, who mocked Moses and Israel, rather than simply critiqued another Jewish group.[110]

The language of Jesus' woes[111] against scribes and Pharisees (Matt 23:13-29// Lk 11:42-47) reflects the regular conventions of ancient polemical rhetoric.[112] In a detailed study, Overman has demonstrated that the language of Matt 23, the harshest of the passages, is not ancient anti-Judaic language, but the language of other sectarian Jewish sources like *1 Enoch, 2 Baruch* or *4 Ezra* against the establishments of their day that they viewed as corrupt.[113] Even lawlessness was a charge sectarian communities regularly leveled against those outside.[114] Josephus estimates only 6000 Pharisees in Jewish Palestine,[115] surely far less than one percent of the population.[116] It is thus irrational to assume that being anti-Pharisaic made one anti-Jewish.[117]

Josephus testifies that some aristocrats exploited popular piety for personal reasons, and that those who valued popular support dare not appear to fall short in such piety.[118] As Davies and Allison point out, "hypocrisy belongs to the human condition and so can always be found in the enemy camp"[119] as well as one's own. Yet the Gospel writers at least sometimes turn this criticism into a moral warning for their own communities (fairly explicit in Matt 24:51).[120] Indeed, in one of the most polemical contexts, Jesus even agrees that many of the ethical teachings of the scribes and Pharisees are good, simply critiquing them for not living up to them (Matt 23:2-3).

Impure Purists

Pharisees were known for their concern for purity in matters such as tithing and eating. It is presumably here that, as in the Gospel traditions, Pharisees found Jesus' different behavior most objectionable. One may note, for example, the complaints against disciples eating with unwashed hands (Mk 7:1-2). It is also here that Jesus particularly lambasts them, emphasizing inward purity more than outward purity (comprising most of the heart of the "Q" material in Matt 23:23, 25-27//Lk 11:39-44).[121] Many Pharisees may have agreed with the value of inward purity, yet maintained the importance of outward, levitical purity as well. Jesus' emphasis on the kingdom might explain his more radical perspective, laying even heavier weight than usual on the central principles of the law.

A Hyperbolic Pharisee

In our earliest sources, Jesus critiques the Pharisees with the sort of wit that characterized the environment of Jewish scribal polemic. For example, in an undoubtedly original saying[122] in "Q" Jesus denounces a hyperbolic Pharisee who tithes meticulously on mint and other debated substances while neglecting the principles of God's law such as justice and love (Matt 23:23//Lk 11:42). As we have noted, Pharisees were known to be careful about tithing (cf. also Lk 18:12). Consequently they sought to determine which substances counted as foodstuffs, hence were covered under the Old Testament agrarian tithe.[123] Later rabbis agreed to tithe on dill[124] and cummin[125] but eventually excluded mint.[126] First-century Shammaites doubted that black cummin need be tithed, in contrast to Hillelites.[127]

In their eagerness to avoid violating any portion of the law, the ultrastrict Pharisees Jesus addresses here (perhaps a hyperbolic, *reductio ad absurdum* construct) tithe even the most disputable of substances. Believing that they were showing their faithfulness to God's law by examining its every detail, they would not have thought of themselves as neglecting the law's broader principles. Jesus, however, insisted that their commendable attention to the former had neglected the latter.[128] Pharisees would have understood Jesus' insistence on some matters of the law being weightier than others.[129]

Consistent with such "Q" material, even material found only in Matthew (who has reasons in his own milieu to highlight Jesus' conflict with Pharisees) sounds as Jesus should have sounded in his original setting. Immediately after denouncing Pharisaic preference for tithing over mercy, Jesus illustrates their inconsistency in Matt 23:24 with a characteristically witty illustration, again portraying a superscrupulous Pharisee more attentive than Pharisaic legal rulings required.

In this saying, Jesus complains that they "strain out a gnat yet swallow a camel!" Again, he probably portrays a hyperbolic, superscrupulous Pharisee. If a fly fell into one's drink, an observant Jew might hope to strain it out before it died, lest it contaminate the drink (cf. Lev 11:34). But Pharisaic legal experts decided that any organism smaller than a lentil (such as a gnat) was exempt.[130] Passionate for purity, this Pharisee goes beyond the apparent letter of the law.[131]

Nevertheless, these hyperbolic Pharisees were so inconsistent, Jesus said, that they concerned themselves with purity issues as trifling as a gnat while ignoring a much larger purity issue in swallowing a camel whole. Biblical law explicitly deemed camels unclean for eating (Lev 11:4). Gnats appear in ancient illustrations as the prototypically smallest of creatures[132] and notably inconspicuous;[133] by contrast, camels were the largest animal in Palestine.[134] In addition to such features of Palestinian Jewish background, the saying probably reflects an Aramaic original. Jesus' contrast involves a pun that works in his Aramaic speech, but not in our Greek translation: "You . . . strain out a gnat but swallow a camel!" In Aramaic the words *gamla* ("camel") and *kamla* or *kalma* ("gnat," "mosquito," "louse") sound almost the same.[135]

Unwashed Hearts

Jesus complains that Pharisees insist on cleaning the outside of the cup, but do not first clean their hearts (Matt 23:25-26//Lk 11:39-41). In using this image, he alludes to a debate that was raging between two schools of Pharisees precisely in his own generation, although he is employing the image figuratively.[136]

The two Pharisaic schools, Shammaites and Hillelites, divided over whether one should purify the inside or the outside of a cup first. The Shammaite school of Pharisees was less concerned whether one cleansed the inner or outer part first. By contrast, the Hillelite Pharisees thought that the outside of cups was typically unclean anyway and thus, like Jesus, insisted on cleansing the inner part first.[137]

On the surface, Jesus' statement challenges Shammaite practice (though for the effect of the metaphor); that the Shammaites predominated in Jesus' time but not after 70 supports the saying's authenticity.[138] Other features also support the saying's authenticity. That Luke's version (Lk 11:41) reads "give in char-

ity" rather than "cleanse" suggests an original Aramaic saying like the one Matthew records; the former (which fits Luke's theology of charity, and could be
construed as abrogating purity laws) represents the Aramaic *zakkau,* the latter
(which fits the saying itself) represents the Aramaic *dakkau.*[139] But Jesus' ultimate challenge goes beyond ritual purity practices to the point he illustrates:
the heart comes first (Mk 7:18-23).

Corpse-impurity

In Mk 5:41, Jesus touched a corpse, bringing it to life. Whatever the other
sources for impurity, touching a corpse caused one to contract even greater impurity.[140] Although dead creatures in one's fluid (Matt 23:24) and flowing blood
(cf. Mk 5:25-34) produced impurity, corpse-uncleanness (Matt 23:27-28//Lk
11:44) was more severe, extending seven days.[141] In Jewish tradition, if so much
as one's shadow touched a corpse or a tomb, one contracted impurity.[142]

Jesus complains that the Pharisees are like hidden tombs that defile people
through contact without the people even realizing it (Lk 11:44). Matthew's version of the saying claims that the tombs are whitewashed to make them look respectable (Matt 23:27). Jesus may have originally alluded to the practice in the
spring of using whitewash to warn passersby and Passover pilgrims to avoid
unclean tombs lest they become impure and hence barred from the feast,[143] an
idea consistent with the parallel in Luke.[144] (Matthew highlights instead the
whitewash's function as a beautifying agent to cover the tomb's corruption.)[145]
Some scholars think that Jesus also may have intended a play on words between
the terms for tomb *(qeber)* and inward part *(qereb).*[146]

We should not overplay the contrast with the Pharisees here, as if all of
them would have disagreed completely with Jesus regarding purity, or he would
have challenged all of them equally regarding spiritual purity.[147] Some Pharisees may have agreed with Jesus' emphasis on inner rather than outer purity
(Mk 7:15), but they normally stated it only in private[148] (perhaps out of fear that
people would stop observing the practices literally).[149]

Relationship to Jesus' Kingdom Message

What sorts of behavior might Jesus specifically have in mind when he denounces Pharisees and scribes (scribes in Mk 12:38-40)? He denounces vices
such as economic injustice (Mk 12:40), hypocrisy and misplaced priorities
(merely outward righteousness; Mk 12:40; Matt 23:23-28//Lk 11:39-42, 44), and
seeking one's own honor (Mk 12:38-39).[150] Pharisees would in fact have largely

agreed with Jesus' principles here, even if not all lived up to them (just as not all religious people today who agree with them live up to them).

In view of Jesus' end-time kingdom ethic, he may have demanded more than many teachers in his day, however. He apparently believed that the urgency of the kingdom demanded priorities different from those of most of his contemporaries; secondary issues of uncleanness and even some aspects of sabbath observance could be suspended in light of the urgency of the hour. Most Jews agreed when they regarded a situation as a matter of life and death;[151] some Torah teachers allowed a prophet to temporarily suspend even a duty in the Torah for the sake of an emergency.[152]

Most teachers apparently did accept marks of their status,[153] as Jesus implies in this denunciation. But as we noted earlier, Jesus emphasizes that the time of eschatological inversion has come, and it will overturn even the marks of religious and intellectual honor in which people boast. The right way instead would be the way that he would model: absolute trust in, dependence on and submission to the will of God, depending on God's power to bring life even from death.[154] That Jesus would be martyred through the agency of the world's elite was itself a sign that God's kingdom would favor not the elite of this age but the broken who depended solely on God.

Killing the Prophets

Even religious people, even God's own people, might kill prophets. In Matt 23:29-31//Lk 11:47-48, in a context addressed to scribes and/or Pharisees (Matt 23:29; Lk 11:46; cf. Lk 11:42), Jesus recalls the widespread early Jewish tradition that their ancestors had killed the prophets.[155] More recent prophetic figures, from Onias[156] to Jesus' predecessor John, had shared this very fate.

In the context, Jesus challenges the hypocrisy of those who honor the prophets by caring for their tombs (Matt 23:29//Lk 11:47), yet perhaps like their ancestors will kill the prophet who has come to them.[157] Their behavior proves that they are spiritually not "descendants of the prophets," but rather "descendants of those who killed them"; descendants who walked in their ancestors' ways would also reap their ancestors' judgments (Ex 20:5).[158]

After this denunciation, Jesus warns that his generation will face all the reserved judgment due for the martyrdoms from Abel to Zechariah (Matt 23:35// Lk 11:51). Jesus probably chooses as examples here the first and final martyrs of the biblical record (many treated the Writings, including 2 Chronicles, as the final section of Scripture).[159] The blood of Abel, a prototypical martyr[160] and figure for the beginning,[161] had cried for vengeance against his fraternal slayer (Gen 4:10).[162] Jesus' second example is probably the Zechariah of 2 Chron

24:20-22, martyred in the Temple.[163] According to a Jewish tradition preserved in later sources, Zechariah's blood, like Abel's, had cried against his murderers for vengeance; in this tradition Zechariah's blood invited the massacre of many priests.[164]

Jesus suggests climactic bloodguilt on that generation (Matt 23:35//Lk 11:51), a sentiment that makes particularly good sense if Jesus saw himself as a special agent of God and expected martyrdom.[165] The Gospel writers who recorded this earlier "Q" saying undoubtedly viewed this judgment as fulfilled in 70 CE. As Zechariah's blood had once desecrated the priestly sanctuary and so invited judgment,[166] so might the blood of the priests in 66 CE as the "abomination that brings about desolation" (Mk 13:14; Matt 24:15).[167] (That the shedding of innocent blood invited judgment was a biblical theme continued in Jewish tradition,[168] and one had to take special pains to protect the sanctuary from bloodshed.)[169] The murder of Zechariah in the temple (Matt 23:35//Lk 11:51) recalls their murder of the very prophets whose tombs they build (Matt 23:29-31// Lk 11:47-48).[170]

Jesus the Wounded Prophet

Jesus apparently expected his conflicts with established teachers and authorities to escalate in Jerusalem. While the Pharisees were centered there and they do appear in the context of Matt 23:29-31//Lk 11:47-48 (treated above), Jesus' expectation of hostility in Jerusalem appears too broad to focus exclusively on them. The "Q" saying in Matt 23:37//Lk 13:34 displays Jesus' love for his people and laments that, despite the Galilean crowds, Israel as a whole had not quickly embraced his (and John's) vision of repentance. Whereas we noted earlier Jesus' lament over the Galilean villages of Chorazin and Bethsaida, this new lament[171] suggests that Jerusalem, the center of the Jewish world, was also the object of his concern. For a prophet, neglect might constitute rejection no less than persecution did, but Jesus apparently expects some persecution as well.

In Matt 23:37//Lk 13:34, Jesus again recalls the Jewish tradition that Jerusalem killed the prophets, at the same time noting Jerusalem's unwillingness to heed him. This connection coheres with Jesus' sense of his mission including martyrdom as in other evidence in the Gospels (a matter to which we turn in ch. 20). Although Matthew understandably locates the saying during the passion week in Jerusalem, Luke's context would also recall Jesus' physical vulnerability to his enemies on Israel's behalf (Lk 13:32).

In the same saying (Matt 23:37//Lk 13:34), Jesus wished to gather his people under his wings. This apparently unusual claim recalls the familiar Jewish image of God sheltering his people under his wings.[172] (Jewish teachers also came to speak of one who converted a Gentile as bringing him or her under the wings of the Shekinah.)[173] Perhaps recalling the experience of God in some other Jewish sources,[174] Jesus' love for Jerusalem here gives way to the brokenhearted pain of their rejection and/or their judgment.

For Luke, Jesus' grief and his promise that they will see him later (Lk 13:34-35) precedes, hence is fulfilled in, the triumphal entry (Lk 19:41); Matthew places it among the woes of coming judgment after that entry, but in so doing transforms this into a promise of future hope (cf. Matt 10:23).[175] Although Luke's context might be more original in this case, Matthew's sense probably does fit the restoration prophet emphasis of Jesus' ministry. Perhaps as in some early Jewish teaching,[176] Israel's repentance was the goal of history, and her salvation was contingent on her repentance.[177]

Conclusion

The early traditions strongly suggest that Jesus and some Pharisees had disagreements over such matters as how to observe the sabbath properly. Each side was convinced that it understood Scripture more accurately, and, if Jesus' words in various strata of the tradition are any indication, harsh words were exchanged. Jesus denounces the Pharisees, masters of ritual purity, for their spiritual impurity, and compares experts in the law with those who murdered the prophets.

But while Pharisees and scribes may have provided many of Jesus' conflicts in the Gospels, his expectation of martyrdom in Jerusalem reflects a wider failure to receive his mission. (As we will argue later, he could expect martyrdom there primarily through the involvement of Jerusalem's priestly elite, not the Pharisees.) Like John, Jesus would face martyrdom, and apparently envisioned this martyrdom as divine necessity. Israel was not yet repenting adequately before the coming judgment.

CHAPTER 17

Jesus the Prophet

"The prevailing opinion has been that Jesus acted as a prophet and was recognized as an eschatological figure. The social historian recognizes traits that support another role. The figure that immediately comes to mind is that of the popular philosopher known as the Cynic."

BURTON MACK[1]

"Jesus cannot be considered simply a teacher. The miracles do not require us to think that he was an eschatological prophet, but they are compatible with that view."

E. P. SANDERS[2]

"Jesus had aims which engaged with the destiny of Israel. He was not simply a wisdom teacher."

KIM HUAT TAN[3]

In considering Jesus as a prophet, I subsume under this title several more specific categories sometimes offered by others: eschatological prophet; charismatic holy man and healer; and founder of a renewal movement. While these categories can be reasonably distinguished (and certainly existed separately for various ancient Jewish figures), they coalesce in Jesus and all do fit the general, earlier biblical rubric "prophet."

That a follower of John who also drew crowds should have been considered a prophet is hardly surprising.[4] The gospel tradition identifies John as the expected Elijah at various points (e.g., Mk 1:6; 9:13; Lk 1:17; Matt 17:12-13), but elsewhere more subtly reserves this image, alongside that of the new Moses, for Jesus (e.g., Lk 4:24-27; 9:8, 30-35, 61-62; Jn 1:21; 6:14-15).[5] Unlike the Baptist, Jesus apparently claimed that his ministry was actually introducing (not merely presaging) the kingdom, and all strata of gospel tradition confirm that Jesus performed miracles like those of Elijah and Elisha.[6] (The category also makes some sense of tradition behind Josephus' description.)[7] That the early Christian movement was also intensely prophetic[8] likewise may point to the prophetic character of its founder.[9]

Most scholars believe that Galileans followed Jesus as a prophet,[10] even if scholars continue to debate which sort of prophetic models are most relevant. Many people in Jesus' day undoubtedly followed charismatic leaders.[11] Although scholars increasingly concur that the historical Jesus was a "charismatic leader" in some sense, they dispute whether he was "(with Vermes) a charismatic healer like Hanina ben Dosa and Honi the Circle-Drawer or (with Hengel, Theissen and others) a charismatic prophet."[12] Given the fluidity of such distinctions in antiquity and the Gospel portrayal of Jesus as legal teacher, healer, and prophet, one must ask why we are forced to choose among these options. Observers probably approached him in terms of whichever role they needed him to fill, although this probably meant in practice that most people approached him as a charismatic signs-prophet (cf. Mk 1:34; 3:10; 6:4, 15; 8:28; Matt 21:11, 46; Lk 24:19).

Those who insist that because Jesus was a sage he was not a prophet[13] assume exclusive modern categories that would not have held among Jesus' contemporaries.[14] Scholars often thus reject the forced choice between Jesus being a sage or a prophet; he could have been both.[15] As Vermes' work on Honi and Hanina suggests, some popular charismatic teachers looked more like prophets, and despite more scribal teachers' objections, the line between popular teachers and prophets may have remained thin for many.[16]

Modern scholars who insist that if Jesus were a sage he could not be an eschatological figure ignore the intensely eschatological orientation of Palestinian Judaism as a whole in Jesus' day;[17] nor can teachers and revolutionaries always be distinguished.[18] Most such forced-choice logic represents the strict imposition of modern categories on much more fluid concepts of charismatic leaders held by people in first-century Jewish Palestine.[19]

Sign-prophets

Jesus' prophetic activity was distinctive in many respects,[20] but comparisons with other prophetic figures of his day help us identify some elements of his ministry that also fit his Palestinian Jewish milieu. Popular prophets[21] include both those who led movements[22] and "solitary popular prophets," such as

Joshua ben Hananiah.[23] The former were often perceived as prophets of deliverance, whose claims evoked Moses or Joshua; the latter resembled the majority of prophets in ancient Israel.[24]

Apparently many people hoped for a new deliverance like the exodus; Josephus complains about several who viewed themselves as eschatological sign prophets, and it is possible that these were simply his most conspicuous examples. Probably, then, first-century Jewish Palestine's most popular figures were the prophets of deliverance, leading messianic movements and modeling their ministries after Moses and Joshua.[25] Some of their promised activities may evoke Moses, signalling their attempts to secure eschatological deliverance.[26] (Eschatological signs were likely widely anticipated. Many Jewish people probably expected not only significant signs before the final deliverance and special miracles at the end[27] but pondered the promised signs of the Messianic era offered by Isaiah, Ezekiel, and other biblical prophets.)[28]

First-century sign-prophets evoking Moses or Joshua included Theudas, who tried to part the Jordan, and a Jewish-Egyptian false-prophet, who expected Jerusalem's walls to collapse before him.[29] Some of these sign-prophets may have envisioned themselves as possible messiahs; Josephus, who tells us about them, had good reasons to play down messianic claims (although he does fail to brand them "brigands" as he normally does revolutionaries).[30] Some of their followers undoubtedly understood them in such terms, and they could not help but recognize that their followers did so.[31]

No less than these prophets who sought to evoke a new Moses, Jesus was an "eschatological" prophet, a prophet of God's impending reign. Accounts of Jesus' miracles accord well with his interpretation of them in light of Is 35:5-6 (Matt 11:5//Lk 7:22); that is, he interprets them eschatologically as blessings of the future kingdom in the present.[32] Most recognize that in the Gospels, Jesus' miracles function as signs of the kingdom (explicit also for exorcisms in Matt 12:28//Lk 11:20).[33] Subsequent Christian sources similarly associate the Christian movement with an eschatological renewal of signs (e.g., Acts 2:17-18).

Jesus' miracles differed from those of the "sign prophets" after him denigrated by Josephus.[34] Although some of these figures announced a major eschatological sign, they did not perform them.[35] Unlike them, Eric Eve notes, Jesus "healed and exorcized, but seems not to have promised a particular spectacular sign."[36] The only sign attributed to him that resembles Moses was feeding people in the wilderness,[37] not plagues or conquest; most of his signs were benevolent acts of healings.

Theissen and Merz appear representative of many scholars today in concluding that while Jewish wonder-workers offer closer parallels than pagan ones do, they differ significantly from Jesus (especially in working only through prayer and lacking eschatological miracles).[38] No other source reports as many miracles concerning an individual as the Gospels do regarding Jesus.[39] More-over, Jesus stands alone among prior miracle-workers in using healings and ex-orcisms to indicate the coming of the eschatological order.[40]

Jesus as Healer and Exorcist

Although the evidence is limited concerning most particular miracles, all of the many ancient sources that comment on the issue agree that Jesus and his early followers performed miracles: Q, Mark, special material in Matthew and Luke, John, Acts, the epistles, Revelation, and non-Christian testimony from Jewish and pagan sources.[41] Underlining further the point, Mark would hardly have invented the idea that Jesus could not heal where faith was lacking (Mk 6:5).[42]

The testimony is not limited to Christian sources. The most explicit non-Christian sources available on this point, the rabbis[43] and Celsus[44] are clear. (Many of these later non-Christian sources attribute the miraculous works to sorcery, probably the earliest anti-Christian explanation for Christian mira-cles.)[45] Earlier than these, Vermes has argued persuasively that the miracle claim for Jesus in Josephus is authentic, based on Josephus' style.[46] Josephus calls Jesus a "wise man," who also worked "startling deeds," a term by which Josephus also depicts the miracles worked by the prophet Elisha.[47] This una-nimity is striking given the conversely unanimous silence in Christian, Jewish and even Mandean tradition concerning any miracles of respected prophetic figures like John the Baptist.[48]

The evidence for Jesus as a miracle-worker is stronger for this claim than for most other specific historical claims we could make about earliest Chris-tianity; miracles characterized Jesus' historical activity no less than his teaching and prophetic activities did.[49] Because miracle claims attach to a relatively small number of figures in antiquity (itinerant or not), there is little reason to suppose that Jesus would have developed a reputation as a wonder-worker if he did not engage in such activities.[50] As Gerd Theissen and Annette Merz put it, "Just as the kingdom of God stands at the centre of Jesus' preaching, so healings and exorcisms form the centre of his activity."[51] That particular stories would be preserved is also not surprising. If followers would preserve his teachings, how much more would they (and especially those who experienced recoveries) spread miracle reports![52]

The "Third Quest" is more respectful toward the Gospels' miracle tradition than the so-called first and second quests were;[53] scholars who treat Jesus as prophet and miracle-worker appear to be the mainstream.[54] Thus, regardless of their philosophic assumptions about divine activity in miracle claims,[55] most scholars today grant that Jesus' contemporaries viewed him as a healer and exorcist.[56] E. P. Sanders regards it as an "almost indisputable" historical fact that "Jesus was a Galilean who preached and healed."[57] Using traditional historical-critical tools, John Meier finds many of Jesus' miracles authentic.[58] Raymond Brown notes that "Scholars have come to realize that one cannot dismiss Jesus' miracles simply on modern rationalist grounds, for the oldest traditions show him as a healer."[59] Otto Betz regards it as "certain" that Jesus was a healer, a matter that "can be deduced even from the Jewish polemic which called him a sorcerer."[60] The miracles are central to the Gospels, he notes, and without them most of the other data in the Gospels are inexplicable.[61] Israeli scholar David Flusser notes that the picture of Jesus in the Synoptics is consistent and Jewish, hence reliably attests to Jesus as "a Jewish miracle-worker and preacher."[62] Even Morton Smith argues that miracle-working is the most authentic part of the Jesus tradition,[63] though he explains it along the magical lines urged by Jesus' and his movement's early detractors.[64]

The emphasis on healings and exorcisms seems fairly distinctive to Jesus (fitting a positive use of the dissimilarity criterion regarding his environment, though healing and exorcism continued among many of his subsequent followers). By way of contrast, most types of miracles reported in Josephus' accounts show little interest in healings.[65] Stories of postbiblical miracles are not very common outside Josephus,[66] and healings are particularly rare.[67]

That Jesus would draw a following performing such signs is not at all surprising. Once word of Jesus as *healer* spread, one cannot doubt that people throughout Galilee would flock to him.[68] People in antiquity traveled long distances to reach healing sanctuaries,[69] and one may compare the masses flocking to the hot springs at Tiberias in Galilee[70] and similar sites[71] to recover their health.[72]

Because of the philosophic questions involved, it is not possible to address Jesus' miracles further here without considerably expanding this book. I have therefore devoted a separate book to this subject, deferring further discussion on the issues of ancient miracle reports (especially the plausibility of eyewitness claims about them in historical narrative) and their interpretation to that book. I have treated most of the Gospels' individual miracle reports in my commentaries,[73] so anyone apt to complain that I have omitted prior discussion of them need only examine this work elsewhere. In the later book regarding miracles I will focus on the broader question of miracle reports and the extent to which they can be held to reflect or develop eyewitness material.

Limited Parallels with "Charismatic Sages"

As we noted in an earlier chapter, Vermes has clearly and helpfully shown that one need not look to more geographically distant Gentile healing traditions for the historical Jesus. Our limited material reports some Jewish signs-workers in Palestine, including in Galilee. Nevertheless, the postbiblical parallels should not be pressed too far.[74] While Honi (Onias) was undoubtedly known for getting answered prayer regarding rain,[75] most of the details we hear about him surface only in Amoraic tradition — perhaps half a millennium after he lived.[76] At the very least, much of the rabbinic characterization of Honi appears to be later. Thus, for example, we do not know if "Honi the Circle-Drawer" actually drew a circle around himself, as in the rabbinic legend (but not Josephus),[77] or merely prayed for rain. Eric Eve contends that, against Vermes, it is not clear that Honi represents a class of people beyond himself.[78]

Vermes' other chief example in rabbinic sources, Hanina ben Dosa, is usually assigned to the first century.[79] Like Jesus he was a Galilean, though he is the only other Galilean we know of to whom signs are attributed.[80] He appears several times in early-third-century sources,[81] where he could tell when he prayed whether the sick would recover or not,[82] and where a lizard who bit him as he prayed died.[83] Later material about Hanina is much more abundant, yet was transmitted and developed over the course of three or four centuries.[84]

Moreover, even if the tradition is reliable, it differs from Jesus: whereas Jesus was itinerant, people came to Hanina for prayer, and few of the divine interventions mentioned involve healing.[85] In their respective sources, Hanina was a petitioner of numinous or divine power, whereas Jesus was its bearer.[86] We cannot know much about other Galilean folk-healers, but Jesus was clearly no ordinary one.[87] Honi and Hanina are the natural places to start when looking for the Jewish context of Jesus' miracles, but the parallels they offer are more limited than we would like.

Elijah-like Signs

Nevertheless, Vermes' suggestion of a Palestinian Jewish model for Jesus appeals ultimately to a source earlier than Honi or Hanina. The miracles of Jesus resemble especially those of Elijah, Elisha, and Moses in the Hebrew Bible.[88] Jesus and his early followers, like some other Jewish wonder-workers,[89] may have deliberately emulated these models; the use of such patterns is probably deliberate (for Jesus; for those who reported the tradition orally; and for those who recorded the pattern in the Gospels and Acts). Unlike other models that some propose, these biblical examples are clearly earlier than our early Christian accounts and were clearly known to Jesus, his audience, and to those who told, wrote, and heard about him.

We need not place Jesus' emulation of Elijah (a sign-working prophet) and acting as an *end-time* prophet in contradictory categories. As we noted at much

greater length in an earlier chapter, people were looking for Elijah precisely because they were expecting the end, with which Elijah was associated (Mal 4:5-6;
Sir 48:10).

The Model of Moses

Elijah was not Judaism's only model for conceptualizing a central end-time
prophet. As we have noted in our discussion of sign-prophets above, some
prophets sought to emulate a new, eschatological Moses. In contrast to his silence about Elijah figures in this area, Josephus seems quite interested in
(though disparaging of) these purported prophets whose activities evoke Moses.[90] As we have noted, one such figure tried to part the Jordan, and another
expected Jerusalem's walls to collapse before him (like those of Jericho of old).[91]

As with the case of Elijah (Mal 4:5), a prophecy of Scripture generated the
expectation of this new prophetic figure. Deut 18:15, 18, promised a new
prophet like Moses, a promise that Jesus' contemporaries commonly applied to
the near future. Thus the Qumran Scrolls at least sometimes linked their expected "prophet" with the prophet like Moses text of Deuteronomy.[92] At least
some Qumran sectarians apparently associated this mission also with the future anointed ruler.[93]

Likewise, Samaritan expectation, though idiosyncratic and preserved only
in much later sources, may also preserve a more widespread tradition concerning the prophet like Moses.[94] Samaritans apparently (if our sources reflect
this early period) rejected prophets (or at least the Jewish tradition of prophets) between Moses and the final prophet, a prophet like Moses, the *Taheb* or
"restorer."[95]

Although the rabbis apparently rarely interpret Deut 18:15-18 eschatologically,[96] many compared the future redeemer to the former one, i.e., to Moses.[97]
The hidden Messiah tradition often connects the Messiah with Moses, who was
also hidden before he was revealed.[98] The related expectation of a new exodus
persisted as late as the rabbis,[99] but was already present in so-called Deutero-
Isaiah.[100] The expectation of a new Moses could be compatible with expectations of an eschatological leader. In fact, a wide range of Jewish tradition emphasized Moses' role as "king" (Deut 33:5).[101]

Together such backgrounds help us to picture the various ways that Jewish
observers could have understood charismatic leaders of their day in light of
contemporary end-time expectations. One need not appeal primarily to geographically distant categories (such as urban Hellenistic Cynics) to explain Jesus, when models of Jewish charismatic miracle-workers and, more often, of
end-time prophets were closer at hand. These models, and especially the model

of an end-time Moses leading an eschatological exodus, are also compatible with gospel traditions about Jesus' claims to special authority.

Prophetic Acts

Jesus acted like a prophet in various ways. Like one prophetic figure a generation later (Joshua ben Hananiah) or like Jeremiah centuries earlier, Jesus announced judgment on the temple. Like Jeremiah, he offered a dramatic symbolic action to draw attention to the temple's problematic status.

Likewise, Jesus chose twelve disciples as the nucleus for a renewal movement. This action is consistent with a prophet of restoration who anticipated God's restoration of his people, as evidenced in his promise that the twelve would sit on twelve thrones judging Israel. He also announced judgment on Israel, and offered various sayings that were more characteristic of prophets than sages.

Challenging the Temple

I treat here only briefly Jesus' overturning tables in the Temple, because I will revisit it in connection with Jesus' passion. But as a prophetic sign it coheres well with Jesus' prophecies of the Temple's impending destruction, inviting some discussion at this point.

Of all Jesus' actions, his challenge by overturning tables in the Temple came closest to appearing as a revolutionary challenge to the political order. Nevertheless, this action was plainly a prophetic declaration rather than the challenge of a revolutionary leader seeking a following.[102] Revolutionary messianic figures typically drew followings in the wilderness, attempting to build support (preferably armed support) before striking; Jesus, by contrast, acted under the nose of the Roman authorities and calculated his martyrdom. His act in the Temple was undoubtedly more symbolic than efficacious. Jesus acted against only a small area in the crowded outer court (the entire area of which was 300 meters by 450 meters).[103] Further, he neither "recleansed" the Temple daily, although the sellers had undoubtedly set up their tables again, nor continued his disruption long enough to permit the intervention of the Temple's Levite police or, had a riot begun, the Romans.[104]

Rather than inciting revolution, Jesus' action fits the conception of a kingdom established by God's direct intervention (a view attested in some apocalyptic sources and the Qumran documents); like some of his contemporaries, Jesus undoubtedly expected a kingdom "in which a temple, whether new or cleansed, would be useful."[105] Some of his contemporaries apparently expected God rather than mortals to supply the eschatological sanctuary.[106] We would add that Jesus probably differed from most of these contemporaries in expecting a future temple that would at least include a spiritual temple (as in other Qumran texts) founded on himself.[107]

The Twelve as a Nucleus of a Renewed Remnant for Israel

Jesus' choice of twelve disciples identifies him as leader of a renewal movement for Israel, again suggesting at the least his prophetic interests (and possibly more). Although Jesus had many disciples, he selected a core group of twelve (e.g., Mk 3:14; 1 Cor 15:5) to communicate a symbolic point. Jesus presumably selected this number to function as representatives[108] for the righteous remnant of the eschatological people of God.[109] This is probable because it appears analogous to twelve select leaders in Qumran texts,[110] as is widely noted.[111]

Twelve naturally was frequently understood to symbolize the twelve tribes of Israel, and many contemporary interpreters understood other references to "twelve" in this manner.[112] Jewish people sometimes opined that ten of the twelve tribes were lost and would be restored only in the end time;[113] many thus believe that Jesus' choice of "twelve" apostles signified the imminence of the end-time regathering of God's scattered people.[114] The twelve apostles may be viewed as akin to the twelve patriarchs (cf. Rev 21:12, 14), or to the princes of the tribes (cf. Num 2:3-29; 7:11, 18-78; 17:6), who would rule over the tribes at the time of their eschatological restoration (Matt 19:28//Lk 22:30).[115]

The designation "the Twelve" undoubtedly is authentic Jesus tradition. Later Gentile Christians would not have invented "Q" material like the twelve's rule over Israel (Matt 19:28//Lk 22:30, which does not suit typical Gentile Christians' theology).[116] The designation "twelve" was established tradition well before the writing of the Gospels (1 Cor 15:5), despite the likelihood that those who passed on the tradition knew that one of Jesus' own disciples betrayed him.[117] The criterion of embarrassment makes it highly unlikely that the later church invented a disciple betraying Jesus, and the historical tradition of the betrayal by someone in Jesus' inner circle makes unlikely any invention of that circle. The variations in the lists among New Testament documents are slight, but the variations may also testify to the idea of a group of "Twelve" more widely known than a standardized list of names.[118] Thus Luke both in Acts 1:13 and in Lk 6:16 has "Judas son of James" rather than Mark's "Thaddeus" (Mk 3:18).[119]

The existence of the "twelve" suggests a role for Jesus beyond that of prophet, however. That Jesus expects the twelve to rule, but is himself their leader, suggests that he claimed to be more than an average prophet (Matt

19:28//Lk 22:30). (In the next chapter, we shall explore other evidence supporting this suggestion.)

Jesus' Community on the Rock?

A wide range of scholars believe that Jesus' choice of *twelve* disciples supports
the notion that Jesus, like some other Jewish groups, planned a community.[120]
A more debated saying, but one worth considering, is Jesus' blessing of Peter
the "rock," with a promise to build his community on him (a passage discussed
briefly in ch. 14). The particular stream of Protestant interpretation that dominated twentieth-century New Testament scholarship not surprisingly doubted
the authenticity of Matt 16:17-19 (especially the specifically Matthean blessing
of Peter). For some the skepticism guarded against Catholic theology,[121] but
others simply objected (correctly) that Matthew alone reports these lines. Yet
for all we know, it could belong to "Q" and Luke simply chose not to follow it
here; we cannot know. Likewise, we need not assume that Mark and "Q" are
Matthew's only possible sources.

If one follows Mark's sequence, this material in Matthew may seem intrusive, and one may argue that Matthew himself has placed an earlier tradition of
Peter's commendation (the existence of which is probably implied by Peter's
central role in the early church)[122] in this particular narrative.[123] But no other
suitable place for commending a Petrine revelation exists in the tradition; certainly after the resurrection commendations on such a revelation would be beside the point.[124] More likely, Luke may have simply followed Mark, who omits
it, and Mark's punchy narrative style and emphatic theme of discipleship failure
were better served by omitting it if he knew of it.[125] Matthean wording[126] may
be more common where Matthew follows oral tradition rather than Mark.[127]

Apart from its single attestation, such a saying to Peter is plausible, and
more recent interpreters have shown less skepticism. Davies and Allison, for
example, argue for authenticity on the following grounds (which I merely summarize here):[128] (1) Evidence in Paul (especially Gal 1:11-21); (2) Semitisms;
(3) indications of Palestinian provenance by comparison with the Qumran
scrolls; (4) the criterion of consistency; (5) the criterion of dissimilarity (gates
of hades, keys of the kingdom, and binding and loosing are not distinctively
Christian;[129] the promise to Peter is not pre-Christian Jewish); (6) geographical
setting; and (7) the weakness of the objections to the contrary.

There is little about the saying that is not characteristic of Jesus elsewhere
or that fails to fit a Palestinian Jewish environment. Commissionings (Mk 6:7-
11; Matt 10:5-16//Lk 10:3-16) and beatitudes (Matt 5:3-11//Lk 6:20-22; Matt 11:6//
Lk 7:23; Matt 13:16//Lk 10:23) appear elsewhere in Jesus' words and certainly

elsewhere in early Judaism.[130] Jewish teachers sometimes pronounced blessings on those who gave correct responses, as Jesus does here.[131] Jesus granting Simon Peter the chief rank among the disciples best explains his multiply attested leadership role both in the gospel tradition and in the apostolic church.[132]

Although the passage as a whole is not multiply attested, some of its elements are. This passage calls Peter's father Jonah,[133] but apparently independent tradition preserves a similar name for Peter's father, "John" (Jn 1:42; 21:15). That Jesus gave him his nickname, "Peter," is also multiply attested (Jn 1:42, using the Aramaic equivalent). That Jesus gave Simon this nickname also fits Jesus' authority as a teacher and biblical naming traditions. It is also not a common name,[134] hence more apt to be a symbolic nickname ("rock")[135] than the sort of name usually given by parents. That "Peter" translates the multiply attested Aramaic version "Kephas" (Jn 1:42), including in undisputed and pre-Gospel letters of Paul (1 Cor 1:12; 3:22; 9:5; 15:5; Gal 1:18; 2:9, 11, 14), points to very early tradition. Many scholars contend that the persistence of the Aramaic nickname suggests that Jesus may have been its author.[136]

Nearly every other element of the blessing (not least the blessing formula itself) is at home in a Palestinian Jewish setting, as I and others have shown elsewhere.[137] The element most crucial for our point about Jesus' continuing mission, however, is Jesus' promise to build his "community" on the rock (coherent with an image in "Q").[138] Some scholars doubt that Jesus could have spoken of a "church," of followers after his departure.[139] But this doubt presupposes that Jesus did not expect a period between his initial mission and the end of the age, whereas many of his extant sayings suggest otherwise.[140] (One could also envision an eschatological community after the end; Qumran texts allow both possibilities.) Albright and Mann go so far as to suspect that confessional polemics are often at work in excluding the passage, noting that "a Messiah without a Messianic Community" would have been "unthinkable" to contemporary Judaism.[141]

Not only did various leaders plan communities to carry on their work;[142] a Jewish renewal movement might have employed the same language Jesus did. The Essenes described themselves as the *qahal*,[143] the Hebrew word for God's congregation in the exodus narrative, which the Greek versions translate as *ekklēsia*, or "church."[144] Jesus likewise depicts his community as the true, faithful remnant of Israel in continuity with the covenant community of Israel;[145] this image coheres with his choice of twelve persons to lead the renewal movement. (What marked it as new was Jesus' specific designation, "*my* community.")[146] This term had a later Christian sense, but also a familiar Jewish sense based on the Greek version of the Old Testament (neither of which would have made sense to uninitiated Gentiles).[147] The language of "building up" this community echoes biblical language and was at home in Judaism.[148]

In favor of Jesus planning for his followers to carry on his work is another disputed, though in this case multiply attested, tradition.[149] Scholars dispute whether Jesus sent out his disciples in ministry during his own ministry, as the Gospels suggest; but just such missions would have better prepared them for the rapid expansion of the movement that historically followed under their leadership.[150] Moreover, teachers often trained leading disciples in part by giving them practice among themselves and with others. Various elements in the "Q" version of the sending fit well the criterion of Jewish environment better than the later Gentile church (e.g., Matt 10:16//Lk 10:3).[151] Indeed, even some elements attested in only one extant location (such as the admonition to freely give as they had freely received, Matt 10:8) fit this criterion.[152]

Judging the Twelve Tribes (Matt 19:28//Lk 22:30)

To the twelve who forsook their livelihoods to follow Jesus' call Jesus promises that they will sit on thrones judging the twelve tribes of Israel (Matt 19:28//Lk 22:30).[153] Some scholars suggest that this Q promise must be authentic, preceding the betrayal by Judas.[154] The "Twelve" continued even after Judas' betrayal (1 Cor 15:5), but one would expect any later prediction pretending to be prophecy and addressed to the Twelve to stress the condition of perseverance, given the church's knowledge of Judas's failure.[155] Further, though later Christians might conceivably have invented a tradition about their apostles reigning, they surely would not have limited their rule to Israel.[156] Given Mark's skepticism about the first disciples (perhaps about disciples in general), it is not difficult to see why he would have omitted this promise, even if this is the point at which it appeared in the tradition. Stylistic evidence also favors an early tradition.[157]

Judgment on Israel

Just as Jesus founded a renewal movement to summon Israel to repentance, he also warned of impending judgment on his people if they failed to repent. (He and John the Baptist were not the only teachers of their day to pose such stark alternatives; the Dead Sea Scrolls testify that the community that produced them viewed itself as Israel's righteous remnant, and the rest of the nation as headed for judgment.) Thus Jesus prophesied to Israel as well as founded a prophetic movement to carry on the mission.

Prophetic Sayings, Especially Regarding the Temple

Jesus undoubtedly viewed himself as a prophet, not just a sage. This observation is suggested not only in his proclaiming the kingdom, working signs or confronting Jerusalem's temple authorities, but in some of his clearly prophetic sayings. For example, Jesus' woes against Galilean villages like Chorazin and Bethsaida are surely authentic (as we have noted), yet they also clearly evoke the language of biblical prophets, who sometimes unfavorably compared God's people to Sodom or pronounced judgment through mock laments.[158]

We noted some of Jesus' eschatological teachings in ch. 3. Such teachings about the future generally suggest Jesus' prophetic interests, often with a future role for himself. Most of these hold good claim to authenticity. We have already noted, for example, Jesus' saying in "Q" that his disciples would judge Israel from twelve thrones (Matt 19:28; Lk 22:30). If Jesus' twelve chief disciples held this exalted role, what role might we expect for their teacher (who repeated the common observation[159] that a disciple is not above a teacher)?

Finally, and at greatest length here, Jesus' warning of the Temple's destruction seems surely authentic.[160] It is multiply attested, probably even in "Q," which is likely pre-70 and pre-Markan (Matt 23:38//Lk 13:35). By itself, the "desolation" of the "house" could in principle refer to anything from a royal palace (Jer 22:5) to Israel as God's house (perhaps Jer 12:7), but in the context of Jesus' teachings in the gospel tradition it can only mean the destruction of the Temple.[161] Thus the Temple is "left" (cf. Mk 13:2) "desolate" (Mk 13:14). This interpretation is the most natural in a Jewish context;[162] the Babylonians had also left the Temple[163] and city[164] "desolate."[165]

Mack asserts that, "apart from Mark's passion narrative, there is no indication that Jesus or his early followers looked for the destruction of the Temple,"[166] but few scholars today would find his position consistent with our data.[167] That Jesus actually uttered such a judgment against the Temple a generation before it happened should not be doubted historically. Whereas the later church may have forgotten some of the significance of some of Jesus' words and deeds against the Temple, they nevertheless preserved them: a symbolic act of judgment there (Mk 11:15), the testimony of witnesses the Christians believed to be false (Mk 14:57-58; cf. Mk 15:29; Jn 2:19; Acts 6:14),[168] and (as we noted) "Q" material like the house being left desolate (Matt 23:38//Lk 13:35). Jewish Christians who continued to worship in the Temple (Acts 2:46; 21:26-27) nevertheless remained faithful to a saying of Jesus that they would surely not have created.[169]

Further, those who question the authenticity of Jesus' more specific threat to destroy and rebuild the Temple based on lack of contemporary expectations for the Temple's destruction and renewal have not examined contemporary expectations carefully enough.[170] Granted, Jesus' warnings about the Temple's destruction cannot have been as popular (or likely as explicit in public) as his teaching that God's kingdom was coming. While first-century Jews did not focus on "positive" messages the way many of the most popular preachers in the U.S. today do, most still remained loyal to the Temple and many regarded it as invulnerable.[171] Nevertheless, Jesus was surely not isolated in his perspective.

Some of Jesus' sectarian contemporaries also predicted judgment on the Temple; for instance, if *Testament of Levi* is pre-Christian at this point, it promises the desolation of the sanctuary on account of the priests' uncleanness.[172] The *Testament of Moses,* which accuses priests of polluting the altar,[173] prophesies judgment against the Temple,[174] and because the Roman ruler destroys only part of the Temple in the oracle, the prophecy undoubtedly predates AD 70. In some texts, enemy rulers may want to destroy the Temple,[175] but God will establish it eschatologically.[176]

Likewise, pre-Christian Jewish literature includes many texts about God bringing down a new Temple, a claim that presumably has implications for the old one.[177] (Some scholars even think they find evidence for a Messianic Son of David building the new Temple.)[178] This expectation may help inform how we should understand Jesus' own approach. Jesus hardly expected his own disciples to tear down the old Temple; like some of his contemporaries, as Sanders observes, Jesus expected God to act.[179] The disciples who hear Jesus' warning about the Temple's destruction are said to connect it with the age's end (Mk 13:4) — thus allowing for an imminent Temple from above. As we have observed, this expectation fits the sort of beliefs known to have existed among some of their contemporaries. (Crossan admits that Jesus' threat against the Temple is authentic, yet doubts that it could have been literal.[180] Such an approach, however, while not impossible,[181] runs into more difficulty with the criterion of Jewish environment; a "symbolic" threat against the Temple is much harder to document among Jesus' contemporaries.)

One may also compare a Qumran document from before 70 CE. It accurately warns that the Kittim (by whom they mean the Romans) would carry off the Jerusalem priesthood's wealth.[182] Yet this warning hardly makes the prediction, in a document that must predate 70 CE, a post-70 prediction![183] As David Hill observes,[184]

> that Jesus himself could have made the prediction [of the Temple's destruction] is no more improbable than that Jesus ben-Chananiah should have done so in AD 62 (Jos. *Bell.* VI.300ff.): indeed, the destruction of the Temple was one of the most important elements in post-Herodian messianism, and not every reference to it requires a date after AD 70.

Similar examples could be multiplied.[185]

Similarly Jesus' evocation of the language of the biblical prophets renders superfluous a necessary appeal to prophecy after the event.[186] That the first Temple's previous violations indicated judgment would have made sense to Jesus' contemporaries steeped in biblical tradition,[187] and many, though not all, Jewish teachers in succeeding centuries recognized the destruction of Herod's temple as judgment.[188]

Finally, those writing a retroactive prophecy after an event might be more likely to report the prophecy with literalistic accuracy rather than hyperbole. That is not the case here, for *some* stones were left standing on others;[189] some of these stones in fact still remain, and are rather conspicuous. Most of them are between two and five tons, but one, nearly forty feet long, is close to 400 tons. One would suppose that someone "prophesying" after the event might have taken better account of the concrete evidence against one's literal claim.[190] Whether or not Mk 13 predates 70, the Jesus tradition it reflects surely does.

Similarly, one would also never guess from the passage that the Temple actually was destroyed by fire.[191] Moreover, in a "prophecy" after the event, the earliest sources would probably also have more clearly distinguished between the Temple's demise and Jesus' return (cf. Mk 13:2).[192] Thus one scholar, who doubts that the Synoptics accurately report Jesus' teaching about the imminent end-time, complains that if the Synoptics *are* accurate here, Jesus was "mistaken rather than misreported"[193] — the very sort of conclusion composers of tradition after 70 would have wished to avoid.

Jesus' graphic language of the sacrilege or desecration that would lead to desolation or destruction (Mk 13:14) made sense in its Jewish environment. It alluded to a recurrent biblical and early Jewish judgment motif regarding Israel's history; it provided the ultimate symbol of national and religious humiliation.[194] Jewish people resisted such desecration to the death,[195] except in times of national apostasy, when they might be considered its cause.[196] Even before the first exile, the prophets recognized scattering and tribulation as a judgment designed to bring God's people to repentance (e.g., Deut 4:26-31). In the second century BCE, the Syrian ruler defiled the altar, causing an "abomination," ruining the sanctuary with "desolation" (1 Macc 4:38; cf. 1:54). In the Dead Sea Scrolls, one could profane the Temple by persecuting the righteous there.[197]

While such language informs Jesus' wording more generally, Jesus' particular reference to a desolating sacrilege in the sanctuary (Mk 13:14) suggests a more specific biblical allusion to the Book of Daniel.[198] Noting this allusion might not in itself resolve what Jesus meant by it. When the Book of Daniel refers more than once to the "abomination that would result in desolation," it might, like Israel's larger history, allow for more than a single event.[199] In any case, the end had not come after Antiochus' desecration of the Temple (Dan 11:31; cf. "then" in 12:1), providing ancient interpreters the possibility that another desolation would come (see Dan 12:11-12). Early Jewish interpreters reapplied Daniel's image of final tribulation in new ways, in the Dead Sea Scrolls[200] and apparently other circles,[201] including among some first-century Christians.[202]

End-time Sayings

Although some, as we have noted, doubt that Jesus would have spoken about the future, particularly in images resembling those often found in apocalyptic literature, their skepticism probably reveals more about their presuppositions about Jesus than about the evidence, as Albert Schweitzer pointed out long ago.[203] Jesus' message about the future pervades the tradition and in a first-century context is hardly inherently incompatible with Jesus the sage. Gentile Christians would not have introduced such Jewish imagery, and one doubts that Jewish Christians need have been more inclined to it than their teacher.[204]

Scholars debate whether the Synoptics applied Jesus' predictions of imminent destruction only to the Temple or also to a later end of the age. What is most important for our purposes here, however, is that Jesus spoke about what he expected in the future from his vantage point. Though Jesus' eschatological imagery is not apocalyptic revelation in the strictest sense,[205] it is thoroughly Palestinian Jewish, and reflects motifs common to apocalyptic literature.[206] Even the motifs of imminence and prerequisite signs appear together in apocalyptic texts as well as in this discourse.[207] Disciples may have assembled elements of the tradition before Mark's composition during some crisis of eschatological significance such as Caligula's public intention to have his statue erected in the Temple.[208]

Jesus' "eschatological discourse," which weaves together a prophecy of judgment against the Temple and eschatological imagery, certainly predates the Gospels. Roughly twenty years after Jesus' execution, the earliest New Testament sources already were using many of Jesus' eschatological teachings. Despite limited correspondence in exact wording, Paul's eschatological material in 1 Thess 4–5 (cf. also 2 Thess 2) corresponds so closely in content to eschatological material elsewhere attributed to Jesus that it reads almost like an interpretive summary of it.

The allusions in the earliest extant Christian document (1 Thess 4:13–5:11; cf. 2 Thess 2:1-12) include clouds, gathering of the elect, angel(s), lawlessness, apostasy, defilement of God's temple, the *parousia* (common to Matthew 24 and the Thessalonian correspondence), coming as a thief, unknown times and seasons (Acts 1:7), sudden destruction on the wicked, and so on.[209] (Though some detractors remain, most scholars recognize the correspondences.)[210] Jesus' final discourse in Matthew includes not only Markan and Q material but also special

Matthean elements, yet even some of Matthew's redaction (such as the trumpet in Matt 24:31//1 Thess 4:16; coming as a thief in the night in Matt 24:43//1 Thess 5:2; and the "parousia") appears to echo genuine oral Jesus tradition.

Other explanations for the correlation between Paul and eschatological language attributed to Jesus falter. Paul's and Jesus' eschatological imagery fits their early Jewish environment, but in contrast to the vast array of early Jewish motifs, the degree of correspondence between Paul and Jesus is overwhelming. Thus both Jesus' discourse and Paul in these passages lack many other themes of Jewish apocalyptic (e.g., mutant babies).[211] This coincidence of particular motifs and absence of others also refutes the idea that merely early Jewish-Christian scriptural embellishment rather than Jesus himself would stand behind both the extant Jesus tradition and 1 Thessalonians. The latter probably constitutes our earliest Christian document and derives from a very nonapocalyptic milieu.[212]

The Jesus tradition does not borrow from Paul: that various Jesus traditions all happened to reproduce so much of Paul's correspondence with one church is hardly likely.[213] The same coincidence of motifs refutes the thesis that Paul and the Gospel tradition have a common source in some early Christian prophecy.[214] Given the abundance of prophecy in early Christianity, probably multiple prophecies during the average weekly gathering (cf. 1 Thess 5:20; 1 Cor 14:26-31) and the number of eastern Mediterranean house churches, tens of thousands of prophecies must have been uttered in the early churches before Paul wrote. Why would a particular prophecy or particular set of motifs come to preeminence?[215]

The only genuinely workable explanation for the coincidence and the "you yourselves already know" (1 Thess 5:1-2), hence the meaning of Paul's "word of the Lord" (1 Thess 4:15) and "traditions delivered to you" (2 Thess 2:15), is that the earliest dominical tradition stands behind Paul's Thessalonian correspondence as well as behind the Gospels. With many scholars,[216] I am virtually certain that this material in Paul reflects dependence on Jesus' eschatological teaching — a dependence that confirms both the preservation of such teaching and the likelihood that Jesus was viewed as a prophet. (Paul applies it to the end of the age, though this does not tell us how the Gospel writers after 70 CE might interpret it.) I treat this subject much more extensively in Appendix 4, where I also provide a chart of some of the motifs.

Conclusion

Various prophetic figures appeared in Jesus' day, including sign-prophets portending imminent deliverance and miracle-working charismatics somewhat in the mold of Elijah. Jesus differs from extant examples of both models (focusing on healings and exorcisms), but does function as an eschatological prophet working Elijah-like signs and depending on divine intervention for deliverance. Biblical models of a new Elijah and new Moses may contribute to his construction of his prophetic calling.

Jesus also appears as a prophet in his sayings about judgment on Israel, particularly the Temple, hence (as in the denunciations of some of his Jewish contemporaries) the ruling priestly elite in Jerusalem who had corrupted it. (That Jesus prophetically challenged the elite is also consistent with his martyr's death in Jerusalem.) Many of Jesus' sayings also seem to address the end of the age (or minimally the present order in some dramatic sense). These sayings are sufficiently well-documented to show that Jesus did not content himself merely with uttering wisdom sayings, but also spoke of the future.

Not only what Jesus said, but also what he did, revealed his prophetic character; he engaged in various prophetic acts. These included acting against commerce in the outer court of the Temple, an act that coheres well with his prophecy of judgment against the Temple. He founded a restoration movement within Israel, as symbolized by his choice of twelve leaders for the new community; some evidence even suggests that he spoke of the new community itself and Peter's foundational role in its formation. That he envisioned his twelve key followers as ruling Israel in the future suggests that he also envisioned a role for himself in the kingdom. Some more explicit material, treated in our next chapter, makes this final point even likelier.

Chapter 18

Jesus as Messiah?

"He will be a Jesus, who was Messiah, and lived as such, either on the ground of a literary fiction of the earliest Evangelist, or on the ground of a purely eschatological Messianic conception."

ALBERT SCHWEITZER[1]

"Before his death Jesus proclaimed the kingdom of God, and after his death his disciples proclaimed him to be the Messiah, the king of Israel. Logic strongly suggests that a messianic element was present in Jesus' teaching and activities, if only implicitly, and that this best accounts for this development."

CRAIG EVANS[2]

Many respected scholars, such as Rudolf Bultmann, have thought it unlikely that Jesus believed he was the Messiah.[3] This opinion has not been the consensus in all generations of critical scholarship,[4] however, and today many European and other scholars are more open to the idea that Jesus thought of himself in some such terms. How did Jesus view himself?

Jesus' Self-Identity

As we have already been noting (e.g., chs. 14, 17), some of the gospel tradition's sayings assign to Jesus a central role in God's plan; some of these exceed the expectations for normal prophets. Some have suggested that Jesus experienced early marginalization, helping to explain his predilection for the marginalized.[5] Such factors are certainly possible. One should not, however, in any case infer from such marginalization that Jesus lacked confidence in his role; in our surviving evidence, he exhibits a confidence that he speaks for God, based on his confidence in his relationship with God.

Some of Jesus' sayings, as we have noted, call Israel to moral reformation. This is what we would expect from a prophet in the Israelite tradition. Other sayings, however, give Jesus a more unusual prophetic role, for example, when he insists that a disciple following him immediately takes precedence over burying a dead father. Even here we might possibly attribute the unusual demand simply to eschatological urgency.

But many other prophetic sayings in the same kinds of sources (notably "Q") assign Jesus an important and distinctive role in the kingdom. Thus for example, when Jesus calls "twelve" disciples in organizing a renewal movement for Israel, he calls them to follow *him*. If they will sit on twelve thrones judging Israel (Matt 19:28//Lk 22:30), what should we assume for the role of the one who called them to follow him? John's sayings in "Q" about one who might be viewed as his successor suggest an even more exalted status (see discussion in the following chapter).

Early Belief in Jesus as Messiah

Some doubt that Jesus' earliest followers considered him a Messiah, but this skepticism rejects all the explicit testimony that remains extant in favor of a hypothesis argued virtually from silence.[6] Writing in a Diaspora setting where "anointed one" was unintelligible as a title, Paul, our earliest extant NT writer, sometimes uses "Christ" virtually as Jesus' surname; the idea of Jesus as "Messiah" must certainly predate Paul. Paul's language may suggest that the entire Judean Jesus movement that he knew considered Jesus as "Christ" (Gal 1:22); certainly he shows no awareness of, or need to refute, Jesus-followers who deny Jesus' Messiahship (not even Paul's so-called "Judaizing" opponents do this).[7] The closest explicit evidence we have in the first century for a nonmessianic interpretation of Jesus belongs to Josephus (*Ant.* 18.63), whom no one claims as Jesus' follower.

Other respected scholars have even suggested that Jesus himself drew on biblical passages that lent themselves to a messianic interpretation.[8] Such arguments remain contested, but one observation seems difficult to evade. Given the environment in which Jesus ministered, he had to know that his teachings about the kingdom and some of his actions would lead to speculation about his messianic character.[9] It would not have been possible for him to be ignorant of the frequent connection between Jewish eschatology and biblical expectations of an end-time Davidic ruler and that his growing following and invitations to follow could not but have stirred speculations.[10] In keeping with this observation, we should note the observation of E. P. Sanders and others that the earliest strands of the Jesus tradition indicate that Jesus taught that his disciples would have a role in the Messianic kingdom, a promise that would naturally imply that he attributed to himself the role of God's viceroy.[11]

"King of the Jews" and the Disciples' Perspective

In the Gospels, Pilate ordered Jesus executed on the charge of sedition, for claiming kingship. Most scholars hold that this charge against Jesus as "king of the Jews" (Mk 15:2, 9, 12, 26) is historical.[12] First, it fits what we know of the period. As we shall observe in ch. 21, the priestly aristocracy would arrest and the Romans execute anyone who offered the slightest grounds for suspicion of treason against Rome (grounds that could include reports about acclamations at the triumphal entry, Mk 11:8-10). Likewise, Romans crucified many self-proclaimed kings and their followers.[13]

Moreover, Christians would not have invented the charge "King of the Jews." It does not reflect any traditional Christian confession; Jesus' "you say" in the tradition (Mk 15:2) suggests that it is not even the title the tradition believed that Jesus would have emphasized. More importantly, Christians would have hardly invented the claim that Jesus was crucified on these grounds, since such a claim invited potential repression for themselves as well (cf. Acts 17:7).[14] As broadly as "treason" could be defined in Roman law[15] and especially in Sejanus's Rome,[16] the charge of claiming to be a king on the part of an otherwise unimportant provincial might require little investigation to secure condemnation. Ironically, Pilate, though known from an inscription and from Jewish sources, appears in extant Roman history only as the governor who ordered Jesus' execution.[17]

Once we grant that Jesus was executed on this charge, his immediate context makes skepticism about his messianic claim implausible. Both Pilate (who had Jesus executed) and the earliest extant views of Jesus' followers on the question portray Jesus as a Jewish king. *Yet neither Pilate nor the disciples got the idea from each other; certainly the later church did not get the idea from Pilate.* What source did Pilate and the disciples have in common? Surely Jesus himself is the likeliest source. Or did both Pilate and the disciples, who were privy to more information about Jesus than we are, coincidentally both misinterpret him — the only true interpreters being modern skeptics of the claim? (Modern skeptics, incidentally, must explain away all the early textual evidence for the claims and then argue from the silence that remains.)

His disciples claimed him to be Messiah; his execution as king indicates that others believed that he considered himself Messiah.[18] It is inherently likelier that Pilate and the disciples shared in Jesus a common source for this idea than that the disciples derived it from Pilate or that Pilate got it from renegade disciples who affirmed something that their teacher denied. That Jesus is the common source is a likely inference, and is more than that: it is in fact what our only extant sources claim.

E. P. Sanders thus thinks that many scholars have been too cautious about assuming that Jesus believed he was a king:[19]

> Jesus taught about the *kingdom;* he was executed as would-be *king;* and his disciples, after his death, expected him to return to establish the *kingdom.* These points are indisputable. Almost equally indisputable is the fact that the disciples thought that they would have some role in the kingdom. We should, I think, accept the obvious: Jesus taught his disciples that he himself would play the principal role in the kingdom.[20]

"Messiah" was a Jewish category, not a Gentile one, so the suggestion that the title was invented by later Gentile Christians can be rightly deemed hopeless. "Christ" was a natural way to translate "Messiah" in Greek,[21] hence it translates "anointed one" (not just in the royal sense) regularly in the Septuagint. But as we have noted, because that term in regular Greek usage simply meant "ointment" — an image the royal nature of which was wholly unintelligible to most Greeks[22] — Paul in the Diaspora normally uses it as Jesus' surname rather than as a title,[23] in contrast to the more primitive usage in the Gospels.[24]

A primary objection that scholars traditionally raised against Jesus claiming to be messiah was that the sources portray him accepting the claim only privately and at the end of his ministry. We shall examine this "messianic secret" below, but first should note that even where the Gospels note Jesus as messiah, they qualify the traditional sense of messiahship.

Qualifying "Messiahship": The Triumphal Entry

Jesus did not claim to be "messiah" in what was likely the most common *traditional* sense, that of a warrior king.[25] (We survey some of these diverse, traditional messianic views below, none of which seem precisely what Jesus claimed for himself.) The gospel tradition itself suggests that Jesus, when he accepted the title, would not always accept it in an unqualified way (Mk 8:29-31; cf. 15:2).[26]

Mark portrays Jesus entering Jerusalem in a way that some could construe as royal, yet not as a military challenger to the elite or toward Rome (Mk 11:7-10). Clearly Jesus did enter Jerusalem during this week, and clearly he already enjoyed the reputation of a prophet; *something* like the triumphal entry is therefore inevitable. Yet even beyond such a general statement, we can make a strong case for some further details recorded in the Gospels.

Some scholars doubt much of the historical substance of the triumphal entry narrative; some, for instance, contend that Mark 11:1-11 fits the formal pattern of a legend, in this case, of a king entering his city.[27] Yet historical narrative could be told using the same formal pattern.[28] In favor of the narrative's reliability, Witherington points out that others commandeered animals; the original acclamation (one coming in the Lord's name) hardly reflects later christological confessions; and Psalm 118:26 (cited by the crowds) was genuinely used during Passover, though later Christians probably would not know this (hence would not fabricate it; see more fully below).[29] Others point out that Mark and John may independently attest Jesus entering on a donkey.[30]

Moreover, if Jesus entered the city in a memorable way at all (and there was no other reason to preserve the story), he had to acquire the animal by some means.[31] Correspondingly, if he rode an ass, he himself probably intended the allusion to Zechariah[32] (which Mark seems not to have exploited and perhaps not to have noticed). And why not, if Jesus both read the Hebrew Bible and believed himself the future king (as we have begun to argue)?

Thus, as many scholars today point out, the triumphal entry itself appears to be historical (even if modest in scale).[33] Perhaps the Romans waited so long to execute Jesus because they did not know of the entry, perhaps because the acclamations at his entry would have been ambiguous to most Jerusalemites greeting pilgrims and his entrance was accomplished quickly.[34] The disciples, however, would have remembered the event in great detail, and what Jesus intended to convey to them through the symbolic act is more critical than the immediate understanding of other bystanders. There was no need to be more publicly explicit than this; Jesus would be executed as a messianic pretender soon enough.[35] Only in retrospect would memories of the event be impressed with the meaning subsequent events were thought to instill in them.[36]

It is unlikely that the later church would have thought to create a scene based on the authentic character of the Passover season; Mark's account, adapted by Matthew, thus presumably preserves accurate tradition. The acclamations "Hosanna!" and "Blessed is he who comes in the Lord's name" (Mk 11:9-10) both reflect Psalm 118, part of the Hallel psalms sung during this season.[37] Although in our later sources people officially began singing the Hallel only the night before the first day of Passover,[38] Passover pilgrims could begin arriving, as Jesus did, considerably earlier, and probably were often singing such psalms in advance of the festival.[39] Interestingly, these allusions to the Hallel appear also in the parable of the vineyard and at the last supper, in every case during the Passover season. Nevertheless, none of these citations betrays

any overt connection with Passover (hence do not appear to be deliberate forg-
eries for verisimilitude). These allusions to the Hallel fit the original context so
well (and probably so much better than that of the later church) that they undoubtedly stem from a very early part of the tradition.

Once we conclude that the narrative reflects historical tradition, we must
ask whether it tells us anything about how Jesus and others viewed his identity.
Is it plausible that anyone viewed him in messianic terms at this entry? Crowds
would have been using the Hallel anyway, but though the disciples undoubtedly
knew that, their tradition preserved a particular part of the Hallel especially relevant to Jesus: "Blessed is the one who comes in the name of the Lord" (Mk
11:9). Rendering the connection with Jesus' role more explicit, Mark or his tradition speaks of the coming Davidic kingdom (Mk 11:10). Such features fit the
actual setting better than we might suppose. Hopes for redemption ran high in
the crowded fervor of Jerusalem near Passover, requiring the Roman governor
to increase security during this time. Later Jewish thinkers clearly saw the future redemption prefigured in Passover, the Hallel,[40] and the cry, "Hosanna!"[41]
Thus the arrival of a prophet from Galilee already associated with eschatologically significant acts (e.g., Mk 6:34-44; Matt 12:28//Lk 11:20) could lead the
Galileans in the crowd, who were most familiar with Jesus' works, to acclaim
the imminent restoration of the Davidic kingdom (Mk 11:10).

Yet the triumphal entry was probably not a lengthy event, and probably not
everyone in Jerusalem would have understood it the same way. The Sadducean
aristocrats' position of power depended on them keeping peace between their
people and the Romans.[42] That they did not intervene during Jesus' triumphal
entry suggests a number of possible factors on the historical level: first, the entry probably happened relatively quickly and the priestly aristocrats, most of
whom were occupied on the Temple Mount during this period, were unaware
of these events while they were transpiring. Probably many of those greeting
the royal party did not recognize the entry as messianic, and possibly the messianic commotion did not spread beyond the portion of the crowd already ex-
cited by Jesus' reputation. It is likely the rural Galilean pilgrims more than urban Jerusalemites who hail Jesus as a prophet (cf. Mk 11:9; Matt 21:10-11).[43]

Assuming, as I think we should, that the event itself is historical, we must
ask what Jesus intended the event to convey. In that vein, it is important to note
that the later church or Jesus' Jewish followers could have chosen for Jesus a
more militant steed, but Jesus chose a beast of burden that would convey the
image of Zech 9:9.[44] That knowledge of the Zechariah allusion seems lost on
Mark and perhaps his tradition,[45] as we have noted, suggests the antiquity of
the tradition of Jesus' entry on the animal.[46] Although later teachers and probably Jesus' contemporaries regarded this prophecy as Messianic,[47] it was not
such a popular text that his followers need have grasped the full significance of

his actions immediately. He was hardly the only pilgrim to enter Jerusalem on an ass, though he was probably the only potential messianic figure to do so in the midst of public acclaim. Many scholars who observe the actions believe that Jesus was announcing that he was indeed a king, but not a warrior-king.[48]

The Gospels suggest that Jesus' view of his kingship was not the common political or military understanding, but that not only his enemies but also his disciples initially misconstrued him in accordance with popular expectations associated with the exaltation and deliverance of Israel. Nevertheless, Jesus and the early movement that emphasized his teachings at least found in the diverse concepts of messiahship a nucleus appropriate for partly defining his mission. The diverse views about messiahship we will survey below show that Jesus did have some room for redefining the meaning of the term. Just as Qumran adapted its messianic and eschatological vision in a distinctive manner, Jesus' disciples would have been forced to do the same.[49]

Why a Messianic Secret?

"Secrets," or rather attempts at privacy or at least crowd control, pervade Mark's (and to some extent probably independently John's)[50] story about Jesus. In a number of Gospel accounts about Jesus' ministry, he urged his followers to silence, perhaps to reduce undue pressure from premature popularity. This popularity demanded other measures as well, such as speaking from a boat separate from the crowds (Mk 3:9), praying alone before sunrise (Mk 1:35), taking the disciples apart alone (Mk 6:31-32; 7:24; cf. 8:27), or evading further crowds in one town in order to fulfill his mission elsewhere (Mk 1:38). In this broader context, it would appear that the tradition that he admonished his disciples to silence about his messianic identity in particular (Mk 8:29-30) might guard against even greater dangers than popularity — such as premature exposure to the authorities as a political threat.

Scholars have, however, widely debated the reason for this "messianic secret." In the early twentieth century William Wrede contended that Mark invented the Messianic Secret to explain why some traditions denied that Jesus claimed Messiahship.[51] Most scholars today, however, judge Wrede's thesis to be inadequate because it dismisses too much of the data.[52] Wrede was correct to notice that Jesus did not proclaim himself messiah or even initially welcome the claim that he was messiah. Yet Wrede was not the first person to notice this reticence, nor is his its only explanation; it was noticed already, and certainly explained differently, in antiquity.[53]

Others suggest that Jesus rejects the title initially due to its military connotations;[54] no public acclamation of Jesus' Messiahship could be understood accurately until after the crucifixion and resurrection (Mk 9:9; 15:26).[55] Indeed, some scholars argue that Jesus could be viewed only as Messiah-designate till after the resurrection anyway.[56] Wrede's opinion of a nonmessianic tradition likely falters not only on literary critical grounds but also on the basis of comparative studies. Our limited information on first-century potential messianic claimants may suggest a reticence to declare their identity prematurely; they apparently felt they had to produce some evidence of their messiahship before publicly claiming kingship.[57] (This may have been the case with the "sign-prophets" treated in ch. 17.) In the broader culture, self-testimony may have seemed inappropriate, especially in view of the sentiment against self-boasting in the first-century Mediterranean world.[58] Further, some prominent biblical prophets often worked clandestinely, endeavoring to accomplish their mission without seeking their own honor (e.g., 1 Kgs 11:29; 13:8-9; 21:18; 2 Kgs 9:1-10), partly because they were investing their time especially in a small circle of disciples they were training (1 Sam 19:20; 2 Kgs 4:38; 6:1-3).[59]

Each of these proposals may be helpful, and we shall discuss Jesus' messiahship further below. But because the "secret" of the kingdom extended far beyond Jesus' messiahship (Mk 4:11), solutions addressing only a *messianic secret* may be too narrow.[60] That Jesus offered private teaching to his disciples is no more unusual than that some other teachers of his day did so (as we noted in our discussion of parables in ch. 13).[61]

Since the disciples rather than crowds presumably supply the primary source of information about Jesus for the gospel tradition, these private teachings could have been transmitted as accurately as the public ones. Of course, later generations could easily claim to report "secret" teachings passed on privately for generations (e.g., second-century gnostics). But teachings could be genuinely passed on in schools, and these "private" teachings of Jesus to disciples were kept private only briefly during the course of his ministry. Depending on when some of these events occurred, that could mean that they were kept private only for a matter of months or weeks.[62]

But while this broader context is important, scholars who note the particularity of secrecy about Jesus' messianic identity are also correct. In addition to some of the other arguments above, at least one important reason for allowing claims of his messiahship only toward the end of his ministry was a matter of practical strategy. Messianic acclamations could (and did) lead the authorities to wrongly classify Jesus as a revolutionary and seek his execution; thus Jesus presumably delays his martyrdom until the appropriate time and place (Passover in Jerusalem) by seeking to reduce his activity's explicitly political associations. Undue publicity drew uncontrollable crowds (e.g., Mk 1:45; 2:2; 3:9-10, 20); the crowds and the rumors they might spread could invite further "incriminating charges" that Jesus sought to delay until the appropriate time.[63] As we have also seen elsewhere, Jesus waited on God to establish the kingdom and install the Messiah. Thus he could expect to fill this role himself while rejecting any attempt to claim it for him before God established it.[64]

Such factors surrounding Jesus' ministry explain the "secret" better than Wrede's theory does. The Gospels portray Galilean crowds risking overwhelming Jesus and his disciples, as we noted above. Explicit public teachings about Jesus' role in the kingdom would risk inciting those eager to follow a traditional messiah and hasten Jesus' conflict with the authorities before he was ready. If Jesus knew anything at all about the political situation in Jerusalem, he would know that a public messianic claim would lead to his almost immediate execution; in Mark, it does.[65] Even when traveling to Jerusalem, Jesus does not arm his followers or offer signs of resistance; the Gospel narratives are thus plausible as they stand, offering a plausible reason for Jesus' silence.

Views of Messiahship in Antiquity

To understand why Jesus needed to qualify the definition of messiahship, it is important to understand the range of ideas attached to messiahship in his day. Jesus was not the only teacher to dissent from other messianic views, for the range of views was broad. Most of the views would not fit his ministry (just as others' messianic views would not fit all the messianic paradigms of their contemporaries).

The prophets had foretold an eschatological king and/or dynasty descended from David,[66] a theme that continued in early Judaism.[67] Because the king was the "anointed one,"[68] Jewish people often granted the eschatological anointed king, the king par excellence, the articular title, "the messiah." "Anointed" (for both royal and nonroyal uses) came into the Septuagint regularly as *christos*.[69]

The Gospels provide the impression that Palestinian Jews in general understood the term "messiah" ("anointed one") and expected his coming. Given the term's inadequacy in the Diaspora and in later Christian christology ("son of David" christology is far less prominent than wisdom, lord, and other christologies), it seems unlikely that the Gospels would have simply invented this usage.[70] Yet our first-century evidence on the issue is disparate; some of it, especially texts directed toward Diaspora audiences, make minimal use of the term. But this lack of use may say more about our sources than about first-century Palestinian Judaism's messianic expectations.

Josephus' omission of messianic data is understandable; writing for a Diaspora readership, seeking to minimize Judaism's revolutionary involvement, he has reason to play down messiahs and popular messianic ideals that could have political implications.[71] Josephus may have even toned down David's revolutionary activity and ancestry for the messiah.[72] He elsewhere suppresses Jewish ideas that would present his heritage badly to the Romans and undoubtedly does the same with messiahship, "though certain of the persons whom he describes as brigands and deceivers must really have been messianic pretenders."[73] Yet the nature of such messiahs varied: not all such messiahs were necessarily associated with militant resistance. If the Samaritan prophet, Theudas, or the Egyptian prophet were messianic figures, they looked to a miraculous divine intervention rather than mere military force to establish God's reign.[74]

The failed Bar Kochba revolt of 132-35 CE led to Hadrian's establishment of pagan Aelia Capitolina on the site of Jerusalem. The Romans flayed alive R. Akiba, one of the primary sources for the Mishnaic tradition. It should therefore not surprise us that the earliest rabbinic texts generally preserve a much more cautious approach to messianism, where it has not been suppressed altogether, than later texts that have returned to contemplation on biblical prophecies about the Son of David.[75] Such skepticism is reported of R. Johanan ben Zakkai, who survived the destruction of 70 CE: finish what you are doing before going out to greet a Messianic claimant.[76] But even in the late second century, rabbis still reportedly hoped for the coming of Messiah.[77]

A variety of other texts, however, emphasize messianic hopes.[78] For example, the fourteenth and fifteenth benedictions of the *Amida,* probably rooted in the pre-70 period,[79] long for the restoration of David's house.[80] Likewise, *Psalms of Solomon* 17:32, a pre-Christian source, declares hope in the coming king; the context envisions a warrior messiah (17:21-25). A variety of other Jewish sources from this period[81] address the Messiah and often connect him with the final judgment.[82] Both *4 Ezra* 13 and Enoch's *Similitudes* suggest a preexistent individual Messiah of some sort who will destroy the wicked.[83]

The Davidic Messiah was, by any definition of the type, a future ruler ordained by God with political (not merely spiritual) rule.[84] Nevertheless, views about this Messiah diverged widely. Qumran's "Messianic" expectation apparently encompassed two major eschatological anointed figures, a Davidic Messiah and a high priest.[85] The Hasmoneans had combined priesthood and kingship in the same persons,[86] a combination to which the Zadokite priests who founded the Qumran community strenuously objected.[87] Thus this separatist priestly community emphasized an "anointed" priest as well as a king (cf. Zech 4:14; 6:13).[88] Other texts less clearly connected with the Essene movement also stress the role of the future priest.[89]

In the earliest texts associated with the sort of movement we find at Qumran, Levi and Judah probably fulfill a special role because these two tribes constituted most of Israel as the community knew it,[90] but only from Judah is a salvific figure mentioned.[91] The ruler would come from Judah, not from what the sectarians viewed as the corrupt priestly Hasmonean line.[92]

After this period, however, scholars divide on the interpretation of the Qumran texts: some contend that they support one Messiah,[93] others that they support two Messiahs,[94] others that diversity of opinion existed within Qumran or its documents,[95] or that different documents portray different stages in the community's development of eschatological thought.[96] 1QS 9.11 does conjoin the expectation of a prophet with that of "the Messiahs of Aaron and Israel"; the Damascus Document, however, consistently employs the singular, lending credence to the possibility of diverse views in the texts.[97]

But the title "anointed" may apply to any figure for a leading office, which diminishes the conflict.[98] One "anointed" figure is the rightful high priest (in contrast with the wicked one in the Temple), so only the other anointed figure is the eschatological *king*.[99] Still, the Qumran evidence may suggest diverse approaches to Messianism; the possibly single Messiah of Aaron and Israel in the Damascus Document would imply that at some point Qumran's greatest expectation was a Levitic rather than a Davidic anointed one.[100]

The rabbinic idea of two messiahs,[101] however, derives from different exegesis and probably arises independently from later circumstances.[102] Sufficient Old Testament basis existed to provide midrashic proofs for a suffering Messiah,[103] but it is probably only after the failure of the Bar Kochba revolt that the rabbinic tradition of a suffering Messiah (Messiah ben Joseph) in addition to the triumphant warrior Messiah (Messiah ben David) arose.[104] (The earlier proposal that the Dead Sea Scrolls envision a slain Messiah[105] has been largely rejected.)[106]

A variety of messianic views thus existed. The view articulated by Jesus' followers exists within this range in its Jewish environment, but is distinctive, not derived from any one source. This view does fit, however, what we have seen of Jesus' mission.

Conclusion: Jesus as a King

We have argued that the earliest sources reveal that while Jesus was initially reticent to claim messiahship publicly, and while even his disciples initially misunderstood the character of his messianic claim, Jesus viewed his mission at least partly in messianic terms. He taught that his disciples would have a role in the Messianic kingdom, which implies that he attributed to himself a messianic role.[107] His disciples claimed him to be messiah, and his execution as king indicates that others believed that he considered himself messiah.[108] Neither Pilate nor the disciples got the idea from each other; rather, it derived from a common ultimate source in Jesus himself. For later followers of Jesus to invent such a title for him is inconceivable; it risked persecution against themselves for following one executed for treason.

We noted above E. P. Sanders' view that many scholars have been too cautious about assuming that Jesus believed he was a king.[109] Raymond Brown likewise concludes that some of Jesus' followers may have thought him the Messiah, but that he responded ambivalently because his mission defined the term differently than the popular title would suggest.[110]

Martin Hengel sums up the evidence well. Although many scholars are reluctant to think that Jesus viewed himself as Messiah, most concur that he does not easily fit within merely sage or prophetic categories alone.[111] Jesus' preaching about the kingdom has implications for his own identity;[112] Jesus seems to claim that the kingdom is present in him (Matt 12:28//Lk 11:20).[113] Such teachings cohere well with the secure information that Jesus was executed on the charge of claiming to be Israel's rightful king.[114] Clearly Jesus viewed himself not as simply "*one* 'eschatological prophet' among many."[115]

CHAPTER 19

More Than an Earthly Messiah?

For the "first followers of Jesus . . . what mattered most was the body of instructions that circulated in his name."

BURTON MACK[1]

". . . the type of interpretation that makes Jesus a moralist, a teacher of an enlightened and individualistic morality, for all of its significant historical insights . . . does not even come close to the real figure of Jesus."

POPE BENEDICT[2]

". . . devotion to Jesus as divine erupted suddenly and quickly, not gradually and late. . . . More specifically, the origins lie in Jewish Christian circles of the earliest years."

LARRY HURTADO[3]

As we have noted, the earliest extant sources about Jesus redefine the traditional nature of "messiahship" in light of his mission. While his mission offered what some of his contemporaries might have viewed as a "low christology" in some respects — he was not a warrior messiah consummating an immediate kingdom — our earliest extant sources also offer a "higher christology" than many modern scholars have supposed.

We have already noted Jesus' self-designation, "son of man," which probably connected him with an eschatological role more cosmic than many messianic expectations. As we shall see here, some material in our earliest extant sources — Mark and especially the more sayings-focused "Q" — points to a role for Jesus higher than that normally found in most conceptions of an earthly messiah. Our other extant sources that comment seem to agree.

268

The Eschatological Judge in "Q"

In ch. 11, we noted that John the Baptist announced the coming of someone who would baptize in God's Spirit and fire. In John's Bible, however, only God would pour out the divine Spirit (e.g., Is 44:3; Ezek 39:29; Joel 2:28-29) and fiery end-time judgment. Whether or not John applied this image to Jesus, Q certainly did. Although Mark omits baptism in fire, he still includes baptism in the Spirit, perhaps abbreviating Q.

In ch. 11, we also noted John's claim that he was unworthy to handle the coming one's sandals, i.e., unworthy to be his servant. (Although this saying could be assigned to Mark rather than Q, because I believe that Mark abbreviates "Q" material for his introduction here I believe this saying predates Mark.) Because prophets were servants of God, we pointed out that such an image appears to imply some superhuman or even divine role for the coming one.

In one "Q" parable, Jesus emphasizes his eschatological role. In both Luke and Matthew, Jesus' sermon on ethics climaxes with a parable that provides the authority for his ethics (Lk 6:47-49//Matt 7:24-27). We have already noted that parables are characteristic of Jesus' teaching, not that of his followers; we would thus naturally deem a "Q" parable particularly reliable. In Jesus' parable, whoever builds on his wise words will endure testing,[4] whereas whoever does not will be swept away.

Jesus sounds like more than a mere sage here, especially when we consider how others may have normally told this same parable. An early-second-century teacher, not dependent on Jesus but probably dependent on a common tradition, offered a similar parable. In this parable, one who studies Torah and has good works "may be likened to" one who lays a foundation of stones and then of bricks, so that rising water or rain cannot overturn it. But one who studies Torah and has no good works is like one who builds with bricks on the bottom, so that even a small amount of water overturns it.[5] The language of this example is almost as similar to Matthew's as Luke's version of the parable is.[6] Jesus here refers to his own words in the way that Jewish teachers generally referred to God's law.[7] The label "sectarian"[8] may therefore constitute an understatement!

We also encounter Jesus' exalted role elsewhere in "Q."[9] As we noted in our chapter on Jesus' conflicts, Jesus wished to gather his people under his wings (Matt 23:37//Lk 13:34). This claim, as we noted, recalls a biblical and early Jewish image of God sheltering his people under his wings;[10] Jewish teachers also came to speak of one who converted Gentiles as bringing them under the wings of the Shekinah, the divine presence.[11]

David's Lord in Mk 12:35-37

In Mark, Jesus begins to hint his messianic identity publicly at Mk 12:6;[12] he begins to imply a corresponding identity greater than that of David already in Mk 12:35-37. Jesus is no mere David redivivus, no mere warrior king like David, but one far greater than David. If he is David's "lord," enthroned not simply in Jerusalem but at God's right hand, how can he be his "son"?

While Jesus' teaching could be read as repudiating the messiah's Davidic descent,[13] the real problem here (as Matthew and Luke especially emphasize) seems to be how he can be David's Lord yet at the same time David's son,[14] younger in age yet superior in rank.[15] Jewish teachers often asked didactic questions that functioned as "haggadic antinomy," in which both sides of a question were correct but their relationship needed to be resolved.[16] The messiah, i.e., the "anointed" king, was by definition "son of David" in various circles of Jewish expectation.[17] Yet the title "Lord" describes him far more adequately.[18]

Because the language about being son of David is ambiguous, however, it does not seem very likely that the early Christians would have created a tradition that could be used to challenge Jesus' Davidic descent, hence his messiahship.[19] Jesus' messiahship was precisely a point of debate with their Jewish contemporaries, and Jesus' wording here could be used against his movement's case on that point. Why would Mark, who clearly affirms that Jesus is Christ (Mk 1:1; 8:29; 9:41; 14:61-62) and seems to also affirm that he is son of David (Mk 10:47-48; cf. 11:10), take this risk if not bound here to genuine tradition?

The question of theological precedent or lack thereof does not affect the point. Early Judaism may not have understood Ps 110 in a messianic sense,[20] but the psalm was readily available for Jesus' own use no less than that of his followers, and by speaking of a "lord" of David secondary to Yahweh it naturally enough lent itself to quasimessianic or supermessianic speculation. That it became widespread in a wide range of early Christian circles[21] probably suggests that a common authority stands behind its usage. Thus it seems most likely that the passage reflects Jesus' own teaching.[22]

Whatever the original psalm means, it probably does portray an exaltation greater than that of David historically. If the psalmist spoke to a lord besides Yahweh, a lord who would be enthroned at God's right hand as his vice-regent, then this king was someone greater than an ordinary royal descendant of David.[23] Some in the psalmist's day might have understood the image on the Near Eastern analogy of divine kings.[24]

The context in Mark reinforces the striking nature of the claim, though we cannot know for sure how closely together the sayings were actually spoken. Because Jesus in Mark's preceding passage had cited one text in which the only "Lord" was God (Mk 12:29-30), his emphasis on the subordinate "Lord" of

Psalm 110 (pronounced as if it read the same in public reading and certainly in Greek, despite the difference in Hebrew) would sound striking, especially given the frequent practice of linking texts on the basis of common key words.[25]

Jesus' Special Relation to God

Jesus' special designation of himself as God's "son" in some traditions connotes intimacy, but it lent itself readily to his followers' later use of it as a title for him. Jesus himself at the very least implied a special intimacy with the Father when he addressed God as "Abba" (Mk 14:36),[26] an Aramaic title that carried over into the early church (Rom 8:15; Gal 4:6) and must be original with Jesus.[27] Jesus calls himself "the Son" (of God) in Mk 13:32, a saying unlikely to have been invented, and in a "Q" saying (Matt 11:25-27//Lk 10:21-22).

God as Father[28]

Claiming that Jesus called God "Father" should not be controversial. Nevertheless, by itself it would also not say much about how he viewed himself. Calling God "Father," including in prayer, is not distinctive; it is not even limited to Judaism. Claiming that God or Zeus was father or begetter of humanity was a common Greek idea.[29] Zeus or Jupiter appears as "the Father" in both Greek[30] and Latin[31] texts; is addressed as "Father" in invocations;[32] is "Father of all";[33] father of the gods;[34] father of humanity;[35] and often "father of humans and gods."[36] Zeus could also be portrayed as father of kings[37] or of the virtuous.[38] Stoic thinkers also spoke of God as a father,[39] i.e., "father of all,"[40] father of human beings,[41] and father of humans and deities,[42] by virtue of creation.

Jewish people called God "father" (also an occasional OT title for God),[43] though not all with equal sympathy for the Greek usage. The Diaspora Jewish philosopher Philo speaks of the "supreme father of deities and people" acknowledged by both Greeks and barbarians;[44] Josephus, however, condemns the Greeks' "father" who rules heaven as a tyrant, rejecting Zeus' identification with the true God.[45] Greek-speaking Jews were united, in any case, in regarding God as Father of all,[46] from Philo[47] to the *Sibylline Oracles*;[48] Jewish magical texts could also invoke God as "father of all creation."[49] God was "begetter of gods and humans."[50] Greek-speaking church fathers agreed.[51]

A variety of other Jewish sources also called God "father."[52] The liturgical title that came to dominate in later rabbinic Judaism was "father in heaven."[53] Corporate Jewish and Christian prayers to God as Father are nearly identical.[54] Because Jewish culture generally perceived fathers as wise, benevolent, but authoritative protectors, "father" offered a useful image for God.[55] For most Jewish sources, God is especially Israel's father;[56] for most Christian sources, God is the father of Jesus' followers.

"Abba, Father"

While calling God "Father" was not distinctive, Jesus calls God "Father" frequently, and sometimes addresses him as "my Father" (Matt 11:27//Lk 10:22).[57] He also emphasizes the intimacy of his relationship with his Father (Matt 11:25-27//Lk 10:21-22), which was not the common use of the image either among his people or among Gentiles. This relationship may be most clearly obvious in the title "Abba" (Mk 14:36).[58]

Vermes views Jesus' invocation of his "Father" as "Abba" as in line with other charismatic sages, comparing the grandson of the famous "charismatic" sage Honi the Circle-Drawer.[59] Whereas the German scholar Joachim Jeremias had insisted that Jesus' use of "Abba" for God was unique,[60] Vermes notes that Honi's grandson compares God with an "Abba."[61] The source for this comparison is much later than Jesus, however,[62] and is merely a comparison, not a direct address. If Jeremias' case for uniqueness may be overstated, the address is at least highly distinctive with Jesus. Vermes' appeal to its "charismatic" character may at least reinforce its implications for Jesus' intimate dependence on God.

Because Mark is written in Greek, only selectively reproducing Aramaic words of Jesus, we read Jesus' "Abba" address there only once, in a time of Jesus' intimate and desperate prayer (Mk 14:36). What suggests to us that this language may have been more generally characteristic of Jesus' non-public prayer addresses is its wholesale adoption by many of his followers. Although Paul, like Mark, supplies the Greek translation with the title, he uses the expression in two letters to Greek-speaking churches (Rom 8:15; Gal 4:6). In both cases, he seems to assume that most of the church will be familiar with the term; that one of these instances is to a church he has never visited (Rom 8:15) indicates that the usage was widespread in early Christianity.[63]

In both cases, Paul refers to a mark of the Spirit within Jesus' followers that gives them intimacy with God. In one case, he describes this relationship as the activity of the Spirit associated with God's Son Jesus, so that Jesus' followers are transferred into Jesus' own intimate relationship with the Father (Gal 4:6).[64] What is most significant about this claim for our purposes is that Jesus' movement widely recognized his intimate relationship with the Father.

The Son's Knowledge Limited

Some sayings attributed to Jesus that are almost certainly authentic claim his Sonship in a special sense. For example, in Mk 13:32, Jesus claims that no one knows the day nor the hour, not even "the Son," a saying that is surely authentic.[65] Especially because Scripture already attested that the Lord knows the time (Zech 14:7), the early church would hardly have created a saying limiting divine omniscience to the Father;[66] no circle of first-century Christianity securely known to us would have readily invented such a christological concession. Had early Christians simply needed a saying to address the delay of the parousia, they would more naturally have created a claim that Jesus denied the imminence of the parousia, not that he was ignorant of its timing.[67]

The saying fits a Palestinian Jewish milieu; Diaspora Jews tended to be far less interested in end-time speculation. In the early centuries of this era, some Jewish futurists even set dates for the end of the age,[68] eliciting a strong reaction among more conservative teachers.[69] Although some later rabbis thought that God revealed all things to his angels, those later rabbis who commented on the subject generally doubted that angels knew the time of Israel's deliverance,[70] and angels were rarely viewed as omniscient.[71]

If we accept the saying as authentic, however, it incidentally verifies the view that Jesus called himself the son of God in a distinctive sense, and assigns himself a role among or above the angels.[72]

The Son's Special Relation to the Father

One passage in "Q" (Matt 11:25-27//Lk 10:21-22) attributes to Jesus a relationship with the Father that sounds almost like what we read in the Gospel of John.[73] This is especially true in the particular saying in Matt 11:27//Lk 10:22: "My Father has delegated everything to me, and no one knows the Son except the Father. Nor does anyone know the Father except the Son — and to whomever the Son wishes to reveal him." Such a claim about the exclusivity of divine knowledge involving Jesus resembles contemporary claims about divine wisdom (e.g., Wisd 9:17).

By employing here a term frequently used for passing on tradition[74] the Gospels might contrast Jesus' revelation, which is directly from the Father, with the traditions that sages received from earlier sages. Although this is not a claim to omniscience (as we noted with regard to Mk 13:32),[75] it claims a position of special authority and relationship with the Father. The Father has given Jesus the sole prerogative to reveal him, so that anyone who approaches God a different way will not find him. Some scholars object that this passage sounds too much like something the Gospel of John would say (e.g., Jn 1:18; 14:6). Others respond, however, that if Jesus *never* spoke in terms like these, it would be more difficult to explain where Johannine tradition derived its picture of Jesus.[76]

Some scholars have objected that this exalted Q picture of Jesus and the language used to describe it is gnostic or Greek, hence not from Jesus himself. But the gnostic interpretation falters severely on the phrase "no one knows the Son but the Father" — a claim that denies the very heart of much gnosticism as we know it.[77] Moreover, further investigations have shown that the passage is thoroughly Palestinian Jewish, representing the sort of blend of mystic and apocalyptic thought that clustered around discussions of Israel, divine Wisdom and the law.[78] As Jeremias already pointed out several decades ago, "Language, style and structure . . . clearly assign the saying to a Semitic-speaking milieu."[79] Not all scholars are certain that the saying is authentic,[80] but most today will agree that it is clearly not hellenistic.[81]

But not even all scholars who suspect that the saying originated with Jesus agree on its sense; some suggest Jesus indicates his relationship with God merely by means of analogy with a natural family: "only a father and son really know each other."[82] The analogy interpretation falters on the inadequacy of the image, however: men were in fact generally closer to their wives and friends than to their fathers.[83] Jesus' prayers addressing God as Father and the use of "Son" as a title for Jesus in the indisputably authentic saying in Mk 13:32 also suggest that Jesus here refers to himself as God's unique son.[84] Although other images[85] may also be at work, many scholars believe Jesus describes himself here especially in the language of divine Wisdom.[86] Witherington notes that

> The claim of exclusivity of mutual knowledge of Father and son should be compared to the claims that state only Wisdom knows God and vice versa (cf. Job 28:1-27; Sir. 1:6, 8; Bar. 3:15-32; Prov. 8:12; Wis. 7:25ff.; 8:3-8; 9:4, 9, 11). The middle two clauses suggest that Jesus sees his relationship to the Father in the light of wisdom ideas, and he may see himself as Wisdom incarnate here.[87]

Jesus claimed to be not merely one sage or prophet among many, but the supreme end-time revealer of God's character and purpose.

"Son of God" in Judaism

In the context of our other observations about Jesus' ministry, the title "son of God" surely meant more than simply intimacy, although it included that.

Speaking of God's Messiah as his "Son" may not have been common in early Judaism, but it was certainly intelligible — though in various senses.

Scripture and Jewish tradition apply the "Son of God" title to those who belong to God;[88] to Israel (most commonly);[89] and to a righteous person in general.[90] Angels, too, could be called "sons of God,"[91] although given that angels were not human, and "son of God" bore many other senses, probably no Jew would interpret a human as "God's son" in the angelic sense without an explicit statement to that effect in the narrative.[92] Yet the problem with most "son of God" parallels, both hellenistic and Jewish, is that early Christians controversially proclaimed Jesus as not merely *a* son of God, but *the* Son of God, his beloved and unique Son.[93] How did the early Jesus movement employ the title?

The most appropriate Jewish background of the term when applied to Jesus was the messianic sense. This usage need not rule out figurative nuances of sonship like obedience, submission,[94] intimacy and delegated authority[95] that would be part of the metaphor in a Jewish context. But the notion of special sonship distinct from Israel or the righteous (such as we have seen in Mk 13:32 or Matt 11:27//Lk 10:22) demands something more, and Scripture provided the content. Nathan's oracle in 2 Sam 7:14[96] indicated that God would adopt David's royal descendants (his "house," 2 Sam 7:11), starting with Solomon, as his own sons, perhaps borrowing this special status from Israel (Ex 4:22) and from divine adoption of kings in other ancient Near Eastern cultures.[97]

Ancient Israel's temple cultus came to celebrate this royal promise (Ps 2:7; 89:26-29).[98] The prophets reminded God's people of the qualification of obedience (cf. 2 Sam 7:14b), even suggesting that the royal tree would become a stump and the house a tent until a time of restoration came (Is 11:1; Amos 9:11). But the prophets also recognized the promise to David (e.g., Is 55:3; Jer 33:17-26; Ezek 34:23-24; 37:24-25; Zech 12:10), sometimes fulfilled in his lineage or his ultimate descendant. This promised reign would last forever, so that the king would be, in Isaiah's words, a "mighty God" (Is 9:6-7) — a title applied in the context to YHWH himself (Is 10:21).[99]

Although hope for an eschatological anointed leader or leaders ran high, and the Davidic messiah remained prominent in many expectations, "son of God" was no more a common description of him in this era than people commonly thought of Dan 7 when they used the more generic expression "son of man."[100] But neither was the usage unknown. In at least some circles, 2 Sam 7:14 was interpreted with direct reference to the Davidic messiah as "son of God" (as we may note from some clear Qumran examples).[101] Some other Dead Sea Scrolls texts (like 4Q369 frg. 1, 2.6-7,[102] and, on some views, also 4Q246 col. 2, line 1)[103] have been thought to apply the phrase similarly.[104] Hints may be found that others also understood Ps 2 Messianically in the period of formative Christianity.[105] Early Christians normally applied this Old Testament title especially to the king's enthronement rather than his birth (Rom 1:3-4; Heb 1:5; 5:5; Acts 13:33).

But while Jesus' use of "the son" probably involves messiahship, Jesus' usage noted above also redefines the character of his messiahship. Jesus' distinctive use of the title seems to emphasize more his intimacy with the Father than his royal status, and in some texts particularly underlines a unique and exalted role. Jesus is Israel's messiah, but even more than this, he is the Father's special son.

Who Did Jesus' Movement Think He Was?

We lack direct access to the minds of Jesus' earliest followers in the 30s and (for the most part) the 40s. The first-century documents we do have, however, virtually without exception suggest an exalted role for Jesus that exceeds rather than falls short of contemporary Jewish messianic expectations. All our sources that address the issue distinguish this open recognition about Jesus' exalted identity after the resurrection from the state of affairs before it[106] (see discussion of the "messianic secret" in ch. 18); nevertheless they seem unanimous in their central affirmation. Perhaps Jesus' followers believed that his postresurrection teaching allowed the resurrection to cast a different light on sayings and events that had preceded. We survey some of their texts below (although recognizing that other scholars have treated this material in greater detail).[107] I omit Johannine texts here[108] because John's exalted christology is sufficiently widely recognized as to require little comment.

Who Did Mark Think Jesus Was?

Besides the text about Jesus being David's "Lord" and texts about Jesus' return, addressed earlier, Mark seems to indicate an exalted role for Jesus elsewhere (although it is not his focus). We will note here his understanding of how Jesus functioned as John's successor in light of Scripture, and Mark's report that Jesus claimed to be "Lord of the Sabbath."

In Mk 1:3, Mark quotes Is 40:3 with reference to John the Baptist's mission of preparing the "way of the Lord." This text is presumably earlier than Mark, since not only Matthew and Luke, who follow Mark directly, but also the Fourth Gospel (Jn 1:23), which probably does not, cites the verse.[109] Some even suspect that John himself used this text (Is 40:3) to explain his own sense of mission (as in Jn 1:23).[110] In view of a Qumran parallel, use of this Isaiah text is more plausible in a Palestinian Jewish environment — indeed, especially in John's wilderness — than anywhere else. The Qumran community applied the same Isaiah text to their own mission in the wilderness,[111] especially to their knowledge of the law.[112]

At the very least, the usage tells us Mark's view about Jesus: the one whose way John prepares is none other than the "Lord" himself (Is 40:3).[113] If Mark was at all biblically literate, then, he would have understood that applying this passage to John meant that John was preparing the way for God himself, though in Mark's narrative John prepares the way for Jesus. This connection would fit his inclusion of John's sayings about being unworthy to deal with the "coming one's" sandals, and that the coming one would baptize in God's Spirit, language apparently implying the divine status of the coming one.

Most of all, it is consistent with the quotation that Mark links with this one (Mk 1:2), from Mal 3:1, where again the messenger prepares for God's own coming. In Malachi that messenger is Elijah, sent before the great day of the Lord's judgment (Mal 4:5). Not surprisingly, a few verses after quoting Malachi's promise of God's messenger, Mark describes John coming in the wilderness with a leather girdle around his waist — an image all biblically informed hearers would associate with Elijah (2 Kgs 1:8).[114] If Mark believes that John is Elijah preparing the way of God, and in Mark John prepares for Jesus (cf. Mk 9:11-13), Mark plainly has an exalted view about Jesus.

In Mk 2:28, Jesus claims that the Son of Man is Lord of the Sabbath. Such a claim might not generate hostility.[115] Because the Semitic expression "son of man" usually just means "human being," even some modern commentators have read Jesus' Son of Man statement here as a teaching about persons in general.[116] In the immediately preceding context, Jesus claims that "The Sabbath was made on account of humanity, rather than humanity on account of the Sabbath" (Mk 2:27). Many other Jewish teachers uttered such a sentiment[117] and similar logical constructions.[118] Thus one could infer that Jesus simply claims that the sabbath was made for humans, so humans are "lord" of the sabbath. While such an interpretation may have occurred to Jesus' hearers within the narrative, however, those familiar with his self-designation as "son of man" would find here a self-claim resembling other hints in his teaching. In the context of Mark's larger Gospel, Jesus' identity as "son of man" is clear. Thus David's "lord" was lord of more than David and his kingdom, but lord even of God's sabbath.[119]

Who Did Matthew Think Jesus Was?

Robert Gundry finds Jesus assuming the role of Yahweh in his teaching in Matthew, citing numerous specific examples (Matt 10:32-33; 11:5, 10, 28, 29; 13:41; 16:27; 17:11; 24:31; 25:31).[120] Although not all of these passages require this interpretation, a number do use imagery typically associated with God in Scripture or early Judaism, and it is clear that Matthew believes Jesus to be more than an earthly messiah.

When Jesus invites hearers to accept his "yoke" (Matt 11:29-30), he may allude to the traditional idea of God's law or kingdom as a good yoke.[121] By speaking of God's law or kingdom as Jesus' own, Jesus implicitly claims authority from the Father (cf. the "Q" saying in Matt 11:27) greater than that of Moses himself; other Jewish texts would have spoken only of *God's* yoke here,[122] or of the yoke of God's Torah.[123] Jesus' words clearly evoke the invitation of the sage Joshua ben Sira (Sir 51:23-27):[124]

> Draw near to me, you who are uneducated . . .
> Why do you delay in these matters,
>   when your souls thirst so much? . . .
> Place your neck under the yoke,
>   and let your soul accept training —
>   she is near if you wish to find her.
> Witness with your own eyes that I have labored little,
>   yet have found much rest for myself.

Yet the offered yoke here is not Ben Sira's, but that of divine Wisdom, and Wisdom elsewhere invites the hearer, "Come to me, you who earnestly desire me," and eat and drink of wisdom (Sir 24:19-21). John is not the only Gospel writer with a "wisdom christology" (Jn 1:1-18; 6:35; 7:37).[125] Even Jesus' promise of "rest for your souls" in this passage evokes a divine role; in Scripture, this promise belonged to God's people if they obeyed God (Jer 6:16 MT).[126]

In Matt 1:23, toward the beginning of his Gospel, Matthew calls Jesus "God with us" (Is 7:14). This claim cannot be a mere slip of the pen; because it fits two other strategic texts about Jesus and the divine presence in Matthew, one at the Gospel's conclusion (18:20; 28:20), Matthew surely makes an exalted claim about Jesus here.[127] In Matt 18:20, Jesus implicitly claims to be the divine presence, using language familiar in a specifically Jewish environment. An ancient Jewish saying promised God's presence not only for ten males (the minimum prerequisite for a synagogue),[128] but for even two or three gathered to study God's law.[129] Here Jesus himself fills the role of the Shekinah, God's presence, in the traditional Jewish saying.[130] (Jewish teachers often emphasized God's omnipresence.)[131] For Matthew, Jesus is "God with us" (1:23; 28:20).

Is it plausible that Jesus actually uttered words like these during his earthly ministry, at least privately to his disciples (who understood such words in a more exalted way at a later time)?[132] The theme is multiply attested in the tradition, though more dominant in Matthew (and certainly John).[133] What we can unquestionably say historically is that, contrary to some modern scholarly constructs about them, our early Christian sources offer a consensus about Jesus' identity and, where they address it, his own knowledge of his identity.

Who Did Luke Think Jesus Was?

Luke indicates his views about Jesus in a speech attributed to Peter on the day of Pentecost — the first point at which Luke reports preaching about Jesus after his exaltation. In addition to the image of Jesus baptizing in the Spirit (which Lk 3:16 presumably derives from"Q"), in Acts 2:33 Jesus "pours out" the Spirit, a clear allusion to God pouring out the Spirit in 2:17-18 (the only other passage in Luke-Acts that uses *ekcheō*). Jewish texts also speak of God pouring out wisdom (Sir 1:9) as his gift (Sir 1:10; cf. Acts 2:38).[134] But the most obvious source of the language, in view of the allusion to Acts 2:17-18, is Joel 2:28-29, where *God* pours out the Spirit.

Moreover, Peter interprets the name of the "Lord" (the divine name in Hebrew) in terms of Jesus of Nazareth in Acts 2:21, 38 (interpreting Joel 2:32 by way of Ps 110:1). By concluding that the gift of the Spirit was available to "as many as God would call," Luke clearly echoes the end of Joel 2:32 (3:5 LXX), completing the quotation interrupted in Acts 2:21.[135] That is, having finished his exposition of "whoever calls on the Lord's name" (2:21) by showing that the name on which they must call is Jesus' (2:38), he concludes the quotation in 2:39. The salvific name of God, then, is "Jesus." That other early Christians interpreted the Joel text similarly in the 50s (Joel 2:32 in Rom 10:9, 13)[136] signals that Luke follows an earlier tradition of interpretation.

Who Did Paul Think Jesus Was?

Paul's evidence, ranging from less than two to roughly three decades after the resurrection, offers our earliest NT evidence and a decisive contradiction to the idea that Christians only gradually evolved the idea of Jesus' exalted status.[137] To be sure, Paul's interests were not the same as those of authors who composed later Christian creeds; but for him Jesus was not only human, but also the preexistent Wisdom of Jewish tradition and the exalted Lord.

In the earliest extant Christian document, 1 Thessalonians, Paul might apply to Jesus' appearing some Old Testament language about God's coming.[138] Likewise, the Marana tha invocation of 1 Cor 16:22 indicates Jesus' exalted status, and is taken by many scholars as "clear evidence that in the very earliest days the Aramaic-speaking church referred to Jesus by the title that in the OT belongs to God alone."[139] In other words, the title "is the ascription to Jesus of the functions of deity."[140]

Paul uses wisdom language for Jesus. The language is found in what are often taken to be pre-Pauline formulas, but of which Paul at the least plainly approves.[141] These passages include 1 Cor 8:6, probably also adapting the Shema (the confession of the oneness of Israel's God, the Lord): "To us there is only one God, the Father, from whom is everything . . . and one Lord, Jesus Christ, through whom is everything . . ."[142] Likewise Phil 2:6-7 reads at least something (despite some debate) like this: Jesus "being in God's form did not consider equality with God something to be taken hold of; instead, he emptied himself, taking a slave's form, having embraced human likeness . . ."[143] Like some other passages, this one goes on to apply to Jesus an Old Testament text about God (Phil 2:10-11, using the language of Is 45:23). Many also would count here the wisdom language in Col 1:15-17[144] and other passages. Paul's references to the "day of the Lord Jesus" or "day of Christ" (1 Cor 1:8; 5:5; 2 Cor 1:14; Phil 1:6, 10; 2:16) clearly evoke OT texts about the "day of the Lord" (YHWH).[145]

This summary does not even count the rare passage where many scholars believe that Paul explicitly calls Jesus "God."[146] Nor does it count the many incidental references assuming Jesus' divine status, such as blessings from Jesus along with the Father (in epistolary introductions where a blessing from a deity was conventional)[147] or links with the Father and the divine Spirit.[148]

It is not likely that Paul originated this "wisdom christology" himself. As we have noted, the same wisdom imagery appears for Jesus in Matthew and probably Q (Matt 11:28-30;[149] 23:34; Lk 11:49; cf. Matt 11:19; Lk 7:35), is most developed in John,[150] and is nowhere clearly challenged in extant records of the early Christian movement. Paul shows that preaching a divine/wisdom Christ precedes Mark's adaptation of the Greco-Roman biographic form to appeal to Gentile audiences accustomed to the sort of narrative structure Mark provides.[151] His (and some other early Christians') central proclamation was a briefer outline of the salvific story, and in that story Christ was no mere mortal (e.g., Acts 2:21, 38; 22:16; 1 Cor 8:6; 12:3; Phil 2:6).

The issue is not that later christologies exalt Jesus in contrast to early sources that do not (though later ones like John are clearly more developed). The issue is instead that it is difficult to find any early Christian source that says much about Jesus that leaves him as a mere earthly Messiah. (Even James, which deals little with Christology, speaks of "our glorious Lord Jesus Christ," claiming Jesus' Lordship and perhaps comparing him with the divine "glorious king" in Scripture.)[152] Unless one counts hypothetical reconstructions as evidence, we lack concrete evidence for a first-century Jesus movement that did not exalt him beyond normal earthly messianic status. This observation may

not fit easily into modern theories about the evolution of early Christian christology, but it should not be simply ignored.

At what point might such claims have created tension with other Jewish
groups? Judaism was monotheistic and Palestinian Judaism rejected divinizing
mortals, but it did provide a fertile context for speculation about exalted figures.

Exalted Figures in Early Jewish Thought

Judaism's use of divine language was more fluid in this period[153] than it later
became.[154] (One may compare, for example, hellenistic Jewish application of
divine language to Moses[155] or Palestinian Jewish exalted language for "Melchizedek.")[156] Many portrayed a sort of subordinate but powerful vizier alongside God, sometimes apparently understanding wisdom or the logos in such
terms.[157]

More often, early Judaism seems to have understood wisdom as an aspect
or part of God, merely personified distinctly.[158] Although Jewish Christians'
christology violated the messianic concepts of most other Jews, especially those
later seeking to normativize Judaism,[159] it offered an alternative interpretation
rather than a disavowal of God's unity.[160] Rather than defining what God was in
a metaphysical Greek sense, biblical faith knew God by his acts and words and
distinguished him from all other realities. At some point, early Christians began affirming Jesus' deity within the identity of the God of their Bible, the way
their contemporaries often presented wisdom as a divine attribute. They continued to distinguish this biblical God's identity from all other realities.[161]

As we have noted, Wisdom christology informed early Christian understanding about Jesus already in our earliest sources such as Paul and possibly
"Q." That a first-century Palestinian Jewish movement would within its earliest
decades already hold a consensus that their founder rose from the dead and
somehow embodied or existed as divine wisdom is remarkable. We have no
comparable evidence for the deification (or even belief in the heavenly exaltation) of other first-century Jewish messianic figures. It seems that something
distinctive within the movement, rather than merely following a common first-
century Jewish social pattern, produced this consensus. It is difficult to comprehend how without the authority of Jesus' teaching about his exalted identity
in some form so many monotheistic Jews in the early church would have simultaneously come to emphasize Jesus' exalted character, and, while debating circumcision, food laws, Jerusalem's authority and other points, fail to offer concrete evidence of being deeply divided over this aspect of Christology.[162]

Israeli scholar David Flusser contends that "On the one hand, Christology
developed from Jesus' exalted self-awareness and from what happened to or

was believed to have happened to Jesus and, on the other hand, from various Jewish religious motifs which became connected with Jesus Christ."[163]

Conclusion

Jesus' exalted status appears early in the tradition. Whether or not Jesus' earliest followers developed that status fully in keeping with his own aims, it is unlikely that they derived these perspectives from someone who lacked confidence in his important role in the kingdom. All our concrete evidence, in fact, suggests that Jesus was conscious of a crucial role in God's kingdom plan. To abandon this evidence by overemphasizing one interpretation of the messianic secret is to argue not from concrete information but from the secret's silence. That silence is better explained in terms of a stage in the mission not yet completed, as the Gospels suggest.

But how did Jesus envision his immediate mission in God's kingdom plan? At least part of his understanding of his mission seems wrapped up in his final journey to Jerusalem. This journey and its consequences consume an inordinate amount of space in the Gospels, and for good reason: ancient biographies typically focused on the subject's fate if the subject died a significant death. We will suggest that unless Jesus was extremely naïve about political realities in Jerusalem, his significant death was no accident. His martyrdom was part of his plan.

CHAPTER 20

Confronting and Provoking the Elite

". . . After [Jesus] entered the temple, he started driving out the sellers and their customers active in the temple. He overthrew the moneychangers' tables and the seats of the dove-sellers."

MARK 11:15

"What will the vineyard's owner do? He will come and destroy those tenant workers, and entrust the vineyard to others."

MARK 12:9

Because the Jesus Seminar explains away most conflict in Jesus' life, it omits, as Craig Evans puts it, "a convincing explanation of what led to Jesus' death."[1] We cannot unnaturally isolate the Jesus of the Gospels' sayings from the significant martyrdom that certainly followed them.[2]

In light of the coherence of gospel tradition, Jesus' behavior seems to exemplify his teaching. He was apparently ready for martyrdom, depending solely on the Father for vindication. Overturning tables in the temple was a prophetic act that knowingly shamed the elite, openly inviting retaliation — and ultimately martyrdom.[3] It is thus reasonable to suppose, even apart from the more controversial evidence of his reported sayings, that Jesus came to Jerusalem not only to challenge the "rulers of this age" but also to face martyrdom.[4] (Cf. also our discussion regarding the triumphal entry in ch. 18.)

The Parable of Tenants

In Mk 12:1-12, Jesus in Jerusalem tells a parable about murderous tenants. The parable is likely reliable and in contrast to some other parables probably was told at the point in Jesus' ministry where the Gospel narratives depict it. The story indicates the rising level of the threat against Jesus at this point in his ministry.

The Parable's Authenticity

As we noted in ch. 13, Jesus' parables are generally authentic.[5] Besides this general consideration, this parable also does not appear to be invented based on the details of Jesus' execution, since he was not killed in the city and thrown out (Mk 12:8).[6]

Although understandable in Jerusalem (where Mark has Jesus tell it, perhaps to some who economically identified themselves with the landlords on whose estates tenants worked), this parable offers an accurate depiction of rural life. It makes better sense from a rural teacher like Jesus than from the later Jesus movement, which spread quickly from Jerusalem to other urban centers.

The viticulture is accurate enough, although this accuracy stems from the Isaiah allusions,[7] and little of it would require specialist knowledge. The viticultural details fit the rural Mediterranean world: fences (often a wall of loosely-fitted stones) or hedges protected vineyards from animals[8] and watchmen could use a tower,[9] often "a hut of leaf-covered wood or possibly of stone which served both as a look-out . . . and as a shelter for the vinedressers at harvest time."[10]

Tenant farmers worked the land for its owners, often absentee landlords, and paid the landowners as much as half the resulting produce.[11] This arrangement was familiar enough that later rabbis also told parables of vineyards tended by tenants;[12] they also could tell of an owner uprooting a vineyard that provided no fruit to portray God's judgment on a people who refused to repent.[13]

Probably more telling in favor of its authenticity than its accurate Galilean or rural flavor here, many Semitisms appear in the Markan parable.[14] It may also adapt some elements of early Palestinian Jewish story lines.[15] It does not distinguish the climactic messenger, the "son," from the earlier messengers as sharply as later Christians would distinguish Jesus from the prophets.[16] Given what we know about Jesus, there is no reason that the parable could not stem from him.[17]

The Hallel and Authenticity (Mk 12:10-11)

Against some, various factors argue strongly for the authenticity of even Jesus' concluding reference to Ps 118:22-23 (Mk 12:10-11).[18] For example, Jewish parables typically *did* include a scripture citation;[19] moreover, the citation appears in all three Synoptics (plus Thomas);[20] Jesus draws his citation from the festal liturgy; "stone" might provide a Semitic play on words here with the "son" earlier in the parable;[21] "Have you not read?" is unique to Jesus in the NT;[22] and the collection of stone sayings in a variety of disparate early Christian texts supports a common authoritative source for diverse early Christian groups (Acts 4:11; Rom 9:33; 1 Pet 2:6-8; cf. Lk 19:38, 40, 44).

Most important among these arguments may be dependence on the festal liturgy. These lines belong to the Hallel, a series of Psalms (Ps 113–118) sung during Passover season. A later Gentile church would not have known to add precisely this detail at precisely this time. One could object that these allusions to the Hallel were added to the passion narrative by early Jewish Christians, who probably did continue to observe the Passover (cf. Acts 20:5-6, 16). (The Hallel surfaces even in Mk 14:26, although Mark makes nothing of it.)

But the same circles of early Jewish Christians also had some *reason* to associate Jesus' death with Passover (1 Cor 5:7), and, most importantly here, early Jewish Christians were also the ones with the best access to the authentic traditions. That they merely invented Jesus' execution during the Passover week is unlikely. We know that Jesus was a Galilean executed near Jerusalem; the likeliest time to find Jesus and his Galilean followers in Jerusalem would have been precisely at one of the three major pilgrimage festivals.

We have already argued that Jesus' parables were widely remembered. There is a logical reason for consistently associating *this* particular parable with the passion narrative — namely, that it occurred then. It is this parable that, in our current Gospels, comes closest to unveiling what has been called the "messianic secret."[23] That Jesus would discreetly reserve such a revelation, obscure though it remains, for a public confrontation with Jerusalem's elite might help explain why he was not detained and executed any earlier than he was.

Threatening Judgment on the Elite

In this parable tenants in the vineyard refuse to yield to the owner his share of the produce, and resist his benevolent messengers. So evil do they prove that they kill the owner's son, foolishly assuming that if he has no heir they will come to own the vineyard. By this point in the story, Jesus' audience will have long been ready for the owner to take vengeance on the tenants;[24] like Nathan of old (2 Sam 12:1-7), Jesus uses a parable to invite some hearers to recognize the just verdict of condemnation against them.

That the relationship between God and Israel constitutes the most common theme in early rabbinic parables[25] may be significant here. Because the vineyard probably refers to Israel,[26] the vine-growers refer to the nation's religious leadership (Mk 12:12). Thus while Jesus borrows the imagery of Isaiah, he adapts it so that the primary evildoers represent not Israel but her leaders.

Despite some realistic details, the landowner's behavior here is unrealistically benevolent. Ancients valued the benevolence of landowners toward tenants, but even those who recommended that they be less than insistent on timely payment[27] warned them not to neglect collection of payment lest the tenants default.[28] In antiquity, all sides regarded as treacherous the killing of unarmed messengers, or heralds.[29] As most commentators suggest, the rejected messengers probably depict the biblical prophets;[30] Jewish tradition not only acknowledged but amplified their sufferings.[31]

But even had hearers not recognized the image of God and his prophets here, no one would expect the benevolent landowner to remain benevolent any longer; indeed, normal landlords sometimes even had their own hired assassins to remove troublesome tenants.[32] The state would clearly side with the landlord, and the murderers would die or be enslaved.[33] The landlord would also know by now that the tenants hate him; in antiquity, the way people treated one's messengers is the way they would treat the sender.[34] Ancient cultural conventions were clear: by continuing to appeal to their sense of honor, the landowner has made himself appear a fool; to maintain any vestige of honor, he must retaliate against their repeated shaming of him.[35]

Quite in contrast to expectations, however, the landowner acts with such benevolence that ancient hearers could have regarded his action only as utter folly: he believes that the murderous tenants will at least respect his son as his own representative. This turn of events would raise the suspense for the parable's first-time hearers. Those who respected an authority figure would respect his son,[36] but those who hated that figure might kill his son.[37] Jesus tells about the death of the father's own "beloved" son.[38]

Who is the "son"? The designation "son" is consistent with Jesus addressing God as "Abba" elsewhere (Mk 14:36).[39] What would the "heir" inherit, that the tenants wanted to control? In Scripture, Israel was God's "inheritance."[40] What was the produce due the owner, that the tenants refused to offer? In "Q," "fruit" involved obedient works (Matt 3:10//Lk 3:9; Matt 7:17-19//Lk 6:43-44).[41] Instead of welcoming the benevolent landowner's "son," however, the tenants commit the ultimate act of treachery. Casting him outside the vineyard, they kill him.[42]

In the final week of his ministry, then, Jesus seems ready to begin to unveil the "messianic secret": more than any prophet before him, Jesus stands in a special relationship with God, and his rejection finally spells doom on the land.[43] Even here, however, his self-revelation would remain somewhat obscure to hearers without the larger context of his ministry; a similar Jewish parable portrays the son as Jacob and thereby Israel.[44]

Jesus' brief "interpretation" of the parable involves God's response. As we have observed, Jesus cites Psalm 118:22, familiar at the season from the Hallel: "The stone rejected by the builders has become the chief cornerstone." The cornerstone or topstone[45] to which Jesus refers possibly could allude to the architecture of the temple; some hearers might have recognized that he was comparing the elect community to a temple, as in the Dead Sea Scrolls.[46] Most clearly, however, they would recognize that he was challenging the "builders," here the temple authorities. (On the historical level, this represented especially, though probably not exclusively, the Sadducees.)[47]

Although the challenge was not explicit, conjoined with Jesus' recent overturning tables in the temple it would be plain enough. Jesus had challenged the authorities, whose honor could best be regained, and whose control could best be maintained, by retaliating against him (just as Mk 12:12 implies).

Challenging Israel's Guardians

The parable may imply a special relationship between Jesus and the Father, hence hinting more publicly at what was hitherto part of the "messianic secret."[48] This hint could provoke further concern from the guardians of public order (cf. the report in Mk 14:61).

More obviously, the parable challenged Jerusalem's political elite (Mk 11:27; 12:1, 12). Whereas the Pharisees might disagree or be angry with Jesus and his disciples, they lacked political power in this period to suppress their rivals. Jerusalem's predominantly Sadducean municipal aristocracy, however, was quite another story. Jesus, like many other religious Jews, regarded the priestly authorities as illegitimate rulers, whose way would necessarily be supplanted by the coming kingdom. Indeed, their power was historically linked with Herod (who installed their families in power) and relations with Rome; it perished in the Judean revolt.

Jesus was ready to deliberately challenge this elite, not from the wilderness (like leaders of most prophetic or revolutionary movements), but in Jerusalem, and to depend on God's vindication. In view of the Jewish tradition of Jerusalem rejecting prophets, that city was the appropriate place for a prophet to perish (Lk 13:33).[49] Jerusalem was the center of Jewish restoration eschatology, hence also the appropriate place for a prophet of such eschatology to prepare his kingdom.[50] But as we shall argue, Jesus did not intend to defend himself physically against their retaliation; his conception of the kingdom (exemplified in the present by healings and exorcisms) was not a political one in the sense in which they would understand it.

Did Jesus Foreknow His Death?

Although scholars in the past century have often doubted that Jesus could have predicted his own death,[51] others have demurred, entirely apart from the question of prophetic foreknowledge.[52] As Leander Keck observes, if "Jesus did reckon seriously with the likelihood that he would be put to death violently, then the passion predictions merit another look."[53] Because they do not interpret the significance of his death, Keck argues, they give no indication of being Christian inventions after the fact.[54]

Some protest that "Q" omits passion predictions, since the passion predictions come from Mark,[55] but this objection fails to reckon with several factors. First, for all we know, "Q" could be Mark's source for the idea at least once; sometimes Mark apparently gives an abbreviated version of "Q" material.[56] While this is simply an objection to an argument from silence rather than a positive argument, other objections exist to assuming these predictions to be merely Mark's invention. Thus second, John apparently independently provides passion predictions (Jn 2:4; 8:28; 12:23-24, 32-33). Third, Paul, writing earlier than Mark, confirms the tradition of one passion prediction and explanation that is implied in Jesus' words at the last supper (1 Cor 11:23-25).[57]

Even if one discounts the possibility that God could grant insight to one of his agents concerning his mission (which, as Raymond Brown notes, is merely a philosophical a priori),[58] doubts that Jesus foresaw his death are untenable for several reasons.[59] Good historical reasons exist for supposing that Jesus foresaw his imminent martyrdom, and probably even viewed it as part of his mission.[60]

First, the saying may reflect an early Aramaic construction and three characteristics of Jesus' distinctive style.[61] Second, Jesus shared the common Jewish view that sufferings precede the kingdom,[62] which renders more understandable his own imminent expectation of suffering. Third, he also accepted the Jewish view, confirmed in John's death, that prophets are martyred, and Jesus in a "Q" saying (Matt 23:37//Lk 13:34) linked this tradition of martyred prophets with Jerusalem's failure to accept his own message.[63] (Some also recall that God's suffering servants in the remnant traditions of both Isaiah and Daniel provided sufficient grist for such views,[64] and the Maccabean tradition hallowed martyrdom.)

Fourth, the gospel tradition reports numerous conflicts Jesus had experienced up to this point, the implications of which should have become clearer as he approached the arena of the political powerbrokers in Jerusalem.[65] Fifth, some of Jesus' other sayings, like disciples sharing his cup (Mk 10:38) and his words at the last supper (Mk 14:22, 24), point in the same direction.[66]

But finally and most importantly, Jesus could not but have foreknown his death: Jesus ultimately *provoked* his death, showing his control over its timing, by his apparent assault on an institution by which the priestly aristocracy symbolized their power.[67] No one could directly challenge Jerusalem's municipal aristocracy, which was connected with Roman interests in "stability" and "order," without anticipating severe reprisals, for any such challenge could not but appear to the state's guardians as a threat to the state's political security.

That Jesus' execution as an accused evildoer condemned by the highest court of the land would be instigated by his people's priestly leaders (also Mk 8:31) is one of the striking ironies of the gospel story that must have made it offensive to Jewish people loyal to the religious establishment — hardly the sort of story Jewish Christian apologists would have invented.[68] Minorities in conflict with the priestly political elite in Judea (whether the Pharisees or, to a greater extent, the Essenes and others) could understand it, but it would simply amplify the offense of Jesus' execution for Diaspora hearers. Yet it fits Jesus' own mission: if he expected a prophet's death in Jerusalem, political conditions being what they were he had to expect the elite priests' Sanhedrin and possibly (especially at Passover) the Roman governor to play a role.

It would not be implausible that if Jesus expected to face rejection and death for an offensive message like many earlier prophets, he might also expect God's vindication in swiftly establishing the kingdom,[69] hence (in the perspective of many Palestinian Jews) raising the dead. Kim Huat Tan has shown the plausibility of Jesus speaking of a future, postmortem role for himself based on several factors, the most compelling being the multiplicity of sayings about the resurrection and especially parousia, many with features we normally use to signal authenticity.[70] That Jesus may have expected his own postmortem, resurrected exaltation ahead of that of others would be distinctive — we know of no direct precedents for the view — but would at least be compatible with Jesus' apparent expectation of an interim era in which a community could carry on after him (see ch. 14). (Certainly some other Jewish teachers envisioned an interim eschatological era of some sort.)[71]

That Jesus *rarely* spoke about his impending passion, especially in public, fits the Gospels' picture of him focusing on God's reign rather than himself in public teaching.[72] That the disciples misunderstood such clear teaching (e.g., Mk 8:32) may imply the strength of the more popular messianic category in light of which they interpreted Jesus' mission; it also suggests that the passion prediction, clear as it was, could be construed the way oracles in the ancient Mediterranean were often construed, on the principle that they often appeared obscure until fulfilment.[73] In any case, that Jesus expected his execution seems clear from his course of action.

Provoking Martyrdom

Given the large amount of theological controversy in first-century Palestinian Judaism, it was most likely not mere debates with the Pharisees, but rather Jesus' acts that could be interpreted politically, or as confrontation with the elite, that led to his execution.[74] Against some scholars who have questioned whether Jesus could have predicted his impending death, it seems nearly impossible that he would not have done so: by disrupting public activity in the Temple and publicly challenging the authorities' honor, Jesus virtually provoked it.[75] In our chapter addressing Jesus as a prophet, we briefly addressed his action in the Temple; here we seek to show its connection to his execution.

Merely prophesying the Temple's destruction publicly could invite scourging and the threat of death,[76] and execution would prove an especially appealing solution if a leader already had a significant gathering of followers.[77] The guardians of law and order in the Temple, whose positions depended on keeping peace between the Romans and the people, were permitted to punish violations of the sanctity of the Temple — and only this offense — with death.[78] If Jesus did not violate the inner sanctuary, nevertheless he provoked the antagonism of those who could hand him over to the Romans as a messianic (royal) pretender, an offense the Romans viewed as treason.[79]

Sanders regards Jesus' controversy with the Temple establishment as an "almost indisputable" historical fact.[80] Later Christians would not have invented Jesus' act against the Temple; they maintained their connections with the Temple (Acts 2:46; 21:23-26) and wished to avoid the suspicion that they were subversive (which enemies of temples were considered anywhere in the Empire). Attestation by both Markan and Johannine streams of tradition further supports the tradition's antiquity.[81] It moreover provides the best explanation for Jesus' execution.[82]

This action also coheres with Jesus' prophecy against the Temple.[83] This prophecy is likely authentic (see ch. 17). A few scholars doubt that Jesus predicted the Temple's destruction, attributing that "fiction" to Mark.[84] In so doing, however, they miss several points (noted in ch. 17): the tradition's multiple attestation (cf. Jn 2:19); that the church would not have invented the claim, feeling comfortable attributing the charge especially to false witnesses (Mk 14:58; Acts 6:14); and likely Jesus tradition in 2 Thess 2:4.[85] That the later church felt comfortable attributing the charge about Jesus destroying the temple only to false witnesses (Mk 14:58; cf. Acts 6:14)[86] suggests that it is not an idea that Jesus' earliest followers felt comfortable with, at least not initially.

Jesus' prophecy against the Temple is plausible in his milieu; we have noted that a minority of Jews before 70, mainly sectarian, did oppose the Temple or the establishment that controlled it.[87] Others before 70 CE also predicted the Temple's destruction,[88] and there is no reason to doubt that Jesus did so.[89] Like some of his contemporaries, as Sanders notes, Jesus undoubtedly expected a kingdom "in which a temple, whether new or cleansed, would be useful."[90] Because Jesus' protest in the Temple would have deliberately provoked the authorities to seek Jesus' death,[91] we should also see the act in the Temple as a pivotal event in Jesus' mission.[92]

Describing Jesus' Action

Some scholars doubt that Jesus could have overturned tables without incurring intervention from the guards in the Fortress Antonia. This skepticism would ring true had Jesus led a full-scale riot, but given the enormity of the outer court and the loudness of the crowds thronging it, a small-scale act by a single person might have escaped the attention of the Roman guards, at least in time for their intervention.[93]

Where did Jesus' prophetic action occur? Sanders argues that most trade took place in shops along a street adjoining the Temple, rather than in the sacred precincts themselves.[94] But the narrow street beside the Temple does not appear to have been large enough to hold sufficient sacrificial animals (certainly not all the lambs needed for Passover) and still admit any flow of passersby. Most likely the shops outside the Temple precincts served the tourist industry, whereas the outer court included authorized dealers at festival times.[95] Very few scholars doubt that birds and moneychangers, at least, were in the outer court of the Temple, where they would save pilgrims considerable time in procuring and offering sacrifices.[96]

Of the four Gospels, only John mentions the oxen and sheep, as well as birds, in the Temple (2:14-15).[97] Sanders doubts that cattle would have been held in the Temple proper, given difficulties such as getting them up the stairs.[98] Yet even John's account is not inherently improbable here. One would not need many cattle for sacrifices, but to fulfill biblical requirements one would have needed some,[99] especially during the festivals. These cattle had to be gotten into the Temple somehow.[100] Moreover, archaeologists have now discovered a direct passage from where large animals were brought to the temple courts.[101] John may be more given to theologizing narrative than the Synoptics are, but his information here corresponds with what we know about the Temple.

Why Jesus Challenged the Temple

Within at most a day after Jesus overturned tables and created a disturbance in the Temple, it is likely that the previous activities had resumed. Indeed, without a significant enough band of followers to overpower the Temple guard and Roman garrison and to permanently hold the Fortress Antonia, Jesus would not have expected it to turn out otherwise. (Our few extant examples of sign-prophets acted outside the city proper, not in the midst of the authorities' power.) It is therefore probable that Jesus intended his act in the Temple symbolically in some sense, as many scholars recognize.[102] Throughout the ancient Mediterranean world people recognized the value of symbolic actions,[103] Jeremiah's smashing of a pot in the temple precincts being a particularly relevant case in point (Jer 19:10-14).[104] The meaning of the symbol here, however, has engendered considerable debate. Some proposals have generated little support among current scholarship, for instance the proposal that the Gospels use the Temple cleansing to symbolize the replacement of the cultic system of the Temple with Jesus' new sacrifice for sins.[105] Others, however, merit further discussion.

Economic Exploitation?

Some have proposed that Jesus challenged economic exploitation in the Temple, but the extant evidence for this thesis is not very strong. Jerusalem was the center of a prosperous trade and tourist industry;[106] while the local aristocracy may not have profited directly from mercantile activity in the Temple (see below), they were at the top of a steep economic pyramid (artisans may have been at its bottom) that profited from Jerusalem's economic strength, especially from a tourist industry encouraged and accommodated by the Temple establishment. Profiting from a system that profited everyone need not, however, be construed as economic exploitation, and sacrifices were not at the heart of it.[107]

One Jewish scholar notes the rabbinic tradition that moneychangers worked in the outer court for about one week and received no profit.[108] He admits that in practice some may have abused this system, and that Jesus may have justly reacted against the abuses; but he doubts that the abuses pervaded the system.[109] This tradition that the moneychangers did not profit (at least not exploitively) may well be late, but we lack a specific early one that offers a contrary view.[110] If one tradition is dependable, the commercial use of the court of the Gentiles, turning it into something of a hellenistic agora, began only shortly before the time of Jesus; this practice may have invited criticism from a number of pietists at that time.[111] Again, we cannot be certain how reliable the tradition is.

Some propose that the issue was simply paying money in the Temple.[112] Yet it is difficult to see how the sacrificial system could have been conducted without selling, money and moneychangers.[113] Pilgrims could hardly bring their own sacrifices from the Diaspora, and it would be inconvenient even from Galilee. Despite other professions in lists of unscrupulous means of profit, moneychangers provoked little complaint, and were often persons of high moral reputation and prominence.[114] Given varying city currencies, moneychangers were also necessary, even in the towns of Galilee.[115] Certainly in the Temple, where pilgrims arrived with a wide variety of currency but needed to purchase sacrifices to obey the law, moneychangers were necessary.[116]

Perhaps most importantly, there is little evidence that Jerusalem's aristocracy profited directly from the commercial activity in the Temple, whether from selling or moneychanging. Although polemical texts often complain about the priestly aristocracy, they remain completely silent about them profiting from sales in the Temple.[117] Granted, our texts cannot reveal the motives of those involved in such trade, and some exploitation may have occurred.[118] But this possibility does not constitute evidence that economic exploitation was at the center of the activity in the Temple or of Jesus' protest there.

Defending the Worship of Gentiles?

Gentiles were welcome alongside Israelites in Solomon's temple (1 Kgs 8:41-43). But due to increased sensitivity to purity considerations, by Jesus' day Gentiles were excluded from courts nearer the holiest place.[119] Thus the commercial activity in the outer court, by treating it as less sacred than the courts of women and Israel that were also part of Solomon's outer court, risked marginalizing Gentile visitors' worship of Israel's God.

Merchants did not prevent gentiles from praying, but the Temple's structure expressed an ideology of separation that, as Borg puts it, "excluded gentiles generally," and that Jesus rejected.[120] Thus it is possible that the separation of Gentiles constituted at least one source of Jesus' protest.[121] It is likely that at least Mark understood Jesus' action in this manner; in Mk 11:17 Jesus quotes Is 56:7: "My house shall be called a house of prayer for all nations." Yet while the saying in Mark fits this agenda, it is otherwise unlikely that defense of Gentiles was Jesus' sole reason for challenging the Temple. The other Gospel writers probably surmised this, for it is not the reason emphasized in Matthew and Luke, who both omit Mark's line about God's house being "for all nations."

Judgment on the Temple

Most likely, Jesus' act in the Temple challenged the Jerusalem aristocracy that controlled the Temple system, hence related in some way to Jesus' prophecy of the Temple's impending destruction. Thus when Jesus overturns the tables in Mark he also cites Jer 7:11 concerning the Temple's destruction (Mk 11:17).[122] A symbolic prediction of judgment fits the likelihood that Jesus did predict the Temple's destruction (a likelihood noted earlier in this chapter).

Some who denounced or prophesied against the Temple did so because they opposed the aristocratic priesthood who ran it.[123] Some thus see Jesus' act as a prophetic symbol of ritual cleansing, reacting against the moral defilement there.[124] In its most extreme form, this view portrays Jesus as following Pharisaic purity rules to their logical conclusion;[125] in its more reasonable forms, it portrays Jesus as zealous for the Temple's cleansing, an agenda that he could easily have borrowed from biblical renewal movements or even Scripture (e.g., Mal 3:1-4).

Others concede contemporary denunciations of the Temple hierarchy's uncleanness but note that the Gospels do not emphasize this point;[126] they argue that a concern for purity in the traditional Jewish sense would focus on ritual concerns.[127] They believe that Jesus' action symbolized something more dramatic than the Temple's purification — namely, its destruction.[128]

Sanders argues that Jesus believed that God would directly intervene to establish his kingdom, and that Jesus was preparing for a kingdom "in which a temple, whether new or cleansed, would be useful."[129] Sanders' proposal may well be correct; such an image fits many contemporary ideas about the eschatological Temple (whether supernaturally reconstructed or humanly restored). This hope naturally stirred more prominently after 70 CE[130] but is abundantly attested before Jerusalem's destruction,[131] especially in the Qumran Scrolls.[132] The expected restoration of the vessels, the ark[133] and perhaps its manna[134] also implies a renewed, eschatological temple of some sort.[135]

The proposals of purification and prophecy of judgment are not, however, mutually exclusive; if Jesus believed that the temple institution warranted judgment, he could well have believed that immoral leadership in some sense had defiled it. Many of Jesus' contemporaries emphasized a new or renewed Temple precisely because of the impurity of the priesthood.[136] Purification and replacement are thus not mutually exclusive options.

While Jesus undoubtedly spoke of the destruction of the Temple and apparently envisioned a new, eschatological one, the gospel tradition does not provide clear indication that Jesus' eschatological Temple was purely a physical one. Jesus' contemporaries, including those that expected an eschatological Temple, could also depict the Temple in spiritual terms.[137] One would expect such spiritualized imagery in the Jewish philosopher Philo,[138] but more noteworthy is its appearance in the Dead Sea Scrolls, where the true Temple sometimes symbolizes the community.[139] The use of Psalm 118 in the festal Hallel suggests the authenticity of its citation in the Synoptic tradition (Mk 12:10-11; cf. 11:9-10; 14:26),[140] which in turn might suggest that Jesus himself did intend a new Temple but with himself as the cornerstone.[141] If so, his followers rightly understood that Temple spiritually (1 Cor 3:16; Eph 2:20-22; 1 Pet 2:5; cf. Lk 19:40, 44; Rom 9:32-33).[142]

Before Jesus could become the chief cornerstone, however, he had to be rejected by the builders — the establishment who controlled Herod's temple (Mk 12:10-12). Opposition to the Temple would generate hostility from most of mainstream Judaism,[143] and perhaps even martyrdom at the hands of the authorities.[144] For Jesus to offer this provocation, then refuse to flee Jerusalem or arm his followers, suggests that he intended to face the authorities' hostility.

Jesus and Politics

Various lines of evidence converge to show that Jesus expected his martyrdom, even if his talk about a role in the impending kingdom made that expectation seem less than intelligible to his disciples. These lines of evidence include both considerations above and the likelihood that (as we argued in ch. 18) Jesus viewed himself as king, and that some of his followers viewed him this way at least potentially.

However *Jesus* meant "kingdom" or his role in the kingdom (probably as God's viceroy, hence probably as a messiah), he could not but know that this teaching would sound like (and would at the very least ultimately prove to be) a challenge to the political elite of Jerusalem.

Jesus could have left Jerusalem afterward, yet he chose not to do so; he also could have gathered more followers or armed them, but chose not to do so. (Josephus does not class him with the wilderness "prophets" with armed followings that Josephus so detested.) Jesus did not resist or flee the authorities' retaliation; he therefore must have expected either his imminent death, God's imminent intervention on his behalf, or more likely (if we incorporate all the evidence we have) both. The question is whether he expected God's intervention before his death (preventing it) or afterward (raising him, whether individually, as in the gospel tradition, or along with others eschatologically, as in popular expectation).

Why would Jesus have deliberately exposed himself to martyrdom? As noted above, this was an expected fate of prophets; yet it is also possible that Jesus expected his death to accomplish something on behalf of his people who were not adequately prepared for the kingdom. Some of Jesus' contemporaries believed that martyrs' deaths could atone for Israel (see discussion below); Jesus may have therefore intended to lay down his life on behalf of his people.

Probably the majority of first-century Palestinian Jews waited for God to bring the end rather than advocating direct violence against the oppressors; while not pacifists, they were "very passively hostile."[145] That Jesus did not resist (cf. Jn 18:36: "otherwise my servants would fight"), and that his followers continued his example, suggest that they may have agreed with this eschatological model.[146] Nevertheless, many plausibly believe that Jesus opposed the Judean elite (as in the Gospels, e.g., Mk 12:9, 12; 13:1-2; cf. 12:38-40); Jewish scholar Alan Segal argues that "Jesus was a passionate advocate of political and individual justice who predicted a terrible and imminent end for the evil regime ruling Judea."[147] At the very least, he did not believe that the aristocratic families empowered by Herod a generation earlier[148] were Israel's true and permanent leaders, and he was prepared to face death at their hands partly to make that point.

The Last Supper

As we have noted, the same circles of early Jewish Christians who preserved reminiscences of the Hallel and other early Jewish features also had some reason to associate Jesus' death with Passover (1 Cor 5:7), and early Jewish Christians were also the ones with the best access to the authentic traditions.[149] That they invented Jesus' execution during the Passover week is unlikely. We know that Jesus was a Galilean executed near Jerusalem; the likeliest time to find Jesus and his Galilean followers in Jerusalem would have been precisely at one of the three major pilgrimage festivals. Had Jesus been martyred in Galilee, where Herod's son Antipas rather than a Roman governor ruled, it is unlikely that he would have died on a Roman cross. Unless Jesus was executed immediately after his entry into Jerusalem, therefore, his "last supper" there was presumably near Passover.

Suggested Comparisons for the Last Supper

No one denies that Jesus ate a final meal with his disciples, but this claim by itself is not saying much; if Jesus ever ate with his disciples, the last time he did so was by definition a "final" one. What bears keeping in mind here, however, is that this meal would be a Jewish one, and would likely be especially remembered by his followers by virtue of it being their last table sharing together. In the ancient Middle East and Mediterranean world, sharing a meal bonded its participants in mutual loyalty. Given the tensions we have noted during passion week, and Jesus' apparent plan to both provoke and await martyrdom, that Jesus spoke about his death at such a meal is not at all implausible.

Ignoring closer Jewish parallels, some have found pagan backgrounds for the Lord's Supper,[150] which would represent the creation of the later church rather than the disciples' accurate memories of what happened on the night of Jesus' arrest. For example, some have compared the Lord's Supper to pagan cult meals[151] or even suggested that the hellenistic sacramental meals were read back into the Jewish last supper tradition.[152] Still further removed from a Jewish setting are occasional proposed connections[153] with the Greco-Roman cult of the dead, which honored departed ancestors.[154] Against connections with the cult of the dead is the antiquity of the resurrection tradition (i.e., disciples were not simply "remembering" a departed loved one), and the closer parallel in the biblical paschal tradition.[155] Mention of "memory" in a passover context involved not mere recollection but more of a participatory commemoration.[156]

Greek associations regularly met for common meals,[157] normally dedicated to the association's patron deity (but with little further attention to the deity).[158] Greek meal practice did affect contemporary Jewish banquets, including Passover customs,[159] hence did indirectly influence some customs at the Last Supper; in some respects the hellenistic church also assimilated the Lord's Supper to hellenistic meals.[160] These meals do not provide the most immediate parallels for the earliest form of the Lord's Supper tradition, however. Most scholars also recognize that before the spread of Christianity, hellenistic meals were not sacramental[161] and did not communicate mystical elements of the deity.[162]

Others, helpfully looking closer to Jesus' actual milieu, have compared the Last Supper with Qumran meals.[163] Their meals themselves might reflect some hellenistic influence.[164] Although some have viewed these meals as priestly or eschatological,[165] others contend that the sacral character may be no more than in most Jewish meals,[166] and the eschatological interpretation also remains unclear.[167] Nevertheless, the proposed parallels between the Qumran meals and the Lord's Supper are not strong:[168] the leader presiding over the meal and blessing bread and wine fits all Jewish meals (see below) — like most other characteristics of the meal.[169] Certainly special rules obtained in the Qumran order,[170] but their meals merely show that a concept related to the sacred meal was already present in Palestinian Judaism and that one need not appeal to geographically distant parallels to explain the Lord's Supper.[171]

Some think that Jesus' final meal more resembles the regular weekly gatherings of the *haburoth*,[172] whose Pharisaic purity rules, some think, may have bound them to eating especially among themselves.[173] But again, are meals of associates or students of the sages pervasive and distinctive enough as meals to warrant special attention in connection with the Last Supper?[174] Palestinian Jewish families probably celebrated the more common weekly Sabbath Kiddush from a very early period.[175] Diaspora Jews also apparently assembled for communal meals at times.[176] What most of these meals have in common with the Lord's Supper they also have in common with each other, as simply *standard* Jewish meal or banquet practice.

A Passover Seder

Many of those features of the Last Supper that are distinguishable from regular Jewish meals parallel the Passover meal, a correspondence not surprising in view of the night on which Jesus was betrayed in the tradition.[177] That Jesus followed the more common practices regarding Passover cannot be proved (especially given the uncertain dating of our extant paschal sources),[178] but this proposal is likely, especially in view of the correspondences on points that can be tested.[179] We note some of these below.

Paul's report	Mark's report	Early Jewish setting
At night (1 Cor 11:23)	At night (Mk 14:30)	Passover meal at night[180]
The context of Jesus' "betrayal"[181] (1 Cor 11:23)	The context of Jesus' betrayal (Mk 14:10-11, 18, 21, 41-44)	—
Jesus took bread, gave thanks, and broke it (11:23-24)	Jesus took bread, gave thanks, and broke it (Mk 14:22)	Blessing and breaking bread customary for all Jewish meals
Jesus interpreted elements (11:24-25)	Jesus interpreted elements (Mk 14:22-24)	*Elements were interpreted symbolically at Passover
Jesus interpreted the bread as his body (11:24)	Jesus interpreted the bread as his body (14:22)	*At Passover the bread was interpreted as that of the ancestors' exodus, commemorating an act of deliverance
Jesus identified the cup as a (new) covenant in his blood (11:25)	Jesus identified the cup as his blood of the (new) covenant, poured out for "the many" (14:24)[182]	The blood of a covenant evokes the first covenant with Israel (Ex 24:8), implying the promised new covenant (Jer 31:31) and possibly evoking also the paschal lamb's blood (see other early Christian interpretations in 1 Cor 5:7; cf. Jn 1:29, 36; 1 Pet 1:19)
His followers would eat and drink in memory of him (11:24-25)	Missing in Mark, but in Luke: Jesus' followers would eat in memory of him (Lk 22:19, most MSS)	*Passover annually commemorated the first redemption of Israel (Ex 12:14; 13:3; Deut 16:2-3; Jub. 49:15)
The meal looked forward to his future coming (11:26)	The meal prefigured the future kingdom banquet (Mk 14:25)	Many Jewish people expected a future messianic banquet,[183] and many believed that Passover presaged a final redemption[184]
—	They sang a hymn (Mk 14:26)	*Jewish households sang the Hallel after the meal

Jesus' Words (Mk 14:22-25; 1 Cor 11:23-25)

On the grounds of multiple attestation (Paul as well as Synoptic tradition) Jesus' words about the cup, the bread, his body and blood are among the most secure elements of our traditions about Jesus.[185] Paul's claim that he "received" and "delivered" to the Corinthian church the Lord's Supper tradition (1 Cor 11:23) reflects ancient language, including ancient Jewish language, for the passing on of traditions.[186] Some think that Paul's claim to have received the tradition "from the Lord" (Jesus) means a divine revelation rather than traditions from the Lord's disciples. But other Jewish teachers sometimes claimed to receive a *halakah* from Sinai (i.e., through Moses) even though everyone understood that the tradition was mediated via other authorities.[187] Paul's claim to have received the tradition "from the Lord" (Jesus) thus does not diminish the likelihood that he draws on early Palestinian tradition here.[188] Although variations in the tradition[189] fit the sort of development one might expect on the basis of liturgical and rhetorical usage, a partly recoverable common Aramaic tradition may remain behind the Markan and Pauline versions.[190] Various early linguistic features appear.[191]

Paul attests the Last Supper tradition before Mark was written, indicating that this tradition was already circulating in the first generation of Jesus' followers.

The Sacrificial Purpose for Jesus' Death

The Last Supper was a symbolic act, like the triumphal entry and Jesus' act in the Temple.[192] Whether the specific act of *breaking* bread foreshadowed Jesus' death is difficult to decide; it was customary for the head of the household (or group)[193] to break bread so he could distribute it (Mk 6:41; 8:6, 19-20).[194] Interpreting the elements of the Passover feast (the bread, bitter herbs, etc.) was a standard Passover practice,[195] but instead of using standard explanations Jesus interprets two elements (the two elements representative of food and drink in blessings at Jewish meals) in a strikingly new way.[196]

Because this tradition is thus very early, whatever information it preserves therefore likely tells us much about Jesus' view of his mission.[197] Jesus elsewhere spoke of the martyrs' blood inviting judgment (Matt 23:35//Lk 11:51). But because Jesus invites his followers to share in this act, he may also play on the atoning value of martyrs' deaths (especially attested in 4 Maccabees). Yet Jesus' death appears as more than that of a *mere* martyr in this earliest tradition, whether as the climactic basis of judgment[198] or as the single martyr whose death his followers should commemorate. The probable allusions to Is 52–53 in Jesus' language here[199] tell us a great deal about how Jesus viewed his own death.

Even more probably, many of Jesus' words (such as "flesh," "blood," "poured out") suggest sacrificial terminology,[200] especially since crucifixion itself technically required no blood.[201] The "blood of the covenant" refers to Ex 24:8, where blood was shed to establish God's covenant with Israel (just as most covenants in Israel's history required the shedding of blood).[202] Whether Paul's "new covenant" midrashically interprets the "blood of the covenant" allusion to Ex 24:8 in light of Jer 31:31,[203] or the most likely textual tradition in Mark and Matthew suppresses "new" to heighten the Exodus allusion, this "covenant" must be a new or renewed one, a prophetic image current in Jesus' day.[204] That Jesus intended his death as sacrificial in some sense fits the evidence from Jesus' life for his intended martyrdom[205] (we discuss Jewish sacrificial martyr theology below).

When Jesus claims that the bread "is" his body he is not claiming any biochemical connection between the two. Presumably he means that the bread "represents" or stands for his body in some sense;[206] the disciples presumably would have understood his words here no more literally than they would have taken the normal interpretation of Passover elements, some of which may have been in widespread use this early: "This is the bread of affliction that our ancestors ate when they came from the land of Egypt."[207] (By no stretch of the imagination did anyone suppose that they were re-eating the very bread the Israelites had eaten in the wilderness.)[208] Those who ate of this bread participated by commemoration in Jesus' affliction in the same manner that those who ate the Passover commemorated in the deliverance of their ancestors.[209] The language of Passover celebration assumed the participation of current generations in the exodus event.[210]

Jesus probably followed Passover practice regarding the cup as well. According to tradition, the head of the household, who had been reclining, would now sit up to bless God for the bread before the meal; after the meal, Jesus probably interprets the third or fourth cup.[211] If later codified customs continued earlier basic practice, as is probable in the case of an annual festal tradition, Jesus may have lifted the cup with both hands, holding it in his right hand about a handbreadth above the table.[212] But after partaking of this cup, Jesus utters what resembles a traditional vow of abstention (promising God to abstain from something for a specified period of time),[213] in this case vowing not to drink wine until the coming of his reign.[214] Many Jewish people viewed the kingdom as a banquet (Is 25:6),[215] so Jesus is apparently promising not to drink wine again until his kingdom. 1 Cor 11:26 (which says that the Lord's Supper declares his death "until he comes") recalls this eschatological significance in the Lord's Supper, related to the implications of future redemption many Jewish people saw in the Passover.[216]

After what was normally a few hours of discussion,[217] here perhaps abbreviated, the household would sing the remaining hymns of the Hallel, undoubtedly the "hymn" to which the text refers (Mk 14:26),[218] antiphonally if they could.[219] As we have noted, the Hallel included lines relevant to the passion narrative like, "The stone rejected by the builders has become the chief cornerstone" (Ps 118:22); "O save . . . blessed is the one who comes in YHWH's name" (Ps 118:25-26).

Martyrdom and Atonement in Early Judaism

Jesus' salvific understanding of his death was intelligible in the tradition precisely because it was not isolated, but belonged to a wider framework of understanding about atoning blood sacrifice, suffering, and martyrs' sacrificial death. Greeks understood the notion of expiatory sacrifice,[220] but we need not look so far afield.[221] 4 Maccabees probably offers the closest extrabiblical parallels to atoning martyrdom in the first century.[222] In 4 Macc 17:22, God watched over Israel because the blood of martyrs atoned for the land (cf. also a martyr's prayer that his suffering would substitute for that of Israel in 4 Macc 6:28-29).[223] Indeed, the concept is already present in the much earlier work 2 Maccabees, where martyrs suffer to turn away God's wrath from Israel (7:37-38).[224]

Some contend that Isaiah's suffering servant provides an earlier model for this conception of atonement, followed by Qumran and possibly 4 Maccabees.[225] Like Jesus at the Last Supper, the saying in Mk 10:45 probably alludes to the suffering servant of Isaiah, particularly in Jesus not only serving but offering his "soul" or "life" (Is 53:12) as a ransom or redemption price (cf. Is 53:10-11)[226] on behalf of "the many" (Is 53:11-12; cf. Rom 5:15). Despite the different paths they have taken into Greek, the numerous correspondences between our first extant appearance of this saying in Mark (Mk 10:45) and the language of Isaiah suggest that Isaiah's servant was in view from the start.[227]

In any case, it was natural for Jesus' followers to apply the Jewish understanding of atoning martyrdom to Jesus' death.[228] What is more striking from the standpoint of our historical purpose is that this application appears in our earliest tradition of the Lord's Supper, attested in both Paul and Mark — hence probably stemming from Jesus himself. Jesus intended to be martyred, and apparently believed that his martyrdom would appease God's anger against his people (which was what many expected the death of martyrs to do). In view of Jesus' expectation of impending judgment on the land (Matt 23:34-38//Lk 11:49-51), however, he might view the atonement as particularly efficacious for the new remnant community he was founding.

Conclusion

The best available evidence suggests that Jesus told the parable of the tenants in Jerusalem before his passion. In this parable he implied his impending death at the hands of Jerusalem's elite. He also challenged Israel's guardians in other respects, most publicly and obviously by disturbing order in the Temple's outer court. Against the traditional critical view, Jesus certainly could have predicted his death. In fact, he not only foreknew it — he deliberately provoked it. He could not but have known where his actions would lead if he neither fled nor fought; the priestly aristocrats would have viewed his actions as both an affront to their honor and a challenge to their authority.

Some of the strongest available evidence in the gospel tradition supports Jesus eating a final meal with his disciples, where he further interpreted his impending death. This meal undoubtedly occurred during the Passover season, as in the Gospels (Galileans likely visiting Jerusalem especially during the major pilgrimage festivals). In these words, Jesus offered a key for understanding his actions that were leading to his impending death: Jesus was offering himself as a martyr to turn away God's anger from Israel, as Jewish tradition understood some other martyrs. His death was no unfortunate or unexpected accident.

CHAPTER 21

Jesus' Arrest and Execution

"We should begin our study with two firm facts before us: Jesus was executed by the Romans as would-be 'king of the Jews', and his disciples subsequently formed a messianic movement which was not based on the hope of military victory."

E. P. SANDERS[1]

"Jesus had alarmed some people by his attack on the Temple. . . . It is highly probable, however, that Caiaphas was primarily or exclusively concerned with the possibility that Jesus would incite a riot. He sent armed guards to arrest Jesus, he gave him a hearing, and he recommended execution to Pilate, who promptly complied. That is the way the gospels describe the events, and that is the way things really happened, as the numerous stories in Josephus prove."

E. P. SANDERS[2]

No one doubts that Jesus was executed. Early Christians would not have invented this fate for their leader, a fate that posed considerable risks for them as followers. Likewise, scholars do not routinely suppose that first-generation persecuted groups usually invented elaborate stories of their founders' executions on criminal charges when such founders died a natural death.

Moreover, early Christians are not the only ones to report Jesus' execution, though some other sources (like the Syrian Stoic Mara bar Serapion, who around the year 73 CE blames the Jewish people for Jesus' death) may follow Christian reports. In the early second century, Tacitus attributes the execution to Pilate. Most strikingly, the Jewish historian Josephus in the first century apparently blames both the governor and Jerusalem's aristocrats: "Pilate condemned Jesus to crucifixion, after our leaders had accused him."[3] Josephus' verdict fits not only the reports in the Gospels but also how matters were usually carried out in this period.

Historical Tradition in the Passion Narratives

Before turning to the historical events surrounding Jesus' death, we must again return to the question of sources.[4] What can scholars say about the Gospels' passion story? The basic outline of the passion story is attested earlier in Paul (cf. 1 Cor 11:23-25). The Fourth Gospel also confirms a number of points in the Synoptics, though divergences at some points underline John's independence (though not necessarily his ignorance) of the Synoptic version.[5] Most ancient believers probably heard the story multiple times; even without religious reasons, ancient Mediterranean storytellers regularly repeated the most popular or important stories. If churches celebrated the Lord's Supper as a symbolic reenactment of the Last Supper at some level, as 1 Cor 11:24-26 in its passover context could suggest, the passion story must have been familiar indeed.

Genre of Passion Narratives

First we should address the genre ancient audiences may have perceived in the passion narrative. Naturally in the Gospels readers would approach the passion narrative as related to a common feature of ancient biographies (i.e., the final part narrating the subject's death). Nevertheless, we must also ask about the earlier, independent passion narrative (or perhaps more likely, various passion narrations) that stand behind this portion of the Gospels.

Because both the passion narratives and martyr stories address the unjust death of the righteous, the passion narratives repeat some themes that also appear in the martyr stories (e.g., 2 Macc 6–7; Wisd 2:12-20),[6] as many scholars have properly emphasized.[7] Ancient moralists and historians praised honorable and heroic deaths, whether within or beyond martyr stories.[8] Writers may have also drawn on a stock arsenal of motifs when expanding martyr stories for dramatic purposes.[9] At the same time, analogous story lines need not demonstrate dependence or genetic relationship. Those who stood against the establishment regularly invited repression, so their stories tended to turn out in similar ways.

Important as comparisons with martyr stories are for analysis of the texts, the comparisons involve some limitations. Apart from the fact that both martyr stories and Gospel passion narratives involve a righteous person's unjust death, the parallels may be inadequate to place the Gospel passion stories fully in this genre, especially given the differences.[10] Many features reflect common notions of courage or acting on behalf of others.[11] More specifically, early Jewish Christians probably drew on the Isaian servant songs, which came to be widely applied to Jesus (e.g., Matt 12:17-21; Acts 3:13; 8:32-35; 1 Pet 2:22).[12]

Of the other motifs that both the passion narratives and martyr stories share, many are no more distinctively characteristic of martyr stories than of other ancient literature. For example, where possible, Diogenes Laertius ends his discussions of the lives of eminent philosophers with their death.[13] Martyr stories of course could vindicate their protagonist's devotion and so offered greater impact than other death accounts.[14]

Despite analogies, barely anyone would suggest that Jesus' execution was merely fabricated to fit this genre; as we have noted, early Christians had every reason to avoid fabricating a story that would bring them into repeated conflict with Roman authorities and their own Jewish elite. Further, most biographies that reported their subjects' death did not conclude with martyrdom, and nearly all scholars concur with good reason that the basic kerygma (gospel message) arose shortly after Jesus' execution.[15] Though martyr stories may explain the form in which some cohesive passion narrative or narratives circulated, they would not by themselves indicate their composition to be fiction.

Theissen thus concludes his own analysis, "There is no analogy to the passion narrative in all of ancient literature. Elements of Hellenistic acts of the martyrs and Jewish tales of martyrdom have been melded into something quite new."[16] If he overstates their uniqueness from a formal standpoint, he nevertheless corrects an overemphasis on parallels that explain less than some other scholars would claim. The vast majority of ancient biographies concluded with the subject's death, funeral, and related events.[17] Many biographies focused a significant amount of space on the conclusion of their subjects' lives, especially if the end was central to the subject's achievements.[18] Likewise, if the passion narrative is not simply a martyr story, neither is it a typical Greek apotheosis story; the focus in the Synoptic Gospels is on Jesus' mortal suffering, not a promotion to divinity.[19]

The Historical Foundation for the Passion Narratives

The extreme skepticism expressed by the most radical scholars is surely unwarranted. Burton Mack, for instance, suggests that most scholars have simply gone easy on the passion narratives from faith prejudice.[20] Nevertheless, he shows little familiarity with the evidence cited by such "prejudicial" scholarship,[21] and in dismissing previous scholarship on the passion narratives as uncritical seems unaware of his predecessors who have focused critical attention on the passion narratives.[22] (Mack himself curiously reads the passion narrative more in light of subsequent western history than in light of ancient urban politics.)[23]

In contrast to Mack's position, we have no record of any form of Christianity where the basic structure of the kerygma was missing, whether or not Christians had yet constructed full passion narratives.[24] Other narratives may have figured as much in early Christian ethical preaching, but it is likely that early Christians would have told and retold the passion story, which lay at the heart of their kerygma, and that the Gospel writers would have here a variety of oral and perhaps written traditions from which to draw.[25] Thus Paul has a passion sequence similar to Mark's (1 Cor 11:23; 15:3-5), and if, as is probable, John represents an independent tradition,[26] it is significant that his passion narrative again confirms the outline that Mark follows, conceivably supporting a pre-Markan passion narrative.[27] In preaching one could flesh out the full sequence or omit some of the stories, but the basic outline would remain the same.[28]

Most scholars think that "Q" lacked a passion narrative. But for all we know, as Bart Ehrman points out, Q could "have had a passion narrative; we simply can't know."[29] If multiple versions were available, the Gospel writers would not be bound to any particular one; "Q" could even be one of Mark's sources, as possibly elsewhere.[30] Most scholars who doubt that Q had a passion narrative do not infer from this doubt the premise that Q opposed a passion narrative.[31] Yet as we noted in ch. 4, a few scholars argue from the possible silence in Q that what Q (possibly) lacked, its community did not believe in.

But how could a community believe Jesus' teachings yet ignore his martyrdom? Because some composed dialogues of Socrates, and most of these dialogues do not mention Socrates' death, ought we to doubt that they cared about his martyrdom? Such a supposition does not make sense with other documents in antiquity. This incoherence prompts me to wonder whether some New Testament scholars get away with compounded speculations only because we treat our discipline as purely subjective, so that if enough scholars claim something it becomes a "likely" position, regardless of whether any concrete evidence supports it.

In fact more positive evidence favors the substantial reliability of the passion narratives. Theissen argues for the most part (and sufficiently) persuasively that the pre-Markan passion narrative as a whole was in use by A.D. 40 in Jerusalem and Judea.[32] Thus, for example, Mark preserves names (such as the sons that identify the second Mary and Simon) that serve no recognizable function in his own narrative — but that may well have been recognizable to those who transmitted his early Jerusalem source (Mk 15:21, 40).[33] Place names like Nazareth, Magdala, and Arimathea would mean nothing to audiences outside Palestine.[34] (Regarding Mary Magdalene, who would invent an origin in

Magdala? A Magdala appears often enough in later rabbinic sources,[35] but it was not known by this name outside Palestine.)[36]

Although one normally identifies local persons through their father's name, most persons in the passion narrative (which identifies more people "than elsewhere in the synoptic tradition") are identified by their place of origin instead. This practice makes the most sense in the church's first generation in Jerusalem, when (and where) its leading figures were people from elsewhere.[37] Mark presumes his audience's prior knowledge of Pilate and (more significantly) Barabbas and other insurrectionists, despite Pilate's confrontations with a wide array of revolutionaries.[38] Finally, some central characters in the account remain anonymous, probably to protect living persons who could face criminal charges in Jerusalem, fitting other ancient examples of protective anonymity.[39] Taken together, these arguments seem persuasive.[40]

Evidence does suggest that Mark edited his passion narrative,[41] but such editing no more denies the authenticity of the prior tradition than frequent rewriting of sources by any other ancient author, including the writers of the Gospels elsewhere;[42] thus, for example, Matthew and Luke may agree against Mark at points (e.g., Mk 14:72; Matt 26:75//Lk 22:61).[43] Independent tradition drawn on by Matthew, Luke and John preserves the name of the high priest, but Mark may follow the oldest passion account in omitting his name for political prudence, though Pilate, now deposed and despised, could easily be named in this period.[44] Where John's passion narrative diverges from the Synoptics, it sometimes displays special Johannine interests. At the same time, D. Moody Smith argues that some of its divergences, like Jesus carrying his own cross or the legs of the crucified men being broken, appear more historically likely than the Synoptics.[45] Thus one should not rule out historical tradition even in John's passion narrative.

Another line of evidence also supports the substantial reliability of the picture of Jesus' execution found in the passion narrative: it fits what we know of the period in question. Thus Craig Evans compares Josephus' account of Joshua ben Hananiah, who similarly entered the Temple area during a festival.[46] Like Jesus, he spoke of doom for Jerusalem, the sanctuary and the people, even referring (again like Jesus) to the context of Jeremiah's prophecy of judgment against the Temple.[47] The Jewish leaders arrested and beat Joshua[48] and handed him over to the Roman governor,[49] who interrogated him.[50] He refused to answer the governor,[51] was scourged,[52] and — in this case unlike Jesus (though cf. Mk 15:9) — released.[53] The different outcome is not difficult to account for: unlike Joshua, Jesus of Nazareth was not viewed as insane and already had a band of followers, plus a growing reputation that could support messianic claims.[54] Joshua ben Hananiah could be simply punished in an attempt to deter his continued antisocial behavior; Jesus of Nazareth had to be executed.

The Abandonment of Jesus' Disciples

That Jesus' disciples abandoned him at his arrest fits the criterion of embarrassment. For disciples to abandon their teacher in this way was a betrayal of their bond of intimacy, and in the social order of the day would have been deeply shaming to the teacher.[55] The abandonment could reflect badly on Jesus in terms of status and clearly reflects badly on the disciples; it is surely not the invention of the later church.

This abandonment is also plausible, even for disciples who had seen Jesus' healings and exorcisms and believed that God was with him. Indeed, disciples attracted to kingdom signs of power, such as healings and exorcisms, might readily miss the parallel trajectory that led to the cross. Their expectations of Jesus' mission to Jerusalem could well be different (as Mk 10:32-37, for example, suggests), just as some groups today emphasize only one or the other of these aspects of Jesus' life.

From the perspective of disciples, because God blessed Jesus with healings and exorcisms or even was offering Jesus to Israel as a king was no guarantee that he or they would survive at the hands of a political and religious elite who treacherously apprehended him away from the crowds. Had not God previously deferred Israel's deliverance because of their disobedience? The disciples could retain belief in God and even in the truth of Jesus' mission while believing that something had gone horribly wrong — indeed, what else could they assume? Even if Jesus had emphasized his impending death as part of his mission, the disciples had little motivation to embrace this particular perspective of his, which, from their frame of reference, contradicted his clearer messianic identity. He might simply be discouraged; or perhaps he had come to realize that Israel would prove unworthy, hence God would await a worthier generation for the messiah. Surely God would raise Jesus up at the resurrection of the righteous, but the current mission seemed shattered.

The Betrayers

A minority of scholars doubt the participation of a betrayer in Jesus' arrest,[56] but Romans normally did work through local informers, including in their attested dealings with Christians less a century later.[57] Mark's betrayal narrative (Mk 14:43-52; followed by Matt 26:47-56 and Lk 22:47-53) is paralleled in John (Jn 18:2-12), hence appears to be multiply attested. 1 Cor 11:23 refers to the night that Jesus was "handed over" in connection with his execution, which could well refer to the "betrayal" to the chief priests,[58] although other interpretations are possible.[59]

More critical in recognizing the authenticity of this tradition, however, is the criterion of embarrassment. Just as the loyalty of one's adherents proved a matter for praise,[60] their disloyalty would prove a matter of a teacher's shame.[61] Jesus' followers would hardly invent a betrayer, especially a betrayer he had chosen to be a disciple. (Indeed, the Gospel writers are at pains to emphasize that Jesus foreknew that one of the twelve would betray him.)[62]

The Synoptics highlight the heinousness of this betrayal by their depiction of Judas "kissing" Jesus to identify him. Raymond Brown is correct that we cannot historically establish or refute the historicity specifically of this kiss;[63] but it does make sense. Except when obscured by clouds, the moon would illumine the countryside during Passover;[64] yet others around Jesus, the shade of olive trees and the importance of getting the right person immediately (before resistance or flight could allow his escape) demanded that Judas specify the right person.[65]

Nevertheless, visibility was probably less to the point than trying to make the expedition look more peaceful than it was; the authorities needed to capture only the ringleader and apparently wished to minimize confrontation and bloodshed (cf. Lk 22:38).[66] By having a disciple trusted by his colleagues approach the group, the aristocratic priests might hope to catch the disciples off guard and delay resistance; and these priests may have considered Judas more expendable than their own guards if the ploy failed or Judas actually was leading them to a trap (cf. Matt 27:3-10). Disciples often greeted rabbis with a kiss as a sign of intimacy and respect.[67] That Judas should betray Jesus with an outward gesture of devotion makes the act all the more heinous, and an ancient audience might grasp something of the depth of such betrayal's pain (Lk 22:48).[68]

The Heinousness of Betrayal

The heinousness of the betrayal suggests the depth of Jesus' wounding at this point. His actions suggest that he was prepared to face martyrdom at the hands of the political elite (leading aristocrats and the Roman occupiers that supported them). Yet betrayal by one of his own special disciples that he had called to lead the renewal movement, and to whom he had promised a special place in the kingdom (Matt 19:28//Lk 22:30), likely invited deeper anguish.[69]

Although it sometimes occurred, people in ancient Mediterranean society considered betrayal by a friend far more heinous than any insult by an enemy.[70] The deeper the level of intimacy, the more that trust was a duty, and the more terrible its betrayal.[71] Breach of covenant such as treaties was regarded as terrible;[72] Judas' discipleship and its longstanding implicit covenant of friendship makes his betrayal a heinous act of treachery,[73] and the meal context that immediately precedes the betrayal amplifies the heinousness of the betrayal all the more.

For many, sharing food and drink represented the most important bond of kindness.[74] Those who ate together shared a common bond and were normally assumed to be trustworthy.[75] Hospitality established friendly ties even with strangers and was mandatory in the ancient Mediterranean.[76] Guest-friendships were politically binding,[77] and could effect reconciliation between political partisans at enmity.[78] Injuring or slaying those who had eaten at one's table was a terrible offense from which all but the most wicked would normally shrink;[79] such behavior was held to incur divine wrath.[80] Those who eat together at a table should not betray friendship even by slandering one another.[81] Though rarer due to the normal distribution of power, betraying or slaying one's host, as here, was equally terrible.[82]

Peter's Denials

Jesus' announcement of Peter's betrayal is early tradition, attested in other contexts in Mk 14:30 and Lk 22:31-34.[83] Especially based on the criteria of multiple attestation (in both Markan and Johannine tradition)[84] and embarrassment (probability is against early Christians inventing such a negative story about Peter),[85] the tradition of Peter's denials is very likely historical.[86]

As with the abandonment of the disciples, so with Peter's denials the criterion of embarrassment proves particularly telling; because the loyalty of one's followers reflected positively on one[87] and because early Christian storytellers would seek to provide a positive moral example (ancient historians sought to elucidate edifying morals in their writings; see ch. 8), the account's survival most likely testifies to its historical verity. Three denials might fit a storytelling pattern, particularly that of the pre-Markan passion narrative,[88] but even this detail is probably historical.[89]

The High Priests and Jerusalem's Elite

Jesus' primary lethal opposition in the Gospels is also what makes best sense of his execution in Jerusalem: he offended members of the municipal elite, aristocrats who mediated between Judea and Rome. Even though the Fourth Gospel addresses a later situation after the demise of the Sadducean party (and John does not in fact mention Sadducees), the high priests provide a major part of Jesus' final opposition even in John (Jn 18:3, 35; 19:6, 15, 21).

A few comments on the high priesthood are therefore in order.[90] Elsewhere in the Roman Empire, the title did not always bear the prestige it held in Palestine.[91] Perhaps under foreign influence, Jewish writers came to speak of the priestly aristocracy or high priestly family as "high priests," rather than reserving that title merely for the ruling chief priest, the *kohen hagadol* of the Hebrew Bible.[92] (The Gospels' use of "high priest" for multiple members of the high priestly family is not then inaccurate.) Even Pharisaic tradition respected the office of high priest,[93] though Sadducees dominated it.[94] Jewish high priests held considerable political authority.[95] Contrary to Israelite law, however, Roman officials freely gave and revoked the high priestly office.[96]

The Gospels are not "anti-Jewish" to complain about corruption among the chief priests; that they were corrupt is the perspective of *most* ancient Jewish sources (except for the aristocratic priests themselves,[97] none of whose views anyone else cared to preserve). Thus Josephus experienced the opposition of high priests he considered corrupt.[98] Qumran and others opposed the priestly aristocracy that controlled the Temple; as Overman notes, "For many marginalized groups in this period the problem, in short, was the local leaders and politicians in Roman Palestine."[99] The sum total of our extant sources suggests that corruption and exploitation pervaded Jerusalem's elite no less than that of other elites in antiquity.[100] Most of Jerusalem's municipal aristocracy or Sanhedrin consisted of members of elite priestly families; these ruling families had been promoted to their favored positions by Herod the Great after he eliminated the aristocrats who opposed him (i.e., most of the earlier Sanhedrin).[101]

A *sunedrion* was a ruling council, equivalent to a *boulē,* or a senate.[102] Cities like Tiberias had their own ruling senates composed of the leading citizens.[103] Municipal senates consisted of aristocrats the Romans called *decurions,* and in the eastern Mediterranean "varied in size from thirty to five hundred members."[104] The Jerusalem Sanhedrin was in a sense the municipal aristocracy of Jerusalem; but just as the Roman senate wielded power far beyond Rome because of Rome's power, Jerusalem's Sanhedrin wielded some influence in national affairs, to the degree that Roman prefects and Herodian princes allowed.[105]

Tradition claims that the Sanhedrin included 71 members;[106] yet if it simply represented a body of ruling elders from the municipal aristocracy this may have been at best an average figure.[107] Later tradition claims that they met in the Chamber of Hewn Stone on the Temple Mount;[108] otherwise they met close to the Temple Mount.[109] Our first-century sources, the New Testament and Josephus, include Sadducees and other groups in the Sanhedrin, under high priestly control; later rabbis characteristically but inaccurately portray the Sanhedrin as an assembly of rabbis.[110]

The Sanhedrin in Jesus' day probably consisted largely of members of the Jerusalem aristocracy and wealthy landowners in the vicinity.[111] Sometimes rulers could use sanhedrins, or assemblies, the way some politicians today use committees: to secure the end they wanted without taking full responsibility for that decision. In Josephus, rulers like Herod appointed the Sanhedrin members they wished and obtained the results they wished.[112] Before Herod came to power, the Jerusalem Sanhedrin exercised significant authority.[113] In Pilate's time, without Herod the Great's interference and the Romans expecting local aristocracies to administer the business they could,[114] we should not be surprised that chief priests were a more dominant force. They could convene a sanhedrin,[115] and the priestly aristocracy constituted a large portion of it.[116] Nevertheless, the Sanhedrin had good reasons to seek to please Rome.[117] Less than four decades after the events the Gospels describe, Jerusalem's aristocracy continued to act as a body. When the high priest and the leading Pharisee allegedly acted without the approval of the rest of the assembly, they provoked that assembly's anger.[118]

After examining Josephus' three mentions of "Sanhedrin" and five of *boulē*,[119] Brown concludes that Josephus' portrait of the Sanhedrin is quite close to that of the Gospels and Acts. They judge, consist of "chief priests, scribes, and rulers or influential citizens (=elders)," sentence those found guilty of crimes, and constitute the leading Jewish body with which Roman rulers would deal. Clearly they "played a major administrative and judicial role in Jewish self-governance in Judea."[120]

Annas and Caiaphas in the Passion Narrative

Joseph Caiaphas's involvement with Jesus' trial makes historical sense.[121] Rome now appointed high priests at will, and Jewish piety was not a primary concern in their appointments. Caiaphas held power for nineteen years (18-36 CE), longer than any other high priest in the first century. His tenure suggests his political acumen in keeping the Romans content.[122] In the case of potential threats to the political stability of Jerusalem, of course, that would mean dealing with them swiftly and efficiently. And someone who caused a commotion in the Temple in the dangerously crowded period just before Passover would clearly be perceived as a threat to the public order.[123] Despite his otherwise high opinion of Caiaphas, Sanders thinks the high priest probably wanted Jesus "dead for the same reason Antipas wanted John dead": public order.[124] That Caiaphas and Pilate would have cooperated in the matter is likely; "That is the way the gospels describe the events, and that is the way things really happened, as the numerous stories in Josephus prove."[125]

This information reinforces the suspicion one gets from other nonpriestly sources concerning the character of much of the high priesthood under Rome: Caiaphas was a skilled but probably often ruthless politician. He kept the public peace in a manner that satisfied both Rome and the populace, and in so doing preserved his own position.[126] He was well-to-do,[127] part of the most hellenized elite,[128] and hence had much at stake personally in keeping the peace. It is reasonable to suppose that, even given the purest of concern for their people's welfare — on which their own rose or fell — the priestly aristocracy would regard unrest, hence the popularity of Jesus, as a threat.[129]

Annas held power from 6 to 15 CE and retained considerable political influence until his death in 35; he may have dominated the two high priests (his successors included a son-in-law and five sons) who followed him.[130] Annas appears especially, but plausibly, in John's passion account. Some writers have charged that John's use of the name "Annas" reflects Jewish-Christian tradition but lacks historical foundation, since Annas had long since retired from office.[131] This skepticism, however, reads more into Annas's "retirement" than the historical evidence warrants; it is likely that he continued to exert power within his household (especially if they privately recognized the biblical tradition concerning the lifelong character of a high priest's calling), including through his son-in-law Caiaphas, until his death in 35 CE.[132] In any case, even though it was customary to refer to the entire high priestly family by John's day as "high priests,"[133] John labels only Caiaphas as "high priest," not Annas. Scholars have offered historically plausible arguments for Annas's involvement.[134]

Historical Tradition in the Trial Narrative?

Some have assailed the historicity of Mark's "trial" narrative;[135] others have shown that the arguments against authenticity are at best inconclusive and at worst fallacious.[136] We may quickly and initially dispense with one argument that could be adduced on the issue. Rabbinic sources acknowledge the Jewish trial of Jesus yet not the Roman trial;[137] but the former acknowledgement probably derives from a response to Jewish Christian polemic whereas the latter silence may derive from embarrassment for the need for Roman intervention[138] or from the same polemic. These sources, centuries later than Mark's account of Jesus' trial, cannot be given equal weight with it.

More often considered are claims that the Gospel accounts violate the Sanhedrin's legal procedures or, more compelling, that the Jesus movement would lack access to any information about what would have occurred in any such meeting of Jerusalem's aristocrats.

Violation of Legal Procedures?

Traditionally, writers have most often cited against the gospel account its incompatibility with rabbinic sources concerning proper legal procedures,[139] but this argument is difficult to defend today.[140]

Although various elements of the later Mishnaic code of legal conduct are probably early,[141] it is tenuous to dispute the historicity of the earlier Gospel accounts of the trials (which include traditions more contemporary than those on which the Mishnah is based) based on conflicts with rules in the later Mishnah. First, the Mishnah reports Pharisaic-type idealizations of the law in its own day, recorded at a period over a century later than the latest of the four Gospels; the Mishnah was written almost two centuries later than Jesus' trial.[142] Meanwhile, the Council in Jesus' day was hardly dominated by Pharisees, further calling into question this rabbinic idealization.[143]

Second, rabbinic sources themselves indicate that the aristocratic priests did not always play by the rules (and certainly not by Pharisaic ones).[144] In fact, because elements of proper legal procedure were standard throughout Mediterranean antiquity, the Gospel writers may expect us to *notice* significant breaches of procedure. Unless one presupposes that the aristocratic priests (like later rabbis) would follow careful procedure even in explosive political situations — which is unlikely — an argument from Mishnaic technicalities does not work against the Gospel narrative.[145] Sanders puts the matter best:

> The gospel accounts do present problems, but disagreement with the Mishnah is not one of them. . . . The system *as the gospels describe it* corresponds to the system that we see in Josephus. The trial of Jesus agrees very well with his stories of how things happened.[146]

If judicial corruption or executions for political expediency seem implausible to readers in many contemporary liberal democracies, we would do well to recognize that they seem quite plausible to readers in many parts of the world today.[147]

Further, the "trial" account of Matthew and Mark probably represents what was more technically a preliminary inquiry in which Jesus' interrogators would be even less likely to regard the rules as constraining;[148] a more formal hearing seems delayed until morning (Mk 15:1; Lk 22:66; cf. Jn 18:24). The hearing is not a technical trial in John (Jn 18:19-24, 28).[149] Both the Synoptics and John agree that Jesus was first at the house of the high priest (Mk 14:53-54, 66; Lk 22:54; Jn 18:13-24). Although many regarded trials in the judge's home as unethical,[150] Josephus shows us that such informal trials could suffice for some high priests, who then made recommendations to the Roman governor.[151]

Finally, the Gospel writers probably *intended* to convey breach of procedure, not to pretend that the mock trial and abuse they depict were standard Jewish custom.[152] (Again, we cannot be sure which Mishnah rules would have been respected by first-century Sadducees, but some of these principles were broadly Mediterranean legal ethics.) At this point we should pause to mention possible breaches of procedure (if the laws were early and the Gospel writers or their traditions seek to portray them as breaches of procedure). To the extent that the later sources provide a reliable picture of legal ethics that many in antiquity would have respected and at least considered ideal, probable breaches of legal ethics indicated in the Gospel trial narratives include the following.

First, judges must conduct and conclude capital trials during daylight;[153] this may explain a late, brief, more official meeting around 5:30 a.m., before conducting Jesus to Pilate (cf. Lk 22:66-71; Jn 18:24), but the high priests probably were unconcerned with such details. Further, trials should not occur on the eve of a Sabbath or festival day,[154] as this day is in John's version (Jn 18:28).[155] (Still, officials may have regarded this as an emergency situation. Even Pharisaic interpretation supported executing an extraordinary offender on a pilgrimage festival to warn others not to repeat the crime.)[156] Pharisees, at least, probably would have disapproved of the haste involved in the verdict and execution.[157] Further, the Sanhedrin (or acting members thereof) should not meet in the high priest's palace.[158]

Most obviously, Jewish law opposed false witnesses, reported in the Synoptic passion narratives (Mk 14:57). The biblical penalty for false witnesses in a capital case was execution (Deut 19:16-21), and later Jewish ideals, at least, continued to regard this penalty as appropriate,[159] as did Roman law.[160] Cross-examination of witnesses was standard in Jewish law,[161] and apparently the examiners did their job well enough here to produce contradictions they did not expect (Mk 14:56, 59). (It is not very likely that Mark would invent their honorably accurate cross-examination.) In the end, these witnesses could provide only a garbled account of Jesus' proclamation of judgment against the Temple (Mk 14:58; cf. Jn 2:19; Acts 6:14), which could have seemed to some members of the elite political reason enough to convict him.[162]

If the Gospels imply that the aristocratic priests did not observe the highest standards in legal ethics, they do not here contradict other early Jewish reports about many of the chief priests. Many officials in antiquity abused their authority, and minority Jewish groups felt that the chief priests did so. We have already observed that ancient Jewish sources regularly criticize the high priests of this period for abuse of power,[163] and Josephus, a contemporary source who sometimes defends the high priests, is our most eloquent witness to the corruption that their power bred. In the time of Felix, high priests became so audacious that they sent their own servants to the threshing floors to seize the tithes that would have gone to poorer priests, leading to the death in poverty of some of the latter.[164] Later we read of another aristocratic priest seizing their tithes; his bold servants would beat those who refused to comply.[165] Josephus claims that a Jerusalem aristocrat bribed and persuaded the high priests to attack Josephus, using both Pharisees and priests as agents.[166] Josephus also believes that a Jewish aristocrat, a friend of a high priest, arranged for the high priest's assassination by bandits.[167] Early rabbinic sources confirm the corruption of various high priestly houses.[168] Ancient Jewish sources confirm rather than undermine the Gospels' perspectives here, and the charge that the basic gospel portrait of the trial is anti-Jewish reflects a misunderstanding of first-century Judean politics and intra-Jewish conflict.

Speculation or Source?

While one cannot prove the veracity of the contents of the trial narrative at this remove, skepticism that the first followers of Jesus would have had access to such information[169] also assumes too much. Sources for the substance of the trial narrative may derive from Joseph of Arimathea (Mk 15:43), from connections within the high priest's household (Jn 18:15-16), others who later became disciples or sympathizers (Jn 19:39; cf. perhaps Acts 6:7), or, if one accepts the resurrection narratives, Jesus himself (cf. Acts 1:3).

It seems unthinkable at least that the early Palestinian tradition would have neglected the witness of anyone like Joseph who could have had contacts present at the trial. Matthew and John apparently independently preserve the report that Joseph was a disciple (Matt 27:57; Jn 19:38). Because tradition preserves his name, Brown thinks that Joseph was a disciple, though only later;[170] even if Joseph became a disciple only later, he would still provide a source for the Jerusalem church long before the writing of the Gospels. That leaks from within the Jerusalem council occurred on other occasions in the first century[171] does not prove that such a leak occurred in Jesus' case, but it does challenge the claims of those who suppose such a leak implausible.[172]

Even though Mark may have crafted the material in his own words and for his own purposes,[173] some argue that substantial evidence remains that he accurately preserves "the decisive elements of Jesus' examination before the Sanhedrin in their correct order."[174]

Involvement from the Jewish Elite?

Although Gentile soldiers executed Jesus at Pilate's orders, involvement by the Jerusalem elite is also likely. Contrary to some detractors, this claim can hardly be viewed as anti-Semitic. As we have noted, it appears in Josephus.[175] Moreover, later rabbis attribute Jesus' trial and execution solely to Jewish rather than Roman authorities,[176] though the Gospels' picture of Roman crucifixion is far more plausible.

While it is true that Rome's soldiers attacked eschatological prophets and their followings in the wilderness without explicit involvement from the priestly elite, such cases are not very comparable, and Jesus "did not die on the battlefield."[177] Jesus' actions more closely resemble John — martyred by Herod Antipas[178] — or the later beating of Joshua ben Hanania, initially detained by the chief priests for prophesying the temple's destruction before being handed over to the governor.[179] True, it was Rome that counted "king of the Jews" a seditious claim; but who framed Jesus' nonviolent activities in such a manner for the Romans?[180] Rome would normally expect members of Jesus' own people (especially elite members, who would have the greatest hearing) to perform the function of *delatores,* or accusers, to charge him with sedition.[181] The substance of the events even in John's account matches historical expectations; "It begins with a formal delation . . . and ends with a formal condemnation *pro tribunali*" (Jn 18:29; 19:13).[182]

Together the cleansing of the Temple (which would offend the Sadducean aristocracy) and crucifixion by the Romans suggest the intermediary step of arrest by the priestly authorities; as Sanders observes, conflict with the Romans, crowds, or Pharisees would not explain subsequent events, but the continuing enmity of the chief priests against Jesus' followers (e.g., Acts 4:1-7; 5:17-18; 9:1-2) points to the priestly aristocracy as the main source of opposition.[183] Given high priestly involvement, the Gospel writers are probably not so generous as to have alleged even the pretense of a hearing if in fact they had no tradition that one occurred. Like most modern preachers, the Gospel writers were more interested in applying their text than in creating a wholly new source to be applied. The tradition of Jewish involvement in Jesus' death is also multiply attested as early as what is probably our first Christian document (1 Thess 2:14-15; cf. 1 Cor 1:23).

Some believe that the Romans would have acted without a session from leaders of the municipal aristocracy,[184] but this expectation does not fit the usual Roman manner of delegating preliminaries to local officials. Detractors sometimes protest that if the Sanhedrin genuinely tried Jesus, they would have executed him themselves, avoiding a Roman cross. This objection rests, however, on the highly improbable notion that the Sanhedrin had legal capital authority or, if not, would have lynched a popular prophet during a festival with the governor in town. On local elites' lack of capital authority in the Roman Empire, see Appendix 7.

The Plausibility of Pilate's Role

Philo and especially Josephus are ill-disposed to report good of Pilate;[185] they seem to have felt that the unrest in Judea is better blamed on deceased prefects like Pilate (once supported by the corrupt Sejanus)[186] than left with the Judeans themselves. Even as governor Pilate seems to have been quite unpopular.[187] From a Roman perspective, however, he was a minor official; his only appearance in the Roman historian Tacitus involves his execution of Jesus.[188]

Few historians would dispute that Jesus in fact appeared before Pilate (accepted even by Crossan as unlikely to have been invented);[189] only the governor[190] could order a person crucified. Further, if Pilate wished some semblance of order, he would provide at least a brief hearing. True, Pilate was known for his brutality,[191] and sometimes had reportedly executed Jews without trial.[192] But that Pilate executed Jesus without some form of hearing is improbable. Even apart from the risk of needlessly provoking anyone who followed him as a mere sage, this is the very sort of breach of normal procedure the earliest Christian sources (eager to show Jesus' innocence under true Roman justice) would be most likely to report; yet they mention nothing of the kind.[193]

That Jesus was crucified by the Romans is likewise inevitably historical; Christians would hardly have invented execution at all, but certainly not *Roman* execution, that would have painted them thereafter as subversives in the Roman world.[194] Pilate often went to great lengths to quell so much as public complaints, including violent suppression of a crowd, leading to many deaths.[195] Romans had borrowed an earlier custom of hanging people alive,[196] and the victims of the punishment were disproportionately slaves[197] and the provincial poor.[198] Roman citizens could not be crucified legally, but slaves and provincials could be.[199] Although dangerous criminals,[200] like slaves, were regularly crucified, crucifixions of free persons in Palestine usually involved the charge of rebellion against Rome.[201]

Pilate's Reticence

The Romans usually allowed internal religious matters to be handled by Jewish courts,[202] hence Pilate's reticence to accept the case at first (Jn 18:31a), so long as no capital charge is offered, makes sense on legal grounds. But what is known of Pilate's personality and the situation's political demands has raised questions about this scenario.

The narrative portrays those who brought the charge as quite insistent that Jesus be executed, and this behavior is hardly surprising given the situation portrayed. What is instead striking is Pilate's reticence to pronounce sentence; if no Roman citizens were involved, one might expect most governors to act quickly at the local aristocracy's request.[203] The Gospels show that Pilate did indeed act fairly quickly, but they also report his reluctance to do so.

Thus some scholars question whether the Pilate of the Gospels is "in character" with the Pilate known to us from other sources.[204] Pilate executed people without trial; it was excessive use of capital punishment that ultimately cost him his office.[205] His earlier plundering of the temple treasury to support an aqueduct[206] and particularly his recent issue of coins bearing an insignia of the divine emperor[207] blatantly demonstrated his insensitivity to local Jewish concerns. (Pilate was an ethnocentric colonialist governor, but his injustice is quite believable in view of even harsher cases of provincial exploitation and maladministration.)[208] From what Philo and especially Josephus show us of Pilate's character, any reticence to accept the local leaders' recommendation would be more out of spite for them than out of concern for justice.[209]

Yet this reticence may not be unhistorical.[210] As corrupt as the later governor Albinus was, he dismissed Joshua ben Hananiah from further punishment (after a scourging reportedly bared his bones) once he took him to be insane, hence harmless.[211] The Gospels do have important apologetic reasons for emphasizing Pilate's reticence,[212] but Pilate may have had good reason for political concern if he erred in judgment.[213] Philo notes the anti-Jewishness of Pilate's patron, Sejanus.[214] If Sejanus was executed on October 19, 31 CE,[215] it is not impossible (though not extremely likely) that some premonitions of his impending weakness might have been felt a year and a half earlier at the likely time of Jesus' trial near Passover of 30 CE.[216] If one dates the crucifixion to 33 CE, the second most accepted date, Pilate's position had certainly become much less secure.

More clearly Pilate, like most provincial officials,[217] was probably politically ambitious, hence would not unnecessarily and deliberately generate bad reports about himself.[218] In contrast with many of his peers in office, being only an equestrian left him especially vulnerable apart from Sejanus' patronage.[219] More to the point, Pilate had already incurred the hatred of the Jewish people,[220] and on some other occasions had backed down to pacify them,[221] especially if threatened with appeal to the emperor.[222] Thus Pilate was not only cruel but, like many bullies, fearful of exposure to those in authority over him.[223]

If anything, this situation might require Pilate in time to become more rather than less cooperative with the more powerful of his subjects (cf. Jn 19:12-13); to fail to prosecute a potential revolutionary, accused by the leaders of his own people, could lay Pilate himself open to the charge of *maiestas*.[224] Even the suspicion of treason could be fatal under the current emperor Tiberius,[225] and despite Sejanus' patronage he likely would not risk it. Further, although Jesus may have proved politically innocuous,[226] cooperation with the local aristocracy would be more politically advantageous than concern for this non-Roman provincial; that Pilate survived as governor until 36 CE,[227] long after his patron's demise, suggests that he had belatedly acquired some political savvy. Even a better governor might have executed a non-citizen potential troublemaker with minimal evidence, especially under pressure from local leaders.[228] This was, after all, the provinces, not Rome.

In any case, the hearing before Pilate is brief, and the execution swift (a few hours later).

How Did Pilate View Jesus?

Of the four Gospels, it is ultimately John that supplies us the most plausible explanation of Pilate's reticence to execute an accused "king" (just as he supplies the most plausible reason for the Jerusalem aristocrats' alarm about Jesus in Jn 11:48-50).[229]

Whereas in other extant gospel tradition Jesus reluctantly accepts the charge "king of the Jews" with the words, "That is what you are saying" (Mk 15:2; Matt 27:11; Lk 23:3), in Jn 18:36-37 John transposes Jesus' response into his own idiom, allowing him to explain the sense in which he is and the sense in which he is not "king of the Jews."[230] Jesus declares that his kingdom was not this-worldly; thus his servants would not fight to protect him (Jn 18:36). Jesus shows Pilate that he and his followers invoke a different sort of kingdom. Whatever we make of the scene, it corresponds with historical information we already recognize. As we have noted, E. P. Sanders accepts as two "firm facts" Jesus' execution by the Romans as a professed "king of the Jews," and a messianic movement of Jesus' followers who entertained no anticipation of military triumph. "Jesus was Messiah, but his kingdom was 'not of this world.'"[231]

Jesus' nonresistance (Jn 18:36) was a striking contrast to expected models of treason. What would have been clear from Pilate's more hellenized perspective was the political harmlessness of a sage whose "kingdom" consisted of truth (18:37). As Diaspora readers would readily recognize, an educated Gentile who heard about a "kingdom of truth" would not think of political kingship, but that of philosophers.[232] For example, Stoics claimed to be kings, by virtue of their character fitting them to rule properly;[233] Cynics made the same sorts of claims.[234] (From Plato on, philosophers claimed that they were the citizens best suited to rule the state,[235] writing both essays and briefer discussions about wisdom's role in ruling.)[236] No one took such claims as a threat to the security of the state, because such philosophers rarely if ever genuinely challenged that security.

Although we argued in ch. 2 that Jesus was not a Cynic, a Cynic is not a bad analogy for how Pilate might view him. To a pragmatic Roman governor, Jesus was nothing more than a harmless philosophic sort of sage; a nuisance, perhaps, but surely no genuine political threat. Ironically, whereas Pilate views Jesus as a harmless sage, the Jerusalem aristocracy views him as a threat to Rome's interests (Jn 19:12, 15; cf. 11:49-50). From their inadequate conceptual frameworks, both misconstrue his perception of his own identity. If John's portrayal of their exchange is his interpretation of how Pilate understood Jesus and how Jesus understood himself, it is a very plausible interpretation.

Jesus' Scourging

In the Synoptic tradition Pilate orders the preliminary scourging that, whether with rods or whips, generally preceded crucifixion and other forms of capital punishment.[237] Unlike some lesser forms of beatings, flogging and scourging regularly accompanied the death sentence.[238] In contrast to Jewish synagogue discipline, Romans did not limit the number of lashes, hence sometimes victims not even sentenced to death died or were disabled under cruel supervisors.[239] Indeed, Josephus had opponents scourged "until their entrails were visible"[240] and reports a procurator laying bare a man's bones, though the man survived.[241] This form of scourging also proved more severe than most Roman public corporal disciplines as well (cf. Acts 16:22; 2 Cor 11:25);[242] sometimes this kind of scourging caused death directly.[243] Whereas Romans used rods on free persons and sticks on soldiers, they used scourges on slaves or provincials of equivalent status.[244]

Following custom Jesus was presumably stripped[245] and tied to a pillar or post,[246] then beaten with *flagella* — leather whips "whose thongs were knotted and interspersed" with pieces of iron or bone, or a spike.[247] This torture left skin hanging from the back in bloody strips.[248] Various texts[249] attest the horror with which this punishment was viewed. It was soldiers who normally executed this task in the provinces.[250] Some felt that the *flagellum* was merciful because it so weakened the prisoner as to hasten his death on the cross.[251] That the Gospels mention but do not describe the practice makes them read more like official reports than rhetorical documents with a heavy element of *pathos* at this point.[252]

A scourging is independently attested by John and the Synoptics, although the sequence differs.[253] Moreover, even Paul seems aware of the tradition of Jesus' abuse (Rom 15:3, citing Ps 69:9).[254] Jesus' abuse also fits the criterion of embarrassment; public beatings produced shame as well as physical pain.[255] Given abundant ancient attestation for the abuse of prisoners coupled with the known tendency of humans to abuse power, the gospel account is plausible.[256]

The other abuse reported in the Gospels, such as soldiers ridiculing Jesus' "kingship," is not implausible.[257] That soldiers would take the opportunity to taunt a captive for entertainment should not surprise us; although one cannot prove that they did so, evidence suggests that such events were not unusual.[258] Public abuse of victims, even adorning someone as a king and beating him, occurred on other occasions.[259] Games of mockery included the game of king,[260] and theatrical mimes were common as well.[261]

Although soldiers sometimes scourged the prisoners en route to the crucifixion, the practice is not mentioned in the Gospels, presumably because Jesus was already scourged.[262] Since crucifixion sometimes lasted days,[263] the swiftness of Jesus' death (probably multiply attested: Mk 15:44; Jn 19:33) reinforces the notion that Jesus was already quite weak.[264] Given the unlikelihood that the soldiers would simply show mercy to a condemned prisoner, scholars are probably correct to suppose that Jesus was too weak to carry the cross himself, and that his executioners preferred to have him die on the cross rather than en route to it.[265]

Jesus' Execution

Once Pilate had pronounced sentence, Jesus' crucifixion would follow. We briefly explore the reported involvement of Simon of Cyrene; the certainty of Jesus' crucifixion; Jesus' reported cry of abandonment on the cross; and the tradition that women (rather than Jesus' male disciples) followed him to the cross. The involvement of these women will also provide a transition to the topic of Jesus' burial.

Simon of Cyrene

Since condemned criminals normally carried their own crosses, it would increase the perception of Jesus' shame if he proved too weak to carry his own.[266] The criterion of embarrassment thus suggests that Mark's report that Simon of Cyrene carried the cross (at least once it became clear that Jesus could not) reflects strong earlier tradition.

In such circumstances, that the soldiers would have drafted a bystander is not improbable;[267] one would not expect them to carry the beam themselves if they could "impress" another into service.[268] Most scholars agree that Simon of Cyrene is a historical figure.[269] It does not seem simply part of Markan predictions of scripture fulfillment, and Simon does not bear the cross willingly as a mere invention to fulfill a disciple paradigm.[270] Many Jews lived in Cyrene in North Africa,[271] and archaeology also attests Cyrenians with such names having settled in Jerusalem.[272]

At Jerusalem's festivals, full of pilgrims and immigrants from other parts of the world,[273] one might simply identify oneself by one's place of origin. This would also be true if Simon or his sons remained part of the Christian community (many believe that Mark's tradition recalls his name and that of his sons because he and/or they became Christians)[274] in Jerusalem, which probably transmitted the passion narrative.[275] The passion narrative in Jerusalem, then, rather than any other part of the gospel story, is the right place for Simon to appear.

The Certainty of Jesus' Execution

Few would dispute the claim that Jesus died, since we know of no first-century exceptions to that fate. To claim that Jesus died by crucifixion is also not controversial; as we noted above, Jesus' followers had to work hard to present his execution positively, and would not have invented it. Following a leader crucified for treason made the followers themselves liable to the same charge.[276]

Jesus' crucifixion by the Romans outside Jerusalem is, as Sanders notes, an "almost indisputable" historical fact;[277] Christians would not have invented the crucifixion. Whereas rhetorical historians would elaborate on sufferings at length,[278] the Gospels keep to the point and avoid such elaboration. The full horror of that mode of execution[279] remained vivid enough in the first century that all four evangelists hurry by the event itself quickly.[280]

Nevertheless, what they do report would likely have been seared deep into their communal memory (especially through the testimony of the women bystanders, which, as we note below, is likely historical). Events most readily remembered, according to memory research, are those in which the eyewitness "is emotionally involved";[281] for any sympathizers of Jesus, the crucifixion would constitute a major psychological trauma.

Although some features of crucifixions remained common, executioners could perform them in a variety of manners, limited only by the extent of their sadistic creativity.[282] Executioners usually tied victims to the cross, but in some cases hastened their death by also nailing their wrists (Jn 20:25).[283] Modern depictions of the crucifixion typically sanitize it. Romans crucified their victims naked;[284] Jewish leaders probably would not have demurred,[285] but even if they had,[286] it is unlikely that Pilate's soldiers would have accommodated them in such details.[287] Public nakedness could generate shame,[288] especially for Palestinian Jews.[289] One being executed on the cross could not swat flies from one's wounds, nor withhold one's bodily wastes from coming out while hanging naked for hours and sometimes days.[290] The victim would be elevated enough for crowds to see, though the cross was not normally as high as in modern symbolic portrayals; animals sometimes assaulted the victim's feet.[291]

The writing posted above Jesus' head[292] announces the charge: Jesus was executed as king of Israel (Mk 15:26), a charge that is historically quite probable.[293] As we have noted, reports about Jesus' triumphal entry (Mk 11:8-10) would mark him as a potential royal aspirant (to those so wishing to interpret them); the priestly aristocracy would arrest and the Romans execute anyone who offered the slightest grounds for suspicion of treason against Rome. The title is not a traditional Christian confession; Jesus' "you say" (Mk 15:2) suggests that it is not the title he would have emphasized, and Romans crucified many self-proclaimed kings and their followers on the charge of treason.[294] Other Jewish rebels apparently hoped for kingship,[295] but unless they *desired* repression Christians would have hardly invented the claim that Jesus was crucified on these grounds.[296]

A further datum supports the plausibility of the posting of this charge: on some other known occasions a member of the execution squad apparently would carry in front of or beside the condemned a small tablet *(tabula)* declaring the charge *(titulus),* the cause of execution *(causa poenae),* which he might later post on the cross.[297] That Matthew and Luke (perhaps Q; "this is") and Matthew and John ("Jesus") share some common elements against Mark suggest the prominence of this memory in the common passion tradition.

Jesus' Cry of Abandonment

Jesus' cry of abandonment ("My God, my God, why have you forsaken me?") meets the criterion of embarrassment, if any witnesses at all were present to report it (such as the women reported in the Gospels). Why would the witnesses, or anyone else who wished to honor Jesus, have invented such a cry of despair? Given subsequent Christian beliefs about Jesus, the early church would have hardly fabricated Jesus uttering a complaint about alienation from God,[298] even though he is quoting Psalm 22:1.[299] Mark records the prayer in its fully Aramaic form;[300] Matthew rehebraizes the address (changing "Eloi" to "Eli"), either to conform to frequent early synagogue practice of using Hebrew prayers,[301] or to explain how listeners thought they heard Jesus calling for "Elijah."[302] (These bystanders may have known the Jewish tradition that rabbis in distress sometimes looked to Elijah for help,[303] and assumed that Jesus was doing likewise.)

Women Followers at the Cross

The presence of some of Jesus' women followers is historically likely as well as theologically suggestive (cf. Mk 15:40-41). It is not unlikely that the soldiers would have permitted women followers to remain among the bystanders.[304] First, that Jesus had close women followers could be used by critics as grounds for scandal,[305] and this potential for scandal militates against the invention of this tradition by later Christians.[306] Multiple attestation of their following also supports the tradition (Mk 15:40; Lk 8:1-3; Jn 19:25).

Second, the soldiers might not have recognized who among the crowds constituted Jesus' followers; many people would be present merely to watch the execution.[307] While the women might not stand immediately beside the cross, they could remain within hearing range. But third, soldiers would be less likely to punish women present for mourning; those supposed to be relatives might be allowed near an execution.[308] Ancient Mediterranean society in general allowed women more latitude in mourning,[309] and women were far less frequently executed than men, though there were plenty of exceptions.[310] They might be given latitude especially if some were thought to be Jesus' relatives. Often family members were permitted to gather around the person being crucified.[311]

Jesus' Burial

The presence of women also offers a transition to the next part of Jesus' story. The Gospels note that the women were watching the burial (Mk 15:47); although many tombs existed in the Judean hills, these women must return by themselves early Sunday morning to the same site. Against Crossan,[312] this does not make good sense as simply Christian apologetic to cover up the women's ignorance of the site; burial practices from this period suggest that people kept track of bodies, and immediately after claims of resurrection appearances, others (both followers and critics) would have checked the tomb (see our next chapter). But this observation does underline the care that was taken to locate the right site, albeit initially for later expressions of mourning.

Historical Support for Jesus' Burial

That Jesus was buried is attested in pre-Pauline tradition known to Paul's readers in his own and other congregations (Rom 6:4; 1 Cor 15:4). John and Mark apparently independently attest the historical role of Joseph of Arimathea in the burial: Given early Christian experiences with and feelings toward the Sanhedrin, the invention of a Sanhedrist acting piously toward Jesus (Mk 15:43) is not likely.[313] Neither Mark nor his tradition invents many names; it is also not likely that Joseph of Arimathea (an inconspicuous village) is named simply for the entertainment of Mark's audience. Despite its bias against the Jewish authorities, early Christian tradition preserves burial by one of them (Mk 15:43, 46; Acts 13:29).[314]

Burial was the standard expectation after death in Judea, even in cases of executions when public mourning was forbidden.[315] That Jewish officials would permit and that some pious Jewish leader might aid in Jesus' burial is thus historically quite reasonable. The Romans normally preferred that the bodies of condemned criminals rot on crosses,[316] but biblical law, respected by all the Jewish sects (including the chief priests), prohibited this final indignity, demanding burial by sunset (Deut 21:23).[317] Josephus additionally testifies to this practice.[318] Burial was an essential duty for both Jews[319] and most Gentiles;[320] like most of their contemporaries,[321] Jewish culture regarded lack of burial as a horrible fate.[322]

Because the punishment was in Pilate's hands, the burial would not be simply delegated to the Judean authorities,[323] but it is unlikely that Pilate would be unaware of the Jewish concern for burial. Jewish law required burial even for foreigners passing through their territory,[324] and even the most dishonorable burial for executed, including crucified, transgressors, was burial nonetheless.[325] If Pilate accommodated a demand for execution, he would surely accommodate local sensitivities concerning disposal of the corpse.[326]

Thus Brown is certain that pious Jews, given their views of burial, would not have allowed Jesus to go unburied.[327] "The only surprise," Davies and Allison note (on Matt 27:60), is that Joseph buries Jesus in a family tomb rather than a criminals' burial plot.[328] (Although only Matthew suggests that it was Joseph's own family tomb, his explanation plausibly accounts for how Joseph came by it so quickly.[329] Most burial sites were private, the property of individual families.)[330]

Although Brown is convinced that Jesus was buried and believes that Joseph played a role in this, he doubts that Joseph was a disciple, supposing that this is why the women did not cooperate with him in the burial;[331] but we may well question to what degree the women would have *trusted* a Sanhedrist they did not know at that point. The preservation of his name and other details may suggest that Joseph either followed Jesus at this time (as we think more likely) or, as Brown thinks,[332] that Joseph became a disciple later.

Burial Preparations (Mk 15:42-47)

In the Synoptic chronology Jesus died c. 3 p.m.; after Joseph stopped to secure Pilate's permission (Mk 15:43),[333] perhaps only an hour remained before sundown and the prohibition of work. Although anointing (Mk 16:1) and washing the corpse were permissible even on the Sabbath,[334] some other elements of the burial[335] could be conducted only in the most preliminary manner for the moment, though undoubtedly hastened considerably through the agency of Joseph's servants. Pious Jews would not move the corpse or its members on the Sabbath.[336]

Spices (Mk 16:1) could diminish the stench of decomposition and, in practice, pay final respects to the deceased; they were not, however, used to preserve the corpse,[337] since the bones would be reinterred a year later.[338] Against the traditional Markan account of women coming to anoint the body after the Sabbath (Mk 16:1), some doubt that women would seek to anoint a corpse that had been decomposing that long.[339] This objection to the tradition, however, may point us in precisely the opposite direction. Whereas someone inventing a story about Jesus' burial may have been concerned about such an issue, the tradition fits the time and place it depicts. William Lane Craig observes that "Jerusalem, being 700 meters above sea level, can be quite cool in April" (cf. also Mk 14:54); the body remained in the tomb only a day and two nights, and "a rock-hewn tomb in a cliff side would stay naturally cool."[340] The women may have done what the tradition depicts, precisely in that time and place.

Some other details simply fit what we know about burials more generally. For example, in a Jewish setting, linen shrouds[341] were part of honorable burial (Mk 15:46),[342] specifically for the righteous.[343]

The Site of the Tomb

Golgotha, the site of Jesus' execution (Mk 15:22), was undoubtedly near the current site of the Holy Sepulchre.[344] That traditional location was outside the city walls, but only roughly 1000 feet north-northeast of Herod's palace, where Pilate was staying.[345] All available historical evidence favors the premise that the earliest Christians preserved the accurate site of the tomb. That Jesus' followers would forget the site of the tomb (or that officials who held the body would not think it worth the trouble to produce it after the postresurrection Jesus movement arose) is extremely improbable. James and the Jerusalem church could have easily preserved the tradition of the site in following decades,[346] especially given Middle Eastern traditions of pilgrimage to holy sites.[347]

The modern Protestant "Garden Tomb" is a much later site and cannot represent the site of Jesus' burial;[348] by contrast, the Catholic Holy Sepulcher and tombs in its vicinity date to the right period.[349] The tradition of the latter vicinity is at least as early as the second century (when Hadrian erected a pagan temple there; he defiled many Jewish holy sites in this manner),[350] and probably earlier.

Good evidence exists, in fact, that this site dates to within the first two decades after the resurrection. This is because

(1) Christian tradition is unanimous that Jesus was buried outside the city walls and no one would make up a site inside (cf. Heb 13:12; Jn 19:41)

(2) Jewish custom made it common knowledge that burials would be outside the city walls[351]
(3) the traditional vicinity of the Holy Sepulchre is *inside* Jerusalem's walls, a site that would not have been invented
(4) Agrippa I expanded the walls of Jerusalem, thereby including this area, sometime between 41 and 44 CE[352]

If Joseph of Arimathea owned the ground in which he buried Jesus (perhaps implicit in Mk 15:46, though more explicit in Matt 27:60),[353] the Jerusalem Christians could well have maintained the site, at least until 70, and it apparently remained known by Judeans in the early second century[354] and preserved afterward.[355] Because the site predates 44 CE (the time of Agrippa's death), it must go back to a period of eight to fourteen years after Jesus' burial, during a time in which his closest followers led the growing church in Jerusalem, within walking distance away (Gal 2:1, 9).

Conclusion

Ancient schools and biographers naturally preserved information about prominent persons' deaths, particularly when those persons died significant deaths like martyrdoms. A number of features in the passion narrative meet the criterion of embarrassment, that is, are elements that early Christians would have been embarrassed to invent, such as the abandonment of Jesus' disciples, denial by his chief disciple Peter, and especially betrayal to death by one of his leading disciples after a shared meal.

The passion narrative's portrayal of the political machinations behind Jesus' execution also fits what we know of ancient politics in a province like Judea. Ancient Jewish sources reveal the extent to which other Jewish groups experienced much of the priestly aristocracy as corrupt; Herod had installed many of the aristocratic families dominating the Sanhedrin, and Rome currently installed the high priests. Local elites often repressed potential threats to public order and to their own power. To execute someone, however, they would first need to accuse the troublemaker to the Roman governor, who depended on local accusers for most cases. The chief priests may have viewed their own role more favorably, but the current high priest Caiaphas probably would not have maintained his office for such a long period without a significant measure of political acumen and efficiency in maintaining order.

That local leaders would have handed Jesus over to Pilate fits analogous accounts in our other first-century source, Josephus. Jewish sources portray Pilate as uncooperative and insensitive to local concerns, yet sometimes giving way under pressure. Pilate could well have viewed Jesus as merely a harmless sage of the sort familiar from Greek and Roman cities, but political considerations would likely have favored Jesus ultimately being executed. As in the Gospels, scourging was standard before an execution. The charge on which Jesus was executed, "king of the Jews," represented high treason against the majesty of the emperor, and is almost certainly the charge on which Jesus was executed. The passion tradition that preserves the name of Simon of Cyrene undoubtedly also preserves accurately his role. Plausible eyewitnesses can be suggested for many elements of the tradition; moreover, sources outside the Gospels attest the basic outline and various elements of the tradition.

In short, elements of the passion tradition so frequently match what is historically probable (with many others being plausible) that the general outlines of this source should be embraced with a great degree of confidence. Even the site of Jesus' burial was very likely preserved from within fourteen years of his execution; that being the case, the lack of alternative to the resurrection message in early Christianity suggests an at least equally early tradition of the empty tomb.

CHAPTER 22

The Resurrection

"Do not be shocked! You are seeking Jesus of Nazareth, who was crucified. He has been raised up! He is not here! Look at the place where they deposited him."

MARK 16:6

"A surprising number of people have asked if I plan a trilogy to conclude with The Resurrection of the Messiah. Responding with mock indignation . . . I tell them emphatically that I have no such plans. I would rather explore that area 'face to face.'"

RAYMOND BROWN[1]

Others have already written separate books addressing the resurrection, and I do not intend to add to that literature.[2] My own treatment, then, will be relatively cursory. Further limiting my scope here, I am addressing historical evidence for an event and (to a limited degree) the first witnesses' understanding of the nature of that event, not philosophic questions regarding supernatural causation. In choosing not to address such questions in this chapter, I am not excluding the viability of such questions, but merely limiting my purview here. Those questions are more complex and involve metahistorical issues (grappling with the nature of historiography), and cannot be addressed fully in this book. (I address them in a preliminary way in appendix 8.)

The Traditions

The disciples' experience of Jesus' resurrection generated a much wider range of traditions than remain extant in our sources. Various non-Markan material recurs in Matthew and Luke (e.g., Matt 28:6; cf. Lk 24:6). John's resurrection narratives resemble each of the three Synoptic accounts in different respects, and many scholars believe that he used "traditions which lie behind the Synoptic Gospels, and not the Gospels themselves."[3] Such factors suggest access to non-Markan resurrection traditions or perhaps material in a now-lost ending of Mark,[4] if indeed the ending we have in Mk 16:8 was not the original one (a disputable premise).[5] It is, in fact, difficult to doubt that such other traditions would have existed, given the large number of reported witnesses to the resurrection (cf. 1 Cor 15:5-7).

The witness of women at the tomb is very likely historical, precisely because it was so offensive to the larger culture — not the sort of testimony one would invent. Not all testimony was regarded as being of equal merit; the trustworthiness of witnesses was considered essential.[6] Yet most of Jesus' Jewish contemporaries held much less esteem for the testimony of women than for that of men;[7] this suspicion reflects a broader Mediterranean limited trust of women's speech and testimony also enshrined in Roman law.[8]

Indeed, the male disciples are said not to believe the women (Lk 24:11; even in the late material in Mk 16:11) — an embarrassing tradition that may reflect historical reality at this point.[9] For the early Christians, neither the empty tomb nor the testimony of the women was adequate evidence by itself (cf. Lk 24:22-24); they also depended on the testimony of men for the public forum (1 Cor 15:5-8).[10] The criterion of embarrassment indicates that no one had apologetic reason to invent the testimony of these women, though the Gospel writers may have a profound theological purpose in preserving it. Most thus judge the report that the women were the first witnesses of the resurrection message to be historically accurate.[11]

Some scholars are convinced that one can completely harmonize the stories of the women at the tomb if we grant that the Gospel writers reported only data essential to their distinctive accounts;[12] others, while acknowledging that the conviction of the resurrection is early, doubt that our current Easter stories belong to the earliest stratum of tradition.[13] While harmonization approaches become strained when they misunderstand the liberties literary historians sometimes applied on details (see ch. 8), they do exhibit the virtue of working harder than more skeptical approaches to make the best possible sense of the data we have. They often help us to probe evidence more deeply if used heuristically rather than inflexibly, and are often so used in historiography more generally.[14] (Differing biographies of Lincoln or news reports may conflict in detail, but we do not normally conclude from these divergences that the reporters or biographers were fabricating their stories and hence are completely unreliable sources.)[15]

Whatever the merits of seeking to explain plausibly in such ways some differences among accounts, our approach here will not be to harmonize details but to look for common elements behind the diverse claims.[16] In courts of law and certainly in history, testimonies may vary on details due to memories and perspectives. The substance, however, is normally what is most important.

On any account, two matters are plain and a third likely follows: (1) the differences in accounts demonstrate that the Gospel writers were aware of a variety of *independent* traditions. The likely diversity and number of such traditions precisely here (more so than at many other points in extant gospel tradition) suggest a variety of initial reports, not merely later divergences in an originally single tradition. Sanders rightly contends that "a calculated deception should have produced greater unanimity. Instead, there seem to have been *competitors:* 'I saw him first!' 'No! I did.'"[17] Eyewitness reports often varied on such details, in antiquity as today.[18]

(2) The independence of the traditions thereby underlines the likelihood of details the accounts share in common.[19] These divergent traditions overlap significantly, hence independently corroborate the basic outlines of the story. (3) Given the likely variety of initial reports, explaining the similarities and differences in terms of multiple witnesses surrounding a core historical event appears plausible and indeed probable. This is the same way that we would approach other historical reports from antiquity.[20]

The various resurrection narratives in our Gospels vary considerably in length, focus, and detail. (For example, the variation in length of the Gospels' resurrection narratives[21] may partly reflect the desire to make optimum use of the scroll length, rather than leaving a blank space at the end as sometimes happened.)[22] If "Q" included a resurrection narrative (a thesis that is not necessarily probable but for which we actually lack evidence either way), most of the Gospel writers treated it as merely one among many; given the many witnesses of the risen Christ (1 Cor 15:6), it is hardly surprising that numerous accounts would exist and different Gospel writers would draw on different accounts. The four Gospels differ in detail, but in all four the women become the first witnesses, and Mary Magdalene is explicitly named as one witness among them.[23]

Pagan Origins for the Christian Resurrection Doctrine?

Here, as elsewhere, some scholars have tried to place the source of our basic traditions outside Jewish Palestine.[24] That Mack suggests that the "resurrection myth" first originated in Jesus groups in northern Syria and Asia Minor[25] is historically incredible.[26] Despite divisions in the church over other issues like food laws and later hellenistic questions about the nature of the resurrection, early Christian testimony is unanimous concerning the resurrection and eyewitnesses of the resurrection, including in the pre-Pauline traditions (most notably 1 Cor 15:3-8 with its possible Aramaisms).[27]

Even apart from this observation, bodily resurrection was a Palestinian Jewish idea. It is difficult to conceive of a rapidly hellenizing Gentile church preaching a dying-and-rising mystery deity triggering Palestinian Jewish Jesus people to adopt a pagan idea and then modify it in a Palestinian Jewish direction (including the specifically Jewish language of "resurrection"). It is far more likely that later Gentiles attracted to a growing Jewish cult would have adopted and transformed a Palestinian Jewish understanding of the resurrection.[28]

Supposed pagan parallels to the resurrection stories prove weak; Aune even declares that "no parallel to them is found in Graeco-Roman biography."[29] Whether any "parallels" exist depends on what we mean by a "parallel"; but plainly none of the alleged parallels involves a historical person (or anyone) resurrected in the strict sense. This is probably in part because resurrection in its strict (bodily and permanent) sense was an almost exclusively Jewish belief, and among Jewish people was reserved for the future. Most pagans would have preferred to play down a savior's or demigod's human death.[30] Ancients commonly reported apparitions of deceased persons[31] or deities, and hence occasionally those of persons who had become immortal,[32] but these are not *resurrection* appearances.

Even the appearance of Apollonius of Tyana, which exhibits some parallels with the Gospel accounts,[33] is not an exception. This story appears in a third-century source, after Christian teaching on the resurrection had become widely disseminated; further and more to our present point, Apollonius proves that he has not died, not that he has risen.[34] In another third century CE work probably by the same author, the hero Protesilaos appears to people and lives on; he is said to have "come back to life," though he refuses to explain the nature of this claim.[35] But whatever else his "return" from death might claim, it does not involve bodily resurrection: his body explicitly remains buried.[36] Moreover, even claims like this one made for Protesilaos do not predate the rise and proliferation of the Christian teaching about Jesus' resurrection.[37]

Nor do stories about magical resuscitation of corpses have much in common with the account of Jesus' resurrection (for example, when a witch drills holes in the corpse to pour in hot blood, dog froth, and so forth).[38] Ancient readers never supposed that bodily immortality followed such resuscitations, because they did not connect them with any doctrine like the Jewish notion of eschatological resurrection. Celsus, a second-century critic of Christians, was fully able to distinguish bodily resurrection from "old myths of returning from the Underworld," hence argued instead that Jesus' resurrection was merely *staged,* as commonly with apparent postmortem recoveries in novels.[39]

Most cultures believe in some form of life after death and such cultures fre-

334 | WHAT WE LEARN ABOUT JESUS FROM THE BEST SOURCES

quently accept some form of contact with the spirits of the dead or of some of
the dead. Such phenomena may help explain how some ancient Mediterranean
hearers may have conceived of Jesus' resurrection appearances; but to cite them
as "parallels" to those appearances, as if they define the latter, stretches the category of parallel too far to be useful. These claims do not normally involve
bodily existence. If Jesus' body was eschatologically transformed in advance of
the fulness of the kingdom, how would the disciples know it and proclaim it if
he failed to appear to them?

Mystery Cults as Background?

Some have offered parallels between dying-and-rising deities, especially in the
mysteries, and the early Christian teaching of the resurrection. We must therefore address the alleged parallels first and then turn to what proves a far closer
background for the early Christian teaching of the resurrection and its first ar-
ticulations even in a Greco-Roman setting (see 1 Cor 15:4, 20-28, 35-49).

The Mysteries apparently influenced some Palestinian Jewish thought in late
antiquity, though the exact date is unclear. Numismatic evidence indicates some
presence of the mysteries in Palestine,[40] though among Gentiles and especially in a
later period.[41] Limited mystery language may have infiltrated some forms of
Judaism,[42] but the use of such language is hardly evidence for widespread influence.[43] Pagan accusations that confused Judaism and the Mysteries[44] do not constitute good evidence that Judaism as a whole made that confusion. For example,
Reitzenstein's early-twentieth-century claim that "Even in Trajan's time the Roman
Jewish community still . . . either altogether or in large part worshiped the *Zeus
Hupsistos Ouranios* and the Phrygian Attis together with Yahweh"[45] has turned out
to be nonsense, refuted by subsequent research into Roman Judaism.[46]

The language of the mysteries clearly infiltrated Christian writers of the
second century and later. For example, Tertullian claims that Christianity has
the true mysteries, of which others are poorer and later copies.[47] Such language
becomes much more prevalent in the third and fourth centuries CE.[48] Some of
the "parallels" appear in Christian interpretations of the mysteries, not in the
pagan sources (which naturally kept mysteries more secret). That the Fathers
understood the Mysteries as "imitation démoniaque du Christianisme"[49] may
suggest that they, like many early modern students of these cults, read them
through the grid of their own Christian background, and the ready-to-hand explanation of demonic imitation may have led them to heighten rather than play
down the similarities between the two.

Yet it is in fact likely that by the patristic period some features of the mysteries were being borrowed from Christianity. As they began to lose devotees to

Christians in a later period, the mysteries could have adopted some features of Christian practice; many of the "parallels" in the mysteries are known only from the period in which Christianity's ideas had become widely known.[50]

Suggestions of mystery influence on first-century Christianity are overdrawn. Much of the most specifically mystery vocabulary is lacking in earliest Christianity: Metzger, following Nock, lists such terms as *mustēs, mustikos, mustagōgos, katharmos, katharsia, katharsis, teletē,* and so on.[51] (We treated the Jewish use of the more general term "mystery" in ch. 13.) What is perhaps more significant is the different perspective on the events described by both kinds of religions. As Metzger points out,[52]

> . . . the Mysteries differ from Christianity's interpretation of history. The speculative myths of the cults lack entirely that reference to the spiritual and moral meaning of history which is inextricably involved in the experiences and triumph of Jesus Christ.[53]

In the apostolic and subapostolic literature,[54]

> In all strata of Christian testimony concerning the resurrection of Jesus Christ, "everything is made to turn upon a dated experience with a historical Person [citing Nock]," whereas nothing in the Mysteries points to any attempt to undergird belief with historical evidence of the god's resurrection.

To notice this difference is perhaps to notice the different cultural matrixes in which these cults took root. In contrast to mysteries, a cult rooted in Israelite biblical piety could not neglect concern for salvation-historical acts of God. God's acts could be celebrated annually in cultic ritual (as with the Passover), but they were viewed as unique events secured by the testimony of witnesses, and grounded in corporate piety.[55]

Harvard classicist Arthur Darby Nock points out that, while many of Paul's hearers may have understood him in terms of the mysteries, most of the early Jewish-Christian missionaries like Paul had probably had little firsthand exposure to the mysteries and reflected instead a broader milieu of which the mysteries were only a part.[56] The mysteries played even less a role in the formation of the earliest Jesus movement in Galilee and Judea.

Dying-and-Rising Deities?

One area of special comparison between the mysteries and Christianity, especially in early-twentieth-century literature, involves the matter of salvation and dying and rising gods. Against some, there were stories of dying (and something like rising) deities before the time of Jesus.[57] Descent to the underworld in such texts need not be permanent; deities might visit or even be restored to life.[58] Greeks seem to have been most familiar with Egyptian accounts of dying and rising deities.[59]

But the parallels remain problematic. While there seems to be pre-Christian evidence for the account of Osiris' rescusitation,[60] he is magically revivified, not transformed into an eschatological new creation. His corpse is awakened through the same potencies as exist in procreation, and he remains in the netherworld, still needing protection by vigilant gods, and replacement on earth by his heir.[61] Adonis' death was mourned annually,[62] but his rising is not documented prior to the middle of the second century CE.[63] (Some sources suggest simply seasonal revivification,[64] which, as we argue below, differs greatly from early Jewish and Christian notions and origins of the resurrection.) Attis, too, was mourned as dead,[65] but there is no possible evidence for his resurrection before the third century CE, and aside from the testimony of the Christian writer Firmicus Maternus, no clear evidence exists before the sixth century CE.[66]

Dionysus' return from death[67] is clear enough, but perhaps in the same category as Heracles' apotheosis or the wounding of Ares in the *Iliad*; mortals could be deified and deities could suffer harm.[68] Some also understood him as returning annually for his holy days in the spring.[69] And even Persephone was taken down to the underworld alive (rather than dying), as Orpheus descended alive to rescue his beloved Eurydice.[70] Frazer's scheme of the "dying and rising god," based on patching together elements of disparate stories and famous over a century ago, has thus been largely discredited in more recent times.[71]

A number of earlier New Testament scholars asserted, again perhaps through the grid of their own religious understanding, that the Mysteries must have provided salvation through union with dying-and-rising gods.[72] While there may be some truth in the idea that a god not subject to death could grant immortality, a specialist in mystery cults cautions against finding this pattern as a common element.[73] Much of the evidence is late[74] and/or specifically Christian.[75] More recent writers are therefore generally more cautious about connecting spiritual salvation (when it appears in the mysteries) with the dying deity motif.[76]

In the Eleusinian rites, the *mystēs* received the promise of a happy afterlife, but by being pledged to the goddess, rather than being reborn or by dying and rising with the deity.[77] The cult of Cybele likewise does not support the hypothesis of immortality through a rising deity, as Gasparro notes.[78] The main problem with the view that many members of the early-twentieth-century "history-of-religions" school, eager to produce "parallels" to primitive Christianity, adduced, is that most of the people who turned to the mysteries already believed in some afterlife in the netherworld anyway. At most (in some cults), it was merely a happier afterlife in that world that the gods could guarantee.

Those like Bousset who drew such connections[79] did not take adequate account of the vegetative, cyclical, and seasonal nature of most of the rescusitation rituals.[80] The annual renewal of life in spring is a far cry from the earliest Christian picture of Jesus' *bodily* resurrection rooted in explicit Jewish eschatological hopes. It also differs substantially from Paul's claim that Jesus' eschatological transformation was an event in recent history guaranteed by hundreds of eyewitnesses, including himself. Paul even insists, despite his hellenistic audience, that this perspective is a necessary understanding of resurrection for a true follower of Jesus (1 Cor 15:1-2, 12-19, 29-34). Earlier Palestinian Christianity would not have held a less rigorously Jewish perspective than Paul did.[81]

The "third day" tradition offers potential parallels, though most of these were not very significant.[82] Most importantly, the "third day" was a fairly regular expression for a short period of time (such as "the day after tomorrow"). While the third day is used for resurrection in the later ritual for Attis and perhaps for Adonis, these may be based on Christian precedents.[83] The third day in the cult of Osiris is most significant, but the traditional Jewish view about the corpse, the use of a "third day" for an interval between two events in close succession in the Hebrew Bible, and the inherent likelihood of some coincidence between a brief period in early Christian tradition and one in the Mysteries, qualify its significance considerably. Some other Jewish traditions may also shed light on this idea, but appeal to them must remain tentative because of their uncertain date or because they were not widely enough recognized to have been obvious without explicit qualification.[84]

The fixing of the third day in the pre-Pauline formula in 1 Corinthians 15:4, however, weights the case in favor of a Palestinian Jewish-Christian tradition for Jesus' resurrection prior to any exposure to the cult of Osiris in the hellenistic world.[85] And while gods could often die in the Mysteries, their deaths were not portrayed as triumphant or meaningful as in many early Christian traditions. Further, the gospel narratives suggest that to whatever extent the early Christians might have adapted the language of three days, they historically intended only parts of three days.[86] That is, they interpreted rather than invented the interval.

Jewish Teaching about Resurrection

Jewish hope in the resurrection of the body belonged to the larger framework of hope in an entire new order,[87] the sort of kingdom of God Jesus preached.

Jewish belief in "resurrection" meant not simply the appearance of a ghost from the afterlife; people believed they saw such ghosts after death, often in dreams,[88] but this was a far cry from the end-time raising of the dead affirmed in Dan 12:2-3. Although Jewish views on the character of the resurrection varied (sometimes it involved an angelic or astral existence; see discussion below), it did not simply represent a disembodied afterlife of the soul, which (in some Jewish views) preceded the resurrection.

The Jewish doctrine of the resurrection was not simply an assertion of immortality.[89] Because much of Greek thought in general, like *many* cultures in the world throughout history,[90] addressed the survival of the soul after death,[91] it should not surprise us that the Eleusis cult promised a happy life in the underworld,[92] that Isis promised patronage and protection,[93] and the Dionysiac mysteries may have indicated a happy afterlife.[94] But there is little evidence for any future hopes in the cult of Cybele, and certainly not any linked with Attis.[95] When the early Christian picture of bodily resurrection plainly derives directly from Jewish eschatological teaching, one casts the net rather widely to make all human hopes for afterlife parallel to it.[96]

Pagan afterlife notions and myths of risen deities did provide Gentiles a handle for apprehending aspects of early Christian teaching about the resurrection,[97] but the Christian teaching remains distinctly Jewish in its origin. The teaching can be recognized in some OT texts (probably Is 26:19; most explicitly Dan 12:2)[98] and probably has early antecedents in Israel's history, though personalized eschatology appears in texts only after the Exile.[99]

Not all streams of early Judaism clearly articulate a doctrine of bodily resurrection. The Sadducees denied it;[100] rabbinic texts, which here probably represent the populist Pharisaic consensus, complain about the moral offensiveness of this denial.[101] The evidence we do have from Qumran may support the likelihood that those responsible for the sectarian Dead Sea Scrolls accepted it,[102] though the concrete evidence is scarce.[103] Clearly the Pharisees and their probable successors in the rabbinic movement[104] affirmed the doctrine of the bodily resurrection,[105] almost equating belief in it with belief in the afterlife.[106] The Pharisees were the most popular "sect," according to Josephus, and popular views of the afterlife might be expected to follow an optimistic rather than pessimistic line of thought, though this was not always the case in paganism.

In any case, widepread attestation in a vast range of pre-Christian Jewish sources (2 Maccabees, *Psalms of Solomon, 1 Enoch,* and so forth) indicates that the doctrine was much more widely held than among the Pharisees, representing common Judaism,[107] and as the widespread use of Daniel (especially in the LXX) would almost require (Dan 12:2).[108] Sanders could be right that nearly all religious Palestinian Jews except the Sadducees affirmed the doctrine.[109]

The belief was probably less widely held initially in the Mediterranean Diaspora, though some evidence for it exists.[110] Some hellenistic Jewish writers, while accommodating the idea to hellenistic notions of immortality and the language of deification, also allude to the doctrine of bodily resurrection.[111] Perhaps after rabbinic Judaism consolidated its influence, the doctrine of a literal, bodily resurrection also became standard in much of the Diaspora.[112] Paul's contention with the Corinthian Christians might reflect not only pagan Greek but also first-century hellenistic Jewish aversion to discussion about the resurrection; while many Diaspora Jews would affirm the resurrection and most would know about the doctrine, in the first century it was probably most widespread in Palestine, to the East, and among the least hellenized communities. Such geographic indications simply reinforce other confirmations of our earliest sources' claim that belief in Jesus' resurrection originated in Jewish Palestine and nowhere else.

But Jesus' early followers did not simply adopt the resurrection doctrine wholesale from Judaism without adaptation: traditional Jewish expectation was a collective, future resurrection.[113] The notion of an individual's bodily resurrection fulfilled in history would therefore not arise without additional factors (such as the experience of the disciples) to explain it.

Historical Support for the Resurrection Tradition?

All our early Christian sources unanimously affirm the bodily resurrection of Jesus,[114] although 1 Cor 15 attests that Paul had to deal with some Gentile Christians who could assimilate the Palestinian Jewish doctrine only with difficulty and did not wish to accept it beyond the case of Jesus. (The sense in which resurrection was "bodily" may have also varied, as in early Judaism; we return to this subject below.) Within earliest Christianity, however, there remains no debate about the received tradition that Jesus himself rose bodily, unless one is inclined to count as proof inferences from silence offered by some modern scholars without explicit supporting evidence.

By some point in the second century, gnostics and others who found the notion of a bodily resurrection of any sort incompatible with Platonic metaphysics sought to interpret the early Christian tradition differently,[115] but there is no clear record of detractors in the Jesus movement, even by way of attempts to answer them, in the first century. Such silence is strange when we consider the centrality of the resurrection teaching to all explicitly known forms of the early Christian movement, and how many debates they had on other issues.

Orthodox Jewish scholar Pinchas Lapide, while doubting that the resurrection proves Jesus' messianic or divine identity (connected though this has traditionally been to the resurrection),[116] nevertheless finds the evidence for his resurrection compelling.[117] Many scholars doubt Jesus' historical resurrection on philosophic or other grounds, but Ladd is generally correct that "Those scholars who are unable to believe in an actual resurrection of Jesus admit that the disciples believed it."[118] That is, apart from philosophic questions about what might have happened to the body, the historical evidence indicates that the early eyewitnesses were convinced that they had seen Jesus genuinely alive.

The Missing Body

Because Paul explicitly reports only resurrection *appearances,* some argue that the empty tomb tradition was originally a myth.[119] Weeden, for instance, is among those who doubt that the empty tomb tradition precedes Mark. His claim that there is no "hard evidence that the early church ever knew of Jesus' grave's being empty"[120] suggests that it did not occur to him that anyone would have checked — an idea as unlikely in Roman antiquity as today. Others rightly question whether Mark could have been inventing 16:1-8 as apologetic. Whether one accepts the pre-Markan Semitic expressions some have proposed in the passage, its conclusion with the women's fear and silence is hardly apologetic, and it lacks any mention of corroborating attestation from Joseph of Arimathea or others.[121]

The variant versions of the tomb discoveries in the other Gospels suggest multiple and likely pre-Markan empty tomb traditions. That Paul does not explicitly mention the empty tomb while spending four verses listing witnesses does not mean that he assumed that the body remained in the tomb. First, witnesses of the risen Jesus counted as much stronger evidence (an empty tomb does not by itself reveal what happened to the body), so there was no need to recount the empty tomb in his brief narration of eyewitness evidence.[122]

Further, Paul believed that Jesus was "buried" (1 Cor 15:4; cf. Rom 6:4; Col 2:12), and must therefore have assumed that the risen Jesus left the tomb: as noted above, Palestinian Jewish doctrine of resurrection *meant* transformation of whatever remained of the body. For the same reason, the thesis that Palestinian Jewish disciples and authorities would have simply ignored the tomb after the resurrection appearances strains all credulity. Indeed, many of Jesus' followers might well have visited the tomb immediately after the sabbath (hence before most of the appearances), given the need to show respect to their teacher's body. (As noted in the last chapter, we have archaeological evidence supporting the preservation of the site of the tomb to within roughly a decade of Jesus' burial, when Jesus' followers led the significant Jerusalem church not far from the site.)

Nor is there historical merit to the old "swoon" theory (that Jesus was not yet dead, hence revived enough to act "resurrected" but then died somewhere unknown). Crucified persons did *not* simply revive: Josephus had three friends taken from crosses, and despite medical attention, two died.[123] Further, if one could revive, one would still be trapped within the tomb, which would soon lead to death.[124] Those inventing an empty tomb tradition would hardly have included women as the first witnesses (see comment above), and Eduard Schweizer is right that "Jesus' resurrection could hardly have been proclaimed in Jerusalem if people knew of a tomb still containing Jesus' body."[125]

Failure to find a body could reflect an ancient motif (see especially 2 Kgs 2:16-17; Gen 5:24 LXX),[126] but need not be fictitious; such a narration is appropriate to the belief that the hero was still (or newly) alive, and in the case of the Gospels involves the recent, eyewitness past rather than the distant, legendary past as in most pagan parallels. Admitting historical evidence favoring an empty tomb is not purely the domain of Christian apologetic; for example, without addressing Jesus' resurrection appearances, Vermes, a Jewish scholar closely acquainted with the primary evidence, opines that "the only conclusion acceptable to the historian" must be that the women actually found the tomb empty.[127] Historian Michael Grant likewise contends that "if we apply the same sort of criteria that we would apply to any other ancient literary sources, then the evidence is firm and plausible enough to necessitate the conclusion that the tomb was indeed found empty."[128]

Some suggest that tomb robbers could have stolen the body.[129] If this happened shortly after this messianic figure's martyrdom, and was followed by the disciples all having resurrection appearances, such a coincidence would prove fortuitous indeed for the formation of what became Christianity. But even discounting the improbability of this coincidence in general, most of our evidence for tomb robberies comes from Gentile rather than Jewish areas.[130] Even assuming otherwise, the arguments for this position would remain weak. Whereas tomb-robbers normally carried off wealth, carrying off the body was so rare that it would shock those who heard of it.[131] It is not impossible that someone would steal a body; corpses were used for magic[132] and people suspected that witches sometimes stole bodies for magic.[133] Indeed, corpses that died violent deaths were considered particularly potent for magic.[134] Nevertheless our evidence for the theft of corpses appears in Gentile regions, never around Jerusalem.[135]

At least some opponents of the resurrection claim suggested that this was in fact the fate of Jesus' corpse (Matt 28:13-15).[136] Yet one would not expect disciples guilty of the corpse's theft to maintain the truth of their claim in the face of death, nor others to withhold the body when bringing it forward to challenge the emerging Jesus movement might have secured substantial reward. If the disciples did not protect Jesus while he was alive, surely they would not have risked their lives to rob his tomb after his death.[137] Other factors also militate against supposing that the disciples stole the body. Jewish scholar Geza Vermes notes that "From the psychological point of view, they would have been too depressed and shaken to be capable of such a dangerous undertaking. But above all, since neither they nor anyone else expected a resurrection, there would have been no purpose in faking one."[138] Those who have ever had their beliefs or deep hopes shattered will recognize that Jesus' death should have disillusioned the disciples too much for them to wish to fake a resurrection (which would also be inconsistent if they expected one). Though the corpse remaining in the tomb would have easily publicly refuted a resurrection claim, had the authorities been able to produce it,[139] an empty tomb by itself would not be self-explanatory.

Resurrection Appearances

Witnesses claimed that they had seen Jesus alive from the dead (e.g., 1 Cor 15:5-8); virtually all the narrative accounts also suggest significant conversation with him (rather than merely fleeting appearances). They were so convinced of the veracity of their claims that many devoted their lives to proclaiming what they had seen, and some eventually died for their faith that rested on it. Whatever one makes of what happened at the tomb, clearly the disciples' testimony was not fabricated.[140] Ancients also recognized that the willingness of people to die for their convictions verified at least the sincerity of their motives, arguing against fabrication.[141] People of course die regularly for values that are false; they do *not,* however, ordinarily die voluntarily for what they *believe* is false. Intentional deception by the disciples is thus implausible; as E. P. Sanders notes, "Many of the people in these lists [of witnesses] were to spend the rest of their lives proclaiming that they had seen the risen Lord, and several of them would die for their cause."[142] These disciples plainly believed that Jesus had risen; and not only that, but that they had *seen* him alive.

As noted above, some scholars deny the empty tomb tradition; most, however, affirm that the disciples believed they had seen Jesus alive. For example Sanders, while conceding his agnosticism as to what lay behind the disciples' experiences, concludes, "That Jesus' followers (and later Paul) had resurrection experiences is, in my judgment, a fact."[143] Yet some scholars deny the historical value of even these resurrection appearances; Mack, for example, suggests that before the Gospels we have only Paul's account of "visions."[144] But while the language Paul employs is general enough that it *could* include visionary experiences, he is reporting earlier Palestinian tradition in 1 Cor 15:3-7,[145] and Palestinian Jews did not speak of nonbodily "resurrections" (see discussion of the Jewish resurrection belief above).[146]

Nor would anyone have persecuted the disciples for simply affirming that they had seen someone who had been dead; apart from the *bodily* character of the resurrection — the sort that would leave behind an empty tomb — people would merely assume that they were claiming to have seen a ghost, a noncontroversial phenomenon in antiquity.[147] Ghosts were "phantasms" thought to appear especially at night,[148] but this phenomenon is not what the resurrection narratives report (Lk 24:40).[149] Further, Jesus "appeared" to his followers in Acts 1:3 yet there provided concrete proofs of his physicality (cf. Lk 24:39-40).[150] Finally, Paul himself distinguishes between the Easter appearances and (the more common phenomenon) mere visions (cf. 1 Cor 9:1; 15:8; 2 Cor 12:1-4).[151]

Few alternative proposals seem persuasive as explanations of the disciples' experiences. The pagan thinker Celsus compared Jesus' resurrection appearances with hellenistic epiphanies.[152] In Greek tradition deities periodically "manifested" themselves to mortals, sometimes in sleep and sometimes as apparitions.[153] Yet from the late hellenistic age "epiphanies" of Greek gods usually meant the activity of a deity rather than its appearance;[154] it is primarily these activities that witnesses attest,[155] though additionally appearances in personal dreams and visions occur.[156] Appearances of deities visible to large numbers of people normally belonged to an era many centuries earlier than the writings,[157] in contrast to early Christian reports about Jesus, arising from the beginning of the movement. We also lack Palestinian Jewish parallels to the claims of the resurrection appearances.

Further, very little evidence suggests the plausibility of successive and mass, *corporate* visions (see especially 1 Cor 15:5-7).[158] Conditions in first-century Judea and Galilee were not those that later produced the seventeenth-century messiah Sabbetai Zevi, many of whose followers failed to be deterred by his apostasy,[159] and some even by his death.[160] Aside from different social conditions, knowledge of the Christian belief in Jesus' resurrection and redefinition of messianic models through him could provide later messianic movements a model for redefining the messianic mission in a manner that did not exist prior to Jesus.

I have elsewhere noted some potential parallels not usually exploited in this connection, though with the observation that they are unpersuasive. Josephus claims that people saw heavenly chariots moving through the clouds and surrounding cities,[161] and priests heard voices in the temple. Some scholars plausibly regard these as collective fantasies,[162] but other explanations that could be offered are that they were (1) somehow true (a Postenlightenment perspective might allow for this possibility, though few of us are likely to embrace it); (2) the sun playing tricks on eyes at dusk; (3) propaganda to justify Jerusalem's fall after the event, which Josephus has accepted;[163] or (4) Josephus' own propaganda (he is the only extant witness concerning the witnesses apart from sources dependent on him).[164]

In fact, Josephus may be following a standard sort of report of such events as portents of destruction.[165] Some poetic writers engaged in poetic license;[166] other writers were fairly sober historians citing reports for particular years. Portents included events such as we might regard as natural phenomena today, such as physical deformities at birth, lightning striking temples, comets, and so forth,[167] but also included visions of celestial figures or armies.[168] The armies were sometimes heard rather than seen;[169] sights that were seen were often acknowledged as divine illusions rather than objects physically present;[170] and the apparitions of armies did not draw near anyone.[171] Such reports were normally not verified by citing witnesses, and the historians who report them sometimes express skepticism concerning their value, at times allowing for imagination in their production[172] and at times pointing out that such reports fed on each other among the gullible.[173] Some of what was genuinely seen at a distance may have been misconstrued; thus for example the report of two suns and light at night may reflect an aurora.[174] In any case, this phenomenon of celestial noises and appearances is quite different from meeting again and talking with a person one had personally known, which the Gospel accounts stress.

But the difference again concerns the *resurrection*. To most ancient Mediterranean peoples, the concept of corporal resurrection was barely intelligible; to Jewish people, it was strictly corporate and eschatological.[175] Yet if one grants, from a neutral starting point, the possibility of a bodily resurrection of Jesus within past history, the appearances would follow such an event naturally with or without parallels. In a Jewish framework, Jesus' resurrection within history must also signify the arrival of the eschatological era in some sense.[176]

Early Christian Faith

Why did Jesus' movement survive in contrast to those of Judean prophets like Theudas? It did so in part because Jesus' followers distinctively believed that he remained alive.

Early Christian faith cannot easily be explained by mere visionary experiences, since these alone would not have convinced many disciples that the person they saw had returned to life bodily (whatever that claim would have meant for them). As we have noted, postmortem "appearances" (especially in dreams) were not unusual, and no one would draw the corollary of Jesus as "Lord of humanity" from claims to have seen a dead person who was "alive" only in the sense that anyone after death was believed to remain alive. Hearers would certainly not have been convinced simply because someone said, "In a vision my deceased teacher told me that he is now ruler of the cosmos." If they believed the speaker's experience, they might conclude that the spirit was lying boastfully; that the visionary had misinterpreted a claim about authority over many other deceased spirits; or the like.[177] But the claim of a mere postmortem apparition would not have generated a movement around one believed to be a living Lord, whether its recipients were believed or not.[178]

Yet this claim that Jesus was the exalted Lord was no less pervasive in our early Christian sources than that he was risen; he obviously was not physically present on earth, yet he himself, and not merely a didactic tradition about him, was held to continue to reign in his church. (Indeed, at least Pauline and Johannine Christians linked a continued charismatic experience of the Spirit with their own continuing experience of Christ.) As many scholars today note, a treatment of the historical Jesus, and certainly of early claims about his resurrection, that does not take into account the early church's newborn faith does not provide a cohesive explanation of the evidence.[179] The church's extant resurrection claims are earlier (in Paul) and more consistently documented than Jesus' teachings are, and were undoubtedly the reason that those teachings continued to circulate widely. I suspect that historical Jesus scholarship's fixation on sayings while sometimes neglecting the resurrection claims is a remaining legacy of nineteenth-century liberal Protestant lives of Jesus, reflecting that era's attraction to Jesus' ethics[180] while discounting the earlier documented center of his earliest followers' preaching. Without the disciples' experience of resurrection, one wonders whether his movement (every known form of which held this belief) would have persisted or would have preserved Jesus' sayings in his name to any greater degree than the sayings of countless other sages of his day have survived.[181]

Some might argue that we could explain the disciples' faith in Christ as reigning Lord if the disciples before the crucifixion believed that Jesus was the messiah (which seems fairly likely, although some doubt that they held this belief), hence regarded their faith as vindicated by these apparitions. But not only would such an explanation fail to explain the terminology of "resurrection"; one also wonders to what extent Jesus could function presently as Messiah or Lord if he were merely a ghost. The explanation also conflicts with all our evidence about the more *plausible* emotional state of the disciples depicted in the Gospels, as well as with the antagonistic state of Paul before his belief in Jesus. The disciples might believe Jesus a pious man whose messianic mission nevertheless failed; God might raise up a different messiah in a worthier time.[182] Moreover, why did it happen not to one or two disciples (who then convinced the others) but to all?[183] The interim unbelief of the disciples, which in that culture would dishonor Jesus as well as themselves, meets the criterion of embarrassment.[184]

Of course, one could doubt all the resurrection narratives' claims that Jesus spent time with the disciples, and did not simply appear in their visionary trances. But how would they have known that they were experiencing a *resurrection* appearance and not an apparition? Would they not wish fuller confirmation than what a dream could confer? Would the group as a whole stake their lives on a mere dream or apparition no different in kind from those commonly claimed by those who thought they dreamed about someone deceased?

The *nature* of Jesus' "body" is another question. Paul's "spiritual" body cannot be simply contrasted with a "physical" body; Paul contrasts it with a *psychikos* body adapted for life in the old Adam, not with physicality (1 Cor 15:20-22, 44-48),[185] and means a body transformed and/or ruled by God's Spirit. At the same time, he clearly intends a quite different form of "physicality" than any experience with biological existence would predispose one to understand. This body is immortal, a body of glory rather than of flesh, comparable to stars, hence perhaps angels (1 Cor 15:35-54, esp. 40-43, 50; Phil 3:21).[186]

Whatever its character, though, it must have been somehow "bodily" to qualify as "resurrection" and to distinguish it from other forms of apparitions.[187] Again, whatever it was, it was understood as transformative, and not supposed to leave a corpse behind (cf. 1 Cor 15:51; Phil 3:21). Whether or not one believes the Gospels' empty tomb narratives, one can hardly imagine that the disciples would have proclaimed the "resurrection" without consulting the tomb. One can imagine even less that their detractors would not have done so to silence them.[188] That so many followers had these experiences (hundreds of them reportedly on a single occasion, 1 Cor 15:6) and they also happened to find the tomb empty, as a mere coincidence without relation to some event, strains plausibility.

While I personally believe that Jesus' resurrection provides the most plausible explanation (barring inflexible antisupernaturalism) for the disciples' faith, it also coheres with the larger theological context of Jesus' ministry (for first-century Palestinian Jews, if not necessarily for many modern readers).[189] If Jesus was a prophet of restoration eschatology, resurrection was a common feature of that eschatological expectation. Jesus' followers would thus naturally understand Jesus' resurrection as a foretaste of the promised resurrection of the righteous in Israel (and for some circles, of any righteous Gentiles). (Moreover, resurrection addressed a more general human concern with death, a concern sometimes associated with Adam traditions in Jewish sources.[190] Paul's theological conclusions in this regard were not inevitable, but they were natural.)

It fits Jesus' teachings about a role for himself after his martyrdom.[191] As we have noted, it also cohered with the the christology of the movement that sprang from Jesus: if Jesus was alive in a distinct (indeed, eschatologically resurrected) way, yet clearly not present physically among the disciples, he was exalted[192] and remained active through the church.[193]

Jesus' Mission and the Resurrection

If Jesus went to Jerusalem expecting his death at the hands of the political elite (as we have argued) yet also envisioned a role for himself in the imminent kingdom (as we have also argued), he apparently trusted God to vindicate him. He certainly believed in an eschatological resurrection,[194] so there should be no question that he expected to rise from the dead. By itself, this could explain his sayings about his role in the coming kingdom (e.g., Matt 19:28//Lk 22:30; Son of Man sayings; parousia sayings).[195]

But if Jesus also established a school to carry on after him, he may have envisioned an interim era between his martyrdom and the consummation of the kingdom. If we allow the possibility of his resurrection predictions (e.g., Mk 8:31; Jn 2:19), we can even entertain at least the *possibility* that he envisioned what in fact his disciples just days after his execution believed happened. Whether he expected his resurrection with others or in advance of them, but especially in the latter case, Jesus died expecting God to raise and vindicate him. This posture coheres with both the demands for radical faith (Mk 4:40; 5:36; 6:7-13; 9:23, 29; 11:22-24; Matt 6:25-34//Lk 12:22-32; Matt 7:7-11//Lk 11:9-13) and nonresistance (Matt 5:38-47; 7:1; Lk 6:27-37) found elsewhere in our gospel sources about Jesus.

Was Jesus' faith in God's intervention on his behalf misplaced? We cannot really begin to answer this question without asking a question involving the rest of his ministry. Was God active in Jesus' ministry? Did Jesus cure people simply by giving them confidence (in which case he rose in the experience of his disciples only), or was the God of Israel actually working through him, in which case a yet greater miracle might be deemed possible? Some scholars, grappling with how to translate the disciples' resurrection experience for a modern world, ask whether it should be interpreted in light of modern (non-supernaturalist) premises, or whether such premises should be modified in light of the resurrection?[196]

Any approach to this question in turn raises a philosophic question: is it possible that a deity, if one exists, can do miracles?[197] Can God act in history? I will treat this question only briefly, in appendix 8. (The question of miracles requires a separate book, a sequel to this one, where I can address ancient parallels, the objections of David Hume, and other issues. Even in that sequel, however, my *primary* focus will remain with the historiographic question regarding the plausibility of eyewitness testimony to miracle claims, more than with the philosophic question of divine activity.) While I do not, as I have said, agree with those who rule out of bounds the validity of such a question, my purpose in the main part of this book has been to make a case on other historical grounds without exploring that question here.

We mentioned earlier that Jesus' movement survived in contrast to those of other Judean prophets because his followers distinctively believed that he remained alive. (This distinctiveness invokes a positive use of the dissimilarity criterion.) This belief invites the further historical question: Why did his movement in contrast to other first-century Jewish movements affirm that its teacher rose from among the dead? That question takes us to the heart of the question "What happened at the tomb?" We examine that question in Appendix 8.

Conclusion

However we understand or explain it, a major historical impetus for the spread of Jesus' movement after his martyrdom was a pivotal event that his disciples virtually unanimously (along with at least a few former detractors) understood as his resurrection. Whatever one does with the more controversial question of divine causation, the best evidence suggests that the first witnesses believed that they had seen Jesus alive from the dead. They interpreted Jesus' current life as resurrected life — a foretaste of the new order, not at all comparable with mere ghost apparitions. Moreover, they were convinced enough as to the nature of this life as to stake the rest of their own lives, both in the current age and in the coming one, on Jesus' resurrection. For them, Jesus' resurrection cohered with his message: God was establishing a new order, and Jesus its proclaimer held first place in it. Whether we choose to agree with their faith or not, we cannot easily doubt the depth of their conviction.

Conclusion

In this book, we have worked to establish especially that the basic portrayal of Jesus in the first-century Gospels, dependent on eyewitnesses, is more plausible than the alternative hypotheses of its modern detractors. (The detractors tend to explain away genuine evidence selectively to fit theories rather than to construct theories coherent with the bulk of the evidence.)

We began arguing this case by showing the weakness of some of today's strongest alternatives. We then examined the biographic and historical character of the Gospels, and something of what that would mean for a first-century (as opposed to simply modern) audience. We then focused on the nature of the Gospels' sources, both written and oral, including the character of oral tradition from eyewitnesses in Mediterranean antiquity.

After laying this broader foundation for why we should treat the Gospels as useful sources for reconstructing our historical portrait of Jesus, we surveyed some elements of his mission in those sources, particularly those that could be shown most consistent with Jesus' first-century Jewish environment. The elements surveyed included many of his teachings (e.g., about the coming kingdom and faith in God), his exalted self-identity, his conflict with the Jerusalem authorities, and his apparently voluntary martyrdom in Jerusalem, probably believing that he was inaugurating salvation for his people.

Although scholars may differ with this or that aspect of the portrayal, I believe that on the whole there is much that we can know about Jesus historically, and that the first-century Gospels preserved by the church remain by far the best source for this information.

Zealots and Revolutionaries

What do we know about the "Zealot movement"? Evidence seems to tell against a *unified* revolutionary movement in first-century Palestine.[1] The actual designation "Zealots" applies strictly only to some rather than to most early Jewish revolutionaries; Josephus seems to reserve the title for a limited group.[2]

Josephus portrays the revolutionaries as "brigands," endeavoring to marginalize them from the mainstream Jewish population.[3] Richard Horsley and John Hanson envision the Zealots as peasant brigands in contrast to more educated levels of resistance.[4] Some modern scholars view these peasant brigands before the Jewish revolt in the light of modern studies of social bandits.[5] The revolutionaries and bandits of Jesus' day may have had some support from Galilean villagers; at least the Roman governor Cumanus thought that they did.[6] But it is not clear to what extent Galilean peasants really supported the goals of such bandits, especially in the Lower Galilee whence Jesus came (we discuss revolutionaries and Galilee further in chapters 1 and 12);[7] one should also allow for the impact of some degree of urban unrest.[8] Nevertheless, it seems likely that many bandits circulated among the peasantry.[9]

Much of this brigandage before the first revolt may have been "prepolitical" rather than aimed at an overthrow of Roman domination, an objective that may have grown only toward the beginning of the Jewish War.[10] Brigandage was common in antiquity and inevitably warranted execution if the brigands were captured.[11] Yet revolution was always a possibility. Many dissatisfied persons opted to work within the system, but others likewise hoped for its overthrow, eschatologically or otherwise.[12] Even Josephus informs us that some of the rebels fancied themselves kings (Jos. *Ant.* 17.285), suggesting that the authorities could view the line between revolutionary and messianic sentiment as thin (see Mk 15:2, 18, 26).

Although some Pharisees probably opposed the revolutionary ideal, some scholars believe that they shared a basic (populist) Pharisaic ideology expressed in a more militant manner.[13] This overlap in perspectives may be because Pharisees were close to popular sentiments in general.[14] Most of the revolutionaries' ideas were probably widespread in early Judaism,[15] and eschatological expectation probably fueled all levels of Jewish resistance.[16] Both resentment against Rome[17] and confidence that God would defend those loyal to him[18] were also widespread.

Witherington points out that some Pharisees did "basic training" (Jos. *Life* 11-21) and that revolutionary leaders could send Pharisees in charge of military contingents (Jos. *Life* 197).[19] In the earlier *Wars,* when the material is still politically sensitive, Josephus plays down both Pharisaic involvement in the revolt and Jewish involvement more generally, but in the later *Antiquities* a revolt as early as A.D. 6 appears part of a larger movement toward the revolt of 66-73 (Jos. *Ant.* 18.9-10, 23-25; Acts 5:34-35). Menahem, a figure instrumental in the revolt of 66-73, was descended from Judas the Galilean, a leader in the earlier revolt (Jos. *War* 2.433). Josephus also admits the revolutionaries' theological commitments (Jos. *Ant.* 18.4-5, 23).

In all, the evidence may not support the early use of the title "Zealot" or a single, unified movement (such as Josephus' convenient "Fourth School"). It does nevertheless support the continuing existence of simmering revolutionary sentiments through the early first century, hence the relevance of such sentiments to Jesus' environment.[20]

Mack's Case for a Wisdom Q

To avoid digressing at further length in the text to address Burton Mack's rejection of eschatological elements at the earliest stages of the Jesus movement, I have chosen to revisit some of his argument in this appendix. He contends that Q was *originally* only a sayings-gospel focused on wisdom sayings.[1] How does he know this? He finds two basic arguments to support this position. We will start with his second argument because it depends on the first and can be addressed more quickly. Once one has postulated this original Q and knows what to look for by excluding material that does not fit what one hypothesizes Q must have been, one has a small amount of material left. This material, Mack finds, fits together quite well with reasonable transitions of thought.[2]

It is not surprising that a document consisting largely of one kind of sayings (other sayings having been excluded) should cohere, but one may question just how smooth the transitions from one point to the next actually prove to be. Wisdom collections did not always strive for coherent arrangement, and the wisdom sayings left to Mack's Q1 indeed could have been arranged more topically than they appear to be. (Moreover, some of the material that belongs together topically here already *was* together in the Gospels.) But if one must find convincing transitions, the "seams" Mack finds into which later material was interpolated offer evidence of such transitions in so few instances that they can easily be attributed to coincidence. Mack offers a methodology that is not falsifiable: once one has arrived at a very brief Q1 by other means, one can undoubtedly discern patterns *even* if one decides to completely rearrange the material.

This boils Mack's real arguments for a convincing Q1 Wisdom text down to one argument: a genre of wisdom or sayings collections existed.[3] No one disputes that such a genre existed, nor even that such a genre could have existed among early Christians. But when our extant sources for Q itself include at least a minimal amount of narrative (not to mention sayings other than wisdom sayings), why is it any more reasonable to place an early form of Q in this genre than to place a finished Gospel like Mark or Matthew in it? Perhaps merely because Q, being a hypothetical source, is more easily reshaped with less protest; perhaps also because Q, whose exact contours remain in dispute among various circles of scholars,[4] is less familiar to the average reader of Mack's thesis.

Does Mack have any *specific* evidence that Q was a wisdom or sayings-source? He believes that he does. It helped, he declares, when "Another example of the genre was found, the sayings gospel known as the Gospel of Thomas."[5] "The Gospel of Thomas looked very much like Q," he contends; "35 percent of the sayings in Thomas had parallels in Q."[6] But when he affirms that Thomas looks like the sayings-gospel Q, Mack simply assumes what he claims to prove: that Q *is* a wisdom sayings-gospel. The overlap in content between the two also sheds far more light on Thomas than it sheds on Q. Thomas is, as we have noted, a second-century work, reporting sayings known from the canonical Gospels and/or traditions behind them, including Q.[7] Of course Thomas has resemblances to Q material! (Thomas itself is also not "wisdom" sayings in the same way that, say, Proverbs is.)

But let us say, for the sake of argument, that Q is (or uses) an early sayings-source. It is, after all, apparently *mostly* sayings, so an analogy with sources that are mostly sayings is possible. Why would disciples of an eschatological teacher not have preserved even eschatological sayings in this format?[8] One may exclude the narrative within Q, but on what basis does Mack exclude some (eschatological) kinds of sayings? Even were we to agree with Mack that the eschatological elements from other Jesus traditions were added only later to this hypothetical recension of Q, on what basis must we suppose them less historical? Nor need we assume that those who employ a sayings-source would oppose as incompatible the use of narratives (another issue sometimes raised).

Mack contends for layers in Q, some being late and not authentic to Jesus (though not all who hold to layers in Q agree on which layers are earliest, and not all who do so believe that the later layers are inauthentic). Based on the likelihood that many later agrapha (sayings attributed to Jesus but not found in the canonical Gospels) are inauthentic, Mack argues for late sayings in Q.[9] But most of these questionable sayings occur in documents of the second century or later, including his own sampling of late citations.[10] If one argues for a late layer of sayings as early as Q on the basis of fabrications over a century later, one could as easily argue that *any* sayings from antiquity, including his "bedrock" sayings of Q, are fabrications. Certainly people in subsequent centuries made up sayings; this was not so common, however, in the first generation (as we noted in ch. 10). *All* of Q must be (at the latest) from the first generation to be used in Matthew, Luke, and (I believe) occasionally in Mark.

Mack's idiosyncratic Q community is curious. Assuming that either no eyewitnesses who knew Jesus remained or (closer to his view) that they did not care about transmitting his life and teaching accurately, one still must contend with the relative unity of our sources. First-century documents indicate explicitly that Christians argued about issues like circumcision and food laws, but until the second century we find no evidence that some groups of Jesus people rejected other groups' literary genres or accounts of Jesus' sayings and deeds. To argue that such debates were widespread in the first century is to argue from silence, a silence made more ominous by the record of all sorts of other debates.

Further, for all the redactional differences among the Gospel accounts, they do not reflect very well many of the known debates among second- and third-generation Christians. The best Mack can do to say that Jesus abolished the food laws is Mark 7:15; yet without Mark's explicit interpretive guidance in 7:19 (a remark Matthew not surprisingly omits) we would hardly know that this was Jesus' point. Yet Mark did not simply compose a more appropriate saying to make his case.[11]

Mack claims that Q (i.e., his hypothetical Q1) "challenges the New Testament account of Christian origins by offering another, more plausible account of the first forty years."[12] Aside from the problem of how a hypothetically reconstructed source of wisdom sayings poses a potent challenge to a range of actual early Christian texts presupposing some major elements of common history, one must ask whether Mack's account is indeed "more plausible." The first forty years of Christian origins include most of Paul's undisputed letters, which already identify Christ with divine wisdom and *especially* in the earliest text (1 Thessalonians)[13] indicate considerable eschatological meditation (which can hardly be attributed to Greek influence). As a "Pharisee" (Phil 3:5; this was a largely Judean sect), Paul's perspective was unquestionably rooted in Palestinian Judaism despite his profound ability (akin to that of many other Diaspora Jews) to articulate Jewish beliefs in broader Mediterranean terminology.[14] Most Pauline scholars believe that Paul employs pre-Pauline creeds containing Aramaisms, some Palestinian Jewish doctrines and language such as "resurrection," and even reflects the adoption of some Aramaic phrases into his churches.[15]

Mack's reconstruction assumes a later fusion of a Christ cult and the Q-like Jesus movement,[16] but our earliest written witness for Christianity, Paul, testifies of conflicts with Jerusalem church leaders (originally Jesus' Galilean disciples) over Gentile relations, not over christology (Gal 2:1-14). The christology of our current "Q" is hardly "low" (as noted earlier in the book; e.g., Matt 3:11//Lk 3:16; Lk 6:47-49//Matt 7:24-27; Matt 23:37//Lk 13:34).[17]

Mack assumes that myth gave way to history in a Greco-Roman cultic environment, but the reverse process is far more likely. Myths and legends tend to grow over time, even from historical roots. Few Greek cults constructed histories from their myths, rarely being interested in biographical history. Starting with historical traditions, however, one can understand how mythic interpretation and cultus would arise in Greek culture while interest in history (and later historical writing) was maintained because of the actual origins of the movement. And whereas Palestinian Jewish writers could embellish history, they clearly sought to derive theology from what they believed was history, not from what would have appeared to be mythology created in the Diaspora.

Mack's "original" Q, after "incompatible" material has been excised, runs to about seven pages.[18] This material seems short for a definitive canon of wisdom sayings — at least if one wishes us to suppose that it represents the sum total of what this "community" believed. Why would someone want to turn a wisdom teacher with so little to say into a Messiah anyway, especially in a Palestinian or Diaspora Jewish context?[19]

Overman rightly observed on Mack's earlier work:[20]

> Why is Q the bench mark against which all other recitals of the Jesus story are measured? Why are Pauline traditions or other early gospel traditions not given a similar place in the development of Christian beliefs and practice? In part the answer seems to be that this is due to Mack's implicit preference for the Greek philosophic tradition, oftentimes as over against the traditions of Israel. For example, Jesus and John the Baptist are Cynic-like prophets and not prophets in the mode of Israel's prophetic tradition (p. 86). Within Jesus' social world Israel's Scriptures and the Cynic poet Meleager would have had about equal influence (p. 64).

Because his version of Q is hypothetical, Mack can exercise greater freedom in emphasizing hellenistic while downplaying Jewish parallels. His case, then, runs directly counter to the best of the Third Quest's desire to set Jesus securely in his first-century Galilean Jewish context.

Jewish Biographical Conventions

Penned in Greek probably to Diaspora audiences, the canonical Gospels reflect Greco-Roman rather than strictly Palestinian Jewish literary conventions.[1] That is, as Diaspora works they share more external characteristics with Diaspora or aristocratic Palestinian Jewish biographies in Greek than they do with many of the Palestinian works composed in Hebrew or Aramaic. Such a statement does not detract from the Jewishness of the Gospels; Jewish historical writing in Greek *generally* adopted Greek historiographic conventions.[2]

In contrast to other Greco-Roman biographies, however, the Gospels, like Diaspora Jewish historical texts, retained considerable stylistic and theological influence from the Greek version of the Old Testament. Further, the Gospels vary among themselves as to the degree of their Palestinian character: Matthew and John, whose ideal audiences apparently have closer continuing ties with Palestinian Judaism, probably reflect more Palestinian literary influences than Mark and Luke do.[3] Because of Palestinian Jewish influences in some of the gospel material, we should examine some forms of Palestinian Jewish literature (though apart from Josephus' hellenistic autobiogaphy, none of these are precisely biography).

Some Palestinian Jewish Literature

The methodology of many Hebrew and Aramaic Palestinian Jewish texts concerning historical figures diverges at significant points from that of Greco-Roman historical writing. Since the Palestinian Jewish roots of the Jesus movement affected Diaspora Christianity, a brief consideration of Jewish biographical conventions may be useful in discussing the traditions behind the Gospels. More importantly for our purposes, they may be useful in understanding literary techniques particularly adapted by Matthew and John. Because the differences in genre are more significant, however, I am treating them only in this appendix.

Although many individuals feature prominently in the Hebrew Bible and in early Jewish literature, there are rarely volumes devoted to a person that would be called biography in the sense in which we have discussed the term in ch. 5; usually they are part of larger narratives. Job, Ruth, Judith, Jonah, Esther, Daniel and Tobit each have books about them in the Greek Bible, but the events rather than the lives of the characters dominate the accounts.[4] Of course, the Gospels could draw on biblical narratives focused on persons as well as on the Greco-Roman genre;[5] but we should not overlook the broader availability of the more general biographic category in this period.[6]

The various reports of events in the lives of pious rabbis are too piecemeal to supply parallels to biographies like the Gospels.[7] It remains possible that some of these stories were collected and told together like some of the brief philosophical lives in Diogenes Laertius. Since no such early collections are extant, however,[8] rabbinic sources can add little to our discussion of Jewish "biography." In contrast to Josephus or Tacitus, rabbinic texts are primarily legal, and incidental biographical information tends to serve more purely homiletical than historical purposes.[9]

Nevertheless, some Jewish works, drawing on the Bible and postbiblical Jewish tradition, bear some resemblance to Greek lives; most of these again, however, are in Greek. I shall note Philo's analogies later. One collection called the *Lives of the Prophets,* with genre parallels in the Greek lives of poets, resembles the briefer lives.[10] Josephus' accounts about Moses in his *Antiquities* often follow patterns in hellenistic philosophical biography[11] (though sometimes also novelistic literary conventions);[12] so also his treatment of Abraham,[13] Jacob,[14] Joseph,[15] Samson,[16] Saul,[17] Zedekiah,[18] and the Aqedah narrative,[19] among others.[20] Thus Cohen lists among Jewish works of history owing "more to Herodotus, Thucydides, and Hellenistic historiography than to Kings and Chronicles" both 2 Maccabees and Josephus.[21]

Degrees of Adaptation in Palestinian Works

While all these works differ from the Gospels, observations about broader classes of Jewish narrative literature can provide insight into Jewish storytelling methods. In Aramaic and Hebrew as well as in Greek, texts about the distant past could combine both historiographic and novelistic traits without apology, depending on the nature of the text in question. Especially in Palestinian works, biblical narratives were often adapted by later story-tellers and eventually formalized into separate accounts;[22] story-tellers especially favored Pentateuchal characters for this sort of development.[23]

Although these reworkings are not strictly midrash nor targum,[24] some midrashic or haggadic principles are sometimes at work in their composition.[25] Some works, like Pseudo-Philo's *Biblical Antiquities,* normally follow the biblical text very closely (often virtually quoting the text), though adding many details.[26] Others, like the *Assumption of Moses,* are more novelistic, having very little to do with the biblical text beyond the characters and a basic story line (quite different from our source-bound Gospels). The degree of freedom depended also on the nature of one's work: for example, whereas the Septuagint preserves incidents of patriarchal deception, Philo and apocryphal works often played it down, and Josephus took a middle path.[27] A continuum existed between historical works and novels composed around historical characters, distinguishable by their measure of fidelity to sources the writers accepted as historically accurate, especially Scripture.

As in other Greco-Roman literature, ancient Jewish literature generally permitted variation in detail; when dealing with the distant past, the variations could become quite significant. Although amplification in matters of halakah was sometimes discouraged,[28] the practice was especially frequent in narratives, to answer questions posed by a narrative[29] or to heighten the praise of God or the protagonist[30] (sometimes by fanciful midrash)[31] or to improve the story.[32] Sometimes adaptations highlight particular moral or theological perspectives.[33] Sometimes writers added details for literary purposes, to make a better story;[34] this could include names,[35] sometimes arrived at midrashically or for symbolic value.[36] (This practice is hardly surprising; Greeks also elaborated their sacred stories, filling in details over the centuries.)[37]

One could emphasize a theme already present in one's source by reiterating it where it appeared and occasionally adding it elsewhere.[38] Similarly, negative incidents could be toned down,[39] omitted,[40] or justified[41] in the character's favor. Such adaptations could range from the sort of "twist" on a narrative acceptable in modern journalism to fabricating details to explain what was not said.

Variations in the tradition and/or its editing in these sources were not seen as problematic;[42] a greater degree of freedom in telling the story was permitted then than is standard in historically oriented works today. One scholar notes:

> The discrepancies between the descriptions of the tortures administered to the first son and the others six, here [in 4 Maccabees] and in 2 Mac, indicate no more than that the story circulated in different forms or that each writer claimed his freedom to shape up the narrative in his own way.[43]

There was thus a wide variety of writing techniques available in ancient Jewish as well as broader Greco-Roman writing related to history.

The Gospels as biography and the shorter time of oral transmission informing them differ significantly from these sources. Nevertheless, the permissibility of variation is instructive. Even documents intended to be essentially historical in the events they report could in principle vary in the accuracy of their details.[44] Relevant for observations about variation in the Gospels, paraphrase of sayings was standard Greco-Roman rhetorical practice;[45] Jewish interpreters also regularly employed paraphrase in communicating what they took to be the biblical text's meaning.[46]

The Evangelists made some use of this freedom. We may illustrate with two examples that are not very controversial. One may compare differences among Luke's three narrations of Paul's conversion in Acts; Luke obviously did not see a problem telling the story in slightly different ways on each occasion.[47] Likewise, in the space of one paragraph the Fourth Gospel paraphrases one sentence in two ways (Jn 13:10-11). These writers were more concerned with the basic substance than the particular wording; indeed, orally oriented cultures were accustomed to such variation and not troubled by it the way that modern readers are.[48] Comparing parallel passages in the Gospels underlines this point further, but the differences are within the range we have noted acceptable to ancient biography.

Differences from the Gospels

But we must observe some important differences between the canonical Gospels and the Palestinian Jewish works noted above. First, the period in which oral tradition was transmitted before the Gospels is at most two generations (roughly 65 years till the Fourth Gospel); Jewish expositions on Pentateuchal characters often draw on centuries of legends, useful to fill in gaps in the biblical narratives. Second, haggadic expansion characterized stories about the distant past far more frequently than recent generations (although it could occur in the latter case extremely rarely). Third, unlike many of these works, the canonical Gospels anticipate a Diaspora audience familiar with the genre of biography (and for at least three of these Gospels, the particular subgenre of "gospel about Jesus"). Many of the works above are quite distant from biographies.

Some Jewish writers did compose something like self-contained biographies, though again, not all of them fit the conventions we have discussed. The Jewish philosopher Philo certainly adapts his material, and may provide an example of a sort of Jewish biography.[49] Nevertheless, Philo's expositions of Abraham, Joseph, and Moses idealize the figures only to communicate Philo's philosophical lessons,[50] though this observation does not negate the evidence for his use of hellenistic biographic conventions.[51] Philo was more of a philosopher than a historian, and his works about biblical individuals are philosophic expositions of biographic information rather than biographies proper.

If we compare Philo's works about individuals with the Gospels, we must keep in mind several observations. First, as a Platonist, much of Philo's interest in the "lives" of Pentateuchal characters like Abraham and Noah is allegorical, and Philo's degree of allegorization is barely comparable even to John, much less to the Synoptics.[52] Second, Philo's narration (as opposed to his allegorical interpretation) normally follows his biblical sources rather than simply his imagination.[53] Third, Philo writes about much earlier characters, following the philosophic disposition to allegorize works about characters of the distant, mythical past. In our discussion of ancient historiography we observed that writers normally recognized that their sources about the distant past were less reliable, hence often exercised literary freedoms that they would not employ for the more recent past. Fourth, Philo's overt resistance to genuine historical content (alongside his emphasis on allegorical significance) at some points involves especially "offensive" texts.

Thus, while we may learn from broad analogies with a wide range of literature, the mainstream Greco-Roman biographies of the Gospels' era provide the most fruitful grounds for genre comparison.

APPENDIX 4

Jesus' Sayings about the End

Although we cannot be certain that Jesus' words in the "eschatological discourse" (roughly, Mk 13; Matt 24; Lk 21) were all spoken on that occasion,[1] many of them appear to have been assembled before Mark used them. In any case, it is this collection of sayings, with the largest number of Jesus' future-oriented sayings, where our inquiry will begin.

The list of eschatological sufferings and signs here fits the eschatological conventions of many of Jesus' Jewish contemporaries. The overlap of these sayings with any *specific* non-Christian document, however, is quite limited. More striking is the oft-noted specific overlap with material in 1 Thessalonians 4–5. Just how striking the overlap is becomes obvious when its correspondences are compared with other Jewish lists of eschatological sufferings and signs. These parallels appear not only from Mark and Q, but even in a few specifically Matthean features as well.

Other Lists of Eschatological Sufferings

Lists of eschatological hardships appear in other early Jewish works, such as *Jubilees* 23:16-31; at various points in *4 Ezra* and *2 Baruch;* in the *Testament of Moses* and in *Mishna Sota* 9:15; as well as several other lists preserved in the NT. Some of the signs or hardships listed also appear in noneschatological pagan sources as portents, reported annually by Roman historians.

Most of the pagan portents are missing in this discourse. Roman writers listed wood, stone or statues sweating, bleeding or speaking (perhaps peripherally paralleled in Rev 13:15);[2] raining blood or stones,[3] not quite analogous to *Jubilees'* hail (23:13) or Revelation's hail echoing a plague in Egypt (Rev 8:7; 16:21; Ex 9:18-34); fluid turned to gore,[4] closer to Revelation's waters turned to blood, again echoing a plague in Egypt (Rev 8:8-9; Ex 7:19); and animal prodigies.[5] Pagans also listed animals born malformed or with human parts,[6] and somewhat

361

more commonly mutant babies or other human birth prodigies (even in the days before modern tabloids).[7] The latter appear twice in 4 Ezra (5:8; 6:21-22) and also in a passage in the Sibylline Oracles (2.154-64) dependent on something like eschatological signs in Hesiod (W.D. 181).

Jewish lists of end-time signs are fairly diverse, but typically include sufferings. Many specific examples of hardships or evils appear in only one list, but of those that recur more often (some in other first-century Christian lists as well), a number are lacking in the list in Mark and Matthew (which admittedly is also fairly random). Besides those mentioned above, common signs included sexual immorality;[8] a hypocritical pretense of righteousness;[9] a particular end-time war (rather than merely "wars" in general), modeled after warnings in the biblical prophets;[10] children sometimes challenging parents or elders, whether to turn them to the right way (Jub. 23:16, 19; cf. 1 En. 90:6-7) or as a sign of the evil of the times (m. Sot. 9:15; 2 Tim 3:2); and a reversal of the poor over the rich, again for positive (Jub. 23:20) or negative (2 Bar. 27:3-4) reasons.

Birth Pangs (Mk 13:7-8)

Some other motifs are common to Mk 13 and these sources, including the language of eschatological "distress" (1QM 15.1; 2 Bar. 26:1; 25:3-4). Although these appear throughout the discourse, they are especially noticeable, as one might expect, in the summary list of hardships in Mk 13:7-8. Wars appear in Jubilees (23:13); 4 Ezra (9:3; 13:31); 2 Baruch (27:2-5; 70:3); and elsewhere.[11] Earthquakes appear in 4 Ezra (9:3; cf. 5:8 Syr.; 6:16); 2 Baruch (27:7, after a famine reference; 70:8); Testament of Moses (10:4); and also in texts about a final earthquake (similar to Rev 6:12).[12] Famines appear in Jubilees (23:13); 2 Baruch (27:6; 70:8); and elsewhere.[13] Especially pervasive are various forms of "lawlessness"[14] (to use Matthew's language, Matt 24:12)[15] and apostasy of the righteous.[16] Heavenly signs, which also appear in pagan portent lists[17] but are common judgment imagery in the biblical prophets (e.g., Is 13:9-11; 24:21-23; Joel 2:31), not surprisingly appear in a variety of early Jewish sources.[18]

In some texts the signs may not be strictly "eschatological." Some writers before the Gospels also may have applied some of these afflictions to a period before the final generation (Jub. 23:13 includes plagues, famine, sword, and the context includes apostasy).[19]

A Comparison with an Early Christian Source

Paul's Thessalonian correspondence confirms the antiquity of these eschatological sayings of Jesus.[20] Most scholars accept 1 Thessalonians as the earliest extant Christian document, probably from c. 50 or 51 CE. I also draw on Paul's second letter to the Thessalonians. Although a number of NT scholars reject that letter's authenticity,[21] I, with many other scholars, regard it as simply inconceivable that a pseudepigrapher writing after the temple's destruction in 70 CE would have spoken of an antichrist figure establishing his throne in the temple.[22] Many scholars question the authenticity of 2 Thessalonians because its eschatological schema seems much more detailed than that of 1 Thessalonians; I would argue that early Jewish sources, including Mk 13 itself, often included such tensions between detailed schemas and warnings of imminence.[23] Whether or not the second epistle's author is Paul, however, it seems likely that the author wrote before the temple's destruction in 70, since the letter predicts the man of lawlessness being enthroned and worshiped in the temple (2:3-4), a different outcome than what happened literally.

These early letters appear to indicate that their eschatological material reflects prior tradition attributed to Jesus. In 1 Thessalonians 4:15, Paul appeals to "the word of the Lord" as the basis for his eschatological instruction, in a letter where he has already appealed to instructions he gave them by the authority of the Lord Jesus (4:2).[24] Second Thessalonians, which includes some comparable eschatological material, also appeals to the "traditions" that Paul delivered to the Thessalonians (2:15; cf. 2:2).

Parallels between the eschatological discourse and 1 Thessalonians include, in decreasing order of significance (in view of how common the motifs were in early Judaism and how close the parallels are): an unexpected coming like a "thief in the night" (Matt 24:43; 1 Thess 5:2-4); the trumpet for gathering (Matt 24:31; 1 Thess 4:16); coming on the clouds (Mk 13:26; 1 Thess 4:17); the term *parousia* (Matt 24:3, 27, 37, 39; 1 Thess 4:15; 2 Thess 2:1, 8); unexpected destruction in a time of peace ("Q" material in Matt 24:38-41; Lk 17:27-32; 1 Thess 5:3); birth pangs (Mk 13:8; 1 Thess 5:3); and the exhortation to stay alert (Mk 13:33-37; 1 Thess 5:6). Interestingly some of these correspondences are with Mark; others from "Q"; and others from Matthean redaction, but apparently based on earlier tradition. Parallels with 2 Thessalonians 2 include apostasy (Matt 24:10, 12; 2 Thess 2:3); the temple's desolation (Mk 13:14; 2 Thess 2:4); a false prophet or prophets working signs (Mk 13:22; 2 Thess 2:9); and the "gathering" (Mk 13:27; 2 Thess 2:1). None of these parallels are exclusive to the Thessalonian correspondence, but their relative concentration there is instructive.

Because the Gospels' eschatological discourses are longer than the eschatological sections in 1 and 2 Thessalonians, we should not expect the Thessalonian material to recall every point. But of 28 eschatological motifs I noted in Matthew 24 with parallels somewhere in Jewish or Christian literature,[25] 12 appear in 1 Thessalonians and 8 in 2 Thessalonians. By contrast, I found 5 in *1 Enoch;* 5 in the list of eschatological troubles in *Jubilees* 23; 6 in *4 Ezra;* 5 in

2 *Baruch;* 3 in *Testament of Moses;* 3 in the *Sibylline Oracles;* and one in *m. Sota* 9:15. Although one could count up the statistics differently, and I undoubtedly did not find all possible parallels in these works, these estimates remain significant in view of the mere 15 verses (245 words) in the most relevant section of 1 Thessalonians (4:13–5:9), and the 12 verses (217 words) in the most relevant section of 2 Thessalonians (2:1-12). By contrast, in some of the other sources I drew from large bodies of material.

Thus over 40% of the motifs in the discourse in Matthew 24 appear in 1 Thessalonians, and *over 70% appear in the two sections of the Thessalonian correspondence* if they are taken together. If we omit the motifs that were fairly common in early Judaism, this reduces the Thessalonian parallels, but it almost eliminates our control group of other early Jewish sources. Some motifs, such as Q's "thief in the night" (Matt 24:43; Lk 12:39), recur elsewhere in other early Christian sources (Rev 3:3; 16:15; 2 Pet 3:10) in addition to 1 Thessalonians (5:2-4), but not *outside* Christian sources, reinforcing the picture of a common source for some elements of early Christian eschatology.

If we start from 1 Thessalonians and look for parallels in Matthew 24, the correspondence is even higher (a bit more so if augmented by some other fragments of Jesus tradition, such as the identical expression "times and seasons" in Acts 1:7). We may find *11 out of 15 correspondences, or almost 75%.* Again, one could count the number differently, but it could be calculated even higher than I have suggested: the four elements in 1 Thessalonians that lack exact correspondence (the Lord descending from heaven; the voice of an archangel; the resurrection; and the living being caught up to meet the Lord "in the air") could be viewed as inferences from this tradition. (Thus, for example, Jewish Christians who accepted the resurrection would naturally assume it at the gathering of the elect; a meeting, or *apantēsis,* belongs to the same conceptual and social world as *parousia,* and a gathering to one coming on the clouds would naturally occur "in the air.")[26]

Despite such lacunae, it appears that Paul drew directly on the same eschatological tradition later reported in Matthew and Mark. The same is true for 2 Thessalonians, though again we lack some elements (such as the tantalizing explanation for the letter's "restrainer of lawlessness"). Apart from the obvious motif of the resurrection, I did not find *any* eschatological motifs in 1 Thessalonians that appear elsewhere in early Jewish literature but not in Matt 24 or Mk 13.

The Common Source

One could argue that Mark, "Q," and Matthew all drew on 1 Thessalonians. This argument would need to assume, however, either that both Mark and "Q" were written from Thessalonica (a view held by no one), or that Paul's letters were already collected by the time that they were written, which is unlikely, *especially* for "Q" (a view again held by, so far as I know, no one).

A much more defensible solution would be to argue that indeed Paul and the extant Jesus tradition draw on a common source. What was this source? Some contend that this source was a prophecy, Paul's "word of the Lord" in 1 Thess 4:15.[27] This solution is likelier than dependence on Paul, but proves problematic in a different way. Paul indicates that early Christian prophecy was pervasive, suggesting even the existence of multiple prophets in local Christian congregations (1 Cor 14:29, 32). He limits their prophecies to two or three at a time (14:29-30), but may allow more prophecies so long as the conduct is orderly (14:31).

Even by the time Paul wrote 1 Thessalonians, and even if we limited the total prophecies to three per week in just twenty eastern Mediterranean house churches, we should think of over 3,000 prophecies per year, or perhaps 60,000 early Christian prophecies by the time that Paul wrote. Indeed, given the increase in churches, that number could easily be doubled by the time Mark wrote. The coincidence of motifs between Matthew and Paul is far more dramatic against a control group of pre-70 Christian prophecies (if we had a better sampling of them) than against the control group of early Jewish eschatological motifs. What would make one particular prophecy or group of prophecies so authoritative as to be cited so prominently?

In Paul's own day, Paul himself, who is not shy about appealing to his apostolic authority, distinguishes between Jesus' tradition and his own counsel (1 Cor 7:10-12), even when he regards the latter as inspired (1 Cor 7:40). Further, the material to which Paul alludes in the "word of the Lord" is something he has already taught them, since he claims that they "already know" these things (1 Thess 5:2). If Mark, Q, Matthew and Paul drew on a common prophet, it was likely Jesus himself, or at least some form of Jesus tradition widely accepted as authentic.

Conclusion

Jesus' eschatological discourse naturally shares many eschatological motifs with its broader Jewish environment. Apart from Jesus tradition, however, it does not draw on any single extrabiblical source significantly more than others. But it appears that most of the eschatological material (informing even much that orally stands behind Matthew's redaction of Mark) was already part of the Jesus tradition by the time that Paul dictated the first document in our NT, 1 Thessalonians, roughly two decades after Jesus' public teachings.

Eschatological Themes (highlighting the most important connections)

Themes	Matt 24	Mk 13	Other Jesus Tradition	1 Th 4–5	2 Th 2	1 Tim 4	2 Tim 3	2 Pet 3; etc.	Rev	Earlier Sources
Temple destroyed	24:2; cf. 23:38; 24:15	13:2	Matt 23:38; = Lk 13:35 (Q)?	—	—	—	—	—	—	Some traditions: views on Dan 11:31; 12:11
Temple desecrated	24:15	13:14		—	2:4	—	—	—	11:2?	Some traditions: views on Dan 11:31; 12:11
False Prophets	24:5, 11, 24	13:6		—	2:9	(4:1-3)	(3:13?)	2:1; 3:3		Common motif of end-time woes, and in NT
False prophets' signs	24:24[30]	13:22		—	2:9	—			13:13	
Wars and rumors of wars	24:6-7	13:7-8		—	—	—			6:2-4	
Eschatological war (cf. 1QM)									16:14; 19:11-21	
Eschatological "distress"	24:21, 29	13:19, 24		(3:3)	(1:4, 6)				(1:9); 7:14	Dan 12:1
Famines	24:7	13:8		—	—	—			6:5-6	
Earthquakes	24:7	13:8		—	—	—			Cf. 6:14	
Birth pangs	24:8	13:8		5:3[37]	—	—				Eschatological idiom?[38]
Betrayal	24:10	13:12					—			
Lawlessness	24:12[41]	—	—		2:3, 7-8	—	3:2-5	3:3		Common motif of end-time woes
Apostasy	24:10, 12[42]	13:12			2:3	4:1	—			Common motif of end-time woes
Parousia	24:3, 27, 37, 39	—		4:15; cf. 2:19; 3:13; 5:23[45]	2:1, 8 (cf. 2:9)	—	—			Elsewhere in NT eschatologically, 1 Cor 15:23; Jms 5:7-8; 2 Pet 3:4, 12; 1 Jn 2:28
Vultures gathered	24:28	—	Lk 17:37 (Q)	—	—	—	—		19:17, 21	Conventional image (in all bodies of ancient literature); esp. Ezek 39:17-20
Sun, moon darkened; stars fall	24:29	13:24	(cf. Acts 2:20)	—	—	—	—		6:12-13	Common in OT (e.g., Is 13:9-11; 24:21-23; Joel 2:31)
Tribes mourn when they see him[47]	24:30	—		—	—	—	—		1:7	Zech 12:10

Jub. 23:16-31	4 Ezra	2 Bar.	Test. Moses	M. Sota 9:15	Other	Pagan Prodigies
			6:8-9		*T. Levi* 15:1; expectation of a new temple[28]	
23:21[29]					(Characterized current time, e.g., in DSS)	
					4Q339 (?): *Test. Jud.* 21:9	
					Sib. Or. 3.63-70 implies that an antichrist figure will work signs (cf. *Apoc. Elij.* 5.11), but this may be a Christian interpolation.	
23:13 (evil report; sword)[31]	9:3; 13:31	27:2-5; 70:3			*Sib. Or.* 2.22; 3.204-5, 636-37, 660-61, 76; *Gen. Rab.* 42:4	
23:20,[32] 22-23[33]	13:34[34]				1QM 15.1	
		26:1			1QM 15:1; *2 Bar.* 25:3-4	
23:13[35]		27:6 (plus drought); 70:8			*Sib. Or.* 2.23; *Pesiq. Rab Kah.* 5:9; *Gen. Rab.* 25:3; 40:3; 64:2; *Ruth Rab.* 1:4; *Pesiq. R.* 15:14/15	
	9:3; cf. 5:8 Syr.; 6:16	27:7; 70:8			*Test. Mos.* 10:4[36]	Ovid *Metam.* 15.798; Livy 32.8.3; Appian *C.W.* 1.9.83; Pausanias 7.24.6
					1QH 3.3-18;[39] cf. *1 En.* 62:4[40]	
	5:10; 14:16-17	27:11-12; 69:3	7:3-10	9:15	*1 En.* 91:7	Hesiod *WD* 181-201
23:9, 16-17[43]	Cf. 5:1-2		(8:2-5)[44]		*1 En.* 91:7; *T. Iss.* 6:1; *Naph.* 4:1; *3 En.* 48A:5-6; *Pesiq. Rab Kah.* 5:9; *Pesiq. R.* 15:14/15	
	Cf. 7:38-42				*1 En.* 102:2-3 (end of age); cf. *Sib. Or.* 3.800-4; 5.476-84; 8.190-93, 204	Heavenly signs in Livy 25.7.8; 29.14.3; 32.8.2; 41.21.13; Lucan *C.W.* 1.526-43[46]

Table continues on pp. 368-71

Themes	Matt 24	Mk 13	Other Jesus Tradition	1 Th 4–5	2 Th 2	1 Tim 4	2 Tim 3	2 Pet 3; etc.	Rev	Earlier Sources	
Coming on clouds	24:30; cf. 26:64	13:26; cf. 14:62	(cf. Acts 1:9, 11)	4:17	—	—	—		1:7	Dan 7:13	
Trumpet for gathering	24:31	—	—	4:16 (also 1 Cor 15:52)	—	—	—		(cf. 11:15)	Familiar image (e.g., Is 27:12-13; cf. Ps. Sol. 11:1-4; Shemoneh Esreh 10)	
Gathering[49]	24:31	13:27	—	(4:15-17)	2:1	—	—			Familiar Jewish expectation	
Unknown time	24:36	13:32		5:1-2	—	—	—			One strand of Jewish expectation	
Unknown "times and seasons"	—	—	Acts 1:7	5:2	—	—					
Unexpected destruction	24:38-41	—	Lk 17:26-30, 34-35	5:3	—	—	—				
Compared with the flood	24:37-39	—	Lk 17:27	—	—	—	—	3:5-6; cf. 2:5		1 En. 54:7-10	
Compared with Sodom's destruction[50]	—	—	Lk 17:29	—		—	—	Cf. 2:6; Jude 7			
Coming like a thief in the night[51]	24:43	—	Lk 12:39[52]	5:2-4	—[53]	—	—	3:10	3:3; 16:15		
Stay alert (in an explicitly eschatological context)	24:42; 25:13	13:33-37	Lk 12:37-38; 21:36	5:6		—	—				
Asleep	—	13:36		5:7, 10		—	—				
Wedding imagery	25:1-13		Lk 12:36			—	—		19:7-9	Is 25:6; messianic banquet	
More general: Salvation for those who persevere	24:13	13:13			2:13	—	—			Common NT idea	
Preaching the gospel among nations precedes end	24:14	13:10				—	—			Perhaps Rom 11:25-26; Rev 5:9; 7:9; cf. 2 Pet 3:9, 12, 15?	
"the elect"	24:22, 31	13:20, 22			Cf. 2:13	—	—			Too common for statistical significance	
Parallels from other documents											
Children reproach elders, including parents							3:2				
Other reversals: poor over rich, etc.											
Fornication and impurity							3:4-6?				

Jub. 23:16-31	4 Ezra	2 Bar.	Test. Moses	M. Sota 9:15	Other	Pagan Prodigies
	6:23[48]				For gathering: Ps. Sol. 11:1-4; cf. *Pesiq. R.* 40:7; for war: 1QM 8.9-12	
			,			
	6:25; 9:7-8					
Cf. 23:16;[54] 23:19[55]				9:15[56]	Cf. *1 En.* 90:6-7	
23:20[57]		27:3-4[58]				
23:14		27:11-12		9:15	*Sib. Or.* 3.204[59]	

Themes	Matt 24	Mk 13	Other Jesus Tradition	1 Th 4–5	2 Th 2	1 Tim 4	2 Tim 3	2 Pet 3; etc.	Rev	Earlier Sources	
Hypocritical pretense of godliness							3:5				
Sickness, plague									6:8		
Sleet, hail, frost											
Raining blood or stones											
Fluid turning to gore											
Howling dogs; animal prodigies											
Animals born malformed or with human parts											
Shortened lives											
Premature aging											
No seed or oil									6:6		
Beasts, birds, fish destroyed											
Sufferings on Israel, or persecution of righteous											
Israel repents after suffering	23:39										
Days lengthened (after repentance)	Cf. 24:22[67]	Cf. 13:20[68]									
Sun at night, moon at day											
Blood from wood, stone speaking										13:14-15		
Mutant babies or birth prodigies											
1 Thess material absent from Matt 24											
The Lord descends from heaven with a shout	(descent implied in parousia?)			4:16						Cf. 19:11-14		
With the voice of the archangel	Cf. 24:31, sends angels with trumpet			4:16								
Resurrection	assumed[70]			4:16						20:4-5		
Living caught up with dead to meet the Lord in the air	24:31 lends itself to this inference?			4:17								

Jub. 23:16-31	4 Ezra	2 Bar.	Test. Moses	M. Sota 9:15	Other	Pagan Prodigies
23:21[60]			7:3-4	(9:15)[61]		
23:13,[62] 22[63]					*Sib. Or.* 2.23	
23:13[64]						
						Livy 24.10.7; 25.7.7-8; 26.23.5; 27.37.1; 34.45.7; 35.9.4; 36.37.3; 42.2.4; 43.13.5; 45.16.5; Appian *C.W.* 2.5.36; 4.1.4
						Virg. *Aen.* 4.453-63; Livy 24.44.8; Rev 8:8-9 with Ex 7:19
						Ovid *Metam.* 15.796-97; Livy 24.10.10; 27.11.4; 35.21.4; 41.13.2; 41.21.13; 43.13.3; Appian *C.W.* 4.1.4
						Livy 27.4.11, 14; 32.1.11; 40.45.4; Phaedrus 3.3.4-5
23:11-12, 15						
23:25[65]						
23:18	6:22			9:15		
23:18						
			8:2-5	(9:15)	*Sib. Or.* 3.213-15;[66] *1 En.* 90:6-16	
23:24						
23:27						
	5:4; cf. 7:38-42					
	5:5					Ovid *Metam.* 15.792; Livy 27.4.14; 40.19.2; 43.13.4; Appian *C.W.* 2.5.36; 4.1.4; Lucan *C.W.* 1.556-57; cf. Eurip. *Iph. Taur.* 1165-67
	5:8; 6:21-22				*Sib. Or.* 2.154-64[69]	Livy 27.11.5; 27.37.5; 34.45.7; 35.21.3; 41.21.12; Appian *C.W.* 1.9.83; Herodian 1.14.1; Lucan *C.W.* 1.562-63

John and the Synoptics on Passover Chronology

Some have used Passovers to reconstruct John's chronology[1] and have claimed conflicts between John and the Synoptics, but it seems better (in view of John's usual literary strategies) to read John's final Passover chronology symbolically.[2] Passover began at sundown with the Passover meal. Whereas in the Fourth Gospel Jesus is apparently executed on the day of the Passover sacrifice preceding the evening meal (Jn 18:28; 19:14), the Synoptics present the last supper as a Passover meal, presupposing that the lamb has already been offered in the temple.[3] Both traditions — a paschal last supper and a paschal crucifixion — are theologically pregnant,[4] but we suspect that Jesus, followed by the earliest tradition, may have intended the symbolism for the last supper, whereas John has applied the symbolism more directly to the referent to which the last supper itself was intended to symbolically point.

Many scholars have argued plausibly that John's chronology here is correct,[5] noting that the last supper narrative does not explicitly mention a lamb,[6] that an execution on the first day of the feast was inconceivable, and suggesting that the disciples could have celebrated Passover early, according to a sectarian calendar,[7] or that Mark inserted Passover references for theological reasons.[8] Other details of the Passion Narrative behind Mark, such as the Sanhedrin originally wishing to kill Jesus before the feast (Mk 14:1-2), Simon coming from the fields (15:21, which some take as coming from work), or burial on a "preparation day" (which in Mk 15:42 is preparation for the Sabbath, but some take as preparation for Passover)[9] can support the Johannine chronology. The rabbis also spoke of Jesus' execution on the eve of Passover,[10] although this is a late polemical tradition probably deriving its information from early Christian sources that may reflect John's Gospel or its tradition.

But the priestly aristocracy might act even on Passover to preserve public order, and Pilate would care little for calendrical matters. Likewise, an execution on the day on which the lamb had been eaten would deter crowds no less than one on the day on which they were being slaughtered, if the site of execution were not far outside Jerusalem's walls. The minor details "behind" Mark's Passion Narrative could also be explained in other ways that fit the narrative equally well. Mark could simply be correct that the preparation was for the Sabbath;[11] Simon could come "from the fields" because he has spent the night in a suburb like Bethphage.[12]

The main argument against the Johannine chronology in a conflict between John and the Synoptics is that on most points Mark's narrative seems more dependable for historical detail, John's more expository (although many hold John's chronology to be an exception, especially regarding the duration of Jesus' ministry). Thus many scholars suggest that the Synoptics are correct; the Synoptics certainly portray the last supper as a Passover meal, even on details that their audiences would no longer have recognized as relevant.[13]

Those favoring the Johannine dating respond that, whereas the Synoptics regard the meal as a Passover meal (this is "challenged by no one"), this does not decide the *historical* question;[14] but then why do Mark and Paul, writing earlier than John and even for Gentile audiences, conform the narrative so closely to Passover traditions? And if the Synoptics report the disciples actually keeping the Passover but on a "sectarian" date, would sectarians have observed so many other traditional Paschal customs as the text suggests? Jeremias admittedly depends on later traditions, but what evidence we do have fits the Gospel narratives and can hardly have derived from them. As scholars often note,[15] John certainly had theological reasons to place the death of God's lamb (Jn 1:29) on Passover (Jn 19:36).

One could argue that Jesus (and the Synoptics) and the temple authorities (and John) followed separate calendars;[16] but our evidence for these calendars is relatively scant, and even if such separate calendars existed, why would John prefer that of the temple authorities? How would he expect his post-70 audience to recognize that he was doing so? One attempt to harmonize the Johannine and Synoptic dating, originally associated with a proposal of Annie Jaubert in 1957,[17] has commended itelf to a number of scholars. According to this proposal, Jesus followed a solar calendar like the one used at Qumran, but Jerusalem's official Passover, and the one followed by John, occur afterward. Given sectarian calendars[18] and even calendrical differences among later rabbis due to different witnesses regarding the new moon,[19] it is not *impossible* that Jesus' disciples followed an Essene, sectarian date for the Passover.[20]

But other scholars have raised more persuasive objections against this thesis.[21] For one, would such an important disagreement with the Temple authorities have gone unnoted in the tradition? After all, calendrical matters constituted a major debate in early Judaism, and had they been central to Jesus' conflict with the authorities, one might expect mention of this point. (The exception would be if this information were suppressed by the later church if it had reverted to the common practice. But probability is against their siding with the authorities against their own teacher; other sects would not have done so.) Further, if Jesus followed a sectarian calendar at this Passover, why do John's narratives imply that he did not do so at other festivals (2:13; 7:2; 10:22)?[22] It is also possible that John followed a Palestinian and the Synoptics the Diaspora reckoning of Passover,[23] but this proposal fails to explain the Paschal character of the last supper tradition, the accommodation of Diaspora pilgrims at the festival, and again the inadequacy of supporting evidence in the tradition.

Calendrical differences may allow us to harmonize John and the Synoptics, but most likely, John has simply provided a theological interpretation of Jesus' death, as many commentators (including myself)[24] have argued. This approach would fit the way he *opens* Jesus' ministry with the Temple cleansing so that the shadow of passion week may cover the whole period. If the two accounts must be harmonized, however, the simplest, Ockham's razor solution would be the best; one such possibility is that "Jesus, knowing that he would be dead before the regular time for the meal, deliberately held it in secret one day early."[25] Another plausible suggestion is that Jn 18:28 refers to them eating the *rest* of the feast of unleavened bread,[26] a solution that is linguistically defensible (though not the text's most obvious sense) but does not seem to match the other clues in John's narrative. At the very least John retains enough ambiguity to allow the reading (and, if we lacked the Synoptic passion tradition, to *assume* the reading) that Jesus was crucified on Passover. John probably does know the same tradition as Mark. Whatever the traditions behind the Gospels, however, Mark's and John's approaches at least imply (perhaps for theological reasons) the Passover on different days, yet derive from it the same theology: Jesus' death is a new passover, a new act of redemption (cf. also 1 Cor 5:7).

APPENDIX 6

Roman Participation in Jesus' Arrest?

Some have argued that the Fourth Gospel, unlike the Synoptics, includes Romans in the force that arrested Jesus.[1] Many further find genuine historical tradition in this claim.[2] While Romans were clearly behind the crucifixion, however, it is not likely that they were involved in the initial arrest.

Local aristocracies used local watchmen to constitute their police force, and all that we know about Jerusalem's temple guard (cf. Lk 22:52; Acts 4:1) fits this pattern.[3]

Moreover, although some military terms in John 18:3 can reflect Roman usage, Greek and Roman military terms had long before been transferred to Jewish soldiers.[4] Both *speira* (Jn 18:3, 12)[5] and *chiliarchos* (18:12)[6] appear frequently enough in ancient sources for *Jewish* soldiers. The Jewish uses of the terms would be too familiar from widely read Jewish sources like Judith and Maccabees for John's audience to be sure of Roman involvement without further qualification.[7]

Some are skeptical that Jewish officials like the high priests or their agents would have participated, but as we have argued, these were the very leaders responsible to the Romans for keeping peace; they were the ones most directly scandalized by Jesus' act in the temple; and a diversity of ancient sources testify to their abuse of power against competitors among their own people. The silence of the Synoptics about Roman involvement in the arrest also seems striking, especially given Luke's knowledge of the Roman military and widespread knowledge of a garrison in Jerusalem.[8]

One could argue that the Romans lent the chief priests some troops as they might to the temple police in quelling public disorders,[9] but this suggestion does not square with the evidence. The Roman garrison in the Antonia would have sided with the Levite police in the case of a riot, but they were not simply at the municipal aristocracy's disposal.[10] Further, even if the municipal aristocracy could have commandeered Roman troops at other times, it is unlikely that

375

they would do so during the festival. Pilate, ready to greet petitioners early in the morning, was undoubtedly already in town (albeit asleep),[11] and it is unlikely that the high priests would have secured troops for such a mission without informing him; yet even John (see especially Jn 18:29) reads as if Pilate has insufficient acquaintance with the case to have already dispatched the troops. Indeed, Pilate explicitly assigns responsibility for the arrest to Jesus' own nation and its chief priests (18:35); Jesus likewise speaks of the lack of resistance his followers have offered to "the Jews" (18:36). Catchpole rightly doubts that Judas would have been cooperating with the Romans and that the Romans would have taken Jesus to Annas (whom the Romans had deposed); moreover, retreat before the divine name (18:4-11) may suggest a Jewish reaction.[12] The Roman involvement proposal interprets selectively even the Gospel to which its appeal is made.

John might use ambiguous language, without explicitly claiming Roman troops, to make a theological statement: both Romans and Jews bore responsibility for Jesus' arrest.[13] Again, however, even within the story world of John, it remains unclear that Pilate was involved at this point,[14] hence Roman participation seems unlikely even on the level of Johannine theology.[15]

Capital Authority

Some believe that the Romans would have acted without a session from leaders of the municipal aristocracy,[1] but this expectation does not fit the usual Roman manner of delegating preliminaries to local officials (unless Jesus offered an immediate military threat, which contradicts the evidence we examined in chs. 1, 20-21). Detractors sometimes protest that if the Sanhedrin genuinely tried Jesus, they would have executed him themselves, avoiding a Roman cross. This objection rests, however, on the highly improbable notion that the Sanhedrin had legal capital authority or, if they did not, would have lynched a popular prophet during a festival with the governor in town.

John's Gospel is probably correct to note that the Judean leaders were not legally permitted to put anyone to death (Jn 18:31); the governor held the power of life and death in a province.[2] The local aristocracy would prepare the charges and suggest action, but Pilate had to pronounce sentence. A few scholars think that the Sanhedrin could execute capital sentences,[3] but this proposal does not fit what we know of the way the Romans administered their provinces. Against one contrary suggestion,[4] Acts 23:1-10 constitutes a preliminary inquiry to formulate a charge (22:30; 23:28-29), *not* evidence for capital authority.[5]

Although Theissen recognizes that the Sanhedrin lacked capital authority in Jesus' time,[6] he thinks that the passion narrative presupposes this jurisdiction, and thus reads its own milieu's circumstances of A.D. 41-44, under Agrippa I, into the narrative.[7] Others might employ this lack of capital authority to deny the passion narrative's own evidence that some of the high priests tried Jesus. Such approaches, however, face two major obstacles: First, the logic of the passion narrative actually presupposes that the Sanhedrin *lacks* capital authority; why else would they hand Jesus over to Pilate?[8] Second, Agrippa I, like Herod the Great, was a client *king* and he was on personal terms with the emperor. He was not the municipal aristocracy, and his capital authority did not transfer to them. In the last decade of the first century, Johannine tradition still preserves the Sanhedrin's lack of authority (Jn 18:31-32). An intermediate position is that Romans rarely delegated capital authority, but that Roman governors were authorized to do so.[9] Whatever governors of some provinces may have wished to do, however, it is inconceivable that Pilate would have simply shared this authority with Jerusalem's local aristocracy, given what we know about them and especially all that we know about him.[10]

Later rabbis discussed appropriate grounds[11] and means[12] for execution, but rabbinic literature itself shows that these discussions were primarily theoretical.[13] Some rabbinic tradition traces the loss of Jewish courts' capital authority to 70 CE,[14] other tradition to no later than 30 CE.[15] Although Josephus naturally does not report any precedents unfavorable toward Jewish autonomy, this loss of sovereignty[16] must have begun much earlier. Although Rome delegated the right of the sword to Herod and other client rulers, and although even Diaspora Jewish communities could enforce corporal penalties on their own members,[17] Rome withheld capital jurisdiction from municipal aristocracies who could employ it against citizens loyal to Rome, as we have noted.[18] For this penalty, local rulers needed at least Roman ratification.

Some precedent existed for Romans overlooking past executions, or even human sacrifices, that could be justified by local custom, but they expected such practices to be discontinued.[19] Provable extrajudicial executions were thus not in the political interests of the priestly aristocracy, whose interests typically coincided with preserving security and Roman order. Although councils of subject territories could pronounce a death sentence, they had to bring their sentence before the governor for ratification.[20] Most scholars thus currently recognize that the Sanhedrin lacked the legal authority to execute prisoners in this period.[21] As Roman legal scholar A. N. Sherwin-White notes,[22]

> When we find that capital power was the most jealously guarded of all the attributes of government, not even entrusted to the principal assistants of the governors, and specifically withdrawn, in the instance of Cyrene, from the competence of local courts, it becomes very questionable indeed for the Sanhedrin.

The Sanhedrin could sentence offenders and recommend them for execution, but apart from violating the Temple few Jewish religious charges would receive an automatic capital sentence from the Romans (e.g., Jesus ben Ananias was not executed).[23] It is not impossible that Roman officials might look the other way in the case of some lynchings, but even these could prove problematic if they could generate complaints to Rome.[24] It was in all the leaders' interests for Jesus to be accused by Jerusalem authorities but handed over to the governor for official sentencing.

What Really Happened at the Tomb?

Historical Jesus books often stop short of addressing the resurrection,[1] though the early Christian claim about this event is the reason that most of our other material about Jesus (as opposed to that about most other prophets or Galilean sages of his day) was preserved.[2] Nevertheless, a historian can address the question of the resurrection the way historians today usually address Jesus' miracles (I will address that subject in a separate book): this is what the disciples experienced, without regard for what may have actually happened to Jesus.

Although historians do not rule out intelligent human causation, for the sake of theological neutrality they normally omit the question of divine causation. (For the most part, such neutrality is prudent: theological interpretations of history vary as widely as the theology behind them.) But what happens when divine causation is the most plausible available explanation? While conventional rules for historical discussion may keep us from asking the question within the framework of conventional historiography, they do not mean (much less prove) that the question is philosophically illegitimate. I am many times more conversant with ancient history than I am with modern philosophy,[3] so I venture the question below to provoke consideration of these suggestions, not to offer dogmatic guidance for philosophic procedures.

Must One Rule Out the Possibility of Divine Activity?

One scholar complains that "the vast majority of modern historians" examining the resurrection story "would say that *no evidence at all would ever demonstrate that a unique resurrection took place*," because it cannot be confirmed by scientifically.[4] "Few if any modern historians" would accept the evidence of the first followers' belief to argue that Jesus actually appeared to them in a physical body; "If so, why not believe not only all the miracles of the Old Testament, including the six-day creation, as well as the miraculous giving of the Quran to Muhammad," since "all have credible witnesses"? All who accept Jesus' physical resurrection "as historical fact" are also Christians, which, he claims, suggests bias.[5]

The complaint here is a response to a Christian scholar claiming that an increasing number of New Testament scholars accept Jesus' physical resurrection.[6] The response seems fair if it primarily questions whether truth can be determined by a head count of scholars: most Christian scholars believe in a supernatural resurrection, whereas most non-Christians deny it. Yet it is unfair if it supposes that an appeal to secular scholars settles the question any more than an appeal to Christian scholars does. Scientific and historical epistemology demands evidence — appeal to authority (such as a head count of scholars) is a different epistemology, and tells us more about reigning philosophic paradigms than about historical facts. Naturally those who believe in the resurrection are (with a few notable exceptions) Christians — why would someone *affirm* Jesus' resurrection yet *not* be counted as a Christian? But is a Christian (or Muslim, or other religious) interpretation any more inherently biased than a nonnegotiably "secular" one?[7] Does this attribution of bias justify ignoring scholars with a different perspective or neglecting the evidence they present?

Most of our knowledge of history depends on the reports of witnesses and on evaluating those reports. To take the examples given, we do not have many witnesses concerning an angel revealing the Qur'an to Muhammad (though this lack of witnesses need not rule the claim out). Scripture offers no witnesses to a six-day creation, and the character of the creation narratives differs markedly from any of the genres of our resurrection reports for Jesus, whether Paul's claims or those in the biographies we call Gospels.[8] The comparisons suggest that the objection is not one of genre but that any claim suggesting supernatural activity (in whatever genre it occurs) must be consigned to the same category.

Some accept many miracle accounts (though not necessarily their explanation of supernatural causation) while rejecting those that lack sufficient parallels. Yet this claim that historiography a priori excludes anything "unique"[9] can beg the question of uniqueness' definition. Every historical event is unique in some sense, involving a variety of causes and consequences. In fact, an event like hundreds of people claiming to have seen their miracle-working teacher alive from the dead, and being prepared to die for this claim, was fairly unique at the time of its occurrence.[10] Yet few would deny that this was in fact the experience of these people, however we explain it. The objection to countenancing "unique" events in this case does not mean objecting to what is merely unusual or even unrepeatable[11] (history is not a repeatable scientific experiment), but to what is normally believed to be "impossible" apart from a divine, supernatural, or at least currently inexplicable cause.

This approach necessarily presupposes a specifically naturalistic definition of history, which is hardly neutral, and in fact functions as a circular argument in this case. To ask how many historians rule out the possibility of God acting in history is essentially to return to a head count of historians' religious beliefs. (Here I think our particular scholar might underestimate the proportion of historians who do believe it, but that is beside our point.) Since historiography does not rule out intelligent causation as a historical factor (so long as the intelligence is human), one can rule out the theological question not because it involves causation but because it involves a deity. That is, to presuppose that God did *not* act (because he *can*not act) one must first presuppose (or demonstrate) atheism or deism.

Methodological naturalism as a ground rule for inquiry functions well when exploring natural causes for events; normally we can accept it as a working method. But as a philosophic foundation *philosophic,* thoroughgoing naturalism is only a presupposition, no matter how many people believe it or (more often) use it. One can make normal use of the method to explore natural causes without assuming that one has thereby *disproved* theism (indeed, most of the early Enlightenment scientists who developed this method did so alongside theistic beliefs). Is it philosophically *necessary* to rule out the question of God as a *possible* cause for events (complicated as it may prove to devise tests for such a hypothesis)? If so, are we not simply presupposing (rather than proving) atheism or (as in the case of many of the later Enlightenment thinkers) deism? Intellectually fashionable though such an option may be in many elite circles, there is no reason why atheism or deism must constitute an epistemological assumption (much less that we should claim to have proved atheism or deism because we have started from this assumption).

Most of our other discussions in this book (regarding sayings traditions, biographic genre and so forth) should be agreeable to most historical inquirers regardless of religious or philosophic presuppositions. Discussing the nature of the resurrection, however, cannot so easily skirt the philosophic question. To rule out the possibility of this extraordinarily unusual occurrence despite otherwise persuasive evidence is easier if one rules out plausible supernatural explanations; yet to rule out the possibility of supernatural explanations is likely to prejudge the conclusion of one's case in this instance.

N. T. Wright's monumental work on resurrection (comparable to Raymond Brown's works on the infancy and passion narratives) challenges the perspective of those who claim that Jesus' resurrection is "not amenable to historical investigation."[12] He surveys five senses in which we use the term "history":

1. An event (what happened, whether or not we know it)
2. A significant event (worthy of record)

3. A provable event
4. Historiography (writing about history)
5. "What modern historians can say about a topic" (from a "modern" perspective)

Wright complains that some historical Jesus research proceeds as if rejecting knowledge about Jesus or the resurrection in the fifth sense entails rejection of it in every other possible sense of "history" as well.[13] He contends that some arguments function as smokescreens meant to absolve scholars from engaging the questions seriously. For example, the claim that we lack direct access to what "happened" could be made for much of history.[14] He suggests that ruling out even asking questions about God or Jesus' resurrection is not neutral, but part of the radical Enlightenment's cultural hegemony.[15]

A Legitimate Question?

Some would end the discussion of the "historical Jesus" with the empty tomb, arguing that history cannot pass judgment on whether God really raised Jesus.[16] Whether this claim is true or not depends partly on which of several definitions of "history" one employs: historiography does when possible explore causes, including personal causes, and to a priori exclude God from legitimate consideration as a cause is to presuppose atheism or deism — that is, to begin with a *theological* judgment about the nature of history. That is, it rigs the outcome, especially for those who conflate different meanings of history: "historically" God could not raise Jesus from the dead, since "history" by (one) definition excludes God a priori from the discussion.[17] Likewise, the argument from lack of analogy would problematize much of history, including the rapid rise of the early movement exalting Jesus within Judaism.[18]

Having registered that objection, we must recognize that discerning such causes is not an easy exercise. Moreover, to enable dialogue among all historical inquirers, be they various forms of atheists, agnostics or theists, we typically declare a "truce" and focus on those minimal historical assumptions that we can all agree on. A "neutral," agnostic starting point should allow for the possibility of divine activity without requiring it, and atheists and theists alike should be ready to grant this exploration, at least on the level of dialogue, whatever their personal convictions.

To conclude, however, that Jesus returned immortal after death, and then to attribute that resurrection to divine activity, is to come to a conclusion that is not agnostic. As such, it appears to break the "truce" and end any dialogue on the point, at least the sort of dialogue in which opinions outside the minimal consensus are unwelcome. (Not all dialogue requires consensus, of course, and scholars are often able to disagree charitably about their conclusions.) To observe this feature of the dialogue is not to decide the case, but it helps us understand a factor in making this part of the discussion particularly controversial.

Yet when a scholar denies that resurrection is "verifiable in principle by believer and nonbeliever alike,"[19] definition of the terms "verifiable" and "nonbeliever" are important. That nonbelievers would not accept any verification for resurrection could be true to the extent that the nonbeliever refuses to accept the possibility of divine or supernatural phenomena, but this definition almost treats "nonbeliever" as "anti-believer" in such possibilities, which is not always the case (and not always to the same degree). An agnostic must by definition remain open-minded, and even an atheist might be willing to respond to evidence that challenged their own position, depending on their level of conviction and certainty. (When I was an atheist, I found theism quite unlikely and reckoned that Christianity had only a 2% likelihood of being true, but I was not absolutely immune to challenge. That I am not an atheist now may make the latter point obvious.) Some non-theists might also admit evidence for a highly unusual phenomenon without granting the common theistic explanation for it.

What everyone should agree that one *can* explore historically is whether eyewitnesses claimed that they witnessed Jesus alive from the dead. We have focused on this approach in our discussion of the resurrection narratives. Nevertheless, I believe the question of causation is legitimate as well, although I recognize that some readers will from the outset demur from my conclusions. I believe that a *genuinely* "neutral" interpretation should not disallow the question of suprahuman activity (since disallowing the question commits one in a non-neutral manner to the position that no deity or force could ever resurrect someone). I defend the "supernatural causation" position in more detail in this book's sequel.

At the same time, I recognize that my own belief — that God did act in history in Jesus' resurrection — is a conclusion that de facto defines my own belief as "Christian."[20] (This statement could be qualified; a few scholars have concluded that God did raise Jesus to vindicate him as a prophet, without becoming Christians. But at the least the premise that God acted requires one to be a theist.) This was my conclusion before it was my premise, but in the spirit of full disclosure, I do hold to this Christian conviction now. In my youth, however, I was an atheist who ridiculed Christians as foolish. Out of commitment to what I came to believe was true, I have chosen to wear the label I had once derided as intellectually vacuous. Is my vantage point necessarily more biased than it was before, or than that of others who rule out of court the possibility of divine or other suprahuman explanations?

Yet when I was once a convinced atheist I was not ashamed to state my atheism (I was in fact proud of my "intellectual" position). I will not apologize for holding a different conviction now. Atheists, theists, and other combinations of dialogue partners can still come to the table and dialogue about the evidence, discussing which ways they think the evidence points.[21] Dialogue should include the ability to disagree respectfully without dismissing another's reasoned position as a priori illegitimate because it does not rule out the possibility of a deity or divine agency. I believe that divine activity best explains the resurrection appearances. That some readers who have followed the book to this point will decline to follow in this section is understood; freedom to choose what to agree with in another's argument is part of the character of dialogue.

My Own Journey

Many scholars today appreciate full disclosure of one's personal presuppositions, recognizing that all scholars have some. Like most scholars, I try to do my historical scholarship as a good historian. Many scholars working in historical Jesus research have personal religious commitments (Christian, Jewish, or other); others do not. But we all try to make a case that can be heard and engaged by others who may disagree with us. Having said that, some of us, myself included, would have gone into other disciplines without the element of religious interest in this particular figure. Before acquiring such interest, I did have enormous interest in the rest of the Greco-Roman world. Nevertheless, I was reticent to study Jesus or even ancient Israel because historical study of these subjects connected to modern "religious" discussions in ways that reading about Germanicus or Nero Drusus (or even "the divine Augustus") did not.

When I was an atheist (largely for what I thought were scientific reasons), one of my central (albeit nonscientific) objections to believing anything about Jesus was that eighty percent of people in my country claimed to be his followers, yet most of them apparently lived as if it made no difference for their lives. In an effort to be provocative, I might ask whether western Christians' frequent way of believing the resurrection is as consistent as most non-Christians' way of disbelieving it. Much of western Christendom does not proceed as if the Jesus of the Gospels is alive and continues to reign in his church. In practice, a gulf remains between their affirmation of Jesus' resurrection and their living as if he is humanity's rightful lord, so that a theological affirmation does not translate into their experience. Their "faith" constitutes mere assent to a proposition, rather than sharing Jesus' resurrection life as depicted in Paul's letters. Likewise, their devotional prayer to God often has little emotional connection to the Jesus of the Gospels; the experience of the early church that connected the Synoptics and Paul is not always their own experience. The experience of Christianity in some other parts of the world is more wholistic; indeed, in many locations

Christians even show great interest in Jesus' example and teachings. At the time, however, I had personally witnessed that commitment from only a few persons, whom I thus treated as anomalous.

I reasoned that if I believed that there was truly a being to whom I owed my existence and who alone determined my eternal destiny, I would serve that being unreservedly. But whatever other religion might contain some truth, I concluded that if Christians did not really believe in Jesus, there was surely no reason for myself to do so. When I later encountered the risen Christ in an unsolicited and unexpected personal experience, hence came to the conviction that he (not to mention the God with whom he was associated) was in fact alive, I understood that the reality of Jesus rises or falls not on how successfully his professed followers have followed his teaching, but on Jesus himself.

Such an encounter will naturally be dismissed as purely subjective by those disinclined to accept it, and admittedly, I did not have a physical "resurrection appearance." I offer this information as an explanation by way of full disclosure, not as an argument, since it functions outside the epistemological criteria used in normal academic historical Jesus work. Many historical Jesus scholars who doubt that Jesus is alive have in fact traveled the opposite direction, moving away from traditional Christian conviction. Some have done so as a result of rigid categories (so that rejecting parts of their earlier faith required rejecting the whole); others through accommodating dominant philosophic trends that made faith impossible; others because faith is often genuinely difficult (though, I think, all the more needed) in a world full of suffering; others for historiographic or other reasons. I can only recount my experience openly, as they are welcome to recount theirs, in the hope that we can dialogue further. Our experiences on both sides inform our presuppositions, for those inclined to skepticism as well as for those inclined to faith.

Concluding "Unscientific Postscript" to Appendix 8

Ending with an "unscientific postscript" runs the risk of having readers paint one's entire work and career as unscientific, especially for those who, scanning a conclusion, suppose they have reconstructed the primary theme of the entire book. (Distinguishing between the body of one's arguments and a concluding personal opinion is, however, why we normally reserve such material for a postscript.) For some readers, being able to pinpoint a scholar as Christian, Jewish, atheistic, or as holding some other view absolves the reader of the need to engage her or his arguments. Yet no scholar lacks personal perspectives, whether they are stated explicitly or not. I do not wish to conceal mine, as I believe that I came by them honestly (even if not in ways that would satisfy detractors), and as I believe that they motivate me to seek truth rigorously because I so esteem the subject matter.

But I also confine this discussion especially to this book's end-matter so as to keep the arguments in the main body of the book as rigorous and independent as possible. Some who will dismiss without consideration that research because they disapprove of my personal perspective have, if they would admit it, personal perspectives of their own.

I believe that there remains in some sectors of academia a prejudice against accepting claims about the reliability of many Gospel traditions, a prejudice that may sacrifice genuine objectivity for the sake of objectivity's appearance. Were the Gospels biographies of Greek or Roman religious figures, the prejudice against them would likely be less, but some assume that anything one tries to say about Jesus historically reflects a modern religious bias. I believe that I have highlighted sufficient evidence to show that there is plenty of historical information available about Jesus for those whose interest in studying him is purely historical, without religious considerations.

The concern about religious bias becomes most acute in the discussion of the resurrection, however. While the charge of bias might be leveled either way, that charge is often invoked before the evidence is even allowed to be weighed. Many explain the resurrection in terms of the disciples' visionary experiences; such experiences can be described without prejudice to their objective content.

But if evidence seems to support the historicity of a more objective event, some view the presentation of such evidence as tendentious support for the claim of one religion (especially when an "act of God" seems the most plausible and parsimonious among proposed explanations). Academicians sometimes thus are predisposed to reject such evidence in the name of religious neutrality (and sometimes, with less pretense of "neutrality," a hostility toward supernatural religion inherited from the most extreme phase of the Enlightenment).

If, however, our concern is with history rather than the religious use to which some may put it, we must ask first of all where the evidence points. At this point I will try to more explicitly separate the historical and theological questions, while at the same time showing where they bear on each other.

I have talked with a number of skeptics about Christian faith who, after extended conversation, admitted that their objections to the basic Gospel portrait stemmed from their concern that acknowledging more about Jesus historically would entail greater moral demands on their lives. This prejudice is not, however, the starting point of all skeptics, and was not my starting point when I was a skeptic. I was an atheist for what I felt were intellectually satisfying reasons; whether they were genuinely defensible reasons or not, they were not merely morally pragmatic ones. Because of my epistemological orientation at the time, I would have derided the intelligence of someone who rejected historical data out of moral convenience just as I derided most Christians (who I felt accepted their faith because of their upbringing or existential convenience).

I believe that, on historical grounds, an atheist could affirm most of the historical points we have established in this book. They are historical arguments, and I believe that most "neutral" observers would find them more convincing than not. As an atheist no less than subsequently as a Christian, I did desire to follow evidence, even if it crashed my own convenient philosophic system (which it ultimately did, especially the Neoplatonic part of it); I believe that I would have found arguments such as those in this book convincing.

When I was an atheist, however, my concerns were not the sorts of historical issues we have been addressing in this book. Admittedly, I believe that affirming the plausibility of the gospel narratives would have moved me to consider following Jesus in a much more significant way than I was then following various other thinkers (Greek philosophers and other sources). Yet at that point in my explorations, Jesus was an uncomfortable question I had deferred until later, and I knew Greek mythology far better than I knew biblical stories (I had read less than one chapter of the Bible — namely part of the first one, which from my cosmological standpoint revolted me). Although my primary objection to theism was that I thought that contemporary scientific philosophy could explain the universe without that hypothesis, my primary objection to Christianity in particular was that Christians did not seem to take it seriously. But because I esteemed truth as the highest value, I wanted to remain open-minded.

While one can believe many of the Gospel reports about Jesus without being a Christian, it seems to me more difficult to be a Christian while rejecting nearly all of the Gospel reports about Jesus. (Admittedly, this observation depends on how one defines "Christian." If one defines it broadly as "follower of Jesus," however, it is hard to follow the teachings and example of someone whose teachings and example remain virtually unknown.)

Historical Jesus research is a historical question; all researchers have biases, but academic dialogue allows us to challenge and probe one another's biases and seek some central, securely grounded information about Jesus. Because such conclusions usually include the minimum on which most parties can agree, they usually do not resolve (and often do not address) the questions involved in religious or spiritual quests for Jesus. The approaches and goals differ, and the limitations of historiographic methodology are not limitations that must be embraced by these latter quests. Nevertheless, if the latter quests mean anything that is distinctive with regard to the person of Jesus of Nazareth, they do invite some historical exploration.

Some scholars have argued that the "Jesus" we can reconstruct from history is irrelevant to faith;[22] others demur.[23] While the historical method does not give us a complete picture of Jesus, however, it does call to our attention some emphases in Jesus' message and ministry that we might otherwise have overlooked.[24] Because churches and cultures have too often remade Jesus in our own image, going back to the sources helps to keep us honest. While academic "Jesus research" does this in a different way than pure study of the Gospels (which mostly lacks the former discipline's intractable problem of lacunae in sources), both approaches can highlight important features of Jesus and challenge our biases.

Some Postresurrection Teachings

Historical Jesus books often stop short of discussing the resurrection, and are if anything even less likely to discuss the content of any teaching attributed to the resurrection appearances. Nevertheless, both Paul (1 Cor 15:5-8) and the Gospels (Matt 28:9-10, 16-20; Lk 24:15-51; Jn 20–21) discuss Jesus' resurrection appearances, and the Gospels multiply attest some of the content of his teachings at that time. (Scholars often describe these appearances in terms of the disciples' experiences rather than the nature of the resurrection. Since the point at issue in this particular appendix is the antiquity of the tradition rather than the nature of the resurrection, I leave the question of that approach to the reader's discretion, though I make my own suggestions elsewhere in this work.)

The Gospels differ substantially in detail regarding the precise content of resurrection appearances, differences that could be explained either by freer creation or by multiple sources (or a combination of the two options). In favor of the former option, Matthew and Luke, like many ancient writers, pull together some of their most important themes at the conclusion of their work, suggesting at the least some significant editorial work. In favor of the latter, 1 Cor 15:5-8 does claim a large number of witnesses (on one occasion over five hundred, 15:6). Whatever one's explanation or combination of explanations for the differences, however, some features remain common to both. Here I wish to survey two of these.

A Gentile Mission

Although there are at least hints of a Gentile mission in Jesus' Galilean teaching, two Gospels provide much more explicit teaching on this subject after the resurrection. Some of his earlier Galilean teachings apparently had even limited his mission and that of his followers to Israel, at least in the short run, even in one of the two narratives that note him reluctantly granting the request of a Gentile supplicant (Mk 7:27-29).[1] Even the prohibitive saying in Matt 10:5-6 is undoubtedly authentic: even those early Jewish Christians least inclined to cross ethnic barriers would probably not have invented such a mission saying for Jesus themselves, since Judaism did not oppose making proselytes[2] and sometimes envisioned an end-time ingathering of Gentiles (cf. e.g., Is 19:19-25; 56:3-8).[3] Further, the prohibition does fit a short-term mission during Jesus' ministry and its expectation of some sort of imminent kingdom.

Where then did the early Christian Gentile mission (more proactive than most early Jewish interest in securing proselytes) come from?[4] Early Judaism provides a plausible context for this mission without fully explaining its genesis. A range of Jewish views about Gentiles in the end time existed.[5] Among these views, Jesus' approach was probably among the more positive ones,[6] as we shall note below. But Judaism did not have a concerted *mission* to the Gentiles such as we find in Matthew's or Luke's commissions (or Paul's actual mission).[7] (Some scholars envision a concerted Jewish mission to the Gentiles;[8] they rightly recognize some Jews' interest in making proselytes, but the evidence does not support the sort of centralized effort that other scholars mean by a "missions" movement.)

Most other Jews were either (especially in the Diaspora) not as eschatologically oriented as Jesus' movement or (e.g., at Qumran) not as favorable toward Gentiles. But even if some had shared these characteristics, these beliefs by themselves need not have led directly to a "Gentile mission." The context may make the early Christian Gentile movement plausible, but no single factor in the context readily explains its genesis.

Jesus' Galilean Teachings

It is possible that Jesus' disciples learned about the gentile mission from Jesus before his execution, hearing at least hints that could later be understood as pointing in that direction during his preresurrection teaching. Among the range of his contemporaries' views regarding Gentiles in the end-time, Jesus' appears to have been fairly positive. He apparently believed that some Gentiles would be included in the kingdom, as surely as some of his own people would be excluded. This perspective may be hinted at when he compares Chorazin and Bethsaida unfavorably with Tyre and Sidon (Matt 11:21-22; Lk 10:13-14), which we have argued is authentic Jesus material.[9]

The Q material in Matt 8:11-12//Lk 13:28-29 probably points in the same direction.[10] Although there are differences between Matthew and Luke,[11] both imply that those from the east and west are Gentiles.[12] While Matthew and

Luke both want to validate the Gentile mission in any case, it is unlikely that the saying's contrast is merely between Judean and Diaspora Jews. Few would have expected Diaspora Jews to be excluded from the eschatological banquet with the patriarchs, or would find their inclusion unusual enough to merit mention.[13] This reading of the saying also coheres with one possible reading of Isaian eschatology: an eschatological ingathering, by conversion or submission,[14] combined with the expected "messianic banquet."[15] Among Jesus' teachings, it coheres with a radical, graphic extension of Jesus' principle of eschatological inversion; Gentiles offered a notable hortatory foil for his audiences,[16] comporting with his characteristic appeal to notably graphic illustrations. Among Jesus' practices, it coheres with his practice of table fellowship with outsiders even at the expense of alienating respected members of the religious establishment. Such attitudes on his part would more readily explain why his followers within a matter of decades began a Gentile mission on terms that quickly transcended those of other Jewish groups (e.g., Acts 11:20-21; 15:14-21).

Mark 13:10, in the context of genuine Jesus tradition about eschatology (as we note in ch. 17 and Appendix 4), indicates preaching among the Gentiles. Though the saying does not yet identify Jesus' followers as the agents, the context in Mk 13 certainly implies it (13:9-13). Certainly Isaiah's scheme of Israel's end-time relation to the nations could be approached in a variety of ways (and Acts portrays the early Christians as only gradually understanding even what the postresurrection Jesus meant).[17] Jesus' unusual openness to the Samaritans, suggested perhaps independently in John and Luke,[18] may well suggest that Jesus did have interest beyond Israel. It is probably not mere coincidence that the Gentile mission arose in a movement with a founder already unusually positive toward Samaritans (as well as one who was believed to have risen).

Movement Beyond These Sayings

Nevertheless, graphic statements about Gentiles in the end-time do not constitute a self-evident commission to reach the Gentiles, even if Jesus and his followers believed that the end was at hand. As we have noted, other eschatologically-oriented Jewish movements did not develop Gentile missions.

Something in the nature of Jesus' movement may better explain the genesis of the gentile mission. Jesus holding one view about many Gentiles in the end-time could be a factor, but this perspective was amplified by the movement's particular and rare view of the end-time: based on Jesus' teaching about the kingdom and the subsequent experience of the resurrection, some of Jesus' followers could undertake an end-time Gentile mission. Is it a coincidence that the same movement offered the remarkable claim of Jesus' resurrection (distinguishing him from other first-century figures whose messianic movements failed) and later experienced remarkable success in a new Gentile mission, or is there a plausible connection between the two? Part of the connection was probably the movement's dependence on what they believed was the divine Spirit, but was there anything further in Jesus' teaching that facilitated the gentile mission?

Postresurrection Teaching about a Gentile Mission

Whatever we may say of Jesus' preresurrection teaching, Matthew (Matt 28:19) and Luke (Lk 24:47-48; Acts 1:8) apparently independently (and later Mk 16:15, perhaps derivatively) specifically report a more explicit commissioning to the nations after Jesus' resurrection. John also includes a postresurrection commission, although not explicitly to the nations.[19] One might suppose that the Pauline movement simply inferred the gentile mission from the combination of factors noted above. But would this explain other sectors of early Christianity embracing the mission, and Matthew and Luke both attributing it to Jesus after the resurrection?

Rather than assuming that Paul originated the idea and all other parts of the Christian movement got the idea from him, tracing the idea in some form to the figure behind the movement more easily explains the range of evidence (e.g., Matthew is not very "Pauline"). Some doubt that the commission in the Gospels stems from the risen Jesus,[20] but others think that even Matthew's commission is authentic,[21] although most would view it as heavily edited to emphasize the focal themes of his Gospel.[22] Even if one were to view it as merely inference, it would be an inference that depended on Jesus' teaching and the experience of the resurrection.

One argument against Jesus teaching about the Gentile mission, whether before or after the resurrection, is that it seems difficult to explain why his immediate followers in Acts took so long to catch (or at least, to implement) this vision. Acts is not, however, unintelligible on its own terms. The disciples' slowness to implement the teaching may partly involve misunderstanding; at first reading Isaiah differently, perhaps they expected the Gentiles to stream into Jerusalem, where the apostles were establishing an alternate kingdom. Perhaps they thought that any further mission was best deferred until they had established firmer foundations in Jerusalem. We do not need to look far for analogies to diverse understandings of implementing the commission; much of the church through much of subsequent history (e.g., most Protestants in the two centuries immediately following the Reformation) has given little heed to a commission to the nations, yet no one can argue that the commission was largely unknown.

What none of our sources about Jesus' teaching on Gentiles provide is a Gentile mission conducted along the specific lines of the Pauline mission, i.e., without circumcision.[23] While some of Jesus' followers may have retroactively found hints in Jesus' teaching (cf. Mk 7:15, 19, for food laws), the Gospels are not able to report anything about embracing uncircumcised Gentiles, much as some of the writers may have wished to.[24] In Acts, Luke appeals to Scripture (Acts 15:15-18) but especially to apostolic revelation (9:15; 11:9, 12, 15-17; 15:7-10; 22:21) through the Spirit that Jesus sent. Even the Pauline mission differed from later Gentile Christianity;[25] we need not account for every detail of the church's subsequent development in Jesus' teaching. Nevertheless, it is likely that something Jesus taught disposed many of his followers in this direction.[26] Because he did not historically address particulars like circumcision, however, they became matters of significant debate in the decades that followed.

God's Spirit

Given that Jesus' followers preserved John's teaching about the eschatological outpouring of the Spirit; that they attributed their own pervasively charismatic activity to the eschatological experience of the Spirit; and that our earliest sources for Jesus include some attribution of his own activity to the Spirit (Mk 3:29-30; cf. Matt 12:28//Lk 11:20), it is likely that Jesus did promise his disciples the Spirit at some point.[27] This would follow his continuity with John's message, since Q portrays John announcing his successor baptizing in the Holy Spirit (Matt 3:11//Lk 3:16).

The promise of the Spirit appears, albeit in quite different ways, in Mk 13:11; Lk 24:49 (with Acts 1:4-8); and Jn 14:17, 26; 15:26; 16:13; 20:22. Both John and Luke, probably independently, place the promise both before and after the resurrection. In view of Luke (Acts 1:4-8) and John (Jn 20:21-22), and perhaps implicitly in the second-century addition to Mk 16 (Mk 16:17-18), it is reasonable to suppose that Jesus' postresurrection teaching about the disciples' mission included empowerment by the Spirit.

Thus some key elements of teaching attributed to the risen Jesus in the Gospels plausibly do derive from early traditions about what Jesus' disciples believed that he taught them after the resurrection.

Notes

Notes to the Preface

1. An old adage from a different context is applicable to scholars: where two scholars are gathered, one expects at least three opinions.

2. *A Commentary on the Gospel of Matthew* (Grand Rapids: Eerdmans, 1999), using over 10,000 extrabiblical references from ancient sources; *The Gospel of John: A Commentary* (Peabody: Hendrickson, 2003), using nearly 20,000 extrabiblical references from ancient sources.

3. This problem became most obvious to me when two friends wrote a very fine and well-informed historical Jesus book, yet despite expressing great appreciation for my research, drew on it very rarely. My arguments could have advanced theirs, but they focused almost exclusively on "historical Jesus" books, not commentaries. Unfortunately, as I myself have realized the vast breadth of publications and the difficulty of noting all of them (even in my Acts commentary, which cites over 10,000 works), I realize that I also have failed to find and cite all worthy sources.

4. See e.g., Keener, *Matthew*, 16-32; idem, *John*, 3-76 (though released in 2003, *John* was submitted in 1997 and merely updated afterward). In a small minority of cases, writers have even made the same arguments using precisely the same ancient references I had already cited, sometimes even obscure ones; I will avoid inferring too much from such instances though I have often observed a pattern of commentators recycling earlier commentators' sources without mentioning where they found them. In most cases, however, scholars' arguments give every indication of being independent; overlap is inevitable.

Notes to the Introduction

1. Theissen and Merz, *Historical Jesus*, 91; cf. Wright, "Dialogue," 246.

2. As most scholars recognize, e.g., Charlesworth and Evans, "Agrapha," 491; Dunn, *New Perspective*, 34; Ellis, "Gospels and History," 49; cf. Tuckett, "Sources and methods," 121; Wright, "Dialogue," 246; Frye, "Analogies in Literatures," 287-302 (esp. 302); De Rosa, "Vangeli."

3. I have made use of journal abstracts to increase the number of works I could at least mention, but even here come nowhere close to a comprehensive survey of the literature.

4. Likewise, Matthew omits Mark's overly sweeping summary of Jewish practice (cf. Mk 7:3-4), perhaps reflecting a common practice of Mark's Diaspora audience; even pious Jews may have washed their hands especially for Sabbath or festival meals (*m. Ber.* 8:1-2; *tos. Ber.* 5:25; Davies, *Matthew*, 112).

5. Ehrman, *Misquoting Jesus*, 151-75, addresses theologically motivated changes, especially due to

second- and third-century christological debates; while emphasizing changes, he recognizes that the copying process was mostly conservative (177-78). He addresses changes due to social worlds in 178-205 (e.g., regarding women, 178-86; anti-Jewish passages, 186-95). Most scholars will agree with the information here.

6. Evans, *Fabricating Jesus*, 27-31. On 30 Evans offers the example of Ehrman noting that some later scribes delete "nor the Son" in Matt 24:36 for Christological reasons; Ehrman's observation is of course correct, but "nor the Son" remains unchanged in Mk 13:32. To make such changes problematic for all knowledge of early Christianity more generally may constitute what one of my doctoral professors called a "fundamentalistic," all-or-nothing approach. Copyist changes pose few theological problems except to strict literalist Christians who hold a more typically Islamic view of inspiration. Thus whereas the Qur'an appears to have been standardized early (e.g., Peters, *Origins*, 257), thereafter copied in noble courts, the earliest Christian manuscripts had more royal persecutors than sponsors, and were copied under much freer conditions. Yet such factors trouble most Christians far less than they would trouble many Muslims, due to different understandings of inspiration. Most Christians do not "recite" the New Testament, and their theology generally focuses on the substance rather than details of the texts.

7. Egyptian Judaism was decimated in the Judeophobic conflicts of the early second century; while this state would not preclude some Jews from resettling there, the vast majority of later Christian scribes there would surely have been Gentiles.

8. Nevertheless, this is not the sort of work designed primarily to defuse the nonsense of works like *The DaVinci Code*. I did address this book on a popular level in "Decoding Da Vinci," but I am hoping that most readers of the present book will be able to distinguish between scholarly research and an intriguing but historically fanciful novel. See also Ehrman, *Fiction*.

9. See e.g., the following bibliographies: Evans, *Jesus*; idem, *Life of Jesus Research*; Mills, *Christ and Gospels*.

10. Keener, *John*, 3-139, 289-91, 296-97, 300-7; very briefly, idem, "Genre." See also many others, e.g., Bauckham, *Testimony*; Blomberg, *Reliability*; Vellanickal, "Historical Jesus"; Segalla, "Gesù di Nazaret"; Moloney, "Jesus of History"; works by my doctoral mentor, D. Moody Smith (including Smith, *Johannine Christianity*; idem, *John Among Gospels*; idem, "Problem of History").

11. Interestingly, one of the early objections to John that led to its frequent current exclusion from consideration was its "Greek" ambiance (Harnack, *Christianity*, 21; Schweitzer, *Quest*, 6) — a presupposition no longer often accepted in Johannine scholarship (Brown, *Essays*, 188-90; Charlesworth, "Scrolls and Gospel"; Longenecker, *Christology*, 19-20, 76; Martyn, "Religionsgeschichte"; Davies, "Aspects"; Scroggs, "Judaizing"; Flusser, *Judaism*, 23-24; Keener, *John*, 142-232, esp. 171-232).

12. E.g., Meier, *Marginal Jew*, 1:21-31.

13. With McClymond, *Stranger*, xi; similarly, Meier, *Marginal Jew*, 1:21-31.

14. That is, a historian, as historian, is not intrinsically opposed to a particular community's beliefs about past events, so long as those beliefs are not simply assumed to be identical with past events. Likewise, historical reconstructions are partial and rest on probability, and cannot easily be substituted for a community's beliefs, since the overlap is not likely to be coextensive. Extant historical evidence about events two thousand years ago is too limited to "prove" or "disprove," even to a high degree of satisfaction, every purported event or saying of ancient history, including in the Gospels. Although a historical purist would object on epistemological grounds, some (Evans, "Naturalism," esp. 205) also advocate appeal to other lines of evidence (including theological evidence) in addition to historical evidence. McClymond, *Stranger*, x, emphasizes the compatibility between faith and history (despite their different approaches).

15. Theissen and Merz, *Historical Jesus*, vii.

16. Charlesworth, "Jesus, Literature and Archaeology," 178.

17. Meier, *Marginal Jew*, 1:21-31.

18. See the fuller argument in Keener, *John*, 185-94; also see Safrai, "Literature"; Silberman,

"Use"; Vermes, *Religion,* 8-9; Neusner, *New Testament,* ix; for similar methodological observations, e.g., Levinskaya, *Diaspora Setting,* 16-17. Archaeology often provides earlier attestation of some customs attested later in rabbinic sources (see e.g., Sanders, *Jesus to Mishnah,* 243; Avigad, *Jerusalem,* 171). Parallels to rabbinic sources also exist (pace some of these authors, merely reflecting "common Judaism") in Josephus (see e.g., Goldenberg, "Halakha"; Goldenberg, "*Antiquities* iv"); Philo (Belkin, *Philo,* passim); Qumran (Schiffman, *Law;* idem, "Light"; Mantel, "Oral Law"; cf. Vermes, *Jesus and Judaism,* 100-14; Adler, "Sectarian Characteristics"); haggadic traditions in *L.A.B.* (Feldman, "Antiquities"); and of course in the New Testament (de Jonge, "New Testament," 40-41). Because later rabbis would not have cited Jesus, I argue in these cases, as classicists normally argue with regard to the chance sources that have survived in their discipline, that the alignment of data suggests early ideas or customs that happen to be attested in both places. David Instone-Brewer's work on rabbinic tradition (Instone-Brewer, *Traditions*), following Jacob Neusner's most refined methodology, seems likely to prove most helpful. Most historical Jesus scholars allow rabbinic sources into the discussion, even if they do not use them as extensively (see e.g., the index in Crossan, *Historical Jesus,* 495, citing 11 references from Tannaitic sources and 12 from later Amoraic ones). Some apply them more extensively (e.g., Chilton even makes significant use of later Targumic traditions).

Notes to Section I

1. Schweitzer, *Quest,* 398.
2. Crossan, *Historical Jesus,* xxviii.
3. For some 15,000 sources, see Mills, *Christ and Gospels.*
4. Briefly, see e.g., Gnilka, *Jesus of Nazareth,* 1-12; Wright, *Who Was Jesus?* 1-18; Bockmuehl, *Jesus,* 2-8; Herzog, *Jesus,* 4-33; McClymond, *Stranger,* 7-25; Pikaza, "Jesús histórico"; Moyise, "Jesus and gospels"; Gisel, "Jésus historique"; Marsh, "Quests"; Boccaccini, "Gesù" (for the history in Italy); more extensively, e.g., Wright, *Quest;* Thompson, *Debate.* For articles treating several works, Webb, "Books"; Bond, "Portraits"; Clark, "Search" (on three works); Radermakers, "Goût"; surveying some books summarizing the debate, Goodacre, "Quest." For summaries of the first quest, see Theissen and Merz, *Historical Jesus,* 2-5; Levine, "Introduction," 5-6; more extensively, Schweitzer, *Quest;* Dawes, *Quest;* Paget, "Quests," 138-45; for Victorian "lives," Pals, *Lives;* for the first half of the twentieth century, Weaver, *Historical Jesus;* the second quest, Anderson, *Jesus and Origins,* 149-84; for the first and second quests, Thompson, *Debate,* 90-111. For the third quest, see Borg, *Jesus in Scholarship,* 18-43; Telford, "Trends"; Witherington, *Quest;* Kealy, "Quest"; Powell, *Jesus in History;* Freyne, "Search"; Evans, "Quest"; Herzog, *Jesus,* 18-33; Bird, "Quest"; briefly, Paget, "Quests," 147-48; Theissen and Merz, *Historical Jesus,* 10-11. (I am employing the common language of three quests as a designation of convenience, but it is not strictly accurate; see Weaver, "Introduction," 2; Paget, "Quests," 146.) Although often not considered in the discussions, Heyer, *Jesus Matters,* 73-93, helpfully notes Jewish works about Jesus.
5. Crossan, *Historical Jesus,* xxvii-xxviii, puts the matter quite well (cf. similarly Meier, *Marginal Jew,* 1:3), but then proposes a methodology to circumvent the impasse (pp. xxviii-xxix) that in my opinion fails for lack of adequate attention to the Jewish and, despite his claim, Greco-Roman context.
6. Since Schweitzer, *Quest,* scholars have periodically remarked on how frequently presuppositions shape one's conclusions in Jesus research (e.g., Stanton, *Gospel Truth,* 145).
7. As scholars sometimes observe (e.g., Neufeld, *Recovering Jesus,* 16-18, esp. 18; cf. the integration of major elements in Pikaza, "Jesús histórico").

Notes to Chapter 1

1. Crossan, *Historical Jesus,* xxvii.

2. Though some scholars cite "consensus" by ignoring other scholars; cf. the warning in Poirier, "Consensus," that scholars too often use "consensus" as a rhetorical substitute for an argument.

3. On the Nazi portrait of Jesus as non-Jewish and Aryan, see Head, "Nazi Quest"; Poewe, *Religions and Nazis*; Theissen and Merz, *Historical Jesus*, 163.

4. On whom see e.g., Paget, "Quests," 141.

5. On Schweitzer, *Quest*, see Weaver, *Historical Jesus*, 25-44; more briefly, Heyer, *Jesus Matters*, 33-39; Anderson, *Jesus and Origins*, 18-22; Theissen and Merz, *Historical Jesus*, 5-7; Herzog, *Jesus*, 4-8.

6. On Reimarus, see Schweitzer, *Quest*, 14-26; Heyer, *Jesus Matters*, 21-23; Mullin, *History*, 167; Brown, *Miracles*, 107-10.

7. Charlesworth, "Adumbrations," x (noting Matthew Tindal, 1655-1733). Earlier, cf. John Lightfoot, writing in the 1600s (reprinted as Lightfoot, *Talmud*).

8. Schweitzer, *Quest*, 39-44.

9. Schweitzer, *Quest*, 44-45.

10. For the "rational" phase, see especially Schweitzer, *Quest*, 27-67. Schweitzer thinks that Strauss (68-95) went too far; he also notes how others, like Bruno Bauer, out of his hatred for theologians, ended up unable to grapple with the history of Jesus at all (157). On Strauss, see further Heyer, *Jesus Matters*, 24-25; Paget, "Quests," 143; Rössler, "Mensch."

11. Schweitzer, *Quest*, e.g., 66-67.

12. Schweizer, *Quest*, 191. For Romantics like Renan (treated in *Quest*, 180-92), the thrill of recognition identified authenticity. On the "liberal lives," see further Heyer, *Jesus Matters*, 25-32; Theissen and Merz, *Historical Jesus*, 5; Paget, "Quests," 143-45. Some have observed that the tendency to read all literary works on the analogy of (modern) novels stems from the Romantic period (Malina and Pilch, *Acts*, 3-5).

13. Schweitzer, *Quest*, 326: "They have scarcely altered since Venturini's time, except that some of the cures performed by Jesus" are now treated through modern research on "hypnotism and suggestion."

14. Although Harnack recognized the distinction between apologetics and historical inquiry, he objected to the former primarily because it defended something less than the true faith (*Christianity*, 7).

15. *Christianity*, 149-50, 158. In keeping with his era's values, he emphasizes spiritual devotion (259) and morally active religion (308).

16. *Christianity*, 282. His belief that early Christians expected a higher form of Christianity to emerge (11) assumes that his own brand fits that expectation. He was less optimistic about the spirit of Eastern Orthodoxy (e.g., 244) and certainly Roman Catholicism (e.g., 263, 267).

17. Though following Luther's own approach of effectively finding a canon within the canon (*Christianity*, 292; cf. Poland, *Criticism*, 19-20), Harnack does not seem to mind that Luther would not have accepted his ready reduction of the essential gospel (*Christianity*, 14-15) to ethics (70).

18. *Christianity*, 56.

19. E.g., *Christianity*, 127.

20. E.g., *Christianity*, 139. Harnack recognized the limits of the historical method (*Christianity*, 18), and historical method was admittedly not his primary focus in this work.

21. *Christianity*, 21, thus preferring the Synoptics to John (though scholars today, who also usually prefer the Synoptics at most points, usually view John as one of the most Jewish Gospels; e.g., Smith, "Learned," 218-22; Charlesworth, "Scrolls and Gospel"; idem, "Reinterpreting"; Martyn, "Religionsgeschichte"; Davies, "Aspects"; Braine, "Jewishness"; Flusser, *Judaism*, 23-24).

22. *Christianity*, 201. He allows that Jesus preserved positive aspects of Jewish thought in his teaching (*Christianity*, 47-48).

23. *Christianity*, 16, 176.

24. *Christianity*, 162.

25. *Christianity*, 160.

26. *Christianity,* 12.

27. *Christianity,* 240.

28. See e.g., *Christianity,* 55, 114, 127.

29. For some observations regarding anti-Jewish perspectives in Harnack's work, see Cohen, "Mission and Expansion."

30. Heyer, *Jesus Matters,* 45-47, noting that others now emphasized Jesus as a model of sacrifice. Barth's neoorthodoxy flourished on the same sort of soil that undercut liberalism.

31. Sometimes not as devastating as it could have been. Thus he notes that Reimarus treated his own view as the only one possible (Schweitzer, *Quest,* 19-20); offered a reconstruction contradicting most sources (20-21); had disciples dying for a lie (21); and so forth, yet charitably finds Reimarus' "sole mistake" as political eschatology. Despite Venturini's naïve acceptance of a providentially exorbitant proportion of coincidences in Jesus' life and unwarranted confidence in the power of ancient physicians, Schweitzer is loath to quickly condemn this approach (57).

32. *Von Reimarus zu Wrede: Eine Geschichte der Leben-Jesu-Forschung,* translated (and referred to here) as *Quest.* He distrusts psychologizing exegesis (*Quest,* 311, 400); totemizing Jesus to represent modern values (312, 329); and faulty lines of reasoning about Jesus' claims (342; but cf. 259).

33. Any one missing Jesus' apocalyptic thinking might be at best a brilliant digression from evolutionary progress toward the modern (i.e., Schweitzer's) view (135). He places his own work in historical context so that it can better guide contemporary theology (159; cf. 182), and repeatedly laments the lack of tolerance historically accorded new ideas (e.g., 166-67). Nevertheless, he regards his own writing as scientific rather than popular (191). He regards his historical "either-or's" (e.g., 238) as signs of progress, but forced-choice logic often leads to erroneous conclusions.

34. See the critique in Wink, "Write," 9; from a different perspective, Fiorenza, *Politics;* Marsh, "Quests."

35. Even Weiss, while recognizing some of Jesus' radical demands (*Proclamation,* 107-8), reapplied kingdom imagery (131-32) for a noneschatological society (135; but cf. 136)

36. He incorporated critical conclusions from his era's scholarship into his methodology, although not always consistently; he respected the Markan hypothesis and Q (*Proclamation,* 60) and avoided arguing from the Fourth Gospel (60, 64; but cf. 95-96). While regarding Matthew as late and too catholic (60), thus excluding evidence from Matt 13 (p. 61) and 25 (p. 62), he often uses M or L material as if they were as reliable as Mark (e.g., 72-73, 105). He treats Paul as *later* than Mark's tradition (88), but wrote when Paul was considered less genuinely Jewish, and Mark less genuinely creative, than is now usually believed.

37. Especially in his work's first edition, he reacted against Albrecht Ritschl's liberal theology that essentially identified God's kingdom with the church; cf. e.g., *Proclamation,* 68-69.

38. In Daniel and *1 Enoch, Proclamation,* 116. In Weiss's thinking, Jesus expected to *become* the Son of man, but only God could intervene to bring the kingdom (82-83).

39. *Proclamation,* 85.

40. *Proclamation,* 91.

41. He does occasionally concede the force of both elements of the tradition (*Proclamation,* 67, 73, 74). Moreover, while he denies that there are phases to the kingdom (it is either here or not here, 73), he admits the presence of the kingdom in the breaking of Satan's power (76-79). The parables of Mk 4 and other early tradition invite more respect for the presence of the kingdom in Jesus' teaching than Weiss allows.

42. For example, the kingdom is only "near so as to be touching" in Matt 12:28 (*Proclamation,* 66); other language is merely hypothetical (71).

43. *Proclamation,* 69. He also contends that repentance as a prerequisite for the kingdom (the corresponding lack of which could delay the kingdom) was a later development in Jesus' thought (*Proclamation,* 86), though that view appears commonly enough in ancient Jewish sources (cf. *Jub.* 23:26-27; *Test. Dan.* 6:4; *Sipre Deut.* 43.16.3; *p. Taan.* 1:1, §7; possibly *Test. Mos.* 1:18).

44. *Proclamation,* 128. Weiss believed that the title of Messiah was to be given to Jesus after his exaltation, not during his earthly ministry (121).

45. *Proclamation,* 115.

46. E.g., Sir 23:1; Wisd 2:16; 3 Macc 5:7; 6:8; 7:6; *m. Sot.* 9:15; *tos. Ber.* 3:14; *B.K.* 7:6; *Hag.* 2:1; *Peah* 4:21; *Sipra Qed.* pq. 9.207.2.13; *Behuq.* pq. 8.269.2.15; *Sipre Deut.* 352.1.2.

47. He accepted Mark's temporal priority (87-88). He rejected the use of John alongside the Synoptics (125, 324-25), though partly because it was "written from the Greek standpoint" (6; cf. 35), an assertion with which most Johannine scholars today would take issue, as we have noted.

48. He objected to the extreme conclusions some drew from Markan priority; took the Matthean redaction context of Mk 13 material as original (361); and leaned heavily on an M saying (Matt 10:23; 360) — though scholars today do not follow his approach to Matt 10 (see Heyer, *Jesus Matters,* 48). His criticism of Wrede's "literary" approach (Schweitzer, *Quest,* 331) was short-sighted and deprived him of a valuable ally; Schweitzer viewed the Gospels not as literary works (6) but as gathering disjointed traditions (47, 394; this was an unfortunate "either-or"). He rightly demands observations grounded in the text (353), though his observations are sometimes not (e.g., that at one stage Jesus expects his tribulation to replace that of the disciples, 389).

49. *Quest,* 34.

50. *Quest,* 387. He thinks that Jesus probably did draw on Daniel for the "Son of man," consistent with the later Similitudes (282).

51. *Quest,* 223. He could not recognize apocalyptic and "legalistic" perspectives coexisting (*Quest,* 290); he lacks firsthand acquaintance with rabbinic (367) and other ancient Jewish sources. He does at least recognize some diversity in ancient Judaism, placing both Jesus and John in that context (368); but some of his ideas about Messiahship (e.g., 375) rest on fragmentary evidence, some of which may derive from Christian interpolations. He rightly recognizes Jesus' use of Aramaic (277), but could not anticipate later evidence that Jesus probably also was conversant in Greek.

52. Dunn, *Jesus and Spirit,* 41.

53. Schweitzer, *Quest,* praises Jesus, yet assumes that he erred even concerning his mission (2, 401). (Further on Schweitzer's view of Jesus as a tragic failure, see Heyer, *Jesus Matters,* 33-39. Perhaps Norse mythology and Friedrich Nietzsche helped pave the way for such a tragic hero image; cf. Vidler, *Revolution,* 197.) His solution of an ahistorical faith (Schweitzer, *Quest,* 399) not grounded in Jesus' own message is not consistent with any known representative of the apostolic church, whose early witness to Jesus is all we really have historically.

54. Schweizer, *Quest,* 398-403.

55. Cf. e.g., Silberman, "Apocalyptic Revisited," especially 497-501.

56. Cf. Thompson, *Debate,* 95; Thurman, *Disinherited,* 20-27.

57. Herzog, *Jesus,* 8-12 (covering 1906 to 1953); cf. Kähler, "Movement." Cf. Barth's move away from historicism (Anderson, *Jesus and Origins,* 22-24). This skepticism about biographies of Jesus did not silence the interest of British form critics in this period concerning Jesus' teaching.

58. On Bultmann's approach, see also Anderson, *Jesus and Origins,* 24-48; Heyer, *Jesus Matters,* 52-61; Weaver, *Historical Jesus,* 103-8.

59. For the two-source theory and authorial redaction, see *Theology,* 3.

60. For "Q," see e.g., *Word,* 27, 34, 40, 44-45, 96; for Mark, *Word,* 28, 31, 34, 36, 39, 44, 75-76, 78, 97, 109, 114; for "L," see *Word,* 28, 31, 33, 40, 45, 50, 53-54, 59-60, 73; for "M," see *Word,* 31, 44, 74, 89-90, 94-95. He rejects, however, John as a source for Jesus' teaching (*Word,* 12), and passages like Matt 16:17-19 (*Theology,* 10).

61. He recognized the limitations of the historical method for theology (Thiselton, *Horizons,* 247).

62. For Bultmann's opposition to Nazism, see Perrin, *Bultmann,* 16.

63. Bultmann reasonably portrays the kingdom and repentance in terms of decision (*Entweder-Oder; Word,* 31, 47; *Theology,* 9), but so demythologizes its eschatological value (*Word,* 35; *Theology,*

22-23) that it would have been unrecognizable to the earliest Jesus movement. He recognizes that Jesus understood it eschatologically (*Word*, 38) and that eschatology should not be reinterpreted (*Word*, 122), but appears to change the message more than he thinks. The "future" is now Heidegger's "authentic possibility of being" ("Man and Faith," 96-97); the present is eschatologically significant ("Between Times," 250-51, arguing that this transition occurred within the NT). He doubts that the imminent end plays any part in Jesus' ethics or opposition to legalism (*Word*, 129); the evangelists certainly would not have concurred (Mk 12:38-44 with Mk 13; Matt 23 with Matt 24-25; Matt 4:17 with 5:3-10, 22-26, 29-30; 6:1, 4-6, 14-16, 18-21; 7:1-2, 13-14, 19, 21-27).

64. Schweitzer himself had laid the groundwork for this approach by finding a "mysticism" involving Jesus' "spirit" more relevant for religion proper than historical research was (see James M. Robinson, "Introduction," xi-xxxiii in Schweitzer, *Quest*, xxv).

65. Bultmann's presuppositions were especially existential (*Word*, 11; cf. 31 n. 1) and anthropocentric ("Man and Faith," 92; "Mythology," 5, 9; *Word*, 55; cf. Jesus' God as something within humanity, *Word*, 102-3). Sometimes his understanding of "logical consistency" (*Word*, 156) simply reflects his modern worldview.

66. The greatest influence on his thought is the early Heidegger (Perrin, *Bultmann*, 15; Hasel, *Theology*, 85), who Bultmann thought discovered a picture according with what Bultmann found in the NT ("Mythology," 23-25; Thiselton, *Horizons*, 178-79, 226, 232, 262). He saw existential understanding not as a bias but a necessary perspective, like any other approach to history (Bultmann, "Exegesis," 149; cf. e.g., *Word*, 11; in contrast to Thielicke, who warns about corruption of the Bible by secular philosophy, in Thiselton, *Horizons*, 3). Old liberalism (despite Bultmann, "Mythology," 12-13; Poland, *Criticism*, 26-27, 29) and his logical extension of Lutheranism ("Mythology," 25; Thiselton, *Horizons*, 178-79, 205-26; cf. Poland, *Criticism*, 19-20) also influenced him; for influences from earlier NT scholarship (D. F. Strauss, J. Weiss, W. Bousset) and his approach to miracles as "mythology," see Twelftree, *Miracle Worker*, 33-37.

67. We will address Bultmann's form-critical methods more fully in our treatment of form criticism. The problem was less with some of Bultmann's methods (though Sanders, *Tendencies*, shows abundant problems there) than with his presuppositions about the nature of history.

68. "Mythology," 17-20, 38-39; "Between Times," 250-51.

69. Cf. Thiselton, *Horizons*, 274, 290.

70. The Aryan ideologues of the Reich Church pursued "relevance" in a very different direction, accommodating to some degree the non-Christian Aryan ideologues of the era; certainly they sought to de-Judaize Christianity (see Poewe, *Religions and Nazis*). Schweitzer himself was ready to praise the unique "German temperament" (*Quest*, 1), but without creating an Aryan Jesus (a thesis that he rejects on 329). Most North Americans are aware of how many contemporary churches, both conservative and liberal, selectively interpret and apply Jesus to make him "relevant" for their own contexts.

71. Borg, *Conflict*, 13-14.

72. One that Thiselton attributes to his Neo-Kantian roots (Thiselton, *Horizons*, 260-61).

73. Bultmann, *Word*, 13-14.

74. Certainly he excluded anything he thought "can have originated only" in Hellenistic Christianity (*Word*, 13), though in practice I believe that he defined "can" too broadly and ignored "only." He believes that Jesus usually radicalizes rather than looses the law (*Word*, 84); he regards baptism as adapting a Jewish practice (*Theology*, 39). He even observes Jesus' continuity with Judaism regarding Scripture (*Word*, 61-64) and the need for forgiveness (*Word*, 199).

75. E.g., despite acknowledging parallels between Jesus' prayers and those of the rest of Judaism (*Word*, 181-82), Bultmann tries too hard to distance the two.

76. *Word*, 76.

77. *Word*, 89-90, 92.

78. He is fairly accurate on Jewish eschatology, gathered from non-rabbinic sources (*Word*, 18-22); he recognizes Jesus' rabbinic-type context (*Word*, 57-61) and Judaism's love doctrine (*Word*, 110-

12), and is sometimes careful to employ early material (*Theology*, 14). Bultmann essentially agrees with Judaism in assigning evil to the will and not to creation (*Word*, 49, 102, 210).

79. He relies on misinterpretations of evidence (e.g., *Theology*, 47); archaeology has challenged Judaism's alleged lack of "art" (*Word*, 16), and the later rabbinic movement developed one of the most sophisticated systems of jurisprudence in antiquity (with Cohen, *Law*; against *Word*, 16).

80. He portrays the law as artificial and irrelevant (*Word*, 17), ignoring Jewish interpretation designed to make it relevant. Although correctly noting nonlegalistic elements in Jewish tradition (*Word*, 69-72), he proceeds to ignore them (esp. *Word*, 67-69, 92). While pride in good works (*Word*, 70) may have been arguably more common in Judaism than Sanders allows (see e.g., Gathercole, *Boasting*), it is a more generic human problem. His view of non-scribes as sinners (*Word*, 82) is exaggerated, as are implications of Jewish asceticism (cf. *Word*, 100; contrast Abrahams, *Studies* 1:12).

81. Anderson, *Jesus and Origins*, 47-52. For critiques of the Gnostic redeemer myth's relevance for this period, see e.g., Drane, "Background," 123; cf. Wilson, *Gnostic Problem*, 226; Yamauchi, *Gnosticism*, 70; Goppelt, *Theology*, 2:49; idem, *Judaism*, 174-75; Martin, *Carmen Christi*, 126-28; Keener, *John*, 169.

82. As Crossan puts it, lamenting the diversity of views before offering his own, "It is impossible to avoid the suspicion that historical Jesus research is a very safe place to do theology and call it history, to do autobiography and call it biography" (Crossan, *Historical Jesus*, xxviii).

83. See e.g., Theissen and Merz, *Historical Jesus*, 7-8; Heyer, *Jesus Matters*, 61-72 (including 66-69 on Käsemann and 69-70 on Bornkamm); Herzog, *Jesus*, 12-18. Although descriptions of the "second quest" often omit Jeremias, he played an important role (see Heyer, *Jesus Matters*, 63-66).

84. The division into three "quests" is not, strictly speaking, historically accurate, since it reads all of Jesus research through the prism of particular lines of German scholarship (meanwhile ignoring even some of German scholarship); see Weaver, "Introduction," 2 (citing, more extensively, his *Historical Jesus in the Twentieth Century*); Levine, "Introduction," 6-7; Paget, "Quests," 146; Bird, "Quest"; Claussen, "Historischen Jesus" (exploring whether today's more optimistic "quest" may even be a fourth one). We employ the terminology because it is recognizable.

85. Brandon, *Zealots* (1967).

86. Schweitzer, *Quest*, 17.

87. *Ant.* 18.117-19.

88. E.g., Brandon, *Zealots*, 283. For the history of the revolutionary thesis, see Bammel, "Revolution theory," 11-68. For critiques of such views, see e.g., Cullmann, *State*, 8-49; Hengel, "Revolutionär"; idem, *Zeloten*; Sweet, "Zealots"; Anderson, *Mark*, 41-42; some even contend that the charge of sorcery was a greater issue (on a popular level) than that of revolutionary (Horbury, "Brigand," 183-95). Note also Stanton, *Gospel Truth*, 176 (Q's "love your enemies" is probably authentic). Sanders, *Jesus and Judaism*, 68 regards Brandon as adequately refuted; see his own case on pp. 231-32.

89. Cf. Harvey, *History*, 14-15.

90. Greek and Roman sources (surveyed in Voorst, *Jesus Outside NT*, 19-74) most essentially view Jesus as "a *troublemaker*. He founded and led a superstitious and possibly seditious movement" (74). Charlesworth, *Jesus Within Judaism*, 98, understands Josephus as categorizing Jesus thus: "He was a rebellious person and disturber of the elusive peace; but he was also a wise person who performed 'surprising,' perhaps even wonderful, works, and was followed by many Jews and Gentiles."

91. Thus e.g., Segundo, *Historical Jesus*, 86-103, views the "kingdom" as political and related to the poor.

92. For the political setting of Jesus, note some essays in Stegemann, Malina and Theissen, *Setting of Jesus*; for views regarding Jesus' "political" activity, see e.g., Horsley, "Death," 405-8 (but warning against viewing this in relation to "Zealots," 416, 418-19); Herzog, *Jesus*; Hendricks, *Politics*. For political applications, cf. e.g., Toren, "Significance"; Hauerwas, "Have to Die." Some others think the political dimension of Jesus' teaching not prominent (Broer, "Death," 163); some view it in terms of apocalyptic passive resistance (Segal, "Revolutionary," 211-12).

93. E.g., Josephus increases the prominence of Elisha (whom he associates with political agendas; Höffken, "Elischa"). See further discussion in ch. 8 on agendas in ancient historiography.

94. Sanders, *Figure*, 262.

95. *1 En.* 90:28-29; 11QTemple 29.8-10.

96. 1QM; *Ps. Sol.* 17:33-34.

97. Horsley and Hanson, *Bandits*, 69-76 (esp. 74-75); cf. also Sampathkumar, "Bandits." For a clear ancient case of urban exploitation of the countryside, and consequent revolt, see e.g., Polyb. 1.72.1-2.

98. See Horsley and Hanson, *Bandits*, 77-85; cf. Freyne, *Galilee*, 148.

99. See Horsley, *Spiral*, 319-21, who plausibly infers from this that Jesus was involved in social revolution (though not political violence; 323-26), including challenging the priestly elite (325).

100. Scholars debate which lines of Jos. *Ant.* 18.63-64 are authentic (although there is now wide agreement on most of them), but none of them sound like the false prophets Josephus condemns.

101. Moreover, the authorities' failure to crush Jesus' movement immediately and decisively at its inception (cf. Acts 4:21; 5:40; mercies not likely to have been simply invented by Luke) reinforces the picture in Josephus that makes Jesus' movement appear different from that of Theudas.

102. See also Borg, *Vision*, 137-40; Horsley, *Spiral*, 318-19.

103. Q material in Matt 10:34//Lk 12:51, but applied in Q to family divisions; special Lukan material in Lk 22:36. The saying in Matt 11:12//Lk 16:16 is difficult, especially given its different forms; it might refer to parabolic, *spiritual* "zealots" (as opposed to literal violent ones; Keener, *Matthew*, 339-40; cf. perspectives in Vermes, *Religion*, 140; Papone, "Violenza"; Häfner, "Basileia"), but the matter is disputed.

104. See 1QS 10.17-20; CD 9.3-6; *Let. Aris.* 227; *L.A.B.* 8:10; *Jos. Asen.* 23:9; 29:3; *2 En.* 50:4; *Sipra Qed.* pq. 4.200.3.4-5; *Ex. Rab.* 26:2; Plato *Crito* 49BD; Seneca *Dial.* 3.6.5; 4.32.1; Mus. Ruf. 10, pp. 76.18–78.28; frg. 39, p. 136.10-16; frg. 41, p. 136; Suetonius *Vesp.* 14; Phaedrus 1.29.10-11; Plutarch *Aristides* 25.7; Max. Tyre *Or.* 12 (e.g., 12.9); Hierocles *On Duties. On Fraternal Love* 4.27.20; Marc. Aur. 6.6; Iamblichus *Pyth. Life* 10.51; Fitzgerald, *Cracks*, 103-5; cf. Diog. Laert. 7.1.123; Ps.-Phoc. 77; *Test. Benj.* ch. 5; later among Christians, *Acts of Peter* (8) 28; *Acts of John* 81. Some limited the principle only to Israel (*Sipra Qed.* pq. 4.200.3.6; cf. Stendahl, "Hate").

105. I do not here enter the argument over whether these are personal (cf. Neil, "Sayings," 160-62; Horsley, "Love"; idem, *Spiral*, 318; Freyne, *Galilee*, 154) or corporate (cf. Borg, *Vision*, 139; Vermes, *Religion*, 157) oppressors; they are at least the former, but probably (in view of lack of distinction) both (Moulder, "Enemies"; for a survey of views, see Luz, *Matthew*, 457-59).

106. Jer 26:11, 23; 1 Kgs 18:4; 19:10; 2 Chron 36:15-16; Neh 9:26.

107. See Michel, *Prophet und Märtyrer*; Schoeps, "Prophetenmorde"; Hare, *Persecution*, 137-38; Jeremias, *Theology*, 280; Amaru, "Killing"; also Davies and Allison, *Matthew*, 1:465, citing e.g., *Lives of Prophets* passim (such as 2:1, Schermann 25 p. 81; 6:1, Schermann 17 p. 60; 7:1-2, Schermann 14 p. 51); *Jub.* 1:12; 4QpHos a 2.3-6; Jos. *Ant.* 10.38; *Asc. Isa.* 2.16; 5.1-14; *Tg.* on Is. 28:1; also *4 Bar.* 9:31; *Pesiq. Rab.* 26:1/2.

108. "Put away your sword" appears in both. Borg, *Conflict*, 195, plausibly draws attention to a parallel to the second line of Matthew's saying in Rev 13:10.

109. Craigie, *War*, 32; cf. Borg, *Conflict*, 195-99.

Notes to Chapter 2

1. Crossan, *Historical Jesus*, 421.

2. Mack, *Myth*, 68. He offers further Cynic comparisons on 67-69 (though not identifying Jesus' teaching completely with "a Greek philosophical ethic," he believes such influence was natural "at the end of the Hellenistic age" (69). Cf. also *Lost Gospel*, 203: ". . . its nearest analogy in contemporary pro-

files of the Cynic-sage. This is as close to the historical Jesus as Q allows us to get, but it is close enough for us to reconstruct a beginning of the movement that is both plausible and understandable."

3. Meier, *Marginal Jew,* 3:3. I should note that Funk has offered serious scholarship; it is his output associated with the Jesus Seminar to which Meier objects here.

4. As Allison, *Jesus of Nazareth,* 75, aptly calls it. For a view from within the Seminar, also responding to criticisms, see Miller, *Jesus Seminar.* While most view the Jesus Seminar as the more skeptical fringe of Jesus scholarship, there are some even more skeptical voices who view the Seminar as too conservative (Price, "Database").

5. A frequent complaint (e.g., Wright, "Seminar," 108-10; against Crossan, see Cromhout, "Construct").

6. This is a generalization, since the Jesus Seminar includes a range of scholars, including some we treat or cite separately elsewhere in this book (and even one of my esteemed former professors). Nevertheless, the dominant majority (who control the vote, hence the outcome) are accused of tending in this direction. For some comments on diversity within the group and ambiguities in evaluating the votes, see e.g., the discussion by Witherington, *Quest,* 45-46.

7. Funk et al., *Gospels,* 4; see similar statements about their target cited in Witherington, *Quest,* 44. In other settings Funk admits that the Seminar's reconstructions are fictive, but regards their fiction as socially preferable to the canonical Gospels and their popular understanding (Johnson, *Real Jesus,* 6-9).

8. See Funk et al., *Gospels,* 35.

9. Its effect, in any case, as suggested also in Funk et al., *Gospels,* 36. Okoye, "Seminar," concludes that it is legitimate for the Jesus Seminar to market itself provided that it is clear for whom it speaks (a problem; see discussion below).

10. Witherington, *Quest,* 45-46; see Funk et al., *Gospels,* 257. They contend that 82% of Jesus' words portrayed in the Gospels are inauthentic (Funk et al., *Gospels,* 5), and 84% of his deeds (Funk et al., *Acts of Jesus,* 1).

11. Johnson, *Real Jesus,* 2; more harshly, Johnson, "Quest," 22: "This is not responsible, or even critical scholarship. It is a self-indulgent charade." Others also have criticized the Jesus Seminar as a radical fringe of NT scholarship (e.g., Craig, "Jesus Seminar").

12. Johnson, *Real Jesus,* 3. For listings of scholars participating, along with the sources of their degrees, see Funk et al., *Gospels,* 533-37; idem, *Acts of Jesus,* 537-42; most are NT specialists, but some are not.

13. Wink, "Write," 9.

14. Johnson, *Real Jesus,* 5 (noting more explicitly this statement of the Seminar's methodology on 24).

15. Johnson, *Real Jesus,* 4-5, 9-20.

16. Most of us would agree that Jesus' sayings and parables are often short, shocking, humorous, and so forth; the problem is excluding the reliability of any other sayings, as if any sage spoke *only* in such ways (cf. Funk et al., *Gospels,* 31; cf. idem, *Acts of Jesus,* 9). Likewise, I would agree that such sayings were most memorable (cf. Funk et al., *Gospels,* 28) — though again not that nothing else would be remembered about him or his teaching. I would readily agree that the Gospels relocate sayings to different contexts (cf. Funk et al., *Gospels,* 19), but I would not allow as much free invention as they do.

17. See e.g., Funk et al., *Gospels,* xviii, claiming that this version is free from the biases that plague "other major translations into English," which reflect "ecclesiastical and religious control." Should one assume that those who worked on, say, the NRSV, were not scholars or that most of the translators were biased? At the least, this claim (which sounds ad hominem) is poorly worded.

18. Funk et al., *Acts of Jesus,* 1.

19. As Raymond Brown noted in his back cover endorsement of one 1995 survey of Jesus scholarship (Witherington, *Quest*), in what may have been a backhanded criticism of the Seminar and its kin,

the work "should help dispel the confusion created by media publicity as to where the majority of scholars stand on the relation of Jesus to the Gospel portraits of him."

20. For some scholars complaining about the Seminar's starting bias in rejecting Jesus' eschatological outlook, see e.g., Pearson, "Exposé"; Kee, "Century of Quests."

21. Johnson, *Real Jesus*, 41. Even Koester allows that Jesus' message probably contained eschatological elements (see Koester, "Victim").

22. Wink, "Write," 9.

23. E.g., Kee, "Century of Quests"; cf. Stanton, "Message," 65. This is not to claim that the Jesus Seminar deliberately made Jesus "comfortable"; they themselves quite clearly warn, "Beware of finding a Jesus entirely congenial to you" (Funk et al., *Gospels*, 5).

24. Overman, "Deciphering," 195.

25. As often noted (e.g., Spencer, *Profiles*, 258; Schröter, "Historische Jesus"; Evans, "Quest"). See also Meier's shorter treatment in Meier, "Reflections"; for one consideration of Meier's hermeneutical approach, see Geyser, "Geskiedenis."

26. Meier, *Marginal Jew*, 1:177. For contrasts between Meier's detailed scholarly work and more populist approaches like the Jesus Seminar, see e.g., Meier, "Dividing Lines"; Boswell, "Essay."

27. Cf. Meier, *Marginal Jew*, 1:177; Stanton, *Gospel Truth*, 177; Tuckett, "Sources and methods," 136.

28. Sanders, *Figure*, 183 (cf. 95).

29. Johnson, *Real Jesus*, 25; Sanders, *Figure*, 183; see our ch. 11. This would remain essentially the case even if the vision of the future deliverance in John and other wilderness prophets involved a radical transformation of the present order rather than a cosmic conflagration or resurrection (for this perspective on John, see e.g., Webb, *Baptizer*, 301-4, 381).

30. Crossan, *Historical Jesus*, 237-38.

31. See Kraeling, *John the Baptist*, 139; cf. *ARN* 28, §57B.

32. Cf. Acts 19:1-6; some discussions on Jn 1:6-8.

33. In the Gospel tradition, Elijah was the background for John (Mk 1:6 [with 2 Kgs 1:8]; 9:13; cf. Matt 11:14), *despite* John's lack of signs; they viewed both as prophets (e.g., Mk 6:4; 11:32).

34. Blomberg, "Studying Jesus," 22.

35. The movement may have spread in Judea with an increased Jewish emphasis, but how would later (as opposed to earlier) sources reflecting that emphasis have become property of the Diaspora churches? Portraying Palestinian Jewish features as the earliest makes greater sense, and those who recognize this priority should give much more detailed attention to early Jewish context than the Jesus Seminar's methodology tends to do.

36. Overman, "Deciphering," 194.

37. He emphasizes Cynicism as background in *Historical Jesus*, 72-88, but it is not the book's pervasive theme.

38. *Historical Jesus*, 421-22, in his epilogue. Some accuse Crossan of "closet positivism" (Hal Childs in Rollins, "Crossan"), a charge to which he responds in Crossan, "Knowledge."

39. *Historical Jesus*, 1-102.

40. For example, while I agree that patronage informs a cultural understanding of Jesus' context, eastern Mediterranean benefaction did differ in some respects from the specifically Roman model of political patronage when the latter is used in its narrower, technical sense (cf. Joubert, "Exchange"; Harrison, *Grace*, 15; Gehrke, "Euergetism," 155).

41. *Historical Jesus*, 103-226.

42. *Historical Jesus*, 227-353.

43. *Historical Jesus*, 354-94.

44. *Historical Jesus*, 395-416.

45. I intend this as an observation about Crossan's method, not as a complaint. In a similar man-

ner, in this book I expend considerable space on the Gospels' genre, and do not explore all the Jesus traditions the way I do in more detailed commentaries.

46. Cf. Malina, *Anthropology,* 72-73 (defining "peasant" as non-elite, hence 98%); Horsley and Hanson, *Bandits,* xii, following Sjoberg, *Preindustrial City,* 110.

47. See e.g., Erdkamp, "Agriculture."

48. See Bauckham, *Climax,* 378-83; for the empire more generally, Erdkamp, "Agriculture." Urban areas depended heavily on the countryside (Garnsey and Saller, *Empire,* 119; MacMullen, *Social Relations,* 48-56), although some cities like Corinth do not fit this pattern (Engels, *Roman Corinth,* 27-33, 131-42).

49. Garnsey and Saller, *Empire,* 43-46. On Greek farmers, see Osborne, "Farmers"; on Roman farmers, Rathbone, "Farmers."

50. Grant, *Social History,* 72. For independent subsistence farmers, despite their relative invisibility, see also Garnsey and Saller, *Empire,* 75-77. Independent workers earned small wages (e.g., White, "Finances," 232), and could find extra work only during harvest (Finley, *Economy,* 107); landowners kept their workforce no larger than necessary to maximize profits (MacMullen, *Social Relations,* 42). On day laborers' lack of security, see also Arlandson, *Women,* 92-98.

51. Lee, "Unrest," 127, compares them with a sort of rural client (employing the image more loosely than its narrower political sense).

52. Foxhall, "Tenant" (also noting various kinds of tenancy). For tenant farmers' difficult situation, see also Krause, "Colonatus," 538-39.

53. See especially Garnsey and Saller, *Empire,* 43-46; MacMullen, *Social Relations,* 1-27; Arlandson, *Women,* 92-98 (esp. 98).

54. Phaedrus 1.15. A modern economic historian in fact argues that "Cato gave his chained slaves more bread than the average peasant in Graeco-Roman Egypt could count on as a regular staple" (Finley, *Economy,* 107).

55. MacMullen, *Social Relations,* 13-14.

56. E.g., Apul. *Metam.* 9.35-37. On class prejudice, see e.g., MacMullen, *Social Relations,* 138-41. Some landowners might even send their own slaves or tenants to seize the land of those too weak to protect their interests (MacMullen, *Social Relations,* 7-12; cf. e.g., Philost. *Hrk.* 4.1-2). The drive was toward consolidating rural resources into increasingly "fewer hands" (MacMullen, *Social Relations,* 6).

57. Pliny *Ep.* 9.37.2. (Aristocrats often accumulated land through peasants' debts; Horsley, *Galilee,* 215-21.) One solution he considers is to lease the land for a proportion of produce rather than monetary rent (9.37.3). Pliny would reduce rents also after a bad harvest (10.8.5); what is noteworthy to us is how easily he could *afford* to do so.

58. Pliny *Ep.* 9.20.2.

59. Pliny *Ep.* 3.19.6.

60. Pliny *Ep.* 3.19.7 (insisting that he wants to employ good slaves there who need no chains, since he does not use chained labor).

61. For the deep urban/rural divide in Mediterranean antiquity, cf. MacMullen, *Social Relations,* 15, 32; we discuss this at greater length later in the book.

62. Jos. *Ag. Ap.* 1.60. For details regarding agriculture in Jewish Palestine, see Applebaum, "Economic Life," 646-56.

63. Jos. *Apion* 1.60; Goodman, *State,* 27; Freyne, *Galilee,* 144-45; Horsley, *Galilee,* 189.

64. Jos. *War* 3.42-44.'

65. *P. Maas.* 2:1; Freyne, *Galilee,* 246-47; Borg, *Conflict,* 31-32.

66. Freyne, *Galilee,* 155, 160. Conditions appear to have been much worse in Egypt; see MacMullen, *Social Relations,* 13-14; Finley, *Economy,* 107.

67. Meyers and Strange, *Archaeology,* 56 (suggesting 1600-2000 inhabitants); more recent estimates are even lower (Stanton, *Gospel Truth,* 112; Horsley, *Galilee,* 193), though these match other Galilean villages (Horsley, *Galilee,* 193).

68. Indeed, its insignificance invited attempts at biblical justification (such as Matt 2:23; Davies and Allison, *Matthew*, 1:274).

69. Though Jn 1:46 might reflect local civic rivalry (Barnett, *Reliable*, 64), a common issue in antiquity (MacMullen, *Social Relations*, 58-59).

70. Theissen and Merz, *Historical Jesus*, 164-65.

71. Biblical prophets had depicted prophecies, especially those of the end-time, in agricultural terms (Is 32:13-17; 35:1-2; 44:3-4; Jer 31:28; 51:33; Joel 3:13; Amos 8:1-2; Riesenfeld, *Tradition*, 150).

72. Agreeing here with Freyne, "Servant Community," 111, 124.

73. Although "carpenter" was not another term for teacher (pace Vermes, *Jesus the Jew*, 21-22; Borg, *Vision*, 39; see *p. Hag.* 2:1, §8) one could be both; Shammai was reportedly a carpenter (stories even equip him with a carpenter's measure to beat an unruly Gentile inquirer — cf. *b. Shab.* 31a). Similarly, Herod trained priests as masons for the temple (Jos. *Ant.* 15.390, 421).

74. Jos. *War* 2.68; *Ant.* 17.289.

75. Cf. Grant, *Judaism*, 99; Thurman, *Disinherited*, 18.

76. In view of the correspondence between Lk 4:22 and Matt 13:55, Mark may rework earlier tradition also reflected in Matt 13:55 here.

77. Jewish fathers sought to equip their sons with a trade (Moore, *Judaism*, 2:127; Safrai, "Education," 958; carpentry in *p. R.H.* 1:3, §35; elsewhere in the Mediterranean, MacMullen, *Social Relations*, 97-98), and most trades were learned by apprenticeship (e.g., Lewis, *Life*, 135).

78. Cf. Hengel, *Property*, 26-27; Freyne, *Galilee*, 241.

79. We discuss both later in the book; but for fishermen, cf. Freyne, *Galilee*, 241; Wilkinson, *Jerusalem*, 29-30; Hengel, *Property*, 27. Mark declares that Zebedee's family employed "hired servants" (Mk 1:20; Hengel, *Property*, 27).

80. The Greek school year ran from October to June (Ferguson, *Backgrounds*, 83). While Jesus and his disciples could have traveled more often than that, weather conditions may have limited their travels to some degree. Galilean rains fell on average thirty to fifty days a year, concentrated in the four months from early December to early March, which would make travel during those periods more difficult (though temperatures on the lake in January average between 50 and 65 degrees F; Sanders, *Figure*, 110).

81. Cf. e.g., Malina, *Anthropology*, 71; Scott, *Parable*, 85-86, 92; Oakman, "Peasant," 117-18.

82. E.g., Oakman, "Peasant," 120-21.

83. Cf. Vermes, *Religion*, 6; Witherington, *Christology*, 75.

84. Cf. Cromhout, "Judean," objecting that both the "peasant" (Crossan) and "marginal" (Meier) classifications of Jesus obscure his fundamentally "Judean" character.

85. Hengel, *Leader*, 27-33; Theissen, *Sociology*, 14-15; cf. Kee, *Origins*, 68.

86. See Bowers, "Propaganda," 318-19; Scroggs, "Sociological Interpretation," 172.

87. Crossan, *Historical Jesus*, 421-22; idem, "Jewish Cynic."

88. Crossan, *Historical Jesus*, 421, viewing Jesus as non-Cynic in this (and some other) respects. The qualifications are, however, in my opinion sufficient to greatly weaken his analogy with Cynics.

89. Among all ancient Cynics named, we know of no exceptions. Hard-working farmers often mistrusted philosophers in general as impractical (Alciph. *Farm.* 11 [Sitalces to Oenopion, his son], 3.14) and against farming (Alciph. *Farm.* [Sitalces to Oenopion, his son], 3.14; 38 [Euthydicus to Philiscus], 3.40, §3). Stoics could link rustics with the ignorant (Arius Did. *Epit.* 2.7.11k, pp. 80-81, lines 12-15), though they also could view urban life as a distraction from philosophy (Mus. Ruf. 11, p. 84.10-11).

90. Cf. Fiorenza, *Memory*, 74; Witherington, *Sage*, 117-45; Eddy, "Diogenes."

91. See Overman, *Crisis*, 67.

92. E.g., Diog. Laert. 2.22.

93. Safrai, "Home," 762; see also Safrai, "Education," 965; *Sipre Deut.* 43.3.7.

94. E.g., Boyd, *Sage*, 151-58; Eddy, "Diogenes," 463-67; Evans, *Fabricating Jesus*, 103-19.

95. Crossan, *Historical Jesus*, 421.

96. Cornfeld, *Josephus,* 216. More Gentiles may have also moved there, at least after 135 (see Horsley, *Galilee,* 104). For Christians coming there, cf. e.g., *b. A.Z.* 17a; Herford, *Christianity,* 115; Crocker, "Sepphoris."

97. Jos. *Life* 346-48; cf. 30, 38, 124, 232. For archaeological and literary data on the city, including claims of a later Christian presence there, see Meyers, Netzer and Meyers, "Ornament"; idem, "Bytmydwt"; Crocker, "Sepphoris"; Weiss and Netzer, "Sty"; cf. Boelter, "Sepphoris." Still, Josephus may have minimized contrary elements for the sake of his apologetic (Miller, "Josephus on Cities").

98. E.g., Jos. *Life* 30, 38, 124, 232, 346-48, 373-74. Its pacifism may have stemmed from its historic devastation in a previous revolt in Jesus' childhood (Jos. *War* 2.68).

99. See Avi-Yonah, "Geography," 105; cf. Meyers, "Judaism and Christianity," 76. Note also careful observation of the Sabbath in the other hellenized city, Tiberias (Jos. *Life* 275, 279). For Sepphoris as hellenized but genuinely Jewish, see Reed, *Archaeology,* 100-38; although it was more hellenized than the countryside (Reed, *Archaeology,* 134-35), "Theories accentuating Greek education or Cynic philosophical schools at Sepphoris are equally implausible" (Reed, *Archaeology,* 135). On Galilean Jews as fully Jewish, see also Dunn, "Synagogue," 207-12.

100. Chancey and Meyers, "Sepphoris"; Evans, *Fabricating Jesus,* 114. Cf. also ritual baths there (with Reed, *Archaeology,* 49; also Eric Meyers in Eshel and Meyers, "Pools," though Eshel was more skeptical).

101. *M. Kid.* 4:5, implying that Galilean records had been kept there.

102. *P. Sanh.* 5:1, §3. Rabbis also attest the presence of later followers of Jesus in Sepphoris (*b. A.Z.* 17a; cf. Herford, *Christianity,* 115).

103. Goodman, *State,* 27, 60. Though Sepphoris's theater seated 4000-5000 (Freyne, *Galilee,* 138), that would not seat all the adults of Sepphoris, much less rural "tourists" (Horsley, *Galilee,* 250-51). The limited trade connections (for agriculture, cooking ware and storage containers, see Adan-Bayewitz and Perlman, "Trade") do not suggest a religiocultural continuum (see Freyne, "Ethos"; Horsley, *Galilee,* 250-51).

104. That one of the priestly courses reportedly settled here after 70 CE indicates "that the remnants of temple Judaism found Nazareth 'clean' and unsullied by paganism" (Meyers and Strange, *Archaeology,* 27), though for questions on the tradition see Trifon, "Msmrwt." Vermes, *Jesus the Jew,* 72 (citing *p. Ber.* 7c; *b. Ber.* 34b), thinks that Johanan ben Zakkai settled not far from Nazareth before 70 CE. On ancient Israelite pottery before resettlement in the hellenistic period, see Horsley, *Galilee,* 193; on the proper Hebrew form of the name, see Rüger, "NAZARETH."

105. Miller, "City."

106. Reed, *Archaeology,* 138, suggests that especially his caution regarding Antipas kept him from Sepphoris.

107. Reed, *Archaeology,* 98-99.

108. Horsley, *Galilee,* 177; for relevant estimates of Sepphoris's population, see Horsley, *Galilee,* 166. Sepphoris was probably Roman Galilee's most critical market center (Adan-Bayewitz and Perlman, "Trade").

109. Jos. *Life* 373-75, 382-84, 392.

110. E.g., Diog. Laert. 7.1.121.

111. See Malherbe, "Gentle as Nurse," passim (= also Malherbe, *Philosophers,* 35-48). Many disdained the harsh, uncompromising "hard Cynics" while respecting the more tolerant "soft Cynics" (see Moles, "Cynics," 418; Malherbe, "Gentle as Nurse," 210, 214; Malherbe, *Philosophers,* 20-22, 71-72). Malherbe, *Philosophers,* 14, points out that the Cynic materials themselves display this division.

112. Arius Did. *Epit.* 2.7.11s, pp. 98-99.24-28 (also n. 222 on pp. 127-28, citing esp. Cic. *Fin.* 3.68; Apollodorus Ephillus in Diog. Laert. 6.104, 7.121; Epict. *Diatr.* 3.22). Embarrassed by their Cynic roots, Stoics had moved away from them in many respects (Engberg-Pedersen, *Paul and Stoics,* 76); but first-century Stoics like Seneca and Epictetus celebrated the Cynic model of simplicity, which regained

popularity in the first two centuries BCE and first century CE (Engberg-Pedersen, *Paul and Stoics*, 78; cf. Epict. *Diatr.* 2.22; 4.8.30-32).

113. For comparison of Cynics to dogs, see e.g., Cereidas *frg.* 1; Mart. *Epig.* 4.53.5; Lucian *Phil. Sale* 7, 10; *Runaways* 16; *Peregrinus* 2; Diog. Laert. 6.2.40, 45-46, 60, 77; Athen. *Deipn.* 13.611bc; *Gr. Anth.* 7.63-68, 115 (perhaps also 116); Philo *Plant.* 151; more positively, Dio Chrys. *Or.* 32.62; Paus. 2.2.4; Crates *Ep.* 16; Diogenes *Ep.* 2, 7; Lucian *Dial. D.* 329, 1 (1) Diogenes 1; 425, 2 (22) Charon and Menippus 3; *Dial. D.* 336, 3 (2) The Dead to Pluto against Menippus 1; 420, 4 (21) *Menippus and Cerberus* 1; Philost. *Vit. Apoll.* 6.31-33.

114. Dio Chrys. *Or.* 8.36 (cf. insanity accusations in 9.8; 12.8; 34.2, 4); dogs were associated with indecent acts (Plut. *Exile* 7, *Mor.* 601DE; *p. Taan.* 1:6, §8).

115. See e.g., Philod. *Crit.* frg. 52.2-3; Sen. *Ep. Lucil.* 95.31; 103.2; Mus. Ruf. 10, p. 78.27-29; 14, p. 92.21-22; Epict. *Diatr.* 2.9.3, 5; 4.1.127; 4.5.21; Diog. *Ep.* 28; Marc. Aur. 3.16; 4.16, 28; Porph. *Marc.* 29.463-65; 1 Cor 15:32; 2 Pet 2:12.

116. Thus when Demonax was not Cynic enough to please the Cynics, one accused him of being insufficiently "doggish," to which he responded that his interlocutor was insufficiently human (Lucian *Dem.* 21). When a Stoic kept a rich woman's dog and it wetted him, people mocked him as a Cynic, a dog (Lucian *Posts* 34).

117. E.g., Lucian *Dem.* 48; *Indictment* 7, 11; *Dead/Fisherman* passim, e.g., 15, 37, 42.

118. Lucian *Runaways* 17, 20; *Dial. D.* 374 (20/10, *Charon and Hermes* 10); *Hermot.* 9, 18; *Peregr.* 13; *Tim.* 54-57; Philost. *Ep. Apoll.* 42; cf. Malherbe, "Gentle as Nurse," 216; for the same charge against religious charlatans, e.g., Soph. *Antig.* 1061; Philost. *Vit. Apoll.* 6.41; against other public figures, see e.g., Lysias *Or.* 28.3, §179; Aeschines *Ctes.* 218.

119. Lucian *Indictment* 6; *Runaways* 12.

120. E.g., Lucian *Dem.* 61.

121. Lucian *Runaways* 15.

122. Malherbe, *Moral Exhortation,* 13, 24-25; Stambaugh and Balch, *Environment,* 45-46; cf. Montiglio, "Wandering philosophers."

123. On harsh Cynics, cf. Pliny *N.H.* 7.19.79; Lucian *Runaways* 19, 27. On such Cynics as demagogues, see Lucian *Dem.* 61.

124. *Peregr.* 3, 18; *Runaways* 14; *Phil. Sale* 10. One wept and tore (gently) at his hair, to stir emotion (*Peregr.* 6).

125. *Peregr.* 3, 5; *Runaways* 14, 27; cf. *Icar.* 31.

126. *Peregr.* 31. One imagines that some hearers' motives for listening resembled those of some watchers of horror movies or graphic violence today: the cheap thrill of an adrenaline rush that does not risk one's safety.

127. Lucian *Fisherman* 44. Pliny complains that a severe Cynic like Diogenes lacked normal human feeling (*N.H.* 7.19.79).

128. More positively, they were known for frank speech; see Vaage, "Barking"; Malherbe, "Gentle as Nurse," 208, 213; Diog. Laert. 6.2.51; 6.5.92. Diogenes probably employed his rude wit effectively, humorously attracting attention (see Bosman, "Selling Cynicism").

129. Diog. Laert. 6.2.32.

130. Diog. Laert. 6.2.60, 64; he is unafraid of Alexander also in 6.2.68, and Alexander respects him in 6.2.32. Crates also answers Alexander boldly in Diog Laert 6.5.93.

131. Philost. *Vit. Apoll.* 4.42.

132. Malherbe, *Philosophers,* 12, 24. Some Cynics may not have adopted the entire lifestyle; e.g., Demetrius the Cynic sought to defend someone in court (Tac. *Hist.* 4.40).

133. E.g., Dio Chrys. *Or.* 32.9; Lucian *Dem.* 5, 7; cf. Philost. *Vit. Apoll.* 1.16; 4.40; Malherbe, *Moral Exhortation,* 26 (citing Dio Chrys. *Or.* 8.4-5, 9-16).

134. See Branham, "Humor."

135. If the Qumran community consisted of wilderness Essenes (the dominant, though debated,

view), they provide an even more extreme example of withdrawal from not only society's conventions but from proximity to it. Cynics remained a largely urban phenomenon.

136. See Goodman, *State*, 39.

137. They did exist in antiquity (Collins, *Sibylline Oracles*, 6; Burkert, *Cults*, 31).

138. Boring, *Sayings*, 59-61; cf. Aune, *Prophecy*, 211-14; pace Harnack; Theissen. Strangely, Gerd Theissen contends that wandering Palestinian charismatics known from the Jesus tradition were Paul's opponents (noting the contrast with Paul in Theissen, *Social Setting*, 35-40); yet Paul himself constitutes our best concrete *evidence* for a literal practice of this lifestyle. Many arguments for continuing itinerant prophets in the Gospels themselves are tenuous (cf. e.g., challenges in Tannehill, *Sword*, 139-40; Hill, *Prophecy*, 154; Aune, *Prophecy*, 211-16, 243; Stambaugh and Balch, *Environment*, 105).

139. 1 Sam 7:16-17; 2 Kgs 4:8-10; cf. Hengel, *Leader*, 16-24; Culpepper, *School*, 227.

140. Crates *Ep.* 18, 30.

141. On the prohibition of the bag forbidding begging, see also Deissmann, *Light*, 108-9.

142. Liefeld, "Preacher," 247; Meeks, *Moral World*, 107; also of priests of Cybele, e.g., Babrius 141.1-6. Cynics typically wore rough robes (e.g., Epict. *Disc.* 3.22.10; cf. 4.8.12, 15) and carried only a bag and a staff (Epict. *Disc.* 3.22.10; Crates *Ep.* 16, 23, 33; Diogenes *Ep.* 6, 7, 13, 19, 26, 30, 46; Diog. Laert. 6.1.13; 6.2.22-23, 76; cf. Anacharsis *Ep.* 5). Many of these references also emphasize that Cynics let their beards grow long, but coins indicate that Palestinian Jews in this period generally already had beards, so this feature of Cynic lifestyle would not be relevant to mention. Liefeld, "Preacher," 167-79 treats the distinctive cloaks of many philosophers and religious figures and notes that some kinds of philosophers — not just Cynics — traveled with only one.

143. Liefeld, "Preacher," 260; cf. Overman, *Crisis*, 146-47; Eddy, "Diogenes," 461-62.

144. Cf. Matt 5:40//Lk 6:29; Theissen, *Sociology*, 34-35. This level of deprivation would, however, be more true of rural Egypt than of most of Galilee.

145. 1QS 1.11-13; 6.22-23; Jos. *Ant.* 18.20; *War* 2.122; Philo *Prob.* 76; *Hypothetica* 11.4-5; Fitzmyer, "Jewish Christianity," 243; Mealand, "Community of Goods"; cf. Fabry, "Umkehr."

146. Jos. *War* 2.124-25. Theissen and Merz, *Historical Jesus*, 215-16, note that Jesus' instructions are not Cynic, since these Essene "travel rules" are equally close.

147. E.g., 1 Kgs 18:13; 2 Kgs 4:38; 5:15-19; 6:1. Cf. Meeks, *Moral World*, 106.

148. E.g., Theissen and Merz, *Historical Jesus*, 215-16; Voorst, *Jesus Outside NT*, 172. Voorst, *Jesus Outside NT*, 169-70, n. 65, notes supporters of the Cynic thesis, including Downing, "Context"; idem, "Reflections"; idem, *Cynics*; and detractors, including Tuckett, "Cynic Q"; Betz, "Jesus and Cynics"; Eddy, "Diogenes"; Witherington; Boyd; Robinson, "Blocks."

149. Stanton, "Message," 65.

150. Downing, *Church and Jesus*, 78-79. He is emphatic that *"An abundance of illustrative material does not itself entail a causal connection"* (Downing, *Church and Jesus*, 79; again, 84).

151. Theissen and Merz, *Historical Jesus*, 11.

152. E.g., Hengel, *Judaism*; Lieberman, *Hellenism*; Levine, "Beth-She'arim" (esp. p. 311); Meyers and Meyers, "Sepphoris." For the history of the scholarly dichotomy between Judaism and Hellenism (esp. as used for anti-Judaism, but sometimes, as in the biblical theology movement, also in an apologetic for Christianity and Judaism), see Meeks, "Judaism"; Martin, "Dichotomy."

153. E.g., Feldman, "Hellenism"; connections to the east via a shared Aramaic language in Wasserstein, "Non-Hellenized Jews"; cf. e.g., Philo of Alexandria or Artapanus. Josephus is Judean, but reflects the more hellenized ruling elite (contrast the Qumran scrolls). Alexander, "Hellenism," 72-79, finds little "hellenization" in rabbinic literature (vs. elsewhere in early Judaism), but defines hellenization narrowly, as *educated* Greek, with a rhetorical level of education.

154. Magic and monotheism being the largest exceptions, though even these (and esp. the former) often appear with minimal Jewish influence.

155. Mack, *Myth*, 87 n. 7.

156. Dunn, *New Perspective*, 62. Cf. the insistence in Segundo, *Historical Jesus*, 69, that "Jesus was

a first-century Jew. No one in their right mind would attempt to comprehend him *directly* in terms of cultural categories proper to the Greek world, the Far East, or the modern West."

157. Thus, e.g., even though the version of Q directly behind Matthew and Luke includes both the narrative context and the sayings concerning John the Baptist's proclamation of a coming judge (which represents an exalted figure, perhaps even divine — see ch. 11), and Mack allows it in Q2 (*Lost Gospel*, 82), he necessarily omits it for his "early" Q1 (*Lost Gospel*, 73-80). Wright, *People of God*, 104 n. 41, correctly provides Mack's book *(Myth)* as one "modern example of a hypothesis which constantly dismembers the evidence in the interests of a broad overall scheme."

158. With whom Mack himself is not in complete methodological agreement (*Lost Gospel*, 193).

159. Perhaps especially by way of protest oracles, hellenism may have exerted some influence on Jewish eschatological thought (cf. Glasson, *Influence*, though overstated); Roman yearning for a new golden era in Augustan propaganda may have also contributed (Virg. *Ecl.* 4.4-25; 8.27-28). Nevertheless, the Egyptian Potter's Oracle and prior Egyptian and Asian models for apocalyptic suggest that the influence moved more from east to west (cf. also Baker, "Review of Glasson"). In our period, eschatological material would reflect more a definite Jewish than a purely hellenistic milieu.

160. One Cynic sage is *from* the general region, albeit from a Gentile part of it; we have *no* Jewish Cynics anywhere in antiquity.

161. *Lost Gospel*, 46, 114-15.

162. On the more general nature of most alleged "Cynic" parallels, see also e.g., Witherington, *Sage*, 117-45.

163. Cf. Vermes, *Religion*, 78-90, comparing Jesus' teaching style.

164. See e.g., Diog. Laert. passim.

165. Cf. further Young, *Theologian*, 171-80; Keener, *John*, 503-4.

166. E.g., Mack, *Myth*, 57, 87 n. 7; cf. idem, *Lost Gospel*, 31-32. This dichotomy was a common one in twentieth-century approaches; see Hallbäck, "Apocalyptic."

167. *Lost Gospel*, 228.

168. *Lost Gospel*, 1-2.

169. A contrast for which Mack has predecessors (see Mack, *Lost Gospel*, 31-33).

170. It is only for those whom one does *not* expect to survive the judgment that one provides no model of an ideal community; and it is only if one is certain that history *cannot* continue for more than a few days that one fails to provide an interim ethic or guidance concerning how to live until the end comes. Qumran's duration of imminent expectation originally may have comprised forty years, trusting that the end would come within that generation (CD^{B1} 2.14-15; cf. 4Q171 frg. 1-2, col. 2.7-8).

171. Collins, "Wisdom"; cf. Harrington, "Wisdom Texts." Many think that the mantic form of wisdom found there influenced apocalyptic thought (VanderKam, "Mantic Wisdom"). Aune, *Prophecy*, 113, notes that while most scholars reject wisdom as the source for apocalyptic, both are scribal traditions, weakening the clear boundaries between mantic wisdom and apocalyptic (citing the model of Daniel as interpreter of mysteries). Bedenbender, "Apocalypticism," argues that apocalyptic in general derives especially from prophetic tradition, and only marginally from mantic wisdom.

172. Witherington, *Christology*, 243. Burkes, "Wisdom," even finds elements relevant to apocalyptic in Wisdom of Solomon, but this work is too hellenized for many connections.

173. The fluid categories of ancient charismatic leaders were not always contradictory; logic's law of noncontradiction only works for genuinely contradictory items.

174. Mack, *Lost Gospel*, 126.

175. Mack, *Myth*, 70-73; idem, *Lost Gospel*, 126.

176. On the kingdom in Jewish teaching, see e.g., Meier, *Marginal Jew*, 2:240-69; Chilton, "Kingdom," especially 280; cf. Vermes, *Religion*, 127-30; Neusner, "Kingdom," acknowledging its subordinate function.

177. Lines that he himself *retains* as authentic in his Q1 (*Lost Gospel*, 76). This is not his only inconsistency. For example: like many scholars, he rejects Jesus' foreknowledge of the cross; neverthe-

less, he accepts the saying, "Whoever does not accept his cross and so become my follower," interpreting it only figuratively (*Lost Gospel,* 79). While some Gentiles did employ this image figuratively (Keener, *Matthew,* 434 n. 103), if Jesus spoke these words without expecting his execution, we are forced to assume a large coincidence with what in fact happened to him.

178. Bonsirven, *Judaism,* 133; Jeremias, *Prayers,* 98; idem, *Theology,* 21; Moore, *Judaism,* 2:213; Smith, *Tannaitic Parallels,* 136; Hill, *Matthew,* 136-37; Perrin, *Language,* 28-29; Vermes, *Jesus and Judaism,* 43; Davies and Allison, *Matthew,* 1:595; Luz, *Matthew,* 371. At least some people probably already used the basic form of the *Kaddish* in Jesus' day (cf. Oesterley, *Liturgy,* 72); it is quite difficult to believe that the *Kaddish* adapted the Lord's Prayer instead.

179. Jeremias, *Prayers,* 98; Oesterley, *Liturgy,* 73; Bonsirven, *Judaism,* 133.

180. Lapide, *Hebrew,* 8.

181. Not limited, by the way, to the Cynics (pace the implication for the unprepared reader in *Lost Gospel,* 126). See e.g., Sen. *Ep. Lucil.* 108.13; Diogenes Laertius 7.1.122; and other sources cited in our ch. 21.

182. For God's or his agent's kingdom, cf. 1QSb 4.26; 5.21; 4Q174 f1 2i.10; 4Q200 f6.5; 4Q246 f1ii.5; 4Q252 5.2, 4; 4Q400 f1ii.1, 3; 4Q400 f2.1; 4Q401 f14.i.7; 4Q403 f1i.25; 4Q403 f1iii.10; 11Q13 2.9.

183. Gnostics, for example, moved in the other direction (cf. Smith, *Gnostic Origins*). Those of us who date Matthew after Mark can observe a process of re-Judaization (e.g., Matthew's fairly consistent "kingdom of heaven"), but Matthew can move in this direction because he belongs to a movement that has never lost its Jewishness, and he writes about a genuinely Jewish teacher whom Mark has somewhat (though far from fully) universalized. Sometimes Matthew's "re-Judaization" may depend on genuine oral tradition (e.g., probably Matt 10:5-6; possibly 15:24) or plausible and possibly correct inference (e.g., Matt 14:1; 27:46, in view of 27:47 [see Keener, *Matthew,* 13-14, 315, 398 n. 9, 682-84]).

184. *Lost Gospel,* 220.

185. For family members, cf. e.g., Gen 33:4; Tob 7:6; 10:13; *Jub.* 22:10-11; 26:21; 31:21; Plut. *R.Q.* 6, *Mor.* 265B; Ach. Tat. 1.7.3; it was also extended to close friends (Artem. *Oneir.* 2.2) and others; see Keener, "Kiss."

186. Indeed, even in the pagan world the philosophers emphasized an idea much closer to the early Christian notion of conversion than did the eclectic mysteries (see especially Nock, *Conversion*).

187. Cf. e.g., Burkert, *Cults,* 101; Nock, *Gentile Christianity,* 60-62, 133; Wagner, *Baptism,* 71-72, 102-3; Meeks, *Urban Christians,* 152-53.

188. Epict. *Disc.* 2.9.20; probably Juv. *Sat.* 14.104; *Sib. Or.* 4.162-65; see also e.g., *m. Pes.* 8:8; *tos. A.Z.* 3:11. The debate surrounding the date and influence of Jewish proselyte baptism continues, but I provide further documentation for my position in Keener, *John,* 442-48 (esp. 444-47); see also Abrahams, *Studies,* 1:42; Montefiore, *Gospels,* 1:8; Rowley, "Baptism"; Schiffman, "Crossroads," 128; idem, *Jew,* 26; against it, e.g., Beasley-Murray, *Baptism,* 18-31; Taylor, "Baptism"; Smith, "Baptism," 13-32.

189. Josephus notes Essene lustrations (*War* 2.129), including one when joining the sect (*War* 2.150). Many have viewed Essene baptism as the background for John's and early Christian baptism (e.g., Fritsch, *Community,* 7; Smith, "Baptism"; Brownlee, "Comparison with Sects," 58; Brown, "Scrolls," 4; Bertalotto, "Immersion"; Flusser, *Sage,* 19); others point out that it was merely the first among many lustrations (e.g., Driver, *Scrolls,* 496-506; Ringgren, *Faith,* 221; Milik, *Discovery,* 102-3; Pryke, "John," 483-96; Simon, *Sects,* 75).

190. Such cult meals were common in all sorts of ancient associations (cf. e.g., Wilken, "Collegia," 280-81; Theissen, *Social Setting,* 131-32; Willis, *Meat,* 14); the idea of sacramental meals in the Mysteries may have derived in conjunction with later Christian sacramentalism, however — the Mysteries borrowed many features from the rapidly spreading Christian cult in the third and fourth centuries, which are not attested in earlier sources concerning the Mysteries (cf. e.g., Nock, *Gentile Christianity,* 74; Willis, *Meat,* 18-46, 62). Despite challenges on numerous points, the most thorough treatment of Jesus' Last Supper in a paschal context remains Jeremias, *Eucharistic Words.*

191. *Lost Gospel,* 256-57.

192. Price, *Son of Man,* 247.

193. Price, *Son of Man,* 247.

194. That is not to say that they were absent in Palestine; they probably appear among Gentiles in Caesarea Maritima and Caesarea Philippi, for instance (though our documentation for them is largely much later; see discussion in ch. 22). Yet the Gospels provide no hint that Jesus traveled near the former (in contrast to later believers in Acts), and his time in the latter vicinity appears only once, and there in outlying villages, probably among Jews (Mk 8:27).

195. Future mysteries in Dan 2:18, 19, 22-23, 27-30, 47; 4:9; the mystery involves the *kingdom* in 2:44-45; Nock, *Gentile Christianity,* 30; Gibbard, "Mystery," 109; Caragounis, *Mysterion,* 126.

196. Cf. e.g., Brown, *"Mysterion"*; idem, *Mystery;* Ellis, "Uses," 208; Ramirez, "Misterio."

197. We treat proposed mystery parallels more fully in ch. 22.

198. See *Ant.* 18.116-19.

Notes to Chapter 3

1. Meier, *Marginal Jew,* 3:3.

2. Vermes, *Religion,* 5.

3. Charlesworth, "Jesus and Theology"; Theissen and Merz, *Historical Jesus,* 11; Levine, "Introduction," 11. Freyne, "Search," surveys Jewish, Cynic, and revolutionary pictures of Jesus in the Third Quest. One may also note social approaches (Geyser, "Uitgangspunte"; Stegemann, Malina and Theissen, *Setting of Jesus;* Aarde, "Methods") and archaeology (Charlesworth, *Archaeology;* esp. the articles Charlesworth, "Research and Archaeology"; Freyne, "Archaeology").

4. Borg, "Reflections," 27; Bird, "Quest."

5. Theissen and Merz, *Historical Jesus,* 11, preferring the latter.

6. E.g., Sanders, *Jesus and Judaism;* idem, *Figure;* idem, "Know," 57; Kee, "Century of Quests"; Meier, "Project"; Theissen and Merz, *Historical Jesus,* 240-80; Allison, "Eschatological Jesus"; idem, *Jesus of Nazareth* (esp. 96-171); McGaughy, "Words"; McKnight, *Vision;* Ehrman, *Prophet,* 125-39; Wright, "Seminar," 101-7; Broadhead, "Priests," 140; Pikaza, "Jesús histórico"; cf. Pearson, "Exposé."

7. So Holmén, "Introduction," 4, 8; Tuckett, "Sources and methods," 133; Meier, "Present State"; Bird, "Quest"; De Rosa, "Chi è Gesù"; McKnight, *Death,* 44. Cf. earlier discussion in Keck, *History,* 22-64; Sanders' praise of Vermes and Paula Fredriksen for their emphasis on Jesus' Jewishness (Sanders, "Quest").

8. Vermes, *Religion,* 6.

9. Holmén, "Introduction," 4, 8; Tuckett, "Sources and methods," 133; Bird, "Quest"; for some examples, see Sanders, *Jesus and Judaism;* Charlesworth, *Jesus Within Judaism,* passim; Levine, *Misunderstood Jew;* Evans, "Context"; Tomson, "Jesus and Judaism," 25-40; Lüdemann, *Two Thousand Years,* 4; Wright, "Seminar," 108-10; Bock and Herrick, *Jesus in Context.* The Third Quest does usually also acknowledge diversity within Judaism (cf. Gisel, "Jésus historique").

10. Even this is a generalization of sorts. For example, Wright's treatment of the resurrection gives significant attention to detail.

11. One ancient writer avoided writing about speakers who were his friends, lest he be accused of bias (Philost. *Vit. soph.* 2.33.628). Sanders' work is too important to avoid discussing, and I am reticent to think that students should avoid mentioning their teachers. Nevertheless, I try to balance a student's respect with an observer's critique, in the hopes of minimizing my bias.

12. Cf. this concern e.g., in Borg, *Vision,* 12-14.

13. *Conflict,* 13. Borg is right to raise the question of definition; Borg's own approach does not completely negate Jesus' concern for the future (such as an imminent danger to Israel) per se.

14. *Conflict,* 27-49.

15. *Conflict,* 51-72. This point may be less clear, although it is true that an oppressed group often emphasizes features that reinforce their self-definition as over against oppressors.

16. E.g., *Conflict,* 236.

17. *Conflict,* 237-38. He compares sages in various cultures. See also Borg, *Vision,* 97-124.

18. *Conflict,* 198, 234-37. See also Borg, *Vision,* 150-71; on Jesus as charismatic, see further ibid., 39-56; idem, "Experience."

19. Borg recognizes in *Vision,* 142-43 n. 2 that he and Sanders share this perspective.

20. *Conflict,* 70. Horsley, "Movements," views the earliest Jesus movements (in Mark and Q) as also seeking the renewal of Israel.

21. *Conflict,* 198. Borg envisions this as a crisis within history (201-77; also idem, *Vision,* 162-63). Certainly historical crisis did materialize (exemplified esp. in the temple's destruction).

22. *Conflict,* 232 (like Jeremias, emphasizing "Abba").

23. *Conflict,* 232-33.

24. *Conflict,* 173; cf. idem, *Vision,* 174-76. Although not addressing here the problem that Sanders raises about the new temple, Borg notes that the temple charge (Mk 14:58) "is always attributed to opponents" in the tradition (*Conflict,* 180).

25. E.g., *Conflict,* 73-121. One may contrast Sanders' approach below.

26. *Conflict,* 143, 162. One may contrast Vermes' skepticism that Jesus as a charismatic sage focused much on Torah disputes.

27. *Conflict,* 123-43. He appears to weigh too much on the use of Hos 6:6 in Matt 9:13; 12:7, though he recognizes these texts as Matthean redaction (*Conflict,* 124). In *Vision,* 129-41, he prefers the language of "compassion."

28. *Conflict,* 145-62.

29. *Conflict,* 163-99.

30. *Conflict,* 100-1. One could construe Matt 23:23//Lk 11:42 as requiring something in addition to tithes rather than critiquing tithes, but Jesus does critique a "superscrupulous," hyperbolic Pharisee here, perhaps poking fun at Pharisaic academic attention to details.

31. *Conflict,* 244-45.

32. *Conflict,* 247.

33. E.g., the dismissal of sayings failing only the criterion of coherence (*Conflict,* 16); the negative use of dissimilarity (20-23). He points out the inconsistency of scholars who fail to follow their own criteria to their logical conclusions (22).

34. E.g., Borg, *Conflict,* 3, 17-20, 28-49.

35. E.g., *Conflict,* 76-78.

36. He argues for a non-eschatological Jesus in Borg, *Jesus in Scholarship,* 47-68. For one persuasive eschatological response to Borg, see Allison, *Jesus of Nazareth,* 96-122.

37. Borg, "Disagreement," 240-41, arguing that because N. T. Wright reduces eschatology to Christology, they may not differ so much about eschatology. Others complain about Wright's excessive realization (or demythologization?) of eschatology (Eddy, "(W)Right Jesus," 59-60; Allison, "Victory of Apocalyptic," 140-41). (Wright, however, affirms future bodily resurrection, as Borg himself recognizes ["Disagreement," 230].)

38. For most of Jesus' future message relating to a crisis *within* history, see *Conflict,* 201-27.

39. *Conflict,* 220; in Borg, *Jesus in Scholarship,* 60, he notes that over half of the scholars surveyed (i.e., *eleven versus ten*) doubted that Jesus expected imminent end in his lifetime. He does recognize Jesus as an "eschatological prophet" as the prior consensus (*Vision,* 11-14), though noting that it has been eroded by doubt that Jesus spoke "coming Son of man" sayings (14). Cf. again the warning in Poirier, "Consensus," that scholars use "consensus" as a rhetorical substitute for an argument.

40. Borg, *Jesus in Scholarship,* 18-43, surveys contemporary Jesus scholarship, arguing that only Sanders (19-21) holds to an eschatological Jesus. But Borg's approach is highly selective in whom he covers (Mack, Fiorenza, Borg himself, and Horsley; he summarizes Horsley's approach [29] as trans-

lating the function of apocalyptic into addressing oppression, hence translating eschatology into anti-imperialism). He argues that only a minority of active North American scholars now view Jesus as eschatological (Borg, "Reflections," 20-21), but this would probably be true only if one counts only those "active" in the Jesus Seminar. Patterson, *God of Jesus*, 170-71, also claims that the eschatological consensus has collapsed (true if by consensus we mean near-unanimity; but not all clear if we refer to a strong majority of detailed historical Jesus scholarship).

41. E.g., *4 Ezra* 7:74; later, *Lev. Rab.* 15:1.

42. E.g., *Jub.* 23:26-27 (probably); *Test. Dan.* 6:4; later *Sipre Deut.* 43.16.3; R. Judah in *b. B.B.* 10a. For a plausible combination of the two approaches, see *Sipra Behuq.* pq. 8.269.2.3. For various views side by side, see *b. Sanh.* 97a-98b.

43. See 1QS 9.17-18; *m. Ab.* 3:15 (according to the usual interpretation); *Sipre Deut.* 312.1.1-2; 319.3.1; cf. the discussion in Jos. *Ant.* 13.171-73; *War* 2.162-65.

44. This is certainly the idea of others in Mk 11:10; 15:43. We will address the kingdom in ch. 14.

45. Nearly all scholars accept the authenticity of 1 Thessalonians; scholars divide on 2 Thessalonians, though most accept at least Pauline tradition. I deal with the more controversial question of the dating of 2 Thessalonians later, in appendix 4.

46. For parallels, see again appendix 4.

47. Borg, *Conflict*, 73, 230-31, 305, 373. I will make more of the cross-cultural approach in my following book on the plausibility of eyewitness claims in historical miracle reports.

48. Borg, *Conflict*, 253.

49. *Conflict*, 257.

50. *Conflict*, 260-61.

51. Cf. *Conflict*, 258-59.

52. Vermes has authored several important works, including *Jesus the Jew; Religion; Jesus and Judaism;* for a briefer summary, see Vermes, "Jesus the Jew."

53. *Jesus and Judaism*, 37.

54. Cf. e.g., *Jesus the Jew*, 58-80; idem, *Religion*, 70-74.

55. *Jesus and Judaism*, 30; idem, *Religion*, 46.

56. *Religion*, 8-9.

57. *Jesus the Jew*, 55-57.

58. *Jesus and Judaism*, 31.

59. *Religion*, 11-45.

60. Vermes, *Jesus the Jew*, 80-82.

61. *Religion*, ix-x.

62. *Jesus the Jew*, 36.

63. *Jesus the Jew*, 36.

64. Keener, *John*, 852, 1073.

65. For summaries of this consensus, see Blackburn, "Miracles," 362; Eve, *Miracles*, 16-17; Welch, "Miracles," 360; for examples, see Betz, *Jesus*, 58-60; Sanders, *Jesus and Judaism*, 11; Smith, *Magician*, 16; Meier, *Marginal Jew*, 2:617-45, 678-772; Brown, *Death*, 143-44; Theissen and Merz, *Historical Jesus*, 281-315; Twelftree, *Miracle Worker*. Ehrman, *Prophet*, 197-200, notes that scholars can accept Jesus as an exorcist and healer without passing judgment on whether he acted supernaturally.

66. Vermes, *Jesus and Judaism*, 5. Horsley, *Galilee*, 152-55, suspects Galileans' loyalty to Torah.

67. Most of the fairly rare reports of rabbinic miracles, probably fitting the predominantly halachic character of rabbinic literature, are "rule miracles," i.e., signs to demonstrate the truth of one's legal teaching (Theissen, *Miracle Stories*, 106-12).

68. Thus Eve contends that, against Vermes, it is not clear that Honi represents a class of people beyond himself (Eve, *Miracles*, 274).

69. Cf. Vermes, *Jesus and Judaism*, 5; note also Hengel, *Leader*.

70. Blackburn, "Miracles," 378.

71. Blackburn, "Miracles," 378-79.

72. Eve, *Miracles,* 285. None involved exorcism (Eve, *Miracles,* 294).

73. Jos. *Ant.* 14.22. Cf. Eve, *Miracles,* 277-78, arguing that Josephus' focus is not on this but on his role in the war (Josephus' focus).

74. The only Tannaitic account is *m. Ta'an.* 3:8 (Eve, *Miracles,* 274-75), and Eve notes (Eve, *Miracles,* 275-77) that W. Scott Green and Jacob Neusner both deny reliable information even there.

75. Eve, *Miracles,* 281, notes that this date is uncertain (on 282 conceding, however, that he was probably from the Second Temple period). Amoraic traditions place him in the first century (see Eve, *Miracles,* 287-88).

76. Eve, *Miracles,* 280-81, cites *m. Ber.* 5:5; *Sot.* 9:15 (= *tos. Sot.* 15:5); *Ab.* 3:10-11; *tos. Ber.* 3:20; *Mek.* on Ex 18:21.

77. Eve, *Miracles,* 282-83 (four centuries, on the Bavli); Blackburn, "Miracles," 378 (three centuries, on the Yerushalmi).

78. Theissen and Merz, *Historical Jesus,* 307-8; Blackburn, "Miracles," 379 (who notes that Jesus rarely is said to pray before working a miracle); Eve, *Miracles,* 377-78.

79. Vermes, *Jesus the Jew,* 89; idem, *Jesus and Judaism,* 6, 10, 27-28; cf. Eve, *Miracles,* 377.

80. *Jesus the Jew,* 90.

81. For Elijah and Elisha as examples of healing miracles in Josephus, see Betz, "Miracles in Josephus," 219-20; as models among signs-sages, see Galley, "Heilige."

82. With Cohen, *Maccabees,* 200. Eve, *Miracles,* 385, argues that the only miracle directly attributed to Isaiah in the account was the shadow going up; but Isaiah does play a role in the healing here.

83. E.g., Sir 48:13; *Liv. Pr.* 2:3 (on Jeremiah, in OTP 2:386-87; Schermann, 81-82, §25).

84. *Jesus the Jew,* 95; cf. 94-99.

85. For one survey, see Teeple, *Prophet,* 4-8.

86. Aune, *Prophecy,* 124-25; cf. Brown, *John,* 1:47. This is relevant even if rabbinic evidence for Elijah's role as forerunner (e.g., *b. Erub.* 43ab, bar.) is later (as contended by Faierstein, "Elijah" [see especially 86]; Fitzmyer, "Elijah"; contrast Allison, "Elijah").

87. Among those who never died (Enoch, Moses, "and possibly Ezra, Baruch, and Jeremiah"; Longenecker, *Christology,* 33).

88. See the survey of material in Keener, *John,* 434-36.

89. *Sipre Deut.* 41.4.3; 342.5.2; *b. Men.* 63a; at the redemption of the new exodus in *Ex. Rab.* 3:4; he would punish the Gentiles in *Gen. Rab.* 71:9; involved in the resurrection in *m. Sot.* 9:15; *p. Sheq.* 3:3. Ford, *Revelation,* 179, cites also *Pirke R. Eliezer* 43, 47; *Eliyyahu Rabba* 25ff.

90. E.g., the figures in *b. Suk.* 52b; *Pesiq. Rab Kah.* 5:9; *Song Rab.* 8:9, §3; *Pesiq. Rab.* 15:14/15. (One may compare the priest anointed for war — and perhaps the two messiahs — in these texts with earlier Qumran expectation; see the chapter on christology above.) In late texts of varying date and opinion he is associated with the Messiah (*Lev. Rab.* 34:8; *Deut. Rab.* 6:7; *Song Rab.* 2:13, §4), preceding him (*b. Erub.* 43b; *Pesiq. Rab.* 35:4); coming with him (*Ex. Rab.* 18:12); knowing something about the time of his coming (*b. B.M.* 85b); he is also protective of his coming reign (*Gen. Rab.* 83:4); or Elijah is Phinehas the high priest (*Tg. Ps.-Jon.* on Ex 6:18; cf. *L.A.B.* 48:1). Elijah would also exercise an eschatological halakhic role (mainly in later texts, e.g., *b. Ber.* 35b; *B.B.* 94b; *B.M.* 3a, 30a; *Men.* 45a, bar.), especially (in line with the rabbinic interpretation of Malachi) in determining proper lines of descent (Israelites vs. proselytes, etc.; *m. Ed.* 8:7; *tos. Ed.* 3:4; cf. *Song Rab.* 4:12, §5). Although the bulk of this evidence derives from the more numerous Amoraic texts, some of it is also Tannaitic (e.g., *m. Ed.* 8:7; *Sot.* 9:15).

91. See Aune, *Prophecy,* 124-25; Ford, *Revelation,* 179; 4Q375 frg. 1, 1.1-4.

92. *Jesus and Judaism,* 123-56, 222-37.

93. *Jesus and Judaism,* 143.

94. *Jesus and Judaism,* 157-73.

95. *Jesus and Judaism,* 172, 238-40. Against Smith's view, see e.g., Theissen and Merz, *Historical*

Jesus, 305-7 (protesting the distinction between Jesus' Galilean milieu and magical papyri). Neusner, in "Foreword," xxvii, and idem, *New Testament*, 5, 173, offers perhaps the harshest critique of Smith's magical thesis.

96. *Ant.* 20.97, 170.

97. Josh 3:16-17; 6:20; Jos. *Ant.* 5.18, 27; cf. Ex 14:21.

98. *Jesus and Judaism*, 234.

99. *Jesus and Judaism*, 10-11. For the narrative tradition grounding early Christians historically, cf. Schröter, "Anfänge." Koester, "Cult," appears to go too far, in suggesting that the historical Jesus is not recoverable by studying his sayings, but rather through studying early Christian cult.

100. *Jesus and Judaism*, 61-76.

101. *Jesus and Judaism*, 77-90.

102. *Jesus and Judaism*, 91-119.

103. See e.g., Allison, *Jesus of Nazareth*, 141-51; McKnight, *Vision*; Freyne, "Servant Community," 109-13.

104. Sanders, *Jesus and Judaism*, 91-94; idem, "Know," 57. For John, cf. also Schweitzer, *Quest*, 240; Ehrman, *Prophet*, 185.

105. *Jesus and Judaism*, 95-106.

106. *Jesus and Judaism*, 174-211.

107. *Jesus and Judaism*, 210; for his view on Jesus and repentance, see 106-13. On this point I think that Borg has the stronger case from the Jesus tradition (*Vision*, 163-65).

108. *Jesus and Judaism*, 245-69.

109. *Jesus and Judaism*, 270-318.

110. I do this partly to guard against my own potential bias, though it is rightly said that a disciple is not greater than the teacher (Matt 10:24-25; cf. Jn 13:16), a point that would certainly be true in this case with or without textual support.

111. *Jesus and Judaism*, 65 (concluding that he attacks neither).

112. *Jesus and Judaism*, 141-42.

113. *Jesus and Judaism*, 150.

114. *Jesus and Judaism*, 148-50.

115. *Jesus and Judaism*, 140. He obliterates some of the circular arguments for Matt 12:28//Lk 11:20 referring to the kingdom as present (133-37), although it is not clear that the verb cannot involve the present; it at least may suggest that the kingdom was expected imminently enough so as to affect the present.

116. *Jesus and Judaism*, 138. His question of what made Jesus' movement "uniquely successful" in contrast to the other movements (138; cf. 240) might be answered at least in large measure by the unique resurrection claim concerning him (which we address in ch. 22).

117. *Jesus and Judaism*, 111. His contrast of Jesus' teaching on judgment with that of contemporary Jewish expectation (*Jesus and Judaism*, 116-18) similarly argues too much from the tradition's silence (especially after constricting the gospel tradition's evidence too narrowly).

118. *Jesus and Judaism*, 92-93.

119. *Jesus and Judaism*, 113. Jesus' wording is conformed to John's most clearly in Matt 4:17 (cf. 3:2), but if one accepts Markan priority, it is actually John's wording that Matthew conforms to Jesus' here (cf. Mk 1:4, 15).

120. *Jesus and Judaism*, 203.

121. *Jesus and Judaism*, 67. Cf. Jn 5:14; possible tradition in Jn 8:11. Jesus appears supportive of the temple cult in Mk 1:44.

122. *Jesus and Judaism*, 206.

123. *Jesus and Judaism*, 207, dismisses the relevance of Mk 1:44, which involves impurity rather than repentance.

124. *Jesus and Judaism*, 252-55.

125. *Jesus and Judaism*, 206-7; idem, *Figure*, 230.

126. This is true even in the special Lukan material that might sound closest to it (Lk 3:11-14, demanding radical obedience, but not restitution).

127. *Jesus and Judaism*, 139-40.

128. *Figure*, 94.

129. *Figure*, 230-33. He does show the extent to which it is a Lukan emphasis; but Luke draws the idea from "Q," and the same appeal to word statistics would readily minimize the centrality of "love" for Jesus' teaching.

130. *Jesus and Judaism*, 270-93; idem, *Jesus to Mishnah*, 95-96. Invoking Schweitzer, Sanders rightly criticizes scholarship that too easily produces a Jesus that "agrees with their own version of Christianity" (*Jesus and Judaism*, 330). While an irenical motivation is much wiser than a polemical one, as historians we also struggle to be vigilant against it producing a tendentious lens through which we view historical data. (History produces negative examples as warnings as well as positive ones as models.) Still, Sanders, *Jesus and Judaism*, 94, recognizes that Jesus' movement experienced persecution.

131. See especially *Jesus and Judaism*, 294-318.

132. See especially Holmén, *Covenant Thinking*.

133. Unless we excise it as redactional, based purely on the presupposition that realized and future eschatology must have been incompatible for late first-century Christians, in contrast to Paul several decades earlier. This presupposition conflicts with our other early Christian evidence; I discuss this question in Keener, *John*, 320-23.

134. Although Josephus, writing for a Gentile audience, is naturally coy about future eschatology (if he himself embraced it), his figures evoking Moses would speak of figures who appeared eschatological in early Judaism, even though we cannot be certain how many who expected such deliverance allowed that it might come in stages, rather than God's future kingdom being consummated at once.

Notes to Chapter 4

1. Crossan, *Historical Jesus*, 395, 415.

2. Stanton, *Gospel Truth*, 95.

3. Evans, *Fabricating Jesus*, 56.

4. We have already noted the Jesus Seminar, which includes *Gospel of Thomas* among the "five Gospels." More surprising is the dating of sources in Crossan, *Historical Jesus*, 427-30, assigning *Gospel of Thomas* and the "Cross Gospel" in *Gospel of Peter* a date before 60 CE, *Secret Mark* before Mark in the period 60-80 CE, and Matthew and Luke in the 90s (with the first version of John in the early second century).

5. Evans, *Fabricating Jesus*, 98. DeConick, *Translation*, 7, who does accept a first-century "kernel" to Thomas, warns against "the tendency" of some "to identify" "*Thomas*' theology" with that of Jesus.

6. Evans, *Fabricating Jesus*, 98.

7. Its possibly revisionist portrait of Judas may address only a minor point in the earlier gospel tradition, but this point would fit the broader revisionist agenda and readings of gnosticism.

8. The manuscript we have dates to between 300 and 350 (Porter and Heath, *Gospel of Judas*, 79); the content cannot easily predate the late second century (for its genre as gnostic rehabilitation literature, see Porter and Heath, *Gospel of Judas*, 80-89; for its dependence on NT material, see pp. 90-95). For one summary of the work and what can be known about it, see Perkins, *Introduction to Gospels*, 278-81. The Coptic may undermine scholars' initial "heroic" reading. Judas plays a heroic role in *Toledot Yeshu* (on which see e.g., Heindl, "Rezeption"; contrast the *Gospel of Barnabas*), but this work is still later.

9. Dan Brown's claim of 80 gospels destroyed by Constantine is fiction (happily the most extravagant statements in the *Da Vinci Code* are attributed to one who turns out to be an unreliable charac-

ter). This complaint is not intended to deny early traditions about Constantine's zeal. Eusebius *Life of Constantine* reports that Constantine destroyed idolatrous temples in 3.54-56; banished "false prophets" in 3.63; deprived heretics of meeting places in 3.65; and in 3.66 searched for heretical books (perhaps including magical books, pagan Sibylline prophecies, and so forth).

10. In this chapter, I draw on my treatments especially in *John*, 34-37, 161-69; also idem, "Lost Gospels."

11. *Her.* 3.11.8-9. Indeed, Irenaeus' working canon differs only marginally from the later one, since he failed to use only 3 Jn, Jms and 2 Pet (Chadwick, *Church*, 81). Some even find the fourfold Gospel presupposed in the early second century longer ending of Mark (Parsons, *Acts*, 14, cites Kelhoffer *Miracle*).

12. Contrasting the early established Christian traditions with the so-called gnostic Gospels, Perkins, *Introduction to Gospels*, 293, offers one answer to those wondering if these other works should be welcomed into the canon: "the simplest response is, 'Take a copy of the *Gospel of* (whatever the news flash of the week is) home. Try reading it silently and out loud to someone in your family. Then tell me.'" She notes she has never had any "votes" for their canonicity after that. This argument may presuppose an established Christian tradition, but as we have argued, one did exist before these works were composed.

13. "Gnostic Gospels" may be generally a misnomer (see Perkins, *Introduction to Gospels*, 280-81), though it is difficult to know what else to call them. A significant number of the works in this category, however, have gnostic elements, the point we are making.

14. Charlesworth and Evans, "Agrapha," 491.

15. See Wright, "Apocryphal Gospels"; cf. Burkitt, *Sources*, 17; Dibelius, *Jesus*, 20; Sanders, *Figure*, 64. A non-gospel narrative, *Acts of Paul and Thecla*, may reflect some of the same trends as appear in Montanism; reports of Maximilla's and Priscilla's adherence to Montanus (cf. Euseb. *H.E.* 5.16) resemble that of chaste women in these texts who leave husbands to cleave to ministers of the word.

16. Jeremias, *Unknown Sayings*, 18-19; compare the function of some Jewish haggadic works above.

17. Cf. Aune, *Environment*, 151-53, especially on apocryphal acts; cf. Bauckham and Porter, "Apocryphal Gospels," 71. Koester, "One Jesus," 158-59, overly skeptical about the canonical gospels, finds barely any historical truth in the apocryphal ones. For further discussion of the genre differences between the "canonical" and "apocryphal" gospels, see Aune, *Dictionary of Rhetoric*, 201; Bauckham and Porter, "Apocryphal Gospels," 71.

18. See Wiersma, "Novel."

19. Novels were largely non-referential (Konstan, "Invention," 5-6). The recycling of a story line (cf. Lucian's *Lucius* and Apuleius' *Metam.*) suggests limits to this distinction, but the point is that the novelist cannot be described as "mistaken" about his claims, since (far more than historians and mythographers) the novelist has control over the work's narrative world.

20. Cf. Charlesworth and Evans, "Agrapha," 491-95 (including also some Nag Hammadi works).

21. E.g., Lucian *Hist.* 12, who distinguishes proper biography from falsification and flattery; Plut. *Poetry* 2, *Mor.* 16F, who points to fabricated materials in poetry (quite different from how he describes his sources in the *Lives*). See Mosley, "Reporting," 26; Kany, "Bericht"; Witherington, *Acts*, 25-26.

22. Bowersock's examples of fictionalized history (*Fiction as History*, 21) are distinctly novelistic; historical fictions (like Xen. *Cyr.*; Ps.-Callisth. *Alex.*, the latter four to eight centuries after Alexander) were exceptional and fairly transparent.

23. Carson, *John*, 64-65, following Sternberg, *Poetics*, 23-35.

24. Aune, *Environment*, 151-52; Lalleman, "Apocryphal Acts," 67; Rebenich, "Historical Prose," 307-8; Bauckham, "Acts of Paul"; Keylock, "Distinctness," 210; Krasser, "Reading," 554; Hofmann, "Novels: Christian," 846-48; Perkins, "World." Pervo, "Fabula," compares the apocryphal acts with the *Aesop Romance*. Cf. n. 17, above.

25. Pervo, *Profit*, 130.

26. Hofmann, "Novels: Christian," 847.

27. See Aune, *Dictionary of Rhetoric*, 322. Perhaps the apocryphal acts originated partly through Christians reading romances through Christian lenses, seeing what they could make use of (see Price, "Evolution of Genres").

28. Aune, *Dictionary of Rhetoric*, 10. Pervo, "Hard Act," sees Acts of Paul not as a sequel to Luke-Acts (against Bauckham, "Acts of Paul") but as an attempt to correct it; clearly it rewrites some of Acts' narratives, but this may be for hagiographic development rather than rejection (see Marguerat, "L'héritage"; idem, *"Acts of Paul"*; cf. idem, *Histoire*, 369-91). Although some think Acts of Paul dependent only on Galatians (Rordorf, "Conversion," 142-43, highlighting Acts' details missing in the later work), most have argued otherwise (e.g., Hills, "Acts and *Acts*"; Pervo, "Hard Act"; Bauckham, "Acts of Paul" and idem, "Sequel"; cf. Hills, *"Acts of Paul"*), especially regarding imitation of Acts' perceived primary subject (not so much its content). The particular dating of the post-Lukan acts is more problematic; their relative sequence also occasions debate (e.g., MacDonald, "Relationships," 40; Pervo, "Egging," 55; Stoops, *"Acts of Peter,"* 83-84).

29. On Paul in the apocryphal acts, see Michaels, "Paul in Tradition," especially 692-94. On Paul and Luke's Acts, see esp. Porter, *Paul in Acts*; Harnack, *Acts*, 264-74; Campbell, "Journeys"; cf. Talbert, *Mediterranean Milieu*, 205-6.

30. Justin *1 Apol.* 66.3; 67.3; *Dial.* 103.8; 106.3 (see Stanton, *New People*, 62-63; Abramowski, "Memoirs," pace Koester).

31. *Infancy Story of Thomas* 4.1-5.1.

32. *Infancy Story of Thomas* 2.2-4.

33. *Infancy Story of Thomas* 9.1-3.

34. On apocryphal gospels of various varieties, Aune, *Dictionary of Rhetoric*, 199-203.

35. Against the "alternative gospel theorists," P. Egerton depends on canonical gospels, reflecting even Matthean and Lukan redaction (Charlesworth and Evans, "Agrapha," 514-25; Evans, *Fabricating Jesus*, 85-92, esp. 89; though Aune, *Dictionary of Rhetoric*, 329, who dates it c. 150 CE, allows its independence).

36. Voorst, *Jesus Outside NT*, 209, notes that apart from H. Koester and J. D. Crossan, most scholars remain skeptical.

37. Crossan dates it to the 50s of the first century (*Historical Jesus*, 429). For skepticism regarding its antiquity, see e.g., Allison, *Jesus of Nazareth*, 17.

38. Evans, *Fabricating Jesus*, 79-85. On the Gospel of Peter and its hypothetical "Cross Gospel," see views in Brown, *Death*, 1317-49; Meier, *Marginal Jew*, 1:117-18.

39. Wright, "Apologetic"; cf. Jeremias, *Unknown Sayings*, 17. Most of the Jesus Seminar apparently have not found the Gospel of Peter very historical (see Funk et al., *Acts of Jesus*, 441-48).

40. Charlesworth and Evans, "Agrapha," 511. Voorst, *Jesus Outside NT*, 209, notes that whereas Crossan offers no sustained source-critical analysis supporting its antiquity, critics of this work's antiquity (such as Raymond Brown) do offer source-critical arguments. Ehrman, *Prophet*, 69-70, however, thinks the work depends on "popular traditions" rather than the written Gospels themselves, since it left out so much; nevertheless, he agrees that it is later than they.

41. E.g., the *Acts of Pilate*; so Quarles, "Gospel of Peter," 119, also noting other second-century features; cf. Charlesworth and Evans, "Agrapha," 507.

42. Evans, *Fabricating Jesus*, 83 (citing *G. Pet.* 8.31; 10.38); cf. Theissen and Merz, *Historical Jesus*, 50; Jos. *Ant.* 18.38; *m. Nazir* 3:5; 7:3; *Mekilta Pisha* 1.83-84. Tannaim thought that only imbeciles slept in cemeteries (*tos. Ter.* 1:3). Cf. also the Jewish leaders' confession (7.25; 11.48), noted by Evans, *Fabricating Jesus*, 82-83.

43. Jeremias, *Unknown Sayings*, 18; Burridge, *Gospels*, 249-50; Wright, *People of God*, 410-11.

44. Though Mack, *Lost Gospel*, 6, appeals to the massive number of *agrapha*, most appear in late documents, and even the small number of *agrapha* accepted by Jeremias are at most possibly authentic (Meier, *Marginal Jew*, 1:113; Voorst, *Jesus Outside NT*, 179-85; Charlesworth and Evans, "Agrapha,"

483-91, esp. 487, 491). Our very inability to distinguish accurate and inaccurate agrapha underlines the value of our earlier written documents (Hofius, "Sayings"). See Aune, *Dictionary of Rhetoric,* 28-29, for summary and secondary sources discussing these 266 sayings.

45. Jeremias, *Unknown Sayings,* 26-28; on Thomas, cf. ibid., 18; Stanton, *Gospels,* 129; Chilton, "Thomas," 171; Blomberg, "Thomas," 195-196; idem, "Studying Jesus," 24; Wright, *People of God,* 437-43. See Stanton, *Jesus of Nazareth,* 129-35, who addresses very significant contrasts between the canonical Gospels and the Gospel of Thomas (which itself is closer to our canonical samples than other Nag Hammadi material is). Although the Gospel of Thomas apparently contains Aramaisms of some sort (DeConick, *Recovering,* 243-44; idem, *Translation,* 11-15, argues even for an Aramaic original of the basic core source), like the Synoptics, this claim is not made for most gnostic "gospels."

46. Platonic thought was a key and frequent element; later Egyptian gnosticism also integrated elements of Egyptian paganism. Jewish mysticism may have played a role in gnosticism's formation, despite the anti-Judaism of some segments of gnosticism. Yet some of these circles (especially in the second century) were closer to the "orthodox" and lines were not always clearly drawn (note e.g., Clement of Alexandria).

47. E.g., Aune, *Dictionary of Rhetoric,* 198.

48. Perhaps related to the tradition of Jewish mysticism, to the Greek Mysteries, or to both. Deprecation of the body may also have contributed to deprecation of public knowledge.

49. Note that we are not denying that many traditions *could* be passed on accurately this late (see our discussion about oral tradition later in the book). Rather, we are denying that gnostics *wanted* to use so much of the church's common tradition, at least without introducing more philosophically satisfactory correctives. But gnosticism by its character was more interested in cosmology than in history or historical particularity.

50. Conzelmann, *Theology,* 11; Jonas, *Religion,* 32-33; Bousset, *Kyrios Christos,* 187, 245. For a survey of the view's development, see Yamauchi, *Gnosticism,* 21-24; Ridderbos, *Paul,* 27-28.

51. See Lohse, *Environment,* 255.

52. For gnosticism's debt to earlier Christianity, see Wilson, *Gnostic Problem,* 68, 256; Yamauchi, *Gnosticism,* 20; Burkitt, *Gnosis,* viii; Grant, *Gnosticism,* 13-14. For one recent reading of gnostic development, see Smith, *Gnostic Origins.*

53. Some (not all) of the texts reflect the completed Synoptics (esp. the most popular, Matthew), but never clearly pre-Synoptic tradition (Tuckett, *Nag Hammadi,* 149, 155, 158-59).

54. One might contrast the rabbinic corpus, dating from a period when knowledge of Christianity was inevitable, but which mentions followers of Jesus only fairly rarely (for examples, see e.g., Herford, *Christianity*) and of course includes no Christian documents.

55. MacRae, "Gnosticism"; Evans, "Prologue," 395. Koester, *Introduction,* 2:211, gives *Hypostasis of the Archons* as an example of reworked material.

56. Wilson, "Nag Hammadi"; cf. "The Testimony of Truth," in *NHLE,* 406.

57. Goppelt, *Theology,* 1:17-18; Bruce, "Myth," 92; Brown, *John,* 1:LV; cf. idem, "Thomas," 155-77; Stark, "Empire."

58. See the summary in Yamauchi, *Gnosticism,* 71.

59. Kilpatrick, "Background," 40-41; this is based on an incomplete but representative sampling of Septuagintal vocabulary.

60. Kilpatrick, "Background," 43.

61. See e.g., Wahlde, "Archaeology"; Hunter, "Trends."

62. Funk et al., *Gospels,* 15.

63. See e.g., Tuckett, "Sources and methods," 130 (suggesting that saying 82 may reflect a wider tradition); Charlesworth and Evans, "Agrapha," 502; Barnett, *Jesus and History,* 26-27.

64. Stanton, *Gospel Truth,* 87; Wright, *People of God,* 437-43; Lüdemann, *Two Thousand Years,* 589 (though he dates Thomas as early as 125 CE); cf. Bruce, *Origins,* 155. DeConick argues for Syrian "orthodox" rather than a "gnostic" reading (*Recovering,* 235, 241-42; idem, *Translation,* 5-7); I believe

that this view would lead to the same conclusion regarding the finished work's date (though DeConick, *Recovering*, 240, dates it at 120 CE at the latest). "Gnostic" is admittedly a slippery category.

65. Scholars starting with expertise in gnostic documents tend to be readier to find gnosticizing elements in first-century sources. While elements of later gnosticism were in fact widespread, scholars starting with expertise in public Greco-Roman sources (philosophy, rhetoric, and so forth) tend to distinguish the later, Christian phenomenon of gnosticism from such elements (since later movements regularly develop tendencies of earlier thought).

66. For one recent and pointed critique of using second-century sources, including *Thomas*, for reconstructing the Jesus tradition, see Meier, *Marginal Jew*, 1:112-66; for a critique of the thesis of pre-Christian gnosticism, see Yamauchi, *Gnosticism*.

67. With e.g., Heyer, *Jesus Matters*, 103; Wright, "Seminar," 92. Smith, "Scripture," 14, notes that whereas Matthew and Luke connect intertextually with the Hebrew canon in such a way as to carry on Jewish Scripture, Thomas reflects a "new, esoteric religion."

68. For different proposed genres for Q, see e.g., Aune, *Dictionary of Rhetoric*, 390-92.

69. E.g., Meier, *Marginal Jew*, 1:123-39; Tuckett, "Thomas and Synoptics"; Tuckett, "Thomas: Evidence"; idem, Tuckett, "Sources and methods," 130; Perrin, *Thomas and Tatian*, 185-88; Charlesworth and Evans, "Agrapha," 498-500; Evans, *Fabricating Jesus*, 67-72; McClymond, *Stranger*, 32; cf. Stegemann, "Jesus," 1182. The consensus is summarized e.g., in Blomberg, "Studying Jesus," 23-25. Although an oral tradition approach challenges traditional redactional approaches (DeConick, *Translation*, 16), observations about even probable redaction shift the burden of proof. There are detractors (cf. the "camps" noted in Perrin, *Thomas and Tatian*, 14); at a high level of sophistication, DeConick, *Translation*, 15-24, seeks to balance evidence for independence and dependence. Some (noted in Perrin, *Thomas and Tatian*, 174-75) attribute parallels with M and L material to later stages in Thomas's composition; such an attribution, however, constitutes an appeal to a hypothetical source that assumes what one hopes to prove. Nevertheless, in the final analysis, even among scholars who see some early traditions in Thomas, very few hold that Thomas itself actually predates the Synoptics (see Johnson, *Real Jesus*, 89).

70. Perrin, *Thomas and Tatian*, 3. Perrin contends that Thomas employs mainly written rather than oral sources (*Thomas and Tatian*, 181-83).

71. Admittedly most scholars (including myself) have not done the detailed work on Thomas that specialist Thomas scholars like April DeConick (who has provided substantive and careful analysis of Thomas traditions) has, and my conclusions here are not comparable in documentation to those I offer in the following chapters. DeConick argues for gradual accretions in Thomas, from a bulk of sayings (with many Q parallels, e.g., DeConick, *Recovering*, 243; *Translation*, 7-8) 40-50 CE (for one clear summary, see *Translation*, 10). Her work may offer the best chance of identifying some earlier material in Thomas, if anything can. I am not drawing on it here, however (useful though it might be if correct), for the same reason I do not engage in source-criticism of Mark or "Q" (in contrast to reconstructing Q from the concrete documents Matthew and Luke): the cumulative level of uncertainty seems too risky for the sort of work I am attempting here. That is not to say that scholars should not attempt such hypothetical analyses, only to explain why I am not exploring them in a work like this one. I concede that my own work has been influenced by narrative-critical skepticism about source criticism beyond a certain point (a reaction against some earlier source criticism's excesses).

72. Perrin, *Thomas and Tatian*, 4-5, even contends that most scholars accept a Syrian, or even Edessene, provenance. He also notes (6-7) that many have seen Syriac as the original language, though (7-8) most have thought Greek its original language.

73. Perrin, *Thomas and Tatian*, 49, 57-155, 171; idem, "Overlooked Evidence," 143-44; followed by Evans, *Fabricating Jesus*, 73. Perrin grants the possibility of a different Aramaic dialect, but believes that Syriac explains more of the evidence ("Overlooked Evidence," 139; *Thomas and Tatian*, 19-47, esp. 46). He argues that Syriac's "range of lexicological options" limits the problems of back translation (Perrin, *Thomas and Tatian*, 54). In *Thomas and Tatian*, 155, he notes that in Coptic, there are a total of

269 catchwords; in Greek, 263; but in Syriac, 502; he observes (156) we know of no non-Syriac text that, converted into Syriac, would produce these results.

74. In Syriac, e.g., Ephrem (*Thomas and Tatian*, 158) and Odes of Solomon (159-62); Thomas often uses the *same* puns as Odes of Solomon (162). Such connections are often especially common in collections of *secret revelation* (164-68). Thomas apparently generates the catchwords by the traditional "exegetical principle" of linking keywords (175); sometimes it modifies sayings to create a connection (176-80). DeConick, *Recovering*, 48, attributes such catchwords to oral tradition.

75. Only in Syriac the same term can represent "soul" or the reflexive, relevant to two of three cases in *Thomas* (*Thomas and Tatian*, 156-57); "wealth" and "place," which pun in Syriac, often appear together (157), as do "hate" and "flesh"; "fruit" and "father"; and so forth (157).

76. *Thomas and Tatian*, 156 (noting *Thomas* 10; 11.3; 82; 83.1, 2).

77. *Thomas and Tatian*, 171.

78. *Thomas and Tatian*, 172.

79. A Syriac original explains the divergence between Greek and Coptic versions (Perrin, "Overlooked Evidence," 144-50). Textual evidence survived especially in Egypt, but Perrin's inferential evidence to this effect appears persuasive.

80. Perrin, *Thomas and Tatian*, 15-16. His focus on the Diatessaron's wording (*Thomas and Tatian*, 55) might prejudice the case in favor of finding parallels.

81. Perrin, *Thomas and Tatian*, 16. Others (e.g., Heyer, *Jesus Matters*, 104; DeConick, below) also note Thomas' affinities with the Diatessaron.

82. Evans, *Fabricating Jesus*, 73-76, arguing that the Syrian evidence refutes the attempts of Crossan and others to find an early source here.

83. See discussion in Aune, *Dictionary of Rhetoric*, 127.

84. DeConick, *Translation*, 20-21, thinks that probably "an early form of the *Gospel of Thomas* . . . was known in Syria to Tatian" (quoting 21; cf. *Recovering*, 242-43). But Tatian does not use this source in his harmony; why would it influence him so much? At the same time, a common Syriac tradition behind both (whether shaped by "Thomas" traditions or a gospel tradition that led to both) is plausible (see discussion below).

85. DeConick, *Recovering*, 48, warns that it is difficult to imagine an original Syriac work translated into Coptic in time for a manuscript of 200 CE. We have a fragment of John dating to within possibly a generation of its composition (see Roberts, *Fragment*; also discussion in e.g., Dibelius, *Jesus*, 13; Clark, "Criticism," 27; Metzger, "Papyri," 40), but no translation was needed in that case.

86. Quispel's argument noted in Perrin, *Thomas and Tatian*, 184-85. Most of Perrin's argument (from catchwords and explanations for translation variants) in fact involves a Syriac origin; only a comparatively small part of his argument involves the *Diatessaron* per se. But Perrin, *Thomas and Tatian*, 183-84, correctly observes that the Diatessaron is the *only* known (written) Syriac gospel in the second century.

87. Perrin, "Overlooked Evidence," 151, argues that Thomas reveals "more about early Syriac Christianity than about the oral traditions handed down from Jesus."

88. Perrin, *Thomas and Tatian*, 5-6, notes that the most widespread consensus date has been c. 140 CE (e.g., Heyer, *Jesus Matters*, 104). Stegemann, "Jesus," 1182, suggests that it is no *later* than 140; Lüdemann, *Two Thousand Years*, 589, dates it earlier, c. 125; DeConick, *Recovering*, 240, to no later than 120 CE.

89. Scribal variation of course still occurred, but the basic forms were stable (our early-second-century fragment of John is identical with our received text), and early-second-century patristic sources used Synoptic material. Contrary to what several scholars have argued, a degree of textual fluidity is not a problem identical to a document's thorough expansion (on some views of Thomas) or creation (on others). Even if we accept development of a core in Thomas, even the Western text of Acts includes less revision than we would have to envision for Thomas here.

90. *Gospel of Thomas* 114 (NHL p. 130).

91. Philo *Embassy* 320.

92. Thomas' approach, however, is probably reacting against earlier eschatology; see Tuckett, "Thomas: Evidence"; Allison, *Jesus of Nazareth,* 124. DeConick even argues that the earliest core of Thomas material was eschatological (*Recovering,* 130-55, 236, 239-40; *Translation,* 25-26, 30-31).

93. Cf. the largely black color coding for John in Funk et al., *Acts of Jesus,* 365-440 (though few narratives fare well in that book); idem, *Gospels,* 401-70. Thomas, with more Synoptic-like sayings, fares better (Funk et al., *Gospels,* 471-532).

94. Some treat John's eschatology as wholly realized (e.g., Käsemann, *Testament,* 15-16, 20); a more nuanced position is that it is mostly realized (Schweizer, *Jesus,* 164-68; for some future eschatology, see e.g., Kümmel, *Theology,* 294-95; Lindars, *Behind,* 66; Barrett, *John,* 68-69; Moule, "Factor," 159; Kysar, *Maverick Gospel,* 87, 110; Schlier, "Begriff," 268). Some have sought to find in John's realized eschatology the original point of Jesus (cf. Dodd, *Preaching,* 75; Glasson, *Advent,* 222-25; Robinson, *Coming,* 163), but Jesus' eschatology probably included both elements. Qumran blended realized and future eschatology (Aune, *Eschatology,* 29-44), and even Philo (who tends toward realized eschatology) had hope for Israel's restoration (Sanders, *Jesus and Judaism,* 86).

95. Possibly including the Gospel of the Nazarenes (P. Vielhauer in *New Testament Apocrypha,* ed. Hennecke, 1:144), though this may be a secondary expansion of Matthew into Aramaic (Meier, *Marginal Jew,* 1:116).

96. Talbert, *Gospel,* 8-9. Later Koester came to view the canonical Gospels as "aretalogical biographies."

97. Cf. Hadas and Smith, *Heroes.*

98. Shuler, *Genre,* 15-20; cf. Talbert, *Gospel,* 12-13; Klauck, *Religious Context,* 167-68. A more general proposal of aretalogical biographies (Wills, *Quest*) would be more reasonable.

99. Burridge, *Gospels,* 18-19; Aune, *Dictionary of Rhetoric,* 57 (following Winkler, *Auctor,* 236). Talbert, *Gospel,* 43, cites biographies of immortals (mainly from the second and third centuries), but as he admits, the religious or mythical dimension does not affect genre (cf. Shuler, *Genre,* 21); his evidence for specific cultic biographies (Talbert, *Gospel,* 91-113) is mainly inferential (Aune, "Problem," 37-42).

100. That Aboth and most wisdom literature share the same rhetorical forms (Gottlieb, "Abot") supports the likelihood that many early sages like Jesus spoke and were understood in part as wisdom teachers.

101. Cf. Keener, *John,* 35-36.

102. With Perrin, *Thomas and Tatian,* 9-10; Evans, *Fabricating Jesus,* 76.

103. These could belong to a different source than most of the other shared material, but they fall at the same points in the narrative, with the healing of the centurion's servant virtually immediately following the sermon on the plain/mount. Funk et al., *Acts of Jesus,* 41-49, does find brief narrative segments in the larger "Q."

104. Kelber, *Gospel,* 199-211; Boring, *Sayings,* 201-3, provide examples of this earlier approach. Contrast Gundry, "Genre," 103-7; more fully, Byrskog, *Story as History,* 107-44 (esp. 128-30, noting that oral historiography does not oppose written sources).

105. E.g., episodes from Aesop's life in a collection of his fables (Phaed. 2.9.1-4); cf. the combination of sayings and deeds in Diog. Laert. Sayings could also be reported from separate sources in a biography after narrating the rest of a "life," without implying that the two genres were contradictory (e.g., Plut. *Timoleon* 15.1; Philost. *Lives* 2.5.574); most often biographies included both (Val. Max. 1.pref.1).

106. Cf. Lindenberger, "Ahiqar," 480-82.

107. Although rhetoric teachers formally distinguished sayings-chreiai and action-chreiai, they also formally recognized mixed chreiai, which included both (Theon *Progymn.* 3.22-23); sayings-chreiai also could include both statement and response (*Progymn.* 3.27-28). On combining sayings and narrative, see also Theon *Progymn.* 4.73-79.

108. Richardson and Gooch, "Logia," 52.

109. Stanton, *Gospel Truth*, 77-95; Sanders, *Figure*, 64. Most of the material that is most defensible depends on the canonical Gospels; see Meier, *Marginal Jew*, 1:114-23.

110. With e.g., Behr, "Taught," 32. The fiction of "secret" traditions works much better for originally secretive groups like Pythagoreans (cf. Iamblichus *V.P.* 35.252-53, 258-60) than where something like the public apostolic tradition was already in place. The less widely known a claim was, the more subject to suspicion it would be (Xen. *Ages.* 5.6).

111. See Burridge, *Gospels*, 249-50; Wright, *People of God*, 410-11; also Smith, "Scripture," 13-14 (noting that it cannot be construed, unlike the Synoptics and John, as seeking to continue the biblical story).

112. Charlesworth and Evans, "Agrapha," 526-32; cf. Marcus, *Mark*, 47-51.

113. Cf. Jeffery, *Secret Gospel*, 247: "we were supposed to accept that these two fragments of the Secret Gospel, preserved only in an (allegedly) eighteenth-century copy, represented a text as early as, or even earlier than, any canonical New Testament writing."

114. Stanton, *Gospel Truth*, 93; Neusner, "Foreword," xxvii; cf. Losie, "Gospel." Brown, *Death*, 297, dates it earlier, to c. 125.

115. As late as the 1700s some writers followed the ancient convention of pretending to translate ancient writings seen by no one else (Lefkowitz, *Africa*, 111); for a Gospel forgery from 1860, see Millard, *Reading and Writing*, 53. For one popular retelling of the "Piltdown Man" forgery or hoax that misled many earlier paleontologists for four decades, see Millar, *Piltdown Men* (though Millar favored Grafton Elliot Smith as the culprit, there has been no consensus).

116. Carlson, *Hoax*, 35-40.

117. Carlson, *Hoax*, 49-64; also Jeffery, *Secret Gospel*, 41, 99 (citing others' observations that it provides much more distinctively Clementine vocabulary than Clement's normal passages do).

118. Carlson, *Hoax*, 65-71. Jeffery, *Secret Gospel*, 55-70 (cf. also 71-90), finds there elements of Smith's Anglican liturgical background; it does not fit second-century Alexandrian liturgy, and Smith misunderstood eastern liturgy (cf. 123-48).

119. For this and other features suggesting forgery, see Carlson, *Hoax*, 26-35.

120. Carlson, *Hoax*, 42-47, esp. 46-47; Evans, *Fabricating Jesus*, 96-97. It also contains some obscure information on which Smith had previously published (Carlson, *Hoax*, 71-72). Jeffery, *Secret Gospel*, suggests other cases of Smith's deception (e.g., 127, 134, 147, although these cases might reflect simply a shift in perspective), sexual humor (e.g., 128-29), misreading another culture in light of his own (132-33, 136-44), and agendas powerful enough to seriously distort data (144-45).

121. Jeffery, *Secret Gospel*, 119, 121.

122. See Jeffery, *Secret Gospel*, 49-50, 185-212, 248. Jeffery also notes that the Mar Saba text's portrayal of homosexuality better fits "the 'Uranian' homosexual subculture of nineteenth-century English universities" than its putative context (*Secret Gospel*, 225; the entire argument is 213-25). For the reversal of Smith's own position (and his movement from an Anglo-Catholic to his belief that early Christianity was a conspiratorial construct), see Jeffery, *Secret Gospel*, 149-84.

123. Jeffery, *Secret Gospel*, argues that Smith composed the work to defend homosexual love against traditional Christian views (119-21, 239, 242-43, 247).

124. Jeffery, *Secret Gospel*, 226-39, 241-42, citing Oscar Wilde's *Salomé* (note esp. the seven veils suggested in Smith's document, 229, reflecting an image developed by Wilde, 227-28, and certainly known to Smith).

125. Evans, *Fabricating Jesus*, 97.

126. *Lost Gospel*, 248.

127. A basic principle of persuasion theory is that if one's audience agrees with premise A and one seeks to persuade them of premise B, one may lump A and B together and call the resulting conglomeration "A." Many persuasion theorists regard such doublespeak as unethical (cf. the example of transfer in Brembeck and Howell, *Persuasion*, 235).

128. See e.g., essays in Goodacre and Perrin, *Questioning*. In contrast to my own book, some major works on Jesus research (such as those of E. P. Sanders) rest nothing on the Q hypothesis, some of the authors (including again E. P. Sanders) finding the hypothesis (or significant elements of it) questionable.

129. Cf. the caution of Meier, *Marginal Jew*, 2:177: Q "is a hypothesis, and only a hypothesis"; similarly, Theissen, *Gospels in Context*, 204. Classicists had similar speculative hypotheses, eventually abandoned for lack of evidence (Kennedy, "Source Criticism," 132).

130. E.g., Matt 8:5-13//Lk 7:1-10, following the same "Q" sermon of Jesus.

131. Cf. Dunn, *New Perspective*, 26-27, on the "one document per community" fallacy. For one challenge to the "community" approach, sometimes going further than I would go but certainly arguing better than Mack has argued here, see Bauckham, *Gospels for Christians*.

132. E.g., one would never guess from the two references to John in my first book *(Marries Another)* that I wrote it at the same time as my dissertation on John ("Pneumatology"; by contrast, I cited Matthew over 180 times in *Marries Another*, because Matthew was more relevant to the book's subject).

133. *Lost Gospel*, 1.

134. Cf. e.g., Theissen, *Gospels in Context*, 206, 226, who admits the appearance of John, Jesus' testing in the wilderness, and the centurion's servant; Voorst, *Jesus Outside NT*, 163; Ehrman, *Prophet*, 82. The Jesus Seminar found such basic narratives in Q (Funk et al., *Acts of Jesus*, 41-50), though they accept few of them as authentic to Jesus.

135. *Lost Gospel*, 1-2.

136. Especially the basic narrative frames in Matt 4:1-11//Lk 4:1-12; Matt 8:5-13//Lk 7:1-10; and Matt 11:2-4//Lk 7:18-20. This is not to deny that Matthew and Luke show greater verbal agreement on sayings than on narrative, though even here the agreements are not precise.

137. Others also note that Q is eschatological in orientation (e.g., Smith, "Scripture," 14).

138. Downing compares Q to Cynic *Lives* ("Like Q"; "Actuality"), but this comparison is too narrow (Tuckett, "Cynic Q"; cf. ancient biographies in general, treated later). Indeed, the original "Q" was probably Aramaic, fitting a Jewish and not a Cynic Jesus (see Casey, *Aramaic Approach*, 185, 190). Some doubt the Aramaic Q approach, however (Tuckett, "Q and Aramaic"). Some think that Paul needed to balance Jesus' wisdom sayings with eschatology in Corinth in the 50s (Koester, "Silence," 343-47).

139. Note this objection in Allison, *Jesus of Nazareth*, 123.

140. John Meier notes that some hold that the wisdom layer of Q is early while the prophetic material is later, and others hold the reverse. He registers his skepticism that one can separate Q into genuine chronological strata by such content-critical grounds (Meier, *Marginal Jew*, 1:178-80). See also Voorst, *Jesus Outside NT*, 166, also noting that A. Yarbro Collins and H. Koester find eschatological elements in *every* supposed stratum of Q. DeConick even argues that the earliest core of Thomas material was eschatological (*Recovering*, 130-55, 236, 239-40; *Translation*, 25-26, 30-31), warning that (*Recovering*, 243) "the vogue thesis that the early stratifications of Quelle were nonapocalyptic may need to be reassessed" (cf. further the critique of such trends in *Recovering*, 244-48).

141. Theissen and Merz, *Historical Jesus*, 29.

142. E.g., Theissen, *Gospels in Context*, 204; Meier, *Marginal Jew*, 2:180; Voorst, *Jesus Outside NT*, 164-65; see further Boyd, *Sage*, 136-39; and Witherington, *Sage*, 215 (following R. A. Horsley).

143. Frye, "Analogies in Literatures," 287.

144. For one discussion contrasting serial and cumulative probability, see Torrance, "Probability," 257-58.

145. For additional comments on the discrepancy between Mack's "authentic" data and the supposedly created material four times as large, see Blomberg, "Studying Jesus," 22, who rightly notes the lack of any known historical parallel for "such a radical transformation of a famous teacher . . . in so short a period of time."

146. *Lost Gospel,* 4-5.

147. Given some passages in the Septuagint; see also Suet. *Claud.* 25.4.

148. Sometimes where it does appear in Diaspora texts, as in some Sibylline Oracles or an oracle cited by Josephus, it is applied to a favorite pagan ruler like a Ptolemy or Roman emperor.

149. One might also ask what was so significant about Jesus as a sage for the putative "Q community" to have preserved his sayings. We do know, however, that schools often did preserve the teachings of their founders, so one need not infer messianic beliefs simply from the sayings collection.

150. Indeed, based on internal evidence, Meadors, "Orthodoxy," argues that Q's christology is essentially the same as Mark's.

151. For a recent pointed critique of arguments from silence, see Brown, *Death,* 7-8.

152. Keck, "Ethos," 435-52.

153. Keck, "Ethos," 448. Keck remains correct that Q's apparent lack of passion narrative (perhaps because of its specific focus) need not imply "that its church either had no passion story or no particular interest in it" (cf. also Voorst, *Jesus Outside NT,* 173-74). As Keck emphatically declares, "Not one bit of evidence has been adduced to show that such a conclusion is justified" (Keck, "Ethos," 448).

154. Some other scholars in addition to Mack have questioned whether eschatological and wisdom sayings are compatible; see Crossan, *Historical Jesus,* 265-306. Crossan, "Necessary," 32, envisions differences between the canonical "biographic" gospels and the noncanonical "discourse" gospels as indicating a war between two *types* of gospels.

155. Keck, "Ethos," 448.

156. Keck, "Ethos," 448-49.

157. E.g., Collins, "Wisdom"; Harrington, "Wisdom Texts"; VanderKam, "Mantic Wisdom."

158. Witherington, *Sage,* 211-12.

159. Witherington, *Sage,* 233-36.

160. Witherington, *Christology,* 243, citing the Similitudes of Enoch; on 4Q300, see Schiffman, "4QMysteries."

161. Pace Crossan, *Historical Jesus,* 288-91, who cites only extremely hellenized sources. Crossan likewise contrasts Paul's apocalyptic Jesus with the Corinthians' sapiential one (pp. 228-30), but Paul hardly rejects the sapiential (1 Cor 1:30; 8:5-6); nor does Jesus beginning a ministry distinct from John the Baptist support Crossan's conclusion that Jesus must have rejected John's apocalypticism (pp. 230-38).

162. Cf. also *Lost Gospel,* 183.

163. Cf. e.g., the agreement of Matt 12:28//Lk 11:20 against Mk 3:26-27. Because Mark would abbreviate material for a concise introduction, it is possible that Mark also abbreviates Q in his introduction and follows Q in starting his narrative with John the Baptist. While some scholars, including myself, find such arguments for Mark's use of "Q" persuasive, others demur (e.g., Marcus, *Mark,* 51-53, with reasonable arguments).

164. In fact, Q's theology probably does not differ in significant (seriously conflicting) ways from Mark's (Meadors, "Orthodoxy"; cf. Witherington, *Sage,* 233-36; see esp. Meadors, *Herald*).

165. Overman, "Deciphering," 193.

166. For a fuller list, including second-century sources Pliny the Younger, Lucian, and Celsus; a first-century letter; and rabbinic sources, see Evans, *Fabricating Jesus,* 104-6; Eddy and Boyd, *Legend,* 172-84; Stein, *Messiah,* 25-28; in more detail, see Bruce, *Origins,* 19-65; Voorst, *Jesus Outside NT,* 19-74 for Gentile sources (noting on 74 that most view Jesus as a troublemaker), and 75-134 for Jewish ones; at medium length, Ehrman, *Prophet,* 56-59 (Gentile sources), 59-63 (Jewish ones); Bruggen, *Narratives,* 25-41 (Gentile sources in 25-29; Jewish in 29-41). One place Jesus does *not* appear, contrary to some earlier media reports, is the Qumran scrolls, most of which are too early (Voorst, *Jesus Outside NT,* 75-81).

167. Allison, "Thallus," 405; Evans, "Non-Christian Sources," 454-55. Eddy and Boyd, *Legend,* 172-73, regard this as of minimal value, though probably the earliest extant non-Christian source

about Jesus. Although few pay attention to Tertullian's claim (*Apol.* 5.1-2) that Tiberius heard about Jesus' resurrection and wanted him viewed as a new divinity (the senate was not standing up to Tiberius much in 30 CE), Rizzo, "Tiberio," takes this claim seriously.

168. Theissen and Merz, *Historical Jesus*, 76-80 (suspecting the influence of Syrian Christans, 80); Evans, "Non-Christian Sources," 455-57.

169. Evans, "Non-Christian Sources," 458-64.

170. Evans, "Non-Christian Sources," 454-64.

171. Tac. *Ann.* 15.44. See comment in Eddy and Boyd, *Legend*, 179-85; Evans, "Non-Christian Sources," 464-66.

172. Suet. *Claud.* 25.4 (widely discussed; see e.g., Mattingly, *Christianity*, 30; Leon, *Jews of Rome*, 25; Harris, "References," 353-54; I offer a wider range of interpretations in my Acts commentary at Acts 18:2).

173. With e.g., Eddy and Boyd, *Legend*, 167-68.

174. Though prominent in Josephus' account of Caligula and even Claudius, in Tacitus Agrippa I appears in Tac. *Ann.* 12.23, a passing mention of his death in connection with the annexation of his territory to Syria.

175. Tac. *Ann.* 15.44.

176. See e.g., Just. *Dial.* 69:7; *b. Sanh.* 43a; 107b; Klausner, *Jesus*, 27-28, 49-51, 293; Dalman, *Jesus in Talmud*, 45-50; Herford, *Christianity*, 50-62; Gero, "Polemic"; Yamauchi, "Magic," 90-91; Horbury, "Brigand"; Bruggen, *Narratives*, 37-41; Voorst, *Jesus Outside NT*, 104-34; Stanton, *Gospel Truth*, 156-58; Ehrman, *Prophet*, 62-63.

177. Probably due to his target audience's displeasure with it in Rome (cf. Tac. *Ann.* 15.44; Suet. *Claud.* 25.4).

178. See Witherington, *Christology*, 83. Sanders, *Jesus and Judaism*, 395, n. 13, finds Jesus less influential than John in Josephus, but this tendency should take account of the reduction of the messianic element.

179. See Feldman, "David."

180. On his likely mention of Jesus, see e.g., Thackeray, *Josephus*, 125; Klausner, *Jesus*, 55ff; Cornfeld, *Josephus*, 510; Meier, "Jesus in Josephus"; idem, "Testimonium"; Whealey, "Josephus"; Gramaglia, "*Testamonium*"; Paget, "Observations"; Vermes, *Jesus the Jew*, 79; Charlesworth, *Jesus within Judaism*, 90-98; idem, "Jesus, Literature, and Archaeology," 189-92; Sanders, *Figure*, 50; Dubarle, "Témoignage"; Martínez, "Reevaluación"; Ehrman, *Prophet*, 59-62; Theissen and Merz, *Historical Jesus*, 64-74; Voorst, *Jesus outside NT*, 81-104; Elledge, "Sources"; Evans, "Non-Christian Sources," 466-68; Eddy and Boyd, *Legend*, 190-98; Flusser, *Sage*, 12. For earlier bibliographies of views, see Winter, "Bibliography"; Feldman, "Bibliography."

181. To my knowledge, Bruggen, *Narratives*, 30-37, is the most effective defender of this option.

182. Betz, *Jesus*, 9-10; Feldman, "Methods," 591.

183. Voorst, *Jesus Outside NT*, 93.

184. See here Charlesworth, *Jesus within Judaism*, 95-96; idem, "Jesus, Literature, and Archaeology," 191-92; Evans, "Non-Christian Sources," 468; Eddy and Boyd, *Legend*, 193-94.

185. Vermes, *Jesus the Jew*, 79.

186. The gospel tradition suggests a less emphatic hostility, but at least a mistrust, on the part of some of Jesus' siblings (Mk 3:21, 31; Jn 7:5), presumably including James, who appears to have shifted his approach after Jesus' resurrection (1 Cor 15:7). The tradition is not likely to have invented their initial mistrust, since the respect of one's family was a normal part of honor.

187. Theissen and Merz, *Historical Jesus*, 93.

188. Theissen and Merz, *Historical Jesus*, 93.

189. Theissen and Merz, *Historical Jesus*, 93. One cannot therefore postulate Bar Kochba as a fiction, since contemporary sources leave no doubt about him (cf. e.g., Pileggi, "Bar-Kochva Letters").

190. Eddy and Boyd, *Legend*, 167-68.

191. Flusser, *Sage*, 1.

192. Flusser, "Ancestry," 154.

193. Kennedy, "Source Criticism," 130.

194. See Kleve, "Did Socrates Exist?"

195. See e.g., Charlesworth and Evans, "Agrapha," 491; Dunn, *New Perspective*, 34; Ellis, "Gospels and History," 49; De Rosa, "Chi è Gesù." From a more theological and narrative vantage point, Pope Benedict views the Jesus of the Gospels as a more coherent figure than scholarly reconstructions about him (Benedict, *Jesus of Nazareth*, xxi-xxii).

Notes to Section II

1. Funk et al., *Gospels*, 16.

2. Allison, *Jesus of Nazareth*, 17. Some date Mark c. 70, but the difference of a year or two does not affect the point under discussion.

3. See our discussion of Luke's preface in ch. 6 (also ch. 9).

4. That is, if we treat Jesus differently, is this difference for historical reasons, or for religious reasons? Is a bias against a religious figure any more objective than a bias for a nonreligious one?

Notes to Chapter 5

1. Stanton, *Gospel Truth*, 139.

2. Aune, "Biography," 125.

3. Cf. Shuler, *Genre*, 25-28; Hirsch, *Interpretation*, 68-126. Although genre categories cannot be applied rigidly, deconstructionist dismissals of their value are also misplaced (see Eddy and Boyd, *Legend*, 318-20).

4. E.g., Quint. *Inst.* 10.1.36; Max. Tyre 26.4; 38.4. Rhetoricians distinguished various categories for literary forms (e.g., Theon *Progymn.* 2.5-33), and ancient editors divided Pindar's poems according to their type of hymn and song, thereby arranging them into books (Race, "Introduction," 1). Of various models for genre criticism in antiquity, Aristotle's prevailed longest (Burridge, *Gospels*, 27-29).

5. Technical rhetorical works often defined specific genres of letters and speeches more strictly than the empirical examples allow. See e.g., examples in Malherbe, "Theorists." Different genres of speeches invited different styles (Dion. Hal. *Demosth.* 45-46);

6. Aune, *Environment*, 23. In spite of elaborate classifications, mixed genres were common in the early imperial period; see idem, "Problem," 10-11, 48; idem, *Dictionary of Rhetoric*, 307 ("Mixtum compositum"); Burridge, *Gospels*, 33-34, 56-61; cf. Selden, "Genre," 39-40; Fuller, "Classics," 189 (summarizing G. Kennedy).

7. E.g., not only novelists but historians strove to develop internally consistent narrative worlds (see Stibbe, *Gospel*, 32-34); among historical writers attempts at consistency of plot and character succeed most often among biographers.

8. Quint. *Inst.* 10.6.1-2. Still, one should also be ready to add improvisations during the speech (10.6.5).

9. Cf. e.g., the opening Virgilic lines of the *Aen.* removed by the final editors (LCL 1:240-41, especially n. 1).

10. Aune, *Environment*, 128. Thus Josephus thoroughly revised an earlier draft of the *War* into better Greek (Jos. *Apion* 1.49-50); less likely, some think the earlier version was an Aramaic draft, probably for Parthian Jews (cf. Hata, "Version"). One could also adapt earlier works; Josephus seems to have employed the *War* as his main source for the comparable portion of the *Antiquities* (Krieger, "Hauptquelle"); 3 and 4 Maccabees adapted material in 2 Maccabees (Gardner, "Mqbym").

11. Thus allowing such literary techniques as foreshadowing (Arist. *Poet.* 15.10, 1454ab; Quint. *Inst.* 10.1.21). Editing provided the writer a chance to craft the material; thus, for example, Epictetus' *Discourses* undoubtedly bear less of Arrian's stamp than the *Encheiridion,* where he organizes and summarizes Epictetus' teachings.

12. Burridge, *Gospels,* 203; Aune, *Environment,* 82, citing Jos. *Apion* 1.47-50; Lucian *History* 16, 48; *Demonax.* Aristotle recommended sketching the plot in outline, then expanding by inserting episodes, and illustrates this with the *Odyssey* (Talbert, *John,* 64, citing Arist. *Poetics* 17.6-11).

13. Aune, *Environment,* 139.

14. Aune, *Environment,* 65; cf. Downing, "Conventions"; idem, "Actuality"; Burridge, *Gospels,* 204-5.

15. Cic. *Ad Att.* 13.21a, 23, 48. While the old source theories concerning proto-Mark and proto-Luke are unfashionable, it is likely that proto-Gospels existed temporarily (though unlikely that they were published); cf. Streeter, *Gospels,* 199-222; Taylor, *Formation,* 6, and Appendix A; Wenham, "Parable."

16. Talbert, "Chance," 230. Some view Acts as a "foundation story" (e.g., Pao, *Isaianic Exodus,* 3).

17. Stanton, *Gospels,* 15-17.

18. Talbert, *Gospel,* 2-3, observing that Strauss, Bultmann (see Bultmann, *Tradition,* 372; idem, "Message," 547) and their followers rejected the biographical category because they confused the two.

19. Mack, *Myth,* 16 n. 6; cf. Marxsen, *Mark,* 16.

20. For a fuller survey, see Burridge, *Gospels,* 3-25.

21. Hennecke, *Apocrypha,* 1:80; Riesenfeld, *Tradition,* 2; Guelich, "Genre." The designation "gospels" appears to date from the mid-second century (Aune, *Environment,* 18, cites Justin *Dial.* 10.2, 100.1; Iren. *Her.* 3.1.1; Clem. Alex. *Strom.* 1.21), though some derive it from Mark's (Kelber, *Story,* 15) or Matthew's usage (Stanton, *New People,* 14-16) and it probably has antecedents in the LXX use of the term (Stuhlmacher, "Theme," 19-25; Betz, "Gospel").

22. Biographies of "divine men" appear only later, and seem to depend on the form of the Gospels; see Dillon and Hershbell, "Introduction," 25-26.

23. Cf. Robbins, *Teacher,* 4-5.

24. So rightly Borchert, *John,* 29-30 (though noting differences between John and the Synoptics, p. 37).

25. Marxsen, *Mark,* 150, thus objects to applying the term "gospel" to Matthew and Luke as well as to Mark, arguing that Matthew is a collection of "gospels" and sermons (Marxsen, *Mark,* 150 n. 106; 205-6), and Luke a "life of Jesus" (Marxsen, *Mark,* 150 n. 106; we would agree regarding Luke). He is uncomfortable with the language of a gospel "genre" (ibid., 25).

26. Aune, *Environment,* 83, cites Quint. *Inst.* 2.42; Cicero *On Rhetorical Invention* 1.27; Sext. Emp. *Against the Professors* 1.263-64 for the three major categories (history, fiction, and myth or legend), though noting that they overlapped in practice (Strabo *Geog.* 1.2.17.35); for distinctions between mythography and history proper, see Fornara, *Nature of History,* 4-12.

27. Luz, *Matthew,* 1:44-45.

28. This view was proposed by K. L. Schmidt, who provided analogies among later folk literatures of various cultures; he is followed also by Kümmel, *Introduction,* 37; cf. Hunter, *Message,* 30; Deissmann, *Light,* 466.

29. Downing, "Literature"; Aune, *Environment,* 12, 63; Burridge, *Gospels,* 11, 153. Rhetorical principles influenced narrative techniques; see e.g., Dowden, "Apuleius."

30. Koester, *Introduction,* 1:108; Kodell, *Luke,* 23; cf. Perry, *Sources,* 7. This estimation becomes even clearer in view of Luke's architectonic patterns (for which see Goulder, *Type and History;* Talbert, *Patterns;* idem, *Luke;* Tannehill, *Luke;* idem, *Acts*).

31. E.g., contrast the popular "Life of Aesop" with the more literary *Agricola.*

32. E.g., Socratics *Ep.* 18, Xenophon to Socrates' friends; Diogenes Laertius includes compilations of traditions, but from a variety of sources. Greeks employed diaries fairly early (Rüpke,

"Ephemeris"); many Roman aristocrats kept personal "memoirs" even in the Republic (Rebenich, "Historical Prose," 313-14); Greeks also published such "memoirs" (Kennedy, "Source Criticism," 136-37). Perhaps "Q" may be understood in such terms; cf. Papias *fr.* 6 (Euseb. *H.E.* 3.39), on the hypothesis that Papias' "Matthew" is our "Q" (cf. Filson, *History*, 83; rejected by Jeremias, *Theology*, 38). Downing, "Like Q," compares Q with a Cynic "Life" (cf. Mack, *Lost Gospel*, 46); contrast Tuckett, "Cynic Q."

33. For an example of extant nonelite biography, see Aune, *Dictionary of Rhetoric*, 433-37, on the "Life of Secundus."

34. Justin *1 Apol.* 66.3; 67.3; *Dial.* 103.8; 106.3 (as noted earlier, see Stanton, *New People*, 62-63; Abramowski, "Memoirs," pace Koester).

35. See Robbins, *Teacher*, 62-67; Stanton, *New People*, 62-63. See earlier Kennedy, "Source Criticism," 128-30, comparing early memoirs about Socrates.

36. This is not to deny the Synoptics' substantial dependence on tradition, but tradition is not so dominant (as writers sometimes sound as if they are suggesting; e.g., Jones, *Parables*, 36) as to violate pursuit of literary coherence.

37. Of the necessary six parts Aristotle identifies in tragedy, the Gospels may include plot and character, but lack song (Arist. *Poetics* 6.9, 1450a), whereas nearly all poets include all these characteristics (*Poetics* 6.11).

38. Most Greek tragedies reflected and developed earlier tradition; thus in *Helen* Euripides follows the *Recantation of Stesichorus* (which violates the natural reading of Homer), yet to harmonize this tradition with Homer must have Menelaus and Helen meet up in Egypt and return to Sparta in time for Telemachus' arrival in the *Odyssey*. But such constraints were often much more general than with historical works or biography (cf. how closely Matthew or Luke follows Mark).

39. I treat this question more extensively in my book on miracles intended as a sequel to this one.

40. It coopted something closer to a biographic form (focused on the individual) primarily in later times (e.g., Philostratus's *Heroikos*), perhaps as a pagan response to the Gospels.

41. E.g., *Apocrit.* 2.12-15 (a polemical work, possibly by Porphyry); Mack, *Myth*, 11, 322-23.

42. I explore the "novel" thesis more fully in my Acts commentary, where I show that Acts includes far too many correspondences with extrinsic history to qualify as any kind of novel.

43. See Burridge, *Gospels*, 245; Aune, *Dictionary of Rhetoric*, 285; Porter, "We Passages," 550-52; Marguerat, *Historian*, 29; Soards, "Review," 309. Boyd-Taylor, "Adventure," argues that the Septuagint's changes to Esther's story move it in the direction of a Greek romance.

44. Bowie, "Readership," 443; Stephens, "Who Read Novels?" 414. Given the relative chronology, Bowersock, *Fiction as History*, 143, thinks that the Gospels inspired Gentile novels rather than the reverse (but see n. 45 below); more generally, Merkelbach, "Novel and Aretalogy," 290, suggests that religious aretalogies helped generate the new genre of novel.

45. Although writers like Apuleius and Achilles Tatius are a century or more after our period, the nineteenth century view of Greek novels as late (fifth or sixth centuries) is no longer tenable (Aune, *Environment*, 150). Thus elements in Char. *Chaer.*, (Ps)Plut. *L.S.* (*Mor.* 771E-775E, though all five are brief), earlier Petron. *Sat.*, Jos. *Asen.*, and earlier still Judith and the Ninus Romance suggest that the general genre was already established in the New Testament period.

46. Cf. e.g., Lindenberger, "Ahiqar." Yet even historical novels from the hellenistic era often exhibited some measure of historical accuracy (cf. Anderson, "3 Maccabees"; Miller, "Introduction," viii), though it varied considerably (e.g., if Judith reflects this genre at all, Jdt 4:3 reflects a serious anachronism). Even a pure novel like Apul. *Metam.* may include some autobiographical hints (e.g., 11.30).

47. E.g., Lucian *History* 12; Plut. *Poetry* 2, *Mor.* 16F; see Mosley, "Reporting," 26; Kany, "Bericht"; cf. Aune, *Environment*, 79 (who both notes the distinction and recognizes some overlap). As noted earlier, this observation is not to deny some degree of overlap among categories in historical content, but to note that what distinguishes the two genres is the nature of their truth claims (Carson, *John*, 64-65, following Sternberg, *Poetics*, 23-35).

48. See e.g., Aune, *Environment*, 151-53; Bauckham, "Acts of Paul"; Keylock, "Distinctness," 210.

49. Some scholars have suggested some overlap in the Gospels, though acknowledging that the degree varies from Gospel to Gospel (e.g., Freyne, *Galilee,* 11). Bowersock, *Fiction as History,* 124, notes parallels between novels and the Gospels, which he believes were generated by the latter. But even if one argued for some influence of novels on the form of the Gospels, Paul attests the basic "gospel story" before our extant Gospels, and, as we note above, the Gospels reflect authentic Palestinian Jewish environment.

50. With e.g., Porter, "We Passages," 550.

51. Most notably Xenophon's *Cyr.* and Ps.-Callisth. *Alex.;* note also two fictitious eyewitness accounts of the Trojan War (Merkle, "True Story," 183-84; Schmeling, "Spectrum," 23); the *Life of Aesop* in Wills, "Aesop Tradition," 224-25. In contrast to Philost. *Vit. soph.* (if by the same Philostratus), Philost. *Vit. Apoll.* is novelistic (with Kee, *Miracle,* p. 288), though it does reflect accurate geography until leaving the Roman world (Jones, "Apollonius' Passage," treating it as a "travel romance"). Many scholars think that Philostratus' main "source" for Apollonius' life, Damis, is a fiction of either Philostratus (Jones, "Apollonius' Passage"; Klauck, *Religious Context,* 170) or an earlier pseudepigrapher (though cf. Conybeare, "Introduction," vii). All of these works involve historical or legendary characters centuries earlier, whose eyewitnesses no longer remained in living memory. Jewish examples are more numerous, e.g., *L.A.E.* or *Joseph and Aseneth* or, to a lesser extent, *Testaments of the Twelve Patriarchs;* but despite some apparent dependence on earlier tradition, they do not reflect the massive use of sources evident in Matthew and Luke, nor are they claims about a historical person within living memory of some eyewitnesses, like the Gospels (on genre issues, see also appendix 3).

52. Cf. also Hengel, "Problems," 212. I might find an exception in Lucian's and Apuleius' recycling of a common story line about one Lucius, but neither expects his audience to embrace the work as a true account. Even John, whose sources are difficult to discern, overlaps enough with the Synoptics in some accounts and clearly in purpose to defy the category of novel.

53. Cf. the interesting parallels between Acts and "institutional history" in Cancik, "Historiography." Cancik ("Historiography," 673) and others are right to recognize the influence of Acts' genre on Luke, but the Gospel's focus on a single person still makes it a "life"; no rule prohibited an overlap between biography and history. See our chapter 6 on Luke-Acts.

54. As in Longus proem 1-2.

55. See Wiersma, "Novel."

56. Alexander, "Fiction and Genre," 392-94. Many novels used known centers like Ephesus or Tyre, but much of (later) Heliodorus' *Ethiopian Story* and Antonius Diogenes' *Wonders Beyond Thule* fit Alexander's point here. Of course, such exotic claims appear in some widely read histories (e.g., the gold-digging giant ants in Dio Chrys. *Or.* 35.23-24 probably allude to Hdt 3.102-5). The one possible analogy for an "exotic" location proposed for Luke-Acts, Philip's encounter with the African court official (Acts 8:26-39), does not fit novelistic expectations (Keener, "Official").

57. E.g., Longus is a countryman who knows the correct fauna of Lesbos, though much of his knowledge would apply to any eastern Mediterranean setting (and he apparently lacked firsthand acquaintance with trapping techniques; Arnott, "Realism," 211).

58. E.g., on cities (Saïd, "City," noting that some that were interested in cities used widely known information).

59. For this plot commonality, see e.g., Fusillo, "Novel," 838-39; Konstan, *"Apollonius* and Novel," 173; see further this emphasis in Konstan, *Symmetry.* "Romantic" themes included surviving dramatic adventures like shipwrecks (cf. e.g., Whitehouse, "Shipwreck on Nile").

60. One may compare works such as the *Acts of Paul and Thecla* or *Acts of Jn* 53-64, 73-80, where elements of the romance story line are followed, except that the women become devotees of the male teacher in chastity, devoted not to sexual love but to God's word. See Hofmann, "Novels: Christian," 847-48; Eddy and Boyd, *Legend,* 338-39; cf. Aubin, "Reversing Romance," 260-62 (noting the subversion of conventional gender assumptions); Thomas, "Fluidity," 277.

61. Talbert, *Gospel,* 17.

62. Most obviously, Apul. *Metam.* In contrast to most, Murgatroyd, "Ending," understands Apul. *Metam.* 11 as parody.

63. Kee, *Miracle*, 193, for other propagandistic narratives in the Isis cult. It is hardly true, however, that the genre as a whole was centered around religious propaganda (Kee, *Miracle*, 193-94). For more Isis aretalogies, see Horsley, *Documents*, 1:10-21.

64. Dio Cass. 1.1.1-2; Fornara, *Nature of History*, 120-33; Palmer, "Monograph," 3, 29, citing e.g., Cic. *Fam.* 5.12.5; Polyb. 1.4.11; 3.31.13; cf. also Dion. Hal. *Demosth.* 47. Burridge, *Gospels*, 149-51 includes entertainment among the function of many biographies. Some fiction did occur at times in ancient biography (Chance, "Fiction"), especially when the subject lived centuries earlier (Lefkowitz, *Africa*, 82).

65. As we have noted above, most *literary* characteristics of novels can also be found in ancient historiography (see Burridge, *Gospels*, 245; Aune, *Dictionary of Rhetoric*, 285; Marguerat, *Historian*, 29; Soards, "Review," 309; cf. Rothschild, *Rhetoric of History*, 291-92).

66. E.g., Aune, *Environment*, 36; see further below.

67. So e.g., Aune, *Environment*, 46-76; idem, *Dictionary of Rhetoric*, 204; Stanton, *Jesus of Nazareth*, 117-36; Robbins, *Teacher*, 10; Burridge, "People," 121-22; idem, "Biography, Ancient"; Cross, "Genres," 402-4; Frickenschmidt, *Evangelium als Biographie*; Ytterbrink, *Biography* (for Luke); "Gospels: forms," 948; Perkins, *Introduction to Gospels*, 2-11; Dunn, "The Tradition," 173-74; cf. Barr and Wentling, "Biography and Genre"; Berschin, "Biography," 653; for aretalogical biography, see Wills, *Quest*. See even Crossan, "Necessary," 27 (though he does not seem to view them as very reliable). Some of these writers (e.g., Stanton, *Gospels*, 19) reverse an earlier skepticism toward the biographical proposal (see Stanton, *New People*, 64, frankly; idem, "Reflection," 544-49 [in 1972 still affirming the consensus, but critically]; cf. Aune, "Problem," answered in Talbert, *Mediterranean Milieu*, 57-63). Cf. Hodgson, "Valerius Maximus."

68. Robbins, *Teacher*, 2-3.

69. Stanton, *New People*, 63; idem, *Gospel Truth*, 137.

70. One might choose to classify different sorts of biographies based on the nature of their primary characters, but this is a separate issue from classifying the larger literary genre of works about the public "life" *(bios)* of a particular person. Biographies of a divine man, while closest to the *subject* matter of the Gospels, seem to begin appearing around the early third century CE, hence by normal standards of historiography are likelier to have been influenced by, than to have influenced, the content of the gospel tradition. The earlier Christian models were widely known by that period.

71. I leave aside the issue of novels, which I address separately (showing their differences from the Gospels). Most such novels were in any case romances about two individuals.

72. See e.g., Culpepper, *John*, 64-66. Some later examples of this form may borrow the gospel form (see Dillon and Hershbell, "Introduction," 25). Other followers of ancient teachers were often deeply interested in their lives from soon after their death, writing about them whether or not expressing this interest in biographic form. See Kennedy, "Source Criticism," 134 (noting that Plato began writing about Socrates within a decade of Socrates' death).

73. Such as those of Plutarch, Tacitus and Suetonius, and Josephus' autobiography.

74. Such as Cornelius Nepos in the late second century BCE.

75. For criteria for genre, see Burridge, *Gospels*, 109-27; for pre-Christian Greco-Roman biographies, 128-53; for later ones, 154-90.

76. *Gospels*, 191-219 on the Synoptics, and 220-39 on John. Although I am citing from the original Cambridge University Press edition, he interacts more fully with subsequent works in his second edition published by Eerdmans (2004).

77. Burridge, *Gospels*, 118, 199, 225-26; an ancient "book" was about what one could listen to in a setting, perhaps about two hours (Burridge, "People," 141). For length in distinguishing genre, see e.g., Arist. *Poet.* 24.4, 1459b.

78. Talbert, "Review," 715; cf. also Stanton, *New People*, 64.

79. See Cancik, "Gattung"; Byrskog, *Story as History,* 45.

80. Dihle, "Biography," 381. Eddy and Boyd, *Legend,* 324-30, point out elements of both biography and historiography. For historical features in John, see Bauckham, *Testimony,* 93-112 (on 95 noting also my observations in Keener, *John,* 11-37). Marcus, *Mark,* 65-66, points to historical characteristics in Mark's work (still something like a *bios*).

81. Dihle, "Biography," 379.

82. Dihle, "Biography," 383-84. Suetonius does admittedly straddle both genres (Rolfe, "Introduction," xvii).

83. Only Luke might appear more questionable, because it is paired with Acts, which is increasingly recognized as a historical monograph. See our chapter on Luke-Acts.

84. Burridge, *Gospels,* 149-52, 185-88. For the divergence see further Barr and Wentling, "Biography and Genre," 81-88, although I would not regard all their examples as biographies.

85. For substantial overlap between the biography and history (as well as other) genres in antiquity, see Burridge, *Gospels,* 63-67.

86. E.g., Kennedy, "Source Criticism," 136.

87. Fornara, *Nature of History,* 34-36, 116. For history's focus on notable deeds, see Fornara, *Nature of History,* 29-46.

88. Fornara, *Nature of History,* 116.

89. Fornara, *Nature of History,* 185, distinguishes primarily by noting that biography used only the features of history relevant to expounding character, whereas "characterizing anecdotes . . . were unsuitable to history." He contends that biography became more like history in early-second-century works like Tacitus's *Agricola* and Suetonius's *Lives* (Fornara, *Nature of History,* 186).

90. By the third century CE some philosophic "biographies" included information on lives of a philosopher's disciples as well as himself, but this may have followed Christian models (Dillon and Hershbell, "Introduction," 25-26), such as Luke-Acts.

91. Fornara, *Nature of History,* 36. At times this approach could produce distortion, but it need not do so (Fornara, *Nature of History,* 64-65).

92. Lucian *History* 7. Plut. *Alex.* 1.1-3 suggests that biographies might leave out what histories could include to remain more concise.

93. See Fornara, *Nature of History,* 185.

94. Plut. *Alex.* 1.1-3.

95. Hose, "Historiography: Rome," 423, noting that the boundaries between these genres were fading; cf. Suetonius in Rolfe, "Introduction," xvii.

96. Aune, "Biography," 125; cf. 64-65; Witherington, *Sage,* 339. Shuler, *Genre,* regards his subject (Matthew) as primarily encomium, or laudatory, biography; but such a *specific* genre probably did not exist (Burridge, *Gospels,* 88), since encomiastic elements were common in many biographies. Penner, *Praise,* 135, argues that encomium now dominated biography; for a brief treatment of encomium, see Aune, *Dictionary of Rhetoric,* 145-47 (esp. 145).

97. With Kennedy, "Source Criticism," 139.

98. Kennedy, "Source Criticism," 139-41.

99. Cf. C. B. R. Pelling, "Plutarch's method of work in the Roman Lives," *JHS* 99 (1979): 74-96; Kaesser, "Tweaking the Real."

100. Kennedy, "Source Criticism," 141. Kennedy notes (141) that the Gospels rely on simpler tradition, but nevertheless deems useful this comparison with hard data.

101. Rolfe, "Introduction," xvii.

102. Theissen and Merz, *Historical Jesus,* 114.

103. See e.g., Barr and Wentling, "Biography and Genre," 81-88 (though I would not classify all these works as biographies; all the non-novelistic ones have recollections).

104. Talbert, "Monograph or *Bios*," 72. Ps.-Callisthenes mixes both historical and fictitious sources, plus adds his own fictions (e.g., *Alex.* 1.23), 450-750 years after the supposed events (it must

have been completed by the time of its Latin translation in the fourth century; cf. Fusillo, "Pseudo-Callisthenes"). Bowersock's examples of fictitionalized history (*Fiction as History,* 21) are also distinctly novelistic.

105. It is more like a historical novel, a relatively rare form of novel in this period (as we have noted).

106. Burridge, *Gospels,* 246 (citing Diod. Sic. Bk. 17); Balch, "ΜΕΤΑΒΟΛΗ ΠΟΛΙΤΕΙΩΝ," 143 (citing Dion. Hal. *Ant. rom.* 4.41-85).

107. Plut. *Alex.* 70.3.

108. While acknowledging parallels with biography, Bruggen, *Narratives,* 75 (writing before Burridge), overplays the differences, but all his contrasts involve *modern* biography.

109. E.g., Plut. *Caesar* 1.1-4.

110. Drury, *Design,* 29.

111. Cf. e.g., the accidental repetition in Plut. *Alex.* 37.4; 56.1. This contrasts with the more chronological practice of historians (e.g., Thucyd. 2.1.1; 5.26.1), although even most historians tended to follow events to their conclusion and not simply strict chronology (Dion. Hal. *Thucyd.* 9; *Letter to Gnaeus Pompeius* 3).

112. E.g., Suet. *Aug.* 9; *Calig.* 22.1; *Nero* 19.3; Görgemanns, "Biography." When interested in chronology, Suetonius cites not biographers but historians (*Calig.* 8.3).

113. For examples of these "Peripatetic" biographies, see Aune, *Environment,* 34, 63-64 (e.g., the lives of Aesop, Homer, Secundus, and Herakles); cf. ibid., 82. The list in 4Q339, col. 1, line 2 is chronological.

114. Aune, *Environment,* 31-32. Dischronologizing was not problematic to ancient readers; thus the writer of 4 Macc is aware that the mother's speech should occur at a certain point in his narrative, and says so (12:7; cf. 2 Macc 7), but chooses to recount it later. Cf. the four categories of ancient biography in Ferguson, *Backgrounds,* 307.

115. Stanton argues that our only actual example of a purely Peripateic biography is not chronological (Stanton, *Jesus of Nazareth,* 119-21); he contends that of extant biographies, only Tacitus' *Agricola* is genuinely chronological. Topical arrangement suited episodic narratives about a person (Hemer, *Acts in History,* 74). Although historical writing and thus biography (Suetonius, Plutarch, *Life of Aesop,* etc.) involved some chronology, it was not the most *significant* feature of any kind of ancient biography.

116. Cf. 4Q158; see Wise, "Introduction to 4Q158"; on events in the Torah more generally, see Kaunfer and Kaunfer, "Time and Torah."

117. *Harmony of the Gospels* 21.51.

118. Papias in Eusebius *H.E.* 3.39. An aged person might recall many events provided he were permitted to recite them randomly rather than in order (Sen. *Controv.* 1.pref.4).

119. Eddy and Boyd, *Legend,* 433-35.

120. Stanton, *Jesus of Nazareth,* 125; idem, *Gospel Truth,* 139; Burridge, *Gospels,* 205, 208; in John, see Burridge, *Gospels,* 229-30. Characterization is in fact central in ancient biographies (Fornara, *Nature of History,* 185).

121. E.g., Corn. Nep. 4 (Pausanias), 1.1; Suet. *Calig.* 44. Many elite biographers were rhetoricians, who knew how to describe a person's character directly to make a case (*Rhet. Her.* 4.50.63). Josephus adapts some biblical characters, adding virtues (e.g., Feldman, "Jehoram"); Matthew reduces Mark's unbelief to "little faith" (Matt 6:30; 8:26).

122. Theophrastus even provides, in graphic and often humorous ways, thirty basic character types (such as a flatterer or one overly talkative) that offer various kinds of examples (*Char.* passim). At other times the storytelling was certainly sufficient. Even in Greece's ancient epic poetry, the stark character of a wrathful Achilles, proud Agamemnon, or clever Odysseus is impossible to miss. Ancient literature abounds with developed examples of dysfunctional relationships; for example, Dido in Virgil's *Aeneid* appeared exceptionally susceptible to Aeneas because she had never recovered from

her first lover's death. In contrast to some later psychologizing approaches, some ancient biographers proved reluctant to speculate concerning their characters' inner thoughts, but this again is not a rule (see Arrian *Alex.* 7.1.4).

123. Contrast Xen. *Symp.* 1.1, who notes that he wants to recount not only the zealous deeds of Socrates, but also those done in more childlike, carefree moments.

124. Burridge, *Gospels,* 150; cf. Dihle, "Biography," 367-74.

125. Robbins, *Teacher,* 110-11.

126. Corn. Nep. 16 (Pelopidas), 1.1.

127. So Polyb. 10.21.8, contrasting depiction of someone in his history with an earlier biography he had written about the same person.

128. Burridge, *Gospels,* 151, 180; for apologetic autobiography, cf. e.g., Jos. *Life* 336-67; 2 Cor 11:8-33; Gal 1:11-24; D Lamour, "L'organisation." Autobiographic writing in some form appears as early as ancient Egypt (Simpson, *Literature,* 401-27); on the genre of autobiography, see further Lyons, *Autobiography;* Aune, *Dictionary of Rhetoric,* 79-81.

129. Burridge, *Gospels,* 68-69.

130. Vermes, *Jesus and Judaism,* 19; cf. Levinskaya, *Diaspora Setting,* 2; Hemer, *Acts in History,* 79-90.

131. Polyb. 8.8 (noting a contrast with many writers).

132. Polyb. 3.4.1.

133. E.g., Arrian *Alex.* 4.7.4; 4.8.1-4.9.6.

134. E.g., Corn. Nep. 11 [Iphicrates], 3.2; Suet. *Jul.* 52 with 53; 73-75 with 76.1; *Dom.* 3.2. For Plutarch, see Lavery, "*Lucullus*"; honoring subjects could but need not produce distortion (Fornara, *Nature of History,* 64-65). Rhetorical conventions appeared in ancient biography, but more in rhetorical biographers like Isocrates (see Burridge, "Biography"). Forensic speech, where a primary object was legal victory, was naturally another story (e.g., Dion. Hal. *Lysias* 8).

135. Plut. *Cimon* 2.4-5. Thus although Plutarch praises Cato extensively in *Cato Major,* he criticizes his mistreatment of slaves (5.1, 5) and notes that Cato mocked Romans who were too fond of Greek culture and ways (12.4).

136. Philost. *Vit. soph.* 2.21.602-3. One might be thought biased when writing about close friends (Philost. *Vit. soph.* 2.33.628), but Tacitus wrote freely of his father-in-law (*Agricola;* see below). (Compare Pliny's recommendation in *Ep.* 3.3.5: "The affection I have for him has not blinded my judgement, as it is in fact based on it.") One pupil reportedly did omit *some* of his teacher's sayings, but because they were rhetorically inappropriate (Philost. *Vit. soph.* 2.29.621); and omission is not fabrication.

137. Eunapius *Lives* 461 (on Iamblichus, who is supernatural in 459); Plut. *Marcus Cato* 5.1, 5; 12.4; for writers' style, Dion. Hal. *Thucyd.* 1. One could also disagree with the dominant view of one's school (e.g., Sen. *Ep. Lucil.* 117.6).

138. *Mem.* 4.8.11.

139. Cf. later Iamblichus *V.P.* passim.

140. See e.g., Sen. *Ep. Lucil.* 108.17, 20, 22; 110.14, 20; Musonius Rufus 1, 36.6-7 (Pythagoras's disciples could not disagree, but this was considered noteworthy — Valerius Maximus 8.15. ext. 1). Occasionally pupils could even turn against their teachers (Eunapius *Lives* 493), but in such a case they would no longer claim the teacher's authority for the source of their teaching.

141. Eunapius *Lives* 484.

Notes to Chapter 6

1. There are notorious debates regarding how to translate these verses. My point is merely to convey the general sense; rendering them differently would not alter the point I make by citing them.

2. Johnson, "Luke-Acts," 406.

3. Hengel, *Acts and History*, 61.

4. In this chapter I draw heavily on material in my forthcoming Acts commentary, as well as on the more concise survey in Keener, "Luke-Acts and Historical Jesus."

5. Cf. Palmer, "Monograph," 3; Parsons, "Unity: Rethinking," especially 45-48.

6. See e.g., Goulder, *Type and History*; Talbert, *Patterns*; Tannehill, *Luke*; idem, *Acts*.

7. E.g., Barrett, *Acts*, lxxviii-lxxix; Marshall, "Treatise," 180; Verheyden, "Unity," 47; Penner, *Praise*, 59.

8. Burridge, *Gospels*, 246 (citing Diod. Sic. Bk. 17); Balch, "ΜΕΤΑΒΟΛΗ ΠΟΛΙΤΕΙΩΝ," 143 (citing Dion. Hal. *Ant. rom.* 4.41-85).

9. Dibelius, *Studies in Acts*, 123-37; Cadbury, *Acts in History*, passim.

10. For Acts as history (often including the more specific proposal of historical monograph), see Palmer, "Monograph"; Schmidt, "Influences," 59; Plümacher, "Luke as Historian," 398; idem, *Lukas*, 33-38 (comparing mission speeches), 137-39; idem, *Geschichte*, 1-32; idem, "Cicero und Lukas," 772-73; idem, "Monographie"; Bovon, *Theologian*, 5; Johnson, *Acts*, 3-7; Marguerat, *Histoire*, 49 (although noting overlap with biography); Eckey, *Apostelgeschichte*, 20-31; Flichy, *L'oeuvre de Luc*; idem, "État des recherches," 28-32 (reviewing recent research); Rothschild, *Rhetoric of History*, 296; Stagg, *Acts*, 17; Fitzmyer, *Acts*, 127; Cross, "Genres," 404-6; Tuckett, *Luke*, 29; Ehrman, *Introduction*, 133; deSilva, *Introduction*, 349-351; Balch, "ΜΕΤΑΒΟΛΗ ΠΟΛΙΤΕΙΩΝ," 141-42, 149-54 (political history); idem, "Genre," passim, especially 11-19; "Gospels: forms," 948-49; Barnett, *Birth*, 195-96; Guijarro Oporto, "Articulación literaria"; Litwak, *Echoes*, 36; Kisau, "Acts," 1297; cf. Fuller, "Classics," 189 (summarizing G. Kennedy). Sterling, *Historiography*, 318 n. 39, lists as supporters also Conzelmann, *Acts*, xl; Hengel, *Acts and History*, 14, 36-37; Schneider, *Apostelgeschichte*, 1:122; Pesch, *Apostelgeschichte*, 1:23.

11. Johnson, "Luke-Acts," 406. Penner, *Praise*, 4, likewise summarizes that most scholars hold "the most obvious generic identification for" Acts, namely "ancient historiographical writing." Even in 1985, Callan could write that "It has long been almost taken for granted that Luke-Acts is a historical work" ("Preface and Historiography," 576, noting that Talbert's biography proposal had reopened the question).

12. Hengel and Schwemer, *Between Damascus and Antioch*, 11.

13. Johnson, *Acts*, 3-5; Hengel, *Acts and History*, 61.

14. Thucyd. 1.22.2.

15. Plümacher, "Luke as Historian," 398.

16. See Plümacher, "Mission Speeches," 251-66; as in idem, "Missionsreden"; idem, "Luke as Historian," 398; Horsley, "Speeches," 613. Novelists usually preferred livelier narration, though Pervo, "Direct Speech," may be right to note the dominance of direct speech in novels.

17. See discussions in e.g., Horsley, "Speeches"; Soards, *Speeches*, 183; Aune, *Environment*, 124-25.

18. Witherington, *Acts*, 808-9.

19. On Luke's prologue as fitting for historical works, see e.g., Callan, "Preface and Historiography"; van Unnik, "Once More Prologue"; Johnson, "Luke-Acts," 406, 407; Porter, "We Narratives," 550; Aune, *Environment*, 80; Penner, *Praise*, 219-22; Rothschild, *Rhetoric of History*, 93-94; Flichy, *L'oeuvre de Luc*.

20. Alexander, *Preface*, 42-101; idem, "Preface." Luke's preface resembles scientific prefaces in structure and similar linguistic usage, although some other features lack parallels in the scientific preface tradition (Alexander, *Preface*, 147).

21. To modestly suggest Luke's scientific background or that hellenistic schools provide an important type of setting for reconstructing Luke's usage (Alexander, *Preface*, 211-12) is not problematic on the thesis that Acts is a historical work. Genuine technical treatises did seek to deal in information, not fiction (cf. Alexander, "Formal Elements," 23-24; Sallmann, "Literature").

22. Adams, "Preface," 177-78, warns that, given the scarcity of extant examples, the scientific prefaces we have might not be representative. Moreover, Adams argues ("Preface," 181-83) that Alex-

ander's argument from preface length depends on Thucydides as representative for history, whereas Luke's falls within the usual historical prefaces (as a proportion of the entire work).

23. Aune, *Dictionary of Rhetoric*, 371, and idem, *"Prooimion,"* points out that parallels are equally close, including some specific wording, in Plutarch *Dinner*, which is *not* scientific.

24. With Callan, "Preface and Historiography," 577. For topics in prefaces, see Alexander, *Preface*, 31-34.

25. Aune, *Dictionary of Rhetoric*, 370.

26. Alexander, *Context*, 16.

27. Alexander, *Context*, 12-13 (though she believes that Acts also contains fictional elements that ancients would have recognized as such, p. 13). She does not believe that the preface by itself must identify Luke-Acts as historiography, though it certainly distinguishes it from genres such as epic (Alexander, *Context*, 21-42).

28. Alexander, *Context*, 17-18.

29. Alexander, *Context*, 41-42.

30. Alexander, *Context*, 41.

31. E.g., Rothschild, *Rhetoric of History*, 93-94; Penner, *Praise*, 219-22, and others noted above.

32. This is a conventional expectation; see Quint. *Inst.* 4.1.34; also *Rhet. Alex.* 29, 1436a, lines 33-39; Polyb. 3.1.3-3.5.9 (esp. 3.1.7); 11.1.1-5; Dion. Hal. *Lysias* 24; *Thucyd.* 19; Cic. *Or. Brut.* 40.137 ; Virg. *Aen.* 1.1-6; Sen. *Controv.* 1.pref.21; Dio Chrys. *Or.* 38.8; Aul. Gel. Pref. 25; Soranus *Gynec.* 1.intro.2; 1.1.3; Philost. *Vit. Apoll.* 7.1; 8.1.

33. Callan, "Preface and Historiography," 577; cf. similarly Hemer, "Alexandria Troas," 98.

34. Callan, "Preface and Historiography," 577, citing Lucian *Hist.* 7-14 (also in 39-40).

35. This is "Luke's own explicit statement of purpose" (Aune, *Environment*, 136).

36. Callan, "Preface and Historiography," 578, also noting that Herodotus just says he wrote so the past may be remembered (Hdt 1.1); Thucydides does not specify (1.1.1). For the quest for truth in historical works, see also Adams, "Preface," 186, and sources he cites.

37. Callan argues that after the fourth century BCE, usefulness becomes a dominant purpose for writing history (Callan, "Preface and Historiography," 579); but in the first century BCE some historical writers stopped emphasizing utility as their purpose and emphasized instead that they simply would write a "true account of something" (Callan, "Preface and Historiography," 579-580). But chronological typology cannot afford to be as strict as Callan seems to suggest, especially given our narrow range of extant sources. In the second century CE, Lucian advises that historical prologues note the usefulness of the work (Lucian *Hist.* 53).

38. One could have more than one objective (e.g., Jos. *Ant.* 1.4, citing two objectives). Thus 2 Maccabees abridges a larger work (2 Macc 2:23, 26, 28) to provide a more pleasurable narrative (2:24-25; cf. 2:27) and to profit readers (2:25).

39. Moessner, "Arrangement," 158, emphasis his.

40. Rothschild, *Rhetoric of History*, 67-69 (among the elements found in various historical prologues; I have listed those relevant to Luke, which is most of them).

41. Penner, *Praise*, 219-21.

42. With e.g., Johnson, "Luke-Acts," 406; Meier, *Marginal Jew*, 1:383. In a different form, legal documents could also be dated by rulers' period of rule (e.g., *P. Tebt.* 104, lines 5-8). Luke cannot do so frequently because his sources do not provide chronological information (and adding such links to his sources based on inferences, to make them seem more precise, would risk introducing possible mistakes, such as many find already in Lk 2:1-2 and Acts 5:36-37).

43. See e.g., Talbert, *Mediterranean Milieu*, 203-8; Hemer, *Acts in History*, 108-220 (see esp. 108-58); Campbell, "Journeys"; Harnack, *Acts*, 264-74. I treat the question much more thoroughly than here in two introductory chapters in my Acts commentary.

44. See Mealand, "Historians and Style." Although he shares some LXX verbs, the stylistic level of his verbs falls between a high level of Koine and Dionysius' atticizing (Mealand, "Verbs").

45. Rosner, "Biblical History," 81, after noting the common features on 65-81.

46. Jervell, "Future," 110-11; on Luke-Acts as salvation history, see also Thielman, *Theology*, 113-16.

47. Jewish historical writing by this period employed Hellenistic conventions (Cohen, *Maccabees*, 194; cf. in general Attridge, "Historiography," 326; Eisman, "Dio and Josephus").

48. E.g., Acts 25:14-22. From the outcome (for this Lukan example, see esp. Acts 25:26-27) many ancient historians would have felt free to infer and reconstruct the substance of the scene (cf. e.g., Tac. *Ann.* 14.35, 57; 15.59; Quint. Curt. 3.2.11-16; Jos. *Ant.* 19.38-45, 53-58, 78-83), as is often suspected in Luke's case (e.g., Witherington, *Acts*, 119-20; Jervell, *Apostelgeschichte*, 586). The case of Acts 5:36-37, more often cited, is of a conversation that took place much earlier, and to which none of the Jerusalem church would have been privy (though Paul might have known the general content of the speech).

49. Such as Lk 2:2 (with e.g., Hengel and Schwemer, *Between Damascus and Antioch*, 326-27; deSilva, *Introduction*, 369; Conzelmann, *Primitive Christianity*, 30). Some scholars propose possible solutions even here (e.g., Ramsay, *Bethlehem*, x, 107-96 passim; Robertson, *Luke*, 118ff; Bock, *Luke*, 903-9; Hayles, "Correct"; Marshall, *Luke*, 104; Brindle, "Census"; Thorley, "Census"; Haacker, "Erst"; cf. Porter, "Census").

50. Fornara, *Nature of History*, 47. See also Aune, *Environment*, 81-82, noting the interview of eyewitness (Polyb. 4.2.2); other sources, when traveling to the scenes in question (Hdt 2.52; Polyb. 3.48.12; 4.38.11; 10.11.4); and reading accounts of eyewitnesses (Polyb. 28.4.8; 38.4.8). For ancient historians' use of oral history, depending on whatever sources provided the best access to events, see Byrskog, *Story as History*, 305.

51. Hdt 1.1.

52. Fornara, *Nature of History*, 47-48 (citing Thucyd. 1.22.2; 5.26). Thucydides notes that he procured (and investigated) reports of speeches from others who heard them (1.22.1-2), and sometimes had to evaluate conflicting claims of eyewitnesses (1.22.2-3).

53. Diod. Sic. 1.4.1. He also claims to have consulted records (1.4.4-5). While granting Diodorus' travels to some locations, Oldfather, "Introduction to Diodorus," xiii, doubts that Diodorus visited either Mesopotamia or Athens; his skepticism concerning Mesopotamia is plausible (though certain only with respect to Nineveh), but his argument regarding Athens is from silence (i.e., what Diodorus does not mention).

54. Appian *Hist. rom.* pref. 12.

55. Philost. *Vit. soph.* 2.23.606.

56. *Vit. soph.* 1.22.524. On other occasions his research came up empty, but he incidentally confirms that he had done some (*Vit. soph.* 2.5.576). Likewise, the later historian Herodian insisted that he accepted nothing secondhand without tracking down all the facts (1.1.3). According to later tradition, even mythographers traveled from one city to the next gathering their various oral traditions (Philost. *Hrk.* 48.11; Maclean and Aitken, *Heroikos*, xc-xci). Likewise, Artem. *Oneir.* 1.pref. emphasized gathering oral reports in addition to reading all the works of his predecessors.

57. Polyb. 12.4c.3 (LCL 4:316-17). Polybius' emphasis on investigation appears throughout 12.4c.1-5.

58. Polyb. 12.4c.4-5. He severely criticizes Timaeus for neglecting travel to the locations about which he writes (12.25e.1), complaining that written sources alone are not sufficient (12.25e.7) or even the most critical part of historical study (12.25i.2). It was possible, however, to visit places, consult witnesses, and still prove mistaken (12.4d.1-2, also on Timaeus). Like a historian researching recent events, a prosecutor preparing a case might do research, such as tracking down eyewitnesses (e.g., Lysias *Or.* 23.2-8, §§166-67).

59. Even here, ancients sometimes found local oral sources that purported to have survived over the centuries (e.g., Paus. 1.23.2). Nevertheless, scholars today often question such local oral information from a much earlier period (Pretzler, "Pausanias and Tradition").

60. E.g., Philost. *Vit. soph.* 2.23.606 (who unsuccessfully tried to evaluate conflicting reports this way in 2.5.576), in contrast to his lack of interviews for earlier information.

61. Aune, *Environment*, 81 (citing Hdt 2.52; Polyb. 3.48.12; 4.38.11; 10.11.4).

62. Polyb. 3.33.17-18 (citing here a bronze tablet of Hannibal).

63. Polyb. 12.9.2; cf. also Plut. *Demosth.* 2.1-2. Urban centers tended to provide better access to documentary sources and those whose memories preserved events (*Demosth.* 2.1). For plausibility and probability as criteria in ancient historical writing, as in ancient rhetoric more generally, see Rothschild, *Rhetoric of History*, 62-64.

64. Meister, "Historiography: Greece," 421. For the preference for oral sources, see also the discussion in Aune, *Environment*, 81.

65. Consulting distant records would be even more difficult (cf. Pucci Ben Zeev, "Capitol"), though this is different from consulting people orally when one traveled to a region, as Luke may have done.

66. Fornara, *Nature of History*, 56. By its nature, earlier (rather than recent) history necessarily depended on earlier historians (Pliny *Ep.* 5.8.12).

67. Fornara, *Nature of History*, 61 (citing Suet. *Caesar* 56).

68. E.g., Abbott, *Acts*, 131-4; Ramsay, *Luke the Physician*, 26; Rackham, *Acts*, xvi; Williams, *Acts*, 22-30; Spencer, *Acts*, 12-13; Dunn, *Acts*, x; Fitzmyer, *Acts*, 50; Le Cornu, *Acts*, xxvii-xxviii; Chance, *Acts*, 4; Parsons, *Luke*, 8; Fusco, "Sezioni-noi"; Botermann, "Heidenapostel"; Riesner, "Zuverlässigkeit," 38-39; Jervell, *Apostelgeschichte*, 66, 82. Significant detractors nevertheless remain (e.g., Barrett, "Acts and Corpus").

69. Nor did he pretend to have done so; Luke includes the "we" sparingly, not pervasively or even commonly.

70. On the value of participation in ancient historiography, see e.g., Byrskog, *Story as History*, 58-64, 153-57.

71. See e.g., Dibelius, *Studies in Acts*, 136; Fitzmyer, *Theologian*, 11-16; Kurz, *Reading Luke-Acts*, 112-13.

72. With e.g., Hengel and Schwemer, *Between Damascus and Antioch*, 7; Neil, *Acts*, 22-23.

73. While Luke's and Paul's theological perspectives differ, the differences have too often been overstated, especially in Vielhauer, "Paulinism"; see critiques in Borgen, "Paul to Luke"; Donfried, *Thessalonica*, 90-96; Porter, *Paul in Acts*, 189-206.

74. Many also argue that the style is not distinguishable from the bulk of Luke's work (e.g., Dibelius, *Studies in Acts*, 104, 136).

75. Robbins, "We-Passages"; idem, "Land and Sea."

76. See Fitzmyer, *Theologian*, 16-22; Hemer, "First Person Narrative"; and especially Praeder, "First Person Narration," 210-14 (refuting Robbins' specific parallel claims).

77. Usually with narrators centuries before their own time (e.g., Plut. *Dinner* 1, Mor.146BC; 4Q537; *1 Enoch*; *4 Ezra*; *2 Bar.*; etc.).

78. For the prefaces (which include first-person usage) prefiguring the "we" narratives, see Cadbury, "We in Luke-Acts"; Dupont, *Sources*, 167.

79. Fusillo, "Novel," 840.

80. Also in biography (e.g., Philost. *Vit. soph.* 2.21.602-4); see discussion of historians' first- and third-person narration in Keener, *John*, 918.

81. Nock, *Essays*, 828; see also Porter, *Paul in Acts*, 24-27.

82. E.g., Cadbury, "We in Luke-Acts"; Dibelius, *Studies in Acts*, 135-37; Dupont, *Sources*, 164-65; Packer, *Acts*, 3; Munck, *Acts*, xliii; Hanson, *Acts*, 21-24; Neil, *Acts*, 22-23; Dunn, *Acts*, x; Spencer, *Acts*, 12-13; Fitzmyer, *Acts*, 103.

83. Alexander, *Preface*, 128.

84. See Alexander, *Preface*, 128-30. The term *anōthen* could also mean "thoroughly," but here presumably means "from an early point," paralleling "from the beginning" (Bauckham, *Eyewitnesses*,

123); "from the beginning" appears in histories to claim the presence of eyewitnesses from the start (Bauckham, *Eyewitnesses*, 119-22).

85. Moessner, "Poetics," 85-97. Cf. also Hemer, *Acts in History*, 322 (noting that Cadbury thought this involved even participation, a reasonable surmise only in Acts and not the Gospel).

86. Moessner, "Poetics," 97; idem, "Prologues," 413. The closest parallel is Jos. *Ag. Ap.* 1.54, 213ff, where Josephus uses the same language to underline that he is thoroughly immersed "in the events, traditions, and reports," hence can evaluate the various claims.

87. Witherington, *Acts*, 27. Witherington, *Acts*, 27, 32-34, places Luke closer to a Polybius than to many other historians. Still, most writers would not have the resources to travel as *much* as Polybius, and the limitations of the "we-narratives" suggest that Luke's travel, too, was limited, though this section specifies only the period that Luke was with *Paul* during the events he narrates.

88. See comments above, especially Nock, *Essays*, 821-32 (esp. 828; cited by various commentators). Although there is no consensus, most scholars favor an eyewitness source behind the we-narratives, and probably a majority identify the "we" author with Luke (see discussion in the excursus in my Acts commentary at Acts 16:10).

89. As Bruggen, *Narratives*, 65-66, notes, it does not require Luke to have been an eyewitness for the events of the Gospel.

90. *BDAG* cites for this sense Dion. Hal. *Pomp.* 6.3; Max. Tyre 16.3h; Jos. *Ant.* 18.342; 19.125; *Ag. Ap.* 1.55; Papias 2:2; 12:2; and Lk 1:2. The original apostolic tradents implied in Lk 1:2 knew Jesus' entire public ministry (Acts 1:21-22; cf. Gerhardsson, *Memory*, 280-88). The term here includes more than the twelve (Acts 1:21-22; Bauckham, *Eyewitnesses*, 389; cf. Lk 24:33; Dillon, *Eye-Witnesses*, 291).

91. Alexander, *Preface*, 34-36 (on the convention of *autopsia*, see Alexander, *Preface*, 34-41). Herodotean history uses the word this way more than Thucydidean history does (Alexander, *Preface*, 38; cf. Adams, "Preface," 189), and often with an emphasis on distant locations (Alexander, *Preface*, 121; as Judea would have seemed to Luke). She suggests that the use for the author's presence at events in Jos. *Ag. Ap.* 1.55 depends on Polyb. 3.4.3 (against Polybius' normal usage). (In principle, at least, Luke could depend on the same passage as Josephus, but in reality probably was less apt to know Polybius.)

92. Byrskog, *Story as History*, 48-49 (arguing on 49 that Alexander focuses too much on the term, whereas leading classicist experts on autopsy in ancient historiography emphasize the centrality of the *practice*).

93. Byrskog, *Story as History*, 49-53, addresses Heraclitus and others; 53-57, Herodotus; 58-59, Thucydides; 59-62, Polybius (note esp. Polyb. 4.2.1-2 on p. 60); 62-63, Josephus (noting *Ag. Ap.* 1.47).

94. Byrskog, *Story as History*, 63, noting Livy as the exception, most following the Greek preference. He notes (63) that Dion. Hal. *Ant. rom.* 1.6.2 "praises Fabius Pictor and Cincius Alimentus . . . for relating with great exactness only the events at which they themselves had been present."

95. Byrskog, *Story as History*, 93-94.

96. Byrskog, *Story as History*, 94 (for it not always being possible, he cites Polyb. 12.4c.4). Byrskog, *Story as History*, 94-98, deals with the use of oral sources in Herodotus, Thucydides, and Xenophon; he notes (98) the more unusual defense of some that oral sources were even better than autopsy (Isoc. *Panathen.* 150; Strabo 2.5.11), but suggests (98-99) that more commonly they were appreciated as supplementing autopsy. For documents' use of eyewitnesses in historians, see Byrskog, *Story as History*, 149-53.

97. Byrskog, *Story as History*, 122 (excepting Livy). Of course, Dionysius of Halicarnassus and others covering long periods of history could not depend on immediate oral history for most of it, as they themselves recognized. For apologetic use of autopsy (as in Josephus), see Byrskog, *Story as History*, 214-22.

98. Byrskog, *Story as History*, 63-64, citing Pliny *Ep.* 6.16 (esp. 6.16.22); 6.20. For the *Annals* Tacitus would have access to witnesses starting in the period of Nero's later years (Byrskog, *Story as History*, 64), though our extant text of *Ann.* ends soon after.

99. Alexander, *Preface,* 120. Historians considered this the best evidence (Aune, *Environment,* 81, citing Hdt 2.99; Polyb. 12.27.1-6; 20.12.8; Lucian *Hist.* 47).

100. Most extensively, see Rothschild, *Rhetoric of History,* 213-90, noting this authenticating technique.

101. As Maddox, *Purpose,* 21, 186, emphasizes, "confirmation" is a primary purpose of Luke-Acts; *asphaleia* is the climactic, final word of Luke's preface.

102. E.g., Isaeus *Pyrr.* 40; Dion. Hal. *Ant. rom.* 7.43.2; Jos. *Ag. Ap.* 2.107; cf. *Ag. Ap.* 1.50-52, 56. The less widely known a claim was, the more subject to suspicion it would be (Xen. *Ages.* 5.6).

103. E.g., Eurip. *El.* 361-62; Demosth. *Letter* 5.1; Cic. *Att.* 2.11; Sen. *Ep. Lucil.* 47.1; *P. Oxy.* 32; Apul. *Metam.* 1.26.

104. E.g., Cic. *Att.* 1.10, 13; 4.1; 8.14. This method could be quick; a letter from Caesar in Britain reached Cicero in less than a month (Cic. *Quint. fratr.* 3.1.8.25). Despite modern postal service those of us traveling to and from many parts of Nigeria, Kenya and Cameroon in recent years have still carried mail for acquaintances.

105. For financial sharing, see e.g., Rom 15:25-27; 1 Cor 16:1-2; 2 Cor 8-9; cf. the shared expense later in Lucian *Peregr.* 13.

106. Sterling, *Historiography,* 135.

107. Sterling, *Historiography,* 136. Greeks themselves recognized that Egyptian culture predated and influenced their own.

108. Sterling, *Historiography,* 137-225. Josephus' rival Justus probably provides one example no longer extant (see Rajak, "Justus of Tiberias," 92). For apologetic in hellenistic Jewish narrative writers, see further Holladay, *Theios Aner,* 234 and passim.

109. Wandrey, "Literature: Jewish-Hellenistic," 696; cf. Ferguson, *Backgrounds,* 349.

110. Sterling, *Historiography,* 226-310. More generally, others also emphasize Josephus' apologetic objectives (e.g., Feldman, "Apologist of World"; in defending himself, Vogel, "Vita 64-69"; Lamour, "L'organisation"). Others offered briefer monographs of apologetic history, e.g., Philo's *Flaccus;* see Meiser, "Gattung." Its discourses help support this conclusion. In contrast to Luke's work, *Flaccus* is more rhetorical and focuses on the blame aspect of epideictic, with abundant overt editorializing.

111. See especially Sterling, *Historiography,* 311-89; for others, see Mason, *Josephus and New Testament,* 196-97; Kee, *Every Nation,* 11-12; Johnson, *Acts,* xii.

112. See Holladay, "Acts and Fragments" (also arguing that Acts shares with these works the heroic characterization of the central heroes). See comment below on Luke's use of the OT.

113. To make such a claim was not to claim canonicity, although canon was apparently an open question among many Jewish groups. See the discussion of such questions in Smith, "Scripture."

114. E.g., Sumney, *Opponents,* 86.

Notes to Chapter 7

1. Penner, *Praise,* 179.

2. Fornara, *Nature of History,* 104. Although I start with extreme quotes, and Penner and Fornara represent different poles of approaches to ancient historiography, both positions are more nuanced than one might gather solely from the brief excerpts above.

3. It is to such elements that those who object to the historical value of ancient historians often point. These factors must be (and will be) noted, but should not be used to ignore evidence for historians' interest in sources. Neither the historical nor the rhetorical elements need exclude the other.

4. On this point, see e.g., Morgan-Wynne, "Traditionsgrundlage."

5. See e.g., Mosley, "Reporting," 26; Hemer, *Acts in History,* 63-70; Byrskog, *Story as History,* 179-84; Eddy and Boyd, *Legend,* 330-34; see e.g., Jos. *Ant.* 20.156-57; cf. *Life* 336-39. On how history was

written, see also Keener, *John*, 17-25, much of which I have also incorporated into the larger discussion here.

6. Of course, they did not define accuracy at all the points the way modern historians do, writing what they thought were probable inferences into their narratives (instead of identifying them as possible reconstructions, as we do today) and allowing rhetorical considerations in composition foreign to modern historiography (see e.g., our discussion on speeches). But on matters of historical events, they did indeed value such accuracy.

7. Mosley, "Reporting," 12-14; on Strabo and Plutarch, 16; for Greek historians in general, see 11-18.

8. Mosley, "Reporting," 20-22 (cf. Tac. *Ann.* 4.10-11; 13.20; in Pelling, "Historiography," 716); among Romans in general, see Mosley, "Reporting," 18-22. Roman historians often appear less careful with facts than Greeks (Cary and Haarhoff, *Life*, 263) and sometimes focused more on "trends" than details (Fornara, *Nature of History*, 88-89); but Luke, writing Greek in the Eastern Mediterranean, undoubtedly is nearer the Greek model.

9. E.g., Jos. *Ag. Ap.* 1.26; Dion. Hal. *Thuc.* 8.

10. Jos. *Life* 336-39; Diod. Sic. 21.17.1; Lucian *Hist.* 24-25; see especially discussion of Polybius below. Those who claimed the superiority of their own works, however, could risk the charge of impudence from detractors (Jos. *Life* 359); the charge of falsehood served polemical agendas well.

11. Diod. Sic. 1.37.4, 6.

12. So Plut. *Mal. Hdt.* 3-7, *Mor.* 855C-856B (though in defense of Herodotus, Plutarch's other extant sources may have followed a *favorable* bias; Plutarch may have his own bias because of Herodotus' critique of Boeotia, Plutarch's homeland). Penner, *Praise*, 169, notes that Plutarch resented Herodotus' "pro-barbarian" approach. Perhaps more plausibly than Plutarch, cf. Dion. Hal. *Pomp.* 3, on Thucydides' grudge against Athens.

13. Polyb. 10.21.8; but see discussion on biographies in our genre chapter.

14. Thus Antiphon's report about Alcibiades is suspect, Plutarch opines, because Antiphon hated him (*Alc.* 3.1).

15. Arist. *Poet.* 9.2, 1451b; thus poetry is more philosophical, conveying general truths, whereas history conveys specific facts (9.3, 1451b). Pliny *Ep.* 9.33.1 notes that historians, unlike poets, care about the authority of their sources.

16. Alexander, "Fiction and Genre," 382-85.

17. Dion. Hal. *Ant. rom.* 1.1.2-4; 1.4.2.

18. Arrian *Ind.* 7.1.

19. As is clear, for example, in his correspondence with Suetonius and especially Tacitus.

20. Pliny *Ep.* 8.4.1.

21. Pliny *Ep.* 7.17.3.

22. Pliny *Ep.* 5.5.3; 5.8.5. Even rhetorical historians writing essays on earlier historians' rhetoric might emphasize the importance of truth-telling (Dion. Hal. *Thuc.* 55).

23. Pliny *Ep.* 9.19.5.

24. Pliny *Ep.* 7.33.1, 3.

25. Narrated in *Ep.* 7.33.4-9.

26. *Ep.* 7.33.10. Likewise, eager to have his own account of Vesuvius in Tacitus' work, he even writes in historic style in Pliny *Ep.* 6.16, 20 (so Augoustakis, "*Nequaquam*"). As it turns out, we know far more about Pliny from his own letters than any other source (except a biography) could have provided.

27. Fornara, *Nature of History*, 116-19.

28. Fornara, *Nature of History*, 135.

29. Fornara, *Nature of History*, 138-39, citing Cic. *De or.* 2.15.62-63.

30. Fornara, *Nature of History*, 72.

31. Fornara, *Nature of History*, 100.

32. Fornara, *Nature of History,* 104. If a history was too biased, it was probably the weakness of the particular historian (Fornara, *Nature of History,* 91).

33. At least insofar as we may infer from the number of copies preserved in Egypt; see Stephens, "Who Read Novels?" 411, 415-16.

34. See e.g., Cueva, "Longus and Thucydides."

35. Dio Chrys. *Or.* 18.10.

36. Jos. *Ag. Ap.* 1.18.

37. On his method, see Meister, "Herodotus," 267 (including his personal observation and interviews with informed locals; cf. 2.28.1; 125.6; 4.76.6; 8.65.6). Herodotus did recognize that historical data was inseparable from the discourses that transmitted it (Byrskog, "History," 279).

38. At least as early as Cicero (*Leg.* 1.1.5), people viewed Herodotus as the "first" historian and western narrative writer (Meister, "Herodotus," 269). Some have compared Herodotus with the Pentateuch (Van Seters, "Primeval Histories"; cf. idem, *Search*), but the differences are considerable (Blenkinsopp, *Pentateuch,* 39-41; on 42 he suggests that Israelite historiography may have anticipated Herodotus), and narratives earlier than 1-2 Kgs may have some earlier parallels in the Greek heroic tradition.

39. Rainey, "Herodotus' Description."

40. Meister, "Herodotus," 267-68.

41. Meister, "Herodotus," 268, notes his "methodological principle": "I am obligated to report that which is reported, but I am not obligated to believe everything" (7.152); he often reports conflicting traditions without passing judgment either way.

42. See fully Meister, "Herodotus," 268-69.

43. E.g., Val. Max. 1.8.7, which he justifies as believable because it is in his sources (importantly for our discussion, however, he does not invent the story). For the special case of "signs," see my book on miracle accounts (intended as a sequel to this one).

44. See e.g., Meister, "Historiography: Greece," 421. Certainly Suetonius, who was in many other respects a good historian, failed to sift his sources and includes much gossip (Cary and Haarhoff, *Life,* 272).

45. Plut. *Arist.* 19.5-6, challenging Hdt 9.85.

46. Plut. *Them.* 25.1-2. Cf. also *Cam.* 6.1-2 (citing Livy 5.22); *Alex.* 31.3; Philost. *Vit. soph.* 1.21.516.

47. Plut. *Alex.* 20.4-5.

48. Livy 3.8.10.

49. Paus. 1.3.3 (LCL 1:15, 17).

50. *Ant.* 19.68, 106-7.

51. He could regard as inauthentic speeches which reflected conditions that don't fit the alleged author's time (here, "before his prime") — e.g., Dion. Hal. *Din.* 11. He used stylistic criteria to evaluate authenticity, when other factors were not compelling (*Lysias* 11; cf. *Demosth.* 57).

52. E.g., that he fails to evoke the full horror of war at points (Dion. Hal. *Thuc.* 15), in contrast to the more rhetorical historians. But Dio Chrys. *Or.* 18.10 rates Thucydides first, above Theopompus and far beyond Ephorus.

53. Dion. Hal. *Thuc.* 19 (LCL 1:512-13); see Thucyd. 1.1.1-2; 1.21.2; 1.23.1-2. For some other cases of hyperbole in historical writing, see Thucyd. 8.96.1 (cf. 2.94.1); Polyb. 1.4.5; Tac. *Hist.* 1.2; cf. also, for us less surprisingly, in epic treatments of history (Sil. It. 9.183; cf. Josh 10:14), in prosecutorial rhetoric (Cic. *Verr.* 2.5.72.189) and in fiction (Xen. *Eph.* 1.1; Philost. *Hrk.* 24.2).

54. Thucyd. 1.3.2-3. Likewise, Homer does not speak of "barbarians" because Greeks had not yet distinguished themselves from others in this manner (Thucyd. 1.3.3).

55. Thucyd. 1.10.1-2.

56. E.g., Diog. Laert. 1.23: "But according to others"; 6.1.13; 8.2.67-72; Plut. *Lyc.* 1.1; Philost. *Vit. soph.* 1.21.516; 2.5.576; *p. Sot.* 9:13, §2.

57. E.g., Sall. *Jug.* 67.3.

58. See Meister, "Herodotus," 268, on Hdt 7.152.

59. *Hist.* 60 (LCL 6:71).

60. Polyb. 34.4.3. He also suggests that the *Odyssey* mixes myth with truth (34.4.1).

61. Polyb. 34.4.2. Sophists made a pastime out of noting logical and chronological problems in Homer (e.g., Maclean and Aitken, *Heroikos*, l-li, citing Philost. *Hrk.* 23.5-6; 25.10-13).

62. Dion. Hal. *Thuc.* 8 (LCL 1:478-79); this is an ideal, not the writer's exceptionless practice.

63. Hdn 1.1.1-2.

64. Hdn 1.1.3. My point is not that Herodian achieved this ideal (certainly he did not strive for chronological precision; see Whittaker, "Introduction," xxxix-xl), but that it was in fact the ideal.

65. E.g., Philost. *Vit. soph.* 2.21.603 (of his own teacher, 2.21.602); the biographer Eunapius *Lives* 461 (of Iamblichus, whom Eunapius considered supernatural, 459-61).

66. E.g., Livy 3.8.10.

67. Aul. Gel. 10.12.8-10. Some could also caution readers not to be too skeptical of something that otherwise appeared implausible (Sall. *Catil.* 3.2; Plut. *Cam.* 6.4).

68. Arrian *Alex.* 4.28.1-2.

69. Polybius' moralistic agenda (emphasized e.g., in Penner, *Praise*, 145; see our chapter on historians' *Tendenz*) need not require fabricating events. Penner, *Praise*, 157, shows how Timaeus' critique of Aristotle, who is useful as a positive moral model, invites Polybius' enmity (noting Polyb. 12.7.2-6; 12.8.1-2).

70. Polyb. 12.3.1-12.15.12.

71. Polyb. 12.7.6.

72. Polyb. 12.4a.1. Cf. Penner, *Praise*, 118, who notes: "if every historian who accuses another of being a dramatic and rhetorical historian is doing so to garner support for his or her own version of events, then the line dividing a Polybius from an Ephorus, Theopompus, Ctesias, or Phylarchus is much thinner than one might be led to believe from the initial comments." Polybius "condemns tragic history but then resorts to it himself." Still, we should note that even in our extant sources, the level of rhetorical embellishment appears to be a matter of degree (as Penner, *Praise*, 179, also acknowledges). Polybius does what Timaeus does, but he apparently does not do it nearly as much as Timaeus does.

73. Fornara, *Nature of History*, 48. Others suggest that Timaeus defended western Greeks' contributions to Greek civilization, providing an "apologetic edge" which Polybius felt compelled to challenge (Sterling, "Historians," 502).

74. Likewise, when Josephus thinks the perspective of some other historians distorted, he criticizes them for failing in their objective to write history properly (*War* 1.7); they undoubtedly responded polemically in kind.

75. Polyb. 12.3.1-2.

76. Polyb. 12.4c.2-5.

77. Polyb. 12.4d.1-2.

78. Polyb. 12.28.12.

79. Polyb. 12.9.1-12.11.7. Polybius condemns those who make up or pass on hearsay about distant lands that cannot be verified (Polyb. 3.38.3), a genuine practice of some.

80. Polyb. 12.7.1. These rhetorical techniques are certainly in common use by Luke's era, although (again) even orators could use such techniques without inventing "facts." Penner, *Praise*, 235-47, argues that epideictic techniques were common in Jewish apologetic historiography.

81. Polyb. 12.7.6.

82. Polyb. 12.15.12.

83. Polyb. 15.34.1.

84. He reports graphic bloodshed (15.33), but claims that unlike some other writers, he avoids amplifying it for sensationalism (15.34). By Luke's day, both Polybius' "critical" approach and the "sensational" approach had left a mark on historiographic practices (see Rothschild, *Rhetoric of History*, 93-95).

85. Polyb. 2.56.7.

86. Polyb. 2.56.10. No one, however, will ensure that Polybius' own speeches are verbatim recollections.

87. Polyb. 2.56.11. The entire digression against Phylarchus starts in 2.56.1-16 (including criticism for excess accommodation of tragic conventions, 2.56.1-11), followed by examples of his sensationalism in the matter at hand in 2.57.1–2.63.6. Poetic treatments of historical events (e.g., Silius Italicus; Lucan) enjoyed more freedom of expression (cf. Pliny *Ep.* 8.4.1).

88. Polyb. 12.11.7-8.

89. Polyb. 12.12.1-3.

90. Polyb. 2.56.1-2. Penner, *Praise,* 153-55, complains that Polybius uses an ethnic plausibility criterion against Phylarchus: by evoking sympathy for the dishonorable Mantineans against the honorable Achaians, Phylarchus violates probability. Sympathetic portrayal of opponents appears commonly in ancient epics (the Trojans in the *Iliad;* Dido in the *Aeneid*), and rhetorical historians use it to heighten tragic pathos (cf. e.g., Dion. Hal. *Ant. rom.* Bk. 3; 9.39.1-6; Livy 21.1.3; cf. discussion in Keener, *John,* 216-17); indeed, Lucian criticizes historians who praise their own leaders while slandering the other side as engaging merely in panegyric (*Hist.* 7). But it is clear that Polybius has his ethnic biases; cf. similarly Plutarch's *Malice of Herodotus.* Ancient and modern judicial rhetoric do infer probability based on past behavior; ancient and modern historians do the same, except that modern historians would be explicit about their inferences rather than simply writing them into their narratives. We would agree with Polybius that historical reconstruction necessarily includes inferred probabilities; we would prove more critical of the ethnographic basis for some of his assumptions, but that is why we must take into account ancient (or modern) historians' perspectives. It is not inference from probability that differs, but the way we narrate those inferences and the particular assumptions (based on differing perspectives) that inform those inferences.

91. Polyb. 2.56.3.

92. Polyb. 2.56.4.

93. Tac. *Hist.* 1.1. Cf. similarly Jos. *Ant.* 20.154, criticizing some of his contemporaries.

94. We might suspect the long-reigning Augustus as offering an exception; but later Suetonius and Tacitus are critical even regarding Augustus, and rival views did survive.

95. Historical distance multiplied the possibility of gratuitous errors, such as 4 Macc 4:15 (Antiochus Epiphanes was Seleucus' younger brother rather than his son, though the mistake is readily understandable). Of course, modern historians also prefer reports closer in time to the events recounted (e.g., Robeck, *Mission,* 293-94, 296).

96. Indeed, as W. D. Davies points out (*Invitation,* 115-16), probably only a single lifespan "separates Jesus from the last New Testament document" (cf. similarly Sanders, *Tendencies,* 28; Benoit, *Jesus,* 1:33).

97. E.g., Xen. *Apol.* 2; *Ages.* 3.1; Dion. Hal. *Thuc.* 7; Plut. *Demosth.* 11.1; Arrian *Alex.* 1, pref. 2-3; 6.11.8; Corn. Nep. 23 (Hannibal), 13.3; 25 (Atticus), 13.7; 17.1; cf. Philost. *Hrk.* 7.9; 8.2, 6-7; Sen. *Nat. Q.* 3.25.8; 4.3.1. Cf. Xen. *Hell.* 6.2.31 (refusing to believe a report until an eyewitness was available). Aune, *Environment,* 81, cites for this also Hdt 2.99; Polyb. 12.27.1-6; 20.12.8; Lucian *Hist.* 47 (and Polybius' somewhat self-serving view that participants made the best historians — 3.4.13; 12.25g.1; 12.28.1-5); Alexander, *Preface,* 34, notes that one recurrent claim was "that the best history was written on the basis of personal experience."

98. Jervell, "Future," 118.

99. See Jos. *Life* 357; *Ag. Ap.* 1.45-49, 56; *War* 1.2-3.

100. Thucyd. 1.22.3. For gist generally being reliable in memory even where details are not, see Bauckham, *Eyewitnesses,* 333-34 (citing memory studies).

101. In a forensic setting, see e.g., Lysias *Or.* 20.22, §160.

102. Fornara, *Nature of History,* 48. For accuracy in certain kinds of ancient Mediterranean oral traditioning over the span of one or two generations, see Keener, *Matthew,* 27-30; idem, *John,* 54-65;

but for failure to learn accurately from purported travels, see Strabo 2.5.10; Hengel, "Geography of Palestine," 31.

103. Eunapius *Lives* 460. Suetonius depends more heavily on older written records than interviews of more recent persons (Rolfe, "Introduction," xviii). The Greek method preferred interviews, but even Romans could write about contemporary figures (e.g., Pliny *Ep.* 9.19.5).

104. Xen. *Hell.* 3.1.2; those who attribute the Gospel of Matthew to one of the Twelve yet accept its dependence on Mark (like R. Gundry; see his *Matthew*, 609-22) could adduce that case as a further example.

105. Eunapius *Lives* 453; for anthropological confirmation, see Lord, *Singer*, 138.

106. E.g., Jos. *Ag. Ap.* 1.45-47; Xen. *Symp.* 1.1 (Todd, "Introduction," 376, is skeptical because Xenophon nowhere places himself in the narrative, but this argument is questionable; Todd concurs that the characters and discussion match external evidence, 376-78; this is also Xenophon's style, since he does not report his presence in *Anab.* until it is relevant to the narrative); Xen. *Anab.* 2.5.41; 3.1.4-6; Thucyd. 2.103.2; 5.26.1; Polyb. 31.23.1-31.24.12; 38.19.1; 38.21.1; 38.22.3; Caesar *C.W.* passim, e.g., 1.1; *Gall. W.* passim, 1.7; 2.1; 3.28; 4.13; 5.9; 6.4; 7.17; Philost. *Vit. soph.* 2.23.606.

107. Jos. *Ant.* 20.266.

108. Jos. *Life* 359-60. Criticizing someone should best be done while they remain alive or, if they have died, only shortly afterward (Pliny *Ep.* 9.1.3-4). Bede *Comm. Acts* pref. (trans. p. 5) contends that Luke wrote while eyewitnesses remained alive.

109. Jos. *Life* 361-66. This also suggests that if Josephus embellished his story with some details, the eyewitnesses accepted that embellishment as relatively minor, fitting acceptable historical canons. Undoubtedly the portrayal was also not to their detriment; Josephus was careful to praise surviving political figures like Agrippa and any member of the Flavian dynasty.

110. Jos. *Ag. Ap.* 1.45.

111. Jos. *Ag. Ap.* 1.46. Naturally, Josephus would be happy to enforce a criterion that excluded his competitors but not himself. Yet Josephus hardly invented this criterion, useful as it proved in his case.

112. Jos. *Ag. Ap.* 1.47.

113. Jos. *Ag. Ap.* 1.49.

114. Jos. *Ag. Ap.* 1.56.

115. Jos. *Life* 357. Josephus is not above depicting a scene, such as the suicide of the Sicarii at Masada, where he lacks potential eyewitnesses (unless we think of the two women who escaped), but he might have protested that this represented a special scene rather than a consistent pattern.

116. See e.g., Mosley, "Reporting," 26.

117. E.g., Diod. Sic. 1.6.2.

118. Pliny *Ep.* 5.8.12-13 (considering earlier times more praiseworthy).

119. E.g., Livy 7.6.6; 25.11.20; Plut. *Mal. Hdt.* 20, *Mor.* 859B. "Modern insights" (like bloodletting!) might be preferred to ancient ones, however (Sen. *Ep. Lucil.* 95.22).

120. E.g., Thucyd. 1.21.1; Livy 6.1.2-3; 7.6.6; Diod. Sic. 1.6.2; 1.9.2; 4.1.1; 4.8.3-5; Dion. Hal. *Ant. rom.* 1.12.3; *Thuc.* 5; Paus. 9.31.7; Jos. *Ag. Ap.* 1.15, 24-25, 58; cf. Bowersock, *Fiction as History*, 1-2. Some also considered the earlier period qualitatively different because of divine activities (Hesiod *W.D.* 158-60, 165; Arrian *Alex.* 5.1.2); by contrast, others mistrusted its reports precisely because of such unusual events (Thucyd. 1.23.3).

121. Dion. Hal. *Thuc.* 5-7; cf. Plut. *Thes.* 1.3; Keener, *John*, 20. At least the early period was regarded as unusual (Thucyd. 1.23.3). This constitutes a major problem for treating Mark's Gospel as "mythical" (so Dibelius, *Tradition*, 278-79, though he does not regard Mark's *material* as mythical).

122. E.g., Thucyd. 1.21.1 (complaining in 1.21.2 that people make ancient events greater than they were); again, see Keener, *John*, 20.

123. They often tried to distinguish between accurate and inaccurate sources, when a consensus view was available (cf. Livy 1.1.1).

124. Some sources, like the *Life of Aesop,* may simply string together all available popular traditions into a narrative; these traditions had grown over six centuries (see Drury, *Design,* 28-29).

125. E.g., Livy 4.29.5-6; 23.47.8; cf. (more skeptically) Lucian *Hist.* 60.

126. See e.g., Thucyd. 1.21.1-2; Dion. Hal. *Ant. rom.* 1.39.1; 1.41.1 (cf. Dion. Hal. *Ant. rom.* 1.84.4); Dion. Hal. *Thuc.* 6; Philost. *Vit. soph.* 2.1.554.

127. Plut. *Thes.* 1.3. Arrian accepts but explains on rationalistic grounds some old legends (*Alex.* 2.16.6). Cf. Kennedy, "Source Criticism," 139, citing Quint. *Inst.* 2.4.18-19 and the 133 cases of cautious attribution in Livy's first 10 books.

128. See Dio Cass. 62.11.3-4; Aune, *Environment,* 83; Fornara, *Nature of History,* 134-36.

129. Ancients noticed tensions in regularly read sources just as we do; even mythographers might note chronological and other tensions within a text (Maclean and Aitken, *Heroikos,* il-l (citing Philostratus *Hrk.* 23.5-6; 25.10-13).

130. Polyb. 3.32.4.

131. Dion. Hal. *Ant. rom.* 9.22.1-5.

132. Polyb. 3.20.1-5; 3.32.5. Polybius insisted on providing the longest-range historical context possible, both early (3.6.1-3.7.3, e.g., 3.6.10) and subsequent (9.2.5).

133. Plut. *Themist.* 27.1, though admitting uncertainty. Thucydides sought to take into account the relative dates of his sources (1.3.2-3); with some sense of relative chronology, Tac. *Dial.* 16, dates Ulysses and Nestor (purportedly early thirteenth century BCE) about a millennium before Alexander and Demosthenes (fourth century BCE).

134. Polyb. 3.33.18; Plut. *Alex.* 46.2; *Demosth.* 5.5; Philost. *Vit. soph.* 2.1.562-63.

135. Arrian *Alex.* 7.14.4-6; Dio Cass. 62.11.3-4; cf. Athen. *Deipn.* 5.215-16, 219ab. The same criterion could apply, however, in fictitious composition or historical reconstruction based on plausibility (cf. Arist. *Poet.* 15.4-5, 1454a; Theon *Progymn.* 1.46-52; 2.79-81; 8.2-3).

136. Thucyd. 1.10.1-2, evaluating the *Iliad.*

137. For probability arguments, see e.g., Arist. *Rhet.* 1.15.17, 1376a; *Rhet. Alex.* 7, 1428a.19-23; Dion. Hal. *Ant. rom.* 11.34.1-6; Kennedy, *Classical Rhetoric,* 20-21; Anderson, *Glossary,* 37. For examples, see Lysias *Or.* 4.5-6, §101; 7.12-18, §§109-10; 12.27-28, §122; 19 passim (e.g., 19.24, §154); Isaeus *Astyph.* 14-15; *Pyrr.* 27; Demosth. *Fals. leg.* 120; *Pant.* 23; Jos. *Ag. Ap.* 2.82.

138. Dion. Hal. *Ant. rom.* 4.6.1. See also Polyb. 3.20.1-5; 3.47.6; 3.48.7-9; Dion. Hal. *Ant. rom.* 3.35.5-6; Plut. *Themist.* 25.1-2; 27.1; cf. Paus. 9.31.7; Plut. *Isis* 8, *Mor.* 353F; and Theon's reasons for thinking the account of Medea murdering her children implausible (*Progymn.* 5.487-501; cf. 3.241-76; 4.112-16, 126-34).

139. Arrian *Alex.* 6.28.2. Hearsay without eyewitness testimony is much less credible (Arrian *Ind.* 15.7).

140. Cook, *Interpretation,* 14. For Celsus' approach to the Gospels as unhistorical, see also pp. 26-27 (2.13).

141. Cook, *Interpretation,* 336-37.

142. Cook, *Interpretation,* 337.

143. Wright, *People of God,* 426.

144. See e.g., Venter, "Reviewing History."

145. There is some debate whether the "teacher" refers only to the founder (Brownlee, "Messianic Motifs," 13-15) or also to his successors in an office (e.g., Aune, *Prophecy,* 132; later Qumran sources suggest this, Buchanan, "Office"); some have also portrayed him as an eschatological figure (Wacholder, "Teacher"); as messianic (Allegro, "References," 175-77; the priestly Messiah, Rosenberg, "Moreh"); as not messianic (Smyth, "Scrolls and Messiah"; Brown, "Messianism," 72-75); earlier, a particular Zealot figure (Roth, "Teacher"); other particular figures (cf. Murphy-O'Connor, "Judah"); or one whose identity is unknown (Burgmann, "Lehrer"). There is today debate even how many other documents at Qumran genuinely derive from this sect. For Jesus' pervasive centrality in extant early Christian Christology, see Hurtado, *One God;* Keener, *John,* 289-310.

146. The Qumran sect emphasized inspired interpretation yet preserved authentic memory of their founding Teacher (Stuhlmacher, "Theme," 13; cf. Keener, *John*, 977-82), albeit not at length. Historical references tend to be generalized, whether because they did not matter or because their audience understood the referents (Callaway, "Reflections").

147. Or most of it; over-Platonized versions had other interests, and Burkitt, *History*, 289, aptly titles ch. 9: "Marcion, or Christianity without History."

148. See Martin, "Mithraism"; cf. Mattingly, *Christianity*, 5. Mithraism flourished in the Roman Empire only in a period long after the Gospels were written.

149. Metzger, "Considerations," 15, 19-20.

150. With Hemer, *Acts in History*, 63-70.

151. Vermes, *Jesus and Judaism*, 139, opines that Josephus produced Judaism's "*best* historiography"; certainly he is our main source for postexilic Jewish history (Hengel, *Acts and History*, p. 7); he was also known to early Christians (e.g., Iren. *frg.* 32). Much has been written on early Jewish historiography (see e.g., Mor and Rappaport, *Bibliography*). Suet. *Vesp.* 5, speaks of Josephus' influence (probably ultimately dependent on Josephus on this point).

152. Jos. *Ant.* 19.60.

153. *Ant.* 19.61, 108. Somewhat like Luke, Josephus cites his sources directly far less often than many other extant historians did.

154. E.g., *Ant.* 16.183-84.

155. Cohen, "Josephus and Scripture," argues that Josephus exercises more freedom and stylizes more in *Ant.* Bks. 1-5 than afterward — i.e., more in the "ancient" period.

156. Sometimes *L.A.B.* dramatically rewrites an account (e.g., Begg, "Ceremonies"), but usually depends on the biblical text for events. Feldman, "*Antiquities*," 76, argues that in narrative style *L.A.B.* is closer to Acts than to Josephus.

157. See e.g., Penner, *Praise*, 113; Niehoff, "Two Examples." Sometimes other Jewish authors omit it and Josephus tries to explain it (Feldman, "Command").

158. See Höffken, "Reichsteilung." In Jos. *Ant.* 6.203, he may amplify, or follow tradition in doing so (contrast 1 Sam 18:27, his source, where the LXX reduces the number in the Hebrew).

159. Cf. e.g., Attridge, *History in Josephus*, 44-50; followed by Newell, "Suicide Accounts," 285.

160. For sample analyses of many of his accounts, see e.g., Begg, "Abimelech"; idem, "Deeds"; idem, "Jotham"; idem, "Rape of Tamar"; and the scores of other works (trying to list all of them would needlessly swell my bibliography) by L. Feldman and C. Begg on this subject (I cite merely a sampling, but a fuller one, in Keener, *John*, 15, 24-28).

161. I reserve treatment of them for my commentary on Acts; but cf. briefly Keener, *John*, 69-75. These differed from sayings traditions (Keener, *John*, 62-64).

162. Bellemore, "Josephus, Pompey and the Jews," suggests that Josephus depended on more Roman sources and fewer Jewish sources in the later *Antiquities* than in the *War*.

163. E.g., *Ant.* 12.127. Probably Josephus depends on Nicolas as his main source from Antiochus IV through Herod I (e.g., Stern, *Authors*, 1:229).

164. *Ant.* 14.9; 16.183-84. Josephus also writes from a Jewish perspective that differs from Nicolas' Greco-Syrian one (Wacholder, "Nicolas"). Josephus sounds less favorable to Herod in *Ant.* than in *War*.

165. Jos. *Ant.* 20.156-57, 260, 262, 266. That the historians he had in mind probably made the same claims need not trouble him; though reporting various perspectives as a rhetorical technique, ancient authors rarely reckoned with the multivalence of perspectives the way postmodernists would today. Josephus sometimes legitimates his own historical work (vis-à-vis that of other historians) by citing tradition (Gillet-Didier, "*Paradosis*").

166. He specifically condemns a rival historian for lack of accuracy (*Life* 336), and compares him to a forger of contracts (*Life* 337-39). In this instance, however, for all we know, Josephus might be the one lying. Josephus' claim not to have added anything may be conventional (Feldman,

"Hellenizations: Abraham," 133, citing Dion. Hal. *Thuc.* 5, 8; Lucian *Hist.* 47) and certainly does not fit his adaptation of biblical narratives in his *Ant.* (see again articles by Begg and Feldman noted above).

167. *Ag. Ap.* 1.45-49.

168. E.g., *Ag. Ap.* 1.48-49.

169. *Ag. Ap.* 1.49. On note-taking, cf. comments in our chapter on oral tradition.

170. *Ag. Ap.* 1.50.

171. But cf. Mason, "Contradiction."

172. At one point (Jos. *Ant.* 20.16) he appears to claim not only that Herod, brother of Agrippa I, removed a high priest, but that the authority to remove high priests continued among his descendants; whereas elsewhere Josephus is clear that Agrippa II (Agrippa's son, not Herod's) ultimately assumed this role. Perhaps Josephus meant only that the right continued among Herod's *relatives,* though his *apogonois* here normally means "descendants." Herod replaces priests in 20.103; Agrippa II does so in 20.179, 196, 203.

173. Sometimes the apparent mistakes might instead betray deliberate literary connections (see the argument in Sievers, "Name"), but this approach does not explain all of them.

174. *Ant.* 20.53.

175. He provides only a later summary of what he already recounted, in 20.101.

176. His account of Caligula's death reflects a source different from and impossible to harmonize with Suetonius' (Scherberich, "Sueton und Josephus").

177. Josephus, like Herodotus, fared much better on narrative than speeches by our standards (cf. Mosley, "Reporting," 11-22); he is heavily influenced by rhetoric (see Botha, "Rhetoric and Josephus").

178. Safrai, "Description in Works," especially 320-21.

179. Cf. e.g., Jos. *Ant.* 18.206, which, at least in text as we have it, misconstrues Germanicus' relationship to Tiberius.

180. Sometimes there is considerable debate, e.g., surrounding Felix's full name (e.g., Hemer, "Name of Felix"; Bruce, "Name of Felix"; Kokkinos, *"Gentilicium"*).

181. For proposed problems in Josephus' summaries, see e.g., McLaren, "Summary Statements."

182. He defends both Rome to his people and his people to Rome (as widely noted, e.g., Neusner, *Politics to Piety,* 2; Crossan, *Historical Jesus,* 93).

183. Nearly three centuries before this time an Italian city used the same excuse of being forced by a few troublemakers (in that case, their leaders), and escaped punishment (Livy 24.47.6). Still, experiences and observations in northern Nigeria have given me more respect for the possibility of a few extremists ultimately provoking wider conflict.

184. Cf. e.g., Pastor, "Strata."

185. Although some think that he emphasizes the Pharisaic connection due to the changed political landscape. Williams, "Josephus on Pharisees," attributes to Josephus the full force of his anti-Pharisaic passages (by denying them to Nicolaus of Damascus); he may have followed much of Pharisaism without having officially joined (Mason, "Was Josephus a Pharisee?").

186. With e.g., Ferguson, *Backgrounds,* 387.

187. Ferguson, *Backgrounds,* 387.

188. See e.g., Syon, "Gamla"; Cotton and Geiger, "Yyn"; Mazar, "Josephus and Excavations"; Safrai, "Education," 995; Feldman, "Introduction: Josephus," 45-46; Thackeray, *Josephus,* 49; Riesner, "Gate"; Pixner, "Gate"; Pixner, Chen, and Margalit, "Zion."

189. Safrai, "Description in Works," especially 320-21.

190. Feldman, "Introduction: Josephus," 45-46; Mazar, "Josephus and Excavations," 325-29.

191. *War* 5.166. McRay, *Archaeology and NT,* 117-18.

192. McRay, *Archaeology and NT,* 140.

193. McRay, *Archaeology and NT,* 144 (noting esp. *War* 1.415; *Ant.* 15.341; cf. *Ant.* 18.57; *War* 2.172).

194. Y. Yadin in Shanks, "BAR Interviews Yadin," 19.

195. Thackeray, *Josephus,* 49; Mosley, "Reporting," 23-24. Broshi suggests that the sources for

much of Josephus' accurate information included Roman military commentaries (Broshi, "Credibility of Josephus"; see esp. *Life* 348, 352; *Ag. Ap.* 56, on p. 381). Newell, "Suicide Accounts," argues for conventional forms in Josephus' suicide accounts, the battle suicides probably simply following the form; the evidence may not be sufficient to verify this suggestion, but Josephus does use tragic pathos like other rhetorical historians. Given his own experience, it is not surprising that he digresses to lament (e.g., *War* 5.19), though quickly returning to the subject with the notice that the rules of history prohibit such lamentation (*War* 5.20).

196. In *Ant.* 1.17; 20.154-57, 260-62; *War* 1.9-12, 30; 7.454-55; *Ag. Ap.* 1.47; *Life* 65.

197. *Ag. Ap.* 1.50-51; Mosley, "Reporting," 23-24, noting that Josephus composed speeches freely, but he has many firsthand sources (e.g., *Ant.* 14.144-45, 189, 219, 224, 228).

198. Most notably, for literary purposes Luke brings the Nazareth pericope forward and makes it programmatic (Lk 4:16-30; Mk 6:1-4).

199. Following the model of Dionysius and Isocrates. In the *War* Josephus is closer to the model of Thucydides and Polybius (Attridge, *History in Josephus*, 44-50; followed by Newell, "Suicide Accounts," 285). The more popular level of the Gospels invites less *rhetorical* embellishment, though no less interest in popular storytelling techniques for shaping and communicating the material.

Notes to Chapter 8

1. Rothschild, *Rhetoric of History*, 291.

2. As is often noted, e.g., Marguerat, *Histoire*, 19-20. Biblical scholars, including conservative scholars, also note this caveat concerning ancient Israelite history (e.g., Dillard and Longman, *Introduction*, 23-25; Arnold, *Samuel*, 23).

3. On the divergence of ancient genre categories from their modern namesake descendants, see e.g., Hunter, "Genre."

4. Josephus either has some very detailed sources (which is possible at many points) or is one of the more creative historians extant.

5. On ancient speech composition, often following the gist of sources when possible and composing "appropriately" when necessary, see e.g., discussions in Hammond, "Speeches"; Fornara, *Nature of History*, 143-54, 160-61 (more negatively regarding the distant past, 166-67); Gempf, "Speaking," 264.

6. Dio Chrys. *Or.* 18.10.

7. It is possible that they could be more relevant for John, where I have treated them (*John*, 53-80; cf. now also Bauckham, *Testimony*, 106-12, who draws firmer conclusions than I did).

8. Keener, *John*, 53-80; idem, *Acts* (Peabody: Hendrickson, forthcoming), introduction, ch. 8.

9. Cf. Tac. *Agr.* 10, where Tacitus assumes that his predecessors embellished details precisely where they lacked accurate information. Cf. similarly Acts 25:14-27; where are Luke's witnesses (note also Witherington, *Acts*, 119-20)? Luke could infer the basic substance of the encounter, however, from the outcome (Acts 25:23-27). This historical approach is not defective, just different from our own; modern historians simply take account of it when reading ancient historians, so as to reproduce their essential information in ways more amenable to modern approaches.

10. Josephus can infer (or guess) what was said in private based on what happened in public (e.g., *War* 2.319). Even Tacitus, perhaps the historian of the early empire most respected today, sometimes indulges in reporting characters' thoughts and fears (e.g., Tac. *Hist.* 2.74); he probably does so more often than Luke, precisely because Tacitus is more rhetorically sophisticated than Luke is. For plausibility and probability, as well as accuracy, as criteria for good ancient history writing, see Rothschild, *Rhetoric of History*, 62.

11. E.g., Luke constructed symposia material and arranged events in his travel narrative (though he normally follows the sequence of his sources more than expected for a biography). Likewise, he

may infer and elaborate a scene in Acts 25:14-27, as noted above; viewing such elaboration as deception or misinformation is anachronistic, because ancients expected such elaboration, and often even much more than Luke provides (compare the much longer speeches in most histories).

12. Lucian *Hist.* 12.

13. Lucian *Hist.* 24-25.

14. Penner, *Praise*, 107, notes that A. J. Woodman and T. P. Wiseman have argued that ancient historians invented even events (though conceding the resistance of most classicists to such claims). The statement may be true in some cases, but our evidence suggests that it was hardly the norm.

15. Thus Dibelius, *Studies in Acts*, 136-37, compares Luke's freedom on details with that of other ancient historians.

16. Alexander, "Fiction and Genre," 385-91.

17. Cic. *Quint. fratr.* 1.1.8.23. W. Miller, "Introduction," viii, also takes Xen. *Cyr.* as historical romance, including history but allowing "many liberties with the facts of history"; yet (p. x) he notes it provides much valuable history and culture.

18. Bosworth, "Pseudo-Callisthenes," opines that genuinely historical material in Ps.-Callisth. *Alex.* is minimal, though some of his fictitious material precedes him.

19. On Ps.-Callisthenes, see Fornara, *Nature of History*, 64-65, 72.

20. Plut. *Alex.* 70.3. His own romantic description of Darius' death (Plut. *Alex.* 43.2) is missing in Arrian (*Alex.* 3.21-23), but was evidently not his own invention (the LCL note, 7:352 n. 1, cites Quint. Curt. 5.13, 28; Diod. 17.73).

21. Kennedy, *NT Interpretation*, 8-10; Satterthwaite, "Rhetoric," 340-42; Litfin, *Proclamation*, 124-26; Aune, *Environment*, 12-13.

22. Cic. *Brut.* 11.42.

23. Fornara, *Nature of History*, 136-37 n. 57. Dio Cass. 1.1.1-2 does complain that some of his predecessors have compromised accuracy for rhetorical style.

24. Marguerat, *Histoire*, 19-20, 25; idem, *Historian*, 12-13.

25. Because he writes at a more popular level, Luke may have less polished rhetoric and more adventure. Again, this is not to suggest that Luke or his contemporaries fabricated events; but the narrative tastes of Luke's audience were no doubt an important factor in his selection and presentation of events.

26. See Rothschild, *Rhetoric of History*, passim, noting especially her conclusion on 291. Penner, *Praise*, 137, observes the influence of the *narratio* on all prose writing.

27. Rothschild, *Rhetoric of History*, 65-66, arguing that they treated them as cases to be defended, though not as actual defense speeches.

28. Observed, e.g., by Meister, "Historiography: Greece," 421.

29. See most fully Rebenich, "Historical Prose." Roman historiography varied stylistically (Rebenich, "Historical Prose," 312).

30. Winterbottom, "Rhetoric."

31. Penner, *Praise*, 129.

32. Pliny *Ep.* 1.16.4. History was a form of discourse distinct from others (e.g., forensic rhetoric or philosophy; e.g., Philost. *Ep. Apoll.* 19).

33. Pliny *Ep.* 2.11.17.

34. Rothschild, *Rhetoric of History*, 62; cf. Penner, *Praise*, 217.

35. Rothschild, *Rhetoric of History*, 62-64.

36. Rothschild, *Rhetoric of History*, 69.

37. Rothschild, *Rhetoric of History*, 69-70.

38. Rothschild, *Rhetoric of History*, 88-91.

39. Cadbury, Foakes Jackson and Lake, "Writing History," 13.

40. Fronto *Ad Ant. Imp.* 2.6.1-2.

41. Pliny *Ep.* 5.5.3.

42. Witherington, "Addendum," 29-31; idem, *Acts*, 41-42.

43. Dion. Hal. *Demosth.* 47 (LCL 1:418-19). *Let. Aris.* 322 claims that it should provide greater pleasure than "mythographers" do.

44. Thucyd. 1.1; Polyb. 1.4.5; 39.8.7. For Thucydides, the *uniqueness* of events established their significance (Grene, *Political Theory*, 83).

45. See Burridge, "Biography." But biographies were rarely as partisan as forensic speech, where a primary object was legal victory (e.g., Dion. Hal. *Lysias* 8).

46. Rothschild, *Rhetoric of History*, 93.

47. Rothschild, *Rhetoric of History*, 95. The function of audience is significant here: among the Gospels, even Luke's audience would not expect extensive rhetorical elaboration and pathos to the degree one finds in more dramatic historians, although they were apparently more comfortable with abundant signs claims than the audiences of many elite historians were.

48. Even Theopompus' weaknesses should not be exaggerated; he did genuine research (Meister, "Theopompus").

49. For his general accuracy, see e.g., Mosley, "Reporting," 20-22. Tacitus complained of the decline in imperial historiography but ranked himself among the earlier, superior historians (Marincola, "Tacitus' Prefaces"); for annotated bibliographies on Tacitus, see e.g., Benario, "Recent Works" (688 sources between 1974 and 1983); Benario, "Work" (709 works on Tacitus from 1994 to 2003).

50. Witherington, "Addendum," 29-31; cf. also 23-32.

51. Rothschild, *Rhetoric of History*, 81.

52. Dion. Hal. *Ant. rom.* 1.1.2-4; 1.4.2.

53. Litwak, *Echoes*, 37, noting what he is not implying.

54. E.g., Jos. *Ag. Ap.* 1.24-25; see discussion of Polybius' standard in this chapter.

55. Lucian *Hist.* 22-23.

56. We should, of course, take into account that Lucian is writing satire (Rothschild, *Rhetoric of History*, 81); his critiques are thus meant to entertain, possibly exaggerating others' offenses.

57. *Hist.* 7. He does not rule out praise and blame or moral evaluation; rather (*Hist.* 59, LCL) "Eulogy and censure will be careful and considered, free from slander, supported by evidence, cursory" — "not in court" (hence, not forensic exaggerations). The rhetorical historian Theopompus, by contrast, "impeached nearly everybody in a quarrelsome spirit" so "that he was a prosecutor rather than a recorder of events."

58. Lucian *Hist.* 8 (trans. LCL 6:13).

59. *Hist.* 40 (LCL 6:55).

60. *Hist.* 40. One must, he emphasized, tell the truth, no matter how offensive to one's own contemporaries; thus one would win praise in future generations (*Hist.* 61-62). As particular models of good historians, he offers Xenophon and Thucydides (both contemporaries of the events they report), who would not let personal bias make them change facts; "public interest" and truth take priority over personal enmity or friendship (*Hist.* 39).

61. *Hist.* 9 (LCL 6:15). Rejecting history's entertainment value altogether — contrary to most of his own (nonhistorical) works — is a stringent standard not shared by all historians (as their pleasant readability suggests); but he affirms history's edifying value, i.e., moral lessons, which flow from truth (e.g., *Hist.* 59). Usefulness and pleasure were not mutually exclusive objectives.

62. Dionysius of Halicarnassus, for example, emphasized rhetoric in the writing of history (see Fox, "Dionysius").

63. Cf. also Botha, "Rhetoric and Josephus."

64. While usually maintaining the biblical story line, he occasionally augments it with subsequent traditions and often reshapes it for apologetic purposes. E.g., even his use of speeches in 1 Macc tends to reveal more adaptation than creation (Gafni, "Maccabees," esp. pp. 126-27).

65. Pliny *Ep.* 5.8.9.

66. Pliny *Ep.* 5.8.10-11.

67. Polyb. 3.4.1 (LCL).

68. Polyb. 10.21.8 (LCL). Of course, even orators praising the emperor claimed objectivity; e.g., Fronto *Ad Ant. Imp.* 2.2 declares that it was not his praise of the emperor, but the emperor's virtues, that had produced admiration. Nor is Polybius always objective in his history. But the point is that Polybius sought to be substantially more objective in history than in pure epideictic. Indeed, historians often praised both sides in a war, thereby amplifying pathos and the credit due the victor.

69. Dio Cass. 1.1.1-2.

70. Rolfe, "Introduction," xix.

71. See e.g., Suet. *Rhet.* passim. Penner, *Praise,* 137, contrasts the epiphany in Suetonius' account of Caesar crossing the Rubicon with Caesar's own account; but a century and a half (well beyond the living memory of eyewitnesses) is sufficient time for legends to grow, and Suetonius' dependence on such sources does not require his own fabrication.

72. See Tac. *Dial.* passim. On Tacitus' rhetorical prowess, see Moore, "Introduction," ix (citing Pliny *Ep.* 2.1.6; 2.11.17). Tacitus does develop dramatic scenes and dialogues.

73. Patristic writers were often embarrassed by the poor Greek and lack of rhetoric in the New Testament, though we should point out that they wrote after the rise of, hence may have been influenced by the standards of, the Second Sophistic. Most educated Greeks found first-century Christian writings in general vulgar (Townsend, "Education," 148-49, citing late-second-century CE Tatian *Or. to Greeks* 26-30). This would create a problem for those for whom inspiration demanded also good rhetoric (Dion. Hal. *Thuc.* 34, though acknowledging that Thucydides was a good historian; cf. Philost. *Hrk.* 25.4, 8, which praises Homer's inspiration, yet critiques his accuracy in 24.1-2; 25.10-17).

74. Penner, *Praise,* 220; cf. Moessner, "Poetics," 97-112.

75. Satterthwaite, "Rhetoric," 337 (summarizing the conclusions of his chapter). Cf. also the positive evaluation in Bultmann, *Tradition,* 366.

76. Pervo, *Profit,* 6, citing Julian *Letter* 36.423d, who lists it with Matthew as inferior.

77. Blass, Debrunner and Funk, *Grammar,* §464; Aune, *Dictionary of Rhetoric,* 347; cf. Cadbury, "Commentary on Preface." Lk 1:1-4 also includes five p-words, as Plutarch employs seven of them in his preface to *Septem sapientium convivium* 146C (Aune, *Dictionary of Rhetoric,* 33); divided in two parts, Luke's prologue employs "three matching phrases" (Aune, *Environment,* 116-17).

78. See Rothschild, *Rhetoric of History,* passim.

79. Parsons, "Progymnasmata," 56-61 (esp. 61, citing the much later Nicolaus 4.18-19).

80. Aune, *Dictionary of Rhetoric,* 382 (noting that Aug. *De doctrina Christ.* 4.41 also observed its rareness in the NT).

81. Parsons, "Progymnasmata," 43-44, further arguing (44-63) that Luke probably had learned from the sort of rhetorical exercises preserved for us in the handbooks. Cf. further the high evaluation of Luke's rhetorical skill in Asso, "Raconter." For an example of some fairly obvious and common rhetorical techniques in one Lukan speech, see Keener, "Rhetorical Techniques."

82. Cf. similarly Barrett, *Acts,* xxxv (with Plümacher); for Acts as popular historiography, also Verheyden, "Unity," 55 (citing further Barrett, "First Testament," 101; *Acts,* 2:li). Of course, antiquity lacked "professional historians" (Rebenich, "Historical Prose," 289).

83. See Rebenich, "Historical Prose," 288. Polybius, in fact, opined (presumably against his competition) that most historians lacked proper qualifications (Polyb. 12.25e.2).

84. Alexander, *Context,* 41.

85. E.g., Pliny *Ep.* 2.5.7; 3.13.4; 4.14.3; 6.33.7-8; 7.9.7; 8.21.1; 9.29.1-2; Cic. *Or. Brut.* 46.156; 47.157; *Fam.* 13.27.1.

86. Ekphrasis (with a sort of set-piece description nowhere found in Luke) does appear in narrative works (Rusten, *"Ekphrasis"*; Bowie, "Second Sophistic," 1377; see discussion in Aphth. *Progymn.* 12. On Ecphrasis, 46S, 36-37R); it often appears in ancient fiction (see e.g., Shea, "Stage," 70). Homer's detailed depiction of Achilles' shield (*Il.* 18.468-608) offered the standard for descriptiveness, and other writers (e.g., Aeschylus *Eum.* 39-59; Eurip. *Ion* 82-183) used such accounts long before ekphrasis

is attested as a rhetorical exercise in the Second Sophistic (Fantuzzi, "Ekphrasis," 873; e.g., Ps.-Lucian *Hipp.* 8).

87. Such as Thersites being "bandy-legged, lame in one foot," in Hermog. *Progymn.* 10. On Ecphrasis 22 (trans. Kennedy, 86).

88. A standard practice; see e.g., Aphth. *Progymn.* 12. On Ecphrasis, 47-49S, 39-41R.

89. Fronto *Ad Ant. Imp.* 2.6.4-15.

90. Fronto *Ad Ant. Imp.* 2.6.6.

91. Athen. *Deipn.* 15.682B.

92. Dion. Hal. *Comp.* 18. Dion. Hal. *Thuc.* 15 complains that Thucydides often portrays successfully the abject cruelty and sufferings involved in war, but at other times fails to evoke the appropriate horror involved. But some historians protested if narration of such scenes exceeded necessary details of history (Polyb. 15.34.1).

93. The initial influence of the Second Sophistic was already in some sense underway when Luke wrote, though it had probably not yet affected members of his social circle. Bowie, "Second Sophistic," 1377, dates it to the period c. 60-230 CE, though some scholars begin it later. Even in the first century BCE, however, some writers already advocated the literary use of old Attic Greek rather than Koine (see e.g., Kennedy, "Survey of Rhetoric," 18; Rowe, "Style," 156), by which standards Luke usually falls short, though less so than most other first-century Christian writers.

94. Fronto *Ad Verum Imp.* 2.1.14.

95. On the grand style, see e.g., Dion. Hal. *Demosth.* 15; Cic. *Or. Brut.* 5.20-6.21; Pliny *Ep.* 3.13.4; 6.33.7-8; 7.12.4; 9.26.1 ; 9.26.10; Aul. Gel. 6.14; Longinus *Sublime;* Fronto *Ad M. Caes.* 3.16.2; Menander Rhetor 1.1, 335.21-22; 2.1-2, 368.9; 2.1-2, 369.8-9; 2.6, 399.21-22; 400.7-9; Keener, *John,* 48-49; Cronjé, "Περὶ ὕψους."

96. This is not to deny any kind of dramatic elements; see Plümacher, *Lukas,* 80-136.

97. Still, "signs" do appear in histories (Plümacher, *Geschichte,* 33-84).

98. Plümacher, *Geschichte,* 33-84.

99. Pathos does appear; see e.g., Acts 20:19, 31, 37; some also argue that Israel's failure to respond is viewed as tragic (so Tannehill, "Rejection," esp. 98-99, 101; cf. Tannehill, "Tragic Story"). But such occasions are minor compared to sources more steeped in Greek tragic conventions (even some descriptions in Tacitus are more "tragic-pathetic," e.g., *Ann.* 5.9), and come nowhere close, for example, to a Phylarchus.

100. Penner, *Praise,* 134.

101. Even in the telling of the story in Acts 8:26-40 (see Keener, "Official").

102. For Acts as a "popular" history, see also Barrett, *Acts,* xxxv; Verheyden, "Unity," 55.

103. Some of this section employs material from Keener, *John,* 14-16, albeit augmented and rearranged.

104. As often noted (e.g., Ehrman, *Introduction,* 133). Ancient historians used history to shed light on their own times, as many do today; Aune, *Environment,* 62, cites especially Isoc. *Nic.* 35; *Demon.* 34; Polyb. 1.1.2; Livy 1, *pref.* 10-11; Plut. *Aem. Paul.* 1.1; Lucian *Dem.* 2.

105. General textbooks on (human) "world history" would be excluded from this principle of focus, but even introductory textbooks focusing on such broad topics as "western civilization" or "Asian history" implicitly accept the legitimacy of focusing on a theme or people in historical study.

106. For their theological as well as historical interest, see e.g., Osborne, "History." This is true even of Luke, who comes closest to the style of Greco-Roman historiography (e.g., Marshall, "Luke as Theologian"; idem, *Historian and Theologian;* Martin, *Foundations,* 53-56; Tuckett, *Luke,* 13-14; Green, "History/Writing"; Hotze, "Zeugen"; Marguerat, *Histoire,* 28-29, 36-37, 42, 59-63, especially 91; Rothschild, *Rhetoric of History,* 59, 295).

107. See at length e.g., Hemer, *Acts in History,* 79-85; see also Mason, *Josephus and New Testament,* 63.

108. I borrow the phrase from Penner, *Praise,* 129 (cf. also the idea on 179).

109. See e.g., Marshall, *Historian and Theologian,* 47, critiquing Perrin for his outdated understanding of historiography. Thus, e.g., Cicero's depiction of Dionysius (in *Tusc.* Bk. 5) probably is shaped partly by the author's concerns for Caesar's rise (Verbaal, "End of Liberty").

110. Litwak, *Echoes,* 37 (noting that it is impossible in any era to write history without a perspective).

111. Jos. *Ant.* 20.154.

112. *Ant.* 20.155-56.

113. *Ant.* 20.157.

114. Luke's primary audience is undoubtedly Christian, but his appeals to the public forum suggest that he wishes his history to be at least acceptable to outsiders (cf. Acts 26:26).

115. Penner, "Discourse," 73-77.

116. E.g., Polyb. 36.9.1-17. Cf. Momigliano, *Historiography,* 71-73. For Polybius' appreciation for history's political value, see Fornara, *Nature of History,* 113.

117. On whose biases cf. Wade-Gery, "Thucydides," 1519, adding that "Perhaps no good historian is impartial." Dion. Hal. *Pomp.* 3 thinks Thucydides more biased (in his case against Athens, which had exiled him) than Herodotus was; but he accuses him of focusing on Athens' failings, not of inventing them.

118. Livy 1, *pref.* 10.

119. Often noted, e.g., Mason, *Josephus and New Testament,* 60-71, 77-81; cf. ibid., 196-98; Crossan, *Historical Jesus,* 93; for Josephus' pro-Flavian propaganda, see Saulnier, "Josèphe."

120. Thus Xenophon, while largely accurate in what he reports in the *Hellenica,* proves biased by what he omits of Thebes' greatness (Brownson, "Introduction to *Hellenica,*" ix-x), though he remains our "best authority" for the period (xi).

121. Cf. the respective roles of Pompey and Caesar in Lucan *Civil War* passim (even Homer portrayed the Trojans appealingly enough for Romans to latch onto the Trojan line as their own). That military success did not always determine history's favor is clear: Greece, with its rich culture, influenced Rome no less (and perhaps more) than Rome influenced Greece.

122. E.g., Albans in Dion. Hal. *Ant. rom.* book 3; plebeians and patricians in Dion. Hal. *Ant. rom.* 9.39.1-6; Romans and Carthaginians in Livy 21.1.3; or (outside history) the evenhandedness of Homer's portrayal of Greek and Trojan heroism in the *Iliad,* which allowed such later works as Euripides' *Trojan Women* and the Roman adoption of Aeneas (e.g., Virg. *Aen.*).

123. E.g., Hdt. 2.4, 32, 50, 58, 77, 82.

124. Meister, "Herodotus," 268. This approach did not commend him to everyone (cf. e.g., Plut. *Mal. Hdt.*).

125. Burridge, *Gospels,* 182-84. So also characters in history, e.g., Marcius as the greatest general of his era, yet with fatal character flaws (Dion. Hal. *Ant. rom.* 8.60.1-2; 8.61.1-3).

126. Lucian *Hist.* 7. Such poetic descriptions are inappropriate within history (*Hist.* 8), though praise is permissible within careful bounds (*Hist.* 9).

127. Plut. *Mal. Hdt.* 3 (*Mor.* 855C).

128. Polyb. 9.9.9-10.

129. Pliny *Ep.* 3.5.20, on his late uncle. In other genres, cf. Aesop's *Fables* (e.g., 172); Pindar *Encomia* frg. 121; Theophr. *Char.* proem 3; Philost. *Vit. soph.* 2.1.554; Athen. *Deipn.* 1.10e; 3 Macc 2:5; Pearl, *Theology.*

130. Aeschines *Embassy* 75-76; Lysias *Or.* 2.61.196; *Rhet. Alex.* 1429b.6-22; Cic. *Sest.* 68.143; Max. Tyre 6.5. See the treatment of examples in rhetoric in *Rhet. Alex.* 8, 1429a.21-1430a.13; cf. also Anderson, *Glossary,* 86-88; Kennedy, "Survey of Rhetoric," 21; Demoen, "Paradigm." The intellectual orator Maximus of Tyre opines that history preserves the memories of humanity and so "guards its virtues" (Max. Tyre 22.5, trans. Trapp).

131. See Men. Rhet. 2.4, 392.28-31.

132. On the hortatory value of history in Roman historians, see Fornara, *Nature of History,* 115-16.

For moralizing elements in ancient historiography, Marguerat, *Histoire*, 28-29 cites examples from Dionysius, Livy, Sallust and Plutarch.

133. E.g., Dion. Hal. *Ant. rom.* 1.2.1.

134. Polyb. 1.1.1 (LCL). On Polybius' moral and political objectives, see also Fornara, *Nature of History*, 113 (who notes on 115-16 that Romans emphasized this even more).

135. Tac. *Agr.* 1.

136. Moore, "Introduction," xiii.

137. E.g., *Hist.* 59.

138. Val. Max. 2.pref. (LCL).

139. E.g., Polyb. 1.35.1-10; Diod. Sic. 31.10.2; Dion. Hal. *Ant. rom.* 7.65.2; Tac. *Ann.* 4.33; Dio Cass. 1.5.4; Arrian *Alex.* 4.10.8; Corn. Nep. 16 (Pelopidas), 3.1. For narrative asides in histories and biographies, see Sheeley, *Asides*, 56-93.

140. See e.g., Dobbeler, "Geschichte"; Kooij, "Death of Josiah"; Reinmuth, "Zwischen Investitur"; Bergren, "Nehemiah"; Borgen, "Reviewing and Rewriting."

141. See e.g., Polyb. 2.56.13; 3.32.2. Ancient historians did not, as some contend, ignore lines of cause and effect (Rajak, *Josephus*, 102).

142. Dion. Hal. *Ant. rom.* 5.56.1; Polyb. 3.31.11-13.

143. For *paradeigmata* to make moral points in speeches, see Dion. Hal. *Ant. rom.* 6.80.1; *Rhet. Alex.* 8.1429a.21-1430a.13; Cic. *Sest.* 48.102; cf. also Kennedy, "Survey of Rhetoric," 21.

144. On such historical "paradigms" see also Diod. Sic. 37.4.1; Hdn. 3.13.3.

145. Dion. Hal. *Ant. rom.* 1.6.3-5; cf. Diod. Sic. 15.1.1; 37.4.1.

146. Philo *Abr.* 4; Jos. *Ag. Ap.* 2.204; 1 Cor 10:11.

147. E.g., 4 Macc 1:7-8. Rabbis sometimes employed earlier rabbis' behavior as legal precedent. For disciples imitating teachers, see also Jos. *Life* 11; *b. Ber.* 62a; Kirschner, "Imitatio"; Abrahams, *Studies* 2:138-154; Xen. *Mem.* 1.2.3; Sen. *Controv.* 9.3.12-13; Lucian *Peregr.* 24; Philost. *Vit. Apoll.* 5.21; 1 Cor 4:16.

148. See Avioz, "Lot."

149. For a more detailed study of Josephus' adaptation of Isaac, see Feldman, "Isaac."

150. See Feldman, "Joseph."

151. See Feldman, "Moses." Hata, "Moses within Anti-Semitism," emphasizes the apologetic value of Josephus' portrayal of Moses against anti-Semites.

152. See Levison, "Ruth."

153. See Feldman, "Samuel."

154. See Jos. *Ant.* 10.24-35; Begg, "Illness"; Feldman, "Hezekiah."

155. See Jos. *Ant.* 9.1-17; Begg, "Jehoshaphat"; Feldman, "Jehoshaphat."

156. See Begg, "Josiah"; Feldman, "Josiah."

157. See Feldman, "Daniel."

158. See Feldman, "Nehemiah."

159. See Feldman, "Jeroboam."

160. See Feldman, "Ahab."

161. Noah appears positive but Feldman, "Noah," thinks that Josephus reduced his role because he was ancestor of the Gentiles (though Josephus does not transfer Noah traditions to Moses the way later rabbis did). In idealizing characters into various types, Josephus may have also used standard hellenistic typologies for women characters (Sarah as the good wife, Potiphar's wife as evil, etc.; Amaru, "Women").

162. Cicero felt that historical monographs were ideal for glorifying their subjects, and Plümacher includes a work of Cicero's and 2 Maccabees as examples of monographs fulfilling this function (Plümacher, *Geschichte*, 15-32; idem, "Cicero und Lukas," 772-73). Naturally this is also a dominant element in biography (Penner, *Praise*, 135).

163. Polyb. 3.4.1.

164. Polyb. 8.8.3-6. He finds it appalling that Theopompus praises Philip while depicting his despicable deeds; one may forgive historians who are slightly wrong, but not those driven by severe bias (Polyb. 8.8.8-9); fairness is the standard (8.8.7). He sometimes digresses in asides to give lessons related to the events narrated (1.35.1-10). But while Theopompus was one of the major "rhetorical" historians, he did genuine research (Meister, "Theopompus").

165. Polyb. 10.26.9.

166. Pliny *Ep.* 5.8.1-2. Cf. Pindar *Encomia* frg. 121.

167. Aeschines *Embassy* 75-76. Classical orators, for example, had long praised those who imitated their ancestors' valor in battle (Lysias *Or.* 2.61, §196) and summoned their hearers to imitate their ancestors' wisdom (Aeschines *Embassy* 75).

168. Fornara, *Nature of History,* 36. At times this approach could produce distortion, but it need not do so (Fornara, *Nature of History,* 64-65).

169. E.g., Corn. Nep. 11 (Iphicrates), 3.2; Arrian *Alex.* 4.7.4; 4.8.1-4.9.6; Plut. *Cim.* 2.4-5; much more fully, see Keener, *John,* 16 (cf. idem, *Matthew,* 51 n. 157).

170. Likewise, Suet. *Jul.* 52 (like much of the work) is full of scandal about Julius, but 53 praises him. After recounting his noble deeds (e.g., *Jul.* 73-75), Suetonius concludes that his negative actions "so turn the scale, that it is thought that he abused his power and was justly slain" (76.1, LCL 1:99).

171. Suet. *Nero* 19.3 (LCL 2:115).

172. Pliny *Ep.* 3.3.5.

173. E.g., Pliny *Ep.* 6.27.1-2.

174. For example, some Socratic ideas appear in Xenophon's Cyrus (e.g., *Cyr.* 3.1.17; Xenophon's other works reveal his admiration of Socrates), though the *Cyropaedia* is not a true historical work or biographic work in the later sense (Cic. *Quint. fratr.* 1.1.8.23 argues that Xenophon's *Cyropaedia* was intended to teach proper government, not primarily to report historical truth).

175. Cf. Seneca the Elder *Historical Fragments* 1, who divided Rome's history into ages corresponding to human maturation. Contrary to some modern interpretations of ancient historiography, some ancient historians did think in terms of cause and effect, though not all of these were divine (e.g., Polyb. 2.56.13; 3.6.1-3.7.3; 3.31.11-13; 3.32.2).

176. E.g., the interpretation of a head found beneath Rome (Dion. Hal. *Ant. rom.* 4.59.2; 4.61.2; Plut. *Cam.* 31.4; Dio Cass. frg. in Zonaras 7.11). Perhaps they inadvertently dug into part of an old burial site (though our sources claim a freshly severed head), but their interpretation became the dominant memory.

177. Xen. *Anab.* 5.2.24.

178. Meister, "Herodotus," 269. The line between "objective" (Herodotus, Thucydides) and "confessional" (OT; Luke) historiography may often be thinner than one would surmise from Marguerat, *Histoire,* 42.

179. With e.g., Konkel, *Kings,* 328.

180. Frei, "Apologetics," 56, notes that this view was also influential in eighteenth-century England.

181. Squires, "Plan," 38, citing Diod. Sic. 1.1.3.

182. Dion. Hal. *Ant. rom.* 8.56.1.

183. Hebrew Scripture likewise affirmed God's providence in all events, even in acts of disobedience to God (Eichrodt, "Faith in Providence," 19-20).

184. Sometimes using it to justify reporting apparently supernatural phenomena (*Ant.* 17.353; cf. 17.350-52).

185. See Squires, *Plan,* 15-17 on Dionysius; 18-20 on Josephus; and 20-36 on Luke; for the nature of providence in hellenistic history, see 38-46, in Josephus, 46-51, in Luke-Acts, 52-77 (where see also Brawley, *Centering on God,* 86-106); for tempering divine determinism with free will, see 154-60 on hellenistic historians, 160-66 on Josephus and 166-85 on Luke-Acts. See also Marguerat, *Histoire,* 36-37; for Luke's interest in providence, 59-61.

186. E.g., Philo *Creation* 1-2, 157; *Let. Aris.* 168; Jos. *Ant.* 1.15. Even in an earlier era, Israel's historical interests contrasted with many surrounding cultures' "extra-temporal myths" (De Vaux, *Israel*, 272), though the contrast should not be overdrawn as if only Israelites cared about history (see Frahm, Jansen-Winkeln, and Wiesehöfer, "Historiography"; Millard, Hoffmeier, and Baker, *Historiography in Context*); cf. Van Seters, "Historiography" for some possible parallels with Greek historiography.

187. Thus some for example compare Luke's work with OT historical works to argue that Luke intended to write history (Rosner, "Biblical History," 81).

188. E.g., Philo *Creation* 1-2: Moses refused to invent fables. Philo did, however, allegorize embarrassing portions (as not literal, not just in addition to literal), and some did so more liberally than he. In *Ant.*, Josephus treated the biblical narratives as real history (though he treated the text with freedom).

189. Wright, *People of God*, 471.

190. See Dunn, *New Perspective*, 15-34, especially 29; regarding the connection between Jesus' mission and the church, cf. Aarde, "Historiese Jesus."

191. Aune, *Environment*, 62 (citing especially Isoc. *Nicocles* 35; *Demon.* 34; Polyb. 1.1.2; Livy 1, *pref.* 10-11; Plut. *Aemilius Paulus* 1.1; Lucian *Demonax* 2). An interpretive framework and even nonhistoric genre need not obscure all historical data; e.g., *Sib. Or.* 5.1-50 recites recent history accurately from its author's conceptual standpoint (i.e., including legends he assumes to be historical), despite some confusion (cf. 5.460-63).

192. Vermes, *Jesus and Judaism*, 20.

193. With Eddy and Boyd, *Legend*, 398-99.

194. Dunn, *Acts*, xvi.

195. With e.g., Marconi, "Interpretation"; Levinskaya, *Diaspora Setting*, 2; Hemer, *Acts in History*, 86-90.

196. E.g., viewers in the U.S. can get a more global perspective from the BBC than from most U.S. media outlets. One newsmagazine here, to which I no longer subscribe, failed to mention war in the Democratic Republic of Congo until the estimated death toll passed three million; I never saw even mention in that magazine of the smaller Congo, in which my wife was a refugee. Such omissions certainly distort perspectives for readers dependent on these sources; yet no one would accuse that newsmagazine of having deliberately fabricated whatever data that it did report.

197. For example, Luke's emphasis on Paul going to the Gentiles is hardly a Lukan creation (cf. Botermann, "Heidenapostel"; cf. Rom 1:14; 11:11-14) even if the way he recounts this going creates a characteristic pattern.

198. Vermes, *Jesus and Judaism*, 19; cf. Levinskaya, *Diaspora Setting*, 2; Hemer, *Acts in History*, 79-90. The shaping of gospel tradition does not exclude tradition to be shaped; cf. Levine, "Word," 510: despite adaptation, much of the Gospels' "general depiction of Jesus' words and deeds has good claims to credibility."

199. Meister, "Historiography: Greece," 421.

200. Cf. Lüdemann, *Acts*, 22, 218, 363, on Acts.

201. Hengel and Schwemer complain (Hengel and Schwemer, *Between Damascus and Antioch*, 6-7) that in modern NT scholarship, "The real danger in the interpretation of Acts (and the Gospels) is no longer an uncritical apologetic but the hypercritical ignorance and arrogance which — often combined with unbridled fantasy — has lost any understanding of living historical reality." For an argument against the usual unreliability of ancient historiography, see e.g., Eddy and Boyd, *Legend*, 330-34 (observing on 333 that most of the critiques offered against ancient historians apply to modern historians as well).

202. Penner, "Discourse," 77-78, warns that historians reinforced power grids of society, reflecting political philosophy. While this was true of elite historians, apologetic historians like Josephus could seek to advance the cause of their minority (in his case, of his fellow Jews, though with special

sympathy for other aristocratic males). Modern historians may be more generally suspicious of these sorts of biases, but are not immune to them.

203. Penner, *Praise,* 179.

204. Penner, *Praise,* 217, correctly emphasizes the centrality of plausibility and arrangement, but goes too far when (Penner, *Praise,* 179) he suggests that "Completely fabricated accounts may in fact be better *historia*" than accurate ones, insofar as they fulfilled their rhetorical function. As we have noted, the genre included a factual as well as rhetorical component, and could be judged by both standards.

205. Penner, *Praise,* 107, prefers postmodern critics' approach to the traditional classicist approach, which he complains has been too resistant to the postmodern critique. For recent appreciative responses to radical postmodern skepticism regarding historiography (each offering some fundamental critiques without rejecting all of postmodernism's elements), see McKnight, *Death,* 6-42; Eddy and Boyd, *Legend,* 15-24. Using ancient historians' biases to negate all factual content may read our postmodern milieu's agendas of radical perspectivalism into the ancient writers no less than the pure "historicizing" approach does. In a sense, it allows the rejected historicist paradigm to continue to set the agenda: if a text does not correspond at *all* points with history as strictly defined today, it is unreliable as a substantial historical source. Particular configurations of facts may produce political fictions, but not in the same sense in which novels are fictitious. Otherwise (at an extreme level) we would have to relinquish attempts at historical claims, unable to arbitrate, for example, between genuine histories of the Nazi Holocaust and the unfounded and dangerous claims of Holocaust deniers (cf. discussion in Beckwith, "History & Miracles," 89-91).

206. Lüdemann, *Acts,* 22. Of course, ad hominem arguments about motives are risky in academic discourse, especially when Lüdemann, too, has agendas (Lüdemann, *Acts,* 383, condemns the fanaticism of Christianity, which on his reading has led to perhaps twenty million deaths).

207. Lüdemann, *Acts,* 22.

208. Lüdemann, *Acts,* 218.

209. *Ant.* 19.346. One may well wonder about the frequency of nocturnal woodland creatures in large public theaters during daylight! Because this omen provides a probable connection with Jos. *Ant.* 18.195, it could easily be Josephus' addition to provide cohesiveness to his narrative, the way Luke, who usually follows Mark's sequence, departs from it for his Nazareth pericope.

210. Rothschild, *Rhetoric of History,* 69.

Notes to Chapter 9

1. Pliny *N.H.* pref. 17, 22 (LCL 1:13, 15).

2. See e.g., Foster, "Introduction," xxxi, who argues that though Livy is sometimes uncritical, he is our only source, hence our best source, "for long stretches of Roman history." Josephus is, for all his weaknesses, our best source for postexilic Jewish history (Hengel, *Acts and History,* 7).

3. E.g., Sil. It. 9.66-177. They could provide such insights, they believed, through inspiration (Val. Flacc. 3.15-17; Sil. It. 9.340-45; cf. also Nagy, "Prologue," xxx; Maclean and Aitken, *Heroikos,* xxxix), through which they could also reveal the divine purposes in history (Sil. It. 1.19).

4. Dion. Hal. *Ant. rom.* 1.1.1; see Keener, *John,* 22-23; for historians ideally using sources, see also Marguerat, *Histoire,* 30. Pervo, *Dating Acts,* 6-7, correctly notes that writers did not always acknowledge their sources, as long as they rewrote the material (citing Josephus' rewrite of Ex 7:8-12 in Jos. *Ant.* 2.284-87); but we should note that it is rare to find elite historians who never mention their predecessors when such existed.

5. Pliny *Ep.* 9.33.1.

6. Suet. *Jul.* 9.3. Suetonius employed primarily written sources, hence had more information for earlier rather than later figures (Rolfe, "Introduction," xviii).

7. Dio Cass. 1.1.1-2.

8. The practice is not limited to historical genres, being found also among mythographers and novelists (though novelists are more prone to free creation and sometimes may have invented their sources). Even a novelist might occasionally remember to provide the story world verisimilitude by providing a source (Apul. *Metam.* 9.30; Philost. *V.A.* 3.27). In other genres, cf. *Contest of Homer and Hesiod* 323; Parth. *L.R.* 11.1-3; 14.5. Ovid's account of Lichas's end (*Metam.* 9.225) diverges from Soph. *Wom. Tr.* 777-82; Ovid claims dependence on prior tradition, but his emphasis on metamorphoses at least accounts for which tradition he prefers! With a much earlier historical person, Philostratus (*Vit. Apoll.* 1.2) claims that he gathered information from cities (i.e., local, century-old traditions); from others' accounts and from his letters; and also (1.3) from Damis's memoirs. As we have noted, Conybeare, "Introduction," vii-viii, treats Damis as a genuine but not entirely reliable source; by contrast, Jones, "Apollonius' Passage," views him as Philostratus' invention.

9. E.g., Num 21:14; Josh 10:13; 2 Sam 1:18; 1 Kgs 14:19, 29; 15:7, 23, 31; 16:5, 14, 20, 27; 22:39, 45; 2 Kgs 1:18; 8:23; 10:34; 12:19; 13:8, 12; 14:15, 18, 28; 15:6, 11, 15, 21, 26, 31, 36; 16:19; 20:20; 21:17, 25; 23:28; 24:5; 1 Chron 27:24; 29:29; 2 Macc. 2:24-25. Rabbis, too, often emphasized citing sources for traditions (e.g., *m. Ab.* 6:6; *b. Nid.* 19b).

10. E.g., Dion. Hal. *Ant. rom.* 1.6.1; Arrian *Alex.* 6.2.4; Plut. *Alex.* 30.7; 31.2-3; 38.4; and further below. For details from Tiberius' time, Tacitus cites generally "historians of that era" (*Ann.* 5.9).

11. Some are more probable and objective than others. Cf. Cook, "Plutarch's Use," for what may be a substantive stylistic source indicator in Plutarch.

12. E.g., Dion. Hal. *Ant. rom.* 1.87.4; 3.35.1-4; 8.79.1; Livy 9.44.6; 23.19.17; 25.17.1-6; Appian *Hist. rom.* 11.9.56; 12.1.1; Plut. *Alex.* 31.3; 38.4; *Demosth.* 5.5; 29.4-30.4; *Themist.* 25.1-2; 27.1; 32.3-4; Paus. 2.5.5; 2.26.3-7; Arrian *Alex.* 4.9.2-3; 4.14.1-4; 5.3.1; 5.14.4; 7.14.2; 7.27.1-3; Hdn. 7.9.4; 7.9.9; Corn. Nep. 7 (Alcibiades), 11.1; 9 (Conon), 5.4; *p. Sot.* 9:13, §2; see further Livy LCL 12:320 n. 2; mythographers in Apollod. *Bib.* 1.4.3; 1.5.2; 1.9.15, 19; 2.3.1; 2.5.11; Ovid *Fasti* 6.1-2, 97-100. When unsure which is best, one simply cites various sources (e.g., Philostratus *Vit. soph.* 2.4.570).

13. Arrian *Alex.* 1, *pref.* 1-2.

14. Arrian *Alex.* 3.3.6.

15. Philost. *Vit. soph.* 2.5.576.

16. Nor can one object that Philostratus, writing lives of sophists, was simply unaware of appropriate rhetorical conventions!

17. I.e., thereby implying far more than the five sources he has named for the "majority."

18. Plut. *Alex.* 46.1-2, adding that the minor divergence does not affect our view of his hero's character (the main point for him).

19. E.g., Diod. Sic. 4.4.1-5.

20. Cf. Damon, "Source to *Sermo*," on Livy 34.54.4-8 (contrasting Tacitus' freer composition in *Ann.* Bks. 1, 14), if this redaction critical approach proves durable.

21. See Hemer, *Acts in History,* 65. See e.g., Val. Max. 5.7.ext. 1; 6.8.3 (though Valerius confuses sources more often than most, especially when commenting on an earlier period).

22. E.g., Philost. *Vit. soph.* 2.4.570; in a different genre, cf. Ovid *Fasti* 6.1-2, 97-100.

23. Cf. e.g., Tacitus, who naturally does not need to cite many sources on his father-in-law in the *Agricola.*

24. E.g., 1 Esdras blends Chronicles, Ezra, and Nehemiah with some midrash. Josephus does not state most of his extrabiblical sources (Nicolaus of Damascus being an important exception; see the source critical analysis in Bellemore, "Josephus, Pompey and Jews"); even Livy can mention that there are many while citing only one (Livy 42.11.1).

25. Schmidt, "Stellung"; Kümmel, *Introduction,* 37; see discussion in e.g., Keener, *Matthew,* 17. "High" literature influenced "low" literature, creating an overlap of style (Burridge, *Gospels,* 11, 153; Aune, *Environment,* 12, 63; Downing, "Relevance").

26. E.g., Dion. Hal. *Ant. rom.* 1.6.1, 3; sometimes earlier oral traditions probably also surface later

in rabbinic literature (see e.g., Keener, *John,* 189-90). Oral and written traditions sometimes overlapped (Jeremias in Hennecke, *Apocrypha,* 1:95).

27. E.g., Cic. *Nat. d.* 3.16.42 (concerning Hom. *Od.* 11.600ff; see especially Cicero LCL 19:324-25, n. a); Diog. Laert. 1.48 (Solon into Hom. *Il.* 2.557).

28. Possibly Hierocles in Stobaeus; Malherbe, *Moral Exhortation,* 85. Jewish scribes, however, rarely practiced redaction criticism on Scripture (despite an occasional fourth-century Palestinian Amora; cf. *Lev. Rab.* 6:6; 15:2).

29. Gundry, "Genre," 102; Witherington, *Christology,* 22; contrast the older approach of Dibelius, *Tradition,* 3.

30. Polyb. 12.25d.1.

31. Polyb. 12.25e.1, 25i.2.

32. Cf. e.g., the many contemporary histories of Nero noted in Jos. *Ant.* 20.154.

33. Pliny *N.H.* pref. 18.

34. *N.H.* pref. 17. Some emphasized the value of crediting one's sources (Vitruvius *Architecture* 7.preface.10-17; Pliny *N.H.* pref. 21), though sometimes noting that most of their sources had not done so (Pliny *N.H.* pref. 21-23).

35. The majority view (so Fitzmyer, *Acts,* 59).

36. Fuller, "Classics," 182, notes G. Kennedy's observation that the plural (rather than the dual) requires minimally three, and grammatically each produced their own narration.

37. Aune, *Environment,* 121, doubts the certainty of this premise, given the conventionality of the statement; but other historians who used this convention did have sources (even if one regards "many" as hyperbolic) — i.e., the convention is not a fiction. Aune himself notes that Hellenistic prefaces often mentioned predecessors (*Environment,* 90); for the mention of sources in prefaces, see Alexander, *Preface,* 32-34; mention of many sources can also occur after concluding a discussion (as in Diog. Laert. 4.1).

38. Kennedy, "Source Criticism," 134-35, suggests as early as 45 CE based on Euseb. *H.E.* 2.14-15, but Eusebius' tradition here seems questionable. More plausibly, Theissen, *Gospels in Context,* 203-34, especially 220-21, 230-32, dates "Q" (though not necessarily a narrative, it might fit Luke's term) in the 40s, though this is uncertain. Certainly we cannot rule out even some early Palestinian written sources, given evidence for sufficient literacy there (Millard, *Reading and Writing,* esp. summary in 227-29; idem, "Literacy"; Head, "Note on *Reading*"); scribes (cf. Millard, *Reading and Writing,* 168, 176; Bucking, "Training") could also be paid to take dictation.

39. E.g., Jos. *War* 1.1-2, 7; *Ant.* 20.154-57 (cf. 20.262); Wardle, *Valerius Maximus,* 67, cites Livy pref. 2; Sall. *Hist. Fr.* 3, 7; Tac. *Hist.* 1.1.2-3; *Ann.* 1.1.2 (comparing also Hecataeus fr. 1; Cato *Orig.* frg. 77; Asinius Pollio frg. 4). Outside history, see e.g., Longin. *Subl.* 1.1.

40. E.g., Val. Max. 1.pref. Only after praising his predecessors does Quintilian note that he will differ from them on some points (Quint. *Inst.* 3.1.22).

41. E.g., Dion. Hal. *Thuc.* 5.

42. Mason, "Chief Priests," 127, following Sterling, *Historiography,* 343-45; Parsons, *Luke,* 47. Cf. *epicheireō,* which appears elsewhere in Luke-Acts for futile or mistaken efforts (Acts 9:29; 19:13), and an adjective.

43. Robbins, "Claims of Prologues," 73-75, 83, arguing that Luke instead intends to provide a continuous account "from the beginning to Rome." Aune, *Dictionary of Rhetoric,* 371, also doubts that Luke criticizes his predecessors' accuracy.

44. Xen. *Apol.* 1-2 (though citing for this new emphasis a specific informant, *Apol.* 2).

45. Aul. Gel. pref. 10 (preferring their style), 11-12 (preferring his selectivity). Cf. also this explanation (of greater selectivity) in 2 Macc 2:24-25 (conciseness was a narrative virtue, Theon *Progymn.* 5.39-40).

46. Nicolaus *Progymn.* 1. pref. 1.

47. One could refute sources based on rhetorical criteria (e.g., Theon *Progymn.* 3.241-244) and claim superiority in arrangement over one's predecessors (Artem. *Oneir.* 3.pref.).

48. Moessner, "Poetics," 97-112.

49. Danker, *New Age*, 4 (comparing Ovid *Metam.* 7.520); Tannehill, *Luke*, 9-10; Penner, *Praise*, 220; Parsons, "Progymnasmata," 52 (noting arrangement for clarity in Theon *Progymn.* 87.13; Quint. *Inst.* 4.2.83; but also acknowledging preference for exact sequence in *Rhet. Alex.* 30, 28-31; *Rhet. Her.* 1.9.15; and Theon's disapproval of accidental confusion of sequence in *Progymn.* 80.26-29). Certainly historical prefaces were supposed to promise that they would be easy to follow (Lucian *Hist.* 53).

50. Because Luke's sources, whose sequence he usually follows meticulously in his Gospel, control his arrangement there but are probably not entirely chronological, Luke's purposeful sequencing of a continuous narrative is probably more effective chronologically in Acts. On his sequential approach to putative sources, cf. also Morton and MacGregor, *Structure*, 27; Perry, *Sources*, 19-20.

51. Biography need not be chronological (see Görgemanns, "Biography"; Stanton, *Jesus of Nazareth*, 119-21; cf. even 4Q158; Augustine *Harm. G.* 21.51; for Mark, see Papias in Euseb. *H.E.* 3.39); cf. e.g., the accidental repetition in Plut. *Alex.* 37.4; 56.1. See somewhat more detailed discussion in Keener, *John*, 12-13.

52. Pliny *Ep.* 1.1.1; Thucyd. 2.1.1; 5.26.1 (although even most historians tended to follow events to their conclusion and not simply strict chronology; Dion. Hal. *Thuc.* 9; *Pomp.* 3). Rhetoricians emphasized order (e.g., Anderson, *Glossary*, 116).

53. See Balch, "Full History," 229-39 (against Moessner); Penner, *Praise*, 163. But cf. Dion. Hal. *Ant. rom.* 3.18.1.

54. E.g., Diod. Sic. 1.4.4; 1.6.2.

55. In most Lukan texts one could interpret the term either way (Acts 18:26; 22:3; 23:15, 20; 24:22; 26:5), but Acts 18:25 seems to imply primarily "accuracy" (possibly implying the same for 18:26, but 18:26 may play on the other nuance of the term), and the texts about Pharisaic scrupulousness (22:3; 26:5; cf. 18:25-26) probably specify "accuracy," in view of similar descriptions of Pharisaic learning in Josephus (*Ant.* 17.41; 19.332; *War* 1.110; 2.162; *Life* 191). For other groups with "accurate" interpretation, see e.g., *Ant.* 12.49, 104; perhaps *Ant.* 1.14; *Ag. Ap.* 2.144, 149; for non-Jewish laws, *Ag. Ap.* 2.227, 257. Josephus' clearest parallel to Luke might be *Ag. Ap.* 2.287, but by itself this passage could be interpreted either way.

56. E.g., Alciph. *Court.* 13, frg. 6, ¶19; in a history, Diod. Sic. 1.6.2 (writing as accurately as possible given his subject's antiquity). Similarly, Herodian applies *akribeias* to his "careful" research (though we do not consider Herodian particularly precise; Whittaker, "Introduction," xxxix-xl); Josephus, too, promises to treat everything with accuracy (*akribē, Ant.* 1.17; cf. 1.214), though we may think this an exaggeration; he also promises to narrate with accuracy in contrast to those whose histories are falsified (*War* 1.2, 6, 9, 22; *Life* 358, 360, 365, 412); cf. his use for Thucydides (*Ag. Ap.* 1.18). Josephus surely concurs that Scripture speaks accurately (*Ant.* 1.82; cf. *War* 1.17; *Ag. Ap.* 1.29).

57. For more detailed discussion, see e.g., Duling and Perrin, *New Testament*, 11-16; France, *Matthew*, 34-38; Carson, Moo and Morris, *Introduction*, 26-38; Stein, "Synoptic Problem."

58. E.g., Whittaker, "Introduction," lxi-lxii.

59. Frye, "Analogies in Literatures," 287-90.

60. For analogous constructions in classics, with the same needs for caution against excessive speculation, see Kennedy, "Source Criticism," 132.

61. See especially Farmer, *Problem*; cf. Longstaff, *Conflation*, 218; Murray, "Conflator"; Frye, "Analogies in Literatures," 304-12 (and 273 on abridgement). For proto-Matthew see Lowe and Flusser, "Theory"; a smaller number have also contended for something like Lukan priority (e.g., Lindsey, *Rabbi*, 84; Young, *Parables*, 129-63; cf. Lindsey, "Approach"), though this thesis has so far gained few adherents outside Israel (cf. Ådna, "Attitude").

62. See Senior, *Matthew*, 17-19; Davies and Allison, *Matthew*, 1:98-114; Tuckett, *Griesbach Hypothesis* (with conclusion on 186).

63. Davies and Allison, *Matthew,* 1:73-74; cf. Marcus, *Mark,* 41-44. The abbreviation is, however, less often theologically motivated than supposed in the heyday of redaction criticism (e.g., Held, "Miracle Stories," 169; on expansion, pp. 193-206).

64. See Gundry, *Old Testament,* 9-28; cf. Stanton, *New People,* 353-63. Sometimes he follows the MT sequence but the LXX wording (e.g., in 19:18-19; cf. Hagner, *Matthew,* 557). Gundry, *Old Testament,* 174-85 also argued that the eclectic text-types behind citations found in all three Gospels fit only the trilingual milieu of first-century Palestine; while we would contend for common oral tradition in the earliest community on this point, Gundry suggests this material goes back to Matthew the tax collector's notes (p. xii). Rabbis also used eclectic text-types (see Goulder, *Midrash,* 27); they are most obvious in Matthew where Matthew's redactional hand is clearest (see Soares Prabhu, *Formula Quotations,* 63-106; cf. Cope, *Scribe,* 121-22). For a survey of views regarding the source of Matthew's quotations, see Hagner, *Matthew,* lvi.

65. E.g., Davies and Allison, *Matthew,* 1:115-24; Voorst, *Jesus Outside NT,* 156-63.

66. Probably from the German *Quelle,* "source," which Weiss abbreviated to "Q" in 1890 (Stanton, *Gospel Truth,* 63). But some find this origin questionable (Voorst, *Jesus Outside NT,* 155 n. 41, following Schmitt, "Siglum").

67. Cf. e.g., Edwards, *Concordance;* idem, *Theology of Q;* more problematically, Mack, *Myth,* 69, 84; idem, *Lost Gospel,* 6, 73-80. As we have noted, Mack and others create an "early" recension of Q that fits their hypothetical reconstruction of early Christianity, but this approach is circular, as most scholars acknowledge (see Overman, "Deciphering," 193; Witherington, *Sage,* 215; Johnson, *Real Jesus,* 52-53; Meier, *Marginal Jew,* 2:177-80; Stanton, *Gospel Truth,* 73-74; Theissen, *Gospels in Context,* 204; Catchpole, *Quest,* 6). Q probably was edited a number of times, and the Gospel writers may have employed Q in various stages of its editing (cf. Koester, *Introduction,* 2:46), but reconstructing these editions is in most cases speculative. For some recent studies on Q (some more historically based, others more speculative), see e.g., Lindemann, *Q and Jesus;* also Lindemann, "Q and Jesus."

68. Apart from the "Q Seminar," this skepticism probably characterizes the majority of Gospels scholarship: e.g., Stanton, *Jesus of Nazareth,* 5; idem, *Gospel Truth,* 73-74; Keck, "Ethos," 448; Voorst, *Jesus Outside NT,* 164-65; Overman, "Deciphering," 193; Theissen, *Gospels in Context,* 204; Catchpole, *Quest,* 6; Meier, *Marginal Jew,* 177-80; Johnson, *Real Jesus,* 52-53. Many earlier scholars were also reticent to define Q too narrowly; cf. Burkitt, *History,* 123; idem, *Sources,* 42-43; Dodd, *Parables,* 39; idem, *More Studies,* 70; Cadbury, *Making,* 98; Jeremias, *Theology,* 38-39; cf. Koester, *Introduction,* 2:46, for the likely suggestion that Q was used in various stages of redaction. See especially the caution of Sanders, *Tendencies,* 276-79.

69. Stanton, *Jesus of Nazareth,* 5; Hengel, *Atonement,* 35; Aune, *Prophecy,* 213; Keck, "Ethos," 448; Witherington, *Christology,* 223; idem, *Sage,* 211-12. As noted earlier, Q's theology probably does not differ significantly (in contradictory ways) from Mark's (Meadors, "Orthodoxy"; cf. Witherington, *Sage,* 233-36; see esp. Meadors, *Herald*). This is not to deny that "Q" has a distinctive *Tendenz* distinguishable from Mark (Kloppenborg, "Q and Jesus").

70. For Galilee's centrality, see Reed, *Archaeology,* 170-96 (esp. 196).

71. Dunn, *New Perspective,* 27 (also attributing its apparent lack of passion narrative to its formation before Jesus' death — though I would argue that, given the multiplicity of passion traditions, we would not know if one of them *were* "Q"; Matthew and Luke mainly follow Mark, however). It could have been passed on by Galilean disciples now in Jerusalem (cf. Gal 1:17-19).

72. E.g., Burkitt, *History,* 123; Dodd, *Parables,* 39; idem, *More Studies,* 70.

73. E.g., Betz, *Jesus,* 22.

74. Cf. the questions of Gundry, "Genre," 105 n. 31; Petrie, "Q"; Perry, *Sources,* p. 11. For one survey of recent approaches to the question of "minor agreements" between Matthew and Luke against Mark (not all opposed to the two-source hypothesis), see Friedrichsen, "Agreements."

75. Where Matthew's topical order (he likewise rearranges Mark, in contrast to Luke's proce-

dure) does not account for a variation; cf. also Schweizer, *Jesus*, 124-25; Tuckett, *History*, 34-39. Ellis, "Criticism," 35, however, doubts this common sequence.

76. Dunn, *New Perspective*, 122.

77. See Casey, *Aramaic Approach*, 185-90. As we have noted, however, some question the Aramaic Q approach (Tuckett, "Q and Aramaic").

78. Drury, *Design*, xi, 121; Farrer, "Q"; Abogunrun, "Debate"; Goulder, "Q," 234; Farmer, *Problem*; Longstaff, *Conflation*, 218; Murray, "Conflator"; Thompson, *Advice* (common traditions); Lowe and Flusser, "Synoptic Theory"; Young, *Parables*, 129-63; Sanders and Davies, *Synoptic Gospels*, 91, 112; Linneman, "Gospel of Q," 7-11.

79. Some have vigorously contested this position, advocating Q (cf. Martin, "Q"; Grant, "Clock"; idem, *Hellenism*, 120; Tuckett, "Relationship"; see especially idem, *History*, 1-39).

80. Linnemann, *Criticism*; idem, *Problem*. Nevertheless, we remain confident that the Synoptics share too much common ground with Mark, while simultaneously reflecting a far broader knowledge of abundant tradition outside Mark (cf. also Jn 21:25), to deny some measure of interdependence.

81. One must start somewhere. Admittedly, Mark Goodacre has rightly pointed out to me that use of such a default position risks uncritically perpetuating some academic presuppositions (for his own and others' able case against Q, see Goodacre, *Synoptic Problem*, 122-61; Goodacre and Perrin, *Questioning*). While the Q hypothesis seems most plausible to me based on my previous work through the Synoptics (e.g., based on Luke's different treatment of Mark and the shared material with Matthew that should include Matthew's use of Mark; and Luke surely had more than two sources available, Lk 1:1), Luke's use of Matthew would change the sources to which I gave first preference in following chapters but would not, I think, radically change the outcome in this book (most of Mark and, by definition, all of our "Q" being available in Matthew). The wide divergence of Luke's account of Judas' demise (Acts 1:18-19) from Matthew's (Matt 27:3-10) is also easier to explain from separate sources than from Luke's direct use of Matthew.

82. Theissen, *Gospels in Context*, 203-34, especially 220-21, 230-32; pace Mack, *Myth*, 84. Theissen and Merz, *Historical Jesus*, 29, suggest that it probably originated in Palestine in the 40s and early 50s (hence by early in Paul's ministry).

83. The material where we cannot check them is traditionally loosely called "M" and "L" material, though usually no longer held to represent a single source.

84. Commonalities between John and Synoptic tradition besides Mark and Q also support the existence of oral traditions (see Stein, "Agreements"). If the "M" material is oral, Matthew may be able to adapt it more freely, however (cf. Brooks, *Sayings Material*).

85. Witherington, *Sage*, 343. Cf. Johnston, "Evangelists," who even compares it to a manual produced by a committee; and Jones, *Parables*, 36, who uses the dominance of tradition to question the current biographical, literary-whole approach to the Gospels. Jones, *Parables*, 52-54 emphasizes Matthew's conservatism with his sources and failure to rewrite them, challenging traditional redaction-critical assumptions.

86. Note especially the climactic rehearsal of some major themes in Matt 28:18-20.

87. Diod. Sic. 1.37.4, 6; Dion. Hal. *Ant. rom.* 1.6.1-3 explicitly note that they provide additional information from different sources that some previous historians lacked. Technical historians sometimes cite sources by name (e.g., Dion. Hal. *Ant. rom.* 1.6.1); more popular-level Jewish sources generally do not, however, so from Matthew's silence we can infer nothing about Mark's or "Q's" anonymity.

88. See Hill, *Matthew*, 31-34; Davies and Allison, *Matthew*, 1:124-25; Luz, *Matthew*, 48; Brown, *Death*, 59-61.

89. Meier in Brown and Meier, *Antioch and Rome*, 55. The oral development of sources does not challenge the existence of written sources. Against the idea that an apocalyptic community like the earliest Christians would not care about writings (hence all written Gospel sources must be late), one need simply compare the early Qumran texts (cf. Boyd, *Sage*, 125). Concern for history also makes

sense in a Jewish covenant context in which people believed God was revealed in history (Wright, *People of God,* 426).

90. For example, though countless allusions in Homer (e.g., *Od.* 12.69-72) were developed later, they are often so incomplete by themselves that it is clear that Homer alludes to commonly known fuller stories he does not record.

91. Euseb. *H.E.* 3.39. Papias does not here claim Mark's dependence on Matthew (though neither does he claim the reverse).

92. Hengel, *Studies in Mark,* 50-53; Boyd, *Sage,* 229-37; on geographic errors, cf. Hengel, "Geography of Palestine," 33 n. 19 (pace Theissen, *Gospels in Context,* 236-37). Cf. the uncontested nature and wide geographic distribution of this authorship claim in Oden and Hall, *Mark,* xxi-xxviii (and its widely used title). Goulder, *Midrash,* 32, thinks that Matthew treats Mark as authoritative because of the tradition that it derives from Peter.

93. See Sanders, *Tendencies,* 19, 46-87, 88-189, 272; cf. Stein, "Criteria," 238-40; Frye, "Analogies in Literatures," 283-84.

94. In Jewish sources, cf. e.g., *ARN* 7, §21 B (for a pseudonymous claim to have personally witnessed something that earlier tradition simply reports). For a halachic example, cf. Hoenig, "Kinds of Labor." Amplification and embellishment are thus more characteristic of the apocryphal Gospels than the earlier canonical ones (Carmignac, "Pré-pascal").

95. Cf. Blomberg, "Thomas," 195, especially on the Gospel of Thomas (whose additions primarily reflect gnostic themes); it was especially abbreviated to streamline. Likewise, Matthew frequently abbreviates Marcan pericopes. Lucian *Lucius or Ass* probably epitomizes (see 7, 24, 38, 44, 54, with Apul. *Metam.* 2.11; 6.29; 9.39; Loeb notes); Virgil would write freely and then condense his own work (Suet. *Vergil* 22).

96. Theon *Progymn.* 4.37-42, 80-82. Even oracles, which were considered divine utterances, could be expanded; see Aune, *Prophecy,* 58.

97. Theon *Progymn.* 3.224-40; cf. Longinus *On the Sublime* 11.1; Hermog. *Progymn.* 3. On Chreia, 7; Aphthonius *Progymn.* 3. On Chreia, 23S, 4R. In *Progymn.* 2.115-23, Theon compares elaborations in earlier historical sources. Elaboration was especially useful for rebuttal (*Progymn.* 1.172-75).

98. Longin. *Subl.* 11.1; cf. Men. Rhet. 2.3, 379.2-4; for other adaptations for the sake of sound, see Dion. Hal. *Lit. Comp.* 9. For a more detailed discussion of amplification, see Anderson, *Glossary,* 26-29, 48-49 (with full reference to the sources).

99. *Rhet. Alex.* 22, 1434b.8-11 (to omit these condenses the work, 22, 1434b.15-17). One could condense by abbreviating larger ideas into single words; avoiding unnecessary connectives; and recapitulating only at the end (22, 1434b.11-18).

100. Hermog. *Progymn.* 3. On Chreia, 7; Aphth. *Progymn.* 3. On Chreia, 23S, 4R; 4. On Maxim, 9-10.

101. E.g., Begg, "Blanks," on Jos. *Ant.* 9.29-43 and 2 Kgs 3:4-27 Josephus exercised a degree of both freedom and fidelity in his handling of *biblical* history (see e.g., Begg, "Jotham"), so one might expect the Gospels to represent the same mixture, albeit not necessarily in the same degree of each. As we have noted, even the most rhetorically proficient of the Gospel writers (Luke) was less intent on rhetorical embellishment than Josephus, who was among the more rhetorically lavish historians.

102. Theon *Progymn.* 5.39-43, 52-53; Phaedrus 2, *prol.* 12-13; 3, *epil.* 8-9; 4, *epil.* 7-9; Philost. *Hrk.* 29.6; in speeches, e.g., Diog. Laert. 7.1.20; Dion. Hal. *Thuc.* 55; *Demosth.* 18, 20, 24; *Lysias* 5; Philost. *Vit. soph.* 2.4.569. One could, however, be too brief at times (Phaed. 3.10.59-60; Dion. Hal. *2 Amm.* 2).

103. Cf. e.g., Dion. Hal. *Comp.* 2-4. For one conspicuous example of rearrangement in the Gospels, cf. Matt 21:12-13, 19-22; Mk 11:13-25.

104. Dion. Hal. *Comp.* 9.

105. Theon *Progymn.* 4.73-79, on adding narrative to a fable or the reverse (although the narrative is added as a parallel, not as a setting, for the fable), though one might expect more restraints for historical narrative. Maxims could be added to narratives (*Progymn.* 5.388-425) or preexisting narra-

tives combined to relate two or more of them at once (5.427-41). The alternative to such arrangement was to simply recite narrative episodically; most readers found it acceptable, though it did not conform to more elite fashions (Drury, *Design,* 30; cf. Smith, *Magician,* 109).

106. Cf. the discussion of catch-words in Gerhardsson, *Memory,* 145-49, 153; in the Gospels, cf. Bultmann, *Tradition,* 325-26. One matter reminding the narrator of another was a common rhetorical technique for transition (Quint. *Inst.* 9.2.60-61). One might compare the rabbinic hermeneutical technique of *gezerah sheva* or the probable catchwords in Thomas (apparently too thoroughgoing, however, to reflect purely oral arrangement rather than a significant element of composition).

107. See especially Lyons, *Autobiography,* 29-32. Lyons advises reading such texts critically, not completely rejecting their historical value (ibid., 66).

108. Often later biographers simply repeat what earlier biographers said (e.g., Dion. Hal. *Lysias* 1); many sources simply repeated earlier ones verbatim (Pliny *N.H.* pref. 22).

109. Aune, *Environment,* 82. Even with regard to human memory in general, details are not always reliable, although the gist tends to be (see Bauckham, *Eyewitnesses,* 333-34, citing memory studies); Bauckham applies this to the consistency of the gist of Peter's denial among varying Gospel accounts, despite "variation in inessential detail" (Bauckham, *Eyewitnesses,* 344-45).

110. E.g., Cic. *De or.* 2.45.189; Dion. Hal. *Lysias* 7.

111. Plut. *Alex.* 70.3.

112. Stanton, *Gospel Truth,* 8.

113. Shuler, *Genre,* 11-12; cf. Bowersock, *Fiction as History,* 1-27. See especially Lucian *Hist.* 7-13; in *True Story* 1.4 he complains that novelizers failed to recognize how obvious their "lies" (a frequent polemical charge in antiquity) were. The later historian Herodian shares this criticism (Hdn. 1.1.1-2) — despite his own rhetorical adjustments (cf. Whittaker, "Introduction," xxxviii-xxxix)! The complaint appears even in mythography (cf. Philost. *Hrk.* 24.1-2), though we may expect that the practice was more common there.

114. See e.g., Whittaker, "Introduction," xlv-lii.

115. Such haggadic adaptation appears in both midrash and folk literature (Wright, "Midrash," 129). Penner, *Praise,* 247-60, contends that Jewish historians rewrote the past, as may be seen in their treatment of the exodus tradition.

116. Cf. Greek elaboration of sacred stories in Maclean and Aitken, *Heroikos,* li-lii.

117. Still, Hellenistic historians like Josephus remain closer to the biographic literary model even for older figures, while nevertheless incorporating old legends and expansive techniques. Polyb. 34.4.1-3 argues that the *Odyssey* mixed history and myth, but notes (34.4.2) that the goal of history, unlike that of myth, is truth.

118. Cf. e.g., Charles, *Jubilees,* lxxxv; Lock, *Pastoral Epistles,* 8-9; Scott, *Pastoral Epistles,* 8.

119. See Anderson, "4 Maccabees," 555; though even here the Gospels are not writing philosophy the way the writer of 4 Macc is. Scholars differ whether 2 Macc is a novel or dramatized history (Penner, *Praise,* 136-37, noting that all agree that 1 Macc is history); I believe it belongs closer to the latter, at least insofar as we regard the intention of the author (who was abridging another source; 2 Macc 2:24-25).

120. Even this parallel is imperfect; whereas Josephus' interests were less philosophic than Philo's or 4 Maccabees', he had obligations to elite rhetorical and literary interests that the Gospels (including Luke) for the most part lacked.

121. For surveys, see e.g., Duling and Perrin, *New Testament,* 20-23; Spivey and Smith, *Anatomy,* 64-65; Carson, Moo and Morris, *Introduction,* 38-45; Osborne, "Redaction Criticism."

122. Dio Cassius *R.H.* 1.1.1-2 explicitly affirms the contrary. Thus, for example, Matthew's account of Judas' death is so Matthean that Gundry, *Matthew,* 553 admits that one might think it Matthew's "wholesale creation" — were it not for Acts 1:15-20. For specific characteristics of Matthean style (useful for redaction criticism) see e.g., Davies and Allison, *Matthew,* 1:74-96; but on dangers of inaccurate use of stylistic criteria, see Jones, *Parables,* 12.

123. Kennedy, "Source Criticism," 138-39, on sections of Livy; more generally, Aune, *Environment*, 65, 139; cf. Downing, "Conventions"; idem, "Actuality"; Burridge, *Gospels*, 204-5.

124. Jones, *Parables*, 13-14. Jones introduces further complications: what if Matthew's version of Mark is an oral tradition based on but differing from our text of Mark (*Parables*, 29-30, 39)?

125. See Payne, "Midrash and History," 209.

126. Phaedrus 2, *prologue* 8-12. Matthew often edits Mark's style (Burridge, "Gospels and Acts," 526), and Luke does so even more often.

127. See Dunn, *New Perspective*, 118-19; Robbins, "Writing," 146-55 (esp. 155). Stylistic, ideological, and legal factors all affected the editing of other works, such as the Mishnah (Kulp, "Patterns").

128. Kennedy, "Source Criticism," 143 (cf. Fuller, "Classics," 187, citing Kennedy's observation that ancients did not usually look up their sources, but quoted from memory or notes).

129. Stanton, *New People*, 23.

130. Cf. Theon *Progymn.* 1.46-52; 2.79-81; 8.2-3; Arist. *Poetics* 15.4-6, 1454a; in a history, see e.g., Dio Cassius *R.H.* 62.11.3-4.

131. Vermes, *Religion*, 153-54.

132. See e.g., Blomberg, "Studying Jesus," 42; cf. Draper, "Didache." Note further the Semitic parallelism pervading Jesus' sayings, probably more emphatic in Matthew (cf. Hagner, *Matthew*, xlviii).

133. See especially Theissen, *Gospels in Context*, 88 n. 70, who concludes that Matthew at points improves Mark's historical accuracy. Josephus sometimes "corrects" the OT based on other OT passages — Höffken, "Reichsteilung."

134. Vermes, *Religion*, 17-19.

135. On the publication of ancient literary works, see the introductory chapter on this subject in my forthcoming Acts commentary (ch. 1 of the introduction); less fully, Keener, *John*, 5-7, and sources noted there. The use of successive drafts might help account for the phenomena that earlier and bolder critics sometimes attributed to "proto-Matthew," "proto-Luke" and so forth.

136. Josephus seems to have followed his own *War* at points in his later magnum opus, the *Antiquities* (Krieger, "Hauptquelle"); 4 Maccabees adapted material from 2 Maccabees (see Gardner, "Mqbym").

137. Aune, *Environment*, 139.

138. Aune, *Environment*, 65; cf. Downing, "Conventions"; idem, "Actuality"; Burridge, *Gospels*, 204-5. Agreements between Matthew and Luke against Mark in Markan material suggest that Luke felt free to adapt his dominant source in light of his larger repository of oral tradition and written information. Some sources could be oral, and the writers could have even drawn on the written sources from memory (see our subsequent chapter on oral traditions).

139. Pliny *N.H.* pref. 22. Pliny went so far as to append bibliography to each of his volumes (explained in Pliny *N.H.* pref. 33). Lucian reworked a story line later attested in Apul. *Metam.* (see Macleod, "Introduction," 47 and 50, following Photius); his *Dialogues of Courtesans* bears some resemblance to Alciphron's *Letters of Courtesans;* Livy reworked much of earlier historians, and biographers had a limited number of sources they could use. For Jewish examples of borrowing, see e.g., *Sib. Or.* 2.56-148 (from Ps.-Phoc.); 2 Peter's use of Jude.

140. Sen. *Suas.* 3.7. The elder Seneca lamented that even obvious, unethical plagiarism could go undetected because of auditors' negligence (*Suas.* 2.19; McGill, "Seneca on Plagiarizing"). Lucian expected his audience to recognize the literary works he satirized (*True Story* 1.2).

141. This practice may have been more common for Jewish religious texts in other genres; cf. e.g., 2 Peter's use of Jude, or the borrowing in *Sib. Or.* 2.56-148 from Ps.-Phoc.

142. The nature of literary borrowing changed dramatically in the modern period, after England's copyright law of 1709 (Frye, "Analogies in Literatures," 275, noting the frequency of conflation before that time).

143. Cf. Gal 2:9; Acts 2:42; see discussion in the following chapter.

Notes to Chapter 10

1. Funk et al., *Gospels*, 25.

2. Davies, *Invitation*, 115-16.

3. Some early-second-century fathers even preferred oral tradition, though cf. the preference for written sources in Eunapius *Lives* 459-60, when an event seemed incredible.

4. Antisthenes in Diog. Laert. 6.1.5 (LCL).

5. For the coexistence of literacy and orality, see the example in Aune, *Dictionary of Rhetoric*, 325: "Greek schoolchildren who used to memorize from written texts of the poets in order to recite them without the written text" (Plato *Protagoras* 325E).

6. Byrskog, *Story as History*, 110-11. Eddy and Boyd, *Legend*, 280, note that oral history has taken a more optimistic view of memory than the dominant contemporary perspective in psychology and sociology. For one discussion of the issues in psychological memory studies, see Bauckham, *Eyewitnesses*, 325-41.

7. See Harvey, *Listening*, 53 (citing Sen. *Ep. Lucil.* 100.2). Among early Christians, note the oft-cited prejudice of Papias (frg. 3.4, Holmes).

8. Lewis, *History*, 43; Vansina, "Afterthoughts," 110; cf. Yamauchi, "Homer," on very general historical events behind Homer. Some scholars argue that ancient writers may have modified written texts more often than oral traditions; hence Matthew and Luke may have adapted Mark more freely than the whole process of oral tradition modified Jesus' sayings (Gundry, "Genre," 102; Witherington, *Christology*, 22; cf. Diog. Laert. 1.48). I am not so confident that this is correct in matters of detail and wording, but am confident about the early persistence of the "gist."

9. Lord, *Singer*, 138. Witherington, *Christology*, 8, 17-20, points to significant differences between the gospel tradition and oral Balkan folklore traditions.

10. See Harvey, *Listening*, 41. On the retention of "gist" in eyewitness memory even when details are inaccurate, see Bauckham, *Eyewitnesses*, 333-34.

11. Dunn, *New Perspective*, 112 (with 110), 118, 122; cf. Lord, "Oral Literature" (but also the response in Talbert, "Oral and Independent"). On the frequent lack of verbatim recall, and often re-creation, see e.g., Moniot, "Historiography," 56-57; performances are adapted to new audiences (Bazin, "Past," 70-71). The variation is typically greater in prose than in verse (Kennedy, "Source Criticism," 143).

12. Cf. e.g., Hoeree and Hoogbergen, "History"; Aron-Schnapper and Hanet, "Archives"; on rote memorization in traditional Quranic education, cf. Wagner and Lotfi, "Learning." Limitations do, however, exist, especially over time (e.g., Iglesias, "Reflexoes"; Harms, "Tradition"; Raphael, "Travail"). For a recent and thoroughly documented case for the potential reliability of oral transmission of gospel materials in light of more general knowledge about oral transmission, see Eddy and Boyd, *Legend*, 239-68 (esp. 252-59).

13. Used in academic African historiography since the 1950s (Moniot, "Historiography," 50), needed to reconstruct practices before modern western influences (Horton, "Possession," 14). Westerners' prior neglect often reflects ethnocentric prejudices (Chrétien, "Exchange," 77). For oral history in NT scholarship, see Byrskog, *Story as History*, 33-40.

14. With e.g., Eddy and Boyd, *Legend*, 395 (on events no older than 80-150 years), citing various sources.

15. Henige, "History," 103, rightly warns of the fanciful excesses caused by using theory to interpret evidence in reconstructing history behind oral tradition. Eddy and Boyd, *Legend*, 260-64, suggest that even folklore traditions about historical characters may often preserve more of the substance than western critics have often assumed, but their focus is more recent history.

16. Cf. West, "Rhapsodes." The frequency of literary fragments scattered throughout the papyri (cf. Avi-Yonah, *Hellenism*, 248) attests to the commonness of their usage.

17. Xen. *Symp.* 3.5-6.

18. Dio Chrys. *Or.* 36.9 (LCL 3:431). Although we cannot confirm this report, the culture that Dio reports apparently did exist (cf. *CIG* 2.2077 in the LCL note).

19. See Finkelberg, *"Cypria"* (doubting that texts always develop from fluid to rigid).

20. Today, it is said that all "true" Dulong can remember their epics, even though recounting them all fully can take several days (Yamamori and Chan, *Witnesses*, 22).

21. Dunn, *New Perspective*, 110.

22. Dunn, *New Perspective*, 112. Such flexibility is also consistent with what is known of memory (Bauckham, *Eyewitnesses*, 344-45). Certainly Roman literature was generally orally performed in this period, affecting its rhetorical shape (see Schmidt, "Public recital"); but cf. the warning of Gerhardsson, "Exegetisk disciplin," against overestimating our knowledge of precisely how the Gospels were orally performed.

23. Dunn, *New Perspective*, 114.

24. Dunn, *New Perspective*, 46-53; cf. idem, "The Tradition," 174-82.

25. Dunn, *New Perspective*, 119; cf. Byrskog, *Story as History*, 110.

26. Cf. Fuller, "Classics," 173-76 (esp. 174, 176), agreeing with G. Kennedy on the complexity of oral tradition beyond the traditional "two sources."

27. Crosby, "Introduction to Fragments."

28. Pliny *N.H.* pref. 17.

29. E.g., Paus. 1.23.2; cf. also Maclean and Aitken, *Heroikos*, xc-xci. Cf. e.g., Xen. *Cyr.* 1.2.1 for an example of long informal traditioning by storytelling and song. Some scholars express misgivings about Pausanias' oldest oral information (cf. Pretzler, "Pausanias and Tradition").

30. E.g., to the voyage of the Argonauts in *Od.* 12.69-72; cf. Apollonius Rhodius; Valerius Flaccus.

31. See Charlesworth, *Pseudepigrapha and NT*, 1-3; cf. Bailey, "Tradition."

32. Eunapius *Lives* 453 (writing it down fixed it and prevented further changes). Even first-century writers recognized that centuries of oral transmission could produce variations in ancient documents (Jos. *Ag. Ap.* 1.12).

33. Cf. Hermog. *Progymn.* 4. On Maxim, 8-10. (By the strictest definition, "maxims" might be unattributed; cf. the later Nicolaus 5. On Maxim, 25.) On boys learning these and *chreiai,* see also Anderson, *Glossary*, 126-27 (citing Sen. *Ep. Lucil.* 33.7).

34. Cf. Vermes, *Jesus the Jew*, 27, who thinks (undoubtedly rightly) that Jesus as a Jewish teacher presumably taught in such forms.

35. E.g., Plut. *Sayings of Kings and Commanders, Mor.* 172B-194E. Many of these sayings also occur in other sources, as the Loeb footnotes indicate (Plutarch LCL 3:8-153). Such compilations of maxims were used in the *progymnasmata,* school rhetorical exercises in which the sayings were adapted (Malherbe, *Moral Exhortation,* 109, 117), and in the process their sense was learned (for the importance of learning maxims, cf. Isoc. *Demon.* 12, Or. 1; Arist. *Rhet.* 2.21.15, 1395b; Petron. *Sat.* 4; Sir. 18:29; Plut. *Poetry* 14, *Mor.* 35EF; also Epicharmus *Gnomai* C.1-15 in *Select Papyri* 3:440-43); often they upheld aristocratic social values (Sinclair, *"Sententia"*).

36. E.g., Sen. *Ep. Lucil.* 94.27-28; also Aune, *Environment,* 34, on Plato's sayings, gathered into *Gnomologia* (maxim collections) only in the fifth century CE. Some also professed to know during what incidents various sayings were uttered, however (e.g., Plut. *Themistocles* 11.2).

37. Theon *Progymn.* 4.73-79; cf. 5.388-441. Early humanist exegetes like Calvin apparently agreed (Blomberg, *Reliability,* 52, citing Calvin's harmony of the Gospels).

38. Frye, "Analogies in Literatures," 291. The same may be noted for ancient speakers like Lucian, who gave orations in multiple locations (Harmon, "Introduction"); Dio Chrysostom also reused his own speeches (cf. Crosby, "Introduction to Discourse 66").

39. E.g., Diog. Laert. 2.72, 6.2.51; Plut. *Agesilaus* 21.4-5.

40. Cf. Hermog. *Progymn.* 3. On Chreia, 6-7; Aphthonius *Progymn.* 3. On Chreia, 23S, 4R; Nicolaus *Progymn.* 4. On Chreia 19-20; 5. On Maxim, 26. Biographers sometimes expressed confidence during which incidents in their subject's life a particular saying was given (Plut. *Themist.* 11.2).

Not all *chreiai* were as brief as the most basic form (cf. Robbins, "Chreia," 3), however, and the examples in the Gospels are the elaborated rather than basic form usually used in rhetorical exercises (see Mack and Robbins, *Patterns*, 196-97). One should not infer too much from hellenistic forms in the gospel tradition (Mack, *Myth*, 179; cf. Guenther, "Greek"); Palestine was hellenized; the Gospels are written in Greek (probably especially for Diaspora audiences); others besides Cynics employed such forms (see Boyd, *Sage*, 160; Wright, *People of God*, 427-35; Theissen, *Gospels in Context*, 120); and the formal pattern for elaborating chreiai seems restricted to rhetorical handbooks (Hester, "Epideictic," 302, n. 1, citing chreia expert Edward O'Neil). For one discussion of chreiai, comparing the use by Jesus, philosophers and rabbis, see Hezser, "Verwendung"; for chreiai as analogous to the gospel tradition's narrative units, cf. also Byrskog, "Chreia."

41. Bultmann, *Tradition*, 88-89, may be too optimistic at how quickly such traditions may have grown in a relatively short span of time; his evidence (e.g., Sir 29:1-6) does not adequately support his conclusions. His evidence on 194 presupposes a longer period of time than is likely in the transmission and then redaction of gospel traditions.

42. *ARN* 22, §46 B, on R. Akiba and Ben Azzai; *m. Ab.* 3:9, 17 (R. Hanina ben Dosa and R. Elazar ben Azariah).

43. Cf. Diog. Laert. 2.60; Ariston 1 in Plut. *Sayings of Spartans, Mor.* 218A; Themistocles 2 in Plut. *Sayings of Kings and Commanders, Mor.* 185A, and Alexander in Dio Chrys. *Or.* 2; Alcibiades 1 in Plut. *Sayings of Kings and Commanders, Mor.* 186D, and a Spartan in *Mor.* 234E; Plut. *Marcus Cato* 2.4; the story in Philost. *Vit. soph.* 1.485; Athen. *Deipn.* 550; and Diog. Laert. 4.37 (Philost. LCL 14-15 n. 2); note also Musonius Rufus *frg.* 51, p. 144.3-7, 10-19. See Aune, *Environment*, 35, on the transference of Greek *chreiai*, because "they tended to represent what was useful rather than unique" (Malherbe, *Moral Exhortation*, 100).

44. E.g., Pliny *Ep.* 6.29.5 (regarding Pollio, a century to a century and a half earlier).

45. Thus many of M. Cato's maxims were translated from Greek (Plut. *Cato Major* 2.4). A saying attributed to both Musonius and Cato (Mus. Ruf. frg. 51, p. 144.3-19) could be misattributed, or could have been recycled (perhaps more than once).

46. Pace Funk et al., *Gospels*, 22-23.

47. Still, some of them, such as Dibelius, *Tradition*, 62, and especially Taylor, *Formation*, passim, saw much of the tradition as essentially historical; Bultmann, *Tradition*, passim, was more radical.

48. Davies, *Invitation*, 115-16; cf. similarly Sanders, *Tendencies*, 28.

49. Benoit, *Jesus*, 1:33.

50. Witherington, *Christology*, 14, citing also Müller, *Traditionsprozess*.

51. Theissen and Merz, *Historical Jesus*, 105; Stein, "Criteria," 225-28; Stanton, *Gospel Truth*, 60-61; Wright, *People of God*, 421.

52. Theissen, *Gospels in Context*, 25-29. Cf. also the presence of Semitisms (e.g., Jeremias, *Theology*, passim; Witherington, *Christology*, 11), though the earliest traditioning community also spoke Aramaic (Meier, *Marginal Jew*, 1:178-80). Translation could be very literal (Young, *Parables*, 180), but Josephus' claim to have written the Bible in Greek (*Apion* 1.1) includes much interpretation.

53. With e.g., Jeremias, *Promise*, 30; Martin, "Healing," 15; France, "Exegesis in Practice," 257; Carson, "Matthew," 201.

54. Missing from Mark, the no less Israel-exclusive claim in Matt 15:24 looks suspiciously like Matthean wording (Gundry, *Matthew*, 313); but Jeremias, *Promise*, 27 insists that its Aramaic construction suggests its antiquity (cf. also Wilson, *Gentile Mission*, 14). A stronger argument in its favor is that it hardly fits Matthew's own perspective (Anderson, *Mark*, 191; cf. Vermes, *Jesus and Judaism*, 55; Matt 28:19); it would at least seem to belong to his community's tradition, which he must answer.

55. The offputting remark about dogs (Mk 7:27) surely predates our extant Gospels (Montefiore, *Gospels*, 1:167).

56. E.g., 1 Sam 17:43; Hom. *Il.* 8.527; 9.373; 11.362; 20.449; 22.345; *Od.* 17.248; 22.35; for the female version, see Hom. *Od.* 11.424; 18.338; 19.91. The insult undoubtedly alluded to dogs' unsociable behav-

ior (cf. Prov 26:11; Mart. *Epig.* 1.83; Plut. *Exile* 7, *Mor.* 601DE; Philo *Gig.* 35; *Mek. Kaspa* 2.23-26; *p. Taan.* 1:6, §8; *Pesiq. Rab Kah.* 7:6). Commentators who suggest that Jewish people regularly called Gentiles "dogs" (e.g., Brandon, *Zealots,* 172-73; Theissen, *Gospels in Context,* 62 n. 1) might make too much of relatively scant references (cf. Smith, *Tannaitic Parallels,* 167; on associations with Rome, cf. Hayward, "Targum to Genesis 27")

57. On the "gist," see e.g., Bauckham, *Eyewitnesses,* 333-34, 344-46.

58. Presumably memory works in a basically similar way in all cultures; my point in noting the cultural difference is simply that we would not expect an oral culture's eyewitness memory to be *less* dependable than modern western memory. Following the approach in oral history studies (which favors net transmission), some scholars also challenge the minimalist western approach to memory (Eddy and Boyd, *Legend,* 280-81). For applications from the use of memory in cultural studies more generally, cf. Strecker, "Perspektive."

59. Bauckham, *Eyewitnesses,* 326, 333, 344.

60. Bauckham, *Eyewitnesses,* 327, 333-34, 345.

61. Bauckham, *Eyewitnesses,* 330, 334-38, 350.

62. Bauckham, *Eyewitnesses,* 331.

63. Bauckham, *Eyewitnesses,* 331.

64. Bauckham, *Eyewitnesses,* 331-32. Those who complain that emotional involvement would render a witness incapable of reporting true information would have to discount testimony from those involved in war, concentration camps, and so forth (Bauckham, *Eyewitnesses,* 492-505; Eddy and Boyd, *Legend,* 397-98).

65. Bauckham, *Eyewitnesses,* 332.

66. Bauckham, *Eyewitnesses,* 334.

67. Bauckham, *Eyewitnesses,* 341-46.

68. Thucyd. 1.22.2-3 (LCL 1:38-39).

69. *Controv.* passim. Kennedy, "Source Criticism," 143, argues that, given the ancient emphasis on memory and the use of commonplaces in declamations, Seneca's recollection of declamation pieces is more credible than some critics have allowed.

70. Tacitus also claims to remember long dialogues years later (*Dial.* 1), but to some degree this is a literary device (cf. Justin *Dial.,* though this also may reflect some genuine dialogue or composite of dialogues; cf. Barnard, *Justin Martyr,* 23-24, 39-40; Williams, *Justin,* xi-xix); while such a dialogue may have occurred, "Maternus" in the dialogue speaks for Tacitus's own views.

71. Some mnemonic claims attributed to much earlier periods (Val. Max. 8.7.ext. 16: Cyrus' knowledge of all his troops' names or Mithridates' of the 22 languages of his subjects) are less credible (these plus L. Scipio's memory of all the Roman people's names appear also in Pliny *N.H.* 7.24.88).

72. Sen. *Controv.* 1.pref.2.

73. Sen. *Controv.* 1.pref.19.

74. Sen. *Controv.* 1.pref.19. Also in Sen. *Controv.* 1.pref.19, he notes an ambassador who the next day greeted all the members of the Senate and the gathered townspeople by name.

75. Philost. *Vit. soph.* 1.11.495. On other exploits of the aged in antiquity, see Keener, *John,* 102-3.

76. *Rhet. Her.* 3.16.28.

77. Ancient theories on how memory worked varied (see Arist. *Mem.;* Plato *Meno* 81CD; Philost. *Vit. soph.* 1.22.523); Cicero expounded on mnemonics (*De or.* 2.351; Olbricht, "Delivery and Memory," 163). Philo (Boccaccini, *Judaism,* 192-94) and Pseudo-Aristeas (Boccaccini, *Judaism,* 194-98) stress memory, blending Greek language with Jewish memorial traditions concerning God's historic acts. For ancient memory techniques, see e.g., *Rhet. Her.* 3.22.35; Small, *Wax Tablets;* Walde, "Mnemonics"; Kennedy, *Classical Rhetoric,* 98; Byrskog, *Story as History,* 163-65; on the importance and nature of memory in antiquity, see further Byrskog, *Story as History,* 111-12, 160-65; for memory cultivation, Byrskog, *Story as History,* 110-11; for exceptional memories in premodern sources, Eddy and Boyd, *Legend,* 283.

78. Quint. *Inst.* 11.2.1-51. In first-century BCE Roman courts, each defense speaker had "only" three hours (Cic. *Brutus* 93.324); by the second century CE, Tacitus laments that the time was normally just one or two hours, curbing eloquence (*Dial.* 38).

79. Satterthwaite, "Rhetoric," 344; cf. Olbricht, "Delivery and Memory" (esp. 159, 163, citing *Rhet. Her.* 1.3-5; Cicero *De Oratore* 2.351); Heath, *Hermogenes*, 7; Eunapius *Lives* 502. Ancient rhetoricians praised this skill (Aeschines *Embassy* 48, 112).

80. Watson, "Education," 310.

81. Pliny *Ep.* 2.3.3. For other praises of orators' memory, see e.g., Pliny *Ep.* 6.11.2. Pliny also gladly reports the failure of his nemesis to be able to memorize his speeches (Pliny *Ep.* 6.2.2).

82. Sen. *Controv.* 1.pref.17.

83. Sen. *Controv.* 1.pref.18.

84. Eunapius *Lives* 494. Dio Chrys. *Or.* 18.19 advises reciting model speeches from memory, if possible. Naturally this would be easier for a speech heard recently; thus Lucian *Peregr.* 3 (LCL 5:5, 7) promises to repeat verbatim, as best as he can, the words of a Cynic he heard the previous day. Knowing basic Cynic style may have helped him with his recall.

85. Philost. *Vit. soph.* 1.22.524.

86. As in Philost. *Vit. soph.* 1.22.524, above.

87. See Dunn, *New Perspective*, 43, 114-15. He notes the emphasis on communal memory in traditional Middle Eastern culture (Dunn, *New Perspective*, 45-46, citing K. Bailey's decades of observations). By contrast, Byrskog, *Story as History*, 69-70, doubts the relevance of the communal memory of the disciples for gospel tradition, since only a few are named and specified. He focuses on several like Peter (71-73) and the women (73-78; esp. Mary Magdalene, 78-81). Certainly tradition associates the twelve with this role (Acts 1:21-22), among others.

88. Philost. *Vit. soph.* 1.24.529. One may compare long-term ethnic conflicts in various regions of the world today.

89. See e.g., Quint. *Inst.* 1.3.1; Plut. *Educ.* 13, *Mor.* 9E; Mus. Ruf. *frg.* 51, p. 144.3-7; Diog. Laert. 6.2.31; Eunapius *Lives* 481; Watson, "Education," 310, 312; Heath, *Hermogenes*, 11.

90. On their learning see Quint. *Inst.* 2.4.15; Jeffers, *World*, 254, 256; memorizing poets in Aune, *Dictionary of Rhetoric*, 143.

91. Mus. Ruf. *frg.* 51, p. 144.3-7 (though it is either misattributed or, more likely, Musonius recycled an earlier saying of Cato — 144.10-19).

92. Theon *Progymn.* 2.5-8.

93. Jeffers, *World*, 256. On memorization in ancient education, see e.g., Quint. 1.3.1; Plut. *Educ.* 13, *Mor.* 9E; Mus. Ruf. *frg.* 51, p. 144.3-7; Diog. Laert. 6.2.31; Eunapius *Lives* 481; Koester, *Introduction*, 1:93; Ferguson, *Backgrounds*, 84; Heath, *Hermogenes*, 11; Watson, "Education," 310, 312; for memorizing examples, see Theon *Progymn.* 2.5-8.

94. Isoc. *Demon.* 18, Or. 1.

95. Jeffers, *World*, 256.

96. Aul. Gel. 8.3. Students apparently did sometimes doze during philosophic lectures (cf. Fronto *Eloq.* 4.3); one sophist struck a hearer for sleeping (Philost. *Vit. soph.* 2.8.578).

97. E.g., Lucian *Alex.* 61, employing *paradidōmi.* This term was applicable to passing down a founder's teachings (Lucian *Alex.* 61; Iambl. *Pyth. Life* 28.148) or practices (Iambl. *Pyth. Life* 28.149); passing down traditional practices from ancestors (Thucyd. 1.85.1); and passing down information in a historian (Dio Chrys. *Or.* 18.10). "Receive" and "pass on" could apply to transmitting information (although allowing stylistic adaptation along the way, Philost. *Vit. soph.* 2.29.621).

98. Dio Chrys. *Or.* 18.10.

99. Culpepper, *School*, 193; Aul. Gel. 7.10.1; Socrates *Ep.* 20.

100. Diog. Laert. 10.1.12, on Epicurus, according to Diocles; on followers of Pythagoras, cf. Culpepper, *School*, 50.

101. Alexander, "IPSE DIXIT," 112.

102. Alexander, "IPSE DIXIT," 112-13. Those who remained part of the school would not normally criticize the founder's teachings (Alexander, "IPSE DIXIT," 110), although schools' beliefs (whether Stoicism or Platonism) evolved over the centuries. Schools with less original tradition eventually composed more (Alexander, "IPSE DIXIT," 113-14; cf. 121), but this accrued gradually over centuries, and would probably not normally be substantial in the first two generations, within living memory of eyewitnesses.

103. Plato probably composed dialogues freely, keeping to what he believed the spirit of Socrates' teaching rather than exact conversation (Kennedy, "Source Criticism," 132-33, 136). Plato is not like the Synoptic tradition in this regard, however; producing literary compositions (whether Plato's dialogues or finished gospels) probably involved more "permanent" adaptations than the bulk of individual retellings about a popular teacher. Nevertheless, despite Plato's freedom in composing dialogues, he and Xenophon do share some common topics (such as love by the soul greater than that of the body (Xen. *Symp.* 8.12), and it is likely that Xenophon does not depend directly on Plato, but both go back to the historical Socrates and the first reports (Marchant, "Introduction," ix-xv, suggesting that Plato retained much of the historical Socrates, yet presents him differently in different works). That Xenophon has a *Symposium* and an *Apology* like Plato could suggest that he deliberately offers a variant perspective, or that the speeches of these occasions had become well known.

104. See e.g., Val. Max. 8.15.ext. 1; Sen. *Ep. Lucil.* 108.17, 20, 22; 110.14, 20; Mus. Ruf. 1, 36.6-7; Philost. *Vit. Apoll.* 7.22. Especially among rabbis, correcting a teacher was rare (*ARN* 1A); against striving with one's teacher, see *Num. Rab.* 18:20; against offering legal decisions in front of one's teacher, *p. Shebi.* 6:1, §8 (it merited death: *Sipra Shemini Mekhilta deMiluim* 99.5.6; *b. Erub.* 63a; *Tem.* 16a; *Lev. Rab.* 20:6-7).

105. E.g., *ARN* 25A; *p. Bik.* 3:3, §9; *Gen. Rab.* 22:2; for rank for esteemed Jewish sages, see e.g., *tos. M.K.* 2:17; *Sanh.* 7:8; *b. Hor.* 13b, bar; *p. Sanh.* 1:2, §13; *Taan.* 4:2, §§8-9. If a pupil ever needed to point something out to the teacher, this should be done respectfully (e.g., Fronto *Ad Verum Imp.* 2.3); a pupil who contradicted a teacher might need to be reconciled to him (Philost. *Vit. Apoll.* 5.38). Later, one who despised a rabbi despised one's help (*b. Shab.* 119b); risked losing eternal life (*Pesiq. Rab.* 11:2); by stinginess toward rabbis (*b. B.B.* 75a) or speaking ill of them after their death (*b. Ber.* 19a) might inherit hellfire; offending rabbis might yield deadly judgment (cf. *b. B.K.* 117a; *B.M.* 84a; *Erub.* 63a; *Tem.* 16a).

106. Culpepper, *School,* 177.

107. Lucian *Hermot.* 1.

108. Iambl. *V.P.* 35.256; Philost. *Vit. Apoll.* 1.14; 2.30; 3.16. Certainly their handing them down secretly only by memory (Iambl. *V.P.* 32.226) is portrayed as unusual. In one fictitious account, a disciple memorized all that his teacher taught (Philost. *Vit. Apoll.* 1.19). Pythagoras' teachings were said to be concisely formulated like laws (Max. Tyre *Or.* 25.2), which would be more easily memorized.

109. Iambl. *V.P.* 20.94.

110. Diod. Sic. 10.5.1; Iambl. *V.P.* 29.165; on their memories, see further ibid., 29.164; 35.256. See note above on mnemonic techniques.

111. Iambl. *V.P.* 31.188.

112. Cf. e.g., by Thompson, Wenger, and Bartling, "Recall," 210 (noting that it becomes unnecessary beyond a certain point; this source was supplied to me by M. Bradley, then a student at Duke); Bauckham, *Eyewitnesses,* 334.

113. See e.g., Philost. *V.A.* 5.21; Liefeld, "Preacher," 223; Robbins, *Teacher,* 64. Some writers emphasized that an internal inclination to virtue was superior to imitation (Philo *Abr.* 6, 38).

114. Eunapius *Lives* 458.

115. Philost. *Lives* 1.22.524.

116. Jos. *Apion* 2.204.

117. Jos. *Life* 11. Amoraim underlined this principle with stories of rabbis who imitated even their masters' toilet habits and home life (*b. Ber.* 62a).

118. E.g., Xen. *Mem.* 1.2.3; Sen. *Ep. Lucil.* 108.4. Writers cared about both the words and "deeds" of characters (e.g., Xen. *Cyrop.* 5.1.1; *Mem.* 1.5.6; 4.4.10; on this pairing see further Keener, *Matthew*, 255, 540; the apparently contrary statement of Eunapius *Lives* intro. 452-53 refers in context to casual activities only — cf. Xen. *Symp.* 1.1).

119. See Gamble, "Literacy," 646; cf. Millard, *Reading and Writing*, esp. 184-209. Although some have argued against overplaying the orality/literacy divide (Malina, "Criticism," 98, as cited in Botha, "Cognition," 37) some others warn against playing it down too much (Botha, "Cognition").

120. *Rhet. Alex.* 36, 1444a.16-28; Sen. *Controv.* 1.pref.17; 3.pref. 4-6; probably Eunapius *Lives* 494. Some, however, did not use notes (Val. Max. 7.3.5; Sen. *Controv.* 1.pref.18), presumably including Galilean sages like Jesus.

121. E.g., Cic. *Brut.* 24.91 (remarking on the laziness of those who fail to write them out); Pliny *Ep.* 2.5.1-2; 5.8.6; 5.20.3; 7.17.5; cf. *Ep.* 2.19.2, 4; 3.13.1; 4.5.3; 4.26.1-3. This observation reinforces the point, however, that many orators spoke from memory.

122. Gempf, "Speaking," 299, citing especially Quint. *Inst.* 11.2.2. Some took notes even during school declamations (Sen. *Suas.* 3.2).

123. Zeno in Diog. Laert. 7.1.20.

124. Shorthand existed (Richards, *Letter Writing*, 65-72) but was not widely available; it became popular only in the second century, and in circles different from those represented among Jesus' disciples (see Maehler, "Tachygraphy," 1468).

125. Cf. Montanari, "Hypomnema," on hypomnema as notes or memory aids (though after the Hellenistic period they often represent a running commentary on texts, p. 72).

126. Cf. Cic. *Fin.* 3.3.10; 5.5.12; Aul. Gel. *pref.* 2, 22.

127. Cf. Sen. *Ep. Lucil.* 108.6; Arius Did. *Epit.* 2.7.11k, p. 80 line 36-82.1; Lucian *Hermot.* 2; see also Kennedy, "Source Criticism," 131, on Socrates (citing Diog. Laert. 2.122; more cautiously, Plato *Theaetetus* 143A; *Symp.* 173B; *Parmenides* 126C); Stowers, "Diatribe," 74, on Arrian's notes on Epictetus; cf. Iambl. *V.P.* 23.104 on Pythagoreans. Cf. the brief discussion of Plutarch's notebooks in Cherniss, "Introduction," 398-99. Notes could derive from other sources as well; an intellectual might in several days fill five notebooks with extracts from sixty "books" (including brief speeches; Fronto *Ad M. Caes.* 2.10.2). I am reusing and augmenting here some material from Keener, *John*, 55-56.

128. Gempf, "Speaking," 299; Quint. *Inst.* 11.2.2, 25.

129. Lutz, "Musonius," 7, 10.

130. Kennedy, "Source Criticism," 129. Even Aristotle's "books" are simply his regularly revised lecture notes (Kennedy, "Source Criticism," 131), though the extant versions are well-organized (Cic. *Fin.* 3.3.10; 5.5.12). Meeks, "Hypomnēmata," 159-60, views Kennedy's contribution regarding notes here as important.

131. For instance, the notes *(hypomnēmata)* of rhetorical lectures by the fifth-century BCE teachers Corax and Tisias, made by themselves or by their students, were published (Kennedy, *Classical Rhetoric*, 19).

132. Oldfather, "Introduction to Epictetus," xii-xiii. Even in the *Encheir.*, where Arrian organizes and summarizes his master's teaching, Epictetus' character dominates.

133. Epict. *Diatr.* 1.preface (LCL 1:4-5). Regarding the preservation of style, Xenophon in an earlier period (with less exacting standards) reports that all who write about Socrates reproduce his same lofty style (*Apol.* 1). As noted above, Aristotle organized his teachings into both popular, random and (those now extant) more formally arranged books (Cic. *Fin.* 3.3.10; 5.5.12).

134. Quint. *Inst.* 1.pref. 7-8 (LCL 1:8-9). Other teachers also had problems with people pirating their books and publishing them before they could nuance them properly (Diod. Sic. 40.8.1). When recounting such exploits to my students, I often add facetiously, "Don't do that to me!"

135. Gerhardsson, *Memory*, 160-62; cf. Safrai, "Education," 966.

136. See Millard, "Literacy"; Head, "Note on *Reading.*"

137. In Matthew's Gospel, this tax-collector is even Matthew (Matt 9:9), one of the twelve (Matt 10:3; Mk 3:18). This particular claim is distinct from the question of who wrote the Gospel of Matthew.

138. See Eddy and Boyd, *Legend,* 250, noting Papias' testimony in Euseb. *H.E.* 3.39.16. Interestingly, even Crossan's approach to the passion story implies that some of Jesus' disciples were learned (so Strijdom, "Unconventionality").

139. Fuller, "Classics," 179. This concession is also highlighted in Eddy and Boyd, *Legend,* 251-52.

140. Watson, "Education," 312.

141. Jos. *Life* 8; *Apion* 1.60; 2.171-73, 204. Josephus' statements on Jewish literacy, like that in *m. Ab.* 5:21, may reflect the literate elite, with much of the population learning Torah orally (Horsley, *Galilee,* 246-47); but there were undoubtedly reasons others considered Judeans a "nation of philosophers" (Stern, *Authors,* 1:8-11, 46-50; Gager, *Anti-Semitism,* 39), and "The synagogue was a comparatively intellectual milieu" (Riesner, "Synagogues in Jerusalem," 209). Philo (Boccaccini, *Judaism,* 192-94) and Pseudo-Aristeas (Boccaccini, *Judaism,* 194-98) also stress memory, blending Greek language with Jewish memorial traditions concerning God's historic acts.

142. See Riesner, "Education élémentaire"; idem, *Jesus.*

143. *Sipre Deut.* 48.1.1-4; Goodman, *State,* 79; cf. *Sipre Deut.* 4.2.1, 306.19.1-3; *b. Ber.* 38b; *p. Meg.* 4:1, §4; Gerhardsson, *Memory,* 113-21, 127-29, 168-70; Zlotnick, "Memory." Because Meir was Akiba's student, his anonymous traditions were assumed to stem from Akiba (*p. Ber.* 2:1, §4).

144. R. Akiba in *Sipre Deut.* 48.2.6. Traditional Israelite learning had emphasized the transmission of wisdom while also allowing individual learning (cf. Shupak, "Learning Methods").

145. See Gerhardsson, *Memory,* 124-25.

146. E.g., *tos. Yeb.* 3:1; *Mek. Pisha* 1.135-36; *Sipre Deut.* 48.2.6; *ARN* 24 A; *Pesiq. Rab Kah.* 21:5; *b. Suk.* 28a; *p. Sheq.* 2:5; cf. *m. Ed.* 1:4-5; *Sipra Behuq.* pq. 13.277.1.12; see further Moore, *Judaism,* 1:99; Urbach, *Sages,* 1:68; Gerhardsson, *Memory,* 122-70; idem, *Origins,* 19-24; Riesenfeld, *Tradition,* 14-17. When the proper attribution was unknown, this was sometimes stated (*p. Ter.* 8:5).

147. Cf. net transmission in the less formal Middle Eastern village settings (Dunn, *New Perspective,* 45-46).

148. See documentation cited in Keener, *Matthew,* 25-29. Greek and Roman philosophers also could do the same (Philost. *Vit. soph.* 1.22.523), even using poetry to reinforce their teaching for early students (Sen. *Ep. Lucil.* 108.9-10), though not advanced ones (ibid. 108.12; poetry and song involved memorization, Apollod. *Bib.* 1.3.1; Sen. *Controv.* 1.pref.2, 19). Various repetition devices aided memory (Harvey, *Listening,* 45, following Stanford, *Sound of Greek,* 83-85; also Harvey, *Listening,* 56). For the effectiveness of long-term memorization by a certain amount of repetition, see discussion of Pythagoreans above.

149. Dunn, *New Perspective,* 115 (including "parataxis, rhythmic speech, repetition, multiple existence, and variation").

150. Many also observe that the later rabbinic method hardly arose *ex nihilo* after 70 CE (e.g., Hagner, *Matthew,* 1:xlix; Boyd, *Sage,* 121).

151. Gerhardsson, *Memory,* 136-48, 173; Goulder, *Midrash,* 64-65. Similar sayings thus could appear in different words (*m. Shab.* 9:1; *A.Z.* 3:6).

152. Simeon ben Azzai in *Sipra VDDen.* pq. 2.2.3.1, 3.

153. *P. Sot.* 5:6, §1; cf. *p. Ket.* 3:1, §4. Of course, the rabbi may have issued several different opinions on a subject in his lifetime; cf. *p. B.K.* 2:6, §3. Sometimes rabbis also seem to have told stories as fictitious homiletic illustrations rather than wishing to be understood as drawing on previous traditions (cf. e.g., *Sipre Deut.* 40.7.1).

154. Theon *Progymn.* 1.93-171; cf. e.g., Epict. *Disc.* 1:9.23-25 with the Loeb note referring to Plato *Apol.* 29C, 28E (LCL 1:70-71). Diod. Sic. 20.1-2 allowed limited "rhetorical embellishment" in composing speeches for historical works (Aune, *Environment,* 93).

155. Philost. *Lives* 2.29.621.

156. See Small, "Memory."

157. Bauckham, *Eyewitnesses*, 333-34 (citing memory studies); he applies this to variation in detail among the different Gospels that nevertheless preserve the essential substance of events (such as Peter's denials; Bauckham, *Eyewitnesses*, 344-45). See also Eddy and Boyd, *Legend*, 275-85 and the many memory studies they cite.

158. Davies, "Aboth," 156.

159. Draper, "Didache."

160. Sanders, *Figure*, 193.

161. Cf. similarly Eddy and Boyd, *Legend*, 269-306. Witherington, *Christology*, 181, argues that if any historical tradition stands behind the sending of the twelve, Jesus' disciples were already communicating his teaching during his lifetime.

162. Others before him, such as Dibelius, *Tradition*, 39, had already drawn less sustained comparisons between rabbinic and gospel traditioning.

163. Smith, "Tradition," critiques Gerhardsson's reading of later rabbinic traditioning into the Jesus tradition from three main angles: third-century rabbinic literature cannot represent pre-70 Pharisaism's transmission techniques; Pharisaism would not represent all of first-century Judaism anyway; and the NT data simply does not fit this kind of traditioning. He is right on all these points, but characteristically overstates his case; Gerhardsson's own case is overstated, but he does provide more useful evidence than Smith allows. Neusner, "Foreword," has retracted his earlier severe critique of Gerhardsson, blaming it on Morton Smith's influence.

164. See Bailey, "Tradition." Cf. e.g., Xen. *Cyrop.* 1.2.1 for an example of long informal traditioning by storytelling and song.

165. Bailey, "Tradition"; also noted in Aune, *Dictionary of Rhetoric*, 326.

166. See Hurtado, *Lord Jesus Christ*, 79-153; Keener, *John*, 297-98, 300-3.

167. His most characteristic basis for ethics was union with the risen Christ rather than the sayings tradition (cf. Pfitzner, "School"), so such attestation is more incidental than pervasive.

168. 1 Cor 9:14 (see Dungan, *Sayings*, 3-26, esp. 16-21); 11:2, 23; 15:3; 1 Thess 4:1-2; cf. 1 Cor 7:10-12; 1 Thess 4:15; 2 Thess 2:15; cf. perhaps Rom 6:17 (writers employed terms like "receiving" and "passing on" for both teachings, e.g., Philost. *Lives* 2.29.621; Iamblichus *V.P.* 28.148; 32.226; and customs, e.g., Thucyd. 1.85.1; Iamblichus *V.P.* 28.149). That these were generated by Christian prophecy is extremely unlikely; see our treatment of prophecy in Appendix 4. Many also find Jesus tradition in Rom 12–14 (e.g., Thompson, *Clothed*; Riesenfeld, *Tradition*, 13), although many of these paranetic themes were more widespread (Gerhardsson, "Path," 81, argues that paranesis was probably not the dominant reason for preserving the Jesus tradition). 1 Thess 2:14-16 resembles some "Q" material (Donfried, *Thessalonica*, 203).

169. This includes Jesus' life (see Wenham, "Story") and teachings (Taylor, "Quest," noting that Paul more often gave them in person; Eddy and Boyd, *Legend*, 216-28; see esp. Dungan, *Sayings*). For the eschatological Jesus tradition, see Appendix 4.

170. Stanton, *Gospel Truth*, 97. On Jesus' divorce saying in Paul, see esp. Dungan, *Sayings*, 83-131.

171. Dunn, *New Perspective*, 119.

172. Theissen, *Gospels in Context*, 3-4. Given the differing genres of "lives" and letters, it is not surprising we lack more Jesus traditions in the letters (see Stuhlmacher, "Theme," 16-19; Gerhardsson, "Path").

173. Dungan, *Sayings*, 150. While we should definitely reckon with Diaspora aspects of Paul's presentation (with Meeks, Malherbe, and others, including myself in Keener, *Corinthians*), this should not be played off against Palestinian features in Paul (e.g., Davies, Sanders) or hellenistic features in the finished Gospels.

174. Pace Koester, *Gospels*; idem, "Gospels." Oral traditions of Jesus' sayings continued to circulate even after the written Gospels were in existence, however; see Jn 21:25; Papias' collection; Hengel, "Problems," 213; Hagner, "Sayings."

175. With Davids, "Tradition," 89-90. Citing Byrskog, Bauckham, and Hengel, Riesner, "Rück-kehr," notes the welcome shift back toward an emphasis on eyewitnesses in Gospels scholarship.

176. See e.g., Sanders, *Jesus and Judaism,* 11 ("almost indisputable"), 98-101 (esp. refutation of Vielhauer in 99-100); Meier, "Circle of Twelve"; Ehrman, *Prophet,* 186-87; Charlesworth, *Jesus within Judaism,* 137; Neufeld, *Recovering Jesus,* 152-53. On Peter as a witness, see Byrskog, *Story as History,* 71-73.

177. Cf. Ex 24:13; 33:11; Josh 1:1; 1 Kgs 19:16-21; CD 8.20-21; *Mek. Pisha* 1.150-53; *Tg. Jon.* on 1 Sam 19:23; 2 Kgs 6:1; 9:1, 4. Cf. Wilkins, *Discipleship,* 43-91.

178. Jos. *Life* 11-12.

179. The focus of "apostolic" witness in Acts is the resurrection, but Acts 1:21-22 indicates that intimate familiarity with Jesus' public ministry was also important.

180. Historians normally did seek to consult with families of relevant individuals (see the sources in Byrskog, *Story as History,* 82-83), so consulting with James (Byrskog, *Story as History,* 86-88) and even Mary (Byrskog, *Story as History,* 89-90), if she remained alive, is plausible.

181. For the women, especially Mary Magdalene, see also Byrskog, *Story as History,* 73-81.

182. Eddy and Boyd, *Legend,* 286-91. This emphasis persisted later; see e.g., Papias in Euseb. *H.E.* 3.39.3-4 (Bauckham, "Eyewitnesses and Traditions"); much later, Bede, *Acts,* p. 5, preface to Acts.

183. Bauckham, "Eyewitnesses and Traditions." While I deeply appreciate most of Bauckham's work, however, I believe that he may go too far behind our data in identifying particular names with particular traditions (cf. also Tuckett, "Review"; Keener, "Review of Bauckham," 132).

184. See my more extensive discussion in Keener, *John,* 81-139 (where I argue for his eyewitness identity). For an eyewitness tradition or source of some sort, see (among many others who could be named) Kysar, *John,* 12; Borchert, *John,* 89-90; O'Day, "John," 500; Smith, *John* (1999), 400; Witherington, *Wisdom,* 15-17; Braun, *Jean,* 301-30; Hengel, *Question;* Muñoz Léon, "Discípulo"; idem, "Juan"; Carson, Moo, and Morris, *Introduction,* 138-51; Bauckham, *Testimony,* 33-91. See the thorough list of scholarly positions in Charlesworth, *Disciple,* 197-211.

185. Stein, "Criteria," 225-28; Wright, *People of God,* 421; Stanton, *Gospel Truth,* 60-61. They also avoided harmonizing their portrayal of early Christianity. As Wright, *People of God,* 454, notes, after recounting Luke's recital of Ananias and Sapphira, church divisions, and the separation of Paul and Barnabas, the mythical claim to early Christian uniformity was the invention of Eusebius, not of first-century Christians still close to the events.

186. Gundry, *Old Testament,* 191; cf. Pfitzner, "School"; Thompson, *Clothed;* Richardson and Gooch, "Logia," 52.

187. See Theissen, *Gospels in Context,* 25-59.

188. Davids, "Tradition," 89-90; France, *Evidence,* 100-1; cf. Blomberg, "Studying Jesus," 22; pace Koester, *Gospels;* idem, "Gospels." Ancients also regarded eyewitnesses as generally more reliable (e.g., Jos. *Life* 357; *War* 1.2-3; *Apion* 1.46-49; Arrian *Alex.* 6.11.8; *Indica* 15.7; Corn. Nep. 23 [Hannibal], 13.3; 25 [Atticus], 13.7; 17.1), especially if they knew both sides of the story (Jos. *Apion* 1.49, 56).

189. Gundry, *Old Testament,* 191, also emphasizing the lack of "Pauline terminology in the gospels" and Paul distinguishing his teaching from Jesus'.

190. E.g., Hill, *Prophecy,* 163, 172; cf. *P. Oxy.* 1 in Jeremias, *Unknown Sayings,* 106-11.

191. Cf. Stein, "Criteria," 225-228; Goetz and Blomberg, "Burden of Proof"; Bartnicki, "Zapowiedzi"; Eddy and Boyd, *Legend,* 364-76 (cf. esp. 368 for this issue among historians generally).

192. Cf. *Acts of Paul* 3:1/*Thecla* 1.

193. Pace Beare, "Sayings," 181; Bultmann, *Tradition,* 163; Boring, "Oracles," 501-2; Boring, *Sayings;* Miller, "Prophets"; Price, *Son of Man,* 29. Boring, *Sayings,* 77 thinks that prophets contributed to the Jesus tradition because they valued it; yet the opposite is far more likely: they valued it enough to retain it as a distinct standard for evaluating prophecies. Boring, *Sayings,* 110 may be less far afield when he contends that early Christian prophets often adapted rather than simply created Jesus material (cf. Hill, *Prophecy,* 163); but lack of adequate formal criteria undercut his attempts to argue that

Christian prophets transmitted and adapted Jesus material. As he himself concedes, some prophetic material must stem from Jesus the prophet (Boring, *Sayings*, 138-39).

194. See Aune, *Prophecy*; Hill, *Prophecy*; Bauckham, "Parables"; Dunn, "Prophetic Sayings"; Eddy and Boyd, *Legend*, 298-305. Some suggest that it occurred occasionally but rarely (Theissen and Merz, *Historical Jesus*, 110-11, for divine "I" sayings, in Matt 23:34/Lk 11:49; Matt 18:20; and often in John; Sanders, *Figure*, 62-63). The position in Sanders, *Figure*, 62-63 sounds more conservative than the language in Sanders, *Tendencies*, 27-28.

195. Cf. e.g., Hill, *Prophecy*, 160-170; Aune, *Prophecy*, 243-44; Stanton, *Gospel Truth*, 97. The prejudice against anonymous oracles might also count against the prophetic generation of Synoptic Jesus material, as does the relative scarceness of material attributed to Jesus outside the Gospels (Stanton, *Gospels*, 159). Given his prophetic activity, could not Jesus himself be responsible for genuinely prophetic material in the tradition (cf. Hill, *Prophecy*, 180-81)?

196. See e.g., Witherington, *Christology*, 3-7.

197. Witherington, *Christology*, 181. For arguments for the likelihood that Jesus, like most teachers, would have sent his disciples to carry on some of his work before his death, see Keener, *Matthew*, 312-13.

198. Price, *Son of Man*, 29; for this present distortion among many of Kimbangu's followers, see Kalu, *African Pentecostalism*, 70, 78-79. Price regards Gerhardsson's rabbinic analogy (which most do regard as too rigid) as anachronistic (Price, *Son of Man*, 28); yet it is less anachronistic than a speculative reconstruction stemming from solely modern premises would be. I use the Kimbangu analogy for other purposes in my book on miracle claims, but for reasons we have noted, it falters as an analogy for passing on first-century tradition.

199. Indeed, many of Kimbangu's "closest disciples were also arrested" (Gray, "Christianity," 158). This repression of Kimbangu is among the disgraceful acts of the colonial administration.

200. Kimbangu's church was divided theologically, and especially after the death of his son Joseph Diangienda in 1992 (about 40 years after his own death; Gondola, "Kimbangu," 767). Contrast the view of Jesus already in Paul's letters spanning roughly 20-30 years after Jesus' death (see ch. 19).

201. Price, *Son of Man*, 28.

202. From different perspectives, see e.g., Duling and Perrin, *New Testament*, 16-20; Carson, Moo and Morris, *Introduction*, 21-25.

203. I deal with these more fully in Keener, *John*, 65-68.

204. See Wright, *People of God*, 342.

205. E.g., Bultmann, *Tradition*. Most of Bultmann's "laws" of tradition were adequately refuted by Sanders, *Tendencies*.

206. E.g., Dibelius, *Tradition*; Jeremias, *Theology*; Taylor, *Formation*.

207. See Sanders, *Tendencies*; on critics discovering differing results from the same criteria, cf. also e.g., Van Oyen, "Criteria."

208. The criteria of multiple attestation and embarrassment, respectively. The latter seems more widely used today than earlier, although it overlaps with the positive use of the criterion of dissimilarity.

209. See France, "Authenticity"; and discussion below.

210. So Wright, *People of God*, 341-42.

211. Dunn, *New Perspective*, 35-42.

212. Frye, "Analogies in Literatures," 287.

213. E.g., Hill, *Matthew*, 58; more forcefully, Theissen, *Gospels in Context*, 5; at length, Porter, *Criteria*, though not all of his new criteria seem helpful, either.

214. Ael. Arist. *Defense of Oratory* 78, §25D.

215. Tuckett, "Sources and methods," 134; Holmén, *Covenant Thinking*, 33-34. For some questions about the application of this criterion, see e.g., Eve, "Meier and Miracle."

216. Arrian *Alex*. 7.14.4-6.

217. E.g., Sanders, *Jesus and Judaism,* 236-37; Johnson, *Real Jesus,* 130; Holmén, *Covenant Thinking,* 35. In a different culture, compare Confucius *Analects* 168 (16.4) with 387 (7.28); even the most unified documents deconstruct (see comments in Keener, *John,* 38-39, 901 n. 19).

218. Lutz, "Musonius," 12-13.

219. See this complaint in Theissen and Merz, *Historical Jesus,* 115 (who also note that this criterion "underestimates" potential development in Jesus' thought); Tuckett, "Sources and methods," 133.

220. On the latter point, see Holmén, *Covenant Thinking,* 34-35; Tuckett, "Sources and methods," 136; cf. Tan, *Zion Traditions,* 237. For the value of a cohesive story, see Hays, "Victory," 158. Witherington, "Wright quest," praises Wright for reading Jesus in light of the passion narrative.

221. Cf. also Pope Benedict, *Jesus of Nazareth,* xxi-xxii.

222. Sanders, "Know," 60 n. 12; Levine, "Introduction," 10-11.

223. Sanders, "Know," 51-53, calling it the criterion of "against the grain"; Eddy and Boyd, *Legend,* 408-12.

224. See e.g., Borg, *Conflict,* 20-23; Sanders, *Jesus and Judaism,* 16, 145; Meier, *Marginal Jew,* 1:173; Brown, *Death,* 19; Stanton, *Gospel Truth,* 143; Young, *Theologian,* 257; Tuckett, "Sources and methods," 133; Theissen and Merz, *Historical Jesus,* 115; Ehrman, *Prophet,* 92 (cautiously); Levine, "Introduction," 10-11; Holmén, "Doubts about Dissimilarity"; idem, *Covenant Thinking,* 20-31 (esp. 29-30); Kazen, "Imagery," 87; Broadhead, "Priests," 125; Dunn, *New Perspective,* 58; Bird, "Quest"; cf. Mealand, "Dissimilarity Test"; Mack, *Lost Gospel,* 193.

225. I noted it in Keener, *Matthew,* 29-30.

226. Sanders, "Know," 60 n. 12. Theissen and Merz, *Historical Jesus,* 115, denounce this emphasis on uniqueness as "dogmatics disguised."

227. See Theissen and Merz, *Historical Jesus,* 11 (noting that virtually all Third Questers mistrust the dissimilarity criterion).

228. Dunn, *New Perspective,* 59-60.

229. Dunn, *New Perspective,* 57-78 (on 68 citing this advice from Keck, *Future,* 33).

230. Stein, *Messiah,* 48.

231. Tuckett, "Sources and methods," 133.

232. With e.g., Theissen and Merz, *Historical Jesus,* 116; Tuckett, "Sources and methods," 133. Ancient historians could also test a report's probability according to coherency with known customs of the report's day (e.g., Dion. Hal. *Ant. rom.* 9.22.1-5).

233. See Holmén, "Introduction" (esp. 1-13), allowing for some discontinuity as well as continuity (2). See likewise Neufeld, *Recovering Jesus,* 46; McKnight, *Death,* 44.

234. Holmén, "Introduction," 4, 8.

235. Holmén, "Introduction," 9. Some seek to explore Jesus' impact on his followers (e.g., Piovanelli, "Charismatic Authority").

236. Holmén, "Introduction," 2; this is more helpful in explaining his ultimate rejection (Holmén, *Covenant Thinking,* 34-35; Tuckett, "Sources and methods," 136). Many note both continuity and discontinuity (e.g., Schlosser, "Jésus de Nazareth").

237. Holmén, *Covenant Thinking,* 35.

238. See Keener, *John,* 283-310; especially Hurtado, *Lord Jesus Christ;* Marshall, *Origins.*

239. Blomberg, "Studying Jesus," 22.

240. I do argue that Matthew re-Judaized tradition for a Jewish audience, but he could do so (and had a Jewish audience) precisely because Jesus was known to be a Palestinian Jew, and Jewish believers in Syria had maintained many of the early traditions. Conservative Syrian Jews would have hardly welcomed and appropriated an obviously non-Jewish tradition that needed to be re-Judaized.

241. Overman, "Deciphering," 194.

242. Aramaisms could also indicate a rural Syrian milieu, but the first churches (and extant Christian authors) in Syria were mostly urban, and in urban centers (including, from an early period, the Jerusalem church) the one language nearly all members could share was Greek. Aramaisms thus

suggest the Galilean tradition or on other occasions the bilingual milieu of the earliest eastern churches; both explanations point to tradition earlier than our extant Greek Gospels. In a later document like Thomas, they could point to indigenous Syriac Christianity, by then no longer restricted mostly to bilingual and Greek-speaking urban centers.

243. Witherington, *Christology*, 11; cf. Barrett, *Jesus and Tradition*, 6.

244. Young, *Parables*, 180.

245. Witherington, *Christology*, 16-17; Riesner, "Ursprung," 507. Some forms of Greek and Roman rhetoric also employed rhythm (Cicero *Orator* 23.77; 50.168-69.231), but obviously not in Aramaic.

246. See Black, *Aramaic Approach*, and others. Thus, e.g., some suggest a connection between "salt" and "manure" in Lk 14:34-35, citing Aramaic *tabbala* (seasoning) and *zabbala* (manure; Manson, *Sayings*, 132); or between "perfect" in Matt 5:48 and "merciful" in the parallel text in Lk 6:36 (Robinson, *Trust*, 32); in beatitudes, Jeremias, *Sermon*, 15-16.

247. Cf. e.g., step parallelism in Matt 7:7-11//Lk 11:9-13 (Bailey, *Poet*, 48; cf. Manson, *Sayings*, 32; Jeremias, *Theology*, 25; Tannehill, *Sword*, 46-47). Black also suggests that some of the comparable beatitudes are parallel lines from others (*Aramaic Approach*, 156-58, 192).

248. See Horsley, *Galilee*, 247-49; cf. Millard, *Reading and Writing*, 85-102 (esp. 91-102).

249. E.g., Mussies, "Vehicle"; Van der Horst, "Funerary Inscriptions"; Millard, *Reading and Writing*, 102-17; cf. p. *Sot.* 7:1, §4.

250. Dalman, *Jesus-Jeshua*, 3; on Greek-speakers in Jerusalem, see Hengel, *Pre-Christian Paul*, 54-62. Because most of Jesus' teachings in the Synoptics appear to have been delivered to Galilean villagers, they probably reflect Aramaic, but because he also taught in urban Jerusalem, the scholars who suggest that he sometimes taught in Greek (Porter, "Teach"; idem, "Greek in Galilee," 154; cf. Argyle, "Semitism"; pace Draper, "Greek") may also be correct. For discussion of Jesus' language through Dalman, see Schweitzer, *Quest*, 270-78.

251. Witness especially Ezra 4:8–6:18; 7:12-26; Dan 2:4–7:28; 2 Macc 15:36; also the Elephantine papyri in Egypt.

252. Segert, "Review" (1972), 274, doubted that the Aramaic materials originated with the sectarians themselves, but if we grant that they authored many of the documents found at Qumran (a point of some debate today), there is no reason to distinguish sectarian documents by language. At least a substantial portion, probably the majority, of *1 Enoch* was composed in Aramaic (Rost, *Judaism*, 139; Charlesworth, *Pseudepigrapha and Research*, 98), though this need not have originated at Qumran.

253. Bruce, *Acts: Greek*, 399, even suggests that Josephus' first draft of the *War* addressed Babylonian Jews in Aramaic. If so, that draft was quite different in substance from the Hellenized audience the current form presupposes; Josephus may think just of style editors to catch Aramaic interference in his Greek unacceptable by purist standards in Greece and Rome.

254. Wilcox, "Influence," 1094. We cannot be sure how far the extant written form may be from what was spoken (Wise, "Palestinian Aramaic," 237).

255. Levine, *Hellenism*, 80-84; Millard, *Reading and Writing*, 85-102 (esp. 91-102).

256. Wilcox, "Influence," 1094-98, especially 1095.

257. Meier, *Marginal Jew*, 1:267-68; Deissmann, *Light*, 64; Black, "Language," 305; Jeremias, *Theology*, 4; Segert, "Languages."

258. Dibelius, *Jesus*, 25.

259. See Meier, *Marginal Jew*, 1:178-80.

260. More adaptation might occur in the "translation" into Greek (although Josephus claims in *Apion* 1.1 that he "translated" [lit., "wrote in Greek"] his *Antiquities* from the Hebrew Bible, he clearly exercised stylistic and apologetic freedom where he felt necessary; the degree of "translation" is not quite clear, e.g., Jos. *War* 1.3; cf. *Ant.* 1.7; 20.263-64; see Townsend, "Education," 148; Hata, "Version").

261. Pace Burkitt, *Sources*, 20.

262. As Meier, *Marginal Jew*, 1:255-68, concurs; cf. Argyle, "Greek." Horsley's case (Horsley, *Doc-*

uments, 5:5-40) against Nigel Turner's "Jewish Greek" (Turner, "Second Thoughts," 46-47; cf. Nock, "Vocabulary," 138-39; Malherbe, *Social Aspects,* 35-36) does not dispute the presence of Semitisms or other features of bilingualism, but that a separate dialect is in view (pp. 6, 40). Most bilinguals are less fluent in their second language, which may be the culture's dominant language (Horsley, *Documents* 5:23-24).

263. Stanton, *Gospel Truth,* 139.

264. Jos. *Life* 11; among later rabbis, cf. e.g., *b. Ber.* 62a; Kirschner, "Imitatio"; Gerhardsson, *Origins,* 16-17.

265. E.g., *tos. Pisha* 2:15-16; *Sipre Deut.* 221.1.1; *p. B.M.* 2:11, §1; *Nid.* 1:4, §2; *Sanh.* 7:2, §4; *Yeb.* 4:11, §8.

266. Jos. *Apion* 2.171, 173-74, 204. To a lesser degree, cf. the broader Greco-Roman principle of imitation among disciples (Quint. *Inst.* 1.2.26; Philost. *V.A.* 5, §21; and sources above) and children (Isoc. *Nicocl./Cypr.* 57, *Or.* 3.37; Quint. *Inst.* 1.1.5; 1.3.1-3; 1 Cor 4:16). For the importance of imitating virtuous fathers or elder brothers in Judaism, see e.g., *L.A.B.* 20:6; 4 Macc 9:23.

267. Cf. Liefeld, "Preacher," 223; Robbins, *Teacher,* 64.

268. See Bauckham, *Eyewitnesses,* 350, 472-508 (e.g., comparing taped interviews of Holocaust survivors on 493-505).

269. Bauckham, *Eyewitnesses,* 347-51.

270. Disciples could readily adapt both the Jesus tradition and Cynic tradition, both highly critical of the social establishment, to fit this form (cf. Theissen, *Gospels in Context,* 115; Wright, *People of God,* 427-35), but this does not imply that *chreiai* represent a strictly Cynic form or that the stories were composed under Cynic influence. Synoptic pericopes fit both Greco-Roman and Jewish forms (Theissen, *Gospels in Context,* 120-22, especially p. 120 n. 143; cf. Guenther, "Greek," though Greek rhetorical forms may have prevailed less in first-century Palestine than he thinks); the specifically Cynic position of Mack, *Myth,* 179, 186-87, is thus too narrow, as is his attribution of Q to "Cynic-like" circles (Mack, *Myth,* 69, 84; cf. Downing, "Like Q"; idem, "Actuality"; but also the critique in Overman, "Deciphering," 193; Tuckett, "Cynic Q"; Witherington, *Christology,* 184; Blomberg, "Studying Jesus," 21; Boyd, *Sage,* 160). On the *chreia* as a basic narrative unit in the tradition, see further Byrskog, "Chreia."

271. Cf. Robbins, "Chreia," 3; Mack and Robbins, *Patterns,* 196-97. Jewish forms of transmitting tradition often closely resembled broader Greco-Roman patterns.

272. Burridge, *Gospels,* 203.

273. See e.g., Plut. *Agesilaus* 21.4-5; Lucian *Demonax* 12-62 (e.g., 39, 44); Alsup, "Function"; Robbins, "Pronouncement Stories"; Poulos, "Pronouncement Story"; Barrett, "Anecdotes," 119-26; Aune, *Dictionary of Rhetoric,* 111, 378-79; the chreia in Stenger, "Apophthegma"; in Jewish contexts, cf. e.g., 1 Kgs 3:16-28; 10:3; *tos. A.Z.* 6:7; *Sanh.* 13:5.

274. These seem to have been substantially rarer in strictly Jewish works, perhaps due to the genres commonly involved; cf. VanderKam, "Pronouncement Stories" (nineteen examples, mainly in *Test. Job* and Ahiqar); Greenspoon, "Pronouncement Story"; and especially Porton, "Pronouncement Story," who alone deals with the Jewish equivalent of "sage" narratives found in the Greek parallels. Yet Porton may underestimate the value of the rabbinic texts, which cite Scripture as in the Gospel narratives (see Theissen, *Gospels in Context,* 120 n. 143). These do admittedly become dominant especially in the Amoraic period, however, probably due to the primarily halakic character of Tannaitic texts preserved. In rabbinic controversy-dialogues (e.g., *b. R.H.* 32b), the rabbis debate pagan interlocutors in general (e.g., *b. Bek.* 8b; *Sanh.* 39a; *p. Meg.* 1:11, §3; 3:2, §3; *Pesiq. Rab Kah.* 1:2; 4:7; *Num. Rab.* 4:9; 9:48; *Eccl. Rab.* 2.8, §2), pagan philosophers (*tos. A.Z.* 6:7; *b. A.Z.* 54b, bar.; *Bek.* 8b-9a; cf. *b. Sanh.* 39a), including "Epicureans" (possibly used in its general denigrating sense of those who denied divine providence and judgment; *tos. Sanh.* 13:5; *p. Sanh.* 10:1, §7; cf. *m. Ab.* 2:14, expounded in *b. Sanh.* 38b), Sadducees (*b. Erub.* 101a), Samaritans (*p. Yeb.* 1:6, §1), and *minim* (schismatics) in general (*b. Sanh.* 38b, 39a, 43a; *Hul.* 84a; perhaps *b. Yoma* 56b-57a; Herford, *Christianity,* 226-27, also lists *Eccl. Rab.* 30:9, 53cd; *b. Hul.* 87a; *Shab.* 152b; *Suk.* 48b; cf. Bagatti, *Church,* 98ff.

275. E.g., Gundry, *Old Testament,* 190.

276. E.g., Witherington, *Christology,* 28-29; Theissen, *Gospels in Context,* 60.

Notes to Section III

1. I distinguish "should" from "do"; if the critical minimum is defined by what *every* scholar would accept, the critical minimum is virtually nothing. The outcome depends on the criteria employed, but the vast majority of scholars do accept more than "nothing"!

2. As Hays, "Victory," 158, notes, one of the most brilliant aspects of N. T. Wright's approach is his synthesis of material into a cohesive whole. Various approaches have produced competing cohesive explanations, of course. We have tried to focus on some of the most secure and certain elements.

Notes to Chapter 11

1. Kraeling, *John the Baptist,* 157.

2. Taylor, *Immerser,* 321. She rightly notes that Jesus' disciples continued this practice.

3. Sanders, *Figure,* 95.

4. E.g., Dodd, *Tradition,* 274; Stauffer, *Jesus,* 65; Lane, *Mark,* 52; Kraeling, *John the Baptist,* 55 (summarizing the position of Lohmeyer [1932] and K. Grobel [1941]); Freyne, "Servant Community," 111.

5. Cf. Jos. *Ant.* 18.117.

6. Crossan contends that Jesus beginning a ministry distinct from John the Baptist suggests that Jesus must have rejected John's apocalypticism (*Historical Jesus,* 230-38). Yet the very purpose of training advanced disciples was for them to be teachers as well; they did not have to await the mentor's death to begin ministry! More scholars recognize Jesus' continuity with John (below).

7. E.g., Meyer, "Judgment"; Michaels, *Servant,* 1-24; Chilton, "Announcement"; Sanders, *Figure,* 94; Taylor, *Immerser,* 314 (summarizing her argument in that section); Webb, "Relationship," especially 214-29; Ehrman, *Prophet,* 185; Allison, "Continuity"; Dapaah, *Relationship.* For Jesus remaining pro-John, see also Spencer, *Profiles,* 54-58; France, "Jesus the Baptist?" 105-7 (France contending that even the subsequent groups remained on good terms).

8. Webb, "Relationship," 229. For a survey of "historical John" research, see Webb, "Relationship," 179-86.

9. Funk et al., *Acts of Jesus,* 51.

10. Feldman, "Methods," 591.

11. E.g., Abrahams, *Studies* 1, 30-35 (contrast the inauthentic Slavic additions in Josephus LCL 3:644-45). Robert Webb ("Josephus on John"; idem, *Baptizer,* 39-41, 87), persuasively argues that Josephus' account is mostly accurate, though shaped by his perspective.

12. See also discussion of competition in Keener, *John,* 388-91, and the (often more extensive) sources cited there.

13. See Meier, "John in Josephus," 234; cf. Liefeld, "Preacher," 146 n. 31.

14. Theissen, *Gospels in Context,* 39; Theissen and Merz, *Historical Jesus,* 101. For the Jordan's possible theological significance (evoking redemptive history), see e.g., Webb, "Relationship," 189. The particular site is uncertain (Hoppe, "Baptized").

15. Hos 2:14-15; 11:5-11; Is 40:3; later interpreters properly understood such passages as applicable to the time of Israel's restoration (e.g., *Ps. Sol.* 11:1).

16. Cf. Theissen, *Sociology,* 48-50. For revelation and purification there, cf. discussion in Najman, "Wilderness."

17. Acts 21:38; Matt 24:26; Jos. *Ant.* 20.189; *War* 2.259, 261-62; cf. Beasley-Murray, *Mark Thirteen,*

84. Apart from new exodus connotations, this was the only place for such large and potentially politically subversive movements (cf. *Ant.* 18.118) to safely gather.

18. As in Jn 1:23, the Baptist may have employed this text to convey his own sense of mission (Robinson, *Studies,* 13).

19. 1QS 8.13-14; cf. Brownlee, "Comparison," 71; Brown, "Scrolls," 4; Evans, "Typologies," 50-52. In their case, this applied especially to their knowledge of the law (1QS 8.15-16). Some argue for the relevance of Is 40:3 to revolutionary movements in the wilderness (cf. Schwartz, "Voice"), though others contend that the new exodus paradigm (cf. Longenecker, "Wilderness") was more influential.

20. 1QS 8.13-14; 9.19-20; Bruce, "Qumran and Christianity," 177; Witherington, *Christology,* 36; cf. Scobie, "John the Baptist," 68; Minde, "Absonderung"; Evans, "Typologies," 52 (noting other wilderness prophets).

21. Josephus also portrays the Essenes as ascetics (*War* 2.120) and evidence suggests that he baptized near them (see Jeremias, *Theology,* 43). But if John was ever an Essene (Betz, "Essene"), it was not during his public ministry — Essenes did not accept those who differed from them in any respects (see Pryke, "John"). Against some who have produced wild theories relating the Essenes to Christianity (e.g., Trudinger, "Gospel"; Thiering, *Hypothesis*), most scholars recognize both similarities and differences (Charlesworth, *Jesus Within Judaism,* 72, 75).

22. E.g., Heb 11:38; Rev 12:6; *Ps. Sol.* 17:17; *Song Rab.* 2:13, §4; Tac. *Ann.* 14.23.

23. To avoid digressing lengthily here, I refer the interested reader to my more extensive discussion of the nature of John's baptism in Keener, *Matthew,* 120-22; idem, *John,* 442-47.

24. Webb, *Baptizer,* 377-78, noting that John's movement was more passive, and his followers consequently were spared, in contrast to some other movements of the time.

25. See Webb, *Baptizer,* 87-88, helpfully.

26. Commentators often note the wordplay (e.g., Manson, *Sayings,* 40; Argyle, *Matthew,* 36; Fenton, *Matthew,* 56; Gundry, *Matthew,* 47; Hagner, *Matthew,* 50). Prophets had often used witty wordplays (Amos 8:1-2; Micah 1:10-15; Jer 1:11-12), and Scripture already used stones to symbolize God's people (Ex 24:4; 28:9-12; Josh 4:20-21; 1 Kgs 18:31; cf. also Evans, "Typologies," 60) or covenants (Gen 31:46; Josh 4:20-24). Bringing stones to life may have been an image for the impossible (Neh 4:2; MT 3:34). For how the language would sound to both Greek and Jewish hearers, see also Keener, "Human Stones."

27. E.g., Is 1:10; Jer 23:14; Ezek 16:46-56; Amos 2:4–3:2; 9:7.

28. At the very time salvation comes for some (Israel), judgment (often fiery hell) comes for others (e.g., *1 En.* 96:1-3; *Sipre Deut.* 307.3.2; 324.1.5; *Ex. Rab.* 30:24; cf. *Sib. Or.* 4.42).

29. Not all of John's imagery was uniquely Palestinian, of course; for example, everyone knew of the threshing floor (Pliny *N.H.* 18.54.195), and I have argued that the viper imagery he employs (Matt 3:7//Lk 3:7) was widespread (see e.g., Keener, "Brood of Vipers"; not cited there, cf. Modestinus *Dig.* 48.9.9).

30. E.g., Ps 1:4; Is 17:5-6, 13; 29:5-6; 33:11; 41:15-16; Jer 15:7; Hos 13:3; Joel 3:13; Zeph 2:2; cf. Ex 15:7; Jer 4:11-13; 13:24; Amos 8:1-2.

31. *4 Ezra* 4:30-32; fire in *Jub.* 36:10; cf. further fire in 1QM 14.1; *Test. Ab.* 12:4-14A; *Sib. Or.* 3.760-61; 5.274; *Num. Rab.* 4:1; cf. *Sipre Deut.* 312.1.1; 343.5.2; Jms 5:7-8; Rev 14:15.

32. *1 En.* 48:9.

33. Ex 15:7; Ps 1:4; 35:5; 83:13; Is 17:13; 29:5; Dan 2:35; Hos 13:3; Mal 4:1; *Sipre Deut.* 312.1.1; 343.5.2; cf. earlier Canaanite poetry (in IAB 2, *ANET* 140). People used chaff for various purposes, of which the most prominent was fuel (*CPJ* 1:199; *Gen. Rab.* 83:5; cf. Hepper, *Plants,* 41; cf. straw in *Pesiq. Rab.* 10:4; straw was otherwise worthless, *Num. Rab.* 18:17).

34. CD 2.4-6; *1 En.* 103:8; *Sib. Or.* 4.43, 161, 176-78; 2 Thess 1:6-7; *Ex. Rab.* 15:27; cf. also the references in Davies and Allison, *Matthew,* 1:310. For the conflation of water ("baptism") and fire metaphors, see the many references in Davies and Allison, *Matthew,* 1:316, who also cite texts linking fire and water in judgment (Ps 66:10-12; Is 30:27-28; 43:2; 66:15-16; *Sib. Or.* 3.689-92; Jos. *Ant.* 1.70) and as a

river or flood of fire (e.g., Dan 7:10; 1QH 3.29-36; *1 En.* 67.13; *Sib. Or.* 2.196-205, 252-54; 3.54, 84-87; *4 Ezra* 13:10-11).

35. E.g., villagers carried grain to village threshing floors, though large estates worked by tenants would have their own (Lewis, *Life*, 123). Archaeologists have recovered winnowing shovels, and the procedure is well-known (see Hepper, *Plants*, 90-91).

36. Kraeling, *John the Baptist*, 42; Ladd, *Theology*, 37; cf. Is 29:5-6; 33:11.

37. E.g., *ARN* 41 A; cf. also 36 A.

38. 4 Macc 9:9; 12:12; *tos. Sanh.* 13:5; probably *1 En.* 108:5-6; *L.A.B.* 38:4; *Asc. Isa.* 1:2; *3 En.* 44:3; *tos. Ber.* 5:31; *b. R.H.* 17a; *p. Hag.* 2:2, §5; *Sanh.* 6:6, §2; cf. Diod. Sic. 4.69.5; Plut. *Divine Vengeance* 31, *Mor.* 567DE. Although Luke does not reject future eschatology in his effort to contextualize for Greek readers (Acts 17:31-32; 23:6; 24:15; contrast e.g., Jos. *Ant.* 18.14, 18; *War* 2.163; Philo *Sacr. Abel & Cain* 5, 8), Matthew's emphases retain more of their original Jewish flavor here (cf. Milikowski, "Gehenna"; Goulder, *Midrash*, 63).

39. Cf. 1QS 4.13-14; *Gen. Rab.* 6:6; most sinners in *tos. Sanh.* 13:3, 4; *Pesiq. Rab Kah.* 10:4; *Pesiq. Rab.* 11:5; cf. 2 Macc 12:43-45.

40. *Num. Rab.* 18:20; other texts are unclear, e.g., *Sipre Num.* 40.1.9; *Sipre Deut.* 311.3.1; 357.6.7; *ARN* 16 A; 32, §69 B; 37, §95 B. Twelve months is a familiar duration (*b. Shab.* 33b; *Lam. Rab.* 1:11-12, §40).

41. Greek mythology spoke of Tartarus for the worst offenders (a parallel used by some Diaspora Jews, *Sib. Or.* 1.10, 101-3; 2.291, 302; 4.186; 5.178; *L.A.B.* 60:3, most MSS; *Test. Sol.* 6:3), but the Semitic term "Gehinnom" predominates in Palestine and other Aramaic sources (among many other examples, e.g., *3 En.* 44:3; *m. Ab.* 1:5; *Sipre Deut.* 333.5.2; *ARN* 25A; 41A; *Pes. Rab Kah.* 5:2; 9:1; Sup. 2:2; 3:2; *b. Ber.* 28b; *Shab.* 104a; *Erub.* 19a; *Yoma* 87a; *Gen. Rab.* 9:9; 20:1; *Tg. Job* on 2:11; *Tg. Is.* on 53:9; 66:24; *Tg. Hosea* on 14:10), and is rare (though occasionally borrowed, *Sib. Or.* 4.186) in Greco-Jewish ones.

42. On John proclaiming the expected one, see Webb, *Baptizer*, 261-306.

43. The Gospels do not claim that he offered that association publicly.

44. Bruce, "Matthew," 84; Flowers, "En Pneumati"; cf. Dunn, "Spirit," 695; Keener, "Spirit," 491; Is 4:4. This interpretation does not preclude John from envisioning such a "purifying wind" as also God's Spirit; the expression "holy Spirit" was a familiar one, and John's contemporaries in the wilderness associated the Spirit with purification (see e.g., Keener, "Pneumatology," 65-69). We have already noted that the tradition of John's preaching included Semitic wordplays.

45. In John's image, the judge burns chaff already separated from the wheat; thus Webb, *Baptizer*, suggests that John saw his ministry as already having separated the two.

46. Cf. e.g., Diog. Laert. *Lives* 6.2.44; *b. B.B.* 53b. Davies and Allison, *Matthew*, 1:315 cite also *b. Kid.* 22b, bar.; *Pes.* 4a; *Sipre* on Num. 15:41; Plaut. *Trin.* 2.1; Lachs, *Commentary*, 45 adds *Mek. Ex.* 21:2; *b. B.M.* 41a; *Erub.* 27b; *Ket.* 96a; *p. B.M.* 7:9, plus Roman custom.

47. E.g., Ex 24:13; 33:11; Deut 1:38; 2 Kgs 2:2-6; 3:11; 4:12, 43; 5:20; 6:3, 15, 17; 8:4; *tos. B.M.* 2:30; *ARN* 25A; *b. Ber.* 7b; *Gen. Rab.* 22:2; 100:10; cf. Diog. Laert. 7.1.12; 7.5.170.

48. *B. Ket.* 96a, cited in Davies, *Sermon*, 135; cf. Daube, *NT and Judaism*, 266. "Loosening" (Mk 1:7; Lk 3:16) and "carrying" (Matt 3:11) the sandals convey the same sense of servility, hence communicate the same point despite the variation in wording (cf. data in Daube, *NT and Judaism*, 266; they might also reflect the same Aramaic verb — cf. Manson, *Sayings*, 40).

49. For the prophets in general, see e.g., 2 Kgs 9:7, 36; 10:10; 14:25; 17:13, 23; 21:10; 24:2; Ezra 9:11; Is 20:3; Jer 7:25; 25:4; 26:5; 29:19; 35:15; 44:4; Dan 3:28; 6:20; 9:6, 10; Amos 3:7; Zech 1:6; cf. *ARN* 37, §95 B; for David, see 2 Sam 3:18; 7:5, 8, 19-21, 25-29; 1 Kgs 3:6; 8:24-26, 66; 11:13, 32, 34, 36, 38; 14:8; 2 Kgs 8:19; 19:34; 20:6; 1 Chron 17:4, 7, 17-19, 23-27; 2 Chron 6:15-21, 42; Ps 78:70; 89:3, 20; 132:10; 144:10; Is 37:35; Jer 33:21-22, 26; Ezek 34:23-24; 37:24-25; cf. *ARN* 43, §121 B; for Moses, see Ex 14:31; Num 12:7-8; Deut 34:5; Josh 1:1-2, 7, 13, 15; 8:31, 33; 9:24; 11:12, 15; 12:6; 13:8; 14:7; 18:7; 22:2, 4-5; 1 Kgs 8:53, 56; 2 Kgs 18:12; 21:8; 1 Chron 6:49; 2 Chron 1:3; 24:6, 9; Neh 1:7-8; 9:14; 10:29; Ps 105:26; Dan 9:11; Mal 4:4; cf. *L.A.B.* 30:2; *ARN* 43, §121 B. Cf. also the patriarchs (Gen 26:24; Ex 32:13; Deut 9:27; Ps 105:6; 2 Macc. 1:2; *Jub.* 31:25;

45:3; *Test. Ab.* 9:4 A; *2 Bar.* 4:4; *ARN* 43, §121 B) and Israel as a whole (Lev 25:42, 55; Deut 32:43; Is 41:8-9; 42:1, 19; 43:10; 44:1-2, 21; 45:4; 48:20; 49:3; Jer 30:10; 46:27-28; Ezek 28:25; 37:25; *2 Bar.* 44:4; *tos. B.K.* 7:5; *ARN* 43, §121 B; *Gen. Rab.* 96 NV; *p. Kid.* 1:2, §24; cf. Tob 4:14 MSS). Slaves of rulers exercised high status; see e.g., Epict. *Disc.* 1.19.19; 4.7.23; Sherk, *Empire,* 89-90; Deissmann, *Light,* 325ff passim.

50. E.g., Anderson, *Mark,* 72-73; Taylor, *Mark,* 157.

51. Webb, "Relationship," 201. For fuller discussion, see our chapter on "beyond Messiah"; also Wright, *People of God,* 248-59; Hayman, "Monotheism"; Bock, *Blasphemy,* 112-83.

52. Some scholars see a contradiction here (e.g., Kraeling, *John the Baptist,* 130; Mason, *Josephus and New Testament,* 159), but certainly the early compiler(s) of "Q" did not see any conflict.

53. Many of those Jesus touched and healed in these narratives were ceremonially unclean, limiting normal physical contact with them (cf. some limitations imposed by even blemishes; Lev 21:23; *m. Bek.* 7; CD 5.6-7; 15.15-16; 1QM 7). Some therefore suspect that John objected to Jesus' violation of ritual purity regulations (cf. Johnson, *Function,* 133). In view of the narratives themselves, however, most scholars who accept both accounts regarding John believe that it was the discrepancy between John's promise of fire-baptism and Jesus' ministry of "mere" healings that disturbed him (Dibelius, *Jesus,* 77; Ladd, *Theology,* 42; Bruce, *Time,* 20; Gundry, *Matthew,* 206; Witherington, *Christology,* 43; Davies and Allison, *Matthew,* 2:244; Hagner, *Matthew,* 300; Meier, *Marginal Jew,* 2:132).

54. Meier, *Marginal Jew,* 2:135.

55. Witherington, *Christology,* 42-43, 165; Sanders, *Figure,* 94; Wink, "Reply." See Meier, *Marginal Jew,* 2:832-37 for a thorough and convincing case that the raising of the dead claim goes back to Jesus (for the authenticity of the section, see also pp. 130-37).

56. Goppelt, *Judaism,* 77; Jeremias, *Parables,* 116; Borg, *Vision,* 165. Because these verses are likely authentic, Sanders thinks the historical Jesus probably did see his miracles in terms of Isaiah 35, hence either that he was fulfilling the prophets' hopes or that their eschatological promises would soon be fulfilled (Sanders, *Figure,* 168; cf. also Witherington, *Christology,* 44).

57. Thus e.g., Stanton, *Gospel Truth,* 186-87 (citing 4Q521; 11QMelch 18). I believe that the language of 4Q521 is not messianic but divine (cf. discussion also in Kvalbein, "Wunder"; idem, "Wonders").

58. Several scholars argue that 4Q521 may blend imagery from Is 35 with Is 61 and other precedent, perhaps Elijah's miracles (for discussion, see Wise and Tabor, "Messiah at Qumran"; Tabor, "4Q521"; Collins, "Works"; adding possibly Is 53:5, see Evans, "Apocalypse," esp. p. 696). Many scholars likewise find an echo of Is 61:1 alongside Is 35:5-6 in Jesus' saying here.

59. Davies and Allison, *Matthew,* 2:244.

60. Meier, *Marginal Jew,* 2:130 accepts the sayings, but noting the divergent wording of the narrative, suspects that the wording for the setting may be secondary. Nevertheless, Matthew and Luke agree on the basic content of the narrative structure, as Meier concurs, so either oral tradition or a written narrative must provide the framework for these otherwise isolated sayings. Jesus worded his sayings for memorization and transmission, but his followers felt more freedom to retell narratives in their own words (see our chapter on oral tradition). The narrative structure also makes historical sense (see Davies and Allison, *Matthew,* 2:244).

61. Fitzmyer thinks "coming one" alludes to Mal 3:1-4 (cf. Lk 3:15-17); Witherington thinks if this suggestion is correct then Jesus replaces that model with a more Isaianic one, but also stresses one of Fitzmyer's other suggestions, a background in Zech 9:9 LXX and Qumran texts (1QS 9.11; 4QPBless 3; Witherington, *Christology,* 43). Flusser, *Sage,* 26, thinks that "coming one" refers to Dan 7:13; although this fits Jesus' use of "Son of man," "coming" is not an uncommon designation. What may be most significant for our purposes is that the title appears characteristic to John in the tradition (Matt 3:11//Lk 3:16//Jn 1:15, 27; Matt 11:3//Lk 7:19-20; though cf. Matt 11:14; Jn 11:27; Heb 10:37; perhaps 2 Jn 7).

62. Although Herod Antipas was only a tetrarch, he would have been the first royal personage to come to most of Jesus' Galilean hearers' minds (Theissen, *Gospels in Context,* 36). Similarly his palace, consisting of multiple buildings, could be described as "houses" (Jos. *Life* 66; Theissen, *Gospels in*

Context, 36); or perhaps Jesus alludes to the fact that Antipas had another fortress palace at Machaerus, where John was imprisoned (Jos. *Ant.* 18.119; cf. Mk 6:17; France, *Matthew,* 194).

63. This need not mean that Antipas was a primary target of Jesus' hostility (cf. Jensen, "Antipas").

64. People who proved too weak for the test that awaited them were compared with the weakness of tall papyrus reeds, easily moved simply by the wind (1 Kgs 14:15; 2 Kgs 18:21; 3 Macc 2:22; cf. Is 42:3; *Ps. Sol.* 8:5; Matt 12:20; Babrius 36; a later example in Manson, *Sayings,* 68). For a survey of other interpretations (including Aesop's fable, *Reed,* later recurring in rabbinic texts; cf. Flusser, *Sage,* 30), see Theissen, *Gospels in Context,* 27. Some scholars' interpretations presuppose that Jesus here depicts John as a reed, but the text indicates Jesus depicts a reed as what John was *not.*

65. Cf. e.g., Gundry, *Matthew,* 207; Theissen, *Gospels in Context,* 26.

66. Theissen, *Gospels in Context,* 28-41.

67. Theissen, *Gospels in Context,* 33-34; Theissen and Merz, *Historical Jesus,* 101.

68. Cf. Theissen, *Gospels in Context,* 39-41.

69. At the least this made Jesus the Messiah (Jeremias, *Eucharistic Words,* 130).

70. Cf. Edgar, "Messianic Interpretation," 48; Manson, *Sayings,* 69; Mal 4:5-6. The formula quotation resembles those in Qumran (Davies and Allison, *Matthew,* 2:249 cite CD 1.13; 19.16; 16.15; 4QFlor 1.16; 4QCatena a 1-4.7; 5-6.11; 1QpHab 3.2, 13-14; 11QMelch. 2.15), which *might* suggest transmission in a source sympathetic toward the Baptist before "Q," or may have echoed the language of wilderness sectarians appropriate to speaking of John. But it is not unfamiliar elsewhere in gospel tradition.

71. Hill, *Prophecy,* 46; Stanton, *Gospel Truth,* 167-68.

72. This is a central argument for Crossan, *Historical Jesus,* 237-38, who thereby seeks to oppose Jesus to John's apocalyptic message.

73. Mark, omitting this passage from "Q," apparently relocates the quotation to Mk 1:2. If Matthew reflects "Q" material, Jesus called John "Elijah" here (Matt 11:14), but Matthew probably draws on Mk 9:13 (which he makes more explicit in Matt 17:12-13).

74. "To what shall I compare" (Matt 11:16//Lk 7:31) is traditional language among Jewish sages (e.g., *Sipre Num.* 93.1.3; *Sipre Deut.* 357.18.2), as may be comments about a wicked eschatological generation (e.g., *m. Sot.* 9:15; *Pesiq. Rab Kah.* 5:9).

75. Extolling one by contrast with another could demean the other, or it could simply be a way of praising the former by way of the latter's greatness. For the latter option, see Dion. Hal. *Demosth.* 33; Fronto *Ad Ant. Imp.* 1.2.4; Men. Rhet. 1.2, 353.9-10; 2.1-2, 376.31-377.2; 2.3, 378.18-26; 2.3, 380.21-22, 30-31; 2.6, 402.26-29; 2.6, 403.26-32; 2.6, 404.5-8 (402-4 involve praise of bride and groom); 2.10, 417.5-17; Hermog. *Progymn.* 8. On Syncrisis 19-20; Aphth. *Progymn.* 10. On Syncrisis, 43-44S, 32-33R, pp. 114-15; Philostratus *Hrk.* 27.4; 37.2; 38.1; more fully, Keener, *John,* 916-17, 966-69, 1183-84; Anderson, *Glossary,* 121.

76. *ARN* 28, §57B. The editor of Kings included superlative (and technically incompatible) praise of two different kings (2 Kgs 18:5; 23:25); the editor of Joshua likewise probably spoke hyperbolically in affirming that God had never listened to such a human entreaty before (Josh 10:14; cf. Ex 8:13; 2 Kgs 6:18).

77. Kraeling, *John the Baptist,* 139.

78. It might also be relevant that "least in the kingdom" is, in another sense, not an insult; the least is the greatest in the kingdom because God evaluates disciples according to their faithfulness in deferring all honor to him (Matt 18:1-4; 20:26-27; Mk 10:43-44; Lk 9:48). But that is probably not the point here (cf. Matt 5:19).

79. *B. Ber.* 34b; *Sanh.* 99a; *Shab.* 63a; earlier attested in Acts 3:24; cf. *Tg. Jon.* on 2 Sam 23:1, 3; *Tg. Jon.* on 1 Kgs 5:13.

80. Crossan, *Historical Jesus,* 260.

81. That is, even where their ministries differ, Jesus affirms John's ministry (Spencer, *Profiles,* 54-58).

82. Kraeling, *John the Baptist,* 11-12; cf. Aune, *Prophecy,* 135; idem, *Environment,* 56.

83. Cf. Jeremias, *Parables,* 160. Nevertheless, later rabbis severely curtailed the applicability of the text and limited it to minors in a certain age range (cf. *m. Sanh.* 8:1-2; *b. Sanh.* 72a, bar.). I treat the context of this passage more fully in Keener, *Matthew,* 340-43; I omit the rest of that discussion to keep my treatment here brief.

84. Jos. *Ant.* 18.116-19. Josephus, whose narrative involves many Herodians, usually calls this one Antipas, yet sometimes, like Mark, calls him "Herod" (Jos. *Ant.* 18.104-6, 117, 243-255).

85. See Jos. *Ant.* 18.240-55. Josephus, unlike Mark, notes that Antipas's divorce was Herodias's idea, which Theissen admits fits hellenistic custom (Theissen, *Gospels in Context,* 84); that Josephus clearly dislikes strong women is no reason to dispute his report that Herodias, sister of the powerful Agrippa I, was one. Herodias' divorce of her husband (Jos. *Ant.* 18.136) fits Greek custom but also royal behavior more generally (e.g., Jos. *Ant.* 18.361).

86. Meier, *Marginal Jew,* 2:171-76; cf. also Taylor, *Immerser,* 246-47.

87. E.g., Herod Philip's name — Theissen, *Gospels in Context,* 87; but cf. Hoehner, *Antipas,* 155-56.

88. Theissen, *Gospels in Context,* 81-97. In any event, the narrative as a whole seems to derive from a pre-Markan source (see Manson, *Servant-Messiah,* 40; Lane, *Mark,* 215).

89. See Hoehner, *Antipas,* 303-6. Given the sheer numbers of early Christian converts, some contacts with the Herodian court are not unlikely (cf. Lk 8:3; Acts 13:1). Although most Palestinian Christians seem to have been from the ranks of the relatively poor (Rom 15:26), there is no reason to doubt that there were some exceptions (cf. Lk 8:3; Acts 6:7; 13:1; Jn 18:16; perhaps Mk 15:41, 43).

90. Mark's title "king" (Mk 6:14) may be given loosely (cf. Jos. *War* 1.208-11; Sanders, *Judaism,* 542 n. 69), and could be understandable in a Galilean context (cf. comments in Theissen, *Gospels in Context,* 36), but perhaps is intended ironically, in view of what that solicited title later cost Antipas (Jos. *Ant.* 18.240-54).

91. Kraeling, *John the Baptist,* 89.

92. The Gospels call him "Philip," Josephus by the more general title "Herod"; but Herod the Great sometimes gave various sons the same name (if they had different mothers), and elsewhere showed a liking for the name "Philip." Herod Philip was son of Herod the Great and Mariamne II (Hoehner, *Antipas,* 133-36; pace Anderson, *Mark,* 168).

93. Jos. *Ant.* 18.136; cf. *Ant.* 17.341.

94. Jos. *Ant.* 18.38; Horsley, *Galilee,* 65.

95. Cf. Jos. *Ant.* 18.118; Kraeling, *John the Baptist,* 85, 90-91, 143-45; Stanton, *Gospel Truth,* 174; Hengel, *Leader,* 36.

96. Jos. *Ant.* 18.113-14, 124-25. Popular sentiments that the loss reflected divine judgment on Antipas for John's execution fit the sort of popular expectations of judgment attested elsewhere as well (e.g., Tac. *Ann.* 13.17). A father's retribution for a son-in-law's mistreatment of a daughter also fits cultural expectations (Alciphron *Fishermen* 6 [Panopê to Euthybolus], 1.6).

97. See Pliny *N.H.* 5.15.72; Wandrey, "Machaerus," 92; Piccirillo, "Machaerus."

98. See Glueck, *Rivers,* 192.

99. Cf. Kraeling, *John the Baptist,* 9-10, 92-93.

100. Mk 6:24; Manns, "Fouilles"; Riesner, "Täufer." Readers in the eastern Mediterranean would probably assume this arrangement (Corn. Nep. preface 6-7).

101. Theissen, *Gospels in Context,* 91-99 thinks this is a legendary motif cohering with other attempts to depict the Herodian women's loose morals. His examples, however, may without much difficulty illustrate that such lewdness could and *did* happen at aristocratic banquets (cf. even usual Roman banquets in Dupont, *Life,* 285; cf. the twelve-year old boy in Boring et al., *Commentary,* 97), arguing against his own position. That Herodian women's lives were probably "no more corrupt than

those of other members of their class" (p. 96) may not be saying much (cf. Rawlinson in Hill, *Matthew*, 244; for evidence of Herodian women's wealthy lifestyle, cf. e.g., Shoemaker, "Earring").

102. Cf. Jos. *Ant.* 18.137; Hoehner, *Antipas*, 155-56; Theissen, *Gospels in Context*, 90-91; Kraeling, *John the Baptist*, 87. Philip died c. 33-34 (Jos. *Ant.* 18.106).

103. Cf. Lane, *Mark*, 221; Nineham, *Mark*, 175; Hoehner, *Antipas*, 157; Esth 1:11.

104. Anderson, *Mark*, 166.

105. Cf. stories in Livy 39.42.8-39.43.5; Val. Max. 2.9.3; Seneca *Controv.* 9.2 (hypothetical); Appian *C.W.* 4.4.20; Plutarch *M. Cato* 17.2-3 (while drunk); Tac. *Ann.* 14.57, 59, 64; Suet. *Calig.* 32.1; Dio Cass. *R.H.* 62.14.1; ordering deaths during a feast, Jos. *Ant.* 13.380 (cf. Sil. It. 11.51-54); bringing heads in Val. Max. 9.2.1; Seneca *Controv.* 10.3.1; 10.3.5; Seneca *Suasoriae* 6.20; Pliny *Nat. Hist.* 33.14.48; Quintus Curtius 7.4.40; Arrian *Alex.* 4.17.7; Tac. *Hist.* 2.16; Suet. *Aug.* 13.1; Plut. *Caesar* 48.2; *Cicero* 49.1; *Sulla* 32.2; Jos. *Ant.* 20.98. For displaying heads after executions, see Polyb. 11.18.6; Cic. *Phil.* 11.2.5; Sall. *Jug.* 12.5; Val. Max. 9.9.1; Sil. It. 2.202-5; 15.813-14; Appian *C.W.* 1.8.71-72; 2.12.86; Tac. *Hist.* 1.49; 2.49; 3.62; Suet. *Galba* 20.2; Herodian 3.7.7; 5.4.4; 8.5.9; 8.6.7; 2 Kgs 10:6-7.

106. Jos. *Ant.* 18.240-44. Such behavior was known to enrage other rulers as well (Plut. *Themistocles* 29.5).

107. Jos. *Ant.* 18.252-54; Kraeling, *John the Baptist*, 86; Lane, *Mark*, 211.

108. As noted earlier in the book, Sanders doubts that repentance was as central to Jesus' teaching as John's (Sanders, *Figure*, 231-32; cf. idem, *Jesus and Judaism*, 109), but the same appeal to word statistics could deny the centrality of love in his message despite the explicit claim in Mk 12:29-30. Although Jesus may have used the *term* less than John, examples of radical conversion show the centrality of the concept in his ministry (e.g., Mk 2:14-17), and Luke's emphasis on the term does not negate the occasional use of "repentance" earlier in the tradition (Matt 11:20-21//Lk 10:13); and the idea that Jesus did not set out many "stipulations and conditions" for the Kingdom (Sanders, *Figure*, 234) needs serious nuancing (cf. e.g., Mk 10:17-25). John undoubtedly influenced Jesus (e.g., Michaels, *Servant*, 1-24; see discussion above), and Sanders himself accepts that Jesus must have mostly agreed with the message of the prophet who baptized him (*Figure*, 94; see further Chilton, "Repentance"). Jesus clearly was not interested only in encouraging disciples; his message was for the whole people (Borg, *Conflict*, 70; contrast Sanders, *Jesus and Judaism*, 112-13, but cf. Sanders, *Jesus and Judaism*, 118).

109. For substantial continuity between John and Jesus in their eschatological message, see e.g., Schweitzer, *Quest*, 240; Sanders, *Jesus and Judaism*, 91-94; Sanders, "Know," 57; Ehrman, *Prophet*, 185.

110. Sanders, *Jesus and Judaism*, 11; idem, *Figure*, 94; idem, "Know," 57; Meier, *Marginal Jew*, 2:100-5; Stanton, *Gospel Truth*, 164-66; Webb, "Relationship," 214-18; pace Bultmann, *Tradition*, 251. Although Matthew and Luke could draw from Mark, this narrative is probably also in Q (Meier, *Marginal Jew*, 2:103), and Mark may well have drawn from it.

111. Theon *Progymn.* 5.52-56.

112. Taylor, *Immerser*, 321 (see also 294-99).

113. Cf. Stauffer, *Jesus*, 65. The lack of water in many places in Galilee could explain its absence in much of his itinerant ministry (cf. Kraeling, *John the Baptist*, 174), though not around the lake of Galilee.

Notes to Chapter 12

1. In these and subsequent introductory quotations from Gospels, I have paraphrased where I believed this would help communicate the sense in English. Because of variant forms between Matthew and Luke, I have cited one or the other even though preferring those presumed to be from "Q."

2. For the value of his using his Galilean Jewish context, see e.g., Osiek, "Jesus and Galilee"; Freyne, *Galilean*; idem, "Jesus and Archaeology"; Sawicki, *Crossing Galilee*; Race, "Influence"; Schuler,

"Archaeology." On Galilee, see further discussions in Freyne, *Galilee*; Freyne, *Galilee and Gospel*; Horsley, *Galilee*.

3. Theissen and Merz, *Historical Jesus*, 101.

4. Flusser, *Sage*, 2.

5. For the deep urban/rural divide in Mediterranean antiquity, cf. MacMullen, *Social Relations*, 15, 32; Lee, "Unrest," 128; Longus 2.22; Alciph. *Farm.* 11 (Sitalces to Oenopion, his son), 3.14 (cf. 38 [Euthydicus to Philiscus], 3.40, ¶3); *Fish.* 4 (Cymothoüs to Tritonis), 1.4, ¶4; Philost. *Hrk.* 4.6-10. Roman law treated country dwellers as less educated (Robinson, *Criminal Law*, 17), and the urban elite expressed surprise at educated rural persons (Pliny *Ep.* 7.25.4-6).

6. E.g., *m. Ned.* 2:4. In later sources, see also *p. Hag.* 3:4, §1; for Judean sources with antipathy toward Galilee, see discussion in Vermes, *Jesus the Jew*, 46-57; Freyne, *Galilee*, 1-2.

7. Again, partly reflecting the urban/rural divide. Pharisees seem to have been primarily an urban movement (cf. also perhaps Jos. *Ant.* 18.15), whereas the Jesus movement began as a primarily rural movement (becoming urbanized shortly after the resurrection and only later penetrating into the rural areas outside Palestine; cf. Judge, *Pattern*, 60-61; Schmeller, "Weg").

8. *Tos. Demai* 1:10. It may be true that particular customs did predominate in some regions: most cities and regions in the Empire had some idiosyncratic traditions (e.g., Paus. 2.1.1).

9. This is not to deny abundant evidence that Jesus' movement also continued to flourish in Galilee; see Saunders, "Synagogues"; Meyers, "Judaism and Christianity," 69, 71. Much earlier, Julian repeatedly calls Christians "Galileans" (see in Stern, *Authors*, 502-72, passim); cf. Epict. *Diatr.* 4.7.6. But while some construct a Galilean "community" for "Q," its Galilean features likely simply represent authentic Jesus tradition (Dunn, *New Perspective*, 27), whether composed in Galilee or not.

10. With e.g., Dunn, "Synagogue," 207-12.

11. Freyne, *Galilee*, 2 (citing Grundmann, *Jesus der Galiläer*, from 1941). Schürer's construct is now recognized as fallacious (Reed, *Archaeology*, 53-54). Most readers will not need to be reminded of the dominant ideology in the time and place in which Grundmann was writing. Larger worldviews have long shaped constructs of Galilee (see Moxnes, "Construction").

12. Freyne, *Galilee*, 169.

13. Freyne, *Galilee*, 170; idem, "Jesus and Archaeology"; Reed, *Archaeology*, 52.

14. See Reed, *Archaeology*, 100-38. For the contrast between Sepphoris' elite and the countryside, see Reed, *Archaeology*, 134-35.

15. Freyne, *Galilee*, 143-44. For an earlier period, see especially 1 Macc 5:15; cf. also Syon, "Evidence." Gentile sites cluster on Galilee's *perimeter* (Reed, *Archaeology*, 51-52).

16. Goodman, *State*, 41-53; Stambaugh and Balch, *Environment*, 93; cf. Overman, "Archaeology."

17. Vale, "Sources."

18. See Chancey, *Myth*; idem, "How Jewish?"; Eddy and Boyd, *Legend*, 116-19 and the sources they cite (esp. Jonathan Reed; Mark Chancey; Sean Freyne; and Eric Meyers).

19. See Levine, *Hellenism*, 94-95; Strange, "Galilee," 395-96; Chancey, *Galilee*; Gregory, "Galilee."

20. Goodman, *State*, 31-32.

21. Meyers, "Regionalism"; cf. Crossan, *Historical Jesus*, 19.

22. Goodman, *State*, 88-89. Hellenization was limited before Antipas (see Chancey, "Milieu"; idem, *Galilee*; the approval of Chancey in Gregory, "Galilee"). I would probably allow for more hellenization (and certainly Greek language) than Chancey does, but his research remains invaluable and challenges wrong-headed assumptions of radical hellenization.

23. Horsley, *Galilee*, 250-51, also commenting on the lack of public baths in the villages. Public baths were a necessity for urban hellenists (e.g., Diog. Laert. 6.2.40; Mart. *Epig.* 12.82; Paus. 2.3.5; Apul. *Metam.* 2.2; Yegül, "Complex"; among Palestinian Jews, cf. *tos. Ber.* 2:20; *B.K.* 9:12).

24. A portrayal that would probably be necessary to sustain the Cynic thesis.

25. Cf. already Jeremias, *Promise*, 35. Those who wish to place Jesus in a hellenistic context have

inappropriately exaggerated the cultural influence of these two cities on the surrounding countryside; see more correctly Horsley, *Galilee*, 174-81, who rightly cites Jos. *Life* 374-75, 384 and other evidence.

26. Freyne, *Galilee*, 216-17; cf. e.g., *b. Erub.* 53b.

27. Although most of the texts cited by Vermes, *Jesus the Jew*, 54, do not support his case, *m. Ned.* 2:4 does. The Palestinian Amoraic account of Johanan ben Zakkai's rejection in Galilee might also be instructive (Vermes, *Jesus the Jew*, 56-57).

28. Cf. e.g., Jos. *Ant.* 20.43; Malinowski, "Tendencies"; Horsley, *Galilee*, 152-55; cf. Mayer, "Anfang"; Manns, "Galilée"; Meyers and Strange, *Archaeology*, 37-38, 45; Dunn, "Synagogue," 207-12. Indeed, they may have been more strict with respect to some traditional customs than Judea was (*m. Pes.* 4:5; cf. especially in upper Galilee, Meyers, "Regionalism").

29. E.g., Akiba (*p. R.H.* 4:6, §1). That halakhic customs varied is clear (e.g., *p. Ket.* 4:14, §1, following *m. Ket.* 4:14; *p. Ned.* 2:4, §3).

30. Freyne, "Relations"; Freyne, *Galilee*, 178-90 (the exception being Sepphoris, Jos. *Life* 348-49).

31. Freyne, *Galilee*, 150-52.

32. See e.g., Reed, *Archaeology*, 44-51; Dunn, "Synagogue," 207-12.

33. Cf. Reed, *Archaeology*, 44-45; Reich, "Jars"; Safrai, "Home," 741; Avigad, "Flourishing," 59; idem, *Jerusalem*, 183; cf. Schwank, "Wasserkrüge"; Magen, "Yrwslym"; Gal, "T'syyt."

34. Reed, *Archaeology*, 49-51 (esp. 49 on Sepphoris). Cf. Jn 2:6.

35. Reed, *Archaeology*, 49; on 45-47, he deals with the usefulness of these in identifying Jewish sites; on 47-49, Jewish burial practices. See also Eric Meyers in Eshel and Meyers, "Pools" (with Eshel being more skeptical); Reich, "Baths." Roman secondary burial (of ashes in urns or boxes) may have influenced the custom (Levine, *Hellenism*, 67; McCane, "Burial Practices," 174), but Jewish bone burial remains distinctive and limited especially to this period.

36. Reed, "Contributions," 53.

37. Berlin, "Life."

38. Vermes, *Jesus and Judaism*, 5, 153 n. 8; Davies, *Setting*, 450; Liefeld, "Preacher," 144.

39. See Freyne, "Religion." For Galilean loyalty to Jerusalem, see especially Jos. *Life* 198.

40. Goodman, *State*, 93-118; cf. Freyne, "Religion." The Pharisees on the whole were probably centered in Jerusalem rather than in Galilee (Vermes, *Jesus the Jew*, 56-57; Neusner, *Crisis*, 38; but cf. perhaps Jos. *Ant.* 20.43), and their immediate successors settled in Jamnia, which was also in Judea.

41. Goodman, *State*, 107. (The rabbis' idealism concerning tithes probably also did not commend itself to more agrarian peasants; see Goodman, *State*, 178.)

42. Technically he was from Gamala across the Jordan (Jos. *Ant.* 18.4; Witherington, *Christology*, 88-89).

43. Vermes, *Jesus the Jew*, 46-48; Vermes, *Jesus and Judaism*, 4-5 (especially on Upper Galilee). Zeitlin and some others even argued that Josephus used "Galilean" as a revolutionary rather than geographical title; Zeitlin, "Galileans"; Loftus, "Note"; cf. idem, "Revolts" (though he could be correct about continuing Hasmonean sympathies).

44. Armenti, "Galileans"; Freyne, "Galileans"; Bilde, "Galilaea."

45. E.g., his military praise in Jos. *War* 3.41.

46. Freyne, *Galilee*, 162.

47. Freyne, *Galilee*, 195; Witherington, *Christology*, 88-90.

48. Although Josephus claims three million residents in Galilee in 67 CE (*Life* 235; *War* 3.43), Avi-Yonah, "Geography," 109, suggests that his 60,000 recruits from there may suggest a likelier population of perhaps 750,000 (*War* 2.583).

49. Some others offer still lower estimates; Hoehner, *Antipas*, 291-95, suspects roughly 200,000 (about 266 persons per square mile). Multiplying the number of known settlements (from literary or archaeological sources) by Galilee's population density in the late nineteenth century, Goodman, *State*, 32, suggests 300,000. But these lower estimates may depend too much on extant information,

underestimating how much evidence has been lost. Galilee seems to have been densely populated with villages (Freyne, *Galilee*, 144, citing the 204 villages in Jos. *Life* 235).

50. Freyne, *Galilee*, 171.

51. Reed, *Archaeology*, 215-16.

52. Freyne, *Galilee*, 144-45, citing Jos. *Life* 58; cf. Freyne, "Galileans."

53. Goodman, *State*, 120; Horsley, *Galilee*, 251. Freyne, "Ethos," argues for some limited trade connections but notes that this does not indicate a cultural or religious continuum.

54. Freyne, *Galilee*, 146-47.

55. Reed, *Archaeology*, 97-99.

56. Meyers and Strange, *Archaeology*, 56 (suggesting 1600-2000 inhabitants); more recent estimates are even lower (Stanton, *Gospel Truth*, 112; Horsley, *Galilee*, 193), though these match other Galilean villages (Horsley, *Galilee*, 193).

57. Indeed, its insignificance invited attempts at biblical justification (such as Matt 2:23; Davies and Allison, *Matthew*, 1:274).

58. Though Jn 1:46 might reflect local civic rivalry (Barnett, *Reliable*, 64), a common issue in antiquity (MacMullen, *Social Relations*, 58-59). Even Jesus' invitation to a wedding in Cana in John 2 fits the sites' relative proximity (on which see e.g., Charlesworth, "Research and Archaeology," 39; Richardson, "Khirbet Qana"), despite John's failure to emphasize this point; for further discussion, see Keener, *John*, 495-96.

59. Theissen and Merz, *Historical Jesus*, 164-65. See e.g., Mk 1:9, 24; 10:47; 14:67; 16:6; Matt 2:23; Lk 2:4; Jn 1:45-46; 18:5-7; Acts 2:22; 3:6; 10:38; and a possibly derogatory title for the movement in Acts 24:5.

60. Stanton, *Gospel Truth*, 115.

61. Davies and Allison, *Matthew*, 1:378, following Meyers and Strange, *Archaeology*, 58.

62. Sanders, *Figure*, 103; Stanton, *Gospel Truth*, 115; Horsley, *Galilee*, 194. The more current, lower estimates appear to be more likely (this village is no more well known to Josephus' readers in *Life* 403 than any other in the vicinity), but more information may force us to revise the estimates.

63. Some believed that coming from a famous city was necessary for happiness (Plut. *Demosth.* 1.1); Plutarch thinks that life in a famous city is necessary only if one needs exposure (*Demosth.* 2.1; cf. Jn 7:3-4).

64. See Farmer, "Peter and Paul," 46-50. Those located near there may have also been interested (cf. Jn 1:44).

65. See *m. B.B.* 1:5; Davies and Allison, *Matthew*, 1:378.

66. Theissen, *Gospels in Context*, 50; note especially the miracle-working Jacob of Capernaum. On the application of some rabbinic uses of *minim* to Christians, see e.g., the sources cited in Keener, *John*, 197-203, 211-12.

67. Charlesworth, *Jesus Within Judaism*, 109, 111-12; Loffreda, "Scoperte"; Strange and Shanks, "House," 26-37; Hengel, *Property*, 27; Blue, "House Church," 138. Some other scholars, however, find the tradition and supporting archaeological evidence to be relatively late (Taylor, "Capernaum").

68. In 1910, Burkitt, *Sources*, 14, expressed skepticism that anyone would invent Galilean towns missing in the OT, like Capernaum and nearby Chorazin. One might argue the same for Cana (Jn 2:1-2; Keener, *John*, 495-96), though (with a few exceptions) I have deliberately excluded John from this work's consideration.

69. Theissen, *Gospels in Context*, 49.

70. Mk 8:22, 26; Jos. *Life* 399; *War* 2.168; *Ant.* 18.28; Pliny *N.H.* 5.71; Ptolemy *Geography* 5.16.4.

71. Euseb. *Onom.* 333; perhaps *b. Men.* 85a, but cf. *tos. Men.* 9:2. In a much later period, see Yeivin, "Ark," 75; Goodenough, *Symbols*, 193-99; Turnheim, "Decoration."

72. Adinolfi, "Lago."

73. Arav and Rousseau, "Bethsaïde."

74. Charlesworth, "Sketch," 97. The presence of Greek culture in Bethsaida may also help explain

Jn 12:21 (Charlesworth, "Sketch," 97-98); that the town remained in another tetrarchy officially outside Antipas' "Galilee" until 34 CE might also allow for Decapolis Greeks to know Philip (Theissen, *Gospels in Context*, 50).

75. Theissen, *Gospels in Context*, 51 n. 73. Rejection after a miracle may be a form of negative acclamation, but otherwise is virtually unparalleled outside early Christian texts (Theissen, *Miracle Stories*, 72).

76. Witherington, *Christology*, 166.

77. Acts 21:3-6; 27:3; Theissen, *Gospels in Context*, 52.

78. Witherington, *Christology*, 166.

79. So Bultmann, *Tradition*, 112. Also pace Bultmann, the prophecy looks back on only the Galilean ministry as completed, and that only in Matthew's redaction (Theissen, *Gospels in Context*, 51 n. 73).

80. Greek sources suggest that they may not always have been of the highest reputation (Horsley, *Documents* 5:100), although around the Lake of Galilee the demands of local economy probably would outweigh any influence from imported perspectives.

81. Freyne, *Galilee*, 241. Cf. *ILS* 7486; Wilkinson, *Jerusalem*, 29-30; Hengel, *Property*, 27.

82. Horsley, *Galilee*, 194.

83. Safrai, "Home," 747. Cf. fishing implements found in Bethsaida (Arav, "Bethsaida"). Cf. also the abundance of small boats available for crossing the sea from one town to another (Jos. *Life* 163-64); on the recovered Galilean fishing boat (26.5 by 7.5 by 4.5 feet), see Riesner, "Neues"; Wachsmann, "Galilee Boat"; Stone, "Galilee Boat"; Andiñach, "Barca"; Peachey, "Kinneret Boat."

84. Neusner, *Beginning*, 23. A custom of eating fish on the Sabbath (Safrai, "Home," 747) may have obtained this early, though Galileans near the lake surely ate fish much more regularly.

85. Horsley, *Documents* 5:99. Among the poor elsewhere, smoked fish could rank "the most popular item" in a general market's sales for a day (*P. Oxy.* 520; Lewis, *Life*, 136).

86. Some aspects of this "M" parable, of course, reflect Matthew's stylistic adjustments, probably including weeping and gnashing of teeth, which appears in "Q" (Matt 8:12//Lk 13:28), but which Matthew apparently transfers to various other sayings as well (Matt 13:42, 50; 22:13; 24:51; 25:30).

87. Davies and Allison, *Matthew*, 2:393-94.

88. Cf. also Lachs, *Commentary*, 58. Wilkins, *Discipleship*, 43-91, finds characteristics of master-disciple relationships in some OT relationships, most convincingly the prophetic groups (Samuel's and Elisha's mentorship) and, less demonstrably, the scribal tradition (cf. perhaps CD 8.20-21).

89. Witherington, *Christology*, 129-30.

Notes to Chapter 13

1. Charlesworth, *Jesus Within Judaism*, 20.

2. Many, like Witherington, *Sage*, 345-46, rank Jesus among the former.

3. See e.g., *m. Ab.* 1-3.

4. E.g., Freyne, *Galilee*, 249-50; Hengel, *Leader*, 42-50; Smith, *Magician*, 22-23; cf. Vermes, "Jesus the Jew," 118.

5. E.g., Jeremias, *Theology*, 77; Vermes, *Jesus and Judaism*, 30-31; cf. Borg, *Vision*, 97-124.

6. Safrai, "Education," 965; cf. idem, "Home," 762; *Sipre Deut.* 43.3.7; 48.2.4, 6; Liefeld, "Preacher," 89-133. Cf. the related Greek tradition of traveling philosophers (see Diog. Laert. 2.22; Liefeld, "Preacher," 26-59). Liefeld uncovers little evidence for itinerant rabbis before 70 (p. 119), but this is hardly surprising given the scarcity of evidence for rabbis before 70 in general.

7. Cf. Meeks, *Moral World*, 117; Hengel, *Leader*, 55-56.

8. Vermes, *Religion*, 54. Jesus may have admittedly made little of traditional covenant boundaries (Holmén, "Covenant"; idem, *Covenant Thinking*). Even apocalyptists, who clearly were not compos-

ing midrash, include midrashic sections and elements (Aune, *Prophecy,* 113, noting the midrash on Is 24:17-23 in *1 En.* 54:1–56:4 and 64:1–68:1).

9. Cf. Jos. *Apion* 2.178; Philo *Legat.* 115, 210, cited by Vermes himself (*Religion,* 186).

10. All of the above scholars would differ from Mack, *Myth,* 64, who (against our evidence concerning first-century Galilean Judaism) suggests that Jesus employed only wisdom thought and may have been as conversant in the Cynic thought of Meleager as in the Bible.

11. Chilton and Evans, "Scriptures"; on allusions, see Allison, "Allusive Jesus." Jesus may have been eclectic in his approach; it often seems unclear which of various Jewish interpretive approaches he followed at given times (so Meier, "Historical Law").

12. Although elders and synagogue "rulers" undoubtedly welcomed scribal exposition when available (cf. Acts 13:15), in Galilee these leaders were probably frequently simply the village equivalent of municipal aristocracies, the most respected community leaders.

13. Hill, *Prophecy,* 50.

14. See Davies, *Setting,* 422-25; Stein, *Method and Message,* 1-3; Carlston, "Maxims"; Meeks, *Moral World,* 117; Cohen, *Maccabees,* 122; Vermes, *Religion,* 50-70, 76-119. For Jesus' Jewish teaching techniques, e.g., in the "sermon on the mount/plain," see e.g., Kennedy, *Classical Rhetoric,* 126; Songer, "Sermon"; Stevens, "Sermon."

15. E.g., Freyne, "Servant Community," 111; Charlesworth, *Jesus Within Judaism,* 44; Eve, *Miracles,* 384-86; Ehrman, *Prophet,* 139; especially Holmén, *Covenant Thinking,* relevant to conflict narratives (treated in a subsequent chapter).

16. E.g., Tarfon's "May I bury my sons," *tos. Hag.* 3:33; *Shab.* 13:5; *Sipra V. D. Deho.* par. 4.7.3.2; *b. Shab.* 16b-17a, 116a; *p. Yoma* 1:1. Ancients also observed that artists, writers and thinkers each had their own style (Fronto *Ad Verum Imp.* 1.1.1-3); various schools also had "their own sectarian idiolect" (Alexander, "IPSE DIXIT," 121).

17. See Jeremias, *Theology,* 22-37; Tannehill, *Sword;* Stein, *Method and Message,* 13-32.

18. Scholars often comment on the meaning of this distinctive trait; see Jeremias, *Theology,* 35-36; cf. Hill, *Prophecy,* 64-66; Aune, *Prophecy,* 164-65; Witherington, *Christology,* 186-88; Marshall, *Origins,* 43-44. Oath formulas sometimes appear in solemn sayings, including among Gentiles (e.g., Mus. Ruf. 2, p. 38.17; 3, p. 42.2, 11); but "Amen" is Aramaic (and Hebrew), limiting the range of available cultural parallels. The doubled "Amen" in John is presumably emphatic (cf. *Pes. Rab Kah.* 16:4), perhaps used by John for emphasis but potentially also recalling a rarer usage of Jesus.

19. Some elements of his style in the Gospels may reflect the usual patterning of oral tradition (Dunn, *New Perspective,* 115), or a teaching style designed to be recalled accordingly.

20. Cf. Gottlieb, "Abot." For many of Jesus' sayings as proverbial, see e.g., Damschen, "Proverbs," 81. Riddles also appear in classical sources (Gärtner, "Riddles").

21. E.g., *m. Ab.* 2:8; *ARN* 36 A; further examples elsewhere in this book. Greek and Roman audiences were also comfortable with these figures of speech (cf. *Rhet. Alex.* 11, 1430b.16-19, *Rhet. Her.* 4.33.44; Cicero *Orator* 40.139; Quint. *Inst.* 8.6.73-76; Arist. *Rhet.* 3.11.15; Demetrius *Style* 2.124-27; 3.161; further Anderson, *Glossary,* 122-24), though this rhetoric may have been disseminated more commonly in the marketplace (cf. e.g., *PGM* 36.69, 134, 211-12, 320) than in deliberative speeches. For examples of hyperbole, see e.g., Dion. Hal. *Demosth.* 18 with *Isaeus* 20; Philost. *V.A.* 8.7; Philost. *Hrk.* 48.11. Use of shock to gain hearers' attention appeared in Cynics (Diog. Laert. 6.2.34) but could be useful rhetoric more generally (Dion. Hal. *Lysias* 24), and appears in Jewish circles (cf. tales in Young, *Theologian,* 171-80).

22. Cf. Stein, *Method and Message,* 8-12; Witherington, *Sage,* 3.

23. See further examples below; in the later Targumim, see Chilton, "Targum and Gospels," 245-47, esp. 246.

24. See *m. Ab.* 3:17; *Suk.* 2:10; *tos. Ber.* 1:11; 6:18; *B.K.* 7:2-4; *Hag.* 2:5; *Sanh.* 1:2; 8:9; *Sipra Shemini Mekhilta deMiluim* 99.2.5; *Behuq.* pq. 2.262.1.9; *Sipre Num.* 84.2.1; 93.1.3; *Sipre Deut.* 1.9.2; 1.10.1; 308.2.1; 308.3.1; 309.1.1; 309.2.1; *ARN* 1, 2, 6, 8, 9, 11, 14, 16, 19, 23, 24, 27, 28, 31A; 2, §10; 4, §14; 8, §24; 9, §24; 12,

§29; 13, §§30, 32; 18, §§39-40; 30, §63; 32, §§69, 70B; 35, §77; *b. Sanh.* 107a; *Pesiq. Rab Kah.* 1:2; 3:8; 14:5; 27:6; *Pesiq. Rab Kah.* Sup. 1:11; 3:2; 7:3; *Eccl. Rab.* 9:8, §1; cf. Bultmann, *Tradition,* 179; Johnston, "Parabolic Interpretations," 531, 630.

25. See *tos. Suk.* 2:6; *Sipra Shemini Mekhilta deMiluim* 99.2.2; *Behuq.* pq.3.263.1.5, 8; *Sipre Num.* 84.1.1; 86.1.1; 89.4.2; *Sipre Deut.* 3.1.1; 11.1.2; 26.3.1; 28.1.1; 29.4.1; 36.4.5; 40.6.1; 43.8.1; 43.16.1; 45.1.2; 48.1.3; 53.1.3; 306.4.1; 306.7.1; 309.5.1; 312.1.1; 313.1.1; 343.1.2; 343.5.2; *p. Taan.* 2:1, §11; *Lev. Rab.* 27:8; cf. Johnston, "Parabolic Interpretations," 531; Vermes, *Religion,* 92; Smith, *Tannaitic Parallels,* 179; Jeremias, *Parables,* 101.

26. Fields do figure prominently as settings in rabbinic parables, though their meaning is ad hoc rather than standard (Johnston, "Parabolic Interpretations," 596). But whereas royal courts appear only in a few parables attributed to Jesus (Matt 18:23; 22:2 [some contrast here Lk 14:16]; cf. Matt 25:34; Lk 14:31; 19:12), they are common in rabbinic parables, where the king represents God: e.g., *tos. Ber.* 6:18; *Suk.* 2:6; *Mek. Beshallah* 6.8-9; *Shirata* 2.131ff; 3.30, 65; 4.54ff; *Amalek* 2.22-23; *Bahodesh* 5.2-3, 82-83; 6.114ff; 8.72ff; *Sipra Shemini Mekhilta deMiluim* 99.2.2, 5; *Behuq.* pq. 2.262.1.9; pq. 3.263.1.5; *Sipre Num.* 84.2.1; 86.1.1; *Sipre Deut.* 3.1.1; 8.1.2; 11.1.2; 28.1.1; 29.4.1; 36.4.5; 43.8.1; 43.16.1; 45.1.2; 48.1.3; 312.1.1; 313.1.1; 343.5.2; *ARN* 2; 16; 19; 24; 25A; 2, §10; 8, §24B; 34, §77. Cf. Neusner, *Beginning,* 23.

27. Earlier biblical prophets had also depicted judgments, especially those of the end-time, in agricultural terms (Is 32:13-17; 35:1-2; 44:3-4; Jer 31:28; 51:33; Joel 3:13; Amos 8:1-2; Riesenfeld, *Tradition,* 150).

28. It appears also further to the east, but complaints about late traditions in the Gospels usually look for hellenistic, not other Middle Eastern, elements. Our published first-century Gospels are in Greek but reflect earlier traditions.

29. Boring et al., *Commentary,* 89, compares Aesop *Fables* 172, but while this example illustrates the widespread use of agricultural images in antiquity, it differs from Jesus' and rabbinic parables. While it offers a moral lesson as any narrative would, it does not provide symbolic correspondences as frequently as in Jesus' parables (e.g., the mustard seed represents the kingdom).

30. Johnston, "Patristic Parables," 226. This in spite of the fact that Greek models and even story lines (e.g., in Aesop's fables) did affect rabbinic parables (Stern, *Parables,* 7; cf. also Mack, *Myth,* 160 n. 18). Greeks borrowed the ancient near eastern form of story parables called fables (already attested in the Sumerian period; see Perry, "Introduction," xxviii-xxxiv; Babrius 2.introduction 1-6). Hesiod used animal fables as riddles too obvious to require explanation (*WD* 202-11), and Aesop's fables were known as early as Aristophanes in the late fifth century BCE (*Birds* 651-53). Yet Greeks typically called these stories "fables," not parables (Theon *Progymn.* 3).

31. With many, e.g., Theissen and Merz, *Historical Jesus,* 337-39. Although demurring from this consensus, Mack, *Myth,* 61, acknowledges it. I affirm the excellent work of Snodgrass, *Stories;* it appeared too late for my use here, but readers can find fuller interaction with secondary literature there than I provide in my brief treatment here.

32. Cf. also *1 En.* 1:2-3.

33. 1 Kgs 5:12 (4:32); Ezek 17:2; and Ps 78:2 (Stern, *Parables,* 290 n. 10).

34. Also Jos. *Ant.* 8.148-49; cf. Jesus' questions (e.g., Mk 11:29). See further Stein, *Method and Message,* 35-36; Manson, *Sayings,* 29; Gerhardsson, "Meshalim"; Vermes, *Religion,* 90.

35. Stern, *Parables,* 9-10; cf. Scott, *Parable,* 7-11.

36. A variety of forms also appear in Jesus' and rabbinic parables. Johnston, "Parabolic Interpretations," 520-26 classifies Tannaitic parables into groups including example stories (pp. 520-22); short similes and metaphors (pp. 522-23; pace Dodd, these usually are called *mashal* and have standard parable formulas); and parabolized fables (pp. 523-24). The example stories in the Gospels all appear in Luke (Lk 10:30-37; 12:16-21; 16:19-31; 18:10-14; perhaps 14:7-11, 12-14; Johnston, "Parabolic Interpretations," 636 n. 4) and example stories may be distinct from normal parables; but Bultmann's distinction between similitudes and parables is untenable ("Parabolic Interpretations," 636).

37. E.g., Quint. *Inst.* 5.11.1; *Rhet. Her.* 4.34.45-46; 4.49.62; Virg. *Ecl.* 3.104-7.

38. Pace Mack, *Myth*, 157-58, who merely summarizes Greco-Roman rhetoric's use of the term *parabolē* and then applies it directly to Jesus' parables. Aristotle used *parabolē* for brief comparisons rhetoricians used as proofs, generally similes; he called genuine stories (like most of Jesus' parables) *logoi* instead, though later rhetoricians also applied the term to narrative illustrations (Stern, *Parables*, 10).

39. Young, *Parables*, 1.

40. Hill, *Prophecy*, 58-59.

41. E.g., *1 En.* 1:2-3; 37-71; cf. Hermas *Sim.* 3.1-10; Hammershaimb, "Lignelser"; Witherington, *Christology*, 243.

42. E.g., 4Q302a (a wisdom parable); *Test. Job* 18:7-8.

43. Before the period of the Gospels, see e.g., Sir 1:24; 3:29; 20:20; 39:2; 47:17; cf. Sir 18:29.

44. E.g., *m. Sot.* 9:15; *Mek. Pisha* 1.82-84; *b. Ber.* 61b.

45. E.g., Stewart, "Parable Form"; Cave, "Parables," 387; Johnston, "Observations," 355; Sandmel, *Judaism*, 105; Barth, "Ethik"; Maisonneuve, "Parables"; Goulder, *Midrash*, 47-69; Scott, *Parable*, 14; Young, *Parables*, 317-18; D'Angelo, "Background"; Vermes, *Religion*, 97.

46. See Johnston, "Parabolic Interpretations," 628-33. For comparisons between rabbinic and Jesus' parables, see also briefly Newman, "Parables" (following Johnston); for comparisons and contrasts, see Porton, "Parable," 207-9.

47. Vermes, *Religion*, 97; cf. Young, *Parables*, 3. Few parables are attributed to the earliest teachers noted in rabbinic texts, perhaps because these teachers appear so infrequently. Three items attributed to Hillel are not very developed; 11 come from ben Zakkai's generation; 33 from the next generation (10 from R. Gamaliel II alone); 39 from the next; and 93 from the next (49 of which come from two rabbis); see Johnston, "Parabolic Interpretations," 498-500; Vermes, *Religion*, 97 n. 21. Unlike Jesus and perhaps some other early wisdom sages, among the rabbis they occur in predominantly midrashic (exegetical) rather than narrative contexts (see Johnston, "Parabolic Interpretations," 632; Scott, *Parable*, 15-16; Vermes, *Religion*, 114-15; for exceptions, see Johnston, "Parabolic Interpretations," 503). Even in Aramaic contexts, rabbinic parables appear in Hebrew (excepting some vernacular conversation in them; Young, *Parables*, 40-42).

48. Pace the astonishing argument from silence in Jeremias, *Parables*, 12. A story about R. Eliezer in the early second century (see Herford, *Christianity*, 137-45, 388; Moore, *Judaism*, 2:250; Dalman, *Jesus in Talmud*, 36-37) indicates the rabbinic disdain for using Jesus' teaching, and in the vast majority of rabbinic sources he is simply ignored.

49. With Abrahams, *Studies* 1:106; Johnston, "Parabolic Interpretations," 43.

50. Taylor, *Formation*, 104; Johnston, "Parabolic Interpretations," 635. Rabbinic parables were sometimes attributed to different authors (Young, *Parables*, 179), probably in part due to their reuse by other rabbis; recycling earlier story lines was a sign of respect for the story's content (e.g., Terence *Eunuch* 30-43 argues that recycling characters is acceptable).

51. E.g., Mk 4:3-20, 26-32; 12:1-9; 13:28; Matt 20:1; Lk 12:16; 13:6; cf. Neusner, *Beginning*, 23.

52. Johnston, "Parabolic Interpretations," 633-34. As Scott, *Parable*, 39 observes, Jesus' parables employ traditional mythemes but function counterculturally, hence as "antimyth."

53. Johnston, "Parabolic Interpretations," 508 (but cf. 626).

54. E.g., Stein, *Method and Message*, 44-45; Dodd, *Parables*, 11; Vermes, *Religion*, 90-91; see more fully Payne, "Authenticity of Parables"; idem, "Sower." Pace Mack, *Myth*, 146-47, who resorts to suggesting that most scholars accept authenticity from motives of convenience! Mack, *Lost Gospel*, 34 seems correct to observe that few parables (at least in the sense of story parables) appear in Q (unless Mark heavily mined Q's parables, but the evidence for such a suggestion, such as Matthew and Luke omitting Mk 4:32's "large" branches, is quite limited), but works from the assumption that only Q (and a hypothetical early layer at that) is largely authentic. Yet even his own portrait of Jesus as a wisdom teacher should have allowed parables. (Even the Jesus Seminar accepts many parables as authentic — Blomberg, "Studying Jesus," 20.) Some story parables clearly do appear in Q (e.g., Matt 7:24-27//Lk

6:47-49), and it contains many briefer metaphors. For the sake of argument I am doing little with special Lukan parables, although they again fit Middle Eastern village life far better than they fit the milieu of the subsequent church (see Bailey, *Poet;* idem, *Peasant Eyes*).

55. Johnston, "Parabolic Interpretations," 621-24, 639.

56. Young, *Parables,* 179.

57. Such as those fitting standard rhetorical principles governing expanding or condensing narratives, noted earlier.

58. Bailey, *Peasant Eyes,* xiii.

59. Carson, "Matthew," 409-10, following P. B. Payne's Ph.D. dissertation.

60. Crisler, "Acoustics," 134-37.

61. Johnston, "Parabolic Interpretations," 502. Perry, "Introduction," xi shows that Greeks had also collected fables for rhetorical purposes by the first century.

62. Cf. our discussion in ch. 9 regarding freedom to rearrange materials.

63. Young, *Parables,* 179; cf. Johnston, "Parabolic Interpretations," 621-24.

64. E.g., Johnston, "Parabolic Interpretations," 507. On the presence of interpretations with the vast majority of ancient parables, see also Snodgrass, *Stories,* 59.

65. Davies and Allison, *Matthew,* 2:397-99 represent an exception to neglect of these sources. Although they tentatively deny authenticity, in the authoritative tradition of Jeremias, they rightly refute traditional reasons for rejecting authenticity, recognizing that Jewish parables could include interpretations. We believe it likely that Jesus explained the parables to his disciples and that the disciples who preserved the traditions of the parables themselves (it is doubtful that the crowds provide the tradition's source) would have transmitted the interpretations as well.

66. E.g., Phaedrus 1.4.1; 1.5.1-2; 1.8.1-3; 1.9.1-2; 1.10.1-3; 1.11.1-2; 1.12.1-2; 1.13.1-2; 1.15.1-3; 1.16.1-2; 1.17.1; 1.18.1; 1.19.1-2; 1.20.1-2; 1.21.1-2; 1.23.1-2; 1.24.1; 1.25.1-2; 1.26.1-2; 1.27.1-2; 1.28.1-2; 1.29.1-3; 1.30.1; 1.31.1-2; 2.2.1-2; 2.5.1-6; 2.6.1-3; 3.1.7; 3.5.1; 3.7.1; 3.8.1; 3.9.1; 3.16.1-2; 4.1.1-3; 4.5.1-2; 4.8.1-2; 4.9.1-2; 4.12.1-2; 4.20.1; 4.23.1; 5.5.1-3; 5.7.1-3.

67. E.g., Phaedrus 1.1.14-15; 1.7.4-5; 1.14.18-19; 1.22.10-13; 2.1.11-12; 2.3.7; 2.4.25-26; 2.6.14-15; 3.2.1; 3.3.1-3; 3.6.10-11; 3.11.7; 3.12.8; 3.14.12-13; 3.17.13; 4.3.5-6; 4.4.12-13; 4.6.11-13; 4.7.25-26; 4.10.4-5; 4.11.14-21; 4.17.7-8; 4.24.3-4; 4.25.23-25; 5.2.14-15; 5.3.11-13; 5.4.7-12; 5.6.7; 5.8.6-7; 5.9.5; 5.10.10.

68. Phaedrus 3.10.1-8, 51-60; 4.13. Some of these morals are clearly redactional, added by the authors to apply the oral traditions (e.g., Phaedrus 2.2.2; 2.3.4; 3.3.14-17; 3.6.10; 3.19.1). Phaedrus suggests that slaves like Aesop originally used fables because they dare not express their views openly (3.prologue 33-40; though Phaedrus' emphasis may be influenced by his own experience with Sejanus — 3.prologue 41-44). Other attached lessons, however, may well be part of the original fables (cf. e.g., Babrius 4.6-8; 6.16-17; 11.10-12; 18.15-16). Most importantly, ancient auditors would have no reason to assume that the interpretations were added, hence tellers of stories could add morals as easily as their editors could.

69. E.g., perhaps Prov 30:4, 18-19, 21-31; cf. *Test. Job* 36-38:5.

70. Johnston, "Parabolic Interpretations," 561-62, 565-66, 638; Vermes, *Religion,* 92-99. On implications for authenticity, see also Blomberg, "Parables," 234-35.

71. Stern, *Parables,* 24.

72. Explicit explanations appear in less than half the parables in the Mishnah, Tosefta and Babylonian Talmud, but in more in other sources, averaging about 76%, especially in later Tannaitic strata but not unknown in any sources (Johnston, "Parabolic Interpretations," 566-67, 637-38; cf. McArthur and Johnston, *Parables,* 139-46). Jones, *Parables,* 79, suggests that the form of the interpretation in Matt 13:18-23 may deliberately echo Zechariah's vision interpretations.

73. Cf. scene explanations in apocalypses, e.g., *Test. Ab.* 12-13A. For this reason some scholars have wrongly thought that Jesus used parables only to reveal and that Mark, the first Gospel writer, misrepresented him (Wrede, *Messianic Secret,* 62; cf. Via, *Parables,* 9; Filson, *History,* 105).

74. Among Greeks, we may note that Plato wished to keep his teaching obscure to outsiders

(Diog. Laert. 3.63); Pythagoras and others sometimes followed the same practice (Diog. Laert. 8.1.15; Boring et al., *Commentary,* 92, adds Iambl. *Life of Pythag.* 23.104). Even most itinerant Greek teachers spent more of their time instructing disciples indoors than lecturing publicly, although members of the general public were welcome to attend (Liefeld, "Preacher," 205-6); unwritten teachings further provided "insiders" a superior status (cf. Botha, "Voice"); some of Epicurus' teachings, while not secret, were penetrable only by his advanced students (Culpepper, *School,* 112); philosophers might also choose to communicate in metaphor obvious only to insiders (e.g., Aul. Gel. 13.5.5-12).

75. E.g., the laws of creation, concealed from most of humanity (cf. e.g., Deut 29:29; *1 En.* 4:1-3; 41:1-8; 49:2; 52:2; 59:1-3; 103:2; 106:19; Wisd 7:21; 1QH 13:13-14; 1QM 14.14; *2 Bar.* 48:3), or "hidden things"/"mysteries" in the righteous' teachings, concealed from the wicked (Wisd 2:22; Ps.-Phoc. 229).

76. E.g., 1QpHab 7.4-5, 13-14; 1QH 2.13-14; 9.23-24; 11.9-10, 16-17; 12.11-13; 1QS 8.1-2, 12; 9.13, 17-19; 4Q418; cf. 1QS 5.11-12; 11.3-5; 1QM 3.9; 17.9; cf. *4 Ezra* 14:45-47. Wright, *People of God,* 394 regards Mk 4 as essentially apocalyptic revelation in which Jesus replaces the angelic revealer; but this proposal is again too narrow in view of other forms of revelation mentioned above.

77. Jewish teaching considered too esoteric for popular consumption (in general, e.g., *b. Pes.* 119a; *Pesiq. Rab.* 22:2) includes especially accounts of the throne-chariot (*tos. Hag.* 2:1; *b. Hag.* 13a, bar; 14b, bar; *Shab.* 80b; *p. Hag.* 2:1, §3-4; cf. 4Qs140), and the creation (*m. Hag.* 2:1; *tos. Hag.* 2:1, 7; *ARN* 39A; *b. Hag.* 15a, bar.; *p. Hag.* 2:1, §15; *Gen. Rab.* 1:5, 10; 2:4; *Pesiq. Rab Kah.* 21:5; *2 En.* 24:3).

78. I.e., *1 En.* 37-71.

79. Cf. Vermes, *Religion,* 92.

80. Young, *Parables,* 21. Many have criticized his distinction; see e.g., Brown, *Essays,* 321-33; recently Snodgrass, "Prophets," 62-64.

81. Following Arist. *Rhet.* 2.20; 3.4. As Johnston, "Parabolic Interpretations," 578, after a massive analysis of Tannaitic parables, wryly observes against Jülicher, "the rabbis evidently felt no obligation to conform to Aristotelian canons defining parable or allegory. . . ." Witherington, *Sage,* 189 notes that even Aristotle does not truly support the distinction; "What Aristotle in fact says is that the difference between simile and metaphor is slight *(mikron)* — The Art of Rhetoric 3.4, 1406b)!"

82. See the history of responses to Jülicher and his critic Fiebig in Johnston, "Parabolic Interpretations," 27-52.

83. Johnston, "Parabolic Interpretations," 119-20 (noting again Fiebig as the critic).

84. Johnston, "Parabolic Interpretations," 75.

85. Johnston, "Parabolic Interpretations," 77; cf. Young, *Parables,* 25. Funk's structuralist schema for interpretation worked fairly well on the parables he chose but did not work well with Tannaitic parables (Johnston, "Parabolic Interpretations," 545); for a critique of Funk's parable-as-metaphor view, see Stern, *Parables,* 11-12; cf. Scott, *Parable,* 46 (though Scott, *Parable,* 419 notes that the narrative is "primary and can never be replaced by its supposed meaning"). Against some contemporary writers, subversion is also not implicit in the parable genre itself; rabbinic parables more often reinforce conventional values (Johnston, "Parabolic Interpretations," 633-34). Witherington (among others) argues persuasively that Jesus' parables should be examined in the context of other Jewish parables (*Sages,* 183-90) rather than as purely polyvalent literary entities (*Sages,* 147-83; cf. also Gerhardsson, "Frames").

86. Bailey, *Peasant Eyes,* xxi. The danger of excessive allegorization may appear in some contemporary approaches as well (see the argument of Snodgrass, "Allegorizing").

87. Stern, *Parables,* 11. Vermes, *Religion,* 96, for example, notes that R. Meir took four different men as examples and supplied an interpretation for each, just like Jesus in the Gospels (*tos. Sot.* 5:9).

88. Johnston, "Parabolic Interpretations," 601-2; also McArthur and Johnston, *Parables,* 140-43.

89. Johnston, "Parabolic Interpretations," 606.

90. Johnston, "Parabolic Interpretations," 636-37. Recent research on metaphor also tends to undermine Jülicher's and Jeremias's skepticism concerning allegory; allegorical language "is no more

avoidable in the New Testament parables than it is in the Old Testament prophetic oracles" (Jones, *Parables*, 68).

91. Johnston, "Parabolic Interpretations," 608, 638-39; Witherington, *Christology*, 72; cf. Scott, *Parable*, 44; at greater length, see Blomberg, *Interpreting Parables*.

92. Stambaugh and Balch, *Environment*, 69; Jeremias, *Parables*, 157-58; Safrai, "Home," 733; Scott, *Parable*, 87.

93. 2 *Bar.* 70:2.

94. *Gen. Rab.* 83:5.

95. E.g., *4 Ezra* 4:30-32; this was essentially the end of the age (*Test. Job* 4:6; cf. *Gr. Ezra* 6:1). Cf. *1 En.* 54:6; 98:3 MSS; *4 Ezra* 7:36. For judgment as harvest, see also Jer 50:16; 51:33; Joel 3:13.

96. *M. B.B.* 4:8-9; Vermes, *Religion*, 107; for later rabbinic texts cf. Lachs, *Commentary*, 229.

97. Jeremias, *Parables*, 198; cf. Smith, *Tannaitic Parallels*, 139.

98. E.g., *Pesiq. Rab.* 23:6; cf. Jeremias, *Parables*, 199; *Gen. Rab.* 39:10. (Jewish teachers sometimes naturally used the pearl as a parable of Torah teaching; *ARN* 18A.)

99. The rhyming *kînâ* meter suggests authenticity (see Jeremias, *Theology*, 27; cf. Dalman, *Jesus-Jeshua*, 228); for a fuller defense of probable authenticity see Fortna, "Equal," who also contrasts the realism of Matt 20:1-7 with the unthinkable, hence dramatic, conflict of 20:8-15.

100. *Sipra Behuq.* pq. 2.262.1.9 (Neusner 3:354). Probably the story line is older than its occurence in this Tannaitic commentary. Some think that Matthew's version deliberately contradicts this older parable (Smith, *Tannaitic Parallels*, 50-51), flouting conventional values (Johnston, "Parabolic Interpretations," 633-35; cf. Young, *Parables*, 262-66). Jeremias cites a fourth-century parable he thinks dependent on Jesus here (*Parables*, 138-39); the parable speaks of laborers receiving equal wages for different tasks, but it was because some (representing a diligent rabbi who died young) had worked harder (*Parables*, 37; cf. Young, *Parables*, 261-62; Vermes, *Religion*, 105-6; Davies and Allison, *Matthew*, 2:70-71). Boring et al., *Commentary*, 120 cites *Tanchuma Ki teze* and Midr. Ps. 37:13.

101. Cf. *m. Kil.* 4:1-8:1.

102. Some argue that other Palestinian texts support the plausibility of various details of the text (e.g., the way idle workers are hired), reflecting an authentic Palestinian source (cf. Manns, "L'arrière-plan").

103. Cf. *m. Peah*, passim.

104. *M. Ab.* 2:14. "Master of labor" in this saying probably serves a function analogous to "Master of the House" who oversees labor in 2:15, attributed to R. Tarfon in the early second century.

105. Goodman, *State*, 34, from Tannaitic evidence.

106. See Horsley and Hanson, *Bandits*, 59; Horsley, *Galilee*, 207-9.

107. See Lewis, *Life*, 122-23.

108. Goodman, *State*, 38-39. Unemployed day laborers were common (see Jeremias, *Parables*, 139; Horsley and Hanson, *Bandits*, 58-59; Applebaum, "Economic Life," 657; Stambaugh and Balch, *Environment*, 91-92). As in Matt 20:8, employers paid wages in the evening (Lev 19:13; Deut 24:14-15; Jeremias, *Parables*, 136; Goodman, *State*, 39).

109. By the second century, the demand for laborers during the harvest allowed day laborers to receive almost the wages of a skilled worker (Lewis, *Life*, 123; he finds three and a half drachmas in *P. Oxy.* 1049).

110. Lewis, *Life*, 208, addressing the situation in Egypt, for which we have the most documentation. Even with wages in Palestine likely being higher than in Egypt, the landowner has probably been generous to all the harvesters (cf. one farm where workers during normal season were paid only two loaves of bread per day — Lewis, *Life*, 69).

111. The unusual abundance of the leaven probably points to the kingdom exceeding normal human analogies (Jeremias, *Parables*, 147; cf. Meier, *Matthew*, 149; Gundry, *Matthew*, 268; Hagner, *Matthew*, 390; on the precise figures, see Davies and Allison, *Matthew*, 2:423).

Notes to Chapter 14

1. With e.g., Sanders, *Jesus and Judaism*, 139-40. Cf. also others, e.g., Giesen, *Herrschaft*.

2. I am grateful for dialogue with Richard Horsley on this topic, which helped clarify my thinking. As we have observed, ancient historiography and biography could have political as well as theological agendas; that many of Jesus' followers during his own ministry had both agendas (and did not readily separate them) seems quite likely.

3. Pace Mack, though the kingdom is not dominant by that language in early Jewish texts, it is frequent (see Meier, *Marginal Jew*, 2:240-69; Chilton, "Kingdom," esp. 280; idem, *"Regnum"*; cf. Vermes, *Religion*, 127-30; Neusner, "Kingdom," acknowledging its subordinate function). The *idea* is pervasive, and the language is present.

4. Frequently acknowledged, e.g., Dodd, *Parables*, 34; Perrin, *Teaching*, 24; Betz, *Jesus*, 33; Boring et al., *Commentary*, 54; see especially Meier, *Marginal Jew*, 2:240-43; but contrast Aalen, "Reign."

5. E.g., *m. Ber.* 2:2; *Sipra A.M.* pq. 13.194.2.1; *Sipra Qed.* pq. 9.207.2.13; *Sipre Deut.* 313.1.3; 323.1.2; *tos. B.K.* 7:5; see Bonsirven, *Judaism*, 176; cf. Ps 145:2; 146:10. Reciting the Shema accepted this yoke (*m. Ber.* 2:2; *b. Ber.* 61b; *Deut. Rab.* 2:31).

6. E.g., Is 9:6-7; 24:23; 52:7; Zech 14:9; Wisd 5:16 (even despite its hellenistic approach); *Jub.* 1:28; *Ps. Sol.* 17:5; *2 Bar.* 73:1; *Sib. Or.* 3.767; 4Q246 col. 2, line 5; 4Q554 Col. 3, lines 14-21, especially 20-21; *Test. Mos.* 10:1; *Mek. Shir.* 10.42-45; *Sipra Behuq.* pq. 8.269.2.3; *Tg. Is.* on 40:9. Pace Crossan, this kingdom belongs more to an apocalyptic than a sapiential frame of reference (Freyne, *Galilean*, 136-37). For further data, cf. Moore, *Judaism*, 1:423; 2:309; Bonsirven, *Judaism*, 176-77; Laurin, "Immortality"; Young, *Parables*, 193; *Tg.* on Ezek 7:7, 10 in Boring et al., *Commentary*, 53.

7. See e.g., Oesterley, *Liturgy*, 65, 70.

8. E.g., Dan 4:26; 3 Macc. 4:21; *1 En.* 6:2; 1QM 12.5; Rom 1:18; Lk 15:18; *m. Ab.* 1:3; *tos. B.K.* 7:5; *Sipra Behuq.* pq. 6. 267.2.1; *Sipre Deut.* 79.1.1; 96.2.2.

9. E.g., *Sipra Qed.* pq. 9.207.2.13; *p. Kid.* 1:2, §24; Matt passim. This is commonly pointed out, both by scholars of Judaism (e.g., Bonsirven, *Judaism*, 7; Marmorstein, *Names*, 93; Moore, *Judaism*, 1:119) and by NT scholars (e.g., Goppelt, *Theology*, 1:44).

10. E.g., *Test. Ab.* 8:3, A; *Tg. Is.* on 40:9.

11. Witherington, *Christology*, 242.

12. With e.g., Niskanen, "Kingdoms"; Witherington, *Christology*, 242; Evans, "Daniel's Visions."

13. Some view the fourth beast as Greek but Rome as partaking in it (Caragounis, "Culture"), but the view may depend on the interpreters' period. Cf. the Kittim, who in at least the earliest Qumran scrolls might be pre-Roman enemies (Rowley, "Kittim"; Avi-Yonah, "War," 5; Treves, "Date," 420; Michel, *Maître*), though many take the Scrolls' Kittim as Romans (Rabin, "Jannaeus"; Burrows, *Scrolls*, 123-142; idem, *More Light*, 194-203; Dupont-Sommer, *Writings*, 167-68; Charlesworth, *Pesharim*, 109-10; Bolotnikov, "War"; Vermes, "Elements"; cf. the redactional approach in Eshel, "Sny"), quite plausibly (cf. 4QpNah 1.3; 1QpHab 3.11; 4Q161, frg. 8, 9, 10; 4Q491 A frg. 10, col. 2, lines 8-12; frg. 13, line 5); some take them more generally (Carmignac, "Kittim" [though *originally* Macedonians]; North, "War," 86-87; Van der Ploeg, *Rouleau*, 24-25; Gaster, *Scriptures*, 388), most plausibly (1QM 1.2, 4, 6; 11.11; 15.2; 18.2-3; perhaps 1QpHab 2.12-14; 3.4, 9; 4.5). The meaning could vary among documents depending on their date (Yadin, *Scroll of War*, 25).

14. On the four kingdoms, see 4Q554 col. 3, lines 14-21; *2 Bar.* 39:5-7; *4 Ezra* 12:11; *Sib. Or.* 8.6-11; *Sipre Deut.* 317.4.2; 320.2.3; *Pesiq. Rab Kah.* 5:2; *p. Taan.* 2:5, §1; *Song Rab.* 7:1, §1; *Midr. Teh.* on Ps 40, §4; Collins, "Eschatologies," 330-31; for early Christian readings, note especially Pfandl, "Interpretations." Cf. the similar Hellenistic-Roman perspective in Mendels, "Five Empires"; and, more relevantly, four ages of metals from Hesiod to Persian sources and Daniel (Lucas, "Origin").

15. With e.g., Sanders, *Jesus and Judaism*, 146-48, 151-54, 231-32; Allison, "Eschatology"; Meier, *Marginal Jew*, 2:289-397; cf. Burkitt, *Sources*, 69; Schweitzer, *Quest*, 223-397.

16. Charlesworth, *Jesus Within Judaism*, 43.

17. So e.g., Dodd, *Parables*; Jeremias, *Parables*; Young, *Parables*, 221; Vermes, *Religion*, 147-49; Borg, *Conflict*, 249; see also Meier, *Marginal Jew*, 2:398-506.

18. E.g., Kümmel, *Promise*, 19-25; Black, *Aramaic Approach*, 208-11; Nineham, *Mark*, 69; cf. Carson, "Matthew," 117.

19. E.g., Dodd, *Parables*, 44; Argyle, *Matthew*, 42; though cf. Matt 21:34.

20. Cf. Mk 14:42; see France, *Matthew*, 90. Somewhat analogous warnings in biblical prophets (Is 13:6, 9; Ezek 30:3; Joel 1:15; 3:14; Obad 15; Zeph 1:7, 14) may connote a prophetic eschatological enthusiasm, but in context can also indicate that nearer judgments foreshadow the imminent end (e.g., Joel's locusts).

21. That this "Q" saying appears in the midst of the same Markan material in both Matthew and Luke suggests (on the Q hypothesis or something like it) that Mark drew on "Q" as a source here.

22. Matthew undoubtedly changes "finger" to God's "Spirit," with Gundry, *Matthew*, 235; Schweizer, *Matthew*, 287; Witherington, *Christology*, 201; Davies and Allison, *Matthew*, 2:340; Allison, *Moses*, 237; pace Rodd, "Finger"; Dunn, *Jesus and Spirit*, 45-46. See my fuller argument from Matthew's context in Keener, *Matthew*, 364. Given Luke's emphases, he would not likely remove an explicit reference to God's Spirit here.

23. See discussion in Evans, "Inaugurating," noting here the coherence of Jesus' exorcisms with his kingdom teaching.

24. It is possible to read it thus; see e.g., Dodd, *Parables*, 28 n. 1; Witherington, *Christology*, 202; Meier, *Marginal Jew*, 2:413-23.

25. Cf. Sanders, *Jesus and Judaism*, 134-36; idem, *Figure*, 177.

26. Ladd, *Kingdom*, 48.

27. Theissen, *Miracle Stories*, 278-79.

28. Cf. Sanders, *Jesus and Judaism*, 134-35; pace Barrett, *Spirit and Tradition*, 59; Betz, *Jesus*, 59-60.

29. The association of the Spirit with miracles other than prophecy does appear in early Judaism, but it was comparatively rare (cf. Menzies, *Development*, 57).

30. Witherington, *Christology*, 204. It should be admitted, of course, that the prayer was probably preserved in multiple forms through its usage, problematizing specific redactional analysis at the textual level.

31. Crossan, *Historical Jesus*, 294. Arguments that Matthew simply created the Lord's Prayer and Luke followed him (Goulder, "Prayer," 45; Tilborg, "Prayer," 104-5) can array little specific support (see Brown, "Prayer," 869-73). Some allow that Jesus prayed component parts but opine that wisdom followers assembled them (e.g., Taussig, "Prayer"; O'Neill, "Prayer"), but this view fails to account for the coherence of the prayer as a whole against the background of Jewish liturgy; its appearance as a whole in Matthew, Luke and the Didache; the possibility that Jesus would have taught his followers a specific prayer; and the failure of most of its constituent parts to appear as prayers elsewhere in the tradition.

32. For the Kaddish, see Bonsirven, *Judaism*, 133; Jeremias, *Prayers*, 98; idem, *Theology*, 21; Moore, *Judaism*, 2:213; Smith, *Tannaitic Parallels*, 136; Hill, *Matthew*, 136-37; Perrin, *Language*, 28-29; Vermes, *Jesus and Judaism*, 43; Davies and Allison, *Matthew*, 1:595; Luz, *Matthew*, 371; for the Eighteen Benedictions, see Bivin, "Prayers."

33. Crossan, *Historical Jesus*, 293-95.

34. Luke's context may suggest a present application (the kingdom inaugurated through the Spirit; see Lk 11:11-13), but the "Spirit" in Lk 11:13 is likely Luke's specification of Q's more general "good gifts," since Matthew has little reason to play down the Spirit. Jesus' original Palestinian Jewish audience, familiar with the Kaddish, would surely have construed this part of the prayer eschatologically.

35. Thus Sanders observes that the prediction's nonfulfilment, requiring clarification or even revision, supports its authenticity (Sanders, *Figure*, 181-82).

36. It may stand, together with (if not part of) Mk 13:26-27//Matt 24:30-31, behind 1 Thess 4:15-17.

Paul adapts "Son of Man" to "Lord," the preferred title for Jesus in his circles, and the Synoptics, written later, clarify that only "some" would remain alive. But even in Paul's early writings, it seems clear that Jesus' promise was of a *potentially* imminent parousia, not one that would necessarily arrive immediately (Witherington, *End*, 45-58).

37. E.g., Stein, *Method and Message*, 60-79; Ladd, *Theology*, 70-80; Aune, *Eschatology*, 3-4; Dunn, *Jesus and Spirit*, 89; Harvey, *History*, 91; Perrin, *Teaching*, 73-74 (noting the modification in Dodd's own approach); Davies and Allison, *Matthew*, 1:389; Witherington, *End*, 51-74; Meier, *Marginal Jew*, 2:10, 289-506; Stanton, "Message," 57-61; Theissen and Merz, *Historical Jesus*, 275; cf. Young, *Parables*, 193. Sanders, *Figure*, 177-78, grudgingly concedes this possibility, but remains doubtful that any authentic passage clearly teaches the kingdom's presence.

38. See e.g., Brown, *Death*, 473-80; Keener, *John*, 289-90; Witherington, *Christology*, 104, 116; cf. Sanders, *Jesus and Judaism*, 234, 307; messianic-type associations in Charlesworth, *Jesus within Judaism*, 139. See our chapter 18 on Jesus' messiahship.

39. Cf. e.g., Matt 19:28//Lk 22:30; Mk 8:38. Historically, in the larger context of his ministry, Jesus' preaching of the kingdom has implications for his role (see Beasley-Murray, "Kingdom," 27-32).

40. See Witherington, *End*.

41. For transitional periods, see e.g. (some from Aune, *Revelation*, 1104-8), *1 En.* 91:8-17; 93:3-10; *4 Ezra* 7:26-44, especially 7:28-29; 12:34; *2 Bar.* 29:3–30:1; 40:3; 72:2–74:3; *Sipre Deut.* 34.4.3; 310.5.1; *b. Sanh.* 97-99; perhaps *Sib. Or.* 3.741-59 with 3.767-95; 4Q171 frg. 1-2, col. 2, lines 7-8.

42. Cf. e.g., Culpepper, *School*, 123.

43. Cf. Flusser, *Judaism*, 35.

44. See Sanders, *Jesus and Judaism*, 20-22, 104; Borg, *Conflict*, 70; Hunter, *Gospel According to Paul*, 38; Witherington, *End*, 84-92.

45. Vermes, *Religion*, 214-15.

46. Albright and Mann, *Matthew*, 195; Davies and Allison, *Matthew*, 2:609-15.

47. Albright and Mann, *Matthew*, 195; cf. Hunter, *Message*, 53.

48. Davies and Allison, *Matthew*, 2:609-15.

49. Albright and Mann, *Matthew*, 121; Brown, Donfried and Reumann, *Peter*, 92; Harrington, *Matthew*, 29. Christian usage of *ekklēsia* clearly originated in a Jewish context, outside which the language would make no sense.

50. E.g., Bultmann, *Theology*, 1:24; Perrin, *Language*; Tannehill, *Sword*, 56; Borg, *Conflict*, 248-63 (see esp. 257, 261); cf. Bultmann, *Mythology*, 137-38. Borg, *Conflict*, 11-12 questions Perrin's use of "apocalyptic" for a concept that is not in fact apocalyptic.

51. See Sanders, *Jesus and Judaism*, 7, 27, 125-27; cf. also Meier, *Marginal Jew*, 2:242; somewhat less helpfully, Scott, *Parable*, 57.

52. Cf. also Thompson, *Debate*, 95; Thurman, *Disinherited*, 20-27.

53. Goldingay, "Expounding," 354.

54. The exceptions are Heb 2:6; Rev 1:13; 14:14, all reflecting OT language and explicable without allusion to Jesus' frequent self-title (though they might reflect cognizance of it).

55. With e.g., Jeremias, *Theology*, 260-62.

56. Walker, "Origin of Concept," 490 (the same article appears as "Concept").

57. See Díez Macho, "Hijo del Hombre," illustrating from the Palestinian Targums.

58. Vermes, *Jesus the Jew*, 163-68, shows that *bar nasha* can mean "that one," which in turn could function as a circumlocution for "I" (some others are less convinced, e.g., Jeremias, *Theology*, 261 n. 1; esp. Chilton, *Approaches*, 75-76). For "that one" as "I," see e.g., *p. Hag.* 2:1, §9; *Ket.* 4:14, §1; *Suk.* 5:1, §7; *Taan.* 1:4, §1; 4:5, §11; for "you," see *Pesiq. Rab Kah.* 9:1. But Vermes probably limits the usage too much to focus solely on it.

59. Witherington, *Christology*, 257-58; idem, *End*, 170.

60. See e.g., Marshall, "Son of Man Sayings," 350-51.

61. With e.g., Cullmann, *Christology*, 138; roughly 100 times in the Hebrew Bible.

62. Vermes, *Jesus the Jew*, 163-68. Even such a phrase as "that one" could refer to significant personages; it became a title for Pythagoras among Pythagoreans (e.g., Iambl. *V.P.* 18.88; 35.255).

63. Burkitt, *Sources*, 66-68; Montefiore, *Gospels*, 1:44; Vermes, *Jesus the Jew*, 160-91; Leivestad, "Exit," 266-67; cf. Cullmann, *Christology*, 138; Chilton, *Approaches*, 75-109. It addresses a prophet in Ezekiel (cf. also the later *Apoc. Elij.* 1:1).

64. Lindars, "Re-Enter." Hamerton-Kelly, *Pre-Existence*, 41 differentiates the use in Daniel (for Israel), the Similitudes (for an exalted Enoch) and *4 Ezra* 13 (for a Messiah), but argues (in keeping with his focus) that all suggest preexistence.

65. E.g., Manson, *Servant-Messiah*, 72-73; Brown, *Death*, 514; Witherington, *Christology*, 239; Wade, "Son of Man"; Hooker, *Message*, 71-72; Bruce, *Time*, 27; cf. Wright, *People of God*, 292; Lohse, *Mark's Witness*, 44. Many focus on Daniel but supplement with the Similitudes as a probable source (e.g., Brown, *Death*, 509-14; Witherington, *Christology*, 235-36; Hagner, *Matthew*, 215). Daniel was more widely known than the Similitudes, though early Christians easily could have known both.

66. *1 En.* 46:3-4; 48:2; 60:10; 62:5, 7, 9, 14; 63:11; 69:26-27, 29; 70:1; 71:13-14, 17. Many scholars find background for the Gospels' usage here, e.g., Burkitt, *Sources*, 66ff; Bonsirven, *Judaism*, 189; Tödt, *Son of Man*; Sandmel, *Judaism*, 88-89; Ladd, *Theology*, 145-58; Lindars, "Re-Enter"; idem, *Son of Man*, 99; Boccaccini, *Judaism*, 219; Collins, "Son of Man"; Charlesworth, *Jesus within Judaism*, 40. Against this, see e.g., Vermes, *Jesus and Judaism*, 89-99. Some think this usage also reflected in *4 Ezra* (cf. *4 Ezra* 13:1-56; Boring et al., *Commentary*, 143; Collins, "Son of Man"); this connection, however, is less clear, and stems from a period after the gospel tradition was widespread.

67. Some date them to the early second century CE (Hindley, "Date") or even Medieval period (Black, "Parables"); most, however, date them earlier (see e.g., Charlesworth, *Pseudepigrapha and NT*, 89; idem, *Jesus within Judaism*, 39-40; Thompson, "Son of Man"). Some think the title in the Similitudes reflects the Christian usage (Agouridis, "Son of Man"; contrast Thompson, "Son of Man"); some view the Similitudes as anti-Christian polemic, reflecting a different Son of Man (Jas, "Hénoch").

68. E.g., Casey, "Son of Man in Similitudes"; Ricciardi, "Henoc"; Charlesworth, *Pseudepigrapha and NT*, 18, 88-89; Hamerton-Kelly, *Pre-Existence*, 41; against this, see e.g., Luke, "Son of Man." Some argue (plausibly but hypothetically) that Enoch becomes the Son of Man (*1 En.* 71:14) only in later redaction (Schreiber, "Menschensohn"); E. Isaac (OTP 1:50) argues that "son of man" for Enoch in this passage is a different Ethiopic construction than in the earlier uses.

69. Cf. Cullmann, *Christology*, 140-41.

70. *1 En.* 48:6.

71. *1 En.* 48:5.

72. *1 En.* 48:4.

73. *1 En.* 48:9.

74. *1 En.* 48:10.

75. *1 En.* 69:26-29. Thus many view the title as messianic (McNamara, *Judaism*, 107-8). Enoch could be or become a superhuman figure himself (as in some other Enoch literature), like Abel in some sources or (in the rabbis) Elijah.

76. So Collins, "Son of Man" (reading *4 Ezra* 13 as a similar attestation of this first-century interpretation of Daniel). Cf. the view that Messiah and Son of Man had been merged by the first century (Davies, *Paul*, 279).

77. Thus *1 En.* 46:3 also alludes to the "Ancient of Days" (Dan 7:9, 13, 22). Possibly even indisputably early portions of *1 Enoch* draw on this part of Daniel (see Glasson, "Son of Man Imagery").

78. Chilton, *Rabbi Paul*, 45.

79. So Burkitt, *Sources*, 67, and Bright, *History*, 457, contrasting the Similitudes.

80. See e.g., Riesenfeld, *Tradition*, 38; on the conception of corporate personality, for an early study, see Robinson, *Personality*. Koch, "Menschensohn," treats it as not messianic, but a single heavenly figure representative for humanity. Witherington, *Christology*, 241, provides a messianic reading of Daniel's "Son of Man," but not all his arguments are compelling.

81. Vermes, *Jesus the Jew*, 169-76, notes that Daniel's "son of man" did acquire messianic significance, but not (he argues) as a title. See sources noted above. Certainly Justin's Trypho in the second century read Dan 7 messianically (*Dial.* 31-32; Barnard, "Old Testament," 404; idem, *Justin Martyr*, 48; Shotwell, *Exegesis*, 73), but this may reflect only Justin's language (Higgins, "Belief," 301-2). In later rabbinic discussion, see Moore, *Judaism*, 2:335-37. Stauffer, *Jesus*, 163-64, suggests deliberate suppression.

82. E.g., Higgins, *Son of Man* (e.g., 53, 118); Borg, *Vision*, 14; idem, *Conflict*, 221-27; Boring, *Sayings*, 239-50; Donahue, *Christ*, 184; Crossan, *Historical Jesus*, 238-55; Koester, *Introduction*, 2:88-89.

83. Many scholars have concluded this: cf. e.g., Bowman, *Intention*, 125-42; Jeremias, *Theology*, 260-76; Kümmel, *Theology*, 106; Gerhardsson, *Origins*, 57; Riesenfeld, "Background," 94-95; Hill, *Prophecy*, 183; Marshall, "Son of Man Sayings"; idem, *Origins*, 63-82; France, "Authenticity," 113; Davies and Allison, *Matthew*, 2:43-50; Witherington, *End*, 170; Bruce, *Time*, 27-28; Bock, "Words," 91; Charlesworth, *Jesus within Judaism*, 42. The negative use of the criterion, by contrast with our approach here, has come in for serious challenges in recent years (Meier, *Marginal Jew*, 1:173; Brown, *Death*, 19; Stanton, *Gospel Truth*, 143; Young, *Theologian*, 257).

84. Cf. Stanton, *Jesus of Nazareth*, 160-61; Witherington, *Christology*, 234-45; Brown, *Death*, 509-14; pace Crossan, *Historical Jesus*, 238-55.

85. See Manson, *Servant-Messiah*, 72-74 (emphasizing corporate personality); Riesenfeld, *Tradition*, 38 (noting corporate personality between king and people); Witherington, *Christology*, 245, 269; Hooker, *Message*, 71-72. Doeve, *Hermeneutics*, instead finds suffering through a midrashic connection with the suffering servant (cf. the favorable review in Boismard, "Review"). Bowman, *Intention*, 142-153, thinks Jesus added the suffering aspect to the conventional apocalyptic usage.

86. Matthew also interprets the title in view of Daniel 7 (see Davies and Allison, *Matthew*, 2:50-52). Kazen, "Imagery," 87, 108, thinks that Jesus and his movement preserved both corporate and individual aspects of the image.

87. Bultmann, *Word*, 58. See also our earlier argument supporting this claim.

88. See Hengel, *Leader*, 1-2, 27-33.

89. Schweizer, "Discipleship," 88; cf. Sanders, *Jesus and Judaism*, 11.

90. Schweizer, "Discipleship," 88; cf. Ladd, *Theology*, 107; Betz, *Jesus*, 71; see Matt 23:8-10; our chapters on Jesus' self-understanding (esp. chs. 18-19).

91. Davies, *Sermon*, 133; Kingsbury, *Matthew*, 62; Gundry, *Matthew*, 62; Garland, *Matthew*, 48. Examples of teachers seeking disciples appear more frequently in the Greek tradition (e.g., Aul. Gel. 5.3.6; cf. Robbins, *Teacher*, 89-94); but these examples are normally "radical" teachers, exceptions to the customary Greek as well as Jewish tradition. Finding little rabbinic precedent for summoning disciples or promising to make disciples into something they are not (Robbins, *Teacher*, 104), Robbins locates the Jewish component of those elements' origin here especially in the divine call in biblical tradition (e.g., p. 115, citing Gen 12:1-2), alongside the Socratic model in Greek tradition (*Teacher*, 117-18; cf. also Philo, 94-95; and Josephus, 97). It is said that Hillel pursued laborers to get them to study Torah (not just as disciples to become rabbis, however) and receive eternal life (*ARN* 26, §54B).

92. E.g., *m. Ab.* 1:6, 16; *ARN* 3, 8 A; Socrates *Ep.* 4; Diog. Laert. 7.1.3.

93. Malina, *Anthropology*, 78; cf. *m. Ab.* 1:6, 16.

94. Culpepper, *School*, 222.

95. Cf. Matt 10:6; 15:24 (which is unlikely to have been invented, even by Matthew); Lk 19:10; Witherington, *Christology*, 131.

96. Jewish people told stories of pagans relinquishing their wealth on converting to Judaism (*Sipre Num.* 115.5.7), and Greek philosophers told stories of converts to philosophy who abandoned wealth to become disciples (Diog. Laert. 6.5.87; Diogenes *Ep.* 38). Such stories reflected well on the teacher the students left all to follow (e.g., Diogenes *Ep.* 9).

97. Disciples were often adolescents, but tradition suggests that at least some of Jesus' were married by this point (see Mk 1:30).

98. Cf. Safrai, "Education," 965.

99. On Akiba, Sandmel, *Judaism*, 246-47; Witherington, *Women*, 10; on others, *Gen. Rab.* 95 MSV. Later teachers assumed such long separations consensual (*p. Ket.* 5:7, §2; cf. *Eccl. Rab.* 7:6, §2).

100. *M. Ket.* 5:6; Safrai, "Home," 763.

101. Cf. *Sipre Deut.* 48.2.4, 6.

102. Some would have also viewed Jesus' demands in such cases as violating the law itself (cf. Holmén, *Covenant Thinking*, 187-99).

103. In both the Hebrew Bible and later Jewish literature (Manson, *Sayings*, 131; cf. e.g., *Ex. Rab.* 51:8).

104. *Let. Aris.* 228; Jos. *Apion* 2.206; Ps.-Phoc. 8. Whereas Roman culture emphasized paternal authority, later rabbis emphasized children's filial responsibility (Harris, "Aging").

105. *M. B.M.* 2:11; *p. Hag.* 2:1, §10. One who received the sages could be counted as if one had received God himself (Jeremias, *Theology*, 254; Smith, *Tannaitic Parallels*, 154), a saying similar to Jesus' in Matt 10:40; Lk 10:16; Jn 13:20 (perhaps both reflect the broader Jewish principle of "agency"; cf. also Ex 16:8; 1 Sam 8:7).

106. Deut 13:6; 33:9; 2 Macc 7:22-23; cf. Gen 22:2-12; 4QTest. 16-17; *Test. Job* 4:5/6. Jewish texts hence extolled those Gentiles who forsook the acceptance of their families by turning to Israel's God (*Jos. Asen.* 12:12/11). The Qumran sectarians, distinct from mainstream Jewish society, did require separation from family and other outsiders (4Q477 frg. 2, col. 2.6, 8).

107. Being perceived as antifamily was a much greater danger then than it is today (cf. Derrett, *Audience*, 39).

108. Cf. Jos. *Ant.* 4.26-28, 34, 58.

109. E.g., Hengel, *Leader*, 13-15; Sanders, *Jesus and Judaism*, 252, 254, who interpret the passage quite differently. (Witherington, *Christology*, 118 does, however, see a parallel in Iamblichus *Pythag.* 17.73.) Hengel envisions an eschatological context for the demand (cf. Matt 10:34-35//Lk 12:51-53; Hengel, *Leader*, 13); McCane briefly suggests an imminent eschatology in the direction of Schweitzer ("Dead," 42-43); Holmén, *Covenant Thinking*, 187-99, argues that Jesus rejected honor of parents as a path-marker.

110. Cf. Ps.-Phoc. 147-48.

111. See further Hengel, *Leader*, 7-8; Davies and Allison, *Matthew*, 2:56 n. 168; Vermes, *Religion*, 29. For such a figurative death, cf. Lk 15:24, 32; Sir 22:11-12; Philo *L.A.* 1.106; *Jos. Asen.* 8:9; *p. Ber.* 2:2, §9; *Taan.* 3:8, §2; *Gen. Rab.* 39:7; *Eccl. Rab.* 9:5, §1; Sen. *Ep. Lucil.* 60.4; perhaps *4 Ezra* 7:92; Lucretius *Nat.* 3.1046; Epict. *Disc.* 1.5.4; 1.13.5; Dio Cass. 45.47.5; Iambl. *Pyth. Life* 17.73-75; 34.246; Philostratus *Vit. Apoll.* 1.9; sources in Buchanan, *Consequences*, 201; Zeller, "Life"; Le Cornu, *Acts*, 574; Klauck, *Religious Context*, 225 (alienation in *CIL* 1.1012, 6.140); some later texts on the second death (e.g., *Tg. Qoh.* on 9:5; Abrahams, *Studies* 2:44; McNamara, *Targum*, 123).

112. Cf. Gundry, *Matthew*, 153; McCane, "Dead," 41. The suggestion of an original mistranslation from the Aramaic such as "Let the waverers or gravediggers bury their dead" (Abrahams, *Studies* 2:183; Black, *Aramaic Approach*, 207-8; Schwarz, "*Nekrous*"), perhaps based on public responsibility for the burial of the poor or unidentified (cf. Moore, *Judaism*, 2:176), seems less probable; cf. Gundry, *Matthew*, 154. Hengel, *Leader*, 7; Sanders, *Jesus and Judaism*, 254 take the saying as eschatologically conditioned rather than proverbial.

113. Sir 22:12; Jdt 16:24; Safrai, "Home," 782; *Apoc. Mos.* 43:3; cf. *b. Sanh.* 47b; Jn 11:19-20; Sandmel, *Judaism*, 200-1; though cf. *Life of Adam* 51:2.

114. E.g., Jos. *Life* 204.

115. Bailey, *Peasant Eyes*, 26; cf. Vermes, *Religion*, 29. Cf. similarly the curse in *PGM* 40.3-4 against a father who apparently robbed his own daughter's tomb: "May he not . . . bury his parents," i.e., may he die before them; a parent's final request might be burial by her son (thereby guaranteeing that he outlived her, Ap. Rhod. 1.280-83). Cf. also Char. *Chaer.* 3.5.4-6; 8.6.10, requesting the son not to depart until the father has died. For burial as a metonymy for death, cf. *Pesiq. Rab.* 22:6.

116. See McCane, "Dead"; for the custom, see also *m. Sanh.* 6:6. McCane, "Bones," contrasts Jewish ossuaries and later Christian reliquaries. A year's mourning period also appears in Eurip. *Alcestis* 336 (cf. 430-31); cf. Sen. *Ep. Lucil.* 63.13.

117. Cf. Hengel, *Leader*, 13.

118. Hengel, *Leader*, 11-12; cf. Jer 15:17; 16:2, 5-8; Ezek 24:16-18; Hos 1:2.

119. *Let. Aris.* 228; Jos. *Apion* 2.206; Ps.-Phoc. 8; Moore, *Judaism*, 2:132.

120. Tob 4:3-4; 6:14; 1 Macc 2:70; 4 Macc 16:11; cf. *Test. Job* 39:10/39:7; Hengel, *Leader*, 8; Sanders, *Jesus and Judaism*, 253-55; Harvey, *History*, 60; compare also Beare, *Matthew*, 214. Burial of the dead was an urgent duty throughout Mediterranean antiquity (e.g., Tob. 1:17-20; 2:7-10; 2 Macc 4:49; 13:7; 1QM 7:2; Ps-Phocyl. 99-101; 1 *En.* 98:13; Jos. *Apion* 2.201; Eurip. *Suppliants* passim; Plut. *Nicias* 6.5-6; Epict. *Disc.* 4.7.31; Diog. Laert. 6.2.52; Char. *Chaer.* 1.5.25; 4.1.3), and failure to bury one's father was a heinous offense (Demosth. *Against Aristogeiton* 54). Even a priest should bury a corpse if no one else was available to bury it (Sanders, *Figure*, 225-26).

121. *M. B.M.* 2:11; *p. Hag.* 2:1, §10; cf. Diod. Sic. 10.3.4. Also, when no son was available, a leading disciple would bury a teacher, as with John's disciples in Mk 6:29: Diog. Laert. 6.2.78; Diod. Sic. 10.3.4. That one should honor one's teacher as one honors God (*m. Ab.* 4:12) was a graphic way of increasing the honor due a teacher without diminishing that due God.

122. Cf. Lk 3:23, again not something an age-honoring culture would have invented.

123. Bailey, *Peasant Eyes*, 29. Josephus claims that even his command of Galilee at the young age of thirty aroused envy (*Life* 80).

124. Cf. e.g., *m. Ber.* 3:1.

125. E.g., Sir 3:7-8; Sent. Syr. Men. 9-10, 20-24, 94-98; Ps.-Phoc. 8, 180; *Let. Aris.* 228, 238; Jos. *Apion* 2.206; Philo *Drunkenness* 17; *Spec. Laws* 2.234-36; *Free* 87; *Sib. Or.* 1:74-75; *Jub.* 7:20; 35:1-6, 11-13; *Test. Ab.* 5:3B; *Mek. Pisha* 1.28; *Bah.* 8.28-32; *Sipre Deut.* 81.4.1-2.

126. Deut 13:6; 4 Macc 2:10-12; Jos. *Apion* 2.206; Ps.-Phoc. 8; *b. Meg.* 3b.

127. Jos. *Life* 12.

128. See Black, *Aramaic Approach*, 139-40; Hengel, *Property*, 24; Jeremias, *Theology*, 6 n. 2; Flusser, *Judaism*, 153; Davies and Allison, *Matthew*, 1:643.

129. The theme is amplified in Luke (e.g., Lk 5:28; 14:33; cf. Acts 2:44-45; 4:32-35), whether based on additional oral tradition (as is likely in Lk 3:11) or simply seeking to clarify and sharpen the emphasis already present in Mark.

130. *B. Ber.* 28b, bar.; *Tamid* 32a; cf. Lk 3:10; Acts 2:37; 16:30, though at least some of these references probably reflect Luke's patterning (following his use of Mk 10:17 in Lk 18:18).

131. It leaves itself open to various interpretations, for which reason Matthew changes it (Matt 19:17; cf. Gundry, *Matthew*, 385; Goulder, *Midrash*, 41; Moule, *Mark*, 80).

132. Most mainstream Jewish teachers probably assumed — as later teachers codified — that one should not give away all one's possessions lest one be reduced to poverty oneself (Lane, *Mark*, 367; Jeremias, *Jerusalem*, 127; one might make an exception if necessary to serve one's parents — Bonsirven, *Judaism*, 147).

133. For the dangers of wealth, see e.g., 1 *En.* 63:10; 94:8; 96:4; 97:8; 1QS 10.18-19; 11.2; CD 4.17; 8.7; Sir 31:8-11; *Let. Aris.* 211; Jos. *War* 2.250; *Ant.* 4.190; *m. Ab.* 2:7; *Sipre Deut.* 43.3.1-2, 5; 318.1.1-4. Some other Jewish writers even oppose the uselessness of worldly wealth with the true treasure of the world to come, just as Jesus did: 1 *En.* 100:6; *m. Ab.* 4:1; 6:9; *b. B.M.* 114b; *Gen. Rab.* 67:5.

134. E.g., scribes changing "camel" to "rope" (Metzger, *Textual Commentary*, 169). Some commentators speculated that the "needle's eye" referred to a low gate in Jerusalem peasant homes into which a camel could enter if it cast off its load; there is no evidence, however, for such a gate in this period, and a "needle's eye" meant then essentially what it means today (cf. *m. Shab.* 6:3). See Filson, *Matthew*, 210; most fully, Bailey, *Peasant Eyes*, 166.

135. Jesus apparently maintained a base of operation in Capernaum (from which most of Galilee was in walking distance — Overman, *Crisis*, 67) and did not reject property altogether, or demand

communal property like the Essenes. He did, however, apparently view possessions as intrinsically worthless (see discussion in the next chapter), demanding radical dependence on the heavenly Father.

136. Abrahams, *Studies* 2:208; Dalman, *Jesus-Jeshua*, 230; Jeremias, *Parables*, 195; Bailey, *Peasant Eyes*, 166, citing *b. Ber.* 55b; *B.M.* 38b.

137. Cf. *b. Ket.* 67a.

138. The expression persists as late as Qur'an 7.40, though this reference (involving eternal life) might evoke the tradition of Jesus' usage.

139. Vermes, *Religion*, 85 (noting that even Bultmann, *Tradition*, 105 accepts it!).

140. Jeremias, *Parables*, 218-19; idem, *Theology*, 242.

141. E.g., Polyb. 15.33. Nevertheless, crosses did also become a natural metaphor for sufferings (e.g., Apul. *Metam.* 7.16; 10.9; cf. Sen. *Dial.* 1.3.10; 7.19.3) or the pain of grief (Apul. *Metam.* 9.31) or anxiety (Apul. *Metam.* 9.23); for other nonliteral usages, cf. Epict. *Disc.* 3.26.22.

142. Manson, *Sayings*, 131; Bruce, *Message*, 19; Klaasen, *Anabaptism*, 88.

143. Cf. *1 En.* 108:10; *2 Bar.* 51:15-16; *m. Ab.* 4:17; *ARN* 32, §71B; *b. Tamid* 32a; *Lev. Rab.* 3:1; *Deut. Rab.* 11:10; *Eccl. Rab.* 4:6, §1; Daube, *NT and Judaism*, 137. Cf. the funeral meter rhythm here in Jeremias, *Theology*, 26.

144. *Sipre Deut.* 175.1.3 (cf. Ex 20:24 with 1 Kgs 18:32).

145. They would also be abundantly supplied in this age (cf. *b. Men.* 44a, bar.), presumably because believers would share with others in need (Mk 10:29-30), with persecution being a major cost in this age (Mk 10:30); cf. Acts 2:44-45; 4:32-35; Kee, *Community*, 109-10; Lane, *Mark*, 372; Tannehill, *Sword*, 147-52; Rhoads and Michie, *Mark*, 92.

146. Cf. also Lk 18:14; Jms 1:9; 4:10. For the authenticity of the saying, see Jeremias, *Parables*, 107.

147. Cf. Is 2:9-12, 17; 5:15; 10:33; 13:11; 52:13; 66:2; also Ezek 17:24; 21:26.

148. Cf. *1 Macc* 2:62-63 (on Antiochus Epiphanes). By the late first century teachers were reportedly claiming that one became exalted over (i.e., proficient in) Torah by humbling oneself before it (as well as the reverse — *Gen. Rab.* 81:2); Hillel reportedly claimed that his humiliation was his exaltation and the reverse, citing Prov 25:7 (*Ex. Rab.* 45:5), if this is authentic rather than borrowed (cf. dependence on the same proverb in Lk 14:9-10).

149. See *1 En.* 46:5-6; 104:2; 1QM 14.10-11, 14-15; *4 Ezra* 6:20-24; *2 Bar.* 83:5; *Test. Jud.* 25:4; *Sib. Or.* 3.350-55; *tos. Taan.* 3:14; *ARN* 5; 9; 28A; *Sipra Behuq.* pq. 3.263.1.8; *Pesiq. Rab Kah.* 9:1; *b. Pes.* 50a; *Yoma* 87a; *p. Sanh.* 6:6, §2; *Gen. Rab.* 21:1; *Lev. Rab.* 13:3; 36:2; in Jesus' sayings, cf. Jeremias, *Parables*, 221-22; for the sayings in Luke, Tannehill, *Luke*, 109-10.

150. Vermes, *Religion*, 148.

151. See e.g., Deut 15:7-11; Tob 4:7; CD 14.13-16; Jos. *Apion* 2.283; *m. Ab.* 1:5; *tos. B.K.* 11:3; *B.M.* 3:9; *Demai* 3:16.

152. "Woes" appear more commonly in "Q" than in Mark, but do appear in the latter (Mk 13:17; 14:21), and probably do reflect one rhetorical form (in the prophetic lament and mock lament) that Jesus adapted.

153. See e.g., Witherington, *Women*; Beavis, "Origins"; Ilan, "Studies." I treat ancient gender ideologies elsewhere (Keener, *Paul*; idem, "Marriage," 687-91), but cannot resolve the issue adequately without a separate book, so I do not stake the case for Jesus' ministry to the marginal on this claim.

154. Tax collectors apparently also heeded John (Matt 21:31-32), although the "Q" saying above associates them particularly with Jesus. Cf. further Lk 15:1; 18:10-14.

155. Sanders, *Jesus and Judaism*, 178; cf. Capito in Philo *Leg. Gai.* 199-202. Ancients might even slay fellow citizens who had allied themselves with enemy conquerors (Diod. Sic. 19.66.6).

156. E.g., *tos. Demai* 2:17; 3:4; *b. Bek.* 31a, bar.

157. E.g., *b. Sanh.* 25b; *p. Hag.* 2:2, §5; Abrahams, *Studies* 1:54; Jeremias, *Theology*, 110; idem, *Jerusalem*, 311. They were as unclean as lepers, communicating impurity to a house by entering it (*p. Hag.* 3:6, §1; cf. *b. Hag.* 26a). Malina and Rohrbaugh, *Gospels*, 83 do point out that though tax gatherers ren-

der a Pharisee's house unclean (*m. Toh.* 7:6), so would *any* nonobservant person who handled things in the person's home (in this case, to assess wealth).

158. Cic. *De Offic.* 1.42.150; Diogenes *Ep.* 36 to Timomachus; Epict. *Disc.* 3.15.12; Tac. *Ann.* 13.50-51 (abuse even in indirect taxation); MacMullen, *Social Relations,* 16; Best, *Temptation,* 139. Overman, *Crisis,* 126 includes some of these references plus Dio Chrys. *Or.* 14.14, and among Jewish sources, *m. Ned.* 3:4; *Toh.* 7:6.

159. Sanders, *Jesus to Mishnah,* 46-47; see Jos. *War* 2.405; cf. Herrenbrück, "Zöllner"; Hoehner, *Antipas,* 77-78. In some areas of Palestine much of the grain (or perhaps the land on which it was grown) belonged to Caesar (Jos. *Life* 71, Upper Galilee); some belonged to members of the aristocracy like Bernice (*Life* 118-19).

160. Cf. Lk 3:12-13; Carmon, *Inscriptions,* 105, 226; Cic. *Verr.* 2.3.10.26; perhaps Cic. *Ad. Quint.* 1.1.2.7; 1.1.11.32-33.

161. Hoehner, *Antipas,* 78; cf. Philo *Leg. Gai.* 199. Abuses by tax farmers before and during this period in rural Egypt reportedly included torturing and killing for the sake of locating tax fugitives (Philo *Spec. Laws* 3.30; Lewis, *Life,* 161) or beating an old woman because her relatives were behind on taxes (*BGU* 515, A.D. 193).

162. Lewis, *Life,* 161-63; a drachma was close to an average worker's daily wage. Such situations remain common at customs stations in many parts of the world today, sometimes evaded by bribes.

163. Many contend that those who paid both taxes and tithes were paying between 30 and 40% (Stern, "Province," 332; Neusner, *Beginning,* 22; Hoehner, *Antipas,* 75-77; Wilkinson, *Jerusalem,* 25; Borg, *Conflict,* 31-32; idem, *Vision,* 84-85).

164. *P. Graux* 2; *P. Thead.* 17; Lewis, *Life,* 164, citing *P. Oxy.* 2669; *P. Ryl.* 595; *SB* 7462, and most significantly *PSI* 101, 102. Most would not have time, but traditional tax farmers could legally search almost anything but the person of a Roman matron, and seize undeclared property (Quint. *Declamations* 359; Lewis, *Life,* 142). Interestingly, the problem continued into the Byzantine period, when Copts fled exorbitant taxes by joining monasteries; see Bianquis, "Egypt," 164.

165. Gundry, *Matthew,* 166.

166. E.g., Stern, "Province," 333; Manson, *Sayings,* 253-54; Lane, *Mark,* 101-2; Anderson, *Mark,* 104; Witherington, *Christology,* 78; contrast Ramsay, "Roads and Travel," 394, who reasonably doubts that customs officers would incur such hatred. For customs toll receipts, cf. e.g., *P. Grenf.* 2.50 c; *P. Ryl.* 197 a; *Select Papyri* 2:28-29.

167. Boundaries of cities and tetrarchies charged customs duties, raising the price of imported goods (Applebaum, "Economic Life," 686; Lewis, *Life,* 140; *IGRR* 1.1183); on Roman customs dues, see Duncan-Jones, "Dues." Tolls and customs tariffs were usually less than 3% for a given city, and the money collected went not to Rome itself but to municipal treasuries overseen by the municipal aristocracies with whom Rome was allied (Stambaugh and Balch, *Environment,* 74; cf. Lewis, *Life,* 141). Customs officers demanded written declarations of travelers' possessions and searched baggage (Casson, *Travel,* 290-91) and may have collected some other government revenues as well (Stern, "Province," 333).

168. Galilean townspeople undoubtedly preferred their municipal aristocracies to Rome and resented direct taxation of their resources far more than commercial tolls that profited Galilee, though those inclined to accept no ruler but God may have classed them together. Some tax-collectors may have become benefactors to local populations (Jos. *War* 2.287-88; cf. Sanders, *Figure,* 228-29; but note that this tax collector had much to lose, and is mentioned in *addition* to the leading men). While *publicani* did not collect direct taxes in this period, they could be involved in tolls and other indirect taxes (Andreau, "Publicani," 181).

169. On the sort of people envisioned in Lk 14:23, see Rohrbaugh, "City," 144.

170. See e.g., Sanders, *Jesus and Judaism,* 174-75; Charlesworth, *Jesus Within Judaism,* 44. Sanders, *Jesus and Judaism,* 205 suggests that this pattern may represent Jesus' "priority of grace to repentance," though warning that the difference vis-à-vis his contemporaries would not invite violence. Mack,

Myth, 80, by contrast, attributes the meal stories to an etiological legend based on the Christ cult ritual outside the Q community. His supposition that a later hellenistic meal is read into the narratives fails to explain (1) why hellenistic storytellers would have done so much research to construct Palestinian Jewish details for the last supper (see comment later in this book); (2) why the narratives, which make sense in their own milieu given the frequency of discussions during meals, focus on conflicts but show little more interest in details of the meal settings themselves except that people ate there; (3) why one should appeal to meals as a common gathering in hellenistic culture (Mack, *Myth*, 81) but not in Jewish Palestine; and (4) given the commonness of banquets, why even a Greek meal connoted a specifically cultic focus. A better case could be made for Luke's hellenistic construction of his symposium section (Lk 14:1-24) to which Luke connects eating with sinners (Lk 15:1), but even this is not cultic per se.

171. See Holmén, *Covenant Thinking*, 209.

172. Cf. e.g., *Jub.* 35:27; 45:5; Eurip. *Cycl.* 125; Xen. *Cyrop.* 8.7.14; discussion in Keener, *John*, 913.

173. Cf. Jeremias, *Eucharistic Words*, 236; Borg, *Vision*, 101. Inviting scholars for dinner was good — one would be blessed on their account (*ARN* 11, §27B; *p. Ter.* 8:7; Urbach, *Sages*, 1:434; Jeremias, *Parables*, 126).

174. E.g., Jeremias, *Parables*, 132; idem, *Theology*, 118; Lane, *Mark*, 103.

175. Sanders, *Jesus and Judaism*, 176-99; Witherington, *Christology*, 73.

176. Later rabbis did look askance at them (*m. Ab.* 3:11; *b. Pes.* 49b) and apparently felt that they communicated uncleanness to scrupulous Pharisees (*m. Demai* 2:2; *M.S.* 3:3; *Hag.* 2:7; *Toh.* 4:5, 8:3, 5; *tos. Ahilot* 5:11); they probably looked down on those uneducated in the law no less than segments of the modern intelligentsia tend to be impatient with the "masses" (cf. *m. Ab.* 2:6, 3:11; *ARN* 36A; *b. Ber.* 61a; *Pes.* 49b, including baraitot). Conversely, the rabbis tolerated them (*m. Git.* 5:9; Urbach, *Sages*, 1:632-34) and viewed them negatively primarily in relation to the Law as the rabbis had come to understand it (Urbach, *Sages*, 1:633).

177. Exorbitant tithes were probably favored by the priestly aristocracy and others besides Pharisees; cf. e.g., Jos. *Ant.* 4.240. Taxes rendered tithes more difficult (*Pesiq. Rab Kah.* Sup. 4:2); later teachers became particularly adamant against eating untithed food even inadvertently (e.g., *Gen. Rab.* 60:8; *Lam. Rab.* 1:3, §28).

178. Simon, *Sects*, 15; cf. *m. Kid.* 4:14.

179. See e.g., *m. Sanh.* 10:1.

180. *1 En.* 100:7-9; *Sir* 12:4; *Ps. Sol.* 2:34; 13:1; 14:6-7; *Sib. Or.* 3.304. (Though it can include any human who sins, as in, e.g., *Test. Ab.* 10:13A; *4 Ezra* 7:138-40, Pharisaic opposition in this context demands a stronger sense of the term here.)

181. See Best, *Temptation*, 139.

182. Mark neglects the opportunity to portray the Pharisees as class-conscious snobs (a portrayal that would have put off Mark's readers and thus could have suited Mark's purpose well).

183. See e.g., *m. Dem.* 2:2-3; *tos. Demai* 3:6-7; *ARN* 32, §72 B. On the untithed food of *amme haaretz*, see also *m. Dem.* 2:2; 4:5; *Maas.* 5:3; *M.S.* 3:3; *b. Bezah* 35b; *Ned.* 20a; 84b; *Pes.* 42b; eating it could be regarded as deathworthy in late sources (*Lam. Rab.* 1:3, §28).

184. Goodman, *State*, 77. We do not argue here that they intended to follow a *priestly* level of purity, as some have argued; see Sanders, *Jesus to Mishnah*, 131-254 (esp. 166-84). While the conflict stories in their current form may represent later developments (Sanders, *Jesus and Judaism*, 265) and Markan arrangement (Hooker, *Message*, 22; Dewey, "Structure," 400; idem, *Debate*, 115-16), Christian origins are not comprehensible without some early conflicts (cf. Gal 1:13-14; 1 Thess 2:14-15; Montefiore, *Gospels*, 1:42); in these narratives Jesus clashed with Pharisees over issues that were defining features of Pharisaism (Stambaugh and Balch, *Environment*, 100-1); and first-century Palestinian Jewish groups frequently clashed seriously (albeit generally not violently).

185. Sir 6:7-12; 12:13-18; 13:1; *Let. Aris.* 130; *m. Ab.* 1:6-7; 2:9; *Sipre Deut.* 286.11.4; *ARN* 16, §36B; Ps.-Phoc. 134; 1 Cor 15:33.

186. Syr. Men. Sent. 148-53, 333-35; cf. Sir 12:4, 7; Borg, *Conflict*, 78-95.

187. Discussion was a common feature of banquets (e.g., Jos. *Life* 222), and sages desired edifying talk (Sir 9:15; *m. Ab.* 3:2; *ARN* 26, 29A; 32, §68B; 35, §81; *p. Taan.* 3:11, §4), including at meals (*p. Hag.* 2:1, §9; 2:2, §5; Safrai, "Education," 968-69).

188. Because it would be hard to make restitution (e.g., *tos. B.M.* 8:26).

189. Abrahams, *Studies* 1:58.

190. *Pesiq. Rab Kah.* 24:12; Young, *Theologian,* 145.

Notes to Chapter 15

1. Granted, not all "later followers" were sedentary (witness e.g., Syrian monasticism), but I think in terms of first-century churches known to us (e.g., Corinth and Rome).

2. Vermes, *Religion,* 148.

3. Qumran's eschatological perspective probably helped shape their radicalism regarding possessions (Murphy, "Disposition").

4. For a comparison with some other ancient views of wealth, see Keener, *Matthew,* 229-30. Jesus did not establish a council to enforce his teachings on possessions as at Qumran, but his teachings were countercultural and radical, comparable to Qumran's. Witherington, *Sage,* 124, notes that Jesus' Jewish emphasis on depending on God also differs in content from a Cynic emphasis on self-dependence. Jesus may use hyperbole, the *point* being that compared to eternal things, possessions were worthless. Subsequent Christendom has rarely heeded the point even as hyperbole.

5. E.g., *m. Ab.* 2:8.

6. *4 Ezra* 7:77; *2 Bar.* 14:12; 24:1; 44:14; cf. further Tob 4:8-10; 12:8; *Test. Levi* 13:5; *Gen. Rab.* 9:9; 53:5; *Ex. Rab.* 31:2; *Lev. Rab.* 34:16; *Eccl. Rab.* 1:3, §1; *Song Rab.* 7:14, §1; Marmorstein, *Merits,* 20; Sandmel, *Judaism,* 190-91; Guelich, *Sermon,* 327; cf. Col 1:5; 1 Pet 1:4; *Gr. Ezra* 1:14. Second-century tradition declared that a first-century king who gave to the poor dispensed with earthly treasures to gain heavenly ones (*tos. Peah* 4:18). For "treasuries" in heaven in a more cosmic sense, cf. e.g., *2 En.* 5:1-2; 6; *3 En.* 10:6.

7. Jewish law addressed possibly theoretical cases of persons who were half-slave and half-free or jointly owned by two persons (*m. Ed.* 1:13; *Git.* 4:5; *Pes.* 8:1; *tos. Ker.* 1:17; *b. Arak.* 2b; *B.K.* 90a; *Git.* 43a; *Hag.* 2a; *Kid.* 90a; *Yeb.* 66a); divisions of estates at inheritances could encourage such situations (cf. *P. Grenf.* 1.21). This seems to have been an uncommon situation (cf. Acts 16:16), but Jesus' observation seems to have typically obtained: the slave naturally preferred one master to the other (Groenewald, "Mammon"; Beare, *Matthew,* 183; cf. Lysias *Or.* 4.1, §100; 4.6, §101; Dio Chrys. *Or.* 66.13).

8. See Black, *Aramaic Approach,* 139-40; Hengel, *Property,* 24; Jeremias, *Theology,* 6 n. 2; Flusser, *Judaism,* 153; Davies and Allison, *Matthew,* 1:643. It appears negatively in e.g., *Tg. Jon.* on 2 Sam 14:14; *Tg. Isa.* on Isa 5:23.

9. Cf. Sir 34:7; Meier, *Matthew,* 66.

10. For *qal vaomer,* see e.g., *tos. Ber.* 4:16-17; 6:19; *B.K.* 7:6; *Ed.* 3:4; *Kil.* 5:6; *Maas.* 2:2; *Shab.* 15:16; *Peah* 3:8; *Ter.* 6:4; *Mek. Pisha* 1.38; 2.36-37; 7.48; 7.61; 9.45; 13.105; 16.119, 126; *Besh.* 1.54; 2.73; 7.128; *Bah.* 5.90; 11.64, 109; *Nez.* 1.101; 2.17; 3.43, 69, 128; 10.47, 67; 12.5; 16.92; 18.79, 80, 83, 97; *Kaspa* 2.26; 5.51, 80, 103; *Shab.* 1.14; 2.41; *Sipra VDDen.* par. 2.3.4.3; par. 3.5.3.2; par. 5.10.1.1; *VDDeho.* pq. 12.53.1.3; *Sav* pq. 8.80.1.2; par. 9.90.1.3, 8; pq. 17.96.1.1; *Sav M.D.* par. 98.8.5, 7; 98.9.5; *Sh. M.D.* 99.3.9; and other sources in Keener, *John,* 716-17.

11. Cf. "Whoever has a morsel in his basket and says What shall I eat to-morrow? is among those of little faith" (*b. Sota* 48b in Abrahams, *Studies* 2:106; cf. *Mek.* 16:4 in Smith, *Tannaitic Parallels,* 137).

12. See e.g., *Mek. Vay.* 5.11-14, 84; *b. Pes.* 24b; 118b; *Sot.* 48b; cf. Abrahams, *Studies* 2:191; Held, "Miracle Stories," 293; Lachs, *Commentary,* 133. "Of little faith" is acceptable Greek but the term appears only in Semitic literature before the Gospels (Jeremias, *Theology,* 161; Black, *Aramaic Approach,*

132), suggesting that even the term may have been early in the Jesus tradition (as in this "Q" saying), though Matthew's Semitic usage probably expands it (Matt 8:26; 14:31; 16:8; 17:20).

13. See most fully Abrahams, *Studies* 1:18-29.

14. Later rabbis often discussed the question of the "greatest" commandment; see Hagner, *Matthew*, 646.

15. I.e., no commandment was so "light" that it could be ignored (*m. Ab.* 4:2; *Sipra Qed.* pq. 8.205.2.6; *Sipra Behor.* par. 5.255.1.10; *Sipre Deut.* 96.3.2; *ARN* 35, §77B; Matt 5:19; Jms 2:10-11).

16. Both philosophers like Philo (Wolfson, *Philo,* 2:277, at length) and the rabbis came to regard some commandments as "weightier" — more significant — than others (*Sipra VDDeho.* par. 1.34.1.3, par. 12.65.1.3; *ARN* 1, §8B; *b. Men.* 43b; cf. Matt 23:23; Johnston, "Least of Commandments," 207). Cf. the Ten Commandments (Vermes, "Phylacteries") and the prohibition of idolatry (*b. Kid.* 40a; *p. Ned.* 3:9, §3).

17. Bonsirven, *Judaism,* 29; Smith, *Tannaitic Parallels,* 174; for a later example, Montefiore and Loewe, *Anthology,* 111. Love for neighbor had long been a fundamental principle of Jewish ethics (*m. Ab.* 1:12, attributed to Hillel; *Jub.* 36:4, 8).

18. *Sipra Qed.* pq. 4.200.3.7; *Gen. Rab.* 24:7.

19. Cf. the observation of Smith, *Tannaitic Parallels,* 138.

20. The context of Lev 19:18 applies it to foreigners as well as Israelites (19:33-34; cf. also Lk 10:27; *Test. Iss.* 7:6; perhaps *Jub.* 7:20; 20:2; 36:4; *m. Ab.* 1:12), although not all interpreters applied the principle thus (*ARN* 16A; such a theme is absent in Greek literature — Boer, *Morality,* 62-72); some sectarians seem to have applied it especially among themselves (CD 6.20-21; Jos. *War* 2.119; cf. Jn 13:34-35); more fully on traditional Jewish interpretations of Lev 19:18, see Neudecker, "Neighbor"; for love of neighbor in Essene circles, see Södig, "Feindeshass." More distant Greek parallels (e.g., Diog. Laert. 8.10 in Thom, "Highways," 111) are less helpful in this instance, since Jesus here directly depends on Torah.

21. *Test. Iss.* 5:2; 7:6; *Dan* 5:3; Philo *Decal.* 108-10; cf. Philo *Every Good Person Is Free* 83; Jos. *Ant.* 3.213.

22. *Gezerah sheva* (perhaps borrowed from hellenism, but notably common in Jewish interpretation; e.g., Mek. *Nez.* 10.15-16, 26, 38; 17.17; *Pisha* 5.103; cf. CD 7.15-20; Keener, *John,* 305, 1184, for further sources).

23. With Diezinger, "Liebesgebot"; Flusser, *Judaism,* 479. Philo headed the most essential laws under the two categories of Godward and humanward (*Spec. Laws* 2.63; see more fully Sanders, *Jesus to Mishnah,* 70; Sanders, *Judaism,* 192-95; in the rabbis, Sanders, *Jesus and Judaism,* 249).

24. E.g., *ARN* 27A; 24, §49B; Philo *Decal.* 154; 4 Macc 2:7-9; cf. Goulder, *Midrash,* 25; Vermes, *Religion,* 44.

25. Cf. Vermes, *Religion,* 43. In Mark the scribe repeats the same words and Jesus appreciates the answer — though the scribe is quoting Jesus. The unnaturalness of the construction might support the Lukan tradition in which the scribe answers directly as being the earlier form (Lk 10:26-27, though Vermes thinks that this is an artificial link for the Samaritan parable; Vermes, *Religion,* 109). But because it in any case reflects Jesus' own view as well, even if the view stems from the scribe, the latter might have known it from prior teaching.

26. E.g., Paul's triad of virtues with love as the greatest (1 Cor 13:13; cf. 1 Thess 1:3; 5:8; Gal 5:5-6; without noting hope, Eph 1:15; 3:17; Col 1:4; 1 Thess 3:6; 2 Thess 1:3; Phlm 5; passim in the Pastorals).

27. Cf. Meier, *Matthew,* 257.

28. Cf. Manson, *Sayings,* 80; on the difference between Matthean and Pauline emphases here, see Mohrlang, *Matthew and Paul,* 45.

29. The Nash papyrus attests the special importance of the Shema already in the first or second century BCE (see Sanders, *Jesus to Mishnah,* 68).

30. Cf. also the derivative form in *GThom* 6.3 (see Chilton, *Approaches,* 123-49).

31. E.g., Tob 4:15; *Let. Aris.* 207; Philo *Hypothetica* 7.6; Syr. Men. Sent. 245-51. Although the *idea*

in the positive form existed in Judaism (Sir 31/34:15; *ARN* 26A; 29, §60B; *Tg. Ps.-Jon.* on Lev 19:18), the lack of the form more explicitly suggests to Vermes authenticity of Jesus' saying by the criterion of dissimilarity (Vermes, *Religion,* 41); the change, however, is slight. Alexander, "Rule," compares the similar traditions regarding Hillel's and Jesus' teaching.

32. E.g., Isoc. *Demon.* 21, *Or.* 1; *To Nicocles* 38, *Or.* 2; *Nicocles/Cyprians* 49, 3.37; Diog. Laert. 1.36, 59 (Thales, Solon); Pub. Syr. 2; Sen. *Controv.* 1.1.5; in Stoicism, see Epict. *Disc.* 1.11.25; Hierocles *Duties. Fraternal Love* 4.27.20; Van der Horst, "Hierocles," 157.

33. Confucius *Analects* 43 (5.13); Jochim, *Religions,* 125.

34. *B. Shab.* 31a. Some suggest a Hebrew wordplay here (Zipor, "Talebearers").

35. Later rabbinic material would not have depended on Matthew or Jesus for this summary, though one can debate whether it originates here with Matthew or Jesus, both of whom knew their Jewish context (in Matt 22:40, Matthew adds it to Mark, perhaps from here; Lk 6:31 omits this summary ending). Interestingly, though, cf. Confucius *Analects* 44 (15.23).

36. Usually regarded as authentic (see e.g., Carter, "Enemies"; Holmén, *Covenant Thinking,* 251-74; Wink, "Passivity").

37. Cf. Holmén, *Covenant Thinking,* 167-68 (though the supposed implication "that the law is inadequate," 168, could be explained instead as respectfully building a fence around the Torah).

38. The precise history of its transmission may be debated; cf. (too recently for inclusion in Keener, *Marries Another*) e.g., Collins, *Divorce* (cf. Keener, "Review of Collins"); Force, "Encore." Placing Jesus' sexual ethic in the context of eschatological urgency (e.g., Levine, "Word," 523) also bears consideration.

39. Cf. (esp. with reference to Matthew) e.g., Dobschütz, "Rabbi," 33; Filson, *Matthew,* 206; Argyle, *Matthew,* 51-52; Swidler, *Women,* 231 n. 225; Gundry, *Matthew,* 377; Ilan, *Women,* 142; Overman, *Crisis,* 82, 279. For the Pharisaic debate, see *m. Git.* 9:10; *Sipre Deut.* 269.1.1. The more liberal interpretation appears in Jos. *Ant.* 4.253 (relevant for a hellenistic audience).

40. CD 4.20-5:2; 11QT 56.18-19, prohibiting royal polygamy. Many have thought that the Qumranites applied this passage to prohibiting divorce as well as polygamy (Schubert, "Ehescheidung," 27; Mueller, "Divorce Texts"), but the Qumran texts themselves prohibit explicitly only polygamy here (Keener, *Marries Another,* 40-41; cf. Vermes, "Matrimonial Halakah"; Nineham, *Mark,* 265). A few rabbis, who allowed polygamy but felt it was not the ideal (cf. *m. Ab.* 2:7; *b. Yeb.* 65a), also appealed to Genesis (*ARN* 2, §9B).

41. *M. Yeb.* 6:6, drawing different applications. See further Keener, *Paul,* 114-15; Ilan, *Women,* 125, on Jewish precedents for women drawn from the Eve story.

42. Many Jewish speculations about the future kingdom also viewed it as a sort of recapitulation of the beginning (*4 Ezra* 8:52-54; *Test. Levi* 18:10-12; *Test. Dan* 5:12; *m. Ab.* 5:20).

43. Sanders, *Jesus and Judaism,* 257.

44. I treat this subject more thoroughly in Keener, *Marries Another,* passim; idem, *Matthew,* 190 92, 462-69; and in some more popular essays.

45. Cf. e.g., Jos. *Apion* 1.167.

46. Cf. e.g., *m. M.S.* 4.10-11; *Ned.* 1:1-2; 8:7; *tos. M.S.* 5:2; *Ned.* 1:1-2; Carmon, *Inscriptions,* 75, §167; Mazar, "Splendors," 59; Fitzmyer, *Essays,* 93-100; McNamara, *Judaism,* 200-2; Sanders, *Jesus to Mishnah,* 53. Others suggest this passage refers to vowing not to perform an act (Zeitlin, "Korban") or an oath uttered by a son in anger from which Pharisees would not release him (Bligh, "Qorban"). Matthew's wording is more polemical than Mark's.

47. Some scholars contend that the only kind of vow that one school of Pharisaism in Jesus' day would not release was a vow to the temple (Falk, *Pharisee,* 98-99; cf. Black, *Aramaic Approach,* 139). One could also prohibit others from using one's property (say, eating his figs) by declaring them dedicated to the temple or perhaps "as if they were" so dedicated, hence, "forbidden to you" (*m. Ned.* 3:2; Baumgarten, *"Korban"*; Sanders, *Jesus to Mishnah,* 54-55).

48. See Sanders, *Jesus to Mishnah,* 57.

49. See e.g., Sir 3:8; Syr. Men. Sent. 9-10, 20-24, 94-98; Ps.-Phoc. 8, 180; *Let. Aris.* 228, 238; Jos. *Apion* 2.206; Philo *Ebr.* 17; *Spec. Laws* 2.234-36; *Prob.* 87; *Sib. Or.* 1.74-75; 2.275-76; *Jub.* 7:20; 29:14-20; 35:1-6, 11-13; *Mek. Pisha* 1.28; *Bah.* 8.28ff; *Sipre Deut.* 81.4.1-2.

50. See Sir 3:7; Jos. *Life* 204; *Test. Ab.* 5B; *Test. Jud.* 1:4-5; *b. Kid.* 31ab; *Pesiq. Rab.* 23/24:2.

51. Cf. Sir 3:12-15; Montefiore and Loewe, *Anthology,* 500-6; Montefiore, *Gospels,* 2:226; Derrett, *Law,* 110; *Pesiq. Rab.* 23/24:2; cf. Prov 28:24. Hagner, *Matthew,* 431 cites *tos. Ned.* 1.6.4 for a vow taking precedence over a biblical commandment, but notes that in later times honor of parents took precedence over a vow (*m. Ned.* 9:1).

52. E.g., *ARN* 37A; 45, §124B.

53. E.g., *Contest of Homer and Hesiod* 322; *Homeric Hymn* 25.4-5; Pindar *Threnoi* fr. 137 (in Clem. Alex. *Strom.* 3.3.17, using *olbios*); Polyb. 26.1.13 (using *makarios*); Mus. Ruf. frg. 35, p. 134; *Apoll. K. Tyre* 31; Babr. 103.20-21; Philost. *Hrk.* 4.11; Porph. *Marc.* 16.276-77; Aune, *Prophecy,* 61, 64; Guelich, *Sermon,* 63-66. For *makarios* in Stoic and Christian literature, see Vorster, "Blessedness."

54. See e.g., Ps 40:4; 41:1; 65:4; 84:4-5, 12; 94:12; 112:1; 119:1-2; 128:1; Is 56:2; Jer 17:7; Dan 12:12; Bar 4:4; with a different term, Jdt 13:18; 14:7; 15:10. The term *makarios* appears 66 times in the LXX, including 25 times in the Psalms (including 1:1; 2:12; 31:1-2=32:1-2), 11 times in Sirach (14:1-2, 20; 25:8-9; 26:1; 28:19; 31:8; 34:15; 48:11; 50:28) and 4 times in Proverbs (Prov 3:13; 8:34; 20:7; 28:14).

55. E.g., *1 En.* 99:10; *2 En.* 42.6-14; 44:5; *Ps. Sol.* 4:23; 5:16; 6:1; 10:1; 17:44; 18:6; *4 Macc* 7:15, 22; 10:15; 17:18; 18:9; *Jos. Asen.* 16:14/7; 19:8, MSS; *Sipra VDDeho.* par. 5.44.1.1; *b. Ber.* 61b; *Hag.* 14b; *Hor.* 10b, bar. At Qumran, see 4Q525 (see Roo, "4Q525"; Brooke, "Beatitudes"; Viviano, "Beatitudes"; Viviano, "Qumran"; Viviano, "Publication"). In early Christianity, *makarios* appears about 50 times in the NT and 40 times in the Apostolic Fathers; this includes Lk 1:45; 6:20-22; 7:23; 10:23; 11:27-28; 12:37-38, 43; 14:14-15; 23:29; in Acts, only 20:35 and 26:2 (Luke-Acts comprises 34% of NT uses).

56. Jeremias, *Sermon,* 15-16; cf. Black, *Aramaic Approach,* 156-58.

57. *Test. Zeb.* 8:1; Dalman, *Jesus-Jeshua,* 226.

58. Jeremias, *Theology,* 24 (citing a three-beat rhythm).

59. Some commentators note that the salt deposits of the Dead Sea are so impure that they leave unsalty "salt" when the the real salt eventually dissolves, or that salt could be mixed with so many impurities "as to become useless" (Davies and Allison, *Matthew,* 1:473 on Pliny *N.H.* 31.82). (Cf. Hellestam, "Saltet": one could accidentally get magnesium salt with one's cooking salt; the former tasted bitter and was used only on roads to hold down weeds and dust.) But Jesus may refer here to a more graphic, inconceivable situation of real salt losing its taste (cf. Hill, *Matthew,* 115; Vermes, *Religion,* 83).

60. R. Tarfon in *b. Bek.* 8b (Dalman, *Jesus-Jeshua,* 229; Lachs, *Commentary,* 82; Vermes, *Religion,* 83). In that society everyone knew that mules are half-breeds (Babrius 62) and are consequently sterile (e.g., Livy 26.23.5; Appian *C.W.* 1.9.83; 2.5.36; *Sipre Deut.* 119.2.3; *Gen. Rab.* 41:6), hence lacking afterbirth.

61. Manson, *Sayings,* 154; Vermes, *Religion,* 19-20 n. 11.

62. *B. Sanh.* 107ab; *p. Sanh.* 2:6, §2; *Gen. Rab.* 47:1; *Lev. Rab.* 19:2; *Num. Rab.* 18:21; *Song Rab.* 5:11, §4.

63. *P. Sanh.* 2:6, §2; *Song Rab.* 5:11, §3; cf. *Ex. Rab.* 6:1. The Greek letter *iota* used here might be a rough equivalent; cf. the play on the Latin "i" in Mart. *Epig.* 2.93. Rulers were known to prescribe a capital sentence against those found chiseling out a single letter of their inscriptions (Dio Chrys. *Or.* 31.86 in Boring et al., *Commentary,* 57); the 22 letters of the alphabet were prepared to testify against Israel's transgressions of Torah (*Lam. Rab.* Proem 24).

64. In the Greek of this period, "great" could mean "greatest," as translators frequently recognize in Matt 22:36 (cf. Mussies, "Greek," 1042).

65. E.g., *m. Ab.* 2:8.

66. E.g., *Sipra VDDeho.* par. 1.34.1.3; 12.65.1.3; Dalman, *Jesus-Jeshua,* 64; Flusser, *Judaism,* 496; cf. Matt 23:23.

67. This tradition, at least, is wider than the later rabbis (see *Let. Aris.* 228; Jos. *Apion* 2.206; Ps.-Phoc. 8).

68. E.g., Urbach, *Sages*, 1:350; Keener, *Marries Another*, 116; see Johnston, "Least of Command-ments."

69. *M. Ab.* 2:1; cf. *Sipre Deut.* 96.3.2; 115.1.2; *ARN* 2 A.

70. *ARN* 35, §77 B; *Sipre Deut.* 48.1.3; cf. *m. Kid.* 1:10; *ARN* 28 A.

71. See Moore, *Judaism*, 1:467-68.

72. *M. Hor.* 1:3; *Sipre Deut.* 54.3.2; *ARN* 27 A; 1, §8 B; cf. Jms 2:10; *Test. Asher* 2.2-8.

73. *Sipra Qed.* pq. 8.205.2.6; *Behuq.* par. 5.255.1.10; more fully, Keener, *Marries Another*, 115-17.

74. See *Test. Iss.* 7:2; *Reub.* 4:8; *b. Nid.* 13b, bar.; *Shab.* 64ab; *p. Hallah* 2:1, §10; *Lev. Rab.* 23:12; *Pesiq. Rab.* 24:2; further, Keener, *Marries Another*, 16-17. Jesus may read Ex 20:14 in light of Ex 20:17.

75. Note Essenes in Jos. *War* 2.135; *Ant.* 15.370-71; Philo *Every Good Man Free* 84; Vermes, *Religion*, 35; cf. Black, *Scrolls*, 94, 120. Apparently, however, not all Essenes agreed (Sanders, *Jesus to Mishnah*, 53; McNamara, *Judaism*, 197). Meier, "Oaths," thinks that Jesus went beyond his Jewish contemporaries on this point.

76. Cf. *m. Ned.* 1:1; *Naz.* 1:1; Vermes, *Religion*, 34-35; Schiffman, *Law*, 137-38; Sanders, *Jesus to Mishnah*, 53-54; Keener, *Matthew*, 194.

77. As noted earlier, for resemblance with the Kaddish, which would not depend on Jesus' prayer; see e.g., Bonsirven, *Judaism*, 133; Jeremias, *Prayers*, 98; idem, *Theology*, 21; Moore, *Judaism*, 2:213; Smith, *Tannaitic Parallels*, 136; Hill, *Matthew*, 136-37; Perrin, *Language*, 28-29; Vermes, *Jesus and Judaism*, 43; Davies and Allison, *Matthew*, 1:595; Luz, *Matthew*, 371; pace Meier, *Marginal Jew*, 2:361-62 n. 36; Lachs, *Commentary*, 118.

78. Many compare the Jewish maxim: "By the measure by which a man metes it is measured to him" (judgment in the present era in *m. Sot.* 1:7; *b. Sot.* 8b; *Pesiq. Rab.* 39:2; more fully, Smith, *Tannaitic Parallels*, 135; Dalman, *Jesus-Jeshua*, 225; Davies and Allison, *Matthew*, 1:670; Bivin, "Measure"). Perhaps only one stream of Jewish tradition applied it to the day of judgment as Jesus does (cf. Rüger, "Ruch"), but it is at least implied elsewhere: a person judged mercifully by another ("with the scale weighted in my favor") prayed that God would also judge the other mercifully at the judgment (*ARN* 8A).

79. Possibly a figure of speech; attested in *b. 'Arakin* 16b; *b. B.B.* 15b (Vermes, *Religion*, 80; other texts in Lachs, *Commentary*, 137), if it is not a polemical distortion of Jesus' teaching.

80. *Sipre Num.* 88, cited in Smith, *Tannaitic Parallels*, 138; Lachs, *Commentary*, 142.

81. E.g., *Sipre Deut.* 173.1.2; *b. Sanh.* 101a; at Qumran, cf. Schiffman, *Law*, 97-98; Davies, *Sermon*, 79; Brown, "Scrolls," 4. See further discussion in Keener, *Matthew*, 453-54.

82. Keener, "Heavenly Court"; idem, *Matthew*, 182-84 (with fuller documentation; cf. also *Tg. Ps.-Jon.* on Deut 5:31); Lachs, *Commentary*, 92, 94. Matthew's context (Matt 5:25) reinforces this likelihood even though the explicit rabbinic sources are later.

83. See e.g., Dalman, *Jesus in Talmud*, passim; idem, *Jesus-Jeshua*, passim; Jeremias, *Theology*, passim; Lachs, *Commentary*, passim; Keener, *Matthew*, passim.

84. See Holmén, *Covenant Thinking*, 221-51 (for Jesus' contacts with the unclean, see 233-37).

85. "Q" notes the cleansing of lepers (Matt 11:5//Lk 7:22). Jewish law forbade touching lepers (Lev 5:3), quarantined lepers from regular society (Lev 13:45-46; Jos. *Ant.* 3.261, 264), and people avoided contact with them (2 Kgs 7:3; Jos. *Ant.* 9.74; *Apion* 1.229, 233, 281; *Sipra Negaim*; *Sipra Mesora* par. 1-5). Nevertheless, Davies and Allison, *Matthew*, 2:11 show (from *m. Negaim* passim) that their isolation was not total.

86. Mark's phrase *pēgē tou haimatos* (Mk 5:29) refers in the LXX to an impure genital flow in every occurrence (Lev 12:7; 20:18), as does his *rhusei haimatos* (Mk 5:25; Lev 15:19, 25; 20:18). Strict pietists sought to avoid unnecessarily exposing themselves to this impurity (e.g., Jos. *Ant.* 3.261; *m. Niddah*), even if it was impossible for married men to avoid that state totally (Sanders, *Judaism*, 228-29) and menstruation did not require quarantine (Levine, "Responsibility," 389-90). At least in rab-

binic theory any strict Jewish man must learn whether a woman who touched his clothing was unclean and therefore had rendered him unclean (*m. Toh.* 5:8). Davies and Allison, *Matthew,* 2:128 list Jewish texts displaying restriction or abhorrence regarding women's menstruation (Ezek 36:17; CD 4.12-5.17; 11QTemple 48.15-17; Jos. *War* 5.227; *Apion* 2.103-4; *m. Zab.* 4:1).

87. In support of the authenticity of Mk 7:15, see Holmén, *Covenant Thinking,* 245-49.

88. Cf. Saldarini, *Community,* 134, 139.

89. Even in Matt 9:20-21, Levine, "Responsibility," 384 doubts that Matthew indicates or implies *vaginal* bleeding. Because Matthew's verb appears in the LXX only with respect to vaginal bleeding (Lev 15:33), I am skeptical of this interpretation. Even if it is correct, however, Jesus touches the leper in Matthew (Matt 8:3).

90. Many might agree with his emphasis on inward purity, yet insist that this emphasis did not relieve one of the responsibility of pursuing outward purity as well.

Notes to Chapter 16

1. If we compare these other teachers with modern academicians, in the hope of portraying them as simply dialoguing dispassionately, without any emotional commitment to the outcome, I fear that we idealize academicians. I suspect that I am not the only academician frustrated when those we consider populist demagogues hijack public discourse while we academicians languish isolated in the academy.

2. See Sanders, *Jesus to Mishnah,* 95-96. Mack, *Myth,* 375, attributes the conflict narratives to Mark's imagination.

3. Sanders, *Figure,* 217.

4. Cf. Lk 3:7.

5. Vermes, *Jesus and Judaism,* 31.

6. It is his interest in Jerusalem that dictates most of his references to Pharisees, though his interest in the sects is probably not geographically based (cf. *Life* 11-12). He claims to have joined the Pharisees in Jerusalem (*Life* 12), but writes after Jerusalem's destruction, which Pharisees, unlike Sadducees, seem to have survived amply.

7. Horsley, *Galilee,* 150-52, 256; Witherington, *Christology,* 61, 66 (with some possible evidence in Jos. *Ant.* 20.34-49).

8. Vermes, *Jesus the Jew,* 56.

9. Simon son of Gamaliel, presumably a Pharisee, is among the Jerusalem leaders interested in events in Galilee and sending persons there (*Life* 190, 309). Three of the four sent were Pharisees (though one, like Josephus, was both a Pharisee and a priest; *Life* 197).

10. See Freyne, *Galilee,* 181. Horsley, *Galilee,* 144-46, challenges the contention that they made pilgrimage three times annually; but he undoubtedly overstates the rarity of visits from Judeans and Galileans.

11. Such as in Mk 7:5; 8:11; 10:2; Mark does place Mk 12:13 in Jerusalem. It would not account for the more readily Galilean settings of many of these stories in the Gospels (local synagogues, meals with tax gatherers, or a grainfield) that seem inseparable from the conflict itself.

12. Pharisees did exercise power freely in an earlier period (see e.g., Jos. *Ant.* 13.405).

13. See especially Sanders, *Jesus and Judaism,* 294-318.

14. Apart from the complaint in Jn 12:19 and synagogue influence in 12:42, the Pharisees explicitly appear in the Fourth Gospel after ch. 9 almost exclusively in summaries of the Jerusalem leadership (11:47, 57; 18:3; though cf. 11:46). The priestly elite, by contrast, dominates (Jn 12:10; 18:3, 10, 13, 15, 16, 19, 22, 24, 26, 35; 19:6, 15, 21).

15. Witherington, *Christology,* 60. Morton Smith and (at least in his earlier works) Jacob Neusner have argued that Pharisaism was much less significant in the pre-70 period, and that Josephus magni-

fied it in his later *Antiquities*, when Pharisaism was more popular. But cf. *War* 2.163, and note that Josephus may have had apologetic reason to downplay the Pharisees' role in his earlier *War* (Witherington, *Christology,* 83-84, following Dunn).

16. One could postulate a *Sitz im Leben* for polemic against a Pharisaic faction within the church in the late 40s (Acts 15:5), but would such polemic generate stories about enemies of the earthly Jesus, and if traditionaries took that much liberty, would they not introduce current controversies like circumcision?

17. Theissen, *Gospels in Context,* 230-31. Theissen's evidence for Pharisaic toleration in the 60s (Jos. *Ant.* 20.200-1; cf. *War* 2.162; *Life* 191) and late 50s (Acts 23:9) is fairly secure, as is his evidence for some hostility in the 30s (Acts 7:54-60; Gal 1:13, 23). His evidence for hostility in the early 40s (Acts 12:2 with Jos. *Ant.* 19.332; *Gospels in Context,* 231-32) is less secure. Luke's portrayal of Pharisaism seems more ambivalent than hostile (cf. Gowler, *Host, Guest,* 177-296; Mason, "Chief Priests," 134-42; Ziesler, "Luke and Pharisees"; Brawley, *Luke-Acts and Jews,* 84-106; even Harnack, *Acts,* xxiv-xxv), but this could reflect his characters' experience with Pharisaism rather than his pro-Pharisaic bias: what evidence we do have from him coheres with what we have from Josephus against the traditional critical expectation of conflict in the 40s-60s.

18. This is our *earliest* extant Christian mention of Pharisees, unless one dates Mark before the mid-50s. For Paul's involvement in the persecution, see also 1 Cor 15:9; Gal 1:13, 23.

19. Some find here an interpolation (Bruce, *Thessalonians,* 49-51; Setzer, *Responses,* 16-19), but more scholars today are skeptical (Collins, "Integrity"; Donfried, *Thessalonica,* 198-99; Witherington, *End,* 101; Stowers, *Rereading of Romans,* 177, citing esp. Hurd, "I Thess. 2:13-16"). There is no textual evidence for an interpolation, so the interpolation proposal appears suspiciously like "content criticism"; the passage may reflect pre-Pauline tradition later reported in the Synoptics (see Wenham, "Apocalypse," 361-62; Donfried, *Thessalonica,* 203).

20. This punishment may have been rarer in Diaspora courts (cf. *p. Mak.* 1:8, §1). If our later rabbinic sources shed light on earlier tradition here, it could apply to technical blasphemy (cursing with God's name, *Pesiq. Rab.* 22:6), breaking ritual law (*tos. Tem.* 1:1), including violating festivals (*p. Besah* 5:2, §11; cf. *m. Pes.* 7:11), or breaking a Nazirite vow (*m. Naz.* 4:3). But one could also be beaten for more questionable infractions (as Akiba presumably was in *Sipra Qed.* pq. 4.200.3.3; but the punishment is not corporal in the parallel in *Sipre Deut.* 1.3.2), including questionable teaching (*Pesiq. Rab Kah.* 4:3; *Gen. Rab.* 7:2; *Num. Rab.* 19:3, 19; *Eccl. Rab.* 7:23, §4; *Pesiq. Rab.* 14:9). At least Hillelite Pharisees may have supported the later custom of making certain the person was warned before flogging him (*p. Ter.* 7:1) and being conservative on the offenses for which flogging was appropriate (*b. Pes.* 24b). The flogging could be repeated more than once if necessary, in extreme cases (*b. Ker.* 15a; *Pes.* 24a).

21. Hare, *Persecution,* 44; cf. Acts 5:40. Some rabbinic accounts suggest that beatings could be justified if one could demonstrate that the transgressor violated Torah (though much later, cf. the tradition in *Pesiq. Rab Kahana* 4:3; *Pesiq. Rab.* 14:9).

22. Hare, *Persecution,* 45-46. Davies and Allison, *Matthew,* 2:183 note reports of floggings in synagogues (Matt 10:17; 23:34; Acts 22:19; Euseb. *H.E.* 5.16) but suggest that, if rabbinic reports are relevant here, the language may be used loosely (perhaps instrumentally) for discipline at the order of synagogue officials, since it took place outside the synagogue building proper (citing *m. Mak.* 3:12, on the reasonable assumption that the person was not bound to a pillar and whipped inside).

23. Borg, *Conflict,* 139-43; Witherington, *Christology,* 66.

24. Cf. Jos. *War* 1.110; 2.162; *Life* 191.

25. See e.g., Sanders, *Jesus to Mishnah,* 84-89.

26. Vermes, "Jesus the Jew," 118, attributing this lack of halakic concern to Galileans in general.

27. Vermes, "Jesus the Jew," 119.

28. Le Cornu, *Acts,* 388, cites 4QpNah ff3 + 4i.6-8; Jos. *Ant.* 13.372ff; *War* 1.88ff, 96-98.

29. E.g., *Life* 272-75, 302-3. Cf. other violence in *Ant.* 20.180, 206-7; *War* 2.441-42.

30. E.g., 1QpHab 8.8-12; 9.4-7; 12.5; 4QpNah 1.11; cf. also sources in Le Cornu, *Acts*, 388 (adding 1QpHab 1.13; 5.9-10; 8.16; 9.2, 9-10; 11.4-5; 12.2-3; 4Q171 2.18-19; 4.8). The "Wicked Priest" has been identified (for example) with Jonathan (Rost, *Judaism*, 163); John Hyrcanus (Brownlee, "Messianic Motifs," 13-15); or "the false priesthood of the Temple at any time between the Maccabean period and the fall of the Hasmonean dynasty" (Fritsch, *Community*, 83-84). Some have identified the "Young Lion" of 4QpNah 1.5 with Alexander Jannaeus (Allegro, "Light," 92; Eisenman, *Maccabees*, 35); opined that a specific identification is impossible (Rowley, "4QpNahum"); or (utterly implausibly) even identified him with Pontius Pilate (Thiering, *Hypothesis*, 70). As the original teacher of righteousness became a model for the future one (CD 6.10-11) and the title probably applied to all his successors (Buchanan, "Office"), the identity of the original "Wicked Priest" may have applied to the priesthood in perpetuity. Overman, *Crisis*, 224 cites 4QMMT as a sample of halakic debates at Qumran. Some scholars find clues of Essene antagonism toward Pharisaism (Roth, "Subject Matter of Exegesis," 65; idem, "Reference"; Dupont-Sommer, *Manuscrits*, 33; Flusser, *Sage*, 46-47) or Pharisaic or rabbinic opposition to the Essenes (Lieberman, "Light," 396-400). The rabbis nevertheless reflect legal or cultural traditions often shared with Qumran, though reasons for those parallels are debated (e.g., Baumgarten, "Qumran Studies," 256; Neusner, "Testimony"; Schiffman, *Law*).

31. Conflicts with Sadducees, e.g., Jos. *Ant.* 18.17; *m. Yad.* 4:7; *tos. Hag.* 3:35; *Nid.* 5:3; *ARN* 5A; 10B; *b. Nid.* 33b; *Suk.* 48b. As with Jesus, conflicts with Sadducees sometimes involved purity (e.g., *m. Yad.* 4:7; cf. *Nid.* 4:2).

32. Harvey, *History*, 51.

33. Stanton, *New People*, 98-102.

34. Holmén, *Covenant Thinking*, 37-87 (for the most prominent cases, see 53; for developments in the Maccabean period, see 76). For earlier critiques of Sanders' suspicion of conflict in the tradition, see e.g., the important essay of Dunn, "Pharisees," and sources he cites.

35. Holmén, *Covenant Thinking*, 88-332.

36. Holmén, *Covenant Thinking*, 90-106.

37. Holmén, *Covenant Thinking*, 98-99. I doubt that Jesus was actually "indifferent" toward sabbath practice (as Holmén concludes on 105), which was grounded in creation and was one of the ten commandments; but Jesus lacked the rigor of his critics in application.

38. Holmén, *Covenant Thinking*, 221-51 (for food laws, 237-50); cf. Regev, "Individualism." Holmén argues that Jesus was uninterested in purity; I would argue that Jesus instead dealt with it effectively by removing rather than merely separating from it.

39. Holmén, *Covenant Thinking*, 275-329 (esp. 280-84). Holmén regards such behavior as challenging the law (330), but I would see it as a matter of priority rather than rejection. He also argues that Jesus' teaching on divorce and oaths prove harsher than the law (157-87); but Jesus' contemporaries did not regard it as against the law to be stricter than the law (hence, the Pharisaic fence around the law).

40. Holmén, *Covenant Thinking*, 106-28.

41. Holmén, *Covenant Thinking*, 128-57 (on fasting as a pious act stemming from this period, see 129; on its distinctive Jewishness, 133).

42. Holmén, *Covenant Thinking*, 200-20 (esp. 205).

43. Holmén, *Covenant Thinking*, 220.

44. See Lk 19:9, though this is an especially Lukan interest (Lk 13:16, 28; 16:23-30). Cf. the notion that all of Israel (except the worst transgressors of the covenant) would be saved (*m. Sanh.* 10:1).

45. Holmén, *Covenant Thinking*, 251-74.

46. Holmén, *Covenant Thinking*, 331-33.

47. Holmén, *Covenant Thinking*, 335.

48. Holmén, *Covenant Thinking*, 337. He doubts that contemporary Judaism emphasized the "new covenant" much, apart from possibly the Damascus Document (Holmén, *Covenant Thinking*, 336).

Notes to Pages 227-29 | 517

49. Holmén, *Covenant Thinking,* 338 (noting that he sometimes relaxed and sometimes radicalized it; but that he avoided the path markers).

50. E.g., *tos. Shab.* 1:13; see further Abrahams, *Studies* 1:129-35; Safrai, "Religion," 804-7; Sanders, *Judaism,* 208-11; in Asia Minor, see Trebilco, *Communities,* 17-18; I also discussed Sabbath practices in general in Keener, *Matthew,* 353-55.

51. See Sanders, *Jesus to Mishnah,* 7-8.

52. See Sherk, *Empire,* 252-53, §198.

53. See e.g., Hor. *Sat.* 1.9.68-69; Sen. *Ep. Lucil.* 95.47; Gager, *Anti-Semitism,* 57; Whittaker, *Jews and Christians,* 63-71; Jewish people were also well aware of Roman hostility toward the Sabbath (*p. Hag.* 2:1, §8). Hellenistic Jews emphasized it (Kraabel, "Judaism," 142) and created apologetic for it (e.g., Aristob. *frg.* 5 in Euseb. *P.E.* 13.12.9-16).

54. E.g., *Jub.* 2.

55. *Jub.* 2:21, 30.

56. *P. Ned.* 3:9, §3; cf. *Lev. Rab.* 3:1. Later rabbis regularly extolled the Sabbath (e.g., *Gen. Rab.* 10:9-11:10; *Pesiq. Rab.* 23:7-8); some even suggested that the Messiah would come if all Israel kept the Sabbath together (*Ex. Rab.* 25:12).

57. Jos. *Apion* 2.175. Josephus heavily emphasizes sabbath observance (cf. e.g., Weiss, "Sabbath"). Second-century rabbis also expected at least some children to study Torah under a teacher on Friday evenings (Safrai, "Education," 954, cites *m. Shab.* 1:3; *tos. Shab.* 1:12).

58. Jos. *Life* 279.

59. E.g., *tos. Ket.* 1:1; *b. Shab.* 12b; see further Westerholm and Evans, "Sabbath," 1031-32.

60. 1 Macc 2:34-38, 41. Neikiprowetzky, "Sabbat," contends that the situation of war helped generate sabbath casuistry. One could also kill a threatening animal (*p. Shab.* 14:1, §2).

61. *M. Pes.* 6:2 (Akiba); *tos. Pisha* 5:1; with regard to warfare, Jos. *Life* 159, 161 (other peoples had also observed holy days that disallowed offensive warfare; e.g., Xen. *Hell.* 6.4.16; Thucyd. 5.54.2-4; 5.75.5; 5.82.2-3; 8.9.1; Ovid *Fasti* 3.811-12). The later practice of a Sabbath goy (e.g., *Deut. Rab.* 1:21; for sheep-tending, *tos. Shebiit* 2:20; *p. Shebiit* 3:3, 34c) would not have been viewed favorably (CD 11.2; *m. Shab.* 16:8; *tos. Shab.* 13:9; cf. Ex 20:10; Deut 5:14).

62. Sanders, *Jesus to Mishnah,* 13; cf. Falk, *Pharisee,* 149, on *tos. Shab.* 17:14; see further, e.g., *m. Yoma* 8:6; *tos. Shab.* 12:12-13; *p. Erub.* 10:11; *M.S.* 2:1, §4; *Shab.* 6:3; further discussion in Keener, *Matthew,* 357-58. Later rabbis preferred death to Sabbath violation if to pagans the latter would imply apostasy (*b. Sanh.* 74b).

63. See Keener, *John,* 716-17. Against many commentators, Jesus may not even be opposing Sabbath law in Jn 5:17-18 (see Keener, *John,* 645-47).

64. Vermes, *Religion,* 13.

65. Probably true today as well as earlier in history. Levine, "Theory," rightly observes that scholars sometimes use their models (in the case she discusses, sociological ones) to arrive at a Jesus perfectly amenable to modern liberals.

66. E.g., *p. Meg.* 1:6, §2; such punishment had biblical warrant (e.g., Num 15:32-36).

67. Sanders, *Jesus to Mishnah,* 18-19.

68. See CD 10.14-11.18, prohibiting talk of work (10.19) and lifting dust (11.10-11); cf. Jos. *War* 2.147-49, prohibiting even defecation; *Jub.* 50:1-13 and comments in Finkelstein, *Making,* 205-11; 4Q251, frg. 1; 4Q265 frg. 7, 1.6-9); those who forgot the Sabbath were apostate (1Q22, 7-8; *Jub.* 1:10). Some argue the Scrolls represent broader Jewish tradition before Akiba (Kimbrough, "Sabbath"), but parallels in Philo may suggest that the more lenient customs, while not universal, predate the Tannaim (see Belkin, *Philo,* 192-203).

69. *Jub.* 50:8.

70. *Jub.* 50:12-13.

71. Contrast pagans who associated the Sabbath and fasting (e.g., Mart. *Epig.* 4.4.7; Suet. *Aug.* 76; Strabo 16.2.40), perhaps confusing the Sabbath with Yom Kippur.

72. See Sanders, *Jesus to Mishnah*, 18; Sanders, *Judaism*, 367, citing CD 12.3-6.

73. See Sanders, *Jesus to Mishnah*, 22-23, 90; Sanders, *Jesus and Judaism*, 266. The Pharisees tolerated all sorts of disputes, including concerning varied interpretations of Sabbath law (cf. Riesenfeld, *Tradition*, 117-18).

74. E.g., *tos. Shab.* 16:22; *b. Shab.* 5b, bar., early second century.

75. E.g., *tos. Shab.* 16:21; cf. *b. Shab.* 18b.

76. The priestly Sadducean aristocracy appears to have clashed with both Essenes (1QpHab 8.8-12; 9.4-7; 12.5; 4QpNah 1.11) and Pharisees (Jos. *Ant.* 18.17; *m. Yad.* 4:7; *tos. Hag.* 3:35; *Nid.* 5:3; *ARN* 5A; 10B; *b. Nid.* 33b; *Suk.* 48b).

77. See Keener, *Matthew*, 351-54; cf. also Borg, *Conflict*, 139-43.

78. Jos. *Life* 302; but this provoked a backlash of the common people in Josephus' defense (*Life* 303).

79. Besides Holmén, noted above, see Borg, *Conflict*, 145-62.

80. Public prayer and study of Torah must have consumed some of each Sabbath (Jos. *Apion* 1.209; 2.175). Even in more hellenized cities, around 6 p.m. Friday evening religious Jews left secular activities, including political assemblies, and began their Sabbath dinner (Jos. *Life* 279). Most Jewish people seem to have observed traditional limits on Sabbath day's journeys (CD 10.20-21; Acts 1:12; cf. *Num. Rab.* 2:9; *Ruth Rab.* 6:4; for circumventing by means of Sabbath residences, e.g., *p. Maas.* 2:3; *m. Erub.* passim). Bowker (*Pharisees*, 39) suggests that the Pharisees made use here of their permitted Sabbath-day's journey (something Sadducees apparently prohibited), about 1100 meters (2000 cubits, based on Num 35:5; *m. Sot.* 5:3; *m. Erub.* 4:3; 5:7; *b. Erub.* 45a; *Suk.* 44b; Lake and Cadbury, *Commentary*, 10); perhaps seeing Jesus take his disciples to the fields, they confronted them there. Davies and Allison, *Matthew*, 2:307 cite *b. Shab.* 127a for a rabbi in the field on the Sabbath. Witherington, *Christology*, 67 suggests that Mk 2:24 does not actually identify the Pharisees' location (Matthew is more explicit, but elsewhere abbreviates accounts by omitting clarifying details, e.g., omitting messengers in 8:5-8; 9:18-19). Wheat was ready for harvest and gleaning in April (Stauffer, *Jesus*, 84).

81. Sanders, *Jesus and Judaism*, 198, 265; idem, *Jesus to Mishnah*, 1, 20-21; Anderson, *Mark*, 109.

82. Jeremias, *Theology*, 278-79; Stauffer, *Jesus*, 85, 207. Powerful Jerusalemites could send aristocratic delegations, which could include Pharisees, to Galilee (Jos. *Life* 21, 28-29, 72-73, 196).

83. Casey, "Culture," accepts the account as authentic; Sanders, *Jesus to Mishnah*, 21; idem, *Jesus and Judaism*, 265 accepts the exchange as authentic, rejecting only its narrative frame.

84. Prohibited in *m. Shab.* 7:2; though cf. *m. Peah* 2:7-8; Davies and Allison, *Matthew*, 2:307 cite Philo *Vit. Mos.* 2.22; *p. Shab.* 9c. Essenes (probably the strictest Jewish Sabbath-keepers) forbade so much as scooping up drinking water in a vessel (CD 11.1-2)!

85. On normal days one could glean, picking heads of standing grain (Deut 23:25). Whereas the law forbade *preparing* food on the Sabbath (Ex 16:22-30; 35:3; Jos. *War* 2.147; CD 10.9), they were not technically "preparing" it; and the law certainly did not forbid *eating* it (cf. Jos. *Life* 279).

86. Contrary to pagan views (Strabo 16.2.40; Mart. *Epig.* 4.4.7; Suet. *Aug.* 76; cf. Sevenster, *Anti-Semitism*, 130-32), Jewish tradition even prohibited fasting on the Sabbath (CD 11.4-5; *Jub.* 50:12-13; Sanders, *Jesus to Mishnah*, 13 cites Jdt 8:6; Jos. *Life* 279; *m. Taan.* 1.6).

87. Cf. Borg, *Conflict*, 154.

88. Cf. Borg, *Conflict*, 152-53.

89. Sanders, *Jesus to Mishnah*, 20.

90. Borg, *Conflict*, 153; cf. *ARN* 32, §72B.

91. Because the high priest *thought* that David had companions with him (1 Sam 21:2-5), his actions indicate the kind of exceptions that both David and the high priest thought appropriate whether or not David was lying (he probably was). Matt 12:5-6 adds an analogy to which Jesus' detractors could have offered less objection (cf. Saldarini, *Community*, 129).

92. *M. Yoma* 8:6; cf. *p. A.Z.* 2:2, §3.

93. *M. Shab.* 14:4; cf. *m. Shab.* 6:2.

94. *Tos. Shab.* 12:12.

95. *M. Eduy.* 2:5; *Shab.* 22:6; *Yoma* 8:6; Lachs, *Commentary*, 199-200 adds *Mek.* on Ex. 31:13.

96. Cf. this entire discussion in Sanders, *Jesus to Mishnah*, 13; idem, *Figure*, 208.

97. Cf. Danker, *New Age*, 77; Sanders, *Jesus to Mishnah*, 21; Rhoads and Michie, *Mark*, 84.

98. *Tos. Shab.* 16:22; cf. Sanders, *Figure*, 268.

99. Acts 5:34-40; 23:6-9; Jos. *Ant.* 20.200-1.

100. Stanton, *New People*, 98.

101. *P. Shab.* 1:4.

102. Falk, *Pharisee*, 118-27, limits this probably too narrowly to Shammaites, although as the dominant majority before 70 they probably did comprise the bulk of his Pharisaic opposition.

103. E.g., *tos. Yoma* 5:12; *b. Sot.* 41b-42a; *Pes.* 113b; in Odeberg, *Pharisaism*, 63.

104. *M. Sot.* 3:4; *ARN* 37A; 45, §124B; *b. Sot.* 22b, bar.; *p. Sot.* 5:5, §2. See further Moore, *Judaism*, 2:193; Sandmel, *Judaism*, 160-61; cf. Rubenstein, "Hypocrites." For love as a motivation superior to fear, see also *b. Sota* 31a.

105. *B. Yoma* 72b.

106. Cf. Bonsirven, *Judaism*, 58.

107. *B. Sanh.* 103a; *Yoma* 86b; Moore, *Judaism*, 2:190 (citing, e.g., *b. Sot.* 41b; 42a).

108. Davies and Allison, *Matthew*, 3:260-67 (on Matt 23, the harshest of the critiques).

109. Cf. e.g., 1QS 1.22-24; CD 4.13, 16; 19.14; as the "congregation of Belial," see 1QH 2.22-23.

110. See e.g., Jos. *Ag. Ap.* 2.89-111; Tac. *Hist.* 5.5; Diod. Sic. 34.3; Raspe, "Manetho on Exodus."

111. It is difficult to deny that Jesus authentically uttered at least some "woes" (Matt 11:21//Lk 10:13).

112. See especially Johnson, "Slander." Thus, for example, Josephus complains that the accusations of a particular opponent of Judaism merely prove the accuser's ignorance and inferior moral character (*Apion* 2.3); the accuser, he opines, is like a dog or an ass (2.85).

113. Overman, *Gospel*, 16-23; cf. McKnight, "Critic."

114. Overman, *Gospel*, 17-18, including Qumran (1QpHab 7.1-5; Overman, *Gospel*, 24-25), 1 *En.* 99:10-12 and *Psalms of Solomon* (ibid., pp. 26-27). In 2 *Baruch* the law reveals who is wicked (41:3; 51:4; 54:14; ibid., p. 27), as in 4 *Ezra* (9:36-37; ibid., pp. 27-28). Josephus regards the Pharisees as the law's most accurate interpreters (*War* 1.110; 2.162; *Life* 191; *Ant.* 17.41; cf. Acts 22:3; 26:5), further suggesting that this was a focus of debate within post-70 Judaism (ibid., pp. 68-71).

115. Jos. *Ant.* 17.41-42. Josephus is further known to inflate numbers (cf. Feldman, "Introduction: Josephus," 45-46; Safrai, "Description in Works," esp. 320-21).

116. Avi-Yonah, "Geography," 109-10, argues for a population of about 2,800,000 for pre-70 Jewish Palestine; some estimate at about 2.5 (Jeffers, *World*, 213) or 3 million (Stambaugh and Balch, *Environment*, 83). But estimates vary between one and six million (McRay, *Archaeology and NT*, 123).

117. Boccaccini, *Judaism*, 215.

118. Jos. *Life* 291.

119. Davies and Allison, *Matthew*, 3:271.

120. See more fully Keener, *Matthew*, 536-37; cf. Bauer, "Characters," 366; Luz, *Matthew*, 76; Viviano, "World." Some Christian preachers have caricaturized ancient Pharisaic piety to avoid the demands Jesus' condemnations otherwise would make on Christians today (see the critique of this caricature in Odeberg, *Pharisaism*).

121. Matt 23:6-7//Lk 11:43 overlaps with Mk 12:38-39.

122. This saying undoubtedly goes back to an original Aramaic saying of Jesus; Luke's "rue" (Lk 11:42) translates an Aramaic word that resembles the Aramaic term for "dill" (Matt 23:23; Argyle, *Matthew*, 175; Borg, *Conflict*, 100). "Cummin" is a Semitic term (Smith, *Tannaitic Parallels*, 7).

123. Cf. Jeremias, *Jerusalem*, 254.

124. Probably *m. M.S.* 4:5.

125. *M. Demai* 2:1.

126. Cf. Goulder, *Midrash,* 22. Hepper, *Plants,* 132-33 argues that the text refers to the horse-mint (*M. longifolia;* the traditional spearmint entered this region only later).

127. *M. Uktzin* 3:6; for this information, see Sanders, *Jesus to Mishnah,* 48. By the second century, rabbis exempted "rue" (Lk 11:42) from requirement for tithe, suggesting to some that Matthew may preserve the more original wording here (*m. Sheb.* 9:1; McNamara, *Judaism,* 204; Gundry, *Matthew,* 463, who usually favors Luke).

128. See Odeberg, *Pharisaism,* 43.

129. *Sipra VDDeho.* par. 1.34.1.3, par. 12.65.1.3; *ARN* 1, §8B; *b. Men.* 43b; cf. Johnston, "Least of Commandments," 207. Some texts offered summaries of fundamental principles (e.g., Deut 10:12-13; Mic 6:8).

130. Sanders, *Jesus to Mishnah,* 32.

131. Cf. Sanders, *Jesus to Mishnah,* 38. Some (Schweizer, *Matthew,* 441; Gundry, *Matthew,* 464; Lachs, *Commentary,* 370, citing *b. Hul.* 67a; cf. *Shab.* 20a) also claim that Pharisees strained everything "through a cloth." While this practice may have occurred (on the use of cloths and other filters in antiquity, see e.g., Hurschmann, "Filter"), it appears unclear how widespread it was in this period.

132. Ach. Tat. 2.21.4-5; 2.22.

133. Babrius 84.

134. Cf. *b. Ket.* 67a. Jesus uses a camel in a graphic image in Mk 10:25 whereas Babylonian sages used an elephant; possibly Jesus shared the camel image with other Judean teachers (cf. Abrahams, *Studies* 2:208; Dalman, *Jesus-Jeshua,* 230; Jeremias, *Parables,* 195; Bailey, *Peasant Eyes,* 166). That Jesus there uses a camel as hyperbole for something impossibly large is consistent with his usage here.

135. Black, *Aramaic Approach,* 175-76; Stein, *Method and Message,* 13; Chilton, *Approaches,* 119. Prophets had often used puns to foretell judgment (the Hebrew of Amos 8:2; Mic 1:10-15; Jer 1:11-12).

136. The Mishnah regularly distinguishes between inner and outer parts of vessels with respect to cleanness (McNamara, *Judaism,* 197, cites *m. Kel.* 25:1-9; *Par.* 12:8; *Toh.* 8:7), and some discussions of cleanness go back to the first-century disputes between the schools of Shammai and Hillel (*b. Shab.* 14b, bar.).

137. Neusner, "Cleanse," 492-94; *m. Ber.* 8:2. Cf. *b. Ber.* 51a; Sanders, *Jesus to Mishnah,* 39; though cf. also the skepticism here of Maccoby, "Washing."

138. Neusner, "Cleanse," 495, thinks that the Gospel writers after 70 did not understand the original application. Yet while Matthew probably writes after 70, his own learning in the law probably predates 70, and he may have known earlier Pharisaic views. Given Jesus' larger range of teachings on purity, he undoubtedly intended his saying metaphorically, as Matthew infers.

139. Black, *Aramaic Approach,* 2; Burney, *Origin,* 9; Argyle, *Matthew,* 176. Luke, who may have known translations from both versions, may have adopted the version most useful to him (utility supplying the dominant ancient Jewish criterion for text criticism). By contrast, Gundry, *Matthew,* 466 suggests an original play on words by Jesus himself.

140. Touching a bier (Lk 7:14) would also have this effect.

141. Num 19:11-14; Jos. *Ant.* 18.38; *m. Kel.* 1:4. Pharisees extended this further than Sadducees (*m. Yad.* 4:7; cf. *ARN* 41A).

142. Sanders, *Jesus to Mishnah,* 34, 232. Cf. CD 12.15-17 (wood, stone, nails, or dust in a room); 4QMMT section B, lines 72-74 (a piece of a bone); Maccoby, "Corpse"; for later exceptions, probably following the purported cleansing of Tiberias (on which see e.g., Levine, "Purification"), cf. e.g., *b. Bek.* 29b; *Ber.* 19b; *B.M.* 114b. In "cases of doubt" (e.g., *Sipra Taz.* pq.1.123.1.6), as in Lk 10:30-32, the priest and Levite might well avoid the possible corpse (cf. Borg, *Conflict,* 104-5; Sanders, *Jesus to Mishnah,* 41-42), in practice if not in theory (cf. *ARN* 11A); though cf. *p. Nazir* 7:1, §§7, 15; Abrahams, *Studies* 1:110.

143. *M. M.K.* 1:2; *M.S.* 5:1; *Shek.* 1:1; *b. B.M.* 85b; *p. M.K.* 1:2, §7; for other warning markers see *tos. M.S.* 5:13.

144. Argyle, *Matthew*, 176; Schweizer, *Matthew*, 442; Meier, *Matthew*, 271; Sanders, *Jesus to Mishnah*, 39.

145. Borrowing the image from Ezek 13:10-12. Luke's form of the saying is thus probably closer to the original wording (Gundry, *Matthew*, 466; Borg, *Conflict*, 113-14), although Jesus may have originally alluded to the way first-century Jews treated the exterior of the very common limestone ossuaries to beatify them (Lachs, "Matthew 23:27-28"). Flusser, *Sage*, 45, argues that Essenes called Pharisees "whitewashed" (CD 8.12; 19.25), and a Sadducean sympathizer denounced them as "painted" (*b. Sot.* 22b).

146. Abrahams, *Studies*, 2:30, citing similar puns in Ps 5 and Jer 5:16.

147. This is not to suggest that ancient Judaism simply conflated ritual and moral impurity (see Himmelfarb, "Impurity and Sin"; Klawans, "Impurity"; idem, "Idolatry"); Klawans, "Purity," 283, argues that only Qumran actually identified the two (in 275, he argues that the rabbis normally distinguish impurity from sin).

148. *Pesiq. Rab Kah.* 4:7; *Pesiq. Rab.* 14:14; Jeremias, *Theology*, 211. On the authenticity of Mk 7:15, see Holmén, *Covenant Thinking*, 245-49 (supporting it).

149. Cf. Philo *Migr. Abr.* 89-93; probably Ps.-Phoc. 228. This could be a temptation especially in the Diaspora, as later Gentile Christianity could be used to illustrate.

150. I treat these in greater detail in Keener, *Matthew*, 540-54.

151. E.g., suspending the sabbath for defensive warfare (1 Macc 2:34-38, 41).

152. *Sipre Deut.* 175.1.3.

153. E.g., remains of synagogues suggest seating by rank: the elders sat on the raised platform with the Torah scroll, facing the congregation (*tos. Meg.* 4:21; Lachs, *Commentary*, 367). In the same way esteemed sages were granted special rank (*tos. Sanh.* 7:8; *b. Hor.* 13b, bar; *p. Sanh.* 1:2, §13; *Taan.* 4:2, §§8-9). Most of the people respected sages and their disciples (Goodman, *State*, 77-78), and honors for rabbis seem to have grown in time (cf. e.g., Neusner, *Sat*, 76, 101). Later rabbis believed that the whole town must mourn when a sage died (*tos. M.K.* 2:17); disciples served rabbis (*ARN* 25A; *Gen. Rab.* 22:2) and could not give legal rulings in the presence of their own teachers (*Sipra Shemini Mekhilta deMiluim* 99.5.6; *Pesiq. Rab Kah.* 26:6/7).

154. The Eighteen Benedictions also emphasize God's "power" to raise the dead. They do not, however, connect this power with the martyr tradition of offering oneself completely as a sacrifice for martyrdom.

155. In Scripture, see e.g., 1 Kgs 18:4, 13; 2 Chron 25:16 (esp. relevant for Matthew's context); Jer 26:20-23; for more general persecution, Amos 2:12; 7:12-13; Is 30:10. Jewish tradition amplified prophetic martyrology further (e.g., Jos. *Ant.* 10.38; *1 En.* 89:51; *Jub.* 1:12; *Liv. Pr.* passim; see Urbach, *Sages*, 1:560; Michel, *Prophet und Märtyrer*; Schoeps, "Prophetenmorde"; Hare, *Persecution*, 137-38; Jeremias, *Theology*, 280; Manson, *Sayings*, 126-27; Tilborg, *Leaders*, 46-72; Amaru, "Killing"; Davies and Allison, *Matthew*, 1:465), as did later Christian (the interpolation in *Sib. Or.* 2.248) and Islamic (Qur'an 4.155; 5.70) tradition.

156. Jos. *Ant.* 14.22-24; this is rabbinic literature's "Honi the Circle-Drawer" (*m. Ta'an.* 3:8).

157. So also Jeremias, *Theology*, 146. The "tombs" of Matt 23:29//Lk 11:47 may appear here by means of a verbal link with Matt 23:27//Lk 11:44 (early Christians undoubtedly linked Jesus' sayings as Jewish interpreters linked biblical texts). Veneration of holy persons' and ancestral tombs is an ancient practice in the Middle East (Diod. Sic. 17.17.3; Dion. Hal. *Ant. rom.* 8.24.6; 11.10.1; Argyle, *Matthew*, 176; Hill, *Matthew*, 313), but Judean care for prophets' tombs seems to have particularly flourished around Jesus' time (Jeremias, *Theology*, 146 n. 2; Schweizer, *Matthew*, 442-43). Herod's and Hyrcanus' detractors accused them of violating David's tomb (near Jerusalem; Neh 3:16; *ARN* 35A; *tos. B.B.* 1:11; cf. Acts 2:29; see Jos. *Ant.* 7.392-94; 13.249; 16.179-84; *War* 1.61) whereas others reported only his monument for David (Jos. *Ant.* 16.183-84); notable monuments for others who were deceased also appear in this period (*Ant.* 18.108; 20.95; Carmon, *Inscriptions*, 120, 252, §255).

158. Cf. Keener, "Brood of Vipers," 9-10.

159. The order of the Hebrew canon was not yet fixed in this period (though cf. Beckwith, *Canon*, 211-22; Nowell, "Order"); unlike codices, scrolls could not normally accommodate all the Tanakh in any case. Nevertheless, this saying apparently reflects a milieu following a Hebrew rather than a Septuagint sequence adopted by later Christians (an observation that *might* be counted in favor of the saying's antiquity).

160. E.g., *L.A.B.* 16:2; *Test. Ab.* 13:2A; 11:2B; *Life of Adam* 23; *Apoc. Mos.* 2-3; 40:4-5; *1 Clem.* 3; *Asc. Isa.* 9:8.

161. *Test. Iss.* 5:4.

162. See also Heb 11:4; 12:24; *Jub.* 4:3; *1 En.* 22:6-7; *ARN* 31A; *Gen. Rab.* 22:9. Jewish tradition naturally amplified the judgment on Cain (e.g., *Jub.* 4:31-32; *Test. Benj.* 7:3-5; *ARN* 41A; *Gen. Rab.* 97 NV). Blood crying out for vengeance becomes an accepted principle (*Sib. Or.* 3.310-13; *Pesiq. Rab.* 24:1; cf. Deut 21:9; Aqhat in *ANET* 154; *1 En.* 9:1-2).

163. So e.g., Gundry, *Matthew*, 471-72; France, *Matthew*, 330-31; Urbach, *Sages*, 1:559; Lachs, *Commentary*, 372. By calling his father "Berechiah," Matthew probably conflates this Zechariah with the prophet who wrote the book of Zechariah (see Gundry, *Matthew*, 471; for conflation of these two Zechariahs in later Jewish tradition, see Davies and Allison, *Matthew*, 3:319; for later Byzantine conflation surrounding Zechariah, see Puech and Zias, "Tombeau"). But that Matthew's conflation here is accidental is no more likely than in the transformation of "Amon" and "Asa" into "Amos" and "Asaph" in Matt 1:7-8, 10.

164. *B. Git.* 57b; *p. Taan.* 4:5, §14; *Pesiq. Rab Kah.* 15:7; *Lam. Rab.* 2:2, §4; 4:13, §16; *Eccl. Rab.* 3:16, §1; 10:4, §1; cf. Urbach, *Sages*, 1:559. The tradition appears in later sources, but our largest body of texts (rabbinic literature) includes less haggadah in the earlier collections, and Jesus' words in Q (Matt 23:35; Lk 11:51) may well presuppose a tradition like this one.

165. Even Matthew's report that Jesus invited his opponents to "fill up" their ancestors' propheticidal deeds (Matt 23:32) may reflect early traditional language (cf. 1 Thess 2:16; Hort, *Judaistic Christianity*, 90).

166. *Lives of Prophets* 23:1; *Sipra Behuq.* pq. 6.267.2.1; *p. Taan.* 4:5, §14; *Pesiq. Rab Kah.* 15:7; *Lam. Rab.* 2:20, §23.

167. Cf. Jos. *Ant.* 20.165-66; Krieger, "Feuer." After 70, Jewish prayers also confessed that Israel's sins had brought on the calamity of exile (noted by Neusner, *Beginning*, 19-20, although he disagrees with their verdict). While some sources blame Rome or Israel as a whole, Josephus joins some of the Gospels in blaming the religious leaders (Hearon, "Read"). Later rabbis used this model to chart their own course for Israel (see e.g., Rubenstein, "Narrative").

168. *Sib. Or.* 3.312; *Test. Zeb.* 2:2; *b. Shab.* 33a; *Yoma* 9b.

169. E.g., 2 Chron 23:14-15; cf. Matt 27:6. Shrines often functioned as sanctuaries of refuge (Ex 21:14; 1 Kgs 2:28-29; Diod. Sic. 11.89.6-8; 16.58.6; 17.41.8), and bloodshed there both revealed the wickedness of the killers, inviting judgment (e.g., Diod. Sic. 13.90.1; 17.13.6; Paus. 7.24.6; Jos. *Apion* 2.57), and desecrated the shrine (e.g., Dio Cass. *R.H.* 51.15.5; Diod. Sic. 14.4.6-7; 38/39.17.1).

170. Typically in the Mediterranean world people honored the sanctity not only of sanctuaries but also of ancestral tombs (Dion. Hal. *Ant. rom.* 11.10.1; Appian *R.H.* 8.12.89); thus, for example, destroying such tombs was hideous (Jos. *Apion* 2.58).

171. Jesus here utters another lament (the Aramaic fits the rhythm of a funeral dirge — Manson, *Sayings*, 126; Minear, *Hope*, 107). In contrast to the woes earlier in Matthew's context (Matt 23:13-29), Jesus' words in Matt 23:37 represent a true lament (cf. Baum, *Jews and Gospel*, 54).

172. E.g., Ex 19:4; Deut 32:11; Ps 17:8; 36:7; 63:7; 91:4; *1 En.* 39:7; *Sipre Deut.* 296.3.1; 306.4.1; 314.1.1-6; *Pesiq. Rab.* 4:1.

173. Cf. *2 Bar.* 41:4; *ARN* 12A; *Sipra Qed.* pq. 8.205.1.4; *Sipre Num.* 80.1.1; *b. A.Z.* 13b; *Shab.* 31a; *Gen. Rab.* 47:10; *Song Rab.* 1:1, §10; 1:3, §3; *Pesiq. Rab.* 14:2 (probably these sources develop Ruth 2:12). For the expression in general, cf. *3 En.* 7:1.

174. Jer 8:21-22; 9:1, 10; *Lam. Rab.* Proem 24; Stern, *Parables*, 126-27; contrast Gentile Christian

tradition as early as the second century (cf. Bokser, "Justin," 205-6). Judaism never forgot the biblical picture of God's special love for Israel (see e.g., the sources in Montefiore and Loewe, *Anthology,* 58-85).

175. Glasson, *Advent,* 96-98; Goppelt, *Judaism,* 96; Aune, *Prophecy,* 176; Patte, *Matthew,* 329.

176. Cf. e.g., Ezek 36:33; Amos 9:8-12; Tob 13:6; *Jub.* 1:15-18; Rom 11:25-27; *b. Sanh.* 97b.

177. Cf. Allison, "Prophecy."

Notes to Chapter 17

1. Mack, *Myth,* 67. Mack emphasizes the incompatibility of Jesus' wisdom teaching with apocalyptic in *Lost Gospel,* 31.

2. Sanders, *Jesus and Judaism,* 173. Jewish texts sometimes connected healing with eschatology, but there was no automatic connection (Eve, *Miracles,* 263-66, 379).

3. Tan, *Zion Traditions,* 237.

4. Cf. Vermes, *Religion,* 73-74; Ehrman, *Prophet,* 185.

5. Cf. Robbins, *Teacher,* 54. Nortjé, "Traditions," plausibly harmonizes these images by viewing Jesus as a John redivivus: John and Jesus may have both carried on functions of the eschatological Elijah.

6. Cf. Meier, *Marginal Jew,* 2:1044-45. In view of Q tradition (Mt 11:4-5//Lk 7:22), Jesus probably viewed his miracles as special eschatological signs fulfilling Scripture (especially Is 35; see e.g., Witherington, *Christology,* 171; Sanders, *Figure,* 167-68).

7. Jos. *Ant.* 18.63 (compare the language for Elisha in *Ant.* 9.182). In a negative vein, the rabbinic sources also preserve this tradition of Jesus as miracle-worker (Meier, *Marginal Jew,* 2:621; Vermes, *Religion,* 5). Such sources make it one of the best-attested features of Jesus' ministry. Guyénot, "Apostle," thinks that Jesus viewed John as Elijah and Israel's redeemer; less daringly, Bostock, "Elisha," suggests that Jesus (as John/Elijah's successor) views himself as Elisha.

8. See e.g., 1 Cor 14; cf. numerous treatments of the prophetic Spirit in early Christianity, including in Fee, *Presence;* Forbes, *Prophecy;* Aune, *Prophecy;* Menzies, *Development;* Keener, *Spirit.*

9. I do not, however, refer here to the scholarly reconstruction of "wandering charismatics" (Theissen, *Sociology,* 8-16; Gager, "Review," 176), which seems questionable (for my objections, see ch. 2; somewhat more fully, *Matthew,* 57).

10. See e.g., Jeremias, *Theology,* 78-80; Hill, *Prophecy,* 50-69; Aune, *Prophecy,* 153-69; Borg, *Vision,* 150-71; idem, "Disagreement," 240; Harvey, *History,* 36-65; Theissen and Merz, *Historical Jesus,* 240-80; Allison, *Jesus of Nazareth;* Ehrman, *Prophet;* McKnight, *Vision;* Broadhead, "Priests," 140-41.

11. Cf. Vermes, *Jesus and Judaism,* 5; cf. Hengel, *Leader.* Horsley, *Galilee,* 152-55 also suspects Galileans' loyalty to Torah (but see our ch. 12). From a Pharisaic standpoint such suspicions would be justified, but most undoubtedly saw themselves as loyal to Torah as they understood it.

12. Sanders, *Jesus to Mishnah,* 3. Borg, *Vision,* 15 correctly acknowledges that Jesus was "a charismatic who was a healer, sage, prophet, and revitalization movement founder"; yet he denies that Jesus was an *eschatological* prophet (ibid., 14, basing his view of the majority primarily on a very selective poll — 20 n. 25).

13. E.g., Mack, *Myth,* 57, 87 n. 7; cf. idem, *Lost Gospel,* 31-32. This dichotomy, already found in Schweitzer (who opted for prophet), was an important part of twentieth-century history of interpretation (Hallbäck, "Apocalyptic").

14. Others also question the validity of this contrast (e.g., Van Oyen, "Criteria"), just as sages and mystics were not incompatible (Sterling, *Ancestral Philosophy,* 99-113), and apocalyptic and wisdom overlapped (Aune, *Prophecy,* 113).

15. E.g., McClymond, *Stranger,* 43; Sigal, *Halakah,* 154 (both proto-rabbi and "a charismatic prophet-figure"); Pikaza, "Jesús histórico"; cf. Tan, *Zion Traditions,* 237.

16. Though Josephus allowed for prophecy, the establishment (reflected in Josephus and at a more advanced stage in the rabbis) seems reticent to speak of full-fledged "prophets" in their era (see e.g., Keener, *Spirit*, 14-15 [but cf. 17]; in Josephus, Leiman, "Josephus and Canon"; Bamberger, "Prophet," 305; Best, "Pneuma," 222-25). By contrast, followers of popular prophets either disagreed or, more likely, believed that they lived on the edge of the eschatological era (cf. eschatological expectation at Qumran in Aune, *Eschatology*), a view prone to the sort of political unrest the establishment would wish to avoid.

17. Cf. Horsley and Hanson, *Bandits*, 25.

18. Cf. Horsley and Hanson, *Bandits*, 119.

19. Cf. Robbins, *Teacher*, 114; Sanders, *Figure*, 153; Witherington, *Sage*, 201.

20. See Eve, *Miracles*, especially 384-86.

21. Besides these categories, Webb, *Baptizer*, also lists "clerical prophets" (317-22, including John Hyrcanus); "sapiential prophets" (322-32, including Essenes [322-26]) and Pharisees (326-32).

22. Webb, *Baptizer*, 333-39. On these and other types of prophets, see also e.g., Grappe, "Prophètes."

23. Webb, *Baptizer*, 339-42.

24. Webb, *Baptizer*, 348, following here Horsley, "Prophets," here 462.

25. Jos. *Ant.* 20.97 (Moses and esp. Joshua), 170 (Joshua); see detailed discussion in Gray, *Figures*; more briefly, Bauckham, *Testimony*, 215-21 (with the caveat on 216); Webb, *Baptizer*, 348; Eve, *Miracles*, 324; earlier discussion in Barnett, "Prophets" (= idem, "Sign Prophets"); idem, "Eschatological Prophets." Cf. Rev 11:6. The idea of a new Moses became still more prevalent in later sources, e.g., *Pesiq. Rab Kah.* 5:8; *b. Ber.* 12b; *Ex. Rab.* 1:5; 2:6; 15:11; 19:6; *Lev. Rab.* 27:4; *Num. Rab.* 11:2; *Deut. Rab.* 9:9; *Ruth Rab.* 5:6; *Eccl. Rab.* 1:9, §1; 3:15, §1; *Song Rab.* 2:9, §3; *Pesiq. Rab.* 15:10; 52:8; cf. *tos. Ber.* 1:10; *p. Ber.* 1:5, §8; Longenecker, *Christology*, 39-40.

26. See Keener, *John*, 270-71; Eve, *Miracles*, 115-16, 324. On these sign prophets, see initially Barnett, "Prophets"; now Evans, "Josephus on Prophets"; and especially Gray, *Figures*, 112-44. Gray contends, probably rightly, that (137) only the cases of Theudas and the Egyptian genuinely evoke the exodus and conquest traditions; but even these two examples offer sufficient evidence to suggest that such views circulated in first-century Judea (whether already in Jesus' day or perhaps even evoking some early views about him). Philo's miracles focus especially on "the distant Mosaic past" (Eve, *Miracles*, 84), like most early Jewish miracle reports (Eve, *Miracles*, 377, though noting that they were not cessationist).

27. E.g., Sir 33:1-8/36:1-8; cf. 2 Thess 2:9. Eve, *Miracles*, 263-66, 379, notes that early Jewish sources could connect miracles with eschatology (citing 4Q521; *Jub.* 23:23-31), but warns (266) that the association was not "automatic."

28. Consistent with such images, some later rabbis taught that signs offered by biblical signs-prophets anticipated the signs that would take place in the messianic era (*Pesiq. Rab Kah.* 9:4; cf. related ideas in Marmorstein, *Names*, 175).

29. Cf. Sanders, *Jesus and Judaism*, 138, 171; Meeks, *Prophet-King*, 163-64; Horsley, "Prophets."

30. See Hill, *Prophecy*, 28-29; cf. Betz, *Jesus*, 68.

31. The portrayal of at least some of the apparent revolutionaries in first-century Palestine as "social bandits" has much to commend it (see Keener, *Matthew*, 59-60).

32. Cf. Harvey, *History*, 115; Witherington, *Christology*, 171; Sanders, *Figure*, 167-68. Qumran also may have combined the very texts to which Jesus alluded here, perhaps suggesting a Palestinian tradition (Evans, "Apocalypse," 696; LeCornu, *Acts*, 1388; though cf. Kvalbein, "Wunder"; idem, "Wonders").

33. See Blackburn, "Miracles," 372-74; Evans, *Fabricating Jesus*, 141; see further Twelftree, *Miracle Worker*, passim; earlier, Ladd, *Kingdom*, 47. At least one other ancient Jewish source appears to associate God's reign with exorcism (4Q510 1.4-5; Vermes, *Religion*, 130), by implying that demons feared God's greater power, but the explicit association was apparently not common.

34. Eve, *Miracles,* 324, emphasizes that those reported by Josephus are apparently all later than Jesus.

35. Theissen and Merz, *Historical Jesus,* 308-9. Many scholars have built on the category of "sign prophets" (see early Barnett, "Prophets"). Eve, *Miracles,* 296-325 (esp. 324), thinks them a disparate group, despite Josephus lumping them together; but he might underestimate common factors.

36. Eve, *Miracles,* 385 (noting that healings and exorcisms were "not that essential to the prophetic role," since even most OT prophets did not perform them). On these sign-prophets not performing miracles, especially healings and exorcisms, see also Eve, *Miracles,* 321.

37. Cf. Hoehner, *Antipas,* 206; Bammel, "Feeding"; Witherington, *Christology,* 91, 100

38. Theissen and Merz, *Historical Jesus,* 307-8; Blackburn, "Miracles," 379 (who notes that Jesus rarely is said to pray before working a miracle); Eve, *Miracles,* e.g., 386. Nevertheless, the various Jewish proposals are closer than the significantly later Gentile accounts of Apollonius (see Koskenniemi, "Apollonius"; Evans, "Apollonius"); the stories exhibit some features more characteristic of the Middle East (Williams, *Miracle Stories,* 22-26, 32-33), hence may have taken their current form "in the first three or four decades of the new movement" (Williams, *Miracle Stories,* 168).

39. Theissen and Merz, *Historical Jesus,* 290.

40. Theissen and Merz, *Historical Jesus,* 309.

41. See also Theissen and Merz, *Historical Jesus,* 297-301.

42. So also Funk et al., *Acts of Jesus,* 85; Montefiore, *Gospels,* 1:119.

43. Yamauchi, "Magic," 90-91, cites *b. Sanh.* 43a; *tos. Hul.* 2:22-23; cf. Vermes, *Jesus the Jew,* 79.

44. See e.g., Cook, *Interpretation,* 36-39 (also Porphyry on 138).

45. Cf. *b. Sanh.* 107b; in paganism, Cook, *Interpretation,* 36-39, 138. Although rabbinic sources do not recite the charge before the late second century (Flusser, *Judaism,* 635), Sanders, *Jesus and Judaism,* 166, rightly notes that the charge concerning Jesus must be early; "Why answer a charge that was not levelled?" (see Mk 3:22; cf. Jn 8:48).

46. Jos. *Ant.* 18.63 in Vermes, "Notice"; idem, *Jesus the Jew,* 79; see also Meier, *Marginal Jew,* 2:621; Theissen and Merz, *Historical Jesus,* 74 (arguing that Josephus seeks to report about Jesus with the same neutrality he used concerning John and James); Voorst, *Jesus Outside NT,* 102.

47. *Ant.* 9.182.

48. See Stauffer, *Jesus,* 10-11 (though the Mandean and Islamic evidence he cites is too late for actual historical relevance). For Jesus as a worker of miracles (attributed by his detractors to magic), see e.g., Qur'an 5.110. The issue never arises clearly in Paul (except with respect to his own miracle-working), though cf. Wenham, "Story," 307-8.

49. See e.g., Twelftree, "Miracles"; idem, *Miracle Worker.*

50. Theissen and Merz, *Historical Jesus,* 113. Miracles are also not widely attached to messianic figures or to the majority of prophets. Using criteria of coherence and dissimilarity, Eve, *Miracles,* 386, argues for the authenticity of Jesus' distinctive ministry of healing and exorcism.

51. Theissen and Merz, *Historical Jesus,* 281 (see more fully 281-315). On miracles as fundamental to Jesus' historical activity, see Twelftree, "Miracles"; idem, *Miracle Worker.*

52. Wright, "Seminar," 114 (suggesting that the reports would rapidly assume a standard form, as they were told and retold).

53. Noted by Meier, "Present State."

54. See e.g., Meier, "Project"; Tan, *Zion Traditions,* 237; Flusser, "Love," 154; Theissen and Merz, *Historical Jesus,* 113, 281-315; Kee, "Century of Quests"; Pikaza, "Jesús histórico"; Rusecki, "Kryteria."

55. Ehrman, *Prophet,* 197-200, notes that scholars can accept Jesus as an exorcist and healer without passing judgment on whether he acted supernaturally. For cross-cultural perspectives on healing, see e.g., Pilch, "Insights"; Pilch, "Sickness," 183; Pilch, *Healing,* 19-36 (esp. 35); for shaman analogies, e.g., Craffert, "Healer" (critiquing Crossan); Davies, "Prophet/healer"; idem, *Healer;* cf. Borg, *Conflict,* 73, 230-31, 305, 373. I will treat this cultural context to philosophic approaches further in my forthcoming work on miracles in first-century Christian narratives.

56. For summaries of this consensus, see Blackburn, "Miracles," 362; Eve, *Miracles*, 16-17; Welch, "Miracles," 360.

57. Sanders, *Jesus and Judaism*, 11. Certainly the Gospels portray Jesus' miracles as "an essential part of that ministry" (Filson, *History*, 105).

58. *Marginal Jew*, 2:678-772; for historical evidence supporting Jesus as a miracle worker, see *Marginal Jew*, 2:617-45; see also Twelftree, *Miracle Worker*; Blomberg, *Gospels*, 127-36.

59. Brown, *Death*, 143-44.

60. Betz, *Jesus*, 58.

61. Betz, *Jesus*, 60.

62. Flusser, "Ancestry," 154.

63. Smith, *Magician*, 16.

64. Neusner, in "Foreword," xxvii, and idem, *New Testament*, 5, 173, offers perhaps the harshest critique of Smith's magical thesis. The charge of magic against Jesus (hardly invented by Jesus' followers) may stem from the earliest gospel tradition (Stanton, "Magician," 175-80).

65. Eve, *Miracles*, 52 (concluding his discussion of miracle in Josephus, 24-52). Like Josephus, Philo overlaps with the Gospels primarily in miracles of provision (Eve, *Miracles*, 84-85).

66. Eve, *Miracles*, 244. They do appear more in later Amoraic haggadah.

67. Eve, *Miracles*, 253, 378. He acknowledges some exorcists, but questions whether they were common (*Miracles*, 378). (Given the different focus of most of the other surviving first-century documents, I would not be so sure.) He also notes rightly that some exorcists have magical associations (*Miracles*, 378).

68. Cf. Sanders, *Figure*, 154, who thinks "fairly certain" that "healing, especially exorcism," was the basis for his fame; cf. Theissen, *Miracle Stories*, 72.

69. Casson, *Travel*, 130-35, 193-94.

70. See e.g., Jos. *War* 2.614; 4.11; *Life* 85; Pliny *N.H.* 5.15.71; *Pesiq. Rab Kah.* 11:16; *Eccl. Rab.* 10:8, §1.

71. Jos. *War* 1.657; Pliny *N.H.* 2.95.208; 5.15.72; Hirschfeld and Solar, "Hmrhs'wt"; idem, "Baths"; Schürer, *History*, 157.

72. The springs of Tiberias were well-known (e.g., *b. Sanh.* 93a; 108a; *Shab.* 40b; 147a; *p. Ned.* 6:1, §2; *Gen. Rab.* 76:5; other references in Urbach, *Sages*, 1:393; Sandmel, *Judaism*, 201).

73. E.g., the leper (Keener, *Matthew*, 259-63); the centurion's servant (*Matthew*, 263-70); the paralytic lowered (in Mark) through the roof (*Matthew*, 288-91); the dead girl and bleeding woman (*Matthew*, 301-5); miraculous feedings (*Matthew*, 402-5, 418-19; idem, *John*, 663-71) and water-walking (*Matthew*, 406-8; idem, *John*, 671-75).

74. For brief critiques of Vermes and Borg on the close relevance of charismatic teachers like Hanina and Honi, see Witherington, *Christology*, 153, 182-83; Chilton, *Approaches*, 45.

75. Jos. *Ant.* 14.22. Cf. Eve, *Miracles*, 277-78, arguing that Josephus' focus is not on Onias' rain-making but on his role in the war (which is not coincidentally Josephus' focus in general). Rain-making is the only miracle common to both Honi and Hanina, and is absent from Jesus' ministry (Blackburn, "Miracles," 378-79).

76. The only Tannaitic account is *m. Ta'an.* 3:8 (Eve, *Miracles*, 274-75), and W. Scott Green and Neusner both deny reliable information even there (Eve, *Miracles*, 275-77).

77. One could use drawing a circle for an ultimatum (Livy 45.12.5; Val. Max. 6.4.3).

78. Eve, *Miracles*, 274.

79. Eve, *Miracles*, 281, notes that this date is uncertain (on 282 conceding, however, that he was probably from the Second Temple period). Amoraic traditions place him in the first century (see Eve, *Miracles*, 287-88).

80. Blackburn, "Miracles," 378.

81. Eve, *Miracles*, 280-81, cites *m. Ber.* 5:5; *Sot.* 9:15 (= *tos. Sot.* 15:5); *Ab.* 3:10-11; *tos. Ber.* 3:20; *Mek.* on Ex 18:21.

82. *M. Ber.* 5:5.

83. *Tos. Ber.* 3:20.

84. Eve, *Miracles,* 282-83 (four centuries, on the Bavli); Blackburn, "Miracles," 378 (three centuries, on the Yerushalmi); see further Avery-Peck, "Piety," 164.

85. Eve, *Miracles,* 285. None involved exorcism (Eve, *Miracles,* 294).

86. Eve, *Miracles,* 289, 295. He also argues (292-93) that the Mishnah's category for Hanina, "men of deed" (*m. Sot.* 9:15), need not specify miracle-workers, noting that the semantic range of "deed" is much broader than "miracle."

87. Eve compares Mexican folk-healer Pedrito Jaramillo, who stood out above other folk-healers of his era (Eve, *Miracles,* 357-59, 379).

88. See also e.g., Meier, "Project"; Strelan, *Strange Acts,* 27; cf. Eve, *Miracle,* 377.

89. For models among signs-sages, see Galley, "Heilige."

90. See Keener, *John,* 270-71; Eve, *Miracles,* 115-16, 324. On these sign prophets, see initially Barnett, "Prophets"; and now especially Gray, *Figures,* 112-44.

91. Cf. Sanders, *Jesus and Judaism,* 138, 171; Meeks, *Prophet-King,* 163-64; Horsley, "Prophets."

92. See e.g., Villalón, "Deux Messies," 62-63; Barrett, *Acts,* 208; citing 1QS 9.10-11; 4QTest (= 4Q175) 5-7; Marshall, "Use of OT," 548; cf. also Teeple, *Prophet,* 51-52; Xeravits, "Moses Redivivus" (suggesting also 11QMelch 2.15-21). Some also mention 1 Macc 14:41; and Mosaic-type attempted prophets in Josephus (e.g., *Ant.* 20.97). Poirier, "Return," thinks Qumran texts envisioned an eschatological prophet and an eschatological priest, corresponding to Moses and Elijah. The Scrolls may also apply the role (and Deut 18:15-18) to the teacher of righteousness, who may have originally filled this role for them (cf. Aune, *Prophecy,* 126; cf. Teeple, *Prophet,* 51-52).

93. A Qumran scroll links the Mosaic prophet (4Q175 1.5-8) with the star from Jacob (Num 24:15-17; 4Q175 1.9-13). This association does not suggest "literary dependence so much as that Qumran and NT authors breathed the same air of eschatological expectation" and used the same Bible (Brooke, "4Q175," 1207). Although the text is "messianic" (see e.g., Villalón, "Deux Messies," 62-63), its messianic figure might not be *the* Messiah in the usual early Jewish sense; the testimonia may address the multiple messianic figures held by the sect (cf. Vermes, *Scrolls,* 247-48).

94. See e.g., Bruce, *Time,* 39; Simon, *Hellenists,* 61, 73. Gaster, *Scriptures,* 393, notes that the Samaritans used the same testimonia for the Taheb as appear in Qumran testimonia (cf. Gaster, *Scriptures,* 444-46, citing Deut 5:25-26; 18:18-19; Num 24:15-17; Deut 33:8-11; Josh 6:26).

95. Bruce, *History,* 37-38; idem, *Time,* 39; on this reading, the prophetic figure of Jos. *Ant.* 18.85-87 might be viewed as the Taheb. On the Taheb (a Mosaic, not Davidic, figure), see *Memar Marqah* 2.40.28; 4:12 (in Boring et al., *Commentary,* 264-65); Teeple, *Prophet,* 63-64; MacDonald, *Samaritans,* 362-63; Bruce, *History,* 37-38; Longenecker, *Christology,* 34; Brown, *John,* 1:172; Dexinger, "Taheb-Vorstellung"; see further Keener, *John,* 610, 619-20.

96. Aune, *Prophecy,* 125-26. Interpreters could apply it to Joshua. Holladay, "Background," and idem, "Jeremiah," suggests that Jeremiah viewed himself in these terms; others compare Elijah (e.g., Konkel, *Kings,* 303). Many prophets may have followed aspects of Moses' model or calling, but Moses remained special (Num 12:6-8; Deut 34:10-12).

97. *Pesiq. Rab Kah.* 5:8; *Num. Rab.* 11:2; *Ruth Rab.* 5:6; *Eccl. Rab.* 1:9, §1; cf. *Pesiq. Rab Kah.* 27:5; *Eccl. Rab.* 3:15, §1; *Tg. Neof.* on Ex 12:42 (but *Tg. Ps.-Jon.* on Ex 12:42 is simpler); Jeremias, "Μωυσῆς," 857-62; Mauser, *Wilderness,* 55-56. Rabbis also compared others to Moses (e.g., *Gen. Rab.* 100:10).

98. Commentators cite *1 En.* 48:6; *4 Ezra* 13:52; Justin *Dial.* 8.4; 110.1; for rabbinic documentation see Vermes, *Jesus the Jew,* 137-39. See further *1 En.* 62:7; *Pesiq. Rab Kah.* 5:8; *Num. Rab.* 11:2; *Ruth Rab.* 5:6; *Song Rab.* 2:9, §3; *Pesiq. Rab.* 15:10; Glasson, *Moses,* 103. Most rabbinic attestation is late, but the basic tradition surely does not derive from inferences from earlier Christian sources like John or Justin's *Dialogue with Trypho.*

99. See e.g., *Pesiq. Rab Kah.* 27:5; *b. Ber.* 12b; *p. Ber.* 1:5, §8; *Ex. Rab.* 1:5; 3:4; 15:11; 19:6; 32:9; *Lev. Rab.* 27:4; *Pesiq. Rab.* 52:8; cf. *tos. Ber.* 1:10; *Eccl. Rab.* 2:15, §2; probably in CD 5.19 (but cf. 7.21); 4Q389 frg. 2.

See more fully Longenecker, *Christology*, 39-41; cf. Qumran imagery in Hatina, "Exile," 349. In some late texts the Messiah would lead home the exiles of Israel (*Pesiq. Rab.* 31:10), i.e., in a new exodus.

100. See e.g., Glasson, *Moses*, 15-19; cf. e.g., Is 12:2 (with Ex 15:2); Is 40:3; 52:4, 12; 63:11-14; Hos 2:14-15; 11:1, 11. On exodus typology in the OT, see extensively Daube, *Exodus Pattern*, passim. N. T. Wright has argued most extensively for Israel's exile as the backdrop for restoration eschatology (cf. also Evans, "Exile"; McKnight, *Vision*); but some contend that the early Jewish data (Pitre, *Tribulation*; Bird, *Gentile Mission*, 39-44) or the NT applications (Bock, "Trial," 119) are more complex.

101. For Moses as king, see Jos. *Ant.* 4.327; *L.A.B.* 9:16; 20:5; Meeks, *Prophet-King*, 107-17, 147-50, 177-79, 181-96, 236.

102. Bammel, "Poor," 124-26.

103. Witherington, *Christology*, 109-10.

104. Cf. Borg, *Conflict*, 171-73; Sanders, *Jesus and Judaism*, 270.

105. Sanders, *Jesus and Judaism*, 232-33; cf. Brown, *Death*, 458. For the eschatological Temple, cf. e.g., Tob 13:10; 14:5; *1 En.* 90:28-29; 91:13, Eth.; *Sib. Or.* 3.657-60, 702, 772-74; 11QTemple cols. 30-45 (which depicts a temple much larger than the current Herodian one — Broshi, "Dimensions"); most extensively, Sanders, *Jesus and Judaism*, 77-90, who emphasizes (pp. 86-87) that precise expectations varied. After the Temple's destruction most Palestinian Jews certainly longed for an imminent new one; cf. e.g., the coin in Carmon, *Inscriptions*, 81, 178; the fourteenth benediction of the 'Amida; *tos. R.H.* 2:9; *Shab.* 1:13; and synagogue mosaics as late as the sixth century (Dequeker, "Zodiaque").

106. E.g., *Jub.* 1:17; *2 Bar.* 4:3; 32:4 (to the extent that the language is intended literally; cf. *Test. Mos.* 2:4, which applies this image to the *first* sanctuary; the fourteenth benediction in Oesterley, *Liturgy*, 65).

107. Cf. Aune, *Prophecy*, 175. For the Temple as the community, cf. 1QS 5.5-6; 8.5, 8-9; 9.6; perhaps CD 2.10, 13; 3.19. See e.g., Flusser, *Judaism*, 37-39, 44; Gärtner, *Temple*, 16-46 (who cites also 4QpIsa d, frg. 1; 1QpHab 12.1ff); Driver, *Scrolls*, 539; Bruce, "Gospels," 76; Wilcox, "Dualism," 93-94; Sanders, *Jesus and Judaism*, 376-77; though cf. Caquot, "Secte." The Temple Scroll even structures the new Temple after Israel's camp in the wilderness (cf. Yadin, "Temple Scroll," 42). The same concept may appear in a more individualized form in Philo *Praem.* 123; cf. *Herm.* 1.*vis.* 3 (especially if the tower may be identified with the temple by way of *1 En.* 89:49-50). Gärtner, *Temple*, 30-42, argues for it also in 4QFlor, but this perspective has been seriously challenged (McNicol, "Temple"; Schwartz, "Temples").

108. Contrary to some who share this perspective, however, "their significance" could be "evocative and not constitutive"; see Richardson, *Israel*, 61.

109. E.g., Jeremias, *Theology*, 234-35. Thus they mark Jesus' movement as a renewal movement within Judaism (e.g., Charlesworth, *Jesus within Judaism*, 138), a frequent scholarly understanding of the earliest Jesus movement (cf. e.g., Horsley, "Movements").

110. E.g., 1QS 8.1-2; 4Q259 2.9; cf. also 1QM 2.1-3; 5.2; 4Q159 frg. 2-4, lines 3-6; 4Q164.4-5; especially (with 1QS 8.1) 4Q259 2.9. For "twelve" in Qumran and other literature, see also Geyser, "Tribes," 392.

111. See Bruce, "Gospels," 75-76; Harrington, *God's People*, 39; Sanders, *Jesus and Judaism*, 104; Evans, "Typologies," 59-60; cf. Jervell, *Luke and People of God*, 82, 89. For the eschatological hope for the twelve tribes, see Sanders, *Judaism*, 291 (citing e.g., 1QM 2.2-3; 11QT 8.14-16; 57.5-6).

112. Even the twelve signs of the zodiac (e.g., Philo *Mos.* 2.112, 124-26; *Rewards* 65; *Pesiq. Rab Kah.* 16:5; *Pesiq. Rab.* 4:1; 29/30A:6; cf. Jos. *War* 5.217)!

113. Jeremias, *Theology*, 235; Sanders, *Jesus and Judaism*, 96-97; *Esth. Rab.* 2:14; though contrast some in *m. Sanh.* 10:5; *tos. Sanh.* 13:12.

114. Cf. Jeremias, *Theology*, 235; Sanders, *Jesus and Judaism*, 98-106.

115. Bauckham, "James," 430 (citing the views of Spencer and Daube, not his own).

116. Sanders, *Jesus and Judaism*, 11 ("almost indisputable"), 98-101 (esp. refutation of Vielhauer in 99-100); Witherington, *Christology*, 126-27; Meier, "Circle of Twelve"; Ehrman, *Prophet*, 186-87; Charlesworth, *Jesus within Judaism*, 137; on the embarrassment, Zwiep, *Judas*, 47.

117. Cf. possibly 1 Cor 11:23; whether this verse refers to Judas' betrayal (Fee, *Corinthians*, 549, given the last supper context) or not (Hays, *1 Corinthians*, 198; Smith, *Symposium*, 188, citing Rom 4:25; 8:32; perhaps Is 53:6, 12b) is debated.

118. Sanders, *Jesus and Judaism*, 101. Such a standardized list would be difficult in any case in the earliest period, given the frequent use of multiple names (see e.g., Acts 1:23). On the list, see detailed discussion in Bauckham, *Eyewitnesses*, 97-108 (esp. 97-101).

119. Luke might follow Q here, Matthew (Matt 10:3) preferring Mark on this point. Although the lists could include different persons at this point, they could also reflect differing traditions of the names of the same person, since individuals often had multiple names in antiquity (e.g., *P. Oxy.* 494.32; 1273.3, 49; *CPJ* 2:140, §§248-49; 2:143, §261; 2:145, §§269-70; 2:146, §274; 2:147, §275; 2:147, §276; 2:151, §298; 2:153, §304; 2:154, §311; 2:156, §321; 3:9, §453; *CIJ* 1:24, §30; 2:111, §879).

120. See Sanders, *Jesus and Judaism*, 20-22, 104; Borg, *Conflict*, 70; Hunter, *Gospel According to Paul*, 38; Witherington, *End*, 84-92.

121. The polemical basis in arguing for or against authenticity, strictly irrelevant to exegesis or historical endeavor, is in any case a moot point. Luz (who rejects the passage's authenticity for other reasons) is probably correct that the text nowhere implies that Peter would be institutionally succeeded by anyone (Luz, "Primacy Text").

122. E.g., 1 Cor 1:12; 9:5; 15:5; Gal 2:7.

123. Cullmann, "Πέτρος," 105.

124. Most critical scholars denied the authenticity of this Matthean material (in contrast to its Markan framework — cf. Montefiore, *Gospels*, 1:182) until studies confirmed its early Palestinian character; the most common theory then became that it represented a postresurrection saying (Cullmann, *Peter*, 166-67, 180; Meier, *Matthew*, 179). Cullmann located it in the Passion story (*Peter*, 184); see Gundry's reasoned critique (Gundry, "Framework"). The debate has somewhat receded along with the polemics that supported it; most NT scholars, including both Roman Catholics and Protestants, concur that Peter died in Rome but doubt that Matt 16:18 intended the authority later claimed by the Popes (Pelikan, "Sees," 60). Hagner, *Matthew*, 465-66, also supplies arguments for authenticity; on Jesus' intention for the church, cf. also Bowman, *Intention*, 191-225.

125. Cf. Ellis, *Matthew*, 128-29; Weeden, *Mark*, 43; Weber, "Notes 1961"; idem, "Notes 1962." Feuillet, "Primauté," suggests that Mark omitted it because he depended on Peter, who was too humble to emphasize it.

126. Gundry, *Matthew*, 330-31.

127. Some deny the likelihood of this logion because it differs from other sayings of Jesus (Goppelt, *Theology*, 1:213), whereas others find its elements in the earliest strata of Jesus tradition (Michaels, *Servant*, 301-2). The passage has three strophes of three lines apiece (Meier, *Matthew*, 179; Gundry, *Matthew*, 331). Some compare the saying's structure to Matthew's love of Semitic parallelism (Gundry, *Matthew*, 331), but others point to the Semitic language as indicating an early tradition (Ellis, *Matthew*, 129-30; Harrington, *Matthew*, 68; Cangh and Esbroek, "Primauté"; Young, *Theologian*, 203 n. 2; cf. Jesus' use of beatitudes, etc., in pre-Matthean tradition). Some who doubt the saying's authenticity nevertheless accept it as pre-Matthean (Carroll, "Peter"; Bornkamm, "Authority," 111).

128. Davies and Allison, *Matthew*, 2:609-15.

129. In 1987, Duling, "Binding," doubted the authenticity of "binding and loosing" because it violated the criterion of dissimilarity, though acknowledging that it fit that of Jewish environment; because I rank the latter criterion much more highly I believe that it cancels the former out.

130. E.g., an angel blesses Aseneth for receiving revelation (*Jos. Asen.* 16:14/7) and a rabbi would praise his disciples (*m. Ab.* 2:8). Revelatory eschatological knowledge also appears in 1Q27 1.7

131. Young, *Theologian*, 199.

132. Some scholars cite against the passage's reliability Peter's lack of corresponding prominence in the early church (Beare, *Matthew*, 353), an argument that (if true) could be turned on its head (why would the early church have created a saying that they knew was untrue in their time?). Other schol-

ars more reasonably find evidence for a measure of Peter's prominence in the early church (1 Cor 1:12; 9:5; Gal 1:18; 2:9; 1 Pet 1:1) and question how he would have obtained this prominence unless he were close to Jesus and somehow appointed to lead the other members of the Twelve (Sanders, *Jesus and Judaism,* 105).

133. Some suggest symbolic value here (Matt 12:41; 16:4; cf. Gundry, *Matthew,* 332-33), *perhaps* playing off the traditional and similar name we note in John. The imaginative suggestion that "bar-Jona" represents an Akkadian (!) loanword for terrorist identifying Peter as a Zealot or outlaw (cf. Cullmann, *State,* 16; Theissen, *Sociology,* 11) has little to commend it (see Brown, Donfried and Reumann, *Peter,* 88 n. 203).

134. Williams, "Names," 104 (noting that it never occurs in this period); for a possible occurrence in 4Q130.8-9, see Charlesworth, "Peter." The name "Petros" might appear rarely and later in some Aramaic Jewish texts (*Gen. Rab.* 92:2; *Ex. Rab.* 52:3).

135. Many scholars point to Abraham's role in Is 51:1-2, as well as to some very late (possibly *too* late; cf. also Witherington, *End,* 89; Arnéra, "Rocher") rabbinic expositions on it (Ford, "Abraham"; Cullmann, "Πέτρος," 106; Ellis, *Matthew,* 129-30; Bruce, *Time,* 60; cf. Chevallier, "Pierre"; Manns, "Halakah"); others object that the differences are too great (Hagner, *Matthew,* 470). Witherington, *End,* 89 suggests the foundation of a new temple, citing the language of *m. Yoma* 5:2 (cf. Jn 7:37-39). The Qumran sect was also founded on a "rock," a refuge against death (1QH 6.23-28; Driver, *Scrolls,* 519; Witherington, *End,* 89; cf. 1QS 8.7; Hill, *Matthew,* 261).

136. Cf. Sanders, *Jesus and Judaism,* 146-47; Cullmann, *Peter,* 19 n. 14.

137. My own argument appears in Keener, *Matthew,* 426-30.

138. The image is fairly consistent with Jesus' portrayal of his teachings as a "rock" in Lk 6:47-49// Matt 7:24-27.

139. Boring, *Sayings,* 213-14.

140. Cf. e.g., Mk 4:15-20, 26-32; 13:5-13 (vs. 13:14-27). (See more fully our discussion in ch. 14.)

141. Albright and Mann, *Matthew,* 195; cf. Hunter, *Message,* 53.

142. This included teachers who were founding schools of thought (cf. e.g., Culpepper, *School,* 123).

143. Albright and Mann, *Matthew,* 121; Brown, Donfried and Reumann, *Peter,* 92; Harrington, *Matthew,* 29.

144. Frequently noted, e.g., Bultmann, *Theology,* 1:38; Foakes Jackson and Lake, "Development," 327-28; Lake and Cadbury, *Commentary,* 54; Richardson, *Theology,* 285; Meeks, *Urban Christians,* 79; Davies and Allison, *Matthew,* 2:629; cf. 1 Macc 2:56; Jos. *Ant.* 3.84, 188, 292, 300, etc.

145. Ridderbos, *Paul,* 328; Bruce, *Books,* 84; Klaasen, *Anabaptism,* 112-16.

146. Ladd, *Theology,* 110; France, *Matthew,* 255.

147. *Ekklēsia* could include any gathering (cf. Deissmann, *Light,* 112-13), even an army (Dion. Hal. *Ant. rom.* 6.94.1). Most often in regular Greek usage it meant the "citizen assembly" of a local community (e.g., Acts 19:32, 39), including in Republican Rome (Dion. Hal. *Ant. rom.* 6.87.1; 7.17.2; 11.50.1) and Jerusalem (Jos. *War* 4.162; 7.412).

148. Biblical tradition had often spoken of "building up" the community of God (e.g., Ruth 4:11; Ps 51:18; 69:35; 147:2; Jer 1:10; 24:6; 31:4, 28; Ladd, *Theology,* 109; cf. Prov 9:1); Qumran texts indicate that the usage remained familiar among Jesus' contemporaries (4QpPs 37.3, 16; Jeremias, *Theology,* 168), although there *God* was the builder of his community (Gundry, *Matthew,* 336).

149. With shorter Markan (Mk 6:7-11) and longer "Q" forms (cf. Matt 10:7-8, 12-13, 15-16//Lk 10:3, 6, 9, 12).

150. Sanders, *Figure,* 123-24 doubts the disciples misunderstood as much as Mark implies or proved as independent as Matt 10 implies; otherwise it would be difficult to reconcile the two pictures. Yet even in Mark Jesus *expects* the disciples to exercise more faith, and it is only the especially difficult cases (like Mk 9:18-19, 28-29) that stump them. Disciples were known to sometimes fall short of their masters' faith (cf. 2 Kgs 5:20; 6:15-17; the later story about Levi ben Sisi and two generations after him

in *p. Taan.* 3:8, §2). Since Matthew does not report the results of their mission, it would actually be Mark (if either of them) who would be exaggerating their success (cf. Malina, *Windows,* 131).

151. Jewish texts contain similar statements in which the sheep represent Israel or the pious among them (*1 En.* 90.6-17; *Tanh. Toledot* 5; Vermes, *Religion,* 89). Nevertheless, Jesus drives home the point still more graphically: his sheep are actually *sent* among the predators (Vermes, *Religion,* 89).

152. See *b. Bek.* 29a; *D.E.* 2.4; Dalman, *Jesus-Jeshua,* 226; Lachs, *Commentary,* 180; cf. *m. Ab.* 1:3; *Sipre Deut.* 48.2.7; *p. Ned.* 4:4.

153. Although possibly a free-floating tradition (the context differs in Matthew and Luke), Wenham, *Rediscovery,* 101-34 suggests that it was transmitted as part of Jesus' eschatological discourse.

154. Manson, *Sayings,* 217.

155. Sanders, *Jesus and Judaism,* 100; idem, *Figure,* 190; Witherington, *Christology,* 140-41.

156. Cf. the probable reapplication to the whole church even in Rev 21:12-14.

157. Martin, *James,* 8-9.

158. For Sodom (Matt 10:15; 11:23//Lk 10:12), e.g., Is 1:9-10; 3:9; Jer 23:14; Lam 4:6; Ezek 16:46-56; Amos 4:11; cf. Sir 16:8; *Jub.* 36:10; 3 Macc 2:5; *tos. Sanh.* 13:8; *Shab.* 7:23; *Sipra Behuq.* par. 2.264.1.3; *Sipre Deut.* 43.3.5. For woes, see e.g., Is 18:1; 33:1; Jer 13:27; 48:46; Ezek 16:23; Hab 2:15; cf. both in Lam 4:6.

159. See Dalman, *Jesus-Jeshua,* 229.

160. On the authenticity of the eschatological discourse, see Wenham, *Rediscovery;* idem, "Apocalypse"; Pitre, *Tribulation,* 231-53, 264-91, 348-77.

161. Certainly this is the immediate context in Matthew; see Matt 24:15; Meier, *Matthew,* 274; Baum, *Jews and Gospel,* 54; cf. Matt 21:13; Jer 12:7; Tob 14:4.

162. The Temple was also "your house" (Jdt 9:13). Later Jewish teachers even used a bilingual play on words to identify Jeremiah's mission with the Temple's "desolation" (*Pesiq. Rab Kah.* 13:12, same Greek term as here); for them, the house left desolate was plainly the Temple (*p. Taan.* 4:5, §11), and exile under a foreign power inevitably followed the "desolation" of their city (*4 Bar.* 5:28).

163. Jos. *Apion* 1.154.

164. *Apion* 1.132.

165. Israel saw itself rising or falling with its Temple (Jer 7:3-15); the restored Temple is a symbol of Israel's restoration and glory in Ezekiel 40–44.

166. Mack, *Myth,* 10 n. 4.

167. Mack, *Myth,* 327 thinks the attribution of Mark 13's eschatological sayings to Jesus is part of Mark's fiction. Kelber, "Conclusion," 168-72, contends that Mark, being anti-Temple, must be post-70; Marxsen, however, believes Mark sees in the Temple's destruction a herald of the imminent end (Marxsen, *Mark,* 168, 189). But while most Jews would have viewed the Temple as invulnerable before 66, some thought otherwise (see text).

168. Only *GThom* 71 attributes the statement to Jesus himself, and this version is clearly late and gnosticizing (Aune, *Prophecy,* 173). Nevertheless Sanders, *Jesus and Judaism,* 73-74 is probably right to suggest that this reflects an authentic (though probably misinterpreted) saying; it is multiply attested and not the sort of threat one would have made up later (also Theissen, *Gospels in Context,* 113, 194; at length on Jesus' temple prediction, see Sanders, "Temple"). If the four-beat rhythm in the proposed Aramaic reconstruction is accurate, it may indicate that Jesus originally offered this teaching privately to the disciples (cf. Jeremias, *Theology,* 22-23).

169. Cf. Hare, *Persecution,* 6.

170. See Sanders, *Jesus and Judaism,* 365 n. 5.

171. Cf. Borg, *Conflict,* 165-70. This was true even in the Diaspora; see e.g., *Let. Aris.* 100-1; Philo *Spec. Laws* 1.76; cf. 4 Macc 4:9-12.

172. *Test. Levi* 15:1; cf. 14:6. This work has at least Christian interpolations, though one need not assume one here.

173. *Test. Moses* 5:4.

174. *Test. Mos.* 6:8-9.

175. *Sib. Or.* 3.665.

176. *Sib. Or.* 3.657-60. John J. Collins apparently regards this material as pre-Christian (*OTP* 1:358).

177. Sanders, *Figure,* 262 cites the repeated expectation of this new Temple (e.g., *1 En.* 90:28-29; 11QTemple 29.8-10; cf. the hope of restoration in the seventeenth benediction of the Amida).

178. Witherington, *End,* 92 (following Juel, *Messiah,* 204), because some interpreters already took 2 Sam 7:13-14 as Messianic (see 4QFlor).

179. Sanders, *Figure,* 259.

180. Crossan, *Historical Jesus,* 359.

181. Jesus could have envisioned the new Temple in partly or wholly "spiritual" forms, or a spiritual present one in addition to a future literal one; Qumran attests belief in a spiritual present temple as well as an eschatological literal one.

182. 1QpHab 9.6-7. Scholars debate the identity of the Kittim in the earliest scrolls, but they surely at least included the Romans in the later ones (cf. 4QpNah 1.3; 1QpHab 3.11; 4Q161, frg. 8, 9, 10; 4Q491 A frg. 10, col. 2, lines 8-12; frg. 13, line 5; see e.g., Dupont-Sommer, *Writings,* 167-68; Charlesworth, *Pesharim,* 109-10).

183. Fritsch thinks that the probable Damascus Essenes were less anti-Temple than the Qumran community, based on CD 13.27; 9.46; 8.11ff (*Community,* 84); cf. also Davies, "Temple." Essene opposition sheds light on another point in the Gospels: that Jesus also respected (Matt 5:23-24; 23:16-21) and taught in (Mk 12:35) the Temple does not conflict with his announcement of judgment against it (Mk 13:2); even Essenes reportedly sent sacrifices to the Temple (Jos. *Ant.* 18.19).

184. Hill, *Prophecy,* 62-63.

185. Aune, *Prophecy,* 174-75 lists many of Jesus' predecessors and contemporaries who prophesied against the Temple or made similar claims: e.g., the Egyptian prophet expected Jerusalem's walls to collapse (Jos. *Ant.* 20.169-70; cf. *War* 2.261-63); Josephus himself claimed to predict the fall of Jotapata (*War* 3.406) and cites an ancient oracle predicting the Temple's fall (*War* 6.96-110; 4.388; he may refer to a biblical oracle, however).

186. Robinson, *Redating,* 27, following Dodd; cf. Taylor, *Formation,* 73.

187. E.g., *Ps. Sol.* 2:1-10; 17:5; cf. *Song Rab.* 8:12, §1.

188. E.g., Jos. *War* 6.288-315; *Pesiq. Rab.* 26:6; cf. *Apoc. Ab.* 27:3-7; Goldenberg, "Explanations." Nevertheless, in keeping with prior biblical tradition, they saw the Temple's destroyers as ignoble (Jos. *War* 6.95; *Gen. Rab.* 37:4) and warranting judgment (Urbach, *Sages,* 1:91-92). Gentile Christians after the first century often saw in the Temple's demise God's rejection of Judaism, vengeance for Christ's death, or the present impossibility of fulfilling the law (Lampe, "A.D. 70," 153-71; cf. Justin's hostility in *Dial.* 16.3-4; Bokser, "Justin," 205-6); apart from judgment for Christ's death (in Matt 23:29–24:2, yet with future hope in 23:39; cf. Lk 13:33-35), these associations are absent in the first-century Gospels.

189. Danker, *New Age,* 198; Kaufman, "Eastern Wall," 115; cf. the language of Hag 2:15.

190. Sanders, *Figure,* 257.

191. Cf. what most scholars take as Matthean redaction in Matt 22:7, probably after 70 CE. See also Beasley-Murray, *Mark Thirteen,* 24; Meier, *Matthew,* 277, 283; Gundry, *Matthew,* 475; Davies and Allison, *Matthew,* 3:335. For portents of the temple's destruction (cf. esp. Josephus' post-70 perspective), see Bedenbender, "Kampf."

192. Thus Kümmel, *Promise,* 101-2 sees the Temple prophecy as originally referring to the end of the age rather than to a historical event (cf. Ellison, *Mystery,* 19ff). "Since the destruction of the temple and the holy city is a theme of Jewish apocalyptic, Jesus' prophecy is generally and quite correctly regarded as eschatological" (Aune, *Prophecy,* 175; citing also Bultmann). But Borg also seems correct when he suggests that Jesus prophesied judgment rather than constructed an elaborate apocalyptic schema (Borg, *Conflict,* 181), though I believe that he is wrong to deny Jesus' eschatological worldview in other respects (see Witherington, *Christology,* 30 n. 111).

193. Glasson, *Advent*, 75.

194. 1 Macc 3:45; 3 Macc 1:29; 2:14; *2 Bar.* 5:1; *Test. Asher* 7:2; *tos. Suk.* 4:28; CD 4.17-18; cf. Ps 74:3-4, 7; Is 63:18.

195. Philo *Embassy to Gaius* 209-10.

196. Jos. *Ant.* 10.37-38; *Ps. Sol.* 1:8; *Apoc. Ab.* 27:7.

197. In Jerusalem, "the Wicked Priest did abominable works and defiled the sanctuary of God" (1QpHab 12.7-9); because this Qumran passage interprets Hab 2:17, which refers to bloodshed, it probably refers to the persecution of the followers of the Teacher of Righteousness (cf. 1QpHab 12.6 and context).

198. Cf. Daube, *NT and Judaism*, 418-20; Hill, *Prophecy,* 63; Beale, "Daniel," 5:129.

199. Daniel's image in at least one or two texts referred to the events surrounding Antiochus Epiphanes, who claimed to be deity and oppressed Israel (Dan 8:13; 11:31, 36-39; 1 Macc 1:54-56; 6:7; cf. Jos. *Ant.* 12.253; *Jub.* 23:21); another text, however, associates the same phenomenon with the cutting off of some sort of anointed ruler (cf. Payne, *Appearing*, 146), and this could be closer to the time of Jesus (Dan 9:26). The latest possible date of Daniel is the second-century BC (given a Qumran Daniel manuscript of that date); nevertheless, calculating the "seventy sevens" from the time of the decree to which Daniel refers could (depending on how one counts) bring one to the early first century. This calculation probably increased eschatological speculation among Jesus' contemporaries (Beckwith, "Date"; on Daniel's popularity then, cf. Jos. *Ant.* 10.268-81; 12.322; Mason, *Josephus and New Testament,* 47). Many scholars today think that Daniel applied only to the Maccabean desecration (e.g., Aalders, "Gruwel"; Colunga, "Abominación"), but both the Qumran pesharim and texts like *Lives of Prophets* 12:11 (§19 in Schermann, p. 63) indicate that Jesus' contemporaries freely applied such images for their own era.

200. In the Dead Sea Scrolls the period of tribulation extended forty years (CD 20.14-15; for reinterpretation after delay, see 1QpHab 7.13-14).

201. E.g., *b. Sanh.* 97a; *Pesiq. Rab Kah.* 5:9; *Song Rab.* 2:13, §4; *Pesiq. Rab.* 15:14/15; 34:1; 36:1-2; see Bonsirven, *Judaism,* 212-13. Jewish speculation concerning the end-time regularly reapplied Daniel's figures in various manners (see Bruce, "Qumran and Christianity," 177; Russell, *Apocalyptic,* 198-201; cf. *Ruth Rab.* 5:6).

202. Revelation seems to reapply Daniel's tribulation period to the period between Jesus' first and second comings (Rev 12:1-6, 10); some scholars have understood Matthew 24 similarly (cf. Davies and Allison, *Matthew,* 3:369; Keener, *Matthew,* 577-78).

203. See Schweitzer, *Quest,* passim; cf. Sanders, *Jesus and Judaism,* 8. Jeremias, *Unknown Sayings,* 33-34 doubts the authenticity of agrapha in Papias because they resemble Jewish apocalyptic more than the Gospels (earthly fertility, etc.); but whether or not these agrapha are authentic, such grounds for excluding them appear unwarranted. Similar imagery appeared in Jesus' Bible (e.g., Amos 9:13; Is 35:1-2; Joel 2:24), and if Jesus could draw on other eschatological images (e.g., Mk 14:25, perhaps evoking the eschatological banquet of Is 25:6; cf. Matt 8:11) and treat the Hebrew Bible as a unified book (Matt 23:35// Lk 11:51) there is no reason he *could* not have embraced biblical images even different from those most frequently found in his canonical sayings.

204. Cf. Bruce, "Matthew," 288; Beasley-Murray, *Future;* idem, *Mark Thirteen,* 1-18.

205. We do not have a description of Jesus' heavenly revelations. That Jesus had visionary experiences may be likely, but Quarles, "Mystic," is right to question the portrayal of Jesus as a merkabah mystic (in Chilton, *Rabbi Jesus*); Jesus' known activity does not specifically fit Merkabah mystic practices, and there is no focus on securing visions of the throne-chariot. (Segal's argument for Paul's preconversion experience seems more plausible.) One might compare elements of a testament (cf. e.g., *Jub.* 36:1-11; *2 En.* 2:2; *Test. Twelve Patriarchs*) or more generally a farewell discourse, which often includes eschatological or sometimes apocalyptic features (see Robbins, *Teacher,* 175). A sage's imminent death often provides the occasion for paranesis (Perdue, "Death"; Jos. *Ant.* 4.177-93). On testaments, see Saldarini, "Deathbed Scenes"; Kolenkow, "Genre"; Collins, "Testamentary Literature"; Endres, *In-*

terpretation, 199-201; McNamara, *Judaism*, 89-92; on farewell speeches, see also Stowers, *Letter Writing*, 55-56; Kurz, "Addresses." Neusner, "Death-Scenes," is correct, however, that the analogy is largely formal; the Gospels' christology necessitates radically different content.

206. Mark could have combined disparate elements of the Jesus tradition (Beasley-Murray, "Second Thoughts"), and may combine apocalyptic with antiapocalyptic motifs (cf. Tagawa, "Marc 13"). After commending Beasley-Murray for a brilliant defense of Mark 13's authenticity, Perrin responds that many "non-Markan" terms common to Revelation appear in this chapter (Perrin, *Teaching*, 130-31); but the data he marshals for his objection merely confirm the pre-Markan character of the text and the distinctive vocabulary of Jewish eschatology. Likewise, an argument for prophetic language similar to Revelation (Boring, *Sayings*, 186-95) does not call into question authenticity if one concedes (as Boring elsewhere does) that Jesus himself spoke as a prophet.

207. Ford, *Abomination*, 28. From the earliest sayings of Jesus, imminence would take effect only after the signs were fulfilled (Bruce, *Apostle*, 230).

208. E.g., Ford, *Abomination*, 23; most fully, Theissen, *Gospels in Context*, 125-65. Caligula's attempt to establish his image in Jerusalem's temple (Jos. *Ant.* 18.259-308; 19.1-20; *War* 2.184-85; Philo *Leg. Gaius* 115-16, 188, 346; Tac. *Ann.* 12.54; cf. Dio Cass. *R.H.* 59.4.4; Bilde, "Statue"; Stern, "Province," 354-59; Benko, "History," 51-53) undoubtedly fueled renewed expectations of the final oppressor, and Jewish tradition recalled him harshly long after his demise (*b. Sot.* 33a; *Song Rab.* 8:9, §3). Philo appropriately charges that Gaius Caligula was zealous for "lawlessness" *(paranomia)*, because he regarded himself as law (*Embassy* 119); some who heard of Caligula's plans sought to rescue themselves from lawlessness (*Embassy* 190).

209. Although it is far from clear, some other material in 1 Thessalonians may also echo the dominical tradition (Riesenfeld, *Tradition*, 17; cf. Dibelius, *Paul*, 93). The "catching up" may reflect an agraphon (Frame, *Thessalonians*, 171; Morris, *Thessalonians*, 141; Jeremias, *Unknown Sayings*, 14; cf. Neil, *Thessalonians*, 97) or a midrashic implication of the explicit gathering (Wenham, "Apocalypse," 348; cf. Marshall, *Thessalonians*, 130); the descent may derive from OT theophany language (see Scott, "Clouds," 132).

210. See especially Waterman, "Sources" (citing 24 parallels, mostly compelling); Wenham, *Rediscovery*; cf. also Hunter, *Predecessors*, 49; Stanley, *Resurrection*, 82; Barrett, *Jesus and Tradition*, 12; Riesenfeld, *Tradition*, 13; Minear, *Commands*, 164-65; Mounce, "Eschatology"; Lane, *Mark*, 449; Beasley-Murray, *Revelation*, 42; Ridderbos, *Paul*, 65; Hill, *Prophecy*, 130; Plevnik, "1 Thess 5"; Robinson, *Coming*, 113-14; Davies, *Paul*, 139; Marshall, *Thessalonians*, 126, 134; Sanders, *Jesus and Judaism*, 144-45; Crossan, *Historical Jesus*, 243-47; Keener, *Matthew*, 565-66; cf. Conzelmann, *Theology*, 165; in 2 Thess 2, see besides those above D. Wenham, *Rediscovery*, 176-80; Milligan, *Thessalonians*, lxi n. 1.

211. *4 Ezra* 5:8; 6:21; *Sib. Or.* 2.154-64, following Hesiod *Works and Days* 181. On Jesus' discourse, see e.g., Gundry, *Matthew*, 478.

212. Glasson, *Advent*, 175 and Robinson, *Coming*, 105-7; they rightly find a source for much of the material in the LXX, especially Is 26-27, but miss the one authority behind early Christian eschatology that could combine these varied motifs (cf. similarly Wenham, "Apocalypse," 348-49).

213. Goulder, *Midrash*, 166 characteristically thinks Matthew derives the trumpet from 1 Thess 4:16 (cf. Dodd, *Parables*, 154-55, on 1 Thess 5:2-8 with Lk 21:34-36), but this gives Paul's correspondence too preeminent and early a role in early Christianity (probably before Christians even collected his letters).

214. Pace Koester, "One Jesus," 196; Best, *Thessalonians*, 189-93; Boring, *Sayings*, 11, 34 n. 41; Aune, *Prophecy*, 253-56.

215. Prophecies could be written down and preserved (*Test. Job* 51:4/3); but it does not appear to have been the norm (cf. Aune, *Prophecy*, 244). (Further, oracles were far more likely to be heavily redacted than didactic traditions were; cf. Collins, "Introduction to Oracles," 320.) Apart from Revelation, we lack much concrete evidence in early Christianity for recording such prophecies or, with rare exceptions, for their widespread geographic circulation.

216. The cumulative evidence is, as Ford, *Abomination,* 22 puts it, virtually "conclusive." See also Waterman, "Sources," and the many other writers noted above.

Notes to Chapter 18

1. Schweitzer, *Quest,* 398. Schweitzer favored the latter opinion, against Wrede (who favored the former).

2. Evans, "Activities," 27. He notes that the Roman governor had Jesus executed as a king (23-24) and that Jesus expected to drink wine with them "anew" in the kingdom (Mk 14:25 [cf. 1 Cor 11:26]; p. 21).

3. Bultmann, *Word,* 9. He was in a sense right to observe that Jesus was not a traditional messianic figure (*Theology,* 27).

4. Schweitzer, *Quest,* 330-98; cf. Weiss, *Proclamation,* 115, 128-30 (Jesus believed God would make him Messiah when God established the kingdom).

5. See Aarde, *Fatherless,* 154 (who also emphasizes Jesus' relationship with God as his Father, an emphasis noted below); cf. Capps, *Biography.*

6. For one example of this extreme approach, see Mack, *Lost Gospel,* 4-5. Did later Gentile Christians assign Jesus to a category they could hardly have created, when they often failed to comprehend even what "anointed one" meant in Judaism?

7. 2 Cor 11:4 does not define "another Jesus" as a non-messianic one, and the opponents plainly do view him as "Christ" in 2 Cor 11:13, 23. We might encounter this problem later, in 1 Jn 2:22, but this perspective seems to involve people who have left the dominant Jesus movement (2:19), whether to accommodate the demands of the synagogue (the setting often assigned to John's Gospel; cf. Rev 2:9; 3:9) or for an early form of docetism (cf. 1 Jn 4:2; 5:6; later, Ignatius *Trall.* 9-10; *Smyrn.* 3; *Ep. Barn.* 5; Justin *Dial.* 103.7).

8. Davies and Allison, *Matthew,* 2:594-601 (noting esp. 2 Sam 7).

9. Marshall, *Origins,* 54-56; Witherington, *Christology,* 272-73.

10. Meyer, "Deed," 171-72.

11. Sanders, *Jesus and Judaism,* 234; cf. Beasley-Murray, "Kingdom," 27-32.

12. So even Winter, *Trial,* 108-9.

13. Jos. *Ant.* 17.285, 295; Brown, *Death,* 968. As Fredriksen, *Christ,* 123, notes, whether or not Jesus claimed a messianic title, "he certainly died as if he had."

14. Harvey, *History,* 13-14; Stanton, *Gospel Truth,* 173.

15. Blinzler, *Trial,* 213, citing *Dig.* 48.4.1-4.

16. E.g., Dio Cass. 57.4.5-6; 57.9.2; 57.19.1; 57.23.1-2.

17. Tac. *Ann.* 15.44.

18. Sanders, *Jesus and Judaism,* 321-22. Jesus' execution as a royal pretender leads many scholars to this conclusion (e.g., Witherington, *Christology,* 104, 116; Stanton, *Gospel Truth,* 173-87).

19. Sanders, *Figure,* 242, suggests that Jesus' view of his royalty may not have been that he was a messiah, but rather that he was God's eschatological viceroy. These figures, however, are easily coalesced.

20. Sanders, *Jesus and Judaism,* 307. The same conclusion is argued from a variety of data; cf. e.g., Chilton, "Announcement," 168. Raymond Brown likewise concludes that some of Jesus' followers may have thought him the Messiah, but that he responded ambivalently because his mission defined the term differently than the popular title would suggest (Brown, *Death,* 473-80; cf. Marshall, *Origins,* 89-90).

21. Outside the Septuagint, Diaspora Judaism rarely used the term, however; even *Sib. Or.* 2.45 is a Christian interpolation. The most obvious exception would be disputes about "Chrestus" in Rome

cited by Suetonius (see above in ch. 4), but if this refers to Jesus, the title could have been introduced mainly by Christians.

22. Meeks, *Urban Christians,* 94; Hooker, *Message,* 13, 65; Ladd, *Criticism,* 96.

23. Morris, *Romans,* 37.

24. Ladd, *Theology,* 140-41.

25. Cf. *Ps. Sol.* 17:21-25.

26. Mk 14:61-62 accepts a messianic title, but cf. more ambiguously Matt 26:63-64; for a combination, Lk 22:67-70.

27. Cf. Catchpole, "Entry."

28. Witherington, *Christology,* 104.

29. Witherington, *Christology,* 105. On authenticity, see also Losie, "Entry."

30. So Keck, *History,* 120.

31. A donkey could cost between two months' and two years' wages, depending on its age and condition. If a farmer had two, however, he sometimes rented one out (Lewis, *Life,* 130).

32. Sanders, *Figure,* 254.

33. See arguments in Tan, *Zion Traditions,* 138-43. In employing the title "triumphal entry" I defer to common usage rather than evaluating its proposed relationship to Roman triumphs.

34. For the suggestion of a limited-scale event, cf. Catchpole, "Entry"; Sanders, *Jesus and Judaism,* 306.

35. Cf. Sanders, *Jesus and Judaism,* 308; pace Borg, *Vision,* 186 n. 9.

36. Keck, *History,* 120 (comparing the significance of Luther's 95 theses, recognized only after the event, and noting that Jesus' failure to explicitly claim kingship prevented this entry from being useful against him at his trial).

37. See *m. Pes.* 5:7; 9:3; 10:5-7; *tos. Pisha* 8:22; *b. Pes.* 117a; cf. Mk 14:26; cf. Moore, *Judaism,* 2:42; Jeremias, *Eucharistic Words,* 255-56; Barclay, *Child,* 42; Safrai, "Religion," 809; Stendahl, *School,* 65; at other feasts, e.g., *m. Suk.* 3:10; 4:8; *tos. Suk.* 3:2; *b. Shab.* 21b, bar.; *Suk.* 38b.

38. *Tos. Suk.* 3:2; *Pesiq. Rab Kah.* Sup. 2:8.

39. Pilgrims often sang en route to festivals (Sanders, *Judaism,* 128-29). Many parents would undoubtedly begin rehearsing it with their children long before then; one might compare the extended prologues to holidays today, except with less mercantile incentive. Second-century rabbis applied to the Hallel the same rules applied to other liturgy (*tos. Meg.* 2:2).

40. Jeremias, *Eucharistic Words,* 256-57 and n. 3.

41. "O save!" which had become an acclamation of praise (Moore, *Judaism,* 2:48; Lane, *Mark,* 398).

42. Cf. Smallwood, "Priests"; Horsley, "Priests"; Sanders, *Jesus and Judaism,* 315.

43. With e.g., Malina and Rohrbaugh, *Gospels,* 128-29; Graves and May, *Preaching Matthew,* 81-82; Keener, *Matthew,* 495. The divisions between rural and urban, and between Galilee and Jerusalem, were important in this period; see Keener, *John,* 228-31.

44. Cf. Judg 10:4; 1 Kgs 1:44; cf. discussion in Sanders, *Figure,* 254; Witherington, *Christology,* 106. An ass was of lower status than a horse (Babrius 76.18-19); later, *Pesiq. Rab.* 36:1 provides the Messiah with a truly royal mount (the four creatures of Ezek 1).

45. Knowledge of Zech 9:9 could have enabled him to avoid a difficult periphrastic expression (Gundry, *Old Testament,* 197-98).

46. Evans, "Hope," 375, points out that Mark, in contrast to Matthew and John later, makes no explicit connection to the Zechariah text (though he suggests that Zecharian imagery pervades Jesus' own mission in the passion narrative, 388).

47. *B. Sanh.* 98a; 99a; *Gen. Rab.* 75:6; Edgar, "Messianic Interpretation," 48-49; Lachs, *Commentary,* 344.

48. Moule, *Mark,* 87; Gundry, *Matthew,* 409; Sanders, *Figure,* 242; cf. Borg, *Vision,* 174; Luciani,

"Seguidores." Duff, "March," suggests that Mark ironically inverts the Gentile custom of triumphal entry into a conquered city and also Zechariah's images of a divine warrior.

49. Klein, "Messianism," 201, relates Jesus to the priestly and royal Messiahs at Qumran, but we argue here from analogy only that Messianic concepts were gradually adapted to the communities and social situations they addressed.

50. Although John's Jesus repeatedly hints at his exalted status, in public he often avoids being explicit, speaking in riddles (cf. Jn 2:9, 19-22; 3:13; 7:25-27; 10:34-36; 12:16; 14:21-22; 16:29-30; 18:19-23, 33-37). See Keener, *John,* 76-77, 290, 397, 545-46, 771-72, 824, 870; cf. Smith, *John* (1999), 210; for riddles in John, see Thatcher, *Riddles;* for riddling in the Jesus tradition more generally, Thatcher, *Riddler.*

51. Wrede, *Messianic Secret,* 17-18, 228.

52. E.g., Ellis, "Composition"; Burkill, *Light,* 1-38; idem, "Strain"; Anderson, *Mark,* 46; Wright, *People of God,* 104.

53. See e.g., Chrys. *Hom. Jn.* 3.

54. Cullmann, *State,* 26.

55. Hurtado, *Mark,* xxiii; Marshall, *Origins,* 89-90.

56. Longenecker, *Christology,* 68-73.

57. See Witherington, *Christology,* 265-67. For supporters of various views or aspects of the "messianic secret," see more fully Keener, *Matthew,* 261-63.

58. Cf. Isoc. *Nicocles/Cyprians* 46, *Or.* 3.36; Plut. *Praising Oneself Inoffensively, Mor.* 539A-547F, especially 15, *Mor.* 544D; Quint. *Inst. Or.* 11.1.17-19; Lyons, *Autobiography,* 44-45, 68-69. On the relevance of avoiding self-boasting to Jesus' mission, see also Neyrey, "Shame of Cross," 127.

59. Keener, *Matthew,* 262.

60. Compare "mysteries" in apocalyptic texts, especially in Daniel and the Dead Sea Scrolls (e.g., 1QS 5.11-12; 9.18; 11.3-5; 1QM 3.9; 14.14; 17.9; 1QH 12.11-13, 20; 13.2, 13-14; other sources in our discussion of parables). For the sake of brevity here, we refer to Gibbard, "Mystery," 109-11; Brown, *"Mysterion"*; idem, *Mystery;* Ellis, "Uses," 208; Longenecker, *Exegesis,* 41-42; and especially Caragounis, *Mysterion.*

61. See full documentation in Keener, *Matthew,* 378-79; also Eunapius *Lives* 371-72, 468. Suspense was a rhetorical technique (e.g., Cic. *Verr.* 2.5.5.10-11) but is less relevant here.

62. Schweitzer, *Quest,* 386, thinks that Peter (by his "confession") and Judas betrayed the messianic secret; although the latter is possible, neither is certain.

63. See Rhoads and Michie, *Mark,* 87. On a literary level, one may add the obduracy of disciples, particularly in Mark, as a foil for Jesus (in John, cf. Braun, "Vie").

64. Thompson, "God," 54.

65. See Rhoads and Michie, *Mark,* 87; cf. Augustine *Tractates on John,* 113. Times can dictate discretion; a pagan who claimed his teacher divine had to be very discreet when Christian emperors were in power (Eunapius *Lives* 461). Such observations are hardly new; Chrys. *John,* hom. 3, recognizes the messianic secret and thinks it was the model for Paul's missions strategy in Acts 17:31.

66. E.g., Is 9:7; Jer 23:5. That the eschatological ruler would be a restoration after the Davidic rule had been cut off was suggested by preexilic prophets (Jesse's "stump" in Is 11:1; Amos 9:11; on the authenticity of the latter, see discussion at Acts 15:16-18 in my Acts commentary).

67. *Ps. Sol.* 17.21; 4Q252 frg. 1, col. 5, lines 1-4; *b. Sanh.* 97b-98a; *p. Suk.* 5:1, §7; *Gen. Rab.* 88:7; *Song Rab.* 2:13, §4; *Pesiq. Rab.* 15:14/15; *Tg.* on Jer 30:9. See Fitzmyer, *Essays,* 113-26; Longenecker, *Christology,* 109-10; Kee, *Community,* 126, especially on the Dead Sea Scrolls.

68. A concept that made more sense in some ancient Near Eastern (esp. Egyptian and Hittite) than Hellenistic settings; see De Vaux, *Israel,* 104; cf. *ANET* 338 (though this is merely ritual anointing).

69. For texts that could be regarded as messianic by some of Jesus' contemporaries, see e.g., Ps 2:2; 18:50 [17:51]; 132[131]:10, 17.

70. In all of Pauline literature, for example, "son of David" christology appears only in Rom 1:3; 2 Tim 2:8.

71. Cf. e.g., Witherington, *Christology*, 83.

72. Cf. Feldman, "David."

73. Kraeling, *John the Baptist*, 52. Some professed signs-prophets also sought kingship in broader Mediterranean culture (Diod. Sic. 34/35.2.5-6, 22-23).

74. See Freyne, *Galilee*, 194-95, on *Ant.* 18.85-87; 20.97-98, 169-71; *War* 2.261-66; Acts 5:36; 21:38; cf. also Crossan, *Historical Jesus*, 158-68.

75. Cf. Moore, *Judaism*, 2:346. Rivkin, "Messiah," 65, contrasts the set belief in the world to come and the resurrection with the greater flexibility on Messianic belief after the revolt. Horsley and Hanson, *Bandits*, 110-31 do, however, point out that popular attempts to rule often focused on commoners rather than a revived Davidic dynasty.

76. *ARN* 31, §67 B.

77. *Sipre Deut.* 34.4.3 (resurrection in the Messianic era); *p. Ket.* 12:3, §13 (R. Meir); speculation flourished again in the Amoraic period (e.g., *b. Meg.* 12a); the Davidic Messiah remained later (e.g., *Tg. Jer* on 30:9). Aberbach, "Hzqyhw," thinks that "Hezekiah" was sometimes a code-name for R. Judah when some still thought him the Messiah.

78. For groups that emphasized biblical messianic hopes, see Horsley and Hanson, *Bandits*, 102-10. 4Q521 frs. 2, 4, col. 1, line 1, suggests a global or even cosmic (though this may be hyperbole) role for the Messiah.

79. There is debate as to how widespread or regular their recitation was in this period, but they are surely some of the earliest samples of postbiblical Jewish prayer we have (cf. discussion in e.g., Schiffman, "Crossroads," 151; Oesterley, *Liturgy*, 54-67; Levine, "Synagogue," 19).

80. Horsley and Hanson, *Bandits*, 109. In a later period redemptive work suggested genealogical correctness rather than Davidic descent being primary; cf. Kaufmann, "Idea."

81. *4 Ezra; 2 Bar.; Test. Twelve Patriarchs;* cf. perhaps the recently discovered inscription in Yardeni, "Prophecy."

82. See Wittlieb, "Bedeutung."

83. Collins, "Son of Man."

84. Wächter, "Messianismus," stresses this political aspect of Jewish expectations, distinguishing them from the early Christian view defined by Jesus' mission. That Jesus did not inaugurate an immediate earthly kingdom is one of the primary objections to his Messiahship in contemporary Jewish scholarship; cf. Berger and Wyschogrod, *Jewish Christianity*, 18-19; Klausner, *Jesus*, 414; Borowitz, *Christologies*, 21.

85. E.g., 1QSa 2.11-17; 4Q174 3.11-12. Evans, "Messianism," 701-2, finds thirty Qumran texts describing "anointed" individuals, with the royal Messiah probably in CD 12.23-13.1; 14.19 (=4Q266 frg. 18, 3.12); 19.10-11; 20.1; 1QS 9.11; 1QSa 2.11-12, 14-15, 20-21; 4Q252 frg. 1 v. 3-4; 4Q381 frg. 15.7; 4Q382 frg. 16.2; 4Q458 frg. 2, 2.6; 4Q521 frg. 2 + 4, 2.1; 4Q521 frg. 7.3. The "firstborn" of 4Q369 frg. 1, col. 2.6-7 probably evokes biblical messianic language.

86. E.g., 1 Macc 14:41-42, with the functions of ruler, priest, commander, and possibly prophet sought for Simon Maccabeus.

87. See the Wicked Priest of 1QpHab 8.8-10; 9.4-7; 11.5-6; 12.5; and the role of Zadokites in the community. The view that the Teacher of Righteousness is modeled after Judas Maccabee (Eisenman, *Maccabees*, 35) has not garnered much support.

88. Evans, "Messianism," 703, lists OT precedent for the two messiahs (Jer 33:15-18; Hag 2:1-7; Zech 4:11-14; 6:12-13; 4Q254 frg. 4 alludes to Zech 4:14).

89. *Test. Reub.* 6:8; *Test. Jud.* 21:1-2; cf. *Test. Sim.* 5:5 with 1QM. On Melchizedek as eschatological priest, see Puech, "Manuscrit." He was not likely the ruling messiah, however (Collins, "Messiah before Jesus," 34).

90. See *Jub.* 31:12-17 and 31:18-20; cf. similarly *Test. Iss.* 5:7; *Test. Dan* 5:4, 10; *Test. Naph.* 5:3-5; 8:2.

Schniedewind, "King," roots the dual messianic expectation in the Chronicler's ideal leadership pattern (especially 1 Chron 17:14).

91. *Jub.* 31:18-20; see Noack, "Qumran and Jubilees," 201.

92. See Charles, *Jubilees,* xiv (although we may date Jubilees somewhat earlier than he suggests on xiii).

93. Higgins, "Priest," 333; idem, "Messiah," 215-19; Laurin, "Messiahs," 52. *Test. Benj.* 11:2 seems to support a figure from both Judah and Levi (perhaps reflecting a Jewish-Christian desire to derive one of Jesus' parents from Levi, cf. Lk 1:5, 36). The Scrolls conflate various anointed figures (e.g., 4Q174 3.10-13; 4Q252 frg. 1, 5.1, 3; 11Q13 2.15-20).

94. Aune, *Prophecy,* 123 (citing *Test. Reub.* 6:5-12; *Test. Levi* 18:2-9; 1QS 9.10-11; 1QSa 12-17; cf. CD 19.10-11; 20.1); Villalón, "Deux Messies," 53-63, especially 63; Burrows, *More Light,* 297-311 (or maybe three, 311); Jóczwiak, "Mesjanizm" (or even three); Jonge, "Anointed," 141-42; Brown, "Messianism," 54-66. In "Theory," 56, Brown still thought there were probably two Messiahs, but noted that not all texts were clear or represented the same period.

95. Smith, "Variety"; Abegg, "Messiah."

96. Longenecker, *Christology,* 114; Driver, *Scrolls,* 468-69; Priest, "Mebaqqer"; cf. Priest, "Messiah." Wcela, "Messiah(s)," finds in the Damascus Document (CD 12.23-13.1; 14.19; 19.10-11; 20.1; cf. 7.17-21) one military Messiah with a priest who could be an Aaronic Messiah (342); 1QS 9.11 has two Messiahs, but often a priestly companion to the Messiah is in view, and the Damascus Document probably sees both as one individual (347). Cf. Smith, "Begetting," 224, who thinks both anointed ones may be "survivals of the same figure," but is not certain that either is eschatological or messianic.

97. CD 12.23-13.1 (albeit with an emended misspelling of משיח); 14.19 (not all the word is clear, but the relevant ending is); 20.1; also the warrior Messiah of 1QM 11.7-8. Puech, "Apocalypse," considers 4Q521 an "apocalypse messianique" (but contrast Bergmeier, "Beobachtungen"); García Martínez, "Textos," finds a messianic king (4Q252, 285, 521), priest (4Q540) and heavenly figure (4Q246).

98. LaSor, "Messiahs," 429; Gaster, *Scriptures,* 392; Bruce, *History,* 122. Stefaniak, "Poglady," thinks Qumran stressed eschatology more than messianology; this is probably right, unless the Messiah was a righteous Teacher redivivus.

99. Silberman, "Messiahs," 82, questioning whether the expectation is even eschatological in the final sense. Perhaps the title originally applied to the first Teacher of Righteousness.

100. Cf. the priest's precedence to the "Messiah" in 1Q28a 2.19-20; "Moses God's anointed ['messiah']" in 4Q377 frg. 2, 2.5; 1Q22 lines 11-12 even adds Eleazar to Joshua in Deut 31:7, to couple priest and ruler figures; see also the "anointed priest" in 4Q376 frg. 1, col. 1 line 1. Some much later rabbis also spoke of a priest "anointed for battle," i.e., an eschatological priest to accompany the troops, along with the Davidic Messiah (*b. Yoma* 73b; *Song Rab.* 2:13, §4).

101. For the suffering and triumphant Messiahs, see e.g., *3 En.* 45:5; for a suffering Messiah, see e.g., the various views offered in *b. Suk.* 52a; *p. Suk.* 5:2, §2; *Pesiq. Rab.* 31:10; 34:2; 36:1-2, and see data listed in Torrey, "Messiah"; for a Messiah suffering for Israel's sins, cf. *Pesiq. Rab.* 36:1-2; 37:1; for a servant Messiah, cf. *2 Bar.* 70:9. The doctrine of two Messiahs continued in ninth-century Karaite doctrine (possibly from Essene roots?); cf. Wieder, "Messiahs."

102. Driver, *Scrolls,* 465-66, thinks the rabbinic picture could shed light on the Scrolls, but this proposition takes too little account of their traditions' divergent dates. Kuhn, "Messias," 208, points out that the Scrolls subordinate the political Messiah to the priestly one, but rabbinic literature offers no parallel to this (though *Jub.* 31 and some other texts might).

103. E.g., Dan 9:26, which is probably messianic in the context of 11Q13 2.18; see Rosenberg, "Messiah," who (less accurately) predicates the prominence of Qumran's Levitic Messiah on the decease of the Davidic one. Brownlee, "Servant," argues that 1QIs(a) applies the suffering servant of Is 52-53 to the "anointed" community as a whole (he and Reider, "MSHTY," debate the Hebrew back and forth on 27-28). Justin argues from the Scriptures for a suffering Messiah and in his account persuades Trypho (Justin *Dial.* 39; 90.1; Higgins, "Belief," 304, regards Trypho's concession as unusual).

104. So Vermes, *Jesus the Jew*, 140; Yamauchi, "Concord," 165-66 (this seems more reasonable than Berger's attribution of the doctrine to typology; cf. "Themes"). If a tradition of testing the Messiah existed (e.g., Bar Kochba by his sense of smell, *b. Sanh.* 93b), it may have arisen the same way (Rivkin, "Meaning," 397, thinks instead that the Pharisees used this tradition in their opposition to Jesus).

105. In 4Q285, fr. 5, line 4; e.g., Tabor, "Messiah" (among others).

106. Vermes, *Religion*, 211 n. 1; idem, "Forum"; idem, "Messiah Text"; Bockmuehl, "Messiah"; Abegg, "Hope"; Martone, "Testo"; Abegg, "Introduction to 4Q285"; Evans, "Messianism," 703. Collins, "Servant," doubts that 4Q541 (on a suffering sage/priest) is messianic. The same may be said for a rising messiah in the "Gabriel's Revelation" inscription; Israel Knohl's reading of lacunae conveniently supports his earlier book (soundly critiqued in e.g., Collins, "Essene Messiah"), but differs from epigrapher Ada Yardeni's reading, and will probably not prevail (correspondence from Craig Evans, July 23, 2008).

107. See Sanders, *Jesus and Judaism*, 234; cf. Beasley-Murray, "Kingdom," 27-32. Cf. Meyer, "Ministry," 352 (emphasis his): *"Jesus understood himself as the climactic and definitive fulfiller of the hopes of Israel."*

108. Sanders, *Jesus and Judaism*, 321-22. Jesus' execution as a royal pretender leads many scholars to this conclusion (e.g., Witherington, *Christology*, 104, 116; Stanton, *Gospel Truth*, 173-87).

109. Sanders, *Figure*, 242.

110. Brown, *Death*, 473-80; cf. Marshall, *Origins*, 89-90.

111. Hengel, "Messiah," 344. On 346 he notes claims like Jesus' warning against taking offense at him (Matt 11:6//Lk 7:23) and that he was greater than Solomon or the temple (Matt 12:42//Lk 11:32).

112. Beasley-Murray, "Kingdom," 27-32 (indicating Jesus' Messiahship).

113. Hengel, "Messiah," 345.

114. Hengel, "Messiah," 347.

115. Hengel, "Messiah," 348.

Notes to Chapter 19

1. Mack, *Lost Gospel*, 1-2.

2. Pope Benedict, *Jesus of Nazareth*, 186.

3. Hurtado, *Lord Jesus Christ*, 650.

4. The storm could represent any test, but some suggest that, in the context of Jesus' message, it points especially to the final Test, the day of judgment (e.g., Jeremias, *Sermon*, 8-9; cf. the test of the final tribulation in Jeremias, *Parables*, 169). The ultimate storm here may recall the flood that Jesus elsewhere uses to prefigure the final day (Matt 24:37-39//Lk 17:26-27; Schweizer, *Matthew*, 191, citing also Ezek 13:10-16; cf. *1 En.* 94:7).

5. *ARN* 24A; a similar example in Bultmann, *Tradition*, 202.

6. Cf. Gundry, *Matthew*, 135.

7. Jeremias, *Parables*, 194; Argyle, *Matthew*, 64; Luz, *Matthew*, 452.

8. A demand to follow Jesus rather than other teachers (Meeks, *Moral World*, 138, regarding some of Jesus' other teachings in Matthew).

9. For Q's "high" Christology (i.e., Jesus is venerated as in other early Christian circles), see especially Hurtado, *Lord Jesus Christ*, 217-57.

10. E.g., Ex 19:4; Deut 32:11; Ps 17:8; 36:7; 63:7; 91:4; *1 En.* 39:7; *Sipre Deut.* 296.3.1; 306.4.1; 314.1.1-6.

11. Cf. *2 Bar.* 41:4; *ARN* 12A; *Sipre Num.* 80.1.1; *Gen. Rab.* 47:10; *Pesiq. Rab.* 14:2.

12. See e.g., Kingsbury, *Christology*, 150. One could also argue that this occurs slightly earlier, at the triumphal entry (Burkill, "Strain").

13. So Grant, *Gospel*, 193.

14. Schweizer, *Matthew*, 427.

15. Moule, *Mark*, 99; the usual rule seems to have been that the father honors a son of higher rank when in public settings (Aul. Gel. 2.2).

16. Jeremias, *Theology*, 259; France, *Matthew*, 321.

17. Lane, *Mark*, 435; cf. Ps 89:27; Is 9:7; 11:1; Jer 23:5-6.

18. Harrington, *Matthew*, 90; Argyle, *Matthew*, 170; Meier, *Matthew*, 260.

19. So e.g., Gundry, *Old Testament*, 200; Witherington, *Christology*, 190; pace Weeden, *Mark*, 133. Witherington, *Christology*, 190-91 responds to arguments against authenticity, noting e.g., that the play on words works in Aramaic as well as in Greek (*amar marya le mari*; but is a play on words central in the passage anyway?); there is no clear indication that Son of God displaces Son of David here (noting the antinomy above); and this is not the only place where Jesus takes the initiative (Mk 8:27-30) or speaks allusively (cf. Matt 11:5-6//Lk 7:22-23).

20. Whether some Jewish people were interpreting Ps 110 messianically before Jesus is debated (Longenecker, *Exegesis*, 73 argues that some were), but Jesus' specific application of the psalm here is new in any case, both by allowing "lord" to bear a meaning much higher than a Davidic king, and by applying it to himself by implication.

21. Including some allusions, see e.g., Acts 2:34-35; 7:55; Eph 1:20; Col 3:1; Heb 1:3, 13; 8:1; 10:12; 12:2; Mk 16:19; Justin *1 Apol.* 45.

22. Probably against Christian polemic, later rabbis applied Ps 110:1 to Abraham (e.g., *b. Ned.* 32b; *Gen. Rab.* 46:5; *Lev. Rab.* 25:6; *Midr. Ps.* 110); cf. Justin's polemic against an application to Hezekiah (*Dial.* 32; cf. Williams, *Justin*, 175).

23. The language of divine adoption of kings appears elsewhere in the ancient Near East; thus the enthronement decree in Ps 2:7 resembles those in Assyrian and other texts (cf. *ANET* [1955], 267, 370, 383; Dahood, *Psalms*, 1:11-12; Gordon, *Near East*, 254), and an adoption formula (de Vaux, *Israel*, 112).

24. Cf. Hanson, *Unity*, 154. The early Christian picture of Jesus' "Lordship" perhaps used Ps 110:1 at the earliest stage, and also draws on OT pictures of Yahweh; cf. further Marshall, *Origins*, 97-111; Hurtado, *Lord Jesus Christ*, 109-18.

25. For this practice, see e.g., CD 7.15-20; *Mek. Nez.* 10.15-16, 26, 38; 17.17; *Pisha* 5.103. Paul also uses the method (with e.g., Plag, "Übernahme"), though Hays, *Echoes*, 12, correctly observes that the use of catchwords is a general method, not specifically rabbinic (for the narrower rabbinic sense, see Chernick, "Restraints").

26. See Hengel, *Son*, 63; also a point emphasized in Pope Benedict's portrayal of Jesus (*Jesus of Nazareth*).

27. Jeremias, *Prayers*, 57 (followed by e.g., Martin, *Worship*, 34-35; Bruce, *Books*, 56; cf. Hunter, *Predecessors*, 50) may have overstated the case for the title's uniqueness, but his detractors on the issue have focused on exceptions rather than the preponderance of evidence (e.g., Vermes, *Jesus the Jew*, 210-13; a rare analogy hardly constitutes proof of vocative appellation; Jeremias himself noted this exception ["Abba," 204, on *b. Taan.* 23b], explaining it differently).

28. Many studies have been done on this motif; e.g., in Luke's Gospel, see Chen, *Father*.

29. I provide surveys of the "father" title for God or deities in Keener, *Matthew*, 217-18; idem, *John*, 401-2, 877-79.

30. E.g., *I. Eph.* 101-4; Hom. *Il.* 2.371; 8.69, 245, 397; 10.154; 11.66, 80, 201, 544; 14.352; 15.637; 16.250, 253; 17.46, 645 (quoted in Longin. *Subl.* 9.10); 22.60, 209; 24.461; *Od.* 4.340; 5.7; 7.311; 12.63; 13.51; 14.440; 15.341; 16.260; 17.132; 18.235; 24.376, 518; Hesiod *W.D.* 169; Aeschylus *Prom.* 40, 53, 947, 984; *Suppl.* 139; Eurip. *Med.* 1352; Aristoph. *Wasps* 652 ("our father"); Hipponax frg. 62; Pindar *Nem.* 5.33; *Ol.* 1.57a; 2.28; 7.87-88; 14.12; *Pyth.* 3.98; 4.23; Aratus *Phaen.* 15; Pliny *Ep.* 1.7.1 (quoting Hom. *Il.* 16.250); Dio Chrys. *Or.* 12.75; Max. Tyre 11.12; *Orph. H.* 15.7; 19.1; as *gennētōr*, e.g., Aeschylus *Suppl.* 206 (in a literal genetic way for the Danaids; such mythological examples of descent from Zeus could be multiplied, e.g., Philost. *Hrk.* 39.3).

31. E.g., Virg. *Aen.* 1.691; *Georg.* 1.121, 283, 328, 353; 2.325; Val. Flacc. 1.498; 3.249; Catullus 64.21;

Sil. It. 3.137, 163; often as "omnipotent father," Virg. *Aen.* 1.60; 3.251; 4.25; 6.592; 7.141; 7.770; 8.398; 10.100; 12.178; Ovid *Metam.* 1.154; 2.304, 401; 3.336; 9.271; as *genitor*, Virg. *Aen.* 12.843; Val. Flacc. 1.531; Sil. It. 4.417; 17.475; Statius *Silv.* 5.3.207; *Theb.* 5.146; Fronto *De Fer Als.* 3.8.

32. E.g., Hom. *Il.* 3.276, 320, 350, 365; 7.179, 202, 446; 8.236; 12.164; 13.631; 15.372; 17.19, 645; 19.270; 21.273; 24.308; *Od.* 12.371; 20.98, 112, 201; 21.200; 24.351; Soph. *Oed. tyr.* 202; Aristoph. *Acharn.* 223-225; Pindar *Nem.* 8.35; 9.53; 10.29; *Isthm.* 6.42; Ap. Rhod. 4.1673; Aratus *Phaen.* 15-16 (esp. 15); Sil. It. 10.432; Dio Chrys. *Or.* 36.36; see further discussion in Keener, *Matthew*, 217-18. So addressed by other gods, e.g., Hom. *Il.* 8.31; 22.178; *Od.* 8.306; 12.377 (even when they are his siblings, because it remains his title — e.g., *Il.* 5.757, 762; 19.121; *Od.* 13.128).

33. E.g., Hom. *Il.* 8.31 ("father of us all," by a deity); (Ps.) Dion. *Epideictic* 2.262; Hor. *Ode* 1.12.13-18; Plut. *S.K., Alexander* 15, *Mor.* 180D; Dio Chrys. *Or.* 74.27 (supplying "father" from the context); cf. Dio Chrys. *Or.* 36.35; Macrob. *Sat.* 4.5.4 (using Virg. *Aen.* 6.123; van der Horst, "Macrobius," 226); syncretistically, *PGM* 22b.1-5. Among the philosophically inclined, see Plato *Tim.* 28C; Plut. *Plat. Q.* 2.1, *Mor.* 1000E-1001C (esp. 2.1, 1000E); *T.-T.* 8.1.3, *Mor.* 718A; Max. Tyre 2.10; 11.5, 9.

34. E.g., Hom. *Il.* 1.503, 534, 578-79; *Phaedrus* 1.2.13; Virg. *Aen.* 9.495; Ovid *Metam.* 2.848; 9.245; Val. Flacc. 4.1; Catullus 64.298, 387; Ovid *Fasti* 3.285; Sil. It. 5.70; 17.342. Thinkers could also call God "father of himself" (Iambl. *Myst.* 8.2), i.e., "self-begotten" (cf. *PGM* 1.342-43; 13.62; *Sib. Or.* 1.20; 3.12). He is also "god of fathers" (Epict. *Diatr.* 3.11.5).

35. Hor. *Ode* 1.12.49; Plut. *Alex.* 27.6; Dio Chrys. *Or.* 12.74; Max. Tyre 41.2. Among Stoics, see Cleanthes *Hymn to Zeus* (Stob. *Ecl.* 1.1.12). The trees could also call Zeus their "father," as their creator (Babr. 142.3).

36. E.g., Hom. *Il.* 1.544; 4.68; 5.426; 8.49, 132; 11.182; 15.12, 47; 16.458; 20.56; 22.103, 167; *Od.* 1.28; 12.445; Hesiod *W.D.* 59; *Theog.* 457, 468, 542; *Shield of Heracles* 27; Ovid *Metam.* 14.807; Diod. Sic. 1.12.1; Dio Chrys. *Or.* 2.75; Philost. *Vit. Apoll.* 4.30; even Philo *Spec. Laws* 2.165; cf. *Phaedrus* 3.17.10; for "father of gods and king of humans," Virg. *Aen.* 1.65; 2.648; 10.2. Philosophers, perhaps especially Platonists, gave a philosophic interpretation of Homer's phrase (Cornutus 9, p. 9.1 Lang [Grant, *Gods*, 78]; Max. Tyre 35.1; Iambl. *V.P.* 8.38). The conjunction of fatherhoods appears pre-Homeric, paralleled at Ugarit (Gordon, *Civilizations*, 233).

37. Dio Chrys. *Or.* 4.27.

38. Dio Chrys. *Or.* 4.19-21.

39. E.g., Mus. Ruf. 8, p. 64.14; Epict. *Diatr.* 1.6.40.

40. Stoics in Diog. Laert. 7.1.147; Marc. Aur. 10.1 ("begetter" of all).

41. E.g., Cleanthes *Hymn to Zeus* (Stob. *Ecl.* 1.1.12); Sen. *Ep. Lucil.* 110.10; Epict. *Diatr.* 1.9.4-5, 6, 7; 1.13.3-4; 3.22.82. Cf. Mus. Ruf. 18a, p. 112.23-25 (in van der Horst, "Musonius," 309). Sen. *Dial.* 1.1.5 refers specifically to a good man (cf. Epict. *Diatr.* 1.19.9).

42. Mus. Ruf. 16, p. 104.30; Epict. *Diatr.* 1.3.1; 1.19.12; Dio Chrys. *Or.* 4.22.

43. See Jeremias, *Prayers*, 12; especially Chen, *Father*, 73-111.

44. *Spec. Laws* 2.165.

45. Jos. *Ag. Ap.* 2.241.

46. E.g., *Apoc. Mos.* 35:2 (God so addressed by angels).

47. *Creation* 135; *Conf.* 170; *Moses* 2.238; *Decal.* 32, 51, 105, 107; *Spec. Laws* 1.14, 22, 32, 41, 96; 2.6, 165; 3.178, 189; *Virt.* 64, 77, 218; *Praem.* 24; *Cont.* 90; *Aet.* 13; *Leg.* 115, 293; cf. perhaps *Q. Gen.* 2.60. For the Logos as father of humanity, cf. *Conf.* 41.

48. God as "begetter" in *Sib. Or.* 3.296, 604, 726; 5.284, 328, 360, 406, 498, 500.

49. *PGM* 22b.1-26 (*Pr. Jac.* 22.4-5).

50. *Sib. Or.* 3.278; cf. *Spec. Laws* 2.165.

51. E.g., Theoph. 1.4; Athenag. 13; 27.

52. See Wisd 2:16; 3 Macc 5:7; 6:8; 7:6. For one survey, see Chen, *Father*, 113-43; note also observations in Levine, *Misunderstood Jew*, 42-44.

53. E.g., *m. Sot.* 9:15; *tos. Ber.* 3:14; *B.K.* 7:6; *Hag.* 2:1; *Peah* 4:21; *Sipra Qed.* pq. 9.207.2.13; *Behuq.*

pq. 8.269.2.15; *Sipre Deut.* 352.1.2; *b. Ber.* 30a, bar.; 30b; 32b; 35b; 57a; *Shab.* 116a; 131b; *Pes.* 85b; 112a; *R.H.* 29a; *Yoma* 76a; *Suk.* 45b; *Meg.* 13a; 14a; *Sot.* 10a; 12a; 38b; *B.B.* 10a; *Sanh.* 94a; 101b; 102a; 102b; *A.Z.* 16b; *Zeb.* 22b; *p. Sanh.* 10:2, §8; *Pesiq. Rab Kah.* 24:9; *Lev. Rab.* 1:3; 7:1; 35:10; *Song Rab.* 7:11, §1; *Tg. Neof.* 1 on Deut 33:24; *Tg. Ps.-Jon.* on Ex 1:19 (with note in trans. p. 163 n. 38). The phraseology must predate later rabbinic sources (cf. Mk 11:25; Lk 11:13), but in the NT appears especially in Matthew, the source closest to rabbinic usage (Matt 5:16, 45, 48; 6:1, 9, 14 [= Mk 11:25], 26, 32; 7:11 [= Lk 11:13], 21; 10:32-33; 12:50; 15:13; 16:17; 18:10, 14, 19, 35; 23:9).

54. Goshen-Gottstein, "God the Father" (excepting Jesus' special sonship).

55. Boer, *Fatherhood,* 25.

56. *Jub.* 1:25, 28; Tob 13:4; Wisd 11:10; *Jos. Asen.* 12:14 MSS; *Test. Job* 33:3 MSS, 9; cf. *Test. Ab.* 16:3, 20:12, 13 A; *Pr. Jos.* 1. For the righteous as a child of God, see Wisd 2:13, 16.

57. If one counts references in Matthew, Luke, and John, one could add over thirty more instances, but while it is implied in Mark's "Abba," it does not appear as "my Father" in Mark.

58. The supposition that it goes back specifically to the Lord's Prayer (e.g., Hunter, *Predecessors,* 50; Ridderbos, *Galatians,* 158), however, remains undemonstrated (see e.g., Lull, *Spirit in Galatia,* 67).

59. *Jesus and Judaism,* 41-42.

60. Jeremias, *Prayers,* 57, 60, 109-10; Bruce, *Time,* 21-22.

61. Vermes, *Jesus the Jew,* 210-13; idem, *Jesus and Judaism,* 42; Borg, *Vision,* 45.

62. Vermes (*Jesus and Judaism,* 42) cites *b. Taan.* 23b. Besides being late, the exceptions are quite rare (see Klausner, *Jesus,* 378; Stanton, *Gospel Truth,* 153).

63. Syriac versions also sometimes use "Abba" even though it was foreign to normal Syriac (Jeremias, *Prayers,* 64-65). That the Gentile churches may have treated it as an ecstatic palindrome (Aune, "Magic," 1550) is rendered less probable by the translation accompanying it (Rom 8:15; Gal 4:6).

64. For "Abba" in Paul as an echo of the "Jesus tradition," see e.g., Dunn, *Theology,* 192-93; Dunn, "Tradition," 168. Many associate it more specifically with the Lord's Prayer, since Jesus taught this prayer to his followers (e.g., Cullmann, *Worship,* 13; Hunter, *Predecessors,* 50; Ridderbos, *Galatians,* 158; Stuhlmacher, *Romans,* 129), but it could have stemmed from his example. Cf. Jn 10:14-15; 16:13-15 (with 15:15).

65. Pace Bultmann, *Tradition,* 159. Vermes, *Religion,* 160 doubts that Jesus believed the Father would hide anything from him; but is it not less likely that the *church* believed he would? Further, his argument that God consults rather than withholds information from his angels (ibid. n. 9) is too sweeping; in Jewish literature God did not reveal everything (including about the time of the end) even to them. Thus most accept the verse's point, though some reject its wording (Dunn, *Jesus and Spirit,* 34-35; cf. Barrett, *Jesus and Tradition,* 25).

66. So also Wenham, *Bible,* 46; Gundry, *Matthew,* 218, 492; Stanton, *Gospel Truth,* 153; cf. Glasson, *Advent,* 93.

67. Witherington, *Christology,* 229-30.

68. See e.g., Bonsirven, *Judaism,* 178; Morris, *Apocalyptic,* 46-47; cf. *Test. Ab.* 7.16B; *Gr. Ezra* 3:3-4.

69. E.g., *b. Pes.* 54b, bar.; *Sanh.* 97a; *Num. Rab.* 5:6; see Moore, *Judaism,* 2:231; Daube, *NT and Judaism,* 289-90; cf. *2 Bar.* 21:8.

70. *B. Sanh.* 99a; Blau and Kohler, "Angelology," 586.

71. *4 Ezra* 4:52.

72. Witherington, *Christology,* 232 (comparing divine Wisdom). Perrin, *Language,* 86, relates the absolute use of "Son" here to the same sayings-source behind Matt 11:25-27/Lk 10:21-22.

73. Among the Gospels, "Son of God" becomes particularly prominent in John and Matthew. Kingsbury, *Matthew,* 40-83, sees "Son of God" as Matthew's primary christological title; Hill, "Son," challenges this centrality of the title.

74. Cf. Manson, *Sayings,* 79; Jeremias, *Theology,* 59.

75. Cf. Vermes, *Jesus and Judaism,* 48.

76. So e.g., Hagner, *Matthew,* 317-18; pace Bousset, *Kyrios Christos,* 83-85.

77. Witherington, *Christology*, 224.

78. E.g., Stauffer, *Jesus*, 165-66; Grant, *Gnosticism*, 152; Suggs, *Christology*, 71-108; Yamauchi, *Gnosticism*, 35; Witherington, *Christology*, 221-22.

79. Jeremias, *Theology*, 57; cf. idem, *Prayers*, 45-48; idem, *Message*, 24.

80. Dunn, *Jesus and Spirit*, allows that Jesus may have spoken the passage but remains uncertain. Vermes, *Religion*, 162, while agreeing that the Q logion behind Matt 11:25-27//Lk 10:21-22 has a Palestinian origin, doubts its authenticity because he says receiving and transmitting revelation (here and Matt 16:17) is foreign to Jesus' teaching. But if Jesus' contemporaries could apply this language to the mysteries of Wisdom (and Vermes admits they could; cf. also n. 12, where he cites 1QS 1.9; 5.9; 8.1; 9.13; CD 15.13; 1QpHab 2.2-3; 7.5-6; 4Q 381 1.1-2), Vermes can exclude the possibility of Jesus the sage speaking likewise only by circularly excluding the evidence of this passage. If, as we argue, Jesus spoke also as a prophet, the language of "revealing" ought not be excluded.

81. E.g., Davies and Allison, *Matthew*, 2:283.

82. Jeremias, *Theology*, 58-61; idem, *Message*, 25; Borg, *Conflict*, 232. One might appeal here to Wisd 2:13, 16, 18 (cf. 7:27), in which Wisdom makes people "children" of God; but while this may constitute a primary background, it does not limit how Jesus could have reapplied the expression, especially if he functions here as the divine revealer, hence as Wisdom herself. A Jewish audience would recognize Wisdom as God's child; partly because Wisdom was a female figure (cf. the term's gender but also her figurative portrayals, e.g., Prov 8–9), partly because later rabbis usually reserved the "son" image for Israel, Wisdom/Torah became God's "daughter" (e.g., *Sipre Deut.* 345.2.2; *b. Sanh.* 101a; *Pesiq. Rab Kah.* 26:9).

83. Schweizer, *Matthew*, 271.

84. Gundry, *Matthew*, 217-18.

85. Such as a new Moses (Davies and Allison, *Matthew*, 2:283-87).

86. Cf. Davies and Allison, *Matthew*, 2:296-97; Deutsch, *Wisdom*, 143.

87. Witherington, *Christology*, 227. Suggs, *Christology*, probably did overstate the case in Matthew (see Pregeant, "Wisdom Passages"), but it should not for that reason be dismissed entirely. Davies and Allison, *Matthew*, 2:222-25, 231 find the language of "exclusive and reciprocal divine knowledge" in the figure of Moses (Ex 33–34; Num 12; Deut 34; also Allison, "Notes"). They acknowledge the Wisdom language in the context, but seek to keep both backgrounds by noting the idea of the king as embodying a living law (Davies and Allison, *Matthew*, 2:228-29, citing three references in Stobaeus and Moses as living Torah in Philo *Mos.* 1.162; cf. 2.3-5). We suspect, however, that Wisdom language, which is closer and more widespread in this exalted form, would strike Jesus' hearers first.

88. Hengel, *Son*, 21-23.

89. See (some from Longenecker, *Christology*, 97), e.g., Ex 4:22-23; Hos 11:1; Is 1:2; 30:1; 63:16; Jer 3:19-22; Tob 13:4; Sir 4:10; *Ps. Sol.* 13:9; 17:27-30; 18:4; *Jub.* 1:24-25; 2:20; 1QH 9.35-36; Wisd 11:10; *m. Ab.* 3:15; *Sipra Behuq.* pq. 2.262.1.9; *Sipre Deut.* 43.16.1; 45.1.2; 96.4.1; 308.1.2; 352.7.1; *ARN* 35, §77; 44, §124 B; *b. Shab.* 31a, 128a; *Pesiq. Rab Kah.* 9:5; 14:5; *Ex. Rab.* 46:4-5; *Num. Rab.* 5:3; 10:2; *Deut. Rab.* 1:6; 3:15; 7:9; *Lam. Rab.* proem 23; *Lam. Rab.* 3:20, §7; *Pesiq. Rab.* 27:3. Besides these, cf. the singular in Ex 4:22; Hos 11:1; Wisd 18:13; *Sipre Deut.* 43.8.1; *b. Shab.* 31a; *Yoma* 76a; *Ex. Rab.* 15:30; *Lev. Rab.* 10:3; *Num. Rab.* 16:7; *Deut. Rab.* 2:24; 10:4; *Lam. Rab.* proem 2; *Lam. Rab.* 1:17, §52; *Song Rab.* 2:16, §1; *Pesiq. Rab.* 15:17.

90. Wisd 2:13, 16, 18; 5:5; cf. 4Q416 fr. 2 (+4Q417) 1.13 (in Wise, Abegg and Cook, *Scrolls*, 384); 4Q418 frg. 81, line 5; Vermes, *Jesus the Jew*, 195-97. Favorite members of Israel, e.g., Moses, could be called God's "son" (*Sipre Deut.* 29.4.1, a parable; cf. possibly 1 *En.* 105:2, but it probably [106:1] refers to Enoch's son). In later rabbinic texts, a heavenly voice identifies a beloved rabbi as his son (*b. Ber.* 7a; *p. M.K.* 3:1, §6; cf. *b. Ber.* 19a; *Suk.* 45b; *p. Taan.* 3:10, §1). On "charismatic rabbis," see Vermes, *Jesus the Jew*, 210-11; but Witherington, *Christology*, 153, correctly notes that the expression when applied to "charismatic rabbis" is not used as distinctively as in early Christianity.

91. Vermes, *Jesus the Jew*, 200.

92. Later rabbinic polemic explicitly emphasizes that the "son" of Dan 3:25 was merely an angel (*p. Shab.* 6:9, §3).

93. So also Hengel, *Son,* 24, on Greek usage.

94. Hooker, *Preface,* 55-65, sees this sense (which is plausible) rather than Messiahship in Paul, but the options are not mutually exclusive (cf. Rom 1:4).

95. See Harvey, *History,* 172-73.

96. Cf. 1 Chron 17:13; 22:10; 28:6.

97. Dahood, *Psalms,* 11-12; cf. De Vaux, *Israel,* 109; Harrelson, *Cult,* 86-87.

98. See Bright, *History,* 225.

99. Cf. Jer 23:5-6, but note Jer 33:16; Zech 12:8. Given the prevalence of ascribing divinity to kings in parts of the ancient Near East (De Vaux, *Israel,* 111; even Akenaton in "The Amarna Letters," 483-90 in *ANET,* passim), one sin to which Israel's and Judah's rulers had not succumbed (De Vaux, *Israel,* 113), one may question whether Isaiah would have risked implying that God would be Israel's ultimate Davidic king if that was not what he meant (pace Berger and Wyschogrod, *Jewish Christianity,* 43; on the structure cf. De Vaux, *Israel,* 107; Kitchen, *Orient,* 110). This idea admittedly lacks parallels elsewhere in the Hebrew Bible, but explicit Messianic material is scarce in it to begin with. (*Tg.* Is. on 9:6 deliberately alters the grammar to distinguish the Davidic king from the Mighty God.)

100. Before the Qumran texts, in fact, scholars generally agreed that first-century Judaism did not employ "son of God" as a messianic title, in contrast to some Old Testament usage (see Conzelmann, *Theology of Luke,* 76-77; Jeremias, *Parables,* 73; Montefiore, *Gospels,* 1:85; Stevens, *Theology,* 104-5). Bultmann, *Theology,* 50, does recognize its use in OT messianic vocabulary before its later hellenistic "mythological" sense.

101. 4QFlor 1.10-11; 1QSa 2.11-12; see Longenecker, *Christology,* 95; Stanton, *Gospels,* 225; García Martínez, "Sonship"; further on 4QFlor, see Brooke, "4Q174." Vermes, *Jesus the Jew,* 198-99, rightly notes that 1QSer(a) (=1Q28a) 2:11-12 is not as clear as 4QFlor; Hengel, *Son,* 44, also cites a Daniel apocryphon as yet unpublished at the time of his book. 4Q174 3.10-11 uses 2 Sam 7:11-14 in an explicitly messianic context (4Q174 3.11-13; the passage may also stress, as Bergmeier, "Erfüllung," argues on 4Q174 2.17-3.13, the eschatological elect and their temple).

102. See Evans, "Son"; idem, "Prayer of Enosh" (including 4Q458); Abegg, "Introduction to 4Q369," 329.

103. Collins, "Son of God"; and, noting also the close parallels with Lk 1:33-35, both Evans, "4Q246" and Kuhn, "Son of God." Fitzmyer, "4Q246," applies it positively to a coming ruler, but not in a messianic sense.

104. Recovery of the context in the latter case (4Q246 1.5-9; 2.2-3) suggests to some that 4Q246 is simply polemic against pagan claims for divine sonship (Fabry, "Texte"; Cook, "4Q246").

105. Cf. Bons, "Psaume 2." *Ps. Sol.* 17:23 uses Ps 2:9 in a messianic passage, although "son" (2:7) is not mentioned. Gero, "Messiah," finds "son of God" in *4 Ezra* (cf. also 13:37, 52), but more scholars think the Greek behind the passage read "servant" (Jeremias, *Parables,* 73 n. 86); the Ethiopic, an Arabic version, and the Armenian omit "Son" (OTP 1:537, note *e*).

106. See Hurtado, "Homage."

107. See especially Hurtado, *Lord Jesus Christ.*

108. For elaboration, see e.g., Keener, *John,* 281-320, 360-63, and passim on relevant passages.

109. This is not certain; simply because John writes a story independently of Mark does not mean that he had not heard Mark (in fact, I believe that he almost surely had heard Mark). His independent telling, however, increases the likelihood of multiple attestation here.

110. Robinson, *Studies,* 13. Although Mark freely blends texts (Is 40:3; Mal 3:1) in the standard Jewish manner (linking them by means of the common phrase, "prepare the way," Longenecker, *Exegesis,* 138), naming the more well-known prophet in his composite quotation, Matthew simplifies Mark's citation by including only the quotation actually from Isaiah (cf. Meier, *Matthew,* 23).

111. 1QS 8.13-14; cf. Brownlee, "Comparison with Sects," 71; Brown, "Scrolls," 4.

112. 1QS 8.15-16.

113. Is 40:3-5 depict readying roads for the king's arrival, hence the coming of God's kingship (cf. 52:7); heralds would go before him announcing the good news as he led his people forth (60:6; 61:1).

114. As commentators regularly note (e.g., Hooker, *Message*, 9; Hengel, *Leader*, 36).

115. Saldarini, *Community*, 131 suggests an allusion to Lev 23:3, a "Sabbath to the Lord," i.e., Yahweh. Equally speculatively, Witherington, *Christology*, 246 (who regards Mk 2:28 as redactional summary — p. 67) suggests a contrast with the evil figure who changes times and law in Dan 7:25 (cf. Jos. *Ant.* 10.276).

116. E.g., Montefiore, *Gospels*, 1:44; Borg, *Conflict*, 155.

117. Cf. Smith, *Tannaitic Parallels*, 138; Jeremias, *Theology*, 18; Vermes, *Religion*, 24; pace Witherington, *Christology*, 68.

118. E.g., 2 Macc 5:19; 2 *Bar.* 14:18; *Deut. Rab.* 3:1; *Pesiq. Rab.* 23:9. Witherington, *Sage*, 169 suggests that Jesus' statement in Mark 2:27 may counter the sort of saying that appears in *Jub.* 2:18ff.

119. Cf. Pope Benedict, *Jesus of Nazareth*, 110-11, engaging Neusner, *Rabbi*.

120. Gundry, *Old Testament*, 214.

121. E.g., God's yoke (*Ps. Sol.* 7:9); that of the law (Jer 5:5; 2 *Bar.* 41:3; *m. Ab.* 3:5; *Sipra Sh.* pq. 12.121.2.5; *Sipre Deut.* 344.4.2); and that of his kingdom (*m. Ber.* 2:2, 5; *Sipra Behar* par. 5.255.1.9, 11).

122. Smith, *Tannaitic Parallels*, 153.

123. Davies and Allison, *Matthew*, 2:289.

124. Pace Stanton, "Salvation"; idem, *New People*, 366-77; and Gundry, *Matthew*, 220, though Gundry's own evidence points to Matthew's changes of Sirach.

125. Cf. Hamerton-Kelly, *Pre-Existence*, 68; Meier, *Matthew*, 127.

126. Hagner, *Matthew*, 323 sees in 11:28 an allusion to Yahweh giving rest (Ex 33:14) that goes beyond Wisdom. This is possible, but the language can be explained simply as an allusion to divine Wisdom.

127. Ridderbos, *Paul and Jesus*, 102; cf. Ellis, *Matthew*, 28; Danker, "Perspectives."

128. 1QS 6.3, 6; CD 13.2-3; *B. Ber.* 6ab; *Meg.* 23b; *p. Meg.* 4:4, §5; Reicke, *Era*, 121.

129. *M. Ab.* 3:2, 6; *Mek. Bahodesh* 11.48ff; cf. *m. Ber.* 7:3.

130. Which presumably predates Jesus'/Matthew's saying, since the rabbis would not likely borrow it from Christian sources (cf. Smith, *Tannaitic Parallels*, 152-53; Meier, *Matthew*, 206; Barth, "Law," 135; Sievers, "Shekhinah"). Cf. Ziesler, "Presence," comparing Jesus' presence with Yahweh's in the Old Testament.

131. E.g., *Sib. Or.* 3.701; 3 *En.* 18:24; *m. Ab.* 2:9, 13; 3:14; *tos. Peah* 1:4; 3:8; *Shab.* 7:22, 25; 13:5; *R.H.* 1:18; *Taan.* 2:13; *B.K.* 7:7; *Sanh.* 1:2; 13:1, 6; 14:3, 10; *Sipra VDDen.* pq. 2.2.4.2; 4.6.4.1; *Sipra Sav Mekhilta deMiluim* par. 98.7.7; *Shemini Mekhilta deMiluim* 99.1.4, 5, 7; 99.2.2, 3; 99.3.9, 11; 99.5.13; *Sipra Qed.* par. 1.195.2.3; pq. 7.204.1.4; *Sipra Emor* pq. 9.227.1.5; *Behuq.* pq. 5.266.1.1; *Sipre Num.* 11.2.3; 11.3.1; 42/1/2; 42.2.3; 76.2.2; 78.1.1; 78.5.1; 80.1.1; 82.3.1; 84.1.1; 84.5.1; 85.3.1; 85.4.1; 85.5.1; *Sipre Deut.* 1.8.3; 1.9.2; 1.10.4; 2.1.1; 11.1.1; 21.1.1; 24.3.1; 26.4.1; 28.1.1; 32.3.2; 32.5.8; 33.1.1; 37.1.1, 3; 38.1.1, 3.

132. Davies and Allison, *Matthew*, 2:790, with most scholars (e.g., Stanton, *Gospel Truth*, 60), regard the saying "as an utterance of the risen Lord" (i.e., not "authentic" in the sense of deriving from Jesus before the resurrection). At the same time they concede that they cannot be dogmatic; was Paul the only person to speak "of being spiritually present with others"? But Matt 18:20 means far more than 1 Cor 5:3-5 (which, pace Fee, *Corinthians*, 205, communicates merely *epistolary* presence — cf. 1 Thess 2:17; Col 2:5; Isoc. *Nic./Cypr.* 51-52, *Or.* 3.37; Sen. *Ep. Lucil.* 32.1). If Jesus did offer this saying in anticipation of his resurrection, he communicated a point to his disciples the full impact of which they were unprepared to grasp.

133. One may exclude this saying from the words of the historical Jesus (e.g., Flusser, *Judaism*, 515) if one a priori assumes that wisdom christology (here, Shekinah christology) originated among Jesus' followers after his departure; but one must exclude a number of Jesus' sayings (e.g., Matt 23:34; 24:36) to support this approach. Witherington, *Sage*, contends that wisdom christology originated

with Jesus; while the thesis does not match traditional modern theories of christology's evolution, those theories have problems with earlier Pauline evidence.

134. Wisdom was often portrayed as water (Philo *Flight* 166; *Worse* 117; *Sib. Or.* 1.33-34; cf. Sir 24:21). This connection is relevant to this passage because wisdom sits by God's throne (Wisd 9:4) and a stream of wisdom teaching did identify God's Spirit with his wisdom (Wisd 9:17; cf. Wisd 1:6-7; 7:22; for Philo, Isaacs, *Spirit*, 54-55; cf. also Keener, *John*, 963-64).

135. As is widely agreed (Haenchen, *Acts*, 184 n. 5; Dupont, *Salvation*, 22; Zehnle, *Pentecost Discourse*, 34; Pao, *Isaianic Exodus*, 231-32; Marshall, "Use of OT," 536, 543).

136. See especially Hurtado, *Lord Jesus Christ*, 198-99, who suggests that this belongs to a very early ritual of confessing Jesus (cf. 1 Cor 1:2; 12:3). Paul elsewhere applies earlier biblical language for God to Jesus, e.g., Is 45:22-23 in Phil 2:10-11.

137. Cf. e.g., Knights, "Faces."

138. See Glasson, *Advent*, 161-79; followed also by Robinson, *Coming*, 140-41.

139. Fee, *Corinthians*, 839.

140. Ladd, *Theology*, 416-17. See further Longenecker, *Christology*, 136. Vermes, *Jesus the Jew*, 114, plausibly objects that "Mar" is also a human form of address, appropriate for rulers, and suggests (p. 127) that in the earliest traditions, the title was probably applied to Jesus as a teacher. Yet a *prayer* to "Come" (rather than a prayer to God to send him) suggests more. This tradition was undoubtedly established before Paul; why else would he teach a Diaspora congregation an Aramaic prayer?

141. Although 1 Cor 8:6 may represent the Corinthian position (Willis, *Meat*, 84-87, 95), Paul himself clearly accepts Wisdom Christology (1 Cor 1:30; cf. Willis, *Meat*, 96; Hamerton-Kelly, *Pre-Existence*, 130).

142. Paul modifies Hellenistic (see Nock, *Gentile Christianity*, 34; Koester, *Introduction*, 1:162; Conzelmann, *1 Corinthians*, 145) — both Stoic (Moffatt, *1 Corinthians*, 106; Hamerton-Kelly, *Pre-Existence*, 130; Meeks, *Urban Christians*, 91) and Platonic (cf. Grant, *Gods*, 48; Horsley, "Formula") — and Hellenistic Jewish (Lohse, *Colossians*, 50; cf. *Sib. Or.* 3.277-78; Grant, *Gods*, 84-85) language here; his wording probably represents an adaptation of the Shema (Goppelt, *Theology*, 2:83; Héring, *1 Corinthians*, 69; Bruce, *Corinthians*, 80), which is attested early, e.g., the Nash papyrus (2d century BCE); *m. Ber.* 2:5.

143. Some have seen elements of an Adam Christology (e.g., Martin, *Carmen Christi*, 116-18; idem, "*Morphē*"; Hunter, *Predecessors*, 43; Johnston, *Ephesians*, 41; Beare, *Philippians*, 80; Ridderbos, *Paul*, 74; Furness, "Hymn"); others have denied it (e.g., Glasson, "Notes," 137-39; Wanamaker, "Philippians"; Bornkamm, *Experience*, 114) or held that Paul revised an earlier Adam Christology (Barrett, *Adam*, 71). Regardless of possible allusions to Adam as God's image (e.g., Philo *Creation* 69; *4 Ezra* 8:44; 9:13; *Life of Adam* 37:3; 39:3; *Apoc. Moses* 10:3; 12:2; 33:5; *m. Sanh.* 4:5; *b. Sanh.* 38a, bar.; *Gen. Rab.* 8:10; *Eccl. Rab.* 6:10, §1), Wisdom was God's image in the ultimate sense (Wisd. 7:26; Philo *Plant.* 18; *Confusion* 97; 147; *Heir* 230; *Flight* 101; *Dreams* 1.239; 2.45; *Spec. Laws* 1.81), which this text distinguishes from the human sense (Phil 2:7-8), especially in presenting Jesus' divinity (cf. Phil 2:10-11 with Isa 45:23). Paul here assumes Christ's preexistence (Hamerton-Kelly, *Pre-Existence*, 156-68; against Talbert, "Problem"); on other christological hymns stressing Christ's preexistence, see Martin, *Carmen Christi*, 19.

144. This passage is frequently regarded as hymnic (e.g., Schweizer, *Colossians*, 63; Lohse, *Colossians*, 41; Beasley-Murray, "Colossians," 170; Martin, "Hymn"; Schweizer, "Christ in Colossians"; Pöhlmann, "All-Prädikationen"; McCown, "Structure"; Gibbs, *Creation*, 95; Hamerton-Kelly, *Pre-Existence*, 168-69; cf. O'Brien, *Colossians*, 40-42, who accepts it as a hymn but thinks it may be Pauline) and as containing Wisdom traditions (Bandstra, "Errorists," 332; Johnston, *Ephesians*, 58; May, "Logos," 446; Manns, "Midrash"; Kennedy, *Epistles*, 156-57; Longenecker, *Christology*, 145; Moule, *Birth*, 167; Glasson, "Colossians"). Prose rhetoric could reuse hymns (Menander Rhetor 2.4.393.9-12); nevertheless, it also could employ a "grand" (an epideictic style for the sublime) or even rhythmic style

without necessarily entailing hymns (cf. Dion. Hal. *Lit. Comp.* 25; Cicero *Orator* 20.67; 50.168-69.231; Fronto *Ad M. Caes.* 3.16.1-2; Rowe, "Style," 154; Harvey, *Listening*, 4).

145. Is 13:6, 9; Ezek 13:5; 30:3; Joel 1:15; 2:1, 11, 31; 3:14; Amos 5:18, 20; Obad 15; Zeph 1:7, 14; Mal 4:5. 2 Thess 2:2 in context implies the same (cf. 2 Thess 2:1); cf. 2 Pet 3:10, 12.

146. Especially in Rom 9:5. With varying degrees of certainty, see Sanday and Headlam, *Romans*, 233-38; Cullmann, *Christology*, 313; Cranfield, *Romans*, 2:467-68; Longenecker, *Christology*, 138; Harris, *Jesus as God*, 143-72; Moo, *Romans*, 565-68; Jewett, *Romans*, 567-68. That the language is praise may make Paul's interest devotional rather than dogmatic (Burridge and Gould, *Jesus*, 94), but this does not appreciably lessen the import. In Pauline literature, cf. also Tit 2:13.

147. E.g., Rom 1:7; 1 Cor 1:3; 2 Cor 1:2. In other ancient literature, see e.g., Pliny *Ep.* 10.1.2; Fronto *Ad M. Caes.* 3.9.1; Horsley, *Documents* 2, §21, pp. 63-67; so also the Jewish "wish-prayer" *shalom*; early interpreters recognized the connection (e.g., Theodoret of Cyr *Comm. 1 Cor.* 166), as have some modern ones (e.g., Hunter, *Predecessors*, 80; Aune, *Environment*, 193; Kelly, *Peter*, 45). Some have found early prayers to Jesus on Palestinian Jewish ossuaries (Sukenik, "Records"; Gustafsson, "Graffiti," assigning them to the early 40s; but c. 50 CE may be closer [Bruce, *Documents*, 95], hence not far removed from Paul's time).

148. Texts like 1 Cor 12:4-6 and especially 2 Cor 13:13[14], which many see as proto-trinitarian (see discussion in Fee, *Presence*, 839-42; Thrall, *2 Corinthians*, 920-21; Thiselton, *Corinthians*, 934; Grieb, "People"; Watson, "Identity").

149. Cf. Sir 24:19; 51:23-28; Meier, *Matthew*, 127; cf. Hamerton-Kelly, *Pre-Existence*, 68; Stein, *Method and Message*, 3; on Sir 51, contrast Stanton, "Salvation"; cf. Gundry, *Matthew*, 220. Multiple points of contact likely suggest that Sir 51 is in view, though by itself this could support a sage christology and not just a wisdom christology.

150. See e.g., Keener, *John*, 300-2, 350-63; Witherington, *Sage*, 368-80; Epp, "Wisdom"; Dunn, "John," 314-16.

151. I would argue that if anything Mark tones down the divine Christ for the genre of philosophic-type biography, to appeal to a hellenistic audience, rather than that divine christology in the NT reflects a late and hellenistic theology.

152. Jms 2:1 (lit., "lord of glory," as in 1 Cor 2:8, treated as an adjectival genitive); cf. Ps 24:7-10.

153. Although our best evidence for this is later, Simon, *Sects*, 94-95, argues that some strands of first-century Judaism also hypostatized divine attributes as distinct. On Jewish monotheism in this period, see especially Hurtado, *One God*; Bock, *Blasphemy*, 112-83 (on exalted figures); more briefly, e.g., Wright, *People of God*, 248-59; Ashton, *Understanding*, 159.

154. Later Judaism became far more precise in its definition of monotheism, perhaps under the influence of Maimonides' use of Aristotelian metaphysics borrowed from Muslim Arabs (which affirmed a monotheism so rigorous that it could define even divine attributes as entities distinct from the Deity; Moore, *Judaism*, 1:437). Even later Judaism, however, regarded Gentile (as opposed to Jewish) adherence to Trinitarian views as *Shittuf* (partnership) rather than idolatry (cf. Falk, *Pharisee*, 33-35; Borowitz, *Christologies*, 32; Berger and Wyschogrod, *Jewish Christianity*, 33; Schoeps, *Argument*, 16-17).

155. Cf. Moses in the probably Hellenistic Jewish long version of Orphica 25-41 (though missing in the short version); Aristob. *frg.* 4 (in Euseb. *P.E.* 13.13.5); Meeks, *Prophet-King*, 103-6.

156. E.g., 11Q13 2.10 (using Ps 82:1); perhaps a divine king appears in 4Q491 manuscript C, frg. 11, 1.18, but probably it is meant in a relative sense.

157. See Hayman, "Monotheism," though he probably overstates the case for the pervasiveness of dualistic monotheism. Cf. Fauth, "Metatron"; Abrams, "Boundaries"; Alexander, "3 Enoch," 235; for other discussions of Metatron, see e.g., Orlov, "Name"; Septimus, "Mttrwn."

158. With Bauckham, *Crucified*, 2-4, 27-28, who believes Jesus in early Christian texts functions like wisdom, being within the unique divine identity (26-42).

159. Pritz, *Nazarene Christianity*, 110; Flusser, *Judaism*, 620, 624. Barrett, *John and Judaism*, 48-49, thinks rabbinic teaching on God's unity reflects some polemic against Christianity.

160. See e.g., Albright, *Stone Age,* 304; Johnson, *Possessions,* 45.

161. For detailed argument, see most fully Bauckham, *Crucified,* 2-15, 26-42; cf. Dunn, *Theology,* 35; Wright, *Paul,* 63-72.

162. The only evidence we could find of groups claiming to be Christian yet playing down Jesus' deity would come from mirror-reading, which is notoriously fallible (see esp. Sumney, *Opponents*). Witherington concludes, in *Christology,* that Jesus would not have claimed deity in a way that confused him with the Father, which is how his contemporaries would have heard a claim to deity. At the same time, Witherington continues, some of Jesus' claims, including the claim to be David's Lord, suggest that he held a more transcendent self-image, so he believes that Raymond Brown is correct in thinking that Jesus would have been comfortable even with the Johannine exposition of his identity had he confronted it (Witherington, *Christology,* 276, citing Brown, "Know," 77-78). Stuhlmacher, "Son of Man," appeals to other evidence for Jesus' awareness of deity in some sense.

163. *Judaism,* 620.

Notes to Chapter 20

1. Evans, "Activities," 24, 27.

2. With e.g., Witherington, "Wright quest" (praising this aspect of N. T. Wright's work). Evans, "Non-Christian Sources," 472, notes that whereas Burton Mack supposes that Mark's linkage of Jesus' teaching and signs to his death is fictitious, these elements also appear together in Josephus' brief sketch of Jesus (*Ant.* 18.63-64). While not everyone who spoke like Gandhi or Martin Luther King, Jr., was martyred, and while Gandhi and King (unlike Jesus) did not provoke martyrdom deliberately, there remains an intrinsic relationship between their message and their martyrdom.

3. For Jesus' prophetic act and confrontation with the elite probably leading to his martyrdom, see also e.g., Mk 11:18; Borg, *Vision,* 176-84; Broadhead, "Priests," 142.

4. Tan, *Zion Traditions,* 234. Keck, *History,* 124, sees Jesus going to Jerusalem to fulfill his costly mission, but no indication that he went to confront the authorities there.

5. Some cite in its favor the appearance of the parable in *Gospel of Thomas* 65 (e.g., Charlesworth, *Jesus Within Judaism,* 139-40); because I consider Thomas' version secondary, however, I will not appeal to it here.

6. Charlesworth, *Jesus Within Judaism,* 141 (also noting the neglect of the burial in the parable, in contrast to widespread early Christian tradition [e.g., 1 Cor 15:4]; p. 142).

7. Which need not be secondary, pace Nineham, *Mark,* 311; 4Q500.1 may conjoin Is 5's vineyard with the temple and possibly even Ps 118, as here (cf. Brooke, "4Q500"; Baumgarten, "4Q500"). The absence of this allusion in *GThom* 65 could indicate that the original Jesus tradition lacked this detail, but the Gospel of Thomas may as easily have omitted it — its original point certainly would not fit Thomas's redactional *Tendenz,* whereas Mark had little reason to invent an allusion that was too subtle for most of his own readers to catch (see also Snodgrass, *Tenants;* Gundry, *Matthew,* 425; Carson, "Matthew," 452, following Snodgrass, "Husbandmen," for doubts that GThom preserves the original form). Still, the *basic* triadic outline of Thomas's parable might vindicate Dodd's defense of this form (*Parables,* 100).

8. Ps 80:12-14; Virg. *Georg.* 2.371-79; Lewis, *Life,* 125.

9. 2 Chron 26:10; Is 1:8; Gundry, *Matthew,* 425.

10. Anderson, *Mark,* 272; see further Jeremias, *Parables,* 74-75. On the care of vineyards, including irrigation, see more fully Hepper, *Plants,* 96-97; for ideal sites, see Colum. *Trees* 4.1-5.

11. Klausner, *Jesus,* 181; Anderson, *Mark,* 272; on tenants leasing plots of land, see Stambaugh and Balch, *Environment,* 68, who cite Varro *Agric.* 1.17.2-3; Columella *Agric.* 1.7; Pliny *Ep.* 3.19; 9.37. In Palestine, see Kloppenborg, "Growth"; for examples of tenant farmers elsewhere, e.g., *CIL* 8.25902 (*Empire,* ed. Sherk, pp. 250-51); Deissmann, *Light,* 33. Grain legally belonged to the landowner until the

lessees had paid their rent (Lewis, *Life,* 123). (Meier, *Matthew,* 243 thinks that the landowner here demands *all* the produce in this parable, mirroring the absolute demands of God's reign; but "*his* fruit" simply means the portion the tenants had contracted to deliver to him.) Despite Matthew's eschatological uses for harvest imagery (3:10-12; 13:39) and "drawn near" (4:17), "proper time" (21:41) need not be eschatological (cf. 24:45), probably referring to harvest in early summer (cf. Jos. *Apion* 1.79).

12. E.g., *Pesiq. Rab Kah.* Sup. 1:11.

13. *Gen. Rab.* 38:9. Johnston, "Parabolic Interpretations," 594, points out that in rabbinic parables, the landlord always represents God, although the share-cropping tenants variously represent Israel (*ARN* 16:3A) or groups of the righteous (the patriarchs, tithe-payers — *Sipre Deut.* 312; *Ex. Rab.* 41:1), or people who should learn Torah (some of whom do and others do not — *Deut. Rab.* 7:4). Servants in rabbinic parables are more ad hoc: they could represent Israel, Israel's pious, Israel's poor, or Israel's prayerful, but also Gentiles, Egypt, and other referents (Johnston, "Parabolic Interpretations," 590).

14. Hengel, "Gleichnis," followed also by Lane, *Mark,* 417 n. 9.

15. Young, *Parables,* 298-301 compares *Sipre Deut.* 312, in which a king finally expelled wicked tenants from his field after his own son was born; and especially *Seder Eliyahu* 30/28 (a passage with an early-second-century attribution), in which a wicked guardian killed his son (p. 301), depicting God's identification with his people in anthropomorphic terms (p. 304). I suspect that the latter parallel, lacking both tenants and vineyard, is too distant, but Young is right to compare the shock value in both illustrations (p. 303).

16. Stanton, *Gospel Truth,* 154.

17. See further arguments in Hagner, *Matthew,* 619.

18. Ignoring these factors, Vermes, *Religion,* 104 rejects the citation as anti-Jewish church polemic, but the saying itself is hardly anti-Jewish.

19. So Stern, *Parables,* 197 on this parable, though many of Jesus' parables lack such allusions.

20. Young, *Parables,* 293-94.

21. Gundry, *Matthew,* 429, following Black. Jesus may read *habonim* ("builders") as if from *bun,* "understand," rather than from *bnh,* "build," hence apply it to the scribes (Stern, *Parables,* 196); Young, *Theologian,* 219 suggests a play among "sons" *(banim),* "builders" *(bonim),* and "stones" *(avanim).* Early Christians naturally accommodated the quotation to the LXX (Perrin, *Teaching,* 132), although Jesus probably did address the Jerusalem aristocracy in Greek.

22. Gundry, *Old Testament,* 200. See Mk 2:25; 12:10, 26; cf. Matt 12:5; 19:4 (apparently added to Mark); 21:16; Lk 10:26. The phrase may correspond to "Is it not written" (Mk 11:17), though "It is written" was a common scripture citation formula (Josh 8:31; 2 Kgs 23:21; 2 Chron 23:18; 25:4; 31:3; 35:12; Ezra 3:2, 4; 6:18; Neh 8:15; 10:34, 36; Dan 9:13; CD 1.13; 5.1; 7.10; 11.18, 20; 1QS 5.15, 17; 8.14; *Test. Zeb.* 3:4; *m. Git.* 9:10; *Sanh.* 10:1; *Mek. Pisha* 1.76-77; *Sipre Deut.* 56.1.2b; Fitzmyer, *Essays,* 7-16).

23. Cf. Gundry, *Matthew,* 427; Kingsbury, *Christology,* 150. See discussion below and in ch. 18.

24. Pace Scott, *Parable,* 249-50, the tenants are not "expected" to challenge the landowner's honor; custom demands rather that they accept their socially inferior status and act accordingly. While ancient peasants undoubtedly enjoyed their plight no more than other peasants, they would not have identified with the foolish tenants in this story, nor do the actions of these tenants represent a Galilean peasant revolt (Gundry, *Matthew,* 425, following Rostovzeff, *History,* 1.269-73; cf. Snodgrass, *Stories,* 293; pace Dodd, *Parables,* 97; Jeremias, *Parables,* 74-75).

25. Johnston, "Parabolic Interpretations," 625.

26. Is 5:2; cf. 3:14; Ezek 17:6; Hos 9:10; *3 Bar.* 1:2; *Mek. Pisha* 1.162; *Sipre Deut.* 15.1.1; *Pesiq. Rab Kah.* 16:9; *Ex. Rab.* 30:17; 34:3; *Song Rab.* 2:16, §1; 7:13, §1; Jeremias, *Parables,* 70, 76-77.

27. *Colum. Rust.* 1.7.1-2. Later rabbis emphasized treating vineyard tenants fairly (*b. Ber.* 5b). Details would be specified in legal contracts (e.g., *P. Oxy.* 1631, from 280 CE), and receipts would be issued for rent paid in produce (e.g., *P. Amh.* 104, from 125 CE).

28. *Colum. Rust.* 1.7.2.

29. Cf. e.g., Hom. *Il.* 7.275-82; Appian *R.H.* 8.8.53; although some had killed royal tax-collectors (1 Kgs 12:18; *Gen. Rab.* 42:3; *Lev. Rab.* 11:7). The slaughter of a group of ambassadors (Jos. *Life* 56-57) or of successive messengers (*Life* 50-52) appeared morally hideous.

30. Cf. Matt 5:12//Lk 6:23, 26; Matt 23:31, 34//Lk 11:49-50; 1 Kgs 18:4, 13; 2 Chron 24:20-22; Neh 9:26; Jer 26:21-23; *1 En.* 89:51-53; *Jub.* 1:12; CD 7.17-18.

31. Cf. Jos. *Ant.* 10.38; *Mart. Is.* 5:1-14; *Liv. Pr.* 1:1 (OTP 2:385)/§24 in Greek of Schermann, p. 75, line 1; 2:1 (Schermann §25, p. 81.2); 6:1 (Schermann §17, p. 60); 7:1-2 (Schermann §14, p. 51). The killing may allude in the narrative world especially to the Baptist (cf. Petersen, *Criticism,* 69); many see in the two sendings the former and latter prophets (cf. Scott, *Parable,* 241). Young, *Parables,* 288 prefers the Lukan and GThom versions, thinking Matthew's (and Mark's) killings represent a later allegorical stage; but Mark is probably our earliest form.

32. For accounts of landholders' use of violence to expand their holdings (the basis for hereditary wealthy), see especially MacMullen, *Social Relations,* 6-12.

33. Hence in a later Jewish parable, those who have killed a royal (i.e., divine) messenger fear retribution (*Gen. Rab.* 42:3; *Lev. Rab.* 11:7; cf. *Ruth Rab.* Proem 7). The Romans likewise enslaved a whole people for killing one of their representatives (Eustathius, *Paraphrase of Dionysius Periegetes* in *Geographi Graeci Minores* 2.p.253, lines 8-10, in Sherk, *Empire,* 37); cf. Lk 21:24.

34. Cf. Matt 10:40; Lk 10:16; *tos. Taan.* 3:2; *m. Ber.* 5:5; also Scott, *Parable,* 249. This is entirely aside from how peasants in general viewed landowners in general (Oakman, "Peasant," 119); this landowner is so benevolent by contrast to most that in an ancient context he may have appeared favorably.

35. Scott, *Parable,* 250.

36. Herodian 4.1.3.

37. Virg. *Aen.* 10.492.

38. Because "beloved" sometimes represents "only" (see Keener, *John,* 412-16, esp. 415; this conclusion also fits the "heir" of Mk 12:7), it heightens the story's *pathos* and suspense; most families had several children, but this father had only one heir (Young, *Theologian,* 217-18).

39. Charlesworth, *Jesus Within Judaism,* 152-53.

40. Also *Jub.* 1:21; *Ps. Sol.* 14:5; cf. 1QM 12.12.

41. This sort of fruit may also be implied in Mk 11:14, since Mark frames Jesus' prophetic act in the temple with the cursing of the fig tree.

42. "Come, let us kill him" (Mk 12:7) reflects Gen 37:20 LXX, hence an allusion to the envy of Joseph's brothers against the one "sent" by their father (Gen 37:13-14), who became their deliverer (cf. Acts 7:9-16).

43. Cf. Gundry, *Matthew,* 427; Kingsbury, *Christology,* 150.

44. Jeremias, *Parables,* 73. "Son" usually represents Israel in rabbinic parables (Johnston, "Parabolic Interpretations," 587; e.g., also *Ex. Rab.* 15:30; *Lev. Rab.* 2:5; 10:3; *Num. Rab.* 16:7; *Deut. Rab.* 7:9; 10:4; *Lam. Rab.* 1:17, 52; 2; *Song Rab.* 2:16, §1; 5:16, §3), a natural usage (cf. e.g., Ex 4:22-23; Hos 11:1; Is 1:2; Jer 3:19-22; Sir 4:10; *Ps. Sol.* 13:9; 17:27-30; 18:4; *Jub.* 1:24-25); but even in rabbinic parables, special servants within Israel are sometimes intended (e.g., *Sipre Deut.* 29.4.1; *p. M.K.* 3:1, §6). Stern, *Parables,* 192-95, who doubts that Jesus would have foreseen his death, suggests that the son is John the Baptist, whose death at best foreshadows that of Jesus. But in the context of Jesus' ministry (especially the recent entry and act in the temple) a self-reference is most likely even before interpretation in Christian tradition (cf. also Hagner, *Matthew,* 619).

45. Cf. McKelvey, "Cornerstone," for the former; Gundry, *Matthew,* 429; Jeremias, "Γωνία," 792-93 for the latter.

46. 1QS 8.5, 8-9; 9.6; CD 2.10, 13; Gärtner, *Temple,* 16-46; Flusser, *Judaism,* 37-39; Wilcox, "Dualism," 93-94. The psalm itself has a temple context (Ps 118:19-20, 27), though it is not clear that the stone refers to it.

47. A later rabbinic tradition plausibly explains the rejected cornerstone as David, repudiated by Saul (Hilton and Marshall, *Gospels,* 60; Young, *Theologian,* 219).

48. Kingsbury, *Story*, 81-84.

49. On the authenticity of Lk 13:31-33, see Tan, *Zion Traditions*, 59-69. Comparing prophets like Amos and Jeremiah, Freyne, "New Reading," suggests that Jesus challenged the center; Borg and Crossan, "Collision Course," believe that Jesus went to Jerusalem to challenge Rome and its allies.

50. Cf. Freyne, "Servant Community," 109.

51. E.g., Wrede, *Messianic Secret*, 82-92; Bultmann, *Word*, 213; idem, *Theology*, 3, 29 (but cf. *Word*, 214-15).

52. Schweitzer, *Quest*, 387-93; Meyer, "Ministry," 352; Keener, *Matthew*, 431-35 (where I offer most of the following arguments); Stuhlmacher, "Readiness"; and especially helpfully Brown, *Death*, 1468-91; Tan, *Zion Traditions*, 57-80; McKnight, *Death*, passim.

53. Keck, *History*, 118.

54. Keck, *History*, 118. If Jesus expected his death, however, is it not possible that he also interpreted it (see discussion below)?

55. Bultmann, *Word*, 29-30.

56. Mk 1:7-13 with Matt 3:7-4:11//Lk 3:7-4:12; Mk 3:28-30 with Matt 12:28//Lk 11:20.

57. E.g., Keener, *Matthew*, 630. Theissen and Merz, *Historical Jesus*, 432-35, draw connections with the last supper, which they interpret in a way hypothetically relevant to the temple cleansing.

58. See Brown, *Death*, 1468.

59. Granted, the Gospel writers had literary and theological reasons to include such predictions in their Gospels: many people believed that prophets and wise men could sense their impending death (see Aune, *Prophecy*, 178; Boring et al., *Commentary*, 105, 155; cf. Tac. *Ann*. 6.46, 48); further, ancient narratives regularly extol heroes who could face suffering or danger bravely (e.g., Livy 5.46.2-3; Plut. *Sayings of Spartans*, Anonymous 35, *Mor*. 234AB; Dion. Hal. 7.68.2-3; Jos. *Ant*. 3.208; 4.322; 6.126-27). From a literary perspective, one might object to a *deus ex machina* or other denouement not anticipated in the plot itself (Arist. *Poetics* 15.10, 1454ab). But noting incentive to record information (without which biographers and historians would not have recorded anything) is not the same as providing an argument that it has been invented.

60. Brown, *Death*, 1468-91; Witherington, *Christology*, 250.

61. Jeremias, *Theology*, 282; Hill, *Prophecy*, 61.

62. Cf. e.g., *Jub*. 23:11-25, especially 23:13; 36:1; 1QM 15.1; *Sib. Or*. 3.213-15; *4 Ezra* 8:63-9:8; 13:30; *2 Bar*. 26:1-27:13; 69:3-5; *Test. Mos*. 7-8; *m. Sot*. 9:15; *b. Sanh*. 97a; *Pesiq. Rab Kah*. 5:9; *Eccl. Rab*. 2:15, §2; *Lam. Rab*. 1:13, §41; *Song Rab*. 8:9, §3; *Pesiq. Rab*. 15:14/15; 34:1.

63. Cf. Hill, *Prophecy*, 57; Aune, *Prophecy*, 157, 159, 173; Theissen and Merz, *Historical Jesus*, 429; for the influence of John's death, see also Kraeling, *John the Baptist*, 157. See especially Tan, *Zion Traditions*, 57-80, particularly 79-80 (also defending the authenticity of Lk 13:31-33 on 59-69).

64. Freyne, *Galilean*, 166. Nevertheless, a specific appeal to Isaiah's servant tradition (also e.g., Adinolfi, "Servo"), like a suggestion concerning Daniel's son of man tradition (Schaberg, "Predictions"), is less certain than the more general appeal to martyred prophets.

65. Although overstating the case, Adinolfi, "Servo," is correct that the growing conflicts with his contemporaries could have indicated to Jesus his impending martyrdom (Hill, *Prophecy*, 61).

66. Jeremias, *Theology*, 277-86; Dodd, *Parables*, 57; Stauffer, *Jesus*, 171-73.

67. See e.g., Keener, *Matthew*, 432, 497-98; Theissen and Merz, *Historical Jesus*, 431-32 (noting on 432-33 that the act in the temple is historically reliable, and fits Jesus' prophecy against the temple).

68. In Acts 13:27, proclamation to a Diaspora Jewish audience somewhat mitigates the leaders' guilt based on ignorance (Foakes-Jackson, *Acts*, 117; O'Neill, *Theology*, 86; Pillai, *Interpretation*, 34). Despite some tensions, later Christians are also unlikely to have invented such a harsh rebuke of Peter (cf. Schweizer, *Mark*, 165 and Anderson, *Mark*, 213, both overstating the case; pace Weeden, *Mark*).

69. Brown, *Death*, 514.

70. Tan, *Zion Traditions*, 222. He also notes Jewish beliefs in returned prophets like Elijah (Mal

4:5; *4 Ezra* 6:26; *Test. Zeb.* 10:2-3; p. 221), early expectations of the parousia (222), and Matt 19:28//Lk 22:30b (p. 223).

71. For transitional eschatological eras, see e.g., *1 En.* 91:8-17; *3 En.* 45:5; *Sib. Or.* 3.741-59 (preceding 3.767-95); *Sipre Deut.* 34.4.3; 310.5.1; 343.7.1; *b. A.Z.* 3b; *Pesiq. Rab Kah.* 3:16; 27:5; *Gen. Rab.* 88:5; see further discussion and sources in Bonsirven, *Judaism,* 212-13; Aune, *Revelation,* 1104-8; Moyise, *Old Testament,* 66-67; Beasley-Murray, *Revelation,* 288; Rissi, *Time,* 116; Morris, *Apocalyptic,* 44-45.

72. Hengel, *Atonement,* 34.

73. E.g., Soph. *Oed. Rex* 439; *Wom. Tr.* 1169–73; Dio Cass. 62.18.4; Diod. Sic. 16.91.2-3; Arrian *Alex.* 7.26.2-3; Jos. *War* 1.80.

74. Young, *Parables,* 296; Sanders, *Jesus to Mishnah,* 94; Vermes, "Jesus the Jew," 120; Broadhead, "Priests," 142; on the confrontation, cf. also Horsley, *Spiral,* 325. Granted, he was not as immediate a political threat as eschatological prophets promising the collapse of Jerusalem's walls or the parting of the Jordan, given Roman attacks against them (Jos. *Ant.* 20.167-72; *War* 2.258-63; Broer, "Death," 159-60). His followers did not appear a threat even for some time after his execution. Nevertheless, his activity suggested at least a minor or potential political threat.

75. E.g., Keener, *Matthew,* 432; Theissen and Merz, *Historical Jesus,* 431-33. This tells against the thesis that the Temple cleansing occurred at the Festival of Tabernacles six months before this Passover (Sanders, *John,* 287; Manson, *Sayings,* 78); his enemies would not have allowed him to live this long.

76. Jer 26:11; Jos. *War* 6.300-9; Sanders, *Jesus and Judaism,* 302; see Winkle, "Model."

77. Sanders, *Jesus and Judaism,* 303.

78. Jos. *War* 6.124-26; *Ant.* 15.417; Carmon, *Inscriptions,* 76, 167-68; cf. O'Rourke, "Law," 174; Segal, "Penalty"; pace Rabello, "Condition," 737-38.

79. This is not to say, with Hamilton, "Cleansing," that Jesus' act in the Temple would have recalled royal appropriation of funds; see the critique by Witherington, *Christology,* 113-14. The mishnaic claim of execution without trial for violating the Temple (*m. Sanh.* 9:6; Segal, "Death Penalty") might have been wishful thinking (cf. Acts 21:31); perhaps more likely, Jesus' act in the outer court may have been marginal enough to "violation" to require a hearing. He did not enter a prohibited precinct (a profanation punishable also elsewhere, e.g., Hesiod *Astron. frg.* 3).

80. Sanders, *Jesus and Judaism,* 11.

81. Witherington, *Christology,* 109-10.

82. Broadhead, "Priests," 142.

83. See Sanders, *Jesus and Judaism,* 364 n. 4. This prophecy is usually regarded as historical as well (e.g., Broadhead, "Priests," 141-42). One could argue that later Christians composed the narrative to fit Jesus' prophecy of judgment against the Temple (so M. Goguel, critiqued in Sanders, *Jesus and Judaism,* 364 n. 4, who employs the criterion of coherence in a positive manner) or the reverse, but various lines of evidence, some of which we have noted, support the authenticity of the central account.

84. Mack, *Myth,* 10 n. 4.

85. On 2 Thess 2 see my comments in *Matthew,* 565-66. That the later church would have grown more eschatologically oriented than Jesus is inherently unlikely, and that they would have invented 2 Thess 2:3-4 after 70, when the Temple was destroyed, is hardly likely.

86. Jn 2:19 further attests this tradition, though published long enough after the Temple's demise to appear safely on Jesus' lips.

87. E.g., 1QpHab 9.6-7; *Test. Mos.* 5:4; 6:8-9 (the content renders unlikely the *Testament of Moses'* composition after the event); if genuinely early, cf. *Test. Levi* 15:1. In more detail, see Keener, *Matthew,* 561.

88. E.g., Jos. *War* 6.300-9. See also *Test. Mos.* 6:8-9, which is very likely pre-70, because only part of the Temple is burned, and the final tribulation follows almost immediately (7:1). The envisioned invasion may be 6 CE, but probably stems from when more of Herod's sons still held some power (6:7).

See other examples in Keener, *Matthew,* 561-62. Later rabbinic tradition, while praising the Temple, acknowledged its inadequacy to withhold judgment if Jerusalem was engaging in sin (e.g., *p. Taan.* 4:5, §13, which may compare the amount of bird offerings to mikvaoth, but attributes Jerusalem's destruction to fornication).

89. See Hill, *Prophecy,* 62-63; Aune, *Prophecy,* 174-75; Sanders, *Jesus and Judaism,* 365 n. 5; further documentation in Keener, *Matthew,* 561-62. The tradition about a rabbi in Jesus' day fasting to prevent the Temple's destruction (Brown, *John,* 1:122) is probably too late and apocryphal to provide independent evidence.

90. Sanders, *Jesus and Judaism,* 232-33; cf. Brown, *Death,* 458. For the eschatological Temple, cf. e.g., Tob 13:10; 14:5; *1 En.* 90:28-29; 91:13, Eth.; *Sib. Or.* 3.657-60, 702, 772-74; 11QTemple cols. 30-45 (which depicts a temple much larger than the current Herodian one — Broshi, "Dimensions"); most extensively, Sanders, *Jesus and Judaism,* 77-90, who rightly emphasizes (pp. 86-87) that precise expectations varied. Many expected God to build the sanctuary, however (e.g., *Jub.* 1:17; *2 Bar.* 4:3; 32:4), to the extent that the language is intended literally (cf. *Test. Mos.* 2:4, which applies this image to the *first* sanctuary; fourteenth benediction in Oesterley, *Liturgy,* 65).

91. With e.g., Stanton, *Gospel Truth,* 180-83.

92. Pace Vermes, *Religion,* 185 n. 1. Witherington, *Christology,* 109, suggests an expectation that the messiah would claim special authority regarding the Temple, but his texts (Jos. *War* 6.285-86; *Ant.* 18.85-87) may merely link eschatological prophecy with the restoration of a temple.

93. Borg, *Conflict,* 171-73; Witherington, *Christology,* 109-10.

94. Sanders, *Judaism,* 87.

95. Philo *Spec. Laws* 1.166-67 claims that priests inspected all the animals, but his apologetic testimony may not be firsthand.

96. Sanders, *Judaism,* 88.

97. Despite extra Johannine symbolism in many narratives, there is little reason to find it here (for the unlikelihood of potential symbolism, see e.g., discussion in Keener, *John,* 521 n. 268).

98. Sanders, *Judaism,* 87-88.

99. E.g., Lev 1:3-9; 4:2-21; 8:2; 22:21; also on special occasions, as in Lev 9:4, 18; 22:23; Num 7:3-88. See also Chilton, *Approaches,* 164.

100. I treat Sanders' objections to John's narrative on this point more fully in Keener, *John,* 521.

101. Charlesworth, *Jesus Within Judaism,* 117.

102. E.g., Borg, *Vision,* 174-76; Catchpole, "Entry," 334; Bammel, "Poor," 124-26; Sanders, *Jesus and Judaism,* 70.

103. E.g., the Egyptian "Potter's Oracle" (in Aune, *Prophecy,* 76-77, 100); Apul. *Metam.* 2.28. Cynics also engaged in deliberately provocative behavior to jolt observers from their ingrained traditions (Meeks, *Moral World,* 54-55).

104. Symbolic actions appear most often in the biblical prophets (Aune, *Prophecy,* 100).

105. Cf. Neusner, "Cambiavalute."

106. E.g., Avigad, "Flourishing"; Sanders, *Judaism,* 124.

107. Holding down the prices of sacrifices may have allowed more to be bought and invited more pilgrims, hence was also good for the local economy (Sanders, *Judaism,* 90).

108. Abrahams, *Studies,* 1:86, citing *m. Shek.* 1:3; cf. Haenchen, *John,* 1:183; Barrett, *John,* 197. In fact the text he cites refers particularly to activities surrounding the half-shekel tax due some time before Passover (Wilkinson, *Jerusalem,* 118); yet one should not be surprised if similar accommodations surrounded the major pilgrimage festivals.

109. Abrahams, *Studies,* 1:87. He cites the merchandising around the Church of the Holy Sepulchre at Easter and notes that such does not characterize Christianity as a whole (*Studies,* 1:88).

110. Unless we count the Gospels as supporting the exploitation view, but counting them as such presupposes rather than demonstrates the explanation in question.

111. Witherington, *Christology,* 110 and Chilton, *Approaches,* 162, following Eppstein.

112. Chilton, *Approaches*, 165-66, appealing to "house of trade" (Jn 2:16).

113. Cf. O'Day, "John," 543.

114. Goodman, *State*, 57-59. They could make profit by changing buying and selling rates (*m. Shek.* 4:2).

115. Goodman, *State*, 57. For their necessity in view of the broader Mediterranean variety of coinage, see Finley, *Economy*, 167.

116. Sanders, *Jesus and Judaism*, 63-65.

117. Sanders, *Judaism*, 88.

118. Second-century sages warned against those who dealt with sacred merchandise such as Torah scrolls for profit rather than for God's honor (*tos. Bikkurim* 2:15). According to tradition some patrician sages profited from the sale of ritually pure merchandise in the Temple (Engle, "Amphorisk," 120).

119. Jos. *Apion* 1.103. This practice was expected to continue in the eschatological temple (Zech 14:21; 4Q174, 3.2-4). Similarly, because of their periodic impurities women were always excluded from the court of Israel, though allowed past the outer court when they were not impure (Jos. *Apion* 2.104).

120. Borg, *Conflict*, 175.

121. E.g., MacGregor, *Pacifism*, 19; Glasson, *Advent*, 149-50; in Mark, Matera, *Kingship*, 147. Sanders, *Jesus and Judaism*, 67-68 doubts that concern for Gentiles was central enough in Jesus' ministry for this to be persuasive.

122. For evidence, see e.g., Keener, *Matthew*, 500-1. Jesus' act recalled Jeremiah's activity in the Temple (Winkle, "Model"; cf. Aune, *Prophecy*, 136).

123. E.g., 1QpHab 9.6-7; *Test. Levi* 15:1; *Test. Mos.* 5:4; 6:8-9; see Keener, *Matthew*, 561, 613. Apocalyptic texts frequently critique the priesthood (see Freyne, *Galilee*, 187-89).

124. Witherington, *Christology*, 115, comparing Neh 13:4-9, 12-13. See also Evans, "Action," opposing Sanders' view, below. Borg, *Conflict*, 163-99, emphasizes Jesus' opposition to his contemporaries' understanding of holiness.

125. Stauffer, *Jesus*, 67.

126. Sanders, *Jesus and Judaism*, 65, cites Mal 3:3; *Ps. Sol.* 8; CD 5.6-8. He doubts that the temple system as a whole was corrupt (*Judaism*, 90-91); but the complaints (against the top leaders) are multiply attested in various streams of early Jewish tradition (cf. Jos. *Ant.* 20.181, 206; 1QpHab. 9.4-5; *Test. Levi* 14:1; 2 *Bar.* 10:18; *tos. Minhot* 13.21 in Avigad, *Jerusalem*, 130; cf. Stauffer, *Jesus*, 67).

127. Sanders, *Jesus and Judaism*, 68. Qumranites applied requirements for ritual purity of the sanctuary even to Eden (4Q265 fr. 7, 2.11-17).

128. E.g., Sanders, *Jesus and Judaism*, 66, 70-76; Harvey, *History*, 131-32; Aune, *Prophecy*, 136.

129. Sanders, *Jesus and Judaism*, 233. On the new temple, see Sanders, *Jesus and Judaism*, 77-90.

130. A coin from 132 CE, during the Bar Kochba revolt, indicates the hope for a restored Temple after 70 (Carmon, *Inscriptions*, 81, 178, §§178-79), as do many texts (e.g., 2 *Bar.* 4:3; 32:4; *tos. R.H.* 2:9; *Shab.* 1:13; *p. Ber.* 1:5, §5; *Gen. Rab.* 65:23; *Num. Rab.* 14:8; 15:10; *Lam. Rab.* proem 33); cf. also the plea for Jerusalem's rebuilding in the fourteenth benediction of the Amida (Oesterley, *Liturgy*, 65) and surrogate temple features in synagogues (e.g., Friedman, "Features"). Worship may have continued on the site of the temple until 135 (Clark, "Worship").

131. E.g., *1 En.* 90:28-29; Tob 13:10; 14:5; *Sib. Or.* 3.657-60, 702, 772-74. The Aramaic may diverge from the Ethiopic of *1 En.* 91:13, but the reconstruction of the Aramaic is problematic, so *1 En.* 91:13 probably also refers to the future temple.

132. 11QTemple cols. 30-45; 4Q174, 3.2; 4Q509, 4.2, 12; 4Q511, frg. 35, line 3; notes in Maier, *Scroll*, 98-116; Yadin, "Temple Scroll," 41; Lincoln, *Paradise*, 149; Broshi, "Dimensions."

133. Cf. 2 Macc. 2:4-7; 2 *Bar.* 6:7-9; 4 *Bar.* 3:10-11, 19; 4:4; *Lives Pr.* 2:15, Schermann p. 83 (25, Jeremiah); Rev 11:19; *m. Shek.* 6:1-2; *Yoma* 5:2; *tos. Kip.* 2:15; contrast Jer 3:16.

134. Cf. 2 Macc 2:8; 2 *Bar.* 29:8; 4 *Bar.* 3:11; *Mek. Vay.* 3.42ff; 5.63-65; perhaps 4Q511 frg. 10, line 9; commentaries on Rev 2:17.

135. The Samaritan hope seems to have drawn this conclusion; see Kalimi and Purvis, "Hiding"; cf. Collins, "Vessels"; MacDonald, *Samaritans*, 365; Bowman, *Documents*, 89.

136. Thus in the Scrolls (Flusser, *Judaism*, 43; probably, e.g., also in 4Q176 frg. 1, 2, col. 1, lines 2-3). Bryan, "Hallel," rightly argues that the renewal of the Temple suggests its purification rather than its rejection.

137. In Roman literature, cf. perhaps Tac. *Ann.* 4.38.2 (Sinclair, "Temples").

138. E.g., Philo *Rewards* 123, where the wise man's mind is God's *oikos*.

139. E.g., 1QS 8.5, 8-9; 9.6; CD 3.19A; 2.10, 13B; 4Q511 frg. 35, lines 2-3; more fully, Gärtner, *Temple*, 20-46; Flusser, *Judaism*, 37-39; Bruce, "Gospels," 76; Wilcox, "Dualism," 93-94; McNamara, *Judaism*, 142; already applied by NT commentators, e.g., in Kelly, *Peter*, 90; Goppelt, *Theology*, 2:11; and by Sanders, e.g., in *Judaism*, 376-77; but cf. suggested qualifications in Caquot, "Secte." The claims for 4QFlor (e.g., Gärtner, *Temple*, 30-42) have proved less persuasive (McNicol, "Temple"; Schwartz, "Temples"). The eschatological Temple in 11QTemple follows the design of Israel's camp in the wilderness (inlay article in Yadin, "Temple Scroll," 42).

140. See Keener, *Matthew*, 492; *m. Pes.* 5:7; 9:3; 10:5-7; *tos. Pisha* 8:22; *Suk.* 3:2. The *Midrash Hallel*, by contrast, is too late a composition (see Costa, *"Midrash Hallel"*) for use here.

141. As often in diverse early Christian traditions, Mk 12:10; Acts 4:11; Eph 2:20; 1 Pet 2:6-7; cf. 1 Cor 3:10-11; Rev 21:14.

142. Cf. also Herm. 1.3.2, 5-6; 3.9, with the tower/temple in *1 En.* 89:49-50; Keener, "Human Stones," 34-35. Aune, *Prophecy*, 175, argues that Jesus probably intended the eschatological remnant community, as in the Qumran Scrolls.

143. See Sanders, *Jesus and Judaism*, 69, 270, citing Jos. *Ant.* 18.262; Philo *Embassy* 159, 192, 194, 212-15; *Let. Aris.* 92-99. Cf. Case, *Origins*, 56.

144. Cf. Sanders, *Jesus and Judaism*, 302-303, citing Jer 26:8; Jos. *War* 6.300-9.

145. Segal, "Revolutionary," 211.

146. Segal, "Revolutionary," 211-12.

147. Segal, "Revolutionary," 212. Some doubt that the political element was prominent in Jesus' teaching (Broer, "Death," 163; cf. Jensen, "Antipas," doubting Jesus' hostility toward Antipas); others underline his "political" activity (Horsley, "Death," 405-8; idem, "Abandoning"; Segundo, *Historical Jesus*, 71-85; Herzog, *Jesus*). Part of the issue may be how one defines "political"; Segal's apocalyptic picture here seems to strike a fair balance. Cf. Segundo, *Historical Jesus*, 85: Jesus was not a "professional politician," but human activity cannot be separated from the political in a more general sense.

148. Jos. *Ant.* 14.175; 15.2.

149. Later rabbinic tradition also suggests his execution near Passover (*b. Sanh.* 43a), but this tradition is probably derivative.

150. Among the most remote and idiosyncratic suggestions is that of Morton Smith, who connects magical traditions in which recipients feeding on the substance of a magician are united with him (Smith, *Magician*, 122-23).

151. E.g., Bousset, *Kyrios Christos*, 131.

152. Bultmann, *Mythology*, 153; Mack, *Lost Gospel*, 220.

153. Cf. Moffatt, *1 Corinthians*, 170. More relevant would be comparison with teachers like Epicurus who instituted monthly memorial meals in their honor (Diog. Laert. 10.18 in Boring et al., *Commentary*, 149-50), *minus* the pagan associations with sacrifices for the dead. More distantly, cf. rabbinic phrases used in naming the deceased: "May so-and-so be remembered [before God] for good" (Lachs, *Commentary*, 401 cites *b. B.B.* 21a; *Shab.* 13b; cf. *m. Yoma* 3:9), perhaps more relevant to Mk 14:9.

154. For this cult of the dead, cf. e.g., *CIL* 6.911; *ILS* 4966 in Sherk, *Empire*, 234; Plut. *R.Q.* 86, *Mor.* 285A.

155. E.g., Bruce, *Corinthians*, 111-12; Gregg, "Antecedents"; Davies, *Paul*, 252; Martin, *Worship*, 147.

156. See Hofius, "Supper," 103-11; cf. Ex 13:3; Deut 16:3, 12. The language of Passover celebration assumed the participation of current generations in the exodus event (e.g., *m. Pes.* 10:4-5; *tos. Pisha* 8:18; *b. Ber.* 14b). For this meal as a reenactment in the way that Passover was, see e.g., Snyder, *Corinthians*, 158.

157. Angus, *Mystery-Religions*, 127; Wilken, "Collegia," 280-81; Theissen, *Social Setting*, 131-32; Willis, *Meat*, 14.

158. Willis, *Meat*, 47-61. Some associations, however, gathered for specifically religious purposes (e.g., Cic. *De Senect.* 13.45; Horsley, *Documents* 1:5-9; Cole, *Theoi Megaloi*, 36-37), and cultic meals were also standard in pagan festivals (e.g., Burkert, *Religion*, 107).

159. Bokser, "Description," 6-7; cf. Pines, "Darkness."

160. Cf. Justin *1 Apol.* 66; Tert. *Apol.* 39.15; Pliny *Ep.* 10.96. Minor assimilation begins as early as the Pauline churches (Guthrie, *Orpheus*, 268; cf. Caird, *Age*, 96). Paul's *kuriakos*, "of the Lord," may allude to typical Roman usage for "imperial" (Deissmann, *Light*, 357). But early attestation of parallels often come from early Christian writers who interpreted the Mysteries through the grid of their own experience (cf. Campbell, *Iconography*, 323), as an "imitation démoniaque du Christianisme" (Benoit, "Mysteres," 79-81), and the rites remained quite distinct (Metzger, "Considerations," 15).

161. A small following of Dionysus (Henrichs, "Identities," 160) and Mithraism (which gained prominence in the Empire after Paul; Nock, *Gentile Christianity*, 133; Metzger, "Considerations," 13-15) may have been the exceptions which ultimately affected other Mysteries and the later Christian sacramental view.

162. Nock, *Gentile Christianity*, 74; Willis, *Meat*, 18-46, 62; Kane, "Cult Meal," 349-51; pace Willoughby, *Initiation*, 85, 136-37, 161; Goodenough, *Church*, 22; Godwin, *Religions*, 28.

163. Fritsch, *Community*, 123-24; Cross, *Library*, 235.

164. Cf. Culpepper, *School*, 168; Donceel-Vouté, "Coenaculum."

165. Some scholars have proposed that these meals followed rules for priestly purity (Gnilka, "Gemeinschaftsmal"; Gärtner, *Temple*, 10), were sacrificial sacred meals (Delcor, "Repas"; cf. 1Qap Gen^ar 21.20-22), were annual and sacramental (Groh, "Meal") or foreshadowed eschatological meals (Harrison, "Rites," 32-33; Schiffman, "Meals"; idem, *Law*, 191-210; Simon, *Sects*, 77-78; Harrington, *God's People*, 41-42).

166. Sutcliffe, "Meals"; Schiffman, *Law*, 191-97. The meal in 1QS 6 is "pure" because consecrated by the community and the priestly blessing, but is not cultic food; the text merely indicates that a newcomer cannot partake until he has surrendered his own wealth and labor to the community, preventing free handouts.

167. 1QSa's Messianic banquet could simply evoke the common practice of the community rather than the latter evoking the former.

168. E.g., the claim that only men participated at each is based on inference about Qumran practice in general, not just meals, and an inference about the Last Supper that certainly did not obtain in house churches. Jeremias contends that Essene meals are more different from than similar to the Lord's Supper (*Eucharistic Words*, 31-36).

169. Van der Ploeg, "Meals"; Driver, *Scrolls*, 506-16; Lach, "Uczta."

170. 1QS 6.4-5, 20-21.

171. One might also compare the sacred communal meals of the Therapeutae (Philo *Cont.* 82), although these too are in the Diaspora.

172. Oesterley, *Liturgy*, 167.

173. See Neusner, *Beginning*, 27. Among schools of sages in Palestine, study companions often ate together as well (*ARN* 18, §40B; this may have been partly to save time, *ARN* 14, §34B).

174. Indeed, Jeremias contends that *haburoth* meals are undocumented (Jeremias, *Eucharistic Words*, 29-31).

175. Oesterley, *Liturgy*, 79 (citing *tos. Ber.* 5:1). Jeremias, *Eucharistic Words*, 28, doubts this, but one may compare echoes of the Kiddush blessing in *Did.* 9.2-3, which far more likely betray Jewish li-

turgical influence than influence later rabbinic tradition. Later sources indicate that one could also share Sabbath meals in common with other families (e.g., *p. B.B.* 1:5, §2).

176. *Ant.* 14.215-16, cf. 14.260-61; Sanders, *Jesus to Mishnah*, 78; idem, *Figure*, 202; Rabello, "Condition," 707.

177. Jeremias, *Eucharistic Words*, 50-51 contends that Jewish people drank wine only on special occasions, but even if one merely factors in the regular Sabbath Kiddush meals (e.g., *tos. Ber.* 3:8; Tannaitic tradition in *b. B.K.* 69b; *Pes.* 102a, bar.; later, *b. Shab.* 23b; *Taan.* 24a; Safrai, "Home," 747; cf. *Jub.* 2:21), which he concedes, they drank it quite regularly (cf. blessings over wine in meals in 1QS 6.4-5; *b. Ber.* 33a; 51a). He is, however, probably correct to emphasize that of the many kinds of wines available (on which cf. e.g., *b. A.Z.* 30a; Paul, "Classifications"), *red* wine was used on Passover, augmenting Jesus' symbolism (*Eucharistic Words*, 53, 290; *tos. Pes.* 10:1).

178. Many individual elements of the Passover traditions are undoubtedly early, although some scholars have overstated the case (Segal, *Passover*; Finkelstein, "Documents"; Wright, "Midrash," 417; Safrai, "Religion," 809; for some older source critical suggestions on the Pesach Haggadah, see Finkelstein, *Making*, 13-120). As a whole, however, it is later; most doubt that it belongs to the first century (Stemberger, "Pesachhaggada"; Hauptman, "Haggadah"; Manns, "Pâque" [suggesting anti-Christian polemic in it]; for the current consensus, see Kulp, "Origins"); Leonhard, "Älteste Haggada," doubts that it predates the tenth century. Yet a prayer recorded in Hippolytus *Apostolic Tradition* apparently adapts tradition preserved in the Passover Haggada (Kinsella, "Transformation").

179. Cf. e.g., Jeremias, *Eucharistic Words*, passim; Stein, *Messiah*, 203-5; Carmichael, "Haggadah," 343-44. The generally stricter Shammaite school (regarding Passover, e.g., *b. Shab.* 18b, bar.) prevailed in his day, but our records were preserved by more lenient, rather than stricter, practitioners. While Smith, *Symposium*, provides excellent insight on hellenistic banquet settings, he too quickly dismisses Passover as the original setting of the Last Supper tradition (4, 295 n. 5, citing a study from 1967 and another from 1976). While acknowledging strong arguments for the Passover connection (Theissen and Merz, *Historical Jesus*, 423-26), Theissen and Merz doubt the connection because the Lord's Supper was not annual and they prefer Johannine chronology (426-27). But cultic adaptations can evoke earlier rituals without imitating every point, and I have argued elsewhere that John (who also symbolically adapts the passion tradition elsewhere) diverges from historical chronology precisely here.

180. Cf. Ex 12:8, 12; *tos. Pes.* 5:2; 10:9. Banquets were, however, commonly at night whether on Passover or not.

181. Some construe Paul's claim as involving God "handing" Jesus over to death; this interpretation is certainly plausible (Rom 4:25; 8:32; cf. LXX Is 53:6, 12; cf. the Passover lamb in 1 Cor 5:7). Given the abundance of other parallels to the passion tradition, however, an allusion to Judas' betrayal here remains likelier than not.

182. Luke specifies that the covenant is the "new covenant" (Lk 22:20), i.e., of Jer 31:31-34.

183. E.g., Is 25:6; 2 *Bar.* 29:4; perhaps 1QSa 2.11-12, 19-21.

184. E.g., *tos. Ber.* 1:10-11.

185. Sanders, *Figure*, 263; cf. Bornkamm, *Experience*, 135; Collins, *Corinthians*, 430.

186. Jos. *Ant.* 13.297, 408; *m. Ab.* 1:1. This language was also intelligible in a broader milieu (Socratics 20; Lucian *Alexander the False Prophet* 61; Iambl. *Pyth. Life* 28.148-49; 32.226; 36.265-66; Cornutus in Van der Horst, "Cornutus," 168-69; Klauck, "Presence," 60-62; cf. Sen. *Ep. Lucil.* 40.3; Conzelmann, *1 Corinthians*, 195-96). Though the hellenistic world did not usually join the terms together (Metzger, "Considerations," 17-18 n. 84), it sometimes did (Philostratus *Vit. soph.* 2.29.621, where they allow for rhetorical improvement). Against the likelihood that Paul's source was his own vision (Maccoby, "Eucharist") are the correspondences with genuine paschal custom; the unlikelihood that Mark (who includes other correct paschal details, such as a hymn after the meal, Mk 14:26) derives the tradition from Paul's vision (for the same reasons we argued against the eschatological sayings deriving from 1 Thess 4–5, in ch. 17); and the implausibility of an analogous argument regarding

Jesus' divorce saying in 1 Cor 7:10-12. Moreover, unlike other cult aetiologies Paul appeals to a tradition of a specific historical event referring to a particular night (Klauck, "Presence," 64).

187. E.g., *m. Ed.* 8:7; *ARN* 25A; *b. Kid.* 30a; *Meg.* 19b; *Naz.* 56b; *Pes.* 110b; *Shab.* 108a, bar.; *Eccl. Rab.* 1:10, §1; cf. Hillel as a disciple of Ezra in *Sanh.* 11a, bar.; *Sot.* 48b; *Song Rab.* 8:9, §3.

188. Gerhardsson, *Memory,* 321; De Beus, "Traditie"; Davies, *Paul,* 248; cf. Cullmann, *State,* 73.

189. See e.g., Sanders, *Jesus and Judaism,* 15.

190. Jeremias, *Eucharistic Words,* 187; Tan, *Zion Traditions,* 202. Paul may even draw the Last Supper tradition from a larger passion story already available to him (see Borgen, "Nattverd-tradisjonen"), although scholars must evaluate the evidence for this possibility more thoroughly. The appearance of *agrapha* (Just. *Dial.* 35; Syr. Didaskalia 6.5.2 in Jeremias, *Unknown Sayings,* 76) in Paul's context (1 Cor 11:19) may support this thesis.

191. Although the LXX expresses the phrase differently, "poured out" may translate the Hebrew in Is 53:12. "For many," a Semitism which very likely dates to the first decade of Jesus tradition (see Jeremias, *Message,* 45), may represent *rabbim* in this section of Isaiah (Jeremias, *Eucharistic Words,* 227), which Jeremias applies not only to Israel but to the nations (*Eucharistic Words,* 230-31; cf. Is 52:14-15). "Blood of the covenant" seems to suit first-century Palestinian Aramaic (Emerton, "Mark XIV.24").

192. Sanders, *Figure,* 263; cf. Theissen and Merz, *Historical Jesus,* 432-34.

193. Not merely nuclear families, but associations of people could band together for one passover offering (*tos. Pisha* 9:1).

194. Cf. Safrai, "Religion," 802.

195. Jeremias, *Eucharistic Words,* 56.

196. Some scholars even suggest that early Christians recited the Passion Narrative in this context as a new Passover haggadah, recalling Paul's phrase: "proclaim the Lord's death until he comes" (Bruce, *Corinthians,* 113; idem, *Message,* 16). Because the standard haggadah comes from a later period, this proposal may exaggerate, but it draws attention to a legitimate connection with paschal interpretation.

197. Curiously, Bultmann, *Theology,* 46-47, concedes that the expiatory understanding of Jesus' death may be early, and (47) that it would not have been unnatural in Judaism. Nevertheless, he disallows this understanding in Jesus' own message (Mk 10:45; 14:24), raising the question what evidence he *would* accept as compelling against his theory.

198. If we may presume that interpretation from his generation being most guilty in Matt 23:34-35//Lk 11:49-50 (counting against the generation also Jesus' martyred followers sent by him).

199. E.g., Cullmann, *State,* 64-65; Gundry, *Matthew,* 528; pace Hooker, *Servant,* 80-82. Collins, "Messiah before Jesus," 34, argues that the early Christian application of vicarious atonement elements of Isaiah's servant to Jesus goes beyond traditional messianic expectations.

200. Some scholars think "This cup is the covenant" rather than "This is my blood" is the earlier form of wording (e.g., Dibelius, *Tradition,* 207) whereas others defend the reverse position (e.g., Davies, *Paul,* 244-50, esp. 246). In any case, "blood" in some form is multiply attested (Mk 14:24; Lk 22:20; 1 Cor 10:16; 11:25, 27). Crossan, *Historical Jesus,* 366 compares "poured out" with the language of libation; a common Mediterranean practice, it appears in the OT (for a metaphorical usage with blood, cf. 2 Sam 23:16-17). For the term's potential sacrificial connotations (e.g., Lev 1–7, 16) relevant to Passover, see e.g., Gundry, *Matthew,* 528; Carson, "Matthew," 537; Hagner, *Matthew,* 2:773. On "the many" and "poured out" together, cf. Is 53:11-12. Certainly Matthew understood it as sacrificial: his "for the remission of sins" (probably borrowed from John's ministry in Mk 1:4) appears in Targum Neofiti with reference to sacrifices (McNamara, *Targum,* 129).

201. Romans sometimes fixed criminals to crosses with rope (Xen. *Eph.* 4.2; Jeremias, *Eucharistic Words,* 220-22).

202. McNamara, *Targum,* 127-28 is surely right that the words here derive from Ex 24:8 and are possible in Palestinian Aramaic; *Tg. Ps.-Jon.* on Ex 24:8 (later) interprets the act with regard to atone-

ment for Israel. *M. Pes.* 10:6 uses the Passover wine as a metaphor for the blood of the covenant in Ex 24:8 (e.g., Hill, *Matthew*, 339; Carson, "Matthew," 537). And while allusions to Jer 31:31-34 and Is 53:11-12 are probable in this narrative, the Ex 24:8 allusion is the most explicit (Allison, *Moses*, 257-58).

203. Cf. Heb 8:8; farther removed, Just. *Dial.* 11.

204. Among the Qumran sect (e.g., CD 6.4-5, 19; 8.21; 20.12; Flusser, *Judaism*, 44-50; Black, *Scrolls*, 91; cf. Gemés, "Aliança") and others (*Sipra Behuq.* pq.2.262.1.13; cf. Lichtenberger and Schreiner, "Neue Bund"). Holmén, *Covenant Thinking*, 335-37, finds more direct evidence for it in Jesus' teaching.

205. For the coherence of Jesus' martyr ideology and actions, see Meyer, "Expiation Motif," 33.

206. Martin, *Worship*, 153 argues this from the Greek and Aramaic, though McNamara, *Targum*, 127-28 is surely right that the words here derive from Ex 24:8 and are possible in Palestinian Aramaic (cf. Gundry, *Matthew*, 528; pace Deissmann, *Light*, 337, who reads the term for covenant here primarily in light of Greco-Roman usage for wills). Some suggest that Jesus being *in* his body at the time he uttered the words further militates against interpreting the bread as literally equivalent to his body (Moffatt, *1 Corinthians*, 168).

207. Related to Deut 16:3 (cf. Stauffer, *Jesus*, 117).

208. Nevertheless, one can see how even the metaphor (which could sound like cannibalism) would have revolted Jewish hearers (Jn 6:52; *1 En.* 98:11; Vermes, *Religion*, 16), and even most Greeks and Romans (e.g., Herod. *Hist.* 1.123, 129; Mart. *Epig.* 10.4.1; 11.31.2), though apparently some cultures demurred (Sext. Emp. *Outlines of Pyrrh.* 3.207; Herod. *Hist.* 1.73, 119; 3.99). One can also envision how outsiders could have eventually construed the language as cannibalism (later, cf. Athenag. *Plea* 3; Theoph. 3.4, 15; Tert. *Apol.* 4.11; 7.1; Visotzky, "Overturning").

209. At this point, the date of various parts of the Passover liturgy is irrelevant, since this pattern was already laid down in Scripture (see Ex 12:14; 13:3; Deut 16:2-3). Paul might even think of somehow acting out elements of the gospel narrative (at least in eating and drinking), somewhat analogous to Passover practice. He might possibly even refer to portraying the crucifixion vividly in Gal 3:1; his language there could, however, suggest simply an appeal to rhetorical vividness (Anderson, *Rhetorical Theory*, 162; Polyb. 2.56.8; Jos. *Ant.* 20.123) as well as to Paul's crucified life (Gal 2:20; 2 Cor 4:10-12).

210. E.g., *m. Pes.* 10:4-5; *tos. Pisha* 8:18; *b. Ber.* 14b. For various conceptions of the memorial value of Jewish rituals among various ancient Jewish groups, see Boccaccini, *Judaism*, 231-39 (Josephus on 242-45).

211. See e.g., Cohn-Sherbok, "Note"; though Sigal, "Note," argues for the second. The tradition of the four cups (e.g., *m. Pes.* 10:1; *tos. Ber.* 4:8; *p. Shab.* 8:1, §3; *b. Pes.* 108a-109a; *Gen. Rab.* 88:5; *Ex. Rab.* 6:4; Safrai, "Home," 748; cf. Salaman, "Haggadah") may precede the superstitious practice of avoiding drinking an even number of cups, though later teachers harmonized these practices (*b. Pes.* 109b). (One *could* drink more than the four required cups — *b. Pes.* 107b-108a; *p. Meg.* 3:5, §1.) The custom probably borrows or is related to the Greek use of cups to signal stages in banquets (Boring et al., *Commentary*, 147 cites Diod. Sic. *Library of History* 4.3.4; *IG* 12 3.330, 670).

212. See Jeremias, *Eucharistic Words*, 110; *Pesiq. Rab.* 9:1.

213. Cf. Num 6:4; 30:2; 11QTemple 53-54; Acts 23:12; *m. Ab.* 3:13; *Gen. Rab.* 92:5; *b. Pes.* 2a, bar. On kinds of vows, cf. McNamara, *Judaism*, 197.

214. Jeremias, *Eucharistic Words*, 182-85; Kümmel, *Promise*, 31; Palmer, "Vow"; cf. Ziesler, "Vow."

215. See e.g., *1 En.* 62:14; *3 En.* 48A:10; *2 Bar.* 29:4; *m. Ab.* 3:16-17; 4:16; Johnston, "Parabolic Interpretations," 593-94; for eschatological abundance of wine, see Joel 3:18; Hos 2:22; Amos 9:13-14; *1 En.* 10:19; *2 Bar.* 29:5; *Sib. Or.* 3.622.

216. Bruce, *Corinthians*, 114. Lane, *Mark*, 508, suggests that Jesus abstained from the fourth cup, having participated in and interpreted the third cup which signified redemption in the Passover liturgy (cf. Lachs, *Commentary*, 408; also Stauffer, *Jesus*, 117, though he places the vow after the first cup — p. 115).

217. That discussion should focus on the significance of Passover would fit what we know of later

Passover tradition and conform to the desires of the sages for edifying talk (Sir 9:15; *m. Ab.* 3:2; *ARN* 26, 29A; 32, §68B).

218. With Daube, *Exodus Pattern,* 45; Ellington, "Translation"; Meier, *Matthew,* 321; Carson, "Matthew," 538; Hagner, *Matthew,* 2:774. Most Mediterranean banquets emphasized music over lectures (Sir 35:3-4; cf. Plut. *Table-Talk* 1.1.5, *Mor.* 614F-615A).

219. Brown, *Death,* 123 thinks Mark's audience would think instead of Christian hymns (Eph 5:19; Col 3:16). Yet even if most of the later Paschal liturgy was not in use or common use in this period, praise was standard in eating the Passover (*Jub.* 49:6; cf. Philo *Spec. Laws* 2.148). The exact sequence of the Hallel in the liturgy was probably not standardized by Jesus' day (cf. the differences among later rabbis in *tos. Pisha* 10:9; *b. Pes.* 118a).

220. Hengel, *Atonement,* 9, 19. For Greeks on atoning martyrdom, cf. Robbins, *Teacher,* 187 (following Williams, *Death,* 137-254).

221. If one looks further afield, sacrificial atonement is certainly early (see e.g., Gurney, *Aspects,* 48; Pfeiffer, *Ras Shamra,* 38; Kitchen, *World,* 86).

222. Cf. Hill, *Matthew,* 289; Mack, *Myth,* 105; Witherington, *Christology,* 252. In early Judaism, see 4 Macc 6:27-30; 9:7, 24; 17:21-22; cf. 1 Macc 2:50; 2 Macc 7:9, 37; 1QS 8.3-4; *Test. Mos.* 9; *Mek. Pisha* 1.105-13; see also the helpful list in McKnight, *Death,* 168-69.

223. On martyrdom as a sacrifice, cf. further also Thoma, "Martyrer"; on both expiatory martyrdom and glorification here, see Grappe, "Christologie."

224. Cf. *Test. Moses* ch. 9; Daube, *NT and Judaism,* 11. The prayer in 2 Macc 7 offers the closest proximate background for Jesus' saying at the last supper (with Schenker, "Martyrium"). Vicarious atonement also appears in Tannaim of the early second century — Kim, "Atonement" (summarized on 143-45). In general, though, the association of Jesus' death with sacrifice is closer to the pre-70 priestly understanding of atonement than to that of later rabbis (cf. Neusner, "Repentance"). (Beyond martyrdom specifically, the Qumran community believed that God had chosen them to atone for errant Israel, probably grounding this understanding of atonement in Isaiah — so Bruce, *Time,* 30, citing 1QS 8:6-7, 10; 1QSa 1:3.)

225. See e.g., Bruce, *Time,* 30. Cf. perhaps later the rabbis' "Messiah son of Joseph" (Mitchell, "Atonement").

226. If Is 53 is in view, the ransom may satisfy God's own anger, as in Is 53:10-12. But some argue that the "ransom" incorporates Is 43:3-4, where the price is a redemption price for liberation from captivity (Witherington, *Christology,* 254, 256, suggesting ransom from Satan's grasp).

227. Pace Hooker, *Servant,* 74-79; idem, *Message,* 93; Anderson, *Mark,* 257. For the sake of space we abbreviate the argument here, but many scholars see Isaiah's servant in the saying (e.g., Taylor, *Atonement,* 14; Cullmann, *Christology,* 64-65; Argyle, *Matthew,* 154; Higgins, *Son of Man,* 43; Jeremias, *Theology,* 292-93; Albright and Mann, *Matthew,* 243; Ridderbos, *Paul and Jesus,* 31; Moulder, "Background," 127; Gundry, *Matthew,* 404; Hagner, *Matthew,* 2:582; Davies and Allison, *Matthew,* 3:95-97; Stuhlmacher, "Readiness," 396-97, 409; with less conviction, Kümmel, *Promise,* 73; Bruce, *Time,* 29-30), though some, like Hill, *Matthew,* 289 and Witherington, *Christology,* 254, find general language from the Isaian servant without Is 53:11-12. The Dead Sea Scrolls later apply "the many" of Isaiah and Daniel to themselves, "the elect" in a sectarian way (1QS 6.6-21; Albright and Mann, *Matthew,* 244; Gundry, *Matthew,* 404), but the rabbis retain Isaiah's use for the covenant community (Albright and Mann, *Matthew,* 245; cf. Lane, *Mark,* 384). For what it is worth, early Christians certainly came to apply Is 53 to Jesus (Lk 22:37; Acts 8:32-35; Jn 12:38; Justin *1 Apol.* 50). Among others, McKnight, *Death,* 207-39, doubts Jesus' (albeit not his followers') connection of his death to the servant, preferring the Son of man model (which is admittedly more dominant overall in Jesus' language). But these models are not mutually exclusive, and the use of one prophetic model may make the other all the more plausible, given evident echoes in our Gospels; the servant comes only after the messianic secret.

228. Flusser, *Judaism,* 619; for a survey of various scholarly views, see McKnight, *Death,* 47-75.

Mack, *Myth*, 302, thinks that Mark tones down Paul's emphasis on Christ cult and sacrifice "toward a more primitive notion of martyrdom."

Notes to Chapter 21

1. Sanders, *Jesus and Judaism*, 294.

2. Sanders, *Figure*, 269.

3. Jos. *Ant.* 18.64; see Theissen and Merz, *Historical Jesus*, 94; Evans, "Non-Christian Sources," 466.

4. Most of this material also appears in Keener, *Matthew*, 607-11; idem, *John*, 1067-76.

5. I have argued elsewhere that John's passion account deliberately plays on the more traditional passion story, for theological reasons; see Keener, *John*, 875, 901, 918-19, 1048, 1100-3, 1133-34 (cf. 820, 1053); idem, "Genre," 323.

6. Cf. Sisti, "Figura"; *Acts of the Alexandrian Martyrs* in *CPJ* 2:55-107, §§154-59.

7. E.g., Dibelius, *Tradition*, 201; Donahue, "Temple," 65-66; Weeden, *Mark*, 66; Nickelsburg, "Genre"; Aune, *Environment*, 52-53; Robbins, *Teacher*, 173, 188; Doran, "Narratives." The tradition places Jesus especially within the rejected prophet tradition (cf. Robbins, *Teacher*, 186).

8. Epameinondas 2 in Plut. *S.K., Mor.* 192C; cf. accounts of Socrates' brave end (Xen. *Apol.* 1).

9. Cf. e.g., the mother in Maccabean accounts with the Spartan mother Argileonis in Plut. *S.S.W., Mor.* 240C. Cf. Robbins, *Teacher*, 185, following Nickelsburg, "Genre," 156 on the tradition of a righteous sufferer vindicated by God.

10. Boring, et al., *Commentary*, 156 lists contrasts with the Maccabean martyr accounts: the Gospels avoid sensationalistic details, interpretive speeches by Jesus, a Stoic lesson contrasting reason with emotions (Plut. *W.V.S.C.U.* 2; 4 Macc. 8:15; though this feature says more about the social context of the Maccabean audience than about any larger genre per se), and "vengeful threats." On the diversity of Jewish martyr stories, see Henten, "Martyrologie."

11. Some features characteristic of martyr stories (in e.g., Boring, et al., *Commentary*, 152) simply reflect the common pattern of ancient law and Jewish resilience, more than a specific borrowing of literary motifs. (This is not to deny that the *recording* of such details augments the hortatory value of the narratives.) To a lesser degree the ancient Mediterranean champion tradition might also provide a context for the concept (e.g., Hom. *Il.* 3.69-70, 86-94, 253-55; 7.66-91, 244-73; Ap. Rhod. 2.20-21; Dion. Hal. *Ant. rom.* 3.12.3-4; Virg. *Aen.* 10.439-509; 11.115-18, 217-21; 12.723-952; Livy 1.24.1-1.25.14; 7.9.8-7.10.14; Aul. Gel. 9.13.10; in the Hebrew Bible, 1 Sam 17; 2 Sam 2:14-16; cf. Gordon, *Civilizations*, 262).

12. Cf. e.g., Jeremias, *Theology*, 292-93; Davies and Allison, *Matthew*, 3:95-97; other references in Keener, *Matthew*, 487.

13. E.g., with Cleanthes in 7.5.176.

14. A legendary figure might even receive a legendary martyrdom (cf. *Life of Aesop*, end, in Drury, *Design*, 29).

15. Jewish accounts stress martyrdom as an example of commitment, but despite the use of Jesus' death as a model, summaries of the earliest gospel (e.g., 1 Cor 15:3-4) suggest their very early kerygmatic function as well.

16. *Gospels in Context*, 123.

17. Burridge, *Gospels*, 146-47, 179-80. While the rest of the Gospels foreshadow this climax, that is also the case in some contemporary biographies (Burridge, *Gospels*, 199).

18. Burridge, *Gospels*, 198, has 26% for Philostratus; Mons Graupius consumes 26% of Tac. *Agricola*, and the Persian campaign 37% of Plut. *Agesilaus* (p. 199).

19. Boring, et al., *Commentary*, 151, contrasting the Markan passion with Philost. *V.A.* 7.14.

20. Mack, *Myth*, 249; for his arguments, see pp. 249-68. For a critique of Crossan's approach to the passion narrative (depending on the late Gospel of Peter), see Evans, "Passion," especially analo-

gies with Justin *1 Apol.* 16.9-13 and Mk 16:9-20 in pp. 163-65. Crossan's idea that the biographic passion and resurrection narratives developed from exegesis and (most astonishingly) lament (Crossan, *Birth*) substitutes speculation for the way we would read any other biographic death report stemming from within living memory of eyewitnesses.

21. Mack cites Jeremias (whom he designates a "conservative" scholar, *Myth,* 254) only three times, and never Blinzler, Hengel or other more conservative continental scholars (much less conservative North American scholars). For one survey of scholarly research regarding Jesus' death, see Horsley, "Death."

22. Perry, *Sources,* published as early as 1920; cf. Lietzmann's skepticism on some points in 1931 ("Prozess").

23. Mack strangely connects imperialism with the early Christian focus "on crucifixion as the guarantee for apocalyptic salvation" (*Lost Gospel,* p. 255). This unusual proposal confuses suffering on behalf of justice (e.g., Martin Luther King, Jr.) with inflicting suffering unjustly (e.g., the Klan). It also confuses how the central gospel message has been exploited or (most often) ignored in history with what it actually teaches; this interpretation actually supports (by assuming the interpretive validity of) the misinterpretation of those who exploited the Gospels rather than clarifying their error. Without supporting evidence, he provides this climactic conclusion as fact, though the assertions in the rest of his book offer little support for (or even discussion of) this conclusion! For a nuanced survey of varied postcolonial approaches in biblical studies, and a very different reading of Mark, see Samuel, *Reading* (for approaches, 14-34).

24. Dibelius, *Tradition,* 178-217, thinks that "the passion story is the only piece of Gospel tradition which in early times gave events in their larger connection."

25. Thus Jewish scholars with no faith commitment to the narratives may also suggest that other Gospels draw on pre-Markan passion material (e.g., Flusser, *Judaism,* 575-87, though he may presuppose Lukan priority here, an approach currently rarely accepted outside Israel).

26. E.g., Kollmann, *Kreuzigung,* sees Jn's passion narrative as independent from the Synoptics, though using a tradition. I believe that it is an independence that betrays knowledge, however; for deliberate playing off the standard Synoptic (or pre-Synoptic) version of the passion, see Keener, *John,* 875, 901, 918-19, 1048, 1100-3, 1133-34 (cf. 820, 1053).

27. Brown, *Death,* 53-55, 77-80.

28. Brown, *Death,* 54.

29. Ehrman, *Prophet,* 82.

30. Cf. Mk 1:12-13 with Matt 4:1-11//Lk 4:1-12; Mk 3:26-27 with Matt 12:27-29//Lk 11:19-22.

31. See e.g., Keck, "Ethos," 448; Voorst, *Jesus Outside NT,* 173-74.

32. Theissen, *Gospels in Context,* 166-99; cf. Pesch, "Jerusalem," who argues that the passion narrative was the oldest tradition in the Jerusalem church. (Hengel seems right, however, that Pesch is too optimistic in his ability to reconstruct sources; "Problems," 209 10.)

33. Theissen, *Gospels in Context,* 176-77.

34. Theissen, *Gospels in Context,* 179. We might add here that the Galilean names may have meant little to most of the Jerusalem church as well, who may have preserved them for the same reasons that Mark did.

35. *B. Nid.* 33a; *Pesiq. Rab Kah.* 11:16; *Gen. Rab.* 5:9; 13:15; 94:4 MSS; *Num. Rab.* 12:4; cf. the association with promiscuity in the late *Lam. Rab.* 2:2, §4. For excavations at Magdala, see Reich, "H'rh"; Aviam, "Magdala"; Shanks, "Hometown"; for its devastation in 67 CE, see Pahlitzsch, "Magdala." For harbor remains of this and other Galilean towns, see Nun, "Ports."

36. Magdala's common Greek name appears to have been Tarichaeae (Avi-Yonah, "Geography," 96; regularly in Josephus, e.g., *Life* 96, 127, 132, 143, 151, 156-57, 159, 162-63, 168, and perhaps 30 more times), known as a Galilean city with a fishing industry, elements of Greek culture, but also fierce Jewish patriotism (see Freyne, *Galilee,* 172-73).

37. Theissen, *Gospels in Context,* 180. When a narrative introduces someone foreign, it often

gives the place of birth (e.g., App. *C. W.* 1.14.116); lists of names from disparate places typically list the places (e.g., Ap. Rhod. 1.40, 49, 57, 77, 95, 105-6, 115, 118, 139-40, 146-47, 151-52, 161, 177, 207).

38. Theissen, *Gospels in Context*, 171, 182-83. Livy occasionally cites a name as if familiar despite lack of previous mention (e.g., 40.55.2), perhaps incompletely following a source. Dodd, *Tradition*, 120, thinks the question of treason relevant in Palestine only before 70 CE; but this argument is questionable: to be sure, the issue fits Tiberius's time very well, but it would remain relevant after 70.

39. Theissen, *Gospels in Context*, 186-88. Some view the fleeing young man of Mk 14:51-52 only in terms of his symbolic significance in the narrative (Crossan, "Tomb," 147-48; Fleddermann, "Flight"; Kelber, *Story*, 77), but Theissen is probably right to find genuine tradition from the early Palestinian church here (*Gospels in Context*, 186; cf. Dibelius, *Tradition*, 182-83; Stauffer, *Jesus*, 121).

40. Some of Theissen's other arguments (*Gospels in Context*, 189-97) are weaker.

41. For Markan structuring, see e.g., Beavis, "Trial."

42. Brown suspects that Mark may have acquired some of his style from frequent recitation of the passion narrative (*Death*, 56, comparing the way some modern evangelists acquire their style from Bible translations); further, Mark may have rephrased the narrative in his own words, especially where his sources were oral. One should see most fully the 1994 essay by Marion Soards (Soards, "Passion Narrative"), who makes a strong case both that Mark uses a source and that we probably cannot separate the tradition from the redaction. Brown, *Death*, 554 also emphatically challenges some earlier redaction-critical studies on the trial narrative in Mk 14:55-64 (cf. perhaps Donahue, "Temple"), complaining that though "Mark used earlier material . . . *our best methods do not give us the ability to isolate confidently that material in its exact wording, assigning pre-Markan verses and half-verses* from the existing, thoroughly Markan account" (emphasis his).

43. Dewey, "Curse," 102-3. Also Jn 13:38.

44. Theissen, *Gospels in Context*, 172-74; cf. Philo *Embassy* 299-304.

45. Smith, "Issues and Problem," 263-65.

46. Jos. *War* 6.300-1; Evans, "What," 108; idem, "Jesus ben Ananias"; see also Vermes, *Jesus and Judaism*, ix; Sanders, *Figure*, 267.

47. Jer 7:34 in *War* 6.301 (cf. Jer 7:11 in Mk 11:17). On the opposition Jeremiah faced for his "unpatriotic" prophecies, cf. e.g., Jer 26:6-24; Jos. *Ant.* 10.89-90. A man inside Tyre likewise reportedly prophesied its judgment and faced the charge of being a traitor (Diod. Sic. 17.41.7-8, which may be legendary or repeat Alexander's propaganda).

48. *War* 6.302.

49. *War* 6.303.

50. *War* 6.305.

51. *War* 6.305. Such refusal to answer may be perceived as heroic, evoking the Jewish martyr tradition (although it was not exclusively Jewish; cf. e.g., Boring et al., *Commentary*, 304; Xenophon *Mem.* 4.8.4; Tacitus *Ann.* 15.60; Zeller, "Philosophen").

52. *War* 6.304.

53. *War* 6.305.

54. Cf. Sanders, *Figure*, 267. A number of followers would be deemed necessary to provide a substantial threat (Xen. *Mem.* 1.2.10).

55. Malina, *Windows*, 18. Thus Josephus praises himself by emphasizing the loyalty of the Galileans to him (Jos. *Life* 84), though as an aristocrat he would have disdained "populist" support had he lacked it. Betrayal by one's own troops, whom one ought to have been able to trust, was tragic (Corn. Nep. 18 [Eumenes], 10.2). Abandonment by one close to a person (such as a relative) would create scandal and generate mass abandonment (Corn. Nep. 14 [Datames], 6.3) and in time of great danger such traitors merited death (Corn. Nep. 14 [Datames], 6.8; 9.5).

56. Cohn, *Trial*, 83 (though citing a rabbinic tradition that "high priests were wont to engage in undercover activity"); Lüdemann, "Betrayal."

57. Pliny *Ep.* 10.96-97; Hdn 7.3.2; Judge, *Pattern*, 71.

58. E.g., Moffatt, *1 Corinthians,* 168; Fee, *Corinthians,* 549. This view seems likely because the association of the betrayal with that night and the last supper fits too closely our extant passion tradition to likely be coincidental. Paul uses the verb differently in Rom 4:25 and 8:32, but then uses it differently from either of these uses in the same verse (1 Cor 11:23).

59. "Handing over to the Romans" was also dramatic enough that it could figure in the tradition (e.g., Mk 10:33-34). It could also mean "handed over by God," as in Rom 4:25; 8:32 (Smith, *Symposium,* 188; Hays, *1 Corinthians,* 198). Some argue that "handing over" in Rom 4:25 reflects Is 53:12 LXX (Hays, *1 Corinthians,* 198), which the Gospels may have used if they had no information to contradict it (Harvey, *History,* 24-25); in context Is 53 reads more naturally as if *God* handed the servant over.

60. E.g., Jos. *Life* 84.

61. Betrayed trust reflected badly only on the betrayer, however, if the betrayed had taken appropriate precautions (Polyb. 8.36.4).

62. Matt 26:21; Mk 14:17-21; Lk 22:21; Jn 6:70-71; 13:11. Some doubt this tradition, however (e.g., Maldamé, "Trahison").

63. Brown, *Death,* 255.

64. On moonlight's adequacy, cf. e.g., Virg. *Aen.* 7.9; Polyb. 7.16.3.

65. Cf. Gundry, *Matthew,* 537.

66. In cases of lesser danger, Romans often settled for executing ringleaders of a revolt rather than a whole populace (e.g., Dion. Hal. *Ant. rom.* 3.40.3; 5.43.2); the Jewish officials would probably be still more inclined toward mercy to fellow-Jews.

67. E.g., Lane, *Mark,* 525; Wilkinson, *Jerusalem,* 126; Anderson, *Mark,* 323; Keener, "Kiss," 629. Cf. kissing of respected teachers or others (even pupils) who brought one great joy (1 Esd 4:47; *tos. Hag.* 2:1; *ARN* 6A; 13, §32B; *b. Hag.* 14b; *p. Hag.* 2:1, §4; *Hor.* 3:5, §3; *R.H.* 2:9, §2; *Sot.* 13a; *Pesiq. Rab Kah.* 1:3; *Eccl. Rab.* 6:2, §1; 9:5, §1; *Pesiq. Rab.* 23/24:2; Ap. Rhod. 1.313; Arrian *Alex.* 4.11.3; Epict. *Disc.* 1.19.24; Char. *Chaer.* 2.7.7).

68. Cf. 2 Sam 20:9; Prov 27:6. Robbins, *Teacher,* 189 cites Dio Chrys. *Or.* 3.86, 114: the king depends on his friends' loyalty and learning them to be his enemies is his greatest pain. Greek and Roman texts often enough regard the treachery of deceitful betrayal as deplorable (e.g., Polyb. 1.7; 3.52; Jos. *War* 2.450-454).

69. The Gospels explain that Jesus foreknew Judas' betrayal when he chose him; it may be questioned, however, whether even this foreknowledge would have done more than cushion the pain. Against our expectations of what Jesus' followers would have invented about him, the gospel tradition portrays Jesus in genuine anguish before facing the cross (Mk 14:32-41, esp. 14:34-36; cf. Lk 12:49-50).

70. E.g., Lysias *Or.* 6.23, §105; 8.5-6, §112; Char. *Chaer.* 5.6.2 *(philos);* Corn. Nep. 14 (Datames), 6.3; 11.5; Sir 22:21-22; *Test. Jud.* 23:3; cf. Derrett, *Audience,* 69. This remained true even if one's life were at stake (Babr. 138.7-8); refusing to betray a friend or spouse was honorable (Athen. *Deipn.* 15.965F, item 25; Sen. *Controv.* 2.5.intro.). Treachery and betrayal warranted death (Valerius Maximus 9.6).

71. Cic. *Pro Amer.* 40.116.

72. E.g., App. *R.H.* 6.8.43; 6.9.52; 6.10.60.

73. Cf. e.g., disgust for traitors against their peoples in Xen. *Hell.* 1.7.22; Cic. *Fin.* 3.9.32; Virg. *Aen.* 6.621; Livy 1.11.6-7; 5.27.6-10 (though cf. Livy 4.61.8-10); Val. Max. 1.1.13; Sen. *Controv.* 7.7.intro.; such behavior invited the hatred of even one's family (Livy 2.5.7-8; Corn. Nep. 4 [Pausanias], 5.3). Loyalty to country might take precedence even over hospitality-friendship (Xen. *Hell.* 4.1.34; Corn. Nep. 13 [Timotheus], 4.4), but disloyalty to friends remained despicable (e.g., *Rhet. Alex.* 36, 1442.13-14).

74. Xen. *Cyrop.* 8.2.2-3.

75. Xen. *Cyrop.* 8.7.14.

76. Eurip. *Cycl.* 125. For hospitality, see e.g., Hom. *Il.* 9.199-220; *Od.* 1.118-20, 123-24; 3.345-58; 4.26-36; 9.176; *Rhet. Her.* 3.3.4; Cic. *Offic.* 2.18.64; *Part. Orat.* 23.80; Epict. *Disc.* 1.28.23; Tob 5:10-15; 7:8-9; 10:6-10; Ps.-Phoc. 24; *m. Ab.* 1:5, 15; 3:12; *tos. Demai* 3:9; see further Koenig, *Hospitality,* 16.

77. E.g., Lysias *Or.* 12.14, §121; 18.10, §150; Plut. *Coriol.* 10.3; Cic. *Fam.* 13.19.1; 13.25.1; 13.36.1; Corn.

Nep. *Gen.* 5 (Cimon), 3.3; *Ex. Rab.* 28:1. This was true even over several generations (Hom. *Il.* 6.212-31; Cic. *Fam.* 13.34.1), and could require the guest-friend to avenge his host (Philostratus *Hrk.* 46.2-3). Still, though it could be inherited, it could shift along with political interests (Marshall, *Enmity,* 18-21, 39-42).

78. E.g., Plut. *Cicero* 26.1.

79. E.g., Hom. *Il.* 21.76; *Od.* 4.534-35; 11.414-20; 14.404-5; Hes. *W.D.* 327; Eurip. *Cycl.* 126-28; *Hec.* 25-26, 710-20, 850-56; Ap. Rhod. 3.377-80; Ovid *Metam.* 1.144; 10.225-28; Livy 25.16.6. This principle included providing protection from other enemies (Ovid *Metam.* 5.44-45; Corn. Nep. *Gen.* 2 [Themistocles], 8.3).

80. Hom. *Od.* 21.26-28; Livy 39.51.12. Nevertheless, some warned that too much trust even of friends could prove dangerous (Hes. *W.D.* 370-72).

81. Aeschines *Embassy* 22, 55. For a guest to act unkindly was deceptive treachery (Catullus 64.176).

82. Eurip. *Ch. Her.* 1034-36 (even in subsequent generations!); Cic. *Ag. Piso* 34.83; by seeking the host's wife, Ovid *Her.* 17.3-4. On kindness due a host, see Cic. *Ag. Verr.* 2.2.47.117.

83. Dewey, "Curse," 106.

84. See Brown, *Death,* 611-13.

85. See Brown, *Death,* 615.

86. See more fully Brown, *Death,* 614-21.

87. E.g., Jos. *Life* 84, again.

88. See the discussion in Brown, *Death,* 11-12; he also acknowledges that basic historical fact could be retold in an imaginative manner (*Death,* 620-21).

89. See the discussion in Brown, *Death,* 613-14.

90. I have taken these comments largely from Keener, *Matthew,* 613-16; cf. also comments in Basser, "Priests"; Reid, "Sacrifice," 1048-49; Keener, "Mistrial."

91. Cf. Lewis, *Life,* 47; Reicke, *Era,* 147.

92. E.g., 1QM 2:1; Jos. *War* 2.243, 316, 320, 342; 410-11; 4.151, 315; *Life* 197; Mk 2:26; Acts 4:6; Stern, "Aspects," 601, 603; Sanders, *Figure,* 327-32; Jeremias, *Unknown Sayings,* 51.

93. E.g., *m. Hor.* 3:1; *p. Sanh.* 2:1, §2; Acts 23:5-6.

94. On the Sadducees, see Meier, *Marginal Jew,* 3:389-411 (most relevantly here, 393-99). Some, however, believe Sadducean dominance of the priestly aristocracy is generally overstated (e.g., Porton, "Sadducees," 1052). Though some aristocrats were not Sadducees (some, like Gamaliel, were Pharisees), nearly all the Sadducees belonged to the aristocracy (see Sanders, *Judaism,* 318, 332). Probably a priestly sect, they may have been the well-to-do priests who had remained loyal to the Zadokite line during the Maccabean era (while other Zadokites fled to Qumran and elsewhere — cf. 1QS 5.2; 6.3-4; CD 5.5), returning to positions of power under the Romans (e.g., Baumbach, "Sadduzäerverständnis"; Lohse, *Environment,* 74). Later rabbinic tradition links them with "Boethusians" under the special charge that they denied the resurrection from the dead (*ARN* 5 A; 10 B; cf. *m. Ber.* 9:5; Bowker, *Pharisees,* 53-76). Other grounds also separated these aristocrats from the dominant views that were followed in rabbinic practice (*m. Nid.* 4:2; *Yad.* 4:7; *tos. Nid.* 5:2; *Suk.* 3:1). Probably claiming to take Scripture as their only authority, Sadducees felt no obligation to embrace Pharisaic traditions (Jos. *Ant.* 18.16; cf. Neusner, *Beginning,* 27-28; Sanders, *Jesus to Mishnah,* 107). Nevertheless, powerful Pharisees and others had to work alongside them before 70.

95. See Smallwood, "Priests." Even some Gentiles recognized this status (Diod. Sic. 40.3.5-6).

96. Thus Quirinius installed Annas (Jos. *Ant.* 18.26); Vitellius retired Caiaphas after Pilate's recall to Rome (Jos. *Ant.* 18.95).

97. For one defense of the motives of the elite priests regarding Jesus' execution, focused on their perspectives from "the pinnacle of their social world," see Borg, *Vision,* 180-82 (quote from 181).

98. Jos. *Life* 216. He especially regards the chief priests as corrupt during the period of Agrippa II (59-65 CE; Sanders, *Figure,* 324; see e.g., Jos. *Ant.* 20.206-7), but this specification may reflect his own

uncomfortable experiences, and may suggest a broader corruption within the aristocratic ranks from which such priests were drawn. For Josephus' negative view of the Sadducees, see Baumbach, "Sadducees"; of some high priests (but not their office), Thoma, "Priesthood" (attributing it to Josephus' pro-Hasmonean tendencies).

99. Overman, *Crisis,* 329; cf. also Perkins, "Resurrection," 431.

100. Perhaps in part because I believe that religion often fails to transform human nature (the way it should at its best), I am less sympathetic to their piety than is Sanders, *Figure,* 336. They probably acted in their own self-interest, as well as for the peace, in relations with the Romans (Horsley, "High Priests"). The charges may be stylized, sectarian polemic, as Sanders suggests (and against the priesthood in general he may be right — *Judaism,* 182-89), but one should not dismiss too readily the reasons for the pervasive polemic (cf. 1QpHab. 9.4-5; *Test. Levi* 14:1; *2 Bar.* 10:18; *tos. Minhot* 13.21 in Avigad, *Jerusalem,* 130; Avigad, "Burnt House," 71; Hengel, *Property,* 23); corrupt priesthoods were common targets of polemic in the ancient Near East through the first century (Crocker, "Priests"; cf. Plut. *Lysander* 26.1-3; Libanius *Declamation* 44.43). I address below e.g., the servants of the later Ananias who beat poorer priests to seize their tithes (Jos. *Ant.* 20.181, 206).

101. Jos. *Ant.* 14.175; 15.2. It is thus not surprising that the interests of this class were allied with those of Herod (Horsley, *Liberation,* 51).

102. "Sanhedrin" is a broad rather than restrictive term, applicable also in Greek texts to an informal assembly of advisors (Diod. Sic. 13.111.1) or, frequently, to Rome's "senate" (e.g., Diod. Sic. 40.1.1; Dion. Hal. *Ant. rom.* 5.70.5; 6.30.2; 6.81.1; 6.85.2; 8.69.2; 9.32.5; 10.2.6; 12.1.14; 12.6.2 [4]; in these texts it appears interchangeably with *boulē,* a more common term, e.g., Dion. Hal. *Ant. rom.* 5.71.1; 6.1.1; 6.21.1; 6.81.4). Usage was broad; a *boulē* traditionally could constitute a local council (Aristoph. *Knights* 475, 653) but also a leader's war council (Hom. *Il.* 2.84).

103. Jos. *Life* 64, 69, 169, 313, 381; such assemblies were distinguishable from the larger citizen assembly (Jos. *Life* 300). Officials could also assemble their own administrative "councils" from among their friends (e.g., Jos. *Life* 368).

104. Jeffers, *World,* 186.

105. Overman, *Crisis,* 372-73, 385 regards the Sanhedrin as a Roman political institution, although conceding that "some of the local Jewish elite may have been involved." Yet in cities like Jerusalem Rome ruled through municipal aristocracies — here, pro-Roman Jewish aristocrats.

106. *M. Sanh.* 1:6; cf. later *Tg. Neof.* 1 on Ex 15:27. Cf. also Josephus' Galilean council of 70 in *War* 2.570; *Life* 79, and that of the Zealots in *War* 4.336, both undoubtedly following the standard contemporary model; the models probably ultimately derive from Mosaic tradition (Ex 24:9; Num 11:16, 24; cf. Ezek 8:11). Josephus also assumed a council of seven judges as a lower court in every city (*War* 2.571; *Ant.* 4.214). An odd number to break a tie made sense; as in Roman law (Dion. Hal. *Ant. rom.* 7.64.6), a tie vote would yield acquittal.

107. Brown, *Death,* 348-49 reasonably doubts that an exact list of 71 members existed in the first century, suggesting that it merely included elders from distinguished families alongside chief priests, representatives of whom were expected to appear. It is in any case doubtful that all members were expected to be present on all occasions (especially at an emergency meeting on the night when people had eaten or would the next evening eat the Passover).

108. *M. Midd.* 5:4; *Sanh.* 11:2; *tos. Shek.* 3:27; *b. Yoma* 25a; *Gen. Rab.* 70:8; *Num. Rab.* 19:26; *Eccl. Rab.* 1:1, §1. A location near the temple is not surprising; at times other peoples' leaders could use temples (the senate in Cic. *Fam.* 8.4.4).

109. Cf. Jos. *War* 5.144; Wilkinson, *Jerusalem,* 86-87; Brown, *Death,* 350. For bibliography on the Sanhedrin, see Safrai, "Government," 418 (the section on the Sanhedrin is pp. 379-400). Josephus generally prefers the term "sanhedrin," "assembly," in the *Antiquities,* and *boulē,* "council," in the *War.*

110. Cohen, *Maccabees,* 156. Later rabbinic portraits of the Sanhedrin include more striking anachronisms than this (e.g., depicting leaders of the Sanhedrin in biblical times, *b. Ber.* 3b; *Gen. Rab.* 74:15; *Ex. Rab.* 1:13; *Pesiq. Rab.* 11:3). Some of the "scribes" may have been Pharisees, but Pharisees were

not dominant in the Sanhedrin (Brown, *Death*, 350-52), despite Josephus' possible favoritism toward them (Jos. *Ant.* 18.15, 17; cf. *Life* 1, 12 and in *Ant.* passim; Brown, *Death*, 353-56). A few scholars have opted for two Sanhedrins — the religious Sanhedrin of the rabbis and the political Sanhedrin attested in first-century sources; one scholar defending the rabbinic picture has even argued that the Gospels and Acts are late sources on this matter, with changes into the fourth century (Mantel, *Sanhedrin*; for this proposal's untenability, see Sutcliffe, "Review"). But it is anachronistic to reject all our first-century portraits on the basis of later, idealized rabbinic accounts, and few scholars have accepted the double Sanhedrin thesis (see Blinzler, *Trial*, 15, 140; Brown, *Death*, 343-48).

111. In contrast to rabbinic (and probably Pharisaic) ideals in which judges who proved themselves locally could be promoted to the Sanhedrin (*tos. Shek.* 3:27).

112. See Sanders, *Figure*, 482-83; cf. *Ant.* 15.173; 20.216-18.

113. Jos. *Ant.* 14.177.

114. Cf. Jos. *War* 2.331, 405; *Ant.* 20.11.

115. Jos. *Ant.* 20.200.

116. Cf. Sanders, *Figure*, 484-87; Jos. *War* 2.331, 336; *Ant.* 17.160, 164; 20.216-17; probably the municipal aristocracy in *Ant.* 14.91, 163, 167, 180; *Life* 62.

117. Cf. e.g., Kennard, "Assembly."

118. Jos. *Life* 309.

119. Jos. *War* 2.331, 336; 5.142-44, 532; *Ant.* 20.11, 200-1, 216-17; *Life* 62.

120. Brown, *Death*, 342-43. Levine, *Hellenism*, 88-90, argues that the Jerusalem Sanhedrin was probably simply an ad hoc group in some texts.

121. Cf. e.g., Borg, *Vision*, 180. Winter, *Trial*, 39, doubts that Caiaphas was much involved with the trial. But while Luke also knows of Caiaphas (Lk 3:2; Acts 4:6), only Matthew and John (Matt 26:3, 57; Jn 18:13-14, 24, 28) connect him explicitly with Jesus' trial, which strongly suggests independent traditions attesting Caiaphas's role. On Annas and Caiaphas in John, see Brown, *Death*, 404-11.

122. Schnackenburg, *John*, 2:348; Sanders, *Figure*, 265.

123. So Vermes, *Religion*, ix-x, though he doubts that Jesus saw himself in messianic terms (p. 5).

124. Sanders, *Figure*, 265.

125. Sanders, *Figure*, 269. Rome held the high priests responsible for controlling the masses (Jos. *War* 2.232-44), and the high priests moved against potential threats to public order when they thought it best to do so (Jos. *War* 6.300-9; *Ant.* 20.199-203; Sanders, *Figure*, 266-67).

126. Stauffer, *Jesus*, 102. (Stauffer, *Jesus*, 54, thinks that Caiaphas "held his peace" when Pilate introduced standards into Jerusalem; but Jos. *Ant.* 18.57-59 is unclear.)

127. See the so-called Caiaphas family tomb, very debated (Riesner, "Familiengrab"; Reich, "Inscriptions"; Reich, "Name"; Evans, "Caiaphas Ossuary"). Even if it did not belong to Caiaphas himself, it probably belonged to aristocratic priests (see Horbury, "Ossuaries") and so illustrates the point; for health advantages of Jerusalem's upper class, cf. Zias, "Remains."

128. On pagan features of the tomb (see note above), see Greenhut, "Tomb"; idem, "Cave."

129. E.g., Case, *Origins*, 56; cf. Winter, *Trial*, 43. The aristocracy undoubtedly considered their method of silencing Jesus successful; Rome regarded Palestine as quiet during Tiberius's reign (Judge, *Pattern*, 23, citing Tac. *Hist.* 5.9).

130. Quirinius installed Annas as high priest in 6 CE (Jos. *Ant.* 18.26), but Valerius Gratus deposed him in 15 CE (Jos. *Ant.* 18.34). Yet because Jewish law mandated the high priesthood for life, many Jews may have still considered Annas the appropriate official to decide important cases like this one (Ellis, *Genius*, 255).

131. Winter, *Trial*, 33.

132. After Vitellius, legate of Syria, deposed Caiaphas in 36 CE, he replaced him with Jonathan son of Annas (Jos. *Ant.* 18.95); in time all five sons of Annas followed in office, suggesting that Annas had in fact exercised considerable influence (Jos. *Ant.* 20.198; on his power, see further Reicke, *Era*, 142-43).

133. E.g., 1QM 2:1; Jos. *War* 2.243, 316, 320, 342, 410-11; 4.151, 315; *Life* 197; Mk 2:26; 11:27; 14:1; Jn 7:32; Acts 4:23; 5:24; 9:14, 21.

134. John's independent report about Annas may well reflect historical tradition; it is not derived from John's theology (see Blinzler, *Trial*, 88-89; Dodd, *Tradition*, 93-94). John has no specific reason to preserve the names of high priests (Matt 26:3, 57; Lk 3:2 mention Caiaphas; Lk 3:2 briefly mentions Annas; neither name appears in Mark), but if he would preserve any, Caiaphas, who actually was high priest at the time of the hearing, would make most sense; his audience already anticipates Jesus confronting Caiaphas (Jn 11:49).

135. E.g., Winter, *Trial*; idem, "Trial"; Cohn, *Trial*, 98; Zeitlin, "Trial."

136. Goppelt, *Judaism*, 84ff; Sherwin-White, *Society*, 34ff; cf. idem, "Trial"; Catchpole, *Trial*, 271; Blinzler, *Trial*, 117-21; Corley, "Trial."

137. Stauffer, *Jesus*, 225.

138. So Stauffer, *Jesus*, 225.

139. E.g., Grant, "Review"; Cohn, *Trial*, 98, 105.

140. For surveys of views concerning the legality of Jesus' trial, see e.g., Brown, *Death*, 330-31.

141. Abrahams, *Studies*, 2:129.

142. Brown, *Death*, 357-63; Blinzler, *Trial*, 138-43.

143. Cf. Anderson, *Mark*, 326; pace Cohn, *Trial*, 105.

144. Cf. Klausner, *Jesus*, 337.

145. Those with power (Roman governors, Herod, Agrippa I) usually executed whom they chose (Sanders, *Jesus and Judaism*, 317); others with more limited power undoubtedly exercised what they could.

146. Sanders, *Judaism*, 487.

147. Noted also by Perkins, "Resurrection," 431.

148. See e.g., Cullmann, *State*, 42, 46; Argyle, *Matthew*, 206; Reicke, *Era*, 146; Hagner, *Matthew*, 797.

149. Some find here that John's account is easier to envision historically than Mark's; see Sanders, *Jesus and Judaism*, 317-18; also, e.g., Meier, *Matthew*, 330; Catchpole, *Trial*, 271.

150. Romans regarded it a crime to try and condemn one in a private rather than public setting, especially the judge's home rather than his tribunal (Cic. *Ag. Verr.* 2.3.23.56; Sen. *Controv.* 9.2.4; cf. Tac. *Ann.* 2.40).

151. Sanders, *Figure*, 67.

152. Cf. Hooker, *Message*, 86; Rhoads and Michie, *Mark*, 120-21. Brown, *Death*, 433 observes that "ancient literary accounts of famous trials" usually include polemic or bias.

153. *M. Sanh.* 4:1. Cf. Pompey's interpretation of Roman law in Aul. Gel. 14.7.8.

154. Cf. *m. Sanh.* 4:1; *Yom Tob* 5:2; *tos. Yom Tob* 4:4; Philo *Migr.* 91. Blinzler, *Trial*, 143-44, thinks rules against meeting on the *eve* of a holy day are later. Some Roman laws opposed certain kinds of trials on holidays (*Lex Irnitana* tablet 10 A, chap. 92; Metzger, *Outline*, 16-17) and may have required advance notice as well (10 A, chap. 90; though Metzger, *Outline*, 60, thinks this applies to postponements).

155. Some argue for sectarian calendars (Pixner, "Zion," 318; cf. Jaubert, *Date*; idem, "Calendar"; critiquing Jaubert on *Jubilees*, Ravid, "Calendar"; for other objections, Benoit, *Jesus*, 1:87-93) and other means of reconciling the two chronologies (e.g., Shepherd, "Date"; ingeniously, Busada, "Calendar"); some prefer John's chronology (Brown, *Essays*, 207-17). With many, I have argued that John's chronology is at this point more symbolic than that of the Synoptics (Keener, *John*, 1100-3).

156. Commentators (e.g., Dalman, *Jesus-Jeshua*, 98; Lane, *Mark*, 529-30; Stauffer, *Jesus*, 209) cite *m. Sanh.* 11:4; *tos. Sanh.* 11:7. This differs from the Roman practice (Cic. *Pro Caelio* 1.1; Sen. *Controv.* 5.4; Suet. *Tib.* 61; cf. Acts 12:3-4). The offenders included those regarded as false prophets, among others (Hill, *Prophecy*, 52).

157. If the Mishnah provides any indication of their view, Pharisaic scruples also required a day

to pass before issuing a verdict of condemnation (*m. Sanh.* 4:1). But the Sadducees may have generally preferred speedier executions than the Pharisees thought appropriate (cf. *m. Mak.* 1:6); certainly they favored stricter punishments (Jos. *Ant.* 20.199). Later rabbis preferred longer deliberation in capital cases (cf. e.g., *Tg. Neof.* 1 on Lev 24:12; Num 9:8; 15:34; 27:5; *Tg. Ps.-Jon.* on Lev 24:12; Num 9:8; 15:34; 27:5). Qumran scrolls differ from rabbinic practice on this issue (Rothstein, "Testimony").

158. Cohn, *Trial*, 98 cites *b. A.Z.* 8b; *Sanh.* 41b; *Shab.* 15a.

159. Jos. *Ant.* 4.219; 11QTemple 61.7-11; *m. Mak.* 1:7; *tos. Sanh.* 6:6; *Sipre Deut.* 190.5.1.

160. Ferguson, *Backgrounds*, 51; cf. the penalty in Sen. *Controv.* 5.4, if genuine. So also reportedly Egyptian custom (Diod. Sic. 1.77.2). Diod. Sic. 12.12.2 thus considers particularly merciful a law which merely shames false witnesses so much that they flee a city.

161. E.g., Sus 48-62; *m. Ab.* 1:9; *Sanh.* 5:1-4; *tos. Sanh.* 6:3, 6; *Sipre Deut.* 93.2.1; 149.1.1-2; 189.1.3.

162. Brown, *Death*, 458; Stanton, *Gospel Truth*, 180-83. Greek rhetoric often preferred arguments from probability and internal consistency (which were frequent, e.g., Demosth. *On the Embassy* 120; *Against Pantaenetus* 23; Arist. *Rhet.* 1.15.17, 1376a; Dion. Hal. *Ant. rom.* 3.35.5-6; 11.34.1-6; Jos. *Apion* 1.219-20, 267, 286; 2.8-27, 82, 148; *Life* 342, 350; Acts 26:8) to witnesses (see Kennedy, *Classical Rhetoric*, 20-21), though the effective testimony of witnesses was nevertheless adequate to convict (Dion. Hal. *Ant. rom.* 8.78.3).

163. E.g., 1QpHab 9.4-5; Jos. *Life* 216; *Ant.* 20.181, 206; *Test. Levi* 14:1.

164. *Ant.* 20.181.

165. *Ant.* 20.206. Perhaps Josephus' literary model was 1 Sam 2:14-16, but the behavior of many Medieval church leaders, not to mention quite a few since that time, confirms the more widespread temptation of sacerdotal power.

166. *Life* 192-93, 196-98, 216.

167. *Ant.* 20.163.

168. E.g., Avigad, *Jerusalem*, 130, citing *tos. Minhot* 13:21; *b. Pes.* 57:1.

169. E.g., Sanders, *Jesus and Judaism*, 299.

170. Brown, *Death*, 1230.

171. Jos. *Life* 204.

172. Those of rank, like Joseph, would often have had friends aware of plots even if they themselves were not present (cf. e.g., Corn. Nep. 4 [Pausanias], 5.1; 14 [Datames], 5.3). Even the Roman senate's inner secrets often leaked out, in contrast to the practice of the earliest times (Valerius Maximus 2.2.1a).

173. See Donahue, *Christ*, 98-99; idem, "Temple," 62-65; Dewey, "Curse," 97-100.

174. Schubert, "Criticism," 401; see pp. 385-402.

175. Also emphasized by Evans, "Non-Christian Sources," 466.

176. See *b. Sanh.* 43a and the discussion in Herford, *Christianity*, 78-90.

177. Broer, "Death," 159-60, 163.

178. Jos. *Ant.* 18.118.

179. Jos. *War* 6.303-5. For the latter, see also Broer, "Death," 165-66, who adds also violations of the temple (166-67).

180. Broer, "Death," 164-65.

181. Harvey, *History*, 16, citing e.g., Pliny *Ep.* 10.97; cf. Ferguson, *Backgrounds*, 51. On *delatores*, see e.g., O'Neal, "Delation."

182. Sherwin-White, *Society*, 47. For even fuller detail, see Malina and Rohrbaugh, *John*, 249.

183. Sanders, *Jesus and Judaism*, 286; cf. Borg, *Vision*, 179-82; for the temple cleansing as a Jewish issue, Broer, "Death," 161, 166-67. Rabbinic attestation of a religious trial of Jesus (Stauffer, *Jesus*, 225; cf. Herford, *Christianity*, 78-83) is late and probably derivative, hence we do not admit it as independent evidence; but a Jewish hearing is essential for other reasons such as these. Even Winter, who emphasizes an arrest and agenda set by Romans (*Trial*, 30, 147), recognizes that Pilate would have expected the high priest's aides to prepare the case (*Trial*, 29).

184. Cohn, *Trial,* 109; Flusser, *Judaism,* 589.

185. Cf. Brown, *Death,* 697. Smallwood, "Historians," concludes that Philo is even more accurate than Josephus when reporting the same historical events (in this case, concerning Caligula).

186. Still despised in a later period, e.g., in Juv. *Sat.* 10.66, 76, 89-90, 104; Phaed. 3, *prol.* 41-44; cf. also Brown, *Death,* 694 on Philo *Flacc.* 1; *Embassy* 160-61.

187. Cf. rumors circulating in Lk 13:1 and Bailey, *Peasant Eyes,* 75. Brown, *Death,* 695-705 ultimately concludes, as we do, that most of the Gospel portrait fits what we know of Pilate from the other sources once all has been taken into account.

188. Tac. *Ann.* 15.44; also mentioned outside the Gospels and Acts in 1 Tim 6:13.

189. Crossan, *Historical Jesus,* 372.

190. The "governor" in Judea in this period was technically a "prefect," rather than the later term "procurator" as in Tac. *Ann.* 15.44; the Gospels simply use the general title "governor," which could have covered either. Literary sources employ the later term "procurator," but an inscription supports the earlier title (see Brown, *Death,* 336-37; Evans, "Pilate Inscription," 804). For the responsibilities of a governor, see e.g., Just. *Dig.* 1.16.4-13 in Jones, *History,* 180-83.

191. E.g., Jos. *Ant.* 18.85. Much of the following section is adapted from Keener, *Matthew,* 662-67.

192. Philo *Embassy to Gaius* 299, 302.

193. With Harvey, *History,* 17.

194. Although the severest form of execution Pharisaic law acknowledged on the basis of the Hebrew Bible was stoning (*b. Sanh.* 49b-50a), Jewish rulers had used crucifixion before the Roman period. Under Roman rule, however, all official, public executions belonged to the Romans (see Appendix 7). Even the Essenes toned down capital sentences from Moses' law (CD 12.2-5), while also detesting Gentile executions in the holy land (CD 9.1).

195. Jos. *War* 2.176-77; *Ant.* 18.60-62.

196. E.g., Arrian *Alex.* 6.30.2.

197. Livy 22.33.1-2; Suet. *Dom.* 10; Cic. *Ag. Verr.* 2.5.66.169; Sen. *Controv.* 3.9 excerpts.

198. E.g., Phaed. 3.5.10 (for throwing a stone at a rich man).

199. Stauffer, *Jesus,* 131. For the outrage at scourging, executing, and (worst of all) occasionally crucifying Roman citizens, see Cic. *Verr.* 1.5.13; 2.1.3.7-9; 2.3.3.6; 2.3.24.59; 2.4.11.26; 2.5.66.169.

200. Suet. *Julius* 4.

201. Harvey, *History,* 12; Overman, *Crisis,* 380-81, 387; e.g., Jos. *War* 2.75, 241, 253, 306; 3.321; 5.449; *Ant.* 20.102. It also appears as a fitting end for other military enemies (e.g., Diod. Sic. 2.1.10; 25.5.2; Jos. *Ant.* 12.256; 13.380) and for the most horrid crimes (Apul. *Metam.* 3.9); it was the epitome of a horrible way to die (Sen. *Ep. Lucil.* 101.10-12).

202. See Jos. *Ant.* 14.235, 260-61; cf. Jos. *Apion* 2.73; Acts 18:13-15; Judge, *Pattern,* 68.

203. Cf. Harvey, *History,* 17; Sanders, *Figure,* 274; Borg, *Vision,* 179; for an impoverished provincial condemned to death without trial, cf. e.g., Apul. *Metam.* 9.42.

204. Winter, *Trial,* 54-55, 60; Borg, *Vision,* 179.

205. Philo *Embassy* 302; Jos. *Ant.* 18.88-89; Sanders, *Figure,* 274. On governors being tried for abusing power, especially executing innocent people (particularly Roman citizens), see Pliny *Ep.* 2.11, in Jones, *History,* 192-95.

206. Others viewed this act as misappropriation of funds (Jos. *War* 2.175-76; cf. *Ant.* 18.60; *The Suda* in Sherk, *Empire,* 75); Pilate, however, probably assumed he followed safe Roman precedent, since public funds were often used for aqueducts and other projects (Frontinus *De aquis* 2.89-101, 116-18, in Jones, *History,* 207; Jos. *Life* 199) — though not from Jerusalem's temple. Romans, however, also complained when designated funds in a public treasury were redirected (App. *C.W.* 2.6.41; Lysias *Or.* 25.19, §173; 27.7, §178; 27.16, §179; Plut. *Cicero* 17.2; *Caesar* 35.2-4); they would have been angriest had he profited himself, which sometimes happened (Catullus 10.7-13). A governor who violated a temple treasury could be banished (Tac. *Ann.* 14.18).

207. Stauffer, *Jesus,* 72; Thompson, *Archaeology,* 308-9.

208. E.g., Cic. *Verr.* 1.1.2; 1.4.12; 2.3.22.55; 2.3.28.69; *Sest.* 25.55; many Judean governors as presented by Josephus, e.g., *Ant.* 20.106-17, 162-63, 215, 253-57; *War* 2.223-45, 272-79.

209. Cf. Benoit, *Jesus,* 1:141-42. Some first-century writers complained about societal injustice (e.g., Sen. *Ep. Lucil.* 95.30).

210. On the consistency of Pilate's behavior, cf. e.g., Hoehner, "Significance," 121-25.

211. Jos. *War* 6.305.

212. See Keener, *John,* 1106; idem, *Matthew,* 666.

213. The danger of making a harmless leader into a martyr occasionally even exempted one from scourging (Lucian *Passing of Peregrinus* 14). The baraita in *b. Sanh.* 43a suggesting special caution regarding Jesus' conviction "because he was close to the kingdom" would be a Jewish deterrent but could have actually aggravated Roman hostility. It is, however, probably derived from later debate with Jewish Christians.

214. Philo *Flacc.* 1.

215. Stauffer, *Jesus,* 132; Lane, *Mark,* 556-57 n. 34; Baum, *Jews and Gospel,* 72; cf. Sherk, *Empire,* 75-77.

216. This is admittedly at best an unlikely guess, rather than a direct inference from our sources which, unanimously hostile to Sejanus, suggest that most of those who disagreed with him in Rome would have been more circumspect than to *say* so.

217. See Reicke, *Era,* 138, 175.

218. Cf. Malina, *Windows,* 115-16.

219. On the equestrian order, see e.g., Jones, *History,* 134-40.

220. E.g., Jos. *War* 2.169-77; *Ant.* 18.55-62.

221. Philo *Embassy* 301-2; Jos. *War* 2.171-74; *Ant.* 18.59.

222. Philo *Embassy to Gaius* 304-5. Cf. Jn 19:12.

223. Winter, *Trial,* 53-54.

224. Blinzler, *Trial,* 236; Smallwood, *Jews,* 169.

225. Cf. e.g., Tac. *Ann.* 2.50; 3.38; Bks. 4-5 passim (e.g., 4.17-21, 30, 60, 66, 69-70, 74; 5.3-6; Dio Cass. *R.H.* 57.9.2; 57.19.1; 57.23.1-2). Among Romans treason was the greatest crime (Dion. Hal. *Ant. rom.* 8.80.1).

226. Cullmann, *State,* 46-47.

227. Jos. *Ant.* 18.89 (though Krieger, "Problematik," doubts Josephus' reasons for Pilate's dismissal).

228. Harvey, *History,* 17. Historically and socially, one who challenged the status quo of either Jerusalem's priestly elite or the Romans would likely face such consequences (Hanson and Oakman, *Palestine,* 94-95).

229. Keener, *John,* 851-52; idem, "Truth"; Winter, *Trial,* 37.

230. Bruce, "Trial," 14; cf. Bammel, "Trial," 420. I treat this passage further in Keener, *John,* 1109-14; idem, "Truth."

231. Sanders, *Jesus and Judaism,* 294; the entire sentence is italicized in the original. A messianic claim could be indictable only if construed as treason (Sanders, *Jesus and Judaism,* 55).

232. Cf. Epict. *Disc.* 3.22.49; Plut. *Flatterer* 16, *Mor* 58E.

233. Sen. *Ep. Lucil.* 108.13; Plutarch *Flatterer/Friend* 16, *Mor.* 58E; Diogenes Laertius 7.1.122; see also Cicero *Fin.* 3.22.75; Horace *Sat.* 1.3.125 (ridiculing Stoics); Arius Didymus *Epit.* 2.7.11m, pp. 88-89.26-29; 90-91.1-6; Grant, *Paul,* 30. This rested on their definition of kingship by nature (Musonius Rufus 8, p. 66.13-16, 21-26; cf. Dio Chrysostom *Or.* 1.14; 4.24-25). Cf. Chrysippus' approach in Engberg-Pedersen, *Paul and Stoics,* 75-76; on Mus. Ruf., see Klassen, "Law."

234. E.g., Maximus of Tyre *Or.* 36.5.

235. E.g., Plato *Rep.* 5.472; Cicero *Fin.* 3.22.75; Quintilian *Inst.* 2.17.28; Musonius Rufus 8, p. 66.5; Dio Chrysostom *Or.* 49.4-14; Iamblichus *Pyth. Life* 27.129; 35.250.

236. E.g., Xenophon *Mem.* 2.1.6-7; Aristotle *Pol.* 3.2.5, 1277a; Isocrates *To Nicocles* 10-11, 29, *Or.* 2; Plutarch *Uneducated Ruler, Mor.* 779D-782F; *Sayings of Romans,* Cato the Elder 8, *Mor.* 198F; *Sayings*

of Kings, Cyrus 2, *Mor.* 172E; Dio Chrysostom *Or.* 62.1; cf. Prov 8:15; Sir 9:17–10:26; the symposium section of *Let. Aris.; Sipre Deut.* 161.2.1. Many cultures have shared this concern (e.g., Confucius *Analects* 244-85).

237. E.g., Jos. *War* 2.306-8; 5.449; Livy 2.5.8; 9.24.15; 10.1.3; 26.40.13; 41.11.8; Polyb. 11.30.2; Cic. *Verres* 5.62.162; Dion. Hal. 3.40.3; 5.43.2; 7.69.1; 9.40.3-4; 12.6.7; 20.16.2; 20.17.2; Quintus Curtius 7.11.28; App. *R.H.* 3.9.3; Arrian *Alex.* 3.30.5; Tac. *Hist.* 3.77; Lucian *Dead Come to Life/Fishermen* 2; Klausner, *Jesus,* 350.

238. Brown, *John,* 2:874. On forms of beatings, see Rapske, *Custody,* 124-25.

239. Commentators cite *Dig.* 18.19.8.3; Cic. *Verres* 2.4.39.85; Philo *Flacc.* 75 (see Blinzler, *Trial,* 222-23). I have borrowed most of the information on scourging from Keener, *Matthew,* 672-73.

240. Jos. *War* 2.612.

241. *War* 6.304.

242. *Test. Jos.* 2:3; *Dig.* 47.21.2. For *coercitio* as part of preliminary examinations, cf. Lake and Cadbury, *Commentary,* 282-83. Josephus adapts such discipline (*Life* 335).

243. Bruce, *Commentary,* 445; cf. e.g., Cic. *Ag. Piso* 34.84.

244. *Dig.* 48.19.10; 68.28.2; Blinzler, *Trial,* 222.

245. Stripping before execution was standard (e.g., Polyb. 11.30.1-2; Dion. Hal. 7.69.2; Hdn. 8.8.6; Jos. *Apion* 1.191; 2.53; *m. Sanh.* 6:3; *b. Sanh.* 45a, bar.), as before public beatings (Longus 2.14; Aul. Gel. 10.3.3; Cic. *Verr.* 2.4.40.86; Herodes *Mime* 5.20).

246. Plaut. *Bacchides* 4.7.25; Artem. *Oneir.* 1.78 in Blinzler, *Trial,* 222; see also *m. Mak.* 3:12. One could also be scourged, presumably across the breast, while bound to the cross itself (Dio Cass. *R.H.* 49.22.6).

247. Apul. *Metam.* 7.30.154; *Codex Theodos.* 8.5.2; 9.35.2; Goguel, *Jesus,* 527; Blinzler, *Trial,* 222.

248. Klausner, *Jesus,* 350; Blinzler, *Trial,* 222.

249. E.g., Hor. *Sat.* 1.3.119; Cic. *In Defense of Rabirius* 5.15-16; Brown, *Death,* 851.

250. Cf. Suet. *Calig.* 26; Blinzler, *Trial,* 222.

251. Wilkinson, *Jerusalem,* 151.

252. Goguel, *Jesus,* 527.

253. Brown, *Death,* 852. Because John's scourging occurs earlier in the narrative's sequence, some scholars argue that John represents a lesser form of scourging than the form that took place in the Synoptics, perhaps as an inquisition rather than the first stage of execution (cf. Bruce, "Trial," 15; Blinzler, *Trial,* 224; Bammel, "Trial," 440-41, though Blinzler and Bammel go too far in separating this scourging from the crucifixion historically). In any case, the same historical event stands behind them; and the distinctions may well have eluded the Gospel writers' original audiences anyway (Brown, *Death,* 851).

254. Johnson, *Real Jesus,* 120.

255. Dupont, *Life,* 126-27.

256. Davies and Allison, *Matthew,* 3:600. Public abuse of prisoners, even adorning one as a king and beating him, occurred on other occasions; see comment below.

257. Even the mockery at the cross, challenging Jesus to "save," is plausible as a play on his Semitic name, a common method of mockery (cf. Paschke, "Namen").

258. See Brown, *Death,* 877.

259. Commentators cite Philo *Flacc.* 36-39; *CPJ* 154, 158; Plut. *Pompey* 24; Dio Cass. 15.20-21; cf. also Winter, *Trial,* 102-3; Josephus's mock funeral (*Life* 323); those in Alexandria were especially to be expected (cf. Hdn 4.9.2-3). Robbins, *Teacher,* xxvi, 189 helpfully supplies another parallel from Persian behavior at the Sacian festival (Dio Chrys. *Or.* 4.67-70), though he lays too much emphasis on this to the exclusion of other parallels.

260. Livy 36.14.4; Corn. Nep. 14 [Datames], 3.1-4; some commentators cite Pollux *Onomasticon* 9.110; cf. also Hdt. *Hist.* 1.114; Hor. *Odes* 1.4.18.

261. For a full survey of games of mockery, see Brown, *Death,* 874-77.

262. Valerius Max. 1.7.4; Dion. Hal. *Ant. rom.* 7.69.1; Blinzler, *Trial,* 244.

263. Jos. *Life* 420-21.

264. Klausner, *Jesus,* 353.

265. Cf. Goguel, *Jesus,* 530-31; Lane, *Mark,* 562; Davies, *Matthew,* 197; Brown, *Death,* 914.

266. John emphasizes instead Jesus carrying his own cross (19:17); although Jesus may have begun doing so initially, John's descripton fits his theology (cf. his emphasis on Jesus laying down his life, Jn 10:15, 17-18; and remaining in control of the passion's details, e.g., Jn 13:26; Keener, *John,* 820, 875, 901, 918-19, 1048, 1053, 1100-3, 1133-34).

267. That Simon was coming in from the "field" (Mk 15:21) cannot mean that he was coming from work — first, work was prohibited on the feast day (Lev 23:7-8) and second, one would hardly finish working in the fields at 9 a.m. The expression may thus mean that Simon had miscalculated his transportation and arrived from Cyrene late for the feast (cf. e.g., Acts 20:16; Sen. *Ep. Lucil.* 53.1-3; 57.1; though the most difficult travel season — cf. e.g., Acts 27:9; Jos. *War* 1.279-80; 2.203; 4.499; Ach. Tat. 8.19.3 — had probably ended a month before); more likely, it simply means "from outside the city" (Dalman, *Jesus-Jeshua,* 100-1), where he had spent the night, perhaps in a nearby town.

268. Brown, *Death,* 914 questions whether the Romans would force someone when Josephus says they did not force subjects to break their own laws (*Apion* 2.73), but this objection lays too much weight on Josephus' propaganda; Josephus employs legal precedents apologetically (cf. Rajak, "Charter"). Soldiers sometimes abused the right of requisition (Livy 43.7.11; 43.8.1-10; Apul. *Metam.* 9.39; Herodian 2.3.4; 2.5.1; *P. London* 3.1171, *ILGS* 5.1998=*SEG* 17.755 in Sherk, *Empire,* 89, 136; *P.S.I.* 446; Jones, *History,* 197; Llewelyn, *Documents* 7:80-85; cf. *p. Ḥag.* 2:1, §8). On the Roman administration's use of local transport services, see e.g., the *kanon* in Horsley, *Documents* 1:36-45; most fully, Llewelyn, *Documents* 7:58-92.

269. Brown, *Death,* 913.

270. Sanders, "Simon," 56-57.

271. Cyrene was as much as a quarter Jewish (Jos. *Ant.* 14.115-18; cf. *Apion* 2.44; Caird, *Age,* 21; Brown, *Death,* 915) and its Jewish community is well-known (Acts 2:10; 11:20; 13:1; see especially Applebaum, *Cyrene;* Yamauchi, "Cyrene").

272. Archaeologists have uncovered the grave of an "Alexander son of Simon," a Cyrenian Jew, near Jerusalem (Lane, *Mark,* 563). This would fit the Jerusalem-based passion narrative Theissen suggests behind Mark, where Simon's sons seem to have been familiar (Mk 15:21; Theissen, *Gospels in Context,* 176-77; some cite Rom 16:13 for Rome). Given the commonness of names like "Alexander" and "Simon" we need not assume that the same Cyrenian is in view, but the tomb at least illustrates the authenticity of the picture of Cyrenian Jews with such names in Jerusalem.

273. Acts 2:5-11; Jos. *War* 1.253; *Ant.* 17.254; Safrai, "Temple," 898.

274. E.g., France, *Matthew,* 395; Brown, *Death,* 913.

275. See Theissen, *Gospels in Context,* 166-99.

276. Happily, most Roman officials initially seem to have understood them as a deviant form of Judaism worshiping someone dead, rather than a political threat (cf. e.g., Acts 25:19, if we do not read this as simply Luke's apologetic).

277. Sanders, *Jesus and Judaism,* 11.

278. E.g., Polyb. 2.56.7 (cf. 15.33). See discussion of the method in Quint. *Inst.* 4.2.113 (on Cic. *Verr.* 5.62).

279. E.g., Apul. *Metam.* 3.9; 6.32; Char. *Chaer.* 3.3.12.

280. Matthew, for example, "disposing of it in a participial clause" (Bruce, "Matthew," 328). It was established rhetorical practice to hurry most quickly over points that might disturb the audience (Theon *Progymn.* 5.52-56).

281. Bauckham, *Eyewitnesses,* 331-32. Those who complain that emotional involvement would render a witness incapable of reporting true information would have to discount testimony from

those involved in war, concentration camps, and so forth (Eddy and Boyd, *Legend,* 397-98; cf. Bauckham, *Eyewitnesses,* 492-505).

282. Hengel, *Crucifixion,* 25; see e.g., Apul. *Metam.* 8.22. Thus positions varied, but for evidence for one probably common position, see Tzaferis, "Crucifixion," 52-53. Before the Roman conquest, following hellenistic (e.g., Jos. *Ant.* 12.256) and Persian (Esth 9:25; De Vaux, *Israel,* 159) practice, Jewish executions had also adopted hanging by crucifixion (e.g., Jos. *War* 1.97; *Ant.* 13.380; 4QpNah 1.7-8; *Sipre Deut.* 221.1.1; *p. Sanh.* 6:6, §2; cf. 11QTemple 64).

283. See Artem. *Oneir.* 2.56; Plautus *Mostellaria* 2.1.12-13; Lucan *C.W.* 6.545, 547; *m. Shab.* 6.10; Lane, *Mark,* 564; Jn 20:25; cf. Lk 24:39. Cf. Diod. Sic. 25.5.2 (if *prosēloō* here means "nailed," as it often does); also the skeleton recovered at Givat ha-Mivtar — Bruce, "Trial," 18, though original reports about the ankle nail(s) have been revised (Stanton, *Gospels,* 148; Kuhn, "Gekreuzigten"); on the wrists, see Yamauchi, "Crucifixion," 2; Tzaferis, "Crucifixion," 52.

284. Artem. *Oneir.* 2.61; Brown, *Death,* 870 adds Dion. Hal. *Ant. rom.* 7.69.2; Val. Max. *Facta* 1.7.4; Jos. *Ant.* 19.270.

285. Rabbinic tradition indicates that even most later rabbis allowed men to be executed naked (*m. Sanh.* 6:3; *Sot.* 3:8; *b. Sanh.* 45a, bar.).

286. Some later rabbis explaining the proper way to carry out theoretical executions allowed men a loincloth (*m. Sanh.* 6:3; Blinzler, *Trial,* 253).

287. Brown, *Death,* 870 thinks the Gospels might "reflect a local concession," noting that Jos. *War* 2.246 and *Ant.* 20.136 do not mention Celer's disrobing; but this would be an argument from silence. (Brown, *Death,* 953, citing Melito of Sardis *On the Pasch* 97 in favor of nakedness and *Acts of Pilate* 10.1 in favor of a loincloth, ultimately doubts that we can know either way.) Nakedness was probably the rule of thumb (in public Roman punishments, e.g., Dion. Hal. *Ant. rom.* 7.69.2; in non-Roman executions, e.g., Jos. *Apion* 1.191; 2.53).

288. E.g., Juv. *Sat.* 1.71; Plut. *R.Q.* 40, *Mor.* 274A; Diog. Laert. 2.73; but contrast Plato *Rep.* 5.452C; Dio Chrys. *Or.* 13.24.

289. E.g., Gen 3:7, 10-11; *Jub.* 3:21-22, 30-31; 7:8-10, 20; 1QS 7.12; *tos. Ber.* 2:14; *Sipre Deut.* 320.5.2.

290. Klausner, *Jesus,* 350.

291. The upright stakes were 10 feet at the highest, more often closer to six or seven feet so that the victim hung barely above the ground, with a seat *(sedile)* in the middle (Blinzler, *Trial,* 249; Reicke, *Era,* 186). Romans could employ high crosses to increase visibility for significant public executions (Suet. *Galba* 9.1), and given the reed here (Mk 15:36), Jesus may have been slightly higher than usual (Blinzler, *Trial,* 249); Brown, *Death,* 948-49, guesses seven feet.

292. Matt 27:37; Lk 23:38; cf. Jn 19:19. The location of the charge identifies the shape of the cross as in Christian tradition, rather than the T or X-shaped crosses also used; mass executions sometimes simply employed scaffolds (on various forms of crucifixion, Brown, *Death,* 948 cites e.g., Sen. *Consol.* 20.3; Jos. *War* 5.451; on the four-armed cross, the *crux immissa,* Iren. *Haer.* 2.24.4; Tert. *Ad nationes* 1.12.7).

293. So even Winter, *Trial,* 108-9.

294. Jos. *Ant.* 17.285, 295; Brown, *Death,* 968.

295. Jos. *War* 2.443-44; *Ant.* 17.285; Harvey, *History,* 13 n. 12.

296. Harvey, *History,* 13-14; Stanton, *Gospel Truth,* 173; cf. Acts 17:7. Surely the apolitical Markan community would have been an unlikely source for the invention (cf. Kee, *Origins,* 120-21).

297. Cullmann, *State,* 42-43; Reicke, *Era,* 186; Brown, *Death,* 963 cite Suet. *Calig.* 32.2; *Domit.* 10.1; Dio Cass. *Hist.* 54.3.7; 54.8; Tert. *Apol.* 2.20; Euseb. *H.E.* 5.1.44; cf. *b. Sanh.* 43a. The posting of the accusation on the cross is not well-attested, either because those describing crucifixion had already mentioned it being carried (Bammel, "Titulus," 353) or because the practice was not in fact standard, although, given the variations among executions, it is in no way improbable (Harvey, *History,* 13). Blinzler, *Trial,* 254, thinks the tablet was "in black or red letters on a white ground."

298. E.g., Stauffer, *Jesus,* 140; Gundry, *Old Testament,* 203; Jeremias, *Theology,* 189. Boring et al.,

Commentary, 157-60 rightly contrasts Jesus' pain here with the standard traditions of glad martyrs (2 Macc 6:18–7:42; Jos. *War* 2.119-20; *b. Ber.* 61b), adding that Matthew's signs, Luke's psalm of trust (Lk 23:46 citing Ps 31:5) and certainly John work to alleviate some of the starkness of Mark's portrait.

299. Jesus' contemporaries recognized in the psalm a plea for mercy (cf. *Mek. Shirata* 3.75ff, Lauterbach 2:28), which accords with Jesus' most recent recorded prayer (Mk 14:35-36), a prayer that also fits the criterion of embarrassment (though the likeliest potential witnesses are said to be dozing). "My God" implies continuing trust (Kingsbury, *Christology,* 130), and Jesus had to know that Psalm 22 went on to declare the psalmist's vindication (22:22-24; cf. e.g., Meier, *Matthew,* 349); given the practice of Jewish Scripture citations, Jesus may have even quoted more than the sample preserved (cf. Stauffer, *Jesus,* 140). Nevertheless, we would expect free invention to have emphasized the vindication, not the note of apparent despair.

300. Perhaps following an early Palestinian tradition that conformed Jesus' cry to the Targum.

301. Cf. e.g., evidence in Bar-Asher, "Formules." Nevertheless, this Hebraism had come over into Aramaic. Cf. also the use of "Eli" in Qumran's hymns.

302. *Eliyahu;* Jeremias, *Theology,* 5 n. 2; cf. Anderson, *Mark,* 346. Matthew's inference here could be correct (pace e.g., Cope, *Scribe,* 104).

303. Rabbinic tradition emphasizes that Elijah (who had never died in the OT — 2 Kgs 2:11) would periodically rescue sages in distress or aid them in their needs (cf. *b. A.Z.* 17b; *Taan.* 21a; *p. Ket.* 12:3, §6; *Pesiq. Rab Kah.* 18:5; *Gen. Rab.* 33:3; Dalman, *Jesus-Jeshua,* 205-6; cf. Bamberger, "Prophet," 308). Although rabbinic tradition is often later, its congruence with independent gospel tradition here likely suggests its antiquity in this case.

304. Pace Barrett, *John,* 551. Women relatives were typically allowed, for example, to visit a man in prison (e.g., Lysias *Or.* 13.39-40, §133).

305. See e.g., Liefeld, "Preacher," 239-40; Ilan, "Attraction." With very few exceptions, women could not be disciples in Jewish Palestine (Swidler, *Women,* 97-111; Keener, *Paul,* 83-84). Although there were apparently some exceptions in the Diaspora, rigorous training in Torah was apparently normally restricted to boys (Safrai, "Education," 955).

306. Witherington, *Women,* 117; Sanders, *Figure,* 109.

307. On crowds present, see e.g., Morris, *John,* 807.

308. E.g., Witherington, *Women,* 94, 187 n. 103.

309. See e.g., Jos. *Ant.* 4.320 (Israelite society); Hom. *Il.* 18.30-31, 50-51; 19.284-85; Soph. *Ajax* 580; Eurip. *M. Her.* 536; Thucyd. 2.34.4; Cic. *Ad Fam.* 5.16.6; Diod. Sic. 17.37.3; Dion. Hal. 7.67.2; 8.39.1; Livy 26.9.7; Valerius Maximus 2.6.13; Pomeroy, *Women,* 44; Dupont, *Life,* 115. Ancients did, however, expect both parents of a crucified person to mourn (*Sipre Deut.* 308.2.1).

310. Cf. e.g., Val. Max. 5.4.7 (cited in Rapske, *Custody,* 247); 9.2.1; Polyb. 5.56.15 (mob action); Jos. *Apion* 2.267 (on Athenian execution of women); Ovid *Metam.* 13.497 (among captives; cf. Polyb. 5.111.6, in a camp).

311. Lane, *Mark,* 576, citing *tos. Git.* 7:1; *p. Git.* 48c; Witherington, *Women,* 94, 187 n. 103; cf. also *Sipre Deut.* 308.2.1.

312. Crossan, "Tomb," 152.

313. Brown, *Death,* 1240; Davies and Allison, *Matthew,* 3:647.

314. Davies and Allison, *Matthew,* 3:647; contrast *Mart. Poly.* 17.2. Acts 13:29 can be construed as burial by his *enemies* among the rulers (13:27) who also sought his execution (13:28), but is summary language; Luke (who offers this summary) also knows of Joseph as righteous (Lk 23:50-53). On the reliability of Mark's burial story, including the account of Joseph of Arimathea, against Crossan, see also O'Collins and Kendall, "Joseph of Arimathea."

315. We would therefore question the view attributed to J. D. Crossan (by Ostling, "Jesus," as cited in Craig, "Rise?" 142), namely that Jesus' corpse was merely covered with a little dirt and probably eaten by wild dogs (being eaten by birds or dogs was the normal fate of the unburied, e.g., Hom. *Il.* 11.395; Aeschylus *Suppl. Maidens* 751-52, 801-2; other sources in Keener, *Matthew,* 582, 695). This view

seems unduly skeptical that Pilate would have accommodated Jewish burial practices, especially if he was not personally committed to affirming Jesus' guilt.

316. Petron. *Sat.* 112; Brown, *Death,* 962, 1208 cites also Phaedrus *Fables of Aesop* Perotti's Appendix 15.9; Hor. *Ep.* 1.16.48. Llewelyn, *New Documents* 8:1-3, §1, cites a slave left to hang so animals could eat him.

317. See further Jos. *War* 4.317; Safrai, "Home," 774.

318. *War* 4.317.

319. E.g., Gen 23:3-20; 50:12-14, 25-26; Sir 38:16-17; Tob 1:17-20; 2:7-10; 4:3-4; 6:14; 1QM 7.2; Acts 8:2; Jos. *Apion* 2.205, 211; *Test. Job* 39:10/7.

320. Soph. *Antig.* 43-48; Diod. Sic. 20.84.3; Plut. *Nicias* 6.5-6; Diog. Laert. 6.2.52; Paus. 1.32.5; Char. *Chaer.* 4.1.3; Philostratus *Hrk.* 33.33; cf. Plut. *Solon* 21.1. See further discussion of burials (with numerous other sources, both Jewish and Gentile), in Keener, *John,* 1157-59.

321. E.g., Hom. *Il.* 23.65-71; *Od.* 11.71-76; 21.363-64; 22.476; Eurip. *Ch. Her.* 588-90; *Hec.* 47-50; *Ph. M.* 1447-50; *Suppliants,* passim; Diod. Sic. 15.35.1; Philostratus *Hrk.* 19.7; it was necessary to enter the netherworld (Hom. *Il.* 23.71; Virg. *Aen.* 6.365-66; Heliod. *Ethiop.* 6.15).

322. Eccl 6:3; *Jub.* 23:23; Jos. *War* 5.514; *Sib. Or.* 3.643; *Eccl. Rab.* 3:2, §2.

323. If a Jewish court rather than a Roman one rendered the verdict (cf. Jos. *Ant.* 5.44; *b. Sanh.* 47b), Jewish people may have usually buried condemned criminals in a shameful common grave reserved for that purpose (cf. *m. Sanh.* 6:5; *tos. Sanh.* 9:8; Daube, *NT and Judaism,* 311; idem, "Gospels," 342), which some think likely here (cf. McCane, "Shame," 452). Jewish custom expected the gathering of the bones to the place of one's ancestors a year later (*m. Sanh.* 6:6), meaning that the bones were kept track of even in the "common" grave, not scattered (Brown, *Death,* 1209-11; cf. Stauffer, *Jesus,* 209). If one objects that the handing over custom is late, one might suppose the same for the regular use of common graves for the executed.

324. Jos. *Apion* 2.211; cf. Tannaim in Crane, "Burying."

325. Jos. *Ant.* 4.202, 264-65. Honorable burials were, however, important to most people (e.g., Corn. Nep. 10 [Dion], 10.3; Aul. Gel. 15.10.2).

326. The paucity of crucifixion victims in tomb excavations may suggest that the case was more difficult with mass executions (and that the numbers of individuals crucified were a tiny proportion of the population), but the skeleton from Givat ha-Mivtar shows that some were buried. A case where Jewish officials had any input would undoubtedly require burial, if the officials had any concern for demands of the written Torah.

327. Brown, *Death,* 1240.

328. Davies and Allison, *Matthew,* 3:648.

329. To bury Jesus in his own tomb fits the situation of haste and location, but also suggests a special love normally reserved for family members or those equally esteemed (cf. 1 Kgs 13:30-31). Further, archaeological evidence for the tombs in this area may suggest that the tomb belonged to a person of some material substance (Craig, "Rise?" 148; cf. Wahlde, "Archaeology," 581).

330. Safrai, "Home," 779-80; among Gentiles, e.g., Stambaugh, *City,* 197. At least one crucifixion victim shows that such bodies could be released to families or persons with means (Charlesworth, *Jesus Within Judaism,* 123; idem, "Jesus, Literature and Archaeology," 193), and the gospel story does make sense here.

331. Brown, *Death,* 1218.

332. Brown, *Death,* 1230.

333. Joseph may have sought the audience while Jesus was dying, but Mk 15:43-45 sounds as if Jesus expired before Joseph sought permission and Pilate confirmed the death.

334. *M. Shab.* 23:5. Washing the corpse was standard preburial practice in Mediterranean antiquity (e.g., Hom. *Il.* 18.345, 350; 24.582; Eurip. *Ph. M.* 1667; Virg. *Aen.* 6.219; 9.487; Ovid *Metam.* 13.531-32; Apul. *Metam.* 9.30; Acts 9:37), and anointing appears to be frequent as well (e.g., Hom. *Il.* 18.350-51; 24.582; Virg. *Aen.* 6.219; Mart. *Epig.* 3.12; *Test. Ab.* 20:11A); for ointments in embalming, e.g., Hdn.

4.2.8; Hagner, *Matthew,* 758 cites *P. Oxy.* 736.13; Artemidorus 1.5; Gen 50:2 LXX. For the practice in other cultures, see Mbiti, *Religions,* 329.

335. See Safrai, "Home," 776-77 for samples of these.

336. *M. Shab.* 23:5. The Sabbath interrupted various activities that could be resumed after its completion (e.g., 2 Macc 8:27-28).

337. For the use of spices at funerals, see Jos. *Ant.* 17.199; *War* 1.673; *m. Ber.* 8:6; Safrai, "Home," 776; Meyers and Strange, *Archaeology,* 97-98.

338. Cf. *m. Sanh.* 6:6; *m. Pes.* 8:8; *M.K.* 1:5; Meyers and Strange, *Archaeology,* 28. On ossuaries in this period, see e.g., Evans, *Ossuaries;* for a possible contrast between ossuaries and later Christian reliquaries, see McCane, "Bones."

339. Weeden, *Mark,* 104.

340. Craig, "Tomb," 184.

341. Some would regard as relevant here scientific debate surrounding the authenticity of the Shroud of Turin. On the one hand, the radiocarbon dating seems against it (Stanton, *Gospel Truth,* 119-20, noting the three independent Carbon 14 tests, each claiming 95% certainty); the colors are known from Medieval artists' pigments (cf. Thompson, *Debate,* 238-43, who surveys both sides); and the shroud is first confirmed at a time "when many dubious 'relics' were flooding the West" (Meier, "Reflections," 106; for arguments for the shroud's earlier history, see Long, "Edessa"; idem, "City"). One also wonders why Jesus' allies would have put coins of Pilate over his eyes (McRay, *Archaeology and NT,* 221). On the other, traces of Palestinian plant fibers and early-first-century Judean burial customs could suggest some elements of accurate portrayal (Borkan, "Authenticity," also noting scientific evaluations regarding the contamination of the radiocarbon sample). Whether or not authentic, the shroud's details apply specifically to Jesus (Habermas, *Evidence,* 156-59, 167; Stevenson and Habermas, *Verdict*). If the Shroud dates from 1260 to 1390 as the radiocarbon tests suggest, it suggests remarkable technology; but the historical case for Jesus being wrapped in a shroud in no wise depends on that shroud's authenticity.

342. Finegan, *Archeology,* 213. For information on wrapping in shrouds, see Safrai, "Home," 777.

343. *Test. Ab.* 20:10A; *Life of Adam* 48.1; *Apoc. Moses* 40.1-3; *b. Ber.* 18b; cf. white wrappings in *L.A.B.* 64:6; *Gen. Rab.* 96:5.

344. The rock-hewn tomb (Mk 15:46) and soil for a garden (Jn 19:41) both fit local topography (Wahlde, "Archaeology," 578-79).

345. Reicke, *Era,* 185.

346. Brown, *Death,* 1280-81.

347. Admittedly evidence for early veneration there is lacking, perhaps because the body was not there (Craig, "Rise?" 148-49, 152; cf. Wedderburn, *Resurrection,* 63-65, somewhat ambivalently).

348. Tomb architecture changed radically after Jerusalem's fall (Goodenough, *Symbols,* 1:84-89), and the skull shape of the Protestant tomb is later than the first century (Brown, *Death,* 938-39).

349. On the latter, see Brown, *John,* 2:899; idem, *Death,* 1279-83; Charlesworth, *Jesus Within Judaism,* 124; McRay, *Archaeology and NT,* 206-17; cf. Blinzler, *Trial,* 251-52; Smith, "Tomb"; Ross, "Church"; Riesner, "Golgotha." On the former, see Frantzman and Kark, "Gordon."

350. Finegan, *Archeology,* 164; see further discussion of the tradition in Skarsaune, *Shadow,* 183-86; cf. possibly Belayche, "Mont du Temple," though it probably reflects a minority opinion.

351. *4 Bar.* 7:13; Wilkinson, *Jerusalem,* 146. This custom was not specifically Palestinian Jewish, hence would also be assumed in the Diaspora (see e.g., Walbank, "Graves," 250; Stambaugh, *City,* 194).

352. Jos. *Ant.* 19.326-27. See e.g., Brown, *Death,* 1282; Charlesworth, *Jesus Within Judaism,* 123-24; Wahlde, "Archaeology," 579; cf. Blinzler, *Trial,* 251-52; for archaeological data, see also the notes in Cornfeld, *Josephus,* 338-40, on Jos. *War* 5.148-55.

353. See further Keener, *Matthew,* 694. John is the least clear of the Gospels on the tomb belonging to Joseph (Jn 19:41-42).

354. For Eusebius' report (believable in *most* of its details) that this was among the Judean holy

sites desecrated by Hadrian (for whom Jewish and Christian holy sites were probably indistinguishable), see Finegan, *Archeology,* 164.

355. Talbert, *John,* 246, cites Euseb. *Life of Constantine* 3.26; Bordeaux Pilgrim; Cyril of Alexandria *Catechetical Lectures* 13.39; 14.5, 22; 18.

Notes to Chapter 22

1. Brown, *Death,* xii.

2. E.g., Wright, *Resurrection;* for various approaches to the subject of Jesus' resurrection, see Davis, Kendall, and O'Collins, *Resurrection;* for alternative views on the *nature* of the resurrection, see the discussion in Wright and Crossan, "Resurrection"; cf. also the summary of views in Schutte, "Resurrection." I will not address spurious "scholarship" like Cameron's "documentary" of the "Jesus tomb"; for responses, see e.g., Freyne, "Tomb"; Hoppe, "Tomb"; Gieschen, "Tomb"; Rasimus, "Évaluation" (as fiction); Riesner, "Jesus-Grab"; López, *Family Tomb;* especially Meyers et al., "Tomb" (with mostly negative responses to the documentary except from James Tabor; see esp. Meyers' critique). Scholarly circles tending to be skeptical of information in the Gospels did not prove friendly to the film, either (Hoffmann, "Faccidents").

3. See Lindars, "Composition," 147. He believes that John utilized his material creatively (Lindars, *Behind,* 76). Dodd, *Tradition,* 148, contends that John's resurrection narratives represent discrete units of tradition woven by the Evangelist into a seamless whole.

4. Wenham, "Narratives"; Gundry, *Matthew,* 590-91.

5. The sudden ending in Mk 16:8 fits some ancient narration patterns; though in some cases, e.g., *L.A.B.,* the ending may be lost, one may also compare abrupt original endings, e.g., in some of Plutarch's works (*Fame of Athenians* 8, *Mor.* 351B; *Fort. Alex.* 2.13, *Mor.* 345B; *Fort. Rom.* 13, *Mor.* 326C; *Uned. R.* 7, *Mor.* 782F); Isoc. *Demon.* 52, *Or.* 1; Demetrius *On Style* 5.304; Lucan *C.W.* 10.542-46; Herodian 8.8.8. See especially Magness, *Sense,* for more ancient literary parallels; for consistency with Markan style, especially a final *gar,* cf. Boomershine and Bartholomew, "Technique." An abbreviated conclusion allows Mark to retain the centrality of the cross without actually playing down the resurrection (cf. also Thompson, *Debate,* 225), because he points to resurrection appearances beyond his narrative (e.g., Anderson, *Mark,* 353; Rhoads and Michie, *Mark,* 42; Hooker, *Message,* 120; cf. Mk 14:28; 16:7). Farmer, *Verses,* even makes a noteworthy case on external (pp. 3-75) and internal (pp. 79-103) grounds that Mk 16:9-20 has more support for being the original ending than often accepted, though few concur.

6. CD 9.21-22; 10:1.

7. See e.g., Jos. *Ant.* 4.219; *m. Yeb.* 15:1, 8-10; 16:7; *Ket.* 1:6-9; *tos. Yeb.* 14:10; *Sipra VDDeho.* pq. 7.45.1.1; cf. Lk 24:11; Keener, *Paul,* 162-63; Baumgarten, "Testimony of Women"; Hooker, *Message,* 119. Some, though not all, condemned listening to women more generally (e.g., Jos. *Ant.* 18.255; *Sent. Syri ac Menander* 118-21, 336-39). Nevertheless, Maccini, *Testimony,* 63-97 rightly notes the responses are more diverse than in legal contexts. Ilan, *Women,* 227 thinks that in practice the non-Pharisaic legal system "often" required women's witness; even if this is overstated, women could testify concerning various matters, and some views of 1QSa 1.10-11 suggest that Qumran was more open to the practice than Pharisees were (Ilan, *Women,* 163-66). Although Josephus tends to downplay women's roles in the biblical narrative, he highlights some like Abigail (Begg, "Abigail").

8. Hesiod *WD* 375; Livy 6.34.6-7; Babrius 16.10; Phaedrus 4.15; Avianus *Fables* 15-16; Justin. *Inst.* 2.10.6 (though contrast the earlier Gaius *Inst.* 2.105); Plut. *Publicola* 8.4; Gardner, *Women,* 165; Kee, *Origins,* 89. Many men regarded women as gullible (cf. Philo *Prob.* 117; Juv. *Sat.* 1.38-39).

9. Vermes, *Jesus the Jew,* 40-41; cf. *L.A.B.* 9:10. Our earliest version of Mark lacks a narrative that would address this point, so Luke's could be the earliest we have (as we have noted, there were probably multiple reports of the resurrection appearances in any case).

10. Cf. Stauffer, *Jesus,* 151; Dunn, *Jesus and Spirit,* 126. Dunn also notes the tradition that stresses

Peter first (1 Cor 15:5; cf. Lk 24:34; Dunn, *Jesus and Spirit*, 126), which Farmer and Kereszty, *Peter and Paul*, 46, regard as a pro-Petrine tradition. It probably simply reflects omission of the women.

11. See e.g., Byrskog, *Story as History*, 192-94; Wedderburn, *Resurrection*, 57-61.

12. E.g., Hodges, "Tomb." C. L. Blomberg notes here Wenham, *Enigma*; Harris, *Raised*, 69-71; Ladd, *Resurrection*, 91-93.

13. E.g., Dibelius, *Jesus*, 139.

14. Eddy and Boyd, *Legend*, 424 (following Bogart and Montell, *Memory*, 77), compare conflicting reports of the 1881 lynching of the McDonald brothers, one reporting the young men hanging "from a railroad crossing" and the other from a pine tree. Amazingly, later discovered photos confirmed both accounts as true — apparently the victims were moved to a more public venue after their murder. Cf. Bruggen, *Narratives*, 91.

15. See Eddy and Boyd, *Legend*, 423-24.

16. Some ancient historians and biographers already recognized the value of this principle when dealing with sources conflicting on details (cf. e.g., Plut. *Alex.* 38.4).

17. Sanders, *Figure*, 280.

18. See e.g., Thucyd. 1.22.3.

19. With, e.g., Boyd, *Sage*, 277-78.

20. One might compare the different accounts of Callisthenes' death from eyewitnesses, which nevertheless agree that he was indicted, publicly scorned, and died (Arrian *Alex.* 4.14.3, writing centuries after the event).

21. Luke 24 is long, though recapitulated briefly in Acts 1; Mk 16:1-8 and Matthew 28 are quite brief; John includes both Judean and Galilean appearances.

22. Diog. Laert. 6.2.38. Josephus seems once caught unexpectedly by the end of his scroll (Jos. *Apion* 1.320); Matthew, approaching the length limit of his standardized scroll, may hasten to his conclusion; Luke may have sufficient space remaining to provide further detail before his closing. John's "second" conclusion (ch. 21) fits the Gospel if John employed a scroll of standardized length, but by early in chapter 20 it would be clear to either the Fourth Gospel's author or a later disciple how much space would remain at chapter 20's completion.

23. For what it is worth, also *Gospel of Peter* 12:50–13:57. Ancient sources more often than not left women unnamed (see Ilan, "Distribution"), but Mary is abundantly documented in the resurrection traditions (Mk 16:1; Matt 28:1; Lk 24:10).

24. Price, "Easters," finds parallels in pagan narratives; I will address such comparative literature for signs in my subsequent book on miracles.

25. Mack, *Lost Gospel*, p. 2.

26. The attachment of geographical attributions to specific traditions is likewise speculative (cf. Theissen, *Gospels in Context*, 16).

27. Smith, "Appearance," divides the evidence for Jesus' resurrection, noting that some texts depict his vindication as appearance and others as exaltation. Playing these elements off against each other as contradictory, though, is fallacious logic (especially since they often occur together in the same documents; 1 Cor 15:5-8, 20, 25; Phil 2:9; 3:10; Lk 24; Acts 1:3-11; Mk 16:14, 19; probably Jn 20:17, addressed in Keener, *John*, 1193-95).

28. Witherington, *Sage*, 139, likewise critiques Mack's (*Myth*, 73) dismissal of Jewish elements in the Jesus tradition (corban, levirate marriage, sabbath, fasting, eschatology, etc.), which underlies Mack's doubt that Jesus engaged Jewish institutions. The idea that the Jewish elements of the tradition are later accretions is precisely counter to any natural reading of the evidence.

29. See Aune, "Problem," 48.

30. See Boring et al., *Commentary*, 151; Philost. *V.A.* 7.14.

31. E.g., Apul. *Metam.* 8.8; 9.31; *ARN* 40A. One supposed divine apparition turned out to be a conjured ghost of a gladiator (one of low class; Eunapius *Lives* 473). Likewise, although the biblical tradition reported only apparitions of angels in dreams, both pagan (e.g., Hom. *Il.* 23.65, 83-85; Eurip.

Hec. 30-34, 703-6; Virg. *Aen.* 1.353-54; 2.268-97, 772-94; 4.351-52; 5.721-23; Ovid *Metam.* 11.586-88, 635, 650-73; Apul. *Metam.* 8.8; 9.31; Plut. *Bravery of Women, Mor.* 252F) and Jewish (*ARN* 40A; *Pesiq. Rab. Kah.* 11:23; *p. Hag.* 2:2, §5; *Ket.* 12:3, §7; *Sanh.* 6:6, §2; cf. *Acts of Paul* 11.6) dreams often included apparitions of deceased persons.

32. E.g., Plutarch's reports of Romulus more than half a millennium earlier (in Talbert, *Gospel*, 41; cf. Plut. *Camillus* 33.7). Boring et al., *Commentary*, 163-64 cites Romulus' apotheosis appearance to Proculus Julius in Livy 1.16.2-8; Plut. *Romulus* 28; *Numa* 11.3; Ovid *Fasti* 2.500-9, and notes that Justin *1 Apol.* 21 made an apologetic comparison between Jesus' resurrection appearances and pagan understanding of imperial apotheosis.

33. Philost. *V.A.* 8.31; Sanders, *Jesus and Judaism,* 320.

34. Blackburn, "ΑΝΔΡΕΣ," 193.

35. Philost. *Hrk.* 58.2.

36. Philost. *Hrk.* 9.1. He visits both Hades and the world of the living (11.7), but visits his wife only in Hades (11.8). Others also returned from Hades without immortality (e.g., in the much later Antonius Diogenes *Thule* 109ab) or lived during the night while remaining corpses during the day (*Thule* 110b).

37. See Bowersock, *Fiction as History,* 108-13; even his mid-first-century parallel does not indicate a bodily resurrection (it may simply mean "a brief tryst with his wife," 112, as in earlier sources; see Petronius *Sat.* 129.1).

38. Lucan *C.W.* 6.667-775; cf. Antonius Diogenes *Thule* 110b. Resuscitation stories are common but most simply claim *apparent* deaths (Bowersock, *Fiction as History,* 99-100, 104-8; more convincing are OT parallels), which often invite suspense on behalf of characters with whom readers have begun to identify; see e.g., Xenophon *Eph.* 3.5-7; *Apoll. K. Tyre* 25-26; Iamblichus *Bab. St.* 3-6 (Photius *Bibliotheca* 94.74b-75a); earlier, Menander *Aspis* 343-87.

39. Bowersock, *Fiction as History,* 117-18; cf. discussion of apparent deaths in novels in Perkins, *"Scheintod"* (who connects it with Christian resurrection).

40. Avi-Yonah, "Sources," 60; Flusser, "Paganism."

41. The influence of a third-century CE Mithraeum in Caesarea (on the Mithraeum see Bull, "Medallion"; Lease, "Mithraeum"; Flusser, "Paganism," 1099) is unclear, since Caesarea was of mixed population and the date is much later than our period (cf. Charlesworth, *Pseudepigrapha and NT,* 82).

42. Cf. arguments in Philonenko, "Initiation"; idem, "Mystère," 65-70; Petuchowski, "Mystery."

43. Willoughby, *Initiation,* 225-62 tries to compare Philonic language with the conversion language of the Mysteries, but like Godwin, *Religions,* 78-83, tends to generalize too much. More nuanced is the approach of Wolfson, *Philo,* 1:27-36 (and cf. 1:101; Philo adapts their language but denounces them as religious alternatives).

44. Russell, "Mysteries," 338; cf. Reitzenstein, *Religions,* 174-84.

45. Reitzenstein, *Religions,* 175

46. On Roman Judaism, see more fully Leon, *Jews of Rome;* Donfried and Richardson, *Judaism.*

47. *Apol.* 47.14.

48. Eliade, *Rites,* 120.

49. Benoit, "Mystères," 79-81.

50. Metzger, "Considerations," 10-11; Eliade, *Rites,* 115. The proposed similarities between Mithraism and Christianity (cf. Gervers, "Iconography," though qualifying on p. 598; cf. Gager, *Kingdom,* 132-34; note the contrast stressed by Mattingly, *Christianity,* 5) also come from the later period in which both had become popular. Deman, "Mithras," for instance, notes the later link between the twelve apostles and the twelve signs of the zodiac; but the twelve apostles in earliest Christian tradition stem from the twelve tribes (though Judaism had already linked the tribes with the zodiac in that period). The closest true parallels address only later Gentile Christianity, as it assimilated into a broader Roman cultural context. The alleged "suffering" of Mithras is speculative (so Klauck, *Religious Context,* 141-42).

51. Metzger, "Considerations," 11.

52. Metzger, "Considerations," 20.

53. Manson, *Sayings,* 64-65 stresses the moral contrast between the Mysteries (where moral ideals were irrelevant) and Christianity (cf. Carcopino, *Life,* 138-39). For many differences, see also Calderón, "Cultos de misterios."

54. Metzger, "Considerations," 15.

55. Cf. Nock, "Vocabulary," 136, for Christianity's "Oriental" nature but lack of "Oriental" trappings. This is not to suggest that many other Greco-Roman cults could not be distinguished from one another, but rather to point out that the originating cultural matrix of Christianity was different enough, and earliest Christianity's monotheism rigorous enough, to disallow the degree of assimilation that could characterize most of the cults.

56. Cf. Nock, *Gentile Christianity,* 31; Cadbury, *Acts in History,* 28; Meyer, "Mysteries," 724.

57. Just as fertility fled the earth during Demeter's search for Persephone in the Eleusinian myth (with roots perhaps even as early as Neolithic times, in Burkert, *Religion,* 160), so it flees during the absence of the Hittite deity Telepinus (*ANET* 126-28), the Canaanite Baal (*ANET* 129-42; Bright, *History,* 118; Albright, *Yahweh,* 125-27), and perhaps the man Aqhat (*ANET* 149-55; esp. Ginsberg's note on p. 155). The same theme appears in the late second millennium BCE story of Ishtar's descent to the netherworld (*ANET* 108 lines 76ff; cf. reverse 34ff). It seems likely that a much older story line or lines stand behind all the regional variations. Some have even claimed that Marduk died and rose again in some sense (Klausner, *Paul,* 103), but I have not found this in *Enuma Elish* (in Heidel, *Genesis,* 18-60).

58. In the epic of Gilgamesh (*Gilg.* 6.97-99; *ANET* 84), Ishtar forces Anu to comply with her demands by threatening to smash the doors of the netherworld and to raise up the dead so that they outnumber the living, and similarly addresses the gatekeeper of that world in the tale of her descent there (*ANET* 107, *Descent* lines 12ff). In a tale perhaps dating to the first half of the second millennium BCE or earlier, Inanna is put to death (though she is a goddess), but after three days and nights she is restored, as the food and water of life are sprinkled sixty times on her corpse (*ANET* 52-57, especially 55).

59. E.g., Maximus of Tyre *Or.* 2.5; cf. also Plutarch *Isis,* passim.

60. For divergent traditions and their antiquity, see Wagner, *Baptism,* 115-20. Cf. his rescue in "The Theology of Memphis" (tr. J. A. Wilson), 4-6 in *ANET,* 5; his apotheosis to immortality among other gods (Diod. Sic. 1.20-22); his return to life in Plut. *Isis* 35, *Mor.* 364F. Osiris is euhemerized in Manetho *Aeg.* frg. 1.1. Serapis assumes some such functions, though not for the masses (Dunand, *Religion Populaire,* 89-92).

61. Wagner, *Baptism,* 119; on Nile water, see pp. 127-35. The patching together of his parts either reflected or produced a more widespread story line (e.g., Ovid *Metam.* 6.401-11); Greeks also told of severed divine genitals creating life (Uranus' form the Furies, Apollod. *Bib.* 1.1.4). Some Greeks treated Osiris and Isis as genuine historical characters (Manetho *Aegyptiaca fr.* 1.1, in Armenian Euseb. *Chronica* 1.p. 93).

62. E.g., Plut. *Nicias* 13.7.

63. Wagner, *Baptism,* 171-207, especially p. 195; cf. Klauck, *Religious Context,* 120-28 (esp. 121-22). The Adonis tradition itself was Semitic and imported into Greek religion from an early period (Burkert, *Religion,* 176-77 thinks perhaps as early as the sixth century BCE). Cf. Ovid *Metam.* 10.710-39; Callim. *Iambi* 3.193.37; Philostratus *Hrk.* 45.6; in the Greek bucolic poets, e.g., *Women at the Adonis Festival* (third century BCE), a lament for Adonis perhaps by Bion, and *The Dead Adonis* (*Greek Bucolic Poets* LCL pp. 176-95, 386-95, 480-83). Cf. Daphnis (Müller, "Daphnis"); earlier mourning for Tammuz in *Gilgamesh* 6.46ff ("The Gilgamesh Epic," tr. E. A. Speiser, 72-99 in *ANET* 72-99).

64. Apollod. *Bib.* 3.14.4, where Persephone and Aphrodite originally had a time-share agreement about Adonis (probably derived from the Persephone myth about the custody battle between Hades and Demeter, e.g., Apollod. *Bib.* 1.5.3); cf. Iamblichus *Myst.* 1.11.

65. E.g., Lucian *Dialogues of Gods* 233-34 (20/12, *Aphrodite and Eros* 1); *Gout* 30-32; *Syrian God-*

dess 6, 15; Ps.-Lucian *Affairs of the Heart* 42. Nevertheless, Attis appears as a deified mortal in Lucian *Parliament of Gods* 9.

66. Wagner, *Baptism,* 219, 229; for the typical story, see Vermaseren, *Cybele,* 91; for the antiquity of the cult more generally, see Bremmer, "Attis."

67. Cf. Otto, *Dionysus,* 79-80, 103-19.

68. E.g., Hom. *Il.* 5.339-42, 382-404, 855-59, 870; on the death of Pan in Plut. *Mor.* 419.17, see Borgeaud, "Death."

69. Fragments of dithyrambic poetry (c. 1 BCE) in *SP* 3:390-93.

70. E.g., Apollod. *Bib.* 1.5.3; cf. Guthrie, *Orpheus,* 31. On Persephone further, see Zuntz, *Persephone* (with archaeological data); Stroud, *Demeter;* less helpfully (from a more speculative, psychoanalytic perspective), Downing, *Goddess,* 30-50.

71. See documentation in Gasparro, *Soteriology,* 30 n. 16. On the imagination of early comparative religionists, see Lessa and Vogt, *Reader,* 7.

72. E.g., Conzelmann, *Theology,* 11; cf. Case, *Origins,* 111; Bultmann, *Christianity,* 158-59; Ridderbos, *Paul,* 22-29.

73. Burkert, *Cults,* 100: "This multiplicity of images can hardly be reduced to a one-dimensional hypothesis, one ritual with one dogmatic meaning: death and rebirth of 'the' god and the initiand." Casadio, "Emasculation," however, thinks that the category remains valuable.

74. E.g., Apuleius, whom Dunand, "Mystères," 58 interprets thus.

75. E.g., Firmicus Maternus *De Errore Profanarum Religionum* 22 (in Grant, *Religions,* 146).

76. E.g., Davies, *Paul,* 91; for caution about dying-and-rising deities, see further Donfried, *Thessalonica,* 41 (following MacMullen, *Paganism,* 55); Nock, *Gentile Christianity,* 29; Klauck, *Religious Context,* 151-52; Mettinger, "Rising."

77. Wagner, *Baptism,* 87. Thus Heracles sought initiation so he could capture Cerberus in Hades (Apollod. *Bib.* 2.5.12).

78. Gasparro, *Soteriology,* 82.

79. *Kyrios Christos,* 57.

80. For the vegetative association see e.g., Ovid *Metam.* 5.564-71; Gasparro, *Soteriology,* 29, 43-49; Ruck, "Mystery," 44-45; Guthrie, *Orpheus,* 55-56.

81. Cf. Metzger, "Considerations," 19-20; Ring, "Resurrection," 228.

82. Some Greeks may have also thought of "three days" in terms of some burial traditions (cf. Thucyd. 2.34.2, for honoring Athenian war dead).

83. Bousset's Hellenistic parallels (*Kyrios Christos,* 58) have been deemed unconvincing (cf. Nock, *Gentile Christianity,* 105-6; Jeremias, *Theology,* 304; Fuller, *Formation,* 25). Many think that the LXX is a more likely source (Hos 6:2; Jon 1:17; cf. 1 Cor 15:4; Nock, *Gentile Christianity,* 108), though it is unlikely that the early Christians would have noticed elements favoring it had the "third day" not been their initial experience. (Later rabbis associated Hos 6:2 with the resurrection of the dead; see *p. Sanh.* 11:6, §1; cf. McArthur, "Day," 83-84.)

84. Some later traditions suggest the retention of the soul for three days after death (until the soul sees the body begin to decompose; *Gen. Rab.* 100:7; *Lev. Rab.* 18:1; though cf. Dola, "Interpretacja") or require three days of purgatory before preparation to appear before God (*3 En.* 28:10; cf. *Apoc. Zeph.* 4:7) or that one should confirm the actuality of the person's death within three days (Safrai, "Home," 784-85). This might possibly fit a broader idea expressed in three days of mourning (Ap. Rhod. 2.837).

85. Metzger, "Considerations," 18-19.

86. E.g., Ignatius *Trall.* 9; Augustine *On the Trinity* 4.6, 10 (ACCS, 238). The third day can mean "after three days," as in *L.A.B.* 11:1-3; or *parts* of each of three days (Scott, *Customs,* 260; *p. Kil.* 2:2, §1, on *tos. Kil.* 1:16); in either case it means "soon" (Gen 40:12-13, 18-19; Ex 3:18).

87. For the concrete connection with a new creation, see e.g., Moltmann, "Resurrection"; Wright, "Resurrection."

88. *ARN* 40A; *Pesiq. Rab. Kah.* 11:23; *p. Hag.* 2:2, §5; *Ket.* 12:3, §7; *Sanh.* 6:6, §2; *Eccl. Rab.* 9:10, §1; cf. *Acts Paul* 11.6; among Gentiles, see Hom. *Il.* 23.65, 83-85; Eurip. *Hec.* 30-34, 703-6; Virg. *Aen.* 1.353-54; 2.268-97, 772-94; 4.351-52; 5.721-23; Ovid *Metam.* 11.586-88, 635, 650-73; Plut. *Sulla* 37.2; *Br. Wom., Mor.* 252F; Apul. *Metam.* 8.8; 9.31; cf. Hom. *Od.* 4.795-839; 19.546-49; Appian *Hist. rom.* 8.1.1; Arrian *Alex.* 7.30.2.

89. Mack makes Jesus' resurrection purely mythical (Mack, *Myth*, 112-13) by wrongly equating immortality in the Wisdom of Solomon with resurrection in 2 Maccabees, wrongly interpreting eschatological *narratives* about Christ's resurrection as if they were eschatological allegory, and wrongly taking the Spirit in a purely hellenistic sense instead of its Jewish usage easily demonstrable in early Christianity (on this last point, see e.g., Keener, *Spirit*, 6-48; Turner, *Spirit*, 1-18).

90. Some utterly unrelated cultures also supply examples of resurrection legends (e.g., the Sonjo myth in Mbiti, *Religions*, 251), although without the historical attestation surrounding the case of Jesus. But *given the transcultural interest in life after death,* one need not suppose an organic connection among all such accounts except when they are geographically close and the story line is substantially similar.

91. E.g., Hdt. *Hist.* 2.123; Plato *Phaedo* 64CD; 80DE; *Phaedrus* 245C; *Laws* 8.828D; *Rep.* 10.611BC; Aristotle *Soul* 1.4, 408b; Diog. Laert. 8.5.83; see further sources in e.g., Keener, *John*, 553-54.

92. Burkert, *Cults*, 21; Grant, *Hellenism*, 11-12; Mylonas, *Eleusis*, 268-69; Wagner, *Baptism*, 87.

93. Wagner, *Baptism*, 112.

94. Burkert, *Religion*, 293-95; idem, *Cults*, 21-22.

95. Gasparro, *Soteriology*, 84-106, 125; Wagner, *Baptism*, 255-56.

96. The idea of astral immortality (Cumont, *After Life*, 91-109; cf. Reitzenstein, *Religions*, 64-65; Avi-Yonah, *Hellenism*, 40-41) is much broader than the Mysteries and thus should not be directly linked to them (Gasparro, *Soteriology*, 98). The doctrine of bodily resurrection might appear in the Hebrew Bible earlier than it is attested in Persian texts (Yamauchi, *Persia*, 456-57, 461; cf. 409; for immortality, however, cf. Olmstead, *History*, 40, 100-1). Some, however, do date Persian apocalyptic ideas earlier (see e.g., Rennie, "Zoroastrianism").

97. Cf. Lewis, *Life*, 100.

98. See Ferguson, *Backgrounds*, 439. Some add Ezek 37; some (see e.g., Bronner, "Resurrection Motif") find even broader antecedents. Others argue that before Dan 12, most biblical images of return to life were simply metaphors (so Léon-Dufour, *Resurrection*, 19), though one might ask how we would know that. On Is 26, see e.g., Raharimanantsoa, *Espérance*, 408-26; for Dan 12:2, see 426-47; for national resurrection (as in Hos 6:1-3; Ezek 37:1-14), 363-408 (on Ezekiel, 378-408). For one survey of early and late evidence, arguing for a decisive shift with 2 Macc 7, see Bauer, "Tod."

99. Cf. Wifall, "Status."

100. Jos. *Ant.* 18.16-17; *War* 2.165. Osborne, "Resurrection," 932, cites also some hellenistic works (4 Macc; Wisd 2:23-24; 3:1-4; Philo *Creation* 135; *Gig.* 14; perhaps also *1 En.* 103:4); and, as denying even immortality, Sirach (17:27-28; 30:17; 37:26; 39:9; 44:8-15; 46:19).

101. Rabbinic texts often emphasize that the Sadducees, unlike Pharisees, denied the teaching, hence held no place in the coming world (e.g., *m. Sanh.* 10:1; *ARN* 5A; 10, §26B; cf. *b. Sanh.* 90b). The doctrine of the resurrection was particularly relevant in the context of martyrdom (2 Macc 7:9, 11; 14:46); those inclined to defend the honor of martyrs hence took serious offense at the denial (rabbinic texts also suggest moral consequences for denying resurrection and judgment, which they viewed together).

102. See Puech, *Croyance*; idem, "Messianisme"; idem, "Resurrection Faith," 643-58, esp. 646-58; Charlesworth, "Resurrection," 145-53; Sanders, *Judaism*, 370; cf. Ulrichsen, "Troen." The supposed resurrection of the Teacher of Righteousness is based on inference from a reconstructed text (cf. 4QpPs 37 frg. 2.2-4 in Dupont-Sommer, *Writings*, 272), which most other scholars have reconstructed quite differently.

103. See especially fragments in 4Q521; also "Pseudo-Ezekiel" (4Q385-386) in Dimant, "Resur-

rection"; Hogeterp, "Resurrection." Some contrary claims (e.g., "Essenism and Christianity," Lightfoot, *Colossians,* 397-419, offering various contrasts with the Essenes) predate the discovery of the Scrolls (depending on e.g., Jos. *Ant.* 18.18).

104. E.g., Stemberger, "Auferstehungslehre"; in the Targums, see e.g., *Tg.* on Hos 14:8; McNamara, *Targum,* 136.

105. This is true though Josephus, adapting his depiction of Jewish "sects" to Greek schools like Pythagoreans and Middle Platonists, depicts the Pharisaic confidence in more acceptable hellenistic terms suggesting reincarnation (Jos. *Ant.* 18.14; *War* 2.163; 3.374; *Apion* 2.218). Cf. Luke's portrayal of Paul in Acts 23:6; 24:15.

106. They condemned a few others for its denial besides explicit Sadducees, e.g., *p. Sanh.* 10:2, §11. Other texts regularly defend the resurrection long after the Sadducees themselves had ceased to be an issue (e.g., *Lev. Rab.* 27:4; *Lam. Rab.* 3:23, §8), but that the rabbis would engage in "textbook apologetics" (not uncommon in some more traditional religious circles today) would not be surprising, given the variety of hypothetical legal situations they also surveyed.

107. E.g., *Ps. Sol.* 3:12; 15:12-13; *1 En.* 22:13; 61:5; 2 Macc 7:9, 14, 23, 29; *2 Bar.* 30:1; 51:1-6; *L.A.B.* 3:10; 25:6-7; *Test. Ab.* 7:16B; cf. *Test. Jud.* 25:1-4; *Zeb.* 10:2; *Apoc. Ezek.* introduction; though contrast *Jub.* 23:31. See more fully Osborne, "Resurrection," 933 (who adds to those above *1 En.* 46:6; 51:1-2; *Ps. Sol.* 13:9-11; 14:4-10; *4 Ezra* 4:41-43; 7:32-38; *2 Bar.* 49:2–51:12; 85:13). Compare also the graffito in Greek at Beth She'arim: "Good fortune in your resurrection" (Finegan, *Archeology,* 208). The Second Benediction of the Amida, affirming the resurrection, is likely early and was undoubtedly recited beyond Pharisaic circles (cf. Charlesworth, "Resurrection," 154-55).

108. Some have suggested that even the use of ossuaries for secondary burial in the first century might support the widespread character of belief in the bodily resurrection (Rahmani, "Glwsqmwt"; cf. Goodenough, *Symbols,* 1:164-77), but this premise is open to question (Fine, "Burial"; Regev, "Ossuaries"), especially given the Sadducean ossuaries (cf. e.g., Evans, "Caiaphas Ossuary"; Horbury, "Ossuaries"). Levine, *Hellenism,* 65-67, argues that ossuaries are irrelevant to belief in the resurrection (they could adapt the Roman custom of secondary burial of cremated ashes). Ossuaries belong especially to the Roman Imperial period and the pre-Israelite Chalcolithic period (see Silberman, "Ossuary").

109. Sanders, *Jesus and Judaism,* 237; cf. Wright, *People of God,* 320-34; Schuller, "Resurrection."

110. Some evidence exists in contemporary Egyptian Judaism, but Philo himself never mentions the doctrine (Wolfson, *Philo,* 1:404). In Palestine, the Samaritans may well have accepted it, though our evidence here is late (see MacDonald, *Samaritans,* 376). For Rome c. 100 CE, Boring et al., *Commentary,* 289, cites *CIJ* 1.348-50. The belief may have flourished in the Persian diaspora, given the compatibility of some Persian conceptions (although their date remains debatable).

111. Ps.-Phoc. 102-5.

112. See Garte, "Resurrection."

113. Collins, "Apotheosis," 97.

114. One cannot, however, cite the widespread use of crosses on early ossuaries, which probably are simply markings for the placement of the lids (Smith, "Cross Marks").

115. Cf. e.g., in Iren. *Haer.* 2.29; Wright, *Resurrection,* 534-51. Pagels, "Mystery," finds gnostics who affirmed resurrection in some sense; cf. the Nag Hammadi *Treatise on Resurrection* 1.4 for resurrection in "spiritual flesh" (what is superior to flesh). But cf. *Gospel of Philip* 2.56.25-57.23 (*Nag Hammadi Library,* 134).

116. See Rivkin, "Meaning," 398.

117. See the review in Kennedy, "Resurrection."

118. Ladd, *Theology,* 320. Cranfield, "Resurrection," 389-90, argues that alternative proposed explanations (deception or mistake) are weak.

119. Cf. Dibelius, *Tradition,* 191, though he admits that on Jewish presuppositions a resurrection

meant "that the body of Jesus had not remained in the grave," hence does not claim that Paul did not *believe* the tomb was empty.

120. Weeden, *Mark*, 102.

121. Boyd, *Sage*, 275.

122. By *itself*, the empty tomb would prove nothing except that Jesus' body was missing; once combined with resurrection appearances, however, it sent a different message to Jesus' followers that the expected eschatological event had begun (cf. Wright, *Resurrection*, 688).

123. Jos. *Life* 420-21. Cf. death a month after a beating, due to swelled intestines (Philost. *Lives* 2.10.588). Apul. *Metam.* 10.11 cites a drug to simulate death (cf. also Diog. Laert. 8.2.61), but his book is full of magic herbs that can do almost anything, here accommodating the story line (cf. the similar plot device in Ach. Tat. 3.15-21; 5.18.2; 7.6.2).

124. Char. *Chaer.* 1.4.11-12; 1.8.

125. Schweizer, *Jesus*, 48. For a fuller defense of the empty tomb traditions, see Craig, "Tomb"; idem, "Historicity"; idem, "Rise?" 146-52; idem, *Assessing*, passim, especially 351-78; Ladd, "Resurrection"; on the bodily character of the resurrection, see Craig, "Resurrection," 47-74.

126. See Boring et al., *Commentary*, 162-63; Robbins, *Teacher*, 192. Celsus compared the empty tomb with Cretan myths of Zeus' tomb (Cook, *Interpretation*, 54), but it in contrast to that myth Jews insisted on burial, the earliest tradition attests to Jesus' burial (1 Cor 15:4), and such recent historical claims are not comparable to local myth traditions about the distant past.

127. Vermes, *Jesus the Jew*, 41. For the evidence all pointing to the tomb being empty, see also Perkins, "Resurrection," 442.

128. Grant, *Jesus*, 176; cited in Habermas, *Evidence*, 114. Wedderburn, *Resurrection*, 21, notes that to exclude Jesus' resurrection from historical analysis gives "the impression of an unwarranted special pleading" (having noted Lüdemann's critiques against Barth on 16-17).

129. Which many scholars think were common enough to warrant the fear (Kysar, *John*, 296; Beasley-Murray, *John*, 371); cf. Iamblichus *Bab. St.* 7 (Photius *Bibliotheca* 94.75a). Many tomb inscriptions threatened curses on tomb violators (Jeffers, *World*, 45); Cyrus' tomb reportedly bore the warning not to rob it, for it held little wealth (Plut. *Alex.* 69.2).

130. An edict against stealing corpses found in Nazareth might not be from Nazareth (Giovannini and Hirt, "L'inscription," arguing also that it stems from the Augustan period). Given the small size of Nazareth, however, if it were to hail from Nazareth, it would probably be a response to Christian proclamation (cf. Wright, *Resurrection*, 708-9).

131. Char. *Chaer.* 3.3 (which also emphasizes the tragedy of a missing corpse); cf. also Xenophon *Eph.* 3.8-9; perhaps *Apoll. K. Tyre* 32 (though cf. 44).

132. Lewis, *Life*, 96. Some would have considered these practices simply folk cures (see e.g., Pliny *N.H.* 28.2.4-7; Pliny himself [28.2.8] rejects these approaches).

133. E.g., Ap. Rhod. 4.51-53; Lucan *C.W.* 6.538-68, 626; Ovid *Her.* 6.90; see especially the tale of Telephron in Apul. *Metam.* 2.30; in other cultures, e.g., Mbiti, *Religions*, 261.

134. *PGM* 1.248-49; 2.49-50; 4.342-43, 1390-95, 1402-3, 2211-17; 57.5-6; 58.5-9; 67.21; 101.1-3; these ghosts were more malevolent (Plut. *Cimon* 1.6; 6.5-6). If Jesus' enemies considered him a magician (Mk 3:22), some Jewish leaders may have even anticipated the theft of the body as in Matt 27:64. In less severe cases, tombs generally settled for divine threats against robbers (e.g., *IG* 3.1417 in Grant, *Religions*, 9). Both tying rope from a cross (Pliny *N.H.* 28.11.46) and iron pounded through the hands (Lucan *C.W.* 6.547) were used in witchcraft (as a superstitious cure in *m. Shab.* 6:10; *p. Shab.* 6:9, §2).

135. Rightly pointed out to me by William Lane Craig in personal correspondence (Aug. 16, 2007), challenging and correcting my earlier citation of pagan parallels for stealing corpses for witchcraft (Keener, *Matthew*, 699 n. 284; idem, *John*, 1181, citing e.g., Ap. Rhod. 4.51-53; Lucan *C.W.* 6.538-68, 626; Ovid *Her.* 6.90; Apul. *Metam.* 2.30).

136. Stauffer, *Jesus*, 144-45, who suspects the question also stands behind Jn 20:15 (where it is not clear), points out that the theory continued to circulate in later times (Just. *Dial.* 108; Tert. *Spec.* 30).

137. Grave-robbing was not only impious (e.g., Plut. *Mor.* 173B), but a capital offense (e.g., *SEG* 8.13 in Sherk, *Empire*, 52, §27). For the sanctity of tombs, see e.g., Plut. *Themist.* 9.4; cf. Jos. *War* 4.531-32; *Apion* 2.58.

138. Vermes, *Jesus the Jew*, 40. On Matthew's guards, see Keener, *Matthew*, 696-97, 713-15.

139. Their failure to produce it is an important argument (noted in Wedderburn, *Resurrection*, 61-63, albeit ambivalently). It would need to be fairly soon to be fully recognizable, however.

140. Sanders, *Figure*, 280.

141. Dio Cass. 58.4.5-6; 63.11.2-12.1. Josephus cites Jews' willingness to die for the law (*Apion* 1.42-43).

142. Sanders, *Figure*, 279-80. Some have contrasted the later apostasy (though not necessarily recantation) of some of the original witnesses to Joseph Smith's golden plates.

143. Sanders, *Figure*, 280.

144. Mack, *Myth*, 308; earlier, cf. cross-cultural, "ecstatic visionary experiences" in Perrin, *Bultmann*, 47. Likewise, against the unanimous witness of extant evidence, from earliest to latest, he supposes that the resurrection was a late myth originated by Christians not in Jewish Palestine but in northern Syria and Asia (*Lost Gospel*, 2). Evidence for early tradition for the site of the tomb (noted in our previous chapter), the largely Palestinian evidence for Jewish belief in the resurrection, the extreme unlikelihood of a Diaspora movement becoming more Palestinian or Judaized in the anti-Judaism of parts of the Greek East, and so forth render his suggestion incredible.

145. See e.g., Dibelius, *Tradition*, 18-20; Gerhardsson, *Memory*, 299-300; Barrett, *Jesus and Tradition*, 1-2; Conzelmann, *1 Corinthians*, 251; Hunter, *Predecessors*, 15-17; Fuller, *Formation*, 10-11; Webber, "Note"; Fee, *Corinthians*, 722.

146. For the disciples genuinely meaning "resurrection," see e.g., Bryan, "Saying"; idem, "Mean."

147. E.g., Dio Cass. 42.11.2-3; Lucan *C.W.* 1.11; Plut. *Cimon* 1.6; 6.6; Ach. Tat. 5.16.1-2; cf. Thom, "Highways," 104-5 for the Pythagorean view. Deities also sent phantom images made only of cloud (e.g., Apollod. *Epitome* 1.20; 3.5).

148. Plut. *Brutus* 36; *Caesar* 69.5, 8; *Cimon* 6.5.

149. Sanders, *Figure*, 278. Some contended that the particular identity of ghosts was difficult to distinguish, since they interchanged their appearances (Philost. *Hrk.* 21.1).

150. Although the second-century date makes the work's value here questionable, we may also note postresurrection conversations of Jesus in the anti-Gnostic *Epistula Apostolorum*.

151. Goppelt, *Times*, 18-19. For the incompatibility of mere apparitions with a "resurrection" claim, see also Evans, "Traditions," p. 56.

152. Cook, *Interpretation*, 58-59.

153. E.g., Eurip. *Bacch.* 42, 53-54; Plut. *Cicero* 14.3; Ael. Arist. *Or.* 48.41; Apul. *Metam.* 11.3; Ach. Tat. *Clit.* 7.12.4; Char. *Chaer.* 2.2.5; 2.3.5; Philostratus *Hrk.* 2.8; 18.1-2 (see further Maclean and Aitken, *Heroikos*, xxvi); reports in Grant, *Religions*, 9-13, 123; in unrelated cultures, see e.g., Mbiti, *Religions*, 105-12 passim; for more concrete effects of angelic manifestations in hellenistic Jewish tradition see Tob 12:19, 22; 2 Macc 3:24-26 (cf. God in 2 Macc 3:30).

154. Nilsson, *Piety*, 106; Diod. Sic. 5.62.4; 11.14.3-4; Dion. Hal. *Ant. rom.* 8.56.1-3.

155. Cf. Grant, *Gods*, 66, 54-55, 64-65.

156. E.g., *PDM* 14.74-91, 95, 98-102, 169.

157. So e.g., Plut. *Coriol.* 3.4 (writing of the time of Tarquin, 3.1); or, less dramatically, the appearance of the Dioscuri's stars (Plut. *Lysander* 12.1; 18.1).

158. E.g., Schweizer, *Jesus*, 48-49. Against hallucinations, see Schweizer, *Parable*, 84. The "cognitive dissonance" comparison with a tiny flying saucer cult proves not analogous: that cult reinterpreted a prophecy that did not materialize, rather than testifying that an unexpected event had happened (Wright, *Resurrection*, 699). A sounder historical analogy would be all the first-century Jewish movements whose founders died — yet those movements ended (Wright, *Resurrection*, 700).

159. Grayzel, *History*, 516; Bamberger, *Story*, 240.

160. Scholem, *Sabbatai Sevi,* 920; Greenstone, *Messiah,* 225-30.

161. Jos. *War* 6.297-99; cf. 2 Kgs 6:17; 2 Macc 3:24-26; 4 Macc 4:10-11; *Sib. Or.* 3.805-8.

162. Horsley and Hanson, *Bandits,* 182-84.

163. Somewhat similarly, Saulnier, "Josèphe," suggests that Josephus borrows the tradition from Flavian propaganda.

164. Tac. *Hist.* 5.13.2-7 likely depends on Jos. *War* 6.288-315.

165. E.g., Aul. Gel. 4.6.2.

166. E.g., Lucan *C.W.* 1.526-57 (most obviously regarding Charybdis; 1.547-48); 572-73 (a giant Fury stalking the city and shaking the snakes in her hair).

167. E.g., many of the portents listed in Livy 21.62.5; 24.10.7-10; 25.7.7-8; 26.23.4-5; 27.4.11-14; 27.11.2-5; 29.37.1-5; 29.14.3; 32.1.10-12; 33.26.7-8; 34.45.6-7; 35.9.2-3; 35.21.3-6; 36.37.2-3; 40.45.1-4; 41.21.12-13; 43.13.3-6; 45.16.5; Lucan *C.W.* 1.562-63.

168. E.g., Livy 21.62.4-5; 24.10.10; 42.2.4; Plut. *Themistocles* 15.1; Hdn. 8.3.8-9.

169. App. *C.W.* 4.1.4 (43 BCE); one of the portents in Livy 24.44.8 (213 BCE); Caesar *C.W.* 3.105; Philostratus *Hrk.* 56.2.

170. E.g., Livy 24.10.11; 24.44.8. If I correctly interpret Livy's summaries, in some cases some reported seeing figures at another location when those present at that location could not confirm them.

171. Livy 21.62.5.

172. E.g., Livy 21.62.1; Hdn. 8.3.8 (though he concludes that it is credible, 8.3.9).

173. Livy 21.62.1; 24.10.6; 27.37.2; 29.14.2; cf. Lucian *Peregrinus* 39-40.

174. See the LCL note on Livy 29.14.3; cf. some discussion in Strothers, "Objects." Flames seen in the sky (e.g., Livy 32.8.2); showers of "stones" (36.37.3); a rainbow in a clear sky (41.21.12); meteors (e.g., Livy 43.13.3); a comet shining for seven nights (Suet. *Jul.* 88) and many other phenomena are also plausible in this manner. Some reports, of course, were simply fabricated by someone.

175. E.g., Collins, "Apotheosis," 97. It was often associated with the messiah (*Sipre Deut.* 34.4.3; *p. Ket.* 12:4, §8) or the age to come (Schiffman, "Crossroads," 140, on *b. Sanh.* 90a, bar.).

176. E.g., Acts 1:3-6; "from among the dead ones" (Rom 1:4; cf. 1 Cor 15:20; Gal 1:4; Heb 6:5).

177. Two centuries later, as pagan alternatives to Christian claims circulated, worship of deceased but active heroes was common. Already in the Gentile world of the apostolic period, apotheosis was the common explanation for old "heroes" like Heracles and Asclepius; they were no longer considered dead. But as the Jesus movement allowed only one God, they also allowed only one risen Lord.

178. Lapide, *Resurrection,* accepted the evidence for the resurrection of Jesus as compelling (Jesus being a prophet of God), but did not view him as Messiah. This position is exceptional, but of course much easier than arguing Jesus' Lordship without the resurrection.

179. Many note that the church's early faith invites explanation, challenging scholarship that ignores our earliest Christian literary evidence, Paul's letters (e.g., Barnett, *Jesus and History,* 25, 39-50). As Schweizer, *Parable,* 16, puts it, "we certainly cannot assess Jesus separately from the impact he made"; or as Dunn, *New Perspective,* 15-34, notes, attempts to screen out the faith of the Gospel writers as bias miss the point: early Christian faith flowed from the faith-stimulating impact of Jesus (see esp. 29). Although personally agnostic regarding what happened, Wedderburn, *Resurrection,* 39-47, is convinced that *something* must have happened to generate the disciples' faith. On the belief in Jesus' messiahship resting on resurrection belief (without which the disciples would be extraordinarily hailing an executed leader as Israel's continuing deliverer), see Wright, *Resurrection,* 553 (more generally, 553-83). But for the warnings of some against extrapolating back from the faith that Jesus evoked (pace Dunn), see Schröter, "Begründer."

180. Supposedly (but not usually actually) unique. The emphasis on uniqueness allowed its proponents to maintain that they still followed what they regarded as "essential" in Christianity.

181. Cf. Keck, *History,* 127-28.

182. Just as some later rabbis believed that Hezekiah had nearly become the Messiah (e.g., *b.*

Sanh. 94a; *Song Rab.* 4:8, §3), though some have applied this designation to R. Judah (Aberbach, "Hzqyhw").

183. Excepting Judas, whose betrayal, as we noted, was undoubtedly not invented (given the criterion of embarrassment).

184. See our comments on the abandonment of Jesus' disciples in ch. 21.

185. Ladd, *Theology,* 370; Ladd, *Last Things,* 82-83; Fee, *Corinthians,* 786; Gundry, "Physicality," 216-17; Keener, *Corinthians,* 132. On Diaspora Jewish application of such language regarding Adam and the other man in the creation narratives, see e.g., Philo *L.A.* 1.31-32; Isaacs, *Spirit,* 78; Pearson, *Terminology,* 17-20; Horsley, *Corinthians,* 211-12; Horsley, "Resurrection"; though Genesis itself (esp. Gen 2:7 LXX) supplies much of this background (cf. Fee, *Corinthians,* 785, n. 42; Barrett, "Significance," 113; both terms together in Jos. *Ant.* 1.34).

186. Keener, *Corinthians,* 131. Some early Jewish sources, including Dan 12:2-3, seem to portray the resurrection as angelic or like stars (*1 En.* 43:3; *2 Bar.* 51:10; perhaps *1 En.* 51:5; 104:2-4; *2 En.* 22:8-10; Ps.-Phoc. 104; *Pr. Jac.* 19); cf. Fletcher-Louis, *Angels,* regarding the partly angelomorphic character of the resurrection in Luke-Acts. This perspective may contrast or stand in tension with the more corporal conception in e.g., *2 Bar.* 49:2–50:4; *Gen. Rab.* 95:1; 100:2.

187. "Resurrection" in Judaism was bodily by its nature (Dan 12:2) — otherwise it was something other than "resurrection" (see Wright, *Resurrection,* 85-206, first brought to my attention by C. L. Blomberg).

188. As noted, Jewish tradition regarding criminals' graves would keep the corpses separate so they could be reburied at the end of a year. This may help explain why we do not have many Palestinian Jewish mass graves from the period.

189. Contrast forced-choice logic in Bultmann's theological approach: since John presents Jesus' resurrection in unity with the cross, the resurrection cannot be an authenticating miracle as Paul and other sources from the apostolic church claim ("Mythology," 36-37).

190. E.g., *4 Ezra* 3:7, 20-22; 4:30; 7:118-19; *2 Bar.* 17:2-3; 23:4; 48:42-43; 56:5-6 (but cf. 54:15, 19); *Life of Adam* 44:3-4; *Sifre Deut.* 323.5.1; cf. more nuanced discussion in Davies, *Paul,* 32-34; Barrett, *Adam,* 14-15; Scroggs, *Adam,* 18-20; Hayman, "Fall."

191. See Tan, *Zion Traditions,* 221-23, on the authenticity of this material (e.g., Matt 19:28//Lk 22:30).

192. See e.g., discussion in Keener, *John,* 1194-95; more fully, my forthcoming commentary on Acts at Acts 1:9-11.

193. Several bridges may have provided coherence between the pre-resurrection teacher Jesus and Paul's experiential "union" with Christ, including the experience of the Spirit (related to Jesus reigning in his church; this experience may be dominant); any Jesus tradition concerning indwelling in John's last discourse (attested only in John, but who might have independent tradition on this point, if not dependent on Pauline theology; cf. Keener, *John,* 998, 999 n. 114); and/or Paul's conversion as narrated by Luke, where the risen Jesus identifies with his church (Acts 9:4; see Kim, *Origin*). But the expected corporate character of the resurrection (Dan 12:2), conjoined with Jesus' accomplished resurrection, could also naturally lead to a partly realized eschatology in which Jesus' followers would share some of the resurrection life.

194. Concerning Mk 12:18-27, where Jesus defends it, see e.g., Schweizer, *Parable,* 87; Witherington, *Christology,* 15 n. 58.

195. For the dependence of the parousia on the resurrection, see Plevnik, "Parousia," especially 277.

196. Theissen and Merz, *Historical Jesus,* 504, 508.

197. Treatments of the subject often recognize this question in addition to the historical one (e.g., Wedderburn, *Resurrection,* 97 [who also notes philosophy's uncertainty regarding human postmortem survival, 129-35]); the philosophic objection is ancient (*Apocrit.* 4.24). History *as* history cannot decide whether an event is a miracle (a theological and philosophic judgment), but it can address

whether or not an event literally happened (see Habermas, *Evidence*, 25). For a philosophic response, see Houston, *Miracles*, 210-23.

Notes to Appendix 1

1. Mason, *Josephus and New Testament*, 206; Borg, *Conflict*, 27-28; idem, *Vision*, 90; cf. Kingdon, "Zealots."

2. Now widely held: Horsley and Hanson, *Bandits*, 214-17; cf. pp. 190-243; Baumbach, "Zeloten"; Smith, "Zealots"; Borg, "Zealot"; idem, *Conflict*, 35-36; Sanders, *Judaism*, 281-83.

3. Crossan puts Josephus' bias best (*Historical Jesus*, 93): "Nobody from the highest aristocracy on either side is guilty of anything."

4. Horsley and Hanson, *Bandits*, 220-41; cf. Crossan, *Historical Jesus*, 217.

5. Horsley and Hanson, *Bandits*, 190 distinguish the Sicarii themselves from peasants and social bandits, relating them to a line of teachers of resistance (pp. 194-97). They suspect Judas the Galilean may have advocated martyrdom rather than violence (pp. 197-98), but this is unclear.

6. Jos. *War* 2.228-29; note, however, that the villagers *could* not have caught everyone (cf. Deut 21:1).

7. Pace Crossan, *Historical Jesus*, 304-5; Horsley and Hanson, *Bandits*, 48-50, 69-70; Oakman, "Peasant," 131. Horsley and Hanson, *Bandits*, 71 contend that the common people asked for justice against Herod when he killed the bandits, citing Jos. *Ant.* 14.168, but Josephus seems to refer to *relatives*. Villagers did protect bandits who robbed a servant of Caesar (p. 72, citing Jos. *Ant.* 20.113-17; *War* 2.228-31), and *War* 2.253 may also be relevant, but Josephus himself does not indicate that the "inhabitants" ravaged by the brigands were nobles. The drowning of nobles is significant (*War* 1.314-16, 326; *Ant.* 14.431-33), but *Ant.* 20.255-56 does not explicitly differentiate "Jews" as gentry from the "masses." Jos. *War* 2.235-38 may well be relevant, but one wonders whether the elders in *Ant.* 14.167 are peasants, since the speaker is a Pharisee. The nuancing of Crossan, *Historical Jesus*, 170 (their social location between the powerful and powerless) may be helpful.

8. Cf. Donaldson, "Bandits."

9. Cf. Horsley and Hanson, *Bandits*, 77-85.

10. Horsley and Hanson, *Bandits*, xiii-xiv, 250-51; Crossan, *Historical Jesus*, 194; Horsley, *Galilee*, 259. Josephus' sources regarding brigands appear weak for 6-44, though he reports some uprisings (cf. also Mk 15:27); but after 44 he supplies many reports of bandits with heavy followings (*War* 2.228, 235, 238, 253; *Ant.* 20.121, 124, 161; Horsley and Hanson, *Bandits*, 66-69).

11. See Lewis, *Life*, 204.

12. Sanders, *Judaism*, 35-43.

13. Simon, *Sects*, 44; cf. Neusner, *Beginning*, 26-27; see especially Jos. *Ant.* 18.4, 23-25. Falk, *Pharisee*, 57-58, 120-25 even decides (too narrowly) that the Zealots were Shammaites. Sanders is undoubtedly right that the "Fourth Philosophy" was "largely Pharisaic in opinion," except that their "members would accept no master but God (*Antiq.* 18.23; *War* 2.118)" (Sanders, *Judaism*, 13-14; cf. pp. 280-84, 408-11). Hengel, *Zeloten*, sees them as a religiously motivated movement; Giblet, "Mouvement," believes they saw themselves as more religious than political. While assuming specific religious beliefs, the nationalists did not represent an organized religious group (Salomonsen, "Nogle"). Applebaum, "Zealots," regarded the revolutionary movement as a natural response to the Roman situation. Evidence at Masada indicates the Sicarii's religious commitment (Cornfeld, *Josephus*, 489, 499).

14. Josephus disparages "brigands" of all sorts except in the one case where he need not do so, the speech he creates for Eleazar (Sanders, *Judaism*, 6-7); but Josephus belonged to the elite.

15. Horsley and Hanson, *Bandits*, xv.

16. Cf. Horsley and Hanson, *Bandits*, 19, 76.

17. Horsley and Hanson, *Bandits*, xv; Borg, *Conflict*, 36-47.

18. Sanders, *Judaism*, 241.

19. Witherington, *Christology*, 83. Josephus may have assumed command of many brigands himself; see the evidence in Horsley, *Galilee*, 266-67.

20. Wright, *People of God*, 179-80; Witherington, *Christology*, 84-87.

Notes to Appendix 2

1. Not all scholars who hold this thesis deny that Jesus also uttered eschatological sayings. While I do not find the evidence for their position persuasive, my reason to treat the topic in a historical Jesus book is Mack's use of their thesis rather than the thesis itself.

2. *Lost Gospel*, 106-7.

3. *Lost Gospel*, 34-36.

4. Some seem fairly certain of Q's shape (e.g., Edwards, *Theology of Q*), but contrast e.g., Stanton, *Jesus of Nazareth*, 5; Keck, "Ethos," 448.

5. Mack, *Lost Gospel*, 16.

6. *Lost Gospel*, 34.

7. Mack also recognizes Thomas's dependence on sayings in Q (e.g., *Lost Gospel*, p. 182).

8. We do find recycled eschatological traditions in apocalyptic literature. Moreover, even those who contend that the eschatological "layer" in Q is a later addition (and, in Mack's case, an inauthentic one) nevertheless recognize that eventually Q (before the composition of Luke and Matthew) included eschatological sayings. Why would eschatological sayings become possible at a second "layer" yet violate genre conventions at a layer that could not have been significantly earlier (given the potential time frame between Jesus' day and an established predecessor to Luke and Matthew)?

9. *Lost Gospel*, 6.

10. *Lost Gospel*, 192.

11. For a full-scale, coherent and scholarly reevaluation of the Gospels' treatment of the Jesus tradition, see especially the six volumes of *Gospel Perspectives*, although many less conservative studies will also concur with the substance of many of their critiques.

12. *Lost Gospel*, 238.

13. Mack apparently accepts this letter as Pauline (*Lost Gospel*, 231).

14. Paul proceeds less in this direction than do many of his contemporaries such as Philo or Josephus.

15. Most significantly *Abba* and *Marana tha*; cf. also *anathema* and *Kephas*. Such phrases reveal the importance the earliest Jesus movement attached to Jesus' relationship with (and teaching about) the Father; his Lordship and return; the role of Peter and the earliest, Aramaic traditions.

16. Cf. here Overman's critique of Mack's distinctions between Galilean Jesus movements and hellenistic Christ cults in his *Myth*: the social experiences of Galilean and Diaspora Christians would not have been that dissimilar (Overman, "Deciphering," 194).

17. For a case that veneration of Jesus belongs to the Jesus movement's earliest stages, see Hurtado, *Lord Jesus Christ*.

18. *Lost Gospel*, 74-79 and parts of 73 and 80.

19. Cf. Meier, *Marginal Jew*, 1:177, on some minimalist Jesus scholarship more generally.

20. Overman, "Deciphering," 193-94.

Notes to Appendix 3

1. Bultmann, *Tradition*, 369, exaggerated their hellenistic character (though allowing some Palestinian tradition); contrast Barrett, *Jesus and Tradition*, 6. Aune explains Gospel biography by delib-

erately "oversimplifying" it as exhibiting "Hellenistic form and function with Jewish content" (*Environment*, 22). Hellenistic narrative techniques were standard in Jewish documents written in Greek (e.g., Cohen, *Maccabees*, 43).

2. Greek conventions for praising heroes or deities were also sometimes transferred to Jewish heroes; cf. e.g., van der Horst, "Children."

3. This is not to deny that the latter depend on ultimate Palestinian sources (Hengel, "Problems," 238-43, for example, supports the ancient tradition of Mark's dependence on Peter), but to argue that they articulate their Gospels for a more pluralistic milieu.

4. Stanton, *Jesus of Nazareth*, 126; Aune, *Environment*, 37.

5. Hengel, "Problems," 219-20.

6. The suggestion that ancient Near Eastern models provided the later Greek emphasis on individual characters (cf. Dihle, "Biography," 366-67) is overstated.

7. Against Bultmann, *Tradition*, 57. Gerhardsson, *Memory*, 181-89, comments on narrative in rabbinic tradition, since disciples learned from their teachers' lives as well as from their words; but as Gundry ("Genre," 101) points out, this still does not correspond to what we have in the gospels, nor to the enormous tradition which must stand behind them.

8. Neusner, *Biography*, is skeptical even of the attributed sayings. There is certainly nothing comparable to the early-nineteenth-century collection of tales In Praise of the Baal Shem Tov (available in English in Ben-Amos and Mintz, *Baal Shem Tov*).

9. Neusner, *Legend*, 8.

10. Aune, *Environment*, 41-42.

11. Van Veldhuizen, "Moses," 215-24.

12. Silver, "Moses" (on Jos. *Ant.* 2:243-53 and Artapanus in Euseb. *P.E.* 9.27). Runnalls, "Campaign," suggests that Josephus indirectly challenged Artapanus' account; but the use of the same tradition demonstrates the inroads that hellenism had made into Moses haggadah (cf. Rajak, "Moses"); Aristobulus (second century BCE) *frg.* 4 (Euseb. *P.E.* 13.13.5) possibly divinizes him with the vision of God. Some Jewish writers may adapt Orphean and Heraclean motifs (cf. Philonenko, "Juda"), and some euhemeristically identify pagan figures with biblical ones (e.g., Ps.-Eupolemus in Euseb. *P.E.* 9.17.9).

13. Feldman, "Abraham," 150.

14. Feldman, "Jacob."

15. Aune, *Environment*, 107.

16. Feldman, "Samson." Roncace, "Samson," critiques Feldman's portrayal of Samson.

17. Feldman, "Saul."

18. Begg, "Zedekiah," argues that Josephus portrays him as something of a tragic hero, following Aristotelian conventions.

19. Feldman, "'Aqedah." Joshua may become a Jewish Pericles (Feldman, "Joshua"). See other citations from Feldman above.

20. E.g., Feldman, "Concubine"; Höffken, "Hiskija." Naturally, there is some disagreement regarding specifics, e.g., Roncace, "Deborah"; Feldman, "Roncace's Portraits."

21. Cohen, *Maccabees*, 194; cf. in general Attridge, "Historiography," 326; cf. Eisman, "Dio and Josephus." Even his apology for his "substandard" Greek fits rhetorical conventions for lowering audience expectations and may be compared with Anacharsis' reported apology to the Athenians (Anacharsis *Ep.* 1.1-6). Other hellenistic Jewish historians probably employed similar techniques (cf. Rajak, "Justus of Tiberias," 92); earlier still, cf. the liberties 1 Esd 1:23-30 takes with 2 Chron 35:20-25 (Kooij, "Death of Josiah").

22. See e.g., Fisk, "Bible": Harrington, "Bible." Harrington, "Bible," 242-43, does not think these reworkings constitute a distinct genre, since some (like Jubilees and Assumption of Moses) purport to be apocalypses, while others (he gives Chronicles as an example) purport to be straightforward historical narrative.

23. Cf. *Jubilees*; *Life of Adam and Eve*; *Assumption of Moses*; *History of Joseph* (of uncertain date); *L.A.B.* (which proceeds through 2 Sam 1); *Testaments of the Twelve Patriarchs*; *1-3 Enoch* (especially the Book of Noah in *1 Enoch*); 1QNoah (related to *1 En.* 8:4; 9:4; 106:9-10; see Fitzmyer, *Scrolls*, 16); 4QAmram; Genesis Apocryphon; cf. Yadin, "Commentaries," 66-68, 66-67. Some of those from Qumran are probably pre-Qumranian (Milik, "Écrits").

24. Harrington, "Bible," 242.

25. On *Life of Adam and Eve*, cf. Johnson, "Adam," 252; Ps-Philo's *L.A.B.* borrows lines from other passages of Scripture. Goulder, *Midrash*, 30, is probably right when he argues that midrash is creative, but seemed to the rabbis who engaged in it as if they were deriving all their data from inferences in the text; in many cases, however, antecedent interpretive traditions may be verified from other sources (e.g., postbiblical traditions in Theodotus; cf. Fallon, "Theodotus," 786). Haggadic traditions were probably more easily remembered than halakic ones (Gerhardson, *Memory*, 147).

26. On the nature of Jubilees' revision of Genesis and Exodus, see Vanderkam, "Jubilees." Hellenistic writers like Hecataeus and Manetho had adapted earlier history to meet the contemporary needs, and it is not surprising that Jewish writers of this period sometimes did the same (Mendels, "History").

27. Freund, "Deception."

28. *ARN* 1 A. What would have been considered *explanatory* amplification of the words of sages was, however, part of the scribe's traditional vocation (Meeks, *Moral World*, 117, on Sir 39:1-2).

29. E.g., Demetrius the Chronographer (third century BCE), *frg.* 5 (Euseb. *P.E.* 9.29.16); *Jub.* 4:1, 9; 12:14; 13:11; 27:1, 4-5 (Esau and Jacob, vs. Isaac and Jacob); *p. Ket.* 12:4, §8 (fanciful midrash).

30. 2 Macc 2:1-8 (expanding Jeremiah's mission); *Jub.* 29:14-20 (rhetorically contrasts Jacob's respect for his parents with Esau's disrespect); *Test. Job* 9-15 (see OTP 1:832); *Test. Jos.* 3:1; cf. Josephus' expansion of Philistine casualties (*Ant.* 6.203; cf. 1 Sam 18:27, though the LXX reduced them). Cf. Jael in *L.A.B.* 31 (Burnette-Bletsch, "Jael").

31. *Pesiq. Rab Kah.* 4:3 ("the rabbis" on Solomon); *Gen. Rab.* 43:3; *Ex. Rab.* 10:4; *Pesiq. Rab.* 49:5; cf. Artapanus on Pharaoh's behavior toward Moses in light of 1 Sam 18:17, 21-25 (Euseb. *P.E.* 9.27.7). Genre conventions also could dictate amplifications; Joseph and Asenath, a Hellenistic romance, incorporates features ideal in such romances.

32. *Jub.* 11:14-15; 13:18, 22; possibly 4Q160, frg. 3-5, 7; *Tg. Ps.-Jon.* on Gen 50:26; *Ps.-Jon.* on Ex 13:19.

33. Endres, *Interpretation*, 214-19.

34. See n. 32 above.

35. *Jub.* 11:14-15; *Liv. Pr.* 19 (Joad) (§30 in Schermann's Greek text); Jos. *Ant.* 8.231; *L.A.B.* 40:1 (in *L.A.B.* in general, cf. Bauckham, "'Midrash,'" 67; in Jewish sources more generally, Pilch, "Naming"); cf. Plut. *Alex.* 20.4-5 (questioning Chares' report).

36. See Rook, "Names," on patriarchal wives in *Jubilees*.

37. See the discussion in Maclean and Aitken, *Heroikos*, li-lii.

38. As *L.A.B.* does in its polemic against idolatry (Murphy, "Idolatry").

39. *L.A.B.* 12:2-3 (Aaron's sin with the golden calf). *Test. Job* 39:12-13 (OTP)/39:9-10 (Kraft) and 40:3/4 seems concerned to soften God letting Job's children die for his test.

40. *Jub.* 13:17-18 (conflict between Lot's and Abram's servants), 14:21–16:22 (omitting Sarah's problems with Hagar, though they surface in 17:4-14), 29:13 (omits Jacob's fear); *Test. Zeb.* 1:5-7 (Zebulon did not act against Joseph). In *Jubilees* (e.g., Abram passing off his sister as his wife), see Wintermute, "Jubilees," 35-36; in Josephus, cf. Aune, *Environment*, 108; in Greco-Roman literature, see Shuler, *Genre*, 50 (following Cic. *Part. or.* 22). The same tendency of tradition may be noted in the Chronicler's omission of David's and Solomon's sins reported in Samuel-Kings (cf. e.g., Williamson, *Chronicles*, 236). On the golden calf in Josephus, see Jos. *Ant.* 3.79-99 (esp. 95-99; despite *War* 4.3). Philo and Ps.-Philo omit the command to destroy Canaan's nations, and Josephus ex-

plains it in a manner intelligible to Romans (Feldman, "Command"; for Philo, see also Berthelot, "Conquest").

41. CD 4.20-5.3 (David's polygamy, behavior that the Qumran community otherwise disapproved; also 11QT 56.18); *Jub.* 19:15-16 (Rebekah, in light of current morality); 27:6-7 (how Jacob could leave his father); 28:6-7 (Jacob's sororal polygyny); 30:2-17 (Simeon and Levi), 41 (Judah and Tamar both made more innocent, especially Judah); 1Qap Gen^ar 20.10-11 (Sarah rather than Abraham proposes the pretense that she is his sister); *Jos. Asen.* 23 (Levi and Simeon); *Test. Jud.* 8-12 (whitewashing Judah, and to a lesser extent Tamar, though Judah confesses it as a lesser sin; cf. the improvement of both in *Tg. Neof.* 1 on Gen 38:25; *Tg. Ps.-Jon.* on Gen. 38:25-26); *Test. Iss.* 3:1 (cf. Gen 49:15); *Tg. Ps.-Jon.* on Gen. 49:28 (all twelve patriarchs were equally righteous).

42. Cf. the variant forms of some sayings in Ahiqar (OTP 2:482).

43. Anderson, "4 Maccabees," 555. Here the freedom is probably that of the author of 4 Maccabees, who appears to expand earlier sources, whereas 2 Macc probably stays closer to its sources, since it is an abridgement.

44. Cf. Robinson, *Problem,* 60.

45. See Theon *Progymn.* 1.93-171; Hock, "Education," 202-3; cf. Gerhardsson, *Memory,* 136-48.

46. Cf. e.g., 4Q422, a homiletic paraphrase of Genesis (Elgvin, "Section"); see further below on rewritings of biblical history. Chilton, "Transmission"; idem, "Development," suggests that Gospel traditions were transmitted and developed in ways similar to Targumic traditions. For the view that John developed Jesus' message in a manner analogous to the Targums, which included interpretive amplification but sought fidelity to the meaning, see Taylor, *Formation,* 116.

47. Dunn, *Acts,* 117 (though noting the identical core, 121). Explanations vary (e.g., Hedrick, "Paul's Conversion/Call," 432; Marshall, *Acts,* 167; see esp. Tannehill, *Acts,* 10), but variation on details seems not to have been problematic. Retellings could selectively omit some details (e.g., Char. *Chaer.* 2.5.10-11).

48. Eddy and Boyd, *Legend,* 429-30. The exception might be if one needed grounds for polemic against a particular document (as in *Apocrit.* 2.12-15).

49. For the comparison, see e.g., Wills, "Aesop Tradition," 225; cf. Keener, "Review of Lincoln" (regarding potential liberties in the Fourth Gospel, not the Synoptics).

50. Stanton, *Jesus of Nazareth,* 127.

51. Cf. e.g., Canevet, "Remarques" (Moses as commander-in-chief). Like other hellenistic Jewish writers, Philo adjusts biblical accounts where necessary to suit his idealization of virtues; cf. Petit, "Exemplaire." Philo can nevertheless prove accurate when reporting events surrounding more recent personages (Smallwood, "Historians").

52. For such reasons, I regard Philo as less comparable than, say, Plutarch's lives or Josephus' autobiography, particularly for the Synoptics (John may be closer, but even John does not go anywhere as far as Philo).

53. Even his postbiblical information (e.g., Philo *Abr.* 71-72; *Migr.* 177; *Mos.* 1.20-24) often derives from Alexandrian Jewish tradition rather than pure invention (we have some examples of this information attested elsewhere, including in Acts 7).

Notes to Appendix 4

1. E.g., Matthew's primary source for Matt 24 is Mark, but he supplements at relevant points with "Q" (e.g., in 24:28 = Lk 17:37; 24:38-41 = Lk 17:26-30, 34-35; 24:43 = Lk 12:39), and perhaps at some points by other tradition (his "trumpet" also parallels Pauline language).

2. Ovid *Metam.* 15.792; Livy 27.4.14; 40.19.2; 43.13.4; Appian *C.W.* 2.5.36; 4.1.4; Lucan *C.W.* 1.556-57; cf. Eurip. *Iph. Taur.* 1165-67.

3. Livy 24.10.7; 25.7.7-8; 26.23.5; 27.37.1; 34.45.7; 35.9.4; 36.37.3; 42.2.4; 43.13.5; 45.16.5; Appian *C.W.* 2.5.36; 4.1.4.

4. Virg. *Aen.* 4.453-63; Livy 24.44.8.

5. Ovid *Metam.* 15.796-97; Livy 24.10.10; 27.11.4; 35.21.4; 41.13.2; 41.21.13; 43.13.3; Appian *C.W.* 4.1.4.

6. Livy 27.4.11, 14; 32.1.11; 40.45.4; cf. Phaedrus 3.3.4-5.

7. Livy 27.11.5; 27.37.5; 34.45.7; 35.21.3; 41.21.12; Appian *C.W.* 1.9.83; Herodian 1.14.1; Lucan *C.W.* 1.562-63.

8. *Jub.* 23:14; *2 Bar.* 27:11-12; *m. Sot.* 9:15; cf. perhaps *Sib. Or.* 3.204.

9. *Jub.* 23:21; *Test. Moses* 7:3-4; *2 Tim* 3:5; cf. *m. Sot.* 9:15.

10. E.g., 1QM 15.1; *Jub.* 23:22-23 (cf. 23:20); *4 Ezra* 13:34.

11. Cf. *Sib. Or.* 2.22; 3.204-5, 636-37, 660-61, 756; *Gen. Rab.* 42:4.

12. E.g., *1 En.* 1:6-8; 53:7; *4 Ezra* 6:13-16; *Test. Moses* 10:4; Bauckham, "Earthquake."

13. *Sib. Or.* 2.23; *Pesiq. Rab Kah.* 5:9; *Gen. Rab.* 25:3; 40:3; 64:2; *Ruth Rab.* 1:4; *Pesiq. R.* 15:14/15.

14. Wickedness in *4 Ezra* 5:10; 14:16-17; *2 Bar.* 27:11-12; 69:3; *Test. Moses* 7:3-10; *m. Sot.* 9:15; *1 En.* 91:7; cf. Hesiod *W.D.* 181-201.

15. Although this is typically Matthean language (Matt 7:23; 13:41; 23:23), it also appears in the eschatological tradition behind 2 Thessalonians (2 Thess 2:3, 7).

16. 1Q22 frg. 1.i.7-8; 4Q390 frg. 1.7-9; *Jub.* 23:9, 16-17; *1 En.* 91:7; *T. Dan* 5:4; *Iss.* 6:1; *Naph.* 4:1; *Zeb.* 9:5; *3 En.* 48A:5-6; *Sipre Deut.* 318.1.10; *Pesiq. Rab Kah.* 5:9; *Pesiq. R.* 15:14/15; cf. *4 Ezra* 5:1-2.

17. Livy 25.7.8; 29.14.3; 32.8.2; 41.21.13; Lucan *C.W.* 1.526-43. Comets (e.g., Appian *C.W.* 2.10.68; Lucan *C.W.* 1.529) were esp. noteworthy.

18. *1 En.* 102:2-3 (end of age); cf. *Sib. Or.* 3.800-4; 5.476-84; 8.190-93, 204; *4 Ezra* 7:38-42.

19. The transition between the present age (i.e., the time between the Flood and the End) and the final generation (probably beginning in *Jub.* 23:14-25, which intensifies the judgments) seems unclear.

20. Many have noted the parallels: see especially Waterman, "Sources" (citing 24 parallels, mostly compelling); Wenham, *Rediscovery*; cf. also Hunter, *Predecessors*, 49; Barrett, *Jesus and Tradition*, 12; Hill, *Prophecy*, 130; Sanders, *Jesus and Judaism*, 144-45; Crossan, *Historical Jesus*, 243-47; Allison, *Jesus of Nazareth*, 125; for 2 Thess 2, see also Wenham, *Rediscovery*, 176-80. The cumulative evidence is, as Ford, *Abomination*, 22 puts it, virtually "conclusive."

21. E.g., Koester, *Introduction*, 2:242; Bailey, "Thessalonians"; Grant, *Paul*, 6; cf. the mediating approach in Donfried, *Thessalonians*, xxiii-xxvi, 51-53.

22. See Kümmel, *Introduction*, 189 (267 in 1975 ed.); Robinson, *Redating*, 53-54. The precise date of Paul's execution in the 60s is debated, but if someone other than Paul wrote 2 Thessalonians, it was presumably someone who knew Pauline tradition well and wrote before 70. The tensions between an imminent return (attributed to 1 Thessalonians) and one preceded by signs (2 Thessalonians) are no greater than within Jesus' eschatological discourse itself. Favoring Paul's authorship, see arguments in e.g., Kümmel, *Introduction*, 187-90 (264-69 in 1975 ed.); Best, *Thessalonians*, 50-58; Milligan, *Thessalonians*, xxxix, lii-lxii, lxxvi-xcii; Neil, *Thessalonians*, pp. xix-xxvi; Frame, *Thessalonians*, 19-20, 39-54; Marshall, *Thessalonians*, 23-25; Morris, *Thessalonians*, 29-31; Bruce, *Thessalonians*, xxxix; Ford, *Abomination*, 195; Carson, "Pseudonymity," 862; cf. Mealand, "Extent."

23. Many Jewish teachers emphasized that Israel's obedience could hasten the end (e.g., Tob 13:6; *T. Zeb.* 9:7; *Sipre Deut.* 41.4.3; 43.16.3; *b. B.B.*10a; *Nid.* 13b, bar.; *Sanh.* 97b; *y. Taan.* 1:1, §7; *Ex. Rab.* 25:12; *Deut. Rab.* 3:2; *Song Rab.* 2:5, §3; 4:8, §3; 5:2, §2; cf. Acts 3:19; 2 Pet 3:12), whereas others preferred fixed schemes, whether able to be determined or known only to God (e.g., *Sipra Behuq.* pq. 8.269.2.3; *b. Abod. Zar.* 9ab; *Sanh.* 97ab; *Lev. Rab.* 15:1; *Lam. Rab.* proem 21). Some reconciled the two by claiming that the redemption was scheduled but would come early if Israel were obedient (*Song Rab.* 8:14, §1). Some set dates (see e.g., Bonsirven, *Judaism*, 178; cf. *Test. Ab.* 7B; *Gr. Ezra* 3:3-4), a position countered by more conservative rabbis (e.g., *b. Pes.* 54b, bar.; *Sanh.* 97a; *Num. Rab.* 5:6; see Daube, *NT and Judaism*, 289-90; cf. *2 Bar.* 21:8). Later rabbis reported both the multiplicity of dates and prerequisites for

the Messiah's coming alongside warnings against speculating when he would come (*b. Sanh.* 97a-98b). Various texts speak of God delaying the end (*1 En.* 60:5; *4 Ezra* 7:24; cf. *2 Bar.* 85:12) to grant time for repentance.

24. Although it is less convincing, some of this other material may also echo the dominical tradition (Riesenfeld, *Tradition*, 17; cf. Dibelius, *Paul*, 93).

25. When I initially collected such parallels, I had been considering a dissertation on the topic, an idea relinquished once I realized how many others have addressed the same topic. Because my study was incomplete, I probably underestimated the parallels in non-Christian Jewish works, but the differences are nevertheless illustrative.

26. Some view the "catching up" as an agraphon (Jeremias, *Unknown Sayings*, 14); others plausibly prefer a midrashic implication of the explicit gathering (Wenham, "Apocalypse," 348); the descent may derive from OT theophany language (see Scott, "Clouds," 132).

27. Cf. Koester, "One Jesus," 196; Boring, *Sayings*, 11, 34 n. 41. Prophecies could be written down and preserved (*Test. Job* 51:4/3); but it does not appear to have been the norm (cf. Aune, *Prophecy*, 244). Further, oracles were far more likely to be heavily redacted than didactic traditions were (cf. Collins, "Introduction to Oracles," 320).

28. *1 En.* 90:28-29; 11QTemple 29:8-10; cf. the hope of restoration in the seventeenth benediction of the *Amida*; cf. 1QpHab 9.6-7 (the Jerusalem priesthood); Joshua ben Ananiah in Josephus *War* 6.300ff.

29. Apparently the final generation.

30. This fits the theme of not seeking signs (Matt 12:38; 16:4), the real sign being Jesus' resurrection (12:39-40), and a future appearing (24:30), in response to the disciples' question (24:3).

31. In period between the Flood and the End.

32. One judgment among many, the righteous youths seeking to force their elders to return to the way of righteousness.

33. Nations against Israel, more relevant. This includes the most cruel of peoples and much bloodshed (23:23).

34. But this may be part of a Christian interpolation (God's Son in 13:32, 37).

35. In period between the Flood and the End.

36. Cf. also the final earthquake, e.g., *1 En.* 1:6-8; 53:7; *4 Ezra* 6:13-16; *Test. Moses* 10:4; Rev 6:12; Bauckham, "Earthquake."

37. But apparently applied differently, to the final judgment (wrath in the day of the Lord, 1 Thess 5:2, 9).

38. Probably this early (cf. 1QH 3.3-18). If not, nevertheless a common image for anguish in OT portrayals of judgment (Ps 48:6; Is 13:8; 21:3; 26:17; 42:14; Jer 4:31; 6:24; 13:21; 22:23; 30:6; 31:8; 48:41; 49:22, 24; 50:43; Hos 13:13).

39. If it refers to the community's suffering.

40. Maybe final judgment rather than tribulation before it. *4 Ezra* 4:42 applies to birth pangs for the resurrection in the realm of the dead.

41. The term *anomia* appears only in Matthew (Matt 7:23; 13:41; 23:28; 24:12) in the Gospels (disregarding the cognate in Lk 22:37, from Is 53:12 LXX).

42. One could apply Matt 24:12 to the moral coarsening of society, but in context apostasy of those who already "love" (24:12) and need to "persevere" (24:13) is likelier.

43. The world and esp. Israel (note the covenant in 23:16, 19, 23).

44. The wicked torture the righteous to seek their apostasy.

45. The nuance attaching to a royal dignitary is probably amplified by the use of *apantēsis* in 1 Thess 4:17.

46. E.g., comets (Appian *C.W.* 2.10.68; Lucan *C.W.* 1.529).

47. That the tribes mourning (Zech 12:10) is conjoined with Dan 7:13 in both Rev 1:7 and Matt

24:30 suggests a common source in which they were linked, or that Revelation drew directly on the form of Jesus tradition found in the Gospels (cf. Rev 3:3).

48. For war, rather than gathering.

49. Cf. also *Did.* 9.4; 10.5; 16:6-7.

50. Sodom is a frequent image in ancient Jewish texts, including elsewhere in the NT; I focus on eschatological destruction (though cf. also Matt 10:15; 11:23-24; Lk 10:12; Rev 11:8).

51. Both 1 Thess 5 and 2 Pet 3 apply this to "the day of the Lord."

52. In a different context.

53. 2 Thess 2:2 mentions the "day of the Lord," but emphasizes its prerequisites rather than its un-expectedness (cf. 1 Thess 5:2); the two emphases often appear together in collections of early Jewish traditions.

54. But here the children are right in doing so, because of parents' sin; it could be inversion of the normal moral order (cf. 23:26), but is probably reproaching ancestors for bringing judgments.

55. Elders and younger ones in conflict, along with poor vs. rich, small vs. great — again to return them to the way (23:20).

56. Children shame elders, in a negative portrayal of social inversion.

57. Positive.

58. Negative.

59. "Adulterous" kings, in the "beginning" of the eschatological time (197-98).

60. Using God's name, "but not with truth."

61. Unless the line is a later interpolation, the Empire falling "into heresy" (Danby, p. 306) cannot be post-Constantinian, given the early-third-century date of the Mishnah.

62. In the period between the Flood and the End.

63. A great final plague.

64. In the period between the Flood and the End.

65. Gray-haired infants, etc.

66. But this is fulfilled first of all in the exile (*Sib. Or.* 3.265-281).

67. But this probably refers to shortening of *number* of days, not their length.

68. But this probably refers to shortening of *number* of days, not their length.

69. Following Hesiod *Works and Days* 181; common in Roman lists of "prodigies."

70. This may be assumed from the sort of Jewish eschatology relevant to first-century Christian works reporting Jesus' resurrection.

Notes to Appendix 5

1. Estimates for the year of crucifixion usually settle on 30 or 33 CE, with preference for the former (Blinzler, *Trial*, 72-80; Brown, *Death*, 1373-76; Meier, *Marginal Jew*, 1:402), including by myself (for the latter, see e.g., Duriez, *Year*). Still, because of potential early Jewish observational mistakes the astronomical evidence for any date remains indeterminate (Sanders, *Figure*, 284).

2. With Borchert, "Passover," 316; Yee, *Feasts*, 68. Much of what follows is adapted from Keener, *Matthew*, 622-23.

3. This makes harmonization difficult (though Story, "Chronology," thinks John agreed with Synoptic chronology here).

4. Cf. e.g., Byron, "Passover"; Boring et al., *Commentary*, 147.

5. E.g., Oesterley, *Liturgy*, 158-67; Stauffer, *Jesus*, 143; Grappe, "Essai"; Wilkinson, *Jerusalem*, 125; Meier, *Marginal Jew*, 1:395-401; Brown, *Death*, 1351-73; McKnight, *Death*, 270-72.

6. Later tradition also permits apostates to partake of the meal except the lamb (Stauffer, *Jesus*, 210), but this prohibition is probably irrelevant here.

7. Reicke, *Era*, 179-82; Meier, *Marginal Jew*, 1:396. See our fuller discussion of Jaubert's thesis below.

8. Jewett, *Chronology*, 27; cf. Meier, *Matthew*, 316.

9. Theissen, *Gospels in Context*, 167.

10. *B. Sanh.* 43a, bar. ("on the eve of Passover").

11. Mk 15:42. Despite disagreement on the relation to the festival, most commentators agree that the crucifixion occurred on a Friday (Brown, *Death*, 1350-51). Even by the third century rabbis were not unanimous about trying and executing someone on a Sabbath (*p. Sanh.* 4:6, §2).

12. On the Sanhedrin wishing to kill Jesus before the feast, see comment on Matt 26:1-2, in Keener, *Matthew*, 617.

13. Jeremias, *Eucharistic Words*, 20-23, 62-84; Hagner, *Matthew*, 772-73; cf. Hill, *Matthew*, 336-37.

14. Bornkamm, *Experience*, 132.

15. E.g., Higgins, "Eucharist," 208-9.

16. E.g., Morris, *John*, 785.

17. Jaubert, *Date*.

18. Cf. *Jub.* 49:10, 14; Herr, "Calendar." The calendar of Jubilees may have had some impact on public policy in the second century BCE (Wirgin, *Jubilees*, 12-17, 42-43) and has some parallels with later rabbinic calendrical halakah (Grintz, "Jubilees," 325), but in contrast to what became mainstream Judaism preserves the older solar calendar (Morgenstern, "Calendar"; cf. Marcus, "Scrolls," 12), for which some even (probably wrongly) label it pre-Hasmonean (Zeitlin, "Jubilees," 224; cf. Zeitlin, "Character," 8-16). Opposition to the lunar calendar is implied even in its creation narrative (*Jub.* 2:9-10; cf. 6:36). This places Jubilees much closer to Qumran thought than to Pharisaism (e.g., Brownlee, "Jubilees," 32; Baumgarten, "Beginning"; Grintz, "Jubilees," 324); Rivkin, "Jubilees," even thinks that Jubilees writes polemically against the Pharisaic calendar, but that could be later.

19. *M. R.H.* 2:9.

20. Cf. Driver, *Scrolls*, 330, 335; Simon, *Sects*, 151; Stauffer, *Jesus*, 115; Bruce, *Documents*, 57; Bruce, "Gospels," 78; Morris, *John*, 785; cf. Svensson, "Qumrankalendern" (John tried to harmonize Qumran's with the dominant lunar calendar). Cf. the carefully conceived work of Busada, "Calendar."

21. E.g., Benoit, *Jesus*, 1:87-93; Abegg, "Calendars," 183.

22. Cf. Brown, *Essays*, 207-17, arguing that John reports the real date, whereas the Synoptics report Jesus' Last Supper a day early.

23. Shepherd, "Date." Carson, "Matthew," 529 also mentions other proposals, e.g., that Pharisees and Sadducees followed divergent calendars (Strack-Billerbeck) or that the Galileans followed the Pharisaic (and Synoptic) one and Judeans the Sadducean (and Johannine) one (though Josephus places most Pharisees in Jerusalem). But I suspect that a major difference in *observance* in the Temple would have left more trace in extant first-century sources concerning feasts (like Josephus).

24. E.g., Keener, *John*, 899, 1100-3, 1129-31.

25. France, *Matthew*, 365. One cannot argue this, however, from the lack of mention of purification or lamb; these would be taken for granted (everyone in the Roman Empire expected animal sacrifices and purifications for festivals), and it would be their *omission* that would have required comment (Sanders, *Figure*, 251).

26. See Blomberg, *Reliability*, 238, 254 (citing esp. Smith, "Chronology of Supper"; Carson, *John*, 589-90, 622; Geldenhuys, *Luke*, 649-70; and linguistic data in Billerbeck, *Kommentar*, 837-38), taking the "high" Sabbath as a Sabbath that falls on a festival (19:31), and John's "preparation" (19:14) as for the sabbath (cf. Mk 15:42) and merely during Passover (Jn 19:14). If we did not have the Synoptic tradition, however, no one would pursue such expedients; the language more naturally suggests the preparation was for Passover as well as the sabbath. This is not to deny that John may depend on historical tradition here (with this as possibly the most workable suggestion), but to suggest that he at least exploits the ambiguity to present Jesus as the passover lamb (1:29; 19:36).

Notes to Appendix 6

1. Many see a Roman "cohort" in John (e.g., Rensberger, *Faith,* 90; O'Day, "John," 801-2; Kaufman, "Anti-Semitism"), and argue that John correctly preserves the tradition that only (Cohn, *Trial,* 78) or, more commonly, additionally (e.g., Anderson, *Mark,* 327; Stauffer, *Jesus,* 119) Romans were involved in the arrest.

2. E.g., Winter, *Trial,* 44; Bruce, "Trial," 9.

3. Stambaugh and Balch, *Environment,* 34. Many scholars see the temple police rather than Romans here (e.g., Ridderbos, *John,* 575).

4. E.g., Jos. *Life* 242. See further Catchpole, *Trial,* 149; Blinzler, *Trial,* 64-65; Bammel, "Trial," 439-40; cf. Wilkinson, *Jerusalem,* 126-27. For knowledge of Gentile military imagery in 1QM, see (favoring Greek imagery) Avi-Yonah, "War," 1-3; Delcor, "Guerre," 380; Atkinson, "Setting," 294; (favoring Roman) Yadin, *Scroll of War,* 138, 161; Vermes, *Scrolls,* 123.

5. Catchpole, *Trial,* 149, cites here Jdt 14:11; 2 Macc 8:23; 12:20, 22; Jos. *Ant.* 17.215. Greek often used more general terms to translate Roman military ones (see e.g., Tully, "Στρατάρχης").

6. In the LXX, 25-30 times (e.g., Ex 18:21, 25; Num 1:16; 31:14, 48-54; Deut 1:15; Josh 22:14, 21; 1 Chron 13:1; 15:25). Catchpole, *Trial,* 149, notes here 1 Macc. 3:55; Jos. *War* 2.578; *Ant.* 17.215; Mk 6:21. Cf. also Bammel, "Trial," 439-40.

7. Even when Josephus refers to a Roman *speira* on the temple roof — the sense of which ought to be obvious — he must limit it with *Romaikē* (*War* 2.224; 5.244; Catchpole, *Trial,* 149).

8. Blinzler, *Trial,* 64-65.

9. Cf. e.g., Hunter, *John,* 166; Hurtado, *Mark,* 233.

10. Pace, e.g., Bernard, *John,* 2:584.

11. The governor normally arrived with extra troops to control the Passover crowds if necessary (cf. *War* 2.224-26; *Ant.* 20.109-10); the crowds grew most restless at the pilgrimage festivals (Jos. *War* 1.88; cf. *War* 2.42, 254-56).

12. *Trial,* 149-50.

13. Cf. Brown, *Death,* 250. Cullmann, *State,* 43-44, assigns legal responsibility to the Romans but moral responsibility (perhaps too much) to the Jerusalem authorities.

14. Brown, *Death,* 250-51.

15. See fuller discussion in Keener, *John,* 1080-81.

Notes to Appendix 7

1. Cohn, *Trial,* 109; Flusser, *Judaism,* 589.

2. Jos. *War* 2.117; cf. *b. Shab.* 108a.

3. Winter, *Trial,* 10-15; Smallwood, *Jews,* 150.

4. Winter, *Trial,* 75-90.

5. Even though profanation of the Temple (cf. Acts 21:28-29) was the one charge for which the Romans permitted local executions; cf. O'Rourke, "Law," 174; Sanders, *Judaism,* 61. Paul's Roman citizenship could shield him under normal circumstances (Rabello, "Condition," 738), but not for profaning a temple (Jos. *War* 2.224; Hesiod *Astron. frg.* 3).

6. Theissen, *Gospels in Context,* 191.

7. Theissen, *Gospels in Context,* 189-93. The execution R. Eliezer ben Zadok allegedly witnessed in his childhood (*m. Sanh.* 7:2; *tos. Sanh.* 9:11) probably would have stemmed from the reign of Agrippa I (Bruce, "Trial," 12; cf. Acts 12:1-3).

8. Cf. also Catchpole, *Trial,* 247.

9. O'Rourke, "Law," 174-75.

10. Brown, *Death,* 339 correctly observes that executions required ratification by the Sanhedrin

in Jos. *Ant.* 14.167; while this datum is undoubtedly relevant, we should note that it describes the time of Herod the Great, not direct Roman rule. The Gospels involve the period of Roman rule.

11. E.g., *Sipre Deut.* 154.2.1.

12. E.g., *b. Sanh.* 49b-50a.

13. Unless secret executions (cf. Winter, *Trial*, 70-73) were practiced; but Pharisaic requirements for evidence were so strict that executions must have remained very rare under the later rabbis, if they even held sufficient influence as to get away with carrying them out at all.

14. *Sipre Deut.* 154.1.1; *b. Sanh.* 37b. The date appears indeterminate in *Sipra Qed.* par. 4.206.2.9.

15. E.g., *p. Sanh.* 1:1, §3; 7:2, §3. Safrai, "Government," 398 cites also *b. Shab.* 15a; *A.Z.* 8b. This was the widespread view at the turn of the twentieth century (Abrahams, *Studies,* 1:73; Sanday, *Criticism,* 127).

16. For so it would be viewed (Ep. Jer. 14).

17. Blinzler, *Trial*, 164; Winter, *Trial*, 12-13.

18. E.g., Morris, *Luke,* 319.

19. Plut. *R.Q.* 83, *Mor.* 283F (although he notes that Romans had themselves offered such sacrifices).

20. Blinzler, *Trial*, 164-68; Ramsay, *Church*, 293.

21. E.g., Benoit, *Jesus,* 1:135; Lane, *Mark,* 530; Stewart, "Procedure"; Sanders, *Jesus to Mishnah,* 17; Bruce, "Trial," 12-13. Cf. the implications of Jos. *Ant.* 20.200.

22. *Society,* 36; see more fully 32-43.

23. Brown, *Death,* 363-72.

24. Sanders, *Jesus to Mishnah,* 17.

Notes to Appendix 8

1. Sanders, *Figure,* 276-80, addresses it carefully, but begins by conceding that "The resurrection is not, strictly speaking, part of the story of the historical Jesus, but rather belongs to the aftermath of his life."

2. For insistence that historical Jesus research is incomplete without addressing this question, see Bockmuehl, "Resurrection," 102-18; for insistence on incorporating the theological question, see Geivett, "Epistemology." Keck, *History,* 127-28, rightly points to the evidence that the early Jesus movement focused on his resurrection more than on his words alone.

3. For a philosophic response (developing Pannenberg), see Houston, *Miracles,* 210-23; more briefly, Charlesworth, "Resurrection," 170-71; idem, "Conclusion," 227.

4. Segal, "Resurrection," 135 (emphasis his).

5. Segal, "Resurrection," 136. Segal's appeal to Paul is more helpful, but I focus on his objection here because it makes explicit a wider methodological problem sometimes ignored in current academic discussion.

6. Habermas, "Trend," 91-92, shows that the majority of scholars writing on the resurrection now view bodily resurrection as the likeliest option, quite a dramatic increase over the views a generation earlier.

7. Here I do not mean a "neutral" one ready to follow wherever the evidence leads, but, as the context of this argument should suggest, someone committed to the philosophic a priori that supernatural activity is impossible (an approach that reflects either atheistic or deistic premises, although not all its advocates would recognize or articulate this).

8. The closest parallels usually cited for the biblical creation narratives are early-second-millennium BCE Mesopotamian creation narratives; Egyptian creation narratives should also be taken into account. Whatever one's other views concerning their point, the *genre* and interests of the biblical creation narratives differ from the form of Greco-Roman biography and historiography we have ear-

lier argued for the Gospels. (The only common elements are a narrative format and focus on divine activity, neither of which is very distinctive.)

9. Cf. e.g., Borg, "Disagreement," 232, allowing for healings and exorcisms but not raising someone long dead, walking on water, or multiplying food.

10. The later parallel with Sabbetai Zevi occurs in a context when the resurrection explanation was already available from pervasive Christian tradition.

11. Although Christians following Paul's theology would affirm that Jesus' resurrection differed in character from other resuscitation accounts (i.e., with an immortal "spiritual" body), many would not see the return of life to a corpse, the primary issue under debate here, as "unique." It appears in the Hebrew Bible, in Jesus' ministry, and in Acts, and claims of such occurrences abound today (albeit with varying degrees of documentation and variation in the plausibility of alternative explanations; see e.g., De Wet, "Signs," 110-11; Lewis, *Healing,* 64-65; Bush and Pegues, *Move,* 52, 57-60, 118-19; Lambert, *Millions,* 109; Chevreau, *Turnings,* 53-56; Khai, "Pentecostalism," 270; Jenkins, *New Faces,* 114; Miller and Yamamori, *Pentecostalism,* 151-53). Again, I reserve full discussion (including more of these claims) for the book on miracles. With Pannenberg, Jesus' resurrection is not unique even in kind if one allows its eschatological context; but this approach necessarily postpones verification and falsification, so (while technically true) it does not affect the matter under discussion here.

12. Wright, *Resurrection,* 12; for his full discussion of historical investigation and Jesus' resurrection, see Wright, *Resurrection,* 3-31, 685-718.

13. Wright, *Resurrection,* 12-13.

14. Wright, *Resurrection,* 15-16.

15. Wright, *Resurrection,* 712-13.

16. Cf. Meier, "Reflections," 106, who apparently does believe that the resurrection occurred, but denies that it is "verifiable in principle by believer and nonbeliever alike."

17. The most thorough work on historiography and the resurrection, one not yet available to me at the time of this work's preparation, is Licona, "Historicity of Resurrection." I mention it here in the hope that further work can take it into account and build on it.

18. Wright, *Resurrection,* 16-17. In contrast to physics and chemistry, history cannot deal only in repeatable events (Wright, *Resurrection,* 685), though one might naturally counter that it normally focuses on "repeatable *kinds* of events."

19. Meier, "Reflections," 106 (though he apparently does himself believe that the resurrection occurred).

20. Cf. Perkins, "Resurrection," 442; Meier, "Reflections," 106.

21. Antony Flew is a notable case of an atheist who turned deist (Flew, *God*); his case is particularly notable because the modern academic world includes many more examples that moved in the other direction (e.g., Bart Ehrman's move toward agnosticism). I believe that particular philosophic premises dominant in the past century of academia drive academicians more naturally toward skepticism (cf. Smith, "Education"; Marsden, *Idea,* 3-7, 13-24), and I personally would attribute this tendency more to cultural plausibility structures than to where I believe the evidence best points.

22. E.g., Johnson, "Quest"; cf. idem, *Real Jesus* (for a summary, see Dowd, "Real Jesus"). Miller, "Orthodoxy," argues that Johnson inconsistently mixes a Jesus of faith (a composite from different Gospels) with an appeal to the earliest, historical Jesus.

23. E.g., Reiser, "Eclipsing"; McEvoy, "Dilemma"; McClymond, *Stranger,* x-xi; Haar, "Quest"; on the importance of Jesus' Jewish character for Christian faith and for dialogue with Judaism, see Levine, *Misunderstood Jew.* For an attempt to enculturate the fruits of Jesus research for India, see e.g., Mathews, "Quest"; for Africa, see e.g., Craffert, "Research." For a postfoundational attempt to integrate the value of historical Jesus inquiry with faith, see Keating, "Epistemology."

24. For example, McClymond, *Stranger,* 140, notes that the sources provide not only the comfortable western interpretation of Jesus as "socially inclusive" or oriented toward "family values," but also "a homewrecker," one who favored the poor, "preached fire-and-brimstone," and "was a totalitarian."

Notes to Appendix 9

1. For Jesus limiting his own mission exclusively or at least mostly to Israel, see Sanders, *Jesus and Judaism*, 11; Ellis, *Matthew*, 49.

2. Witherington, *Christology*, 124.

3. Nevertheless, the saying in Matt 10:5 addresses geography more than ethnicity, restricting the mission primarily to Galilee (see Gundry, *Matthew*, 185; Manson, *Sayings*, 179; cf. Jeremias, *Promise*, 19 n. 3).

4. Some doubt that it originated with Jesus' teaching, though not necessarily regarding it as incompatible with Jesus' teaching (Sanders, *Jesus and Judaism*, 212-21).

5. See Donaldson, *Gentiles*, 52-74.

6. See e.g., Schnabel, "Mission," especially 58; Bird, *Gentile Mission*, passim, esp. 3, 26-29, 172, 177; Simon, "Acts of Philip," 69-70. I leave aside the question of whether he viewed Gentiles as pure during his mission, before an end-time ingathering; many would answer this question less optimistically (see Mk 7:27; more strongly and perhaps traditionally, Matt 15:24-26; note also what seems likely a question [possibly an objection] in Matt 8:8, though not in Lk 7:6).

7. See Bowers, "Propaganda," 320-21; Murphy-O'Connor, "Mission"; McKnight, *Light;* Cohen, "Missionize."

8. E.g., Paget, "Proselytism"; Ker, "Missionary Activity"; Rokéah, "Proselytism."

9. Cf. Theissen, *Gospels in Context*, 52.

10. Pace Sanders, *Jesus and Judaism*, 220; Allison, "East." Strong evidence supports Matt 8:11-12// Lk 13:28-29 as an authentic saying of Jesus (Semitisms and background in Jeremias, *Promise*, 55-62).

11. Matthew may draw Jesus' words here from another context (whether or not the context of Lk 13:28-29 is original) to reinforce the point that this story prefigures the Gentile mission, which Jesus endorsed in advance (France, "Exegesis in Practice," 260).

12. The context is explicit in Matthew; similarly, Luke's addition of "north and south" probably is meant to recall the recent "the queen of the south" and Nineveh (Lk 11:30-31).

13. See also Gundry, *Matthew*, 145.

14. E.g., Is 56:3-8. For the end-time ingathering of Gentiles in Jewish sources, see the data in Jeremias, *Promise*, 56-61; Sanders, *Jesus and Judaism*, 213-15. Theissen, *Gospels in Context*, 45 suggests uncertainly that both Diaspora Jews and Gentiles could be involved.

15. Is 25:6-8 is the biblical source (so also Sanders, *Figure*, 185). Davies and Allison, *Matthew*, 2:27-28 tentatively object that no single passage in the Hebrew Bible has both nations coming to Zion (Is 2:2-4) and then banqueting (25:6-8). This objection, however, ignores the synthetic way Jesus and others of his day read Isaiah; why would Jesus' view of this aspect of the future, in contrast to his eschatology more broadly, be bound to a single text? Even if he drew from only a single text, his understanding of that text would be informed by others. For Jewish expectation of the messianic banquet, see e.g., 4 Macc 13:17; *1 En.* 70:4; *3 En.* 48A:10; *Test. Asher* 7:7; *Test. Benj.* 10:6-9; *m. Ab.* 3:16-17; 4:16; *b. Ber.* 34b; *Sanh.* 98b; *p. Taan.* 4:2, §12; *Gen. Rab.* 62:2; *Ex. Rab.* 45:6; 50:5; *Lev. Rab.* 13:3; *Num. Rab.* 13:2; *Ruth Rab.* 5:6; *Pesiq. Rab.* 41:5, 48:3; cf. Marmorstein, *Merits*, 46, 59, 120, 135; Bonsirven, *Judaism*, 244; Koenig, *Hospitality*, 16. Many find it also at Qumran (1QSa [=1Q28a] 2.11-12, 19-21; Priest, "Messiah"; but contrast Smith, "Begetting," 224).

16. Cf. Matt 5:47; 6:7, 32; 18:17; although these are plausibly directed toward Matthew's Jewish audience, at least one of these sayings is "Q" material (Lk 12:30), hence some of the other examples potentially might be, since Luke has reason not to emphasize them. Matthew includes an earlier prohibition against mission to Gentiles (Matt 10:5), but modifies it by the larger context of his gospel (Matt 10:18; 24:14; 28:19).

17. Pao, *Isaianic Exodus*, 111-46, shows at length that Luke sees Israel's restoration especially through the lens of Isaiah. But given the diverse understandings of Gentiles' fate (Donaldson, *Gentiles*,

52-74), sometimes even from Isaiah, it would not be surprising if Jesus' disciples initially remained confused.

18. Lk 9:52-55; 10:33; 17:16-18 (though Luke has a clear interest in Samaritans, this seems to stem from the Samaritan church, which in turn could have been justified from genuine teachings of Jesus; Acts 1:8; 8:1, 5-25; 9:31; 15:3); Jn 4:1-43. Cf. cautiously Meier, "Samaritans."

19. He refers to "other sheep" (Jn 10:16), who may refer to Gentiles (see Keener, *John*, 818-19); within the narrative world itself Jesus reaches Samaritans, who acknowledge him as "savior of the world" (Jn 4:42; cf. 12:20). He does not specifically articulate a Gentile mission, however, perhaps because of his Jewish focus or perhaps because it was no longer debatable by the time he wrote (Gentiles may have seen themselves as converts to this Jewish movement in any case; cf. Keener, *John*, 175).

20. Cf. e.g., Bultmann, *Tradition*, 289; Bornkamm, *Experience*, 15; Brown, "Mission."

21. E.g., White, *Initiation*, 338-45; Beasley-Murray, *Baptism*, 77-92.

22. See Meier, "Questions"; Brooks, "Design"; cf. Hubbard, *Redaction*; Davies and Allison, "Texts."

23. Bird, *Gentile Mission*, 6, 172, 177.

24. Even in Acts 15, the compromise probably involved treating Gentiles as God-fearers observing levitical laws for strangers in the land, or the Noahide laws. Not everyone would have agreed with Paul's approach of treating them as full proselytes without circumcision.

25. Paul saw his Gentile mission's eschatological role in Israel's history as forcing the rest of Judaism to recognize that it was the Jesus movement that was successfully implementing the eschatological ingathering of Gentiles, hence leading them to faith in Jesus (Rom 11:11-14; cf. Nanos, *Mystery*, 18, 249-50). He would have regarded subsequent Gentile Christianity's anti-Semitism as a failure compromising the direction of his own mission.

26. I say "many" because even Acts suggests that many of the believers in Jerusalem, influenced by their local culture's nationalistic shift under and after Agrippa I, seem to have moved in a different direction. They apparently became increasingly sensitive to the criticisms of Paul's movement (Gal 4:29; 5:11; 6:12; cf. Rom 3:8), including that it might ultimately lead even to Jews abandoning the law (Acts 21:20-21).

27. Matthean redaction adds to the attribution of Jesus' Spirit-empowerment (Matt 12:28), but in a context that already suggested it (Matt 12:24, 32 with Mk 3:29-30); Lukan redaction adds it to Jesus' teaching in Lk 11:13, undoubtedly foreshadowing the Pentecost narrative.

Bibliography of Sources Cited

As an aid to the reader, the listing below is by author, then by short title, followed by the full publishing information.

Aalders, "Gruwel." • Aalders, G. C. "De 'gruwel der verwoesting.'" *GTT* 60 (1960): 1-5.

Aalen, "Reign." • Aalen, Sverre. "'Reign' and 'House' in the Kingdom of God in the Gospels." *NTS* 8 (1962): 215-40.

Aarde, *Fatherless.* • Aarde, Andries van. *Fatherless in Galilee: Jesus as Child of God.* Harrisburg: Trinity Press International, 2001.

Aarde, "Historiese Jesus." • Aarde, Andries van. "Die historiese Jesus, die Jesus-beweging en die vorming van die kerk (The historical Jesus, the Jesus movement and the birth of the church)." *HTS/TS* 51 (3, 1995): 623-44.

Aarde, "Methods." • Aarde, Andries van. "Methods and models in the quest for the historical Jesus: Historical criticism and/or social scientific criticism." *HTS/TS* 58 (2, 2002): 419-39.

Abbott, *Acts.* • Abbott, Lyman. *The Acts of the Apostles. With Notes, Comments, Maps, and Illustrations.* New York: A. S. Barnes & Company, 1876.

Abegg, "Calendars." • Abegg, Martin G., Jr. "Calendars, Jewish." 180-83 in *DNTB.*

Abegg, "Hope." • Abegg, Martin G., Jr. "Messianic Hope and 4Q285: A Reassessment." *JBL* 113 (1, 1994): 81-91.

Abegg, "Introduction to 4Q285." • Abegg, Martin. "Introduction to 4Q285." 291-92 in *The Dead Sea Scrolls: A New Translation.* By Michael Wise, Martin Abegg, Jr., and Edward Cook. San Francisco: Harper SanFrancisco, 1999.

Abegg, "Introduction to 4Q369." • Abegg, Martin. "Introduction to 4Q369." 328-29 in *The Dead Sea Scrolls: A New Translation.* By Michael Wise, Martin Abegg, Jr., and Edward Cook. San Francisco: Harper SanFrancisco, 1999.

Abegg, "Messiah." • Abegg, Martin G. "The Messiah at Qumran: Are We Still Seeing Double?" *DSD* 2 (2, 1995): 125-44.

Aberbach, "Hzqyhw." • Aberbach, Moses. "Hzqyhw mlk yhwdh wrby yhwdh hsny': hqsrym msyhyym." *Tarbiz* 53 (3, 1984): 353-71.

Abogunrin, "Debate." • Abogunrin, Samuel O. "The Synoptic Gospel Debate: A Re-Examination in the African Context." *AJBS* 2 (1-2, 1987): 25-51.

Abrahams, *Studies* 1. • Abrahams, I. *Studies in Pharisaism and the Gospels.* 1st series. Prolegomenon by Morton S. Enslin. Library of Biblical Studies. New York: Ktav, 1967; reprint of Cambridge: Cambridge University Press, 1917.

Abrahams, *Studies* 2. • Abrahams, I. *Studies in Pharisaism and the Gospels.* 2d series. Cambridge: Cambridge University Press, 1924.

Abramowski, "Memoirs." • Abramowski, Luise. "The 'Memoirs of the Apostles' in Justin," 323-35 in *The Gospel and the Gospels.* Ed. Peter Stuhlmacher. Grand Rapids: Eerdmans, 1991.

Abrams, "Boundaries." • Abrams, Daniel. "The Boundaries of Divine Ontology: The Inclusion and Exclusion of Metatron in the Godhead." *HTR* 87 (3, 1994): 291-321.

Adams, "Preface." • Adams, Sean A. "Luke's Preface and Its Relationship to Greek Historiography: A Response to Loveday Alexander." *JGRCJ* 3 (2006): 177-91.

Adan-Bayewitz and Perlman, "Trade." • Adan-Bayewitz, David, and Isadore Perlman. "The Local Trade of Sepphoris in the Roman Period." *IEJ* 40 (1990): 153-72.

Adinolfi, "Lago." • Adinolfi, Marco. "Il lago di Tiberiade e le sue città nella letteratura greco-romana." *SBFLA* 44 (1994): 375-80.

Adinolfi, "Servo." • Adinolfi, Marco. "Il servo di Jhwh nel logion servizio e del riscatto (*Mc.* 10,45)." *BeO* 21 (1979): 43-61.

Adler, "Sectarian Characteristics." • Adler, Yonatan. "Identifying Sectarian Characteristics in the Phylacteries from Qumran." *RevQ* 23 (89, 2007): 79-92.

Ådna, "Attitude." • Ådna, Jostein. "The Attitude of Jesus to the Temple. A critical examination of how Jesus' relationship to the Temple is evaluated within Israeli scholarship, with particular regard to the Jerusalem School." *Mishkan* 17-18 (1992-93): 65-80.

Agouridis, "Son of Man." • Agouridis, S. "The Son of Man in Enoch." *DBM* 2 (6, 1973): 130-47.

Albright, *Stone Age*. • Albright, William Foxwell. *From the Stone Age to Christianity: Monotheism and the Historical Process.* Baltimore: Johns Hopkins, 1946.

Albright, *Yahweh* • Albright, William Foxwell. *Yahweh and the Gods of Canaan.* The Jordan Lectures 1965. Garden City, NY: Doubleday & Company, 1968.

Albright and Mann, *Matthew*. • Albright, W. F., and C. S. Mann. *Matthew.* Anchor Bible. Garden City, NY: Doubleday & Company, 1971.

Alexander, *Context*. • Alexander, Loveday C. A. *Acts in Its Ancient Literary Context: A Classicist Looks at the Acts of the Apostles.* Early Christianity in Context, LNTS 298. London: T & T Clark International, 2005.

Alexander, "3 Enoch." • Alexander, P. Introduction to "3 (Hebrew Apocalypse of) Enoch." 1:223-253 in *OTP.*

Alexander, "Fiction and Genre." • Alexander, Loveday. "Fact, Fiction and the Genre of Acts." *NTS* 44 (3, 1998): 380-99.

Alexander, "Formal Elements." • Alexander, Loveday C. A. "Formal Elements and Genre: Which Greco-Roman Prologues Most Closely Parallel the Lukan Prologues?" 9-26 in *Jesus and the Heritage of Israel: Luke's Narrative Claim upon Israel's Legacy.* Ed. David P. Moessner. Vol. 1 in Luke the Interpreter of Israel. Harrisburg, PA: Trinity Press International, 1999.

Alexander, "Hellenism." • Alexander, Philip S. "Hellenism and Hellenization as Problematic Historiographical Categories." 63-80 in *Paul Beyond the Judaism/Hellenism Divide.* Ed. Troels Engberg-Pedersen. Louisville, KY: Westminster John Knox, 2001.

Alexander, "IPSE DIXIT." • Alexander, Loveday. "IPSE DIXIT: Citation of Authority in Paul and in the Jewish Hellenistic Schools." 103-27 in *Paul Beyond the Judaism/Hellenism Divide.* Ed. Troels Engberg-Pedersen. Louisville, KY: Westminster John Knox, 2001.

Alexander, *Preface*. • Alexander, Loveday. *The Preface to Luke's Gospel: Literary Convention and Social Context in Luke 1.1-4 and Acts 1.1.* SNTSMS 78. Cambridge: Cambridge University Press, 1993.

Alexander, "Preface." • Alexander, Loveday C. A. "The Preface to Acts and the Historians." 73-103 in *History, Literature, and Society in the Book of Acts.* Ed. Ben Witherington, III. Cambridge: Cambridge University Press, 1996.

Alexander, "Rule." • Alexander, P. S. "Jesus and the Golden Rule." 489-508 in *The Historical Jesus in*

Recent Research. Ed. James D. G. Dunn and Scot McKnight. Winona Lake, IN: Eisenbrauns, 2005.

Allegro, "Light." • Allegro, John M. "Further Light on the History of the Qumran Sect." *JBL* 75 (2, June 1956): 89-95.

Allegro, "References." • Allegro, John M. "Further Messianic References in Qumran Literature." *JBL* 75 (3, Sept 1956): 174-187.

Allison, "Allusive Jesus." • Allison, Dale C., Jr. "The Allusive Jesus." 238-47 in *The Historical Jesus in Recent Research.* Ed. James D. G. Dunn and Scot McKnight. Winona Lake, IN: Eisenbrauns, 2005.

Allison, "Continuity." • Allison, Dale C. "The Continuity between John and Jesus." *JSHJ* 1 (1, 2003): 6-27.

Allison, "East." • Allison, Dale C., Jr. "Who Will Come from East and West? Observations on Matt 8.11-12 — Luke 13.28-29." *IBS* 11 (1989): 158-70.

Allison, "Elijah." • Allison, Dale C., Jr. "Elijah Must Come First." *JBL* 103 (2, 1984): 256-58.

Allison, "Eschatological Jesus." • Allison, Dale C. "The Eschatological Jesus: Did He Believe the End Was Near?" *BRev* 12 (5, 1996): 34-41, 54-55.

Allison, "Eschatology." • Allison, Dale C., Jr. "A Plea for Thoroughgoing Eschatology." *JBL* 113 (1994): 651-68.

Allison, *Jesus of Nazareth.* • Allison, Dale C. *Jesus of Nazareth: Millenarian Prophet.* Minneapolis: Fortress, 1998.

Allison, *Moses.* • Allison, Dale C., Jr. *The New Moses: A Matthean Typology.* Minneapolis: Fortress, 1993.

Allison, "Notes." • Allison, Dale C., Jr. "Two Notes on a Key Text: Matthew 11:25-30." *JTS* 39 (1988): 477-85.

Allison, "Prophecy." • Allison, Dale C., Jr. "Matt. 23:39=Luke 13:35b as a Conditional Prophecy." *JSNT* 18 (1983): 75-84.

Allison, "Thallus." • Allison, Dale C., Jr. "Thallus on the Crucifixion." 405-6 in *The Historical Jesus in Context.* Ed. Amy-Jill Levine, Dale C. Allison Jr., and John Dominic Crossan. Princeton Readings in Religions. Princeton: Princeton University Press, 2006.

Allison, "Victory of Apocalyptic." • Allison, Dale C., Jr. "Jesus & the Victory of Apocalyptic." 126-41 in *Jesus and the Restoration of Israel: A Critical Assessment of N. T. Wright's Jesus and the Victory of God.* Ed. Carey C. Newman. Downers Grove: InterVarsity, 1999.

Alsup, "Function." • Alsup, John E. "Type, Placement, and Function of the Pronouncement Story in Plutarch's *Moralia.*" *Semeia* 20 (1981): 15-27.

Amaru, "Killing." • Amaru, Betsy Halperin. "The Killing of the Prophets: Unraveling a Midrash." *HUCA* 54 (1983): 153-80.

Amaru, "Women." • Amaru, Betsy Halperin. "Portraits of Biblical Women in Josephus' Antiquities." *JJS* 39 (2, 1988): 143-70.

Anderson, *Glossary.* • Anderson, R. Dean, Jr. *Glossary of Greek Rhetorical Terms Connected to Methods of Argumentation, Figures and Tropes from Anaximenes to Quintilian.* Leuven: Peeters, 2000.

Anderson, *Jesus and Origins.* • Anderson, Hugh. *Jesus and Christian Origins: A Commentary on Modern Viewpoints.* New York: Oxford University Press, 1964.

Anderson, "3 Maccabees." • Anderson, Hugh. Introduction to "3 Maccabees." 2:509-516 in *OTP.*

Anderson, "4 Maccabees." • Anderson, Hugh. Introduction to "4 Maccabees." 2:531-43 in *OTP.*

Anderson, *Mark.* • Anderson, Hugh. *The Gospel of Mark.* New Century Bible. London: Oliphants (Marshall, Morgan & Scott), 1976.

Anderson, *Rhetorical Theory.* • Anderson, R. Dean, Jr. *Ancient Rhetorical Theory and Paul.* Rev. ed. Contributions to Biblical Exegesis and Theology, 18. Leuven: Peeters, 1999.

Andiñach, "Barca." • Andiñach, Pablo. "Una antigua barca del Mar de Galilea." *Revista Bíblica* 52 (1990): 178-84.

Andreau, "Publicani." • Andreau, Jean. "Publicani." 12:181-84 in *Brill's New Pauly*.

Angus, *Mystery-Religions*. • Angus, S. *The Mystery-Religions and Christianity*. New York: Scribner's, 1925.

Applebaum, *Cyrene*. • Applebaum, Shim'on. *Jews and Greeks in Ancient Cyrene*. SJLA 28. Leiden: E. J. Brill, 1979.

Applebaum, "Economic Life." • Applebaum, Shim'on. "Economic Life in Palestine." 631-700 in *JPFC*.

Applebaum, "Zealots." • Applebaum, Shim'on. "The Zealots: the Case for Reevaluation." *JRS* 61 (1971): 155-70.

Arav, "Bethsaida." • Arav, Rami. "Bethsaida, 1989." *IEJ* 41 (1991): 184-85.

Arav and Rousseau, "Bethsaïde." • Arav, Rami, and J. Rousseau. "Bethsaïde, ville perdue et retrouvée." *RB* 100 (1993): 415-28.

Argyle, "Greek." • Argyle, A. W. "Greek Among the Jews of Palestine in New Testament Times." *NTS* 20 (1973): 87-89.

Argyle, *Matthew*. • Argyle, A. W. *The Gospel According to Matthew*. Cambridge: Cambridge University Press, 1963.

Argyle, "Semitism." • Argyle, A. W. "An Alleged Semitism." *ExpT* 67 (1956): 247.

Arlandson, *Women*. • Arlandson, James Malcolm. *Women, Class and Society in Early Christianity: Models from Luke-Acts*. Peabody: Hendrickson, 1997.

Armenti, "Galileans." • Armenti, Joseph R. "On the Use of the Term 'Galileans' in the Writings of Josephus Flavius: A Brief Note." *JQR* 72 (1, July 1981): 45-49.

Arnéra, "Rocher." • Arnéra, G. "Du rocher d'Esaïe aux douze montagnes d'Hermas." *ETR* 59 (1984): 215-20.

Arnold, *Samuel*. • Arnold, Bill T. *1 & 2 Samuel*. NIVAC. Grand Rapids: Zondervan, 2003.

Arnott, "Realism." • Arnott, W. Geoffrey. "Longus, Natural History, and Realism." 199-215 in *The Search for the Ancient Novel*. Ed. James Tatum. Baltimore, London: The Johns Hopkins University Press, 1994.

Aron-Schnapper and Hanet, "Archives." • Aron-Schnapper, Dominique, and Daniele Hanet. "Archives orales et histoire de institutions sociales." *RevFSoc* 19 (2, April 1978): 261-75.

Ashton, *Understanding*. • Ashton, John. *Understanding the Fourth Gospel*. Oxford: Clarendon Press, 1991.

Asso, "Raconter." • Asso, Philippe. "Raconter pour persuader: discours et narration des *Actes des Apôtres*." *RSR* 90 (4, 2002): 555-71.

Atkinson, "Setting." • Atkinson, K. M. T. "The Historical Setting of the 'War of the Sons of Light and the Sons of Darkness.'" *BJRL* 40 (1957-58): 272-97.

Attridge, "Historiography." • Attridge, Harold W. "Jewish Historiography." 311-43 in *Early Judaism and Its Modern Interpreters*. Ed. Robert A. Kraft and George W. E. Nickelsburg. SBLBMI 2. Atlanta: Scholars Press, 1986.

Attridge, *History in Josephus*. • Attridge, Harold W. *The Interpretation of Biblical History in the Antiquitates Judaicae of Flavius Josephus*. Harvard Dissertations in Religion 7. Missoula, MT: Scholars Press, 1976.

Aubin, "Reversing Romance." • Aubin, Melissa. "Reversing Romance? *The Acts of Thecla* and the Ancient Novel." 257-72 in *Ancient Fiction and Early Christian Narrative*. Ed. Ronald F. Hock, J. Bradley Chance and Judith Perkins. SBLSymS 6. Atlanta: Society of Biblical Literature, 1998.

Augoustakis, "Nequaquam." • Augoustakis, Antonios. "*Nequaquam historia digna?* Plinian Style in *Ep.* 6.20." *CJ* 100 (3, 2005): 265-273.

Aune, "Biography." • Aune, David Edward. "Greco-Roman Biography." 107-26 in *Greco-Roman Lit-*

erature and the New Testament: Selected Forms and Genres. Ed. David E. Aune. SBLSBS 21. Atlanta: Scholars Press, 1988.

Aune, *Dictionary of Rhetoric.* • Aune, David E. *The Westminster Dictionary of New Testament & Early Christian Literature & Rhetoric.* Louisville: Westminster John Knox, 2003.

Aune, *Environment.* • Aune, David Edward. *The New Testament in Its Literary Environment.* LEC 8. Philadelphia: Westminster Press, 1987.

Aune, *Eschatology.* • Aune, David Edward. *The Cultic Setting of Realized Eschatology in Early Christianity.* NovTSup 28. Leiden: E. J. Brill, 1972.

Aune, "Magic." • Aune, David Edward. "Magic in Early Christianity." *ANRW* II (Principat).23.1.1507-1557.

Aune, "Problem." • Aune, David Edward. "The Problem of the Genre of the Gospels: A Critique of C. H. Talbert's *What Is a Gospel?*" 2:9-60 in *GosPersp.* Vol. 2: *Studies of History and Tradition in the Four Gospels.* Sheffield: JSOT Press, 1981.

Aune, "Prooimion." • Aune, David E. "Luke 1.1-4: Historical or Scientific *Prooimion?*" 138-48 in *Paul, Luke and the Graeco-Roman World.* Ed. Alf Christophersen, Carsten Claussen, Jörg Frey and Bruce Longenecker. JSNTSup 217. Sheffield: Sheffield Academic Press, 2002; London: T. & T. Clark, 2003.

Aune, *Prophecy.* • Aune, David Edward. *Prophecy in Early Christianity and the Ancient Mediterranean World.* Grand Rapids: Eerdmans, 1983.

Aune, *Revelation.* • Aune, David E. *Revelation.* 3 vols. WBC 52, 52b, 52c. Dallas: Word, 1997.

Avery-Peck, "Piety." • Avery-Peck, Alan J. "The Galilean Charismatic and Rabbinic Piety: The Holy Man in the Talmudic Literature." 149-65 in *The Historical Jesus in Context.* Ed. Amy-Jill Levine, Dale C. Allison Jr., and John Dominic Crossan. Princeton Readings in Religions. Princeton: Princeton University Press, 2006.

Aviam, "Magdala." • Aviam, Mordechai. "Magdala." 3:399-400 in *OEANE.*

Avigad, "Burnt House." • Avigad, Nahman. "The Burnt House Captures a Moment in Time." *BAR* 9 (6, Nov. 1983): 66-72.

Avigad, "Flourishing." • Avigad, Nahman. "Jerusalem Flourishing — A Craft Center for Stone, Pottery, and Glass." *BAR* 9 (6, Nov. 1983): 48-65.

Avigad, *Jerusalem.* • Avigad, Nahman. *Discovering Jerusalem.* Nashville: Thomas Nelson Publishers, 1980.

Avioz, "Lot." • Avioz, Michael. "Josephus's Portrayal of Lot and His Family." *JSP* 16 (1, 2006): 3-13.

Avi-Yonah, "Geography." • Avi-Yonah, Michael. "Historical Geography." 78-116 in *JPFC.*

Avi-Yonah, *Hellenism.* • Avi-Yonah, Michael. *Hellenism and the East: Contacts and Interrelations from Alexander to the Roman Conquest.* Jerusalem: Institute of Languages, Literature and the Arts, The Hebrew University; University Microfilms International, 1978.

Avi-Yonah, "Sources." • Avi-Yonah, Michael. "Archaeological Sources." 46-62 in *JPFC.*

Avi-Yonah, "War." • Avi-Yonah, Michael. "The 'War of the Sons of Light and Sons of Darkness' and Maccabean Warfare." *IEJ* 2 (1, 1952): 1-5.

Bagatti, *Church.* • Bagatti, Bellarmino. *The Church from the Circumcision.* Jerusalem: Franciscan Printing Press, 1971.

Bailey, *Peasant Eyes.* • Bailey, Kenneth Ewing. *Through Peasant Eyes: More Lucan Parables, Their Culture and Style.* Grand Rapids: Eerdmans, 1980.

Bailey, *Poet.* • Bailey, Kenneth Ewing. *Poet and Peasant: A Literary Cultural Approach to the Parables in Luke.* Grand Rapids: Eerdmans, 1976.

Bailey, "Thessalonians." • Bailey, J. A. "Who Wrote II Thessalonians?" *NTS* 25 (2, Jan. 1979): 131-45.

Bailey, "Tradition." • Bailey, Kenneth Ewing. "Informal Controlled Oral Tradition and the Synoptic Gospels." *AJT* 5 (1, 1991): 34-54.

Baker, "Review of Glasson." • Baker, J. A. Review of "T. F. Glasson. *Greek Influence in Jewish Eschatology. With Special Reference to the Apocalypses and Pseudepigraphs.*" *JTS* 14 (1963): 120-21.

Balch, "Full History." • Balch, David L. "ἀκριβῶς . . . γράψαι (Luke 1:3). To Write the *Full* History of God's Receiving All Nations." 229-50 in *Jesus and the Heritage of Israel: Luke's Narrative Claim upon Israel's Legacy.* Ed. David P. Moessner. Vol. 1 in Luke the Interpreter of Israel, series ed. Moessner and David L. Tiede. Harrisburg, PA: Trinity Press International, 1999.

Balch, "Genre." • Balch, David L. "The Genre of Lk-Acts: Individual Biography, Adventure Novel, or Political History." *SWJT* 33 (1990): 5-19.

Balch, "ΜΕΤΑΒΟΛΗ ΠΟΛΙΤΕΙΩΝ." • Balch, David L. "ΜΕΤΑΒΟΛΗ ΠΟΛΙΤΕΙΩΝ — Jesus as Founder of the Church in Luke-Acts: Form and Function." 139-88 in *Contextualizing Acts: Lukan Narrative and Greco-Roman Discourse.* Ed. Todd Penner and Caroline Vander Stichele. SBLSymS 20. Atlanta: Society of Biblical Literature, 2003.

Bamberger, "Prophet." • Bamberger, Bernard J. "The Changing Image of the Prophet in Jewish Thought." 301-23 in *Interpreting the Prophetic Tradition: The Goldman Lectures 1955-1966.* Ed. Harry M. Orlinski. Cincinnati: Hebrew Union College Press, 1969; New York: Ktav, 1969.

Bamberger, *Story.* • Bamberger, Bernard J. *The Story of Judaism.* New York: The Union of American Hebrew Congregations, 1962.

Bammel, "Feeding." • Bammel, Ernst. "The Feeding of the Multitude." Pp. 211-40 in *Jesus and the Politics of His Day.* Ed. Ernst Bammel and C. F. D. Moule. Cambridge: Cambridge University Press, 1984.

Bammel, "Poor." • Bammel, Ernst. "The Poor and the Zealots." 109-28 in *Jesus and the Politics of His Day.* Ed. Ernst Bammel and C. F. D. Moule. Cambridge: Cambridge University Press, 1984.

Bammel, "Revolution Theory." • Bammel, Ernst. "The Revolution Theory from Reimarus to Brandon." 11-68 in *Jesus and the Politics of His Day.* Ed. Ernst Bammel and C. F. D. Moule. Cambridge: Cambridge University Press, 1984.

Bammel, "Titulus." • Bammel, Ernst. "The *titulus.*" Pp. 353-64 in *Jesus and the Politics of His Day.* Ed. Ernst Bammel and C. F. D. Moule. Cambridge: Cambridge University Press, 1984.

Bammel, "Trial." • Bammel, Ernst. "The Trial before Pilate." Pp. 415-51 in *Jesus and the Politics of His Day.* Ed. Ernst Bammel and C. F. D. Moule. Cambridge: Cambridge University Press, 1984.

Bandstra, "Errorists." • Bandstra, Andrew J. "Did the Colossian Errorists Need a Mediator?" 329-43 in *New Dimensions in New Testament Study.* Ed. Richard N. Longenecker and Merrill C. Tenney. Grand Rapids: Zondervan, 1974.

Bar-Asher, "Formules." • Bar-Asher, Moshé. "Les formules de bénédiction forgées par les sages (étude préliminaire)." *REJ* 166 (3-4, 2007): 441-61.

Barclay, *Child.* • Barclay, William. *Train Up a Child: Educational Ideals in the Ancient World.* Philadelphia: Westminster, 1959.

Barnard, *Justin Martyr.* • Barnard, L. W. *Justin Martyr: His Life and Thought.* Cambridge: At the University Press, 1967.

Barnard, "Old Testament." • Barnard, L. W. "The Old Testament and Judaism in the Writings of Justin Martyr." *VT* 14 (4, October 1964): 395-406.

Barnett, *Birth.* • Barnett, Paul. *The Birth of Christianity: The First Twenty Years.* Grand Rapids: Eerdmans, 2005.

Barnett, "Eschatological Prophets." • Barnett, Paul. "The Jewish Eschatological Prophets." Ph.D. dissertation, University of London, 1977.

Barnett, *Jesus and History.* • Barnett, Paul. *Jesus and the Logic of History.* New Studies in Biblical Theology. Grand Rapids: Eerdmans, 1997.

Barnett, "Prophets." • Barnett, Paul W. "The Jewish Sign Prophets — A.D. 40-70 — Their Intentions and Origin." *NTS* 27 (5, Oct. 1981): 679-97.

Barnett, *Reliable.* • Barnett, Paul. *Is the New Testament Reliable? A Look at the Historical Evidence.* Downers Grove, IL: InterVarsity Press, 1986.

Barnett, "Sign Prophets." • Barnett, P. W. "The Jewish Sign Prophets." 444-62 in *The Historical Jesus* *in Recent Research.* Ed. James D. G. Dunn and Scot McKnight. Winona Lake, IN: Eisenbrauns, 2005.

Barr and Wentling, "Biography and Genre." • Barr, David L., and Judith L. Wentling. "The Conventions of Classical Biography and the Genre of Luke-Acts: A Preliminary Study." 63-88 in *Luke-Acts: New Perspectives from the Society of Biblical Literature Seminar.* Ed. Charles H. Talbert. New York: Crossroad, 1984.

Barrett, *Acts.* • Barrett, C. K. *A Critical and Exegetical Commentary on the Acts of the Apostles.* 2 vols. Edinburgh: T. & T. Clark, 1994-1998.

Barrett, "Acts and Corpus." • Barrett, C. K. "Acts and the Pauline Corpus." *ExpT* 88 (1, 1976): 2-5.

Barrett, *Adam.* • Barrett, C. K. *From First Adam to Last.* New York: Charles Scribner's Sons, 1962.

Barrett, "Anecdotes." • Barrett, D. S. "'One-Up' Anecdotes in Jewish Literature of the Hellenistic-Roman Era." *Prudentia* 13 (1981): 119-126.

Barrett, "First Testament." • Barrett, C. K. "The First Testament?" *NovT* 38 (1996): 94-104.

Barrett, *Jesus and Tradition.* • Barrett, C. K. *Jesus and the Gospel Tradition.* London: S.P.C.K., 1967.

Barrett, *John.* • Barrett, C. K. *The Gospel According to St. John: An Introduction with Commentary and Notes on the Greek Text.* 2d ed. Philadelphia: Westminster, 1978.

Barrett, *John and Judaism.* • Barrett, C. K. *The Gospel of John and Judaism.* Trans. D. Moody Smith. Philadelphia: Fortress, 1975.

Barrett, "Significance." • Barrett, C. K. "The Significance of the Adam-Christ Typology for the Resurrection of the Dead: 1 Co 15,20-22.45-49." 99-122 in *Résurrection du Christ et des Chrétiens (1 Co 15).* Ed. Lorenzo De Lorenzi. Série Monographique de <Benedictina>, Section Biblico-Oecuménique 8. Rome: Abbaye de S. Paul h.l.m., 1985.

Barrett, *Spirit and Tradition.* • Barrett, C. K. *The Holy Spirit and the Gospel Tradition.* London: S.P.C.K., 1966.

Barth, "Ethik." • Barth, M. "Autonome statt messianische Ethik?" Review of David Flusser, *Die rabbinischen Gleichnisse und der Gleichniserzähler Jesus.* Part 1. *Judaica* 37 (1981): 220-33.

Barth, "Law." • Barth, Gerhard. "Matthew's Understanding of the Law." 58-164 in *Tradition and Interpretation in Matthew.* Ed. Günther Bornkamm, Gerhard Barth, and Heinz Joachim Held. Philadelphia: Westminster, 1963; London: SCM, 1963.

Bartnicki, "Zapowiedzi." • Bartnicki, Roman. "Ewangeliczne zapowiedzi meki, smierci i zmartwychwstania w swietle kryteriow autentyeznosci logiow Jezusa." *Collectanea Theogica* 51 (2, 1981): 53-64.

Basser, "Priests." • Basser, Herbert W. "Priests and Priesthood, Jewish." 824-27 in *DNTB.*

Bauckham, "Acts of Paul." • Bauckham, Richard J. "The Acts of Paul as a Sequel to Acts." 105-52 in *The Book of Acts in Its Ancient Literary Setting.* Ed. Bruce W. Winter and Andrew D. Clark. Vol. 1 in The Book of Acts in Its First Century Setting. Grand Rapids: Eerdmans; Carlisle: Paternoster, 1993.

Bauckham, *Climax.* • Bauckham, Richard. *The Climax of Prophecy: Studies on the Book of Revelation.* Edinburgh: T. & T. Clark, 1993.

Bauckham, *Crucified.* • Bauckham, Richard. *God Crucified: Monotheism and Christology in the New Testament.* Grand Rapids: Eerdmans, 1998.

Bauckham, "Earthquake." • Bauckham, Richard. "The Eschatological Earthquake in the Apocalypse of John." *NovT* 19 (3, 1977): 224-33.

Bauckham, *Eyewitnesses.* • Bauckham, Richard. *Jesus and the Eyewitnesses: The Gospels as Eyewitness Testimony.* Grand Rapids: Eerdmans, 2006.

Bauckham, "Eyewitnesses and Traditions." • Bauckham, Richard. "The Eyewitnesses and the Gospel Traditions." *JSHJ* 1 (1, 2003): 28-60.

Bauckham, *Gospels for Christians.* • *The Gospels for All Christians: Rethinking the Gospel Audiences.* Ed. Richard Bauckham. Grand Rapids: Eerdmans, 1998.

Bauckham, "James." • Bauckham, Richard. "James and the Jerusalem Church." 415-80 in *The Book* *of Acts in Its Palestinian Setting.* Ed. Richard Bauckham. Vol. 4 in The Book of Acts in Its First Century Setting. Grand Rapids: Eerdmans; Carlisle: Paternoster, 1995.

Bauckham, "Midrash." • Bauckham, Richard J. "The Liber Antiquitatum Biblicarum of Pseudo-Philo and the Gospels as 'Midrash.'" 3:33-76 in *GosPersp.* Vol. 3: *Studies in Midrash and Historiography.* Ed. R. T. France and David Wenham. Sheffield: JSOT Press, 1983.

Bauckham, "Parables." • Bauckham, Richard. "Synoptic Parousia Parables and the Apocalypse." *NTS* 23 (1976-77): 162-76.

Bauckham, "Sequel." • Bauckham, Richard J. "The *Acts of Paul:* Replacement of Acts or Sequel to Acts?" 159-68 in *The Apocryphal Acts of the Apostles in Intertextual Perspectives.* Semeia 80. Ed. Robert F. Stoops. Atlanta: Scholars Press, 1997.

Bauckham, *Testimony.* • Bauckham, Richard. *The Testimony of the Beloved Disciple: Narrative, History, and Theology in the Gospel of John.* Grand Rapids: Baker Academic, 2007.

Bauckham and Porter, "Apocryphal Gospels." • Bauckham, Richard J., and Stanley E. Porter. "Apocryphal Gospels." 71-79 in *DNTB.*

Bauer, "Characters." • Bauer, David R. "The Major Characters of Matthew's Story: Their Function and Significance." *Int* 46 (1992): 357-67.

Bauer, "Tod." • Bauer, Dieter. "Der Tod von Märtyrern und die Hoffnung auf die Auferstehung." *BK* 57 (2, 2002): 82-86.

Baum, *Jews and Gospel.* • Baum, Gregory. *The Jews and the Gospel: A Re-examination of the New Testament.* London: Bloomsbury Publishing Company, 1961.

Baumbach, "Sadducees." • Baumbach, Günther. "The Sadducees in Josephus." 173-95 in *Josephus, the Bible, and History.* Ed. Louis H. Feldman and Gohei Hata. Detroit: Wayne State University Press, 1989.

Baumbach, "Sadduzäerverständnis." • Baumbach, Günther. "Das Sadduzäerverständnis bei Josephus Flavius und im Neuen Testament." *Kairos* 13 (1971): 17-37.

Baumbach, "Zeloten." • Baumbach, Günther. "Zeloten und Sikarier." *TLZ* 90 (1965): 727-40.

Baumgarten, "Beginning." • Baumgarten, Joseph M. "The Beginning of the Day in the Calendar of Jubilees." *JBL* 77 (December 1958): 355-60.

Baumgarten, "Korban." • Baumgarten, Albert I. "*Korban* and the Pharisaic *Paradosis.*" *JANESCU* 16-17 (1984-85): 5-17.

Baumgarten, "4Q500." • Baumgarten, Joseph M. "4Q500 and the Ancient Conception of the Lord's Vineyard." *JJS* 40 (1989): 1-6.

Baumgarten, "Qumran Studies." • Baumgarten, Joseph M. "Qumran Studies." *JBL* 77 (1958): 249-257.

Baumgarten, "Testimony of Women." • Baumgarten, Joseph M. "On the Testimony of Women in 1QSa." *JBL* 76 (1957): 266-69.

Bazin, "Past." • Bazin, Jean. "The Past in the Present: Notes on Oral Archaeology." 59-74 in *African Historiographies: What History for Which Africa?* Ed. Bogumil Jewsiewicki and David Newbury. SSAMD 12. Beverly Hills, London, New Delhi: Sage, 1986.

Beale, "Daniel." • Beale, Gregory K. "The Use of Daniel in the Synoptic Eschatological Discourse and in the Book of Revelation." 129-53 in *The Jesus Tradition Outside the Gospels.* Vol. 5 in *Gospel Perspectives.* Ed. David Wenham. Sheffield: JSOT Press, 1984.

Beare, *Matthew.* • Beare, Francis Wright. *The Gospel According to Matthew.* San Francisco: Harper & Row, 1981.

Beare, *Philippians.* • Beare, Francis Wright. *A Commentary on the Epistle to the Philippians.* 2d ed. London: Adam & Charles Black, 1969.

Beare, "Sayings." • Beare, Francis Wright. "Sayings of the Risen Jesus in the Synoptic Tradition: An Inquiry into Their Origin and Significance." Pp. 161-81 in *Christian History and Interpretation: Studies Presented to John Knox.* Ed. William R. Farmer, C. F. D. Moule and R. R. Niebuhr. Cambridge: Cambridge University Press, 1967.

Beasley-Murray, Baptism. • Beasley-Murray, George R. *Baptism in the New Testament.* Grand Rapids: Eerdmans, 1962.

Beasley-Murray, "Colossians." • Beasley-Murray, Paul. "Colossians 1:15-20: An Early Christian Hymn Celebrating the Lordship of Christ." 169-183 in *Pauline Studies: Essays Presented to Professor F. F. Bruce on His 70th Birthday.* Ed. Donald A. Hagner and Murray J. Harris. Exeter: Paternoster; Grand Rapids: Eerdmans, 1980.

Beasley-Murray, Future. • Beasley-Murray, G. R. *Jesus and the Future: An Examination of the Criticism of the Eschatological Discourse, Mark 13, with Special Reference to the Little Apocalypse Theory.* London: Macmillan & Company, 1954.

Beasley-Murray, John. • Beasley-Murray, George R. *John.* WBC 36. Waco, TX: Word, 1987.

Beasley-Murray, "Kingdom." • Beasley-Murray, George R. "The Kingdom of God and Christology in the Gospels." 22-36 in *Jesus of Nazareth: Lord and Christ. Essays on the Historical Jesus and New Testament Christology.* Ed. Joel B. Green and Max Turner. Grand Rapids: Eerdmans, 1994.

Beasley-Murray, Mark Thirteen. • Beasley-Murray, G. R. *A Commentary on Mark Thirteen.* London: Macmillan & Company, 1957.

Beasley-Murray, Revelation. • Beasley-Murray, George R. *The Book of Revelation.* NCBC. Greenwood, SC: The Attic Press; London: Marshall, Morgan & Scott, 1974.

Beasley-Murray, "Second Thoughts." • Beasley-Murray, George R. "Second Thoughts on the Composition of Mark 13." *NTS* 29 (1983): 414-20.

Beavis, "Origins." • Beavis, M. A. "Christian Origins, Egalitarianism, and Utopia." *JFSR* 23 (2, 2007): 27-49.

Beavis, "Trial." • Beavis, Mary Ann L. "The Trial before the Sanhedrin (Mark 14:53-65): Reader Response and Greco-Roman Readers." *CBQ* 49 (1987): 581-96.

Beckwith, Canon. • Beckwith, Roger T. *The Old Testament Canon of the New Testament and Its Background in Early Judaism.* Grand Rapids: Eerdmans, 1985.

Beckwith, "Date." • Beckwith, Roger T. "Daniel 9 and the Date of Messiah's Coming in Essene, Hellenistic, Pharisaic, Zealot and Early Christian Computation." *RevQ* 10 (1981): 521-42.

Beckwith, "History & Miracles." • Beckwith, Francis J. "History & Miracles." 86-98 in *In Defense of Miracles: A Comprehensive Case for God's Action in History.* Ed. R. Douglas Geivett and Gary R. Habermas. Downers Grove, IL: InterVarsity, 1997.

Bedenbender, "Apocalypticism." • Bedenbender, A. "Jewish Apocalypticism: A Child of Mantic Wisdom?" *Hen* 24 (1-2, 2002): 189-96.

Bedenbender, "Kampf." • Bedenbender, A. "Kampf der Menschen, Kampf der Götter. Part 1: Die religiösen und ideologischen Auseinandersetzungen im Umfeld des Jüdischen Krieges." *T&K* 28 (108, 2005): 26-48.

Begg, "Abigail." • Begg, Christopher T. "The Abigail Story (1 Samuel 25) according to Josephus." *EstBib* 54 (1, 1996): 5-34.

Begg, "Abimelech." • Begg, Christopher T. "Abimelech, King of Shechem according to Josephus." *ETL* 72 (1, 1996): 146-64.

Begg, "Blanks." • Begg, C. T. "Filling in the Blanks: Josephus' Version of the Campaign of the Three Kings, 2 Kings 3." *HUCA* 64 (1993): 89-109.

Begg, "Ceremonies." • Begg, Christopher T. "The Ceremonies at Gilgal/Ebal According to Pseudo-Philo. *LAB* 21,7-10." *ETL* 73 (1, 1997): 72-83.

Begg, "Deeds." • Begg, Christopher T. "Elisha's Great Deeds According to Josephus (*AJ* 9,47-94)," *Hen* 18 (1-2, 1996): 69-110.

Begg, "Illness" • Begg, Christopher T. "Hezekiah's Illness and Visit According to Josephus." *EstBib* 53 (3, 1995): 365-85.

Begg, "Jehoshaphat" • Begg, Christopher T. "Jehoshaphat at Mid-Career According to *AJ* 9,1-17." *RB* 102 (3, 1995): 379-402.

Begg, "Josiah." • Begg, Christopher T. "The Death of Josiah: Josephus and the Bible." *ETL* 64 (1, 1988): 157-63.

Begg, "Jotham." • Begg, Christopher T. "Jotham and Amon: Two Minor Kings of Judah According to Josephus." *BBR* 6 (1996): 1-13.

Begg, "Rape of Tamar." • Begg, Christopher T. "The Rape of Tamar (2 Samuel 13) according to Josephus." *EstBib* 54 (4, 1996): 465-500.

Begg, "Zedekiah." • Begg, C. "Josephus's Zedekiah." *ETL* 65 (1, 1989): 96-104.

Behr, "Taught." • Behr, John. "Taught by the Apostles." *CHB* 96 (Fall 2007): 31-32.

Belayche, "Mont du Temple." • Belayche, Nicole. "Du Mont du Temple au Golgotha: le Capitole de la colonie d'*Aelia Capitolina*." *RHR* 214 (4, 1997): 387-413.

Belkin, *Philo*. • Belkin, Samuel. *Philo and the Oral Law: The Philonic Interpretation of Biblical Law in Relation to the Palestinian Halakah.* HSS 11. Cambridge: Harvard University Press, 1940.

Bellemore, "Josephus, Pompey and Jews." • Bellemore, Jane. "Josephus, Pompey and the Jews." *Historia* 48 (1, 1999): 94-118.

Ben-Amos and Mintz, *Baal Shem Tov*. • Ben-Amos, Dan, and Jerome R. Mintz, translators and editors. *In Praise of the Baal Shem Tov [Shivhei ha-Besht]: The Earliest Collection of Legends about the Founder of Hasidism.* Bloomington: Indiana University Press, 1970; New York: Schocken Books, 1984.

Benario, "Recent Works." • Benario, Herbert W. "Recent Works on Tacitus: 1974-1983." *CW* 80 (2, 1986): 73-147.

Benario, "Work." • Benario, Herbert W. "Recent Work on Tacitus: 1994-2003." *CW* 98 (3, 2005): 251-336.

Benedict, *Jesus of Nazareth*. • Pope Benedict XVI (Joseph Ratzinger). *Jesus of Nazareth.* Trans. Adrian J. Walker. New York: Doubleday, 2007.

Benko, "History." • Benko, Stephen. "The History of the Early Roman Empire." 37-80 in *The Catacombs and the Colosseum: The Roman Empire as the Setting of Primitive Christianity.* Ed. Stephen Benko and John J. O'Rourke. Valley Forge: Judson, 1971.

Benoit, *Jesus*. • Benoit, Pierre. *Jesus and the Gospel.* 2 vols. Trans. Benet Weatherhead. Vol. 1: New York: Herder & Herder; London: Darton, Longman & Todd, 1973. Vol. 2: New York: The Seabury Press (Crossroad); London: Darton, Longman & Todd, 1974.

Benoit, "Mystères." • Benoit, A. "Les Mystères Païens et le Christianisme." Pp. 73-92 in *Mystères et Syncrétismes.* EHRel 2. Ed. M. Philonenko and M. Simon. Paris: Librairie Orientaliste Paul Geuthner, 1975.

Berger, "Themes." • Berger, David. "Three Typological Themes in Early Jewish Messianism: Messiah Son of Joseph, Rabbinic Calculations, and the Figure of Armilus." *AJSR* 10 (2, 1985): 141-64.

Berger and Wyschogrod, *"Jewish Christianity."* • Berger, David, and Michael Wyschogrod. *Jews and "Jewish Christianity."* New York: Ktav, 1978.

Bergmeier, "Beobachtungen." • Bergmeier, Roland. "Beobachtungen zu 4Q521 f 2, II, 1-13." *ZDMG* 145 (1, 1995): 38-48.

Bergmeier, "Erfüllung." • Bergmeier, Roland. "Erfüllung der Gnadenzusagen an David." *ZNW* 86 (3-4, 1995): 277-86.

Bergren, "Nehemiah." • Bergren, Theodore A. "Nehemiah in 2 Maccabees 1:10–2:18." *JSJ* 28 (3, 1997): 249-70.

Berlin, "Life." • Berlin, Andrea M. "Jewish Life Before the Revolt: The Archaeological Evidence." *JSJ* 36 (4, 2005): 417-70.

Bernard, *John*. • Bernard, J. H. *A Critical and Exegetical Commentary on the Gospel According to St. John.* 2 vols. ICC. Edinburgh: T. & T. Clark, 1928.

Berschin, "Biography." • Berschin, Walter. "Biography: Late Antiquity." 2:653-55 in *Brill's New Pauly.*

Bertalotto, "Immersion." • Bertalotto, P. "Immersion and Expiation: Water and Spirit from Qumran to John the Baptist." *Hen* 27 (1-2, 2005): 163-81.

Berthelot, "Conquest." • Berthelot, Katell. "Philo of Alexandria and the Conquest of Canaan." *JSJ* 38 (1, 2007): 39-56.

Best, "Pneuma." • Best, Ernest. "The Use and Non-Use of Pneuma by Josephus." *NovT* 3 (3, Oct. 1959): 218-25.

Best, *Temptation.* • Best, Ernest. *The Temptation and the Passion: The Markan Soteriology.* SNTSMS 2. Cambridge: Cambridge University, 1965.

Best, *Thessalonians.* • Best, Ernest. *A Commentary on the First and Second Epistles to the Thessalonians.* BNTC. London: Adam & Charles Black, 1977.

Betz, "Essene." • Betz, Otto. "Was John the Baptist an Essene?" *BRev* 6 (6, 1990): 18-25.

Betz, "Gospel." • Betz, Otto. "Jesus' Gospel of the Kingdom." 53-74 in *The Gospel and the Gospels.* Ed. Peter Stuhlmacher. Grand Rapids: Eerdmans, 1991.

Betz, *Jesus.* • Betz, Otto. *What Do We Know About Jesus?* Philadelphia: Westminster; London: SCM, 1968.

Betz, "Jesus and Cynics." • Betz, Hans Dieter. "Jesus and the Cynics: Survey and Analysis of a Hypothesis." *JR* 74 (1994): 453-75.

Betz, "Miracles in Josephus." • Betz, Otto. "Miracles in the Writings of Flavius Josephus." 212-35 in *Josephus, Judaism and Christianity.* Ed. Louis H. Feldman and Gohei Hata. Detroit: Wayne State University Press, 1987.

Bianquis, "Egypt." • Bianquis, T. "Egypt from the Arab conquest until the end of the Fatimid State (1171)." 163-93 in *Africa from the Seventh to the Eleventh Century.* Vol. 3 in *General History of Africa.* Ed. M. El Fasi; assistant editor I. Hrbek. UNESCO International Scientific Committee for the Drafting of a General History of Africa. Berkeley: University of California Press; London: Heinemann Educational Books; Paris: United Nations Educational, Scientific and Cultural Organization, 1988.

Bilde, "Galilaea." • Bilde, Per. "Galilaea og galilaeerne på Jesu tid." *DTT* 43 (2, 1980): 113-35.

Bilde, "Statue." • Bilde, Per. "The Roman Emperor Gaius (Caligula)'s Attempt to Erect His Statue in the Temple of Jerusalem." *ST* 32 (1978): 67-93.

Billerbeck, *Kommentar.* • Strack, Hermann L., and Paul Billerbeck. *Kommentar zum Neuen Testament aus Talmud und Midrasch.* 6 vols. Munich: Beck, 1956.

Bird, *Gentile Mission.* • Bird, Michael F. *Jesus and the Origins of the Gentile Mission.* LNTS 331. London: T&T Clark International, 2006.

Bird, "Quest." • Bird, Michael F. "Is There Really a 'Third Quest' for the Historical Jesus?" *SBET* 24 (2, 2006): 195-219.

Bivin, "Measure." • Bivin, David. "A Measure of Humility." *JerPersp* 4 (1991): 13-14.

Bivin, "Prayers." • Bivin, David. "Prayers for Emergencies." *JerPersp* 5 (1992): 16-17.

Black, *Aramaic Approach.* • Black, Matthew. *An Aramaic Approach to the Gospels and Acts.* Oxford: Clarendon, 1967.

Black, "Language." • Black, Matthew. "The Recovery of the Language of Jesus." *NTS* 3 (1957): 305-13.

Black, "Parables." • Black, Matthew. "The 'Parables' of Enoch (1 En 37-71) and the 'Son of Man.'" *ExpT* 88 (1, 1976): 5-8.

Black, *Scrolls.* • Black, Matthew. *The Scrolls and Christian Origins.* London: Thomas Nelson & Sons, 1961.

Blackburn, "ΑΝΔΡΕΣ." • Blackburn, Barry L. "'Miracle Working ΘΕΙΟΙ ΑΝΔΡΕΣ' in Hellenism (and Hellenistic Judaism)." 6:185-218 in *GosPersp.* Vol. 6: *The Miracles of Jesus.* Ed. David Wenham and Craig Blomberg. Sheffield: JSOT Press, 1986.

Blackburn, "Miracles." • Blackburn, Barry L. "The Miracles of Jesus." 353-94 in *Studying the Historical Jesus: Evaluations of the State of Current Research.* NTTS 19. Ed. Bruce Chilton and Craig A. Evans. Leiden, New York, Cologne: E. J. Brill, 1994.

Blass, Debrunner and Funk, *Grammar.* • Blass, F., and A. Debrunner. *A Greek Grammar of the New*

Testament and Other Early Christian Literature. Trans., rev., Robert W. Funk. Chicago: The University of Chicago Press, 1961.

Blau and Kohler, "Angelology." • Blau, Ludwig, and Kohler, Kaufmann. "Angelology." 1:583-97 in *The Jewish Encyclopedia.* 12 vols. Ed. Isidore Singer. New York: Funk & Wagnalls Company, 1901-1906.

Blenkinsopp, *Pentateuch.* • Blenkinsopp, Joseph. *The Pentateuch: An Introduction to the First Five Books of the Bible.* ABRL. New York: Doubleday, 1992.

Bligh, "Qorban." • Bligh, J. "'Qorban!'" *HeyJ* 5 (1964): 192-93.

Blinzler, *Trial.* • Blinzler, Josef. *The Trial of Jesus: the Jewish and Roman proceedings against Jesus Christ described and assessed from the oldest accounts.* Trans. Isabel and Florence McHugh. Westminster, MD: The Newman Press, 1959.

Blomberg, *Gospels.* • Blomberg, Craig L. *The Historical Reliability of the Gospels.* 2nd ed. Downers Grove, IL: InterVarsity, 2008.

Blomberg, *Interpreting Parables.* • Blomberg, Craig L. *Interpreting the Parables.* Downers Grove, IL: InterVarsity, 1990.

Blomberg, "Parables." • Blomberg, Craig L. "The Parables of Jesus: Current Trends and Needs in Research." 231-54 in *Studying the Historical Jesus: Evaluations of the State of Current Research.* NTTS 19. Ed. Bruce Chilton and Craig A. Evans. Leiden, New York, Cologne: E. J. Brill, 1994.

Blomberg, *Reliability.* • Blomberg, Craig L. *The Historical Reliability of John's Gospel: Issues and Commentary.* Downers Grove, IL: InterVarsity, 2001.

Blomberg, "Studying Jesus." • Blomberg, Craig L. "Where Do We Start Studying Jesus?" 17-50 in *Jesus Under Fire.* Ed. Michael J. Wilkins and J. P. Moreland. Grand Rapids: Zondervan, 1995.

Blomberg, "Thomas." • Blomberg, Craig L. "Tradition and Redaction in the Parables of the Gospel of Thomas." 5:177-205 in *GosPersp.* Vol. 5: *The Jesus Tradition Outside the Gospels.* Ed. David Wenham. Sheffield: JSOT Press, 1984.

Blue, "House Church." • Blue, Bradley. "Acts and the House Church." 119-222 in *The Book of Acts in Its Graeco-Roman Setting.* Ed. David W. J. Gill and Conrad Gempf. Vol. 2 in The Book of Acts in Its First Century Setting. Grand Rapids: Eerdmans; Carlisle: Paternoster, 1994.

Boccaccini, "Gesù." • Boccaccini, Gabriele. "Gesù ebreo e cristiano: sviluppi e prospettive di ricerca sul Gesù storico in Italia, dall'Ottocento ad oggi." *Hen* 29 (1, 2007): 105-54.

Boccaccini, *Judaism.* • Boccaccini, Gabriele. *Middle Judaism: Jewish Thought 300 B.C.E. to 200 C.E.* Foreword by James H. Charlesworth. Minneapolis: Fortress, 1991.

Bock, *Blasphemy.* • Darrell L. Bock, *Blasphemy and Exaltation in Judaism: The Challenge against Jesus in Mark 14:53-65.* Grand Rapids: Baker, 2000. Originally published as *Blasphemy and Exaltation in Judaism and the Final Examination of Jesus.* Wissenschaftliche Untersuchungen zum Neuen Testament, 2nd ser., 106. Tübingen: J. C. B. Mohr (Paul Siebeck), 1998.

Bock, *Luke.* • Bock, Darrell L. *Luke.* 2 vols. BECNT. *Luke 1:1–9:50. Luke 9:51–24:53.* Grand Rapids: Baker, 1994.

Bock, "Trial." • Bock, Darrell L. "The Trial & Death of Jesus in N. T. Wright's *Jesus and the Victory of God.*" 101-25 in *Jesus and the Restoration of Israel: A Critical Assessment of N. T. Wright's* Jesus and the Victory of God. Ed. Carey C. Newman. Downers Grove: InterVarsity, 1999.

Bock, "Words." • Bock, Darrell L. "The Words of Jesus in the Gospels: Love, Jive, or Memorex?" 73-99 in *Jesus under Fire.* Ed. Michael J. Wilkins and J. P. Moreland. Grand Rapids: Zondervan, 1995.

Bock and Herrick, *Jesus in Context.* • Bock, Darrell L., and Gregory J. Herrick, eds. *Jesus in Context: Background Readings for Gospel Study.* Grand Rapids: Baker, 2005.

Bockmuehl, *Jesus.* • Bockmuehl, Markus. *This Jesus: Martyr, Lord, Messiah.* Edinburgh: T&T Clark; Downers Grove: InterVarsity, 1994.

Bockmuehl, "Messiah." • Bockmuehl, Markus. "A 'Slain Messiah' in 4Q Serekh Milhamah (4Q285)?" *TynBul* 43 (1, 1992): 155-69.

Bockmuehl, "Resurrection." • Bockmuehl, Markus. "Resurrection." 102-20 in *The Cambridge Companion to Jesus*. Ed. Markus Bockmuehl. Cambridge: Cambridge University, 2001.

Boelter, "Sepphoris." • Boelter, Francis W. "Sepphoris — Seat of the Galilean Sanhedrin." *Explor* 3 (1977): 36-43.

Boer, *Fatherhood*. • Boer, P. A. H. de. *Fatherhood and Motherhood in Israelite and Judean Piety*. Leiden: E. J. Brill, 1974.

Boer, *Morality*. • Boer, W. Den. *Private Morality in Greece and Rome: Some Historical Aspects*. Mnemosyne: Bibliotheca Classica Batava. Leiden: E. J. Brill, 1979.

Bogart and Montell, *Memory*. • Bogart, Barbara Allen, and William Lynwood Montell. *From Memory to History: using oral sources in local history*. Nashville: American Association for State and Local History, 1981.

Boismard, "Review." • Boismard, Marie-Émile. Review of Doeve, *Hermeneutics*. *RB* 63 (1956): 291.

Bokser, "Description." • Bokser, Baruch. "Philo's Description of Jewish Practices." *The Center for Hermeneutical Studies in Hellenistic and Modern Culture Colloquy* 30. Berkeley, CA: The Center for Hermeneutical Studies in Hellenistic and Modern Culture, 1977.

Bokser, "Justin." • Bokser, Ben Zion. "Justin Martyr and the Jews." *JQR* 64 (2, Oct 1973): 97-122; (3, Jan 1974): 204-11.

Bolotnikov, "War." • Bolotnikov, Alexander. "The Theme of Apocalyptic War in the Dead Sea Scrolls." *AUSS* 43 (2, 2005): 261-66.

Bond, "Portraits." • Bond, Helen K. "Portraits of the Historical Jesus: Review Article." *ExpT* 110 (12, 1999): 407.

Bons, "Psaume 2." • Bons, Eberhard. "Psaume 2. Bilan de recherche et essai de réinterprétation." *RevScRel* 69 (2, 1995): 147-71.

Bonsirven, *Judaism*. • Bonsirven, Joseph. *Palestinian Judaism in the Time of Jesus Christ*. New York: Holt, Rinehart & Winston, 1964.

Boomershine and Bartholomew, "Technique." • Boomershine, Thomas E., and Gilbert L. Bartholomew. "The Narrative Technique of Mark 16:8." *JBL* 100 (1981): 213-23.

Borchert, *John*. • Borchert, Gerald L. *John 1–11*. NAC 25A. N.p.: Broadman & Holman Publishers, 1996.

Borchert, "Passover." • Borchert, Gerald L. "The Passover and the Narrative Cycles in John." Pp. 303-16 in *Perspectives on John: Method and Interpretation in the Fourth Gospel*. National Association of the Baptist Professors of Religion Special Studies Series 11. Ed. Robert B. Sloan and Mikeal C. Parsons. Lewiston, NY: The Edwin Mellen Press, 1993.

Borg, *Conflict*. • Borg, Marcus J. *Conflict, Holiness & Politics in the Teachings of Jesus*. Studies in the Bible and Early Christianity 5. New York: The Edwin Mellen Press, 1984.

Borg, "Disagreement." • Borg, Marcus J. "An Appreciative Disagreement." 227-43 in *Jesus and the Restoration of Israel: A Critical Assessment of N. T. Wright's Jesus and the Victory of God*. Ed. Carey C. Newman. Downers Grove: InterVarsity, 1999.

Borg, "Experience." • Borg, Marcus J. "The Spirit-Filled Experience of Jesus." 302-14 in *The Historical Jesus in Recent Research*. Ed. James D. G. Dunn and Scot McKnight. Winona Lake, IN: Eisenbrauns, 2005.

Borg, *Jesus in Scholarship*. • Borg, Marcus J. *Jesus in Contemporary Scholarship*. Valley Forge, PA: Trinity Press International, 1994.

Borg, "Reflections." • Borg, Marcus J. "Reflections on a Discipline: A North American Perspective." 9-31 in *Studying the Historical Jesus: Evaluations of the State of Current Research*. NTTS 19. Ed. Bruce Chilton and Craig A. Evans. Leiden, New York, Cologne: E. J. Brill, 1994.

Borg, *Vision*. • Borg, Marcus J. *Jesus: A New Vision (Spirit, Culture, and the Life of Discipleship)*. San Francisco: Harper & Row, Publishers, 1987.

Borg, "Zealot." • Borg, Marcus J. "The Currency of the Term 'Zealot.'" *JTS* 22 (1971): 504-12.

Borg and Crossan, "Collision Course." • Borg, Marcus, and J. D. Crossan. "Collision Course. Jesus' Final Week." *Christian Century* 124 (6, 2007): 27-31.

Borgeaud, "Death." • Borgeaud, Philippe. "The Death of the Great Pan: The Problem of Interpretation." *HR* 22 (1983): 254-83.

Borgen, "Nattverdtradisjonen." • Borgen, Peder. "Nattverdtradisjonen i 1. Kor. 10 og 11 som evangelietradisjon." *SEÅ* 51-52 (1986-87): 32-39.

Borgen, "Paul to Luke." • Borgen, Peder. "From Paul to Luke: Observations toward Clarification of the Theology of Luke-Acts." *CBQ* 31 (1969): 168-82.

Borgen, "Reviewing and Rewriting." • Borgen, Peder. "Philo of Alexandria: Reviewing and Rewriting Biblical Material." *SPhilA* 9 (1997): 37-53.

Boring, "Oracles." • Boring, M. Eugene. "How May We Identify Oracles of Christian Prophets in the Synoptic Tradition? Mark 3:28-29 as a Test Case." *JBL* 91 (1972): 501-21.

Boring, *Sayings.* • Boring, M. Eugene. *Sayings of the Risen Jesus: Christian Prophecy in the Synoptic Tradition.* SNTSMS 46. Cambridge: Cambridge University, 1982.

Boring et al., *Commentary.* • Boring, M. Eugene, Klaus Berger and Carsten Colpe, editors. *Hellenistic Commentary to the New Testament.* Nashville: Abingdon, 1995.

Borkan, "Authenticity." • Borkan, Mark. "Ecce Homo? Science and the Authenticity of the Turin Shroud." *Vertices: The Duke University Magazine of Science, Technology, and Medicine* 10 (2, Winter 1995): 18-51.

Bornkamm, "Authority." • Bornkamm, Günther. "The Authority to 'Bind' and 'Loose' in the Church in Matthew's Gospel (1970)." 101-14 in *The Interpretation of Matthew.* 2d ed. Ed. Graham Stanton. Edinburgh: T. & T. Clark, 1995.

Bornkamm, *Experience.* • Bornkamm, Günther. *Early Christian Experience.* New York: Harper & Row, Publishers, 1969.

Borowitz, *Christologies.* • Borowitz, Eugene B. *Contemporary Christologies: A Jewish Response.* New York: Paulist Press, 1980.

Bosman, "Selling Cynicism." • Bosman, Philip. "Selling Cynicism: The Pragmatics of Diogenes' Comic Performances." *CQ* 56 (1, 2006): 93-104.

Bostock, "Elisha." • Bostock, D. Gerald. "Jesus as the New Elisha." *ExpT* 92 (2, 1980): 39-41.

Boswell, "Essay." • Boswell, J. "Review Essay: *A Marginal Jew: Rethinking the Historical Jesus." LTQ* 31 (2, 1996): 167-69.

Bosworth, "Pseudo-Callisthenes." • Bosworth, Albert Brian. "Pseudo-Callisthenes." 1270 in *OCD.*

Botermann, "Heidenapostel." • Botermann, H. "Der Heidenapostel und sein Historiker. Zur historischen Kritik der Apostelgeschichte." *TBei* 24 (2, 1993): 62-84.

Botha, "Cognition." • Botha, Pieter J. J. "Cognition, Orality-Literacy, and Approaches to First-Century Writings." 37-63 in *Orality, Literacy, and Colonialism in Antiquity.* SBLSemS 47. Atlanta: Society of Biblical Literature, 2004.

Botha, "Rhetoric and Josephus." • Botha, Pieter J. J. "History, rhetoric and the writings of Josephus." *Neot* 31 (1, 1997): 1-20.

Botha, "Voice." • Botha, P. J. J. "Living voice and lifeless letters: Reserve towards writing in the Greco-Roman world." *HvTSt* 49 (1993): 742-59.

Bousset, *Kyrios Christos.* • Bousset, William. *Kyrios Christos: A History of the Belief in Christ from the Beginnings of Christianity to Irenaeus.* Trans. John E. Steely. Nashville: Abingdon, 1970.

Bovon, *Theologian.* • Bovon, François. *Luke the Theologian: Thirty-Three Years of Research (1950-1983).* Trans. Ken McKinney. Allison Park, PA: Pickwick Publications, 1987.

Bowers, "Propaganda." • Bowers, Paul. "Paul and Religious Propaganda in the First Century." *NovT* 22 (1980): 316-23.

Bowersock,. *Fiction as History* • Bowersock, G. W. *Fiction as History: Nero to Julian.* Berkeley: University of California, 1994.

Bowie, "Readership." • Bowie, Ewen. "The Readership of Greek Novels in the Ancient World." 435-

459 in *The Search for the Ancient Novel*. Ed. James Tatum. Baltimore, London: The Johns Hopkins University Press, 1994.

Bowie, "Second Sophistic." • Bowie, Ewen Lyall. "Second Sophistic." 1377-78 in *OCD*.

Bowker, Pharisees. • Bowker, John. *Jesus and the Pharisees*. Cambridge: At the University Press, 1973.

Bowman, Documents. • Bowman, John, translator and editor. *Samaritan Documents Relating to Their History, Religion & Life*. POTTS 2. Pittsburgh, PA: Pickwick, 1977.

Bowman, Intention. • Bowman, John Wick. *The Intention of Jesus*. Foreword by Walter Marshall Horton. Philadelphia: Westminster, 1943.

Boyd, Sage. • Boyd, Gregory A. *Cynic Sage or Son of God?* Wheaton, IL: BridgePoint, 1995.

Boyd-Taylor, "Adventure." • Boyd-Taylor, Cameron. "Esther's Great Adventure: Reading the LXX version of the Book of Esther in light of its assimilation to the conventions of the Greek romantic novel." *BIOSCS* 30 (1997): 81-113.

Braine, "Jewishness." • Braine, David D. C. "The Inner Jewishness of St. John's Gospel as the Clue to the Inner Jewishness of Jesus." *SNTSU* 13 (1988): 101-55.

Brandon, Zealots. • Brandon, S. G. F. *Jesus and the Zealots*. New York: Charles Scribner's Sons, 1967.

Branham, "Humor." • Branham, R. Bracht. "Authorizing Humor: Lucian's *Demonax* and Cynic Rhetoric." *Semeia* 64 (1993): 33-48.

Braun, Jean. • Braun, François-M. *Jean le Théologien et son Evangile dans l'Église Ancienne. Études Bibliques*. Paris: Librairie Lecoffre, 1959.

Braun, "Vie." • Braun, François-M. "La vie d'en haut." *RSPT* 40 (1956): 3-24.

Brawley, Centering on God. • Brawley, Robert L. *Centering on God: Method and Message in Luke-Acts*. Louisville, KY: Westminster/John Knox, 1990.

Brawley, Luke-Acts and Jews. • Brawley, Robert L. *Luke-Acts and the Jews: Conflict, Apology, and Conciliation*. SBLMS 33. Atlanta: Scholars Press, 1987.

Brembeck and Howell, Persuasion. • Brembeck, Winston L., and William S. Howell. *Persuasion: A Means of Social Influence*. 2d ed. Englewood Cliffs, NJ: Prentice-Hall, 1976.

Bremmer, "Attis." • Bremmer, Jan N. "Attis: A Greek God in Anatolian Pessinous and Catullan Rome." *Mnemosyne* 57 (5, 2004): 534-73.

Bright, History. • Bright, John. *A History of Israel*. 3d ed. Philadelphia: Westminster, 1981.

Brindle, "Census." • Brindle, Wayne. "The Census and Quirinius: Luke 2:2." *JETS* 27 (1, 1984): 43-52.

Broadhead, "Priests." • Broadhead, Edwin K. "Jesus and the Priests of Israel." 125-44 in *Jesus from Judaism to Christianity: Continuum Approaches to the Historical Jesus*. Ed. Tom Holmén. European Studies on Christian Origins. Library of New Testament Studies 352. London, New York: T&T Clark, 2007.

Broer, "Death." • Broer, Ingo. "The Death of Jesus from a Historical Perspective." 145-68 in *Jesus from Judaism to Christianity: Continuum Approaches to the Historical Jesus*. Ed. Tom Holmén. European Studies on Christian Origins. Library of New Testament Studies 352. London, New York: T&T Clark, 2007.

Bronner, "Resurrection Motif." • Bronner, Leila L. "The Resurrection Motif in the Hebrew Bible: Allusions or Illusions?" *JBQ* 30 (3, 2002): 143-54.

Brooke, "Beatitudes." • Brooke, George. "The Wisdom of Matthew's Beatitudes (4QBeat and Mt. 5:3-12)." *ScrB* 19 (1989): 35-41.

Brooke, "4Q174." • Brooke, George J. "Florilegium (4Q174)." 378-80 in *DNTB*.

Brooke, "4Q175." • Brooke, George J. "Testimonia (4Q175)." 1205-7 in *DNTB*.

Brooke, "4Q500." • Brooke, George J. "4Q500 1 and the Use of Scripture in the Parable of the Vineyard." *DSD* 2 (1995): 268-94.

Brooks, "Design." • Brooks, Oscar S. "Matthew xxviii 16-20 and the Design of the First Gospel." *JSNT* 10 (1981): 2-18.

Brooks, *Sayings Material*. • Brooks, Stephenson H. *Matthew's Community: The Evidence of His Special Sayings Material*. JSNTSup 16. Sheffield: JSOT, Sheffield Academic Press, 1987.

Broshi, "Credibility of Josephus." • Broshi, Magen. "The Credibility of Josephus." *JJS* 33 (1-2, 1982): 379-384.

Broshi, "Dimensions." • Broshi, Magen. "The Gigantic Dimensions of the Visionary Temple in the Temple Scroll." *BAR* 13 (1987): 36-37.

Brown, *Death*. • Brown, Raymond E. *The Death of the Messiah: From Gethsemane to Grave. A Commentary on the Passion Narratives in the Four Gospels*. 2 vols. New York: Doubleday, 1994.

Brown, *Essays*. • Brown, Raymond E. *New Testament Essays*. Garden City, NY: Doubleday & Company, 1968.

Brown, *John*. • Brown, Raymond E. *The Gospel According to John*. 2 vols. AB 29 and 29A. Garden City, NY: Doubleday & Company, 1966-1970.

Brown, "Know." • Brown, Raymond E. "Did Jesus Know He Was God?" *BTB* 15 (1985): 74-79.

Brown, "Messianism." • Brown, Raymond E. "The Messianism of Qumran." *CBQ* 19 (1, Jan 1957): 53-82.

Brown, *Miracles*. • Brown, Colin. *Miracles and the Critical Mind*. Grand Rapids: Eerdmans; Exeter: Paternoster, 1984.

Brown, "Mission." • Brown, Schuyler. "The Matthean Community and the Gentile Mission." *NovT* 22 (1980): 193-221.

Brown, *"Mysterion."* • Brown, Raymond E. "The Semitic Background of the New Testament *Mysterion* (II)." *Bib* 39 (1958): 426-48; 40 (1959): 70-87.

Brown, *Mystery*. • Brown, Raymond E. *The Semitic Background of the Term "Mystery" in the New Testament*. Philadelphia: Fortress, 1968.

Brown, "Prayer." • Brown, Colin. "The Form of the Lord's Prayer." 2:869-73 in *The New International Dictionary of New Testament Theology*. 3 vols. Ed. Colin Brown. Grand Rapids: Zondervan, 1975-1978.

Brown, "Scrolls." • Brown, Raymond E. "The Dead Sea Scrolls and the New Testament." 1-8 in *John and Qumran*. Ed. James H. Charlesworth. London: Geoffrey Chapman Publishers, 1972.

Brown, "Theory." • Brown, Raymond E. "J. Starcky's Theory of Qumran Messianic Development." *CBQ* 28 (1, January 1966): 51-57.

Brown, "Thomas." • Brown, Raymond E. "The Gospel of Thomas and St John's Gospel." *NTS* 9 (2, January 1963): 155-77.

Brown, Donfried and Reumann, *Peter*. • Brown, Raymond E., Karl P. Donfried, and John Reumann, eds. *Peter in the New Testament*. New York: Paramus, Toronto: Paulist Press; Minneapolis: Augsburg, 1973.

Brown and Meier, *Antioch and Rome*. • Brown, Raymond E., and John P. Meier. *Antioch and Rome: New Testament Cradles of Catholic Christianity*. New York: Paulist Press, 1983.

Brownlee, "Comparison with Sects." • Brownlee, William H. "A Comparison of the Covenanters of the Dead Sea Scrolls with Pre-Christian Jewish Sects." *BA* 13 (3, Sept. 1950): 49-72.

Brownlee, "Jubilees." • Brownlee, William H. "Light on the Manual of Discipline (DSD) from the Book of Jubilees." *BASOR* 123 (October 1951): 30-32.

Brownlee, "Messianic Motifs." • Brownlee, William H. "Messianic Motifs of Qumran and the New Testament." *NTS* 3 (1, Nov. 1956): 12-30.

Brownlee, "Servant." • Brownlee, William H. "The Servant of the Lord in the Qumran Scrolls I." *BASOR* 132 (Dec. 1953): 8-15.

Brownson, "Introduction to *Hellenica*." • Brownson, Carleton L. "Introduction" to Xenophon's *Hellenica*. 1:vii-xi in Xenophon. *Hellenica* and *Anabasis*. 3 vols. Trans. Carleton L. Brownson. LCL. Cambridge: Harvard, 1918-1922.

Bruce, *Acts: Greek*. • Bruce, F. F. *The Acts of the Apostles: The Greek Text with Introduction and Commentary*. Grand Rapids: Eerdmans, 1951.

Bruce, *Apostle.* • Bruce, F. F. *Paul: Apostle of the Heart Set Free.* Grand Rapids: Eerdmans, 1977.

Bruce, *Books.* • Bruce, F. F. *The Books and the Parchments.* Old Tappan, NJ: Fleming H. Revell Company, 1963.

Bruce, *Commentary.* • Bruce, F. F. *Commentary on the Book of the Acts: The English Text with Introduction, Exposition and Notes.* NICNT. Grand Rapids: Eerdmans, 1977.

Bruce, *Corinthians.* • Bruce, F. F. *1 & 2 Corinthians.* NCBC 38. Greenwood, SC: The Attic Press; London: Marshall, Morgan & Scott, 1971.

Bruce, *Documents.* • Bruce, F. F. *The New Testament Documents: Are They Reliable?* 5th rev. ed. Grand Rapids: Eerdmans; Leicester: Inter-Varsity Press, 1981.

Bruce, "Gospels." • Bruce, F. F. "Jesus and the Gospels in the Light of the Scrolls." 70-82 in *The Scrolls and Christianity: Historical and Theological Significance.* Ed. Matthew Black. London: S.P.C.K., 1969.

Bruce, *History.* • Bruce, F. F. *New Testament History.* Garden City, NY: Doubleday & Company, 1972.

Bruce, "Matthew." • Bruce, Alexander Balmain. "Matthew." 1:61-340 in *The Expositor's Greek Testament.* 5 vols. Ed. W. Robertson Nicoll. Grand Rapids: Eerdmans, 1979.

Bruce, *Message.* • Bruce, F. F. *The Message of the New Testament.* Grand Rapids: Eerdmans, 1981.

Bruce, "Myth." • Bruce, F. F. "Myth and History." Pp. 79-99 in *History, Criticism and Faith.* Ed. Colin Brown. Downers Grove, IL: InterVarsity Press, 1976.

Bruce, "Name of Felix." • Bruce, F. F. "The Full Name of the Procurator Felix." *JSNT* 1 (1978): 33-36.

Bruce, *Origins.* • Bruce, F. F. *Jesus and Christian Origins Outside the New Testament.* Grand Rapids: Eerdmans, 1974.

Bruce, "Qumrân and Christianity." • Bruce, F. F. "Qumrân and Early Christianity." *NTS* 2 (1956): 176-90.

Bruce, *Thessalonians.* • Bruce, F. F. *1 & 2 Thessalonians.* WBC 45. Waco, TX: Word, 1982.

Bruce, *Time.* • Bruce, F. F. *The Time Is Fulfilled.* Grand Rapids: Eerdmans, 1978.

Bruce, "Trial." • Bruce, F. F. "The Trial of Jesus in the Fourth Gospel." 7-20 in *Studies of History and Tradition in the Four Gospels.* Vol. 1 in *GosPersp.* Ed. R. T. France and David Wenham. Sheffield: JSOT Press, 1980.

Bruggen, *Narratives.* • Bruggen, Jakob van. *Christ on Earth: The Gospel Narratives as History.* Trans. Nancy Forest-Flier. Grand Rapids: Baker, 1998. Kampen: Uitgeversmaatschappij J. H. Kok B.V., 1987.

Bryan, "Hallel." • Bryan, Christopher. "Shall We Sing Hallel in the Days of the Messiah? A Glance at John 2:1–3:21." *SLJT* 29 (1, Dec. 1985): 25-36.

Bryan, "Mean." • Bryan, Christopher. "Did the First Christians Mean What They Said, and Did They Know What They Were Talking About?" *Sewanee Theological Review* 50 (2, 2007): 247-63.

Bryan, "Saying." • Bryan, Christopher. "What Exactly Was It That the First Christians Were Saying?" *Sewanee Theological Review* 50 (2, 2007): 235-46.

Buchanan, *Consequences.* • Buchanan, George Wesley. *The Consequences of the Covenant.* NovTSup 20. Leiden: E. J. Brill, 1970.

Buchanan, "Office." • Buchanan, George Wesley. "The Office of Teacher of Righteousness." *RevQ* 9 (2, 1977): 241-43.

Bucking, "Training." • Bucking, Scott. "On the Training of Documentary Scribes in Roman, Byzantine, and Early Islamic Egypt: A Contextualized Assessment of the Greek Evidence." *Zeitschrift für Papyrologie und Epigraphik* 159 (2007): 229-47.

Bull, "Medallion." • Bull, R. "A Mithraic Medallion from Caesarea." *IEJ* 24 (1974): 187-90.

Bultmann, "Between Times." • Bultmann, Rudolf. "Man between the Times According to the New Testament." 248-266 in *Existence and Faith: Shorter Writings of Rudolf Bultmann.* Ed. Schubert Ogden. New York: Meridian Books, 1960.

Bultmann, *Christianity.* • Bultmann, Rudolf. *Primitive Christianity in Its Contemporary Setting.* Trans. Reginald H. Fuller. New York: Meridian Books, 1956.

Bultmann, "Exegesis." • Bultmann, Rudolf. "Is Exegesis Without Presuppositions Possible?" 145-53 in *New Testament Mythology and Other Basic Writings*. Ed. Schubert Ogden. Philadelphia: Fortress, 1984.

Bultmann, "Man and Faith." • Bultmann, Rudolf. "The Historicity of Man and Faith." 92-100 in *Existence and Faith: Shorter Writings of Rudolf Bultmann*. Ed. Schubert Ogden. New York: Meridian Books, 1960.

Bultmann, "Message." • Bultmann, Rudolf. "The Message of Jesus and the Problem of Mythology." 531-42 in *The Historical Jesus in Recent Research*. Ed. James D. G. Dunn and Scot McKnight. Winona Lake, IN: Eisenbrauns, 2005.

Bultmann, *Mythology.* • Bultmann, Rudolf. *Jesus Christ and Mythology*. New York: Charles Scribner's Sons, 1958.

Bultmann, "Mythology." • Bultmann, Rudolf. "New Testament and Mythology." 1-43 in *New Testament Mythology and Other Basic Writings*. Ed. Schubert Ogden. Philadelphia: Fortress, 1984.

Bultmann, *Theology.* • Bultmann, Rudolf. *Theology of the New Testament*. 2 vols. Trans. Kendrick Grobel. New York: Charles Scribner's Sons, 1951.

Bultmann, *Tradition.* • Bultmann, Rudolf. *The History of the Synoptic Tradition*. 2d ed. Trans. John Marsh. Oxford: Basil Blackwell, 1968.

Bultmann, *Word.* • Bultmann, Rudolf. *Jesus and the Word*. Trans. Louise Pettibone Smith and Erminie Huntress Lantero. New York: Charles Scribner's Sons, 1958.

Burgmann, "Lehrer." • Burgmann, Hans. "Wer war der 'Lehrer der Gerechtigkeit'?" *RevQ* 10 (4, 1981): 553-578.

Burkert, *Cults.* • Burkert, Walter. *Ancient Mystery Cults*. Carl Newell Jackson Lectures. Cambridge: Harvard University Press, 1987.

Burkert, *Religion.* • Burkert, Walter. *Greek Religion*. Tr. John Raffan. Cambridge: Harvard University Press, 1985.

Burkes, "Wisdom." • Burkes, Shannon. "Wisdom and Apocalypticism in the Wisdom of Solomon." *HTR* 95 (1, 2002): 21-44.

Burkill, *Light.* • Burkill, T. A. *New Light on the Earliest Gospel: Seven Markan Studies*. Ithaca: Cornell University, 1972.

Burkill, "Strain." • Burkill, T. A. "Strain on the Secret: An Examination of Mark 11:1–13:37." *ZNW* 51 (1960): 31-46.

Burkitt, *Gnosis.* • Burkitt, F. Crawford. *The Church and Gnosis: A Study of Christian Thought and Speculation in the Second Century*. The Morse Lectures for 1931. Cambridge: Cambridge University Press, 1932.

Burkitt, *History.* • Burkitt, F. Crawford. *The Gospel History and Its Transmission*. Edinburgh: T. & T. Clark, 1907.

Burkitt, *Sources.* • Burkitt, F. Crawford. *The Earliest Sources for the Life of Jesus*. Boston and New York: Houghton Mifflin Company, 1910.

Burnette-Bletsch, "Jael." • Burnette-Bletsch, Rhonda. "At the Hands of a Woman: Rewriting Jael in Pseudo-Philo." *JSP* 17 (1998): 53-64.

Burney, *Origin.* • Burney, C. F. *The Aramaic Origin of the Fourth Gospel*. Oxford: Clarendon Press, 1922.

Burridge, "Biography." • Burridge, Richard A. "Biography." 371-91 in *Handbook of Classical Rhetoric in the Hellenistic Period 330 B.C.-A.D. 400*. Edited Stanley E. Porter. Leiden: Brill, 1997.

Burridge, "Biography, Ancient." • Burridge, Richard A. "Biography, Ancient." 167-70 in *DNTB*.

Burridge, *Gospels.* • Burridge, Richard A. *What Are the Gospels? A Comparison with Graeco-Roman Biography*. SNTSMS 70. Cambridge: Cambridge University, 1992.

Burridge, "Gospels and Acts." • Burridge, Richard A. "The Gospels and Acts." 507-32 in *Handbook of Classical Rhetoric in the Hellenistic Period 330 B.C.-A.D. 400*. Ed. Stanley E. Porter. Leiden: Brill, 1997.

Burridge, "People." • Burridge, Richard A. "About People, by People, for People: Gospel Genre and Audiences." 113-46 in *The Gospels for All Christians: Rethinking the Gospel Audiences.* Ed. Richard Bauckham. Grand Rapids: Eerdmans, 1998.

Burridge and Gould, *Jesus.* • Burridge, Richard A., and Graham Gould, *Jesus Now and Then.* Grand Rapids: Eerdmans, 2004.

Burrows, *More Light.* • Burrows, Millar. *More Light on the Dead Sea Scrolls.* New York: Viking, 1958.

Burrows, *Scrolls.* • Burrows, Millar. *The Dead Sea Scrolls.* New York: Viking, 1955.

Busada, "Calendar." • Busada, Charles. "Calendar and Theology: An Investigation into a Possible Mutable Calendric System in the Fourth Gospel." Ph.D. dissertation, Southeastern Baptist Theological Seminary, 2003.

Bush and Pegues, *Move.* • Bush, Luis, and Beverly Pegues. *The Move of the Holy Spirit in the 10/40 Window.* Ed. Jane Rumph. Seattle, WA: YWAM Publishing, 1999.

Byron, "Passover." • Byron, Brian. "The Last Supper a Passover? The Theological Response." *ACR* 70 (2, 1993): 233-39.

Byrskog, "Chreia." • Byrskog, Samuel. "The Early Church as a Narrative Fellowship. An Exploratory Study of the Performance of the *Chreia.*" *TTKi* 78 (3-4, 2007): 207-26.

Byrskog, "History." • Byrskog, Samuel. "History or Story in Acts — A Middle Way? The 'We' Passages, Historical Intertexture, and Oral History." 257-83 in *Contextualizing Acts: Lukan Narrative and Greco-Roman Discourse.* Ed. Todd Penner and Caroline Vander Stichele. SBLSymS 20. Atlanta: Society of Biblical Literature, 2003.

Byrskog, *Story as History.* • Byrskog, Samuel. *Story as History — History as Story: The Gospel Tradition in the Context of Ancient Oral History.* Boston, Leiden: Brill Academic Publishers, 2002. Originally: Tübingen: J. C. B. Mohr (Paul Siebeck), 2000.

Cadbury, *Acts in History.* • Cadbury, Henry J. *The Book of Acts in History.* London: Adam & Charles Black, 1955.

Cadbury, "Commentary on Preface." • Cadbury, Henry J. "Commentary on the Preface of Luke." 2:489-510 in *The Beginnings of Christianity.* 5 vols. Ed. F. J. Foakes Jackson and Kirsopp Lake. Reprint ed.: Grand Rapids: Baker, 1979.

Cadbury, *Making.* • Cadbury, Henry J. *The Making of Luke-Acts.* London: S.P.C.K., 1968.

Cadbury, "We in Luke-Acts." • Cadbury, Henry J. "'We' and 'I' Passages in Luke-Acts." *NTS* 3 (1956-57): 128-32.

Cadbury, Foakes Jackson and Lake, "Writing History." • Cadbury, Henry J., F. J. Foakes Jackson and Kirsopp Lake. "The Greek and Jewish Traditions of Writing History." 2:7-29 in *The Beginnings of Christianity.* Ed. F. J. Foakes Jackson and Kirsopp Lake. Grand Rapids: Baker, 1979.

Caird, *Age.* • Caird, George B. *The Apostolic Age.* London: Gerald Duckworth & Company, 1955.

Calderón, "Cultos de misterios." • Calderón, Carlos. "Los cultos de misterios y su influencia en el cristianismo." *Kairós* 40 (2007): 51-75.

Callan, "Preface and Historiography." • Callan, Terrance. "The Preface of Luke-Acts and Historiography." *NTS* 31 (1985): 576-81.

Callaway, "Reflections." • Callaway, Philip R. "Reflections on the Language of the 'Historical' Dead Sea Scrolls." *QC* 12 (2-4, 2004): 123-126.

Campbell, *Iconography.* • Campbell, Leroy A. *Mithraic Iconography and Ideology.* ÉPROER 11. Published by M. J. Vermaseren. Leiden: E. J. Brill, 1968.

Campbell, "Journeys." • Campbell, Thomas H. "Paul's 'Missionary Journeys' as Reflected in His Letters." *JBL* 74 (2, June 1955): 80-87.

Cancik, "Gattung." • Cancik, Hubert. "Die Gattung Evangelium. Das Evangelium des Markus im Rahmen der antiken Historiographie." 85-113 in *Markus-Philologie. Historische, literargeschichtliche und stilistische Untersuchungen zum zweiten Evangelium.* Ed. Hubert Cancik. WUNT 33. Tübingen: Mohr Siebeck, 1984.

Cancik, "Historiography." • Cancik, Hubert. "The History of Culture, Religion, and Institutions in

Ancient Historiography: Philological Observations Concerning Luke's History." *JBL* 116 (4, 1997): 673-95.

Canevet, "Remarques." • Canevet, Mariette. "Remarques sur l'utilisation du genre littéraire historique par Philon d'Alexandrie dans la *Vita Moysis* ou Moïse général en chef-prophète." *RevScRel* 60 (3-4, July-Oct. 1986): 189-206.

Cangh and Esbroek, "Primauté." • Cangh, J.-M. van, and M. van Esbroek. "La primauté de Pierre (Mt 16,16-19) et son contexte judaïque." *RTL* 11 (1980): 310-24.

Capps, *Biography*. • Capps, Donald. *Jesus: A Psychological Biography*. St. Louis, MO: Chalice, 2000.

Caquot, "Secte." • Caquot, André. "La secte de Qoumrân et le temple (Essai de synthèse)." *RHPR* 72 (1992): 3-14.

Caragounis, "Culture." • Caragounis, Chrys C. "Greek Culture and Jewish Piety: The Clash and the Fourth Beast of Daniel 7." *ETL* 65 (4, 1989): 280-308.

Caragounis, *Mysterion*. • Caragounis, Chrys C. *The Ephesian Mysterion: Meaning and Content*. CBNTS 8. Lund: C. W. K. Gleerup, 1977.

Carcopino, *Life*. • Carcopino, Jérôme. *Daily Life in Ancient Rome: The People and the City at the Height of the Empire*. Ed. Henry T. Rowell. Trans. E. O. Lorimer. New Haven: Yale University Press, 1940.

Carlson, *Hoax*. • Carlson, Stephen C. *The Gospel Hoax: Morton Smith's Invention of Secret Mark*. Waco: Baylor University, 2005.

Carlston, "Maxims." • Carlston, Charles E. "Proverbs, Maxims, and the Historical Jesus." *JBL* 99 (1980): 87-105.

Carmichael, "Haggadah." • Carmichael, Calum. "The Passover *Haggadah*." 343-56 in *The Historical Jesus in Context*. Ed. Amy-Jill Levine, Dale C. Allison Jr., and John Dominic Crossan. Princeton Readings in Religions. Princeton: Princeton University Press, 2006.

Carmignac, "Kittim." • Carmignac, Jean. "Les Kittim dans la <Guerre des fils de lumière contre les fils de ténèbres>." *NRTh* 77 (7, July 1955): 737-748.

Carmignac, "Pré-pascal." • Carmignac, Jean. "Pré-pascal et post-pascal. Sens et valeur de ces expressions." *EspV* 90 (28, 1980): 411-15.

Carmon, *Inscriptions*. • Carmon, Efrat, ed. *Inscriptions Reveal: Documents from the Time of the Bible, the Mishna and the Talmud*. Tr. R. Grafman. Jerusalem: Israel Museum, 1973.

Carroll, "Peter." • Carroll, Kenneth L. "'Thou art Peter.'" *NovT* 6 (1963): 268-76.

Carson, *John*. • Carson, D. A. *The Gospel According to John*. Leicester, England: Inter-Varsity Press; Grand Rapids: Eerdmans, 1991.

Carson, "Matthew." • Carson, D. A. "Matthew." 8:3-599 in *The Expositor's Bible Commentary*. Ed. Frank Gaebelein. Grand Rapids: Zondervan, 1984.

Carson, "Pseudonymity." • Carson, D. A. "Pseudonymity and Pseudepigraphy." 857-64 in *DNTB*.

Carson, Moo and Morris, *Introduction*. • Carson, D. A., Douglas J. Moo, and Leon Morris. *An Introduction to the New Testament*. Grand Rapids: Zondervan, 1992.

Carter, "Enemies." • Carter, Warren. "Love Your Enemies." *WW* 28 (1, 2008): 13-21.

Cary and Haarhoff, *Life*. • Cary, M., and T. J. Haarhoff. *Life and Thought in the Greek and Roman World*. 4th ed. London: Methuen & Company, 1946.

Casadio, "Emasculation." • Casadio, Giovanni. "The Failing Male God: Emasculation, Death and Other Accidents in the Ancient Mediterranean World." *Numen* 50 (3, 2003): 231-68.

Case, *Origins*. • Case, Shirley Jackson. *The Social Origins of Christianity*. New York: Cooper Square Publishers, 1975; reprint of 1923 ed.

Casey, *Aramaic Approach*. • Casey, Maurice. *An Aramaic Approach to Q: Sources for the Gospels of Matthew and Luke*. SNTSMS 122. Cambridge: Cambridge University Press, 2002.

Casey, "Culture." • Casey, P. Maurice. "Culture and Historicity: the Plucking of the Grain (Mark 2:23-28)." *NTS* 34 (1988): 1-23.

Casey, "Son of Man in Similitudes." • Casey, Maurice. "The Use of the Term 'Son of Man' in the Similitudes of Enoch." *JSJ* 7 (1, 1976): 11-29.

Casson, Travel. • Casson, Lionel. *Travel in the Ancient World.* London: George Allen & Unwin, 1974.

Catchpole, "Entry." • Catchpole, David R. "The Triumphal Entry." 319-34 in *Jesus and the Politics of His Day.* Ed. Ernst Bammel and C. F. D. Moule. Cambridge: Cambridge University Press, 1984.

Catchpole, Quest. • Catchpole, David R. *The Quest for Q.* Edinburgh: T. & T. Clark, 1993.

Catchpole, Trial. • Catchpole, David R. *The Trial of Jesus: A Study in the Gospels and Jewish Historiography from 1770 to the Present Day.* Studia Post-Biblica duodevicesimum. Leiden: E. J. Brill, 1971.

Cave, "Parables." • Cave, Cyril H. "The Parables and the Scriptures." *NTS* 11 (1965): 374-87.

Chadwick, Church. • Chadwick, Henry. *The Early Church.* New York: Penguin Books, 1967.

Chance, Acts. • Chance, J. Bradley. *Acts.* SHBC. Macon, GA: Smyth & Helwys, 2007.

Chance, "Fiction." • Chance, J. Bradley. "Fiction in Ancient Biography: An Approach to a Sensitive Issue in Gospel Interpretation." *Perspectives in Religious Studies* 18 (2, 1991): 125-42.

Chancey, Galilee. • Chancey, Mark. *Greco-Roman Culture and the Galilee of Jesus.* SNTSMS 134. New York: Cambridge University Press, 2006.

Chancey, "How Jewish?" • Chancey, Mark. "How Jewish Was Jesus' Galilee?" *BAR* 33 (4, 2007): 42-50, 76.

Chancey, "Milieu." • Chancey, Mark. "The Cultural Milieu of Ancient Sepphoris." *NTS* 47 (2, 2001): 127-145.

Chancey, Myth. • Chancey, Mark. *The Myth of a Gentile Galilee.* SNTSMS 118. Cambridge: Cambridge University Press, 2002.

Chancey and Meyers, "Sepphoris." • Chancey, M., and E. M. Meyers, "How Jewish Was Sepphoris in Jesus' Time?" *BAR* 26 (4, 2000): 18-33, 61.

Charles, Jubilees. • Charles, R. H. *The Book of Jubilees or The Little Genesis.* London: Adam & Charles Black, 1902.

Charlesworth, "Adumbrations." • Charlesworth, James H. "Foreword: Adumbrations of Some 'Modern' Insights in Historical Research on Jesus from 1774 to 2002." ix-xiii in Walter Weaver. *Jesus and His Biographers.* North Richland Hills, TX: BIBAL Press, 2005.

Charlesworth, Archaeology. • Charlesworth, James H., ed. *Jesus and Archaeology.* Grand Rapids: Eerdmans, 2006.

Charlesworth, "Conclusion." • Charlesworth, James H. "Conclusion: The Origin and Development of Resurrection Beliefs." 218-31 in *Resurrection: The Origin and Future of a Biblical Doctrine.* By James H. Charlesworth, C. D. Elledge, J. L. Crenshaw, H. Boers, and W. W. Willis, Jr. New York: T & T Clark, 2006.

Charlesworth, Disciple. • Charlesworth, James H. *The Beloved Disciple: Whose Witness Validates the Gospel of John?* Valley Forge, PA: Trinity Press International, 1995.

Charlesworth, "Jesus and Theology." • Charlesworth, James H. "The Historical Jesus and Exegetical Theology." *PSB* 22 (1, 2001): 45-63.

Charlesworth, "Jesus, Literature and Archaeology." • Charlesworth, James H. "Jesus, Early Jewish Literature, and Archaeology," 177-98 in *Jesus' Jewishness: Exploring the Place of Jesus within Early Judaism.* Ed. James H. Charlesworth. New York: The American Interfaith Institute, Crossroad Publishing Company, 1991.

Charlesworth, Jesus Within Judaism. • Charlesworth, James H. *Jesus within Judaism: New Light from Exciting Archaeological Discoveries.* ABRL. New York: Doubleday, 1988.

Charlesworth, Pesharim. • Charlesworth, James H. *The Pesharim and Qumran History: Chaos or Consensus?* Grand Rapids: Eerdmans, 2002.

Charlesworth, "Peter." • Charlesworth, James H. "Has the Name 'Peter' been found among the Dead Sea Scrolls?" *QC* 2 (1993): 105-6.

Charlesworth, Pseudepigrapha and NT. • Charlesworth, James H. *The Old Testament Pseudepigra-*

pha and the New Testament: Prolegomena for the Study of Christian Origins. SNTSMS 54. Cambridge: Cambridge University Press, 1985.

Charlesworth, *Pseudepigrapha and Research.* • Charlesworth, James H. *The Pseudepigrapha and Modern Research with a Supplement.* Scholars Press, Chico, CA (SBL), 1981.

Charlesworth, "Reinterpreting." • Charlesworth, James H. "Reinterpreting John. How the Dead Sea Scrolls Have Revolutionized Our Understanding of the Gospel of John." *BRev* 9 (1, 1993): 18-25, 54.

Charlesworth, "Research and Archaeology." • Charlesworth, James H. "Jesus Research and Archaeology: A New Perspective." 11-63 in *Jesus and Archaeology.* Ed. James H. Charlesworth. Grand Rapids: Eerdmans, 2006.

Charlesworth, "Resurrection." • Charlesworth, James H. "Resurrection: The Dead Sea Scrolls and the New Testament." 138-86 in *Resurrection: The Origin and Future of a Biblical Doctrine.* By James H. Charlesworth, C. D. Elledge, J. L. Crenshaw, H. Boers, and W. W. Willis, Jr. New York: T & T Clark, 2006.

Charlesworth, "Scrolls and Gospel." • Charlesworth, James H. "The Dead Sea Scrolls and the Gospel According to John." 65-97 in *Exploring the Gospel of John: In Honor of D. Moody Smith.* Ed. R. Alan Culpepper and C. Clifton Black. Louisville: Westminster John Knox, 1996.

Charlesworth, "Sketch." • Charlesworth, James H. "The Historical Jesus: Sources and a Sketch." 84-128 in *Jesus Two Thousand Years Later.* Ed. James H. Charlesworth and Walter P. Weaver. Faith and Scholarship Colloquies Series. Harrisburg, PA: Trinity Press International, 2000.

Charlesworth and Evans, "Agrapha." • James H. Charlesworth and Craig A. Evans. "Jesus in the Agrapha and Apocryphal Gospel." 479-533 in *Studying the Historical Jesus: Evaluations of the State of Current Research.* NTTS 19. Ed. Bruce Chilton and Craig A. Evans. Leiden, New York, Cologne: E. J. Brill, 1994.

Chen, *Father.* • Chen, Diane Grace. *God as Father in Luke-Acts.* Studies in Biblical Literature 92. New York: Peter Lang, 2006.

Chernick, "Restraints." • Chernick, Michael. "Internal Restraints on *Gezerah Shawah's* Application." *JQR* 80 (3-4, 1990): 253-82.

Cherniss, "Introduction." • Cherniss, Harold. "Introduction" to *Stoic Self-Contradictions.* 13:369-603 in Plutarch, *Moralia.* 15 vols. Trans. Frank Cole Babbitt et al. Loeb Classical Library. London: Wm. Heinemann; New York: G. P. Putnam's Sons, 1927-1976.

Chevallier, "Pierre." • Chevallier, Max-Alain. "'Tu es Pierre, tu es le nouvel Abraham' (Mt 16/18)." *ETR* 57 (3, 1982): 375-87.

Chevreau, *Turnings.* • Chevreau, Guy. *Turnings: The Kingdom of God and the Western World.* Foreword by Rolland and Heidi Baker. Kent: Sovereign World, 2004.

Chilton, "Announcement." • Chilton, Bruce. "Announcement in Nazara: An Analysis of Luke 4:16-21." 2:147-172 in *GosPersp.* Vol. 2: *Studies of History and Tradition in the Four Gospels.* Sheffield: JSOT Press, The University of Sheffield, 1981.

Chilton, *Approaches.* • Chilton, Bruce. *Judaic Approaches to the Gospels.* USFISFCJ, vol. 2. Atlanta: Scholars Press, 1994.

Chilton, "Development." • Chilton, Bruce. "A Comparative Study of Synoptic Development: The Dispute between Cain and Abel in the Palestinian Targums and the Beelzebul Controversy in the Gospels." *JBL* 101 (4, December 1982): 553-62.

Chilton, "Kingdom." • Chilton, Bruce. "The Kingdom of God in Recent Discussion." 255-80 in *Studying the Historical Jesus: Evaluations of the State of Current Research.* NTTS 19. Ed. Bruce Chilton and Craig A. Evans. Leiden, New York, Cologne: E. J. Brill, 1994.

Chilton, *Rabbi Jesus.* • Chilton, Bruce. *Rabbi Jesus. An Intimate Biography.* New York: Doubleday, 2000.

Chilton, *Rabbi Paul.* • Chilton, Bruce. *Rabbi Paul: An Intellectual Biography.* New York: Doubleday, 2004.

Chilton, "Regnum." • Chilton, Bruce. "*Regnum Dei Deus Est.*" 115-22 in *The Historical Jesus in Recent Research.* Ed. James D. G. Dunn and Scot McKnight. Winona Lake, IN: Eisenbrauns, 2005.

Chilton, "Repentance." • Chilton, Bruce. "Jesus and the Repentance of E. P. Sanders." *TynBul* 39 (1988): 1-18.

Chilton, "Targum and Gospels." • Chilton, Bruce. "Targum, Jesus, and the Gospels." 238-55 in *The Historical Jesus in Context.* Ed. Amy-Jill Levine, Dale C. Allison Jr., and John Dominic Crossan. Princeton Readings in Religions. Princeton: Princeton University Press, 2006.

Chilton, "Thomas." • Chilton, Bruce. "The Gospel According to Thomas as a Source of Jesus' Teaching." 5:155-175 in *GosPersp.* Vol. 5: *The Jesus Tradition Outside the Gospels.* Ed. David Wenham. Sheffield: JSOT Press, 1984.

Chilton, "Transmission." • Chilton, Bruce. "Targumic Transmission and Dominical Tradition." 1:21-45 in *GosPersp.* Vol. 1: *Studies of History and Tradition in the Four Gospels.* Ed. R. T. France and David Wenham. Sheffield: JSOT Press, 1980.

Chilton and Evans, "Scriptures." • Chilton, Bruce, and Craig A. Evans. "Jesus and Israel's Scriptures." 281-335 in *Studying the Historical Jesus: Evaluations of the State of Current Research.* NTTS 19. Ed. Bruce Chilton and Craig A. Evans. Leiden, New York, Cologne: E. J. Brill, 1994.

Chrétien, "Exchange." • Chrétien, Jean-Pierre. "Confronting the Unequal Exchange of the Oral and the Written." 75-90 in *African Historiographies: What History for Which Africa?* Ed. Bogumil Jewsiewicki and David Newbury. SSAMD 12. Beverly Hills, London, New Delhi: Sage, 1986.

Clark, "Criticism." • Clark, Kenneth W. "The effect of recent textual criticism upon New Testament studies." 27-51 in *The Background of the New Testament and Its Eschatology: Studies in Honour of Charles Harold Dodd.* Ed. W. D. Davies and D. Daube. Cambridge: Cambridge University Press, 1964.

Clark, "Search." • Clark, Neville. "The Search for Jesus: Review Article." *ExpT* 109 (11, 1998): 345.

Clark, "Worship." • Clark, Kenneth W. "Worship in the Jerusalem Temple after A.D. 70." *NTS* 6 (4, 1960): 269-80.

Claussen, "Historischen Jesus." • Claussen, Carsten. "Vom historischen zum erinnerten Jesus. Der erinnerte Jesus als neues Paradigma der Jesusforschung." *ZNT* 10 (20, 2007): 2-17.

Cohen, "Josephus and Scripture." • Cohen, N. G. "Josephus and Scripture: Is Josephus' Treatment of the Scriptural Narrative Similar Throughout the *Antiquities* I-XI?" *JQR* 54 (4, 1964): 311-332.

Cohen, *Law.* • Cohen, Boaz. *Jewish and Roman Law: A Comparative Study.* 2 vols. New York: The Jewish Theological Seminary of America, 1966.

Cohen, *Maccabees.* • Cohen, Shaye J. D. *From the Maccabees to the Mishnah.* LEC 7. Philadelphia: Westminster, 1987.

Cohen, "Mission and Expansion." • Cohen, Shaye J. D. "Adolf Harnack's 'The Mission and Expansion of Judaism': Christianity Succeeds Where Judaism Fails." 163-69 in *The Future of Early Christianity: Essays in Honor of Helmut Koester.* Philadelphia: Augsburg Fortress, 1991.

Cohen, "Missionize." • Cohen, Shaye J. D. "Did Ancient Jews Missionize?" *BRev* 19 (4, 2003): 40-47.

Cohn, *Trial.* • Cohn, Haim. *The Trial and Death of Jesus.* New York: Ktav, 1977. First English translation from the Hebrew 1967.

Cohn-Sherbok, "Note." • Cohn-Sherbok, Dan M. "A Jewish Note on *to potērion tēs eulogias.*" *NTS* 27 (1981): 704-9.

Cole, *Theoi Megaloi.* • Cole, Susan Guettel. *Theoi Megaloi: The Cult of the Great Gods at Samothrace.* ÉPROER 96. Published by M. J. Vermaseren. Leiden: E. J. Brill, 1984.

Collins, "Apotheosis." • Collins, Adela Yarbro. "Apotheosis and Resurrection." 88-100 in *The New Testament and Hellenistic Judaism.* Ed. Peder Borgen and Søren Giversen. Peabody: Hendrickson, 1997.

Collins, *Corinthians.* • Collins, Raymond F. *First Corinthians.* SP 7. Collegeville, MN: The Liturgical Press, a Michael Glazier Book, 1999.

Collins, *Divorce.* • Collins, Raymond F. *Divorce in the New Testament.* Good News Studies 38. Collegeville, MN: The Liturgical Press, Michael Glazier, 1992.

Collins, "Eschatologies." • Collins, John J. "Eschatologies of Late Antiquity." 330-37 in *DNTB.*

Collins, "Essene Messiah." • Collins, John J. "An Essene Messiah? Comments on Israel Knohl, *The Messiah before Jesus.*" 37-44 in *Christian Beginnings and the Dead Sea Scrolls.* Ed. John J. Collins and Craig A. Evans. Grand Rapids: Baker Academic, 2006.

Collins, "Integrity." • Collins, Raymond F. "A propos the Integrity of 1 Thes." *ETL* 55 (1, 1979): 67-106.

Collins, "Introduction to Oracles." • Collins, John J. Introduction to "Sibylline Oracles." 1:317-26, 354-61 in *OTP.*

Collins, "Messiah before Jesus." • Collins, John J. "A Messiah before Jesus?" 15-35 in *Christian Beginnings and the Dead Sea Scrolls.* Ed. John J. Collins and Craig A. Evans. Grand Rapids: Baker Academic, 2006.

Collins, "Servant." • Collins, John J. "The Suffering Servant at Qumran?" *BRev* 9 (6, 1993): 25-27, 63.

Collins, *Sibylline Oracles.* • Collins, John J. *The Sibylline Oracles of Egyptian Judaism.* SBLDS 13. Missoula, MT: SBL, 1972.

Collins, "Son of God." • Collins, John J. "A Pre-Christian 'Son of God' Among the Dead Sea Scrolls." *BRev* 9 (3, 1993): 34-38, 57.

Collins, "Son of Man." • Collins, John J. "The Son of Man in First-Century Judaism." *NTS* 38 (3, 1992): 448-66.

Collins, "Testamentary Literature." • Collins, John J. "The Testamentary Literature in Recent Scholarship." 268-85 in *Early Judaism and Its Modern Interpreters.* Ed. Robert A. Kraft and George W. E. Nickelsburg. SBLBMI 2. Atlanta: Scholars Press, 1986.

Collins, "Vessels." • Collins, Marilyn F. "The Hidden Vessels in Samaritan Traditions." *JSJ* 3 (2, 1972): 97-116.

Collins, "Wisdom." • Collins, John J. "Wisdom Reconsidered, in Light of the Scrolls." *DSD* 4 (3, 1997): 265-81.

Collins, "Works." • Collins, John J. "The Works of the Messiah." *DSD* 1 (1994): 98-112.

Colunga, "Abominación." • Colunga, A. "La abominación de la desolación (Mat. 24,15)." *CB* 17 (1960): 183-85.

Conybeare, "Introduction." • Conybeare, F. C. "Introduction." 1:v-xv in Philostratus. *The Life of Apollonius of Tyana.* 2 vols. Trans. F. C. Conybeare. LCL. Cambridge: Harvard University Press, 1912.

Conzelmann, *Acts.* • Conzelmann, Hans. *A Commentary on the Acts of the Apostles.* Trans. James Limburg, A. Thomas Kraabel, and Donald H. Juel. Ed. Eldon Jay Epp with Christopher R. Matthews. Philadelphia: Fortress, 1987.

Conzelmann, *1 Corinthians.* • Conzelmann, Hans. *1 Corinthians: A Commentary on the First Epistle to the Corinthians.* Trans. James W. Leitch. Bibliography and references by James W. Dunkly. Ed. George W. MacRae. Philadelphia: Fortress, 1975.

Conzelmann, *Primitive Christianity.* • Conzelmann, Hans. *History of Primitive Christianity.* Trans. John E. Steely. Nashville: Abingdon, 1973.

Conzelmann, *Theology.* • Conzelmann, Hans. *An Outline of the Theology of the New Testament.* New York: Harper & Row, Publishers, 1969.

Conzelmann, *Theology of Luke.* • Conzelmann, Hans. *The Theology of St. Luke.* Trans. G. Buswell. New York: Harper & Row; London: Faber & Faber, 1960.

Cook, *Interpretation.* • Cook, John Granger. *The Interpretation of the New Testament in Greco-Roman Paganism.* Peabody, MA: Hendrickson, 2002; Tübingen: J. C. B. Mohr, 2000.

Cook, "Plutarch's Use." • Cook, Brad L. "Plutarch's Use of λέγεται: Narrative Design and Source in *Alexander.*" *GRBS* 42 (4, 2001): 329-360.

Cook, "4Q246." • Cook, Edward M. "4Q246." *BBR* 5 (1995): 43-66.

Cope, Scribe. • Cope, O. Lamar. *Matthew: A Scribe Trained for the Kingdom of Heaven.* CBQMS 5. Washington, D.C.: The Catholic Biblical Association of America, 1976.

Corley, "Trial." • Corley, Bruce. "Trial of Jesus." 841-54 in *DJG.*

Cornfeld, *Josephus*. • Josephus. *The Jewish War.* Ed. Gaalya Cornfeld with Benjamin Mazar and Paul L. Maier. Grand Rapids: Zondervan, 1982.

Costa, "*Midrash Hallel*." • Costa, José. "Qu'est-ce que le *Hallel*? L'Introduction du *Midrash Hallel*." *REJ* 166 (1-2, 2007): 17-58.

Cotton and Geiger, "Yyn." • Cotton, Hannah M., and Joseph Geiger. "Yyn lhwrdws hmlk." *Cathedra* 53 (1989): 3-12.

Craffert, "Healer." • Craffert, Pieter F. "Crossan's Historical Jesus as Healer, Exorcist and Miracle Worker." *R&T* 10 (3-4, 2003): 243-66.

Craffert, "Research." • Craffert, Pieter F. "Appropriating Historical Jesus Research in Africa." *R&T* 9 (3-4, 2002): 199-24.

Craig, *Assessing*. • Craig, William Lane. *Assessing the New Testament Evidence for the Historicity of the Resurrection of Jesus.* Studies in the Bible and Early Christianity 16. Lewiston/Queenston, Lampeter: Edwin Mellen, 1989.

Craig, "Historicity." • Craig, William Lane. "The Historicity of the Empty Tomb of Jesus." *NTS* 31 (1985): 39-67.

Craig, "Jesus Seminar." • Craig, William Lane. "Rediscovering the Historical Jesus: Presuppositions and Pretensions of the Jesus Seminar." *F&M* 15 (2, 1998): 3-15.

Craig, "Resurrection." • Craig, William Lane. "The Bodily Resurrection of Jesus." Pp. 47-74 in *Studies of History and Tradition in the Four Gospels.* Vol. 1 in *GosPersp.* Ed. R. T. France and David Wenham. Sheffield: JSOT Press, 1980.

Craig, "Rise?" • Craig, William Lane. "Did Jesus Rise from the Dead?" 141-76 in *Jesus Under Fire.* Ed. Michael J. Wilkins and J. P. Moreland. Grand Rapids: Zondervan, 1995.

Craig, "Tomb." • Craig, William Lane. "The Empty Tomb of Jesus." Pp. 173-200 in *Studies of History and Tradition in the Four Gospels.* Ed. R. T. France and David Wenham. Vol. 2 in *GosPersp.* 6 vols. Sheffield: JSOT Press, University of Sheffield, 1981.

Craigie, *War*. • Craigie, Peter C. *The Problem of War in the Old Testament.* Grand Rapids: Eerdmans, 1978.

Crane, "Burying." • Crane, Jonathan K. "Jews Burying Gentiles." *RevRabbJud* 10 (2, 2007): 145-61.

Cranfield, "Resurrection." • Cranfield, C. E. B. "The Resurrection of Jesus Christ." 382-91 in *The Historical Jesus in Recent Research.* Ed. James D. G. Dunn and Scot McKnight. Winona Lake, IN: Eisenbrauns, 2005.

Cranfield, *Romans*. • Cranfield, C. E. B. *A Critical and Exegetical Commentary on the Epistle to the Romans.* 2 vols. ICC. Edinburgh: T. & T. Clark, 1975.

Crisler, "Acoustics." • Crisler, B. Cobbey. "The Acoustics and Crowd Capacity of Natural Theaters in Palestine." *BA* 39 (1976): 128-41.

Crocker, "Priests." • Crocker, P. T. "Corrupt Priests — A Common Phenomenon." *BurH* 26 (1990): 36-43.

Crocker, "Sepphoris." • Crocker, P. T. "Sepphoris. Past History and Present Discoveries." *BurH* 23 (4, 1987): 64-76.

Cromhout, "Construct." • Cromhout, Markus. "J. D. Crossan's Construct of Jesus' 'Jewishness': A Critical Assessment." *APB* 17 (2006): 155-78.

Cromhout, "Judean." • Cromhout, Markus. "What Kind of 'Judean' Was Jesus?" *HTS/TS* 63 (2, 2007): 575-603.

Cronjé, "Περὶ ὕψους." • Cronjé, J. V. "Longinus' Περὶ ὕψους and the New Testament." *APB* 5 (1994): 38-53.

Crosby, "Introduction to Discourse 66." • Crosby, H. Lamar. "Introduction" to the 66th Discourse.

5:86-87 in Dio Chrysostom. *Works.* 5 vols. Trans. J. W. Cohoon (vols. 1-3) and H. Lamar Crosby (vols. 3-5; vol. 3 includes both). LCL. Cambridge: Harvard University Press, 1932-1951.

Crosby, "Introduction to Fragments." • Crosby, H. Lamar. "Introduction" to "Fragments." 5:345 in Dio Chrysostom. *Works.* 5 vols. Trans. J. W. Cohoon (vols. 1-3) and H. Lamar Crosby (vols. 3-5; vol. 3 includes both). LCL. Cambridge: Harvard University Press, 1932-1951.

Cross, "Genres." • Cross, Anthony R. "Genres of the New Testament." 402-11 in *DNTB.*

Cross, *Library.* • Cross, Frank Moore. *The Ancient Library of Qumran and Modern Biblical Studies.* Rev. ed. Grand Rapids: Baker, 1980. Reprinted from Garden City, NY: Doubleday & Company, 1961.

Crossan, *Birth.* • Crossan, John Dominic. *The Birth of Christianity: Discovering What Happened in the Years Immediately After the Execution of Jesus.* San Francisco: HarperCollins, 1998.

Crossan, *Historical Jesus.* • Crossan, John Dominic. *The Historical Jesus: The Life of a Mediterranean Jewish Peasant.* San Francisco: HarperSanFrancisco, 1991.

Crossan, "Jewish Cynic." • Crossan, John Dominic. "Open Healing and Open Eating. Jesus as a Jewish Cynic." *BR* 36 (1991): 6-18.

Crossan, "Knowledge." • Crossan, John Dominic. "Historical Knowledge: A Response to Hal Childs." *PastPsy* 51 (6, 2003): 469-75.

Crossan, "Necessary." • Crossan, John Dominic. "Why Is Historical Jesus Research Necessary?" 7-37 in *Jesus Two Thousand Years Later.* Ed. James H. Charlesworth and Walter P. Weaver. Faith and Scholarship Colloquies Series. Harrisburg, PA: Trinity Press International, 2000.

Crossan, "Tomb." • Crossan, John Dominic. "Empty Tomb and Absent Lord (Mark 16:1-8)." Pp. 135-52 in *The Passion in Mark: Studies in Mark 14-16.* Ed. Werner H. Kelber. Philadelphia: Fortress, 1976.

Cueva, "Longus and Thucydides." • Cueva, Edmund P. "Longus and Thucydides: A New Interpretation." *GRBS* 39 (4, 1998): 429-440.

Cullmann, *Christology.* • Cullmann, Oscar. *The Christology of the New Testament.* Philadelphia: Westminster, 1963.

Cullmann, *Peter.* • Cullmann, Oscar. *Peter: Disciple, Apostle, Martyr.* Philadelphia: Westminster, 1953.

Cullmann, "Πέτρος." • Cullmann, Oscar. "Πέτρα." 6:95-99. "Πέτρος, Κηφᾶς." 6:100-12 in *TDNT.* 10 vols. Ed. Gerhard Kittel and Gerhard Friedrich. Grand Rapids: Eerdmans, 1964-1976.

Cullmann, *State.* • Cullmann, Oscar. *The State in the New Testament.* New York: Charles Scribner's Sons, 1956.

Cullmann, *Worship.* • Cullmann, Oscar. *Early Christian Worship.* Philadelphia: Westminster, 1953.

Culpepper, *John.* • Culpepper, R. Alan. *The Gospel and Letters of John.* Interpreting Biblical Texts. Nashville: Abingdon, 1998.

Culpepper, *School.* • Culpepper, R. Alan. *The Johannine School: An Evaluation of the Johannine-School Hypothesis Based on an Investigation of the Nature of Ancient Schools.* SBLDS 26. Missoula, MT: Scholars Press, 1975.

Cumont, *After Life.* • Cumont, Franz. *After Life in Roman Paganism: Lectures Delivered at Yale University on the Silliman Foundation.* New Haven: Yale University Press, 1922.

Dahood, *Psalms.* • Dahood. Mitchell. *Psalms 1: Psalms 1–50.* AB 16. Garden City, NY: Doubleday & Company, 1966.

Dalman, *Jesus in Talmud.* • Dalman, Gustaf. *Jesus Christ in the Talmud, Midrash, Zohar and the Liturgy of the Synagogue.* New York: Arno, 1973. Reprint of Cambridge: Deighton, Bell, 1893.

Dalman, *Jesus-Jeshua.* • Dalman, Gustaf. *Jesus-Jeshua: Studies in the Gospels.* New York: Macmillan, 1929.

Damon, "Source to Sermo." • Damon, Cynthia. "From Source to *Sermo*: Narrative Technique in Livy 34.54.4-8." *AJP* 118 (2, 1997): 251-66.

Damschen, "Proverbs." • Damschen, Gregor. "Proverbs. III. Classical Antiquity." 12:80-81 in *Brill's New Pauly.*

D'Angelo, "Background." • D'Angelo, T. P. "The Rabbinic Background of the Parables of Jesus." *CathW* 235 (1992): 63-67.

Danker, *New Age.* • Danker, Frederick W. *Jesus and the New Age: According to St. Luke.* St. Louis, MO: Clayton Publishing House, 1972.

Danker, "Perspectives." • Danker, Frederick W. "God With Us: Hellenistic Christological Perspectives in Matthew." *CurTM* 19 (1992): 433-39.

Dapaah, *Relationship.* • Dapaah, Daniel S. *The Relationship between John the Baptist and Jesus of Nazareth: A Critical Study.* Lanham, MD: University Press of America, 2005.

Daube, *Exodus Pattern.* • Daube, David. *The Exodus Pattern in the Bible.* All Souls Studies 2. London: Faber & Faber, 1963.

Daube, "Gospels." • Daube, David. "The Gospels and the Rabbis." *Listener* 56 (1956): 342-46.

Daube, *NT and Judaism.* • Daube, David. *The New Testament and Rabbinic Judaism.* Peabody, MA: Hendrickson, n.d.; London: University of London, 1956.

Davids, "Tradition." • Davids, Peter H. "The Gospels and Jewish Tradition: Twenty Years After Gerhardsson." 1:75-99 in *GosPersp.* Vol. 1: *Studies of History and Tradition in the Four Gospels.* Ed. R. T. France and David Wenham. Sheffield: JSOT Press, 1980.

Davies, "Aboth." • Davies, W. D. "Reflexions on Tradition: The Aboth Revisited." Pp. 129-37 in *Christian History and Interpretation: Studies Presented to John Knox.* Ed. W. R. Farmer, C. F. D. Moule, and R. R. Niebuhr. Cambridge: Cambridge University Press, 1967.

Davies, "Aspects." • Davies, W. D. "Reflections on Aspects of the Jewish Background of the Gospel of John." Pp. 43-64 in *Exploring the Gospel of John: In Honor of D. Moody Smith.* Ed. R. Alan Culpepper and C. Clifton Black. Louisville: Westminster John Knox, 1996.

Davies, *Healer.* • Davies, Stevan L. *Jesus the Healer: Possession, Trance, and the Origins of Christianity.* New York: Continuum, 1995.

Davies, *Introduction.* • Davies, W. D. *Introduction to Pharisaism.* Philadelphia: Fortress, 1967.

Davies, *Invitation.* • Davies, W. D. *Invitation to the New Testament: A Guide to Its Main Witnesses.* Garden City, NY: Doubleday & Company, 1966.

Davies, *Matthew.* • Davies, Margaret. *Matthew.* Readings: A New Biblical Commentary. Sheffield: JSOT Press, Sheffield Academic Press, 1993.

Davies, *Paul.* • Davies, W. D. *Paul and Rabbinic Judaism: Some Rabbinic Elements in Pauline Theology.* 4th ed. Philadelphia: Fortress, 1980.

Davies, "Prophet/healer." • Davies, Stevan L. "The historical Jesus as a prophet/healer: A different paradigm." *Neot* 30 (1, 1996): 21-38.

Davies, *Sermon.* • Davies, W. D. *The Sermon on the Mount.* Cambridge: Cambridge, 1966.

Davies, *Setting.* • Davies, W. D. *The Setting of the Sermon on the Mount.* Cambridge: Cambridge University Press, 1964.

Davies, "Temple." • Davies, Philip R. "The Ideology of the Temple in the Damascus Document." *JJS* 33 (1982): 287-301.

Davies and Allison, *Matthew.* • Davies, W. D., and Dale C. Allison, Jr. *A Critical and Exegetical Commentary on the Gospel According to Saint Matthew.* ICC. 3 vols. Vol. 1: *Introduction and Commentary on Matthew I-VII.* Edinburgh: T. & T. Clark, 1988. Vol. 2: *Commentary on Matthew VIII-XVIII.* Edinburgh: T. & T. Clark, 1991. Vol. 3: *The Gospel According to Saint Matthew.* Edinburgh: T. & T. Clark, 1997.

Davies and Allison, "Texts." • Davies, W. D., and Dale C. Allison, Jr. "Matt. 28:16-20: Texts Behind the Text." *RHPR* 72 (1992): 89-98.

Davis, Kendall, and O'Collins, *Resurrection.* • Davis, Stephen T., Daniel Kendall, and Gerald O'Collins. *The Resurrection: An Interdisciplinary Symposium on the Resurrection of Jesus.* Oxford: Oxford University Press, 1997.

Dawes, *Quest.* • Gregory W. Dawes, ed. *The Historical Jesus Quest: A Foundational Anthology.* Leiden: Deo Publishing, 1999; Louisville: Westminster John Knox, 2000.

De Beus, "Traditie." • De Beus, C. "Paulus en de traditie over de opstanding in I Cor. 15:3 vlg." *NedTT* 22 (1968): 185-99.

DeConick, *Recovering.* • DeConick, April D. *Recovering the Original Gospel of Thomas: A History of the Gospel and Its Growth.* Library of NT Studies 286. London: T&T Clark, 2005.

DeConick, *Translation.* • DeConick, April D. *The Original Gospel of Thomas in Translation: With a Commentary and New English Translation of the Complete Gospel.* Library of NT Studies 287. London: T&T Clark, 2006.

Deissmann, *Light.* • Deissmann, G. Adolf. *Light from the Ancient East.* Grand Rapids: Baker, 1978.

De Jonge, "New Testament." • De Jonge, Marinus. "The New Testament." 37-43 in *JPFC.*

Delcor, "Guerre." • Delcor, M. "La guerre des fils de lumière contre les fils de ténèbres." *NRTh* 77 (4, April 1955): 372-99.

Delcor, "Repas." • Delcor, Mathias. "Repas cultuels esséniens et thérapeutes. Thiases et Haburoth." *RevQ* 6 (1968): 401-25.

Deman, "Mithras." • Deman, A. "Mithras and Christ: some iconographical similarities." 2:507-17 in *Mithraic Studies: Proceedings of the First International Congress of Mithraic Studies.* Ed. John R. Hinnells. 2 vols. Manchester: Manchester University Press, 1975.

Demoen, "Paradigm." • Demoen, Kristoffel. "A Paradigm for the Analysis of Paradigms: The Rhetorical *Exemplum* in Ancient and Imperial Greek Theory." *Rhetorica* 15 (2, 1997): 125-58.

Dequeker, "Zodiaque." • Dequeker, Luc. "Le Zodiaque de la Synagogue de Beth Alpha et le Midrash." *Bijdr* 47 (1986): 2-30.

De Rosa, "Chi è Gesù." • De Rosa, Giuseppe. "Chi è Gesù di Nazaret? Duecento anni di ricerche sul 'Gesù storico.'" *Civiltà Cattolica* 158 (3763, 2007): 17-27.

De Rosa, "Vangeli." • De Rosa, Giuseppe. "Dai Vangeli a Gesù." *Civiltà Cattolica* 158 (3780, 2007): 528-40.

Derrett, *Audience.* • Derrett, J. Duncan M. *Jesus's Audience: The Social and Psychological Environment in Which He Worked.* New York: The Seabury Press, 1973.

Derrett, *Law.* • Derrett, J. Duncan M. *Law in the New Testament.* London: Darton, Longman, & Todd, 1970.

DeSilva, *Introduction.* • DeSilva, David A. *An Introduction to the New Testament: Contexts, Methods & Ministry Formation.* Downers Grove, IL: InterVarsity; Leicester: Apollos, 2004.

Deutsch, *Wisdom.* • Deutsch, Celia. *Hidden Wisdom and the Easy Yoke: Wisdom, Torah and Discipleship in Matthew 11.25-30.* JSNTSup 18. Sheffield: JSOT Press, Sheffield Academic Press, 1987.

De Vaux, *Israel.* • De Vaux, Roland. *Ancient Israel: Its Life and Institutions.* Trans. John MacHugh. New York: McGraw-Hill Book Company, 1961.

De Wet, "Signs." • De Wet, Christiaan Rudolph. "Signs and Wonders in Church Growth." A Thesis Presented to the Faculty of the School of World Mission and Institute of Church Growth, Fuller Theological Seminary, In Partial Fulfillment of the Requirements for the Degree Master of Arts in Missiology. M.A. thesis, Fuller Theological Seminary, School of World Mission, Dec. 1981.

Dewey, "Curse." • Dewey, Kim E. "Peter's Curse and Cursed Peter (Mark 14:53-54, 66-72)." 96-114 in *The Passion in Mark: Studies in Mark 14-16.* Ed. Werner H. Kelber. Philadelphia: Fortress, 1976.

Dewey, *Debate.* • Dewey, Joanna. *Markan Public Debate: Literary Technique, Concentric Structure, and Theology in Mark 2:1-3:6.* SBLDS 48. Chico, CA: Scholars, 1980.

Dewey, "Structure." • Dewey, Joanna. "The Literary Structure of the Controversy Stories in Mark 2:1-3:6." *JBL* 92 (1973): 394-401.

Dexinger, "Taheb-Vorstellung." • Dexinger, Ferdinand. "Die Taheb-Vorstellung als politische Utopie." *Numen* 37 (1, 1990): 1-23.

Dibelius, *Jesus.* • Dibelius, Martin. *Jesus.* Trans. Charles B. Hedrick and Frederick C. Grant. Philadelphia: Westminster, 1949.

Dibelius, Paul. • Dibelius, Martin. *Paul.* Edited and completed by Werner Georg Kümmel. Philadelphia: Westminster, 1953.

Dibelius, Studies in Acts. • Dibelius, Martin. *Studies in the Acts of the Apostles.* Ed. H. Greeven. Trans. M. Ling. New York: Charles Scribner's Sons, 1956.

Dibelius, Tradition. • Dibelius, Martin. *From Tradition to Gospel.* Trans. from the 2nd (1933) German ed. by Bertram Lee Woolf. Cambridge: James Clarke & Company, 1971; Greenwood, SC: The Attic Press, 1971.

Díez Macho, "Hijo del Hombre." • Díez Macho, Alejandro. "La Cristología del Hijo del Hombre y el uso de la tercera persona en vez de la primera." *ScrTh* 14 (1, 1982): 189-201.

Diezinger, "Liebesgebot." • Diezinger, Walter. "Zum Liebesgebot Mk xii,28-34 und Parr." *NovT* 20 (1978): 81-83.

Dihle, "Biography." • Dihle, Albrecht. "The Gospels and Greek Biography." 361-86 in *The Gospel and the Gospels.* Ed. Peter Stuhlmacher. Grand Rapids: Eerdmans, 1991.

Dillard and Longman, Introduction. • Dillard, Raymond B., and Tremper Longman. *An Introduction to the Old Testament.* Grand Rapids: Zondervan, 1994.

Dillon, Eye-Witnesses. • Dillon, Richard J. *From Eye-Witnesses to Ministers of the Word.* AnBib 82. Rome: Biblical Institute Press, 1978.

Dillon and Hershbell, "Introduction." • Dillon, John, and Jackson Hershbell. "Introduction." 1-29 in Iamblichus *On the Pythagorean Way of Life: Text, Translation and Notes.* SBLTT 29, Graeco-Roman Religion Series 11. Atlanta: Scholars, 1991.

Dimant, "Resurrection." • Dimant, Devorah. "Resurrection, Restoration, and Time-Curtailing in Qumran, Early Judaism, and Christianity." *RevQ* 19 (76, 2000): 527-48.

Dobbeler, "Geschichte." • Dobbeler, Stephanie von. "Geschichte und Geschichten. Der theologische Gehalt und die politische Problematik von 1 und 2 Makkabäer." *BK* 57 (2, 2002): 62-67.

Dobschütz, "Rabbi." • Dobschütz, Ernst von. "Matthew as Rabbi and Catechist (1928)." Pp. 27-38 in *The Interpretation of Matthew.* 2d ed. Ed. Graham Stanton. Edinburgh: T. & T. Clark, 1995.

Dodd, More Studies. • Dodd, C. H. *More New Testament Studies.* Grand Rapids: Eerdmans, 1968.

Dodd, Parables. • Dodd, C. H. *The Parables of the Kingdom.* London: Nisbet & Company, 1936.

Dodd, Preaching. • Dodd, C. H. *The Apostolic Preaching and Its Developments.* Grand Rapids: Baker, 1980; London: Hodder & Stoughton, 1936.

Dodd, Tradition. • Dodd, C. H. *Historical Tradition in the Fourth Gospel.* Cambridge: Cambridge University Press, 1965.

Doeve, Hermeneutics. • Doeve, J. W. *Jewish Hermeneutics in the Synoptic Gospels and Acts.* Assen: Van Gorcum & Company, 1954.

Dola, "Interpretacja." • Dola, Tadeusz. "Antropologiczna interpretacja formuly 'zmartwychwstal dnia trzeciego' (Die anthropologische Interpretation der Formel 'auferweckt am dritten Tag nach der Schrift')." *ColT* 53 (1983): 37-52.

Donahue, Christ. • Donahue, John R. *Are You the Christ? The Trial Narrative in the Gospel of Mark.* SBLDS 10. Missoula, MT: Society of Biblical Literature, 1973.

Donahue, "Temple." • Donahue, John R. "Temple, Trial, and Royal Christology (Mark 14:53-65)." 61-79 in *The Passion in Mark: Studies in Mark 14-16.* Ed. Werner H. Kelber. Philadelphia: Fortress, 1976.

Donaldson, "Bandits." • Donaldson, Terence L. "Rural Bandits, City Mobs and the Zealots." *JSJ* 21 (1, 1990): 19-40.

Donaldson, Gentiles. • Donaldson, Terence L. *Paul and the Gentiles: Remapping the Apostle's Convictional World.* Minneapolis: Fortress, 1997.

Donceel-Vouté, "Coenaculum." • Donceel-Vouté, Pauline H. E. "'Coenaculum' — La salle à l'étage du *locus* 30 à Khirbet Qumrân sur la Mer Morte." *Res Orientales* 4 (1993): 61-84.

Donfried, Thessalonica. • Donfried, Karl Paul. *Paul, Thessalonica, and Early Christianity.* Grand Rapids: Eerdmans; London: T & T Clark, 2002.

Donfried and Richardson, *Judaism.* • Donfried, Karl P., and Peter Richardson, eds. *Judaism and Christianity in First-Century Rome.* Grand Rapids: Eerdmans, 1998.

Doran, "Narratives." • Doran, Robert. "Narratives of Noble Death." 385-99 in *The Historical Jesus in Context.* Ed. Amy-Jill Levine, Dale C. Allison Jr., and John Dominic Crossan. Princeton Readings in Religions. Princeton: Princeton University Press, 2006.

Dowd, "Real Jesus." • Dowd, Sharyn. "The Real Jesus: The Misguided Quest for the Historical Jesus and the Truth of the Traditional Gospels." *LTQ* 31 (2, 1996): 179-83.

Dowden, "Apuleius." • Dowden, Ken. "Apuleius and the Art of Narration." *CQ* 32 (2, 1982): 419-35.

Downing, "Actuality." • Downing, F. Gerald. "Actuality versus Abstraction: The Synoptic Gospel Model." *Continuum* 1 (3, 1991): 104-20.

Downing, *Church and Jesus.* • Downing, F. Gerald. *The Church and Jesus: A Study in History, Philosophy and Theology.* SBT, second series, 10. Naperville, IL: Alec R. Allenson, 1968.

Downing, "Context." • Downing, F. Gerald. "The Social Context of Jesus the Teacher." *NTS* 33 (1987): 439-51.

Downing, "Conventions." • Downing, F. Gerald. "Compositional Conventions and the Synoptic Problem." *JBL* 107 (1, March 1988): 69-85.

Downing, *Cynics.* • Downing, F. Gerald. *Cynics and Christian Origins.* Edinburgh: T&T Clark, 1994.

Downing, *Goddess.* • Downing, Christine. *The Goddess: Mythological Images of the Feminine.* New York: Crossroad Publishing Company, 1981.

Downing, "Like Q." • Downing, F. Gerald. "Quite like Q. A Genre for 'Q': The 'Lives' of Cynic Philosophers." *Bib* 69 (2, 1988): 196-225.

Downing, "Literature." • Downing, F. Gerald. "A bas les aristos. The Relevance of Higher Literature for the Understanding of the Earliest Christian Writings." *NovT* 30 (3, 1988): 212-30.

Downing, "Reflections." • Downing, F. Gerald. "Deeper Reflections on the Jewish Cynic Jesus." *JBL* 117 (1998): 97-104.

Downing, "Relevance." • Downing, F. Gerald. "A bas les aristos. The Relevance of Higher Literature for the Understanding of the Earliest Christian Writings." *NovT* 30 (3, 1988): 212-30.

Drane, "Background." • Drane, John W. "The Religious Background." 117-25 in *New Testament Interpretation: Essays on Principles and Methods.* Ed. I. Howard Marshall. Grand Rapids: Eerdmans, 1977.

Draper, "Didache." • Draper, Jonathan. "The Jesus Tradition in the Didache." 5:269-287 in *GosPersp.* Vol. 5: *The Jesus Tradition Outside the Gospels.* Ed. David Wenham. Sheffield: JSOT Press, 1984.

Draper, "Greek." • Draper, H. Mudie. "Did Jesus Speak Greek?" *ExpT* 67 (1956): 317.

Driver, *Scrolls.* • Driver, G. R. *The Judaean Scrolls: The Problem and a Solution.* Oxford: Basil Blackwell, 1965.

Drury, *Design.* • Drury, John. *Tradition and Design in Luke's Gospel: A Study in Early Christian Historiography.* London: Darton, Longman & Todd, 1976.

Dubarle, "Témoignage." • Dubarle, André-Marie. "Le témoignage de Josèphe sur Jésus d'après la tradition indirecte." *RB* 80 (4, 1973): 481-513.

Duff, "March." • Duff, Paul Brooks. "The March of the Divine Warrior and the Advent of the Greco-Roman King: Mark's Account of Jesus' Entry into Jerusalem." *JBL* 111 (1992): 55-71.

Duling, "Binding." • Duling, Dennis C. "Binding and Loosing: Matthew 16:19; Matthew 18:18; John 20:23." *Forum* 3 (1987): 3-31.

Duling and Perrin, *New Testament.* • Duling, Dennis C., and Norman Perrin. *The New Testament: Proclamation and Parenesis, Myth and History.* 3d ed. Fort Worth: Harcourt Brace College Publishers, 1994.

Dunand, "Mystères." • Dunand, Françoise. "Les Mystères Egyptiens." 11-62 in *Mystères et Syncrétismes.* EHRel 2. Ed. M. Philonenko and M. Simon. Paris: Librairie Orientaliste Paul Geuthner, 1975.

Dunand, *Religion Populaire.* • Dunand, Françoise. *Religion Populaire en Égypte Romaine.* ÉPROER 77. Leiden: E. J. Brill, 1979.

Duncan-Jones, "Dues." • Duncan-Jones, R. "Roman Customs Dues: a Comparative View." *Latomus* 65 (1, 2006): 3-16.

Dungan, *Sayings.* • Dungan, David L. *The Sayings of Jesus in the Churches of Paul: The Use of the Synoptic Tradition in the Regulation of Early Church Life.* Philadelphia: Fortress, 1971.

Dunn, *Acts.* • Dunn, James D. G. *The Acts of the Apostles.* Narrative Commentaries. Valley Forge, PA: Trinity Press International, 1996.

Dunn, *Jesus and Spirit.* • Dunn, James D. G. *Jesus and the Spirit: A Study of the Religious and Charismatic Experience of Jesus and the First Christians as Reflected in the New Testament.* London: SCM, 1975.

Dunn, "John." • Dunn, James D. G. "Let John Be John: A Gospel for Its Time." 293-322 in *The Gospel and the Gospels.* Ed. Peter Stuhlmacher. Grand Rapids: Eerdmans, 1991.

Dunn, *New Perspective.* • Dunn, James D. G. *A New Perspective on Jesus: What the Quest for the Historical Jesus Missed.* Grand Rapids: Baker, 2005.

Dunn, "Pharisees." • Dunn, James D. G. "Pharisees, Sinners, and Jesus." 463-88 in *The Historical Jesus in Recent Research.* Ed. James D. G. Dunn and Scot McKnight. Winona Lake, IN: Eisenbrauns, 2005.

Dunn, "Prophetic Sayings." • Dunn, James D. G. "Prophetic 'I'-Sayings and the Jesus tradition: The importance of testing prophetic utterances within early Christianity." *NTS* 24 (1978): 175-98.

Dunn, "Spirit." • Dunn, James D. G. "Spirit." 3:688-707 in *The New International Dictionary of New Testament Theology.* Ed. Colin Brown. Grand Rapids: Zondervan, 1978.

Dunn, "Synagogue." • Dunn, James D. G. "Did Jesus Attend the Synagogue?" 206-22 in *Jesus and Archaeology.* Ed. James H. Charlesworth. Grand Rapids: Eerdmans, 2006.

Dunn, *Theology.* • Dunn, James D. G. *The Theology of Paul the Apostle.* Grand Rapids: Eerdmans, 1998.

Dunn, "The Tradition." • Dunn, James D. G. "The Tradition." 167-84 in *The Historical Jesus in Recent Research.* Ed. James D. G. Dunn and Scot McKnight. Winona Lake, IN: Eisenbrauns, 2005.

Dunn, "Tradition." • Dunn, James D. G. "Jesus Tradition and Paul." 155-78 in *Studying the Historical Jesus: Evaluations of the State of Current Research.* NTTS 19. Ed. Bruce Chilton and Craig A. Evans. Leiden, New York, Cologne: E. J. Brill, 1994.

Dupont, *Life.* • Dupont, Florence. *Daily Life in Ancient Rome.* Trans. Christopher Woodall. Oxford: Basil Blackwell, 1992.

Dupont, *Salvation.* • Dupont, Jacques. *The Salvation of the Gentiles: Essays on the Acts of the Apostles.* Trans. John R. Keating. New York: Paulist Press, 1979.

Dupont, *Sources.* • Dupont, Jacques. *The Sources of the Acts: The Present Position.* Trans. Kathleen Pond. New York: Herder and Herder; London: Darton, Longman & Todd, 1964.

Dupont-Sommer, *Manuscrits.* • Dupont-Sommer, André. *Les Manuscrits de la Mer Morte et le Problème des Origines Chrétiennes.* Paris: Éditions Estienne, 1969.

Dupont-Sommer, *Writings.* • Dupont-Sommer, A. *The Essene Writings from Qumran.* Trans. G. Vermes. Gloucester, MA: Peter Smith, 1973. Earlier: Oxford: Basil Blackwell, 1961.

Duriez, *Year.* • Duriez, Colin. *AD 33: The Year That Changed the World.* Downers Grove, IL: IVP Books, 2006.

Eckey, *Apostelgeschichte.* • Eckey, Wilfried. *Die Apostelgeschichte: Der Weg des Evangeliums von Jerusalem nach Rom.* 2 vols. Neukirchen-Vluyn: Neukirchener Verlag, 2000. Vol. I: 1,1-15,35; Vol. II: 15,36-28,31.

Eddy, "Diogenes." • Eddy, Paul Rhodes. "Jesus as Diogenes? Reflections on the Cynic Jesus Thesis." *JBL* 115 (1996): 449-69.

Eddy, "(W)Right Jesus." • Eddy, Paul R. "The (W)Right Jesus: Eschatological Prophet, Israel's Messiah, Yahweh Embodied." 40-60 in *Jesus and the Restoration of Israel: A Critical Assessment of*

N. T. Wright's Jesus and the Victory of God. Ed. Carey C. Newman. Downers Grove: InterVarsity, 1999.

Eddy and Boyd, *Legend*. • Eddy, Paul Rhodes, and Gregory A. Boyd. *The Jesus Legend: A Case for the Historical Reliability of the Synoptic Jesus Tradition.* Grand Rapids: Baker Academic, 2007.

Edgar, "Messianic Interpretation." • Edgar, S. L. "The New Testament and Rabbinic Messianic Interpretation." *NTS* 5 (1958): 47-54.

Edwards, *Concordance*. • Edwards, R. A. *A Concordance to Q.* SBLSBS 7. Missoula, MT: Society of Biblical Literature and Scholars Press, 1975.

Edwards, *Theology of Q*. • Edwards, R. A. *A Theology of Q: Eschatology, Prophecy, and Wisdom.* Philadelphia: Fortress, 1975.

Ehrman, *Fiction*. • Ehrman, Bart D. *Truth and Fiction in* The Da Vinci Code: *A Historian Reveals What We Really Know about Jesus, Mary Magdalene, and Constantine.* Oxford, New York: Oxford University Press, 2004.

Ehrman, *Introduction*. • Ehrman, Bart D. *The New Testament: A Historical Introduction to the Early Christian Writings.* 3rd ed. New York, Oxford: Oxford University Press, 2004.

Ehrman, *Misquoting Jesus*. • Ehrman, Bart D. *Misquoting Jesus: The Story Behind Who Changed the Bible and Why.* San Francisco: HarperSanFrancisco, 2005.

Ehrman, *Prophet*. • Ehrman, Bart D. *Jesus: Apocalyptic Prophet of the New Millennium.* Oxford: Oxford University Press, 1999.

Eichrodt, "Faith in Providence." • Eichrodt, Walther. "Faith in Providence and Theodicy in the OT (1934)." In *Theodicy in the OT.* Ed. James L. Crenshaw. Philadelphia: Fortress, 1983.

Eisenman, *Maccabees*. • Eisenman, Robert. *Maccabees, Zadokites, Christians and Qumran: A New Hypothesis of Qumran Origins.* StPB. Leiden: E. J. Brill, 1983.

Eisman, "Dio and Josephus." • Eisman, M. M. "Dio and Josephus: Parallel Analyses." *Latomus* 36 (3, 1977): 657-73.

Elgvin, "Section." • Elgvin, Torleif. "The Genesis Section of 4Q422 (4Q ParaGenExod)." *DSD* 1 (2, 1994): 180-96.

Eliade, *Rites*. • Eliade, Mircea. *Rites and Symbols of Initiation: The Mysteries of Birth and Rebirth.* Trans. Willard R. Trask. New York: Harper & Row, Publishers, 1958.

Elledge, "Sources." • Elledge, Casey. "Critiquing Sources for Jesus: Josephus, Tacitus, and Suetonius." Paper presented on April 20, 2007, at The Second Princeton-Prague Symposium on Jesus: Methodological Approaches to the Historical Jesus, April 18-21, 2007.

Ellington, "Translation." • Ellington, John. "The Translation of *humnéo* 'sing a hymn' in Mark 14.26 and Matthew 26.30." *BTr* 30 (1979): 445-46.

Ellis, "Composition." • Ellis, E. Earle. "The Composition of Luke 9 and the Sources of Its Christology." Pp. 121-27 in *Current Issues in Biblical and Patristic Interpretation: Studies in Honor of Merrill C. Tenney Presented by His Former Students.* Ed. Gerald F. Hawthorne. Grand Rapids: Eerdmans, 1975.

Ellis, "Criticism." • Ellis, E. Earle. "Gospels Criticism: A Perspective on the State of the Art." 26-52 in *The Gospel and the Gospels.* Ed. Peter Stuhlmacher. Grand Rapids: Eerdmans, 1991.

Ellis, *Genius*. • Ellis, Peter F. *The Genius of John: A Composition-Critical Commentary on the Fourth Gospel.* Collegeville, MN: The Liturgical Press, 1984.

Ellis, "Gospels and History." • Ellis, E. Earle. "The Synoptic Gospels and History." 49-57 in *Authenticating the Activities of Jesus.* Ed. Bruce Chilton and Craig A. Evans. NTTS 28.2. Leiden: Brill, 1999.

Ellis, *Matthew*. • Ellis, Peter F. *Matthew: His Mind and His Message.* Collegeville, MN: Liturgical Press, 1974.

Ellis, "Uses." • Ellis, E. Earle. "How the New Testament Uses the Old." Pp. 199-219 in *New Testament Interpretation: Essays on Principles and Methods.* Ed. I. Howard Marshall. Grand Rapids: Eerdmans, 1977.

Ellison, *Mystery.* • Ellison, H. L. *The Mystery of Israel: An Exposition of Romans 9–11.* Grand Rapids: Eerdmans, 1966.

Emerton, "Mark XIV.24." • Emerton, John A. "Mark XIV.24 and the Targum to the Psalter." *JTS* 15 (1964): 58-59.

Endres, *Interpretation.* • Endres, John C. *Biblical Interpretation in the Book of Jubilees.* CBQMS 18. Washington, D.C.: Catholic Biblical Association of America, 1987.

Engberg-Pedersen, *Paul and Stoics.* • Engberg-Pedersen, Troels. *Paul and the Stoics.* Louisville, KY: Westminster John Knox; Edinburgh: T. & T. Clark, 2000.

Engels, *Roman Corinth.* • Engels, Donald W. *Roman Corinth: An Alternative Model for the Classical City.* Chicago: University of Chicago, 1990.

Engle, "Amphorisk." • Engle, Anita. "An Amphorisk of the Second Temple Period." *PEQ* 109 (1977): 117-22.

Epp, "Wisdom." • Epp, Eldon Jay. "Wisdom, Torah, Word: The Johannine Prologue and the Purpose of the Fourth Gospel." 128-46 in *Current Issues in Biblical and Patristic Interpretation: Studies in Honor of Merrill C. Tenney Presented by His Former Students.* Ed. Gerald F. Hawthorne. Grand Rapids: Eerdmans, 1975.

Erdkamp, "Agriculture." • Erdkamp, P. "Agriculture, underemployment, and the cost of rural labour in the Roman world." *CQ* 49 (2, 1999): 556-572.

Eshel, "Sny." • Eshel, Hanan. "Sny hrbdym hhystwryym hmtw'dym bmgylt psr hbqwq." *Zion* 71 (2, 2006): 143-52.

Eshel and Meyers, "Pools." • Eshel, H., and E. M. Meyers, "The Pools of Sepphoris — Ritual Baths or Bathtubs?" *BAR* 26 (4, 2000): 42-49, 60-61.

Evans, "Action." • Evans, Craig A. "Jesus' Action in the Temple: Cleansing or Portent of Destruction?" *CBQ* 51 (1989): 237-70.

Evans, "Activities." • Evans, Craig A. "Authenticating the Activities of Jesus." 3-29 in *Authenticating the Activities of Jesus.* Ed. Bruce Chilton and Craig A. Evans. NTTS 28.2. Leiden: Brill, 1999.

Evans, "Apocalypse." • Evans, Craig A. "Messianic Apocalypse (4Q521)." 695-98 in *DNTB.*

Evans, "Apollonius." • Evans, Craig A. "Apollonius of Tyana." 80-81 in *DNTB.*

Evans, "Caiaphas Ossuary." • Evans, Craig A. "Caiaphas Ossuary." 179-80 in *DNTB.*

Evans, "Context." • Evans, Craig A. "Context, family and formation." 11-24 in *The Cambridge Companion to Jesus.* Ed. Markus Bockmuehl. Cambridge: Cambridge University, 2001.

Evans, "Daniel's Visions." • Evans, Craig A. "Defeating Satan and Liberating Israel: Jesus and Daniel's Visions." *JSHJ* 1 (2, 2003): 161-70.

Evans, "Exile." • Evans, Craig A. "Jesus & the Continuing Exile of Israel." 77-100 in *Jesus and the Restoration of Israel: A Critical Assessment of N. T. Wright's* Jesus and the Victory of God. Ed. Carey C. Newman. Downers Grove: InterVarsity, 1999.

Evans, *Fabricating Jesus.* • Evans, Craig A. *Fabricating Jesus: How Modern Scholars Distort the Gospels.* Downers Grove: InterVarsity, 2006.

Evans, "Hope." • Evans, Craig A. "Jesus and Zechariah's Messianic Hope." 373-88 in *Authenticating the Activities of Jesus.* Ed. Bruce Chilton and Craig A. Evans. NTTS 28.2. Leiden: Brill, 1999.

Evans, "Inaugurating." • Evans, Craig A. "Inaugurating the Kingdom of God and Defeating the Kingdom of Satan." *BBR* 15 (1, 2005): 49-75.

Evans, *Jesus.* • Evans, Craig A. *Jesus.* IBR Bibliographies 5. Grand Rapids: Baker, 1992.

Evans, "Jesus ben Ananias." • Evans, Craig A. "Jesus ben Ananias." 561-62 in *DNTB.*

Evans, "Josephus on Prophets." • Evans, Craig A. "Josephus on John the Baptist and Other Jewish Prophets of Deliverance." 55-63 in *The Historical Jesus in Context.* Ed. Amy-Jill Levine, Dale C. Allison Jr., and John Dominic Crossan. Princeton Readings in Religions. Princeton: Princeton University Press, 2006.

Evans, *Life of Jesus Research.* • Evans, Craig A. *Life of Jesus Research: An Annotated Bibliography,* rev. ed. NTTS 24. Leiden: Brill, 1996.

Evans, "Messianism." • Evans, Craig A. "Messianism." 698-707 in *DNTB*.

Evans, "Naturalism." • Evans, C. Stephen. "Methodological Naturalism in Historical Biblical Scholarship." 180-205 in *Jesus and the Restoration of Israel: A Critical Assessment of N. T. Wright's Jesus and the Victory of God*. Ed. Carey C. Newman. Downers Grove: InterVarsity, 1999.

Evans, "Non-Christian Sources." • Evans, Craig A. "Jesus in Non-Christian Sources." 443-78 in *Studying the Historical Jesus: Evaluations of the State of Current Research*. NTTS 19. Ed. Bruce Chilton and Craig A. Evans. Leiden, New York, Cologne: E. J. Brill, 1994.

Evans, Ossuaries. • Evans, Craig A. *Jesus and the Ossuaries*. Waco, TX: Baylor University Press, 2003.

Evans, "Passion." • Evans, Craig A. "The Passion of Jesus: History Remembered or Prophecy Historicized?" *BBR* 6 (1996): 159-65.

Evans, "Pilate Inscription." • Evans, Craig A. "Pilate Inscription." 803-4 in *DNTB*.

Evans, "Prayer of Enosh." • Evans, Craig A. "Prayer of Enosh (4Q369 + 4Q458)." 820-21 in *DNTB*.

Evans, "Prologue." • Evans, Craig A. "On the Prologue of John and the *Trimorphic Protennoia*." *NTS* 27 (3, April 1981): 395-401.

Evans, "4Q246." • Evans, Craig A. "Son of God Text (4Q246)." 1134-37 in *DNTB*.

Evans, "Quest." • Evans, Craig A. "The Third Quest of the Historical Jesus: A Bibliographical Essay." *Christian Scholar's Review* 28 (4, 1999): 532-43.

Evans, "Son." • Evans, Craig A. "A Note on the 'First-Born Son' of 4Q369." *DSD* 2 (2, 1995): 185-201.

Evans, "Traditions." • Evans, Craig A. "In Appreciation of the Dominical and Thomistic Traditions: The Contribution of J. D. Crossan and N. T. Wright to Jesus Research." 48-57 in *The Resurrection of Jesus: John Dominic Crossan and N. T. Wright in Dialogue*, ed. Robert B. Stewart. Minneapolis: Fortress, 2006.

Evans, "Typologies." • Evans, Craig A. "Jesus, John, and the Dead Sea Scrolls: Assessing Typologies of Restoration." 45-62 in *Christian Beginnings and the Dead Sea Scrolls*. Ed. John J. Collins and Craig A. Evans. Grand Rapids: Baker Academic, 2006.

Evans, "What." • Evans, Craig A. "What Did Jesus Do?" Pp. 101-15 in *Jesus Under Fire*. Ed. Michael J. Wilkins and J. P. Moreland. Grand Rapids: Zondervan, 1995.

Eve, "Meier and Miracle." • Eve, Eric. "Meier, Miracle and Multiple Attestation." *JSHJ* 3 (1, 2005): 23-45.

Eve, Miracles. • Eve, Eric. *The Jewish Context of Jesus' Miracles*. JSNTSup 231. London, New York: Sheffield Academic Press, 2002.

Fabry, "Texte." • Fabry, Heinz-Josef. "Neue Texte aus Qumran." *BK* 48 (1, 1993): 24-27.

Fabry, "Umkehr." • Fabry, Heinz-Josef. "Umkehr und Metanoia als monastisches Ideal in der 'Mönchsgemeinde' von Qumran." *ErAuf* 53 (1977): 163-80.

Faierstein, "Elijah." • Faierstein, Morris M. "Why Do the Scribes Say That Elijah Must Come First?" *JBL* 100 (1, March 1981): 75-86.

Falk, Pharisee. • Falk, Harvey. *Jesus the Pharisee: A New Look at the Jewishness of Jesus*. New York: Paulist Press, 1985.

Fallon, "Theodotus." • Fallon, F. "Introduction to Theodotus." 2:785-789 in *OTP*.

Fantuzzi, "Ekphrasis." • Fantuzzi, Marco. "Ekphrasis: Greek." 4:872-75 in *Brill's New Pauly*.

Farmer, "Peter and Paul." • Farmer, William R. "Peter and Paul, and the Tradition concerning 'The Lord's Supper' in 1 Corinthians 11:23-26." 35-55 in *One Loaf, One Cup: Ecumenical Studies of 1 Cor 11 and Other Eucharistic Texts*. The Cambridge Conference on the Eucharist, August 1988. New Gospel Studies 6. Ed. Ben F. Meyer. Macon, GA: Mercer University Press, 1993.

Farmer, Problem. • Farmer, William R. *The Synoptic Problem: A Critical Analysis*. New York: Macmillan, 1964.

Farmer, Verses. • Farmer, William R. *The Last Twelve Verses of Mark*. SNTSMS 25. Cambridge: Cambridge University Press, 1974.

Farmer and Kereszty, Peter and Paul. • Farmer, William R., and Roch Kereszty. *Peter and Paul in* *the Church of Rome: The Ecumenical Potential of a Forgotten Perspective.* Studies in Contemporary Biblical and Theological Problems. New York; Mahwah, NJ: Paulist Press, 1990.

Farrer, "Q." • Farrer, Austin. "Q." *Theology* 59 (1956): 247-48.

Fauth, "Metatron." • Fauth, Wolfgang. "Tatrosjah-Totrosjah und Metatron in der judischen Merkabah-Mystik." *JSJ* 22 (1, 1991): 40-87.

Fee, *Corinthians*. • Fee, Gordon D. *The First Epistle to the Corinthians.* NICNT. Grand Rapids: Eerdmans, 1987.

Fee, *Presence*. • Fee, Gordon D. *God's Empowering Presence: The Holy Spirit in the Letters of Paul.* Peabody: Hendrickson, 1994.

Feldman, "Abraham." • Feldman, Louis H. "Hellenizations in Josephus' *Jewish Antiquities:* The Portrait of Abraham." 133-153 in *Josephus, Judaism and Christianity.* Ed. Louis H. Feldman and Gohei Hata. Detroit: Wayne State University Press, 1987.

Feldman, "Ahab." • Feldman, Louis H. "Josephus' Portrait of Ahab." *ETL* 68 (4, 1992): 368-84.

Feldman, "Antiquities." • Feldman, Louis H. "Josephus' *Jewish Antiquities* and Pseudo-Philo's *Biblical Antiquities*." 59-80 in *Josephus, the Bible, and History.* Ed. Louis H. Feldman and Gohei Hata. Detroit: Wayne State University Press, 1989.

Feldman, "Apologist of World." • Feldman, Louis H. "Josephus as an Apologist of the Greco-Roman World: His Portrait of Solomon." 69-98 in *Aspects of Religious Propaganda in Judaism and Early Christianity.* Ed. Elisabeth Schüssler Fiorenza. UNDCSJCA 2. Notre Dame: University of Notre Dame Press, 1976.

Feldman, "'Aqedah." • Feldman, Louis H. "Josephus as a Biblical Interpreter: The 'Aqedah." *JQR* 75 (3, January 1985): 212-52.

Feldman, "Bibliography." • Feldman, Louis H. "Bibliography." 9:419-21 in Josephus. *Works.* 10 vols. Trans. H. St. J. Thackeray (vols. 1-5), Ralph Marcus (vols. 5-7), Ralph Marcus and Allen Wikgren (vol. 8), and Louis H. Feldman (vols. 9-10, 1965). LCL. Cambridge: Harvard University Press, 1926-1965.

Feldman, "Command." • Feldman, Louis H. "The Command, According to Philo, Pseudo-Philo, and Josephus, to Annihilate the Seven Nations of Canaan." *AUSS* 41 (1, 2003): 13-29.

Feldman, "Concubine." • Feldman, Louis H. "Josephus' Portrayal (*Antiquities* 5.136-174) of the Benjaminite Affair of the Concubine and Its Repercussions (Judges 19–21)." *JQR* 90 (3-4, 2000): 255-92.

Feldman, "Daniel." • Feldman, Louis H. "Josephus' Portrait of Daniel." *Hen* 14 (1-2, 1992): 37-96.

Feldman, "David." • Feldman, Louis H. "Josephus' Portrait of David." *HUCA* 60 (1989): 129-74.

Feldman, "Hellenism." • Feldman, Louis H. "How Much Hellenism in Jewish Palestine?" *HUCA* 57 (1986): 83-111.

Feldman, "Hellenizations: Abraham." • Feldman, Louis H. "Hellenizations in Josephus' *Jewish Antiquities:* The Portrait of Abraham." 133-53 in *Josephus, Judaism and Christianity.* Ed. Louis H. Feldman and Gohei Hata. Detroit: Wayne State University Press, 1987.

Feldman, "Hezekiah." • Feldman, Louis H. "Josephus's Portrait of Hezekiah." *JBL* 111 (4, 1992): 597-610.

Feldman, "Introduction: Josephus." • Feldman, Louis H. "Introduction." 17-49 in *Josephus, the Bible, and History.* Ed. Louis H. Feldman and Gohei Hata. Detroit: Wayne State University Press, 1989.

Feldman, "Isaac." • Feldman, Louis H. "Josephus' Portrait of Isaac." *RSLR* 29 (1, 1993): 3-33.

Feldman, "Jacob." • Feldman, Louis H. "Josephus' Portrait of Jacob." *JQR* 79 (2-3, 1988-1989): 101-51.

Feldman, "Jehoram." • Feldman, Louis H. "Josephus's Portrait of Jehoram, King of Israel." *BJRL* 76 (1, 1994): 3-20.

Feldman, "Jehoshaphat." • Feldman, Louis H. "Josephus' Portrait of Jehoshaphat." *SCI* 12 (1993): 159-75.

Feldman, "Jeroboam." • Feldman, Louis H. "Josephus' Portrait of Jeroboam." *AUSS* 31 (1, 1993): 29-51.

Feldman, "Joseph." • Feldman, Louis H. "Josephus' Portrait of Joseph." *RB* 99 (2, 1992): 397-417; 99 (3, 1992): 504-28.

Feldman, "Joshua." • Feldman, Louis H. "Josephus's Portrait of Joshua." *HTR* 82 (4, 1989): 351-76.

Feldman, "Josiah." • Feldman, Louis H. "Josephus' Portrait of Josiah." *LS* 18 (2, 1993): 110-30.

Feldman, "Methods." • Feldman, Louis H. "Josephus: Interpretive Methods and Tendencies." 590-96 in *DNTB*.

Feldman, "Moses." • Feldman, Louis H. "Josephus' Portrait of Moses." *JQR* 82 (3-4, 1992): 285-328; "Josephus' Portrait of Moses. Part Two." *JQR* 83 (1-2, 1992): 7-50.

Feldman, "Nehemiah." • Feldman, Louis H. "Josephus' Portrait of Nehemiah." *JJS* 43 (2, 1992): 187-202.

Feldman, "Noah." • Feldman, Louis H. "Josephus' Portrait of Noah and Its Parallels in Philo, Pseudo-Philo's *Biblical Antiquities,* and Rabbinic Midrashim." *PAAJR* 55 (1988): 31-57.

Feldman, "Roncace's Portraits." • Feldman, Louis H. "On Professor Mark Roncace's Portraits of Deborah and Gideon in Josephus." *JSJ* 32 (2, 2001): 193-220.

Feldman, "Samson." • Feldman, Louis H. "Josephus' Version of Samson." *JSJ* 19 (2, 1988): 171-214.

Feldman, "Samuel." • Feldman, Louis H. "Josephus' Portrait of Samuel." *AbrN* 30 (1992): 103-45.

Feldman, "Saul." • Feldman, Louis H. "Josephus' Portrait of Saul." *HUCA* 53 (1982): 45-99.

Fenton, *Matthew.* • Fenton, J. C. *Saint Matthew.* Philadelphia: Westminster, 1977.

Ferguson, *Backgrounds.* • Ferguson, Everett. *Backgrounds of Early Christianity.* Grand Rapids: Eerdmans, 1987.

Feuillet, "Primauté." • Feuillet, André. "La primauté et l'humilité de Pierre. Leur attestation en Mt 16,17-19, dans l'Evangile de Marc et dans la Première Epître de Pierre." *NV* 66 (1991): 3-24.

Filson, *History.* • Filson, Floyd V. *A New Testament History.* Philadelphia: Westminster, W. L. Jenkins, 1964.

Filson, *Matthew.* • Filson, Floyd V. *A Commentary on the Gospel According to St. Matthew.* New York, Evanston: Harper & Row, Publishers, 1960.

Fine, "Burial." • Fine, Steven. "A Note on Ossuary Burial and the Resurrection of the Dead in First-Century Jerusalem." *JJS* 51 (1, 2000): 69-76.

Finegan, *Archeology.* • Finegan, Jack. *The Archeology of the New Testament.* Princeton: Princeton University Press, 1969.

Finkelberg, "Cypria." • Finkelberg, Margalit. "The *Cypria,* the *Iliad,* and the Problem of Multiformity in Oral and Written Tradition." *CP* 95 (1, 2000): 1-11.

Finkelstein, "Documents." • Finkelstein, Louis. "Pre-Maccabean Documents in the Passover Haggadah." *HTR* 35 (1942-43): 291-332; 36: 1-38.

Finkelstein, *Making.* • Finkelstein, Louis. *Pharisaism in the Making: Selected Essays.* New York: Ktav, 1972.

Finley, *Economy.* • Finley, M. I. *The Ancient Economy.* Sather Classical Lectures 43. Berkeley: University of California Press, 1973.

Fiorenza, *Memory.* • Fiorenza, Elisabeth Schüssler. *In Memory of Her: A Feminist Theological Reconstruction of Christian Origins.* New York: The Crossroad Publishing Company, 1983.

Fiorenza, *Politics.* • Fiorenza, Elisabeth Schüssler. *Jesus and the Politics of Interpretation.* New York, London: Continuum, 2000.

Fisk, "Bible." • Fisk, Bruce N. "Rewritten Bible in Pseudepigrapha and Qumran." 947-53 in *DNTB*.

Fitzgerald, *Cracks.* • Fitzgerald, John T. *Cracks in an Earthen Vessel: An Examination of the Catalogues of Hardships in the Corinthian Correspondence.* Society of Biblical Literature Dissertation 99. Atlanta: Scholars Press, 1988.

Fitzmyer, *Acts.* • Fitzmyer, Joseph A. *The Acts of the Apostles: A New Translation with Introduction and Commentary.* AB 31. New York: Doubleday, 1998.

Fitzmyer, "Elijah." • Fitzmyer, Joseph A. "More about Elijah Coming First." *JBL* 104 (2, 1985): 295-96.

Fitzmyer, *Essays.* • Fitzmyer, Joseph A. *Essays on the Semitic Background of the New Testament.* 2d ed. SBLSBS 5. Missoula, MT: Scholars Press, 1974.

Fitzmyer, "Jewish Christianity." • Fitzmyer, Joseph A. "Jewish Christianity in Acts in Light of the Qumran Scrolls." 233-57 in *Studies in Luke-Acts: Essays in Honor of Paul Schubert.* Ed. Leander E. Keck and J. Louis Martyn. Nashville: Abingdon, 1966.

Fitzmyer, "4Q246." • Fitzmyer, Joseph A. "4Q246: The 'Son of God' Document from Qumran." *Bib* 74 (2, 1993): 153-74.

Fitzmyer, *Scrolls.* • Fitzmyer, Joseph A. *The Dead Sea Scrolls: Major Publications and Tools for Study.* SBLSBS 8. Missoula, MT: Scholars Press for the Society of Biblical Literature, 1977.

Fitzmyer, *Theologian.* • Fitzmyer, Joseph A. *Luke the Theologian: Aspects of His Teaching.* New York: Paulist, 1989.

Fleddermann, "Flight." • Fleddermann, Harry. "The Flight of a Naked Young Man (Mark 14:51-52)." *CBQ* 41 (1979): 412-18.

Fletcher-Louis, *Angels.* • Fletcher-Louis, Crispin H. T. *Luke-Acts: Angels, Christology and Soteriology.* WUNT 2, Reihe 94. Tübingen: J. C. B. Mohr, 1997.

Flew, *God.* • Flew, Antony, with Roy Abraham Varghese. *There Is a God: How the World's Most Notorious Atheist Changed His Mind.* New York: HarperOne, HarperCollins, 2007.

Flichy, "État des recherches." • Flichy, Odile. "État des recherches actuelles sur les Actes des Apôtres." 13-42 in *Les Actes des Apôtres: Histoire, récit, théologie.* Ed. Michel Berder. XXe congrès de l'Association catholique française pour l'étude de la Bible (Angers, 2003). Lecto divina 199. Paris: Cerf, 2005.

Flichy, *L'oeuvre de Luc.* • Flichy, Odile. *L'oeuvre de Luc: L'Évangile et les Actes des Apôtres,* CaÉ 114. Paris: Cerf, 2000.

Flowers, "En Pneumati." • Flowers, Harold J. "ἐν πνεύματι ἁγίῳ καὶ πυρί." *ExpT* 64 (5, Feb. 1953): 155-56.

Flusser, "Ancestry." • Flusser, David. "Jesus, His Ancestry, and the Commandment of Love." 153-76 in *Jesus' Jewishness: Exploring the Place of Jesus within Early Judaism.* Ed. James H. Charlesworth. New York: The American Interfaith Institute, Crossroad Publishing Company, 1991.

Flusser, *Judaism.* • Flusser, David. *Judaism and the Origins of Christianity.* Jerusalem: Magnes Press, Hebrew University, 1988.

Flusser, "Love." • Flusser, David. "Jesus, His Ancestry, and the Commandment of Love." 153-76 in *Jesus' Jewishness: Exploring the Place of Jesus within Early Judaism.* Ed. James H. Charlesworth. New York: The American Interfaith Institute, Crossroad Publishing Company, 1991.

Flusser, "Paganism." • Flusser, David. "Paganism in Palestine." 1065-1100 in *JPFC.*

Flusser, *Sage.* • Flusser, David, with R. Steven Notley. *The Sage from Galilee: Rediscovering Jesus' Genius.* Introduction by James H. Charlesworth. Grand Rapids, Cambridge: Eerdmans, 2007.

Foakes-Jackson, *Acts.* • Foakes-Jackson, F. J. *The Acts of the Apostles.* MNTC. London: Hodder & Stoughton, 1931.

Foakes Jackson and Lake, "Development." • Foakes Jackson, F. J., and Kirsopp Lake. "The Development of Thought on the Spirit, the Church, and Baptism." 1:321-44 in *The Beginnings of Christianity.* 5 vols. Ed. F. J. Foakes Jackson and Kirsopp Lake. Grand Rapids: Baker, 1979.

Forbes, *Prophecy.* • Forbes, Christopher. *Prophecy and Inspired Speech in Early Christianity and Its Hellenistic Environment.* Peabody, MA: Hendrickson, 1997; Tübingen: J. C. B. Mohr, 1995.

Force, "Encore." • Force, Paul. "Encore les incises de Matthieu!" *BLE* 94 (1993): 315-27.

Ford, *Abomination.* • Ford, Desmond. *The Abomination of Desolation in Biblical Eschatology.* Washington, D.C.: The University Press of America, 1979.

Ford, "Abraham." • Ford, J. Massingberde. "'Thou Art Abraham' and 'Upon This Rock . . .'" *HeyJ* 6 (1965): 289-301.

Ford, *Revelation*. • Ford, J. Massyngberde. *Revelation*. AB 38. Garden City, NY: Doubleday & Company, 1975.

Fornara, *Nature of History*. • Fornara, Charles William. *The Nature of History in Ancient Greece and Rome*. Berkeley: University of California Press, 1983.

Fortna, "Equal." • Fortna, Robert T. "'You have made them equal to us!' (Mt 20:1-16)." *JTSA* 72 (1990): 66-72.

Foster, "Introduction." • Foster, B. O. "Introduction." 1:ix-xxxv in Livy. *Ab Urbe Condita*. 14 vols. Trans. B. O. Foster, Frank Gardner, Evan T. Sage, A. C. Schlesinger. LCL. Cambridge: Harvard University Press, 1919-1959.

Fox, "Dionysius." • Fox, Matthew. "Dionysius, Lucian, and the Prejudice against Rhetoric in History." *JRS* 91 (2001): 76-93.

Foxhall, "Tenant." • Foxhall, Lin. "The Dependent Tenant: Land Leasing and Labour in Italy and Greece." *JRS* 80 (1990): 97-114, Plate 3.

Frahm, Jansen-Winkeln, and Wiesehöfer, "Historiography." • Frahm, Eckart, Karl Jansen-Winkeln, Josef Wiesehöfer. "Historiography: Ancient Orient." 6:415-418 in *Brill's New Pauly*.

Frame, *Thessalonians*. • Frame, James Everett. *A Critical and Exegetical Commentary on the Epistles of St. Paul to the Thessalonians*. ICC. Edinburgh: T. & T. Clark, 1912.

France, "Authenticity." • France, R. T. "The Authenticity of the Sayings of Jesus." 101-143 in *History, Criticism & Faith*. Ed. Colin Brown. Downers Grove, IL: InterVarsity, 1976.

France, *Evidence*. • France, R. T. *The Evidence for Jesus*. Downers Grove: InterVarsity, 1986.

France, "Exegesis in Practice." • France, R. T. "Exegesis in Practice: Two Examples." 252-81 in *New Testament Interpretation: Essays on Principles and Methods*. Ed. I. Howard Marshall. Grand Rapids: Eerdmans, 1977.

France, "Jesus the Baptist." • France, R. T. "Jesus the Baptist?" 94-111 in *Jesus of Nazareth: Lord and Christ. Essays on the Historical Jesus and New Testament Christology*. Ed. Joel B. Green and Max Turner. Grand Rapids: Eerdmans; Carlisle: Paternoster, 1994.

France, *Matthew*. • France, R. T. *Matthew*. TNTC. Grand Rapids: Eerdmans, 1985.

Frantzman and Kark, "Gordon." • Frantzman, Seth J., and Ruth Kark. "General Gordon, the Palestine Exploration Fund and the Origins of 'Gordon's Calvary' in the Holy Land." *PEQ* 140 (2, 2008): 119-36.

Fredriksen, *Christ*. • Fredriksen, Paula. *From Jesus to Christ: The Origins of the New Testament Images of Jesus*. New Haven: Yale, 1988.

Frei, "Apologetics." • Frei, Hans. "Apologetics, Criticism, and the Loss of Narrative Interpretation." 45-64 in *Why Narrative? Readings in Narrative Theology*. Ed. Stanley Hauerwas and L. Gregory Jones. Grand Rapids: Eerdmans, 1989.

Freund, "Deception." • Freund, R. A. "Lying and Deception in the Biblical and Post-Biblical Judaic Tradition." *SJOT* 5 (1, 1991): 45-61.

Freyne, "Archaeology." • Freyne, Sean. "Archaeology and the Historical Jesus." 64-83 in *Jesus and Archaeology*. Ed. James H. Charlesworth. Grand Rapids: Eerdmans, 2006.

Freyne, "Ethos." • Freyne, Sean. "The Ethos of First-Century Galilee." *PIBA* 17 (1994): 69-79.

Freyne, *Galilean*. • Freyne, Sean. *Jesus, A Jewish Galilean: A New Reading of the Jesus-Story*. London, New York: T&T Clark International, 2004.

Freyne, "Galileans." • Freyne, Sean. "The Galileans in the Light of Josephus' *Vita*." *NTS* 26 (3, 1980): 397-413.

Freyne, *Galilee*. • Freyne, Sean. *Galilee, Jesus and the Gospels: Literary Approaches and Historical Investigations*. Philadelphia: Fortress, 1988.

Freyne, *Galilee and Gospel*. • Freyne, Sean. *Galilee and Gospel: Collected Essays*. WUNT 125; Tübingen: Mohr Siebeck, 2000.

Freyne, "Jesus and Archaeology." • Freyne, Sean. "The Historical Jesus and Archaeology." *Explorations* 10 (2, 1996): 6.

Freyne, "New Reading." • Freyne, Sean. "Jesus a Jewish Galilean: A New Reading of the Jesus Story." *Proceedings of the Irish Biblical Association* 28 (2005): 106-23.

Freyne, "Relations." • Freyne, Sean. "Galilee-Jerusalem Relations According to Josephus' *Life*." *NTS* 33 (4, April 1987): 600-609.

Freyne, "Religion." • Freyne, Sean. "Galilean Religion of the First Century c.e. against Its Social Background." *PIBA* 5 (1981): 98-114.

Freyne, "Search." • Freyne, Sean. "In Search of the Real Jesus." *Furrow* 49 (10, 1998): 527-38.

Freyne, "Servant Community." • Freyne, Sean. "Jesus and the 'Servant' Community in Zion: Continuity in Context." 109-24 in *Jesus from Judaism to Christianity: Continuum Approaches to the Historical Jesus*. Ed. Tom Holmén. European Studies on Christian Origins. Library of New Testament Studies 352. London, New York: T&T Clark, 2007.

Freyne, "Tomb." • Freyne, Sean. "An Easter Story: 'The Lost Tomb of Jesus.'" *Doctrine and Life* 57 (4, 2007): 2-6.

Frickenschmidt, *Evangelium als Biographie*. • Frickenschmidt, Dirk. *Evangelium als Biographie. Die vier Evangelien im Rahmen antiker Erzählkunst*. TANZ 22. Tübingen: Francke, 1997.

Friedman, "Features." • Friedman, Theodore. "Some Unexplained Features of Ancient Synagogues." *ConsJud* 36 (3, 1983): 35-42.

Friedrichsen, "Agreements." • Friedrichsen, Timothy A. "The Matthew-Luke Agreements against Mark. A Survey of Recent Studies: 1974-1989." 335-391 in *L'Évangile de Luc: The Gospel of Luke*. Rev. ed. Ed. F. Neirynck. BETL 32. Leuven: Leuven University Press, 1989.

Fritsch, *Community*. • Fritsch, Charles T. *The Qumran Community: Its History and Scrolls*. New York: The Macmillan Company, 1956.

Frye, "Analogies in Literatures." • Frye, Roland Mushat. "The Synoptic Problems and Analogies in Other Literatures." 261-302 in *The Relationships Among the Gospels: An Interdisciplinary Dialogue*. Ed. William O. Walker, Jr. San Antonio: Trinity University Press, 1978.

Fuller, "Classics." • Fuller, Reginald H. "Classics and the Gospels: The Seminar." 173-92 in *The Relationships Among the Gospels: An Interdisciplinary Dialogue*. Ed. William O. Walker, Jr. San Antonio: Trinity University Press, 1978.

Fuller, *Formation*. • Fuller, Reginald H. *The Formation of the Resurrection Narratives*. New York: Macmillan Company, 1971.

Funk et al., *Acts of Jesus*. • Funk, Robert W., and the Jesus Seminar. *The Acts of Jesus: The Search for the Authentic Deeds of Jesus*. New York: Polebridge, HarperSanFrancisco, 1998.

Funk et al., *Gospels*. • Funk, Robert W., Roy W. Hoover, and the Jesus Seminar. *The Five Gospels: The Search for the Authentic Words of Jesus*. New York: Polebridge, Macmillan, 1993.

Furness, "Hymn." • Furness, J. M. "Behind the Philippian Hymn." *ExpT* 79 (6, March 1968): 178-82.

Fusillo, "Novel." • Fusillo, Massimo. "Novel: Greek." 9:837-42 in *Brill's New Pauly*.

Fusillo, "Pseudo-Callisthenes." • Fusillo, Massimo. "Pseudo-Callisthenes." 12:114 in *Brill's New Pauly*.

Fusco, "Sezioni-noi." • Fusco, Vittorio. "Le sezioni-noi degli Atti nella discussione recente." *BeO* 25 (2, 1983): 73-86.

Gafni, "Maccabees." • Gafni, Isaiah M. "Josephus and 1 Maccabees." 116-131 in *Josephus, the Bible, and History*. Ed. Louis H. Feldman and Gohei Hata. Detroit: Wayne State University Press.

Gager, *Anti-Semitism*. • Gager, John G. *The Origins of Anti-Semitism: Attitudes Toward Judaism in Pagan and Christian Antiquity*. New York: Oxford University Press, 1983.

Gager, *Kingdom*. • Gager, John G. *Kingdom and Community: The Social World of Early Christianity*. Englewood Cliffs, NJ: Prentice-Hall, 1975.

Gager, "Review." • Gager, John G. "Review of *Early Christianity and Society: Seven Studies* by R. M. Grant; *Social Aspects of Early Christianity* by A. J. Malherbe; and *Sociology of Early Palestinian Christianity* by Gerd Theissen." *RelSRev* 5 (1979): 174-80.

Gal, "T'syyt." • Gal, Zvi. "T'syyt kly 'bn bglyl hthtwn." *'Atiqot* 20 (1991): 25-26.

Galley, "Heilige." • Galley, Susanne. "Jüdische und christliche Heilige — Ein Vergleich." *ZRGG* 57 (1, 2005): 29-47.

Gamble, "Literacy." • Gamble, Harry. "Literacy and Book Culture." 644-48 in *DNTB*.

García Martínez, "Sonship." • García Martínez, Florentino. "Divine Sonship at Qumran and in Philo." *SPhilA* 19 (2007): 85-99.

García Martínez, "Textos." • García Martínez, Florentino. "Nuevos Textos Mesiánicos de Qumrán y el Mesías del Nuevo Testamento." *Communio* 26 (1, 1993): 3-31.

Gardner, "Mqbym." • Gardner, A. E. "Mqbym g' wmqbym d' whmsbr bymy hmqbym." *Zion* 53 (2, 1988): 291-301.

Gardner, *Women*. • Gardner, Jane F. *Women in Roman Law & Society*. Bloomington: Indiana University Press, 1986.

Garland, *Matthew*. • Garland, David E. *Reading Matthew: A Literary and Theological Commentary on the First Gospel*. New York: Crossroad Publishing Company, 1993.

Garnsey and Saller, *Empire*. • Garnsey, Peter, and Richard Saller. *The Roman Empire: Economy, Society and Culture*. Berkeley and Los Angeles: University of California Press, 1987.

Garte, "Resurrection." • Garte, Edna. "The Theme of Resurrection in the Dura-Europos Synagogue Paintings." *JQR* 64 (1973): 1-15.

Gärtner, "Riddles." • Gärtner, Hans Armin. "Riddles. III. Classical Antiquity," 12:589-91 in *Brill's New Pauly*.

Gärtner, *Temple*. • Gärtner, Bertril. *The Temple and the Community in Qumran and the New Testament: A Comparative Study in the Temple Symbolism of the Qumran Texts and the New Testament*. Cambridge: Cambridge University Press, 1965.

Gasparro, *Soteriology*. • Gasparro, Giulia Sfameni. *Soteriology and Mystic Aspects in the Cult of Cybele and Attis*. ÉPROER, tome 103. Published by M. J. Vermaseren. Leiden: E. J. Brill, 1985.

Gaster, *Scriptures*. • Gaster, Theodor H. *The Dead Sea Scriptures*. Garden City, NY: Doubleday & Company, 1976.

Gathercole, *Boasting*. • Gathercole, Simon J. *Where Is Boasting? Early Jewish Soteriology and Paul's Response in Romans 1–5*. Grand Rapids: Eerdmans, 2002.

Gehrke, "Euergetism." • Gehrke, Hans-Joachim. "Euergetism." 5:154-156 in *Brill's New Pauly*.

Geivett, "Epistemology." • Geivett, R. Douglas. "The Epistemology of Resurrection Belief." 93-105 in *The Resurrection of Jesus: John Dominic Crossan and N. T. Wright in Dialogue*, ed. Robert B. Stewart. Minneapolis: Fortress, 2006.

Geldenhuys, *Luke*. • Geldenhuys, Norval. *The Gospel of Luke*. London: Marshall, Morgan & Scott, 1950; Grand Rapids: Eerdmans, 1951.

Gemés, "Aliança." • Gemés, I. "Aliança no Documento de Damasco e na Epístola aos Hebreus. Uma contribuição à questãa: Qumrân e as origens do Cristianismo." *Rivista Cultura Bíblica* 6 (1969): 28-68.

Gempf, "Speaking." • Gempf, Conrad. "Public Speaking and Published Accounts." 259-303 in *The Book of Acts in Its Ancient Literary Setting*. Ed. Bruce W. Winter and Andrew D. Clarke. Vol. 1 in The Book of Acts in Its First Century Setting. Grand Rapids: Eerdmans; Carlisle: Paternoster, 1993.

Gerhardsson, "Exegetisk disciplin." • Gerhardsson, Birger. "'Performance Criticism' — en ny exegetisk disciplin?" *SEÅ* 72 (2007): 95-108.

Gerhardsson, "Frames." • Gerhardsson, Birger. "If We Do Not Cut the Parables out of Their Frames." *NTS* 37 (1991): 321-35.

Gerhardsson, *Memory*. • Gerhardsson, Birger. *Memory and Manuscript: Oral Tradition and Written Transmission in Rabbinic Judaism and Early Christianity*. ASNU 22. Uppsala: C. W. K. Gleerup, 1961.

Gerhardsson, "Meshalim." • Gerhardsson, Birger. "The Narrative Meshalim in the Synoptic Gospels. A Comparison with the Narrative Meshalim in the Old Testament." *NTS* 34 (1988): 339-63.

Gerhardsson, *Origins*. • Gerhardsson, Birger. *The Origins of the Gospel Traditions*. Philadelphia: Fortress, 1979.

Gerhardsson, "Path." • Gerhardsson, Birger. "The Path of the Gospel Tradition." 75-96 in *The Gospel and the Gospels*. Ed. Peter Stuhlmacher. Grand Rapids: Eerdmans, 1991.

Gero, "Messiah." • Gero, Stephen. "'My Son the Messiah': A Note on 4 Esr 7:28-29." *ZNW* 66 (3-4, 1975): 264-67.

Gero, "Polemic." • Gero, Stephen. "Jewish Polemic in the Martyrium Pionii and a 'Jesus' Passage from the Talmud." *JJS* 29 (1978): 164-68.

Gervers, "Iconography." • Gervers, Michael. "The Iconography of the Cave in Christian and Mithraic Tradition." 579-99 in *Mysteria Mithrae*. Ed. Ugo Bianchi. ÉPROER tome 80. Published by M. J. Vermaseren. Leiden: E. J. Brill, 1979.

Geyser, "Geskiedenis." • Geyser, P. A. "Die Jesus van die geskiedenis: Hermeneutiese uitgangspunte in die ondersoek van J P Meier (The Jesus of history: Hermeneutic premises in the research of J P Meier)." *HTS/TS* 57 (1-2, 2001): 230-46.

Geyser, "Tribes." • Geyser, A. "The Twelve Tribes in Revelation: Judean and Judeo-Christian Apocalypticism." *NTS* 28 (3, July 1982): 388-99.

Geyser, "Uitgangspunte." • Geyser, P. A. "Hermeneutiese uitgangspunte in historiese-Jesus navorsing, Deel 1: Sosiaal-wetenskaplike vooronderstellings." *HTS/TS* 56 (2-3, 2000): 527-48; 56 (4, 2000): 1146-70.

Gibbard, "Mystery." • Gibbard, S. M. "The Christian Mystery." 97-120 in *Studies in Ephesians*. Ed. F. L. Cross. London: A. R. Mowbray & Co., 1956.

Gibbs, *Creation*. • Gibbs, John G. *Creation and Redemption: A Study in Pauline Theology*. NovTSup 26. Leiden: E. J. Brill, 1971.

Giblet, "Mouvement." • Giblet, Jean. "Un mouvement de résistance armée au temps de Jésus?" *RTL* 5 (1974): 409-26.

Gieschen, "Tomb." • Gieschen, Charles A. "The Lost Tomb of Jesus?" *CTQ* 71 (2, 2007): 199-200.

Giesen, *Herrschaft*. • Giesen, Heinz. *Herrschaft Gottes — heute oder morgen? Zur Heilsbotschaft Jesu und der synoptischen Evangelien*. BibUnt 26. Regensburg: Pustet, 1995.

Gillet-Didier, "Paradosis." • Gillet-Didier, Veronique. "*Paradosis*: Flavius Josèphe et la fabrique de la tradition." *REJ* 158 (1-2, 1999): 7-49.

Giovannini and Hirt, "L'inscription." • Giovannini, A., and M. Hirt. "L'inscription de Nazareth: nouvelle interprétation." *ZPE* 124 (1999): 107-32.

Gisel, "Jésus historique." • Gisel, Pierre. "La question du Jésus historique chez Ernst Käsemann revisitée à partir de la 'troisième quête.'" *ETR* 79 (4, 2004): 451-63.

Glasson, *Advent*. • Glasson, T. Francis. *The Second Advent: The Origin of the New Testament Doctrine*. 3d rev. ed. London: Epworth, 1963.

Glasson, "Colossians." • Glasson, T. Francis. "Colossians I 18, 15 and Sirach XXIV." *NovT* 11 (1-2, 1969): 154-56.

Glasson, *Influence*. • Glasson, T. Francis. *Greek Influence in Jewish Eschatology. With Special Reference to the Apocalypses and Pseudepigraphs*. S.P.C.K. Biblical Monographs 1. London: S.P.C.K., 1961.

Glasson, *Moses*. • Glasson, T. Francis. *Moses in the Fourth Gospel*. SBT. Naperville, IL: Alec R. Allenson, 1963.

Glasson, "Notes." • Glasson, T. Francis. "Two Notes on the Philippians Hymn (II.6-11)." *NTS* 21 (1, Oct. 1974): 133-39.

Glasson, "Son of Man Imagery." • Glasson, T. Francis. "The Son of Man Imagery: Enoch XIV and Daniel VII." *NTS* 23 (1, Oct. 1976): 82-90.

Glueck, *Rivers*. • Glueck, Nelson. *Rivers in the Desert: A History of the Negev*. New York: Grove Press, 1960.

Gnilka, "Gemeinschaftsmal." • Gnilka, Joachim. "Das Gemeinschaftsmal der Essener." *BZ* 5 (1961): 39-55.

Gnilka, *Jesus of Nazareth.* • Gnilka, Joachim. *Jesus of Nazareth: Message and History.* Trans. Siegfried S. Schatzmann. Peabody: Hendrickson, 1997.

Godwin, *Religions.* • Godwin, Joscelyn. *Mystery Religions in the Ancient World.* San Franscico: Harper & Row, Publishers, 1981.

Goetz and Blomberg, "Burden of Proof." • Goetz, Stewart C., and Craig L. Blomberg, "The Burden of Proof." *JSNT* 11 (1981): 39-63.

Goguel, *Jesus.* • Goguel, Maurice. *The Life of Jesus.* Tr. Olive Wyon. New York: Macmillan, 1948.

Goldenberg, "*Antiquities* iv." • Goldenberg, David M. "*Antiquities* iv,277 and 288, Compared with Early Rabbinic Law." 198-211 in *Josephus, Judaism and Christianity.* Ed. Louis H. Feldman and Gohei Hata. Detroit: Wayne State University Press, 1987.

Goldenberg, "Explanations." • Goldenberg, Robert. "Early Rabbinic Explanations of the Destruction of Jerusalem." *JJS* 33 (1982): 517-25.

Goldenberg, "Halakha." • Goldenberg, David. "The Halakha in Josephus and in Tannaitic Literature: A Comparative Study." *JQR* 67 (1, July 1976): 30-34.

Goldingay, "Expounding." • Goldingay, John. "Expounding the New Testament." 351-65 in *New Testament Interpretation: Essays on Principles and Methods.* Ed. I. Howard Marshall. Grand Rapids: Eerdmans, 1977.

Gondola, "Kimbangu." • Gondola, Charles Didier. "Kimbangu, Simon, and Kimbanguism." 2:766-67 in *Encyclopedia of African History.* 3 vols. Ed. Kevin Shillington. New York, London: Fitzroy Dearborn (Taylor & Francis Group), 2005.

Goodacre, "Quest." • Goodacre, Mark. "The Quest to Digest Jesus: Recent Books on the Historical Jesus." *RRT* 7 (2, 2000): 156-61.

Goodacre, *Synoptic Problem.* • Goodacre, Mark. *The Synoptic Problem: A Way Through the Maze.* New York: Sheffield Academic Press, 2001.

Goodacre and Perrin, *Questioning.* • Goodacre, Mark, and Nicholas Perrin, eds. *Questioning Q: A Multidimensional Critique.* Foreword by N. T. Wright. Downers Grove, IL: InterVarsity, 2004.

Goodenough, *Church.* • Goodenough, Erwin R. *The Church in the Roman Empire.* New York: Cooper Square Publishers, 1970.

Goodenough, *Symbols.* • Goodenough, Erwin R. *Jewish Symbols in the Greco-Roman Period.* 13 vols. Bollingen Series 37. Vols. 1-12: New York: Pantheon Books, for Bollingen Foundation, 1953-1965. Vol. 13: Princeton: Princeton University Press, for Bollingen Foundation, 1968.

Goodman, *State.* • Goodman, Martin. *State and Society in Roman Galilee, A.D. 132-212.* OCPHS. Totowa, NJ: Rowman & Allanheld, Publishers, 1983.

Goppelt, *Judaism.* • Goppelt, Leonhard. *Jesus, Paul and Judaism.* Trans. Edward Schroeder. New York: Thomas Nelson & Sons, 1964.

Goppelt, *Theology.* • Goppelt, Leonhard. *Theology of the New Testament.* 2 vols. Trans. John E. Alsup. Ed. Jürgen Roloff. Grand Rapids: Eerdmans, 1981-1982.

Goppelt, *Times.* • Goppelt, Leonhard. *Apostolic and Post-Apostolic Times.* Trans. Robert Guelich. Grand Rapids: Baker, 1980.

Gordon, *Civilizations.* • Gordon, Cyrus H. *The Common Background of Greek and Hebrew Civilizations.* New York: W. W. Norton & Company, 1965.

Gordon, *Near East.* • Gordon, Cyrus H. *The Ancient Near East.* New York: W. W. Norton & Company, 1965.

Görgemanns, "Biography." • Görgemanns, Herwig. "Biography: Greek." 2:648-51 in *Brill's New Pauly.*

Goshen-Gottstein, "God the Father." • Goshen-Gottstein, Alon. "God the Father in Rabbinic Judaism and Christianity: Transformed Background or Common Ground?" *JES* 38 (3, 2001): 470-504.

Gospel Perspectives. • *Gospel Perspectives.* 6 vols. Ed. R. T. France and David Wenham. Sheffield: JSOT Press, 1980-1986.

"Gospels: Forms." • "Gospels (literary forms)." 5:947-949 in *Brill's New Pauly.*

Gottlieb, "Abot." • Gottlieb, Isaac B. "Pirqe Abot and biblical wisdom." *VT* 40 (2, 1990): 152-64.

Goulder, *Midrash.* • Goulder, M. D. *Midrash and Lection in Matthew.* The Speaker's Lectures in Biblical Studies 1969-71. London: S.P.C.K., 1974.

Goulder, "Prayer." • Goulder, M. D. "The Composition of the Lord's Prayer." *JTS* n.s. 14 (1963): 32-45.

Goulder, "Q." • Goulder, Michael Douglas. "On Putting Q to the Test." *NTS* 24 (2, January 1978): 218-34.

Goulder, *Type and History.* • Goulder, Michael Douglas. *Type and History in Acts.* London: S.P.C.K., 1964.

Gowler, *Host, Guest.* • Gowler, David B. *Host, Guest, Enemy and Friend: Portraits of the Pharisees in Luke and Acts.* ESEC 2. New York: Peter Lang, 1991.

Gramaglia, "Testamonium." • Gramaglia, P. A. "Il *Testamonium Flavianum.* Analisi linguistica." *Hen* 20 (2, 1998): 153-77.

Grant, "Clock." • Grant, Frederick C. "Turning Back the Clock." *Int* 19 (3, 1965): 352-354.

Grant, *Gnosticism.* • Grant, Robert M. *Gnosticism and Early Christianity.* 2d ed. New York: Columbia University Press, 1966.

Grant, *Gods.* • Grant, Robert M. *Gods and the One God.* LEC 1. Philadelphia: Westminster, 1986.

Grant, *Gospel.* • Grant, Frederick C. *The Earliest Gospel.* New York: Abingdon-Cokesbury, 1943.

Grant, *Hellenism.* • Grant, Frederick C. *Roman Hellenism and the New Testament.* New York: Charles Scribner's Sons, 1962.

Grant, *Jesus.* • Grant, Michael. *Jesus, An Historian's Review of the Gospels.* New York: Charles Scribner's Sons, 1977.

Grant, *Judaism.* • Grant, Frederick C. *Ancient Judaism and the New Testament.* New York: Macmillan, 1959.

Grant, *Paul.* • Grant, Robert M. *Paul in the Roman World: The Conflict at Corinth.* Louisville: Westminster John Knox, 2001.

Grant, *Religions.* • Grant, Frederick C., ed. *Hellenistic Religions: The Age of Syncretism.* The Library of Liberal Arts. Indianapolis: The Bobbs-Merrill Company, The Liberal Arts Press, 1953.

Grant, "Review." • Grant, Frederick. Review of "A. N. Sherwin-White, *Roman Society and Roman Law in the New Testament."* *JTS* 15 (2, 1964): 352-58.

Grant, *Social History.* • Grant, Michael. *A Social History of Greece and Rome.* New York: Charles Scribner's Sons; Oxford: Maxwell Macmillan International, 1992.

Grappe, "Christologie." • Grappe, Christian. "De l'intérêt de 4 Maccabées 17.18-22 (et 16.20-1) pour la christologie du NT." *NTS* 46 (3, 2000): 342-57.

Grappe, "Essai." • Grappe, Christian. "Essai sur l'arrière-plan pascal des récrits de la dernière nuit de Jésus." *RHPR* 65 (2, 1985): 105-25.

Grappe, "Prophètes." • Grappe, Christian. "Jésus parmi d'autres prophètes de son temps." *RHPR* 81 (4, 2001): 387-411.

Graves and May, *Preaching Matthew.* • Graves, Mike, and David M. May. *Preaching Matthew: Interpretation and Proclamation.* St. Louis: Chalice, 2007.

Gray, "Christianity." • Gray, Richard. "Christianity." 140-90 in *The Cambridge History of Africa.* 8 vols. Ed. J. D. Fage and Roland Oliver. Vol. 7: *From 1905-1940.* Ed. A. D. Roberts. Cambridge: Cambridge University Press 1986.

Gray, *Figures.* • Gray, Rebecca. *Prophetic Figures in Late Second Temple Jewish Palestine: The Evidence from Josephus.* New York: Oxford University Press, 1993.

Grayzel, *History.* • Grayzel, Solomon. *A History of the Jews.* Philadelphia: Jewish Publication Society of America, 1961.

Green, **"History/Writing."** • Green, Joel B. "The Book of Acts as History/Writing." *LTQ* 37 (3, 2002): 119-27.

Greenhut, **"Cave."** • Greenhut, Zvi. "Burial Cave of the Caiaphas Family." *BAR* 18 (5, 1992): 28-36, 76.

Greenhut, **"Tomb."** • Greenhut, Zvi. "Discovery of the Caiaphas Family Tomb." *JerPersp* 4 (4-5, 1991): 6-12.

Greenspoon, **"Pronouncement Story."** • Greenspoon, Leonard. "The Pronouncement Story in Philo and Josephus." *Semeia* 20 (1981): 73-80.

Greenstone, *Messiah.* • Greenstone, Julius H. *The Messiah Idea in Jewish History.* Philadelphia: Jewish Publication Society of America, 1906.

Gregg, **"Antecedents."** • Gregg, David W. A. "Hebraic Antecedents to the Eucharistic ἀνάμνησις Formula." *TynBul* 30 (1979): 165-68.

Gregory, **"Galilee."** • Gregory, Andrew. "A Galilee Less Greek than Before?" *ExpT* 118 (7, 2007): 337-38.

Grene, *Political Theory.* • Grene, David. *Greek Political Theory: The Image of Man in Thucydides and Plato.* Chicago: University of Chicago, 1950.

Grieb, **"People."** • Grieb, A. Katherine. "People of God, Body of Christ, Koinonia of Spirit: The Role of Ethical Ecclesiology in Paul's 'Trinitarian' Language." *ATR* 87 (2, 2005): 225-52.

Grintz, **"Jubilees."** • Grintz, Yehoshua M. "Jubilees, Book of." 10:324-26 in *Encyclopaedia Judaica.* 16 vols. Jerusalem: Keter Publishing House, 1972.

Groenewald, **"Mammon."** • Groenewald, E. P. "God and Mammon." *Neot* 1 (1967): 59-66.

Groh, **"Meal."** • Groh, John E. "The Qumran Meal and the Last Supper." *CTM* 41 (1970): 279-95.

Guelich, **"Genre."** • Guelich, Robert. "The Gospel Genre." 173-208 in *The Gospel and the Gospels.* Ed. Peter Stuhlmacher. Grand Rapids: Eerdmans, 1991.

Guelich, *Sermon.* • Guelich, Robert. *The Sermon on the Mount: A Foundation for Understanding.* Waco, TX: Word, 1982.

Guenther, **"Greek."** • Guenther, Heinz O. "Greek: Home of Primitive Christianity." *TJT* 5 (2, 1989): 247-79.

Guijarro Oporto, **"Articulación literaria."** • Guijarro Oporto, Santiago. "La articulación literaria del Libro de los Hechos." *EstBib* 62 (2, 2004): 185-204.

Gundry, **"Framework."** • Gundry, Robert H. "The Narrative Framework of Matthew xvi 17-19. A Critique of Professor Cullmann's Hypothesis." *NovT* 7 (1964): 1-9.

Gundry, **"Genre."** • Gundry, Robert H. "Recent Investigations into the Literary Genre 'Gospel.'" 97-114 in *New Dimensions in New Testament Study.* Ed. Richard N. Longenecker and Merrill C. Tenney. Grand Rapids: Zondervan, 1974.

Gundry, *Matthew.* • Gundry, Robert H. *Matthew: A Commentary on His Literary and Theological Art.* Grand Rapids: Eerdmans, 1982.

Gundry, *Old Testament.* • Gundry, Robert H. *The Use of the Old Testament in St. Matthew's Gospel: With Special Reference to the Messianic Hope.* NovTSup 18. Leiden: E. J. Brill, 1975.

Gundry, **"Physicality."** • Gundry, Robert H. "The Essential Physicality of Jesus' Resurrection according to the New Testament." 204-19 in *Jesus of Nazareth: Lord and Christ. Essays on the Historical Jesus and New Testament Christology.* Ed. Joel B. Green and Max Turner. Grand Rapids: Eerdmans; Carlisle: Paternoster, 1994.

Gurney, *Aspects.* • Gurney, O. R. *Some Aspects of Hittite Religion.* Oxford: Oxford University Press, 1977.

Gustafsson, **"Graffiti."** • Gustafsson, Berndt. "The Oldest Graffiti in the History of the Church?" *NTS* 3 (1, Nov. 1956): 65-69.

Guthrie, *Orpheus.* • Guthrie, W. K. C. *Orpheus and Greek Religion: A Study of the Orphic Movement.* 2d ed. New York: W. W. Norton & Company, 1966.

Guyénot, **"Apostle."** • Guyénot, Laurent. "Jesus as Elijah's Apostle." *DRev* 121 (425, 2003): 271-96.

Haacker, "Erst." • Haacker, Klaus. "Erst unter Quirinius? Ein Übersetzungsvorschlag zu Lk 2, 2." *BN* 38-39 (1987): 39-43.

Haar, "Quest." • Haar, Stephen. "Historical Jesus Studies: A Fertile or a Futile Quest?" *Lutheran Theological Journal* 41 (1, 2007): 27-36.

Habermas, *Evidence.* • Habermas, Gary R. *Ancient Evidence for the Life of Jesus: Historical Records of His Death and Resurrection.* Nashville: Thomas Nelson, 1984.

Habermas, "Trend." • Habermas, Gary R. "Mapping the Recent Trend Toward the Bodily Resurrection Appearances of Jesus in Light of Other Prominent Critical Positions." 78-92 in *The Resurrection of Jesus: John Dominic Crossan and N. T. Wright in Dialogue.* Ed. Robert B. Stewart. Minneapolis: Fortress, 2006.

Hadas and Smith, *Heroes.* • Hadas, Moses, and Morton Smith. *Heroes and Gods: Spiritual Biographies in Antiquity.* Religious Perspectives 13. New York: Harper & Row, Publishers, 1965.

Haenchen, *Acts.* • Haenchen, Ernst. *The Acts of the Apostles: A Commentary.* Philadelphia: Westminster, 1971.

Haenchen, *John.* • Haenchen, Ernst. *A Commentary on the Gospel of John.* 2 vols. Trans. Robert W. Funk. Ed. Robert W. Funk with Ulrich Busse. Hermeneia. Philadelphia: Fortress, 1984.

Häfner, "Basileia." • Häfner, Gerd. "Gewalt gegen die Basileia? Zum Problem der Auslegung des 'Stürmerspruches' Mt 11,12." *ZNW* 83 (1992): 21-51.

Hagner, *Matthew.* • Hagner, Donald A. *Matthew 1–13.* WBC 33A. Dallas: Word, 1993. *Matthew 14–28.* WBC 33B. Dallas: Word, 1995.

Hagner, "Sayings." • Hagner, Donald A. "The Sayings of Jesus in the Apostolic Fathers and Justin Martyr." 5:233-268 in *GosPersp.* Vol. 5: *The Jesus Tradition Outside the Gospels.* Ed. David Wenham. Sheffield: JSOT Press, 1984.

Hallbäck, "Apocalyptic." • Hallbäck, Geert. "From Apocalyptic to Sage: Paradigms of Jesus in the 20th Century." *STK* 77 (3, 2001): 118-25.

Hamerton-Kelly, *Pre-Existence.* • Hamerton-Kelly, R. G. *Pre-Existence, Wisdom, and the Son: A Study of the Idea of Pre-existence in the New Testament.* Cambridge: Cambridge University Press, 1973.

Hamilton, "Cleansing." • Hamilton, Neill Q. "Temple Cleansing and Temple Bank." *JBL* 83 (1964): 365-72.

Hammershaimb, "Lignelser." • Hammershaimb, E. "Om lignelser og billedtaler i de gammeltestamentlige Pseudepigrafer." *SEÅ* 40 (1975): 36-65.

Hammond, "Speeches." • Hammond, Nigel G. L. "The speeches in Arrian's *Indica* and *Anabasis*." *CQ* 49 (1, 1999): 238-253.

Hanson, *Acts.* • Hanson, R. P. C. *The Acts in the Revised Standard Version, With Introduction and Commentary.* Oxford: Clarendon Press, 1967.

Hanson, *Unity.* • Hanson, Stig. *The Unity of the Church in the New Testament: Colossians and Ephesians.* Lexington, KY: The American Theological Library Association, 1963.

Hanson and Oakman, *Palestine.* • Hanson, K. C., and Douglas E. Oakman. *Palestine in the Time of Jesus: Social Structures and Social Conflicts.* Minneapolis: Fortress, 1998.

Hare, *Persecution.* • Hare, Douglas R. A. *The Theme of Jewish Persecution of Christians in the Gospel According to St. Matthew.* Cambridge: Cambridge University, 1967.

Harmon, "Introduction." • Harmon, A. M. "Introduction" to Lucian *Zeus Rants.* 2:89 in Lucian. *Works.* 8 vols. Trans. A. M. Harmon, K. Kilburn, and M. D. Macleod. LCL. Cambridge: Harvard University Press, 1913-1967.

Harms, "Tradition." • Harms, Robert. "Oral Tradition and Ethnicity." *JIHist* 10 (1, summer 1979): 61-85.

Harnack, *Acts.* • Harnack, Adolf von. *The Acts of the Apostles.* New Testament Studies 3. Trans. J. R. Wilkinson. New York: G. P. Putnam's Sons; London: Williams and Norgate, 1909.

Harnack, *Christianity.* • Harnack, Adolf von. *What Is Christianity?* Trans. Thomas Bailey Saunders.

Introduction by Rudolf Bultmann. Fortress Texts in Modern Theology. Philadelphia: Fortress, 1986; reprint from New York: Harper & Brothers, 1957.

Harrelson, *Cult.* • Harrelson, Walter. *From Fertility Cult to Worship.* Garden City, NY: Doubleday & Company, 1969.

Harrington, "Bible." • Harrington, D. J. "The Bible Rewritten (Narratives)." Pp. 239-47 in *Early Judaism and Its Modern Interpreters.* Ed. Robert A. Kraft and George W. E. Nickelsburg. Society of Biblical Literature and Its Modern Interpreters Series 2. Atlanta: Scholars Press, 1986.

Harrington, *God's People.* • Harrington, D. J. *God's People in Christ.* Philadelphia: Fortress, 1980.

Harrington, *Matthew.* • Harrington, Daniel J. *The Gospel According to Matthew.* Collegeville, MN: The Liturgical Press, 1982.

Harrington, "Wisdom Texts." • Harrington, Daniel J. "Ten Reasons Why the Qumran Wisdom Texts Are Important." *DSD* 4 (3, 1997): 245-54.

Harris, "Aging." • Harris, J. G. "Rabbinic Responses to Aging." *HS* 58 (2007): 187-94.

Harris, *Jesus as God.* • Harris, Murray J. *Jesus as God: The New Testament Use of* Theos *in Reference to Jesus.* Grand Rapids: Baker, 1992.

Harris, *Raised.* • Harris, Murray J. *Raised Immortal.* London: Marshall, Morgan and Scott, 1983; Grand Rapids: Eerdmans, 1985.

Harris, "References." • Harris, Murray J. "References to Jesus in Early Classical Authors." 343-68 in *The Jesus Tradition Outside the Gospels.* Ed. David Wenham. Sheffield: JSOT Press, 1984. Vol. 5 in *GosPersp.*

Harrison, *Grace.* • Harrison, James R. *Paul's Language of Grace in Its Graeco-Roman Context.* WUNT 2. Reihe, 172. Tübingen: J. C. B. Mohr, 2003.

Harrison, "Rites." • Harrison, R. K. "The Rites and Customs of the Qumran Sect." 26-36 in *The Scrolls and Christianity: Historical and Theological Significance.* Ed. Matthew Black. London: S.P.C.K., 1969.

Harvey, *History.* • Harvey, A. E. *Jesus and the Constraints of History.* Philadelphia: Westminster, 1982.

Harvey, *Listening.* • Harvey, John D. *Listening to the Text: Oral Patterning in Paul's Letters.* Foreword by Richard N. Longenecker. Grand Rapids: Baker; Leicester: Apollos, 1998.

Hasel, *Theology.* • Hasel, Gerhard F. *New Testament Theology: Basic Issues in the Current Debate.* Grand Rapids: Eerdmans, 1978.

Hata, "Moses within Anti-Semitism." • Hata, Gohei. "The Story of Moses Interpreted within the Context of Anti-Semitism." 180-97 in *Josephus, Judaism and Christianity.* Ed. Louis H. Feldman and Gohei Hata. Detroit: Wayne State University Press, 1987.

Hata, "Version." • Hata, Gohei. "Is the Greek Version of Josephus' *Jewish War* a Translation or a Rewriting of the First Version?" *JQR* 66 (2, October 1975): 89-108.

Hatina, "Exile." • Hatina, Thomas R. "Exile." 348-351 in *DNTB.*

Hauerwas, "Have to Die." • Hauerwas, Stanley. "Why Did Jesus Have to Die?: An Attempt to Cross the Barrier of Age." *PSB* 28 (2, 2007): 181-90.

Hauptman, "Haggadah." • Hauptman, Judith. "How Old Is the Haggadah?" *Judaism* 51 (1, 2002): 5-18.

Hayles, "Correct." • Hayles, D. J. "The Roman Census and Jesus' Birth. Was Luke Correct? Part 1: The Roman Census System." *BurH* 9 (4, 1973): 113-32. "Correct? Part II: Quirinius' Career and a Census in Herod's Day." *BurH* 10 (1, 1974): 16-31.

Hayman, "Fall." • Hayman, A. P. "The Fall, Freewill and Human Responsibility in Rabbinic Judaism." *SJT* 37 (1, 1984): 13-22.

Hayman, "Monotheism." • Hayman, Peter. "Monotheism — A Misused Word in Jewish Studies." *JJS* 42 (1, 1991): 1-15.

Hays, *1 Corinthians.* • Hays, Richard B. *First Corinthians.* Interpretation. Louisville, KY: John Knox, 1997.

Hays, Echoes. • Hays, Richard B. *Echoes of Scripture in the Letters of Paul.* New Haven: Yale University Press, 1989.

Hays, "Victory." • Hays, Richard B. "Victory over Violence: The Significance of N. T. Wright's *Jesus for New Testament Ethics.*" 142-58 in *Jesus and the Restoration of Israel: A Critical Assessment of N. T. Wright's Jesus and the Victory of God.* Ed. Carey C. Newman. Downers Grove: InterVarsity, 1999.

Hayward, "Targum to Genesis 27." • Hayward, Robert. "Targum Pseudo-Jonathan to Genesis 27:31." *JQR* 84 (1993): 177-88.

Head, "Nazi Quest." • Head, Peter M. "The Nazi Quest for an Aryan Jesus." *JSHJ* 2 (1, 2004): 55-89.

Head, "Note on Reading." • Head, Peter M. "A further note on *Reading and Writing in the Time of Jesus.*" *EvQ* 75 (4, 2003): 343-345.

Hearon, "Read." • Hearon, Holly E. "To Read Ourselves as the 'Other.'" *Enc* 63 (1-2, 2002): 109-18.

Heath, Hermogenes. • Heath, Malcolm, translator and commentator. *Hermogenes On Issues: Strategies of Argument in Later Greek Rhetoric.* Oxford: Clarendon Press, 1995.

Hedrick, "Paul's Conversion/Call." • Hedrick, Charles W. "Paul's Conversion/Call: A Comparative Analysis of the Three Reports in Acts." *JBL* 100 (3, Sept. 1981): 415-32.

Heidel, Genesis. • Heidel, Alexander. *The Babylonian Genesis.* 2d ed. Chicago: The University of Chicago Press, 1951.

Heindl, "Rezeption." • Heindl, Andreas. "Zur Rezeption der Gestalt des Judas Iskariot im Islam und im Judentum. Ein Versuch der Annäherung an heikles Thema (Teil II)." *PzB* 16 (1, 2007): 43-66.

Held, "Miracle Stories." • Held, Heinz Joachim. "Matthew as Interpreter of the Miracle Stories." 165-299 in *Tradition and Interpretation in Matthew.* By Günther Bornkamm, Gerhard Barth, and Heinz Joachim Held. Philadelphia: Westminster, 1963.

Hellestam, "Saltet." • Hellestam, S. "Mysteriet med saltet." *SEÅ* 55 (1990): 59-63.

Hemer, Acts in History. • Hemer, Colin J. *The Book of Acts in the Setting of Hellenistic History.* Ed. Conrad H. Gempf. WUNT 49. Tübingen: J. C. B. Mohr (Paul Siebeck), 1989.

Hemer, "Alexandria Troas." • Hemer, Colin J. "Alexandria Troas." *TynBul* 26 (1975): 79-112.

Hemer, "First Person Narrative." • Hemer, Colin J. "First Person Narrative in Acts 27-28." *TynBul* 36 (1985): 79-109.

Hemer, "Name of Felix." • Hemer, Colin. "The Name of Felix Again." *JSNT* 31 (1987): 45-49.

Hendricks, Politics. • Hendricks, Obery M. *The Politics of Jesus: Rediscovering the True Revolutionary Nature of the Teachings of Jesus and How They Have Been Corrupted.* New York: Doubleday, 2006.

Hengel, Acts and History. • Hengel, Martin *Acts and the History of Earliest Christianity.* Trans. John Bowden. London: SCM, 1979; Philadelphia: Fortress, 1980.

Hengel, Atonement. • Hengel, Martin. *The Atonement: The Origins of the Doctrine in the New Testament.* Trans. John Bowden. Philadelphia: Fortress, 1981.

Hengel, Crucifixion. • Hengel, Martin. *Crucifixion in the ancient world and the folly of the message of the cross.* Philadelphia: Fortress, 1977.

Hengel, "Geography of Palestine." • Hengel, Martin. "The Geography of Palestine in Acts." 27-78 in *The Book of Acts in Its Palestinian Setting.* Ed. Richard Bauckham. Vol. 4 in The Book of Acts in Its First Century Setting. Grand Rapids: Eerdmans; Carlisle: Paternoster, 1995.

Hengel, "Gleichnis." • Hengel, Martin. "Das Gleichnis von den Weingärtnern Mc 12,1-12 im Lichte der Zenonpapyri und der rabbinischen Gleichnisse." *ZNW* 59 (1968): 9-31.

Hengel, Judaism. • Hengel, Martin. *Judaism and Hellenism: Studies in their encounter in Palestine during the early Hellenistic period.* 2 vols. Trans. John Bowden. Philadelphia: Fortress, 1974.

Hengel, Leader. • Hengel, Martin. *The Charismatic Leader and His Followers.* Ed. John Riches. Trans. James Greig. New York: Crossroad, 1981.

Hengel, "Messiah." • Hengel, Martin. "Jesus, the Messiah of Israel: The Debate About the 'Messianic

Mission' of Jesus." 323-49 in *Authenticating the Activities of Jesus*. Ed. Bruce Chilton and Craig A. Evans. NTTS 28.2. Leiden: Brill, 1999.

Hengel, *Pre-Christian Paul*. • Hengel, Martin. *The Pre-Christian Paul*. Valley Forge, PA: Trinity Press International, 1991.

Hengel, "Problems." • Hengel, Martin. "Literary, Theological, and Historical Problems in the Gospel of Mark." 209-51 in *The Gospel and the Gospels*. Ed. Peter Stuhlmacher. Grand Rapids: Eerdmans, 1991.

Hengel, *Property*. • Hengel, Martin. *Property and Riches in the Early Church: Aspects of Social History of Early Christianity*. Philadelphia: Fortress, 1974.

Hengel, *Question*. • Hengel, Martin. *The Johannine Question*. Trans. John Bowden. Philadelphia: Trinity Press International; London: SCM, 1989.

Hengel, "Revolutionär." • Hengel, Martin. "War Jesus Revolutionär? Sechs Thesen eines Neutestamentlers." *EvK* 2 (1969): 694-96.

Hengel, *Son*. • Hengel, Martin. *Son of God*. Trans. John Bowden. Philadelphia: Fortress, 1976.

Hengel, *Studies in Mark*. • Hengel, Martin. *Studies in the Gospel of Mark*. Trans. John Bowden. Philadelphia: Fortress, 1985.

Hengel, *Zeloten*. • Hengel, Martin. *Die Zeloten. Untersuchungen zur jüdischen Freiheitsbewegung in der Zeit von Herodes I. bis 70n. Chr.* Arbeiten zur Geschichte des Spätjudentums und Urchristentums, vol. I. Leiden, Cologne: E. J. Brill, 1961.

Hengel and Schwemer, *Between Damascus and Antioch*. • Hengel, Martin, and Anna Maria Schwemer. *Paul Between Damascus and Antioch: The Unknown Years*. Trans. John Bowden. London: SCM; Louisville, KY: Westminster John Knox, 1997.

Henige, "History." • Henige, David. "African History and the Rule of Evidence: Is Declaring Victory Enough?" 91-104 in *African Historiographies: What History for Which Africa?* Ed. Bogumil Jewsiewicki and David Newbury. SSAMD 12. Beverly Hills, London, New Delhi: Sage, 1986.

Hennecke, *Apocrypha*. • Hennecke, Edgar. *New Testament Apocrypha*. Ed. Wilhelm Schneemelcher and R. McL. Wilson. 2 vols. Philadelphia: Westminster, 1963-1965.

Henrichs, "Identities." • Henrichs, Albert. "Changing Dionysiac Identities." 137-60 in *Self-Definition in the Greco-Roman World*. Ed. Ben F. Meyer and E. P. Sanders. Vol. 3 in *Jewish and Christian Self-Definition*. Philadelphia: Fortress, 1982.

Henten, "Martyrologie." • Henten, Jan Willem van. "Einige Prolegomena zum Studien der jüdischen Martyrologie." *Bijdr* 46 (1985): 381-90.

Hepper, *Plants*. • Hepper, F. Nigel. *Baker Encyclopedia of Bible Plants*. Grand Rapids: Baker; Leicester: Inter Varsity, 1992.

Herford, *Christianity*. • Herford, R. Travers. *Christianity in Talmud and Midrash*. Library of Philosophical and Religious Thought. Clifton, NJ: Reference Book Publishers, 1966; reprint of 1903 edition.

Héring, *1 Corinthians*. • Héring, Jean. *The First Epistle of Saint Paul to the Corinthians*. Trans. A. W. Heathcote and P. J. Allcock. London: Epworth, 1962.

Herr, "Calendar." • Herr, M. D. "The Calendar." 834-64 in *JPFC*.

Herrenbrück, "Zöllner." • Herrenbrück, Fritz. "Wer waren die 'Zöllner'?" *ZNW* 72 (1981): 178-94.

Herzog, *Jesus*. • Herzog, William R., II. *Jesus, Justice, and the Reign of God: A Ministry of Liberation*. Louisville, KY: Westminster John Knox, 2000.

Hester, "Epideictic." • Hester, James D. "Placing the Blame: The Presence of Epideictic in Galatians 1 and 2." 281-307 in *Persuasive Artistry: Studies in New Testament Rhetoric in Honor of George A. Kennedy*. Ed. Duane F. Watson. JSNTSup 50. Sheffield: Sheffield Academic Press, 1991.

Heyer, *Jesus Matters*. • Heyer, C. J. den. *Jesus Matters: 150 Years of Research*. Valley Forge: Trinity Press International, 1997.

Hezser, "Verwendung." • Hezser, Catherine. "Die Verwendung der hellenistischen Gattung Chrie im frühen Christentum und Judentum." *JSJ* 27 (4, 1996): 371-439.

Higgins, "Belief." • Higgins, A. J. B. "Jewish Messianic Belief in Justin Martyr's *Dialogue with Trypho." NovT* 9 (4, Oct. 1967): 298-305.

Higgins, "Eucharist." • Higgins, A. J. B. "The Origins of the Eucharist." *NTS* 1 (1955): 200-9.

Higgins, "Messiah." • Higgins, A. J. B. "The Priestly Messiah." *NTS* 13 (1966-1967): 211-39.

Higgins, "Priest." • Higgins, A. J. B. "Priest and Messiah." *VT* 3 (4, October 1953): 321-36.

Higgins, *Son of Man*. • Higgins, A. J. B. *Jesus and the Son of Man*. Philadelphia: Fortress, 1964.

Hill, *Matthew*. • Hill, David. *The Gospel of Matthew*. New Century Bible. Grand Rapids: Eerdmans; London: Marshall, Morgan & Scott, 1972.

Hill, *Prophecy*. • Hill, David. *New Testament Prophecy*. New Foundations Theological Library. Atlanta: John Knox, 1979.

Hill, "Son." • Hill, David. "Son and Servant: An Essay on Matthean Christology." *JSNT* 6 (1980): 2-16.

Hills, "Acts and *Acts*." • Hills, Julian V. "The Acts of the Apostles and the *Acts of Paul." SBLSP* 33 (1994): 24-54.

Hills, "*Acts of Paul*." • Hills, Julian V. "The *Acts of Paul* and the Legacy of the Lukan Acts." 145-58 in *The Apocryphal Acts of the Apostles in Intertextual Perspectives*. Semeia 80. Ed. Robert F. Stoops. Atlanta: Scholars Press, 1997.

Hilton and Marshall, *Gospels*. • Hilton, Michael, with Gordian Marshall. *The Gospels and Rabbinic Judaism: A Study Guide*. Hoboken, NJ: Ktav, 1988.

Himmelfarb, "Impurity and Sin." • Himmelfarb, Martha. "Impurity and Sin in 4QD, 1QS, and 4Q512." *DSD* 8 (1, 2001): 9-37.

Hindley, "Date." • Hindley, J. C. "Towards a Date for the Similitudes of Enoch. An Historical Approach." *NTS* 14 (4, July 1968): 551-565.

Hirsch, *Interpretation*. • Hirsch, E. D., Jr. *Validity in Interpretation*. New Haven: Yale University Press, 1967.

Hirschfeld and Solar, "Baths." • Hirschfeld, Yizhar, and Giora Solar. "Sumptuous Roman Baths Uncovered near Sea of Galilee: Hot Springs Drew the Afflicted from Around the World." *BAR* 10 (1984): 22-40.

Hirschfeld and Solar, "Hmrhs'wt." • Hirschfeld, Yizhar, and Giora Solar. "Hmrhs'wt hrwmyym sl hmt-gdr — slws 'wnwt-hpyrh (The Roman Thermae at Hammath-Gader — Three Seasons of Excavations)." *Qad* 13 (1980): 66-70.

Hock, "Education." • Hock, Ronald F. "Paul and Greco-Roman Education." 198-227 in *Paul in the Greco-Roman World: A Handbook*. Ed. J. Paul Sampley. Harrisburg, PA: Trinity Press International, 2003.

Hodges, "Tomb." • Hodges, Zane C. "The Women and the Empty Tomb." *BSac* 123 (1966): 301-9.

Hodgson, "Valerius Maximus." • Hodgson, Robert. "Valerius Maximus and Gospel Criticism." *CBQ* 51 (3, 1989): 502-10.

Hoehner, *Antipas*. • Hoehner, Harold W. *Herod Antipas*. SNTSMS 17. Cambridge: Cambridge University, 1972.

Hoehner, "Significance." • Hoehner, Harold W. "The Significance of the Year of Our Lord's Crucifixion for New Testament Interpretation." 115-26 in *New Dimensions in New Testament Study*. Ed. Richard N. Longenecker and Merrill C. Tenney. Grand Rapids: Zondervan, 1974.

Hoenig, "Kinds of Labor." • Hoenig, Sidney B. "The Designated Number of Kinds of Labor Prohibited on the Sabbath." *JQR* 68 (4, April 1978): 193-208.

Hoeree and Hoogbergen, "History." • Hoeree, Joris, and Wim Hoogbergen. "Oral History and Archival Data Combined: The Removal of the Saramakan Granman Kofi Bosuman as an Epistemological Problem." *CommCog* 17 (2-3, 1984): 245-289.

Höffken, "Elischa." • Höffken, Peter. "Elischa in seinem Verhältnis zu Elija bei Josephus." *ETL* 81 (4, 2005): 477-86.

Höffken, "Hiskija." • Höffken, Peter. "Hiskija und Jesaja bei Josephus," *JSJ* 29 (1, 1998): 37-48.

Höffken, "Reichsteilung." • Höffken, Peter. "Eine Reichsteilung bei Josephus Flavius. Beobachtungen zu seiner Auffassung von Daniel 5." *JSJ* 36 (2, 2005): 197-205.

Hoffmann, "Faccidents." • Hoffmann, R. Joseph. "'Faccidents.' Bad Assumptions and the Jesus Tomb Debacle." *CSER Review* 1 (2, 2006-7): 32-35.

Hofius, "Sayings." • Hofius, Otfried. "Unknown Sayings of Jesus." 336-60 in *The Gospel and the Gospels.* Ed. Peter Stuhlmacher. Grand Rapids: Eerdmans, 1991.

Hofius, "Supper." • Hofius, Otfried. "The Lord's Supper and the Lord's Supper Tradition: Reflections on 1 Corinthians 11:23b-25." 75-115 in *One Loaf, One Cup: Ecumenical Studies of 1 Cor 11 and Other Eucharistic Texts.* The Cambridge Conference on the Eucharist, August 1988. New Gospel Studies 6. Ed. Ben F. Meyer. Macon, GA: Mercer University Press, 1993.

Hofmann, "Novels: Christian." • Hofmann, Heinz. "Novels: Christian." 9:846-49 in *Brill's New Pauly.*

Hogeterp, "Resurrection." • Hogeterp, Albert L. A. "Resurrection and Biblical Tradition: Pseudo-Ezekiel Reconsidered." *Bib* 89 (1, 2008): 59-69.

Holladay, "Acts and Fragments." • Holladay, Carl R. "Acts and the Fragments of Hellenistic Jewish Historians." 171-98 in *Jesus and the Heritage of Israel: Luke's Narrative Claim upon Israel's Legacy.* Ed. David P. Moessner. Vol. 1 in Luke the Interpreter of Israel. Harrisburg, PA: Trinity Press International, 1999.

Holladay, "Background." • Holladay, William L. "The Background of Jeremiah's Self-Understanding." *JBL* 83 (1964): 153-64.

Holladay, "Jeremiah." • Holladay, William L. "Jeremiah and Moses: Further Observations." *JBL* 85 (1, March 1966): 17-27.

Holladay, *Theios Aner.* • Holladay, Carl R. *Theios Aner in Hellenistic Judaism: A Critique of the Use of This Category in New Testament Christology.* SBLDS 40. Missoula, MT: Scholars Press, 1977.

Holmén, "Covenant." • Holmén, Tom. "Jesus, Judaism and the Covenant." *JSHJ* 2 (1, 2004): 3-27.

Holmén, *Covenant Thinking.* • Holmén, Tom. *Jesus & Jewish Covenant Thinking.* Biblical Interpretation Series 55. Leiden: Brill, 2001.

Holmén, "Doubts about Dissimilarity." • Holmén, Tom. "Doubts about Double Dissimilarity: Restructuring the Main Criterion of Jesus-of-History Research." 47-80 in *Authenticating the Words of Jesus.* Ed. Bruce Chilton and Craig A. Evans. NTTS 28.1. Leiden: Brill, 1999.

Holmén, "Introduction." • Holmén, Tom. "An Introduction to the Continuum Approach." 1-16 in *Jesus from Judaism to Christianity: Continuum Approaches to the Historical Jesus.* Ed. Tom Holmén. European Studies on Christian Origins. Library of New Testament Studies 352. London, New York: T&T Clark, 2007.

Hooker, *Message.* • Hooker, Morna D. *The Message of Mark.* London: Epworth, 1983.

Hooker, *Preface.* • Hooker, Morna D. *A Preface to Paul.* New York: Oxford University Press, 1980.

Hooker, *Servant.* • Hooker, Morna D. *Jesus and the Servant.* London: S.P.C.K., 1959.

Hoppe, "Baptized." • Hoppe, Leslie J. "Where Was Jesus Baptized? Three Alternatives." *BibT* 45 (5, 2007): 315-20.

Hoppe, "Tomb." • Hoppe, Leslie J. "Jesus Family Tomb? Bad Television and Worse Archaeology." *BibT* 45 (3, 2007): 179-83.

Horbury, "Brigand." • Horbury, William. "Christ as brigand in ancient anti-Christian polemic." 183-95 in *Jesus and the Politics of His Day.* Ed. Ernst Bammel and C. F. D. Moule. Cambridge: Cambridge University, 1984.

Horbury, "Ossuaries." • Horbury, William. "The 'Caiaphas' Ossuaries and Joseph Caiaphas." *PEQ* 126 (1, 1994): 32-48.

Horsley, "Abandoning." • Horsley, Richard A. "Abandoning the Unhistorical Quest for an Apolitical Jesus." 288-301 in *The Historical Jesus in Recent Research.* Ed. James D. G. Dunn and Scot McKnight. Winona Lake, IN: Eisenbrauns, 2005.

Horsley, *Corinthians.* • Horsley, Richard A. *1 Corinthians.* ANTC. Nashville: Abingdon, 1998.

Horsley, "Death." • Richard A. Horsley, "The Death of Jesus." 395-422 in *Studying the Historical Jesus: Evaluations of the State of Current Research*. NTTS 19. Ed. Bruce Chilton and Craig A. Evans. Leiden, New York, Cologne: E. J. Brill, 1994.

Horsley, *Documents 1*. • Horsley, G. H. R., editor. *New Documents Illustrating Early Christianity: A Review of the Greek Inscriptions and Papyri Published in 1976*. Vol. 1. North Ryde, N.S.W.: The Ancient History Documentary Research Centre, Macquarie University, 1981.

Horsley, *Documents 2*. • Horsley, G. H. R., editor. *New Documents Illustrating Early Christianity: A Review of the Greek Inscriptions and Papyri Published in 1977*. Vol. 2. North Ryde, N.S.W.: The Ancient History Documentary Research Centre, Macquarie University, 1982.

Horsley, *Documents 5*. • Horsley, G. H. R., editor. *New Documents Illustrating Early Christianity*. Vol. 5: *Linguistic Essays*. North Ryde, N.S.W.: The Ancient History Documentary Research Centre, Macquarie University, 1989.

Horsley, "Formula." • Horsley, Richard A. "The Background of the Confessional Formula in I Cor 8:6." *ZNW* 69 (1-2, 1978): 130-35.

Horsley, *Galilee*. • Horsley, Richard A. *Galilee: History, Politics, People*. Valley Forge, PA: Trinity Press International, 1995.

Horsley, "High Priests." • Horsley, Richard A. "High Priests and the Politics of Roman Palestine. Contextual Analysis of the Evidence in Josephus." *JSJ* 17 (1, 1986): 23-55.

Horsley, *Liberation*. • Horsley, Richard A. *The Liberation of Christmas: The Infancy Narratives in Social Context*. New York: Continuum, 1993.

Horsley, "Love." • Horsley, Richard A. "Ethics and Exegesis: 'Love Your Enemies' and the Doctrine of Non-Violence." *JAAR* 54 (1986): 3-31.

Horsley, "Movements." • Horsley, Richard A. "Early Christian Movements: Jesus Movements and the Renewal of Israel." *HTS/TS* 62 (4, 2006): 1201-25.

Horsley, "Priests." • Horsley, Richard A. "High Priests and the Politics of Roman Palestine. A Contextual Analysis of the Evidence in Josephus." *JSJ* 17 (1986): 23-55.

Horsley, "Prophets." • Horsley, Richard A. "'Like One of the Prophets of Old': Two Types of Popular Prophets at the Time of Jesus." *CBQ* 47 (1985): 435-63.

Horsley, "Resurrection." • Horsley, Richard A. "'How can some of you say that there is no resurrection of the dead?' Spiritual Elitism in Corinth." *NovT* 20 (3, 1978): 203-31.

Horsley, "Speeches." • Horsley, G. H. R. "Speeches and Dialogue in Acts." *NTS* 32 (4, Oct. 1986): 609-14.

Horsley, *Spiral*. • Horsley, Richard A. *Jesus and the Spiral of Violence: Popular Jewish Resistance in Roman Palestine*. Minneapolis: Fortress, 1993.

Horsley and Hanson, *Bandits*. • Horsley, Richard A., and John S. Hanson. *Bandits, Prophets, and Messiahs: Popular Movements in the Time of Jesus*. Minneapolis: A Seabury Book, Winston Press, 1985.

Hort, *Judaistic Christianity*. • Hort, Fenton John Anthony. *Judaistic Christianity*. Ed. J. O. F. Murray. Grand Rapids: Baker, 1980. (Reprint from 1894 ed.)

Horton, "Possession." • Horton, Robin. "Types of Spirit Possession in Kalabari Religion." 14-49 in *Spirit Mediumship and Society in Africa*. Ed. John Beattie and John Middleton. Foreword by Raymond Firth. New York: Africana Publishing Corporation, 1969.

Hose, "Historiography: Rome." • Hose, Martin. "Historiography: Rome." 6:422-426 in *Brill's New Pauly*.

Hotze, "Zeugen." • Hotze, G. "Christi Zeugen bis an die Grenzen der Erde — Die Apostelsgeschichte (Teil 1)." *BL* 72 (1, 1999): 29-35.

Houston, *Miracles*. • Houston, J. *Reported Miracles: A critique of Hume*. Cambridge: Cambridge University Press, 1994.

Hubbard, *Redaction*. • Hubbard, Benjamin Jerome. *The Matthean Redaction of a Primitive Apos-*

tolic Commissioning: An Exegesis of Matthew 28:16-20. SBLDS 19. Missoula, MT: Society of Biblical Literature, 1974.

Hunter, "Genre." • Hunter, Richard. "Literary genre." 7:652-55 in *Brill's New Pauly.*

Hunter, *Gospel According to Paul.* • Hunter, A. M. *The Gospel According to St. Paul.* Philadelphia: Westminster, 1966.

Hunter, *John.* • Hunter, Archibald M. *The Gospel According to John.* The Cambridge Bible Commentary. Cambridge: Cambridge University Press, 1965.

Hunter, *Message.* • Hunter, Archibald M. *The Message of the New Testament.* Philadelphia: Westminster Press, 1944.

Hunter, *Predecessors.* • Hunter, Archibald M. *Paul and His Predecessors.* Rev. ed. Philadelphia: Westminster; London: SCM, 1961.

Hunter, "Trends." • Hunter, Archibald M. "Recent Trends in Johannine Studies." *Expository Times* 71 (6, March 1960): 164-67.

Hurd, "I Thess. 2:13-16." • Hurd, John. "Paul Ahead of His Time: I Thess. 2:13-16." 1:21-36 in *Anti-Judaism in Early Christianity.* Ed. Peter Richardson. Waterloo, Ontario: Wilfrid Laurier University Press, 1986.

Hurschmann, "Filter." • Hurschmann, Rolf. "Filter." 5:426 in *Brill's New Pauly.*

Hurtado, "Homage." • Hurtado, Larry W. "Homage to the Historical Jesus and Early Christian Devotion." *JSHJ* 1 (2, 2003): 131-46.

Hurtado, *Lord Jesus Christ.* • Hurtado, Larry W. *Lord Jesus Christ: Devotion to Jesus in Earliest Christianity.* Grand Rapids: Eerdmans, 2003.

Hurtado, *Mark.* • Hurtado, Larry W. *Mark.* Good News Commentary. San Francisco: Harper & Row, 1983.

Hurtado, *One God.* • Hurtado, Larry. *One God, One Lord: Early Christian Devotion and Ancient Jewish Monotheism.* Philadelphia: Fortress, 1988.

Iglesias, "Reflexoes." • Iglesias, Esther. "Reflexoes sobre o quefazer da historia oral no mundo rural." *Dados* 27 (1, 1984): 59-70.

Ilan, "Attraction." • Ilan, Tal. "The Attraction of Aristocratic Women to Pharisaism During the Second Temple Period." *HTR* 88 (1995): 1-33.

Ilan, "Distribution." • Ilan, Tal. "Notes on the Distribution of Jewish Women's Names in Palestine in the Second Temple and Mishnaic Periods." *JJS* 40 (2, 1989): 186-200.

Ilan, "Studies." • Ilan, Tal. "Women's Studies and Jewish Studies — When and Where Do They Meet?" *JSQ* 3 (2, 1996): 162-73.

Ilan, *Women.* • Ilan, Tal. *Jewish Women in Greco-Roman Palestine.* Tübingen: J. C. B. Mohr; Peabody: Hendrickson, 1996.

Instone-Brewer, *Traditions.* • Instone-Brewer, David. *Traditions of the Rabbis from the Era of the New Testament.* Grand Rapids: Eerdmans, 2004.

Isaacs, *Spirit.* • Isaacs, Marie E. *The Concept of Spirit: A Study of Pneuma in Hellenistic Judaism and Its Bearing on the New Testament.* Heythrop Monographs 1. London: Heythrop College, 1976.

Jas, "Hénoch." • Jas, Michel. "Hénoch et le Fils de l'Homme. Datation du livre des parabies pour une situation de l'origine du Gnosticisme." *RRéf* 30 (3, 1979): 105-119.

Jaubert, "Calendar." • Jaubert, A. "The Calendar of Qumran and the Passion Narrative in John." 62-75 in *John and Qumran.* Ed. James H. Charlesworth. London: Geoffrey Chapman Publishers, 1972.

Jaubert, *Date.* • Jaubert, Annie. *The Date of the Last Supper.* Staten Island: Alba House, 1965.

Jeffers, *World.* • Jeffers, James S. *The Greco-Roman World of the New Testament Era: Exploring the Background of Early Christianity.* Downers Grove, IL: InterVarsity, 1999.

Jeffery, *Secret Gospel.* • Jeffery, Peter. *The Secret Gospel of Mark Unveiled: Imagined Rituals of Sex, Death, and Madness in a Biblical Forgery.* New Haven: Yale University Press, 2007.

Jenkins, *New Faces*. • Jenkins, Philip. *The New Faces of Christianity: Believing the Bible in the Global South*. New York, Oxford: Oxford University Press, 2006.

Jensen, "Antipas." • Jensen, Morten Hørning. "Herod Antipas in Galilee: Friend or Foe of the Historical Jesus?" *JSHJ* 5 (1, 2007): 7-32.

Jeremias, "Abba." • Jeremias, Joachim. "*'Abba* as an Address to God." 201-6 in *The Historical Jesus in Recent Research*. Ed. James D. G. Dunn and Scot McKnight. Winona Lake, IN: Eisenbrauns, 2005.

Jeremias, *Eucharistic Words*. • Jeremias, Joachim. *The Eucharistic Words of Jesus*. Trans. Norman Perrin. Philadelphia: Fortress, 1966.

Jeremias, "Γωνία." • Jeremias, Joachim. "Γωνία, ἀκρογωνιαῖος, κεφαλὴ γωνίας." 1:791-93 in *TDNT*. 10 vols. Ed. Gerhard Kittel and Gerhard Friedrich. Grand Rapids: Eerdmans, 1964-1976.

Jeremias, *Jerusalem*. • Jeremias, Joachim. *Jerusalem in the Time of Jesus*. Philadelphia: Fortress, 1975; London: SCM, 1969.

Jeremias, *Message*. • Jeremias, Joachim. *The Central Message of the New Testament*. New York: Charles Scribner's Sons, 1965.

Jeremias, "Μωυσῆς." • Jeremias, Joachim. "Μωυσῆς." 4:848-73 in *TDNT*.

Jeremias, *Parables*. • Jeremias, Joachim. *The Parables of Jesus*. 2d rev. ed. New York: Charles Scribner's Sons, 1972.

Jeremias, *Prayers*. • Jeremias, Joachim. *The Prayers of Jesus*. Philadelphia: Fortress, 1964.

Jeremias, *Promise*. • Jeremias, Joachim. *Jesus' Promise to the Nations*. Tr. S. H. Hooke. The Franz Delitzsch Lectures for 1953. SBT 24. London: SCM, 1958.

Jeremias, *Sermon*. • Jeremias, Joachim. *The Sermon on the Mount*. Trans. Norman Perrin. Philadelphia: Fortress, 1963.

Jeremias, *Theology*. • Jeremias, Joachim. *New Testament Theology*. New York: Charles Scribner's Sons, 1971.

Jeremias, *Unknown Sayings*. • Jeremias, Joachim. *Unknown Sayings of Jesus*. 2d English ed. Trans. Reginald H. Fuller. London: S.P.C.K., 1964.

Jervell, *Apostelgeschichte*. • Jervell, Jacob. *Die Apostelgeschichte*. KEKNT 17. Göttingen: Vandenhoeck & Ruprecht, 1998.

Jervell, "Future." • Jervell, Jacob. "The future of the past: Luke's vision of salvation history and its bearing on his writing of its writing of history." 104-26 in *History, Literature, and Society in the Book of Acts*. Ed. Ben Witherington, III. Cambridge: Cambridge University Press, 1996.

Jervell, *Luke and People of God*. • Jervell, Jacob. *Luke and the People of God: A New Look at Luke-Acts*. Minneapolis: Augsburg, 1972.

Jewett, *Chronology*. • Jewett, Robert. *A Chronology of Paul's Life*. Philadelphia: Fortress, 1979.

Jewett, *Romans*. • Jewett, Robert. *Romans: A Commentary*. Assisted by Roy D. Kotansky. Ed. Eldon Jay Epp. Hermeneia. Minneapolis: Fortress, 2007.

Jochim, *Religions*. • Jochim, Christian. *Chinese Religions: A Cultural Perspective*. Prentice-Hall Series in World Religions. Englewood Cliffs, NJ: Prentice-Hall, 1986.

Jóczwiak, "Mesjanizm." • Jóczwiak, F. "Mesjanizm w literaturze z Qumran (Le messianisme dans les textes de Qumran)." *RocTK* 10 (1, 1963): 35-42.

Johnson, *Acts*. • Johnson, Luke Timothy. *The Acts of the Apostles*. SP 5. Collegeville, MN: Liturgical Press, 1992.

Johnson, "Adam." • Johnson, M. D. "Introduction to the Life of Adam and Eve." 2:249-257 in *OTP*.

Johnson, *Function*. • Johnson, Luke Timothy. *The Literary Function of Possessions in Luke-Acts*. SBLDS 39. Missoula, MT: Society of Biblical Literature, 1977.

Johnson, "Luke-Acts." • Johnson, Luke Timothy. "Luke-Acts, Book of." 4:403-420 in *ABD*.

Johnson, *Possessions*. • Johnson, Luke Timothy. *Sharing Possessions: Mandate and Symbol of Faith*. Philadelphia: Fortress, 1981.

Johnson, "Quest." • Johnson, Luke Timothy. "The Jesus Seminar's misguided quest for the historical Jesus." *ChrCent* 113 (1, 1996): 16-22.

Johnson, *Real Jesus*. • Johnson, Luke Timothy. *The Real Jesus: The Misguided Quest for the Historical Jesus and the Truth of the Traditional Gospels.* San Francisco: Harper San Francisco, 1996.

Johnson, "Slander." • Johnson, Luke Timothy. "The New Testament's Anti-Jewish Slander and Conventions of Ancient Rhetoric." *JBL* 108 (1989): 419-41.

Johnston, *Ephesians*. • Johnston, George. *Ephesians, Philippians, Colossians and Philemon.* The Century Bible. Greenwood, SC: Attic Press, 1967.

Johnston, "Evangelists." • Johnston, George. "Should the synoptic evangelists be considered as theologians?" *SR/SR* 21 (1992): 181-90.

Johnston, "Least of Commandments." • Johnston, Robert Morris. "'The Least of the Commandments': Deuteronomy 22:6-7 in Rabbinic Judaism and Early Christianity." *AUSS* 20 (1982): 205-15.

Johnston, "Observations." • Johnston, Robert Morris. "The Study of Rabbinic Parables: Some Preliminary Observations." 337-57 in *SBLSP, 1976*. Ed. George MacRae. 1976.

Johnston, "Parabolic Interpretations." • Johnston, Robert Morris. "Parabolic Interpretations Attributed to Tannaim." Ph.D. dissertation, Hartford Seminary Foundation, 1977. Ann Arbor, MI: University Microfilms International, 1978.

Johnston, "Patristic Parables." • Johnston, Robert Morris. "Greek Patristic Parables." 215-29 in *SBLSP, 1977*. Ed. Paul Achtemeier, 1977.

Jonas, *Religion*. • Jonas, Hans. *The Gnostic Religion: The Message of the Alien God and the Beginnings of Christianity.* 2d rev. ed. Boston: Beacon Press, 1963.

Jones, "Apollonius' Passage." • Jones, C. P. "Apollonius of Tyana's Passage to India." *GRBS* 42 (2, 2001): 185-99.

Jones, *History*. • Jones, A. M. H. *A History of Rome Through the Fifth Century.* Vol. 2: *The Empire.* New York: Walker and Company, 1970.

Jones, *Parables*. • Jones, Ivor H. *The Matthean Parables: A Literary and Historical Commentary.* NovTSup 80. Leiden: E. J. Brill, 1995.

Jonge, "'Anointed.'" • Jonge, Marinus de. "The Use of the Word 'Anointed' in the Time of Jesus." *NovT* 8 (2-4, April 1966): 132-48.

Joubert, "Exchange." • Joubert, Stephan J. "One Form of Social Exchange or Two? 'Euergetism,' Patronage, and New Testament Studies." *BTB* 31 (1, 2001): 17-25.

Judge, *Pattern*. • Judge, Edwin A. *The Social Pattern of the Christian Groups in the First Century: Some Prolegomena to the Study of New Testament Ideas of Social Obligation.* London: Tyndale Press, 1960.

Juel, *Messiah*. • Juel, Donald. *Messiah and Temple.* Missoula: Scholars Press, 1977.

Kaesser, "Tweaking the Real." • Kaesser, Christian. "Tweaking the Real: Art Theory and the Borderline between History and Morality in Plutarch's *Lives*." *GRBS* 44 (4, 2004): 361-74.

Kähler, "Movement." • Kähler, Martin. "Against the Life-of-Jesus Movement." 67-84 in *The Historical Jesus in Recent Research.* Ed. James D. G. Dunn and Scot McKnight. Winona Lake, IN: Eisenbrauns, 2005.

Kalimi and Purvis, "Hiding." • Kalimi, Isaac, and James D. Purvis. "The Hiding of the Temple Vessels in Jewish and Samaritan Literature." *CBQ* 56 (4, 1994): 679-85.

Kalu, *African Pentecostalism*. • Kalu, Ogbu. *African Pentecostalism: An Introduction.* Oxford: Oxford University Press, 2008.

Kane, "Cult Meal." • Kane, J. P. "The Mithraic Cult Meal in Its Greek and Roman Environment." 2:313-51 in *Mithraic Studies: Proceedings of the First International Congress of Mithraic Studies.* 2 vols. Ed. John R. Hinnells. Manchester: Manchester University Press, 1975.

Kany, "Bericht." • Kany, R. "Der lukanische Bericht von Tod und Auferstehung Jesu aus der Sicht eines hellenistichen Romanlesers." *NovT* 28 (1, 1986): 75-90.

Käsemann, Testament. • Käsemann, Ernst. *The Testament of Jesus.* Trans. Gerhard Krodel. Philadelphia: Fortress, 1978.

Kaufman, "Anti-Semitism." • Kaufman, Philip S. "Anti-Semitism in the New Testament: The Witness of the Beloved Disciple." *Worship* 63 (5, 1989): 386-401.

Kaufman, "Eastern Wall." • Kaufman, Asher S. "The Eastern Wall of the Second Temple at Jerusalem Revealed." *BA* 44 (1981): 108-15.

Kaufmann, "Idea." • Kaufmann, Yehezkel. "The Messianic Idea. The Real and the Hidden Son-of-David." *JBQ* 22 (3, 1994): 141-50.

Kaunfer and Kaunfer, "Time and Torah." • Kaunfer, Alvan and Elie. "Time and Torah: A Curious Concept Revisited." *ConsJud* 54 (4, 2002): 15-32.

Kazen, "Imagery." • Kazen, Thomas. "Son of Man as Kingdom Imagery: Jesus Between Corporate Symbol and Individual Redeemer Figure." 87-108 in *Jesus from Judaism to Christianity: Continuum Approaches to the Historical Jesus.* Ed. Tom Holmén. European Studies on Christian Origins. Library of New Testament Studies 352. London, New York: T&T Clark, 2007.

Kealy, "Quest." • Kealy, Séan P. "The Third Quest for the Historical Jesus." *PIBA* 19 (1996): 84-98.

Keating, "Epistemology." • Keating, James F. "Contemporary Epistemology and Theological Application of the Historical Jesus Quest." *JJT* 10 (2, 2003): 343-56.

Keck, "Ethos." • Keck, Leander E. "On the Ethos of Early Christians." *JAAR* 42 (1974): 435-452.

Keck, Future. • Keck, Leander E. *A Future for the Historical Jesus.* Nashville: Abingdon, 1971.

Keck, History. • Keck, Leander E. *Who Is Jesus? History in the Perfect Tense.* Minneapolis: Fortress, 2001.

Kee, "Century of Quests." • Kee, Howard Clark. "A Century of Quests for the Culturally Compatible Jesus." *ThTo* 52 (1, 1995): 17-28.

Kee, Community. • Kee, Howard Clark. *Community of the New Age: Studies in Mark's Gospel.* Philadelphia: Westminster, 1977.

Kee, Every Nation. • Kee, Howard Clark. *To Every Nation under Heaven: The Acts of the Apostles.* Harrisburg, PA: Trinity Press International, 1997.

Kee, Miracle. • Kee, Howard Clark. *Miracle in the Early Christian World: A Study in Sociohistorical Method.* New Haven: Yale University Press, 1983.

Kee, Origins. • Kee, Howard Clark. *Christian Origins in Sociological Perspective: Methods and Resources.* Philadelphia: Westminster, 1980.

Keener, "Brood of Vipers." • Keener, Craig S. "'Brood of Vipers' (Mt. 3.7; 12.34; 23.33)." *JSNT* 28 (1, Sept. 2005): 3-11.

Keener, Corinthians. • Keener, Craig S. *1 & 2 Corinthians.* NCamBC. Cambridge: Cambridge University Press, 2006.

Keener, "Decoding." • Keener, Craig S. "Decoding Da Vinci." *MT* (May 2006): 60-64.

Keener, "Genre." • Keener, Craig S. "Response: Genre, Sources, and History." 321-23 in *What We Have Heard from the Beginning: The Past, Present, and Future of Johannine Studies.* Ed. Tom Thatcher. Waco, TX: Baylor University Press, 2007.

Keener, "Heavenly Court." • Keener, Craig S. "Matthew 5:22 and the Heavenly Court." *ExpT* 99 (2, 1987): 46.

Keener, "Human Stones." • Keener, Craig S. "Human Stones in a Greek Setting — Luke 3.8; Matthew 3.9; Luke 19.40." *JGRCJ* 6 (2009): 28-36.

Keener, John. • Keener, Craig S. *The Gospel of John: A Commentary.* 2 vols. Peabody: Hendrickson, 2003.

Keener, "Kiss." • Keener, Craig S. "Kiss, Kissing." 628-29 in *DNTB.*

Keener, "Lost Gospels." • Keener, Craig S. "Why the 'lost gospels' were lost." *CHB* 82 (Spring 2004): 15.

Keener, "Luke-Acts and Historical Jesus." • Keener, Craig S. "Luke-Acts and Historical Jesus." The Second Princeton-Prague Symposium on Jesus: Methodological Approaches to the Historical

Jesus, April 18-21, 2007, Princeton, NJ. To be published in a collection of essays edited by James H. Charlesworth, forthcoming from Eerdmans.

Keener, "Marriage." • Keener, Craig S. "Marriage." 680-93 in *DNTB*.

Keener, *Marries Another.* • Keener, Craig S. *. . . And Marries Another: Divorce and Remarriage in the Teaching of the New Testament.* Peabody, MA: Hendrickson, 1991.

Keener, *Matthew.* • Keener, Craig S. *A Commentary on the Gospel of Matthew.* Grand Rapids: Eerdmans, 1999. Reprinted with new material as *The Gospel of Matthew: A Socio-Rhetorical Commentary.* Grand Rapids: Eerdmans, 2009.

Keener, "Mistrial." • Keener, Craig S. "Mistrial of the Millennium." *CHB* 17 (3, 1998): 38-40.

Keener, "Official." • Keener, Craig S. "Novels' 'Exotic' Places and Luke's African Official (Acts 8:27)." *AUSS* 46 (1, 2008): 5-20.

Keener, *Paul.* • Keener, Craig S. *Paul, Women & Wives: Marriage and Women's Ministry in the Letters of Paul.* Peabody, MA: Hendrickson, 1992.

Keener, "Pneumatology." • Keener, Craig S. "The Function of Johannine Pneumatology in the Context of Late First-Century Judaism." Ph.D. dissertation, New Testament and Christian Origins, Duke University, 1991.

Keener, "Review of Bauckham." • Keener, Craig S. "Review of Richard Bauckham, *Jesus and the Eyewitnesses.*" *BBR* 19 (1, 2009): 130-32.

Keener, "Review of Collins." • Keener, Craig S. "Review of *Divorce in the New Testament.* By Raymond F. Collins." *CRBR 1993.* Vol. 6. Atlanta: Scholars Press, 1994.

Keener, "Review of Lincoln." • Keener, Craig S. Online review of Andrew T. Lincoln, *The Gospel According to Saint John. RBL.* May 2006.

Keener, "Rhetorical Techniques." • Keener, Craig S. "Some Rhetorical Techniques in Acts 24:2-21." 221-51 in *Paul's World.* Ed. Stanley E. Porter. PAST 4. Leiden: E. J. Brill, 2008.

Keener, *Spirit.* • Keener, Craig S. *The Spirit in the Gospels and Acts: Divine Purity and Power.* Peabody: Hendrickson, 1997.

Keener, "Spirit." • Keener, Craig S. "Spirit, Holy Spirit, Advocate, Breath, Wind." 484-96 in *The Westminster Theological Wordbook of the Bible.* Ed. Donald E. Gowan. Louisville, KY: Westminster John Knox, 2003.

Keener, "Truth." • Keener, Craig S. "'What Is Truth?' Pilate's Perspective on Jesus in John 18:33-38." Paper presented at the Society of Biblical Literature, Boston, 2008.

Kelber, "Conclusion." • Kelber, Werner H. "Conclusion: From Passion Narrative to Gospel." 153-80 in *The Passion in Mark: Studies in Mark 14-16.* Ed. Werner H. Kelber. Philadelphia: Fortress, 1976.

Kelber, *Gospel.* • Kelber, Werner H. *The Oral and the Written Gospel.* Philadelphia: Fortress, 1983.

Kelber, *Story.* • Kelber, Werner H. *Mark's Story of Jesus.* Philadelphia: Fortress, 1979.

Kelhoffer, *Miracle.* • Kelhoffer, James A. *Miracle and Mission: The Authentication of Missionaries and Their Message in the Longer Ending of Mark.* Tübingen: Mohr Siebeck, 2000.

Kelly, *Peter.* • Kelly, J. N. D. *A Commentary on the Epistles of Peter and Jude.* Thornapple Commentaries. Grand Rapids: Baker, 1981.

Kennard, "Assembly." • Kennard, J. Spencer, Jr. "The Jewish Provincial Assembly." *ZNW* 53 (1962): 25-51.

Kennedy, *Classical Rhetoric.* • Kennedy, George A. *Classical Rhetoric and Its Christian and Secular Tradition from Ancient to Modern Times.* Chapel Hill: University of North Carolina Press, 1980.

Kennedy, *Epistles.* • Kennedy, H. A. A. *The Theology of the Epistles.* New York: Charles Scribner's Sons, 1920.

Kennedy, *NT Interpretation.* • Kennedy, George A. *New Testament Interpretation through Rhetorical Criticism.* Chapel Hill, NC: University of North Carolina Press, 1984.

Kennedy, "Resurrection." • Kennedy, K. A. "The Resurrection of Jesus." *Studies* 74 (1985): 440-54.

Kennedy, "Source Criticism." • Kennedy, George A. "Classical and Christian Source Criticism."

125-55 in *The Relationships Among the Gospels: An Interdisciplinary Dialogue*. Ed. William O. Walker, Jr. San Antonio: Trinity University Press, 1978.

Kennedy, "Survey of Rhetoric." • Kennedy, George A. "Historical Survey of Rhetoric." 3-41 in *Handbook of Classical Rhetoric in the Hellenistic Period 330 B.C.-A.D. 400*. Ed. Stanley E. Porter. Leiden: Brill, 1997.

Ker, "Missionary Activity." • Ker, Donald P. "Jewish Missionary Activity Under Review." *IBS* 18 (4, 1996): 205-16.

Keylock, "Distinctness." • Keylock, Leslie R. "Bultmann's Law of Increasing Distinctness." 193-210 in *Current Issues in Biblical and Patristic Interpretation: Studies in Honor of Merrill C. Tenney Presented by His Former Students*. Ed. Gerald F. Hawthorne. Grand Rapids: Eerdmans, 1975.

Khai, "Pentecostalism." • Khai, Chin Khua. "The Assemblies of God and Pentecostalism in Myanmar." 261-80 in *Asian and Pentecostal: The Charismatic Face of Christianity in Asia*. Ed. Allan Anderson and Edmond Tang. Foreword by Cecil M. Robeck. Regnum Studies in Mission, Asian Journal of Pentecostal Studies 3. Oxford: Regnum; Baguio City, Philippines: APTS Press, 2005.

Kilpatrick, "Background." • Kilpatrick, G. D. "The Religious Background of the Fourth Gospel." 36-44 in *Studies in the Fourth Gospel*. Ed. F. L. Cross. London: A. R. Mowbray & Company, 1957.

Kim, "Atonement." • Kim, Jintae. "The Concept of Atonement in Early Rabbinic Thought and the New Testament Writings." *JGRCJ* 2 (2001-2005): 117-45.

Kim, *Origin*. • Kim, Seyoon. *The Origin of Paul's Gospel*. Tübingen: J. C. B. Mohr, 1981.

Kimbrough, "Sabbath." • Kimbrough, S. T. "The Concept of Sabbath at Qumran." *RevQ* 5 (4, 1966): 483-502.

Kingdon, "Zealots." • Kingdon, H. Paul. "The Origin of the Zealots." *NTS* 19 (1972): 74-81.

Kingsbury, *Christology*. • Kingsbury, Jack Dean. *The Christology of Mark's Gospel*. Philadelphia: Fortress, 1983.

Kingsbury, *Matthew*. • Kingsbury, Jack Dean. *Matthew: Structure, Christology, Kingdom*. Philadelphia: Fortress, 1975.

Kingsbury, *Story*. • Kingsbury, Jack Dean. *Matthew as Story*. Philadelphia: Fortress, 1986.

Kinsella, "Transformation." • Kinsella, Sean E. "The transformation of the Jewish Passover in an early Christian liturgy. The influence of the Passover *Haggadah* in the *Apostolic Tradition*." *ScEs* 52 (2, 2000): 215-228.

Kirschner, "Imitatio." • Kirschner, Robert. "Imitatio Rabbini." *JSJ* 17 (1986): 70-79.

Kisau, "Acts." • Kisau, Paul Mumo. "Acts of the Apostles." 1297-1348 in *Africa Bible Commentary*. Ed. Tokunboh Adeyemo. Grand Rapids: Zondervan; Nairobi: WordAlive, 2006.

Kitchen, *Orient*. • Kitchen, Kenneth A. *Ancient Orient and the Old Testament*. Chicago: InterVarsity Press, 1968.

Kitchen, *World*. • Kitchen, Kenneth A. *The Bible in Its World*. Downers Grove, IL: InterVarsity, 1978.

Klaasen, *Anabaptism*. • Klaasen, Walter, ed. *Anabaptism in Outline: Selected Primary Sources*. Scottdale, PA: Herald Press, 1981.

Klassen, "Law." • Klassen, William. "The king as 'living law' with particular reference to Musonius Rufus." *SR/SR* 14 (1, 1985): 63-71.

Klauck, "Presence." • Klauck, Hans-Josef. "Presence in the Lord's Supper: 1 Corinthians 11:23-26 in the Context of Hellenistic Religious History." 57-74 in *One Loaf, One Cup: Ecumenical Studies of 1 Cor 11 and Other Eucharistic Texts*. The Cambridge Conference on the Eucharist, August 1988. New Gospel Studies 6. Ed. Ben F. Meyer. Macon, GA: Mercer University Press, 1993.

Klauck, *Religious Context*. • Klauck, Hans-Josef. *The Religious Context of Early Christianity: A Guide to Graeco-Roman Religions*. Trans. Brian McNeil. Minneapolis: Fortress, 2003.

Klausner, *Jesus*. • Klausner, Joseph. *Jesus: His Life, Times, and Teaching*. Trans. Herbert Danby. Foreword by Sidney B. Hoenig. New York: Menorah, 1979; n.p.: Macmillan, 1925.

Klausner, *Paul.* • Klausner, Joseph. *From Jesus to Paul.* Trans. W. Stinespring. New York: Menorah, 1979; n.p.: Macmillan, 1943.

Klawans, "Idolatry." • Klawans, Jonathan. "Idolatry, Incest, and Impurity: Moral Defilement in Ancient Judaism." *JSJ* 29 (4, 1998): 391-415.

Klawans, "Impurity." • Klawans, Jonathan. "The Impurity of Immorality in Ancient Judaism." *JJS* 48 (1, 1997): 1-16.

Klawans, "Purity." • Klawans, Jonathan. "Moral and Ritual Purity." 266-84 in *The Historical Jesus in Context.* Ed. Amy-Jill Levine, Dale C. Allison Jr., and John Dominic Crossan. Princeton Readings in Religions. Princeton: Princeton University Press, 2006.

Klein, "Messianism." • Klein, Ralph W. "Aspects of Intertestamental Messianism." 191-203 in *The Bible in Its Literary Milieu.* Ed. Vincent L. Tollers and John R. Maier. Grand Rapids: Eerdmans, 1979.

Kleve, "Did Socrates Exist?" • Kleve, Knut. "Did Socrates Exist?" *GrBeit* 14 (1987): 123-37.

Kloppenborg, "Growth." • Kloppenborg, John S. "The Growth and Impact of Agricultural Tenancy in Jewish Palestine (III BCE–I CE)." *JESHO* 51 (1, 2008): 31-66.

Kloppenborg, "Q and Jesus." • Kloppenborg, John S. "The Sayings Gospel Q and the Quest of the Historical Jesus." *HTR* 89 (4, 1996): 307-44.

Knights, "Faces." • Knights, Chris. "Jesus' Changing Faces: A Response to Geza Vermes." *ExpT* 113 (6, 2002): 203-5.

Koch, "Menschensohn." • Koch, Klaus. "Der 'Menschensohn' in Daniel." *ZAW* 119 (3, 2007): 369-85.

Kodell, *Luke.* • Kodell, Jerome. *The Gospel According to Luke.* Collegeville Bible Commentary. Collegeville, MN: The Liturgical Press, 1983.

Koenig, *Hospitality.* • Koenig, John. *New Testament Hospitality: Partnership with Strangers as Promise and Mission.* OBT 17. Philadelphia: Fortress, 1985.

Koester, "Cult." • Koester, Helmut. "The Historical Jesus and the Cult of the Kyrios Christos." *HDBull* 24 (3, 1995): 13-18.

Koester, *Gospels.* • Koester, Helmut. *Ancient Christian Gospels: Their History and Development.* Philadelphia: Trinity Press International; London: SCM, 1990.

Koester, "Gospels." • Koester, Helmut. "Written Gospels or Oral Tradition?" *JBL* 113 (2, Summer 1994): 293-97.

Koester, *Introduction.* • Koester, Helmut. *Introduction to the New Testament.* 2 vols. Hermeneia Foundations and Facets Series. Vol. 1: *History, Culture, and Religion of the Hellenistic Age.* Vol. 2: *History and Literature of Early Christianity.* Philadelphia: Fortress, 1982.

Koester, "One Jesus." • Koester, Helmut. "One Jesus and Four Primitive Gospels." 158-204 in *Trajectories through Early Christianity.* By James M. Robinson and Helmut Koester. Philadelphia: Fortress, 1971.

Koester, "Silence." • Koester, Helmut. "The Silence of the Apostle." 339-49 in *Urban Religion in Roman Corinth: Interdisciplinary Approaches.* Ed. Daniel N. Schowalter and Steven J. Friesen. HTS 53. Cambridge: Harvard University Press, 2005.

Koester, "Victim." • Koester, Helmut. "Jesus the Victim." *JBL* 111 (1992): 3-15.

Kokkinos, "Gentilicium." • Kokkinos, Nikos. "A Fresh Look at the *gentilicium* of Felix, Procurator of Judaea." *Latomus* 49 (1, 1990): 126-41.

Kolenkow, "Genre." • Kolenkow, Anitra Bingham. "The Literary Genre 'Testament.'" 259-67 in *Early Judaism and Its Modern Interpreters.* Ed. Robert A. Kraft and George W. E. Nickelsburg. SBLBMI 2. Atlanta: Scholars Press, 1986.

Kollmann, *Kreuzigung.* • Kollmann, Hanjo-Christoph. *Die Kreuzigung Jesu nach Joh 19, 16-22. Ein Beitrag zur Kreuzestheologie des Johannes im Vergleich mit den Synoptikern.* Europäische Hochschulschriften, Reihe 23, Theologie 710. Frankfurt: Lang, 2000.

Konkel, *Kings.* • Konkel, August H. *1 & 2 Kings.* NIVAC. Grand Rapids: Zondervan, 2006.

Konstan, "*Apollonius* and Novel." • Konstan, David. "*Apollonius, King of Tyre* and the Greek

Novel." 173-182 in *The Search for the Ancient Novel*. Ed. James Tatum. Baltimore, London: The Johns Hopkins University Press, 1994.

Konstan, "Invention." • Konstan, David. "The Invention of Fiction." 3-17 in *Ancient Fiction and Early Christian Narrative*. Ed. Ronald F. Hock, J. Bradley Chance and Judith Perkins. SBLSymS 6. Atlanta: Society of Biblical Literature, 1998.

Konstan, *Symmetry*. • Konstan, David. *Sexual Symmetry: Love in the Ancient Novel and Related Genres*. Princeton: Princeton University Press, 1994.

Kooij, "Death of Josiah." • Kooij, Arie van der. "The Death of Josiah According to 1 Esdras." *Text* 19 (1998): 97-109.

Koskenniemi, "Apollonius." • Koskenniemi, Erkki. "Apollonius of Tyana: A Typical θεῖος ἀνήρ?" *JBL* 117 (3, 1998): 455-67.

Kraabel, "Judaism." • Kraabel, Alf Thomas. "Judaism in Western Asia Minor Under the Roman Empire, with a Preliminary Study of the Jewish Community at Sardis, Lydia." Th.D. Dissertation, Harvard Divinity School, 1968.

Kraeling, *John the Baptist*. • Kraeling, Carl H. *John the Baptist*. New York: Charles Scribner's Sons, 1951.

Krasser, "Reading." • Krasser, Helmut. "Light reading." 7:553-55 in *Brill's New Pauly*.

Krause, "Colonatus." • Krause, Jens-Uwe. "Colonatus." 3:538-41 in *Brill's New Pauly*.

Krieger, "Feuer." • Krieger, Klaus-Stefan. "Das reinigende Feuer. Die Zerstörung des Zweiten Tempels in der Darstellung des Josephus." *BK* 53 (2, 1998): 73-78.

Krieger, "Hauptquelle." • Krieger, Klaus-Stefan. "Zur Frage nach der Hauptquelle über die Geschichte der Provinz Judäa in den Antiquitates Judaicae des Flavius Josephus." *BN* 63 (1992): 37-41.

Krieger, "Problematik." • Krieger, Klaus-Stefan. "Die Problematik chronologischer Rekonstruktionen zur Amtszeit des Pilatus." *BN* 61 (1992): 27-32.

Kuhn, "Gekreuzigten." • Kuhn, Heinz W. "Zum Gekreuzigten von Giv'at ha-Mivtar. Korrektur eines Versehens in der Erstveröffentlichung." *ZNW* 69 (1978): 118-22.

Kuhn, "Messias." • Kuhn, Heinz-Wolfgang. "Die beiden Messias in den Qumrantexten und die Messiasvorstellung in der rabbinischen Literatur." *ZAW* 70 (1958): 200-8.

Kuhn, "Son of God." • Kuhn, Karl A. "The 'One like a Son of Man' Becomes the 'Son of God.'" *CBQ* 69 (1, 2007): 22-42.

Kulp, "Origins." • Kulp, Joshua. "The Origins of the Seder and Haggadah." *CBR* 4 (1, 2005): 109-34.

Kulp, "Patterns." • Kulp, Joshua. "Organisational Patterns in the Mishnah in Light of Their Toseftan Parallels." *JJS* 58 (1, 2007): 52-78.

Kümmel, *Introduction*. • Kümmel, Werner Georg. *Introduction to the New Testament*. London: SCM, 1965.

Kümmel, *Promise*. • Kümmel, Werner George. *Promise and Fulfilment: The Eschatological Message of Jesus*. Tr. Dorothea M. Barton. SBT 23. Naperville: Alec R. Allenson, 1957.

Kümmel, *Theology*. • Kümmel, Werner Georg. *The Theology of the New Testament According to Its Major Witnesses — Jesus, Paul, John*. Trans. John E. Steely. Nashville: Abingdon, 1973.

Kurz, "Addresses." • Kurz, William S. "Luke 22:14-38 and Greco-Roman and Biblical Farewell Addresses." *JBL* 104 (1985): 251-68.

Kurz, *Reading Luke-Acts*. • Kurz, William S. *Reading Luke-Acts: Dynamics of Biblical Narrative*. Louisville, KY: Westminster/John Knox, 1993.

Kvalbein, "Wonders." • Kvalbein, Hans. "The Wonders of the End-Time: Metaphoric Language in 4Q521 and the Interpretation of Matthew 11.5 par." *JSP* 18 (1998): 87-110.

Kvalbein, "Wunder." • Kvalbein, Hans. "Die Wunder der Endzeit. Beobachtungen zu 4Q521 und Matth 11,5p." *ZNW* 88 (1-2, 1997): 111-25.

Kysar, *John*. • Kysar, Robert. *John*. Augsburg Commentary on the New Testament. Minneapolis: Augsburg, 1986.

Kysar, *Maverick Gospel.* • Kysar, Robert. *John, The Maverick Gospel.* Atlanta, GA: John Knox, 1976.

Lach, "Uczta." • Lach, J. "Uczta Zrzeszenia z Qumran a Ostatnia Wieczerza (Convivium congregationis Quomranensis cum ultima cena comparatur)." *RuBL* 11 (1958): 489-97.

Lachs, *Commentary.* • Lachs, Samuel Tobias. *A Rabbinic Commentary on the New Testament: The Gospels of Matthew, Mark, and Luke.* Hoboken, NJ: Ktav; New York: Anti-Defamation League of B'Nai B'Rith, 1987.

Lachs, "Matthew 23:27-28." • Lachs, Samuel Tobias. "On Matthew 23:27-28." *HTR* 68 (1975): 385-88.

Ladd, *Criticism.* • Ladd, George Eldon. *The New Testament and Criticism.* Grand Rapids: Eerdmans, 1967.

Ladd, *Kingdom.* • Ladd, George Eldon. *The Gospel of the Kingdom.* Grand Rapids: Eerdmans, 1978; Paternoster, 1959.

Ladd, *Last Things.* • Ladd, George Eldon. *The Last Things.* Grand Rapids: Eerdmans, 1978.

Ladd, *Resurrection.* • Ladd, George E. *I Believe in the Resurrection of Jesus.* London: Hodder & Stoughton; Grand Rapids: Eerdmans, 1975.

Ladd, *Theology.* • Ladd, George Eldon. *A Theology of the New Testament.* Grand Rapids: Eerdmans, 1974.

Lake and Cadbury, *Commentary.* • Lake, Kirsopp, and Henry J. Cadbury. *English Translation and Commentary.* Vol. 4 in *The Beginnings of Christianity.* Ed. F. J. Foakes Jackson and Kirsopp Lake. Grand Rapids: Baker, 1979.

Lalleman, "Apocryphal Acts." • Lalleman, Pieter J. "Apocryphal Acts and Epistles." 66-69 in *DNTB.*

Lambert, *Millions.* • Lambert, Tony. *China's Christian Millions: The Costly Revival.* London, Grand Rapids: Monarch Books, 1999.

Lamour, "L'organisation." • Lamour, Denis. "L'organisation du récit dans l'*Autobiographie* de Flavius Josèphe." *BAGB* 55 (2, 1996): 141-150.

Lampe, "A.D. 70." • Lampe, G. W. H. "A.D. 70 in Christian Reflection." 153-71 in *Jesus and the Politics of His Day.* Ed. Ernst Bammel and C. F. D. Moule. Cambridge: Cambridge University Press, 1984.

Lane, *Mark.* • Lane, William L. *The Gospel According to Mark.* NICNT. Grand Rapids: Eerdmans, 1974.

Lapide, *Hebrew.* • Lapide, Pinchas E. *Hebrew in the Church: The Foundations of Jewish-Christian Dialogue.* Tr. Erroll F. Rhodes. Grand Rapids: Eerdmans, 1984.

Lapide, *Resurrection.* • Lapide, Pinchas. *The Resurrection of Jesus: A Jewish Perspective.* Minneapolis: Augsburg, 1983; London: SPCK, 1984.

LaSor, "Messiahs." • LaSor, William Sanford. "'The Messiahs of Aaron and Israel.'" *VT* 6 (4, Oct. 1956): 425-29.

Laurin, "Immortality." • Laurin, Robert B. "The Question of Immortality in the Qumran Hodayot." *JSS* 3 (1958): 344-55.

Laurin, "Messiahs." • Laurin, Robert B. "The Problem of Two Messiahs in the Qumran Scrolls." *RevQ* 4 (13/1, Jan. 1963): 39-52.

Lavery, "*Lucullus.*" • Lavery, Gerard B. "Plutarch's *Lucullus* and the Living Bond of Biography." *CJ* 89 (3, 1994): 261-73.

Lease, "Mithraeum." • Lease, Gary. "The Caesarea Mithraeum: A Preliminary Announcement." *BA* 38 (1975): 2-10.

Le Cornu, *Acts.* • Le Cornu, Hilary, with Joseph Shulam. *A Commentary on the Jewish Roots of Acts.* Jerusalem: Nitivyah Bible Instruction Ministry, 2003.

Lee, "Unrest." • Lee, Clarence L. "Social Unrest and Primitive Christianity." 121-38 in *The Catacombs and the Colosseum: The Roman Empire as the Setting of Primitive Christianity.* Ed. Stephen Benko and John J. O'Rourke. Valley Forge, PA: Judson, 1971.

Lefkowitz, *Africa.* • Lefkowitz, Mary. *Not Out of Africa: How Afrocentrism Became an Excuse to Teach Myth as History.* New York: BasicBooks, HarperCollins, 1996.

Leiman, "Josephus and Canon." • Leiman, Sid Z. "Josephus and the Canon of the Bible." 50-58 in

Josephus, the Bible, and History. Ed. Louis H. Feldman and Gohei Hata. Detroit: Wayne State University Press, 1989.

Leivestad, "Exit." • Leivestad, Ragnar. "Exit the Apocalyptic Son of Man." *NTS* 18 (3, April 1972): 243-67.

Leon, *Jews of Rome.* • Leon, Harry J. *The Jews of Ancient Rome.* The Morris Loeb Series. Philadelphia: The Jewish Publication Society of America, 1960.

Léon-Dufour, *Resurrection.* • Léon-Dufour, Xavier. *Resurrection and the Message of Easter.* Trans. R. N. Wilson. New York: Holt, Rinehart & Winston; Geoffrey Chapman Publishers, 1974. Originally *Résurrection de Jésus et message pascal.* N.p.: Editions du Seuil, 1971.

Leonhard, "älteste Haggada." • Leonhard, Clemens. "Die älteste Haggada. Übersetzung der Pesachhaggada nach dem palästinischen Ritus und Vorschläge zu ihrem Ursprung und ihrer Bedeutung für die Geschichte der christlichen Liturgie." *ALW* 45 (2, 2003): 201-231.

Lessa and Vogt, *Reader.* • *Reader in Comparative Religion: An Anthropological Approach.* 4th ed. Ed. William A. Lessa and Evon Z. Vogt. New York: Harper & Row, 1979.

Levine, "Beth-She'arim." • Levine, Lee I. "Beth-She'arim." 1:309-311 in *OEANE.*

Levine, *Hellenism.* • Levine, Lee I. *Judaism and Hellenism in Antiquity: Conflict or Confluence?* Peabody, MA: Hendrickson, 1998.

Levine, "Introduction." • Levine, Amy-Jill. "Introduction." 1-39 in *The Historical Jesus in Context.* Ed. Amy-Jill Levine, Dale C. Allison Jr., and John Dominic Crossan. Princeton Readings in Religions. Princeton: Princeton University Press, 2006.

Levine, *Misunderstood Jew.* • Levine, Amy-Jill. *The Misunderstood Jew. The Church and the Scandal of the Jewish Jesus.* San Francisco: HarperSanFrancisco, 2006.

Levine, "Purification." • Levine, Lee I. "R. Simeon b. Yohai and the Purification of Tiberias: History and Tradition." *HUCA* 49 (1976): 143-85.

Levine, "Responsibility." • Levine, Amy-Jill. "Discharging Responsibility: Matthean Jesus, Biblical Law, and Hemorrhaging Woman." 379-97 in *Treasures New and Old: Recent Contributions to Matthean Studies.* Ed. David R. Bauer and Mark Allan Powell. SBLSymS 1. Atlanta: Scholars Press, 1996.

Levine, "Synagogue." • Levine, Lee I. "The Second Temple Synagogue: The Formative Years." 7-31 in *The Synagogue in Late Antiquity.* Ed. Lee I. Levine. Philadelphia: The American Schools of Oriental Research, 1986.

Levine, "Theory." • Levine, Amy-Jill. "Theory, Apologetic, History: Reviewing Jesus' Jewish Context." *ABR* 55 (2007): 57-78.

Levine, "Word." • Levine, Amy-Jill. "The Word Becomes Flesh: Jesus, Gender, and Sexuality." 509-23 in *The Historical Jesus in Recent Research.* Ed. James D. G. Dunn and Scot McKnight. Winona Lake, IN: Eisenbrauns, 2005.

Levinskaya, *Diaspora Setting.* • Levinskaya, Irina. *The Book of Acts in Its Diaspora Setting.* Vol. 5 in The Book of Acts in Its First Century Setting. Grand Rapids: Eerdmans; Carlisle: Paternoster, 1996.

Levison, "Ruth." • Levison, John R. "Josephus's Version of Ruth." *JSP* 8 (1991): 31-44.

Lewis, *Healing.* • Lewis, David C. *Healing: Fiction, Fantasy, or Fact?* London: Hodder & Stoughton, 1989.

Lewis, *History.* • Lewis, Bernard. *History Remembered, Recovered, Invented.* New York: Simon & Schuster, 1975.

Lewis, *Life.* • Lewis, Naphtali. *Life in Egypt Under Roman Rule.* Oxford: Clarendon Press, 1983.

Lichtenberger and Schreiner, "Neue Bund." • Lichtenberger, Hermann, and S. Schreiner. "Der neue Bund in jüdischer Überlieferung." *TQ* 176 (4, 1996): 272-90.

Licona, "Historicity of Resurrection." • Licona, Michael R. "The Historicity of the Resurrection of Christ: Historiographical Considerations in the Light of Recent Debates." Ph.D. dissertation, University of Pretoria, 2008.

Lieberman, *Hellenism.* • Lieberman, Saul. *Hellenism in Jewish Palestine: Studies in the Literary Transmission, Beliefs and Manners of Palestine in the I Century* B.C.E.-*IV Century* C.E. 2d ed. Texts and Studies of The Jewish Theological Seminary of America 18. New York: The Jewish Theological Seminary of America, 1962.

Lieberman, "Light." • Lieberman, Saul. "Light on the Cave Scrolls from Rabbinic Sources." *PAAJR* 20 (1951): 395-404.

Liefeld, "Preacher." • Liefeld, Walter Lewis. "The Wandering Preacher as a Social Figure in the Roman Empire." Ph.D. dissertation, Columbia University, 1967. (Ann Arbor: University Microfilms International, 1976)

Lietzmann, "Prozess." • Lietzmann, Heinrich. "Der Prozess Jesu." *Sitzenberichte der Akademie der Wissenschaft* 14 (1931): 310-22.

Lightfoot, *Colossians.* • Lightfoot, J. B. *Saint Paul's Epistles to the Colossians and to Philemon.* Grand Rapids: Zondervan, 1959; reprint of n.p.: Macmillan & Company, 1879.

Lightfoot, *Talmud.* • Lightfoot, John. *A Commentary on the New Testament from the Talmud and Hebraica,* 4 vols. N.p.: Oxford, 1959; Grand Rapids: Baker, 1979.

Lincoln, *Paradise.* • Lincoln, Andrew T. *Paradise Now and Not Yet: Studies in the role of the heavenly dimension in Paul's thought with special reference to his eschatology.* SNTSMS 43. Cambridge: Cambridge University Press, 1981.

Lindars, *Behind.* • Lindars, Barnabas. *Behind the Fourth Gospel: Studies in Creative Criticism.* London: Talbot Press, 1971.

Lindars, "Composition." • Lindars, Barnabas. "Composition of John XX." *NTS* 7 (January 1961): 142-47.

Lindars, "Re-Enter." • Lindars, Barnabas. "Re-Enter the Apocalyptic Son of Man." *NTS* 22 (1, October 1975): 52-72.

Lindars, *Son of Man.* • Lindars, Barnabas. *Jesus Son of Man: A Fresh Examination of the Son of Man Sayings in the Gospels in the Light of Recent Research.* Grand Rapids: Eerdmans, 1983.

Lindemann, *Q and Jesus.* • Lindemann, Andreas, ed. *The Sayings Source Q and the Historical Jesus.* BETL 158. Leuven: Leuven University Press/Peeters, 2001.

Lindemann, "Q and Jesus." • Lindemann, Andreas. "The Sayings Source Q and the Historical Jesus: Colloquium Biblicum Lovaniense XLIX (2000)." *ETL* 76 (4, 2000): 549-59.

Lindenberger, "Ahiqar." • Lindenberger, J. M. Introduction to "Ahiqar." 2:479-493 in *OTP.*

Lindsey, "Approach." • Lindsey, Robert L. "A New Approach to the Synoptic Gospels." *Mishkan* 17-18 (1992-93): 87-106.

Lindsey, *Rabbi.* • Lindsey, Robert L. *Jesus: Rabbi & Lord. The Hebrew Story of Jesus Behind Our Gospels.* Oak Creek, WI: Cornerstone Publishing, 1990.

Linnemann, *Criticism.* • Linnemann, Eta. *Historical Criticism of the Bible: Methodology or Ideology?* Trans. Robert W. Yarbrough, from *Wissenschaft oder Meinung? Anfragen und Alternativen.* Grand Rapids: Baker, 1990.

Linnemann, "Gospel of Q." • Linnemann, Eta. "The Gospel of Q — Fact or Fantasy?" *TJ* 17NS (1996): 3-18.

Linnemann, *Problem.* • Linnemann, Eta. *Is There a Synoptic Problem? Rethinking the Literary Dependence of the First Three Gospels.* Trans. Robert W. Yarbrough, from *Gibt es ein synoptisches Problem?* Grand Rapids: Baker, 1992.

Litfin, *Proclamation.* • Litfin, Duane. *St. Paul's Theology of Proclamation: 1 Corinthians 1-4 and Greco-Roman Rhetoric.* SNTSMS 83. Cambridge: Cambridge University Press, 1994.

Litwak, *Echoes.* • Litwak, Kenneth Duncan. *Echoes of Scripture in Luke-Acts: Telling the History of God's People Intertextually.* JSNTSup 282. London, New York: T&T Clark International, 2005.

Llewelyn, *Documents 7.* • Llewelyn, S. R., with R. A. Kearsley. *New Documents Illustrating Early Christianity: A Review of the Greek Inscriptions and Papyri Published in 1982-83.* Vol. 7. North Ryde, N.S.W.: The Ancient History Documentary Research Centre, Macquarie University, 1994.

Lock, *Pastoral Epistles.* • Lock, Walter. *A Critical and Exegetical Commentary on the Pastoral Epistles.* ICC. Edinburgh: T. & T. Clark, 1924.

Loffreda, "Scoperte." • Loffreda, Stanislao. "Recenti scoperte a Cafarnao." *RivB* 19 (1971): 221-29.

Loftus, "Note." • Loftus, Francis. "A Note on σύνταγμα τῶν Γαλιλαίων B.J. iv 558." *JQR* 65 (3, January 1975): 182-83.

Loftus, "Revolts." • Loftus, Francis. "The Anti-Roman Revolts of the Jews and the Galileans." *JQR* 68 (2, October 1977): 78-98.

Lohse, *Colossians.* • Lohse, Eduard. *Colossians and Philemon.* Trans. William R. Poehlmann and Robert J. Karris. Ed. Helmut Koester. Hermeneia. Philadelphia: Fortress, 1971.

Lohse, *Environment.* • Lohse, Eduard. *The New Testament Environment.* Trans. John E. Steely. Nashville: Abingdon, 1976.

Lohse, *Mark's Witness.* • Lohse, Eduard. *Mark's Witness to Jesus Christ.* New York: Association Press, 1955.

Long, "City." • Long, John. "The Shroud's Earlier History. Part 2: To the Great City." *BibSp* 20 (4, 2007): 120-28.

Long, "Edessa." • Long, John. "The Shroud's Early History. Part 1: To Edessa." *BibSp* 20 (2, 2007): 46-53.

Longenecker, *Christology.* • Longenecker, Richard N. *The Christology of Early Jewish Christianity.* London: SCM, 1970; Grand Rapids: Baker, 1981.

Longenecker, *Exegesis.* • Longenecker, Richard N. *Biblical Exegesis in the Apostolic Period.* Grand Rapids: Eerdmans, 1975.

Longenecker, "Wilderness." • Longenecker, Bruce W. "The Wilderness and Revolutionary Ferment in First-Century Palestine: A Response to D. R. Schwartz and J. Marcus." *JSJ* 29 (3, 1998): 322-36.

Longstaff, *Conflation.* • Longstaff, Thomas R. W. *Evidence of Conflation in Mark? A Study in the Synoptic Problem.* SBLDS 28. Missoula, MT: Scholars, 1977.

López, *Family Tomb.* • López, René A. *The Jesus Family Tomb Examined: Did Jesus Rise Physically?* Foreword by Darrell L. Bock. Springfield, MO: 21st Century Press, 2008.

Lord, "Oral Literature." • Lord, Albert B. "The Gospels as Oral Traditional Literature." 33-91 in *The Relationships Among the Gospels: An Interdisciplinary Dialogue.* Ed. William O. Walker, Jr. San Antonio: Trinity University Press, 1978.

Lord, *Singer.* • Lord, Albert B. *The Singer of Tales.* New York: Atheneum, 1965.

Losie, "Entry." • Losie, L. A. "Triumphal Entry." 854-59 in *DJG*.

Losie, "Gospel." • Losie, Lynn A. "Mark, Secret Gospel of." 708-12 in *Dictionary of the Later New Testament & Its Developments.* Ed. Ralph P. Martin and Peter H. Davids. Downers Grove, IL: InterVarsity Press, 1997.

Lowe and Flusser, "Theory." • Lowe, Malcolm, and David Flusser. "Evidence Corroborating a Modified Proto-Matthean Synoptic Theory." *NTS* 29 (1983): 25-47.

Lucas, "Origin." • Lucas, Ernest C. "The Origin of Daniel's Four Empires Scheme Re-Examined." *TynBul* 40 (2, 1989): 185-202.

Luciani, "Seguidores." • Luciani, Rafael. "Seguidores y Discípulos del Reino en la praxis fraterna del Jesús Histórico. Un Maestro y muchos hermanos." *ITER* 18 (42-43, 2007): 161-207.

Lüdemann, *Acts.* • Lüdemann, Gerd. *The Acts of the Apostles: What Really Happened in the Earliest Days of the Church.* Assisted by Tom Hall. Amherst, NY: Prometheus Books, 2005.

Lüdemann, "Betrayal." • Lüdemann, Gerd. "Why the Church Invented Judas's 'Betrayal' of Jesus." *CSER Review* 1 (2, 2006-7): 36-37.

Lüdemann, *Two Thousand Years.* • Lüdemann, Gerd. *Jesus after Two Thousand Years: What he really said and did.* With contributions from Frank Schleritt and Martina Janssen. Amherst, NY: Prometheus Books, 2001.

Luke, "Son of Man." • Luke, K. "Enoch and the Son of Man." *ITS* 37 (1, 2000): 46-64.

Lull, *Spirit in Galatia.* • Lull, David John. *The Spirit in Galatia: Paul's Interpretation of Pneuma as Divine Power.* SBLDS 49. Chico, CA: Scholars Press, 1980.

Lutz, "Musonius." • Lutz, Cora E. "Musonius Rufus: The Roman Socrates." *YCS* 10 (1947): 3-147.

Luz, *Matthew.* • Luz, Ulrich. *Matthew 1–7: A Commentary.* Trans. Wilhelm C. Linss. Minneapolis: Fortress, 1989.

Luz, "Primacy Text." • Luz, Ulrich. "The Primacy Text (Mt. 16:18)." *PSB* 12 (1991): 41-55.

Lyons, *Autobiography.* • Lyons, George. *Pauline Autobiography: Toward a New Understanding.* SBLDS 73. Atlanta: Scholars Press, Society of Biblical Literature, 1985.

McArthur, "Day." • McArthur, Harvey K. "On the Third Day." *NTS* 18 (1971): 81-86.

McArthur and Johnston, *Parables.* • McArthur, Harvey K., and Robert M. Johnston. *They Also Taught in Parables: Rabbinic Parables from the First Centuries of the Christian Era.* Grand Rapids: Academie, 1990.

McCane, "Bones." • McCane, Byron R. "Bones of Contention? Ossuaries and Reliquaries in Early Judaism and Christianity." *SecCent* 8 (1991): 235-46.

McCane, "Burial Practices." • McCane, Byron R. "Burial Practices, Jewish." 173-75 in *DNTB.*

McCane, "Dead." • McCane, Byron R. "'Let the Dead Bury Their Own Dead': Secondary Burial and Matt 8:21-22." *HTR* 83 (1990): 31-43.

McCane, "Shame." • McCane, Byron R. "'Where No One Had Yet Been Laid': The Shame of Jesus' Burial." 431-52 in *Authenticating the Activities of Jesus.* Ed. Bruce Chilton and Craig A. Evans. NTTS 28.2. Leiden: Brill, 1999.

Maccini, *Testimony.* • Maccini, Robert Gordon. *Her Testimony Is True: Women as Witnesses according to John.* JSNTSup 125. Sheffield: Sheffield Academic Press, 1996.

McClymond, *Stranger.* • McClymond, Michael J. *Familiar Stranger: An Introduction to Jesus of Nazareth.* Grand Rapids: Eerdmans, 2004.

Maccoby, "Corpse." • Maccoby, Hyam. "The Corpse in the Tent." *JSJ* 28 (2, 1997): 195-209.

Maccoby, "Eucharist." • Maccoby, Hyam. "Paul and the Eucharist." *NTS* 37 (2, 1991): 247-67.

Maccoby, "Washing." • Maccoby, Hyam. "The Washing of Cups." *JSNT* 14 (1982): 3-15.

McCown, "Structure." • McCown, Wayne. "The Hymnic Structure of Colossians 1:15-20." *EvQ* 51 (3, 1979): 156-62.

MacDonald, "Relationships." • MacDonald, Dennis R. "Which Came First? Intertextual Relationships Among the Apocryphal Acts of the Apostles." 11-41 in *The Apocryphal Acts of the Apostles in Intertextual Perspectives.* Semeia 80. Ed. Robert F. Stoops. Atlanta: Scholars Press, 1997.

MacDonald, *Samaritans.* • MacDonald, John. *The Theology of the Samaritans.* Philadelphia: Westminster, 1964.

McEvoy, "Dilemma." • McEvoy, James. "Narrative or History? — A False Dilemma: The Theological Significance of the Historical Jesus." *Pacifica* 14 (3, 2001): 262-80.

McGaughy, "Words." • McGaughy, Lane C. "Words Before Deeds: Why Start with the Sayings." *Forum* 1 (2, 1998): 387-98.

McGill, "Seneca on Plagiarizing." • McGill, Scott. "Seneca the Elder on Plagiarizing Cicero's *Verrines.*" *Rhetorica* 23 (4, 2005): 337-46.

MacGregor, *Pacifism.* • MacGregor, G. H. C. *The New Testament Basis of Pacifism and the Relevance of an Impossible Ideal.* Nyack, NY: Fellowship Publications, 1954.

Mack, *Lost Gospel.* • Mack, Burton L. *The Lost Gospel: The Book of Q & Christian Origins.* San Francisco: Harper San Francisco, 1993.

Mack, *Myth.* • Mack, Burton L. *A Myth of Innocence: Mark and Christian Origins.* Philadelphia: Fortress, 1988.

Mack and Robbins, *Patterns.* • Mack, Burton L., and Vernon K. Robbins. *Patterns of Persuasion in the Gospels.* Sonoma, CA: Polebridge, 1989.

McKelvey, "Cornerstone." • McKelvey, R. J. "Christ the Cornerstone." *NTS* 8 (1962): 352-59.

McKnight, "Critic." • McKnight, Scot. "A Loyal Critic: Matthew's Polemic with Judaism in Theological Perspective." 55-79 in *Anti-Semitism and Early Christianity: Issues of Polemic and Faith*. Ed. Craig A. Evans and Donald A. Hagner. Minneapolis: Fortress, 1993.

McKnight, Death. • McKnight, Scot. *Jesus and His Death: Historiography, the Historical Jesus, and Atonement Theory*. Waco, TX: Baylor University, 2005.

McKnight, Light. • McKnight, Scot. *A Light Among the Gentiles: Jewish Missionary Activity in the Second Temple Period*. Minneapolis: Fortress, 1991.

McKnight, Vision. • McKnight, Scot. *A New Vision for Israel: The Teachings of Jesus in National Context*. Grand Rapids, Cambridge: Eerdmans, 1999.

McLaren, "Summary Statements." • McLaren, James S. "Josephus' Summary Statements Regarding the Essenes, Pharisees and Sadducees." *ABR* 48 (2000): 31-46.

Maclean and Aitken, Heroikos. • Maclean, Jennifer K. Berenson, and Ellen Bradshaw Aitken. *Flavius Philostratus: Heroikos*. SBLWGRW 1. Volume editor: Jackson P. Hershbell. Atlanta: Society of Biblical Literature, 2001.

Macleod, "Introduction." • Macleod, M. D. "Introduction," 8:47-51 in Lucian. *Works*. 8 vols. Trans. A. M. Harmon, K. Kilburn, and M. D. Macleod. Loeb Classical Library. Cambridge: Harvard University Press, 1913-1967.

MacMullen, Paganism. • MacMullen, Ramsay. *Paganism in the Roman Empire*. New Haven: Yale University Press, 1981.

MacMullen, Social Relations. • MacMullen, Ramsay. *Roman Social Relations: 50 B.C. to A.D. 284*. New Haven: Yale University Press, 1974.

McNamara, Judaism. • McNamara, Martin. *Palestinian Judaism and the New Testament*. GNS 4. Wilmington, DE: Michael Glazier, 1983.

McNamara, Targum. • McNamara, Martin. *Targum and Testament*. Grand Rapids: Eerdmans, 1972.

McNicol, "Temple." • McNicol, Allan J. "The Eschatological Temple in the Qumran Pesher 4QFlorilegium 1:1-7." *OJRS* 5 (1977): 133-41.

MacRae, "Gnosticism." • MacRae, George W. "Gnosticism and New Testament Studies." *BibT* 38 (November 1968): 2623-2630.

McRay, Archaeology and NT. • McRay, John. *Archaeology and the New Testament*. Grand Rapids: Baker, 1991.

Maddox, Purpose. • Maddox, Robert. *The Purpose of Luke-Acts*. Studies of the NT in Its World. Edinburgh: T. & T. Clark, 1982. FRLANT; Göttingen: Vandenhoeck & Ruprecht, 1982.

Maehler, "Tachygraphy." • Maehler, Herwig. "Tachygraphy." 1468-69 in *OCD*.

Magen, "Yrwslym." • Magen, Y. "Yrwslym kmrkz sl t'syyt kly-'bn btqwpt hwrdws." *Qad* 17 (4, 1984): 124-27.

Magness, Sense. • Magness, J. Lee. *Sense and Absence: Structure and Suspension in the Ending of Mark's Gospel*. SBLSemS. Atlanta: Society of Biblical Literature, 1986.

Maier, Scroll. • Maier, Johann. *The Temple Scroll. An Introduction, Translation & Commentary*. JSOTSup 34. Sheffield: JSOT Press, 1985.

Maisonneuve, "Parables." • Maisonneuve, Dominique de la. "The Parables of Jesus and the Rabbinic Parables." *SIDIC* 20 (1987): 8-15.

Maldamé, "Trahison." • Maldamé, Jean-Michel. "La trahison de Judas. Psychologie, histoire et théologie." *Esprit & Vie* 117 (166, 2007): 1-13.

Malherbe, "Gentle as Nurse." • Malherbe, Abraham J. "'Gentle as a Nurse': The Cynic Background to I Thess ii." *NovT* 12 (2, April 1970): 203-17.

Malherbe, Moral Exhortation. • Malherbe, Abraham J. *Moral Exhortation, A Greco-Roman Sourcebook*. LEC 4. Philadelphia: Westminster, 1986.

Malherbe, Philosophers. • Malherbe, Abraham J. *Paul and the Popular Philosophers*. Philadelphia: Fortress, 1989.

Malherbe, Social Aspects. • Malherbe, Abraham J. *Social Aspects of Early Christianity*. 2d ed. Philadelphia: Fortress, 1983.

Malherbe, "Theorists." • Malherbe, Abraham J. "Ancient Epistolary Theorists." *OJRS* 5 (2, Oct. 1977): 3-77.

Malina, *Anthropology.* • Malina, Bruce J. *The New Testament World: Insights from Cultural Anthropology.* Atlanta: John Knox, 1981.

Malina, "Criticism." • Malina, Bruce J. "Rhetorical Criticism and Social-Scientific Criticism: Why Won't Romanticism Leave Us Alone?" 72-101 in *Rhetoric, Scripture and Theology: Essays from the 1994 Pretoria Conference.* Ed. Stanley E. Porter and Thomas H. Olbricht. JSNTSup 131. Sheffield: Sheffield Academic Press, 1996.

Malina, *Windows.* • Malina, Bruce J. *Windows on the World of Jesus: Time Travel to Ancient Judea.* Louisville, KY: Westminster/John Knox, 1993.

Malina and Pilch, *Acts.* • Malina, Bruce J., and John J. Pilch. *Social-Science Commentary on the Book of Acts.* Minneapolis: Fortress, 2008.

Malina and Rohrbaugh, *Gospels.* • Malina, Bruce J., and Richard L. Rohrbaugh. *Social-Science Commentary on the Synoptic Gospels.* Minneapolis: Fortress, 1992.

Malina and Rohrbaugh, *John.* • Malina, Bruce J., and Richard L. Rohrbaugh. *Social-Science Commentary on the Gospel of John.* Minneapolis: Fortress, 1998.

Malinowski, "Tendencies." • Malinowski, Francis X. "Torah Tendencies in Galilean Judaism according to Flavius Josephus with Gospel Comparisons." *BTB* 10 (1, Jan. 1980): 30-36.

Manns, "Fouilles." • Manns, Fréderic. "Marc 6,21-29 à la lumière des dernières fouilles du Machéronte." *SBFLA* 31 (1981): 287-90.

Manns, "Galilée." • Manns, Fréderic. "La Galilée dans le quatrième Evangile." *Anton* 72 (3, 1997): 351-64.

Manns, "Halakah." • Manns, Fréderic. "La Halakah dans l'évangile de Matthieu. Note sur *Mt.* 16,16-19." *BeO* 25 (1983): 129-35.

Manns, "L'arrière-plan." • Manns, Fréderic. "L'arrière-plan socio-économique de la Parabole des ouvriers de la onzième heure et ses limites." *Anton* 55 (1980): 258-68.

Manns, "Midrash." • Manns, Fréderic. "Col. 1,15-20: midrash Chrétien de Gen. 1,1." *RevScRel* 53 (2, April 1979): 100-110.

Manns, "Pâque." • Manns, Fréderic. "Pâque juive et pâque chrétienne." *EphLit* 113 (1, 1999): 31-46.

Manson, *Sayings.* • Manson, T. W. *The Sayings of Jesus.* Grand Rapids: Eerdmans, 1979; London: SCM, 1957.

Manson, *Servant-Messiah.* • Manson, T. W. *The Servant-Messiah.* Cambridge: Cambridge University, 1961.

Mantel, "Oral Law." • Mantel, Hugo D. "The Antiquity of the Oral Law." *ASTI* 12 (1983): 93-112.

Mantel, *Sanhedrin.* • Mantel, Hugo. *Studies in the History of the Sanhedrin.* HSS 17. Cambridge: Harvard University Press, 1961.

Marchant, "Introduction." • Marchant, E. C. "Introduction." Vii-xxvii in Xenophon's *Memorabilia* and *Oeconomicus.* Trans. E. C. Marchant. LCL, fourth Xenophon vol. Cambridge: Harvard, 1923.

Marconi, "Interpretation." • Marconi, Gilberto. "History as a Hermeneutical Interpretation of the Difference Between Acts 3:1-10 and 4:8-12." 167-80 in *Luke and Acts.* Ed. Gerald O'Collins and Gilberto Marconi. Trans. Matthew J. O'Connell. New York: Paulist, 1993.

Marcus, *Mark.* • Marcus, Joel. *Mark 1–8: A New Translation with Introduction and Commentary.* AB 27. New York: Doubleday, 2000.

Marcus, "Scrolls." • Marcus, Ralph. "The Qumran Scrolls and Early Judaism." *BR* 1 (1956): 9-47.

Marguerat, "Acts of Paul." • Marguerat, Daniel. "The *Acts of Paul* and The Canonical Acts: A Phenomenon of Rereading." 169-83 in *The Apocryphal Acts of the Apostles in Intertextual Perspectives.* Semeia 80. Ed. Robert F. Stoops. Atlanta: Scholars Press, 1997.

Marguerat, *Histoire.* • Marguerat, Daniel. *La Première Histoire du Christianisme (Les Actes des apôtres).* LD 180. Paris, Geneva: Les Éditions du Cerf, 1999.

Marguerat, *Historian.* • Marguerat, Daniel. *The First Christian Historian: Writing the 'Acts of the*

Apostles.' SNTSMS 121. Trans. Ken McKinney, Gregory J. Laughery and Richard Bauckham. Cambridge: Cambridge University Press, 2002.

Marguerat, "L'héritage." • Marguerat, Daniel. "L'héritage de Paul en débat: Actes des apôtres et Actes de Paul." *FoiVie* 94 (4, 1995): 87-97.

Marincola, "Tacitus' Prefaces." • Marincola, John. "Tacitus' Prefaces and the Decline of Imperial Historiography." *Latomus* 58 (2, 1999): 391-404.

Marmorstein, *Merits.* • Marmorstein, A. *The Doctrine of Merits in Old Rabbinical Literature.* New York: Ktav, 1968. Reprint of 1920 ed.

Marmorstein, *Names.* • Marmorstein, A. *The Old Rabbinic Doctrine of God: The Names and Attributes of God.* New York: Ktav, 1968; reprint of 1927 ed.

Marsden, *Idea.* • Marsden, George M. *The Outrageous Idea of Christian Scholarship.* New York: Oxford University Press, 1997.

Marsh, "Quests." • Marsh, Clive. "Quests of the Historical Jesus in New Historicist Perspective." *BibInt* 5 (4, 1997): 403-37.

Marshall, *Acts.* • Marshall, I. Howard. *The Acts of the Apostles: An Introduction and Commentary.* TNTC. Grand Rapids: Eerdmans, 1980.

Marshall, *Enmity.* • Marshall, Peter. *Enmity in Corinth: Social Conventions in Paul's Relations with the Corinthians.* WUNT 2, Reihe, 23. Tübingen: J. C. B. Mohr (Paul Siebeck), 1987.

Marshall, *Historian and Theologian.* • Marshall, I. Howard. *Luke: Historian and Theologian.* Exeter: Paternoster, 1970.

Marshall, *Luke.* • Marshall, I. Howard. *The Gospel of Luke: A Commentary on the Greek Text.* NIGTC. Grand Rapids: Eerdmans; Exeter: Paternoster, 1978.

Marshall, "Luke as Theologian." • Marshall, I. Howard. "Luke as Theologian." 4:402-3 in *ABD.*

Marshall, *Origins.* • Marshall, I. Howard. *The Origins of New Testament Christology.* 2d ed. Downers Grove: InterVarsity, 1990.

Marshall, "Son of Man Sayings." • Marshall, I. Howard. "The Synoptic Son of Man Sayings in Recent Discussion." *NTS* 12 (4, July 1966): 327-51.

Marshall, *Thessalonians.* • Marshall, I. Howard. *1 & 2 Thessalonians.* NCBC. Ed. Matthew Black. Grand Rapids: Eerdmans, 1983.

Marshall, "Treatise." • Marshall, I. Howard. "Acts and the 'Former Treatise.'" 163-82 in *The Book of Acts in Its Ancient Literary Setting.* Ed. Bruce W. Winter and Andrew D. Clarke. Vol. 1 in The Book of Acts in Its First Century Setting. Grand Rapids: Eerdmans; Carlisle: Paternoster, 1993.

Marshall, "Use of OT" • Marshall, I. Howard. "Acts." 513-606 in *Commentary on the New Testament Use of the Old Testament.* Ed. G. K. Beale and D. A. Carson. Grand Rapids: Baker Academic, 2007.

Martin, *Carmen Christi.* • Martin, Ralph P. *Carmen Christi.* Cambridge: Cambridge University Press, 1967.

Martin, "Dichotomy." • Martin, Dale B. "Paul and the Judaism/Hellenism Dichotomy: Toward a Social History of the Question." 29-62 in *Paul Beyond the Judaism/Hellenism Divide.* Ed. Troels Engberg-Pedersen. Louisville, KY: Westminster John Knox, 2001.

Martin, *Foundations.* • Martin, Ralph P. *New Testament Foundations: A Guide for Christian Students.* Vol. 2: *The Acts, The Letters, The Apocalypse.* Grand Rapids: Eerdmans; Exeter: Paternoster, 1978.

Martin, "Healing." • Martin, Ralph P. "The Pericope of the Healing of the Centurion's Servant/Son (Matt 8:5-13 par. Luke 7:1-10): Some Exegetical Notes." 14-22 in *Unity and Diversity in New Testament Theology: Essays in Honor of George E. Ladd.* Ed. Robert A. Guelich. Grand Rapids: Eerdmans, 1978.

Martin, "Hymn." • Martin, Ralph P. "An Early Christian Hymn (Col 1:15-20)." *EvQ* 36 (4, Oct. 1964): 195-205.

Martin, *James.* • Martin, Ralph P. *James.* WBC 48. Waco, TX: Word, 1988.

Martin, "Mithraism." • Martin, Luther H. "Roman Mithraism and Christianity." *Numen* 36 (1, 1989): 2-15.

Martin, *Morphē.* • Martin, Ralph P. "*Morphē* in Philippians ii.6." *ExpT* 70 (6, March 1959): 183-84.

Martin, "Q." • Martin, W. H. Blyth. "The Indispensability of Q." *Theology* 59 (1956): 182-88.

Martin, *Worship.* • Martin, Ralph P. *The Worship of God.* Grand Rapids: Eerdmans, 1982.

Martínez, "Reevaluación." • Martínez, A. E. "Reevaluación crítica del 'testimonio' de Flavio Josefo acerca de Jesús." *Apuntes* 25 (3, 2005): 84-118.

Martone, "Testo." • Martone, Corrado. "Un testo qumranico che narra la morte del Messia? A propositio del recente dibattito su 4Q285." *RivB* 42 (3, 1994): 329-36.

Martyn, "Religionsgeschichte." • Martyn, J. Louis. "Source Criticism and Religionsgeschichte in the Fourth Gospel (1970)." Pp. 99-121 in *The Interpretation of John.* Ed. John Ashton. Issues in Religion and Theology 9. Philadelphia: Fortress; London: S.P.C.K., 1986.

Marxsen, *Mark.* • Marxsen, Willi. *Mark the Evangelist: Studies on the Redaction History of the Gospel.* Trans. James Boyce, Donald Juel, William Poehlmann with Roy A. Harrisville. Nashville: Abingdon, 1969.

Mason, "Chief Priests." • Mason, Steve. "Chief Priests, Sadducees, Pharisees and Sanhedrin in Acts." 115-78 in *The Book of Acts in Its Palestinian Setting.* Ed. Richard Bauckham. Vol. 4 in The Book of Acts in Its First Century Setting. Grand Rapids: Eerdmans; Carlisle: Paternoster, 1995.

Mason, "Contradiction." • Mason, Steven. "Contradiction or Counterpoint? Josephus and Historical Method." *RRJ* 6 (2-3, 2003): 145-188.

Mason, *Josephus and New Testament.* • Mason, Steven. *Josephus and the New Testament.* Peabody, MA: Hendrickson, 1992.

Mason, "Was Josephus a Pharisee?" • Mason, Steven N. "Was Josephus a Pharisee? A Re-Examination of Life 10-12." *JJS* 40 (1, 1989): 31-45.

Matera, *Kingship.* • Matera, Frank J. *The Kingship of Jesus: Composition and Theology in Mark 15.* SBLDS 66. Chico, CA: Scholars Press for Society of Biblical Literature, 1982.

Mathews, "Quest." • Mathews, J. "The Renewed Quest for the Historical Jesus and Its Implications for Indian Biblical Hermeneutics." *BiBh* 30 (4, 2004): 242-59.

Mattingly, *Christianity.* • Mattingly, Harold. *Christianity in the Roman Empire.* New York: W. W. Norton & Company, 1967.

Mauser, *Wilderness.* • Mauser, Ulrich. *Christ in the Wilderness.* SBT 39. London: SCM, 1963.

May, "Logos." • May, Eric. "The Logos in the Old Testament." *CBQ* 8 (1946): 438-47.

Mayer, "Anfang." • Mayer, Reinhold. "Der Anfang des Evangeliums in Galiläa." *BK* 36 (2, 1981): 213-21.

Mazar, "Josephus and Excavations." • Mazar, Benjamin. "Josephus Flavius and the Archaeological Excavations in Jerusalem." 325-29 in *Josephus, the Bible, and History.* Ed. Louis H. Feldman and Gohei Hata. Detroit: Wayne State University Press, 1989.

Mazar, "Splendors." • Mazar, Benjamin. "Excavations near Temple Mount Reveal Splendors of Herodian Jerusalem." *BAR* 6 (1980): 44-59.

Mbiti, *Religions.* • Mbiti, John S. *African Religions and Philosophies.* Garden City, NY: Doubleday & Company, 1970.

Meadors, *Herald.* • Meadors, Edward P. *Jesus the Messianic Herald of Salvation.* WUNT 2. Reihe 72. Tübingen: Mohr-Siebeck, 1995.

Meadors, "Orthodoxy." • Meadors, Edward P. "The Orthodoxy of the 'Q' Sayings of Jesus." *TynBul* 43 (2, 1992): 233-57.

Mealand, "Community of Goods." • Mealand, David L. "Community of Goods at Qumran." *TZ* 31 (1975): 129-39.

Mealand, "Dissimilarity Test." • Mealand, David L. "Dissimilarity Test." *SJT* 31 (1978): 41-50.

Mealand, "Extent." • Mealand, David L. "The Extent of the Pauline Corpus: A Multivariate Approach." *JSNT* 59 (1995): 61-92.

Mealand, "Historians and Style." • Mealand, David L. "Hellenistic Historians and the Style of Acts." *ZNW* 82 (1-2, 1991): 42-66.

Mealand, "Verbs." • Mealand, David L. "Luke-Acts and the Verbs of Dionysius of Halicarnassus." *JSNT* 63 (1996): 63-86.

Meeks, "Hypomnēmata." • Meeks, Wayne A. "Hypomnēmata from an Untamed Sceptic: A Response to George Kennedy." 157-72 in *The Relationships Among the Gospels: An Interdisciplinary Dialogue.* Ed. William O. Walker, Jr. San Antonio: Trinity University Press, 1978.

Meeks, "Judaism." • Meeks, Wayne A. "Judaism, Hellenism, and the Birth of Christianity." 17-27 in *Paul Beyond the Judaism/Hellenism Divide.* Ed. Troels Engberg-Pedersen. Louisville, KY: Westminster John Knox, 2001.

Meeks, *Moral World.* • Meeks, Wayne A. *The Moral World of the First Christians.* LEC 6. Philadelphia: Westminster, 1986.

Meeks, *Prophet-King.* • Meeks, Wayne A. *The Prophet-King: Moses Traditions and the Johannine Christology.* NovTSup 14. Leiden: E. J. Brill, 1967.

Meeks, *Urban Christians.* • Meeks, Wayne A. *The First Urban Christians: The Social World of the Apostle Paul.* New Haven: Yale, 1983.

Meier, "Circle of Twelve." • Meier, John P. "The Circle of the Twelve: did it exist during Jesus' public ministry?" *JBL* 116 (1997): 635-72.

Meier, "Dividing Lines." • Meier, John P. "Dividing Lines in Jesus Research Today: Through Dialectical Negation to a Positive Sketch." *Int* 50 (4, 1996): 355-72.

Meier, "Historical Law." • Meier, John P. "The Historical Jesus and the Historical Law: Some Problems within the Problem." *CBQ* 65 (1, 2003): 52-79.

Meier, "Jesus in Josephus." • Meier, John P. "Jesus in Josephus: A Modest Proposal." *CBQ* 52 (1, 1990): 76-103.

Meier, "John in Josephus." • Meier, John P. "John the Baptist in Josephus: Philology and Exegesis." *JBL* 111 (1992): 225-37.

Meier, *Marginal Jew.* • Meier, John P. *A Marginal Jew: Rethinking the Historical Jesus.* ABRL. Vol. 1: *The Roots of the Problem and the Person.* New York: Doubleday, 1991. Vol. 2: *Mentor, Message, and Miracles.* New York: Doubleday, 1994. Vol. 3: *Companions and Competitors.* New York: Doubleday, 2001.

Meier, *Matthew.* • Meier, John P. *Matthew.* New Testament Message: A Biblical-Theological Commentary, 3. Wilmington, DE: Michael Glazier, 1980.

Meier, "Oaths." • Meier, John P. "Did the Historical Jesus Prohibit All Oaths? Part 1." *JSHJ* 5 (2, 2007): 175-204.

Meier, "Present State." • Meier, John P. "The Present State of the 'Third Quest' for the Historical Jesus: Loss and Gain." *Bib* 80 (4, 1999): 459-87.

Meier, "Project." • Meier, John P. "The Quest for the Historical Jesus as a Truly Historical Project." *Grail* 12 (3, 1996): 43-52.

Meier, "Questions." • Meier, John P. "Two Disputed Questions in Matt 28:16-20." *JBL* 96 (1977): 407-24.

Meier, "Reflections." • Meier, John P. "Reflections on Jesus-of-History Research Today." 84-107 in *Jesus' Jewishness: Exploring the Place of Jesus within Early Judaism.* Ed. James H. Charlesworth. New York: The American Interfaith Institute, Crossroad Publishing Company, 1991.

Meier, "Samaritans." • Meier, John P. "The Historical Jesus and the Historical Samaritans: What Can Be Said?" *Bib* 81 (2, 2000): 202-32.

Meier, "Testimonium." • Meier, John P. "The Testimonium, Evidence for Jesus Outside the Bible." *BRev* 7 (3, 1991): 20-25, 45.

Meiser, "Gattung." • Meiser, Martin. "Gattung, Adressaten und Intention von Philos 'In Flaccum.'" *JSJ* 30 (4, 1999): 418-430.

Meister, "Herodotus." • Meister, Klaus. "Herodotus." 6:265-271 in *Brill's New Pauly.*

Meister, "Historiography: Greece." • Meister, Klaus. "Historiography: Greece." 6:418-421 in *Brill's New Pauly.*

Meister, "Theopompus." • Meister, Klaus. "Theopompus." 1505-6 in *OCD.*

Mendels, "Five Empires." • Mendels, Doron. "The Five Empires: A Note on a Propagandistic *Topos.*" *AJP* 102 (3, 1981): 330-37.

Mendels, "History." • Mendels, Doron. "'Creative History' in the Hellenistic Near East in the Third and Second Centuries BCE: The Jewish Case." *JSP* 2 (1988): 13-20.

Menzies, *Development.* • Menzies, Robert P. *The Development of Early Christian Pneumatology with Special Reference to Luke-Acts.* JSNTSup 54. Sheffield: Sheffield Academic Press, 1991.

Merkelbach, "Novel and Aretalogy." • Merkelbach, Reinhold. "Novel and Aretalogy." 283-295 in *The Search for the Ancient Novel.* Ed. James Tatum. Baltimore, London: The Johns Hopkins University Press, 1994.

Merkle, "True Story." • Merkle, Stefan. "Telling the True Story of the Trojan War: The Eyewitness Account of Dictys of Crete." 183-196 in *The Search for the Ancient Novel.* Ed. James Tatum. Baltimore, London: The Johns Hopkins University Press, 1994.

Mettinger, "Rising." • Mettinger, Tryggve N. D. "The 'Dying and Rising God'. A Survey of Research from Frazer to the Present Day." *SEÅ* 63 (1998): 111-23.

Metzger, "Considerations." • Metzger, Bruce M. "Considerations of Methodology in the Study of the Mystery Religions and Early Christianity." *HTR* 48 (1, Jan. 1955): 1-20.

Metzger, *Outline.* • Metzger, Ernest. *A New Outline of the Roman Civil Trial.* Oxford: Clarendon, 1997.

Metzger, "Papyri." • Metzger, Bruce M. "Recently Published Greek Papyri of the NT." *BA* 10 (2, May 1947): 25-44.

Metzger, *Textual Commentary.* • Metzger, Bruce M. *A Textual Commentary on the Greek New Testament.* Corrected edition. New York: United Bible Societies, 1975.

Meyer, "Deed." • Meyer, Ben F. "Appointed Deed, Appointed Doer: Jesus and the Scriptures." 155-76 in *Authenticating the Activities of Jesus.* Ed. Bruce Chilton and Craig A. Evans. NTTS 28.2. Leiden: Brill, 1999.

Meyer, "Expiation Motif." • Meyer, Ben F. "The Expiation Motif in the Eucharistic Words: A Key to the History of Jesus?" 11-33 in *One Loaf, One Cup: Ecumenical Studies of 1 Cor 11 and Other Eucharistic Texts.* The Cambridge Conference on the Eucharist, August 1988. New Gospel Studies 6. Ed. Ben F. Meyer. Macon, GA: Mercer University Press, 1993.

Meyer, "Judgment." • Meyer, Ben F. "The Judgment and Salvation of Israel." 426-43 in *The Historical Jesus in Recent Research.* Ed. James D. G. Dunn and Scot McKnight. Winona Lake, IN: Eisenbrauns, 2005.

Meyer, "Ministry." • Meyer, Ben F. "Jesus' Ministry and Self-Understanding." 337-52 in *Studying the Historical Jesus: Evaluations of the State of Current Research.* NTTS 19. Ed. Bruce Chilton and Craig A. Evans. Leiden, New York, Cologne: E. J. Brill, 1994.

Meyer, "Mysteries." • Meyer, Marvin W. "Mysteries." 720-25 in *DNTB.*

Meyers, "Judaism and Christianity." • Meyers, Eric M. "Early Judaism and Christianity in the Light of Archaeology." *BA* 51 (1988): 69-79.

Meyers, "Regionalism." • Meyers, Eric M. "Galilean Regionalism as a Factor in Historical Reconstruction." *BASOR* 221 (February 1976): 93-101.

Meyers and Meyers, "Sepphoris." • Meyers, Carol L., and Eric M. Meyers. "Sepphoris." 4:527-536 in *OEANE.*

Meyers, Netzer and Meyers, "Byt-mydwt." • Meyers, Eric M., Ehud Netzer and Carol L. Meyers. "Byt-mydwt snhsp b'qrwpwlys sl sypwry wbmrkzw psyps mpw'r." *Qad* 21 (1988): 87-92.

Meyers, Netzer and Meyers, "Ornament." • Meyers, Eric M., Ehud Netzer and Carol L. Meyers. "Sepphoris 'Ornament of All Galilee.'" *BA* 49 (1986): 4-19.

Meyers and Strange, Archaeology. • Meyers, Eric M., and James F. Strange. *Archaeology, the Rabbis, & Early Christianity.* Nashville: Abingdon, 1981.

Meyers et al., "Tomb." • Meyers, Eric M., et al., "The Talpiot 'Jesus' Family Tomb." *NEA* 69 (3-4, 2006): 116-37.

Michaels, "Paul in Tradition." • Michaels, J. Ramsey. "Paul in Early Church Tradition." 692-95 in *DPL.*

Michaels, Servant. • Michaels, J. Ramsey. *Servant and Son: Jesus in Parable and Gospel.* Atlanta: John Knox, 1981.

Michel, Maître. • Michel, A. *Le Maître de Justice d'après les documents de la Mer Morte, la littérature apocryphe et rabbinique.* Avignon, Maison Aubanel Père, 1954.

Michel, Prophet und Märtyrer. • Michel, Otto. *Prophet und Märtyrer.* Gütersloh: Verlag Bertelsmann, 1932.

Milik, Discovery. • Milik, J. T. *Ten Years of Discovery in the Wildernes of Judaea.* London: SCM, 1959.

Milik, "Écrits." • Milik, J. T. "Écrits préesséniens de Qumrân: d'Hénoch à Amram." 91-106 in *Qumrân: Sa piété, sa théologie et son milieu.* Ed. M. Delcor. BETL 46. Paris: Gembloux, Leuven University Press, 1978.

Milikowsky, "Gehenna." • Milikowsky, Chaim. "Which Gehenna? Retribution and Eschatology in the Synoptic Gospels and in Early Jewish Texts." *NTS* 34 (1988): 238-49.

Millar, Piltdown Men. • Millar, Ronald. *The Piltdown Men.* New York: Ballantine, 1972.

Millard, "Literacy." • Millard, Alan. "Literacy in the Time of Jesus." *BAR* 29 (4, 2003): 36-45.

Millard, Reading and Writing. • Millard, Alan. *Reading and Writing in the Time of Jesus.* The Biblical Seminar 69. Sheffield: Sheffield Academic Press, 2000.

Millard, Hoffmeier, and Baker, Historiography in Context. • Millard, Alan R., James K. Hoffmeier, and David W. Baker, eds. *Faith, Tradition, and History: Old Testament Historiography in Its Near Eastern Context.* Winona Lake, IN: Eisenbrauns, 1994.

Miller, "City." • Miller, Stuart S. "Sepphoris, the Well Remembered City." *BA* 55 (2, 1992): 74-83.

Miller, "Introduction." • Miller, Walter. "Introduction." 1:vii-xiii in Xenophon's *Cyropaedia.* 2 vols. Trans. Walter Miller. LCL. Cambridge: Harvard, 1914.

Miller, Jesus Seminar. • Miller, Robert J. *The Jesus Seminar and Its Critics.* Santa Rosa, CA: Polebridge, 1999.

Miller, "Josephus on Cities." • Miller, S. S. "Josephus on the Cities of Galilee: Factions, Rivalries and Alliances in the First Jewish Revolt." *Historia* 50 (4, 2001): 453-67.

Miller, "Orthodoxy." • Miller, Robert J. "The Jesus of Orthodoxy and the Jesuses of the Gospels: A Critique of Luke Timothy Johnson's *The Real Jesus*." *JSNT* 68 (1997): 101-20.

Miller, "Prophets." • Miller, Robert J. "The Rejection of the Prophets in Q." *JBL* 107 (1988): 225-40.

Miller and Yamamori, Pentecostalism. • Miller, Donald E., and Tetsunao Yamamori. *Global Pentecostalism: The New Face of Christian Social Engagement.* Berkeley: University of California Press, 2007.

Milligan, Thessalonians. • Milligan, George. *St Paul's Epistles to the Thessalonians: The Greek Text with Introduction and Notes.* London: Macmillan & Company, 1908.

Mills, Christ and Gospels. • Mills, Watson E. *Index to Periodical Literature on Christ and the Gospels.* NT Tools and Studies 27. Leiden: Brill, 1998.

Minde, "Absonderung." • Minde, Hans-Jürgen van der. "Die Absonderung der Frommen. Die Qumrangemeinschaft als Heiligtum Gottes." *BL* 61 (1988): 190-97.

Minear, Commands. • Minear, Paul S. *Commands of Christ.* Nashville: Abingdon, 1972.

Minear, Hope. • Minear, Paul S. *Christian Hope and the Second Coming.* Philadelphia: Westminster, 1954.

Mitchell, "Atonement." • Mitchell, David C. "Messiah ben Joseph: A Sacrifice of Atonement for Israel." *Review of Rabbinic Judaism* 10 (1, 2007): 77-94.

Moessner, "Arrangement." • Moessner, David P. "Dionysius's Narrative 'Arrangement' (οἰκονομία) as the Hermeneutical Key to Luke's Re-Vision of the 'Many.'" 149-64 in *Paul, Luke and the Graeco-Roman World.* Ed. Alf Christophersen, Carsten Claussen, Jörg Frey and Bruce Longenecker. JSNTSup 217. Sheffield: Sheffield Academic Press, 2002; London: T. & T. Clark, 2003.

Moessner, "Poetics." • Moessner, David P. "The Appeal and Power of Poetics (Luke 1:1-4): Luke's Superior Credentials (παρηκολουθηκότι), Narrative Sequence (καθεξῆς), and Firmness of Understanding (ἡ ἀσφάλεια) for the Reader." 84-123 in *Jesus and the Heritage of Israel: Luke's Narrative Claim upon Israel's Legacy.* Ed. David P. Moessner. Vol. 1 in Luke the Interpreter of Israel, series ed. Moessner and David L. Tiede. Harrisburg, PA: Trinity Press International, 1999.

Moessner, "Prologues." • Moessner, David P. "The Lukan Prologues in the Light of Ancient Narrative Hermeneutics. Παρηκολουθηκότι and the Credentialed Author." 399-417 in *The Unity of Luke-Acts.* Ed. Joseph Verheyden. BETL 142. Leuven: Leuven University Press, 1999.

Moffatt, *1 Corinthians.* • Moffatt, James D. *The First Epistle of Paul to the Corinthians.* MNTC. London: Hodder & Stoughton, 1938.

Mohrlang, *Matthew and Paul.* • Mohrlang, Roger. *Matthew and Paul: A Comparison of Ethical Perspectives.* SNTSMS 48. Cambridge: Cambridge University, 1984.

Moles, "Cynics." • Moles, John L. "Cynics." 418-19 in *OCD.*

Moloney, "Jesus of History." • Moloney, Frank J. "The Fourth Gospel and the Jesus of History." *NTS* 46 (1, 2000): 42-58.

Moltmann, "Resurrection." • Moltmann, Jürgen. "The Resurrection of Christ and the New Earth." *CV* 49 (2, 2007): 141-49.

Momigliano, *Historiography.* • Momigliano, Arnaldo. *Essays in Ancient and Modern Historiography.* Middletown, CT: Wesleyan University Press, 1977; Oxford: Basil Blackwell, 1977.

Moniot, "Historiography." • Moniot, Henri. "Profile of a Historiography: Oral Tradition and Historical Research in Africa," 50-58 in *African Historiographies: What History for Which Africa?* Ed. Bogumil Jewsiewicki and David Newbury. SSAMD 12. Beverly Hills, London, New Delhi: Sage, 1986.

Montanari, "Hypomnema." • Montanari, Franco. "Hypomnema." 6:641-43 in *Brill's New Pauly.*

Montefiore, *Gospels.* • Montefiore, C. G. *The Synoptic Gospels.* 2 vols. Library of Biblical Studies. New York: Ktav, 1968; reprint of 1927 ed.

Montefiore and Loewe, *Anthology.* • Montefiore, C. G., and Herbert Loewe, editors and translators. *A Rabbinic Anthology.* New York: Schocken Books, 1974; reprint of London: Macmillan, 1938. New prolegomenon by Raphael Loewe, 1974.

Montiglio, "Wandering Philosophers." • Montiglio, Silvia. "Wandering philosophers in Classical Greece." *JHS* 120 (2000): 86-105.

Moo, *Romans.* • Moo, Douglas J. *The Epistle to the Romans.* Grand Rapids, Cambridge: Eerdmans, 1996.

Moore, "Introduction." • Moore, Clifford H. "Introduction: Life and Works of Tacitus." 1:vii-xiii in Tacitus. *The Histories.* 2 vols. Trans. Clifford H. Moore. LCL. London: Heinemann; Cambridge: Harvard, 1937, 1948.

Moore, *Judaism.* • Moore, George Foot. *Judaism in the First Centuries of the Christian Era.* 2 vols. New York: Schocken Books, 1971. Reprint from Cambridge: Harvard University Press, 1927.

Mor and Rappaport, *Bibliography.* • Mor, Menahem, and Uriel Rappaport. *Bibliography of Works on Jewish History in the Hellenistic and Roman Period, 1976-80.* Jerusalem: Zalman Shazar Center for the Furtherance of the Study of Jewish History, Historicity Society of Israel, 1982.

Morgan-Wynne, "Traditionsgrundlage." • Morgan-Wynne, John E. "2 Corinthians VIII.18f. and the Question of a Traditionsgrundlage for Acts." *JTS* 30 (1, 1979): 172-173.

Morgenstern, "Calendar." • Morgenstern, Julian. "The Calendar of the Book of Jubilees, Its Origin and Its Character." *VT* 5 (1, January 1955): 34-76.

Morris, *Apocalyptic.* • Morris, Leon. *Apocalyptic.* Grand Rapids: Eerdmans, 1972.

Morris, John. • Morris, Leon. *The Gospel According to John: The English Text with Introduction, Exposition and Notes.* NICNT. Grand Rapids: Eerdmans, 1971.

Morris, Luke. • Morris, Leon. *The Gospel According to St. Luke.* Grand Rapids: Eerdmans, 1974.

Morris, Romans. • Morris, Leon. *The Epistle to the Romans.* Grand Rapids: Eerdmans; Leicester, England: Inter-Varsity Press, 1988.

Morris, Thessalonians. • Morris, Leon. *The First and Second Epistles to the Thessalonians.* NICNT. Grand Rapids: Eerdmans, 1959.

Morton and MacGregor, Structure. • Morton, A. Q., and G. H. C. MacGregor. *The Structure of Luke and Acts.* New York: Harper & Row, Publishers, 1964.

Mosley, "Reporting." • Mosley, A. W. "Historical Reporting in the Ancient World." *NTS* 12 (1, Oct. 1965): 10-26.

Moulder, "Background." • Moulder, W. J. "The Old Testament Background and the Interpretation of Mark X.45." *NTS* 24 (1977): 120-27.

Moulder, "Enemies." • Moulder, James. "Who are my enemies? An exploration of the semantic background of Christ's command." *JTSA* 25 (1978): 41-49.

Moule, Birth. • Moule, C. F. D. *The Birth of the New Testament.* New York: Harper & Row, 1962.

Moule, "Factor." • Moule, C. F. D. "A Neglected Factor in the Interpretation of Johannine Eschatology." 155-60 in *Studies in John: Presented to Professor Dr. J. N. Sevenster on the Occasion of His Seventieth Birthday.* Ed. W. C. van Unnik. NovTSup 24. Leiden: E. J. Brill, 1970.

Moule, Mark. • Moule, C. F. D. *The Gospel According to Mark.* Cambridge: Cambridge University Press, 1965.

Mounce, "Eschatology." • Mounce, Robert H. "Pauline Eschatology and the Apocalypse." *EvQ* 46 (1974): 164-66.

Moxnes, "Construction." • Moxnes, Halvor. "The Construction of Galilee as a Place for the Historical Jesus — Part I." *BTB* 31 (1, 2001): 26-37.

Moyise, "Jesus and gospels." • Moyise, Steve. "Jesus, history and the gospels." *AcT* 23 (2, 2003): 167-82.

Moyise, Old Testament. • Moyise, Steve. *The Old Testament in the Book of Revelation.* JSNTSup 115. Sheffield: Sheffield Academic Press, 1995.

Mueller, "Divorce Texts." • Mueller, James R. "The Temple Scroll and the Gospel Divorce Texts." *RevQ* 10 (1980): 247-56.

Müller, "Daphnis." • Müller, Hans-Peter. "Daphnis — ein Doppelgänger des Gottes Adonis." *ZDPV* 116 (1, 2000): 26-41.

Müller, Traditionsprozess. • Müller, Paul-Gerhard. *Der Traditionsprozess im Neuen Testament: Kommunikationsanalytische Studien zur Versprachlichung des Jesusphänomens.* Freiburg: Herder, 1982.

Mullin, History. • Mullin, Robert Bruce. *A Short World History of Christianity.* Louisville: Westminster John Knox, 2008.

Munck, Acts. • Munck, Johannes. *The Acts of the Apostles.* Revised by W. F. Albright and C. S. Mann. AB 31. Garden City, NY: Doubleday & Company, 1967.

Muñoz Léon, "Discípulo." • Muñoz Léon, D. "¿Es el Apóstol Juan el Discípulo Amado? Razones en contra y en pro del carácter apostólico de la tradición joánica." *EstBib* 45 (3-4, 1987): 403-92.

Muñoz Léon, "Juan." • Muñoz Léon, D. "Juan el presbítero y el discípulo amado. Consideraciones críticas sobre la opinión de M. Hengel en sa libro 'La cuestión joánica.'" *EstBib* 48 (4, 1990): 543-63.

Murgatroyd, "Ending." • Murgatroyd, P. "The Ending of Apuleius' *Metamorphoses.*" *CQ* 54 (1, 2004): 319-321.

Murphy, "Disposition." • Murphy, Catherine M. "The Disposition of Wealth in the *Damascus Document* Tradition." *RevQ* 19 (73, 1999): 83-129.

Murphy, "Idolatry." • Murphy, Frederick J. "Retelling the Bible: Idolatry in Pseudo-Philo." *JBL* 107 (2, 1988): 275-87.

Murphy-O'Connor, "Judah." • Murphy-O'Connor, Jerome. "Judah the Essene and the Teacher of Righteousness." *RevQ* 10 (4, 1981): 579-585.

Murphy-O'Connor, "Mission." • Murphy-O'Connor, Jerome. "A First-Century Jewish Mission to Gentiles?" *Pacifica* 5 (1, 1992): 32-42.

Murray, "Conflator." • Murray, A. Gregory. "Mark the Conflator." *DRev* 102 (1984): 157-62.

Mussies, "Greek." • Mussies, G. "Greek in Palestine and the Diaspora." 1040-64 in *JPFC*.

Mussies, "Vehicle." • Mussies, G. "Greek as the Vehicle of Early Christianity." *NTS* 29 (1983): 356-69.

Mylonas, *Eleusis.* • Mylonas, George E. *Eleusis and the Eleusinian Mysteries.* Princeton: Princeton University Press, 1961.

Nagy, "Prologue." • Nagy, Gregory. "The Sign of the Hero: A Prologue." xi-xxxv in *Flavius Philostratus: Heroikos.* Trans., ed. Jennifer K. Berenson Maclean, and Ellen Bradshaw Aitken. SBLWGRW 1 (volume editor: Jackson P. Hershbell). Atlanta: Society of Biblical Literature, 2001.

Najman, "Wilderness." • Najman, Hindy. "Towards a Study of the Uses of the Concept of Wilderness in Ancient Judaism." *DSD* 13 (1, 2006): 99-113.

Nanos, *Mystery.* • Nanos, Mark D. *The Mystery of Romans: The Jewish Context of Paul's Letter.* Minneapolis: Fortress, 1996.

Neikiprowetzky, "Sabbat." • Neikiprowetzky, V. "Le Sabbat et les armes dans l'histoire ancienne d'Israël." *REJ* 159 (1-2, 2000): 1-17.

Neil, *Acts.* • Neil, William. *The Acts of the Apostles.* NCBC. London: Marshall, Morgan & Scott; Grand Rapids: Eerdmans, 1973.

Neil, "Sayings." • Neil, William. "Five Hard Sayings of Jesus." 157-71 in *Biblical Studies: Essays in Honor of William Barclay.* Philadelphia: Westminster, 1976.

Neil, *Thessalonians.* • Neil, William. *The Epistle of Paul to the Thessalonians.* MNTC. London: Hodder & Stoughton, 1950.

Neudecker, "Neighbor." • Neudecker, Reinhard. "'And You Shall Love Your Neighbor as Yourself — I Am the Lord' (Lev 19,18) in Jewish Interpretation." *Bib* 73 (1992): 496-517.

Neufeld, *Recovering Jesus.* • Neufeld, Thomas R. Yoder. *Recovering Jesus: The Witness of the New Testament.* Grand Rapids: Brazos, 2007.

Neusner, *Beginning.* • Neusner, Jacob. *Judaism in the Beginning of Christianity.* Philadelphia: Fortress, 1984.

Neusner, *Biography.* • Neusner, Jacob. *In Search of Talmudic Biography: The Problem of the Attributed Saying.* BJS 70. Chico, CA: Scholars Press, 1984.

Neusner, "Cambiavalute." • Neusner, Jacob. "I cambiavalute ne tempio: la spiegazione della Mishnah." *RivB* 35 (4, 1987): 485-89.

Neusner, "Cleanse." • Neusner, Jacob. "'First Cleanse the Inside.'" *NTS* 22 (1976): 486-95.

Neusner, *Crisis.* • Neusner, Jacob. *First-Century Judaism in Crisis: Yohanan ben Zakkai and the Renaissance of Torah.* Nashville: Abingdon, 1975.

Neusner, "Death-Scenes." • Neusner, Jacob. "Death-Scenes and Farewell Stories: An Aspect of the Master-Disciple Relationship in Mark and in Some Talmudic Tales." *HTR* 79 (1986): 187-96.

Neusner, "Foreword." • Neusner, Jacob. "Foreword." xxv-xlvi in *Memory and Manuscript: Oral Tradition and Written Transmission in Rabbinic Judaism and Early Christianity,* with *Tradition and Transmission in Early Christianity.* By Birger Gerhardsson. Grand Rapids: Eerdmans, 1998.

Neusner, "Kingdom." • Neusner, Jacob. "The Kingdom of Heaven in Kindred Systems, Judaic and Christian." *BBR* 15 (2, 2005): 279-305.

Neusner, *Legend.* • Neusner, Jacob. *Development of a Legend: Studies on the Traditions Concerning Yohanan ben Zakkai.* Studia Post-Biblica 16. Leiden: E. J. Brill, 1970.

Neusner, *New Testament.* • Neusner, Jacob. *Rabbinic Literature & the New Testament: What We Cannot Show, We Do Not Know.* Valley Forge, PA: Trinity Press International, 1994.

Neusner, *Politics to Piety*. • Neusner, Jacob. *From Politics to Piety: The Emergence of Pharisaic Judaism*. 2nd ed. New York: Ktav, 1979.

Neusner, *Rabbi*. • Neusner, Jacob. *A Rabbi Talks with Jesus*. Montreal: McGill-Queen's University Press, 2000.

Neusner, "Repentance." • Neusner, Jacob. "Sin, Repentance, Atonement and Resurrection. The Perspective of Rabbinic Theology on the Views of James 1–2 and Paul in Romans 3–4." *ASDE* 18 (2, 2001): 409-31.

Neusner, *Sat*. • Neusner, Jacob. *There We Sat Down: Talmudic Judaism in the Making*. Nashville: Abingdon, 1972.

Neusner, "Testimony." • Neusner, Jacob. "'By the Testimony of Two Witnesses' in the Damascus Document IX, 17-22 and in Pharisaic-Rabbinic Law." *RevQ* 8 (30/2, March 1973): 197-217.

Newell, "Suicide Accounts." • Newell, Raymond R. "The Forms and Historical Value of Josephus' Suicide Accounts." 278-94 in *Josephus, the Bible, and History*. Ed. Louis H. Feldman and Gohei Hata. Detroit: Wayne State University Press, 1989.

Newman, "Parables." • Newman, Robert C. "Rabbinic Parables." 909-911 in DNTB.

Neyrey, "Shame of Cross." • Neyrey, Jerome H. "'Despising the Shame of the Cross': Honor and Shame in the Johannine Passion Narrative." *Semeia* 68 (1994): 113-37.

Nickelsburg, "Genre." • Nickelsburg, George W. E., Jr. "The Genre and Function of the Markan Passion Narrative." *HTR* 73 (1980): 153-84.

Niehoff, "Two Examples." • Niehoff, Maren R. "Two Examples of Josephus' Narrative Technique in His 'Rewritten Bible.'" *JSJ* 27 (1, 1996): 31-45.

Nilsson, *Piety*. • Nilsson, Martin Persson. *Greek Piety*. Trans. Herbert Jennings Rose. Oxford: Clarendon Press, 1948.

Nineham, *Mark*. • Nineham, D. E. *Saint Mark*. Pelican NT Commentaries. Philadelphia: Westminster; London: SCM, 1977.

Niskanen, "Kingdoms." • Niskanen, Paul. "Kingdoms, Dominions, and the Reign of God." *BibT* 42 (6, 2004): 343-348.

Noack, "Qumran and Jubilees." • Noack, Bent. "Qumran and the Book of Jubilees." *SEÅ* 22-23 (1957-1958): 119-207.

Nock, *Conversion*. • Nock, Arthur Darby. *Conversion: The Old and the New in Religion from Alexander the Great to Augustine of Hippo*. Oxford: Clarendon Press, 1933.

Nock, *Essays*. • Nock, Arthur Darby. *Essays on Religion and the Ancient World I and II*. Selected and ed. by Zeph Stewart. Cambridge: Harvard University Press, 1972.

Nock, *Gentile Christianity*. • Nock, Arthur Darby. *Early Gentile Christianity and Its Hellenistic Background*. New York: Harper & Row, Publishers, 1964.

Nock, "Vocabulary." • Nock, Arthur Darby. "The Vocabulary of the New Testament." *JBL* 52 (1933): 131-39.

North, "War." • North, Robert. "'Kittim' War or 'Sectaries' Liturgy?" *Bib* 39 (1958): 84-93.

Nortjé, "Traditions." • Nortjé, S. J. "John the Baptist and the resurrection traditions in the Gospels." *Neot* 23 (1989): 349-58.

Nowell, "Order." • Nowell, Irene. "Canonical Order." *BibT* 26 (1988): 220-21.

Nun, "Ports." • Nun, Mendel. "Ports of Galilee." *BAR* 25 (4, 1999): 18-31, 64.

Oakman, "Peasant." • Oakman, Douglas E. "Was Jesus a Peasant? Implications for Reading the Samaritan Story." *BTB* 22 (1992): 117-25.

O'Brien, *Colossians*. • O'Brien, Peter T. *Colossians, Philemon*. WBC 44. Waco, TX: Word, 1982.

O'Collins and Kendall, "Joseph of Arimathea." • O'Collins, Gerald O., and Daniel Kendall. "Did Joseph of Arimathea Exist?" *Biblica* 75 (1994): 235-41.

O'Day, "John." • O'Day, Gail R. "The Gospel of John: Introduction, Commentary, and Reflections." 9:491-865 in *The New Interpreter's Bible*. 12 vols. Ed. Leander E. Keck. Nashville: Abingdon, 1995.

Odeberg, *Pharisaism*. • Odeberg, Hugo. *Pharisaism and Christianity.* Tr. J. M. Moe. St. Louis: Concordia, 1964. Swedish ed., 1943.

Oden and Hall, *Mark*. • *Mark*. Vol. 2 in Ancient Christian Commentary on Scripture: NT. Ed. Thomas C. Oden and Christopher A. Hall. Downers Grove: IVP, 1998.

Oesterley, *Liturgy*. • Oesterley, William Oscar Emil. *The Jewish Background of the Christian Liturgy.* Oxford: Clarendon, 1925.

Okoye, "Seminar." • Okoye, James C. "Jesus and the Jesus Seminar." *New Theology Review* 20 (2, 2007): 27-37.

Olbricht, "Delivery and Memory." • Olbricht, Thomas H. "Delivery and Memory." 159-67 in *Handbook of Classical Rhetoric in the Hellenistic Period 330 B.C.-A.D. 400.* Ed. Stanley E. Porter. Leiden: Brill, 1997.

Oldfather, "Introduction to Diodorus." • Oldfather, C. H. "Introduction" to Diodorus Siculus. 1:vii-xxvii in Diodorus Siculus. *The Library of History.* 12 vols. Trans. C. H. Oldfather, Charles L. Sherman, C. Bradford Welles, Russel M. Geer, and Francis R. Walton. LCL. Cambridge: Harvard University Press (Heinemann, in UK), 1933-1967.

Oldfather, "Introduction to Epictetus." • Oldfather, C. H. "Introduction" to Epictetus. *Epictetus: The Discourse as Reported by Arrian, the Manual, and Fragments.* 2 vols. Trans. By W. A. Oldfather. LCL. London: William Heinemann; New York: G. P. Putnam's Sons, 1926-1928.

Olmstead, *History*. • Olmstead, A. T. *History of the Persian Empire.* Chicago: Phoenix Books, The University of Chicago Press, 1959.

O'Neal, "Delation." • O'Neal, William J. "Delation in the Early Empire." *CBull* 55 (2, 1978): 24-28.

O'Neill, "Prayer." • O'Neill, J. C. "The Lord's Prayer." *JSNT* 51 (1993): 3-25.

O'Neill, *Theology*. • O'Neill, J. C. *The Theology of Acts in Its Historical Setting.* 2nd ed. London: S.P.C.K., 1970.

Orlov, "Name." • Orlov, Andrei. "The Origin of the Name 'Metatron' and the Text of 2 (Slavonic Apocalypse of) Enoch." *JSP* 21 (2000): 19-26.

O'Rourke, "Law." • O'Rourke, John J. "Roman Law and the Early Church." Pp. 165-86 in *The Catacombs and the Colosseum: The Roman Empire as the Setting of Primitive Christianity.* Ed. Stephen Benko and John J. O'Rourke. Valley Forge, PA: Judson, 1971.

Osborne, "Farmers." • Osborne, Robin. "Farmers: Greece." 5:354-356 in *Brill's New Pauly.*

Osborne, "History." • Osborne, Grant R. "History and Theology in the Synoptic Gospels." *TJ* 24 (1, 2003): 5-22.

Osborne, "Redaction Criticism." • Osborne, Grant R. "Redaction Criticism." 662-69 in *DJG.*

Osborne, "Resurrection." • Osborne, Grant R. "Resurrection." 931-36 in *DNTB.*

Osiek, "Jesus and Galilee." • Osiek, Carolyn. "Jesus and Galilee." *BibT* 34 (3, 1996): 153-59.

Ostling, "Jesus." • Ostling, Richard N. "Jesus Christ, Plain and Simple." *Time* (Jan. 10, 1994): 32-33.

Otto, *Dionysus*. • Otto, Walter F. *Dionysus: Myth and Cult.* Trans. Robert B. Palmer. Bloomington, IN: Indiana University Press, 1965.

Overman, "Archaeology." • Overman, John Andrew. "Recent Advances in the Archaeology of the Galilee in the Roman Period." *CurBS* 1 (1993): 35-57.

Overman, *Crisis*. • Overman, John Andrew. *Church and Community in Crisis: The Gospel According to Matthew.* NTIC. Valley Forge: Trinity Press International, 1996.

Overman, "Deciphering." • Overman, John Andrew. "Deciphering the Origins of Christianity." Review of *A Myth of Innocence: Mark and Christian Origins,* by Burton L. Mack. *Int* 44 (April 1990): 193-95.

Overman, *Gospel*. • Overman, John Andrew. *Matthew's Gospel and Formative Judaism: The Social World of the Matthean Community.* Minneapolis: Fortress, 1990.

Packer, *Acts*. • Packer, J. W. *Acts of the Apostles.* CBC. Cambridge: University Press, 1966.

Pagels, "Mystery." • Pagels, Elaine H. "'The Mystery of the Resurrection': A Gnostic Reading of I Corinthians 15." *JBL* 93 (2, June 1974): 276-88.

Paget, "Observations." • Paget, James Carleton. "Some Observations on Josephus and Christianity." *JTS* 52 (2, 2001): 539-624.

Paget, "Proselytism." • Paget, James Carleton. "Jewish Proselytism at the Time of Christian Origins: Chimera or Reality?" *JSNT* 62 (1996): 65-103.

Paget, "Quests." • Paget, James Carleton. "Quests for the historical Jesus." 138-55 in *The Cambridge Companion to Jesus*. Ed. Markus Bockmuehl. Cambridge: Cambridge University, 2001.

Pahlitzsch, "Magdala." • Pahlitzsch, Johannes. "Magdala." 8:126-27 in *Brill's New Pauly*.

Palmer, "Monograph." • Palmer, Darryl W. "Acts and the Ancient Historical Monograph." 1-29 in *The Book of Acts in Its Ancient Literary Setting*. Ed. Bruce W. Winter and Andrew D. Clarke. Vol. 1 in The Book of Acts in Its First Century Setting. Grand Rapids: Eerdmans; Carlisle: Paternoster, 1993.

Palmer, "Vow." • Palmer, D. "Defining a Vow of Abstinence." *Colloq* 5 (1973): 38-41.

Pals, *Lives*. • Pals, Daniel L. *The Victorian "Lives" of Jesus*. TUMSR 7. San Antonio, TX: Trinity University Press, 1982.

Pao, *Isaianic Exodus*. • Pao, David W. *Acts and the Isaianic New Exodus*. Grand Rapids: Baker, 2002. Originally in WUNT Series 2 number 130. Tübingen: J. C. B. Mohr (Paul Siebeck), 2000.

Papone, "Violenza." • Papone, Paolo. "Il regno dei cieli soffre violenza? (Mt 11,12)." *RivB* 38 (1990): 375-76.

Parsons, *Acts*. • Parsons, Mikeal C. *Acts*. Paideia Commentaries on the New Testament. Grand Rapids: Baker Academic, 2008.

Parsons, *Luke*. • Parsons, Mikeal C. *Luke: Storyteller, Interpreter, Evangelist*. Peabody: Hendrickson, 2007.

Parsons, "Progymnasmata." • Parsons, Mikeal C. "Luke and the *Progymnasmata*: A Preliminary Investigation into the Preliminary Exercises." 43-63 in *Contextualizing Acts: Lukan Narrative and Greco-Roman Discourse*. Ed. Todd Penner and Caroline Vander Stichele. SBLSymS 20. Atlanta: Society of Biblical Literature, 2003.

Parsons, "Unity: Rethinking." • Parsons, Mikeal C. "The Unity of Luke-Acts: Rethinking the *Opinio Communio*." 29-53 in *With Steadfast Purpose: Essays on Acts in Honor of Henry Jackson Flanders Jr*. Ed. N. H. Keathley. Waco, TX: Baylor University Press, 1990.

Paschke, "Namen." • Paschke, Boris A. "*Nomen est omen*: Warum der gekreuzigte Jesus wohl auch unter Anspielung auf seinen Namen verspottet wurde." *NovT* 49 (4, 2007): 313-27.

Pastor, "Strata." • Pastor, J. "Josephus and Social Strata: An Analysis of Social Attitudes." *Hen* 19 (3, 1997): 295-312.

Patte, *Matthew*. • Patte, Daniel. *The Gospel According to Matthew: A Structural Commentary on Matthew's Faith*. Philadelphia: Fortress, 1987.

Patterson, *God of Jesus*. • Patterson, Stephen J. *The God of Jesus: The Historical Jesus & the Search for Meaning*. Harrisburg, PA: Trinity Press International, 1998.

Paul, "Classifications." • Paul, S. M. "Classifications of Wine in Mesopotamian and Rabbinic Sources." *IEJ* 25 (1975): 42-45.

Payne, *Appearing*. • Payne, J. Barton. *The Imminent Appearing of Christ*. Grand Rapids: Eerdmans, 1962.

Payne, "Authenticity of Parables." • Payne, Philip Barton. "The Authenticity of the Parables of Jesus." 2:329-44 in *Gospel Perspectives: Studies of History and Tradition in the Four Gospels*. 6 vols. Ed. R. T. France, David Wenham, and Craig Blomberg. Sheffield: JSOT Press, University of Sheffield, 1981.

Payne, "Midrash and History." • Payne, Philip Barton. "Midrash and History in the Gospels with Special Reference to R. H. Gundry's *Matthew*." 3:177-215 in *GosPersp*. Vol. 3: *Studies in Midrash and Historiography*. Ed. R. T. France and David Wenham. Sheffield: JSOT Press, 1983.

Payne, "Sower." • Payne, Philip Barton. "The Authenticity of the Parable of the Sower and Its Interpretation." 1:163-207 in *Gospel Perspectives: Studies of History and Tradition in the Four Gospels*. 6

vols. Ed. R. T. France, David Wenham, and Craig Blomberg. Sheffield: JSOT Press, University of Sheffield, 1980.

Peachey, "Kinneret Boat." • Peachey, Claire. "Model Building in Nautical Archaeology. The Kinneret Boat." *BA* 53 (1, 1990): 46-53.

Pearl, Theology. • Pearl, Chaim. *Theology in Rabbinic Stories.* Peabody, MA: Hendrickson, 1997.

Pearson, "Exposé." • Pearson, Birger A. "An Exposé of the Jesus Seminar." *Di* 37 (1, 1998): 28-35.

Pearson, Terminology. • Pearson, Birger A. *The Pneumatikos-Psychikos Terminology in 1 Corinthians: A Study in the Theology of the Corinthian Opponents of Paul and Its Relation to Gnosticism.* SBLDS 12. Missoula, MT: Scholars Press, 1973.

Pelikan, "Sees." • Pelikan, Jaroslav. "The Two Sees of Peter." 57-73 in *The Shaping of Christianity in the Second and Third Centuries.* Ed. E. P. Sanders. Philadelphia: Fortress. Vol. 1 in *Jewish and Christian Self-Definition.* 3 vols. Philadelphia: Fortress, 1980-1982.

Pelling, "Historiography." • Pelling, C. B. R. "Historiography, Roman." 716-17 in *OCD.*

Penner, "Discourse." • Penner, Todd. "Civilizing Discourse: Acts, Declamation, and the Rhetoric of the *Polis*." 65-104 in *Contextualizing Acts: Lukan Narrative and Greco-Roman Discourse.* Ed. Todd Penner and Caroline Vander Stichele. SBLSymS 20. Atlanta: Society of Biblical Literature, 2003.

Penner, Praise. • Penner, Todd. *In Praise of Christian Origins: Stephen and the Hellenists in Lukan Apologetic Historiography.* Foreword by David L. Balch. New York, London: T&T Clark International, 2004.

Perdue, "Death." • Perdue, Leo G. "The Death of the Sage and Moral Exhortation: From Ancient Near Eastern Instructions to Greco-Roman Paraenesis." *Semeia* 50 (1990): 81-109.

Perkins, Introduction to Gospels. • Perkins, Pheme. *Introduction to the Synoptic Gospels.* Grand Rapids: Eerdmans, 2007.

Perkins, "Resurrection." • Perkins, Pheme. "The Resurrection of Jesus of Nazareth." 423-42 in *Studying the Historical Jesus: Evaluations of the State of Current Research.* NTTS 19. Ed. Bruce Chilton and Craig A. Evans. Leiden, New York, Cologne: E. J. Brill, 1994.

Perkins, "Scheintod." • Perkins, Judith B. "Fictive *Scheintod* and Christian Resurrection." *R&T* 13 (3-4, 2006): 396-418.

Perkins, "World." • Perkins, Judith B. "This World or Another? The Intertextuality of the Greek Romances, the Apocryphal Acts and Apuleius' *Metamorphoses*." 247-60 in *The Apocryphal Acts of the Apostles in Intertextual Perspectives.* Semeia 80. Ed. Robert F. Stoops. Atlanta: Scholars Press, 1997.

Perrin, Bultmann. • Perrin, Norman. *The Promise of Bultmann.* Philadelphia: Fortress, 1969.

Perrin, Language. • Perrin, Norman. *Jesus and the Language of the Kingdom: Symbol and Metaphor in New Testament Interpretation.* Philadelphia: Fortress, 1976.

Perrin, "Overlooked Evidence." • Perrin, Nicholas. "NHC II,2 and the Oxyrhynchus Fragments (P.Oxy. 1, 654, 655): Overlooked Evidence for a Syriac *Gospel of Thomas*." *VC* 58 (2004): 138-51.

Perrin, Teaching. • Perrin, Norman. *The Kingdom of God in the Teaching of Jesus.* Philadelphia: Westminster, 1963.

Perrin, Thomas and Tatian. • Perrin, Nicholas. *Thomas and Tatian: The Relationship between the Gospel of Thomas and the Diatessaron.* SBLAcBib 5. Atlanta: Society of Biblical Literature, 2002.

Perry, "Introduction." • Perry, Ben Edwin. "Introduction." Xi-cii in Babrius and Phaedrus. Trans. Ben Edwin Perry. LCL. Cambridge: Harvard University Press, 1965.

Perry, Sources. • Perry, Alfred Morris. *The Sources of Luke's Passion Narrative.* Chicago: University of Chicago Press, 1920.

Pervo, Dating Acts. • Pervo, Richard I. *Dating Acts: Between the Evangelists and the Apologists.* Santa Rosa, CA: Polebridge, 2006.

Pervo, "Direct Speech." • Pervo, Richard I. "Direct Speech in Acts and the Question of Genre." *JSNT* 28 (3, 2006): 285-307.

Pervo, "Egging." • Pervo, Richard I. "Egging on the Chickens: A Cowardly Response to Dennis MacDonald and Then Some." 43-56 in *The Apocryphal Acts of the Apostles in Intertextual Perspectives*. Semeia 80. Ed. Robert F. Stoops. Atlanta: Scholars Press, 1997.

Pervo, "Fabula." • Pervo, Richard I. "A Nihilist Fabula: Introducing *The Life of Aesop.*" 77-120 in *Ancient Fiction and Early Christian Narrative*. Ed. Ronald F. Hock, J. Bradley Chance and Judith Perkins. SBLSymS 6. Atlanta: Society of Biblical Literature, 1998.

Pervo, "Hard Act." • Pervo, Richard I. "A Hard Act to Follow: *The Acts of Paul* and the Canonical Acts." *JHC* 2 (2, 1995): 3-32.

Pervo, Profit. • Pervo, Richard I. *Profit with Delight: The Literary Genre of the Acts of the Apostles.* Philadelphia: Fortress, 1987.

Pesch, Apostelgeschichte. • Pesch, Rudolf. *Die Apostelgeschichte.* 2 vols. EKKNT 5. Zürich: Benziger Verlag, 1986.

Pesch, "Jerusalem." • Pesch, Rudolph. "The Gospel in Jerusalem: Mark 14:12-26 as the Oldest Tradition of the Early Church." 106-48 in *The Gospel and the Gospels*. Ed. Peter Stuhlmacher. Grand Rapids: Eerdmans, 1991.

Peters, Origins. • Peters, F. E. *Muhammad and the Origins of Islam.* Albany: State University of New York, 1994.

Petersen, Criticism. • Petersen, Norman R. *Literary Criticism for New Testament Critics.* Philadelphia: Fortress, 1978.

Petit, "Exemplaire." • Petit, Madeleine. "À propos d'une traversée exemplaire du désert du Sinaï selon Philon (*Hypothetica* VI, 2-3.8): texte biblique et apologétique concernant Moïse chez quelques écrivains juifs." *Sem* 26 (1976): 137-42.

Petrie, "Q." • Petrie, C. Stewart. "'Q' Is Only What You Make It." *NovT* 3 (1-2, Jan.-April 1959): 28-33.

Petuchowski, "Mystery." • Petuchowski, Jacob J. "Judaism as 'Mystery' — The Hidden Agenda?" *HUCA* 52 (1981): 141-52.

Pfandl, "Interpretations." • Pfandl, Gerhard. "Interpretations of the Kingdom of God in Daniel 2:44." *AUSS* 34 (2, 1996): 249-68.

Pfeiffer, Ras Shamra. • Pfeiffer, Charles F. *Ras Shamra and the Bible.* Grand Rapids: Baker, 1962.

Pfitzner, "School." • Pfitzner, Victor C. "The School of Jesus. Jesus-Traditions in Pauline Paraenesis." *LTJ* 13 (2-3, 1979): 22-36.

Philonenko, "Initiation." • Philonenko, Marc. "Initiation et mystère dans Joseph et Asénath." 147-53 in *Initiation: Contributions to the Theme of the Study-Conference of the International Association for the History of Religions,* held at Strasburg, September 17th to 22nd 1964. Ed. C. J. Bleeker. SHR 10. Leiden: E. J. Brill, 1965.

Philonenko, "Juda." • Philonenko, Marc. "Juda et Héraklès." *RHPR* 50 (1, 1970): 61-62.

Philonenko, "Mystère." • Philonenko, Marc. "Un Mystère Juif?" Pp. 65-75 in *Mystères et Syncrétismes.* EHRel 2. Ed. M. Philonenko and M. Simon. Paris: Librairie Orientaliste Paul Geuthner, 1975.

Piccirillo, "Machaerus." • Piccirillo, Michele. "Machaerus." 3:391-393 in *OEANE.*

Pikaza, "Jesús histórico." • Pikaza, Xabier. "El Jesús histórico: Nota bibliográfico-temática." *IgViv* 210 (2002): 85-90.

Pilch, Healing. • Pilch, John J. *Healing in the New Testament: Insights from Medical and Mediterranean Anthropology.* Minneapolis: Fortress, 2000.

Pilch, "Insights." • Pilch, John J. "Insights and models from medical anthropology for understanding the healing activity of the Historical Jesus." *HTS/TS* 51 (2, 1995): 314-37.

Pilch, "Naming." • Pilch, John J. "Naming the Nameless in the Bible." *BibT* 44 (5, 2006): 315-20.

Pilch, "Sickness." • Pilch, John J. "Sickness and Healing in Luke-Acts." 181-209 in *The Social World of Luke-Acts: Models for Interpretation.* Ed. Jerome H. Neyrey. Peabody, MA: Hendrickson, 1991.

Pileggi, "Bar-Kochva Letters." • Pileggi, David. "The Bar-Kochva Letters." *JerPersp* 4 (1, 1991): 9-11.

Pillai, *Interpretation.* • Pillai, C. A. Joachim. *Apostolic Interpretation of History: A Commentary on Acts 13:16-41.* Hicksville, NY: Exposition Press, 1980.

Pines, "Darkness." • Pines, Shlomo. "From Darkness into Great Light." *Imm* 4 (1974): 47-51.

Piovanelli, "Charismatic Authority." • Piovanelli, Pierluigi. "Jesus' Charismatic Authority: On the Historical Applicability of a Sociological Model." *JAAR* 73 (2, 2005): 395-427.

Pitre, *Tribulation.* • Pitre, Brant. *Jesus, the Tribulation, and the End of the Exile: Restoration Eschatology and the Origin of the Atonement.* Tübingen: Mohr Siebeck; Grand Rapids: Baker Academic, 2005.

Pixner, "Gate." • Pixner, Bargil. "The History of the 'Essene Gate' Area." *ZDPV* 105 (1989): 96-104, plates 8-16a.

Pixner, "Zion." • Pixner, Bargil. "Mount Zion, Jesus, and Archaeology." 309-22 in *Jesus and Archaeology.* Ed. James H. Charlesworth. Grand Rapids: Eerdmans, 2006.

Pixner, Chen, and Margalit, "Zion." • Pixner, Bargil, Doron Chen, and Shlomo Margalit. "Mount Zion: The 'Gate of the Essenes' Reexcavated." *ZDPV* 105 (1989): 85-95, plates 8-16a.

Plag, "Übernahme." • Plag, C. "Paulus und due *Gezera schawa:* Zur Übernahme rabbinischer Auslegungskunst." *Judaica* 50 (2-3, 1994): 135-40.

Plevnik, "Parousia." • Plevnik, Joseph. "The Parousia as Implications of Christ's Resurrection (An Exegesis of 1 Thes 4:13-18)." 199-277 in *Word and Spirit: Essays in Honor of David Michael Stanley, S.J., on His 60th Birthday.* Ed. Joseph Plevnik. Willowdale, ON: Regis College, 1975.

Plevnik, "1 Thess 5." • Plevnik, Joseph. "1 Thessalonians 5,1-11: Its Authenticity, Intention and Message." *Bib* 60 (1979): 71-90.

Plümacher, "Cicero und Lukas." • Plümacher, Eckhard. "Cicero und Lukas. Bemerkungen zu Stil und Zweck der historischen Monographie." 759-75 in *The Unity of Luke-Acts.* Ed. Joseph Verheyden. BETL 142. Leuven: Leuven University Press, 1999.

Plümacher, *Geschichte.* • Plümacher, Eckhard. *Geschichte und Geschichten: Aufsätze zur Apostelgeschichte und zu den Johannesakten.* Ed. Jens Schröter and Ralph Brucker. WUNT 170. Tübingen: Mohr Siebeck, 2004.

Plümacher, *Lukas.* • Plümacher, Eckhard. *Lukas als hellenisticher Schriftsteller: Studien zur Apostelgeschichte.* SUNT 9. Göttingen: Vandenhoeck & Ruprecht, 1972.

Plümacher, "Luke as Historian." • Plümacher, Eckhard. "Luke as Historian." Trans. Dennis Martin. 4:398-402 in *ABD.*

Plümacher, "Mission Speeches." • Plümacher, Eckhard. "The Mission Speeches in Acts and Dionysius of Halicarnassus." 251-66 in *Jesus and the Heritage of Israel: Luke's Narrative Claim upon Israel's Legacy.* Ed. David P. Moessner. Vol. 1 in Luke the Interpreter of Israel, series ed. Moessner and David L. Tiede. Harrisburg, PA: Trinity Press International, 1999.

Plümacher, "Missionsreden." • Plümacher, Eckhard. "Die Missionsreden der Apostelgeschichte und Dionys von Halikarnass." *NTS* 39 (2, 1993): 161-77.

Plümacher, "Monographie." • Plümacher, Eckhard. "Die Apostelgeschichte als historiche Monographie." 457-66 in *Les Actes des Apôtres: Tradition, rédaction, théologie.* Ed. Jacob Kremer. BETL 48. Gembloux: J. Duculot, and Leuven: Leuven University Press, 1979.

Poewe, *Religions and Nazis.* • Poewe, Karla. *New Religions and the Nazis.* New York, London: Routledge, 2006.

Pöhlmann, "All-Prädikationen." • Pöhlmann, Wolfgang. "Die hymnischen All-Prädikationen in Kol 1:15-20." *ZNW* 64 (1-2, 1973): 53-74.

Poirier, "Consensus." • Poirier, John C. "On the Use of Consensus in Historical Jesus Studies." *TZ* 56 (2, 2000): 97-107.

Poirier, "Return." • Poirier, John C. "The Endtime Return of Elijah and Moses at Qumran." *DSD* 10 (2, 2003): 221-242.

Poland, *Criticism.* • Poland, Lynn M. *Literary Criticism and Biblical Hermeneutics.* AARAS 48. Atlanta: Scholars Press, 1985.

Pomeroy, *Women*. • Pomeroy, Sarah B. *Goddesses, Whores, Wives, and Slaves: Women in Classical Antiquity.* New York: Schocken Books, 1975.

Porter, "Census." • Porter, Stanley E. "The Reasons for the Lukan Census." 165-88 in *Paul, Luke and the Graeco-Roman World.* Ed. Alf Christophersen, Carsten Claussen, Jörg Frey and Bruce Longenecker. JSNTSup 217. Sheffield: Sheffield Academic Press, 2002; London: T. & T. Clark, 2003.

Porter, *Criteria*. • Porter, Stanley E. *The Criteria for Authenticity in Historical-Jesus Research: Previous Discussions and New Proposals.* JSNTSup 91; Sheffield: Sheffield Academic Press, 2000.

Porter, "Greek in Galilee." • Porter, Stanley E. "Jesus and the Use of Greek in Galilee." 123-54 in *Studying the Historical Jesus: Evaluations of the State of Current Research.* NTTS 19. Ed. Bruce Chilton and Craig A. Evans. Leiden, New York, Cologne: E. J. Brill, 1994.

Porter, *Paul in Acts*. • Porter, Stanley E. *Paul in Acts.* LPSt. Peabody: Hendrickson, 2001. Reprint of *The Paul of Acts: Essays in Literary Criticism, Rhetoric, and Theology.* WUNT 115. Tübingen: J. C. B. Mohr (Paul Siebeck), 1999.

Porter, "Teach." • Porter, Stanley E. "Did Jesus Ever Teach in Greek?" *TynBul* 44 (1993): 199-235.

Porter, "We Passages." • Porter, Stanley E. "Excursus: The 'We' Passages." 545-574 in *The Book of Acts in Its Graeco-Roman Setting.* Ed. David W. J. Gill and Conrad Gempf. Vol. 2 in The Book of Acts in Its First Century Setting. 6 vols. Ed. Bruce W. Winter. Grand Rapids: Eerdmans; Carlisle: Paternoster, 1994.

Porter and Heath, *Gospel of Judas*. • Porter, Stanley E., and Gordon L. Heath, *The Lost Gospel of Judas: Separating Fact from Fiction.* Grand Rapids: Eerdmans, 2007.

Porton, "Parable." • Porton, Gary G. "The Parable in the Hebrew Bible and Rabbinic Literature." 206-21 in *The Historical Jesus in Context.* Ed. Amy-Jill Levine, Dale C. Allison Jr., and John Dominic Crossan. Princeton Readings in Religions. Princeton: Princeton University Press, 2006.

Porton, "Pronouncement Story." • Porton, Gary G. "The Pronouncement Story in Tannaitic Literature: A Review of Bultmann's Theory." *Semeia* 20 (1981): 81-99.

Porton, "Sadducees." • Porton, Gary G. "Sadducees." 1050-52 in *DNTB.*

Poulos, "Pronouncement Story." • Poulos, Paula Nassen. "Form and Function of the Pronouncement Story in Diogenes Laertius' *Lives.*" *Semeia* 20 (1981): 53-63.

Powell, *Jesus in History*. • Powell, Mark Allan. *Jesus as a Figure in History: How Modern Historians View the Man from Galilee.* Louisville, KY: Westminster John Knox, 1998.

Praeder, "First Person Narration." • Praeder, Susan Marie. "The Problem of First Person Narration in Acts." *NovT* 29 (3, 1987): 193-218.

Pregeant, "Wisdom Passages." • Pregeant, Russell. "Wisdom Passages in Matthew." 197-232 in *Treasures New and Old: Recent Contributions to Matthean Studies.* Ed. David R. Bauer and Mark Allan Powell. SBLSymS 1. Atlanta: Scholars Press, 1996.

Pretzler, "Pausanias and Tradition." • Pretzler, Maria. "Pausanias and Oral Tradition." *CQ* 55 (1, 2005): 235-49.

Price, "Database." • Price, Robert M. "Dubious Database. Second Thoughts on the Red and Pink Materials of the Jesus Seminar." *CSER Review* 1 (2, 2006-7): 19-27.

Price, "Easters." • Price, Robert M. "Brand X Easters." *FR* 20 (6, 2007): 13-15, 18-19, 23.

Price, "Evolution of Genres." • Price, Robert M. "Implied Reader Response and the Evolution of Genres: Transitional Stages Between the Ancient Novels and the Apocryphal Acts." *HvTSt* 53 (4, 1997): 909-38.

Price, *Son of Man*. • Price, Robert M. *The Incredible Shrinking Son of Man: How Reliable Is the Gospel Tradition?* Amherst, NY: Prometheus Books, 2003.

Priest, "Mebaqqer." • Priest, John F. "Mebaqqer, Paqid, and the Messiah." *JBL* 81 (1, March 1962): 55-61.

Priest, "Messiah." • Priest, John F. "The Messiah and the Meal in 1QSa." *JBL* 82 (1, March 1963): 95-100.

Pritz, *Nazarene Christianity.* • Pritz, Ray A. *Nazarene Jewish Christianity: From the End of the New Testament Period Until Its Disappearance in the Fourth Century.* StPB. Jerusalem-Leiden: Magnes Press, Hebrew University, E. J. Brill, 1988.

Pryke, "John." • Pryke, John. "John the Baptist and the Qumran Community." *RevQ* 4 (4, 1964): 483-96.

Pucci Ben Zeev, "Capitol." • Pucci Ben Zeev, Miriam. "Polybius, Josephus, and the Capitol in Rome." *JSJ* 27 (1, 1996): 21-30.

Puech, "Apocalypse." • Puech, Émile. "Une apocalypse messianique *(4Q521)." RevQ* 15 (4, 1992): 475-522, plates 1-3.

Puech, *Croyance.* • Puech, Émile. *La croyance des Esséniens en la vie future: Immortalité, résurrection, Vie éternelle? Histoire d'un croyance dans le judaïsme ancien. II. Les données qumraniennes et classiques.* École biblique 22. Paris: Gabalda, 1993.

Puech, "Manuscrit." • Puech, Émile. "Notes sur le manuscrit de 11QMelchîsédeq." *RevQ* 12 (4, 1987): 483-513.

Puech, "Messianisme." • Puech, Émile. "Messianisme, eschatology et résurrection dans les manuscrits de la mer Morte." *RevQ* 18 (70, 1997): 255-98.

Puech, "Resurrection Faith." • Puech, Émile. "Jesus and Resurrection Faith in Light of Jewish Texts," 639-59 in *Jesus and Archaeology.* Ed. James H. Charlesworth. Grand Rapids: Eerdmans, 2006.

Puech and Zias, "Tombeau." • Puech, Émile, and Joseph Zias. "Le tombeau de Zacharie et Siméon au monument funéraire dit d'Absalom dans le vallée de Josaphat." *RB* 110 (3, 2003): 321-35.

Quarles, "Gospel of Peter." • Quarles, Charles L. "The Gospel of Peter: Does It Contain a Precanonical Resurrection Narrative?" 106-20 in *The Resurrection of Jesus: John Dominic Crossan and N. T. Wright in Dialogue.* Ed. Robert B. Stewart. Minneapolis: Fortress, 2006.

Quarles, "Mystic." • Quarles, Charles L. "Jesus as Merkabah Mystic." *JSHJ* 3 (1, 2005): 5-22.

Rabello, "Condition." • Rabello, Alfredo Mordechai. "The Legal Condition of the Jews in the Roman Empire." 10.13.662-762 in *ANRW*. Berlin: Walter de Gruyter, 1980.

Rabin, "Jannaeus." • Rabin, Chaim. "Alexander Jannaeus and the Pharisees." *JJS* 7 (1-2, 1956): 3-11.

Race, "Influence." • Race, M. "Galilee's Influence on Jesus." *BibT* 41 (2, 2003): 73-79.

Race, "Introduction." • Race, W. H. "Introduction." 1-41 in Pindar. *Odes.* 2 vols. Trans. William H. Race. LCL 56, 485. Cambridge: Harvard, 1997.

Rackham, *Acts.* • Rackham, Richard Belward. *The Acts of the Apostles.* 4th ed. Grand Rapids: Baker, 1964. Reprint ed. (First edition, London: Methuen & Company, 1901)

Radermakers, "Goût." • Radermakers, Jean. "Goût d'évangile et quête de Jésus. À propos d'ouvrages récents." *NRTh* 129 (3, 2007): 447-56.

Raharimanantsoa, *Espérance.* • Raharimanantsoa, Mamy. *Mort et Espérance selon la Bible Hébraïque.* Coniectanea Biblica Old Testament Series 53. Stockholm: Almqvist & Wiksell, 2006.

Rahmani, "Glwsqmwt." • Rahmani, L. Y. "Glwsqmwt wlyqwt ʾsnwt bslhy tqwpt byt sny." *Qad* 11 (1978): 102-12.

Rainey, "Herodotus' Description." • Rainey, Anson F. "Herodotus' Description of the East Mediterranean Coast." *BASOR* 321 (2001): 57-63.

Rajak, "Charter." • Rajak, Tessa. "Was There a Roman Charter for the Jews?" *JRS* 74 (1984): 107-23.

Rajak, *Josephus.* • Rajak, Tessa. *Josephus: The Historian and His Society.* Philadelphia: Fortress, 1984; London: Gerald Duckworth & Company, 1983.

Rajak, "Justus of Tiberias." • Rajak, Tessa. "Josephus and Justus of Tiberias." 81-94 in *Josephus, Judaism and Christianity.* Ed. Louis H. Feldman and Gohei Hata. Detroit: Wayne State University Press, 1987.

Rajak, "Moses." • Rajak, Tessa. "Moses in Ethiopia: Legend and Literature." *JJS* 29 (2, 1978): 111-22.

Ramirez, "Misterio." • Ramirez, José M. Casciaro. "El 'Misterio' divino en los escritos posteriores de Qumran." *ScrTh* 8 (1976): 445-75.

Ramsay, *Bethlehem*. • Ramsay, William M. *Was Christ Born at Bethlehem? A Study in the Credibility of St. Luke*. London: Hodder & Stoughton, 1898; reprint: Grand Rapids: Baker, 1979.

Ramsay, *Church*. • Ramsay, William M. *The Church in the Roman Empire*. 5th ed. Grand Rapids: Baker, 1979; London: Hodder & Stoughton, 1897.

Ramsay, *Luke the Physician*. • Ramsay, William M. *Luke the Physician and Other Studies in the History of Religion*. London: Hodder & Stoughton, 1908; reprint, Grand Rapids: Baker, 1979.

Ramsay, "Roads and Travel." • Ramsay, William M. "Roads and Travel (in NT)." 5:375-402 in *Dictionary of the Bible*. 5 vols. Ed. James Hastings. Edinburgh: T. & T. Clark; New York: Charles Scribner's Sons, 1898-1923.

Raphael, "Travail." • Raphael, Freddy. "Le Travail de la memoire et les limites de l'histoire orale." *Annales* 35 (1, Jan. 1980): 127-45.

Rapske, *Custody*. • Rapske, Brian. *The Book of Acts and Paul in Roman Custody*. The Book of Acts in Its First Century Setting, vol. 3. Grand Rapids: Eerdmans, 1994.

Rasimus, "Évaluation." • Rasimus, Tuomas. "Une évaluation critique du film *The Lost Tomb of Jesus*." *LTP* 63 (1, 2007): 113-20.

Raspe, "Manetho on Exodus." • Raspe, Lucia. "Manetho on the Exodus." *JSQ* 5 (2, 1998): 124-54.

Rathbone, "Farmers." • Rathbone, Dominic. "Farmers: Rome." 5:356-358 in *Brill's New Pauly*.

Ravid, "Calendar." • Ravid, Liora. "The Book of Jubilees and Its Calendar — A Reexamination." *DSD* 10 (3, 2003): 371-94.

Rebenich, "Historical Prose." • Rebenich, Stefan. "Historical Prose." 265-337 in *Handbook of Classical Rhetoric in the Hellenistic Period 330 B.C.-A.D. 400*. Ed. Stanley E. Porter. Leiden: Brill, 1997.

Reed, *Archaeology*. • Reed, Jonathan L. *Archaeology and the Galilean Jesus: A Re-examination of the Evidence*. Harrisburg, PA: Trinity Press International, 2000.

Reed, "Contributions." • Reed, Jonathan L. "Archaeological Contributions to the Study of Jesus and the Gospels." 40-54 in *The Historical Jesus in Context*. Ed. Amy-Jill Levine, Dale C. Allison Jr., and John Dominic Crossan. Princeton Readings in Religions. Princeton: Princeton University Press, 2006.

Regev, "Individualism." • Regev, Eyal. "Pure Individualism: The Idea of Non-Priestly Purity in Ancient Judaism." *JSJ* 31 (2, 2000): 176-202.

Regev, "Ossuaries." • Regev, Eyal. "The Individualistic Meaning of Jewish Ossuaries: A Socio-Anthropological Perspective on Burial Practice." *PEQ* 133 (1, 2001): 39-49.

Reich, "Baths." • Reich, Ronny. "They *Are* Ritual Baths." *BAR* 28 (2, 2002): 50-55.

Reich, "H'rh." • Reich, Ronny. "H'rh lpsyps hrwmy mmgdl 'sr lhwp ym-kynrt." *Qad* 22 (1-2, 1989): 43-44.

Reich, "Inscriptions." • Reich, Ronny. "Ossuary Inscriptions from the Caiaphas Tomb." *JerPersp* 4 (4-5, 1991): 13-22.

Reich, "Jars." • Reich, Ronny. "6 Stone Water Jars." *JerPersp* 48 (1995): 30-33.

Reich, "Name." • Reich, Ronny. "Caiaphas Name Inscribed on Bone Boxes." *BAR* 18 (5, 1992): 38-44.

Reicke, *Era*. • Reicke, Bo. *The New Testament Era: The World of the Bible from 500 B.C. to A.D. 100*. Trans. David E. Green. Philadelphia: Fortress, 1974.

Reid, "Sacrifice." • Reid, Daniel G. "Sacrifice and Temple Service." 1036-50 in *DNTB*.

Reider, "MSHTY." • Reider, Joseph. "On MSHTY in the Qumran Scrolls." *BASOR* 134 (April 1954): 27.

Reinmuth, "Zwischen Investitur." • Reinmuth, Eckart. "Zwischen Investitur und Testament. Beobachtungen zur Rezeption des Josuabuches im Liber Antiquitatum Biblicarum." *SJOT* 16 (1, 2002): 24-43.

Reiser, "Eclipsing." • Reiser, W. "The Eclipsing of History?: Luke Timothy Johnson's *The Real Jesus*." *Hor* 24 (1, 1997): 119-25.

Reitzenstein, *Religions.* • Reitzenstein, Richard. *Hellenistic Mystery-Religions: Their Basic Ideas and Significance.* Trans. John E. Steeley. PTMS 15. Pittsburgh: Pickwick, 1978.

Rennie, "Zoroastrianism." • Rennie, Bryan. "Zoroastrianism: The Iranian Roots of Christianity?" *Council of Societies for the Study of Religion Bulletin* 36 (1, 2007): 3-7.

Rensberger, *Faith.* • Rensberger, David. *Johannine Faith and Liberating Community.* Philadelphia: Westminster Press, 1988.

Rhoads and Michie, *Mark.* • Rhoads, David, and Donald Michie. *Mark as Story: An Introduction to the Narrative of a Gospel.* Philadelphia: Fortress, 1982.

Ricciardi, "Henoc." • Ricciardi, Alberto. "1 Henoc 70–71: ¿Es Henoc el Hijo del hombre?" *CuadTeol* 17 (1998): 129-46.

Richards, *Letter Writing.* • Richards, E. Randolph. *Paul and First-Century Letter Writing: Secretaries, Composition and Collection.* Downers Grove, IL: InterVarsity, 2004.

Richardson, *Israel.* • Richardson, Peter. *Israel in the Apostolic Age.* SNTSMS 10. Cambridge: Cambridge University Press, 1969.

Richardson, "Khirbet Qana." • Richardson, Peter. "Khirbet Qana (and Other Villages) as a Context for Jesus." 120-44 in *Jesus and Archaeology.* Ed. James H. Charlesworth. Grand Rapids: Eerdmans, 2006.

Richardson, *Theology.* • Richardson, Alan. *An Introduction to the Theology of the New Testament.* New York: Harper & Brothers, 1958.

Richardson and Gooch, "Logia." • Richardson, Peter, and Peter Gooch. "Logia of Jesus in 1 Corinthians." 39-62 in *The Jesus Tradition Outside the Gospels.* Ed. David Wenham. Sheffield: JSOT Press, 1984. Vol. 5 in *Gospel Perspectives.* 6 vols.

Ridderbos, *Galatians.* • Ridderbos, Herman N. *The Epistle of Paul to the Churches of Galatia.* Grand Rapids: Eerdmans, 1953.

Ridderbos, *John.* • Ridderbos, Herman N. *The Gospel according to John: A Theological Commentary.* Trans. John Vriend. Grand Rapids: Eerdmans, 1997.

Ridderbos, *Paul.* • Ridderbos, Herman N. *Paul: An Outline of His Theology.* Trans. John Richard De Witt. Grand Rapids: Eerdmans, 1975.

Ridderbos, *Paul and Jesus.* • Ridderbos, Herman N. *Paul and Jesus.* Tr. David H. Freeman. Philadelphia: Presbyterian and Reformed, 1974.

Riesenfeld, "Background." • Riesenfeld, Harald. "The Mythological Background of New Testament Christology." 81-95 in *The Background of the New Testament and Its Eschatology: Essays in Honor of Charles Harold Dodd.* Ed. W. D. Davies and D. Daube. Cambridge: Cambridge University Press, 1964.

Riesenfeld, *Tradition.* • Riesenfeld, Harald. *The Gospel Tradition.* Philadelphia: Fortress, 1970.

Riesner, "Education élémentaire." • Riesner, Rainer. "Education élémentaire juive et tradition évangélique." *Hok* 21 (1982): 51-64.

Riesner, "Familiengrab." • Riesner, Rainer. "Wurde das Familiengrab des Hohenpriesters Kajaphas entdeckt?" *BK* 46 (2, 1991): 82-84.

Riesner, "Gate." • Riesner, Rainer. "Josephus' 'Gate of the Essenes' in Modern Discussion." *ZDPV* 105 (1989): 105-9, plates 8-16a.

Riesner, "Golgotha." • Riesner, Rainer. "Golgotha und die Archäologie." *BK* 40 (1985): 21-26.

Riesner, *Jesus.* • Riesner, Rainer. *Jesus als Lehrer: Eine Untersuchung zum Ursprung der Evangelien-Überlieferung.* 2d ed. WUNT 2d series, 7. Tübingen: J. C. B. Mohr, 1984.

Riesner, "Jesus-Grab." • Riesner, Rainer. "Ein falsches Jesus-Grab, Maria Magdalena und kein Ende." *TBei* 38 (4-5, 2007): 296-99.

Riesner, "Neues." • Riesner, Rainer. "Neues vom See Gennesaret." *BK* 42 (1987): 171-73.

Riesner, "Rückkehr." • Riesner, Rainer. "Die Rückkehr der Augenzeugen. Eine neue Entwicklung in der Evangelienforschung." *TBei* 38 (6, 2007): 337-52.

Riesner, "Synagogues in Jerusalem." • Riesner, Rainer. "Synagogues in Jerusalem." 179-211 in *The*

Book of Acts in Its Palestinian Setting. Ed. Richard Bauckham. Vol. 4 in The Book of Acts in Its First Century Setting. Grand Rapids: Eerdmans; Carlisle: Paternoster, 1995.

Riesner, "Täufer." • Riesner, Rainer. "Johannes der Täufer auf Machärus." *BK* 39 (1984): 176.

Riesner, "Ursprung." • Riesner, Rainer. "Der Ursprung der Jesus-Überlieferung." *TZ* 38 (6, 1982): 493-513.

Riesner, "Zuverlässigkeit." • Riesner, Rainer. "Die historische Zuverlässigkeit der Apostelgeschichte." *ZNW* 9 (18, 2006): 38-43.

Ring, "Resurrection." • Ring, George C. "Christ's Resurrection and the Dying and Rising Gods." *CBQ* 6 1944): 216-29.

Ringgren, *Faith*. • Ringgren, Helmer. *The Faith of Qumran.* Philadelphia: Fortress, 1963.

Rissi, *Time*. • Rissi, Mathias. *Time and History: A Study on the Revelation.* Trans. Gordon C. Winsor. Richmond, VA: John Knox, 1966.

Rivkin, "Jubilees." • Rivkin, Ellis. "The Book of Jubilees — An Anti-Pharisaic Pseudepigraph?" *Er-Isr* 16 (1982): 193-198.

Rivkin, "Meaning." • Rivkin, Ellis. "The Meaning of Messiah in Jewish Thought." *USQR* 26 (4, Summer 1971): 383-406.

Rivkin, "Messiah." • Rivkin, Ellis. "The Meaning of Messiah in Jewish Thought." Pp. 54-75 in *Evangelicals and Jews in Conversation on Scripture, Theology, and History.* Ed. Marc H. Tanenbaum, Marvin R. Wilson, and James A. Rudin. Grand Rapids: Baker, 1978.

Rizzo, "Tiberio." • Rizzo, Francesco Paolo. "L'imperatore Tiberio fu favorevole ai cristiani?" *Civiltà Cattolica* 158 (3771-72, 2007): 257-65.

Robbins, "Chreia." • Robbins, Vernon K. "The Chreia." Pp. 1-23 in *Greco-Roman Literature and the New Testament: Selected Forms and Genres.* SBLSBS 21. Atlanta: Scholars Press, 1988.

Robbins, "Claims of Prologue." • Robbins, Vernon K. "The Claims of the Prologues and Greco-Roman Rhetoric: The Prefaces to Luke and Acts in Light of Greco-Roman Rhetorical Strategies." 63-83 in *Jesus and the Heritage of Israel: Luke's Narrative Claim upon Israel's Legacy.* Ed. David P. Moessner. Vol. 1 in Luke the Interpreter of Israel. Harrisburg, PA: Trinity Press International, 1999.

Robbins, "Land and Sea." • Robbins, Vernon K. "By Land and by Sea: The We-Passages and Ancient Sea Voyages." 215-42 in *Perspectives on Luke-Acts.* Ed. Charles H. Talbert. Danville, VA: Association of Baptist Professors of Religion; Edinburgh: T. & T. Clark, 1978.

Robbins, "Pronouncement Stories." • Robbins, Vernon K. "Classifying Pronouncement Stories in Plutarch's *Parallel Lives*." *Semeia* 20 (1981): 29-52.

Robbins, *Teacher*. • Robbins, Vernon K. *Jesus the Teacher: A Socio-Rhetorical Interpretation of Mark.* Minneapolis: Augsburg Fortress, 1992.

Robbins, "We-Passages." • Robbins, Vernon K. "The We-Passages in Acts and Ancient Sea Voyages." *BR* 20 (1975): 5-18.

Robbins, "Writing." • Robbins, Vernon K. "Writing as a Rhetorical Act in Plutarch and the Gospels." 142-68 in *Persuasive Artistry: Studies in New Testament Rhetoric in Honor of George A. Kennedy.* Ed. Duane F. Watson. JSNTSup 50. Sheffield: Sheffield Academic Press, 1991.

Robeck, *Mission*. • Robeck, Cecil M., Jr. *The Azusa Street Mission & Revival: The Birth of the Global Pentecostal Movement.* Nashville: Thomas Nelson, 2006.

Roberts, *Fragment*. • Roberts, C. H. *An Unpublished Fragment of the Fourth Gospel.* Manchester: Manchester University Press, 1935.

Robertson, *Luke*. • Robertson, A. T. *Luke the Historian in the Light of Research.* New York: Charles Scribner's Sons, 1923.

Robinson, "Blocks." • Robinson, James M. "Building Blocks in the Social History of Q." 87-112 in *Reimagining Christian Origins: A Colloquium Honoring Burton L. Mack.* Ed. Elizabeth A. Castelli and Hal Taussig. Valley Forge, PA: Trinity Press International, 1996.

Robinson, *Coming.* • Robinson, John A. T. *Jesus and His Coming.* 2d ed. Philadelphia: Westminster, 1979.

Robinson, *Criminal Law.* • Robinson, O. F. *The Criminal Law of Ancient Rome.* London: Duckworth; Baltimore: The Johns Hopkins University Press, 1995.

Robinson, "Introduction." • Robinson, James M. "Introduction." xi-xxxiii in Schweitzer, *Quest.*

Robinson, *Personality.* • Robinson, H. Wheeler. *Corporate Personality in Ancient Israel.* Philadelphia: Fortress Press, 1980.

Robinson, *Problem.* • Robinson, James M. *The Problem of History in Mark and Other Marcan Studies.* Philadelphia: Fortress, 1982.

Robinson, *Redating.* • Robinson, John A. T. *Redating the New Testament.* Philadelphia: Westminster; London: SCM, 1976.

Robinson, *Studies.* • Robinson, John A. T. *Twelve New Testament Studies.* SBT 34. London: SCM, 1962.

Robinson, *Trust.* • Robinson, John A. T. *Can We Trust the New Testament?* Grand Rapids: Eerdmans, 1977.

Rodd, "Finger." • Rodd, Cyril S. "Spirit or Finger." *ExpT* 72 (1961): 157-58.

Rohrbaugh, "City." • Rohrbaugh, Richard L. "The Pre-Industrial City in Luke-Acts: Urban Social Relations." 125-49 in *The Social World of Luke-Acts: Models for Interpretation.* Ed. Jerome H. Neyrey. Peabody: Hendrickson, 1991.

Rokéah, "Proselytism." • Rokéah, David. "Ancient Jewish Proselytism in Theory and in Practice." *TZ* 52 (3, 1996): 206-24.

Rolfe, "Introduction." • Rolfe, J. C. "Introduction to 'The Lives of the Caesars.'" 1:xvii-xxxi in Suetonius. (*Works.*) 2 vols. Translated J. C. Rolfe. LCL. London: Wm. Heinemann; New York: The Macmillan Co.; Cambridge: Harvard University Press, 1914.

Rollins, "Crossan." • Rollins, Wayne G. "Crossan on the Couch, Along with the Rest of Us: Part One: The Silhouette of a Jesus Scholar from the Perspective of Psychological Realism as Developed by Hal Childs." *PastPsy* 51 (6, 2003): 441-54.

Roncace, "Deborah." • Roncace, Mark. "Josephus' (Real) Portraits of Deborah and Gideon: A Reading of *Antiquities* 5.198-232." *JSJ* 31 (3, 2000): 247-74.

Roncace, "Samson." • Roncace, Mark. "Another Portrait of Josephus' Portrait of Samson." *JSJ* 35 (2, 2004): 185-207.

Roo, "4Q525." • Roo, Jacqueline C. R. de. "Beatitudes Text (4Q525)." 151-53 in *DNTB.*

Rook, "Names." • Rook, John. "The Names of the Wives from Adam to Abraham in the Book of *Jubilees.*" *JSP* 7 (1990): 105-17.

Rordorf, "Conversion." • Rordorf, Willy. "Paul's Conversion in the Canonical Acts and in the *Acts of Paul.*" Trans. Peter W. Dunn. 137-44 in *The Apocryphal Acts of the Apostles in Intertextual Perspectives.* Semeia 80. Ed. Robert F. Stoops. Atlanta: Scholars Press, 1997.

Rosenberg, "Messiah." • Rosenberg, Roy A. "The Slain Messiah in the Old Testament." *ZAW* 99 (2, 1987): 259-61.

Rosenberg, "Moreh." • Rosenberg, Roy A. "Who is the Moreh haṣṢedeq?" *JAAR* 36 (2, 1968): 118-122.

Rosner, "Biblical History." • Rosner, Brian S. "Acts and Biblical History." 65-82 in *The Book of Acts in Its Ancient Literary Setting.* Ed. Bruce W. Winter and Andrew D. Clark. Vol. 1 in The Book of Acts in Its First Century Setting. Grand Rapids: Eerdmans; Carlisle: Paternoster, 1993.

Ross, "Church." • Ross, J.-P. B. "The Evolution of a Church — Jerusalem's Holy Sepulchre." *BAR* 2 (3, September 1976): 3-8.

Rössler, "Mensch." • Rössler, Andreas. "Jesus: ein blosser Mensch." *ZeitZeichen* 9 (1, 2008): 56-58.

Rost, *Judaism.* • Rost, Leonhard. *Judaism Outside the Hebrew Canon: An Introduction to the Documents.* Trans. David E. Green. Nashville: Abingdon, 1976.

Rostovzeff, *History*. • Rostovzeff, M. I. *The Social and Economic History of the Roman Empire*. 2nd ed. Oxford: Clarendon Press, 1957.

Roth, "Reference." • Roth, Cecil. "A Talmudic Reference to the Qumran Sect?" *RevQ* 2 (2, 1960): 261-265.

Roth, "Subject Matter of Exegesis." • Roth, Cecil. "The Subject Matter of Qumran Exegesis." *VT* 10 (1, Jan. 1960): 51-68.

Roth, "Teacher." • Roth, Cecil. "The Teacher of Righteousness." *Listener* 57 (June 27, 1957): 1037-1041.

Rothschild, *Rhetoric of History*. • Rothschild, Clare K. *Luke-Acts and the Rhetoric of History: An Investigation of Early Christian Historiography*. WUNT 2, Reihe, 175. Tübingen: Mohr Siebeck, 2004.

Rothstein, "Testimony." • Rothstein, David. "Same-Day Testimony and Same-Day Punishment in the Damascus Document and Jubilees." *ZABR* 11 (2005): 12-26.

Rowe, "Style." • Rowe, Galen O. "Style." 121-57 in *Handbook of Classical Rhetoric in the Hellenistic Period 330 B.C.-A.D. 400*. Ed. Stanley E. Porter. Leiden: Brill, 1997.

Rowley, "Baptism." • Rowley, H. H. "Jewish Proselyte Baptism and the Baptism of John." *HUCA* 15 (1940): 313-34.

Rowley, "Kittim." • Rowley, H. H. "The Kittim and the Dead Sea Scrolls." *PEQ* 88 (1956): 92-109.

Rowley, "4QpNahum." • Rowley, H. H. "4QpNahum and the Teacher of Righteousness." *JBL* 75 (3, Sept 1956): 188-193.

Rubenstein, "Hypocrites." • Rubenstein, Richard L. "Scribes, Pharisees and Hypocrites. A Study in Rabbinic Psychology." *Judaism* 12 (1963): 456-68.

Rubenstein, "Narrative." • Rubenstein, Jeffrey L. "Bavli Gittin 55b-56b: An Aggadic Narrative in Its Halakhic Context." *HS* 38 (1997): 21-45.

Ruck, "Mystery." • Ruck, Carl A. P. "Solving the Eleusinian Mystery." 35-50 in *The Road to Eleusis: Unveiling the Secret of the Mysteries*. By Robert Gordon Wasson, Albert Hofmann, and Carl A. P. Ruck. New York: A Helen and Kurt Wolff Book, Harcourt Brace Jovanovich, 1978.

Rüger, "ΝΑΖΑΡΕΘ." • Rüger, Hans Peter. "ΝΑΖΑΡΕΘ/ΝΑΖΑΡΑ ΝΑΖΑΡΗΝΟΣ/ΝΑΖΩΡΑΙΟΣ." *ZNW* 72 (3-4, 1981): 257-63.

Rüger, "Ruch." • Rüger, Hans Peter. "'Mit welchem Mass ihr messt, wird Ruch gemessen werden.'" *ZNW* 60 (1969): 174-82.

Runnalls, "Campaign." • Runnalls, Donna. "Moses' Ethiopian Campaign." *JSJ* 14 (2, December 1983): 135-56.

Rüpke, "Ephemeris." • Rüpke, Jörg. "Ephemeris." 4:1022 in *Brill's New Pauly*.

Rusecki, "Kryteria." • Rusecki, M. "Kryteria historycznosci cudów Jezusa." *RocT* 54 (6, 2007): 317-34.

Russell, *Apocalyptic*. • Russell, D. S. *The Method and Message of Jewish Apocalyptic*. Philadelphia: Westminster, 1964.

Russell, "Mysteries." • Russell, Elbert. "Possible Influence of the Mysteries on the Form and Interrelation of the Johannine Writings." *JBL* 51 (1932): 336-51.

Rusten, "Ekphrasis." • Rusten, Jeffrey Stuart. *"Ekphrasis."* 515 in *OCD*.

Safrai, "Description in Works." • Safrai, Zeev. "The Description of the Land of Israel in Josephus' Works." 295-324 in *Josephus, the Bible, and History*. Ed. Louis H. Feldman and Gohei Hata. Detroit: Wayne State University Press, 1989.

Safrai, "Education." • Safrai, S. "Education and the Study of the Torah." 945-70 in *JPFC*.

Safrai, "Government." • Safrai, S. "Jewish Self-government." 377-419 in *JPFC*.

Safrai, "Home." • Safrai, S. "Home and Family." 728-92 in *JPFC*.

Safrai, "Literature." • Safrai, S. "Talmudic Literature as an Historical Source for the Second Temple Period." *Mishkan* 17-18 (1992-93): 121-37.

Safrai, "Religion." • Safrai, S. "Religion in Everyday Life." 793-833 in *JPFC*.

Safrai, "Temple." • Safrai, S. "The Temple." 865-907 in *JPFC*.

Saïd, "City." • Saïd, Suzanne. "The City in the Greek Novel." 216-236 in *The Search for the Ancient Novel*. Ed. James Tatum. Baltimore, London: Johns Hopkins University, 1994.

Salaman, "Haggadah." • Salaman, R. "The Number Four in the Passover Haggadah." *JPJ* 13 (1999): 19-28.

Saldarini, *Community.* • Saldarini, Anthony J. *Matthew's Christian-Jewish Community*. Chicago Studies in the History of Judaism. Chicago: University of Chicago Press, 1994.

Saldarini, "Deathbed Scenes." • Saldarini, Anthony J. "Last Words and Deathbed Scenes in Rabbinic Literature." *JQR* 68 (1977): 28-45.

Sallmann, "Literature" • Sallmann, Klaus. "Technical Literature." 14:195-201 in *Brill's New Pauly*.

Salomonsen, "Nogle." • Salomonsen, Børge. "Nogle synspunkter fra den nyere debat omkring zeloterne." *DTT* 27 (1964): 149-62.

Sampathkumar, "Bandits." • Sampathkumar, P. A. "Bandits and Messiahs: Social Revolts in the Time of Jesus." *Jeev* 30 (175, 2000): 72-89.

Samuel, "Acts of Philip." • Samuel, Simon. "The Acts of Philip and the Tines Andres (Certain Men) of Cyprus and Cyrene: A Remapping of Early Christian Mission Frontiers." 42-71 in *Remapping Mission Discourse: A Festschrift in Honor of the Rev. George Kuruvila Chavanikamannil*. Ed. Simon Samuel and P. V. Joseph. Dehradun, India: New Theological College, and Delhi: ISPCK, 2008.

Samuel, *Reading.* • Samuel, Simon. *A Postcolonial Reading of Mark's Story of Jesus*. LNTS 340. London, New York: T&T Clark, 2007.

Sanday, *Criticism.* • Sanday, William. *The Criticism of the Fourth Gospel*. Oxford: Clarendon Press, 1905.

Sanday and Headlam, *Romans.* • Sanday, William, and Arthur Headlam. *A Critical and Exegetical Commentary on the Epistle to the Romans*. 5th ed. ICC. Edinburgh: T. & T. Clark, 1902.

Sanders, *Figure.* • Sanders, E. P. *The Historical Figure of Jesus*. New York: Allen Lane, Penguin, 1993.

Sanders, *Jesus and Judaism.* • Sanders, E. P. *Jesus and Judaism*. Philadelphia: Fortress, 1985.

Sanders, *Jesus to Mishnah.* • Sanders, E. P. *Jewish Law from Jesus to the Mishnah: Five Studies*. London: SCM; Philadelphia: Trinity Press International, 1990.

Sanders, *John.* • Sanders, J. N. *A Commentary on the Gospel According to St. John*. Edited and completed by B. A. Mastin. Harper's New Testament Commentaries. New York: Harper & Row, Publishers, 1968.

Sanders, *Judaism.* • Sanders, E. P. *Judaism: Practice and Belief, 63 BCE-66 CE*. London: SCM; Philadelphia: Trinity Press International, 1992.

Sanders, "Know." • Sanders, E. P. "How Do We Know What We Know about Jesus?" 38-61 in *Jesus Two Thousand Years Later*. Ed. James H. Charlesworth and Walter P. Weaver. Faith and Scholarship Colloquies Series. Harrisburg, PA: Trinity Press International, 2000.

Sanders, "Quest." • Sanders, E. P. "In Quest of the Historical Jesus." *New York Review of Books* 48 (18, 2001): 33-36.

Sanders, "Simon." • Sanders, Boykin. "In Search of a Face for Simon the Cyrene." 51-63 in *The Recovery of Black Presence: An Interdisciplinary Exploration, Essays in Honor of Dr. Charles B. Copher*. Nashville: Abingdon, 1995.

Sanders, "Temple." • Sanders, E. P. "Jesus and the Temple." 361-81 in *The Historical Jesus in Recent Research*. Ed. James D. G. Dunn and Scot McKnight. Winona Lake, IN: Eisenbrauns, 2005.

Sanders, *Tendencies.* • Sanders, E. P. *The Tendencies of the Synoptic Tradition*. SNTSMS 9. Cambridge: Cambridge University Press, 1969.

Sanders and Davies, *Synoptic Gospels.* • Sanders, E. P., and Margaret Davies. *Studying the Synoptic Gospels*. London: SCM; Philadelphia: Trinity Press International, 1989.

Sandmel, *Judaism.* • Sandmel, Samuel. *Judaism and Christian Beginnings*. New York: Oxford University Press, 1978.

Satterthwaite, "Rhetoric." • Satterthwaite, Philip E. "*Acts* Against the Background of Classical Rhetoric." 337-79 in *The Book of Acts in Its Ancient Literary Setting*. Ed. Bruce W. Winter and Andrew D. Clarke. Vol. 1 in The Book of Acts in Its First Century Setting. Grand Rapids: Eerdmans; Carlisle: Paternoster, 1993.

Saulnier, "Josèphe." • Saulnier, Christiane. "Flavius Josèphe et la propagande flavienne." *RB* 96 (4, 1989): 545-562.

Saunders, "Synagogues." • Saunders, Ernest W. "Christian Synagogues & Jewish-Christianity in Galilee." *Explor* 3 (1, 1977): 70-77.

Sawicki, *Crossing Galilee*. • Sawicki, Marianne. *Crossing Galilee: Architectures of Contact in the Occupied Land of Jesus*. Harrisburg, PA: Trinity Press International, 2000.

Schaberg, "Predictions." • Schaberg, Jane. "Daniel 7.12 and the New Testament Passion-Resurrection Predictions." *NTS* 31 (1985): 208-22.

Schenker, "Martyrium." • Schenker, Adrian. "Das fürbittend sühnende Martyrium 2 Makk 7,37-38 und das Kelchwort Jesu." *FZPhTh* 50 (3, 2003): 283-92.

Scherberich, "Sueton und Josephus." • Scherberich, Klaus. "Sueton und Josephus über die Ermordung des Caligula." *RMPhil* 142 (1, 1999): 74-83.

Schiffman, "Crossroads." • Schiffman, Lawrence H. "At the Crossroads: Tannaitic Perspectives on the Jewish Christian Schism." 2:115-56 in *Jewish and Christian Self-Definition*. 3 vols. Ed. E. P. Sanders. Philadelphia: Fortress, 1980-1982.

Schiffman, *Jew*. • Schiffman, Lawrence H. *Who Was a Jew? Rabbinic and Halakhic Perspectives on the Jewish Christian Schism*. Hoboken, NJ: Ktav, 1985.

Schiffman, *Law*. • Schiffman, Lawrence H. *Sectarian Law in the Dead Sea Scrolls: Courts, Testimony and the Penal Code*. BJS 33. Chico: Scholars Press, 1983.

Schiffman, "Light." • Schiffman, Lawrence H. "New Light on the Pharisees. Insights from the Dead Sea Scrolls." *BRev* 8 (3, 1992): 30-33, 54.

Schiffman, "Meals." • Schiffman, Lawrence H. "Communal Meals at Qumran." *RevQ* 10 (1979): 45-56.

Schiffman, "4QMysteries." • Schiffman, Lawrence H. "4QMysteries^b, A Preliminary Edition." *RevQ* 16 (1993): 203-23.

Schlier, "Begriff." • Schlier, Heinrich. "Zum Begriff des Geistes nach dem Johannesevangelium." Pp. 264-271 in *Besinnung auf das Neue Testament*. Exegetische Aufsätze und Vorträge II. Freiburg: Herder, 1964.

Schlosser, "Jésus de Nazareth." • Schlosser, Jacques. "Jésus de Nazareth, un juif enraciné et libre." *EspV* 115 (120, 2005): 1-8.

Schmeling, "Spectrum." • Schmeling, Gareth. "The Spectrum of Narrative: Authority of the Author." 19-29 in *Ancient Fiction and Early Christian Narrative*. Ed. Ronald F. Hock, J. Bradley Chance and Judith Perkins. SBLSymS 6. Atlanta: Society of Biblical Literature, 1998.

Schmeller, "Weg." • Schmeller, T. "Der Weg der Jesusbotschaft in die Städte." *BK* 47 (1992): 18-24.

Schmidt, "Influences." • Schmidt, Daryl D. "Rhetorical Influences and Genre: Luke's Preface and the Rhetoric of Hellenistic Historiography." 27-60 in *Jesus and the Heritage of Israel: Luke's Narrative Claim upon Israel's Legacy*. Ed. David P. Moessner. Vol. 1 in Luke the Interpreter of Israel. Harrisburg, PA: Trinity Press International, 1999.

Schmidt, "Public recital." • Schmidt, Peter Lebrecht. "Public recital." 12:178-81 in *Brill's New Pauly*.

Schmidt, "Stellung." • Schmidt, K. L. "Die Stellung der Evangelien in der allgemeinen Literaturgeschichte." Pp. 59-60 in *EYXAPIΣTHPION: Studien zur Religion und Literatur des Alten und Neuen Testaments, Festschrift für Hermann Gunkel*. Ed. K. L. Schmidt. FRLANT 19.2. Göttingen: Vandenhoeck & Ruprecht, 1923.

Schmitt, "Siglum." • Schmitt, John L. "In Search of the Origin of the *Siglum* Q." *JBL* 100 (1981): 609-11.

Schnabel, "Mission." • Schnabel, Eckhard J. "Jesus and the Beginnings of the Mission to the

Gentiles." 37-58 in *Jesus of Nazareth: Lord and Christ. Essays on the Historical Jesus and New Testament Christology.* Ed. Joel B. Green and Max Turner. Grand Rapids: Eerdmans; Carlisle: Paternoster, 1994.

Schnackenburg, John. • Schnackenburg, Rudolf. *The Gospel According to St. John.* 3 vols. Vol. 1: Trans. Kevin Smyth. Ed. J. Massingberde Ford and Kevin Smyth. New York: Herder & Herder, 1968. Vol. 2: New York: The Seabury Press, 1980. Vol. 3: New York: Crossroad, 1982.

Schneider, Apostelgeschichte. • Schneider, Gerhard. *Die Apostelgeschichte.* 2 vols. HThKNT 5.1. Freiburg: Herder, 1980.

Schniedewind, "King." • Schniedewind, William M. "King and Priest in the Book of Chronicles and the Duality of Qumran Messianism." *JJS* 45 (1, 1994): 71-78.

Schoeps, Argument. • Schoeps, Hans Joachim. *The Jewish-Christian Argument: A History of Theologies in Conflict.* Trans. David E. Green. London: Faber & Faber, 1965; New York: Holt, Rinehart & Winston, 1963.

Schoeps, "Prophetenmorde." • Schoeps, Hans Joachim. "Die jüdischen Prophetenmorde." 126-43 in *Aus frühchristlichen Zeit: Religionsgeschichtliche Untersuchungen.* Tübingen: J. C. B. Mohr, 1950.

Scholem, Sabbatai Sevi. • Scholem, Gershom. *Sabbatai Sevi: The Mystical Messiah.* Princeton: Princeton University Press, 1973.

Schreiber, "Menschensohn." • Schreiber, Stefan. "Henoch als Menschensohn. Zur problematischen Schlussidentifikation in den Bilderreden des äthiopischen Henochbuches (äthHen 71,14)." *ZNW* 91 (1-2, 2000): 1-17.

Schröter, "Anfänge." • Schröter, Jens. "Anfänge der Jesusüberlieferung: Überlieferungsgeschichtliche Beobachtungen zu einem Bereich urchristlicher Theologiegeschichte." *NTS* 50 (1, 2004): 53-76.

Schröter, "Begründer." • Schröter, Jens. "Der erinnerte Jesus als Begründer des Christentums? Bemerkungen zu James D. G. Dunns Ansatz in der Jesusforschung." *ZNT* 10 (20, 2007): 47-53.

Schröter, "Historische Jesus." • Schröter, Jens. "Der historische Jesus in seinem jüdischen Umfeld: Eine Bestandsaufnahme angesichts der neueren Diskussion." *Bib* 83 (4, 2002): 563-73.

Schubert, "Criticism." • Schubert, Kurt. "Biblical criticism criticized: with reference to the Markan report of Jesus's examination before the Sanhedrin." 385-402 in *Jesus and the Politics of His Day.* Ed. Ernst Bammel and C. F. D. Moule. Cambridge: Cambridge University Press, 1984.

Schubert, "Ehescheidung." • Schubert, Kurt. "Ehescheidung im Judentum zur Zeit Jesu." *TQ* 151 (1971): 23-27.

Schuler, "Archaeology." • Schuler, Mark T. "Recent Archaeology of Galilee and the Interpretation of Texts from the Galilean Ministry of Jesus." *CTQ* 71 (2, 2007): 99-117.

Schuller, "Resurrection." • Schuller, Eileen. "Ideas of Resurrection in Intertestamental Sources." *BibT* 27 (3, 1989): 140-45.

Schürer, History. • Schürer, Emil. *A History of the Jewish People in the Time of Jesus.* Ed. Nahum N. Glatzer. New York: Schocken Books, 1961, 1971. (Abridged from Division I of Schürer's work)

Schutte, "Resurrection." • Schutte, Philippus Jacobus Wilhelmus. "The Resurrection of Jesus: What's Left to Say?" *HTS/TS* 62 (4, 2006): 1513-26.

Schwank, "Wasserkrüge." • Schwank, Benedikt. " 'Sechs steinerne Wasserkrüge' (Joh 2,6)." *ErAuf* 73 (4, 1997): 314-16.

Schwartz, "Temples." • Schwartz, Daniel R. "The Three Temples of 4QFlorilegium." *RevQ* 10 (1979): 83-91.

Schwartz, "Voice." • Schwartz, Daniel R. "Whence the Voice? A Response to Bruce W. Longenecker." *JSJ* 31 (1, 2000): 42-46.

Schwarz, "Nekrous." • Schwarz, Günther. *"Aphes tous nekrous thapsai tous heauton nekrous."* *ZNW* 72 (1981): 272-76.

Schweitzer, Quest. • Schweitzer, Albert. *The Quest of the Historical Jesus.* Introduction by James M. Robinson. New York: Collier Books, Macmillan Publishing Company, 1968.

Schweizer, "Christ in Colossians." • Schweizer, Eduard. "Christ in the Letter to the Colossians." *RevExp* 70 (4, 1973): 451-67.

Schweizer, *Colossians.* • Schweizer, Eduard. *The Letter to the Colossians: A Commentary.* Trans. Andrew Chester. Minneapolis, MN: Augsburg, 1982.

Schweizer, "Discipleship." • Schweizer, Eduard. "Discipleship and Belief in Jesus as Lord from Jesus to the Hellenistic Church." *NTS* 2 (1955): 87-99.

Schweizer, *Jesus.* • Schweizer, Eduard. *Jesus.* Trans. David E. Green. New Testament Library. London: SCM, 1971.

Schweizer, *Mark.* • Schweizer, Eduard. *The Good News According to Mark.* Atlanta: John Knox, 1970.

Schweizer, *Matthew.* • Schweizer, Eduard. *The Good News According to Matthew.* Tr. David E. Green. Atlanta: John Knox, 1975.

Schweizer, *Parable.* • Schweizer, Eduard. *Jesus the Parable of God: What Do We Really Know About Jesus?* Princeton Theological Monograph Series 37. Allison Park, PA: Pickwick Publications, 1994.

Scobie, "John the Baptist." • Scobie, Charles H. H. "John the Baptist." 58-69 in *The Scrolls and Christianity: Historical and Theological Significance.* Ed. Matthew Black. London: S.P.C.K., 1969.

Scott, "Clouds." • Scott, R. B. Y. "'Behold, He Cometh with Clouds.'" *NTS* 5 (1959): 127-32.

Scott, *Customs.* • Scott, Julius J. *Customs and Controversies: Intertestamental Jewish Backgrounds of the New Testament.* Grand Rapids: Baker, 1995.

Scott, *Parable.* • Scott, Bernard Brandon. *Hear Then the Parable: A Commentary on the Parables of Jesus.* Minneapolis: Augsburg Fortress, 1989.

Scott, *Pastoral Epistles.* • Scott, E. F. *The Pastoral Epistles.* MNTC. London: Hodder & Stoughton, 1936.

Scroggs, *Adam.* • Scroggs, Robin. *The Last Adam. A Study in Pauline Anthropology.* Philadelphia: Fortress, 1966.

Scroggs, "Judaizing." • Scroggs, Robin. "The Judaizing of the New Testament." *CTSR* 76 (1, 1986): 36-45.

Scroggs, "Sociological Interpretation." • Scroggs, Robin. "The Sociological Interpretation of the New Testament: The Present State of Research." *NTS* 26 (1980): 164-79.

Segal, "Death Penalty." • Segal, Peretz. "The 'Divine Death Penalty' in the Hatra Inscriptions and the Mishnah." *JJS* 40 (1, 1989): 46-52.

Segal, *Passover.* • Segal, Judah B. *The Hebrew Passover from the Earliest Times to A.D. 70.* London Oriental Series 12. New York: Oxford University Press, 1963.

Segal, "Penalty." • Segal, Peretz. "The Penalty of the Warning Inscription from the Temple of Jerusalem." *IEJ* 39 (1-2, 1989): 79-84.

Segal, "Resurrection." • Segal, Alan F. "The Resurrection: Faith or History?" 121-38 in *The Resurrection of Jesus: John Dominic Crossan and N. T. Wright in Dialogue.* Ed. Robert B. Stewart. Minneapolis: Fortress, 2006.

Segal, "Revolutionary." • Segal, Alan F. "Jesus, the Jewish Revolutionary." 199-225 in *Jesus' Jewishness: Exploring the Place of Jesus within Early Judaism.* Ed. James H. Charlesworth. New York: The American Interfaith Institute, Crossroad Publishing Company, 1991.

Segalla, "Gesù di Nazaret." • Segalla, Giuseppe. "Gesù di Nazaret fondamento storico del racconto evangelico giovanneo." *Teologia* 29 (1, 2004): 14-42.

Segert, "Languages." • Segert, Stanislav. "The Languages of Historical Jesus." *CV* 44 (2, 2002): 161-73.

Segert, "Review" (1972). • Segert, Stanislav. Review of J. A. Fitzmyer's *The Genesis Apocryphon of Qumran Cave I, A Commentary* (2d rev. ed., 1971). *JSS* 17 (2, Autumn 1972): 273-74.

Segundo, *Historical Jesus.* • Segundo, Juan Luis. *The Historical Jesus of the Synoptics.* Vol. 2 of Jesus of Nazareth Yesterday and Today. Trans. John Drury. Maryknoll, NY: Orbis; London: Sheed & Ward; Melbourne: Dove Communications, 1985.

Selden, "Genre." • Selden, Daniel L. "Genre of Genre." 39-64 in *The Search for the Ancient Novel*. Ed. James Tatum. Baltimore, London: The Johns Hopkins University Press, 1994.

Senior, *Matthew*. • Senior, Donald. *What Are They Saying About Matthew?* New York: Paulist, 1983.

Septimus, "Mttrwn." • Septimus, B. "Ht'w sl mttrwn: bsbk lswnwt wnwsh'wt." *Lesonénu* 69 (3-4, 2007): 291-300.

Setzer, *Responses*. • Setzer, Claudia J. *Jewish Responses to Early Christians: History and Polemics, 30-150 C.E.* Minneapolis: Fortress, 1994.

Sevenster, *Anti-Semitism*. • Sevenster, J. N. *The Roots of Pagan Anti-Semitism in the Ancient World.* NovTSup 41. Leiden: E. J. Brill, 1975.

Shanks, "*BAR* Interviews Yadin." • Shanks, Hershel. "BAR Interviews Yigael Yadin." *BAR* 9 (1, Jan.-Feb. 1983): 16-23.

Shanks, "Hometown." • Shanks, Hershel. "Major New Excavation Planned for Mary Magdalene's Hometown." *BAR* 33 (5, 2007): 52-55.

Shea, "Stage." • Shea, Chris. "Setting the Stage for Romances: Xenophon of Ephesus and the Ecphrasis." 61-76 in *Ancient Fiction and Early Christian Narrative*. Ed. Ronald F. Hock, J. Bradley Chance and Judith Perkins. SBLSymS 6. Atlanta: Society of Biblical Literature, 1998.

Sheeley, *Asides*. • Sheeley, Steven M. *Narrative Asides in Luke-Acts*. JSNTSup 72. Sheffield: Sheffield Academic Press, 1992.

Shepherd, "Date." • Shepherd, Massey H. "Are Both the Synoptics and John Correct about the Date of Jesus' Death?" *JBL* 80 (1961): 123-32.

Sherk, *Empire*. • Sherk, Robert K., ed. and trans. *The Roman Empire: Augustus to Hadrian*. Translated Documents of Greece and Rome 6. New York: Cambridge University Press, 1988.

Sherwin-White, *Society*. • Sherwin-White, A. N. *Roman Society and Roman Law in the New Testament*. Grand Rapids: Baker, 1978. Reprint of Oxford: Oxford University, 1963.

Sherwin-White, "Trial." • Sherwin-White, A. N. "The Trial of Christ." Pp. 97-116 in *Historicity and Chronology in the New Testament*. Essays by D. E. Nineham, et al. London: S.P.C.K., 1965.

Shoemaker, "Earring." • Shoemaker, Michael T. "Herod's Lady's Earring?" *BAR* 17 (4, 1991): 58-59.

Shotwell, *Exegesis*. • Shotwell, Willis A. *The Biblical Exegesis of Justin Martyr*. London: S.P.C.K., 1965.

Shuler, *Genre*. • Shuler, Philip L. *A Genre for the Gospels: The Biographical Character of Matthew*. Philadelphia: Fortress, 1982.

Shupak, "Learning Methods." • Shupak, Nili. "Learning Methods in Ancient Israel." *VT* 53 (3, 2003): 416-426.

Sievers, "Name." • Sievers, Joseph. "What's in a Name? Antiochus in Josephus' '*Bellum Judaicum*.'" *JJS* 56 (1, 2005): 34-47.

Sievers, "Shekhinah." • Sievers, Joseph. "'Where Two or Three . . .': The Rabbinic Concept of Shekhinah and Matthew 18:20." *SIDIC* 17 (1984): 4-10.

Sigal, *Halakah*. • Sigal, Phillip. *The Halakah of Jesus of Nazareth According to the Gospel of Matthew*. Lanham, MD: University Press of America, 1986.

Sigal, "Note." • Sigal, Phillip. "Another Note to 1 Corinthians 10.16." *NTS* 29 (1983): 134-39.

Silberman, "Apocalyptic Revisited." • Silberman, Lou H. "Apocalyptic Revisited: Reflections on the Thought of Albert Schweitzer." *JAAR* 44 (3, Sept. 1976): 489-501.

Silberman, "Messiahs." • Silberman, Lou H. "The Two 'Messiahs' of the Manual of Discipline." *VT* 5 (1, Jan. 1955): 77-82.

Silberman, "Ossuary." • Silberman, Neil Asher. "Ossuary: A Box for Bones." *BAR* 17 (3, 1991): 73-74.

Silberman, "Use." • Silberman, Lou H. "Anent the Use of Rabbinic Material." *NTS* 24 (3, April 1978): 415-17.

Silver, "Moses." • Silver, Daniel J. "Moses and the Hungry Birds." *JQR* 64 (2, October 1973): 123-53.

Simon, *Hellenists*. • Simon, Marcel. *St Stephen and the Hellenists in the Primitive Church*. The

Haskell Lectures delivered at the Graduate School of Theology, Oberlin College, 1956. New York: Longmans, Green & Company, 1958.

Simon, *Sects.* • Simon, Marcel. *Jewish Sects at the Time of Jesus.* Philadelphia: Fortress, 1967.

Simpson, *Literature.* • *The Literature of Ancient Egypt: An Anthology of Stories, Instructions, Stelae, Autobiographies, and Poetry.* 3rd ed. Ed. and introduction by William Kelly Simpson. New Haven: Yale University Press, 2003.

Sinclair, "*Sententia.*" • Sinclair, Patrick. "The *Sententia* in *Rhetorica ad Herennium:* A Study in the Sociology of Rhetoric." *AJP* 114 (4, 1993): 561-80.

Sinclair, "Temples." • Sinclair, P. "'These Are MY Temples in Your Hearts' (Tac. *Ann.* 4.38.2)." *CP* 86 (4, 1991): 333-35.

Sisti, "Figura." • Sisti, A. "La figura del giusto perseguitato in *Sap.* 2,12-20." *BeO* 19 (1977): 129-44.

Sjoberg, *Preindustrial City.* • Sjoberg, Gideon. *The Preindustrial City: Past and Present.* New York: Free Press, 1960-1966.

Skarsaune, *Shadow.* • Skarsaune, Oskar. *In the Shadow of the Temple: Jewish Influences on Early Christianity.* Downers Grove, IL: InterVarsity, 2002.

Small, "Memory." • Small, Jocelyn Penny. "Artificial Memory and the Writing Habits of the Literate." *Helios* 22 (2, 1995): 159-66.

Small, *Wax Tablets.* • Small, Jocelyn Penny. *Wax Tablets of the Mind: Cognitive studies of memory and literacy in classical antiquity.* London, New York: Routledge, 1997.

Smallwood, "Historians." • E. Mary Smallwood. "Philo and Josephus as Historians of the Same Events." 114-29 in *Josephus, Judaism and Christianity.* Ed. Louis H. Feldman and Gohei Hata. Detroit: Wayne State University Press, 1987.

Smallwood, *Jews.* • Smallwood, E. Mary. *The Jews Under Roman Rule: From Pompey to Diocletian.* SJLA 20. Leiden: E. J. Brill, 1976.

Smallwood, "Priests." • Smallwood, E. Mary. "High Priests and Politics in Roman Palestine." *JTS* 13 (1962): 14-34.

Smith, "Appearance." • Smith, Dennis A. "Appearance or Disappearance? Early Beliefs about Jesus' Vindication." *FR* 21 (1, 2008): 3-8, 21.

Smith, "Baptism." • Smith, Derwood. "Jewish Proselyte Baptism and the Baptism of John." *ResQ* 25 (1, 1982): 13-32.

Smith, "Begetting." • Smith, Morton. "'God's Begetting the Messiah' in 1QSa." *NTS* 5 (1958-1959): 218-24.

Smith, "Chronology of Supper." • Smith, Barry D. "The Chronology of the Last Supper." *WTJ* 53 (1991): 29-45.

Smith, "Cross Marks." • Smith, Robert Houston. "The Cross Marks on Jewish Ossuaries." *PEQ* 106 (1974): 53-66.

Smith, "Education." • Smith, Christian. "Secularizing American Higher Education: The Case of Early American Sociology." 97-159 in *The Secular Revolution: Power, Interests, and Conflict in the Secularization of American Public Life.* Ed. Christian Smith. Berkeley: University of California Press, 2003.

Smith, *Gnostic Origins.* • Smith, Carl B., II. *No Longer Jews: The Search for Gnostic Origins.* Peabody: Hendrickson, 2004.

Smith, "Issues and Problem." • Smith, D. Moody. "Historical Issues and the Problem of John and the Synoptics." Pp. 252-67 in *From Jesus to John: Essays on Jesus and New Testament Christology in Honour of Marinus de Jonge.* Ed. Martinus C. De Boer. JSNTSup 84. Sheffield: JSOT Press, 1993.

Smith, *Johannine Christianity.* • Smith, D. Moody. *Johannine Christianity: Essays on Its Setting, Sources, and Theology.* Columbia, SC: University of South Carolina, 1984.

Smith, *John* (1999). • Smith, D. Moody. *John.* Abingdon New Testament Commentaries. Nashville: Abingdon, 1999.

Smith, *John Among Gospels.* • Smith, D. Moody. *John Among the Gospels: The Relationship in Twentieth-Century Research.* Minneapolis: Fortress, 1992. Revised as: *John among the Gospels.* 2nd ed. Columbia: University of South Carolina Press, 2001.

Smith, "Learned." • Smith, D. Moody. "What Have I Learned about the Gospel of John?" Pp. 217-35 in *"What Is John?" Readers and Reading of the Fourth Gospel.* Ed. Fernando F. Segovia. SBLSymS 3. Atlanta: Scholars Press, 1996.

Smith, *Magician.* • Smith, Morton. *Jesus the Magician.* San Francisco: Harper & Row, Publishers, 1978.

Smith, "Problem of History." • Smith, D. Moody. "The Problem of History in John." 311-20 in *What We Have Heard from the Beginning: The Past, Present, and Future of Johannine Studies.* Ed. Tom Thatcher. Waco, TX: Baylor University Press, 2007.

Smith, "Scripture." • Smith, D. Moody. "When Did the Gospels Become Scripture?" *JBL* 119 (1, Spring 2000): 3-20.

Smith, *Symposium.* • Smith, Dennis E. *From Symposium to Eucharist: The Banquet in the Early Christian World.* Minneapolis: Augsburg Fortress, 2003.

Smith, *Tannaitic Parallels.* • Smith, Morton. *Tannaitic Parallels to the Gospels.* Philadelphia: Society of Biblical Literature, 1951.

Smith, "Tomb." • Smith, Robert Houston. "The Tomb of Jesus." *BA* 30 (1967): 74-90.

Smith, "Tradition." • Smith, Morton. "A Comparison of Early Christian and Early Rabbinic Tradition." *JBL* 82 (1963): 169-76.

Smith, "Variety." • Smith, Morton. "What Is Implied by the Variety of Messianic Figures?" *JBL* 78 (1959): 66-72.

Smith, "Zealots." • Smith, Morton. "Zealots and Sicarii, Their Origins and Relation." *HTR* 64 (1971): 1-19.

Smyth, "Scrolls and Messiah." • Smyth, Kevin. "The Dead Sea Scrolls and the Messiah." *Studies* 45 (1956): 1-14.

Snodgrass, "Allegorizing." • Snodgrass, Klyne R. "From Allegorizing to Allegorizing: A History of the Interpretation of the Parables of Jesus." 248-68 in *The Historical Jesus in Recent Research.* Ed. James D. G. Dunn and Scot McKnight. Winona Lake, IN: Eisenbrauns, 2005.

Snodgrass, "Husbandmen." • Snodgrass, Klyne R. "The Parable of the Wicked Husbandman: Is the Gospel of Thomas Version the Original?" *NTS* 21 (1975): 142-44.

Snodgrass, "Prophets." • Snodgrass, Klyne. "Prophets, Parables, and Theologians." *BBR* 18 (1, 2008): 45-77.

Snodgrass, *Stories.* • Snodgrass, Klyne R. *Stories with Intent: A Comprehensive Guide to the Parables of Jesus.* Grand Rapids, Cambridge: Eerdmans, 2008.

Snodgrass, *Tenants.* • Snodgrass, Klyne R. *The Parable of the Wicked Tenants.* WUNT 27. Tübingen: Mohr, 1983.

Snyder, *Corinthians.* • Snyder, Graydon F. *First Corinthians: A Faith Community Commentary.* Macon, GA: Mercer University Press, 1992.

Soards, "Passion Narrative." • Soards, Marion L. "Appendix IX. The Question of a Premarcan Passion Narrative." 1492-1524 in *The Death of the Messiah: From Gethsemane to Grave. A Commentary on the Passion Narratives in the Four Gospels.* 2 vols. New York: Doubleday, 1994.

Soards, "Review." • Soards, Marion L. Review of *Profit with Delight,* by Richard Pervo. *JAAR* 58 (2, Summer 1990): 307-10.

Soards, *Speeches.* • Soards, Marion L. *The Speeches in Acts: Their Content, Context, and Concerns.* Louisville, KY: Westminster John Knox, 1994.

Soares Prabhu, *Formula Quotations.* • Soares Prabhu, George M. *The Formula Quotations in the Infancy Narrative of Matthew: An Enquiry into the Tradition History of Mt 1–2.* Rome: Biblical Institute Press, 1976.

Södig, "Feindeshass." • Södig, Thomas. "Feindeshass und Bruderliebe. Beobachtungen zur essenischen Ethik." *RevQ* 16 (1995): 601-19.

Songer, "Sermon." • Songer, Harold S. "The Sermon on the Mount and Its Jewish Foreground." *RevExp* 89 (1992): 165-77.

Spencer, *Acts*. • Spencer, F. Scott. *Acts*. Sheffield: Sheffield Academic Press, 1997.

Spencer, *Profiles*. • Spencer, F. Scott. *What Did Jesus Do? Gospel Profiles of Jesus' Personal Conduct.* Harrisburg: Trinity Press International, 2003.

Spivey and Smith, *Anatomy*. • Spivey, Robert A., and D. Moody Smith. *Anatomy of the New Testament: A Guide to Its Structure and Meaning.* 3d ed. New York: Macmillan Publishing Company; London: Collier Macmillan Publishers, 1982.

Squires, *Plan*. • Squires, John T. *The Plan of God in Luke-Acts.* SNTSMS 76. Cambridge: Cambridge University Press, 1993.

Squires, "Plan." • Squires, John T. "The Plan of God." 19-39 in *Witness to the Gospel: The Theology of Acts.* Ed. I. Howard Marshall and David Peterson. Grand Rapids: Eerdmans, 1998.

Stagg, *Acts*. • Stagg, Frank. *The Book of Acts: The Early Struggle for an Unhindered Gospel.* Nashville, TN: Broadman, 1955.

Stambaugh, *City*. • Stambaugh, John E. *The Ancient Roman City.* Baltimore: The Johns Hopkins University Press, 1988.

Stambaugh and Balch, *Environment*. • Stambaugh, John E., and David L. Balch. *The New Testament in Its Social Environment.* LEC 2. Philadelphia: Westminster, 1986.

Stanford, *Sound of Greek*. • Stanford, William Bedell. *The Sound of Greek: Studies in the Greek Theory and Practice of Euphony.* Berkeley, CA: University of California Press, 1967.

Stanley, *Resurrection*. • Stanley, David Michael. *Christ's Resurrection in Pauline Soteriology.* AnBib 13. Rome: Pontifical Biblical Institute, 1961.

Stanton, *Gospels*. • Stanton, Graham N. *The Gospels and Jesus.* Oxford Bible Series. Oxford: Oxford University Press, 1989.

Stanton, *Gospel Truth*. • Stanton, Graham N. *Gospel Truth? New Light on Jesus and the Gospels.* Valley Forge, PA: Trinity Press International, 1995.

Stanton, *Jesus of Nazareth*. • Stanton, Graham N. *Jesus of Nazareth in New Testament Preaching.* Cambridge: Cambridge University, 1974.

Stanton, "Magician." • Stanton, Graham N. "Jesus of Nazareth: A Magician and a False Prophet Who Deceived God's People?" 164-80 in *Jesus of Nazareth: Lord and Christ. Essays on the Historical Jesus and New Testament Christology.* Ed. Joel B. Green and Max Turner. Grand Rapids: Eerdmans; Carlisle: Paternoster, 1994.

Stanton, "Message." • Stanton, Graham N. "Message and miracles." 56-71 in *The Cambridge Companion to Jesus.* Ed. Markus Bockmuehl. Cambridge: Cambridge University, 2001.

Stanton, *New People*. • Stanton, Graham N. *A Gospel for a New People: Studies in Matthew.* Louisville: Westminster/John Knox, 1993; Edinburgh: T. & T. Clark, 1992.

Stanton, "Reflection." • Stanton, Graham N. "The Gospel Traditions and Early Christological Reflection." 543-52 in *The Historical Jesus in Recent Research.* Ed. James D. G. Dunn and Scot McKnight. Winona Lake, IN: Eisenbrauns, 2005.

Stanton, "Salvation." • Stanton, Graham N. "Salvation Proclaimed: X. Matthew 11:28-30: Comfortable Words?" *ExpT* 94 (1982): 3-9.

Stark, "Empire." • Stark, Rodney. "Christianizing the Urban Empire: An Analysis Based on 2 Greco-Roman Cities." *SocAn* 52 (1, 1991): 77-88.

Stauffer, *Jesus*. • Stauffer, Ethelbert. *Jesus and His Story.* Tr. Richard and Clara Winston. New York: Alfred A. Knopf, 1960.

Stefaniak, "Poglady." • Stefaniak, L. "Poglady mesjanskie czy eschatologiczne sekty z Qumrân. Les opinions de la secte de Qumrân, sont-elles messianiques ou eschatologiques?" *RocTK* 9 (4, 1962): 59-73.

Stegemann, "Jesus." • Stegemann, Ekkehard. "Jesus." 6:1178-1189 in *Brill's New Pauly*.

Stegemann, Malina and Theissen, *Setting of Jesus*. • Stegemann, Wolfgang, Bruce J. Malina, and Gerd Theissen, eds., *The Social Setting of Jesus and the Gospels*. Minneapolis: Fortress, 2002.

Stein, "Agreements." • Stein, Robert H. "The Matthew-Luke Agreements Against Mark: Insight from John." *CBQ* 54 (1992): 482-502.

Stein, "Criteria." • Stein, Robert H. "The 'Criteria' for Authenticity." 1:225-63 in *GosPersp*.

Stein, *Messiah*. • Stein, Robert H. *Jesus the Messiah: A Survey of the Life of Christ*. Downers Grove: InterVarsity, 1996.

Stein, *Method and Message*. • Stein, Robert H. *The Method and Message of Jesus' Teachings*. Philadelphia: Westminster, 1978.

Stein, "Synoptic Problem." • Stein, Robert H. "Synoptic Problem." 784-92 in *DJG*.

Stemberger, "Auferstehungslehre." • Stemberger, Günter. "Zur Auferstehungslehre in der rabbinschen Literatur." *Kairos* 15 (1973): 238-66.

Stemberger, "Pesachhaggada." • Stemberger, Günter. "Pesachhaggada und Abendmahlsberichte des Neuen Testaments." *Kairos* 29 (3-4, 1987): 147-58.

Stendahl, "Hate." • Stendahl, Krister. "Hate, Non-Retaliation, and Love. 1QS x,17-20 and Rom. 12:19-21." *Harvard Theological Review* 55 (1962): 343-55.

Stendahl, *School*. • Stendahl, Krister. *The School of St. Matthew and Its Use of the Old Testament*. Philadelphia: Fortress, 1968.

Stenger, "Apophthegma." • Stenger, Jan. "Apophthegma, Gnome und Chrie. Zum Verhältnis dreier literarischer Kleinformen." *Phil* 150 (2, 2006): 203-21.

Stephens, "Who Read Novels?" • Stephens, Susan A. "Who Read Ancient Novels?" 405-418 in *The Search for the Ancient Novel*. Ed. James Tatum. Baltimore, London: Johns Hopkins University Press, 1994.

Sterling, *Ancestral Philosophy*. • Sterling, Gregory E., ed. *The Ancestral Philosophy: Hellenistic Philosophy in Second Temple Judaism: Essays of David Winston*. BJS 331. SPhilMon 4. Providence: Brown University, 2001.

Sterling, "Historians." • Sterling, Gregory E. "Historians, Greco-Roman." 499-504 in *DNTB*.

Sterling, *Historiography*. • Sterling, Gregory E. *Historiography and Self-Definition: Josephos, Luke-Acts and Apologetic Historiography*. NovTSup 64. Leiden: E. J. Brill, 1992.

Stern, "Aspects." • Stern, Menahem. "Aspects of Jewish Society: The Priesthood and Other Classes." 561-630 in *JPFC*.

Stern, *Authors*. • Stern, Menahem. *Greek and Latin Authors on Jews and Judaism: Edited with Introductions, Translations and Commentary*. Vol. 1: *From Herodotus to Plutarch*. Jerusalem: The Israel Academy of Sciences and Humanities, 1974. Vol. 2: *From Tacitus to Simplicius*. Jerusalem: The Israel Academy of Sciences and Humanities, 1980. Vol. 3: Appendixes and Indexes. Jerusalem: The Israel Academy of Sciences and Humanities, 1984.

Stern, *Parables*. • Stern, David. *Parables in Midrash: Narrative and Exegesis in Rabbinic Literature*. Cambridge: Harvard University Press, 1991.

Stern, "Province." • Stern, Menahem. "The Province of Judaea." 308-76 in *JPFC*.

Sternberg, *Poetics*. • Sternberg, Meir. *The Poetics of Biblical Narrative*. Bloomington: Indiana University Press, 1985.

Stevens, "Sermon." • Stevens, Gerald L. "Understanding the Sermon on the Mount: Its Rabbinic and New Testament Context." *TTE* 46 (1992): 83-95.

Stevens, *Theology*. • Stevens, George B. *The Johannine Theology: A Study of the Doctrinal Contents of the Gospel and Epistles of the Apostle John*. New York: Charles Scribner's Sons, 1894.

Stevenson and Habermas, *Verdict*. • Stevenson, Kenneth E., and Gary R. Habermas, *Verdict on the Shroud*. Ann Arbor: Servant Books, 1981.

Stewart, "Parable Form." • Stewart, Roy A. "The Parable Form in the Old Testament and the Rabbinic Literature." *EvQ* 36 (1964): 133-47.

Stewart, "Procedure." • Stewart, Roy A. "Judicial Procedure in NT Times." *EvQ* 47 (1975): 94-109.

Stibbe, *Gospel.* • Stibbe, Mark W. G. *John's Gospel.* New Testament Readings. London and New York: Routledge, 1994.

Stone, "Galilee Boat." • Stone, G. R. "The Galilee Boat — A Fishing Vessel of New Testament Times." *BurH* 25 (2, 1989): 46-54.

Stoops, "*Acts of Peter.*" • Stoops, Robert F., Jr. "*The Acts of Peter* in Intertextual Context." 57-86 in *The Apocryphal Acts of the Apostles in Intertextual Perspectives.* Semeia 80. Ed. Robert F. Stoops. Atlanta: Scholars Press, 1997.

Story, "Chronology." • Story, Cullen I. K. "The Bearing of Old Testament Terminology on the Johannine Chronology of the Final Passover of Jesus." *NovT* 31 (4, 1989): 316-24.

Stowers, "Diatribe." • Stowers, Stanley K. "The Diatribe." 71-83 in *Greco-Roman Literature and the New Testament: Selected Forms and Genres.* Ed. David E. Aune. SBLSBS 21. Atlanta: Scholars Press, 1988.

Stowers, *Letter Writing.* • Stowers, Stanley K. *Letter Writing in Greco-Roman Antiquity.* LEC 5. Philadelphia: Westminster, 1986.

Stowers, *Rereading of Romans.* • Stowers, Stanley K. *A Rereading of Romans: Justice, Jews, and Gentiles.* New Haven: Yale, 1994.

Strange, "Galilee." • Strange, James F. "Galilee." 391-98 in *DNTB.*

Strange and Shanks, "House." • Strange, James F., and Hershel Shanks. "Has the House Where Jesus Stayed in Capernaum Been Found?" *BAR* 8 (6, 1982): 26-37.

Strecker, "Perspektive." • Strecker, Christian. "Der erinnerte Jesus aus kulturwissenschaftlicher Perspektive." *ZNT* 10 (20, 2007): 18-27.

Streeter, *Gospels.* • Streeter, Burnett Hillman. *The Four Gospels: A Study of Origins Treating of the Manuscript Tradition, Sources, Authorship, & Dates.* Rev. ed. London: Macmillan & Co., 1930.

Strelan, *Strange Acts.* • Strelan, Rick. *Strange Acts: Studies in the Cultural World of the Acts of the Apostles.* BZNW 126. Berlin, New York: Walter de Gruyter, 2004.

Strijdom, "Unconventionality." • Strijdom, Johan M. "The 'unconventionality' of Jesus from the perspective of a diverse audience: Evaluating Crossan's historical Jesus." *Neot* 29 (2, 1995): 313-23.

Strothers, "Objects." • Strothers, R. "Unidentified Flying Objects in Classical Antiquity." *CJ* 103 (1, 2007): 79-92.

Stroud, *Demeter.* • Stroud, R. S. *Demeter and Persephone in Ancient Corinth.* Princeton: ASCSA, 1987.

Stuhlmacher, "Readiness." • Stuhlmacher, Peter. "Jesus' Readiness to Suffer and His Understanding of His Death." 392-412 in *The Historical Jesus in Recent Research.* Ed. James D. G. Dunn and Scot McKnight. Winona Lake, IN: Eisenbrauns, 2005.

Stuhlmacher, *Romans.* • Stuhlmacher, Peter. *Paul's Letter to the Romans: A Commentary.* Trans. Scott J. Hafemann. Louisville, KY: Westminster/John Knox, 1994.

Stuhlmacher, "Son of Man." • Stuhlmacher, Peter. "The Messianic Son of Man: Jesus' Claim to Deity." 325-44 in *The Historical Jesus in Recent Research.* Ed. James D. G. Dunn and Scot McKnight. Winona Lake, IN: Eisenbrauns, 2005.

Stuhlmacher, "Theme." • Stuhlmacher, Peter. "The Theme: The Gospel and the Gospels." 1-25 in *The Gospel and the Gospels.* Ed. Peter Stuhlmacher. Grand Rapids: Eerdmans, 1991.

Suggs, *Christology.* • Suggs, M. J. *Wisdom, Christology and Law in Matthew's Gospel.* Cambridge: Harvard University Press, 1970.

Sukenik, "Records." • Sukenik, E. L. "The Earliest Records of Christianity." *AJA* 51 (1947): 351-65.

Sumney, *Opponents.* • Sumney, Jerry L. *Identifying Paul's Opponents: The Question of Method in 2 Corinthians.* JSNTSup 40. Sheffield: JSOT Press, 1990.

Sutcliffe, "Meals." • Sutcliffe, Edmund Felix. "Sacred Meals at Qumran?" *HeyJ* 1 (1960): 48-65.

Sutcliffe, "Review." • Sutcliffe, Edmund Felix. Review of "H. Mantel, *Studies in the History of the Sanhedrin.*" *HeyJ* 4 (1963): 283-87.

Svensson, "Qumrankalendern." • Svensson, Jan. "Johannespåsken och Qumrankalendern." *SEÅ* 62 (1997): 87-110.

Sweet, "Zealots." • Sweet, J. P. M. "The Zealots and Jesus." 1-9 in *Jesus and the Politics of His Day*. Ed. Ernst Bammel and C. F. D. Moule. Cambridge: Cambridge University Press, 1984.

Swidler, *Women*. • Swidler, Leonard. *Women in Judaism: The Status of Women in Formative Judaism*. Metuchen, NJ: Scarecrow Press, 1976.

Syon, "Evidence." • Syon, Danny. "Numismatic Evidence of Jewish Presence in Galilee before the Hasmonean Annexation?" *IsNumR* 1 (2006): 21-24.

Syon, "Gamla" • Syon, Danny. "Gamla: Portrait of a Rebellion." *BAR* 18 (1, 1992): 20-37, 72.

Tabor, "Messiah." • Tabor, James D. "A Pierced or Piercing Messiah? — The Verdict Is Still Out." *BAR* 18 (6, 1992): 58-59.

Tabor, "4Q521." • Tabor, James D. "4Q521 'On Resurrection' and the Synoptic Gospel Tradition: A Preliminary Study." *JSP* 10 (1992): 149-62.

Tagawa, "Marc 13." • Tagawa, Kenzo. "Marc 13. La tâtonnement d'un homme réaliste éveillé face à la tradition apocalyptique." *FoiVie* 76 (1977): 11-44.

Talbert, "Chance." • Talbert, Charles H. "Reading Chance, Moessner, and Parsons." 229-40 in *Cadbury, Knox, and Talbert: American Contributions to the Study of Acts*. Ed. Mikeal C. Parsons and Joseph B. Tyson. Atlanta: Scholars Press, 1992.

Talbert, *Gospel*. • Talbert, Charles H. *What Is a Gospel? The Genre of the Canonical Gospels*. Philadelphia: Fortress, 1977.

Talbert, *John*. • Talbert, Charles H. *Reading John: A Literary and Theological Commentary on the Fourth Gospel and the Johannine Epistles*. New York: Crossroad, 1992.

Talbert, *Luke*. • Talbert, Charles H. *Reading Luke: A Literary and Theological Commentary on the Third Gospel*. New York: Crossroad Publishing Company, 1982.

Talbert, *Mediterranean Milieu*. • Talbert, Charles H. *Reading Luke-Acts in Its Mediterranean Milieu*. NovTSup 107. Leiden: Brill, 2003.

Talbert, "Monograph or *Bios*." • Talbert, Charles H. "The Acts of the Apostles: monograph or *bios*?" 58-72 in *History, Literature, and Society in the Book of Acts*. Ed. Ben Witherington, III. Cambridge: Cambridge University, 1996.

Talbert, "Oral and Independent." • Talbert, Charles H. "Oral and Independent or Literary and Interdependent? A Response to Albert B. Lord." 93-102 in *The Relationships Among the Gospels: An Interdisciplinary Dialogue*. Ed. William O. Walker, Jr. San Antonio: Trinity University Press, 1978.

Talbert, *Patterns*. • Talbert, Charles H. *Literary Patterns, Theological Themes, and the Genre of Luke-Acts*. SBLMS 20. Missoula, MT: Scholars Press, 1974.

Talbert, "Problem." • Talbert, Charles H. "The Problem of Pre-Existence in Philippians 2 6-11." *JBL* 86 (2, June 1967): 141-53.

Talbert, "Review." • Talbert, Charles H. Review of Richard A. Burridge, *What Are the Gospels? JBL* 112 (4, Winter 1993): 714-15.

Tan, *Zion Traditions*. • Tan, Kim Huat. *The Zion Traditions and the Aims of Jesus*. SNTSMS 91. Cambridge: Cambridge University, 1997.

Tannehill, *Acts*. • Tannehill, Robert C. *The Narrative Unity of Luke-Acts: A Literary Interpretation*. 2 vols. Vol. 2: *The Acts of the Apostles*. Minneapolis: Fortress, 1990.

Tannehill, *Luke*. • Tannehill, Robert C. *The Narrative Unity of Luke-Acts: A Literary Interpretation*. 2 vols. Vol. 1: *The Gospel According to Luke*. Philadelphia: Fortress, 1986.

Tannehill, "Rejection." • Tannehill, Robert C. "Rejection by Jews and Turning to Gentiles: The Pattern of Paul's Mission in Acts." 83-101 in *Luke-Acts and the Jewish People: Eight Critical Perspectives*. Ed. Joseph B. Tyson. Minneapolis: Augsburg, 1988.

Tannehill, *Sword*. • Tannehill, Robert C. *The Sword of His Mouth*. SBLSemS 1. Missoula, MT: Scholars Press, 1975.

Tannehill, "Tragic Story." • Tannehill, Robert C. "Israel in Luke-Acts: A Tragic Story." *JBL* 104 (1, 1985): 69-85.

Taussig, "Prayer." • Taussig, Hal. "The Lord's Prayer." *Forum* 4 (1988): 25-41.

Taylor, *Atonement.* • Taylor, Vincent. *The Atonement in New Testament Teaching.* London: Epworth, 1945.

Taylor, "Baptism." • Taylor, T. M. "The Beginnings of Jewish Proselyte Baptism." *NTS* 2 (Feb. 1956): 193-98.

Taylor, "Capernaum." • Taylor, Joan E. "Capernaum and Its 'Jewish-Christians': A Re-examination of the Franciscan Excavations." *BAIAS* 9 (1989): 7-28.

Taylor, *Formation.* • Taylor, Vincent. *The Formation of the Gospel Tradition.* 2d ed. London: Macmillan & Company, 1960; reprint of 1935 ed.

Taylor, *Immerser.* • Taylor, Joan E. *The Immerser: John the Baptist within Second Temple Judaism.* Grand Rapids: Eerdmans, 1997.

Taylor, *Mark.* • Taylor, Vincent. *The Gospel According to St. Mark.* London: Macmillan & Company, 1952.

Taylor, "Quest." • Taylor, Nicholas H. "Paul and the Historical Jesus Quest." *Neot* 37 (1, 2003): 105-26.

Teeple, *Prophet.* • Teeple, Howard M. *The Mosaic Eschatological Prophet.* JBLMS 10. Philadelphia: Society of Biblical Literature, 1957.

Telford, "Trends." • Telford, William R. "Major Trends and Interpretive Issues in the Study of Jesus." 33-74 in *Studying the Historical Jesus: Evaluations of the State of Current Research.* NTTS 19. Ed. Bruce Chilton and Craig A. Evans. Leiden, New York, Cologne: E. J. Brill, 1994.

Thackeray, *Josephus.* • Thackeray, H. St. John. *Josephus: The Man and the Historian.* New York: Ktav, 1967; reprint of 1929 edition.

Thatcher, *Riddler.* • Thatcher, Tom. *Jesus the Riddler: The Power of Ambiguity in the Gospels.* Louisville: Westminster John Knox, 2006.

Thatcher, *Riddles.* • Thatcher, Tom. *The Riddles of Jesus in John: A Study in Tradition and Folklore.* SBLMS. Atlanta: Society of Biblical Literature, 2000.

Theissen, *Gospels in Context.* • Theissen, Gerd. *The Gospels in Context: Social and Political History in the Synoptic Tradition.* Trans. Linda M. Maloney. Minneapolis: Fortress, 1991.

Theissen, *Miracle Stories.* • Theissen, Gerd. *The Miracle Stories of the Early Christian Tradition.* trans. Francis McDonagh. Ed. John Riches. Philadelphia: Fortress, 1983.

Theissen, *Social Setting.* • Theissen, Gerd. *The Social Setting of Pauline Christianity.* Edited and trans. John H. Schütz. Philadelphia: Fortress, 1982.

Theissen, *Sociology.* • Theissen, Gerd. *Sociology of Early Palestinian Christianity.* Philadelphia: Fortress, 1978.

Theissen and Merz, *Historical Jesus.* • Theissen, Gerd, and Annette Merz. *The Historical Jesus: A Comprehensive Guide.* Minneapolis: Fortress, 1998. Trans. by John Bowden from *Der historische Jesus: Ein Lehrbuch.* Göttingen: Vandenhoeck & Ruprecht, 1996.

Thielman, *Theology.* • Thielman, Frank. *Theology of the New Testament.* Grand Rapids: Zondervan, 2005.

Thiering, *Hypothesis.* • Thiering, Barbara E. *The Gospels and Qumran: A New Hypothesis.* ANZSTR. Sydney: Theological Explorations, 1981.

Thiselton, *Corinthians.* • Thiselton, Anthony C. *The First Epistle to the Corinthians: A Commentary on the Greek Text.* Cambridge, Grand Rapids: Eerdmans; Carlisle: Paternoster, 2000.

Thiselton, *Horizons.* • Thiselton, Anthony C. *The Two Horizons: New Testament Hermeneutics and Philosophical Description.* Grand Rapids: Eerdmans, 1980.

Thom, "Highways." • Thom, Johan C. "'Don't Walk on the Highways': The Pythagorean *Akousmata* and Early Christian Literature." *JBL* 113 (1994): 93-112.

Thoma, "Martyrer." • Thoma, Clemens. "Frühjüdische Martyrer. Glaube an Auferstehung und Gericht." *FreiRund* 11 (2, 2004): 82-93.

Thoma, "Priesthood." • Thoma, Clemens. "The High Priesthood in the Judgment of Josephus." 196-215 in *Josephus, the Bible, and History.* Ed. Louis H. Feldman and Gohei Hata. Detroit: Wayne State University Press, 1989.

Thomas, "Fluidity." • Thomas, Christine M. "Stories Without Texts and Without Authors: The Problem of Fluidity in Ancient Novelistic Texts and Early Christian Literature." 273-91 in *Ancient Fiction and Early Christian Narrative.* Ed. Ronald F. Hock, J. Bradley Chance and Judith Perkins. SBLSymS 6. Atlanta: Society of Biblical Literature, 1998.

Thompson, *Advice.* • Thompson, William G. *Matthew's Advice to a Divided Community: Mt. 17,22-18,35.* AnBib 44. Rome: Biblical Institute Press, 1970.

Thompson, *Archaeology.* • Thompson, J. A. *The Bible and Archaeology.* Grand Rapids: Eerdmans, 1962.

Thompson, *Clothed.* • Thompson, Michael. *Clothed with Christ: The Example and Teaching of Jesus in Romans 12.1-15.13.* JSNTSup 59. Sheffield: JSOT Press, 1991.

Thompson, *Debate.* • Thompson, William M. *The Jesus Debate: A Survey & Synthesis.* Mahwah, NJ: Paulist, 1985.

Thompson, "God." • Thompson, Marianne Meye. "Jesus and his God." 41-55 in *The Cambridge Companion to Jesus.* Ed. Markus Bockmuehl. Cambridge: Cambridge University, 2001.

Thompson, "Son of Man." • Thompson, G. H. P. "The Son of Man: The Evidence of the Dead Sea Scrolls." *ExpT* 72 (4, 1961): 125.

Thompson, Wenger, and Bartling, "Recall." • Thompson, C. P., S. K. Wenger, and C. A. Bartling. "How Recall Facilitates Subsequent Recall: A Reappraisal." *JExpPsyc* 4 (3, 1978): 210-21.

Thorley, "Census." • Thorley, John. "The Nativity Census: What Does Luke Actually Say?" *GR* 26 (1, 1979): 81-84.

Thrall, *2 Corinthians.* • Thrall, Margaret E. *A Critical and Exegetical Comemntary on the Second Epistle to the Corinthians.* 2 vols. Edinburgh: T. & T. Clark, 1994, 2000.

Thurman, *Disinherited.* • Thurman, Howard. *Jesus and the Disinherited.* Richmond, IN: Friends United Press, 1981. Reprint from Abingdon, 1949.

Tilborg, *Leaders.* • Tilborg, Sjef van. *The Jewish Leaders in Matthew.* Leiden: E. J. Brill, 1972.

Tilborg, "Prayer." • Van Tilborg, Sjef. "A Form-Criticism of the Lord's Prayer." *NovT* 14 (1972): 94-105.

Todd, "Introduction." • Todd, O. J. "Introduction." 376-79 in Xenophon. *Symposium* and *Apology.* Trans. O. J. Todd. LCL, third Xenophon vol. Cambridge: Harvard, 1922.

Tödt, *Son of Man.* • Tödt, Heinz Eduard. *The Son of Man in the Synoptic Tradition.* Philadelphia: Westminster, 1965.

Tomson, "Jesus and Judaism." • Tomson, Peter J. "Jesus and his Judaism." 25-40 in *The Cambridge Companion to Jesus.* Ed. Markus Bockmuehl. Cambridge: Cambridge University, 2001.

Toren, "Significance." • Toren, B. van den. "The Political Significance of Jesus: Christian Involvement for the Democratisation of Africa." *AJET* 26 (1, 2007): 65-88.

Torrance, "Probability." • Torrance, Alan J. "The Lazarus Narrative, Theological History, and Historical Probability." 245-62 in *The Gospel of John and Christian Theology.* Ed. Richard Bauckham and Carl Mosser. Grand Rapids, Cambridge: Eerdmans, 2008.

Torrey, "Messiah." • Torrey, Charles C. "The Messiah Son of Ephraim." *JBL* 66 (1947): 253-77.

Townsend, "Education." • Townsend, John T. "Ancient Education in the Time of the Early Roman Empire." 139-63 in *The Catacombs and the Colosseum: The Roman Empire as the Setting of Primitive Christianity.* Ed. Stephen Benko and John J. O'Rourke. Valley Forge, PA: Judson, 1971.

Trebilco, *Communities.* • Trebilco, Paul R. *Jewish Communities in Asia Minor.* SNTSMS 69. Cambridge: Cambridge University, 1991.

Treves, "Date." • Treves, Marco. "The Date of the War of the Sons of Light." *VT* 8 (1958): 419-24.

Trifon, "Msmrwt." • Trifon, D. "H'm 'brw msmrwt hkwhnym myhwdh lglyl 'hry mrd br-kwkb'?" *Tarbiz* 59 (1989-90): 77-93.

Trudinger, "Gospel." • Trudinger, Paul. "St. Paul, the Damascus Road, 'My Gospel,' and Jesus." *Faith and Freedom* 59 (2, 2006): 102-7.

Tuckett, "Cynic Q." • Tuckett, Christopher M. "A Cynic Q?" *Bib* 70 (1989): 349-76.

Tuckett, *Griesbach Hypothesis.* • Tuckett, Christopher M. *The Revival of the Griesbach Hypothesis: An analysis and appraisal.* Cambridge: Cambridge University Press, 1983.

Tuckett, *History.* • Tuckett, Christopher M. *Q and the History of Early Christianity: Studies on Q.* Peabody: Hendrickson, 1996.

Tuckett, *Luke.* • Tuckett, Christopher M. *Luke.* NTG. Sheffield: Sheffield Academic Press, 1996.

Tuckett, *Nag Hammadi.* • Tuckett, Christopher M. *Nag Hammadi and the Gospel Tradition: Synoptic Tradition in the Nag Hammadi Library.* Ed. John Riches. Edinburgh: T. & T. Clark, 1986.

Tuckett, "Q and Aramaic." • Tuckett, Christopher. "Q, Jesus and Aramaic: Some methodological reflections." *PIBA* 26 (2003): 29-45.

Tuckett, "Relationship." • Tuckett, Christopher M. "On the Relationship between Matthew and Luke." *NTS* 30 (1984): 130-41.

Tuckett, "Review." • Tuckett, Christopher. Review of Richard Bauckham, *Jesus and the Eyewitnesses.* *RBL* 12 (2007).

Tuckett, "Sources and methods." • Tuckett, Christopher. "Sources and methods." 121-37 in *The Cambridge Companion to Jesus.* Ed. Markus Bockmuehl. Cambridge: Cambridge University, 2001.

Tuckett, "Thomas and Synoptics." • Tuckett, Christopher. "Thomas and the Synoptics." *NovT* 30 (2, 1988): 132-57.

Tuckett, "Thomas: Evidence." • Tuckett, Christopher M. "The Gospel of Thomas: Evidence for Jesus?" *NedTT* 52 (1, 1998): 17-32.

Tully, "Στρατάρχης." • Tully, G. D. "The στρατάρχης of *Legio* VI Ferrata and the Employment of Camp Prefects as Vexillation Commanders." *ZPE* 120 (1998): 226-32.

Turner, "Second Thoughts." • Turner, Nigel. "Second Thoughts — VII. Papyrus Finds." *ExpT* 76 (1964): 44-48.

Turner, *Spirit.* • Turner, Max. *The Holy Spirit and Spiritual Gifts in the New Testament Church and Today.* Rev. ed. Peabody, MA: Hendrickson, 1998.

Turnheim, "Decoration." • Turnheim, Yehudit. "Some Observations on the Decoration of the Chorazin Pilaster." *PEQ* 119 (1987): 152-55.

Twelftree, *Miracle Worker.* • Twelftree, Graham H. *Jesus the Miracle Worker: A Historical and Theological Study.* Downers Grove, IL: InterVarsity, 1999.

Twelftree, "Miracles." • Twelftree, Graham H. "The Miracles of Jesus: Marginal or Mainstream?" *JSHJ* 1 (1, 2003): 104-24.

Tzaferis, "Crucifixion." • Tzaferis, Vassilios. "Crucifixion — The Archaeological Evidence." *BAR* 11 (1, January 1985): 44-53.

Ulrichsen, "Troen." • Ulrichsen, Jarl H. "Troen på et liv etter døden i Qumrantekstene." *NTT* 78 (1977): 151-63.

Unnik, "Once More Prologue." • Unnik, W. C. van. "Once More St. Luke's Prologue." *Neot* 7 (1973): 7-26.

Urbach, *Sages.* • Urbach, Ephraim E. *The Sages: Their Concepts and Beliefs.* 2d ed. 2 vols. Trans. Israel Abrahams. Jerusalem: Magnes Press, The Hebrew University, 1979.

Vaage, "Barking." • Vaage, Leif E. "Like Dogs Barking: Cynic *Parrēsia* and Shameless Asceticism." *Semeia* 57 (1992): 25-39.

Vale, "Sources." • Vale, Ruth. "Literary Sources in Archaeological Description: The Case of Galilee, Galilees, and Galileans." *JSJ* 18 (2, December 1987): 209-26.

Van der Horst, "Children." • Van der Horst, Pieter W. "Seven Months' Children in Jewish and Christian Literature from Antiquity." *ETL* 54 (4, 1978): 346-60.

Van der Horst, "Cornutus." • Van der Horst, Pieter W. "Cornutus and the New Testament." *NovT* 23 (2, 1981): 165-172.

Van der Horst, "Funerary Inscriptions." • Van der Horst, Pieter W. "Jewish Funerary Inscriptions. Most Are in Greek." *BAR* 18 (5, 1992): 46-57.

Van der Horst, "Hierocles." • Van der Horst, Pieter W. "Hierocles the Stoic and the New Testament." *NovT* 17 (1975): 156-60.

Van der Horst, "Macrobius." • Van der Horst, Pieter W. "Macrobius and the New Testament: A Contribution to the Corpus Hellenisticum." *NovT* 15 (3, July 1973): 220-232.

Van der Horst, "Musonius." • Van der Horst, Pieter W. "Musonius Rufus and the New Testament." *NovT* 16 (4, Oct. 1974): 306-15.

VanderKam, "Jubilees." • VanderKam, James C. "Jubilees — How It Rewrote the Bible." *BAR* 8 (6, 1992): 32-39, 60, 62.

VanderKam, "Mantic Wisdom." • VanderKam, James C. "Mantic Wisdom in the Dead Sea Scrolls." *DSD* 4 (3, 1997): 336-53.

VanderKam, "Pronouncement Stories." • VanderKam, James C. "Intertestamental Pronouncement Stories." *Semeia* 20 (1981): 65-72.

Van der Ploeg, "Meals." • Van der Ploeg, J. "The Meals of the Essenes." *JSS* 2 (1957): 163-75.

Van der Ploeg, *Rouleau*. • Van der Ploeg, J. *Le Rouleau de la Guerre: Traduit et Annoté avec une Introduction.* STDJ 2. Ed. J. Van der Ploeg. Leiden: E. J. Brill, 1959.

Van Oyen, "Criteria." • Van Oyen, Geert. "How Do We Know (What There Is To Know)? Criteria for Historical Jesus Research." *LS* 26 (3, 2001): 245-67.

Van Seters, "Historiography." • Van Seters, John. "Is there any Historiography in the Hebrew Bible? A Hebrew-Greek Comparison." *JNSL* 28 (2, 2002): 1-25.

Van Seters, "Primeval Histories." • Van Seters, John. "The Primeval Histories of Greece and Israel Compared." *ZAW* 100 (1988): 1-22.

Van Seters, *Search*. • Van Seters, John. *In Search of History: Historiography in the Ancient World and the Origins of Biblical History.* New Haven: Yale, 1983.

Vansina, "Afterthoughts." • Vansina, Jan. "Afterthoughts on the Historiography of Oral Tradition." 105-10 in *African Historiographies: What History for Which Africa?* Ed. Bogumil Jewsiewicki and David Newbury. SSAMD 12. Beverly Hills, London, New Delhi: Sage, 1986.

Van Veldhuizen, "Moses." • Van Veldhuizen, Milo. "Moses: A Model of Hellenistic Philanthropia." *RefR* 38 (3, Spring 1985): 215-24.

Vellanickal, "Historical Jesus." • Vellanickal, Matthew. "The Historical Jesus in the Johannine Christological Vision." *Jeev* 26 (152, 1996): 131-45.

Venter, "Reviewing History." • Venter, P. M. "Reviewing history in apocalyptic literature as ideological strategy." *HTS/TS* 60 (3, 2004): 703-23.

Verbaal, "End of Liberty." • Verbaal, Wim. "Cicero and Dionysios the Elder, or the End of Liberty." *CW* 99 (2, 2006): 145-56.

Verheyden, "Unity." • Verheyden, Joseph. "The Unity of Luke-Acts: What Are We Up To?" 3-56 in *The Unity of Luke-Acts* (ed. Joseph Verheyden; BETL 142; Leuven: Leuven University, 1999.

Vermaseren, *Cybele*. • Vermaseren, Maarten J. *Cybele and Attis: the Myth and the Cult.* Trans. A. H. H. Lemmers. London: Thames & Hudson, 1977.

Vermes, "Elements." • Vermes, Geza. "Historiographical Elements in the Qumran Writings: A Synopsis of the Textual Evidence." *JJS* 58 (1, 2007): 121-39.

Vermes, "Forum." • Vermes, Geza. "The Oxford Forum for Qumran Research: Seminar on the Rule of War from Cave 4 (4Q285)." *JJS* 43 (1, 1992): 85-94.

Vermes, *Jesus and Judaism*. • Vermes, Geza. *Jesus and the World of Judaism.* Philadelphia: Fortress, 1984; London: SCM, 1983.

Vermes, *Jesus the Jew.* • Vermes, Geza. *Jesus the Jew: A Historian's Reading of the Gospels.* Philadelphia: Fortress, 1973.

Vermes, "Jesus the Jew." • Vermes, Geza. "Jesus the Jew." 108-22 in *Jesus' Jewishness: Exploring the Place of Jesus within Early Judaism.* Ed. James H. Charlesworth. New York: The American Interfaith Institute, Crossroad Publishing Company, 1991.

Vermes, "Matrimonial Halakah." • Vermes, Geza. "Sectarian Matrimonial Halakah in the Damascus Rule." *JJS* 25 (1974): 197-202.

Vermes, "Messiah Text." • Vermes, Geza. "The 'Pierced Messiah' Text — An Interpretation Evaporates." *BAR* 18 (4, 1992): 80-82.

Vermes, "Notice." • Vermes, Geza. "The Jesus Notice of Josephus Re-Examined." *JJS* 38 (1, Spring 1987): 1-10.

Vermes, "Phylacteries." • Vermes, Geza. "Pre-mishnaic Jewish worship and the phylacteries from the Dead Sea." *VT* 9 (1959): 65-72.

Vermes, *Religion.* • Vermes, Geza. *The Religion of Jesus the Jew.* Minneapolis: Augsburg Fortress, 1993.

Vermes, *Scrolls.* • Vermes, Geza, ed. *The Dead Sea Scrolls in English.* 2d ed. New York: Penguin Books, 1981.

Via, *Parables.* • Via, Dan Otto, Jr. *The Parables: Their Literary and Existential Dimension.* Philadelphia: Fortress, 1967.

Vidler, *Revolution.* • Vidler, Alec R. *The Church in an Age of Revolution: 1789 to the Present Day.* Penguin History of the Church 5. London: Penguin, 1974.

Vielhauer, "Paulinism." • Vielhauer, Philipp. "On the 'Paulinism' of Acts." 33-50 in *Studies in Luke-Acts: Essays in Honor of Paul Schubert.* Ed. Leander E. Keck and J. Louis Martyn. Nashville: Abingdon, 1966.

Villalón, "Deux Messies." • Villalón, José R. "Sources vétéro-testamentaires de la doctrine qumrâninenne des deux Messies." *RevQ* 8 (29.1, June 1972): 53-63.

Visotzky, "Overturning." • Visotzky, Burton L. "Overturning the Lamp." *JJS* 38 (1987): 72-80.

Viviano, "Beatitudes." • Viviano, Benedict T. "Beatitudes Found Among Dead Sea Scrolls." *BAR* 18 (6, 1992): 53-55, 66.

Viviano, "Publication." • Viviano, Benedict T. "Eight Beatitudes at Qumran and in Matthew? A New Publication from Cave Four." *SEÅ* 58 (1993): 71-84.

Viviano, "Qumran." • Viviano, Benedict T. "Eight Beatitudes from Qumran." *BibT* 31 (4, 1993): 219-24.

Viviano, "World." • Viviano, Benedict T. "Social World and Community Leadership: The Case of Matthew 23.1-12, 34." *JSNT* 39 (1990): 3-21.

Vogel, "Vita 64-69." • Vogel, Manuel. "Vita 64-69, das Bilderverbot und die Galiläapolitik des Josephus." *JSJ* 30 (1, 1999): 65-79.

Voorst, *Jesus Outside NT.* • Van Voorst, Robert E. *Jesus Outside the New Testament: An Introduction to the Ancient Evidence.* Grand Rapids: Eerdmans, 2000.

Vorster, "Blessedness." • Vorster, Willem S. "Stoics and Early Christians on Blessedness." 38-51 in *Greeks, Romans, and Christians: Essays in Honor of Abraham J. Malherbe.* Ed. David L. Balch, Everett Ferguson, and Wayne A. Meeks. Minneapolis: Fortress, 1990.

Wacholder, "Nicolas." • Wacholder, Ben Zion. "Josephus and Nicolaus of Damascus." 147-172 in *Josephus, the Bible, and History.* Ed. Louis H. Feldman and Gohei Hata. Detroit: Wayne State University Press, 1989.

Wacholder, "Teacher." • Wacholder, Ben Zion. "Who Is the Teacher of Righteousness?" *BRev* 15 (2, 1999): 26-29.

Wachsmann, "Galilee Boat." • Wachsmann, Shelley. "The Galilee Boat: 2,000-Year-Old Hull Recovered Intact." *BAR* 14 (5, 1988): 18-33.

Wächter, "Messianismus." • Wächter, Ludwig. "Jüdischer und christlichen Messianismus." *Kairos* 18 (2, 1976): 119-34.

Wade, "Son of Man." • Wade, Loron. "'Son of Man' Comes to the Judgment in Daniel 7:13." *JATS* 11 (1-2, 2000): 277-81.

Wade-Gery, "Thucydides." • Wade-Gery, Henry Theodore. "Thucydides." 1516-19 in *OCD*.

Wagner, *Baptism*. • Wagner, Günter. *Pauline Baptism and the Pagan Mysteries: The Problem of the Pauline Doctrine of Baptism in Romans VI.1-11, in Light of Its Religio-Historical "Parallels."* Trans. J. P. Smith. Edinburgh: Oliver & Boyd, 1967.

Wagner and Lotfi, "Learning." • Wagner, Daniel A., and Abdelhamid Lotfi. "Learning to Read by 'Rote.'" *IJSocLang* 42 (1983): 111-21.

Wahlde, "Archaeology." • Wahlde, Urban C. von. "Archaeology and John's Gospel." 523-86 in *Jesus and Archaeology*. Ed. James H. Charlesworth. Grand Rapids: Eerdmans, 2006.

Walbank, "Graves." • Walbank, Mary E. Hoskins. "Unquiet Graves: Burial Practices of the Roman Corinthians." 249-80 in *Urban Religion in Roman Corinth: Interdisciplinary Approaches*. Ed. Daniel N. Schowalter and Steven J. Friesen. Harvard Theological Studies 53. Cambridge: Harvard University Press, 2005.

Walde, "Mnemonics." • Walde, Christine. "Mnemonics." 9:96-97 in *Brill's New Pauly*.

Walker, "Concept." • Walker, William O., Jr. "The Origin of the Son of Man Concept as Applied to Jesus." 156-65 in *The Bible in Its Literary Milieu*. Ed. Vincent L. Tollers and John R. Maier. Grand Rapids: Eerdmans, 1979.

Walker, "Origin of Concept." • Walker, William O., Jr. "The Origin of the Son of Man Concept as Applied to Jesus." *JBL* 91 (4, Dec 1972): 482-490.

Wanamaker, "Philippians." • Wanamaker, Charles A. "Philippians 2.6-11: Son of God or Adamic Christology?" *NTS* 33 (2, 1987): 179-93.

Wandrey, "Literature: Jewish-Hellenistic." • Wandrey, Irina. "Literature: Jewish-Hellenistic." 7:694-99 in *Brill's New Pauly*.

Wandrey, "Machaerus." • Wandrey, Irina. "Machaerus." 8:91-92 in *Brill's New Pauly*.

Wardle, *Valerius Maximus*. • *Valerius Maximus: Memorable Deeds and Sayings*. Trans. and commentary by D. Wardle. Oxford: Clarendon Press, 1998.

Wasserstein, "Non-Hellenized Jews." • Wasserstein, A. "Non-Hellenized Jews in the Semi-Hellenized East." *SCI* 14 (1995): 111-37.

Waterman, "Sources." • Waterman, G. Henry. "The Sources of Paul's Teaching on the Second Coming of Christ in 1 & 2 Thessalonians." *JETS* 18 (1975): 105-13.

Watson, "Education." • Watson, Duane F. "Education: Jewish and Greco-Roman." 308-13 in *DNTB*.

Watson, "Identity." • Watson, Francis. "The Triune Divine Identity: Reflections on Pauline God-language, in Disagreement with J. D. G. Dunn." *JSNT* 80 (2000): 99-124.

Wcela, "Messiah(s)." • Wcela, Emil A. "The Messiah(s) of Qumrân." *CBQ* 26 (3, July 1964): 340-49.

Weaver, *Historical Jesus*. • Weaver, Walter P. *The Historical Jesus in the Twentieth Century: 1900-1950*. Harrisburg, PA: Trinity Press International, 1999.

Weaver, "Introduction." • Weaver, Walter P. "Introduction." 1-6 in *Jesus Two Thousand Years Later*. Ed. James H. Charlesworth and Walter P. Weaver. Faith and Scholarship Colloquies Series. Harrisburg, PA: Trinity Press International, 2000.

Webb, *Baptizer*. • Webb, Robert L. *John the Baptizer and Prophet: A Socio-Historical Study*. JSNTSup 62. Sheffield: JSOT Press, Sheffield Academic Press, 1991.

Webb, "Books." • Webb, Robert L. "Books on the Historical Jesus." *JSHJ* 5 (2, 2007): 205-18.

Webb, "Josephus on John." • Webb, Robert L. "Josephus on John the Baptist. Jewish Antiquities 18.116-119." *Forum* 2 (1, 1999): 141-68.

Webb, "Relationship." • Webb, Robert L. "John the Baptist and His Relationship to Jesus." 179-229 in *Studying the Historical Jesus: Evaluations of the State of Current Research*. NTTS 19. Ed. Bruce Chilton and Craig A. Evans. Leiden, New York, Cologne: E. J. Brill, 1994.

Webber, "Note." • Webber, Randall C. "A Note on 1 Corinthians 15:3-5." *JETS* 26 (1983): 265-69.

Weber, "Notes 1961." • Weber, J.-J. "Notes exégétiques sur le texte 'Tu es Petrus.'" *BEDS* 80 (1961): 541-60.

Weber, "Notes 1962." • Weber, J.-J. "Notes exégétiques sur le texte 'Tu es Petrus.'" *Ami du Clergé* 72 (1962): 113-21.

Wedderburn, Resurrection. • Wedderburn, A. J. M. *Beyond Resurrection.* London: SCM; Peabody: Hendrickson, 1999.

Weeden, Mark. • Weeden, Theodore J., Sr. *Mark — Traditions in Conflict.* Philadelphia: Fortress, 1971.

Weiss, Proclamation. • Weiss, Johannes. *Jesus' Proclamation of the Kingdom of God.* Trans., ed. Richard H. Hiers and David Larrimore Holland. Philadelphia: Fortress, 1971.

Weiss, "Sabbath." • Weiss, Herold. "The Sabbath in the Writings of Josephus." *JSJ* 29 (4, 1998): 363-90.

Weiss and Netzer, "Sty." • Weiss, Zeev, and Ehud Netzer. "Sty 'wnwt-hpyrh bsypwry." *Qad* 24 (3-4, 1991): 113-21.

Welch, "Miracles." • Welch, John W. "Miracles, *Maleficium,* and *Maiestas* in the Trial of Jesus." 349-83 in *Jesus and Archaeology.* Ed. James H. Charlesworth. Grand Rapids: Eerdmans, 2006.

Wenham, "Apocalypse." • Wenham, David. "Paul and the Synoptic Apocalypse." 2:345-375 in *GosPersp.* Vol. 2: *Studies of History and Tradition in the Four Gospels.* Sheffield: JSOT Press, The University of Sheffield, 1981.

Wenham, Bible. • Wenham, John W. *Christ and the Bible.* Downers Grove, IL: InterVarsity, 1977.

Wenham, Enigma. • Wenham, John. *Easter Enigma: Do the Resurrection Stories Contradict One Another?* Exeter: Paternoster; Grand Rapids: Zondervan 1984; Eugene, OR: Wipf & Stock, reprint 2005.

Wenham, "Narratives." • Wenham, David. "The Resurrection Narratives in Matthew's Gospel." *TynBul* 24 (1973): 21-54.

Wenham, "Parable." • Wenham, David. "The Interpretation of the Parable of the Sower." *NTS* 20 (3, April 1974): 299-319.

Wenham, Rediscovery. • Wenham, David. *The Rediscovery of Jesus' Eschatological Discourse.* Vol. 4 of *GosPersp.* 6 vols. Ed. R. T. France and David Wenham. Sheffield: JSOT Press, The University of Sheffield, 1984.

Wenham, "Story." • Wenham, David. "The Story of Jesus Known to Paul." 297-311 in *Jesus of Nazareth: Lord and Christ. Essays on the Historical Jesus and New Testament Christology.* Ed. Joel B. Green and Max Turner. Grand Rapids: Eerdmans; Carlisle: Paternoster, 1994.

West, "Rhapsodes." • West, Martin Litchfield. "Rhapsodes." 1311-12 in *OCD.*

Westerholm and Evans, "Sabbath." • Westerholm, Stephen, and Craig A. Evans. "Sabbath." 1031-35 in *DNTB.*

Whealey, "Josephus." • Whealey, Alice. "Josephus on Jesus: Evidence from the First Millennium." *TZ* 51 (4, 1995): 285-304.

White, "Finances." • White, William, Jr. "Finances." 218-36 in *The Catacombs and the Colosseum: The Roman Empire as the Setting of Primitive Christianity.* Ed. Stephen Benko and John J. O'Rourke. Valley Forge, PA: Judson Press, 1971.

White, Initiation. • White, R. E. O. *The Biblical Doctrine of Initiation.* Grand Rapids: Eerdmans, 1960.

Whitehouse, "Shipwreck on Nile." • Whitehouse, Helen. "Shipwreck on the Nile: A Greek Novel on a 'Lost' Roman Mosaic?" *AJA* 89 (1, 1985): 129-34, plate 28.

Whittaker, "Introduction." • Whittaker, C. R. "Introduction." 1:ix-lxxxvii in Herodian. *History.* 2 vols. Trans. C. R. Whittaker. LCL. Cambridge: Harvard University Press, 1969.

Whittaker, Jews and Christians. • Whittaker, Molly. *Jews and Christians: Graeco-Roman Views.* CCWJCW 6. Cambridge: Cambridge University Press, 1984.

Wieder, "Messiahs." • Wieder, Naphtali. "The Doctrine of the Two Messiahs Among the Karaites." *JJS* 6 (1, 1953): 14-23.

Wiersma, "Novel." • Wiersma, S. "The Ancient Greek Novel and Its Heroines: A Female Paradox." *Mnemosyne* 43 (1-2, 1990): 109-23.

Wifall, "Status." • Wifall, Walter R. "The Status of 'Man' as Resurrection." *ZAW* 90 (1978): 382-94.

Wilcox, "Dualism." • Wilcox, Max. "Dualism, Gnosticism, and Other Elements in the Pre-Pauline Tradition." 83-96 in *The Scrolls and Christianity: Historical and Theological Significance.* Ed. Matthew Black. London: S.P.C.K., 1969.

Wilcox, "Influence." • Wilcox, Max. "Semitic Influence on the New Testament." 1093-98 in *DNTB.*

Wilken, "Collegia." • Wilken, Robert. "Collegia, Philosophical Schools, and Theology." 268-291 in *The Catacombs and the Colosseum: The Roman Empire as the Setting of Primitive Christianity.* Ed. Stephen Benko and John J. O'Rourke. Valley Forge, PA: Judson Press, 1971.

Wilkins, *Discipleship.* • Wilkins, Michael J. *Discipleship in the Ancient World and Matthew's Gospel.* 2nd ed. Grand Rapids: Baker, 1995. First ed.: Leiden: E. J. Brill, 1988.

Wilkinson, *Jerusalem.* • Wilkinson, John. *Jerusalem as Jesus Knew It.* London: Thames & Hudson, 1978.

Williams, *Acts.* • Williams, C. S. C. *A Commentary on the Acts of the Apostles.* New York: Harper & Row, Publishers, 1957.

Williams, *Death.* • Williams, Sam K. *Jesus' Death as a Saving Event: The Background and Origin of a Concept.* HDR 2. Missoula, MT: Scholars Press, 1975.

Williams, "Josephus on Pharisees." • Williams, David S. "Josephus or Nicolaus on the Pharisees?" *REJ* 156 (1-2, 1997): 43-58.

Williams, *Justin.* • Williams, A. Lukyn. *Justin Martyr: The Dialogue with Trypho. Translation, Introduction, and Notes.* Translations of Christian Literature Series I — Greek Texts. New York: Macmillan, 1930.

Williams, *Miracle Stories.* • Williams, Benjamin E. *Miracle Stories in the Biblical Book* Acts of the Apostles. MBPS 59. Lewiston: Edwin Mellen Press, 2001.

Williams, "Names." • Williams, Margaret H. "Palestinian Jewish Personal Names in Acts." 79-114 in *The Book of Acts in Its Palestinian Setting.* Ed. Richard Bauckham. Vol. 4 in The Book of Acts in Its First Century Setting. Grand Rapids: Eerdmans; Carlisle: Paternoster, 1995.

Williamson, *Chronicles.* • Williamson, H. G. M. *1 & 2 Chronicles.* NCBC. Grand Rapids: Eerdmans; London: Marshall, Morgan & Scott, 1982.

Willis, *Meat.* • Willis, Wendell Lee. *Idol Meat in Corinth: The Pauline Argument in 1 Corinthians 8 and 10.* SBLDS 68. Chico, CA: Scholars Press, 1985.

Willoughby, *Initiation.* • Willoughby, Harold R. *Pagan Initiation: A Study of Mystery Initiations in the Graeco-Roman World.* Chicago: University of Chicago Press, 1929.

Wills, "Aesop Tradition." • Wills, Lawrence M. "The Aesop Tradition." 222-37 in *The Historical Jesus in Context.* Ed. Amy-Jill Levine, Dale C. Allison Jr., and John Dominic Crossan. Princeton Readings in Religions. Princeton: Princeton University Press, 2006.

Wills, *Quest.* • Wills, Lawrence M. *The Quest of the Historical Gospel. Mark, John, and the Origins of the Gospel Genre.* London: Routledge, 1997.

Wilson, *Gentile Mission.* • Wilson, Stephen G. *The Gentiles and the Gentile Mission in Luke-Acts.* SNTSMS 23. Cambridge: Cambridge University, 1973.

Wilson, *Gnostic Problem.* • Wilson, R. McL. *The Gnostic Problem.* London: A. R. Mowbray & Company, 1958.

Wilson, "Nag Hammadi." • Wilson, R. McL. "Nag Hammadi and the New Testament." *NTS* 28 (3, July 1982): 289-302.

Wink, "Passivity." • Wink, Walter. "Neither Passivity nor Violence. Jesus' Third Way (Matt 5:38-42// Luke 6:29-30)." *Forum* 7 (1991): 5-28.

Wink, "Reply." • Wink, Walter. "Jesus' Reply to John. Matt 11:2-6/Luke 7:18-23." *Forum* 5 (1989): 121-28.

Wink, "Write." • Wink, Walter. "Write What You See." *FR* 7 (3, May 1994): 3-9.

Winkle, "Model." • Winkle, Rose E. "The Jeremiah Model for Jesus in the Temple." *AUSS* 24 (1986): 155-72.

Winkler, *Auctor*. • Winkler, John J. *Auctor & Actor: A Narratological Reading of Apuleius's The Golden Ass.* Berkeley: University of California Press, 1985.

Winter, "Bibliography." • Winter, P. "Bibliography to Josephus, *Antiquitates Judaicae,* XVIII, 63, 64." *JHistS* 2 (4, 1969-1970): 292-96.

Winter, *Trial*. • Winter, Paul. *On the Trial of Jesus.* SJFWJ 1. Berlin: Walter de Gruyter & Company, 1961.

Winter, "Trial." • Winter, Paul. "The Trial of Jesus and the Competence of the Sanhedrin." *NTS* 10 (1964): 494-99.

Winterbottom, "Rhetoric." • Winterbottom, Michael. "Rhetoric, Latin." 1314 in *OCD*.

Wintermute, "Jubilees." • Wintermute, Orval S. "Introduction to Jubilees." 2:35-50 in *OTP*.

Wirgin, *Jubilees*. • Wirgin, Wolf. *The Book of Jubilees and the Maccabaean Era of Shmittah Cycles.* LUOSM 7. N.p.: Leeds University, 1965.

Wise, "Introduction to 4Q158." • Wise, Michael O. "Introduction" to 4Q158. 199-200 in *The Dead Sea Scrolls: A New Translation.* By Michael Wise, Martin Abegg, Jr., and Edward Cook. San Francisco: HarperSanFrancisco, 1999.

Wise, "Palestinian Aramaic." • Wise, Michael O. "Palestinian Aramaic." 4:237-38 in *OEANE*.

Wise, Abegg and Cook, *Scrolls*. • Wise, Michael, Martin Abegg, Jr., and Edward Cook. *The Dead Sea Scrolls: A New Translation.* San Francisco: Harper SanFrancisco, 1999.

Wise and Tabor, "Messiah at Qumran." • Wise, Michael O., and James D. Tabor. "The Messiah at Qumran." *BAR* 18 (6, 1992): 60-63, 65.

Witherington, *Acts*. • Witherington, Ben, III. *The Acts of the Apostles: A Socio-Rhetorical Commentary.* Grand Rapids: Eerdmans, 1998.

Witherington, "Addendum." • Witherington, Ben, III. "Addendum to W. J. McCoy, 'In the shadow of Thucydides.'" 23-32 in *History, Literature, and Society in the Book of Acts.* Ed. Ben Witherington, III. Cambridge: Cambridge University Press, 1996.

Witherington, *Christology*. • Witherington, Ben, III. *The Christology of Jesus.* Minneapolis: Augsburg Fortress, 1990.

Witherington, *End*. • Witherington, Ben, III. *Jesus, Paul and the End of the World: A Comparative Study in New Testament Eschatology.* Downers Grove: InterVarsity, 1992.

Witherington, *Quest*. • Witherington, Ben, III. *The Jesus Quest: The Third Search for the Jew of Nazareth.* Downers Grove: InterVarsity, 1995.

Witherington, *Sage*. • Witherington, Ben, III. *Jesus the Sage: The Pilgrimage of Wisdom.* Minneapolis: Fortress, 1994.

Witherington, *Wisdom*. • Witherington, Ben, III. *John's Wisdom: A Commentary on the Fourth Gospel.* Louisville: Westminster/John Knox 1995.

Witherington, *Women*. • Witherington, Ben, III. *Women in the Ministry of Jesus: A Study of Jesus' Attitudes to Women and Their Roles as Reflected in His Earthly Life.* SNTSMS 51. Cambridge: Cambridge University Press, 1984.

Witherington, "Wright quest." • Witherington, Ben, III. "The Wright quest for the historical Jesus." *ChrCent* 114 (33, 1997): 1075-78.

Wittlieb, "Bedeutung." • Wittlieb, Marian. "Die theologische Bedeutung der Erwähnung von 'Masîah/Christos' in den Pseudepigraphen des Alten Testaments palästinischen Ursprungs." *BN* 50 (1989): 26-33.

Wolfson, *Philo*. • Wolfson, Harry Austryn. *Philo: Foundations of Religious Philosophy in Judaism, Christianity, and Islam.* 2 vols. 4th rev. ed. Cambridge: Harvard University Press, 1968.

Wrede, *Messianic Secret.* • Wrede, William. *The Messianic Secret.* Tr. J. C. G. Greig. Cambridge: James Clarke & Co., 1971.

Wright, "Apocryphal Gospels." • Wright, David F. "Apocryphal Gospels: The 'Unknown Gospel' (Pap. Egerton 2) and the Gospel of Peter." 5:207-232 in *GosPersp.* Vol. 5: *The Jesus Tradition Outside the Gospels.* Ed. David Wenham. Sheffield: JSOT Press, 1984.

Wright, "Apologetic." • Wright, David F. "Apologetic and Apocalyptic: The Miraculous in the *Gospel of Peter.*" 6:401-18 in *GosPersp.* Vol. 6: *The Miracles of Jesus.* Ed. David Wenham and Craig Blomberg. Sheffield: JSOT Press, 1986.

Wright, "Dialogue." • Wright, N. T. "In Grateful Dialogue: A Response." 244-77 in *Jesus and the Restoration of Israel: A Critical Assessment of N. T. Wright's* Jesus and the Victory of God. Ed. Carey C. Newman. Downers Grove: InterVarsity, 1999.

Wright, "Midrash." • Wright, Addison G. "The Literary Genre Midrash." *CBQ* 28 (2, April 1966): 105-38; 28 (4, Oct. 1966): 417-57.

Wright, *Paul.* • Wright, N. T. *What Saint Paul Really Said: Was Paul of Tarsus the Real Founder of Christianity?* Grand Rapids: Eerdmans, 1997.

Wright, *People of God.* • Wright, N. T. *The New Testament and the People of God.* Vol. 1 in Christian Origins and the Question of God. Minneapolis: Fortress; London: S.P.C.K, 1992.

Wright, *Quest.* • Wright, N. T. *The Contemporary Quest for Jesus.* Facets. Minneapolis: Fortress, 2002.

Wright, *Resurrection.* • Wright, N. T. *The Resurrection of the Son of God.* Christian Origins and the Question of God 3. Minneapolis: Fortress, 2003.

Wright, "Resurrection." • Wright, N. T. "Resurrection and New Creation." *ChSt* 46 (3, 2007): 270-86.

Wright, "Seminar." • Wright, N. Thomas. "Five Gospels but no Gospel: Jesus and the Seminar." 83-120 in *Authenticating the Activities of Jesus.* Ed. Bruce Chilton and Craig A. Evans. NTTS 28.2. Leiden: Brill, 1999.

Wright, *Who Was Jesus?* • Wright, N. T. *Who Was Jesus?* Grand Rapids: Eerdmans, 1992.

Wright and Crossan, "Resurrection." • Wright, N. T., and John Dominic Crossan. "The Resurrection: Historical Event or Theological Explanation? A Dialogue." 16-47 in *The Resurrection of Jesus: John Dominic Crossan and N. T. Wright in Dialogue,* ed. Robert B. Stewart. Minneapolis: Fortress, 2006.

Xeravits, "Moses Redivivus." • Xeravits, Géza G. "Moses Redivivus in Qumran?" *QC* 11 (1-4, 2003): 91-105.

Yadin, "Commentaries." • Yadin, Yigael. "Commentaries on Genesis xlix and Isaiah, from Qumran Cave 4." *IEJ* 7 (1, 1957): 66-68.

Yadin, *Scroll of War.* • Yadin, Yigael. *The Scroll of the War of the Sons of Light against the Sons of Darkness.* Trans. Batya and Chaim Rabin. Oxford: Oxford University Press, 1962.

Yadin, "Temple Scroll." • Yadin, Yigael. "The Temple Scroll." *BAR* 10 (1984): 32-49.

Yamamori and Chan, *Witnesses.* • Yamamori, Tetsunao, and Kim-kwong Chan. *Witnesses to Power: Stories of God's Quiet Work in a Changing China.* Waynesboro, GA; Carlisle, Cumbria: Paternoster, 2000.

Yamauchi, "Concord." • Yamauchi, Edwin. "Concord, Conflict, and Community: Jewish and Evangelical Views of Scripture." 154-196 in *Evangelicals and Jews in Conversation on Scripture, Theology and History.* Ed. Marc H. Tannenbaum, Marvin R. Wilson, and James A. Rudin. Grand Rapids: Baker, 1978.

Yamauchi, "Crucifixion." • Yamauchi, Edwin. "The Crucifixion and Docetic Christology." *CTQ* 46 (1982): 1-20.

Yamauchi, "Cyrene." • Yamauchi, Edwin. "The Archaeology of Biblical Africa: Cyrene in Libya." *ABW* 2 (1, 1992): 6-18.

Yamauchi, *Gnosticism.* • Yamauchi, Edwin. *Pre-Christian Gnosticism: A Survey of the Proposed Evidences.* Grand Rapids: Eerdmans, 1973.

Yamauchi, "Homer." • Yamauchi, Edwin M. "Historic Homer. Did It Happen?" *BAR* 33 (2, 2007): 28-37, 76.

Yamauchi, "Magic." • Yamauchi, Edwin. "Magic or Miracle? Diseases, Demons and Exorcisms." 89-183 in *GosPersp.* Vol. 6: *The Miracles of Jesus.* Ed. David Wenham and Craig Blomberg. Sheffield: JSOT Press, 1986.

Yamauchi, *Persia.* • Yamauchi, Edwin M. *Persia and the Bible.* Foreword by Donald J. Wiseman. Grand Rapids: Baker, 1990.

Yardeni, "Prophecy." • Yardeni, Ada. "A New Dead Sea Scroll in Stone? Bible-like Prophecy Was Mounted in a Wall 2,000 Years Ago." *BAR* 34 (1, 2008): 60-61.

Yee, *Feasts.* • Yee, Gale A. *Jewish Feasts and the Gospel of John.* Zacchaeus Studies: New Testament. Wilmington, DE: Michael Glazier, 1989.

Yegül, "Complex." • Yegül, F. Kret K. "The Bath-Gymnasium Complex." 148-161 in *Sardis from Prehistoric to Roman Times: Results of the Archaeological Exploration of Sardis 1958-1975.* Ed. George M. A. Hanfmann, assisted by William E. Mierse. Cambridge: Harvard University Press, 1983.

Yeivin, "Ark." • Yeivin, Ze'ev. "Has Another Lost Ark Been Found?" *BAR* 9 (1983): 75-76.

Young, *Parables.* • Young, Brad H. *Jesus and His Jewish Parables: Rediscovering the Roots of Jesus' Teaching.* New York: Paulist, 1989.

Young, *Theologian.* • Young, Brad H. *Jesus the Jewish Theologian.* Forewords by Marvin R. Wilson and Rabbi David Wolpe. Peabody: Hendrickson, 1995.

Ytterbrink, *Biography.* • Ytterbrink, Maria. *The Third Gospel for the First Time: Luke within the Context of Ancient Biography.* Lund: Lund University — Centrum för teologi och religionsvetenskap, 2004.

Zehnle, *Pentecost Discourse.* • Zehnle, Richard F. *Peter's Pentecost Discourse: Tradition and Lukan Reinterpretation in Peter's Speeches of Acts 2 and 3.* SBLMS 15. Nashville: Abingdon, for the Society of Biblical Literature, 1971.

Zeitlin, "Character." • Zeitlin, Solomon. "The Book of Jubilees, Its Character and its Significance." *JQR* 30 (1939): 1-31.

Zeitlin, "Galileans." • Zeitlin, Solomon. "Who Were the Galileans? New Light on Josephus' Activities in Galilee." *JQR* 64 (3, 1974): 189-203.

Zeitlin, "'Jubilees.'" • Zeitlin, Solomon. "The Book of 'Jubilees' and the Pentateuch." *JQR* 48 (1957-1958): 218-235.

Zeitlin, "Korban." • Zeitlin, Solomon. "Korban: A Gift." *JQR* 59 (1968): 133-35.

Zeitlin, "Trial." • Zeitlin, Solomon. "The Trial of Jesus." *JQR* 53 (1, 1962): 85-88.

Zeller, "Life." • Zeller, Dieter. "The Life and Death of the Soul in Philo of Alexandria. The Use and Origin of a Metaphor." *SPhilA* 7 (1995): 19-55.

Zeller, "Philosophen." • Zeller, Dieter. "Jesus und die Philosophen vor dem Richter (zu Joh 19.8-11)." *BZ* 37 (1, 1993): 88-92.

Zias, "Remains." • Zias, J. "Human Skeletal Remains from the Mount Scopus Tomb." *'Atiqot* 21 (1992): 97-103.

Ziesler, "Luke and Pharisees." • Ziesler, John A. "Luke and the Pharisees." *NTS* 25 (2, 1979): 146-57.

Ziesler, "Presence." • Ziesler, John A. "Matthew and the Presence of Jesus (2)." *EpwRev* 11 (1984): 90-97.

Ziesler, "Vow." • Ziesler, J. A. "The Vow of Abstinence Again." *Colloq* 6 (1973): 49-50.

Zipor, "Talebearers." • Zipor, Moshe A. "Talebearers, Peddlers, Spies, and Converts: The Adventures of the Biblical and Post-Biblical Roots *rg'l* and *rkyl.*" *HS* 46 (2005): 129-44.

Zlotnick, "Memory." • Zlotnick, Dov. "Memory and the Integrity of the Oral Tradition." *JANESCU* 16-17 (1984-1985): 229-41.

Zuntz, *Persephone*. • Zuntz, Günther. *Persephone: Three Essays on Religion and Thought in Magna Graecia.* Oxford: Clarendon Press, 1971.

Zwiep, *Judas*. • Zwiep, Arie W. *Judas and the Choice of Matthias: A Study on Context and Concern of Acts 1:15-26.* WUNT 2, 187. Tübingen: Mohr Siebeck, 2004.

Index of Authors and Modern Names

Gregory, A., 489n.19, 22
Grene, D., 452n.44
Grieb, A. K., 548n.148
Grintz, Y. M., 598n.18
Grobel, K., 482n.4
Groenewald, E. P., 509n.7
Groh, J. E., 557n.165
Grundmann, W., 489n.11
Guelich, R., 429n.21, 509n.6, 512n.53
Guenther, H. O., 470n.40
Guijarro Oporto, S., 436n.10
Gundry, R. H., 277, 423n.104, 446n.104,
    461n.29, 463nn.64,74, 466n.122, 468n.8,
    470n.54, 477nn.186,189, 482n.275, 483n.26,
    485n.53, 486n.66, 498n.111, 500n.22, 503n.91,
    504n.112, 505n.131, 507n.165, 511n.39,
    520nn.127,131,139, 521n.145, 522n.163,
    529nn.124,126-27, 530nn.133,148, 532n.191,
    534n.211, 536nn.45,48, 540n.6, 541n.19,
    543n.66, 544n.84, 546nn.120,124, 548n.149,
    549nn.7,9, 550nn.21-24, 551nn.43,45,
    559nn.199,200, 560n.206, 561n.227, 565n.65,
    575n.298, 579n.4, 589n.185, 592n.7, 602nn.3,
    13
Gurney, O. R., 561n.221
Gustafsson, B., 548n.147
Guthrie, W. K. C., 557n.160, 583nn.70,80
Guyénot, L., 523n.7

Haacker, K., 438n.49
Haar, S., 601n.23
Haarhoff, T. J., 442n.8, 443n.44
Habermas, G. R., 578n.341, 586n.128, 590n.197,
    600n.6
Hadas, M., 423n.97
Haenchen, E., 124, 547n.135, 554n.108
Häfner, G., 402n.103
Hagner, D. A., 463n.64, 467n.132, 475n.150,
    476n.174, 483n.26, 485n.53, 498n.111,
    502n.65, 510n.14, 512n.51, 529n.124, 530n.135,
    543n.76, 546n.126, 550n.17, 551n.44,
    559n.200, 561nn.218,227, 569n.148, 578n.334,
    598n.13
Hall, C. A., 465n.92
Hallbäck, G., 410n.166, 523n.13
Hamerton-Kelly, R. G., 502n.64,68, 546n.125,
    547nn.141-44, 548n.149
Hamilton, N. Q., 553n.79
Hammershaimb, E., 495n.41
Hammond, N. G. L., 450n.5
Hanet, D., 468n.12
Hanson, J. S., 350, 402n.98, 405n.46,

498nn.106,108, 524nn.17-18, 538nn.75,78,80,
    588n.162, 590nn.2,4-5,7,9-10,15-17
Hanson, K. C., 572n.228
Hanson, R. P. C., 439n.82
Hanson, S., 541n.24
Hare, D. R. A., 402n.107, 515nn.21-22, 521n.155,
    531n.169
Harmon, A. M., 469n.38
Harms, R., 468n.12
Harnack, A., 5-6, 395n.11, 397nn.14-25,
    398nn.26-29, 409n.138, 419n.29, 437n.43,
    515n.17
Harrelson, W., 545n.97
Harrington, D. J., 410n. 171, 426n.157, 501n.49,
    528n.110, 529n.127, 530n.143, 541n.18,
    557n.165, 592n.22, 593n.24
Harris, J. G., 504n.104
Harris, M. J., 427n.172, 548n.146, 580n.12
Harrison, J. R., 404n.40
Harrison, R. K., 557n.165
Harvey, A. E., 401n.89, 501n.37, 505n.120,
    516n.32, 523n.10, 524n.32, 535n.14, 545n.95,
    555n.127, 565n.59, 570n.181, 571nn.193,201,
    203, 572n.228, 575nn.295-97
Harvey, J. D., 468nn.7,10, 475n.148, 548n.144
Hasel, G. F., 400n.66
Hata, G., 428n.10, 456n.151, 480n.260
Hatina, T. R., 528n.99
Hauerwas, S., 401n.92
Hauptman, J., 558n.178
Hayles, D. J., 438n.49
Hayman, A. P., 589n.190
Hayman, P., 485n.51, 548n.157
Hays, R. B., 479n.220, 482n.2, 529n.117,
    541n.25, 565n.59
Hayward, R., 471n.56
Head, P. M., 397n.3, 461n.38, 474n.136
Headlam, A., 548n.146
Hearon, H. E., 522n.167
Heath, G. L., 417n.8
Heath, M., 472nn.79,89,93
Hedrick, C. W., 594n.47
Heidegger, M., 8, 400nn.63,66
Heidel, A., 582n.57
Heindl, A., 417n.8
Held, H. J., 463n.63, 509n.12
Hellestam, S., 512n.59
Hemer, C. J., 434n.115, 435n.130, 437nn.33,43,
    439n.76, 440n.85, 441n.5, 448n.150,
    449n.180, 454n.107, 458nn.195,198, 460n.21
Hendricks, O. M., 401n.92
Hengel, M., 34, 85, 86, 239, 267, 401n.88,
    406nn.78-79,85, 409n.139, 152, 414n.69,

Index of Subjects

Probability, historical, xxvii, 163-64, 445n.90, 447n.137, 450n.10, 570n.162

Pronouncement stories, 160, 481n.274

Prophecy and sayings of the risen Christ, 152-53, 365, 477n.193, 534nn.206,215, 546n.132

Prophets, and Jesus, xxxvi, 34, 36, 153, 172, 183, 203, 238-55, 292, 478n.195, 523nn.12-14

Prophets, wandering/itinerant, 24, 409n.138, 523n.9

Proselyte baptism, 30, 411n.188

Purity, 210, 221-22, 227, 232-34, 294, 485n.53, 514nn.86-90, 516n.38, 520n.138, 521n.147

"Q," date of, 132, 138

"Q" hypothesis, 61, 62, 69, 127, 131-32, 141, 168, 170, 205, 208, 210, 216, 217, 220, 222, 224, 226, 231, 232, 236, 241, 246, 247, 248, 249, 250, 253, 269, 273-74, 279, 280, 286, 288, 306, 324, 332, 361, 363, 364-65, 366, 390, 393, 398n.36, 399n.60, 402n.103, 410n.157, 417n.129, 421nn.68,71, 423n.103, 425nn.128-30,134,137-40, 426nn.149-50,153,163-64, 430n.32, 461n.38, 463nn.66-67,71, 464nn.77-79,81, 476n.168, 485n.52, 488n.110, 489n.9, 492n.86, 495n.54, 500n.21, 506n.152, 513n.85, and passim in remaining notes

"Q," as wisdom document, 26, 27, 61-66, 352-55, 425n.140, 591n.1

Qumran scrolls, 28, 29, 30, 31, 37, 65, 158, 167, 170, 192, 198, 200, 231, 244, 245, 246, 247, 248, 249, 251, 252, 262, 265-66, 276, 287, 294, 297, 301, 311, 338, 373, 408-9n.135, 410n.170, 423n.94, 447n.145, 448n.146, 464n.89, 480n.252, 483n.21, 499n.13, 509n.4, 521n.147, and passim. *See also* references to individual documents and passages in the index of primary sources

Rabbi, Jesus as, 39, 187, 239

Rabbinic Judaism, 9, 338, 400n.78, 600n.13; see further rabbinic sources

Rabbinic sources, xxxvi-xxxvii, 39, 149-50, 187, 189, 192, 194, 216, 219, 228, 313-14, 316, 357, 372, 396n.18, 414n.67, 420n.54, 495n.48, 511n.35, 513n.82, 556n.149, 570n.183, 592nn.7-8, and passim. *See also specific sources in the index of primary sources*

Realized eschatology. *See* Eschatology, realized

Redaction criticism, 135-38, 460n.20, 461n.28, 463n.63, 464n.85, 466n.122, 564n.42, 603n.27

Reductio ad absurdum, 232

Renaissance, 4

Repentance, 43, 44-45, 168, 212, 488n.108, 596n.23

Restoration eschatology, 44, 169, 237, 248-49, 287, 294, 346, 528n.100, 532n.177. *See also* Kingdom; Temple, eschatological

Resurrection, in Judaism, 11, 337-39, 340, 342, 344, 346, 584n.101, 585nn.105-66

Resurrection, alleged pagan analogies, 332-37, 344, 581nn.32,36-39, 584nn.90,96, 588n.177

Resurrection, of Jesus, historical consider-ations, 164, 263, 289, 330-32, 339-48, 379-80, 383, 384, 389, 412n.10, 587nn.144,158, 600nn.1-2

Resurrection body, nature of, 346, 585n.115, 585-86n.119, 586n.125, 589nn.186-87, 600n.6, 601n.11

Revolutionaries, 10-13, 167-68, 196-97, 245, 262, 264-65, 287, 350-51, 524n.31, 530n.133, 590nn.5,7,13

Revolutionaries and Galilee, 181, 350, 490n.43, 590n.5

Rhetoric, 59, 92, 116, 172, 176, 423n.107, 428n.5, 470n.40, and passim (see numerous rhetor-ical sources in the primary sources index)

Rhetoric and ancient historiography, 87, 96, 99, 105-6, 109-25, 134, 429n.29, 443n.53, 445n.90, 449n.177, 454n.92, 457n.164, 459n.204, 465n.101, 475n.154

Rhetoric and the Gospels, 115-18, 450n.199, 453nn.75-81, 454n.99, 465n.101

Rhetoric, of sages, 24, 172, 188, 204, 215, 216, 217, 219-20, 232, 270

Romanticism, 4-5

Rural setting, 20-21, 168-69, 181, 193, 194, 195, 284, 484n.35. *See also* Urban vs. rural

Sabbath, 226, 227, 228-30, 297, 326, 516n.37, 517nn.50,53,56-57,60-63,68,71, 518nn.80,84-86

Sabbetai Zevi, 343, 601n.10

Sadducees, 226, 230, 287, 310, 311, 338, 566n.94, 570n.157, 584n.101, 585n.106

Sage, 39-41, 153, 186-95, 215-16, and passim

Sanhedrin, 310-12, 328, 566n.94, 567nn.102-3, 105-9, 567-68n.110, 568nn.111,120, 599-600n.10

Sayings collections, 58, 62, 142, 186, 191, 352

Sayings, combined with narrative, 59, 62, 65, 142, 403n.16, 423n.107

Scientific (technical) treatises, ancient, 87, 436nn.20-21

Scourging, Jesus', 321-22, 573n.253

"Second Quest," 9-10, 156, 401n.84

Index of Scripture References

Index of Ancient Sources

5.4	411n.182
4Q254	
frg. 4	538n.88
4Q259	
2.9	528n.110
4Q265	
7.1.6-9	517n.68
7.2.11-17	555n.127
4Q266	
frg. 18.3.12	538n.85
4Q285	539n.97
5.4	540n.105
4Q300	426n.160
4Q302a	495n.42
4Q339	367
1.2	434n.113
4Q369	545n.102
frg. 1, 2.6-7	275, 538n.85
4Q375	
frg. 1.1.1-4	415n.91
4Q376	
frg. 1.1.1	539n.100
4Q377	
frg. 2.2.5	539n.100
4Q381	
1.1-2	544n.80
frg. 15.7	538n.85
4Q382	
frg. 16.2	538n.85
4Q385-86 (Pseudo-Ezekiel)	584n.103
4Q389	
frg. 2	527n.99
4Q390	
1.7-9	595n.16
4Q400	
f1ii.1	411n.182
f1ii.3	411n.182
f2.1	411n.182

4Q401	
f14.i.7	411n.182
4Q403	
f1i.25	411n.182
f1iii.10	411n.182
4Q416	
frg. 2 (+4Q417) 1.13	544n.90
4Q418	497n.76
frg. 81.5	544n.90
4Q422	594n.46
4Q458	545n.102
frg. 2.2.6	538n.85
4Q477	
2.2.6	504n.106
2.2.8	504n.106
4Q491 A	
frg. 10.2.8-12	499n.13, 532n.182
13.5	499n.13, 532n.182
4Q491 C	
11.1.18	548n.156
4Q500.1	549n.7
4Q509	
4.2	555n.132
4.12	555n.132
4Q510	
1.4-5	524n.33
4Q511	
10.9	555n.134
35.2-3	556n.139
35.3	555n.132
4Q521	485nn.57,58, 524n.27, 539n.97, 584n.103
frg. 2, 4.1.1	538n.78
frg. 2, 4.2.1	538n.85
frg. 7.3	538n.85
4Q525	512n.55
4Q537	439n.77
4Q540	539n.97
4Q541	540n.106

RABBINIC LITERATURE

TANNAITIC SOURCES

Mekilta (Mek.)

*Mostly following the enumeration in James R. Butts, *The Progymnasmata of Theon the Sophist: a new text with translation and commentary* (Ann Arbor, MI: University Microfilms International, 1989).

8.27-28	410n.159
Georgics	
1.121	541n.31
1.283	541n.31
1.328	541n.31
1.353	541n.31
2.325	541n.31
2.371-79	549n.8

Vitruvius
Architecture

7.pref.10-17	461n.34
Women at the Adonis Festival	582n.63

Xenophon
Agesilaus

3.1	445n.97
5.6	424n.110, 441n.102
Anab. (Anabasis)	446n.106
2.5.41	446n.106
3.1.4-6	446n.106
5.2.24	457n.177
Apol. (Apology)	473n.103
1-2	461n.44
1	474n.133, 562n.8
2	445n.97, 461n.44
Cyr. (Cyropedia)	111, 418n.22, 431n.51,
	451n.17, 457n.174
1.2.1	469n.29, 476n.164
3.1.17	457n.174
5.1.1	474n.118
8.2.2-3	565n.74
8.7.14	508n.172, 565n.75
Hell. (Hellenica)	455n.120
1.7.22	565n.73
3.1.2	446n.104
4.1.34	565n.73
6.2.31	445n.97
6.4.16	517n.61
Mem. (Memorabilia)	76
1.2.3	456n.147, 474n.118
1.2.10	564n.54
1.5.6	474n.118
2.1.6-7	572n.236
4.4.10	474n.118
4.8.4	564n.51
4.8.11	435n.138

Symp.	473n.103
1.1	435n.123, 446n.106, 474n.118
3.5-6	468n.17
8.12	473n.103

Xenophon of Ephesus
Ephesiaca

1.1	443n.53
3.5-7	581n.38
3.8-9	586n.131
4.2	559n.201

Zonaras

7.11	457n.176

INSCRIPTIONS AND PAPYRI

BGU

515	507n.161

CIG

2.2077	469n.18

CIJ (Corpus Inscriptionum Iudaicarum)

1:24, §30	529n.119
1:348-50	585n.110
2:111, §879	529n.119

CIL

1.1012	504n.111
6.140	504n.111
6.911	556n.154
8.25902	549n.11

CPJ (Corpus Papyrorum Judaicorum)

154	573n.259
158	573n.259
1:199	483n.33
2:55-107, §§154-59	562n.6
2:140, §§248-49	529n.119
2:143, §261	529n.119
2:145, §§269-70	529n.119
2:146, §274	529n.119
2:147, §275	529n.119
2:147, §276	529n.119
2:151, §298	529n.119
2:153, §304	529n.119
2:154, §311	529n.119
2:156, §321	529n.119
3:9, §453	529n.119

Elephantine Papyri 480n.251

OTHER NON-MODERN SOURCES

*ANET*² *(Ancient Near Eastern Texts,* ed.
Pritchard, 2nd edition, 1955)

5	582n.60
52–57	582n.58
55	582n.58
72–99	582n.63
84	582n.58
107	582n.58
108	582n.57
126–28	582n.57
129–42	582n.57
140	483n.33
149–55	582n.57
154	522n.162
267	541n.23
338	537n.68
370	541n.23
383	541n.23
483–90	545n.99

Confucius

Analects	147n.18
5.13 (43)	511n.33

7.28 (387)	479n.217
15.23 (44)	511n.35
16.4 (168)	479n.217
(244-85)	573n.236

Enuma Elish	582n.57

Gilgamesh

6.46ff	582n.63
6.97-99	582n.58

IAB

2	483n.33

Qur'an 395n.6, 468n.12

4.155	521n.155
5.70	521n.155
5.110	525n.48
7.40	506n.138

Theology of Memphis	582n.60

Toledot Yeshu	417n.8